A HISTORY OF EUROPE

LAETITIAE SACRUM

A HISTORY OF EUROPE

BY

H. A. L. FISHER

COMPLETE EDITION IN
ONE VOLUME

LONDON
EDWARD ARNOLD & CO.

Printed in Great Britain by
Billing and Sons Ltd., Guildford and Esher

PREFACE

I BEGIN this book with neolithic man and conclude with Stalin and Mustapha Kemal, Mussolini and Hitler. Between these rough and rugged frontiers there are to be found some prospects flattering to human pride which it is a pleasure to recall to memory, the life-giving inrush of the Aryan peoples, the flowering of Greek genius, the long Roman peace, the cleansing tide of Christian ethics, the slow reconquest of classical learning after the barbaric invasions, the discovery through oceanic travel of the new world, the rationalism of the eighteenth, and the philanthropy and science of the nineteenth centuries. One intellectual excitement has, however, been denied me. Men wiser and more learned than I have discerned in history a plot, a rhythm, a predetermined pattern. These harmonies are concealed from me. I can see only one emergency following upon another as wave follows upon wave, only one great fact with respect to which, since it is unique, there can be no generalizations, only one safe rule for the historian: that he should recognize in the development of human destinies the play of the contingent and the unforeseen. This is not a doctrine of cynicism and despair. The fact of progress is written plain and large on the page of history; but progress is not a law of nature. The ground gained by one generation may be lost by the next. The thoughts of men may flow into the channels which lead to disaster and barbarism.

My opening themes are Greece and Rome, barbarism and Christianity. The discovery and colonization of the new world, the rise of nation states and the full development of the capitalistic system, belong to a later but still, having regard to the six thousand years of civilized life upon the planet, relatively recent period. Steam and electricity are more recent still. It is possible that two thousand years hence these two scientific inventions may be regarded as constituting the "Great Divide" in human history.

Book III describes The Liberal Experiment, using the adjective Liberal in no narrow party sense, but as denoting the system of civil, political and religious freedom now firmly established in Britain and the Dominions as well as among the French, the Dutch, the Scandinavian and American peoples. And if I speak of Liberty in this wider sense as experimental, it is not because I wish to disparage Freedom (for I would as soon disparage Virtue herself), but merely to indicate that after gaining ground through the nineteenth century, the tides of liberty have now suddenly receded over wide tracts of Europe. Yet how can the spread of servitude, by whatever benefits it may have been accompanied, be a matter for congratulation? A healthy man needs no narcotics. Only when the moral spine of a people is broken may plaster of Paris become a necessary evil.

For extended bibliographies the reader is referred to the Cambridge Ancient, Mediaeval and Modern Histories, to the authorities cited in J. B. Bury's edition of Gibbon's *Decline and Fall of the Roman Empire*, Lavisse's *Histoire de France*, Stubbs' *Constitutional History of England*, and other standard histories. I have confined myself to drawing attention at the end of each chapter to a few illustrative books, choosing by preference those which are modern and accessible in the English or French languages.

I have to thank my wife, Mr. Leopold Wickham Legg and Mr. David Ogg for their great kindness in reading the proofs; Mr. D. A. Reilly, of All Souls College, for several useful suggestions with respect to the opening chapters; and, for much valuable counsel in the later part of the work, my old friend Sir Richard Lodge, who at eighty years retains unimpaired his remarkable gifts of historical judgment and information.

H. A. L. FISHER.

January, 1936.

CONTENTS

BOOK I

ANCIENT AND MEDIAEVAL

BOOK II

RENAISSANCE, REFORMATION, REASON

CONTENTS ix

BOOK III

THE LIBERAL EXPERIMENT

LIST OF MAPS

BOOK ONE

ANCIENT AND MEDIAEVAL

INTRODUCTION

Our civilization Hellenic. At present Europe is a creditor, formerly it was a debtor. Rome transmits the legacy of Greece. Oriental religions penetrate the west. Christianity the white man's religion. Its severance from Judaism and submission to Greek influence. The Christian test. Its acceptance by Bulgars, Hungarians, and Finns, its rejection by Jews, Arabs, and Turks. Civilization of Europe spiritual not racial. The problem of European unity.

WE Europeans are the children of Hellas. Our civilization, which has its roots in the brilliant city life of the eastern Aegean, has never lost traces of its origin, and stamps us with a character by which we are distinguished from the other great civilizations of the human family, from the Chinese, the Hindus, the Persians, and the Semites. Scholars may explain to us that the languages spoken by the formative races of Europe are akin to Sanscrit and Persian, that the west has borrowed from the east, and the east from the west, and that the interpenetration of east and west has been so complex and subtle and continuous that any attempt to disentangle the European elements in our civilization from those which are foreign and adventitious must be a forlorn enterprise. Nevertheless, the broad fact remains. There is an European civilization. We know an European when we meet him. It is easy to distinguish him from a native of Pekin, of Benares, or of Teheran.

Our civilization, then, is distinct: it is also all-pervading and preponderant. In superficial area Europe is surpassed by Asia, Africa, and America, in population by the vast stable peasantry of Asia, which outnumbers not Europe only, but the rest of the world put together. Yet if a comprehensive survey of the globe were to be made, it would be found that in almost every quarter of it there were settlements of European men, or traces of the operation of the European mind. The surviving aboriginal peoples in the western hemisphere are a small, unimportant, and dwindling element in the population. The African negroes have been introduced by white men as an economic convenience. Northern and southern America are largely populated by colonists from Europe. Australasia is British. The political direction of Africa has fallen, with the ambiguous exception of the lower reaches of the Nile, into European hands. In Asia the case is not dissimilar. The political influences of Europe are apparent, even where they are not, as in India or Palestine, embodied in direct European control. The ideas of nationality and responsible government, of freedom and progress, of democracy and democratic education, have passed from the west to the east with revolutionary and far-reaching consequences.

It is, moreover, to European man that the world owes the incomparable gifts of modern science. To the conquest of nature through knowledge the contributions made by Asiatics have been negligible and by Africans (Egyptians excluded) nonexistent. The printing press and the telescope, the steam-engine, the internal combustion engine and the aeroplane, the telegraph and telephone, wireless broadcasting and the cinematograph, the gramophone and television, together with all the leading discoveries in physiology, the circulation of the blood, the laws of respiration and the like, are the result of researches carried out by white men of European stock. It is hardly excessive to say that the material fabric of modern civilized life is the result of the intellectual daring and tenacity of the European peoples.

Yet this astounding supremacy in the field of scientific discovery has not always existed and may not always continue. Judged by the length of years during which human life has existed on this planet, the intellectual ascendancy of the white European races is a very recent phenomenon. Europe has not always been the tutor, nor Asia always the pupil. There was a time when these relations were reversed, and the men of Europe (the land of the setting sun) were deeply influenced by the far older and more sumptuous civilizations of Babylon and Egypt.

It is not my purpose to discuss the extent to which the civilization of Hellas was influenced by oriental sources. Let it be sufficient to note that an imposing mass of archaeological evidence can now be adduced in support of the proposition that the arts and crafts of the Orient were widely known to the peoples dwelling round the Mediterranean basin long before our earliest written records of Ionian civilization. Yet when the dawn of European literature begins to shine it reveals a society which is not oriental. The Homeric poems are a sufficient proof that round the eastern shores of the Mediterranean there was about 1200 B.C. a distinctive civilization of the west.

From that moment the survival value of the European mind was assured. The civilization of Greece, which was rooted in the religion of the Homeric age, grew from strength to strength. It repelled the might of Persia; and when the free cities of Greece were extinguished by the power of Macedon the influence of Hellenism was spread eastwards to the Indus by the armies of Alexander.

The mantle of the great Macedonian ultimately devolved on the Roman Empire, which for four hundred years defended western civilization against the dangers which assailed it from the barbarians without. But if the Roman legions could hold the frontiers against external foes, they afforded no protection against the penetration of the west by oriental beliefs. The old classical deities gave ground before the cults of Isis and Mithras and the Sun God, and these in turn ceded to Christ.

The founder of Christianity was a Galilean, speaking the Aramaic language, and nurtured in the Jewish traditions; but the Christian religion struck no deep roots in the country of its origin. Almost from the first it became a European creed, winning the souls of the poor as well by its simple Galilean piety and democratic ideals as by its ardent claim, inherited from the Hebrews, to be the one truth and the sole means of salvation from a terrible and impending doom. A religion springing from a Jewish root, but how quickly in the Hellenic atmosphere of the first century severed from the legal rigours of Jerusalem and woven into the texture of Greek thought! The language of its Scriptures was Greek. So, too, remains the distinctive vocabulary of its creed, its ritual, its organization—the words apostle, evangel, church, diocese, bishop, priest, deacon, and countless others, for the Christian Church, even in Rome, was Greek before it was Latin, Greek in its theology, its official language, its local organization. The oriental rite of circumcision, which Paul of Tarsus, the greatest Greek writer of his age, rejected as a fatal obstacle to the spread of the Gospel through the gentile world, drew a clear line of division between two sects which in the Roman mind were at first apt to be confounded. Christian and Jew sprang apart. As time went on, the story of the Crucifixion, told with exquisite simplicity and pathos, and becoming widely known wherever Christians met together, deepened the gulf, and the crime of a handful of priests and elders in Jerusalem was visited by the Christian Churches upon the whole Jewish race. It is thus that St. Mark, the earliest evangelist, appears to many Jews today as being, although without malice, the first of the line of anti-Semite authors.

Here, then, in Christianity as sharply distinguished from Judaism, was a new test, a new principle of organization for European society. To be a Christian was to be admitted, as it were, into the fellowship of the European nations. To be a non-Christian was to be an outcast and an enemy. Much of European history consists in the secular conflict between east and west, which, beginning with the wars of Greece and Persia, was resumed in the form of the long duel between Christianity and Islam, the most recent phase of which was closed by the Treaty of Lausanne in 1923. What famous names are connected with that secular struggle—Urban II and Godfrey de Bouillon, Saladin and Richard Coeur de Lion, St. Louis and the Cid, Soleyman the Magnificent and Prince Eugène, Mustapha Kemal and Venizelos! The action and interaction of the Moslem and Christian world is one of the great themes of European history.

The acceptance of the Christian test as a mark of European fellowship has necessarily determined the relations between the old-established European races and those Asiatic peoples who at one time or another have effected a lodgment in the European continent. The Bulgars, the Hungarians, and the Finns accepted with varying degrees of readiness the European religion. The fact that in language and physical type they bore marks of an oriental and savage origin did not injure them. Religion atoned for an alien origin, and gave them the rights of the European confraternity. It was otherwise with the three oriental races, which continued to maintain upon European soil a non-Christian faith.

The Jews were persecuted, the Arabs by degrees driven from Spain, and the Turks, after a long-drawn struggle, expelled from the Greek mainland and islands, and from all but a small fraction of the Balkan peninsula.

Of these three sharply contrasted peoples only one has exercised a major and permanent influence on European life. The Turks have been barren of ideas, and retained until the present generation the modes of thought and life appropriate to the nomads of the Asiatic highlands. From the Arab peoples mediaeval Europe learnt something of medicine, science, history, and philosophy, which served its turn for the moment and is now superseded. But to the Jews Europe owes the Old Testament, which, being translated into Greek and becoming an accepted part of the Christian canon, has entered more deeply perhaps than any other book into the lives of the western peoples. From this great body of sacred literature, some of it rising to heights of sublime moral beauty, while other parts reflect the morals of a barbarous age, generation after generation of European men have drawn their ideas, not only of an historical order governed by divine providence, but of extreme antiquity, and of the lineaments of oriental society in distant times. The influence of the Old Testament has not been wholly good. If it has given courage and consolation to the saint, it has too often nerved the arm of the persecutor.

Apart from the power of their sacred literature, and despite the cruel persecutions to which they have been exposed, the Jews have achieved for themselves a singular position in the economy of Europe. Dispersed after the conquest of Palestine by the Roman Emperor Titus in A.D. 70, this shrewd and gifted oriental people have spread themselves through the Christian society of the world, and now number some eleven millions in Europe and four millions in America.

For many centuries the gates of mercy were closed upon them. They were regarded as outcasts, debarred from the most honourable callings and responsibilities, and constrained to the pestilential squalors of the ghetto. Always despised, periodically plundered, and in times of public calamity or fear exposed to the blood lust of murderous and ignorant mobs, the Jews of Europe endured through the middle ages unspeakable miseries. The eighteenth century brought the dawn of happier things. As the sunshine of religious toleration spread through central and western Europe the Jews were admitted to civic rights. The hospitality of the Christian state was amply repaid in noble contributions to art, science, and literature. Receiving at last encouragement from the vigorous and thriving populations of the west, the Jew rose to the level of the society around him, educated himself in its spirit, took on its colour, and ministered to some of its needs. Yet the difference between east and west, between Aryan and Semite, between Jew and Gentile, still remained, as sensible after more than eighteen hundred years as when the Hebrews were first driven from their small sunbaked home in Palestine to seek an asylum and a future in the west.

and is liable even yet, as in the violent paroxysm of racial hysteria which has shaken the Germans, to give rise to bursts of savage oppression.

Race, then, has never entered as a unifying factor into European history. The races of Europe have always felt themselves to be different from one another, and have acted as if they were so. Attempts to give to Europe some form of organization or coherence have never been based on racial unity, or limited in scope to the geographical area which we have agreed to describe as European. The Empire of Alexander stretched to India, the Empire of Rome to the Euphrates, the claims of the Pope to the uttermost parts of the earth. The League of Nations, which incidentally supplies Europe with an organization for peace, is so framed as to include Asia and Africa, South America, Canada, and Australasia.

It follows that the kind of civilization which we specifically designate as European reposes not upon a foundation of race, but on an inheritance of thought and achievement and religious aspirations.

To this inheritance every race in Europe has made its distinct and specific contribution. That is why Europe is interesting. Its civilization has a certain character to be distinguished from that of the Semites, the Hindus, or the Chinese, and yet as we examine that character it dissolves under our eyes into a thousand different colours and shades, race differing from race, country from country, shire from shire, the men of Wiltshire sharply opposed in certain particulars to the men of Dorset, and even neighbouring villages eyeing one another as foreigners.

These differences are unresolved. One by one the great attempts to impose a common system upon the energetic self-willed peoples of Europe have broken down. The Roman Empire was foiled by the Germans. The Christian Church, by far the most powerful of the influences which in historical times has worked for union, was ruptured first by the quarrel between the Greeks and Latins, and then by the revolt of the Protestant north. Nor has any system of secular ideas been more successful in obtaining universal acceptance. Europe refused to be unified by the egalitarian plan of the French Revolution. Equally it now declines to accept the iron programme of Russian Communism. Yet ever since the first century of our era the dream of unity has hovered over the scene and haunted the imagination of statesmen and peoples. Nor is there any question more pertinent to the future welfare of the world than how the nations of Europe, whose differences are so many and so inveterate, may best be combined into some stable organization for the pursuit of their common interests and the avoidance of strife.

CHAPTER I

ORIGINS

Geographical and climatic changes. Evidence of craniology. Peasantry of the neolithic and bronze age. The coming of the Aryans. Mixed races of Europe. The Aegean culture of archaic times. Its debt to Babylon and Egypt. Difference between east and west.

IN the last three thousand years there has been little change in the geographical conformation or climatic conditions of Europe. Here and there the sea has gained upon the land, or the land encroached upon the sea. Here and there a harbour has been silted up, a river has changed its course, a hill has subsided. But the broad currents of history have not been and could not be altered by such slight changes as these. In its physical outlines the Europe of the Homeric age was practically the same as the Europe of today.

This has not always been so. Geographical evidence shows that at earlier periods in the world's history the area which is now described as Europe went through transformations remarkable in scale, though effected by minute gradations spread over long periods of time. The climate was now much colder, now much warmer, than that which we experience at the present day. At one time herds of reindeer wandered over France and Britain; at another the shy hunter in the forests of western Europe would track the elephant, the hippopotamus, and the sabre-toothed tiger—animals now to be found only in the tropical or semi-tropical regions of the world. There was an age during which the Scandinavian peninsula, the British Isles, and the greater part of northern Germany were covered by a vast sheet of ice, an age when men might cross the Irish Sea, the German Ocean, and the British Channel dryshod, and walk into Africa or China without the use of oar or sail. In this long period of human history, extending perhaps for three hundred thousand years, there was a time when Europe pushed out a shelf a hundred miles to the west of its present limits, when the Baltic was a fresh-water lake, and the Atlantic had not yet burst into the Mediterranean, nor the Mediterranean established a marine connection with the Black Sea. At one point or other in geological time it would seem that every part of Europe wore an aspect wholly at variance with our present experience of it. The islands of the Aegean were eminences in a stretch of land inhabited by the elephant, the rhinoceros, and the mastodon. The plain of Hungary was a waste of salt water stretching to the Caspian; the Harz mountains were an island; Britain was broken up into a number of little pieces floating in an icy inhospitable sea. The site of imperial Rome was hidden beneath a floor of untravelled waters. Only after many experiments, continued into upper miocene times, were the main lines of Europe, as we now know it, decided.

The new structure of Europe was of capital importance. The waterways opened from the Atlantic into the Mediterranean in the south, and into the Baltic in the north, the establishment of a maritime connection between the Aegean and the Black Sea through the Dardanelles, the Sea of Marmora, and the Bosphorus have given to Europe a climate so temperate and subject to such modest variations of heat and cold as to provide the most favourable physiological stimulus to activity and enterprise. The sea is a source of infinite refreshment. The penetration of the continent of Europe by the long arms of inland seas has not only encouraged intercommunication, with all its consequences for the development of trade and society, but has prevented, at least in that part of Europe which lies west of the Pripet marshes, the social and political stagnation which prevails in the heart of great land continents. But the favours of nature are distributed unequally. The vast plain of Russia is, save on its southern fringes, too remote from the mitigating influences of a great body of temperate sea water to enjoy the benefits of its western neighbours. The cold, dark winters of the Russian plain are inimical to the spirit of activity, vigilance, and criticism. In such a climate man easily becomes the victim of narrowing localism and deadening routine. The gloom of geographical uniformity, combined with a harsh climate, exercises its effect on the mind. An all-pervading spirit of resignation and acquiescence saps initiative and lames resource.

In the western half of Europe man has been assisted both by climate and by geography. Rolling hills or mountain ranges relieve the monotony of the level spaces. Comparatively speaking, the cleansing sea is always a neighbour. Save in northern

Germany there is no long stretch of monotonous plain, and here the plain is comparatively narrow, and bounded on one side by the waters of the Baltic. In all this western part of Europe, nature seems to have been bent on providing every form of variety calculated to refresh and encourage the human race. Hill and valley are intermingled; mountain ranges are intersected by passes, and never so high as to oppose an insuperable barrier to the passage of men. The plains are well watered. In the Scandinavian north, where the winter cold is extreme, there is always the sea and always the mountains. In Greece or Spain, where the summer heat is strongest, it is never, as in India, almost unbearable. Everything facilitates the movement of men, the intermixture of races, and the development of an active habit of thought and enterprise.

Long before the age of history proper, man had made his appearance in Europe. Some think that he came from Africa, others from southern Russia, others again that the original habitat of the human race is to be found in the highlands of Asia. We do not know. But if the origin of man and the course of his early migrations are wrapped in obscurity, we know something of his physical properties, something of the stages of civilization through which he passed, and something of the racial types existing in Europe when he first emerged into the light of history.

At the beginning of the neolithic age, when the great ice sheets had receded from the continent of Europe, and the climate had become tolerable to the human species, it would seem that European men fell into three main types, the Mediterranean, the Nordic, and the Alpine; the Mediterranean and the Nordic agreeing with one another in the important particular of being long-headed, but the Nordic, probably under the stress of climatic influences, being fairer, slower to achieve maturity, and more muscular than the Mediterranean. In sharp contradistinction to these two long-headed races, the one resembling the modern Berber and the other the modern Swede, is a race of round-headed, thick-set people, sometimes, as in the Illyrian Alps, tall and dark, elsewhere, as in the Swiss and French Alps, short and stocky, who appear to have come into Europe from the east, and are known to ethnologists as Alpines from the fact that they are to be found thickly occupying the mountain chains which divide northern from southern Europe. It is not, however, to be supposed that these races were possessed of any developed sense of race consciousness or exclusiveness. Alpine mixed freely with Nordic, Nordic with Mediterranean. Almost everywhere we find evidence of intermediate types, or of survivals from an earlier age. In the British Isles, for instance, "the population was long-headed, and 'intermediate' in character between the two differentiated races, tall, gaunt, and dark in parts of the Scottish Highlands and North Wales, short and almost Mediterranean in parts of South Wales and Ireland, and 'betwixt-and-between' almost everywhere." In Finland, Asiatic broadheads mingled with long-headed men of the Nordic stock.

In a word, as Europe is a patchwork of differing landscapes, so it is a miscellany of differing physical types.

As the ice age came to an end, and mile after mile of Europe was retrieved from frosty desolation, the hunting men of the south came drifting northwards through the evergreens of bay and myrtle and box, through the thick forests of beech and oak, with their flint arrows and spears in pursuit of game. *Homo sapiens* had entered upon his long struggle with nature. Peril and want sharpened his wits and gave him reliance. He learned to spin, to weave, to clothe himself against the cold. By degrees he perfected his weapons against the wild beasts in the forests, exchanging stone for bronze, and bronze for iron. The sail, the wheel, the domestication of animals, three of the most important inventions in human history, belong to this unrecorded period. Gradually the hunter acquired the arts of stock keeping and farming, so that thousands of years before the dawn of history a peasantry was settled upon the soil of Europe, and there, for century after century, bent to the unchanging cycle of the seasons, sowing, ploughing, and reaping, tending the ox, the goat, the sheep, and the pig, practising with such skill as they might command the arts and crafts of weaving and building, carving and pottery, and, since religion is well-nigh universal, worshipping nature in its manifold forms, whether terrible or benignant. Into this passive civilization of scattered huts and villages there was injected somewhere in the course of the second millennium before Christ a new and disturbing force. Out of hither Asia, we know not by what successive waves or driblets, there streamed a people who had tamed the wild horse to the needs of man and had found in the use of iron the convincing secret of the slashing sword. With these two commanding advantages the new race or combination of races imposed itself as a dominating authority upon the archaic Europe of the bronze age and was the exciting cause of new and far reaching developments. Not that the newcomers obliterated the old sedentary population of the continent, or that they were able to efface the primitive beliefs which haunt the imagination of rustic men. That population, those beliefs, endure to this day, but refashioned and overlaid by the higher and more spirited culture of the new tribal aristocracy, which had come so far and moved so fast. What these new peoples called themselves or were called by others when they dwelt in their original home (wherever that may have been) and spoke their original tongue is a mystery, for in historical times they were divided into separate races, which had lost the memory of a common origin: but since they share with the Persians and Indians a common linguistic pedigree, they are called by philologists Indo-Europeans or Aryans. From the mixture of these conquering intruders with the bronze-using peoples of archaic Europe, the races which bear the burden of European history, the Greeks and Latins, the Celts, Teutons, and Slavs, derive their origin. Purity of race does not exist. Europe is a continent of energetic mongrels.

In certain regions, and most notably in the eastern Aegean, civilization had touched high points of luxury and craftsmanship long before the Aryan invasions. The exhumed treasures of Crete and the Cyclades, of Mycenae and the Troad, suffice to show that the human hand has gained nothing in dexterity from the lapse of ages. In Crete, that long and beautiful island, surmounted by the snowy crest of Ida, which of all European islands lies nearest to Egypt, there was for near two thousand years (3000-1400 B.C.) a flourishing civilization which spread its influence far and wide through the lands washed by the Aegean seas or westward to the shores of Sicily.

The ruins of the palace of Minos at Cnossos afford astonishing evidence of the comfort and luxury to be procured in that distant age. The system of heating and draining, and even some of the women's fashions, as depicted in the frescoes, have a thoroughly modern air. The source of Minoan luxury is not obscure. Cnossos, planted at the northern end of the great south road across the island, received and distributed the merchandise of the east. In that distant age this city, which may have contained a hundred thousand inhabitants, acted as a centre of exchange between east and west, playing the same part in the economy of European trade as afterwards devolved on Venice. Then a sudden destruction came upon it. The place was burned and sacked, the town was destroyed. The Minoan dynasty and the Minoan power pass out of history, leaving only among the Greeks a memory of half-magical skill, luxury, and cruelty.

No clue has been discovered to the Minoan script, nor has any book belonging to this age survived the catastrophe of the Greek conquest. The mysterious people, who worshipped a woman, a man, and a child, and for whom the cross appears to have been a religious symbol, cannot speak to us, and could not, so it would seem, speak to the fair-haired Achaeans, who at Mycenae and elsewhere settled in the shell of their castles and palaces. The break seems absolute. Yet it has been suggested, despite the silence of records, that something precious may yet have been handed down to posterity from this brilliant race. The Minoan gems are of exquisite workmanship, and fragments of the art of that distant age, unearthed by the spade in Hellenic times, may have helped to inspire the aesthetic consciousness of Greece in the greatest period of its artistic achievement.

The secret of this rich Aegean culture is to be found in its contact with the yet older and more advanced civilization in the alluvial valleys of the Euphrates and the Nile. Here it is that we find the first evidence of a developed urban life, of temples and priestly corporations, of written records and correspondence, of schools and codes of law, and of a leisured class raised above the urgency of material wants and dedicated to the pursuit of learning. While all Europe was yet rude and unlettered, geometry, astronomy, engineering, and land-surveying were cultivated by the Sumerians of Mesopotamia. Here, too, more than three thousand years before Christ mankind had carried to a point of perfection, as the most recent investigations at Ur of the Chaldees have shown, the arts of the jeweller, the carver, and the cabinet maker. Great centres of culture and wealth are never self-contained. From the Sumerians, shafts of light spread in every direction to the Hittites and Cretans, to the Philistines and Egyptians, and ultimately through many different chan-nels to the Aryan Greeks. Yet, though the west borrowed from the east, a deep chasm divides the settled hieratic society and theocratic governments of Mesopotamia and Egypt from the free world of warriors, minstrels, pirates, and adventurers, which is depicted in the poems of Homer, and out of which, as the wild Greek clans took to city life, the distinctive civilization of the European world was in due course developed.

BOOKS WHICH MAY BE CONSULTED

Christopher Dawson : The Age of the Gods. 1928.

John Joly : The Surface History of the Earth. 1925.

W. J. Sollas : Ancient Hunters and their Modern Representatives. 1924.

V. G. Childe : The Aryans. 1926.

V. G. Childe : The Dawn of European Civilization. 1925.

T. Rice Holmes : Ancient Britain. 1907.

G. Glotz : The Aegean Civilization. 1925.

J. L. Myres : The Dawn of History. 1911.

Arthur Evans : The Earlier Religions of Greece in the Light of the Cretan Discoveries. Frazer Lecture, 1931.

G. Elliott Smith : The Migrations of Early Culture. 1915.

H. J. Fleure : The Peoples of Europe. 1922.

Ebert : Reallexikon der Vorgeschichte. 14 vols. 1924-9.

CHAPTER II

THE DAWN OF HELLAS

The coming of the Greeks. The Homeric age. Geographical features. The city states. Absence of theocracy. Successive stages of political development. Athens and Sparta. The Ionian cities. The colonial movement.

By an astonishing dispensation of fate the one people of genius in the annals of the world is the earliest of the European races to emerge into the full light of history. The Greeks of history believed themselves to be one in race, origin, language, and institution, and in all these respects were misled; but the fact that they thought of themselves as one, and as distinguished by a superior culture from the dark background of the barbarian world around them, is more important than the truth, discerned by modern analysts, that like all the great peoples of the world, the Greeks drew their wealth from many quarters. Who they were and whence ultimately they came, are matters rather of learned conjecture than of certain knowledge. We only know that when the dawn breaks about 1000 B.C. men of Aryan stock are established, as a result of a long series of tribal infiltrations, which may have lasted many hundred years, in the coastlands of Asia Minor, in the islands of the Aegean, and in the land which is now called Greece.

In the western portions of this sunlit corner of the Mediterranean, in the islands, and on the mainland of Greece, the invaders found a civilization long established, and distinguished as far back as the fifteenth century B.C. by an advanced degree of accomplishment in the arts of life. With these older Minoan or Aegean peoples, the Achaeans and Dorians (for such were the names of successive tribal migrations of the Greek-speaking invaders) mingled in varying proportions, taking whatever culture the autochthonous settlers had to give, but everywhere imposing their own rich and flexible language, their political ideas, and their worship of Zeus. But how little do we know of those distant times! No chronicle records the sequence of these early migrations (1200-900 B.C.) and confused struggles, of this widespread displacement and readjustment of peoples, while the

Aegean civilization was broken up under the pressure of immigrants from the north, and the Ionians and others were forced
out of mainland Greece and formed settlements on the coast of
Asia Minor. We do not even know whether the later sovereigns
of Mycenae were Greek. Legend and conjecture must take the
place of true knowledge.

Yet one incomparable monument remains of this period of
vast and adventurous agitation. In Greece everything invites to
the seafaring life, the scant living to be obtained from the sunbaked hills and little level plains, the abundance of small, well-
sheltered harbours, the constellation of islands, forming, as it
were, a pathway between Greece and Asia Minor. The Greeks
took to the sea. They crossed the Aegean, and made settlements
on the further shore, they stole up to the mouths of the Hellespont, challenging, when a challenge was needed, the peoples of
hither Asia. One such encounter (1194-84 B.C.), between a great
Achaean confederacy and the Phrygian inhabitants of Troy, supplied to the minstrels of the Greek world a theme upon which the
poetic imagination of many subsequent generations embroidered
unending tapestries. In the Iliad of Homer the blind poet of
Chios, which embodies, transmutes, and enlarges the poetical
material of the Achaean minstrels, the facts of history are obscured in a haze of legend. The actors take on heroic form, the
gods participate in the struggle and the issue is portrayed as a
contest between the gathered strength of Hellas and an Asiatic
power. To the modern antiquary the Iliad, which depicts in
vivid colours the Aegean civilization of the bronze age, is full
of instruction. In the ruins of Tiryns, the port of Mycenae, he
discovers the regal halls of Homer; but to ancient Greece this
splendid body of epical verse was much more than a repertory
of curious detail; it was the Bible of a vanished and more heroic
world, the book of books, containing the traditions and beliefs
of a race, the testament of that great age of conflict, migration,
and discovery, out of which a triumphant civilization was destined to emerge.

To us this great Ionian poem is precious not only by
reason of its artistic beauty, but also as the earliest surviving
specimen of European speech.[1] Our common culture derives

[1] Though the Homeric poems seem to have assumed their final form
only in the sixth century, the Iliad and Odyssey were probably in existence c. 800 B.C. The society which they depict is much earlier—
c. 1200-1100 B.C.

from Homer. In certain broad particulars his outlook on the world is also ours. Though it seems probable that he spent most of his life on the Asiatic coast, for the Iliad shows him to be familiar with the landscape round Smyrna and Ephesus, and but dimly cognizant of the west, there is no touch of orientalism in the Homeric poems. The scene of action in the Iliad is not laid in the Asiatic hinterland, into which Greek mercenaries had already penetrated, but in the eastern Mediterranean, and always within sight of the foaming seas. The joy of life, a sense of the dignity of man, the eager desire for personal pre-eminence, the cheerfulness, curiosity, and love of adventure, which are characteristics of the Greek genius and were destined to make the fortunes of Europe, are to be found in Homer. Man was essentially proud and free, on happy terms with himself, with the world, and with Olympus. The gods were his friends and partners, very human, amusing men and women, not monstrous animals as in Egypt or India. The King was no eastern despot, but the first in an equal company of princes. Speech was free. Agamemnon, the King, was balanced by Thersites the demagogue.

The landscape of Greece, one of the loveliest in the world, conceals beneath its manifest seductions of line and colour a harsh discipline for man. In the temperate north the seasons melt into one another by insensible gradations, summer is not too hot, winter is not too cold, and the daily flow of human activities proceeds with little interruption through the year. In such climes rivers flow level, or nearly level, with their banks, and woods of well-grown timber clothe the rounded hills or are interspersed with the tillage and spreading pastures of the plain. Greece offers a complete contrast. Here a winter of piercing cold is sharply distinguished from a practically rainless summer, the heat of which is only tempered by the north-north-east winds which blow at that season. In place of rivers in our northern sense there are torrents rushing and brawling during the winter's rains, a silent bed of dry boulders under the long summer drought. Here and there, amid the tumbled mass of barren mountains, there is a small level plain of cultivated soil. But of forest timber there is little. It is a land of olives and tamarisks, of juniper trees and oleanders. The plane, the lime, and the oak are less abundant.

A land thus stinted is a perpetual invitation to plunder and piracy, to colonization and war. The Greek settlers, hibernating through the winter cold, but with the first spring flowers resuming their active life of open air discussion and hard agricultural or mechanical toil, felt the stress of a niggard world. The gaiety of the Greek scene, its sharp mountain outlines cut against a sky of azure, did nothing to soften the uphill struggle with the spectre of want. The frontier foray for sheep and goats, leading perhaps to a regular little summer campaign, was, in these early centuries, as common an incident as the raid of a pirate craft or the more lawful quest for wealth by the peaceful methods of trading. The quest of supplies by war or plunder was a necessary supplement to the tillage and pasturage of the community. It was not so much a crime as a part of state economy. Man must eat to live. If crops ran short, he must steal, fight, or emigrate.

Before any organized colonizing movement had begun (750 B.C. to 550 B.C.) the public life of the Greeks had assumed the form which has given it a permanent value in the education of man. The early settlers had lived in scattered villages, half-nomads, half agriculturalists; but by degrees convenience and defence pointed to concentration. Cities were built, on high, defensible crags, and at a distance from the shore, so that they might not be surprised by a pirate raid; and with a city there was developed a political consciousness of such rare power and intensity that the world has never been able to forget it. The Greek city state owes much to the favouring circumstances of climate and geography. Set in a girdle of hills it lived a life apart from its neighbours, developed its own institutions, and acquired a character so well marked that, despite all the common ties of language and religion, a Spartan, an Athenian, and a Theban could as little be confused as the Marseillais with the Parisian, or the Yorkshire tyke with the Somersetshire yokel.

The aloofness imposed by geography over against the neighbour on the other side of the hill was set off by a closeness of association among the citizens themselves for which we can find no parallel in the northern latitudes of Europe. The Greek citizen lived in the public eye. All day during the fine months he was out of doors, talking with his neighbours, acting as a juror, sitting in the theatre, or carrying on his employment. Never was there a society so favourable to the clash of intellects, the dissemination of scandal, or the development of political liberty and civic pride: never an audience more delighting in eloquence, more keen in criticism, more open to the persuasive arts of the great advocate, never a patriotism more happily tempered, or in its greater moments more passionate and entire. Jealousy and detraction flourished side by side with a degree of political idealism which has never been surpassed.

It is perhaps a consequence of this frank open-air existence that the Greeks escaped the paralyzing control of an organized priestcraft. At no time were they enslaved to a book or to a church, or embarrassed by the quarrels of civil with sacerdotal authorities. Neither the mysteries of Eleusis nor the priests of Delphi were able to crush the free curiosity or luxurious imagination of this quick-witted race. Superstition they had in abundance, some of it dark and primitive, but much of it lightly held and sublimated by the genius of poetry, for they found divinities everywhere, in sky and sea, stream and grove, as well as in the half-legendary figures of their distant past, and peopled Olympus with beings of like passions and appetites with themselves. Indeed, whatever seemed to them to be precious, august, or formidable was likely to receive divine honours—the snakes of Aesculapius, which were regarded by the invalid visitors to Epidaurus as sound ministers of health, no less than the divine Apollo, mediator between earth and heaven, or Aphrodite, that primitive goddess of love, who, long before the Greeks had touched the Aegean shores, had secured her empire over the hearts of Mediterranean men. But more particularly was devotion due to the tutelary god or goddess of the city itself.

Religion, then, entered into patriotism, but not to any great extent into politics. The great wars of ancient Greece were fought not upon religious but upon secular issues. It was not Athena who brought Athens her enemies, but the jealousy of an imperial and ambitious power felt by her rivals in trade and arms.

So in the miniature states of the Greek world there grew up an art and practice of secular politics which, despite social revolutions such as the abolition of slavery, and great changes of scale and power, has still a meaning for modern men. In that lively and mutable society forms of government were quickly made, altered, discarded. Every experiment was possible, every idea was open to discussion. In the comprehensive treatise on Politics in which Aristotle sums up the experience gained from the study of a hundred and fifty-eight Greek constitutions, the world has a manual of political wisdom which can never be obsolete. The roots of European political philosophy are to be found in the practice and speculation of this distant age.

Monarchy, aristocracy, plutocracy, and thereafter tyranny leading to democracy—such, broadly speaking, were the five successive stages in the political development of the Greek city states. A long catalogue, it will be urged, yet marked by one instructive omission. Despotism of the old Asiatic type, theocratic, hereditary and absolute, was absent. The typical Greek tyrant did not, like Napoleon afterwards, or like some Sicilian tyrants in ancient times, cleave his way to power by arms and violence. He came forward as the champion of the oppressed and as the enemy of aristocratic privilege. If he was a despot, he was also a demagogue who broke the crust of custom, promoted commerce and wider relations with foreign states and paved the way for democratic freedom. In the development of Athenian culture and liberty, Peisistratus the enlightened tyrant had his contribution to make as well as Solon, the wise legislator who preceded him, and Cleisthenes the founder of Athenian democracy, who rose to power when the absolutism of the Peisistratid family had done its work.

It was a great step forward in the rational ordering of human affairs when political decisions came to be taken by a majority vote after a peaceful discussion. This discovery, the root of all civilized political life, was made by the cities of Greece, and most notably by Athens, where the institutions of liberty were earliest and most fully developed. There are many points in Athenian democracy, such as the use of the lot, and the ostracism or banishment of prominent men, the popular law courts and the swift rotation of office and responsibility, which bring a smile to the lips of modern critics. How childish, they exclaim, how amateurish, how inconsistent with efficiency! Yet the more closely these things are examined, the more evident does it become that such was the necessary price of political freedom. Democracy was a lottery only made attractive by lavish opportunities of reward. The principle of equal opportunity so logically carried out in Athenian institutions appealed to the sense of justice which is inherent in human nature itself.

and made up for the sacrifice of primitive passion which is involved in the acceptance of majority rule.

To the general course of political development which had now been evolved Sparta offered a notable exception. Ever since their victory over the Messenians at the end of the seventh century the Spartans had been the foremost people in the Peloponnesus. No state enjoyed so high a reputation for the steadfastness of its temper, the simplicity of its living, or the antiquity and harmony of its constitution as this old-fashioned, unwalled city in the rich and secluded valley of the Eurotas. Here it would seem that a great alarm, probably connected with Helot revolts and Messenian risings, had converted a society once easy, luxurious, and artistic to the need of a grim and grinding military discipline founded on the entire abnegation of self. The Spartan citizen, living in the midst of mutinous subjects or hostile serfs, was trained from early childhood to the arts of war. Private luxury was forbidden, weakling children were exposed, even the girls were submitted to gymnastic exercises. The whole state was a military barrack governed on communal principles, and taking no account of private tastes and inclinations. A community ordered on so clear a plan evoked the enthusiasm of contemporary philosophers. Here was primitive and heroic virtue preserved and regulated. Here was a pattern of human character exempt from the weakness bred of liberty. But war is not the true end of human life, and being organized solely for war, Sparta had no contribution to make to the arts of peace. Nor was she apt for far-flung enterprise. The first military power in Greece was too keenly alive to her domestic perils eagerly to respond to the attractions of empire or to venture her famous hoplites in distant fields.

It was not, however, either in Sparta or in Athens, but rather in the brilliant necklace of Ionian cities, which had been strung along the coast of Asia Minor as a consequence of the great migration, that the true centre of Greek civilization was to be found in the seventh and sixth centuries before Christ. In art and philosophy, in trade and civilization, Miletus was a pioneer in that astounding development of the human faculties, speculative, artistic, and practical, which we recognize as distinctively Hellenic. At a time when the rough tribal invaders of the north were destroying the old Mycenaean civilization in the mainland of Greece, the Ionians of Asia Minor and the islands preserved

THE GREEK WORLD.

what was precious in the older culture, and assimilating also the customs of the nearer east, deriving a coinage from the Lydians and a system of astronomy from Babylon and Egypt, made rapid advances in the arts of peace.

The Greek colonial movement was distinguished by a feature which marks it off from the emigration of the present age. A Greek colony was an act of state, often prompted by the desire to rid the city of that part of its population which appeared to be redundant or likely to give trouble, and the colonists were sped on their way, not as individual fortune seekers, but as members of a daughter city and with the circumstance demanded by a solemn and public enterprise. The Delphic Oracle gave its sanction and encouragement to an undertaking which without the goodwill of Apollo or the information available to her priests might have seemed to err from rashness or impiety, and like the Vatican in later times, or the Concert of Europe, delimited the sphere of competing undertakings. Under such favouring circumstances bodies of Greek citizens were despatched to every quarter of the Mediterranean and Pontic coasts.

A string of colonies from Miletus tapped the rich corn lands of southern Russia and the spoils of the fur traders and gold miners of the interior. Cyrene was the key to north Africa, Marseilles to the markets of Gaul, a cluster of thriving colonies, Corinthian Syracuse, Rhodian Gela, Megarian Selinus to the limitless fertility of the Sicilian vales. By the middle of the sixth century the Mediterranean and Pontic coasts from the Ebro to the Dnieper were surrounded with a girdle of Greek cities.

For many centuries it was the habit of Europeans, or rather of that small section of European peoples who lived along the shores of the Mediterranean, to consider that they alone constituted the civilized world. Outside the sacred circle of Hellas they saw nothing but a penumbra of barbaric darkness. Very little was known of further Asia, either in antiquity, or until the voyages of Marco Polo the Venetian were published at the end of the thirteenth century. Even Alexander the Great did not suspect the existence of China. Vast tracts of desert separated the great orderly society of land-owning Chinese from the active mariners and traders of the Mediterranean basin. The two chief civilizations of the planet grew up in mutual ignorance. Dante, reflecting the common view of the geographers of the thirteenth century, places Jerusalem at the centre of the earth.

BOOKS WHICH MAY BE CONSULTED

M. Rostovtzeff : A History of the Ancient World. 2 vols. 1926-7.
Grote : A History of Greece. Condensed and edited by J. M. Mitchell and M. A. B. Caspari. 1907.
J. B. Bury : A History of Greece 1922.
A. E. Zimmern : The Greek Commonwealth. 1911.
G. Glotz : The Greek City. Tr. N. Mallinson. 1929.
Gilbert Murray : History of Ancient Greek Literature. 1897.
Gilbert Murray : Rise of the Greek Epic. 1924.
C. M. Bowra : Tradition and Design in the Iliad. 1930.
C. M. Bowra : Ancient Greek Literature. 1933.
Walter Leaf : Homer and History. 1915.
S. H. Butcher : Some Aspects of the Greek Genius. 1904.
E. Abbott : Hellenica. 1898.
E. Cavaignac : Histoire de l'Antiquité. 3 vols. 1913-9.

CHAPTER III

GREECE AND PERSIA

Lydia conquered by the Persians. The Carthaginian challenge. The Ionian revolt. The Persian War. Real significance of the Greek victory. Rise of the Athenian Empire. Pericles.

UNTIL the sixth century was half spent the Greek world had met no peril more formidable than its own internal dissensions. The dispersion of the Greek race had nowhere been seriously contested. Their settlements in Sicily and Magna Graecia, in Tripoli and in Egypt, had successfully survived the perils of youth. Even in Asia Minor, with its vast hinterland of barbaric peoples, the Ionian coast towns had been permitted a period of almost unmolested prosperity. On the sea, the Phoenicians, a Semitic people, long familiar with the southern routes of Europe, were compelled to admit a rival.

On land the Lydia of Alyattes and his son Croesus owned the fascination of a culture more refined than its own. So long as the Lydian kingdom survived, the hither parts of Asia Minor were probably more open to Greek influence than at any period previous to the conquests of Alexander. Greek travellers frequented Sardis, the Lydian capital. Greek oracles were appealed to and lavishly remunerated by the Lydian monarch. Perhaps if another half-century had been conceded to the kingdom of Croesus the Lydian, Asia Minor would have been largely hellenized. But there supervened one of those catastrophes which abound in the violent history of Asia. Suddenly (546 B.C.), to the surprise of the Greeks, the Lydian Croesus, long regarded as a miracle of wealth and authority, was overthrown and his capital stormed and conquered. The victor was Cyrus (Kurush) the Persian, whose vast empire, not long afterwards to be augmented by the conquest of Egypt, was built on the ruins of Assyrian power. With the disappearance of the Lydian buffer state the Greek world was brought face to face for the first time with an organized and aggressive oriental monarchy. For the next two hundred years the Persian menace was a governing factor in Greek politics. It was a rivalry between east and west, between despotism and liberty, between Iranian fire-worship

25

and the free and various play of Hellenic polytheism. To the generation of Greeks who experienced its opening phases the stakes appeared to be freedom, law, progress. The history of Herodotus, who was a youth during the great days when Hellas repelled the might of Darius the Persian and his son Xerxes, is full of the exaltation caused by the triumph of Athenian democracy over oriental barbarism.

For it so happens that when the clash came Athens had become, thanks to the reforms of Solon and Cleisthenes, a democratic state; and since she was at once the naval and intellectual capital of Hellas, and from her geographical position exposed to the first onset of the invader, it seemed to contemporaries that the force opposed to the legions of Asia was not so much the collective energies of Greece as the power released by the new-found liberties of Athens.

While the drama of the Persian War was proceeding in the east, the Greeks of Sicily were confronted by an oriental power long schooled in trade and commerce, and now embarked on a course of political expansion. The Phoenicians of Carthage were making rapid strides in the western Mediterranean. They were established on the coast of Spain, their influence was predominant in Sardinia, they were at once allied with the pirates of Etruria and in close communication with the Persian court. It is then no mere chance that a Carthaginian attack on the Greeks in Sicily should have coincided with a Persian invasion
480 B.C   of Greece. The glorious year of Thermopylae and Salamis in the east also witnessed the Carthaginian overthrow at the battle of Himera in Sicily. On each front the Greeks were assailed by an Asiatic people; in each case it was the Asiatic power which sustained defeat. Yet though Greece after the victory of Salamis was never subjected to a Persian occupation, nor Sicily after the battle of Himera left undisputed to the Carthaginians, there was no settlement in either sphere. The Persian War dragged on with intermissions until Persia was finally conquered by Alexander the Great. And not all the wealth and military power of the tyrants of Syracuse were able to sweep the Carthaginians out of western Sicily.

The Persian War arose out of the help afforded by Athens and Eretria to a revolt of the Ionian cities of Asia Minor against the satraps of Darius (521-485).

The opening phases of this famous struggle were big with a sense of impending calamity for Hellas. Darius stamped out the Ionian revolt with ruthless thoroughness. Miletus, birthplace of Thales, the parent of European philosophy, was stripped bare of its populace, its men slain, its women and children deported to Susa, and after Asia Minor had been thus cruelly tranquillized and Thrace and Macedonia reduced to the Persian obedience, a powerful armada proceeded eastward to effect the chastisement of Eretria and Athens.

Had Greece been united, the problem of repelling the invader might still have appeared grave and even desperate; but neither then nor at any subsequent time in her history were all the forces of Greece combined under a single leader, with undivided loyalty upon a common enterprise; and in that critical summer of 490 B.C. it fell to nine thousand Athenians only, aided by a small contingent from the little town of Plataea, to assail and beat the Persian army on the famous field of Marathon.

This surprising victory concluded the campaign. Finding Athens defended, the Persian fleet sailed for home, and ten years elapsed before Xerxes, the successor of Darius, was in a position to resume the attack. In that precious decade Athens, inspired by the rare insight of Themistocles, and aided by the discovery of silver at Laureion, fortified the Piraeus and strengthened her navy, so that when the blow fell in 480, she was among the cities of Greece as supreme at sea as was Sparta on land.

The new invasion was marked by every circumstance calculated to alarm the Greeks into comprehensive and concerted measures of defence. The vast Asiatic army, magnified by rumour to a host of five million men, drawn from forty-three races variously armed and accoutred, the bridge of boats across the Hellespont, the canal to pierce the peninsula of Athos— these formidable preparations announced perils transcending all former experience.[1] Yet even so, not all Greece was of one mind. A congress of thirty-one cities summoned to the Isthmus of Corinth was remarkable for the sparse representation of the north. Here some were hostile, others afraid to venture their future. Even Sparta was more concerned with the defence of

[1] The army could not have exceeded 150,500 combatants, 60,000 followers and 75,000 animals (Sir F. Maurice, *Journal of Hellenic Studies*, 1931).

her own position in the Peloponnesus than with measures to arrest the invader on the threshold of Hellas. The Pass of Thermopylae, the gateway into eastern Greece, was held not by an army but by a detachment whose valour and unavailing sacrifice are among the immortal memories of Europe.

When the last of the brave Spartans had paid the toll, the Persians marched into Attica without let or hindrance, for the main body of the Peloponnesians, instead of contesting their advance, were engaged in building a wall across the isthmus. It was then that the Athenians took one of the great resolutions in history. Unsheltered and unprotected on the landward side, with no assurance of Spartan help and with a very clear determination that they would not share the fate of Miletus, they decided to find their salvation on the sea. The population, save a small garrison left in the acropolis, was embarked, and while the old, the women, and the children, were distributed in the neighbouring islands, the valid men of Athens were with the fleet and eager to try conclusions with the enemy. A cowardly decision to retreat to the isthmus was overcome by the arts of Themistocles, the Athenian. To him it is due that the united navy of the Greek allies sailed out to challenge the Persians in the narrow straits between Salamis and the sea.

In this battle, in which two hundred Athenian triremes were supported by smaller but still substantial contingents from Sparta and other members of the Confederacy, the Persians, fighting under the eyes of the great King himself, experienced an irreparable disaster. But though Xerxes withdrew to Asia, his army, after a winter in Thessaly, renewed the offensive in 479. The issue was joined at Plataea. Again the Greeks attacked, the Spartans this time bearing the brunt of the battle, and again the orientals were defeated. Outgeneralled and outfought, their leader Mardonius slain, and their numbers depleted, the army of Asia evacuated Greece, and the great peril, which for more than ten years had hung over the country, was finally overpast. The later stages of the war were fought on the sea or on the soil of Asia.

Marathon, Salamis, Plataea have each been accounted among the world's decisive battles. Decisive indeed they were, but not in the accepted political sense. Had Darius won at Marathon or Xerxes at Plataea, it is difficult to believe that the free and distinctive life of the Greek cities would have suffered a final eclipse.

Susa was far away, and to govern Greece from Susa would have exceeded the resources of any state of the ancient world. The Persians had already seen the wisdom of conferring some form of liberty on the conquered Ionian Greeks, and what was politic in Asia Minor was far more politic in Europe. It may be assumed that the great King, if victorious, would not have been wanting in an obsequious band of Greek supporters. Darius would have restored the tyrant Hippias to the governance of Athens from which he had been ejected. Xerxes would have discovered Thessalian princes or Boeotian oligarchs amenable to his nod. A loose Persian suzerainty exercised through philo-Persian Greeks might have been compatible with the preservation of many of the essential liberties and institutions of Hellas.

But the real significance of the Greek victories in this great decade is to be found not so much in the field of politics as in the domain of spirit. A tiny people had defeated a great empire. Something spiritual had, by the help of the favouring gods, vanquished wealth, numbers, material strength. Insolence had been curbed; the pride of power had received a fall. The goddess Athena had protected her chosen people in the hour of need. The exaltation which ensued bred great designs and a body of achievement in literature and art so astonishing in its beauty, its variety, and the permanence of its human appeal, that of all the elements which have entered into the education of European man, this perhaps has done most for the liberation of thought and the refinement of taste.

The forty-seven years which succeeded the battle of Plataea are marked by the rise of the Athenian empire and by the opening phases of that great movement of the artistic imagination which has secured for Athens the undying gratitude of mankind. It was in this period that Aeschylus, who fought as a hoplite at Marathon, produced the " Persae " and afterwards (in 458) his famous trilogy the " Oresteia." It was now that the genius of Sophocles was first manifested on the Athenian stage. To the Athenians of that golden age everything must have seemed possible after Marathon and Salamis. The Greeks of the Aegean looked to the foremost naval power in Greece for protection, and allowed themselves to be combined in the Confederacy of Delos, which implied acceptance of Athenian leadership and monetary contributions to the support of the fleet. It is given to few victorious peoples to make moderate use of a brilliant fortune, and Athens cannot be acquitted of the charge of having in some directions overstrained her strength and in others exercised it to the oppression of her subject cities. An expedition to Egypt ended in inevitable failure, and the transference in 454 of the Confederate Treasury from Delos to Athens gave rise to the well-founded suspicion that the funds of the Confederacy would be spent on the embellishment of the metropolis. Still, with all deductions it is a brilliant page in the history of Greece. The Persians were again beaten by land and sea at the Eurymedon (468) and in 448 brought to the signature of peace. The acquisition of Thasos, an island rich in minerals, strengthened the financial basis of the Empire. To the islanders who grumbled at the tribute, to the prudent who challenged the expense, the directors of Athenian policy could reply that, popular or no, the Empire had at last realized its mission. It had made the coasts of the Aegean safe for the Greeks.

Moreover, the conduct of Athenian affairs had from 462 onwards fallen into the hands of a visionary of genius. Pericles was a democrat and an imperialist, and was therefore in full sympathy with the two main currents of political thought which prevailed in Athens at that time; but he appears to have had also what is a rarer gift—a clear-cut ideal for his state, not only in its political and economic aspect, but also in relation to human conduct and character and artistic achievement. He wanted the influence of Athens to be widespread, and so planted out Athenian settlers far and wide from the shores of the inhospitable Euxine to the vine-clad hills of southern Italy; but it was also part of his philosophy that the mother city should occupy a position of commanding pre-eminence from the splendour and beauty of her public monuments. In a moment of inspiration he determined to restore the temples of Athens and Eleusis which had been destroyed by the Persians and to make of this act of restoration a demonstration, not merely of Athenian, but of Hellenic magnificence. A great architect and a great sculptor were at hand to serve his ambition. The famous statue of Athena has long since been destroyed, but the sculptured frieze of Pheidias may be seen in the British Museum, and we may still admire the genius of Ictinus, who contrived the exquisite proportions of the Parthenon.

BOOKS WHICH MAY BE CONSULTED

G. B. Grundy : The Great Persian War. 1893.
R. W. Livingstone (ed.) : The Legacy of Greece. 1921.
Cambridge Ancient History, Vol. IV.
Herodotus. Tr. A. D. Godley. (Loeb Classical Library.) 4 vols. 1921-4.
G. Glotz and R. Cohen : Histoire Grecque. 1925.
E. Cavaignac : Histoire de l'Antiquité. 3 vols. 1913-19.

CHAPTER IV

ATHENS AND SPARTA

Causes of the Peloponnesian War. Athens and Sparta. First decade of the war. The Syracusan expedition. The Athenian defeat. Permanent effects. Lustre and fame of Athenian literature.

HARDLY had Athens established herself under the enlightened rule of Pericles as the capital of Hellenic civilization than she was drawn into a war which, though marked by initial success, ultimately led to great disasters and to the extinction of Athenian political influence in the Mediterranean world.

The Athenian empire, the brilliant growth of two generations, shared the fate of every polity which rises by the repression of local liberties. From within it was exposed to the discontents of unwilling subjects, from without to the enmity of jealous rivals. To the more conservative states of Greece there was something alarming in the spectacle of so much power placed at the disposal of a single city. Athens ruled the waves. Her ships convoyed the harvests of the Crimea and Cyprus, of Egypt and Cyrene; they could close and open the Dardanelles, they pressed forward into the waters of the western Mediterranean. The need of finding food for a constantly increasing foreign population enjoined a policy of expansion, and apprehensions such as Japan now inspires in Australia and New Zealand were entertained by the citizens of Sparta and Corinth when confronted by the marine empire of Periclean Athens, so recent in its origin, so swift in its development, so formidable in its possibilities of pressure or offence.

When a war atmosphere is once created the particular circumstances out of which war arises are relatively indifferent. A quarrel broke out between Dorian Corinth and her powerful colony Corcyra. Both parties appealed to Athens for assistance, and Athens found it in her interest to support Corcyra against a strong commercial rival for the markets of the west. A naval battle was fought at Sybota, off the coast of western Greece, in which Athenian ships were engaged on one side and Megarian ships on the other. Then the quarrel widened ominously. Megara

32

and Corinth were members of the Lacedaemonian Confederacy, of which Sparta was the honoured chief. Both were grievously affronted by Pericles. Megara was interdicted from the ports of the Athenian empire. Corinth was wounded through an attack on Potidaea, a tributary ally of Athens, but also a Corinthian colony which had refused, on the demand of Pericles, to dismiss its Corinthian magistrates or to raze its walls. The obstinacy with which Pericles persisted in these severe courses provided so remarkable a contrast to a record of peacefulness spread over fifteen years that strange theories were invented to account for it, as that the woman Aspasia was at the bottom of the Megarian decree, or that the great statesman plunged into war to divert the force of a private attack. It is more probable that his patience gave way, and that, deeming war to be inevitable, he chose his own occasion for precipitating the crisis.

It would be hardly possible to imagine a sharper contrast than that which distinguished the two leading states of Hellas who were now about to enter upon a twenty-seven years' war. A deliberate prudence was the mark of the Spartan, a vivacious and enterprising audacity of the Athenian character. The Spartan loved his home, the Athenian sought adventure far and wide in foreign lands. All the oligarchical parties in the Greek cities looked to conservative Sparta as their natural leader and the principal prop and support of the aristocratic cause. To the democrats, on the other hand, whether on the mainland of Greece or in the islands or in the distant cities of Thrace, Sicily, or Asia Minor, Athens stood out, not indeed as the champion of liberty, but as the exponent of equality at home; so that the war between Athens and Sparta, involving as it did not merely a conflict of interests and customs, but an opposition of political principle, in addition to its own evils, raised the temperature of local factions throughout Greece, and led to revolutions, some of which were shamed by great atrocities.

It might have been expected that a war between peoples so opposed to one another in every particular of character and temperament would in that age of costly battles have been sharp and short. But Sparta was a continental, Athens a maritime power. The Athenians had no army capable of mastering the Spartans on land, and Sparta, during the earlier years of the war, possessed no navy strong enough to try conclusions with the Athenians at sea. In effect Athens was an island. Her treasure, her foodstuffs, her shipbuilding materials came to her from overseas. A revenue-bearing Empire supported her democratic fleet and kept in repair her invulnerable fortifications. A power so equipped was in a strong position. The enemy might ravage the harvests of Attica, but he could neither starve Athens to submission nor compel her against her wish to accept battle on land. At the end of ten years of costly struggle no decisive advantage had been gained. The Athenians had fought a number of successful actions both by sea and land, mainly on the north-western coast of Greece; had established three bases on the Peloponnese, and captured a Spartan force on the island of Sphacteria. These were for Athens important advantages, but they were offset by severe trials, an annual invasion of Attica by a Spartan army, resulting, through the overcrowding of the city, in the great plague of 430, and, six years later, a severe defeat in the plains of Boeotia (battle of Delium) coupled with the loss of Amphipolis, an important and wealthy colony in Chalcidice. Sensible men like Nicias, a wealthy conservative slave-owner, had long seen the folly of a war out of which no material advantage could be gained; but since the death of Pericles in 429 B.C. the control of Athenian policy had fallen into the hands of a new type of politician, rougher, more violent, nearer to the common crowd than the wise aristocrat and philosopher who has given his name to an age of literary and artistic triumphs. To Cleon the leather merchant, and Hyperbolus the lampmaker, a popular war fought to a finish was the wine of life. So the war went on, waged somewhat reluctantly by Sparta, but as a matter of life and death by Corinth and Athens, until in an interval of good sense, and 421 B.C.   through the influence of Nicias, a peace was ultimately signed. But it was one thing to sign a peace and another to secure its observance. Before the ink was dry on the Treaty of Nicias it became clear that some of Sparta's most important allies, notably Corinth, Megara, and Boeotia, refused to be bound, and that Sparta either could not, or would not, hold them to the bond. Still, had the peace mind really prevailed in Athens it would have been an easy task to avoid giving fresh provocation to the principal enemy. But a new and dazzling star had risen above the political horizon in Athens. Alcibiades was young and beautiful, brilliant and persuasive. He had learned from his master Socrates to challenge accepted conventions, and a gay audacity of thought and speech, blending with the natural grace of his person, marked him out in the eyes of the Demos for high responsibilities. In 420 Alcibiades was chosen to be a general, and it is probably due to his restless spirit that Athens sought new allies in the Peloponnese and sent an army into the Argolis to attack Epidaurus, afterwards a famous health resort, but in this connection solely important as the friend of Sparta. The enterprise resulted in failure. The Athenian and Argive armies were routed at Mantinea, and Athens was compelled to look outside the Peloponnese for her next military adventure.

Prominent among the Greek cities in Sicily, and consequently the cause of fear and jealousy among its neighbours, was the Corinthian colony of Syracuse. To wound Corinth by the conquest and occupation of the greatest of her daughter cities was a thought which naturally occurred to the war party in Athens. What indeed might not follow from the acquisition of so great a prize? The mastery of Syracuse might lead to the control of Sicily, and this in turn to the capture of Carthage and a naval supremacy in the western Mediterranean. In 427, moved by the eloquence of Gorgias of Leontini, the Athenians sent an expedition to Syracuse; but the work was done with half a heart, and nothing came of it. Very different was the response given nine years later to the appeal of another Sicilian city. The glowing imagination of Alcibiades was now at play, and on the call of Segesta the greatest armada yet seen in Greek waters set sail from the Piraeus for the west.

There was nothing desperate in this design. An army of thirty thousand Athenians backed by a large fleet was quite capable of taking Syracuse by a prompt and resolute attack; but the Athenians made the fatal mistake of entrusting the chief command to Nicias, who was as inept in his prosecution of the campaign as he was averse from its inception. To his long catalogue of errors, more than to any other cause, the catastrophe which ensued must be ascribed.

There was another blunder which proved to be equally serious. On the eve of the expedition the public mind of Athens had been deeply stirred by the mutilation of certain ancient statues known as the Hermae. To whom, it was asked, was this foul impiety to be ascribed? Alcibiades sailed with the expedition. He had many enemies, he was known to be a freethinker, and during his absence the cloud of detraction thickened till it was resolved to recall him for trial.

Alcibiades, however, was not the man to allow himself to be led like a sheep to the slaughter. He left Sicily, not, however, for Athens but for Sparta, and during the next eight years devoted his great abilities to procuring the humiliation of his native city. It was on his advice that Sparta seized and fortified Decelea, a strong post on the soil of Attica, which enabled her to deprive Athens of the resources derived from the mines and farms of her territory. It was Alcibiades, again, who told the Spartans that if they wished to save Syracuse they must send a general to conduct the defence. His advice was taken, and the skill of Gylippus, assisted by the incompetence of Nicias, brought down upon Athens and upon the whole Athenian connection the greatest disaster which they sustained during the war.

The repercussion of this event was felt throughout the civilized world. Rebellion beginning in Chios spread among the island allies of Athens, but what was even more serious, Persia re-entered the war on the side of Sparta. The scales were now weighted more heavily than ever against the Athenians. While their silver mines were closed, a new source of supply was open to their adversaries. The Spartans had no hesitation in sacri-ficing the Ionian cities to their new allies, and, having discovered in the person of Lysander an admiral distinguished alike for military and political talent, were in a position to drive home their advantage. Meanwhile political and constitutional changes succeeded one another in Athens as the sky lowered or bright-ened. An oligarchy was tried and discarded, and it was under the rule of the demagogues, who declined two fair offers of peace, that Athens experienced that final overthrow of the fleet at Aegospotami which concluded the war. Deprived of her navy and her foreign possessions, and with her fortifications razed to the ground, the city of Pericles tasted the bitterness of frustrated hopes. The victors imposed a government to their liking, and an oligarchy was established in place of that desperate democratic faction which had played so high for victory and lost the stakes.

405 B.C.

The losses of Athens during this long and melancholy struggle were far in excess, having regard to the population of Attica at that time, of those experienced even by the most highly tried country in the great war of 1914-1918. The plague alone is esti-mated to have carried off seventeen thousand soldiers. Forty thousand men were lost in Sicily; and besides these outstanding catastrophes, every year brought its sad tale of casualties, " ships lost by tens and fives and more, and men that died by the thousand and ten thousand." Even if we make allowances for the fact that a considerable proportion of the rowers of the Athenian fleet may have been hired slaves and that there were subject ally contingents and mercenaries in the Athenian army, the casual- ties were formidable. The old aristocratic families, which had played so great a part in the Persian war were extinguished in this baser controversy, and aliens in increasing numbers were inscribed upon the civic rolls, so that, in the words of Isocrates, there was in Athens "a new people." When we reflect upon the brilliant contributions to art, letters, and philosophy which we owe to the Athenians of the fifth century B.C., the destruction through war of a large part of this gifted population must be accounted one of the grave and irretrievable calamities of history.

The needless tragedy of the Peloponnesian war has received more than its fair share of attention from the fact that it forms the theme of one of the world's great historical masterpieces. The genius of Thucydides has conferred immortality upon many a trifling detail attending the declension of Athenian power. The long series of disastrous errors by which the Athenians threw away their great initial advantage is recounted in terms of grave and moving eloquence by this Athenian, writing in exile, but raised above the exile's narrowness by a native austerity and greatness of soul. The story of the revolution in Corcyra, of the plague at Athens in the second year of the war, of the capture of Sphacteria, and of the Syracusan expedition, and the speeches with which the moral issues underlying the conflict are brought before the reader's mind, give to the pages of Thucydides the colour of a tragic drama. Yet in reality it is not the ruin of Athens in the Peloponnesian War which has been important for mankind, but its survival; not its political failures, but its in- tellectual and artistic triumphs. While the deathly struggle with Sparta was proceeding, Socrates, the stonecutter, was challeng- ing the accepted conventions of mankind, and laying the basis of moral and metaphysical science. It was during this same period of agonizing strain that Athenian audiences were crowd- ing to the open-air theatre of Dionysus to delight in the ex- quisite poetry of Euripides, the rationalist, or the brilliant wit of Aristophanes, the critic of rationalism, demagogy, and jingoism. It was in the first year of the struggle that Euripides produced the Medea, in the second that Herodotus completed his History, and, while no less than fourteen out of the twenty-seven years of the war are similarly memorable in the annals of the stage, it has been noted that the two blackest moments were marked each by the production of plays which still preserve their freshness and brilliance for the world. In 413, when the Spartans fortified Decelea and the Athenians were disastrously beaten in a great naval action in the harbour of Syracuse, Euripides produced the Iphigenia in Tauris and the Electra. The fatal year of Aegospotami (405) was similarly distinguished. It is the year of the Bacchae, the beautiful swan song of Euripides, and of the Frogs, perhaps the most delightful of ancient comedies.

The services of Athens to the education of Hellas were recognized and requited. When her fleet had been destroyed at Aegospotami at the end of a long and bitter war, Sparta might have applied to Athens the same terrible penalty which, in a spasm of passionate wrath, Athens had meted out to the little island of Melos. She might have razed the city to the ground, she might have slaughtered or enslaved its inhabitants. In the fierce hatred inspired by Athenian tyranny these cruelties would have been popular and were, in fact, recommended; but Athens was saved by the respect which even Sparta was compelled to feel for the brightest ornament of Hellenic civilization. The city was spared in consideration of her virtues, and not on one occasion only. Seventy years later, when Alexander of Macedon had destroyed Thebes, saving only the house of Pindar, and Athens, which had designed to send help to the Thebans, was exposed to his attack, the same sentiment of homage to the shrine of so much genius interposed its mediation—

> and the repeated air
> Of sad Electra's poet had the power
> To save the Athenian walls from ruin bare.

BOOKS WHICH MAY BE CONSULTED

Thucydides. *Tr.* Crawley. (Everyman's Library.) 1910.

E. Abbott : Pericles and the Golden Age of Athens. 1891.

Grote : A History of Greece.

J. B. Bury : A History of Greece. 1922.

A. E. Zimmern : The Greek Commonwealth. 1911.

Cambridge Ancient History, Vol. V.

B. W. Henderson : The Great War between Athens and Sparta. 1927.

CHAPTER V

GREECE AND MACEDON

Disunion of Greece. Macedon. Philip II. Alexander. The hellenistic age. Religion. Philosophy. The Epigoni. Political legacies of the Macedonian age. Empire worship. Bureaucracy. The divisions of Greece are the opportunity of Rome. Character of the Greeks. Hellenic influences on Christianity.

THE fourth century, which opens with the condemnation and death of Socrates (399 B.C.), is chiefly memorable as the great age of Greek prose writing, and for the rise and spread of the Macedonian empire. The accusation preferred against Socrates, that he did not believe in the gods recognized by the city, that he introduced strange supernatural beings, and that he corrupted the youth, marks the honest fears inspired in vulgar minds by the application of free, logical questioning to the loyalties, conventions, and traditions of a people. For, indeed, Greece was moving swiftly into a new intellectual climate, in which the individual counted for more, and the city for less, and old inhibitions of custom and religion were fast breaking down. Socrates, who taught that life was an art and knowledge the key to it, was behind these changes, and was condemned to drink the cup of death; but it is idle to suppose that the influence of a great liberating mind can be stayed by persecution. The glory of Socrates was enhanced by the tragedy of his end. He was revered as a saint of rationalism and virtue; and the beautiful fabric of the Platonic philosophy is the homage of a pupil to a master, and an imperishable monument to his fame.

Hellenic politics during the sixty-six years which divided the Spartan conquest of Athens from the Macedonian conquest of Greece were marked by a continuation, with some aggravations, of the old evils of the Peloponnesian War. Factions were as furious, fighting was as fierce, but mercenary troops tended to replace citizen levies. So far from profiting from the lessons of the past, Sparta repeated all the faults which had been charged against Athens during her period of domination, with none of her redeeming graces. The old ideal of Panhellenic unity in

opposition to Persia seems to have survived chiefly in the orations of the wise Isocrates. All parties were willing to help themselves from the Persian till and to move at the Persian behest.
Xenophon, a pupil of Socrates and an accomplished gentleman,
thought it no shame to serve with a band of Spartan mercenaries under the Persian Cyrus and afterwards even to fight with
a Spartan army against Athens, the nursing mother of his mind.
When Sparta was opposed to Persia, Athens was Persia's friend,
and an Athenian admiral, commanding a Persian fleet, and
aided by Persian funds, defeated the Spartans at sea and rebuilt
the fortifications of his city. When, on the other hand, Sparta
made friends with Persia, and even went so far as solemnly to
betray to her the interests of the Ionian Greeks (Peace of Antal-
cidas, 387), the attitude of Athens was correspondingly reversed.
The spirit of the soldier of fortune, snatching at luck, wherever
it might be found, dominated the scene.

Isocrates is probably right when he claims that the curse of
Hellenic politics at this time was the desire for empire. Athens,
Sparta, Thebes, Phocis, all in turn, strove for supremacy, and
as each state mounted on the crest of fortune, it was pulled back
into the trough by its jealous rivals. Even Epaminondas of
420?-362 Thebes, the ablest and the most disinterested soldier of his age,
B.C. could not see beyond Boeotia, and was incapable of great
political combinations.

The solution of the Greek question came from an unsuspected
quarter. To the north of Thessaly, in the coastlands round the
Thermaic gulf, there was established a Greek people, rougher
and less civilized than the inhabitants of Athens or Corinth, and
regarded by the southern Greeks much as a Parisian views a
provincial from Brittany or Languedoc. These were the Macedonians, deep drinkers, lusty fighters, passionate in pursuit of
the bear and the wolf through the forests and glens of their
mountain home, and still living in the Homeric stage of civilization, of whom not much that is important can be related until
Philip of the royal house, returning at the age of twenty-four
from Thebes, where he had learned the art of war from Epaminondas, made himself master of his native country. In the
whole range of European history few statesmen have been more
effective than this strenuous clear-sighted man (359-336). Macedonia at the time of his accession was poor, but became, through
the exploitation of the gold-mines of Mt. Pangaeus, the richest

state in Europe. Out of this country, which was scarcely more than a geographical expression (for the wild Illyrian hillmen, though nominally vassals of the crown, were as little congenial to the lowland Greeks as were the highland rievers of the seventeenth century to the farmers in the vales of Perth or Stirling), Philip made a nation and an army—a nation wholesomely compounded, and an army at once national in spirit and professional in aim, and moreover, in its combination of the cavalry with the infantry arm and of light with heavy troops, superior to any force which the states of Hellas could put into the field. The Macedonian phalanx changed the history of the world. It was the creation of Philip. Loyal to their punctual paymaster, the spearmen of Macedonia marched into action in open array and held the enemy while the cavalry charged in upon the wings in wedgelike squadrons and decided the issue.

What would be the attitude of the Greek states towards this new half-barbarian power in the north? Philip was anxious to be friendly. Despite his rough animal nature he reckoned himself to be a Greek, set a value on culture and knowledge (engaging Aristotle of Stagira, the son of a Macedonian court doctor, as tutor to his son), and desired to be accepted as suzerain of a Greek confederacy. A true realist comparing his resources with those of the Greek cities would have advised them to seek his goodwill. Even contemporaries asked whether a captain had not now arisen who could lead the Greeks against Persia, and provide for their hungry and redundant numbers new fields for colonial settlement in Asia Minor. Athens certainly had much to gain from a firm understanding with the master of Macedonia and Thessaly and the conqueror of Thrace: but at this juncture of her history Athenian policy was swayed by an orator who saw in the growing power of the Macedonians a menace to the traditional liberties of Hellas, which must be resisted to the death. The speeches of Demosthenes rank among the classics of political liberty, and cannot even now be read without emotion: but they led only to the bloodstained field of Chaeronea. Here Philip, defeating the joint army of Thebes *338 B.C.* and Athens, made himself by that one blow master of Greece. Two years later the conqueror fell by the hand of an assassin. At a synod of Greek cities at Corinth he had announced his intention of making war upon Persia on behalf of Greece and the gods, of liberating the Greek cities in Asia Minor, and of punishing the barbarians for acts of sacrilege committed in the reign of Xerxes; and it was on the eve of his departure on this vast enterprise that the founder of Macedonia met his end.

Alexander, his son by the violent Olympias, succeeded to his throne and vast ambitions. In a short reign of thirteen years this wonderful young man reasserted the Macedonian authority in Hellas and Thrace, levelled Thebes to the ground, conquered, with his small, mobile, and most effective army, Asia Minor, Syria, Egypt, and Persia, and marched his Macedonian veterans over the Khyber Pass into the plains of India. No military career, not even that of his imitator Napoleon, has exercised a wider influence on history, opening out as it did the whole of hither Asia to Hellenic speech and culture, and bringing to the west a flood of new facts relating to oriental lands and peoples, which is only equalled by those later additions to knowledge which Europe owes to the Crusades. Moreover, it must be recollected that Alexander embarked upon his enterprise as the elected generalissimo of Greece. Steeped in Greek legends and literature, believing himself to be sprung from Achilles, the fair young Macedonian descended upon Asia as the successor of the heroes who fought against Troy; but if he came as the missionary of Hellas, crowning the statue of Achilles at Troy and founding a temple of Zeus at Sardis, he was a missionary untouched by fanaticism. Despite the advice of Aristotle he refused to regard the orientals as an inferior race, nor did he proscribe their religious beliefs. A wise toleration, social, religious, political, informed the government of his conquered provinces. The great landowning nobles of Persia won from him the sympathy and respect which the spectacle of a gentleman and a sportsman never fails to evoke in the hearty nature of the open-air man. While he lost nothing of his conviction of Hellenic excellence, founding, as it is said, seventy Greek cities, and carrying the Iliad as the constant companion of his travels, he wedded his Macedonian paladins to the heiresses of Asia, himself married a Persian princess, and assumed the state of an oriental monarch. In idea his empire was coterminous with the world and founded on the doctrine of the equality of man, a universal society designed to conform to a common standard and subjected to a sovereign who, as the supreme benefactor of mankind, was rightly accorded divine honours, in fine a Holy Greek Empire foreshadowing the Holy Roman Empire

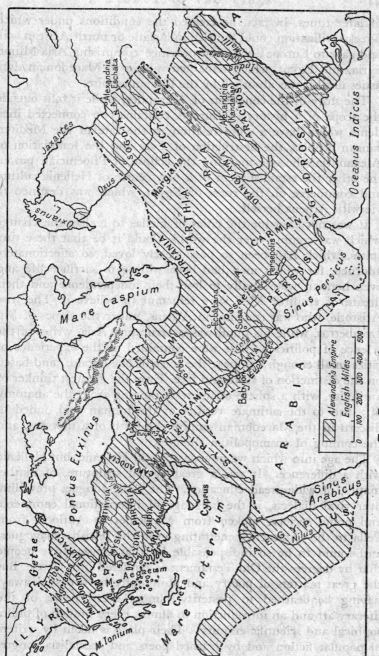

THE EMPIRE OF ALEXANDER THE GREAT.

of later times. In fact, he created the conditions under which Greek civilization could flourish in Asiatic or north African soil, and gave to Europe a vast new province, comprising Asia Minor, Syria, and Egypt, which remained subject to Macedonian dynasties until it was absorbed by the Roman empire.

The story of the conquests of Alexander, while it falls outside the scope of a history of Europe, contains two connected incidents which have a close relation to the fate of the Mediterranean peoples, the destruction of Tyre and the foundation of Alexandria, the one marking the eclipse of Phoenician power, the other the establishment of a new centre of Hellenic culture and commerce on the coast of Egypt, which was destined to vie with Athens herself.

It was not easy for the cities of Hellas to realize the change which was coming over the world. Could it be that these tiny states, which had been so passionately loved, so affectionately adorned, for which men had been willing to sacrifice life and even honour, were finally to lose their independence and their dream of empire? Men were reluctant to believe it. The wise Aristotle, who was teaching in Athens, under the slopes of Mt. Lycabettus, while his pupil was overrunning Asia, writes of the science of politics as if it were contained in the experience of cities small enough " to hear the voice of óne herald," and based on the distinction of slave and free. Even the greatest thinker of antiquity, with a sphere of interests ranging from the anatomy of a fish to the ultimate verities of the human soul, failed to discern in the Macedonian empire the birth of a new era, and the coming of cosmopolitan thought.

384-22 B.C.

The age into which we now pass is still Hellenic, but Hellenic with a difference. It was a great age of sculpture, of mathematics, of widespread education. The Attic tongue, prevailing over rival dialects, is the language of international commerce and polite society, spoken from Marseilles to Antioch, from Pella to the Cataracts, penetrating even the Jewish synagogues, and found to be so indispensable by that conservative people that by degrees the Old Testament is rendered into Greek. But the great masters of poetry and philosophy have passed away, having bequeathed to posterity almost every *genre* of the literary art and an introduction to almost every branch of philosophical and scientific enquiry. Their place is taken by writers of popular fiction and by learned poets and specialists congregating where great libraries are to be found and a government capable of protecting the studious from piracy and the disturbance of war. Under the rule of the Ptolemies and Attalids such libraries were founded at Alexandria and Pergamum, the rival capitals of paper and parchment.

Another feature of this age which is called Hellenistic is that, without being fanatical, men and women are feeling everywhere for religion. It is the property of polytheism to be tolerant, and while the Greeks had preferences in the matter of gods and goddesses, they practised no exclusions. As the old Olympian divinities lost their appeal, new worships and beliefs surged in from the religious east: astrology, magic, the mystery religions with their rites of initiation and purification, the imposing and popular cult, proximately derived from Egypt, of Serapis and Isis. More particularly significant was the worship of Isis, for two centuries the Holy Mother of the Mediterranean world. Isis " all-seeing and all-powerful, the star of the sea, the diadem of life, the law giver and saviour," was the woman's goddess. She was figured as a young matron, crowned with the blue lotus or the crescent moon, bearing the infant Horus in her arms. Not seldom were the statues of Isis made afterwards to serve as images of the Madonna.

For the higher minds there were the religious philosophies of Zeno and Epicurus. In 311 Zeno, a Phoenician from Cyprus, came to Athens and took up the teaching of philosophy in the painted portico or Stoa. He preached the doctrine of a World State ruled by a Supreme Power, all-wise and all-good, of equality and human brotherhood, of conscience and duty, of harmony with the divine purpose only to be obtained through wisdom and virtue, and of an inner peace proof against the outward agitations of fate to be found in a retreat within the fortress of the soul. Little remains of the original writings of this noble thinker, but the hymn of Cleanthes (rendered into English prose by Walter Pater in *Plato and the Platonists*), the Meditations of Marcus Aurelius and the singularly beautiful body of moral teaching which survives in the works of Epictetus, attest the wide and prolonged influence of Stoicism over the best minds and characters of the Pagan world in its decline. Epicurus was the philosopher of happiness, as Zeno of duty.

In the field of politics the Hellenistic period is distinguished by a difference of scale from the centuries which preceded it.

Large kingdoms, vast cities, greater ships and engines of war, imposing private fortunes, are the marks of the new age. The Greek world waxes prosperous on the pillage of the east and the opening of new markets, despite the fact that the sea is infested by pirates, and that few years pass without fighting in some part or other of the Macedonian empire. War, infanticide, and perhaps even malaria take their toll. The true Greek population steadily dwindles, and the cities of Hellas in the first century must have been largely filled by Greek-speaking aliens.

Alexander left no will, and the prize of the Macedonian empire fell to be disputed by his marshals. The tie of race counted for nothing with these able and ambitious adventurers: and the disappearance of the great captain is followed by a long series of wars between Egypt and Syria, and Egypt and Macedonia, until a new power enters the eastern scene, and the vast estate which the Macedonians had squandered in their quarrels was taken over and administered by Rome. Yet, despite the grave drawback of their civil dissensions, the Macedonian dynasts conferred upon European civilization two great services, for the absence of which the world today would be immeasurably the poorer. For a century and a half they defended the fabric of Greek civilization from the Illyrians and Thracians, from the Parthians in the east, and from the pressure of the hungry and savage denizens of the fens and forests of central Europe. Their armour was sometimes pierced: their defence was not always loyal. They had to retreat from India. The Gauls or Galati penetrated to Delphi, crossed into Asia Minor, and at one time threatened to plunge that flourishing region into chaos. Yet in the end the power of these formidable barbarians was checked and confined within territorial limits by princes of the Macedonian house. The Gauls were beaten in Europe by Antigonus Gonatas, "the second founder of Macedonia," and in Asia by Attalus of Pergamum. It is easy to see that the Galatians, to whom St. Paul writes his Epistle, had long been fitted into the fabric of hellenistic society.

318-242
B.C.

Within the irregular frontier which they thus guarded the descendants of Alexander upheld, and often promoted vigorously, the interests of Greek civilization. The Ptolemies, who established themselves in Egypt, if they failed to hellenize the country or even seriously to mitigate the violent superstitions of its native inhabitants, developed in the royal quarter of Alexandria a centre of learning and taste which has exercised a critical influence on the progress of Europe.

Here it was that the masterpieces of Greek thought and poetry were collected and stored in a great library, copied by slaves, and annotated by scholars; here that the Old Testament was translated from Hebrew into Greek, the text of Homer fixed, and the love-story and the pastoral added to the categories of western literature. Here, finally, was born a mystical philosophy founded on the writings of Plato, which has exercised a profound influence on the theology of the Christian Church.

Nor was the vast Asiatic empire which Seleucus and his descendants ruled from the great pleasure city of Antioch to be regarded otherwise than as part of a world in which culture and Greek were synonymous terms. If there was no centre in this so-called Syrian kingdom so predominant in science and letters as Alexandria, there was no part of Egypt so thoroughly hellenized as Syria. The delicate lyrics of Meleager and the simple eloquence of the synoptic gospels attest the vitality of the Greek language in a land where the speech of the common folk was Aramaic.

The Macedonian sovereigns gave to the world a new principle of authority, which was one of the most important of the means of binding the Roman Empire together in the first two centuries of its existence. Alexander and his descendants claimed and received the worship due to divinity. Since they could find no place in the constitution of the Greek city state, they entered with general acclamation the Greek Pantheon. Where better than in worship could a force be found to bind together a heterogeneous kingdom and to give sanctity and legitimacy to a usurping rule? The idea of a universal state appealed to the philosophers, the worship of the monarch excited and satisfied the mob.

Another element important to the future governance of Europe may be traced back to Macedonian times. Statistics and bureaucracy were familiar in Egypt. In this archaic civilization exact knowledge, more particularly with regard to revenue, had long been regarded as a perquisite of government. Here was a regular and minute administration depending on an army of scribes and a mountain of documents. The lessons to be derived from such a spectacle were not lost upon the conquerors of Egypt. If the Romans took their literature from Greece, they borrowed the civil service of their Empire from the valley of the Nile.

It might perhaps have been expected that the Antigonids of Macedonia, whose state proved to be so useful a protection against the barbarians of the north, would have been able to count upon the support and sympathy of the Greek cities. This was not to be. There was no political sentiment deeper in the Greek mind than aversion from monarchy, and Macedon was a monarchical state. Yet though the underlying sentiment of Greece, too often stimulated by Egyptian gold, was anti-Macedonian, the Greeks were at no time prepared with a united mind to resist their suzerain. Athens, among whose democratic leaders the spirit of Demosthenes burned brightly, gave up the struggle just when Achaia and Aetolia were prepared to take it up. The civic attachments, jealousies, and passions, which were at once the spiritual force and political weakness of Hellas, continued to the end. The honourable expedient of federation was tried by the Achaeans, and, in a less hopeful form, by the bandit villages of Aetolia. But federation in any full sense involved sacrifices which no member of a Greek League was prepared to make. The Achaean League, which fought Antigonus and his successor Demetrius II (251-229), was itself the object of a destructive attack by Cleomenes III of Sparta, and neither the brilliance of its leaders nor the value of the political principle upon which it was founded won for it the allegiance of a united country or brought to its counsels the wider vision. So Greece, fretting for home rule, but not sufficiently united within itself effectually to throw off the light yoke of Macedonia, waited for a deliverer, and hailed with expectation and delight the growing influence of Rome.

The peoples who described themselves as Hellenes were quick-witted, hardy, and frugal, and, as Herodotus observed, marked off from the barbarians around them as more intelligent and more emancipated from silly nonsense; but they lived in an insecure world. The barriers against want, plague, war, and revolution were frail and easily overthrown. At any moment plenty might give way to starvation, peace to war. Merely to keep alive required wit and energy. In such a society some virtues which we find easy were very difficult. The Greeks, though an extraordinary people, were not perfect. They exposed their new-born infants. Some of them tortured slaves. Many practised, without

adverse comment, vices which excite our abhorrence. Their religion, which was unfettered by a sacred book, was compatible
with the belief in magic and with a luxuriant growth of primitive
and violent superstitions. A strange callousness to suffering seems
to have been accepted as a necessary, if lamentable, part of the
human lot. Great as was their wealth in political ideas, they
lacked the power of combination, so that the history of their
cities is a long tale of faction, which was apt to degenerate into
that "competition in perfecting the fine art of conspiracies and
atrocities" of which Thucydides writes in his account of the
sedition in Corcyra. They loved freedom, but from time to time,
as in the famous case of Socrates, took fright for the safety of
their cherished conventions and persecuted an honest thinker to
the death.

Yet almost everything which is to be valued in modern civilization is owing to the ancient culture of that part of the Mediterranean world which spoke and thought in Greek—our science
and philosophy, our epic and drama and lyrical poetry, our
standards in sculpture and architecture, our medicine and mathematics, our theory of humane education, the form of our Christian theology, and that ideal of the rule of law which distinguishes western from Chinese civilization. The Greeks loved
beauty and pursued reason. They lived close to nature. Their
taste in art was austere and simple. They thought greatly about
great things. The profound question of the ultimate constitution
of matter, which vexes the minds of modern physicists, was raised
as early as the sixth century B.C. by Thales of Miletus (c. 585), who
regarded the four elements as states of one substance. Our theory
of numbers is to be traced to Pythagoras, our moral science to
Socrates, our biology to Aristotle. The spirit of free enquiry,
which we sometimes describe as rationalism because it leads men
to search by the light of reason for natural causes rather than to
acquiesce in popular superstitions, was distinctively Greek. The
curiosity of the Greeks was lively and universal. No problem
suggested by the contemplation of the mysterious universe was
too remote, too sacred, or too abstruse, to abash their refreshing
audacity. Centuries before Copernicus discovered the heliocen-
tric theory a Greek thinker had inferred that the earth was a
globular body revolving round the sun, and had reached conclusions, differing little from the reality, as to its exact girth.

It has sometimes been contended that while the science and

literature of the modern world derive from the Greeks, the religion of Europe is in its origin essentially Jewish. This states the contrast too strongly. Greece has exercised a profound influence on religion no less than on science and literature. We know little of the life of Jesus. His disciples were not chiefly concerned to record it. When at last, more than a generation after the Crucifixion, Mark took up his pen to write, it was not that he might trace the life course of the Master and Prophet, who had filled his soul with a new enchantment, but that he might reveal Him from the story of the Passion and the Resurrection, and from the recital of His many proofs of miraculous power, as a divine and predestined figure, as the Messiah foretold in Jewish Scriptures, who was come to judge the world and to call sinners to repentance. We cannot, therefore, follow the development of Christ's teaching in chronological order, or reconstruct His life for any given year, month, week, or day. Save for the detailed story of the Passion, we are much at a loss for chronological guidance.

Precious fragments of ethical teaching are contained in the Gospels, and in scattered sayings, some of which have only recently been recovered from a buried library in Egypt; but the spread of Christianity in the Apostolic age was not so much due to the conviction that only the Christian life was perfect as to the belief that in Christ the divine power was manifested. The disciples did not ask their hearers to imitate Christ, but to accept His Messianic authority. They represented Him as healing the sick, casting out devils, working miracles, and preaching repentance, believing in common with many of their generation that the end of the world was at hand and that Jesus was the anointed one, the Man from Heaven, who was sent to recall mankind to righteousness before the Last and terrible Day.

The early disciples did not, then, dream of a permanent universal Church. For them the end of the world was near at hand, the number of the elect necessarily small. They were content to preach the message of their Master in the little Jewish synagogues of Palestine.

Paul of Tarsus, who brought Christianity to the Gentiles, was a Jew of the Dispersion. He belonged to a society which spoke and thought in Greek. The Epistles to the Colossians and Ephesians clearly show that he was acquainted, as indeed could hardly fail to be the case, with the allegories and mysteries of the Greek religion and that he was influenced by them; and since his message was addressed, not to the Jews of Palestine, but to the Gentiles who derived their culture from Greece, the fact that he was a member of two worlds, of the narrow Jewish as of the wider Hellenic brotherhood, served to commend his message to the Greek-speaking city populations of the west. If he never saw Jesus in the flesh, this meant the less for him since in a sudden flash, after persecuting Christians with Jewish fanaticism, he had reached the conviction that the spirit of Christ had entered into possession of his own soul. This burning faith gave wings to his eloquence. Wherever he travelled in his missionary journeys he made converts and established little communities of Christian men and women bound together by ties of worship, self-surrender, and affection. Passing from Asia into Europe, he preached at Salonika, at Athens, at Corinth, and in Rome, everywhere creating intense spiritual excitement, both by his free treatment of the Jewish Law and by the sharp contrast he presented to the current beliefs of pagan society. Under the powerful impulsion of his fervent genius a small Judaic sect, spurned by the priests and scribes of Jerusalem, became a religion so large and human in its appeal that no European race, however rude and brutal, has altogether escaped its spiritual influence.

By the second century the chief seaport towns of the Mediterranean basin, and many upland towns also, contained little groups of Christians, who were now, and even as early as A.D. 65, when Nero singled them out for persecution in Rome, recognized to be distinct from the Jews, with whom they were at first commonly confounded.

With the Jews, however, they had in common a prophetical and exclusive religion. They lived a life apart, based on principles of belief and conduct, upon which they refused to compromise. "We," wrote Justin Martyr, "who formerly rejoiced in uncleanness of life and now love only chastity; who also used magic arts and have now dedicated ourselves to the good and unbegotten God; we who loved resources of money and possessions more than anything, and now actually share what we have and give to everyone who is in need; we who hated one another and killed one another and would not eat with those of another race, and now since the manifestation of Christ have a common life, and pray for our enemies and try to win over those who hate us without just cause." But while the Christians were

d. *c.* A.D. *165*

thus sharply severed from the pagan world it was a source of strength to them that they never regarded their religion as a reversal of human history, but rather as its divinely ordained fulfilment. Christian apologists were equally willing to find authority for their religion in the Jewish Scriptures, in Greek philosophy, and in the prophecies of the Sibyl. It was one of the secrets of the success of the Christian Church that, while it offered salvation to the outcasts of the world, it did not shrink from challenging the wise upon their own ground, nor hesitate to call to its aid the speculations of the ancients. Nothing certain is known of the origin of the Fourth Gospel or of the circumstances in which, it was written. The better opinion appears to be that it was composed by John the Presbyter in Ephesus early in the second century. But whether this be so or not, there is little doubt that the author of this wonderful book, without which the substance of Christian belief would be far other than it is, was influenced by St. Paul and perhaps also by the doctrine of Philo of Alexandria, a learned Jew who evolved from the philosophy of Plato a warrant for the truths of his inherited faith. Philo was the first of a long line of theologians and philosophers who believed that Plato was divinely inspired, and addressed themselves to the congenial task of harmonizing the exalted teaching of the Athenian thinker with the Jewish or Christian message. For nearly thirteen centuries the theology of the Christian Church in the west was moulded by the thought of Plato. There followed an age of intellectual disturbance. The metaphysical and physical writings of Aristotle were restored through the Arabians of Spain. Christian theology was confronted by pagan science, Christian idealism by a philosophy based on experience. There was a moment of anxiety, of free thinking on fundamentals, when even doctors in the Paris University dallied with Pantheism and challenged the orthodox view of the creation of the world. Albert the Great and Thomas Aquinas, two great Dominican doctors, restored the situation by harnessing the new Aristotle to the chariot of the Catholic Church. The teaching of Christ was a sublime and original contribution to the moral improvement of mankind. But it is doubtful whether the Christian religion would have made the conquest of Europe had it not been of all oriental religions the most Greek and the most nearly akin alike to the best thought of the Greek philosophers and to those popular notions of purgatory and puri-

b. 20
B.C. ?

fication, of eternal bliss and eternal torment, of a divine mediator between God and man, and of some sacramental ceremony whereby the sinner might be cleansed of his sin and assured of his salvation hereafter, which were already current among the Greeks, and the basis of solemn religious observance over that wide tract of the Mediterranean basin in which Greek civilization prevailed.

BOOKS WHICH MAY BE CONSULTED

Cambridge Ancient History, Vols. VI. and VII.

D. G. Hogarth : Philip and Alexander of Macedon. 1897.

W. W. Tarn : Hellenistic Civilisation. 1930.

E. Bevan : The House of Seleucus. 1902.

Gilbert Murray : Four Stages in Greek Religion. 1912.

W. S. Ferguson : Greek Imperialism. 1913.

A. E. Taylor : Plato. 1929.

A. E. Taylor : Aristotle. 1919.

C. Bailey : Epicurus. 1926.

W. S. Ferguson : Hellenistic Athens. 1911.

B. Jowett : The Dialogues of Plato. 5 vols. 1892.

J. A. Smith and W. D. Ross : The Works of Aristotle translated into English. 1908-31.

E. Barker : The Political Thought of Plato and Aristotle. 1906.

G. Glotz : Ancient Greece at Work. 1926.

A. D. Nock : Conversion, the Old and New in Religion from Alexander the Great to Augustine of Hippo. 1933.

CHAPTER VI

ROME AND CARTHAGE

Rise of the Roman Republic. Character of its legal and constitutional growth. The Roman conquest of Italy. Cisalpine Gaul and Carthage. Romans and Etruscans. The Punic Wars and conquest of Cisalpine Gaul. Hannibal. P. Cornelius Scipio. Destruction of Carthage. Roman prestige. Growing influence of Rome in the east. Subjection of Macedonia and Greece. Absence of a predetermined plan of conquest.

GREECE looks to the rising, Italy to the setting sun. On the west of the Italian peninsula are wide and fertile plains, ample streams, and sheltered ports. On the east the stiff spine of the Apennines runs close to an inhospitable coast for the greater part of its course, so that, save for the two good Apulian harbours of Brindisi and Otranto, there is little shelter for the mariner against the storms of the Adriatic. Thus a sharp difference established itself between the centre and south of the Italian peninsula. While the southern littoral became the scene of a brilliant Greek culture, and of an immigration which has left a still discernible mark upon the character and appearance of the south Italian people, the Latin heart of the country was sheltered from these alien influences. Between Hellas and the yellow waters of the Tiber there was interposed, apart from the Adriatic, a barrier of rude and difficult hills.

Behind that barrier the Roman Republic, originally a small city state, developed an aptitude for government and war which owed little to the practice and precepts of Greece. A supremacy, greater than that for which Athens, Sparta, and Thebes had in turn striven, came to the Romans as the prize of tenacious warfare and wise discipline, of moderation and good sense, of sound family life and strong legal instincts, and of a certain stern and simple gravity of bearing, which was rooted in the ancient pieties of the homestead and the soil. A sharp revolution, the expulsion of a dynasty of foreign kings in 510 B.C., made upon the Roman memory an impression which was all the deeper because revolutions were not in the Roman fashion. The constitution of the Republic developed slowly, insensibly adapting itself to successive changes of social pressure and the imperious calls of expanding duty.

A system of law gradually developed out of a mass of primitive custom and sacerdotal usage, growing with the enlarging life of the community, helping itself from the decrees of popular assemblies, the edicts of praetors, the opinions of jurisconsults, the systems of philosophers, until it became adequate to the practical needs of the civilized world. Inner social and political discords were solved by protest and compromise, by sagacious, face-saving expedients and constitutional laws rather than by bloodshed or the clash of arms. In the long struggle between the patricians and the plebeians (510-287 B.C.) the successive victories of the plebeian party appear to have left no mortal wound or implacable resentment. Compelled to surrender privilege after privilege the patricians never went into exile nor yielded their claim to render honourable service to the Roman state. Vital liberties were early conquered, as early as the Twelve Tables, *450 B.C* but the Senate, though partially recruited from the Plebs, remained in essence and outlook a patrician body. Domestic tension was never so grave as to sap the patriotism of the Romans or to weaken them in face of a foreign foe.

One by one all her Italian antagonists were made to acknowledge the power of Rome, the Latins of the plain, the mysterious non-Aryan Etruscans within whose kingdom Rome herself was once embodied, the sturdy Samnites of the hills, the formidable Gauls who had sacked Rome in 390, leaving behind them a memory of terror, and finally the Greek cities of the south aided by the phalanx and the elephants of Pyrrhus the Epirot. By the beginning of the third century B.C. Rome was supreme in Italy. But while other cities of the ancient world had conquered and lost, what Rome conquered in Italy she held and welded into a compact state. There was a method in her aggrandizement. She built military roads, such as only the Persian Empire had witnessed, and upon these planted at strategic points fortified cities garrisoned by Roman citizens. Other Italian communities she united by ties of exclusive alliance and carefully graded privilege to herself.

Yet she was not secure. The Gauls, established in the valley of the Po, occupied the largest and richest plain in the Mediterranean basin: but a peril even greater than the Gauls was the naval power of Carthage, disputing the fertile island of Sicily

with the Greeks, contesting Sardinia, and exercising through
her experienced fleets an unchallenged supremacy in the Tyrrhenian Sea.

With this great Semite power, then the commercial capital of
the world, Rome waged a struggle lasting more than 100 years
(264-146 B.C.), which changed the political complexion of Europe.
At the end of this desperate contest, conducted on a scale far
exceeding all previous experience, Carthage was obliterated from
the scroll of history. Her navies were sunk, her empire reft
from her, her proud and populous capital was levelled to the
ground. Rome, entering the contest without a military navy
or a yard of territory beyond the seas, had become by the logic
of war a world power. The commerce of the Mediterranean was
in her hands. Sicily, Sardinia, Spain, Africa had become Roman
provinces. Every part of the widespread Carthaginian Empire
in the west had passed into her control.

Character rather than culture supplied the key to the understanding of these victories. In point of artistic taste and achievement the Etruscans, who invaded Italy from Asia Minor at the
end of the ninth century, and reached their highest point of
power and prosperity three hundred years later, distanced their
rude and virile conquerors. Central Italy is still full of the monuments of a gifted and luxurious aristocracy who spoke a non-
Indo-European language, which we cannot read, who rode and
drove, hunted and farmed, and bequeathed much secret lore
concerning the arts of divination to the great Roman families,
who were proud to reckon an Etruscan among their ancestors.
If there was any Etruscan literature, it has perished long ago,
but the Apollo of Veii and the Orator of Lake Trasimene are
among the glories of European statuary. The Romans of the
young Republic had nothing which could compare with these
masterpieces in terra-cotta, or with the ivories and jewelry of
this accomplished people who, while borrowing freely from the
art of Assyria, Egypt, and Greece, had nevertheless something
distinctive of their own to contribute. It was not then a barbaric Italy which was subdued by the Romans, but as to a third
of its area an Italy already imbued with the arts and crafts of
Hellas and the east. But while Rome was united and tenacious,
the Etruscans suffered from a fatal lack of combination. The
Tarquins were expelled from the Seven Hills on the Tiber
(510 B.C.). The Etruscan navy went down before the Greeks at

Cumae (476). It was permitted that Veii, a principal shrine of Etruscan statuary, should sustain unfriended a war of eighty years against her inveterate enemy. Yet, if Etruria disappeared as an empire, the Tuscans survived as a race, substantially identical with itself through millennia, and now and again, as in the thirteenth and fifteenth centuries, revealing a genius for beauty which touches the summit of human excellence.

The First Punic War ended after twenty-three years of intermittent and disjointed struggle with a peace which transferred the island granary of Sicily from Carthage to Rome. That the contest lasted so long and was productive of no more decisive result may be attributed, partly to the conditions under which the war was waged, and also to a certain indistinctness of aim in the minds of each of the combatants. In days when a warship must be propelled by oars, when only in the summer months could it safely put to sea, and when, in the absence of long-range weapons, the ship which had not been grappled and boarded might easily escape unharmed, swift decisions were not difficult to avoid. Rome had to learn the lessons of salt water; Carthage, experienced at sea, but hampered at home, found difficulty in sparing mercenary troops sufficient for the needs of the Sicilian campaign. Neither party was as yet fully resolved upon a war of destruction. The Romans invaded Africa, but left the army of Regulus without support, and made no attempt to retrieve his defeat. Nor did the Carthaginians make use of their sea power to molest the coasts of Italy. In the end the Romans won, because, having learnt from their adversary a disagreeable and unfamiliar technique, they were able by a supreme effort of private patriotism to build a fleet capable of victory at a moment when Carthage was weary of the contest. *264-241 B.C.*

There followed an interval of twenty-three years which has left its mark upon the history of Europe. In that interval, Rome seized Sardinia, curbed the Illyrian pirates in the Adriatic, effecting in that process, through the conquest of Corcyra, her first lodgment on Grecian soil, and, greatest and most important achievement of all, conquered Cisalpine Gaul and extended her frontiers to the Alps. Not less memorable is the work of Carthage during the same period. Apart from the suppression of a serious revolt in Africa it consisted in the establishment of a new empire in Spain. *241-218 B.C.*

It is then to Carthage that Spain owes its introduction into the political history of Europe. In Spain, with its wealthy mines and factories, its fertile littoral, its numerous population of hardy and warlike tribes distributed in the high central plateau, where the wind is searching and the sun scorches, and the breed of man is tough and wiry, a Carthaginian of genius descried a new source of power for his state and a new base of operations against Rome. Hamilcar Barca, a soldier well proved in the Sicilian War, had determined to dedicate the remainder of his days to a war of vengeance. The idol of the Carthaginian democracy, he obtained a free hand in the Iberian peninsula, and there, in eight years of crowded and brilliant energy, built up a state, a treasury, and an army. A son-in-law and a son continued and consolidated his work. The son was Hannibal. To him, inheriting power in 221 B.C., Hamilcar had bequeathed his gifts, his energies, and his revenge.

Among the captains of the ancient world Hannibal alone in point of genius ranks with Alexander the Great. If he lacked the engaging radiance of the Macedonian, he was his superior in sobriety and concentration of purpose. His daring was extreme, his resource infinite, and his gifts of personal magnetism were such as in passages of extreme hardship and peril evoke and sustain the devotion of an army. He was quick to discern and to profit by the weakness of an adversary. Nothing was too great or too small for his attention.

His plan was simple, audacious, and, had all gone well, of deadly efficiency. It was to pick a quarrel with Rome, which he did by attacking Saguntum, a Spanish town under Roman patronage, and then to march with his African and Spanish levies overland to Italy, and to strike the Republic at the heart. He was not, of course, so foolish as to suppose that he could accomplish his purpose unaided. He counted upon the Cisalpine Gauls, still writhing under their recent defeat, on the cities of Italy presumed to be resentful of Roman dominion, on Philip of Macedon, young, ambitious, headstrong, who might be lured to emulate the career of Pyrrhus under happier circumstances, and to win from the Romans the control of the south.

218-201 B.C. Despite an amazing march, followed by three brilliant and annihilating victories, the plan failed. There was no general rising of the Gauls, no revolt in central Italy, no invasion from Macedonia, no abatement in the resolution of the Roman Senate never to treat with an enemy standing on Italian soil, nor was there from Carthage that measure of support which Hannibal had a right to expect. Yet for years he held the field with his small army of 30,000 in a populous enemy country and against a foe who had the call on forces more than thirty-three times as numerous as his own.

In the ruses and stratagems of war, in the handling of cavalry as well as in the moral gift of leadership which inspires the devoted loyalty of troops, Hannibal was supreme. A magical aura seemed to surround him. Though he had no siege train, and could never have taken Rome by force, he created in his adversaries a paralyzing sense of their inferiority. Again and again, after Lake Trasimene, after Cannae, and when it was known that his brother Hasdrubal had crossed the Alps with Spanish reinforcements, a deadly anxiety clutched at the heart of Rome. But Hasdrubal was beaten at the Metaurus. In truth, ever since Fabius had discerned that the best way of dealing with Hannibal was to avoid engaging him, a Roman victory was only a matter of time.

What finally brought the war to a conclusion was the discovery by Rome of a gifted commander. While Hannibal was overrunning Italy, P. Cornelius Scipio was engaged in evicting the Carthaginians from Spain. The lustre of this considerable achievement, which has fixed the mould of Spanish civilization, gave to Scipio a unique place in the confidence of the Roman people. He was permitted to conduct an expedition to Africa, the surest way of relieving the Italian peninsula of the incubus of a Punic army; in 204 B.C. he crossed the sea, and two years later, meeting Hannibal on the field of Zama, routed his elephants, his foot, and his horse, and secured a peace (201) which stripped Carthage of her overseas possessions and left her the tributary vassal of Rome.

Still, while Carthage remained, a fortified city on the gulf of Tunis with a population of some 700,000 inhabitants, rich, enterprising, industrious, resilient, Rome was uneasy. Fear and jealousy possessed her of a rival whose deadly fault was a too swift recovery from defeat. "Carthage must be destroyed," she began to repeat to herself. The incantation worked, pretexts were found, the apologies and excuses of compliant Semites were brushed aside. Carthage, it was urged, had attacked Massanissa, the Numidian ally of Rome. So fifty-two years after the field of

Zama another Roman expedition crossed to Africa. This time there was to be no weakness. After a long and terrible siege the city of Carthage was stormed and burned to the ground, and Africa incorporated as a province in the dominions of Rome.

The surprising fortunes of the Roman Republic had long been followed with anxiety and wonder by the intelligent peoples of the east. An honourable pedigree was invented for this rude community of formidable super-men, and the Romans learned that they were descended through Aeneas from King Priam of Troy, and linked to the most splendid legends of Hellenic antiquity. As the Punic Wars proceeded, the great qualities of the Roman character, never more brilliantly exhibited than in the dark hours of defeat, impressed themselves with increasing force upon the Greek-speaking world. Was it not to Rome, a Republic, and the inveterate foe of monarchy, that the city states of Greece and Asia Minor might look for the protection of their liberties and the preservation of their alliance, to Rome, which had chastised the Gauls and curbed the Illyrian pirates and was now, after desperate vicissitudes, vanquishing the stubborn oligarchy of Carthage? Such, at least, was the view of Polybius the Arcadian, whose wise history is the capital authority for these critical times, when Rome was bringing east and west into the orbit of her controlling power.

It will readily be imagined that, amid the strain and exhaustion of the Carthaginian struggle, Rome was in no mood to embark upon a course of aggression in the east. Her policy was to foster commercial relations with Egypt, and to grasp the hand of friendship, where it was freely offered, as by the wealthy house of Pergamum, the powerful island state of Rhodes, and the university city of Athens, and by such connections to paralyze the activities of any power who might be tempted to intrude on the western theatre of war.

This policy was successful. Neither Antiochus III of Syria nor Philip V of Macedon was in a position to send a ship or a man to Italy. Each of these eastern friends of Carthage, operating without combination, was defeated in detail and in his own territory, Antiochus in the great slaughter of Magnesia (190 B.C.), Philip in the soldiers' battle at Cynoscephalae. The cumbrous phalanx of spearmen, which had helped Alexander to conquer his vast empire of the east, had shown itself unequal to the Roman legion and the Spanish sabre. Antiochus was compelled to withdraw behind the Taurus, and the hegemony of Asia Minor henceforth devolved upon Rome.

Still the Greeks were unhappy. Home rule they had asked for, and home rule they had received. The Macedonians had been expelled from the key fortresses of Greece, the Romans had been acclaimed as liberators; but the harmony and union of Hellas were no further advanced. Roman commissioners were called in to arbitrate Greek quarrels, making enemies as well as friends with every award, and if it be true that unscrupulous Romans fomented Greek discords, it is no less certain that dis-affected Greeks intrigued secretly with Perseus, King of Mace-donia, as they found him steadily drifting into enmity with Rome.

So the final destruction of Macedonian power after the battle of Pydna in 168 B.C. was followed by the deportation to Italy of the leading Greek sympathizers with the vanquished cause. L. Aemilius Paulus was one of the best of Romans, a soldier, a statesman, a friend of good letters, a character raised above pecuniary temptation; but the vengeance which he exacted after his crowning victory at Pydna lacked nothing in completeness. Every Macedonian notable from the king downwards was de-ported to Italy. A great part of the population was enslaved, the country broken into four fragments, and reduced to such a state of helpless misery that its subsequent conversion into a Roman province was by comparison a blessing.

But the stern lesson was lost on Greece. An insurrection broke out, cruelly conducted, cruelly suppressed; and when the last desperate rally of the Achaean League had been crushed by L. Mummius on the field of Corinth (146 B.C.), and the men of Corinth had been slain and the women and children sold into slavery, and the city had been razed to the ground, Greece at last had a rest of fifty years under her Roman master. Long before this, war, infanticide and malaria had depleted her popu-lation and carried off the descendants of the men who had given her an immortal name and that burning love of liberty which had brought her to her doom.

The subjection during the space of a single lifetime of the whole inhabited world to the rule of Rome struck contem-poraries as being, which indeed it was, the crowning miracle of history. Yet, while the political power of the Roman Republic was felt from Cadiz to the Euphrates, the limits of its deeper influence were more strictly drawn. Upon Sicily and Spain the image of Rome was ineffaceably stamped; but east of the Adriatic the peoples of the Mediterranean remained, as they were before, a world apart, half Greek, half oriental, influencing their conquerors deeply by their refined and more exquisite culture, but receiving nothing in return save a measure of order, discipline, and protection, and not until the mediaeval crusades seriously invaded by the Latin culture of the west.

It would appear that Rome was drawn into empire not indeed in a fit of absentmindedness, but half reluctantly and of no set plan. The successive stages of her conquest of Italy were forced upon her because, as England afterwards experienced in India, an orderly power ringed round by turbulence always finds itself compelled to establish peace and security upon its frontiers. The struggle with Carthage indeed began with a moment of popular war fever, but that was short-lived. Rome went to Spain to cut off Hannibal, to Gaul much later that she might keep open her communications with Spain. There is no substance in the view that commercial and financial interests pushed Rome into conquest and annexation, except possibly in the cases of the destruction of Carthage and Corinth, until the first century B.C., when Pompey's annexation of Syria was probably due to the influence of the equites, the capitalistic class. More particularly did Rome show great reluctance to annex the Hellenistic kingdoms. She broke their power, practically destroyed their capacity to rule the east, and then shirked the task of administration herself. It is a remarkable fact that she had been the dominating power in the eastern Mediterranean for a hundred and fifty years before she finally, after suffering immense inconvenience from chaos and piracy, took over the direct rule of the whole area.

BOOKS WHICH MAY BE CONSULTED

T. Mommsen : History of Rome. *Tr.* W. P. Dickson. 5 vols. 1894.

H. F. Pelham : History of Rome. Outlines of Roman History. 4th Ed. 1905.

D. Randall McIver : The Etruscans. 1927.

G. Dennis : Cities and Cemeteries of Etruria. 1878.

H. Stuart Jones : A Companion to Roman History. 1912.

W. E. Heitland : Short History of the Roman Republic. 1911.

L. P. Homo : L'Italie Primitive et les Débuts de l'Impérialisme Romain. 1925.

Cambridge Ancient History, Vol. VIII.

Tenney Frank : An Economic History of Rome till the End of the Republic. 1927.

CHAPTER VII

REPUBLIC AND EMPIRE

The Roman Senate. Flaws in the Republican constitution. Ill effects of rapid conquest. Maladministration in the provinces. The last century of the Republic. The Gracchi. Idea of Italian freedom. Marius and Sulla. The challenge of Mithradates. Sulla's victories in the east and at home. His proscriptions. The unsolved military and police problems of the later Republic. Pompey. His compact with Caesar and Crassus. Julius Caesar. Early reputation and campaigns in Gaul. Rift with Pompey. Victories and death. The spirit of his rule. Its adaptation to the needs of the time.

THE form of government under which the Romans conquered Italy and weathered the storms of the Punic Wars was, like many constitutions which are the growth of time, one thing in theory and another in practice. In theory sovereignty rested with the assemblies of the Roman people organized in their centuries or their tribes. In practice government was carried on by the Senate, an aristocracy of birth and service, recruited according to established rules from men who had held offices of state or had distinguished themselves in war. It is to this remarkable assembly of patriotic and disciplined citizens that we must principally ascribe the successes of republican Rome. Armies might suffer defeat, fleets might be lost at sea, but the Senate, drawn for the most part from the members of patrician or ennobled families, grave, proud, resolute, accustomed to consider dishonour more terrible than death, never flinched in the hour of danger and created in the Roman colonies and in many of the allied cities of Italy a spirit as courageous and patriotic as their own.

Yet even at this period, when the republican government was working at its best, it was subject to many drawbacks. Of these the gravest was the organization of the executive power, which was neither concentrated in the hands of a single person, nor divided between a soldier and "civilian," nor granted for a term of years. By a singular arrangement, prompted by the strong and continuing fear of monarchy which had existed in Rome ever since the expulsion of its foreign kings, the supreme authority both in peace and war was confided to two annual officers known as consuls, each possessed of plenary power, and each entitled to veto the other's decisions. The evils of such a system, patent at all times, were specially manifest in times of war. No state is so rich in military talent as to be able to furnish an annual supply of excellent generals. The Romans of the third century before Christ, despite their martial habits, were no exception to this rule, and save on those rare occasions which justified the appointment of a dictator, submitted to a system under which good generals were retired too soon and bad generals appointed too often.

Another defect almost equally serious was the absence of any effective machinery for financial administration and control. There was no Board of Finance. The *quaestors*, to whom the management of the public Treasury was confided, so far from being the most experienced, were the least experienced members of the official hierarchy. Living on war plunder, the state could afford to dispense with direct taxation and to farm out its public lands to companies of tax farmers.

Upon a state so governed the burden of an empire descended with an almost unbearable shock. The vast plunder of Africa and Asia, of Macedonia and Greece, produced upon the Roman character the evil effects which suddenly acquired wealth always exerts upon minds unprepared to receive it. The old virtues of rustic simplicity and patriarchal discipline, of honest toil and pecuniary integrity, gave way before the overwhelming temptations of the new luxury. The flower of the Italian yeomanry had been used up in the armies, slaves were abundant, for every Roman victory brought a fresh consignment of slaves to the Roman market, and slavery, here as elsewhere, produced its demoralizing results. In the countryside great ranches tilled by gangs of slaves began to supersede the small holdings which before the terrible devastations of the Hanniballic wars had been the pride and mainstay of Italy. In Rome itself a vast slave population, ministering to the necessities and enjoyments of the free, constituted an invitation to idleness, frivolity, and vice. Moreover, as Rome became the capital and chief money-making centre of the world, it acted as a magnet upon the fortune hunters and adventurers of the Levant. To the influences of Greece, as to those of a civilization admittedly superior, the Romans of this and the succeeding centuries were more particularly open, but it was not the highest part of the Greek message which made the widest appeal in Italy, but rather the superficial cleverness, the attractive and effeminate vices, and the supple adaptability of conscience for which the average Greek of the period was then noted.

With these demoralizing influences abroad it is little to be wondered at that the first experiment of republican government overseas was attended by calamitous abuses. It was the custom of the Senate, on the establishment of a Roman province, to lay down in a written document known as the *Lex Provinciae* the principles in accordance with which the province was to be administered. In general, however, there was the sharpest opposition between the Provincial Law, which was often enlightened and humane, and the administration, which was for the most part characterized by cruel and shameful extortions. In a very short space of time the proconsuls of the Republic bled the provinces white. They ruined Sicily and the province of Asia and carried their depredations through every part of Greece. Neither the law courts nor the Senate were strong enough to check the evil. A fierce hatred of the Italian spread round the Mediterranean basin and threatened the new foundations of his rule.

To the disaffection bred of extortion and misgovernment abroad there was added a long catalogue of formidable evils threatening to shatter the fabric of empire which had been built up under senatorial rule: slave revolts in Sicily and Italy, a fierce faction fight in Rome between the popular and senatorial party which widened out into a bitter and destructive civil war, a dangerous rebellion of the Italian allies, and, reacting fiercely on domestic politics, the pressure of external enemies on every frontier. The last century of the Roman Republic is an age of violent internal convulsions associated with and exasperated by foreign wars. A succession of great captains, a gift of fortune upon which no community has a right to reckon, saved the state again and again, and maintained and greatly extended the boundaries of Roman rule. Gaius Marius ended the Jugurthine war, and by his two great victories over the Teutons and Cimbri saved northern Italy from barbaric invasions for five hundred years. L. Cornelius Sulla reconquered Greece from Mithradates, King of Pontus, and compelled him to restore his Asiatic conquests. The names of Lucullus and of Pompey are associated with a series of brilliant Asiatic campaigns, which left Rome

3

mistress of Syria and Asia Minor, and with no serious enemy in the east save the distant monarchy of Parthia. Gaul was conquered, Britain was invaded by Julius Caesar, yet the age which witnessed these dazzling feats of arms was one of the most unhappy and uncomfortable in Roman history. It was marked, indeed, by a great advance in wealth and luxury, by the growth of huge private fortunes, and by a concern for art, letters, and philosophy which has left an enduring mark upon civilization. It is the age of Lucretius, of Catullus, and of Cicero. Yet the contemporaries of these three fine human spirits had witnessed the clash of contending armies in the streets of Rome, had heard the cries of Sulla's victims as they were beheaded in their thousands in the Campus Martius, and in their walks among the glistening marbles of the sacred city were compelled to endure the grisly spectacle of severed heads, a ferocious but not unusual symptom of a party victory in the last century of the Republic. From these miseries bred of civil discord and external peril Italy was eventually delivered by the foundation of the Empire and by the Augustan Peace.

The first blows in the long domestic struggle were struck by two brothers, well born, for they were the grandsons of Scipio the elder, and well-to-do, but each touched by the spirit of reform and fated to atone for his dreams and ambitions by a violent end.

d. 133
B.C.

Tiberius Gracchus was killed in a vulgar riot by his political enemies of the senatorial party. Ten years later his younger brother Gaius, defeated, disillusioned, and desperate, fell in the same cause. The programme of Tiberius was to restore the decaying agriculture of central Italy by planting out settlers upon the public lands. His object was admirable, but since the proposals for carrying it out involved a widespread disturbance of vested interests, they were hotly resisted by the Senate. It was now that the vehement Tiberius developed a procedure, archaic in form but revolutionary in substance, which threatened to undermine the authority of the Senate and to give a new complexion to the Roman constitution.

In the course of the struggles between the patricians and plebeians during the fourth century there had been developed, over and above the assembly of the whole people voting by tribes (*Comitia Tributa*) and of the more plutocratically organized assembly of the whole people voting by centuries (*Comitia*

Centuriato), which had the right of appointing the chief magistrates, of making the laws, and of deciding on the questions of war and peace, another more democratic legislative body, the *concilium plebis*, which was served by officers known as tribunes of the people. Each of these assemblies was sovereign, but each was hampered by archaic restrictions, meeting only when convened by a magistrate, opining only upon questions which the convening magistrate had laid before them, and with characteristic Roman conservatism giving their votes standing and in groups (centuries or tribes) like the primitive armed levies of the Roman people. It was this cumbrous machinery which first Tiberius and then Gaius set in motion against the Senate. Each was a tribune, and saw that in the exercise of the tribunician power he could submit measures to the *concilium plebis* without reference to the Senate and pass them into law in spite of its resistance. Neither was a stickler for constitutional forms. When the constitution served their purpose it was obeyed; when it presented obstacles it was strained or broken.

Men once embarked on the ocean of political strife are apt to be carried further than they originally intended. In the hands of the younger Gracchus the programme of the popular party went far beyond the agrarian policy which first brought Tiberius into the arena against the Senate. Excellent schemes for colonization overseas were accompanied by plans in which the alloy of political profit was copiously blended with the gold of philanthropy. To conciliate the world of commerce and finance, and at the same time to abase the Senate, the equestrian order were put in charge of the Law Courts and accorded the lucrative privilege of farming the taxes and destroying the prosperity of the province of Asia. The favour of the Italian cities enjoying Latin rights was sought by the offer of the Roman franchise, that of the Roman proletariat by one of those fatal bribes so easy to offer and so difficult to withdraw, a dole of Sicilian corn from the granaries of the state.

Yet despite his skilfully combined programme, his popular gifts, and his ardent industry, the position of Gaius Gracchus was essentially insecure. His activities had been purely civilian. He had no army at his back. He was a tribune of the people, dependent for his office, his authority, and his life on the popular vote. He was elected twice. On the third occasion the *Comitia* turned against him. A private citizen who had made so many enemies as he could hardly hope to survive in that climate of furious hatred when the luck turned.

The idea of the Italian franchise had a great future. Though the Italian allies could seldom expect to vote in Roman assemblies, they learned from the lips of Roman orators to resent their inferior status, and to claim equality with Roman citizens. For a time progress was blocked. The enfranchisement of the despised Italian was opposed by all that was selfish and narrow in the Senate and people of Rome. At last the Italian allies rose in revolt, chose a capital, sketched out a constitution, and involved Rome in a serious war; and then only did the Senate concede a privilege which, once asked, should never have been denied. In the history of political enfranchisement one step leads to another. Out of the policy originally promulgated by the Gracchi there sprang a long series of enfranchising and equalizing measures culminating in the great edict of Caracalla (A.D. 212), which conferred Roman citizenship on all freeborn members of the Roman Empire. Yet though in theory political equality was conceded first to Italy and then to the whole Empire, no organ was created through which the provinces could make an effective use of their rights. The idea of representative government was foreign to antiquity. The first parliament of united Italy met in 1870.

With this one exception of the Italian franchise nothing so far had been done to increase the stability of republican government. A new peril was, in fact, already disclosed, the full bearing of which neither faction could justly measure. The rôle of popular hero, which had been played by the civilian Gaius, had now fallen to a soldier, who had recruited a volunteer army from the lowest class of the community and was universally and rightly regarded as the saviour of his country. Gaius Marius, the hero of the Jugurthine and Cimbrian Wars, the rude soldier from Arpinum, who had been selected to defend Italy from the gravest peril by which it had yet been assailed, and after five years of vigilant soldiering had wiped out the German victories at Arausio on the fields of Aquae Sextiae (102) and Vercellae (101), had the Roman state in the hollow of his hand.

In the plenitude of their thankfulness for these two crowning triumphs there was no political boon which Rome would have denied him. But in the field of home politics Marius was a child, with little in his head save the abasement of the Senate through the demagogic activities of his turbulent friends, so that although he was seven times elected consul, and may thus be regarded as a forerunner of the Emperors, he left no mark on the structure of Roman government. The task which he might have accomplished devolved upon his nephew Caius Julius Caesar.

By a curious accident of history the next great Roman general who might have upset the Republic was a conservative only anxious to preserve it. L. Cornelius Sulla had begun his military career as the lieutenant of Marius in Africa. The two men were 107 B.C opposed to one another in almost every point of circumstance and temper. Marius was a plebeian and a savage, Sulla an aristocrat of fine culture and licentious manners. The art of politics as understood by Marius was a course of violent demagogy directed to no coherent end. Sulla cherished a distinct scheme, articulated in every part, for the restoration of the Senate to the position of ascendancy which it had enjoyed during the Punic Wars. Each was reckless of bloodshed; but whereas the later cruelties of Marius were tinged with insanity, Sulla's butchery was done upon a system. A special cause of rancour envenomed the relations of the two soldiers thus differently disposed, for Sulla had procured the betrayal of Jugurtha, which had given Marius his reputation, and lost no occasion to advertise the fact.

Fourteen years after Marius had won his last great victory in the Cimbrian War, Rome was called upon to face a serious danger in the east. Mithradates Eupator, the King of Pontus, was an oriental of remarkable force and large ambitions who viewed himself as the leader and patron of an Hellenic world burning to free itself from Roman shackles. The territory of this Philhellenic barbarian was attacked by Nicomedes of Bithynia, a client of Rome, and, since satisfaction was refused him, Mithradates declared war upon the Roman Republic. In the challenge of this fiery potentate the Greek cities of the Levant saw an opportunity of wreaking vengeance on the Italians, by whom they had been mercilessly pillaged and oppressed. There was a great massacre in which it is said that a hundred thousand Latin residents in Asia, in Delos, and on the mainland, perished at the hands of outraged or envious Greeks. Asia Minor was won for the King. His armies, generalled by Greeks, occupied Athens and Boeotia. Was the Empire of Alexander the Great to live again and to be ruled from Sinope by an eastern tyrant served by eunuchs and soothed by a harem?

The Roman Senate commissioned Sulla to take up the eastern command, and no better choice could have been made. Sulla was in the prime of life. His military service had been varied and distinguished. As Propraetor in Cilicia he had fought and bargained with orientals. He was the only Roman officer of high mark who had a first-hand knowledge of Asia. But the idea of so great a prize going to a political opponent stirred the fury of the Roman democrats. The tribune Sulpicius Rufus introduced a decree depriving Sulla of his command and appointing Marius, now grown old and impotent, in his place. That was the signal for civil war. At the head of 30,000 men, Sulla marched to Rome, dispersed the disorderly horde of the Marians, and, having executed many prominent democrats and hunted Marius out of Italy, crossed the sea with five legions to deal with Mithradates.

88 B.C.

A lurid light was then thrown upon the extent to which party passion had corrupted the political life of Rome. Sulla's campaign was brilliant. He stormed Athens and the Piraeus, crushed, with infinitesimal loss to himself, the swollen oriental armies of Mithradates in two great battles, and after four years of successful fighting, forced his adversary to a humiliating peace. Yet in all these operations he was acting, not only without the support, but with the active opposition of the government of Rome. In his absence the *populares* had seized the helm; and while Sulla was winning victories in the east, his friends at home were exposed to the remorseless rage of Marius and his associates.

84 B.C.

Then Sulla returned to Italy, rich with spoils and indemnities, and with a well-paid, seasoned army at his heels to deal with his enemies. Mingling force with blandishments, defeating one army, seducing another, he marched to Rome, while two able young members of his party, Gnaeus Pompeius and Marcus Crassus, emerging from their hiding places, created diversions in his favour. Yet even the possession of Rome did not end the war. The democrats had appealed to the Samnites for help, and, while Sulla was engaged in Etruria, an army inspired by the fierce old Samnite spirit marched against Rome, Caius Pontius of Telesia, the national leader of these mountain levies, proclaiming that the tyrant city must be destroyed to her foundations and that the Roman wolves, the bane of Italian liberty, would never be got rid of until their land was laid waste. Sulla

82 B.C.

hurried back, and, just in time, threw his weary legions against
the enemy at the Colline Gate. The fight was long and hard;
but in the end the veterans of the east, aided by the levies of
Crassus, won a decisive victory.

The proscriptions of the victor, undertaken on a scale and
with a fierceness beside which the cruelties of the Marians
seemed mild, inflicted an irreparable harm on the senatorial
cause. Italy could not be made safe for the Senate either on these
or on any other terms. It was easy for Sulla to draw up a new constitution, depriving the assemblies of their initiative, the tribunate of its importance, the equestrian order of their new judicial
privileges, and precluding the continuous exercise of the higher
offices of the state in order that the Senate might shine with an
unchallenged lustre. What neither Sulla nor anyone else could
do was to fight against the stars in their courses. In quiet times
an oligarchical assembly, served by annual magistrates, might
survive the jealousy of the populace and the envy of the world
of business and finance. An ambitious soldier or a great emergency were lethal. Sulla died in 78 B.C. Eight years later
Pompey and Crassus, each in command of a victorious army,
undid his work.

Swiftly, but imperceptibly, the world was slipping into a new
phase of history in which the old forms and methods of the
Roman Republic were no longer effective. In the days before
Marius a Roman army was composed of peasant proprietors enlisted from their farms for a summer campaign and afterwards,
when the fighting was over, well content to return to the
pleasant livelihood which awaited them at home. Levies so composed and so supported constituted no danger to the republican
state. But as the march of Roman conquest advanced and the
military problems confronting the Republic increased in scale,
this old-fashioned domestic way of levying war no longer sufficed. The military reforms of Marius marked a revolution. The
Roman army became in practice a long-service force of professional soldiers. A vast change was imposed by the stern pressure
of circumstance, the implications of which, since they were costly
and unpleasant, were, as often happens when novelty is disagreeable, never boldly faced. The Senate failed to realize that,
unless the Republic controlled the professional armies by making itself responsible for their pay and pensions, the professional

armies would master the Republic. It failed to see that, while an army recruited in the old short-service way from the farms was already provided for, a professional army recruited in the new long-service way was not. It refused to listen to the demands which came from the commanders that the soldiers under their command should receive the guerdon of their services. And since it declined to work out a system of military pensions, it taught the armies to look, not to the state, but to the military chiefs who had promised rewards to the troops under their command, and were alone in a mood and a position to secure them.

One reason, therefore, why the Republic gave way to the Empire was that it provided no solution of the military problem created by the span of its conquests.

Another was its incapacity to police the streets of Rome. The idea of a professional police force, which is at once the friend of the people and the impartial protector of law and order, was alien to the conceptions both of the ancient and of the mediaeval world. Rome knew nothing of the kind. At no time, however, was the capacity of the government to keep order in the streets at a lower point of efficiency than during the period which is described in the letters of Cicero. The republican government in its last days was not only unable to control the commanders of the legions, it was not strong enough to put down the armed gangs of the political factions who were struggling for power in the streets of the capital itself.

Pompey was not one of those men who swing instinctively with the spirit of the masses, or apprehend the approach of great revolutions. By early association he was a member of the *optimate*, or aristocratic, party, but he had affiliations with the democrats, and was fitted by a certain moderation of temper and haziness of view to occupy an arbitral position between the two rival factions. He had no taste for party management, no base absorption in money getting, none of the eloquence or literary culture which gave to Cicero his unique position in the Senate and the Forum. But he was a soldier, a gentleman, and a patriot, well content to be the servant of the Republic on condition that no rival aspired to be its master.

The great opportunity which was given to this able but somewhat enigmatic figure came to him in 67 B.C. He was then called upon by popular acclaim to put down the Cilician pirates, whose depredations had even caused a famine in Rome. The task, estimated to last three years, was accomplished brilliantly and once for all in seven months, but on its heels came a wider and more important commission. The crushing victories of Sulla had failed to satisfy Mithradates of his inferiority. The irrepressible monarch was still in the field, and still capable, despite many reverses, of inflicting upon a Roman army the ignominy of a defeat. Pompey was commissioned to retrieve the situation, and endowed under the Manilian law with the largest powers.

The confidence of the Roman people was not misplaced. The eagles were carried to the Caspian and the Euphrates, Mithradates was driven into the Crimea. Cilicia, Syria, and Bithynia Pontus were annexed to the Republic. In a short five years Pompey had made Rome mistress of hither Asia, leaving behind him the name, not only of a successful general, but of a founder of cities, a friend of civilization, a wise and humane administrator. His work was not seriously disturbed till the coming of Islam.

Fresh from this resplendent achievement, he asked the Senate to confirm his Asian treaties and to make a grant of land to his veterans. His requests were refused. Though he had disbanded his armies, he was still suspect, confronted by that strong spirit of republican puritanism which has been a force in European politics from Cato to Robespierre, and by the vanity of politicians, unable to measure the size of men and events. But what the Senate had refused, the democratic leaders were prepared, upon terms, to grant. He entered (60 B.C.) into a compact with Crassus, the millionaire manager of the democratic party, and with Caesar, his brilliant lieutenant. The consideration for Caesar was a year of the consulate to be followed by five years of the Gallic and Illyrian commands.

No one would have predicted that the youngest member of this triumvirate would outrange Pompey in military renown and change the face of Europe. Save for a year's soldiering in Spain, when he was already past forty, Caesar had no experience in the handling of troops. As an "intellectual" trained under the best Greek masters, as an eloquent advocate in the forum, and a skilful manager of democratic intrigues, he was well known in the capital. His gallantries, his lavish spectacles and entertainments, his debts, were famous, and since he was the nephew of

Marius and son-in-law of Cinna, rumour was prompt to associate him with every dark plot to upset the Republic.

Something of the true scale of the man appeared during his year of consulship. He passed a decree to put down extortion, swept aside constitutional fetters, and showed that he meant to have his way in Rome: but it was eight wonderful campaigns in Gaul which revealed for the first time his full range as a soldier and a statesman. Everything he set out to accomplish was secured. The frontiers of Rome were extended to the ocean and the Rhine, and, so defined, the Gaul of Caesar remains graven this day on the heart of France.

58-51 B.C.

It is no deduction from his renown that the Celtic tribes of Gaul were ill armed, ill disciplined, and honeycombed with rivalries. Caesar knew how to avail himself of every weakness. He could cajole as well as threaten, conciliate as well as coerce. In the early stages of his Gallic war he was helped by the Aedui and the Remi. Later, when his old allies had turned against him, the Gallic cavalry, in the critical fight before Alesia, was routed by a body of German horsemen, whom, with a prompt sense of the military value of these giants of the north, Caesar had enlisted in the Roman army. It was perhaps also a fortunate incident that he first appeared rather as the defender than as the assailant of the Celtic tribes of Gaul, repelling a great popular migration from Helvetia, and then a formidable intrusion from the German forests. But no one can read the sober narrative in which Caesar himself describes his Gallic campaigns without realizing the breadth and audacity of his conceptions, his personal courage, his wonderful combination of patience and velocity, and the fidelity and skill with which he was served. At every extremity of Gaul he gave evidence of Roman power. He crossed the Rhine to impress the Germans, the Channel twice to overawe the Britons, and built a fleet on the lower waters of the Rhine to help the Celtic mariners of the channel to realize that Rome was mistress of the seas. Three great barbarian leaders, Ariovistus, the German, Cassivelaunus, the Briton, and Vercingetorix, the Arvernian noble who headed the last and most formidable rally of the Gauls, went down before him.

It is easy to conceive the thrill of excitement which these conquests must have caused in the Roman world. Southern Gaul had long been overrun by Roman farmers and graziers, moneylenders and contractors. But now a vast territory, contiguous to

the "province," but hitherto little explored, rich in flocks and
herds, suitable for tillage, abounding in potential slaves, and
providing almost inexhaustible opportunities for trade and commerce, was laid open to the Roman view. And beyond Gaul lay
another reservoir of slave labour, the mysterious island of
Britain, long famous for its tin mines, but otherwise little visited
even by the adventurous seamen of Marseilles, and now shown
to be easily accessible to the Roman legions. In comparison with
this spectacular development of exploration and conquest at the
very door of Italy, the distant triumphs of Pompey lost something of their original lustre.

There was, however, in Rome itself a clique of hard-bitten
republicans, in whose eyes the very scale of these achievements
constituted an offence. The *optimates* had never trusted the
mercurial chieftain of the popular party. They hated his hardy
spirit, his mocking defiance of established creeds and customs,
his patent contempt for constitutional pedantries, and after the
Gallic conquests they feared the sharp edge of his sword. They
were therefore resolved that when, on March 1, 49 B.C., the time
should come for Caesar to lay down his proconsular command,
he should for a time at least be depressed to the station of a
private citizen, unprotected by the sacrosanctity of public office.
and deprived of all possibility of public harm.

Into these busy machinations Pompey allowed himself to be
drawn by men whose party passions were probably a good deal
more violent than his own. Detaching himself from Caesar, his
father-in-law and former ally, and perhaps influenced by accidents of personal history, such as the death of Julia, his wife, and
his remarriage to the daughter of a severe republican, Pompey
drifted into the headship of the conservative party. As time proceeded, the quarrel became malignant. Clodius, Caesar's political
agent in Rome, was murdered by Milo, the bravo of the opposite
faction. A reasonable proposal for compromise was rejected by
the Pompeians. It became plain to Caesar that his enemies were
implacable and that they wanted his blood. The long renown of
the Roman Republic, for Pompey was sole consul and the lawful
civil ruler of that ancient state, had no terrors for the master of
the Gallic legions. Crossing the Rubicon in January, 49 B.C., he
marched his famous veterans, amid the acclamations of the
countryside, down the Adriatic coast, drove Pompey out of Italy,
and upset the constitution which had served Rome for five

hundred years and even yet commanded the passionate loyalty
of some of her noblest sons.

Much fighting lay still before Caesar. There were enemy
legions in Spain, in Epirus, in Africa; and Roman republicans
of the iron stamp of Cato were not the men to cede their
cherished ideals without a struggle. But at the end of four years
the favourite of fortune had triumphed over all his enemies in
the field. He had beaten Pompey at Pharsalus, vanquished the
republican levies in Africa and Spain, and even found time to
dally with Cleopatra in Egypt, and to punish a king of Pontus
in his distant home on the Euxine.

Then, in July, 45 B.C., he returned to Rome, bringing to the
task of reorganization the greatest civil intelligence which had
yet been seen in Europe.

Seven months later, at the age of fifty-eight, he fell by the
hands of two republican fanatics.

In that brief space of time Caesar laid the foundations of the
Roman Empire. There were no proscriptions or confiscations.
The new ruler intended himself to be regarded, not as the
victorious head of a vindictive faction, but as the healer of civic
wounds, as the master of a united society. All power, civil and
military, was concentrated in his hands. The commanders of the
legions and the rulers of the provinces were no longer the
nominees of the Senate or assemblies, but the legates of the
great soldier, who, after the crowning victory of Munda, was also
created dictator for life. Yet the old constitution, the centre of so
many loyalties and affections, was still in name preserved. The
Senate, enlarged and diluted, the Comitia, the republican magis-
tracies, continued to function, but as instruments in the hands
of a military commander, who at the same time was consul and
had the sacrosanctity of a tribune for life. Indications were also
given that the supreme power so constituted would be used for
wise and beneficent ends. Decency was restored to the capital by
the dissolution of the factious guilds and the limitation of the corn
dole; but with the recognition of the cogent need for discipline
went a large vision of the wants of Italy. The generous ideas of
the Gracchi were taken up by their political heir, but worked
out with greater prudence and on an ampler scale. The franchise was granted to Cisalpine Gaul. Every city government in
Italy was the better for Caesar's touch.

The world was in need of such a man. There was no outrage
to the civilian conscience in a government which, though
created by the sword and contemptuous of republican forms,
enthroned the civil above the military power. In our age, the
ideals of Caesarism would be sharply challenged by national
sentiment and democratic doctrine. Neither of these great
fashioning forces existed in the civilized world during this century. There were no nations, no democracies, not even a general
intellectual interest in politics, but on the one side an old-
fashioned civic Republic, unable even to police the streets of
Rome, and on the other a vast society of men and women
hungering for peace that it might meditate on religion or philosophy, or taste the sweets of its fast expanding wealth.

BOOKS WHICH MAY BE CONSULTED

T. Mommsen : History of Rome. *Tr.* W. P. Dickson. 5 vols. 1894.

H. F. Pelham : History of Rome. Outlines of Roman History. 4th Ed.
    1905.

Sir Charles Oman : Seven Roman Statesmen. 1902.

J. L. Strachan Davidson : Cicero and the Fall of the Roman Republic.
    1894.

Warde Fowler : Julius Caesar, and the Foundation of the Roman
    System. 1892.

W. E. Heitland : Short History of the Roman Republic. 1911.

Gaston Boissier : Ciceron et ses Amis. 1877.

C. Bailey : Phases in the Religion of Ancient Rome. 1932.

C. Bailey (*ed.*) : The Mind of Rome. 1926.

C. Bailey (*ed.*) : The Legacy of Rome. 1925.

H. D. Leigh and W. W. How : History of Rome to the Death of Caesar.
    1898.

Cambridge Ancient History, Vol. IX.

T. Rice Holmes : The Roman Republic. 1923.

G. Ferrero : Greatness and Decline of Rome. *Tr.* A. E. Zimmern and
    H. J. Chaytor. 5 vols. 1907-09.

Tenney Frank : An Economic History of Rome till the End of the
    Republic. 1927.

CHAPTER VIII

STRENGTH AND WEAKNESS OF THE ROMAN EMPIRE

The end of the Civil War. Actium. Augustus and Virgil. Bounds of the Empire. Absence of a fixed rule of succession. Expansion of the Empire. Romanization of the provinces. Roman tolerance. The age of the Antonines. The third century. Barbaric pressure and imperial defence. Growth of religious interest. Stoicism. Oriental cults. The Christians. Decay of patriotism. Roman education. Its defects and merits. Absence of scientific and technical progress. Gradual impoverishment. Currency. Decline of the population in numbers and quality. The army: its composition and numbers.

THE murder of Julius Caesar plunged everything once more into chaos and uncertainty. There was a war between the Caesarians and the Republicans, and again a war of succession between the Caesarians themselves. The blood of Cicero, the last prophet of the Roman Republic, the greatest orator and humanist of his age, was shed in an orgy of retribution for the crime of the Ides of March. Nor was the quarrel confined to Italy. It extended to every quarter of the Empire, which it threatened to disrupt. Parthians fought at Philippi for Brutus and Cassius. Greeks commanded the pirate fleet of Sextus Pompeius, which for seven years held the seas for the republican cause. The fleets and treasures of Egypt were thrown into the scale in the last deciding phase of the conflict.

Eventually and by slow degrees light broke through the clouds. Octavius, the adopted son and great-nephew of Julius Caesar, was at his great-uncle's death in his nineteenth year; but though young in years, and with little aptitude for the profession of arms, he was old in prudence and heir to a famous name. From the first he determined to have everything, but from the first was wise enough to see that he was not strong enough to have everything at once. Mark Antony, formerly Caesar's Master of the Horse, was, on the date of his patron's murder, sole consul and *de facto* ruler of Italy, and, had the brilliance of a soldier been supported by the gifts of a statesman, his authority would have been difficult to shake. But Antony met more than his match in

63 B.C.-
A.D. 14

78

the youth who was destined to establish on firm foundations the empire of the Caesars. Octavius fought him, treated with him, used him as an ally against Brutus, and then quieted him with the lure of the east, while he employed his own sagacious energies on the problems of Italy, Spain, and Gaul. The seductions of the Levant worked on the emotional temperament of Antony. While the prudent Octavius was deepening his hold on the affections of the Italian people, Antony drifted into the vices, the languors, the credulities of the east. Vast, nebulous ambitions floated before his brain, fostered, perhaps, by Cleopatra, his Egyptian siren, who captured his love and for nine years corrupted his will. He claimed to be the god Dionysus, and, having mastered the east, to extend his domination to Italy. At the sea fight at Actium his dream was shattered. Octavius, with a fleet *Sept. 2,* organized by his friend Agrippa and all the resources of the west *31 B.C.* behind him, was stronger than any power which could then be recruited in the Levant. The consequences of his victory were momentous. The presumption of Cleopatra was avenged by the annexation of Egypt, with its great wealth, its advanced methods of accountancy, business, and finance; and the Roman Empire, which seemed likely to split into an eastern and a western half, was soldered together during those critical centuries, when the establishment of a world state seemed providentially designed to give support to the aspirations for a world religion.

The new government set itself to work to cure the evils which had been bequeathed by two centuries of war. The empire of Augustus, as Octavius now (January 16, 27 B.C.) came to be called, stood for peace and clemency, order and justice. It was a symbol of the new era that thirty-two legions were demobilized and rewarded without confiscations. The frontiers were defended by standing armies, the administration placed upon a business footing by the formation of a bureaucracy, by a statistical survey, and by the introduction, most probably from Egypt, of a regular system of public accounts. Ignorant amateurs were no longer entrusted with unlimited powers to enrich themselves at the expense of the provinces which had been submitted to their charge. The legates of Augustus were experts, flanked by independent financial officers responsible only to the Emperor, and if they proved themselves worthy were continued in their province. So organized the provincial system of the Roman Empire stood the test of centuries and stamped itself deeply on the life of Europe.

It was part of the prudence of Augustus to preserve the forms of liberty so dear to a proud and conservative people. If his person was sacrosanct, it was because at stated intervals he solicited and received at the hands of the people the tribunician power; if his authority was unchallenged, it was because the people had given him the legions, the provinces, and the proconsular authority in Rome itself. His innovations, which were vast, but harmless because they were gradual, were concealed under the guise of a republican restoration, and the master of the civilized world was content to be known as Princeps, the first citizen of a free state.

There has never been a more valuable government than that of this thrifty, respectable, long-headed, and long-lived representative of the Italian middle class. Under Augustus power for the first time became consistently helpful, benign, and even paternal. The odious extortions of the capitalist oligarchy who in the last days of the Republic had ruined the provinces were at an end. The Princeps made war on irreligion and race-suicide and attempted to restore the wholesome morals and immemorial pieties of the Italian race. It was noted of him that he had a full measure of the countryman's superstitions, that he loved truth and hated flattery, that he was discreet in the choice of counsellors, affable to his friends, and intolerant of pride in his associates. Agrippa, the contriver of his victories, and Maecenas, the discerning patron of the arts, gave lustre and variety to his court. A society just escaped from the galling trials of civil war was little disposed to quarrel with a prince so accessible and considerate, or with a system which afforded to every class in the community an honourable career in the public service. The modest Augustus, who was rightly hailed as a saviour of his country, could not escape the divine honours which had actually been accorded to his brilliant uncle; and the worship of the Emperor, gently insinuated into the family and local cults of Rome and with some ostentation practised in the provinces, was soon regarded as a helpful bond of union in a providential state.

Yet, important as was the achievement of Augustus, it would have meant far less for the world but for the image which the spectacle of Roman greatness created in the minds of two writers of genius.

It so happens that Virgil, the inspired poet of Italy, and Livy, the romantic historian of the Roman Republic, were both born

in that Cisalpine region which had so lately been incorporated
in the Roman state—Virgil at Andes, near Mantua, in 70 B.C.,
and Livy at Padua in 59 B.C. But if there was Celtic blood in
either writer, it was compatible with an ardour of Italian
patriotism so strong as to kindle for all time a sense of Roman
virtue and greatness in the imagination of mankind. The beautiful landscape of Italy is painted in the Georgics, the historic
mission of Rome unfolded in the Aeneid. Upon that age these
two wonderful works of a shy poet, nature lover, scholar, savant,
patriot, fell with the force of a revelation. A supreme master of
Latin letters, inviting comparison with Homer himself, had
burst upon the scene, giving lessons to grammarians in language,
to rhetoricians in eloquence, to ritualists in ceremonial, to poets
in music. Moreover, this great artist had a message. He preached
the love of Italy, the mission of Rome, the gospel of patriotic
duty. He discerned in the rise of the Roman Empire a new
hope for the human race, a hope of peace, of order, of civilization. So long dominant was his gospel in Europe that Dante,
writing in the spirit of the great concluding passage of the first
Georgic, assigns Brutus and Cassius, the murderers of Julius
Caesar, to the lowest pit of the Inferno with Judas Iscariot, the
betrayer of Christ.

The empire, as it was finally shaped by Augustus, included
Spain, Gaul, Italy and the Balkans, the north coast of Africa,
Palestine, Syria, and Asia Minor. The Mediterranean was a
Roman lake. Every people who had contributed to the sum of
western civilization was now subjected to Rome. In the north
and north-west, the two quarters from which the pressure of the
barbarian world was most to be feared, the empire was defended
by the Danube and the Rhine, a long river frontier behind which
were ranged in uncalculated numbers the valiant tribesmen of
Germany. The conquest of this tumultuous people, had it been
achieved by Augustus, would have changed the course of European history, for a frontier drawn from the Baltic to the Danube
by the line of the Elbe and the Morava would have been relatively short and easy to defend. But a single military disaster in
a German forest was sufficient to deter the Emperor from further A.D. 9
adventures in a difficult, unexplored, and uninviting land.
    After the loss of Varus and his legions, Augustus resolved to
stand on the defensive. His decision was wise. The world needed

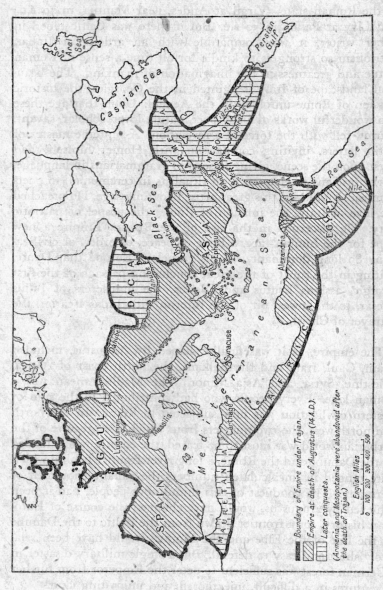

Boundary of Empire under Trajan.

Empire at death of Augustus (14 A.D.)

Later conquests.

(Armenia and Mesopotamia were abandoned after the death of Trajan.)

English Miles
0   100 200 300 400 500

THE ROMAN EMPIRE AT ITS GREATEST EXTENT UNDER TRAJAN.

peace. The laborious pacification of Spain was in itself a task sufficient to employ the energies of the young Empire, and the legions stationed on the Rhine could not be expected at one and the same time to police Gaul and conquer Germany. Yet, however wise and inevitable it may have been, the determination to refrain from a resolute attempt to include the Germans within the Empire was none the less momentous. The long new frontier was not permanently held, and Italy and Gaul were overwhelmed before Rome had civilized its Teutonic conquerors. Six centuries of intellectual darkness were the tremendous penalty consequent upon the premature breakdown of the Imperial defences.

The work of Augustus was continued by his stepson and successor Tiberius, an excellent soldier and administrator, whose reign of twenty-three years, odious as it appeared to the aristocratic *frondeurs* of Rome, did much to consolidate the Imperial system. That the Empire responded to a general need is sufficiently evidenced by its survival despite the almost inconceivable crimes and vices of many of its rulers. The three immediate successors of Tiberius were a madman, a pedant, and a monster. Yet it is probable that the freaks of Caligula, the pedantries of Claudius, and the atrocities of Nero, distasteful as they must have been to the better elements of Roman society, made little impression upon the larger life of the Empire. What was more serious was the absence of any fixed rule of succession. Such was the prejudice against the mere thought of an hereditary monarchy that despite the manifold evils of a system which often remitted the choice of an Emperor to the clamour of the troops and more than once involved the Empire in civil discords, the idea of Caesarism as an autocracy founded on popular election was never lost sight of. The death of Nero, the last representative of the Julio-Claudian house, was the signal for the emergence of four rival Emperors and for a year of anarchy during which a battle was fought in Rome itself which is said to have cost fifty thousand lives. Then ensued a happier century inaugurated by Vespasian (A.D. 69-79), a rude Sabine soldier, and lasting until the death of Marcus Aurelius (A.D. 180), during which the transmission of the supreme power was peaceably effected at first through heredity and afterwards through the sensible practice of adoption. It is to this last practice that Rome owes the choice of Trajan, the great Spanish conqueror of Dacia, of Hadrian, the universal genius, and of Antoninus Pius, the embodiment of

A.D. *14-37*

A.D. *68*

the best virtues of the Italian country gentleman. But these standards were not maintained. The elevation of Pertinax, who was the choice of the Praetorian Guard, set an evil example to every legionary camp on the frontier. The diadem became the prize of ambitious soldiers and its transmission the occasion of civil strife. The results were such as might be expected from a system under which military leaders chosen by distant troops and imposed by violence were suddenly called upon to undertake the greatest political responsibility in the world. The rulers of Rome in the third century were often bad and always insecure. Of the twenty-three Emperors who preceded Diocletian (A.D. 284), all but three died violent deaths.

It was said of the wise Augustus that he left a solemn injunction upon his successors to be content with the existing frontiers of the Empire. All experience, however, shows that nothing is so difficult as to arrest the enterprise of a people once infected with ideas of conquest and exploration. While Christ and His disciples were preaching the gospel of renunciation, the Italians, animated by a spirit as far removed as possible from that of the Galilean, were pushing into new markets, developing new enterprises, exploring new lands, and clamouring for new conquests. Claudius, the boorish, self-indulgent invalid, yielding to the exalted spirit of his times, began the serious conquest of Britain and added Thrace, Mauretania, and Judea to the Roman provinces. Even under Nero, to whom nothing was serious save his own reputation as an actor and a vocalist, places so far distant as the flats of Anglesea and the highlands of Armenia were subjected by Roman arms. To the Flavian Emperors belongs the credit of seizing the strategical importance of Vienna and of connecting the Danube with the Rhine by a chain of fortified posts.

Nor was it until the later part of the second century, under the reign of Marcus Aurelius, the noblest of the Emperors, that the Roman guard at length gave way. In 161 A.D. a horde of barbarians, the Marcomanni from Bohemia, the Quadi from Moravia, forcing the north-eastern barrier of Italy at its lowest and most vulnerable point, besieged Aquileia—a symptom of worse things to come, and a warning to the Italians that they could no longer count upon the Augustan peace.

Meanwhile the Roman legions, defending the Imperial frontiers as they did during the two centuries which followed the battle of Actium, preserved to posterity the priceless gift of Greco-Roman civilization. It is to the respite from external invasion so obtained that we must ascribe the permanent romanization of France and Spain, and that most important though more superficial romanization of Britain which, though almost wholly obliterated by the Saxon conquest of the fifth century, has bequeathed to us the city of London and our Roman roads. Behind the spears and shields of the legions Iberian and Gaulish schoolboys blundered through the Latin Grammar, henceforward the quickest passport to worldly success, as their parents learnt from the conquering people the manner of its baths and theatres, its meals and festivals, its amphitheatres and law courts, or the empty and elegant ritual demanded by its gods. Behind the buckler of Roman valour the knowledge of Latin spread as English has spread in India, or supersedes for the Greek or Italian immigrant to the United States the use of his native tongue. Latin was the avenue to public employment, public dignity, literary renown. The members of the senatorial order, a kind of imperial peerage, spoke Latin and lived as Latins did. The humble German or Briton who waited upon the rich Roman invalid as he took the cure at Wiesbaden or Bath would doubtless furnish himself with some scraps of a vocabulary which the student of Terence and Plautus may recognize today; and upon a higher scale, as new towns sprang up and received colonists from Rome, men of distinguished talent would come forward, a Seneca or a Lucan from Corduba, an Apuleius from the Roman province of Africa, and add to the splendour of Latin letters.

Grim and terrible as was the process of Roman conquest, it brought happiness and prosperity in its train. If some provinces like Rhaetia and Britain were backward, in others, notably in Gaul and southern Spain, the progress was amazing. Here there was developed during the two hundred years of the Augustan peace a flourishing city life which vied with that of Italy itself. Old towns were expanded and glorified, new towns grew up round legionary camps or in response to the needs of expanding commerce, so that the Empire became a great association of municipalities, tending to be assimilated, so far as their rights and privileges went, to the colonies and *municipia* of Italy. To the provincials of Lyons or Toledo, of Autun or Saragossa, Rome was the glass of fashion. The amusements, the occupations, the studies of the capital were followed in the provinces. If a book were popular in Rome, copies would be eagerly awaited by the reading public in Lyons, and many a well-appointed villa in Baetica or Provence must have afforded to the wealthy Italian visitor a cuisine and a library not wholly unworthy of his pleasant country home among the Alban hills.

Tacitus said of his countrymen, " They value the reality of the Empire, but disregard its empty show." It was part of the Roman strength to mingle diplomacy with force, to make no more disturbance of local customs than was necessary, to attack only such forms of religious belief as, like the worship of the Druids, were political in their object, and to preserve old laws and institutions where, as in Egypt or in Sicily, they adjudged them to be good. When the soldiers had done their butchers' work, military predominance was kept in the background. The legions were employed to make roads, to build amphitheatres and aqueducts, and generally to assist in making as rapidly as possible the material fabric within which the common life of a civilized community could proceed; but they were not obtruded. The great legionary camps were on the frontiers, and a traveller might voyage from Marseilles to Boulogne without catching the glint of a Roman helmet. To outward seeming Rome's handsome estate might be held together by nothing but the invisible ties of good humour and good will.

The age of the Antonines was selected by Gibbon as that in which the state of the human race in the west was happier than at any period either before or since. The full weight of the barbaric pressure upon the frontiers had not yet made itself felt. The burden of taxation was still light. A large cultivated middle class enjoyed a rich inheritance of literature in circumstances of great material comfort. Amusements on a lavish scale were provided for the many, the chariot races in the circus, the gladiatorial games and combats of wild beasts in the amphitheatre, an easy access to the public baths. A pleasant intercommunion, unvexed by the modern fanaticisms of creed and race, of nationality, language and colour, spread from one end of the Empire to the other. In the service of Rome, Syrians and Spaniards, Africans and Britons mingled together without difficulty or wounding discrimination. A wide and indulgent tolerance was the mark of the age. The peoples of the Empire were too close to the Romans in race and too quick to assimilate Roman culture ever to be regarded in the light of natural inferiors. The cities were self-governing and much left to themselves. Of religion as such there was no persecution, for the Roman Pantheon was hospitable to every god. Social customs were embodied in the growing fabric of Roman law, local languages—Punic, Lycaonian, Celtic—permitted to coexist with the *lingua franca* of the Empire which was Latin. Cruelty, indeed, existed then as it exists now; but the humanitarian might reflect that the slave trade had died down, that freedmen could win their way to wealth and authority, and that even a slave might exercise an influence as an author in a society where careers were open to talent. Of the ultimate fate of the Empire there were as yet no apprehensions. It was the universal and comforting belief that Roman rule would endure for ever.

A change came with the third century A.D. After the strain of the Marcomannic War certain ominous symptoms made themselves for the first time increasingly evident. Already in the time of Augustus grave anxiety was felt as to the falling birth-rate of Italy. Legislation was attempted, but while the natality of Jews, Egyptians, and Germans steadily advanced, the Italian birth-rate continued to fall. The wastage of almost incessant warfare, the practice of infanticide, the growth of luxury and self-indulgence, the inability of science, as then conceived, to cope with the sanitary problems of large towns, were among the causes which contributed to the depletion of the man power in the two leading countries in the Mediterranean. By the age of Marcus Aurelius there was little left of the virile population of ancient Greece or of the best breeding stocks of Rome and Italy. Even among the Emperors and their relations the will to found large families seems to have been absent. And to these unhappy tendencies there was added a series of devastating plagues, beginning in 166 A.D. with the return of the troops of Avidius Cassius from the east, and observed to be specially fatal to Italians.

It was idle to expect that the defence of the Empire could be entrusted to Italians only. Nor was this in fact ever the practice. Auxiliary troops, drawn from every quarter of the compass, from Palmyra and the Balearic Islands, from Germany and Illyria, had assisted the legions in their vigils and excursions. But after the Marcomannic War it was found that these measures no longer sufficed to meet the growing difficulties of the state. A policy was then for the first time initiated of directly opening

the Empire to colonization. Blocks of barbarian warriors were
invited to settle on the waste places behind the Roman frontiers.
Once inaugurated, the process of infiltration continued. From
the opening of the third century the great traditions of Greek
and Roman civilization were protected almost entirely by troops
of alien origin, living with their wives and families a half-civilian
life in the standing camps along the confines of the Empire.
The most responsible posts in the army and the state might be
filled by men devoid of any drop of Italian blood. The two best
generals of Marcus Aurelius were Syrians. During the third
century one Emperor was a Syrian, another an Arab, a third an
African, springing from a family whose familiar speech was
Punic. The African was Septimius Severus, who was raised to the
purple by the Pannonian legions in 190 A.D., and died in York in
212 A.D. His name should be known in England, for by repairing
Hadrian's wall, between the Solway and the Tyne, he secured
for Britain a century of peace.

　　The third century of the Christian era is memorable for the
work of two great Roman jurists, Ulpian and Papinian, both of
Asiatic origin, and for a late and brilliant flowering of Greek
literature, illustrated by the profound mystical writings, harmonizing Christian belief with Platonic thought, of the Alexandrian philosopher Plotinus. It was an age of great distraction
and unhappiness, during which the pressure of the barbarian
tribes upon the defences of the Empire became increasingly
severe, reaching a climax in the middle of the century when
the Goths, a northern people of fair-haired giants, sacked most
of what was worth plundering in the Balkans, seized the Crimea,
and, after pillaging many flourishing cities in the Euxine and
Asia Minor, crowned their pirate course by burning to the
ground the great Temple of Artemis at Ephesus. It was an age
in which Tarragona, in the heart of Spain, was sacked by a
wandering band of Franks from Germany, when the Alemanni
carried fire and sword through the valleys of the Rhone and Po,
and Antioch, the key of Roman power in the east was held, now
by a King of Persia, and now by a rebel Queen of the desert city
of Palmyra. It was an age also of sharp civil discords, of clashes
between rival emperors and rival armies, the main centre of
power lying throughout with the Pannonian legions, schooled
in the hard life of the Danube frontier, and with the Illyrian

soldiers whom from time to time it was their pleasure to raise
to the purple. Yet grave as were the dangers which assailed the
Roman Empire in the third century, often as it must have
seemed likely to contemporaries either that Gaul would fall
away on the one side, or that the east would pass out of Roman
control on the other, or that the whole Greco-Roman world
would be overwhelmed and ruined by the barbarism of the
north, the task of defence was in fact accomplished. Advanced
positions were, indeed, abandoned. From the Black Forest and
the plain of Transylvania the legions fell back to the Rhine and
the Danube, the old frontiers of Augustus; and it is significant of
the increased insecurity that Aurelian, the brilliant soldier, who   A.D. 270-5
drove the Germans out of Italy and restored Gaul and the east
to a common obedience, thought it prudent to fortify Rome.

Meanwhile in this time of general strain and anxiety the
Mediterranean world was becoming increasingly occupied with
the thought of a life beyond the grave.

The old paganism of the Roman people, which had still a
long life before it in the hill villages of Italy, was a pleasant, un-
moral, tolerant creed, free from the control of clerics or the
vexation of inquisitors, and easily harmonized with those
popular festivals and amusements of which it was, indeed, an
integral part; but it had long since ceased to claim the allegiance
of the finer natures or the better minds. It responded to none
of the deeper needs of conscience. It answered to none of the
claims of intellect. To thinking men and women, philosophy,
which ever since the days of Zeno and Epicurus had become
increasingly occupied with problems of conduct, offered a
stronger and more satisfying diet. Before Christianity had become a European religion, educated people in the Roman Empire
were familiar with the conception of a monotheistic faith and
of a dedicated life.

In the society of the second century the philosopher filled a
definite place, as a spiritual counsellor, a healer of inward distress, performing many functions which were afterwards discharged by the father confessors of the Roman Church. Under
the worst of the Roman tyrants Stoic philosophers had been
found brave enough to speak their minds and to defend the full
dignity of man, and, were reason a sufficient support for human
frailty, Stoicism, the noblest contribution which the pagan

world had to offer to the art and science of righteous living, would have secured for itself a permanent influence in human society.

To Mediterranean men, athirst for colour, imagery, and consolation, a system of austere monotheism and reasoned ethics could never bring full satisfaction. The Roman world turned with increasing interest to the ardent cults of the east, like those of Isis and Serapis, and Mithras, the soldier's god, which offered to all, however humble in station or mean in intellect, the boon of purifying mysteries and the hope of eternal life. It is in reality with these eastern creeds, rather than with the Olympian gods of Homer, that the eventual battle of Christianity was fought. The worshippers of the Egyptian Isis, the Phrygian Cybele, and the Persian Mithras shared many beliefs which were afterwards to be found in the Christian system. They believed in a sacramental union with the divine being, either through a ritual marriage, or more simply through a ceremonial eating of the god's flesh. The old riddle of birth and death, of fertility and decay, of the seed which flowers, and of the flower which returns to seed, was ever present to the religious imagination of the east. A god dying amid wails and lamentations, but resurgent amid cries of welcoming joy, was a central feature in these oriental mystery cults. In such symbolism the devotees of Mithras and of Isis found warrant for a faith in ultimate deliverance from the grave.

It is easy, even were the evidence of monuments less abundant, to account for the wide popularity of such beliefs. No attempt was made to check them. Marcus Aurelius instituted a temple to Mithras on the Vatican hill. Aurelian made sun-worship the official religion of the state. "The worship of Isis," writes Dean Inge, "was organized in a manner very like that of the Catholic Church. There was a kind of Pope, with priests, monks, singers, and acolytes. The images of the Madonna were crowned with true or false jewels, and her toilette was dutifully attended to every day. Daily matins and evensong were said in her chief temples. The priests were tonsured and wore white linen vestments." Before Rome became Christian, it had become clerical, a city of temples and images, of priests and religious processions, of cynic philosophers in cowls and coarse woollen gowns like the begging friars of the middle ages, of astrologers and magicians, such as always thrive amid public misfortunes.

When, under the reign of Diocletian, Rome ceased to be a A.D. 284-305 political capital, it was not perhaps difficult to foresee that one day the place of the absent Emperor would be taken by a Roman priest.

From this pagan effervescence the sectaries of the Christian religion stood austerely apart. As a secret society professing pacifist opinions and refusing to do sacrifice to the Emperor, the Christians were suspect to authority, and from time to time, as under Decius and Valerian, were exposed to severe persecu- A.D. 249-253 tions. The odium which in many quarters now attaches to the opponent of militarism and blood sports, and in a lesser degree to the feminist and the communist, was easily aroused by the spectacle of these eccentric fanatics, who denounced the cruel abominations of the amphitheatre, claimed equal treatment for the woman and the slave, and, spurning the delights of wealth and comfort, professed themselves the sole depositaries of truth. A body offering so strong a challenge to the social and political convictions of the world was bound to be unpopular and to be misunderstood. The Christians were accused of atheism because they did not accept the pagan gods, of misanthropy because they denounced the debased amusements of the people, and of immorality because they were not comprehended. Yet the Church grew steadily, fostered rather than hindered by persecu- tion, which was never sufficiently systematic or continuous to be deadly. By the time of Aurelian Christian beliefs had spread widely through the east, and in Rome itself were firmly rooted, A.D. 270-3 a rival influence to the established worship of the unconquerable sun.

It is perhaps to this growing concern for religion that we should in part ascribe a curious feature of the life and policy of the Empire in the fourth and fifth centuries. The more people thought about the inner life, the less they cared about the out- ward accidents. The more they became involved in the new religious excitements, the less were they attracted by the laborious routine of secular duty. In that mobile cosmopolitan society there was little left of the old flame of Roman patriotism. A new allegiance was beginning to claim an in- creasing number of earnest and valuable men and women in Gaul, in Italy, and in the Greek world. The state offered careers, but had ceased to speak to the soul. As outward difficulties accumulated, government became more costly, more nervous.

and more exacting. The pressure of the state upon the individual increased in a steadily diminishing temperature of
political obedience. The spirit of evasion, of reluctance to pay
the taxes in blood, in money, and in commodities, which the
state demanded, spread through all classes. It was found in the
peasants, in the traders, in the town councils, and it was met by
a policy of repression which converted peasants, traders, and
town councillors into the hereditary bondsmen of a servile
state.

The educational outlook of antiquity was necessarily coloured
by the institution of slavery. Even for the most generous minds
a sharp line was drawn between the small number of studies
and pursuits which a free man might follow without loss of
dignity, and the more utilitarian occupations from which he
would properly shrink. Plato thought that retail trade was degrading. Lucian, while admiring the statues of Praxiteles, was
thankful that he had not been called upon to produce them.
The conception which most generally prevailed was that the
world consisted of a civilized society whose economic needs were
provided by slaves and freedmen, foreigners and mechanics, for
whom nature had ordained a life of service, and who stood outside the charmed circle of the city. It followed that the education of civilized men concerned itself with those branches of
knowledge which ministered to happiness or success in a society
thus circumscribed.

In so far as it was not physical, education was concerned with
the appreciation of poetry, philosophy, and the fine arts. It
trained taste, afforded a discipline in eloquence, and exhibited
the ethical and political lessons of the past. Further it did not
go. Nature, history, and religion found no place in the curriculum. There was nothing in the ordinary education of the
Roman clearly calculated to direct his mind to the grave
social and economic problems which lay around him. In the
first century of the Empire slaves were so abundant that they
revolutionized the agrarian economy of Italy; but no attempt
was made to measure the productiveness of slave as compared
with free labour. Indeed, Varro even goes so far as to advise the
landowner to send freemen rather than slaves to work on un-
healthy land, as the loss of a freeman would be less crippling
than the death of a slave. Again, the steady depreciation of the
currency during the third century was productive of manifold

evils and of a violent remedial measure in the reign of Aurelian, over which men fought and died by the thousand in the streets of Rome. Yet no one put out a theory of currency or realized that bad money drives out good. So little were the elements of economic science understood that Diocletian, one of the wisest of the Emperors, issued an edict fixing prices all over the Empire, and found, as many have found since his day, that not all the laws or penalties in the world can prevent men from buying in the cheapest and selling in the dearest market.

The Eton master of the eighteenth century flogged his boys. The Roman youth of the second and third centuries flogged his masters. A system under which the education of youth is mainly entrusted to slaves cannot be wholesome; yet under favouring circumstances the literary training of a young Roman was probably as good as that which was received by an English boy in the reign of George III. In the sphere of grammar and literary criticism a tradition of scholarly competence long outlived the glories of the Augustan age. The Latin classics were studied with care. An effort, not often successful, was made to teach Greek as a subsidiary language. Education, however, cannot be carried on with success in airless compartments, but depends for its healthy growth upon fresh currents of thought and interest sweeping in from the active intellectual life of the world outside. If great motives vanish from poetry and prose, they will disappear also from the teaching of the young. The singular decay of Latin language and literature, which set in during the third century, was accompanied by a corresponding decline in the serious effectiveness of western education. Here there was no ferment comparable to that exciting influence of Plato and Aristotle, which so long sustained the intellectual life of the University of Athens. The pagan world of the west was ailing for lack of a popular literature. The Christian movement was regarded by its teachers as vulgar, foreign, and remote. It was, perhaps, a misfortune that the dominant intellectual influence in Latin education was that of a master of golden eloquence, for the ghost of Cicero hovered over every class-room. The imitation of his rounded periods became a schoolboy industry, and when the Empire was starving for statesmen and thinkers, the typical product of its schools was a shallow rhetorician.

To this narrow literary convention we may perhaps attribute the great lack of inventiveness in the practical arts which is

characteristic of the Roman people. There was no science after
the reign of Hadrian, there were no technical improvements.
Even in the art of war, so well understood and so brilliantly
practised for many centuries, the Romans were curiously uninventive. The Carthaginians taught them how to handle ships
at sea. The Parthians taught them the value of mounted
archery, the Balearic Islanders the use of the sling, the Goths
the penetrating power of heavily armed cavalry. But with the
exception of the " raven," a moving platform constructed to enable ships to be boarded, which was discovered in the First
Punic War, and Greek fire, which was first put to decisive use
in the sea fight at Actium, no important innovation in the
mechanics of war was discovered by the most warlike of the
Mediterranean peoples. The Roman legion inherited a long
tradition of discipline. It was sturdier than its barbarian opponents, less subject to wild panics, handier in manoeuvre: but it
never enjoyed the mechanical advantages which in modern
times have given to European troops a commanding ascendancy
against uncivilized armies.

Most curious is the fact, only recently brought out by a
French enquirer, that the true art of harnessing draft horses was
unknown to antiquity and only discovered in the west in the
age of Charlemagne. Much as the Greeks and Romans valued
horses, skilful as were their charioteers, they failed to see that no
horse can pull its proper weight if the harness presses against
the windpipe. The industrial consequences of a wrong method
of harnessing were far reaching. The transport of heavy material
by road was made eight times as costly as it need have been, and
the concentration of material for the purposes of large-scale production was proportionately hindered.

Although the Roman Empire was an association of towns,
the Romans were never an industrial people. With some few
exceptions the cities of Italy, Gaul, or Spain did not produce
wealth for the surrounding country, still less did they attempt
to supply a world market. The wealth which was squandered in
Rome during the first century had not been manufactured in
the west, but was derived from the spoils of the conquered east,
and once dissipated, was not replaced. By the reign of Vespasian
the impoverishment of the old senatorial class was already
marked, and though happier times came under the Antonines,
and large fortunes could still be made, the general level of

A.D. 117-
78

A.D. 69-
73

prosperity continued to descend. Gradually the towns shrank in size and population, and being walled to meet the hazards of the third century, lost something of the abundance and expansiveness of their earlier life. The spreading suburbs, with their pleasant gardens and marble villas, were no longer appropriate to those grim times. A stern fortress crowned the hill or dominated the plain. And long before the Roman Empire went down, its cities had adopted the mediaeval livery of fear.

The absence of any organized system of industrial production in Roman society, accompanied as it was by a lack of economic forethought, had serious consequences, of which one example may here be given. The devaluation of the coinage during the third century brought about the ruin of the middle class. In recent times a similar cause has produced a similar effect in one of the most advanced nations in Europe. But deadly as were the immediate effects of the fall of the German mark in 1923, these effects were soon repaired by the productive energies of the German people assisted by the application of capital to industry. The Roman Empire possessed no such powers of recuperation. There was no organized system of credit, no elaborate industrial plant, or skilled industrial or commercial leadership. The conditions under which a great economic reverse could be promptly retrieved did not exist.

More important was a decline in morale, a loss of heart, evident even in the Senate, the body which should have led the Commonwealth in the civic virtues of honour and independence, courage and patriotism. No contrast can be more tragic than the picture which Livy paints of the Roman Senate in the days of its glory during the Punic Wars, and the image of the same assembly abasing itself in servile adulation before the sombre Tiberius, which Tacitus presents to his readers. In that loss of moral dignity and independence we may read the terrible price which Rome was compelled to pay for the civil wars and proscriptions which had decimated her ruling class, and extinguished the flame of republican liberty. Demoralization was not, however, confined to the senators of Rome. Polybius, writing a hundred years before the days of Augustus, had pointed out the disastrous effects of luxury and immorality on the population of Greece. The causes which operated there were present throughout the Mediterranean littoral. Everywhere save in Egypt there was a dearth of men, and everywhere the immediate reason was the same, a reluctance to bring children into the world.

As the old families which had been the mainstay of the Roman state died out, new stocks came to the front, some of them sound and wholesome, but the greater number bearing little resemblance either in character or mentality to the men who fought in the Sabine or Punic Wars. Even in the first century, Juvenal had complained of the alien immigration into Rome. "The Orontes," he writes, " has flowed into the Tiber." The evil denounced by the satirist did not diminish. Apart from the slaves and freedmen, who were for the most part non-Italic, Levantine crews manned the commercial navy, bringing Levantine usurers and merchants into every western mart where money could be made. By the fourth century much alien blood, Greek Asiatic, Punic, Iberian, must have mingled with the native Italian strain in Rome and the largest cities of Italy. The admixture did not help to preserve a high standard of public duty. We receive the impression of an unhappy, superstitious, nervous society, depressed by a sense of calamity, which it has not the calmness or thinking power to diagnose. It is significant that when the armies of Aurelian returned to Europe, bringing with them the terrible eastern plague, no attempt was made to explore the cause or to find a remedy. Analysis was bankrupt. In place of thought, superstition indicated imaginary foes and administered its damaging opiates. When political troubles were unusually grave, as under Decius, it was thought prudent to persecute the Christians.

A.D. 270-5

The fighting spirit which had made the fortunes of the Republic had already by the age of Hadrian deserted the Italians. They were well content that their battles should be fought by Illyrian and Anatolian highlanders or by barbarian mercenaries from beyond the frontiers. In the old republican days, when the fighting was for the most part under the blue Italian sky, in a land of vines and olives, and campaigns were short and plunder was good, war was a national pastime; but life in a legionary camp on the Danube or the Rhine or by the Roman wall in Britain was a different matter. It did not attract the Latin race. The Italians vanished from the legions, which in the fourth century were chiefly composed of and even officered by Germans.

Since the most populous and civilized parts of the Empire had ceased by the beginning of the third century to contribute fighting men to the legions, the number of troops available for frontier defence was far smaller than it should have been, having regard to the total population of the Empire, which in the time of Constantine may have reached 70,000,000. A modern state containing 70,000,000 inhabitants might be expected in a great war to put 6,000,000 soldiers in the field. Of such an effort the Empire was incapable. Even after its reorganization by Diocletian and Constantine the total strength of the Roman army did not exceed 650,000 men, one-third belonging to the mobile force and two-thirds to the garrisons. In view of the length of the frontier to be defended these figures were dangerously low. As the defending force came in the end to be composed mainly of Germans they were such as to lead to inevitable disaster.

BOOKS WHICH MAY BE CONSULTED

H. Stuart Jones : The Roman Empire. 1908.

Rostovtzeff : Social and Economic History of the Roman Empire. 1926.

J. W. Mackail : History of Latin Literature. 1895.

J. W. Mackail : The Aeneid of Virgil. 1930.

W. W. Capes : The Roman Empire of the Second Century; or, The Age of the Antonines. 1876.

J. B. Bury : History of the Later Roman Empire. 2 vols. 1889.

J. B. Bury : Invasion of Europe by the Barbarians. 1928.

Christopher Dawson : The Making of Europe. 1932.

Ferdinand Lot : La Fin du Monde Antique et le Début du Moyen Âge. 1927.

Lefebvre des Noëttes : L'attelage, le cheval de selle à travers les âges. 1931.

W. R. Inge : The Philosophy of Plotinus. 1918.

G. Boissier : La Fin du Paganisme. 2 vols. 1891.

E. Renan : Marc Aurèle. 1882.

L. P. Homo : L'Empire Romain. 1925.

G. Ferrero : Greatness and Decline of Rome. Tr. A. E. Zimmern. 1907.

J. S. Reid : Municipalities of the Roman Empire. 1913.

T. Rice Holmes : The Architect of the Roman Empire. 1928-31.

N. M. P. Nilsson : Imperial Rome. Tr. G. C. Richards. 1926.

T. Mommsen : The Provinces of the Roman Empire. Tr. W. P. Dickson. 2 vols. 1886.

Cambridge Ancient History, Vol. X.

Tenney Frank : Roman Imperialism. 1914.

Tenney Frank : An Economic History of Rome till the End of the Republic. 1927.

4

CHAPTER IX

DIOCLETIAN AND CONSTANTINE

Reforms of Diocletian. Constantine as soldier and organizer. He embraces Christianity. Consequences of the Imperial recognition of the Christian Faith. Close association of Church and State under Constantine. His choice of Byzantium as a capital. East and west drift apart. Less Greek culture in the west. The continuing influence of Latin classics. Difference between the Roman and the Greek church.

THE new despotism was inaugurated by two great Illyrian Emperors, Diocletian and Constantine. To every lover of liberty their work would seem to have grave faults, for it was conceived in a spirit most hostile to individual initiative and executed in an atmosphere poisoned by spies and sycophants. Moreover, the last eight years of Diocletian's reign are marked by a bitter and memorable persecution of the Christians.

A.D. 297-305

Yet, despite these shortcomings, few statesmen have been so successful in giving to the world in which they were born what it seemed to want and was content to preserve. The administrative system of Diocletian governed eastern Rome for a thousand years. The reformed coinage of Constantine[1] lasted till the eleventh century. And the whole course of European history would have been otherwise, had Constantine declined to accept Christianity as an authorized religion, or failed to summon the Council of Nicaea, which defined the doctrine of the divinity of Christ, or had he not, with the instinct of the higher strategy, determined to transfer the capital of the Empire to that old Greek city on the Bosphorus which still bears his name.

Diocletian, who was raised to supreme power by the Pannonian legions in 284, brought an atmosphere of saving novelty into the management of affairs. Through his long reign of twenty years he applied the resources of a powerful and restless mind to the tasks of government. To contemporaries the course of this Dalmatian peasant may have appeared inconsistent and wayward, and too often determined by impulse and superstition. He would build and unbuild, enact and recall his enactment: but

---

[1] A gold aureus or solidus, roughly equalling 12s 6d. of our money.

posterity, regarding not so much the details as the general effect
of his work, sees in him a man of system supervening on a plan-
less state. He introduced centralization, administrative uniformity, the subdivision of powers and provinces. He saw the
importance of severing political and military authority, of a
strict and hierarchical civil discipline in a society which had lost
the gift of political thinking. To him also is due the introduction of those servile forms of ceremonial which for many centuries afterwards continued to characterize the court life of
European princes. In theory the Emperor was still the elected
protector of the people, bound by laws which it was his duty
to obey. In fact, he was an eastern sultan, claiming divine right,
the directing engine of a vast bureaucratic machine with a long
and carefully graded hierarchy of officials depending on his nod.
We pass from the Roman to the Byzantine age.

In another respect also the reign of Diocletian marks an epoch.
He appreciated the fact that the defence of the Empire on four
separate fronts could not be supervised by a single man, that
defence must be mobile, not stationary, and directed from
centres near the frontier, and that an end must be put to the
system of military *pronunciamentos*, which had involved the
Empire in so much chaos and bloodshed. His plan was that the
Empire should be governed by two Augusti, himself and Maxi-
mianus, a Thracian peasant, and that these should be assisted by
two younger men to be known as Caesars, who should succeed
to the purple when the Augusti resigned, as they undertook to
do after twenty years of rule. Rome ceased to be the capital.
The rulers of the Empire held their courts at Trèves and Milan.
at Sirmium and Nicomedeia. Diocletian himself selected Nicomedeia, and from that pleasant Asiatic station undertook to
police the troublesome east.

Ingenious as was the device of entrusting the management of
the Empire to a college of four, it failed to secure the desired
effect. The retirement of the two Augusti in 305 was followed by
a period of civil discord, memorable only at this distance of
time as establishing upon unassailable foundations the name
and the empire of Constantine the Great.

This outstanding man, the bastard son of a well-born Illyrian
officer by an innkeeper at Nish (in modern Serbia), was upon the
death of his father Constantius at York proclaimed Emperor A.D. *306*
by the troops—the precise evil which the reforms of Dio-

cletian had been framed to avert. Disastrous as such elections
had too often been, the instinct of the British legionaries was
here justified. The youth of thirty-two proved himself to be a
consummate commander in the field. After a skilful defence of
the Gallic frontier, he overthrew, in a succession of brilliant engagements, his two rivals, Maxentius, the ruler of Italy, and
Licinius, the Emperor of the East. In all his military career he
never suffered a reverse. The speed and energy of his offensives
were characteristic of a man to whom physical fears were unknown, and the ever present world of spirits supplied cordials of
intoxicating strength. Is it to be wondered that he regarded himself as the favoured son of the victory-bringing God, or that the
despotic system of Diocletian received from his hands additional
aggravations?

Only the strictest regard to the principles of justice and
economy can save such a system from terrible abuses. The
Roman administration in the fourth century, despite many improvements, was still lamentably deficient in justice and knowledge. Great wealth was lightly taxed, moderate fortunes were
crippled by crushing exactions. Owing to the steady depreciation of the coinage, an important part of the revenue was levied
in kind, a system leading on the one hand to irregularity and
extortion, and on the other to a forlorn attempt to fix a money
value to commodities. These things were bad enough. A vicious
fiscal system was not the least among the causes which led to
the downfall of the Roman empire; but what was equally
serious was the all-pervading system of compulsion, by which
the new despotism attempted to secure the upkeep of the state.
The landlord was compelled to act as recruiting officer and tax
collector for his neighbourhood. The peasant was tied to the
soil. The *decurion*, a town councillor, was made responsible for
the contributions due from his municipality and forbidden to
leave his birthplace. Even trade was placed in fetters. Free commercial associations were turned into hereditary castes and
saddled with definite obligations of state service.

More important even than these far-reaching changes were
the two decisions which have given to Constantine a place among
the small number of men who have changed the course of
history. Nobody would be bold enough to contend that this
vigorous and capable soldier was a Christian character. If he did
not actually, as is attested, throw German captives to the beasts,

he certainly put to death his wife and his son. But in a violent age crimes of violence are lightly condoned, and the failings of Constantine were soon overshadowed by the great achievement which caused him to be regarded in the eastern Empire as a thirteenth apostle.

In that rude age the truth of a religion was apt to be measured by its results. If it brought victory to its devotees, it was likely to be true; if defeat, it was probably false. It is to the credit of Constantine that at an early point in his long career, while he was policing the frontier of Gaul, he came to the conclusion that the Cross, a symbol alike of Christ and of the Sun God, was the bestower of victory. In a vision, reported at first hand to Eusebius, and by him recounted, not in his ecclesiastical history, but in a later biography, Constantine saw the standard of the Cross with the legend Ἐν τούτῳ νίκα (By this conquer), and, advancing with the Christian monogram on his banner, won four victories in succession against the forces of his rival Maxentius, and made himself master of Italy (A.D. 312). The secular fortunes of the Christian Church were henceforth assured. Though his baptism was delayed till 337, the conqueror of Maxentius threw the full weight of his influence on the side of the religion which had brought him victory at Turin, at Verona, at the Milvian bridge hard by the very gates of Rome. The Christians had given their proofs. They had survived persecution, they were organized. Active and energetic characters had been drawn into their fold. Constantine made up his mind to enlist the support, to control the activities, and to appease the dissensions of this influential society. It is true that the Christians were a small minority.[1] The barbarians, the legions, the vast proportion of the civilian population of the west, were still pagan. But there was this difference between paganism and Christianity, that while the pagans, with polytheistic hospitality, were willing to receive the Christian God, the Christians regarded the pagan divinities as malignant demons. A Christian bishop could not dispute the power of Apollo to foresee or of Aesculapius to heal. He did not contest the reality of these beings, but he contended that they were false and that it was wicked to consult them. Paganism was more tolerant. To a discerning prince a well-organized and convinced

[1] Bury estimates one-fifth, "History of the Later Roman Empire," p. 366.

minority, fortified by sacred books and a clear-cut creed, might well seem to be a better ally than a superior number of indulgent and variously minded sectaries.

Yet it would appear that even after the crowning mercy of the Milvian bridge the purpose of Constantine was still indistinct. He believed in Christ, but also in the unconquered sun. He tolerated the Christians but retained the office of Pontifex Maximus. His coins bore on one side the emblem of Christianity, on the other an attestation of sun-worship. More than a decade elapsed before soldiers were rebuked for sacrificing to Jupiter or pagan rites were eliminated from official ceremonies.

It can hardly be doubted that the adoption of Christianity as the official religion of the Empire gave a powerful impulse to the enlargement of the Christian community. To pass from Paganism to Christianity was not for many professors of the older creed to enter a climate altogether strange nor to experience a revolution altogether sudden. The process of conversion was gentle and assisted by infinite small gradations of feeling and experience. The sacraments of the new religion recalled the ancient mysteries, its preaching the newer philosophy. The doctrine of a mediator was familiar alike to the Persians and the Neoplatonics. The conception of a Trinity was a well-known religious idea proceeding from the acknowledged fact that three was the perfect number. Abstinence and poverty, ecstasy and calm, were no novelties to the pious adherents of the older creeds. Nor was the idea of the last judgment, with all its terrible consequences, a monopoly of the Christian Faith. The believers in Mithras and the professors of Stoicism were united in holding that the world was destined to perish in flame.

Yet when the pagan had completed his journey he found himself in a world of altered values. Old virtues were disparaged, new virtues, such as chastity, rose in the scale. Poverty was exalted above wealth, faith above works, humility above pride, equality above privilege. The gates of salvation were open to all. A strong inrush of ethical feeling from the underworld pervaded the Empire, dashing itself against the vices and cruelties which were the shadow side of that old civilization, cleansing away many foul impurities, but also obliterating in its passionate course much that in ancient ideals of conduct and expression was noble, temperate, and wise.

From such enthusiasms Constantine, for all his superstition, was exempt. His motto was unity. A church divided against itself would be of little value to the state. So, though he had small personal interest in theological discussions, he was drawn from considerations of policy to be a convener and president of Church councils, a mediator in Church disputes, an influence in the determination of Church dogma. The defeat of the Donatists (a sect of African Puritans) at the Western Council at Arles (314) and of the Arians at the far more important Ecumenical Council at Nicaea (325) were signs of a new association between the Catholic Church and the Roman State, which has coloured the destinies of all Christian peoples. The importance of Constantine's decision is clear; its consequences are variously estimated. To the friends of institutional religion the sovereign who brought the Roman Empire over to Christianity is one of the greatest benefactors of mankind. Others see in that close association of church and state a principal source of the secular pride and ambition which for so many centuries has obscured the original candour of the Christian life.

The second great decision of Constantine was prompted by personal pride blended with military and religious considerations. Like Romulus and Alexander he must build a capital. But he was a son of the Balkans. He knew, as the Austrians knew so well at a later time, how rich in recruits were the wild Illyrian hills of his native home. He was aware that for more than a hundred years the chief danger to the Empire had come from the barbarian tribesmen north of the Danube, and from the oriental monarchies east of the Euphrates. If he were well placed for the defence of the Balkans he saw that he would be in the best position to save the Empire. Already Diocletian had realized that on strategical grounds the capital should be near the frontier between Asia and Europe. Guided by a sure instinct, Constantine, when he had defeated his rival, Licinius, at Chrysopolis, decided on Byzantium, than which no town was better defended by nature or by art.

The new city was to be both Christian and Latin. Christian it remained, Latin it soon ceased to be. The Emperor may have reflected that it was easier to make a Christian capital on the Bosphorus than in a great centre of historic paganism like Rome, where every temple and statue challenged attack or defence. He can as little have foreseen the dominance of the Greek language in Constantinople as that Rome, which he regarded as the chief fortress of paganism, should become the leader of the Christian world.

The eastern city rose like an exhalation. Palaces and mansions, porticos, law courts, and public baths were constructed with feverish celerity. The whole Empire was ransacked for treasures wherewith to decorate the fame of Constantine. While the serpent column reft from Delphi recalled the victory of Plataea, the basilica of the Roman law court crowned with the Persian dome gave to the new Christian churches their characteristic form, a blend of the eastern and the western spirit. On May 11, 330, the work was complete. The new Rome had been built in less than six years.

The foundation of Constantinople marks the beginning of a new era, during which the Greek and Roman worlds drift further and further apart until the unity of the Empire becomes nothing more than a theory and a hope. Roman government as reconstructed by Diocletian and Constantine survived in the east and was not seriously shaken until the Frankish conquest of Constantinople in 1204. Far different was the future of western Europe. Here after a hundred and fifty years of weakened and precarious existence the Empire went down under the German invasions, leaving to the Church the office of preserving as best it might the legacy of ancient culture in a barbaric world.

Much of that ancient culture was lost or rejected. The free spirit of rationality which was characteristic of Hellenism disappeared in a world which had come to believe with St. Augustine that Time was a brief course of passing moments created by God and destined at God's pleasure in the twinkling of an eye to pass away and to give place to eternity. In this frail, uncertain, and crumbling dispensation, so full of wickedness and misery, the Christian held that all mundane interests paled before the awful problem of the soul's salvation. The reward of the righteous was everlasting blessedness. Sinners (including unbaptized infants) would burn for ever in the fires of hell. Sacred books, interpreted by a Providential Church, illumined the path to heaven. Following those lamps, and those alone, and constraining others to pursue the same course, the believer would be saved. False opinion would mean ruin. He must neither dally with it nor suffer it in others. Had not Jesus said, " Compel them

A.D 354.
430

to come in "? On this text St. Augustine founded the doctrine of religious persecution which fenced in the mind of Europe during the centuries of Faith.

Though St. Augustine was saturated with the thought of Plato, as later St. Thomas with the speculations of Aristotle, a first-hand knowledge of Greek language and literature died out in the west. Some time in the course of the third century, by an obscure revolution in literary history, Greek ceased to be used by Roman Christians in the celebration of their rites. In time the language fell under suspicion as a vehicle of heresy. Ovid and Terence were taught. Homer and Aeschylus were forgotten, and the knowledge of Greek, the key to the most original and valuable portion of the ancient culture, was not recovered in the west till the fifteenth century. The consequences were serious both for culture and for religion. The effective unity of the Christian Church was broken on the rock of vocabulary and syntax. Greek Christianity, in a climate of Greek metaphysics and imperial despotism, took one course. Latin Christianity, in an undisciplined and barbaric world, but using the language and sharing the spirit of Roman Law, took another. In the east the church was subject to the state; in the west, under the leadership of the Bishop of Rome, it made pretensions to be an independent, if not a superior authority.

The culture of the Latin Church in the west was founded partly upon the Christian and Jewish Scriptures and partly upon the tradition of Latin learning which was maintained in the schools of rhetoric, and which survived the disappearance of the pagan empire. It is this interfusion of literary influences which characterized the intellectual life of western Europe during the early middle ages, when the Church alone preserved and multiplied manuscripts and schooled its barbarian pupils in the elements of Latin grammar and style. At no time has European civilization been so deeply in the debt of Virgil and Cicero as during the first fierce and gloomy centuries of the Christian Empire, when almost alone they represented, in a society which but dimly apprehended their greatness, the healing spirit of ancient humanism.

In curious contrast to the rationalistic spirit of ancient Greek philosophy, the Greek Church of the East Roman, and afterwards of the Russian Empire, has felt little temptation to challenge secular power or ecclesiastical tradition. No great liberating movements for the improvement of the human lot are traceable to its agency. It has been a department of state, stiff, hieratic, constitutional, and conservative, in art no less than in belief. The annals of the Roman Church in the tumultuous and disorganized west present a very different picture, for here during the long abeyance of the western Empire the Church stood out from the licence of the times as heir to the discipline and influence of Rome.

BOOKS WHICH MAY BE CONSULTED

Christopher Dawson : The Making of Europe. 1932.

N. H. Baynes : Constantine the Great and the Christian Church. (Proceedings of the British Academy, Vol. XV., 1931.)

N. H. Baynes : The Byzantine Empire. 1926.

Ferdinand Lot : La Fin du Monde Antique. 1927.

S. Dill : Roman Society in the Last Century of the Western Empire. 1899.

Charles Oman : Short History of the Byzantine Empire. 1892.

CHAPTER X

THE GERMANIC INVASIONS

Two currents of migration. The east Germans or Goths. They become Arians. The west Germans described by Tacitus. Main characteristics of German society. The impact of the Huns. The Visigoths cross the Danube. Alaric. Dislocation of the western Empire. Continuing prestige of Rome. Gaul in the fifth century. Fall of the Visigothic Kingdom. Vandal conquest of Africa. Attila, his rise and fall. Deposition of Romulus. Theodoric in Italy. Clovis in Gaul. He becomes a Roman Catholic. The darkest age in Britain. The Saxon Conquest. Multiplicity of states. Conversion to Roman Christianity.

So far the history of Europe has been dominated by the three great forces of Hellenic civilization, the Roman empire, and the Christian religion, the first two clearly interlinked, but the last deriving from the east and challenging at many crucial points the conduct, beliefs, and interests of the ancient world. A further influence now comes upon the scene and changes for all subsequent time the course of European history. The Latin world of the west, after successfully defeating and absorbing the continental Celts, is overcome by the Germans.

We know very little of the early history of this remarkable race save that they were originally settled in the Scandinavian north, where some remained to form the parent stock of the present Swedish, Norwegian, and Danish nations, while others wandered through Germany in search of food or warmth, or from mere love of adventure and fighting, until one group of these southward-trending peoples reached the waters of the Rhine, while a second, pursuing a more eastern course, descended ultimately on the Danube and the coast of the Black Sea. It is with these two diverging currents of German migration that the Roman Empire was brought into contact. It was the West Germans who fought with Marius and Julius Caesar, who under Augustus defeated Varus and his legions, and whose habits and institutions are described in one of the classics of ethnology, the *De Origine, situ, moribus et populis Germaniae* of Tacitus. Finally, it is to two West German peoples, the Saxons and the Franks, that we must ascribe the formation of the mediaeval kingdoms of England and France.

The career of the eastern or Gothic branch of this vigorous race[1] differs in certain important particulars from the fortune of its western cousins. The Goths burst later into the sunlight of history,[2] struck harder, and built more swiftly, but their work, though arresting and spectacular, was ephemeral and soon undone. Whereas the Franks and Saxons have left a permanent memorial of their passage through time in two powerful and ordered modern states, the name Gothic, save where it is used in relation to a form of architecture originating in a region which the Goths never controlled, is synonymous with all that is dark, barbaric, and destructive. Yet on two occasions the shaping of Europe seemed likely to be confided to the Goths. In the middle of the third century it might have appeared to contemporaries that the fabric of the Roman Empire was destined to perish under the mighty hammer of this formidable people. With an equal show of probability it might have been contended two hundred years later that from the Gothic kingdoms of Italy and Aquitaine there was destined to proceed a continuous and promising civilization blending the vigour and piety of the Goth with the long inherited culture of the Roman. Yet each of these predictions, had it been made, would have been falsified in the event. The terrible crisis of the third century (235-268) was mastered by the courage and resource of three Illyrian commanders, Claudius II, Aurelian, and Probus; and two centuries afterwards, by the strange irony of fortune, the Goths of the west were undone by their very eagerness to receive the spiritual gifts of the Roman world. The Visigoths who were settled in the Balkan peninsula were the first of all the German peoples to accept Christianity. Ulfila, a great missionary of Cappadocian extraction, translated the Bible into Gothic and so spread the Christian message among his adopted people that Ostrogoths and Visigoths alike accepted the faith, and attempted, as far as their rough natures permitted, to understand its meaning. Unfortunately the sacred message had reached the Goths in its Arian form. The poor barbarians had learned that though Christ was divine, he had been created by God and was inferior to his Father. Many pious divines, many famous statesmen, including Constantine the Great himself, had shared these opinions, first promulgated in Alexandria by the presbyter Arius,

A.D. 310-80

---

[1] Goths, Vandals, Gepids, Burgundians, Lombards, Rugians, etc.
[2] Goths had reached the Black Sea under Caracalla (A.D. 214).

as to the nature of Christ. The Goths can hardly be blamed if they believed what they were told about a mystery so abstruse by leading oracles of contemporary wisdom. But Arianism, despite brilliant spells of official favour, finished in the blackest disgrace. It was condemned by the Council of Nicaea. It was condemned by the Bishop of Rome. It was reprobated by the western clergy in Italy, Gaul and Spain, who represented to congregations unversed in theological subtleties that the Arian was the enemy of Christ (χριστόμαχος) and that Arianism was a challenge to Christ's divinity. In the troubled theological atmosphere of the fifth century, when success in this world and in the world beyond was thought to depend on the accuracy of faith, there was no issue more passionately or widely debated than the nature of the Second Person of the Trinity, which few were fitted to discuss, and none were able to understand.

So the Gothic kingdoms of Italy and Aquitaine, which had been founded by the sword, perished of a heresy, and the more barbarous West Germans, who were converted later, but to the orthodox faith, entered upon a long inheritance of power, with the applause and support of the western Church.

Of these West Germans, Tacitus, writing in the time of Trajan, *c. A.D. 98* has drawn a picture more remarkable perhaps for its moral purpose than for its fidelity to fact. It is the aim of the Roman historian to contrast the idealized simplicity of the German life with the degenerate luxury of Italian society, and to find in the free ways of the noble savage material for the chastisement of civilized man.

It is probable, therefore, that the virtues of the Germans were here exaggerated, as it is certain that no Roman would willingly have exchanged the vivid life of the forum for the lonely clearings, the forbidding forests, and the leaden skies of Germany. Tacitus, however, was right in thinking that the Germans had something new and valuable to give to European civilization. He seems to have divined in this barbaric people a refreshing and renovating power, to have seen that they had the secret of political liberty, which Rome had forgotten, the passion for individual initiative which Rome had suppressed, the habit of rearing large families, which Rome had chosen to neglect and despise. The last of these characteristics gave to the Germans a decisive superiority in the struggles which were to come. Again and again in the course of history the Latin world has had cause to tremble before the irrepressible fecundity of this wholesome and monogamous race.

Save that the West Germans had by the time of Tacitus taken to a settled agricultural life, while the easterners with their waggons and herds were still trekking through pathless forests, one part of the Teuton world much resembled another. The violent, blond, beer-swilling giant with fierce blue eyes and long fair hair, drinking and dreaming, fighting and gambling, singer and song lover, his strong loyalty to chieftain and clan only mastered by his still greater passion for warlike adventure, was a type well known in the fourth century to every legionary camp on the northern frontier. It is true that during two centuries of internecine war and forest clearance the clans of Germany had undergone many changes of size, shape, and appellation. Small clans had disappeared, greater aggregations had been formed round some heroic figure, or in response to some warlike necessity, and then dissolving, as men died or fell, had entered into new combinations. The little tribes mentioned by Tacitus had vanished by the age of Constantine, and were replaced by larger people, the Franks, the Saxons, the Alemans of south Germany. But the main characteristics of German life and society were little changed, and might be found anywhere in central Europe—the chieftain and his chosen band of warrior comrades, the popular assembly of free tribesmen, the ancient royal families, from which kings might be chosen, the great herds of small cattle, the open field tillage of corn and barley, the predial serfs, and the absence not only of towns but even of villages or hamlets with close-set houses and sheltered streets. Yet despite their common origin and similar manners the Germans were wholly devoid of national feeling. Tribe fought with tribe, family with family. By some the Roman Empire was regarded as an enemy, by others as a possible paymaster or host. Accordingly the armies which this fecund race could put into the field at any one time were ludicrously disproportionate to its numbers. If the Roman armies were, as we have seen, dangerously under strength, their German antagonists were not to any marked degree more numerous. It is not, then, to a series of conflicts in which some twenty thousand men were involved on either side that we must look for an explanation of the decline and fall of the Roman Empire. That great structure was not brought down to the ground by a frontal attack, but by a process of infiltration extending over a hundred years which ended by placing the government of Italy, Gaul, Spain, and Africa in German hands.

A wild Mongolian people riding on stout ponies out of central Asia had in the later part of the fourth century made its way over the steppes into south-eastern Europe. Slaying and plundering as they rode, these ugly merciless creatures, known as Huns, swept every obstacle before them like chaff before an eastern gale. Alans, Ostrogoths, and Visigoths felt successively the force of a thrust spreading tremors through the whole German world, and leading to those great but obscurely chronicled movements of the German peoples, which for a time submerged Gaul and Britain, Spain, Africa, and Italy, and bequeathed to mediaeval Germany the heroic memories of the Niebelungenlied.

The first effect of this new disturbing force was felt upon the north-eastern bastion of the Empire. By 376 the Huns had penetrated into Dacia (the beautiful country of Transylvania which has recently passed to the Roumans) and there defeated the Visigoths, who had themselves some years before evicted the descendants of that Roman province, from which Trajan has obtained an undying renown, and modern Roumania a disputed title.

Uprooted from this pleasant home the Visigoths appealed for Roman shelter. They were permitted to cross the Danube and to form an encampment in lower Moesia. Eighty thousand alien immigrants are not easily absorbed even by the best organized community. The Visigoths were uncomfortable, and as discomfort ripened into suspicion and suspicion into hate, they took up arms against their imperial host. The issue was joined on the field of Adrianople (378), when the mailed cavalry of the invaders defeated the imperial army, slew Valens, the Emperor, and established for a thousand years the predominance of the cavalry arm in European warfare.

The man who was called upon to deal with this desperate situation was a fine Spanish soldier, claiming descent from the family of Trajan. Theodosius I, being ready to apply persecution to the support of orthodoxy, has received from ecclesiastical historians the title of "great"; and the Emperor under whose rule the mysteries of Eleusis and the Olympian games were celebrated for the last time deserves a special place in the annals of the Christian Church. But the reputation of Theodosius has a better foundation than the bigotry with which he persecuted the pagans and the heretics. By skilfully converting the Goths into federates of the Empire and providing them with an assured settlement on imperial territory, he purchased a peace of thirteen years for his harassed dominions.

Had Theodosius been succeeded by a son as resolute as himself, it is possible that the Goths might have been converted into loyal and obedient servants of the east Roman state; but there ensued upon his death, at the age of fifty in 395, a calamity from which the Empire never recovered. At this critical juncture two feeble and inexperienced youths, Arcadius and Honorius, were called respectively to rule the eastern and western Empire. The first of these shadow sovereigns was governed by the eunuch Eutropius, the second by the Vandal Stilicho.

Though bound to defend the Empire under the terms of the recent treaty, the Visigoth retained in his Thracian home the heart and speech of a German savage. A cultured visitor from Africa saw the impolicy of admitting these armed and predatory aliens into the body of the Roman state. In a spirited allocution to Arcadius, Synesius of Cyrene pleaded for the formation of a national army to cope with the Gothic peril. The farmer should be called from his farm, the philosopher from his study, the craftsman from his craft, the salesman from his shop, the city drone from his beloved theatre, and all should be enrolled in a force for national defence. The speech, if ever delivered, fell upon idle ears. While Arcadius did nothing effective, the Visigoths elected as their King a fighting man of thirty, Alaric the Bold.

The career of this Christian savage is in many respects of great significance. All through his life Alaric appears to have had for his object not the destruction of the Empire, which would have been to him unthinkable, but his own elevation in the Imperial Service, and the assignment of an attractive settlement to his people. To obtain these ends there was no form of blackmail to which he would not resort, no impiety which he was not prepared to commit. He held Athens to ransom, took Corinth and Sparta, ravaged Thessaly and the Peloponnese, and then, passing into Italy, besieged Rome three times, and finally (410) gave it over to his barbarians to sack.

This great calamity striking a city which for many centuries had been regarded as the pre-ordained centre of human authority on earth created a profound impression of dismay. Was this, then, the result of Christianity, and the vengeance of the ancient shrines? Was this the reward of the Christian Faith? The answer came in the *De Civitate Dei*, begun in 412 and finished in 427. In this, perhaps the greatest of patristic writings, St. Augustine of Hippo replied that over and against the city of man was the city of God, unaffected by material things, without frontiers and embracing the entire body of the faithful all over the world.

Yet the sack of Rome was but a minor element in a great developing calamity. The Gothic attacks on Italy initiated nine years before had only been repelled by the depletion of the imperial garrisons on the Rhine. Sueves, Alans, Vandals (the last an East German people already converted to Arian Christianity) swarmed over the ill-defended frontier of Gaul, and after three years of terrible pillage and slaughter crossed the Pyrenees into Spain. In these three years of memorable anarchy the A.D. whole complexion of the western Empire was changed; for not 406-9 only was its authority finally shaken in Gaul and Spain, but a certain Constantine, raised to the purple by the legions of Britain, took most of the Roman garrison from that island, leaving it by so much the more exposed to the assaults of Saxon pirates in the south, and to the raids of Picts and Scots along the northern border.

This preliminary hurricane was followed by a steady pressure of German tribes westward into Gaul. The Salian Franks occupied Belgium, the Ripuarian Franks took Trèves, the Alemanni encamped in Alsace, the Burgundians founded a kingdom with its capital at Worms, and finally the Visigoths, exchanging Italy for Gaul, settled in the region of Toulouse, and from that centre built up a state which at the point of its greatest extension stretched from the Straits of Gibraltar to the Loire, and from the Atlantic to the Rhone.

The government of Ravenna, for this was now the working capital of the Empire in the west, was never at any time during the fifth century in a position seriously to curb these mass movements of the German peoples. It adopted the policy inaugurated by Theodosius of recognizing as federates of the Empire tribes whom it was inconvenient to attack or impossible to conquer. The principle of forced "hospitality," in accordance with which it had been a time-honoured practice to quarter troops upon

Italian proprietors, was extended to Gaul for the benefit of the Visigoths and Burgundians. A reluctant host was compelled by a reluctant Emperor to cede two-thirds of his property to a barbarian "guest."

The German intruders were well disposed to the polite fiction, which disguised pillage under the name of hospitality, and independence under the respectable banner of federation. To the Visigoths and Burgundians Rome was still a moral power, and Roman civilization an object of ignorant but admiring regard. In the eyes of these barbarians, now faintly tinctured with civility, only a Roman citizen might wear the purple. A Visigoth might marry a Roman princess or acclaim a Roman emperor, but the imperial diadem was not for the rude brow of an alien. A curious mixture of superstitious reverence and defiant hostility marked the relations of Goth and Burgundian to the Roman state. It seemed as if they thought that against Rome there were no talismans other than those which Rome could supply. So among the trophies carried out of Italy by Ataulph, the founder of the Visigothic kingdom in South-Western Gaul, were two Roman persons, the Princess Galla Placidia, sister of the Emperor Honorius, and Attalus, an obscure rhetorician, the first designed for the barbarian's bed, the second as a counter emperor to be used against the court of Ravenna in case of need.

A.D. *411*

For the remainder of the fifth century and until the great Frankish victory at Vouillé in A.D. 507 the social history of Gaul is dominated by the presence within it of these two states of "friendly" or "federate" barbarians. One of the strongest forces in human society is imitation, and once settled in their new homes the Visigoths and Burgundians applied themselves to the study and imitation of the Greco-Roman culture, which nowhere in that age was so fully maintained as in Gaul. The barbarian kings soon discovered that, however much they might despise the effeminacy of Mediterranean men, government could not be carried out in a Latin-speaking country without the employment of ministers and clerks who spoke the Latin tongue or of legists who knew the Roman law. It does not then appear that life was anywhere made intolerable to the Gallo-Roman provincial who lived in the kingdoms of Burgundy or Aquitaine. The great noble farmed and hunted, built and gardened, visited his friends and trifled in his library, enjoying a stately, unruffled existence, as if there were no barbarians to murder the beautiful

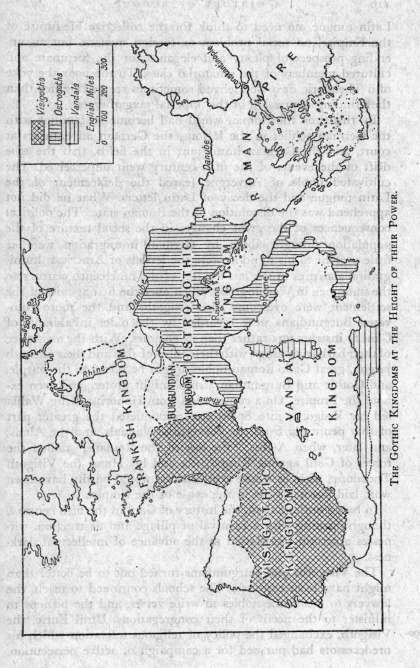

THE GOTHIC KINGDOMS AT THE HEIGHT OF THEIR POWER.

Latin tongue, no need to think for the collective life-future of the Empire, no social problem or foreign menace, but an unending prospect of plenty and elegance for the fortunate and cultured members of the senatorial class. To the poor the yoke of a Theodoric or a Gondebaud sometimes seemed lighter than the grinding oppression of the imperial taxgatherers.

By this time the Roman world had become so familiar with the German soldier in the legions, the German adventurers at court, and the German immigrant in the fields, that the true drift of the events of the fifth century went unperceived. The cultivated noble of Auvergne feared the defacement of the Latin tongue and the decay of Latin letters. What he did not apprehend was the dissolution of the Roman state. The political consequences of the great changes in the social texture of the population brought about by German immigration were as little present to his mind as were the lessons of American immigration statistics in the last quarter of the nineteenth century to the statesmen in Washington. When once the first agonies of the settlement were overcome, the Visigoths and the more cultivated Burgundians were regarded by the older inhabitants of Gaul as instruments rather than as enemies. With the assistance of their barbarian kings, with their robes of skin and their uncouth jargon, great Gallo-Roman nobles might be raised to the purple, and Gothic and Burgundian armies might protect and even extend the Empire. On a commission from Honorius, King Wallia led his Visigoths into Spain and reconquered the greater part of that peninsula from the Sueves, the Vandals, and the Alans; and later, when Aetius, "the last of the Romans," rallied the forces of Gaul against King Attila and his Huns, the Visigoth Theodoric, without whose army success would hardly have been won, laid down his life in the cause of the Empire.

In broad outline, then, the history of Gaul in the fifth century, though opening with a carnival of pillage and destruction, witnesses a certain retardation in the advance of intellectual darkness.

The Visigoths and Burgundians turned out to be better than might have been expected. The schools continued to teach, the lawyers to plead, the nobles to write verses, and the bishops to minister to the needs of their congregations. Until Euric, the Visigoth, exchanged the policy of religious toleration which his predecessors had pursued for a campaign of active persecution, the orthodox Church in Gaul had little to complain of from the presence of two Arian monarchies on Gallic soil. Euric, however, was intolerable. That he was the most powerful and aggressive of the Visigoth monarchs, that he attacked the Bretons and conquered the loyalist province of Auvergne, were errors less heinous in that theological age than his aggressive heresy. At Euric's death whatever store of popularity his house had secured in Aquitaine was effectively squandered, and when the Visigothic army went down before the orthodox Franks on the field of Vouillé, the old inhabitants of southern France looked on with indifference and relief.

Seventy-eight years before this, the Roman government suffered a startling reverse in an unexpected quarter. Africa, the principal source of the Roman corn supply and the seat of a flourishing Italian civilization, had already fired the ambition of two Gothic kings, and was now, on the invitation of a Roman governor, invaded by the Vandals of Spain. To the enfeebled strength of the western empire no blow could be more serious. Under the leadership of Gaiseric, the ablest barbarian chieftain of his age, the Vandals advanced from strength to strength. They took Carthage (439), built a fleet, and in a short time made themselves the greatest naval power in the western Mediterranean. For the first time since the close of the Punic Wars the Roman government was faced with the menace of a navy superior to its own, a navy capable of detaching Sicily, Sardinia, and Corsica, and of bringing an army of pillaging Vandals to loot and ravish, devastate and murder in Rome itself. A succession of treaties (435-442), each more favourable to the invader than the last, failed to convert these Arian barbarians into friendly or even valuable associates of the government in Italy. The Vandals were savages. They destroyed much, they constructed nothing, and of their hundred years of rule in Africa only memories of havoc remain. Yet their intervention in the theatre of European affairs was of critical importance. At the moment when it was most necessary that all the forces of Italy should be concentrated on checking the barbarian advance in Gaul and Britain, they were weakened and dispersed by the necessity of dealing with the formidable pirate state which had established itself in the richest corn-bearing province of the Empire. The consequences were far reaching. They comprise the final loss of Gaul, the withdrawal (442) of the last Roman garrison from Britain, the conquest of the south-eastern portion of the British island by the Saxons, and, on a lower scale of importance, the exodus of Celtic fugitives from the south-western regions of our island, which has given the name of Brittany to the ancient Armorican districts of Gaul.

The Mongolian invasion of eastern Europe, which had been the *primum mobile* in this long chain of shattering experiences for the Empire, had not yet exhausted its effects. It was one of the secrets of the longevity of the Roman state that it made a practice of recruiting from its most formidable enemies. The Franks were employed to defend the Rhine frontier in 407, the Huns to destroy the Burgundian kingdom of Worms in 435. But this policy, though it might be successful as a makeshift, offered no permanent protection against the hungry appetites of restless and fecund nations. In the middle of the fifth century one of the greatest dangers which assailed the Empire proceeded from the Huns, who a few years earlier had proved themselves to be valuable auxiliaries. This people, under the guidance of Attila, one of those remarkable leaders who from time to time arise to fashion the destiny of a race, or startle the world by a sudden revelation of violence or power, succeeded in obtaining for themselves for a period of nineteen years (435 to 454) an ascendancy which extended from the Rhine to the Urals. The eastern Empire paid them tribute; the German peoples of central Europe (Gepids, Ostrogoths, Rugians, and Scirians) entered into their confederacy, submitted to their direction, and influenced their manners.

So vast an aggregation of peoples ruled by a powerful and unscrupulous savage sent a thrill of consternation through Europe. Upon whom would the thunderbolt fall? The western Empire, under the rule of Valentinian, the feeble nephew of the weak Honorius, offered the most tempting prey, and in 450 Attila made up his mind to seize it.

Then a striking illustration was afforded of the gulf which divides courage from strategy, numbers from science, and true political coherence from the magnetism of a name. Attila was no general. His vast and miscellaneous following was no army. His personal ascendancy was no substitute for the organized institutions of a state. The Mongolian invasion of Gaul in 451, dreadful as it appeared in prospect and retrospect, was foiled when Attila turned back from Orleans rather than attack a fortified and well defended city; and the battle of Troyes, which inflicted severe punishment on the retreating army, confirmed rather than decided the issue of the campaign. Nor was the invasion of Italy in the succeeding year marked by any evidence of intelligent design. After a brief spell of pillage and extortion, Attila withdrew north of the Alps, and that so swiftly that the pious have ascribed to the intercession of the Bishop of Rome a course more probably dictated by the prevalence of disease, the failure of supplies, and the intelligence of an advancing army from the east. Two years later the Hun king was in his grave and his empire broken (battle of Nedao, 454) by an insurrection of its German vassals.

From this moment the germanization of the west steadily proceeded. Ostrogoths poured into the Balkan peninsula, creating by their restless and turbulent activities a problem similar to that which had taxed the resources of the eastern Empire a century before. In Italy a succession of phantom and ephemeral emperors reached its close with a pathetic figure, named, by the supreme irony of providence, Romulus Augustulus, who was deposed by Odovacar, the East German master of the troops. A.D. 476 Military revolutions were no novelty in the annals of the Roman Empire, and the act of Odovacar had many precedents. If he assumed the title of king, so, too, had Ataulph and his Visigothic successors. If he had risen to power by claiming for his troops a third part of the lands of Italy, he was entitled to invoke the old practice of hospitality so recently applied in Burgundy and Aquitaine. It is true that he deposed Romulus, but the lad was a usurper, unrecognized in Constantinople, and the deed condoned by the bestowal upon its author of the high imperial title of patrician. What was original in Odovacar's action was not that it was revolutionary, but that it was conservative. He refused to appoint a successor to Romulus, calculating that he would have more elbow room in a united Empire governed from Constantinople as in the days of Theodosius the Great. That unity was in fact and theory preserved until the coronation of Charlemagne as Emperor of the west in 800.

The age immediately succeeding is remarkable for the emergence of two great barbaric figures, Theodoric the Ostrogoth, and Clovis the Frank, the first the founder of a short-lived Gothic monarchy in Italy, the second the creator of the mediaeval monarchy of France. A peculiarity common to each of these dynamic and experienced men, though more clearly marked in the Goth than in the Frank, was a recognition of the continuing authority of the Emperor. Theodoric was sent into Italy to overthrow Odovacar on a commission from the Emperor Zeno, and throughout his long reign (493-526) regarded himself not only as a Gothic king, but also as an Imperial official. Clovis received the insignia of the honorary consulship from Anastasius. But there was one critical difference. Theodoric, by far the more powerful and important figure throughout his life, was an Arian. Clovis became a militant Catholic. To this divergence we may principally ascribe the fact that Theodoric failed and Clovis succeeded in laying the foundations of an enduring state.

Yet a singular interest attaches to the experiment which failed in Italy. In the legends of Germany, Theodoric figures under the name of Dietrich of Bern as a great leader of the German peoples, the Achilles of a German Iliad playing his heroic part in a tempestuous and memorable age. And such a leader he was recognized to be by the Arian sovereigns, Vandal, Visigoth, and Burgundian, with whom he entered into bonds of alliance. The instinct of a people is never wholly wrong. There was a bigness of scale about Theodoric which redeemed many of the grosser vices, and may be set against illiteracy, cruelty, and craft. After three years' hard fighting he eliminated from Italy the Rugian army of Odovacar, and thereafter gave thirty-six years of golden peace to that much harassed land, enlarging its frontiers, encompassing it with a network of protective diplomacy, and holding or winning for it a circle of outlying territories, Provence, southern Germany, the Tyrol, part of Hungary, and Dalmatia, and exercising a kind of suzerainty over Spain. But it is probable that even so he would not have attained to mythical stature but for the fact that he, a German with all the qualities of his race, ruled as the Roman master of Italy, and from that central pivot directed his far-flung operations.

The beautiful city of Ravenna, besides other famous memorials of this age, still shows the tomb of Theodoric the Goth. His court and administration were Latin. He respected the Roman Senate and was studious to restore the ancient monuments of Italy. The folly of attempting to force the Gothic language upon Italy was far from his mind. It was no part of his policy to make changes in law or government, to force the pace of racial assimilation, or to affront the religious prejudices of Rome; he did not legislate, or issue coins without the Emperor's name. He repaired the aqueducts, maintained the public chairs of grammar and rhetoric, and even the Imperial laws which forbade intermarriage between Romans and barbarians; and it was only in his last years, and as an answer to an outbreak of persecution against his co-religionists in the east, that the Arian in him showed his teeth, and that he committed the crime of passion which is charged against the memory of many good deeds. Boethius, the last of the ancient thinkers and poets, whose *De consolatione Philosophiae* was one of the best books generally known to the middle ages, was a benefactor of mankind. His judicial murder is a blot on the A.D. 525 fame of Theodoric.

The reign of Clovis, founder of the Merovingian House and Architect of France (481-511) is marked by three great victories, over Syagrius, King of the Romans, at Soissons in 486, over the Alemanns in Alsace ten years later, and lastly over Alaric, king of the Visigoths, on the field of Vouillé (near Poitiers) in 507. It was after the first of these triumphs, obtained over an officer who was representing the Roman cause in Gaul, that Clovis removed from Soissons to Paris, and there established his capital; after the second that he exchanged paganism for the Catholic faith; after the third that he advanced his kingdom to the Pyrenees, driving the main body of his Visigothic enemies to find in Spain the centre of their power. Whether the conversion of Clovis was due to the influence of his Catholic wife Clotilda, a Burgundian princess, or to his conviction that Christ had delivered the Alemans into his hands, or to a long-headed calculation of political chances, is of little moment compared with the capital fact that in 496 the leader of the Salian Franks, the most renowned of all the Germanic tribes, became a protagonist of the Catholic cause.

The long alliance between the French monarchy and the Roman Church, which ended in 1830 with the flight of the last Bourbon King from the Paris mob, was baptized in the blood of that Alsatian battlefield more than 1,300 years earlier. It was a turning point in the history of Gaul, and indeed of Europe, when the Catholic Church was made supreme from the Mediterranean to the Channel and from the Atlantic to the Rhine, and a barbarian king accepted under the influence of the Church the machinery of government through bishops, count, and city, which was the legacy of later Rome to mediaeval France. A warrior chief had placed himself at the head of a militant church; and in the words attributed by the chronicler to Clovis, as he marched against the Visigoths, " It vexes me to see these Arians hold part of Gaul. Let us attack them with God's aid, and having conquered them, subject their land," we seem to hear a premonitory blast of the trumpet which called the Frankish chivalry to the Crusades, sounded the knell of the Albigensian heretics, and led to the Huguenot emigration from France in the seventeenth century, by which the Protestant countries of Europe were sensibly enriched.

It has been noted that among the consequences of the great tidal wave of Germanic conquest which swept into Gaul at the beginning of the fifth century was the snapping of the connection between Britain and Rome. The province was not formally abandoned. There was no official decision to relinquish territory which for four hundred years had been a source of affluence and pride to the Empire, territory covered by Roman roads, studded with Roman cities and luxurious villas, and long prized not only as a market for slaves, but for its minerals, its agriculture, its watering-places, and its oyster beds. The separation ensued from the force of events which Rome was unable to control. The provincials of Britain were left to their own resources, and before the double danger of the Picts and the Scots in the north and of the Saxon pirates in the south the provincials ultimately succumbed. How fierce or protracted their resistance may have been we can only conjecture.

A.D. 597   What happened in Britain during the hundred and fifty years which elapsed between the final break with Rome and the coming of St. Augustine is shrouded in the deepest mystery. There are no contemporary chronicles or records or any gleam of authentic light. The spade of the archaeologist indicates extensive burnings in many important towns, such as Canterbury, which are thought to point to a violent contest, but may have other interpretations. The Anglo-Saxon Chronicle, which belongs to a much later date, contains so much that is clearly mythical that a tincture of doubt necessarily attaches to those portions of its narrative which may embody authentic facts.

We cannot therefore reconstitute the chain of events through this dark period. It may be that a violent and destructive attack, ruining towns and exterminating, enslaving, or chasing away the provincial population, was followed by a quieter period of steady agricultural settlement. Nothing is certain but the result. When the darkness clears away with the coming of St. Augustine, England is a Saxon and a pagan country.

This astonishing change, pointing to some great unchronicled catastrophe, was quite consistent with the preservation in Britain of those earlier human types which Julius Caesar and Claudius had found in the island. The dark Iberians, who may be traced back to the neolithic age, the fair-haired Goidelic or Gaelic Celts of the Scottish highlands, whose weapons were of bronze, and the later wave (later, as we know, for their weapons were of iron) of the Brythonic Celts, who eventually settled in Wales and Cornwall, survived the shock and are still constituent elements of the British population. What was obliterated by the Saxon conquest was the living influence of Rome, its speech, its religion, its towns, its institutions.

In the shell of this old Roman province was a raw, Teuton, agricultural society, worshipping Odin, speaking a Germanic tongue, and living a life as far as possible removed from the routine of a provincial townsman under the Roman Empire. The Jutes, the Saxons, and the Angles, the three cognate peoples who are found firmly settled in England at the beginning of the seventh century, were quite untouched by Roman influence. Everywhere they lived in townships or villages, cultivated the land in common on the open field system, and retained in their hundred courts those forms of popular government and justice which had attracted the notice of Tacitus in the first century. Conquest, however, had brought in its train one important development. The leader in war had become a king, and traced his pedigree to the gods. He was assisted by a Witan, a body of counsellors.

Yet despite their strong family likeness, the invaders were far from being of the same mind. Vast tracts of marsh and impenetrable forest kept the settlers apart and obstructed communication. The estuary of the Humber was probably in the seventh century a greater obstacle between the north and south of England than are the Pyrenees today between Spain and France. East Anglia was an island surrounded by forest and fen. The Andredsweald, an intricate tract of marsh and forest, divided the North Downs and the South Downs. In a country so full of natural obstacles many years passed before the descendants of the original private adventurers grew together into a state, and many more before any local king dreamed of an all-England monarchy. Accordingly the early history of that part of our island which was colonized by the Saxons is marked by a tangle of internecine wars between various parties of invaders, who, helped by the geography of the country, had formed themselves into separate states. Now a kingdom rose, now it declined in the scale of superiority. The little Jutish kingdom of Kent, then as always the garden of England, and of all portions of our island the most advanced in civilization, saw its best days under Ethelbert, the patron of St. Augustine. Northumbria, quickened by its contact with Celtic Christianity, was supreme till 685, Mercia till the death of Offa in 796. It was while the country was thus distracted by internal rivalries that the Danes opened a new chapter in English history.

Meanwhile England had once again been called into the circle of the Roman Church. Here, as elsewhere, the conversion of the pagan is to be attributed not to any penitential movement of the heart, but to the pressure of the monarchy upon a submissive population. The men of Kent and the Kentish men followed Ethelbert into the Christian fold. In Northumbria, in East Anglia, in Mercia, and in Wessex the story was the same. The creed of the king became the creed of the people. A plain, unquestioning, superstitious people was content to take its religious fashions from the court.

The effect of the conversion was not the less profound and far-reaching by reason of its perfunctory and superficial operation on conscience and conduct. Britain was again knit to the Latin world, taught the advantage of written law, and fitted with an ecclesiastical organization which was strictly modelled on the imperial organization of Rome. The first national assemblies to be held in Britain were church councils. The first code of native laws was drafted in Kent under the influence of Augustine. The parish, which has played so large a part in English life, more particularly in the country, was the gift of the Roman

churchmen to Saxon England. It was characteristic of the downright practical temper of the race that the Celtic form of Christianity, which had been brought from Ireland to Iona, and had
thence with all its wayward graces penetrated to Northumbria,
was not able to survive in the competition with its stern Roman
antagonists. Both on the continent and in England the Saxons
were noted for their submission to the papal see. The Latin
education of the inhabitants of this island, which had been intermitted for a hundred and fifty years, was now begun again under
the ferule of the Roman priest.

BOOKS WHICH MAY BE CONSULTED

C. W. Previté-Orton : Outlines of Mediaeval History. 1924.
L. Halphen : Les Barbares (Vol. V., Peuples et Civilisation, ed. Halphen
    et Saquac. 1926.
A. Rambaud : Histoire de la Russie. 1884.
V. Kluchevsky : History of Russia. Tr. C. J. Hogarth. 5 vols. 1911-31.
T. Hodgkin : Italy and her Invaders. 1931.
T. Hodgkin : Theodoric the Goth. 1891.
S. Dill : Roman Society in the Last Century of the Roman Empire. 1899.
R. G. Collingwood : Roman Britain. 1921.
Sir Charles Oman : A History of England before the Norman Conquest.
    1910.
G. M. Trevelyan : History of England. 1926.
E. Lavisse : Histoire de France, Vol. II. 1903.

CHAPTER XI

THE AGE OF JUSTINIAN

Belief in the necessary continuance of the Empire. The Byzantine state. Justinian and Theodora. Western policy. The reconquest of Italy from the Goths. Effects of the Gothic wars. The destruction of the Gothic kingdom of Italy a mistake. The Lombards. Exhaustion of the eastern Empire at Justinian's death. The causes. Roman law. The Monophysite heresy and its influence in the east. Absolutism and orthodoxy of the Emperor.

THE barbaric conquests in the west, which to the modern eye are significant as leading to the replacement of the Roman Empire by other and more varied forms of political life, were very differently regarded by the Christian contemporaries of Clovis and Theodoric. Learned divines then taught to the full satisfaction of plain men that the world had entered into its sixth and last phase, and that beyond the Roman Empire there was nothing but Antichrist and the final catastrophe of all things. Such was the doctrine of Augustine in the fifth and of Bede in the eighth century, and from such teaching it followed either that the triumphs of the barbarians would be succeeded by an imperial restoration or else that they portended the coming of the judgment day. The one contingency which was ruled out was that the Roman Empire might perish and the world notwithstanding proceed.

Accordingly it is not surprising that in the century succeeding this great upheaval in the west, a serious attempt was made to restore the effective unity of the Empire. While all was fluid and tumultuous in Italy and Gaul, the great fabric of Roman government was still maintained by the civil officials and mercenary armies of the eastern Empire. Here was a corrupt and intriguing court, a centralized but venal bureaucracy, a city mob living for the rival factions of the hippodrome, a church obscurantist, influential and umbrageous, and a line of Emperors owing their authority, not as did the barbarian kings to a divine origin, but as often as not to the workings of intrigue and to the tumultuous acclamations of the soldiers and the crowd. Amid the upheavals of Europe there was within the cincture of Con-

stantinople an assured civilization and an atmosphere in the
conduct of affairs so unwholesome, refined, and persistent that
under the name of Byzantinism it survived both the Latin and
the Turkish conquests, and was only dispersed by the vigorous
blasts of Ottoman nationalism in our own age.

Though it experienced great alternations of fortune, sometimes brilliantly victorious, at other times driven to the lowest
pit of abasement and misery, the east Roman Empire defended
for a thousand years the cause of Greek Christianity in a world
of enemies. Goths, Slavs, Avars, Bulgars, Persians, Saracens
ravaged and despoiled, but failed to upset this enduring fabric of
the ancient world. It persisted through every storm, renouncing
nothing which had once been Roman, cherishing hopeless claims
and outworn pretensions, and yet, despite its rags and tatters, so
vital, that but for the shattering Latin conquest in the thirteenth
century, it might have had strength to uphold the Cross against
the Crescent into modern times. For century after century, this
state, Roman in name and theory, but in reality part Greek and
part oriental, maintained a standard of cultured refinement
which shone like gold against the surrounding gloom. The
classical scholar may smile at the Byzantines, yet they were the
channel through which the rudiments of culture and Christianity were communicated to the Slavs of Russia and the Balkans,
and the instructors of many rude Asiatic peoples in the ways and
institutions of an ordered state.

On the death of the Emperor Anastasius in 518 the throne of
Constantinople passed to an elderly and illiterate Illyrian soldier,
who in later life developed an unpleasant passion for persecuting
Arians. Justin was born in the village of Tauresium near Uskub,
that swiftly contracting region of the Balkans in which Latin
still survived as the spoken tongue. Latin, then, he knew, and
the soldier's trade, but little else. He had, however, a nephew
from the same Latin-speaking region, whom, being childless, he
adopted as his heir, and caused to be instructed in all the accomplishments then thought to be necessary for the formation of the
princely mind. Justinian proved worthy of his uncle's regard.
The young Illyrian peasant was endowed with that rare capacity
for sustained and minute labour which is a sure sign of intellectual strength. Long after others were abed this passionate
worker would be toiling over his files, or would be found rest-
lessly striding down the corridors like a ghost. During Justin's

reign he was the real ruler. Then in 527, a year after Theodoric's death, the heir-apparent, an experienced man in his forty-fifth year, succeeded to his uncle's place.

Before this he had looked into the gutter for a wife, and picked out a diamond. Theodora was the daughter of a Cypriot bear keeper. She had been an actress and a courtesan, had wandered and suffered, and combined in her person every quality of station and experience certain to give offence to respectable people. But though a thousand scandals were woven round her name, though she was violent in her passions and vindictive in her hates, she appears to have been in a sense a noble being, beautiful and witty, with a high courage, a statesman's mind, and the precious gift of womanly compassion. When Constantinople was in the hands of the rioters in 532, and the Emperor and his councillors were in favour of flight, Theodora came forward and saved her husband's throne. "If you wish to protract your life, O Emperor, flight is easy; there are your ships and there is the sea. But consider whether, if you escape to exile, you will not wish every day that you were dead. As for me, I hold with the ancient saying that the imperial purple is a glorious shroud." Her piety was equal to her pluck. The first home for the rescue of fallen women to be erected in Europe is due to this fallen woman, who for twenty-one years shared an Emperor's throne and swayed his policy.

A peace with Chosroes I of Persia, struck in 532 after three years' indecisive fighting, released the energies of Justinian for the great task of imperial recovery in the west. An army under Belisarius, whose shining military talents had been equally proved in the riots at Constantinople and in the Persian War, was sent to Africa to evict the Vandals, and after two pitched battles near Carthage so effectually accomplished his task that nothing more was heard of this barbarous and heretical people, whose fleets had been the terror of the western Mediterranean. Africa returned nominally to the Roman obedience and to undisputed enjoyment of the orthodox faith. But if Justinian expected to extend to the north African littoral a Roman peace he was soon disabused. The Moors, who had seriously strained the powers of the Vandals, began at once to molest the new government in Africa. The western provinces fell into their hands. What remained was only held after two exhausting wars which tested the resources of the best generals of the Empire.

For the moment, however, the Emperor had triumphed beyond all expectations. In a three months' campaign Belisarius had wiped one set of German heretics off the map, and it was reasonable to suppose that with hardly less expenditure of effort he could do equal execution on another. Accordingly the next objective was the Gothic kingdom of Italy, which had just lost a capable ruler by the murder of Amalasuntha, the daughter of Theodoric the Great. Since the murderer was Theodahat, the Gothic king whom Amalasuntha in her need for male support had selected as a colleague, and since the victim was a lady friendly to Roman ways and already in secret relation with the Imperial Court, a convenient pretext was offered for a premeditated invasion.

In September, 535, the brilliant Belisarius was despatched to Sicily with a small army of 7,500 men.

There ensued a struggle of twenty-eight years, during which fortune favoured alternately the Roman, the Gothic, and again the Roman cause. At first Belisarius, despite the exiguous force at his disposal, outmatched his opponents. Sicily fell to him almost without a struggle, Naples after a siege. He found Rome undefended and there successfully maintained himself for a year and nine days against the large but ill-led army of King Vitiges the Goth. So skilful was his management, so well did he compensate for inferior numbers by the efficiency of his mailed cavalry, by the command of the sea, and by a clever use of mounted archers that by 540 he appeared to have broken the enemy's resistance. Vitiges had been trapped into captivity. Ravenna had fallen into the hands of the imperialists. All central and southern Italy was recovered for the Empire. But then, when the Gothic fortunes appeared to be desperate and the great Roman general had returned in triumph to Constantinople, the wheel turned full circle. A young leader of genius, bold, humane, and enterprising, was elected to be king of the Gothic people in 541, and under Totila's inspiring command the Goths recovered all Italy save Ravenna and Ancona, exhibiting qualities of resilience and resource which might have inclined a less tenacious antagonist to thoughts of peace.

Peace Totila was anxious to have and had more than once offered, for he was willing, like Odovacar, to rule Italy as the servant of the Empire and even to pay tribute. But Justinian was determined on victory, and in 551 sent Narses, an elderly

5

Armenian eunuch, with a strong army of 35,000 men to secure it. On the field of Gualdo Tadino, a village in Umbria, Narses, a good soldier and a most prudent statesman, defeated his enemy, using against him that combination of dismounted archers and pikemen which was afterwards employed with success by English commanders against the chivalry of France. Totila was slain in the pursuit, and eleven years afterwards, but not before Italy had been exposed to the horrors of an invasion of Franks and Alemans, the last garrisons of the gallant Gothic army surrendered Brescia and Verona to the foe.

For Italy this long and bitter struggle was an unrelieved calamity. The armies of Belisarius and Narses were Roman only in name, and even more alien to the native population of Italy than the Gothic swordsmen who had been peaceably settled in the country for half a century. Great atrocities were committed on either side, none more notable than the destruction of the whole adult male population (300,000 according to Procopius) of Milan by the Goths and Burgundians in 539. We have pictures, which may perhaps be overdrawn, of the unspeakable misery of the countryside, of populations wasted, of peasants living on chestnuts and grasses and in some instances impelled to acts of cannibalism. For the city of Rome, five times besieged, the results of this calamitous struggle were decisive. At the end of the war the teeming capital with its luxurious public baths, its system of food doles and popular amusements had disappeared. In its place a few thousand impoverished beings, many of them clerics, lingered on among the monuments of ancient greatness, henceforth and for many centuries to come to be girdled by undrained and malarious wastes. No more was there a Roman Senate. The last circus had been held, the last triumph celebrated, the last consul elected. Trade and commerce were extinct, and since the Goths had cut the aqueducts which had given to ancient Rome as good a water supply as any modern city can boast, the reign of mediaeval squalor, which Roman example might have corrected, spread without resistance through the western world.

The conquest of Africa and Italy only spurred Justinian's ambition for further triumphs. "God," he said, "has granted us to bring the Persians to conclude the peace, to submit the Vandals, the Alemans, and the Moors, to recover all Italy and Sicily, and we have good hopes that the Lord will grant us the rest of the Empire which the Romans formerly extended to the limits of the two oceans and lost through indolence."

The satisfaction of these vast ambitions was far beyond Justinian's powers. His conquests in Africa, Italy, and Spain (for here too an imperial force was successful in its capture of seaports) were as impossible to maintain as the recovery of Gaul and Britain was impossible even to initiate.

Moreover, the whole policy of uprooting the Goths from Italy was a great disaster. A better course, both for Italy itself and for the Balkan peninsula, would have been to have supported this brave Teutonic people, as a bulwark against the ruder nations beyond the alpine barrier. As a Gothic envoy said to Belisarius, "We have observed the laws and constitutions of the Empire as faithfully as any of the Emperors of the past. Neither Theodoric nor any of his successors has ever enacted a law. We have shown scrupulous respect for the religion of the Romans. No Italian has ever been forcibly converted to Arianism, no Gothic convert has been forced to return to his old creed. We have reserved all the posts in the Civil Service to the Italians." A Gothic monarchy thus respectful of Italian sentiment and tradition might have saved Italy from the long series of invasions and civil wars to which that unfortunate land was condemned. The Goths were a virile race. They were capable of supplying to the defence of the peninsula those qualities of martial energy which the native population had lost for centuries. It was a profound error to destroy them. Had they been left in peace there might have been no Lombard invasions, no papal state, no revival of the Empire in the west, and the political unity which Italy so painfully achieved in the reign of Queen Victoria might have been realized in the reign of Ethelbert.

Had the Emperor been able to establish a strong government in Italy, the elimination of the Goths might have been effected without evil results. But at no time was the Exarch at Ravenna master of the whole country or able to defend its frontiers against attack. The Lombards, the last great wave of conquering Teutons to sweep down upon the Roman Empire, poured into Italy under their King Alboin and effected a permanent A.D. 568 lodgment in the country. Little good can be said of these fierce Arian barbarians at this early stage of their history, but like all the Teutons they had in them the seeds of discipline and decency, and if the Italian borders had been guarded by Gothic spears the Lombards might have been deflected to the Balkan peninsula. In that event the face of history might have worn a different aspect. With a population largely Teutonic established in the Balkans the eastern question would have assumed another and perhaps easier form.

The ambitious western wars of Justinian were conducted by a state which was never safe from hazards and humiliations. During the reign of this laborious monarch the Huns nearly took Constantinople, the Slavs captured Adrianople, and the Persians sacked the brilliant city of Antioch. The government which was ready to send an army to Spain and even cherished gigantic designs on Gaul and Britain could not secure a Balkan village against marauding barbarians. When every effort should have been concentrated on domestic defence much was fruitlessly expended on distant ventures involving, if Procopius is to be trusted, a loss of ten million lives in Italy and Africa alone. And so Justinian, dying in 565 at the age of eighty-three, left his Empire poorer, weaker, and less Roman than it was when he mounted the throne thirty-eight years before.

It seems that the Cypriot Theodora took a sounder view of the needs of the political situation than her Latin-speaking husband. She saw that the strength of the eastern Empire depended upon the degree to which it could command the resources of Asia Minor, of Syria, and of Egypt, and that no conquests in the west were likely to compensate the government of Constantinople for the loss of the Anatolian highlanders, the Egyptian harvests, and the wealth and sparkling talents of Syria. Yet the maladies of the reign must not wholly be traced to errors of policy. In many respects the Emperor showed a true perception of the problems of his day, and made a courageous and indeed imaginative attempt to cope with them. Realizing the weakness of the barbarians in siege operations, he covered his Asiatic and European dominions with castles, forts, and lines of defence. Since armies were costly and money was difficult to raise, he tried every device which diplomacy could suggest to cajole, to divide, or to undermine his opponents. To some barbarians he would pay regular tribute. Others he would enrol as "federates" in his army or load, perhaps unwisely, with sumptuous hospitality and costly gifts. Lombards were set against Gepids, Avars against Huns, Greek missionaries were scattered far and wide against the heathen. Yet even so the government which began in a blaze of glory steadily declined in strength.

The causes of this progressive exhaustion were partly natural, the great plague of 542, which is reputed to have carried off a third of the population, and the declining energies of the Emperor himself during the last two decades of his long life. But there was a third evil which, being moral, was more serious. The government was cheated by all its agents. Two-thirds of the revenue extorted from the taxpayers failed to find its way to the Treasury. The evil was apparently incurable: against the peculation of his tax-collectors the good laws of Justinian were so ineffectual that a reign begun with promise and continued with ambition closed in an atmosphere of opprobrium and grinding discontent.

Yet there are few rulers in Europe whose work is still so widely remembered as the sovereign who commissioned the building of St. Sophia and that great series of legal compilations, the Codex, the Digest, the Institutes, and afterwards the Novellae, through which the legacy of Roman law has been transmitted to posterity. The numerous buildings, ecclesiastical, municipal, and military, with which Justinian endeavoured to secure or embellish his dominions have been described by the secretary Procopius, to whose brilliant narrative we are also indebted for our principal knowledge of the campaigns of Belisarius his master. Many of these buildings have perished, but there survive a sufficient number both in Europe and hither Asia to impress the traveller with a sense of grandeur and force. The mosaics at Ravenna are famous. More renowned is St. Sophia, whose vast low dome crowning the lovely city of Constantinople exceeds the masterpieces of the Moslem architects who found in its mysterious proportions a challenge to their highest genius.

The final systematization of Roman law by Justinian exercised an immediate and continuous influence in the east and in those regions of Italy which remained under Byzantine control. It was not, however, until the foundation of the famous school of glossators at Bologna at the end of the eleventh century that the study of Justinian's civil code became an active influence in the intellectual history of western Europe. From that moment it would be difficult to overestimate its power as a factor in the moulding of intellectual, social, and political life. The Roman law expressed the ideas of a society more civilized and mature than the western Europe of the early middle ages. It was a society which had evolved clear-cut ideas about private property and possession, family rights and the sanctity of contract, and had come to regard law as a reasoned and intelligible system adapted to the needs of humanity as a whole. A great state with commercial dealings all over the world evolves a law capable of meeting the manifold occasions of its life. The Roman law though influenced by philosophy was close to reality. It was built up not so much by legislation as by custom and by the answers of jurisconsults upon the cases real and imaginary which were submitted to them. And so as western Europe emerged from mediaeval darkness it found in the Corpus Juris of Justinian a revelation of the great thing which European civilization had once been and might again become. The ferment of the mind thus occasioned was immense. Perhaps a faint analogy may be found in the exciting influence at a later stage of human development of Rousseau's *Contrat Social* or Darwin's *Origin of Species.*

All this lay in the future. For the moment the intellectual life of the eastern Empire was not legal but theological. The Council of Nicaea had failed to quench the curiosity of the Greek world as to the difficult problem of the Incarnation. Other questions in connection with this high mystery suggested themselves to ingenious minds, and, being involved in the pretensions of rival sees or attached to the proclivities of different races, excited the fiercest and most intolerant passions. If Nicaea had affirmed the divinity of Christ, it had left open for further examination the delicate matter of determining how the divine substance was related to the human nature. Was there one Nature or two? Was Mary the mother of the human Christ only or of the human and divine as well? In the fifth century no question was more passionately discussed than this of the single or dual nature of Christ, or than the formula by which that union of natures should be most correctly expressed. The controversy lasted long after its original protagonists, Cyril of Alexandria and Nestorius of Constantinople, were laid in their graves, influencing the debates of four Councils of the Church, and continuing, even after the Council of Chalcedon had decided, under the joint influence of Pope and Emperor, for the dual nature in 451, to envenom the impressionable peoples of the east. It followed that however orthodox the Emperor might desire to be, he was forced, if he were a wise man, to take account of the strong bodies of monophysite[1] opinion which were to be found in Constantinople, in Mesopotamia, in Syria, and in Egypt. Some Emperors essayed compromising formulae, others like Anastasius a policy of toleration. No statesman could be indifferent to a question which even excited the dangerous mobs of the hippodrome and threatened to disrupt the Empire.

Justinian was an orthodox bigot against whom it must be remembered not only that he closed the schools of Athens and silenced the voice of philosophy in the Greek world, but that he spent the concluding years of his life in sterile theological speculations and stern repression of heresies. Yet theology was a subject in which the beautiful Theodora had also her opinions. Her sympathies were monophysite, her interests oriental, her political sense enlisted on the side of a theological entente with a movement which defied persecution and was proving increasingly attractive to the peoples of the east. Justinian listened to the counsels of his wife. A substantial measure of toleration was extended to the monophysites, and to the delight of the anti-Roman party a miserable captive Bishop of Rome was compelled in a Council at Constantinople to condemn certain theses which had won the approval of the hated Council of Chalcedon. It was wise of Justinian thus to endeavour to plaster over the cracks which this heresy was driving through the eastern half of his Empire. Yet the cracks remained and steadily widened, weakening the sentiment of allegiance to Constantinople, more especially in Egypt and Syria, preparing, maybe, the way for the Saracen conquests, and so permanent that the Coptic Church in Egypt today stands on the ancient rock of the monophysite faith.

To Justinian it was given to display upon a great theatre and to an admiring world the two spectacles, not hitherto combined, of Roman absolutism and ecclesiastical tyranny. He was, says Agathias, " the first of the Roman Emperors to show himself by word and deed the absolute master of the Romans." Yet a man so jealous, vain, and irresolute, a man for whom no design was too great, no detail too small, no superstition too absurd, and no subject irrelevant or remote, cannot excite admiration. With almost infinite resources of skill and industry he appears to have

[1] *I.e.*, in favour of the single nature of Christ.

lacked the higher gifts of statesmanship, the energetic will, the true sense of proportion, the capacity for taking unpleasant decisions. Few men, whose personality is so uncertain, fill a greater place in history. As for a moment we tread beside him through the corridors of the past we seem to see the shades of night battling with the blood-red sunset of imperial Rome.

BOOKS WHICH MAY BE CONSULTED

J. B. Bury : History of the Later Roman Empire. 2 vols. 1889.
N. H. Baynes : The Byzantine Empire. 1926.
Cambridge Mediaeval History, Vol. IV.
C. Diehl : Byzance—Grandeur et Décadence. 1919.
C. Diehl : History of the Byzantine Empire. *Tr.* G. B. Ives. 1925.
C. Diehl : Une République Patricienne—Vénise. 1915.
O. M. Dalton : Byzantine Art and Archaeology. 1911.
W. G. Holmes : The Age of Justinian. 2 vols. 1905-7.

CHAPTER XII

ISLAM

Early obscurity of Arabia. The Arab conquests of the seventh century. Muhammad, his life and teaching. Rise and progress of Moslem civilization. The mystics of Islam. Shiites and Sunnites. The defence of Europe against Islam by Leo the Isaurian and Charles Martel.

WE have now reached a point at which the history of Europe becomes complicated by the victories of the Moslem religion. For the first six centuries of the Christian era no European statesman had occasion to remember the existence of Arabia. It was a land of mystery, doing a little trade with Syria and Egypt and contributing some mercenaries to the Persian and Byzantine armies, but otherwise as remote and inhospitable as the frozen north. Nothing likely to be reported from this scorching wilderness would be calculated to disturb the bazaars of Damascus or Alexandria. Arabian society was still in the tribal stage, and the hawk-eyed Bedouin tribes might be confidently expected to rob and massacre each other till the crack of doom. Nowhere was there a vestige of an Arabian state, of a regular army, or of a common political ambition. The Arabs were poets, dreamers, fighters, traders; they were not politicians. Nor had they found in religion a stabilizing or unifying power. They practised a low form of polytheism, so low that some finer minds among them, touched perhaps by vague influences from Christianity or Judaism, had begun quietly to challenge it. At Mecca, their principal trading town, only fifty miles removed from the great highway of the Red Sea, they appeared to worship a black stone placed in a temple, called the Caba, or Cube. Such were the impressions likely to prevail about the population of Arabia in the year in which Heraclius, the Byzantine Emperor, concluded his Persian wars.

A hundred years later these obscure savages had achieved for themselves a great world power. They had conquered Syria and Egypt, they had overwhelmed and converted Persia, mastered western Turkestan and part of the Punjab. They had wrested Africa from the Byzantines and the Berbers, Spain from the Visigoths. In the west they threatened France, in the east Constantinople. Their fleets, built in Alexandria or the Syrian ports, rode the waters of the Mediterranean, pillaged the Greek islands and challenged the naval power of the Byzantine Empire. Their successes had been won so easily, the Persians and the Berbers of the Atlas mountains alone offering a serious resistance, that at the beginning of the eighth century it must have seemed an open question whether any final obstacle could be opposed to their victorious course. The Mediterranean had ceased to be a Roman lake. From one end of Europe to the other the Christian states found themselves confronted with the challenge of a new oriental civilization founded on a new oriental faith.

To what causes are we to attribute this sudden and extraordinary outpouring of the Arab race? An answer which is often given is that the Arabs were propelled into the uttermost parts of the earth by the ferment within them of their new religion, and that they rode, battled, and conquered to extend the faith. But this explanation does not accord with the fact that, during the early years of the Arab expansion, the conquerors were at no particular pains to make converts. On the contrary, their success in government largely consisted in the wise policy of toleration which they practised towards Jews and Christians, presenting in this respect the happiest contrast to the persecuting practices of their successors. But if religion was not the primary motive which underlay this extraordinary movement, still less can it be ascribed to consistent design. The Bedouin horsemen did not ride out of Arabia with a clear-cut scheme for the conquest of the world and the establishment of new states. They made their empire as other states have made empires after them, blindly, without set purpose and with no near and immediate project other than plunder. They began by making plundering raids into Palestine and Irak at a time when the defences of those provinces were at their lowest point of efficiency, and finding victory easy and booty rich, they extended their operations. Success, beyond the utmost dreams of ambition, attended their attacks. In 636 they beat the last army of Heraclius at the Yarmak and conquered Syria. In 637 they entered Ctesiphon and mastered Mesopotamia. In 639 they invaded Egypt, and three years later entered Alexandria. Having discovered the weakness of the Empire, they were resolved to exploit it and to hold, administer, and extend their conquests. Not otherwise did the Elizabethan buccaneers throw themselves upon the wealth of the western hemisphere. Yet if religion was not the originating force in the expansion of Arabia, it gave to it a degree of animation and permanence which it would otherwise have lacked. Without the bond of a common religion the Arab horsemen would have lacked the cohesion failing which victories can seldom be won and never secured. Without some inspiration higher than mere appetite they could never have commended their rule to Syrians and Egyptians, Persians and Berbers. No small part of their success was due to the fact that there had been evolved in the heart of Arabia a form of religion which satisfied then, as it continues to satisfy now, the souls of men and women living under the burning skies of Asia and Africa, and that of this religion the Arabs were the armed and exultant missionaries.

The Hedjaz was that part of Arabia most exposed, by reason of its trade, to foreign influences. Here Jews and Christians might sometimes be found, more especially in Mecca, which was the commercial centre of the district and a town of pilgrimage, or at Yathrib, two hundred miles north, one of the few areas in that waterless land where the arts of agriculture were practised by a settled population.

Muhammad (c. 570-632) was born at Mecca of a family neither rich nor distinguished, but of the Kuraishite tribe, which controlled the local sanctuary. As a young man he entered the commercial house of Kadija, a wealthy widow, whom he subsequently married, nor perhaps is it irrelevant to his spiritual development that the pursuit of his calling involved caravan journeys across the desert and opportunities of converse with Christians and Jews. Muhammad was one of those men of whom religious history offers many examples, in whom a passionate animal nature is combined with the temper of a visionary. In many of the conventional virtues of western society he was wholly deficient. He was cruel and crafty, lustful and ignorant, lacking in physical courage and the gift of self-criticism; but despite these grave faults, which became intensified with age and success, he had the ardour of the mystic, the zeal of the ethical reformer, and that absorbing preoccupation with the things of the soul which comes most easily to men in the solitary places of the world. By degrees the mind of this Arab merchant became possessed of certain large religious and ethical ideas. He went into trances, and in these trances visions appeared to him. He had a vision of the one God, of a future life, of the sensual delights of paradise, of the material torments of hell, and of an impending day of retribution in which sinners would be punished. These visions, crude, vigorous, animated, he began to recite (Koran), first of all privately to a circle of intimates, then more widely. Mecca was sharply critical. Was he a madman, an impostor, a poet? Nevertheless he persevered, winning adherents by the flow and vehemence of his invective, by his apocalyptic threats of impending doom, and by the large and attractive appeal of the monotheistic faith and the practice of brotherly love. That he was influenced by Judaism and Christianity is certain; but his information with regard to these two religions, being derived from oral sources only, was dim, fragmentary, and confused. He regarded Christ as a prophet, born of a virgin mother, but neither had the story of the crucifixion reached him, nor yet does he appear to have been aware of the difference between the Jewish and Christian creeds. The Koran is a collection of utterances of an unlettered prophet preaching the message of God to the Arab race.

From the mockeries of his native town Muhammad escaped in 622 to Yathrib, henceforth known as Medinat en Nabi, the city of the Prophet. This is the famous *Hegira*, or flight, which is taken to mark the beginning of the Moslem era. In Medina, which was tormented by rival factions, the Prophet continued his pious labours, preaching the welcome doctrine of concord, of submission (*islam*) to the will of God (*Allah*) and developing many of those practical precepts which govern the conduct of the Moslem world to this day, the five daily prayers, the fasting in the month of Ramadan, the yearly pilgrimage, the abstention from wine. In all this side of his teaching the Prophet showed a shrewd insight into Arab nature. It would be an anachronism to ascribe to him the idea of attempting to impose upon Arabia a universalist religion. With that strong, practical sense which was in him so strongly combined with religious exaltation and self-hypnotism, he aimed at reform rather than at revolution. He did not attempt to change everything, but tolerated polygamy and slavery, institutions too secure to be assailed with success, and even temporized with the symbols of polytheism. Returning to Mecca in 631, after a long struggle marked by acts of brigandage and wholesale murder, he adopted the black stone, and declared that the Caba was the temple of Abraham. Before he died he had founded a little state by the sword, for in the last analysis his Universal God was an Arab, and Mecca was his Holy City.

The new religion had from the first a great political value. Into the wild, lawless, infinitely divided Arab world it brought unity of belief, submission to authority, a tranquillizing daily ritual of prayer and that abstinence from strong drinks which has given to Moslem armies throughout history a special advantage. Moreover, the monotheism of Islam was not so far removed from the monophysite forms of Christianity which were popular in Syria and Egypt as to interpose an obstacle in the way of the Arab conquest of those lands.

So the Moslem civilization spread. Under the Ummayyads its political centre was Damascus, under the Abbasids Bagdad, under the Fatimites Cairo. Syrians and Persians, Turks, Berbers, and Spaniards contributed to bring about the great age of Moslem literature and art which, for four centuries while the European mind was deep sunk in ignorance and sloth, gave to the peoples of Islam the intellectual leadership of the world. The memory of that epoch still survives. Still the Palestinian Arab proudly contrasts the literature of his golden age with the scriptures of the Jew. Still the Nigerian Emir dreams of the pilgrimage to Mecca, and of the day when all the world will acknowledge the true faith. Still from the Atlantic Ocean to the Himalayas the *muezzin* calls the faithful to prayer at sunrise and sunset, the mosques fill with shoeless worshippers, the little children learn the Koran by heart, and in the shaded alcoves of the great Cairene University of Al Azhar groups of white-robed students, seated on the floor, swing back and forth in a mood of fanatical ecstasy, as they intone the sacred words of the polygamous Prophet to whom all wisdom and all modern science were miraculously revealed.

Islam is a religion of warriors and shepherds, which, albeit without a clergy or a regular liturgy, has persisted for 1,300 years and now is thought to number some 300,000,000 adherents. Asceticism after the early Christian manner was not encouraged by the Prophet, who is reputed to have said that "two prostrations of a married Moslem are worth more than seventy of a celibate." Nevertheless Islam, like Christianity, reckons its fraternities of ascetics, its enraptured mystics, its nonconformist sectaries. The harsh creed of the Arabian desert has taken colour and content from the richer civilizations of Syria and Egypt, of Persia, India, and Spain, from which, at different times, it has drawn its votaries. The crude outpourings of the Koran do not exhaust its message. There is in Islam a body of mystical literature, which, in the purity of its religious emotion, vies with the spiritual masterpieces of the Jewish or Christian faith.

The period which succeeds the death of the Prophet, while distinguished for many dazzling achievements in war and policy, is also memorable for the emergence of that deep rift within the Moslem world which still envenoms the relations of the Shiite and the Sunnite sects. Under the able rule of Omar, the second of the Caliphs or Vicars and the true founder of the Arab state, the voice of discontent was silenced by the victories of the Arab generals. But his successor, Othman, was less fortunate, less able, less industrious, and perhaps also, since his government was hotly blamed for its extortions, less well served. A campaign was set on foot in favour of Ali, the son-in-law of the Prophet, which resulted in the assassination of Othman, and in the elevation of Ali to the caliphate in his place. From that moment the Moslem world was sharply sundered into two irreconcilable factions. The title of Ali was disputed by the experienced Moawya, the cousin of the murdered caliph and a member of the Ummayyad house, who, having ruled Syria for seventeen years, was in no mood to surrender the throne of power to the nominee of Medina.

The Shiites or partisans of Ali were strong in Arabia and Irak, the Sunnites adhered to Moawya in Syria and Egypt. The murder of Ali and later of his second son, Hosein, left in the hearts of their votaries a long memory of passionate regret such as has coloured the annals of Ireland and Serbia; but the strength lay with the caliphs of the Ummayyad house who ruled at Damascus. At the cost of two civil wars they established (692) their supremacy over the Arab world.

The divisions between the Shiites and the Sunnites, while temporarily arresting the Moslem offensive, brought no permanent relief to the Byzantine Empire. Its position was challenged in Asia Minor and in the islands. Its capital was exposed to the risk of capture. The defection of those of its Christian

A.D. 634-43

A.D. 643-56

A.D. 661

subjects who exalted the divine as opposed to the human side
of Christ was always to be apprehended. Meanwhile no great
figure appeared upon the Byzantine scene between the death of
Heraclius in 641 and the accession of Leo the Isaurian in 717.
Emperor succeeded emperor, assassination followed assassination. But though the state was shaken by palace revolutions and
civil war and its annals stained by fratricidal intrigues, Asia
Minor and Constantinople were held. The subdivision of the
Empire into military districts or themes, garrisoned by army
divisions and under entire subjection to military officers, may
have helped to this end.

It is a commonplace of history to remark that the Saracen
expansion in Europe was ultimately checked by the victory won
by the Frankish sovereign, Charles Martel, over the great army
of the Viceroy Abdur Rahman on the field of Poitiers in 732.
The numbers engaged on either side in that famous conflict
were high, the conflict between the huge Frankish footmen and
the fiery cavalry of Spain and Africa was fierce and long, the
victory of the Christian army was complete and decisive. But
in the scale of importance the victory of Poitiers does not rank
with the successful repulse by Leo the Isaurian of the formidable Saracen attacks on Constantinople in 717 and 718, not only
because Constantinople was closer to the centre of Moslem
power and therefore more likely, if taken, to be retained, but
also because the Saracens once established in the Byzantine
capital would have found among the rude and imperfect
Christians of eastern Europe a free field for Moslem propaganda.
If the Turkish conquest of Constantinople in the fifteenth century spread the Moslem creed far and wide through the Balkan
peninsula, we may imagine the success which would have
attended a Saracen conquest 700 years earlier, at a time when
the peoples of Russia and the Balkans had received but a faint
initial tincture of Christianity, and were still in a rude disorder
of institutions and beliefs.

In the west the Saracens were confronted by an organized
Christian society inheriting something of the strength of the
Roman Empire, and even had they won the day at Poitiers,
would still have been far removed from the conquest and con-
version of France. In eastern Europe it was otherwise. Here in
Russia and Hungary, or among the Bulgarians and Slavs of the
Balkan peninsula, there was no centre of moral and physical

resistance comparable to the Gallo-Roman Church or to the Frankish monarchy. Had Leo the Isaurian failed to beat off the imposing armada of Moslemah, the Moslem faith might have spread like a prairie fire through the Balkans and the plain of Hungary and northwards and eastwards to the Urals. From this danger the great defence of Constantinople in 718, conducted by a young and capable Emperor, with the aid of stout fortifications, a superior navy, Greek fire, and the timely assistance of a Bulgar army, delivered European civilization. The name of Leo should be remembered. That the Russian Church is Greek and not Moslem today is one of the results, how fortunate we dare not say, which may, without a great stretch of probabilities, be attributed to his great and resounding triumph.

BOOKS WHICH MAY BE CONSULTED

W. Muir. Mahomet and History of Islam. 1894.

D. S. Margoliouth : Mohammed and the Rise of Islam. 1905.

H. Lammens : Islam, Beliefs and Institutions. *Tr.* E. Denison Ross 1929.

R. Bell : The Origins of Islam in its Christian Environment. 1926.

R. A. Nicholson : A Literary History of the Arabs. 1907.

CHAPTER XIII

THE FRANKISH EMPIRE

Long duration of the house of Meroveus. Sources of its authority. Survival of Latin culture in Gaul. Its disappearance in Britain. Decomposition of public power under the Merovingians. Survival of the idea of Frankish unity. Rise of the Carolings. Charles Martel. Christian missions in Germany. The Papacy quarrels with the Greeks and Lombards and invokes the Franks. Pippin and Pope Stephen. Charles the Great. First visit to Rome. Coronation in A.D. 800. Its importance. The Carolingian renaissance. The debt to Ireland and England. Alcuin. The Saxon wars. Central Europe secured for the Latin Church. Strength and weakness of the Frankish Empire. Its dissolution in the ninth century.

THE descendants of King Clovis the Frank were for the most part either cruel and treacherous barbarians or enfeebled debauchees. Yet, despite their atrocities and lusts, their fratricidal enmities and purposeless civil wars, the house of Meroveus endured for nearly 300 years (481-716), outlasting the Valois or the Bourbons, the Stuarts or the Hanoverians, and in this point of endurance presenting the sharpest contrast to the short-lived ruling families of imperial Rome. So strong was the prestige attaching to the stock of Clovis that for seventy-eight years after all effective power had passed into the hands of the mayors of the palace, members of the Merovingian house were still solemnly crowned and accorded honours of a phantasmal royalty. "Nothing," says Einhard, writing of this last period of their rule, " was left the King, except the name of King, the flowing locks, the long beard. He sat on his throne and played at government, gave audience to envoys, and dismissed them with the answers which he had been schooled, or rather commanded, to give. He had nothing to call his own except one estate of small value where he had a residence and a not very numerous retinue. He travelled, when occasion required it, in a waggon drawn by oxen, and driven like a farmer's cart by a cowherd. In this guise he came to the palace or to the annual assembly of his people. The Mayor controlled the administration and decided all issues of policy at home or abroad."

The explanation of this extraordinary reluctance to terminate

145

the life of a bad dynasty is to be chiefly found in the field of religion. If the Merovingians were kings, they were also priests. If they were wicked, they were also holy. No steel must shear their flowing locks, for were they not, as the Frankish song writers knew, descended from the sea god or sea monster who begat Meroveus? An aura of sanctity, far older than Christianity, clung about this national priesthood of the Franks. They did not need the consecration of a Christian bishop to establish their authority, or to commend them to the loyalty of their Frankish warriors. Not that they failed to derive substantial and continuing advantages from the fact that Clovis, the founder, had adopted the faith and obtained the support of the Roman Church. Thereby they were free from the obstacles which confronted the Arian Ostrogoths or Lombards in Italy, or the Visigoths during their government of Toulouse and the first heretical period of their Spanish rule. The only organized and educated body of men, surviving the wreck of the Empire in the west, instead of being inimical, was an ally. They could beat down the Arian and the Jew with the plaudits of the Church, and count every victory as a triumph of the orthodox, of the Roman faith.

Moreover, despite their Teuton origin, the early Merovingian kings were prone to regard themselves as the generals or magistrates of Rome. They accepted Roman insignia, made use of Roman coins, and appear, in the true imperial spirit, to have recognized no frontiers to the extension of their rule. In Constantinople they were, from time to time, regarded as auxiliaries. The Emperor Maurice, in 590, alluding to the ancient concord between the Franks and the Roman people, invoked the aid of Childebert II against the Lombards in Italy.

It is, therefore, easy to see how, despite the Teutonic origin of its Frankish conquerors, the land which is now known as France has remained part of the Latin world. The Franks, though they effected an occupation of Gaul, did not enter upon their inheritance as the enemies of the Gallo-Roman population, but rather as the foes of the Arian Visigoths and Burgundians. It was against these, or against one another, that Clovis and his descendants were chiefly concerned to turn their arms, not against the Roman Church, which they regarded as a friend, nor the Gallo-Roman population which accepted their yoke, nor the Roman Emperor, who, from his distant throne on the Bosphorus, was disposed to regard them as potential allies. After a very few years the Church imposed its Latin culture on the conquerors. Chilperic, the grandson of Clovis, described by Gregory of Tours as the Nero and Herod of his age, composed Latin verses, and in the pride of his new won knowledge, added four Greek letters to the alphabet.

That the continuity of Latin civilization should have been thus secured in Gaul while it was broken in Britain is explained when we consider the comparative weight of the Roman influence in the two countries and the differing circumstances attending their conquest. In Gaul the Roman cities were numerous and comparatively large; in Britain they were few (some fifteen or sixteen in number) and exceedingly small. In the one country the Church was affluent and influential; in the other, as the tiny basilica in Silchester seems to indicate, it was weak and poor. The correspondence of Sidonius Apollinaris, taken in conjunction with the later evidence of Gregory of Tours, proves that in Gaul there was both before and after the Frankish invasion an influential country aristocracy of Gallo-Roman descent. No such aristocracy survived in those parts of Britain which were effectually conquered by the Saxons. But what was equally important was the contrasted character of the two invasions, in Gaul accepted by the larger part of the native population, in Britain fiercely contested, and leading to the replacement of the Latin-speaking Celts of England by their heathen and Teutonic conquerors, to the submergence of the Christian religion and the loss of the Latin speech.

With the Franks, as with the other Teutonic peoples, the old institutions of tribal liberty had failed to survive the ordeal of war. The popular assemblies were no longer held. The king's will, in so far as it was not contested in practice by the nobles, was law. Yet nothing was done to turn these initial advantages to account. The Merovingian kings had no idea of political responsibility or historical tradition. They applied to the Frankish monarchy the principles which in Teutonic society governed the regulation of private property. The inheritance was divided among the sons, and since the sons invariably quarrelled, the country was plagued for five generations by useless civil war.

From these contests, which were inspired by no principle

higher than the violent appetites of an ill-conditioned child may supply, one consequence plainly followed, a progressive degeneration in the art and system of government. As we study the history of Gaul in the Merovingian age we are sensible of a steady decomposition of public power. Privileges are freely granted or freely taken, which are inconsistent with the exercise of state authority.

The tendencies which Sir Henry Spelman, an English jurist of the seventeenth century, summarized under the phrase " the feudal system," begin to make themselves increasingly apparent. The administration of justice, the levy of taxes, the obligation of raising fighting men for the army or the host, tend to fall into the hands of great landed proprietors, civil or ecclesiastical. Grants of " immunities " are made to churches or abbeys, which in effect exclude them from the normal responsibilities and duties of the citizen. The count, who is the public official in the city, may not enter the " immunized " territory to levy taxes, or to administer justice, or to raise men for the host. These functions, if they are still to be performed, belong henceforth to the territorial lord, upon whom, under the vague and ill-defined suzerainty of the king, the exercise of political power is in effect devolved. By the end of the Merovingian period a great part of the land of Gaul had fallen into the hands of the Church.

While this slow decomposition was taking place in the body politic of Frankish Gaul, while the monarchy was becoming weaker, the Church more wealthy, and in consequence more barbarous and corrupt, and the nobility more independent, the fabric of Christian society in the west was menaced by the Saracens, the Avars, and the Slavs. The pressure of foreign danger was sufficient to maintain in the ill-soldered Frankish dominions a sense of unity which the partitions and civil wars of the Merovingian kings were unable to destroy. The frontiers were defended. A term was placed on fresh Teutonic invasions. The strong provincial feelings of Burgundy and Aquitaine, of Neustria and Austrasia (as the western and eastern parts of northern France had by 561 come to be termed), were not allowed altogether to efface the historic image of Rome. Even the fifty years of decadence and disorder which followed the death of Dagobert (638), the last Merovingian king to rule over a united country, failed to obliterate the idea of an undivided monarchy,

Christian, Roman, and Frankish, governing the vast area which was once Gaul.

A new epoch opens with the rise to power of that vigorous and remarkable Teutonic dynasty which obtains an immortal lustre from the great name of Charlemagne. From being weak and contemptible the Frankish monarchy became, under the Carolings, the strongest instrument for government and conquest which Europe had seen since the great days of the Roman Empire. The whole landscape of public affairs was transformed by the strenuous activities of the Austrasian or eastern Franks. The Saracens were driven back into Spain, the Avars blotted from the map, and Pannonia, their latest home, made bare for the reception of the Hungarian people. A Papal state was created in Italy at the expense of the defeated Lombards, with the three important consequences of preventing, until 1870, the establishment of a unified Italian state, of widening the rift between Rome and Byzantium, and of giving to the Papacy a position of political independence, which was thought by some to be a temptation to worldliness and corruption, by others to be essential to its spiritual freedom and authority. These changes were important. To this day we experience their effects. But more important still was the conversion to Christianity of Frisia and Germany and the acceptance by Charlemagne of the Imperial crown from the hands of Pope Leo III on Christmas day, 800. A new world in central Europe was called into the Christian and Roman fold to redress the losses in Syria and Egypt, in Africa and Spain. A conquest for Rome greater than any single conquest since the days of Julius Caesar had been achieved by the co-operation of English and Irish missionaries, Frankish soldiery, and papal encouragement and support.

The Carolings sprang from the border land which has been disputed for centuries between the Latin and Teutonic races. Among the grandees who were prominent in the politics of Austrasia at the beginning of the seventh century were a certain Pippin of Landen in Brabant, and a certain Arnulf, a duke, and subsequently a bishop of Metz. Pippin, who became mayor of the palace, and *de facto* ruler of Austrasia in 622, married his daughter to the son of Arnulf, and seldom can there have been a grander alliance in Austrasia than this union between the daughter of its foremost statesman and the son of a man who was in turn a duke, a bishop, and a saint, but most specially distinguished, if his genealogy can be trusted, for his connections with a Roman senatorial family in Narbonne. The child of this marriage won for himself a place in world history.[1]

Pippin II, Mayor of Austrasia in 681, master of Neustria in 687, a valiant fighter, and a zealous friend of missionary enterprise among the Germans and Frisians, was the father of Charles Martel and the great-grandfather of Charlemagne. Such in brief was the lineage of the illustrious Emperor, who is claimed as a national hero both by the Germans and by the French, but who was in truth neither German nor French as we now understand these terms, but an Austrasian Frank, Teutonic, no doubt, in origin and sentiment, but Latin in discipline, and regarded by himself and his contemporaries as the captain of Roman Christianity in the western world.

Charles Martel, or Charles "the Hammer," the bastard son of Pippin II, reigned over the two kingdoms of Austrasia and Neustria for twenty-six years, defeating all his neighbours in battle, and earning his title of the Hammer by his drastic and probably not unneeded handling of the Gallo-Roman Church. The tall, mail-clad infantry from the east who brought him victory on so many fields had not been softened by the luxuries of the town, and restored to the Frankish name a military lustre which had been lost since the days when Clovis first loosed his untamed Teutons on the fields of Gaul. Of the Hammer's achievements, one, though most insufficiently described, is specially memorable. On an October Sunday in 732 he defeated near Poitiers a great Moslem army under Abdur Rahman, the Arab Governor of Spain, with a loss to the invaders, if the figures of Paul the Deacon can be trusted (as they can not), of 375,000 lives. This resounding victory, though it did not prevent fresh Arab incursions into Gaul, for three years later the Arabs took Arles and Avignon, from each of which cities they were evicted by the Hammer, was nevertheless a decisive deliverance.

It is true that the Arabs would not have been strong enough to capture, still less to hold Gaul, and that quite apart from the

[1] Genealogical Table A.

conspiracies and intrigues which are the web and woof of oriental politics, they were confronted with troubles from the Berbers in Africa and the Christians in Spain. Still, if they could not have conquered, they could have persisted in destructive raids. In particular they could have opposed a serious obstacle to the prosecution of the greatest of all the improvements which was then, with the Hammer's material help, being carried out in Europe.

The conversion of Germany could never have been accomplished by the Frankish clergy in the state to which it had been reduced under the Merovingian régime. It is to the missionaries of Ireland and England, where Christianity shone with a purer light, that we must ascribe the spiritual impulse which prompted the German mission and revived the religious tone of the western Church. We have now reached the time when the British peoples, emerging from their northern mists, make their first great contribution to the advancement of civilized life in the larger world. The long roll of great Englishmen opens at the beginning of the eighth century with the names of a scholar and a missionary. Thus early did the Anglo-Saxons evince their passion for the improvement of mankind through religion and knowledge. The Ecclesiastical History of Bede, a Northumbrian monk, who took all knowledge for his province, retained for at least four centuries a pre-eminent place in the Latin literature of Europe, and is still valued as our prime source of information on the development of Christian society and institutions in Britain. Almost an exact contemporary of this famous polymath was Wynfrith, better known under his later name of Boniface, the apostle of Germany. The work of a missionary among barbarous people, living in dense and distant forests, may leave but little trace on the written memorials of his time. But the salient facts in the career of Boniface are eloquent of ardour and persistence, of capacity and success. Despatched by Pope Gregory II in 719 on a mission to the heathen in Germany, he put himself to school with his compatriot Willibrod, who was engaged upon the conversion of the Frisians; and it was in Frisia, after thirty-five years of unremitting toil, that Boniface found a martyr's death. Meanwhile, labouring always in the service of the apostolic see, but also with the powerful assistance of the Frankish kings, he converted the Hessians and Thuringians, organized the Church in Bavaria, and being appointed to the Archbishopric of Mainz in 748, exercised a general supervision over the Christian communities which, mainly through his efforts, had been fashioned in southern and central Germany. That he was assisted by other valiant workers does not detract from his achievement. In the task of binding Germany to Rome he was a pioneer, and his the decisive and dynamic influence.

In one important particular the conversion of Germany differs from the far earlier movement for the introduction of Christianity into Gaul. The humble Syrian traders who first brought the Christian message to Marseilles came into a highly civilized Roman province. Votaries of an obscure oriental sect, they could offer neither poetry nor metaphysics, neither law nor science, to a society far better instructed in all these matters than they. What they had to propound was a revolutionary way of life round which a new literature, wider and more practical than the old, and offering a fresh range of moral interests, was gradually built up in Greek and Latin. To the cultivated gentlemen of Gaul, even as late as the fifth century, Virgil was more melodious than Prudentius, Cicero more eloquent than Augustine. The new theology had a rival in the old literature, which to many a pious mind seemed to be dangerous just because it was seductive. But in Germany there was no such dualism. There the Christian missions did not at any point conflict with allegiance to an ancient and splendid literature, for Boniface and his fellow-workers preached to rude, unlettered barbarians. It was indeed to the missions and monasteries that Germany owed its knowledge of Latin and an introduction into the culture of the ancient world.

While the Venerable Bede was writing his immortal work in his cell at Jarrow and Boniface was preaching Christ to the wild Thuringians, and Charles the Hammer, but also the missionary, was hammering the bishops and abbots of Gaul, and secularizing their property, events were preparing a fresh rift within the Christian fold, and working up to that alliance between the Papacy and the Frankish kings which transformed the politics of western Europe.

It is part of the wisdom of the Roman Church to accept what it cannot prevent. It accepts and subordinates to its system the ineradicable polytheism of Mediterranean man. The pagan genius became the Christian angel, the pagan Isis the Christian Madonna, the pagan hero became the Christian saint, the pagan festival the Christian feast. And while canonizing this deep-seated popular craving for spiritual helpers and mediators, the Roman Church also welcomed the material modes, be they low or lofty, in which expression was sought to be given to these needs. It accepted statues and paintings, the worship of relics and the pilgrimage to shrines in which relics were placed. In the general debasement of mind and morals which characterized the seventh century this material or superstitious side of the Christian religion was greatly developed. Image worship was prevalent in the Roman, it was still more prevalent in the Byzantine Church. It was open to the critic to observe that the cult of a single God had been left to the Moslem and the Jew.

Such critics were to be found in plenty in the highlands of Armenia and Anatolia. The Paulicians, so called because they appealed to the authority of St. Paul, acknowledged only those principles of conduct for which they found a warrant in the Scriptures. They repudiated the commentaries of the Fathers. They denied the authority of the Church. They rejected the sacraments, the veneration of the Cross, the adoration of the Virgin. In the rigour of their puritanism they anticipated the Protestant reformers of the sixteenth century. It would seem that the Emperor Leo III, who came from the regions in Asia Minor where such beliefs prevailed, was impressed by the message of these highland sectaries. To his austere and soldierly mind the practices which may be summarized in the term " image-worship " were corrupting to the fibre of the body politic. The Empire was not to be saved from the Moslem by monks, relics, and incantations, but by civilian discipline and military valour. In 726 the Isaurian Emperor issued an edict commanding the destruction of images throughout his dominions.

At once a storm arose in Italy. To the many causes of dissension between Greek and Roman churches, the quarrel over the single Nature, the quarrel over the single Will, the claim that the Patriarch of Constantinople was on an equal footing with the Pope of Rome, there was now added the embittering circumstance that a Greek tyrant was seeking to deprive the Italian people of their cherished religious images. A revolt broke out in Ravenna, a Greek exarch was killed; in a council of Italian bishops summoned in 731 by Gregory III the iconoclasts were excommunicated. The defiance of Rome was bold, popular, dangerous. Hopelessly at issue with the Empire, the Popes were compelled to look elsewhere for material support.

The stream of history would have run in different channels if, at this juncture, the Papacy had elected to ally itself steadily with the Lombard monarchy. There was much to be said for such a course. The Lombards, after the first great explosion of cruelty which marked their original settlement in Italy, had shown some aptitude for civilization. They had abjured Arianism and reduced some of their laws to writing, and under the rule of the enlightened Liutprand were making swift advances in the arts of life. Moreover, in a contest with the Greeks, Lombard sympathy could be counted on in advance. From their first entry into Italy in 568 until the peace of 680, the principal thread in Lombard history had been the prosecution of a quarrel with the Greek Empire. That antagonism, though intermitted for the time, was still an underlying condition of Italian politics. No Lombard king could rest content while an inch of Italian soil was held by the Empire, and no Emperor could look upon the Lombards as other than pestilent intruders upon his sacred preserves. A doubt can never have existed in the papal curia but that the Lombards would prove to be zealous and effective allies against the Greek iconoclasts.

Yet the Papacy, showing that fine instinct for secular diplomacy which belongs in a special degree to Italian statesmanship, decided, after some fluctuations of policy, that the Lombards, despite their Catholicism and their improvements in the arts and their hatred of the Greeks, were to be treated not as friends but as enemies. Pavia was too near Rome. If the Lombards became uncontested masters of Italy, the Papacy would be degraded to a Lombard bishopric. Rather than rest upon the support of these warlike neighbours, the Popes decided to appeal to the distant and powerful Franks. In 739 Gregory III sent the keys of St. Peter's tomb to Charles Martel, and asked him to replace the Emperor in the governance of Rome. That offer Charles declined, and two years afterwards the three great political figures on the stage—Leo, Gregory, and Charles—were dead.

The men changed, the policies continued. By the steady suction of circumstance the Pope of Rome and the Frankish king

712-43

were drawn into fateful combination. Pippin the Short, the younger son of Charles, and after the retirement of his elder brother to a monastery the effective ruler of France, was the friend of Boniface the Englishman. To the mayor of the palace, as to the missionary, it was important to venerate the apostolic see, to promote the German missions, and to administer a much-needed correction to the Gallic Church. The piety of Pippin, whether real or assumed, met with its reward. In response to a prudent enquiry as to whether it was right that the real should not also be the nominal ruler, he was assured by Pope Zachary that he might depose the last of the Merovings and assume the crown himself. Pippin acted on that advice. In the cathedral at Soissons, Boniface, the Englishman, anointed him king.

For the enormous services of legalizing the Carolingian monarchy, the Pope was soon in a position to claim a commensurate recompense. The new Lombard king, Aistulf, was distinguished by an imprudent and intemperate ambition to conquer at one and the same time the exarchate and the Roman patrimony. His armies, directed against the imperialists, met with such success as to inspire the liveliest apprehensions in the heart of the Pope. At the invitation of Pippin, and possibly also with the connivance of the Emperor, Pope Stephen crossed the Alps 753 and made a memorable bargain with the Frankish king. He conferred upon him the imperial title of Patrician, anointed him afresh together with his two sons, and bound the Franks to choose their future kings from his descendants alone. In return, Pippin engaged to transfer the cities which the Lombard kings had taken from the Emperor, not to their lawful but iconoclastic master, but to the Roman Republic and to St. Peter. What the Frank promised he performed. In two brief campaigns he wrested from the Lombards all the country which they had won since the death of Liutprand, and made it over to the Papal See.

Thus was founded that extraordinary polity, governed for over eleven hundred years by clerics, and presenting over most of that long period an almost continuous spectacle of disorder. Such was the origin of the Papal States, so long a fatal obstacle to Italian unity and a perpetual invitation to foreign invasion and intrigue. It is perhaps reasonable to conjecture that even in the eighth century some scrupulous minds may have been exercised by the validity of a title resting on nothing better than two violent conquests. If so, a pious and timely forgery allayed such misgivings. It was discovered that the Emperor Constantine had, upon his conversion, made a donation to Pope Sylvester of all Italy and the west. The extravagance of the legend was no bar to its acceptance, even after many centuries, and by men violently hostile to the mundane ambitions of the Church. It is thanks to the forged donation that Constantine is eloquently denounced alike in Hell and Paradise by Dante, the imperialist, more than five hundred years after the pious forger had been sent to his last account.

Pippin died in 768. Among the blessings vouchsafed to Charles, his eldest son, was, as a pious monk once reminded him, the removal by death three years later of his younger brother Carloman. For forty-three years the deadly system of partition, which even Pippin had not been strong enough to discard, was interrupted by fate, and the stage was cleared for the unimpeded action of a powerful character. Charles was worthy of his opportunity. He was bold and yet deliberate, genial and yet exact, popular and yet formidable. A vast appetite for animal enjoyment was combined in him with the cardinal gifts of statesmanship, a spacious vision, strong common sense, a flawless memory, and a tenacious will. It was part of his strength that he attempted nothing impossible, and asked no more of his people than they were able to accomplish. To his Frankish warriors he was the ideal chief, tall and stout, animated and commanding, with flashing blue eyes and aquiline nose, a mighty hunter before the Lord. That he loved the old Frankish songs, used Frankish speech, and affected the traditional costume of his race—the high-laced boots, the cross-gartered scarlet hose, the linen tunic, and square mantle of white or blue—that he was simple in his needs, and sparing in food and drink, were ingratiating features in a rich and wholesome character. Yet if in the habits of daily life he was a Frank to the marrow, in all matters pertaining to culture and religion he was prepared to obey the call and to extend the influence of his Roman priests.

Not many years elapsed before the same political logic which brought about the close conjunction of Pippin with the Papacy worked to a similar conclusion for Charles. Again a Lombard king made an incursion into papal territory. Again a Pope appealed to the Frankish monarch for help, and again that help was accorded. In the second act of the drama, however, the incidents appeared to be heightened and intensified, the actors to be stronger, the dénouement to be more decisive. Didier the Lombard and Charles the Frank were already estranged before Didier made his attack on Ravenna and the Pentapolis and menaced the walls of Rome. Charles had married, and on grounds of personal aversion divorced, the daughter of the Lombard king. Didier had given shelter to the infant nephews and possible rivals of Charles, and pressed the Pope to crown them. Nothing, however, was further from the mind of Pope Hadrian, a proud and steadfast Roman noble, than to purchase by a dishonouring alliance with the hated Lombard the dangerous enmity of the Frank. He appealed to Charles the Roman Patrician (773) and his appeal was not in vain. A great Frankish army marched into Italy and drove Didier off his throne. Nothing was wanting to the completeness of the Frankish triumph, neither the eclipse of the royal line of Lombards after two hundred years of rule in Italy, nor the assumption by Charles, the conqueror, of the Lombard crown, nor the final act of scorn which relegated the last of the Lombard kings to a lifelong imprisonment in a monastery.

In the midst of his Italian campaign Charles was solemnly received by the grateful and submissive ecclesiastics of Rome. He was then thirty-two years of age; upon his fresh and experiencing, but naïvely superstitious, mind the marvels of Rome, its wealth in churches and wonder-working relics, its finished priestcraft, its Gregorian chants and well-ordered ritual, made a profound impression. A visit to Rome more than seven hundred years later drove Luther from the Catholic fold. Upon Charles the reaction of this extraordinary city was otherwise. He found it rich and incomparable in the signs of the favour of God. Here the awestruck visitor would be shown the very ark of the covenant and the heads of St. Peter and St. Paul. Here he could inspect two phials of blood and water from the side of Christ, the purple robe worn by the Saviour of mankind, and part of the cradle in which He lay when the Magi came to adore Him. Here was the very table at which He ate His Last Supper, here His portrait painted by the hand of Luke the Evangelist, or perhaps even, as some were bold to conjecture, by the divine brush of the Creator Himself. Moreover, the whole art and science of

serving God was here better understood than anywhere in those
northern lands with which Charles was familiar. The singing
was more beautiful, the ritual more perfect, the churches richer
and more numerous. Charles determined to bring this Roman
art and science of priestcraft into his Frankish world. Making
a lifelong friend of the Pope, he confirmed, perhaps with
additions, that donation of mid-Italian territory by which his
father had founded the Papal State.

Twenty-six years afterwards a yet graver problem connected
with the Papacy brought Charles again to Rome. If a Pope were
accused by his enemies of simony, adultery, and perjury; if he
were set upon by his enemies in the streets of Rome (as was the
fate of Leo III on April 25, 799) and beaten within an inch of
his life; if then he were rescued by his friends and escorted to
the great Frankish king as he held court at Paderborn, who was
competent to try the issue? To what power was entrusted the
solemn duty of passing judgment on the vicar of Christ?

Certainly, in the view of the wise men of the west, that function did not belong to the beautiful Athenian lady who, having
caused her son Constantine VI to be blinded and imprisoned,
now reigned supreme in Constantinople. Irene, despite her addiction to images, and the enthusiasm of her monkish following,
was no more fit to try the Pope of Rome than her wretched,
image-breaking boy. A woman, least of all a homicidal Greek
woman, could not be Roman Emperor. Thus, in 800, men awoke
to the fact that in the wide world there was neither a valid
Emperor nor yet a valid Pope.

To the mind of that age a world so destitute was given over
to ruin and chaos. Someone there must be to uphold the
Christian Faith, to safeguard the Roman tradition, to preside
over the trial of the dubious Pope, to balance the brilliant and
menacing power of Abdur Rahman, the Caliph of Bagdad, and to
maintain in a comprehensive bond the sacred unity of civilization. That person could only be Charlemagne. It is an illustration of his wide renown that the Patriarch of Jerusalem,
despairing of protection from the eastern Empire, despatched
to him the keys of the Holy Places.

So when, in the late autumn of 800, Charles descended into
Italy, we cannot doubt that over and above the urgent need of
clearing the reputation of the Pope, there was present to his

mind that momentous void in the Roman Empire. A Pope must be purged and an Emperor must be crowned. Yet the precise method of reaching these two ends may have been left to chance. On December 23 Pope Leo asserted his innocence by a solemn oath taken on the Gospels in the Basilica of St. Peter's, to the satisfaction of a great synod of Roman and Frankish clergy. Two days later, as Charles was rising from his knees at the end of the Christmas Mass, the Pope placed upon his head the imperial crown, and the congregation at St. Peter's, apparently not unprepared, shouted, " Karolo piissimo Augusto a Deo coronato vita et victoria." Once more there was a Roman Emperor in western Europe.

It is possible that Charles was chagrined, as his biographer hints, by the sudden mode of his coronation, for no Emperor in the west had ever yet received his crown from the Pope. But the superstructure of papal pretensions built upon that Christmas Day ceremony was in the distant future. What mattered at the time was not the mode, but the fact, of the coronation. The imperial title brought with it neither treasure nor territory. It did not give to Charles authority in Spain, or Britain, or Africa, once flourishing provinces of the Roman Empire; nor a yard of Lombardy, of which he was already king and master; nor yet on the strength of it could he command the service of an additional soldier or ship of war. Yet the revival of the Roman Empire in the west was none the less important, for through it that deep inner sense of unity which persists at the heart of European turmoils, and has given rise to such institutions as the Concert of Europe and the League of Nations, received for many centuries its secular embodiment.

It is one of the highest titles of Charlemagne to fame that he used his great authority to promote the revival of intellectual life on the illiterate continent of Europe. The Carolingian Renaissance lacks all the qualities of charm, freedom, and audacity which distinguished the great liberating movement of the human spirit in the age which divides Petrarch from Galileo. To the orthodox mind of Charles literature was chiefly to be valued as the handmaid of faith. The learned men who were attracted from all quarters to his court were not expected to discover new verities for the service of man. The Holy Scriptures, though often circulating in corrupt and misleading texts, contained the whole key to the truth, the sovereign guide to conduct. These it was the province of the scholar to copy out, and if needful, to amend, to understand himself and to make clear to his pupils; and that a supply of men qualified to perform this learned office might never be lacking, every diocese and monastery of the realm was expected to take up the work of education.

The value of this intellectual movement must not be judged by the quality of Carolingian literature. This, with the exception of Einhard's Life of Charles, does not rise above mediocrity, and shines only by contrast with the preceding darkness. What is important to notice is the new place which, with the advent of Charles, learning and education are made to take in the life of the court and the country, the concentration of foreign men of learning round the person of the king, the travelling academy or school of the palace which follows him even on his campaigns, the equal terms on which he associates with his scholar friends, his strong insistence on literacy as a qualification for a clerical career and for preferment in the Church, the establishment of diocesan and monastic schools, and the encouragement given to the multiplication, correction, and gathering together of books. Far reaching novelties were not to be expected in that age. There was no idea of science, no close observation of the outer world, no instinct for discovery. The prime necessity of the moment was not to invent, but to recover what had been lost, to preserve what had been found, and to reconstitute in the midst of barbarism a literate society.

The task would have been rendered by many degrees more difficult but for the fact that there was one corner of western Europe in which the lamps of learning and literature were still burning with a relative brightness. The islands of Ireland and Britain, though far from peaceful, had been for a century immune from many of the grave calamities which had afflicted the continent. At Armagh and Iona, at Jarrow and York, knowledge and piety shone with a clear, if intermittent, lustre. In these two islands a scholar possessed of a good deal of Latin, a little Greek, and possibly some fragments of Hebrew was not altogether unknown. More particularly in Northumbria, where Roman and Irish influences were found in combination or in conflict, was the care for letters specially evident. It is probable that at the date of Charlemagne's accession the best store of books north of the Alps was the library at York.

It was from York that Charles took his spiritual counsellor. To Alcuin, a Northumbrian of noble lineage, born and educated in that city, there was vouchsafed the greatest educational opportunity ever opened to an Englishman. He was called in to prescribe for the intellectual wants of a great empire fallen from civilization to barbarism. To this task he brought a pure and ardent character, a communicative zeal, and a gift of eloquent but unoriginal writing. He composed complimentary Latin verses, moral and pedagogic treatises, and an extended controversial reply to those Spanish heretics who maintained that Christ was adopted by God. Nobody now reads the tedious writings of Alcuin. Yet he was one of those valuable men who, without being gifted with discovering genius, create by their energy, sociability, and enthusiasm an atmosphere favourable to intellectual advance. His school of the palace set a new standard of culture. To the influence of this robust, studious, and convivial Englishman we may fairly trace the legislation which defines the educational responsibilities of the Church and the episcopal and monastic schools which resulted from it. To him also is due the initiation of that immense labour in the transcription, the emendation, and the preservation of manuscripts, the best and most permanent contribution which that age was able to make to the relief of man's estate. The earliest copies of twelve of the great Latin classics are due to the scribes of the Carolingian Renaissance.

Notable among the achievements of a famous reign was the final inclusion of Germany within the sphere of the Frankish nation and the Roman Church. Since Julius Caesar conquered Gaul there had been no such augmentation of Latin influence in Europe. Einhard, whose brief biography of Charles is justly accounted a model, says not only that he almost doubled the Empire which he received from his father, but that all the tribes between the Rhine and the Vistula were subjected to his rule. The particular mode of his operation was to batter down with a persistence which no rebuff could weaken the two principal obstacles which arrested the advance of Christianity in central Europe. These were the Saxon block in Westphalia, and the Avars, whose barbarous power, enriched

6

by the sack of the Balkan cities, lay athwart the middle Danube. The struggle was long, obstinate, and cruel. Thirty-three years of hard fighting were necessary to the reduction and forced conversion of the Saxons, eight campaigns to the destruction of the Avars, whose hoarded treasures are said to have raised their conquerors from prosperity to affluence. But once done, the work did not require to be done again. The Saxons passed into the Christian fold, the Avars vanished from the map, and the tide of Frankish influence, bearing with it the seeds of Christian and Latin culture, swept slowly but surely eastwards into lands which afterwards came to be known as Poland and Bohemia, Austria and Hungary.

Even had he desired to do so, Charlemagne could never have latinized Germany as Caesar latinized Gaul. That branch of the Saxon race which had not passed into Britain preserved among their untamed forests a fierce attachment to the faith of their ancestors. Under Widukind, their national leader, they offered a desperate resistance to the armed missionaries of the Christian Faith. In the end they suffered a decisive defeat. Their idols were broken, their sacred groves were burned; their independence was forfeit; they were compelled to accept the odious creed of their conquerors at the point of the sword. But notwithstanding they remained true to type. Wotan was nearer than Christ. The Latin outlook on the world, clear, orderly, precise, was never theirs. They preserved their language, and with it the spirit, vague, passionate, and tumultuous, which distinguishes the German from the Latin character.

There is no failure here as some French authors have surmised. The prodigal military energy of this extraordinary reign was not vainly expended. The purpose of the wars of Charlemagne, of his fifty-three campaigns fought upon every front, Danish, Slav, Saxon, Avar, Dalmatian, Lombard, Spanish, was not to give lessons in the Latin spirit, but to defend the orthodox Christians of the west against the enemies who assailed them on every side. The issue was not one between Latin and Teuton, Gallo-Roman and German, but between the Latin Christians of the west, Germans, Gauls, Romans, Spaniards, and the encircling forces of the anti-Christian world. In that struggle Charlemagne emerged the victor. He made central Europe safe for the Roman Church. By admitting the conquered

Saxons and Bavarians into his empire on equal terms with the conquering Franks he made Germany. And if he failed to break the Saracens in Spain, and even suffered a reverse at the hands of the Gascons in the pass of Roncesvalles, his one repulse shone with more glory than many victories through the transforming power of legend, which gave to his campaign in the Ebro Valley the lustre of a crusade, and wove round the name of the fallen Roland interminable garlands of song.

When the great Emperor passed away, his vast dominions fell asunder, and in their severance gave rise to the nations of the west. He did not succeed, fortunately perhaps for Europe, in creating a centralized government strong enough to function in the absence of a dominating mind. His permanent achievements must be sought elsewhere. Mounting the throne at a time when the political future was dark and troubled, when the idea of authority had grown faint, and the lamps of learning and literature were flickering to extinction, he called a vigorous halt to the forces of paganism, anarchy, and ignorance. To him the domain of Latin Christianity owes the geographical shape which it has since retained. To his vigorous impulsion is due a remarkable revival of intellectual activity. The idea of a strong civilized government, concerned to promote religion, to secure justice, to listen to the complaints of all its subjects, to spread education, and to conserve learning, was brought back into western Europe by this eager, vital, and capacious spirit. The central institutions which he alone could infuse with energy did not long survive him; but under the protection of his lengthy reign, dukes and counts and other feudatories made private fortunes and built up for themselves centres of local government and authority, little states capable of defending themselves against hostile attack, and of preserving some part of the legacy of Greece, of Syria, and of Rome.

The keynote of Charlemagne's rule was personal authority but not despotism. A monarch without a paid regular army or a bureaucracy or a settled revenue payable in coin may exercise a widespread influence but cannot play the tyrant. At the great periodical gatherings of notables, the *placita Generalia*, when enquiry was held into the public needs, it was Charlemagne who represented the people at large, and not the officials by whom the poor were too often oppressed. Moreover, without

814

organization no large state can be tyrannically governed, and the Frankish Empire, like every other mediaeval polity, was unorganized. Some necessary steps in decentralization were taken. The government of Italy was handed over to one son (Pippin), that of Aquitaine to another (Lewis). But the Civil Service, if this phrase may be used of administrators who did not regard themselves as belonging to a professional corps, was deficient in numbers, skill, and honesty. The business was unclassified, and since the king insisted on looking into everything, some grave matters passed unnoticed while trivialities attracted an earnest regard. This fundamental absence of method meant that the kingdom was undergoverned, that the imperial edicts or capitularies were imperfectly executed, and that the bishops and counts who conducted the local government were inadequately controlled. For a time the commanding energy of the Emperor mitigated the force of these evils. Constantly travelling from vill to vill, asking questions, redressing grievances, showing himself open and hospitable to all, and when he was unable himself to be present, sending imperial commissaries to represent him, the popular sovereign kept the august fact of government before the eyes of his subjects. Yet all through his reign tendencies, destructive as contemporary nationalism to the workings of effective empire, were gathering in strength. Fiefs, awarded on condition of public service, were becoming hereditary estates. Vassals were becoming independent chieftains. The pious or politic benefactions of the sovereign were building up for the German church a basis of material power so great as permanently to influence the balance of political forces in that country. It is to this reign that we trace the rise of the great abbeys which played so large a part in the development of German agriculture, commerce, and learning. It is to the munificence of Charlemagne that the Archbishops of Köln, Trier, and Mainz owed their princely estates and a position of worldly power and independence which lasted till the days of Napoleon.

Out of the energetic movement of the Frankish Empire Europe emerges in its mediaeval shape. Over against the Greek world ruled from Byzantium, and the Saracen world governed from Bagdad and Cordova, is the vast territory of Latin Christianity stretching from the Ebro to the Carpathians and

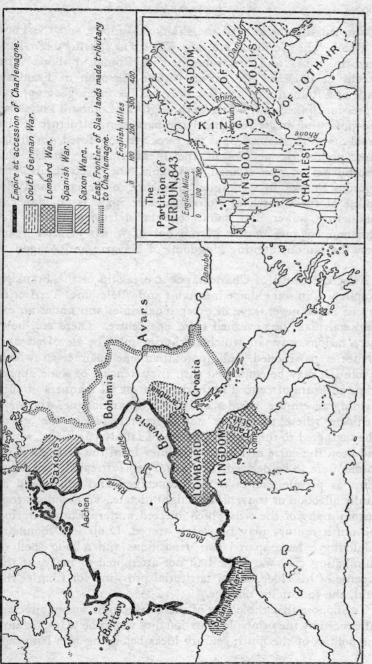

CHARLEMAGNE'S EMPIRE AND (INSET) THE PARTITION OF VERDUN.

acknowledging the rule of the Frankish Empire and the Pope
of Rome. The Germans are now Christians, having been bap
tized in tribes and are submitted to Roman bishops. The
Czechs of Bohemia are drawn within the orbit of Frankish
trade and Roman missionaries. Italy has become a geographical
expression, linked to the Franks through the Lombard kingdom
and possessing in its very heart the paralyzing structure of the
Papal State. In Roman Gaul the races are now fused, the little
dark, prehistoric peoples of the Mediterranean littoral, the
descendants of the Roman emigrants, the lively Celts, the
vigorous Franks, in a common allegiance to the faith and dis
cipline of the Church of Rome. Saracen Spain is no longer a
conquering power, but stands on the defensive against the
Christian colonies of the March out of which in after years
grew the famous fighting kingdoms of Navarre and Aragon.

After the death of Charlemagne a break-up of the Frankish
Empire was in some shape inevitable and wholesome. Territories
so vast could never, save in exceptional times and under an ex
ceptional man, be governed from one centre. There are, how
ever, various ways in which authority may be devolved and
territories partitioned, and more than one manner in which
devolution may be combined with the retention of some appro
priate measure of central authority. But of all manners of sub
dividing an empire, the descendants of Charlemagne, who were
mediocre where they were not degenerate, chose the worst
They adhered to the bad old system of family partitions, which
had been the curse of Frankish politics from the first. As if no
lessons were to be derived from history, they treated their king
doms as private estates to be bequeathed and subdivided as
family affection or convenience might dictate. To this disastrous
custom many of the evils which affected western Europe during
the ninth century may be clearly traced. Louis le Débonnaire
would have been spared two depositions and a long spell of
humiliating civil war if he had not attempted to make, at the
expense of his elder sons, a territorial provision for Charles the
Bald, the son of his old age.

To suppose that the policy of these sovereigns was in any way
influenced by the principle of nationality would be to import into
the politics of the ninth century ideas belonging to a later age

Yet it is true that in the Carolingian partitions of the ninth century we may discern the emergence of the nations of western Europe. After the death of Louis le Débonnaire in 840, civil war broke out between his sons, Charles the Bald, who ruled in Neustria, combining with Lewis the German, who ruled east of the Rhine, against Lothair their elder brother, who had been allotted Austrasia, Burgundy, and Italy. After the great battle at Fontenay, at which Lothair was defeated with huge losses, the three brothers came together at Verdun and agreed to divide their father's inheritance. To Charles the Bald was allotted Neustria, Aquitaine, and the Spanish March, a territory mainly, though not entirely, Romance in speech, and comprising all that part of modern France which is west of the Rhone and the Saône. Lewis the German received Austrasian Francia east of the Rhine, Bavaria, Swabia, Saxony, and Rhaetia, all save the last German-speaking districts, and all save the last comprised in the modern German Reich; while Lothair was assigned a long, inter-mediate, heterogeneous region comprising the two capitals of Aix-la-Chapelle and Rome, and stretching from Friesland to the border of Calabria. It would be possible to contend that Lewis the German ruled over a nation. It would be a tenable proposi-tion to make the same claim for Charles the Bald, despite the fact that he exercised no real authority either in Brittany or in Aquitaine. But the share of the Emperor Lothair, with its mix-ture of Teutonic and Latin populations, is a flat contradiction of the racial principle and a proof that very little importance was attached to it by the members of the Carolingian house.

A subdivision of the Frankish dominions, clear, absolute, and regarded as permanent, would have served the cause of good government. The Partition of Verdun was none of these things. It was provisional, liable to change at every death in the family, and vitiated by the fact that each of the partitioning brothers regarded himself as king of the Franks, as a potential claimant to the undivided inheritance and imperial authority of Charle-magne. Thus, although the idea of unity survived, it was in the form most calculated to weaken effective rule. The Partition of Verdun, so far from inaugurating an era of peaceful govern-ment, was followed by new partitions and fratricidal wars, by a steady decline in the power of the Frankish kings, and a corre-sponding increase in the power of the nobles.

In the western and middle kingdoms the anarchy was appalling. In East Francia or Germany, where the inhabitants were of one stock and language, where the level of civilization was uniform and low, where there was still a large class of freeholders, and the institutions of feudalism were in an early stage of development, the prospect of strong government should have been more favourable. Yet government was no stronger in Germany than it was in France. The tribes of Germany, despite their common origin and speech, were as little prepared to live together in amity as the Athenians and the Spartans. The Saxons, the Franconians, the Bavarians, and the Alemans lived their own law, went their own ways, and were as ready to quarrel among themselves as to follow the king against Danes and Slavs. The kingdoms were partitioned and repartitioned. Even the imperial crown failed to bring good fortune to its holder or to restore the lost sentiment of a common allegiance. There is no more significant fact in the Europe of the ninth century than the fate of Charles the Fat, the third son of Lewis the German. Upon this incompetent descendant of Charlemagne fortune showered every blessing. He was crowned Emperor by the Pope. A chapter of convenient family accidents made him king of Italy, Germany, and France; a ruler, on paper at least, such as Europe had not seen for seventy years. But the man was a craven, his authority a figment, and on his deposition in 887 there was a final break-up of the Carolingian Empire, and save for the bastard Arnulf, a grandson of Lewis the German, who was chosen to rule in East Francia, an end to the long spell of authority exercised by the Carolingian house.

In fairness to these later Frankish kings it should be remembered that all through the ninth century they were assailed by external dangers from the Saracens, the Slavs, and the Northmen. The outskirts of Rome itself were burned by the Saracens in 847. To these pirates who had succeeded in breaking down the guard of the Byzantines and in making themselves masters of Sicily the reply should have been the formation of a strong Frankish navy. Nothing of the kind was attempted; but to Pope Leo IV is due the credit of giving to the Vatican suburb that girdle of fortifications which has earned it the name of the Leonine City. The achievement of the Pope lives in the memory of the Italian people, while the well-meant endeavours of the

Frankish Emperor Louis II to rid southern Italy of its Saracen pests are only known, and that imperfectly, to a handful of learned men.

BOOKS WHICH MAY BE CONSULTED

S. Dill : Roman Society in Gaul in the Merovingian Age. 1926.

O. M. Dalton : Gregory of Tours (The History of the Franks). 1927.

N. D. Fustel de Coulanges : Histoires des Institutions Politiques de l'ancienne France. 1888-92.

F. P. G. Guizot : Histoire de la Civilisation en France. 1851.

H. W. C. Davis : Charlemagne. 1900.

J. B. Mullinger : The Schools of Charles the Great. 1877.

J. Bryce : The Holy Roman Empire. 1904.

M. R. James : Learning and Literature till Pope Sylvester II. (Cambridge Mediaeval History, Vol. III.).

Einhard : Life of Charlemagne. Ed. H. W. Garrod and R. B. Mowat. 1915.

T. Hodgkin : Charles the Great. 1897.

E. Lavisse : Histoire de France, Vol. II. 1903.

CHAPTER XIV

THE ROMAN CHURCH

The Primitive Church. Earliest Popes of Rome. Their credentials. The Papacy helped by the breakdown of the imperial power in the west. The early Christians not social reformers. Effect of the Teutonic invasions on the position of the western clergy. Social and educational work of the western Church. Spread of monasticism.

RELIGIONS are founded by laymen and organized by priests. The early Christian communities were societies of poor men and women banded together for worship, charity, and discipline. The spirit was democratic, universalist, and egalitarian. There was "neither Greek nor Jew, barbarian nor Scythian, bond nor free." In the eyes of God all Christians were equal. A bishop or overseer dispensed alms with the assistance of a deacon, and came to be regarded as the successor of the Apostle or missionary to whom the Church owed its original foundation. Where religion was a common and intimate concern and the body of the faithful was small and ardent no very sharp line was drawn between laity and clergy. A council of presbyters or elders was associated with the bishop in the direction of the Church's affairs.

The story of the development of the Roman Catholic Church from such democratic and simple beginnings may be explained by the common human craving for authority and direction in the conduct of life. As the Roman republic grew into an autocratic empire, so out of the scattered churches of the apostolic age there was gradually evolved the imposing fabric of papal theocracy. The trend of the human spirit being in the direction of despotism, the Church followed where the State had led. Its organization was modelled on that of the Empire. It became, in fact, after the conversion of Constantine, the Roman Empire in its ecclesiastical aspect.

From the logic then prevailing it followed that the Church, like the Empire, must have a supreme head. Councils were difficult to assemble and were better adapted to deal with great emergencies than with the current administration. If the unity of doctrine and practice was to be observed there must be a bishop of bishops, to whom in the last resort all questions of doubt could be referred, a single church dominated by a single head and embracing in its large hospitality all the Christian peoples of the world.

That this primacy should belong to the Bishop of Rome was an opinion more readily entertained by the Italians than by the Patriarchate of Constantinople, by the Christian bishops of Africa, or by the apostolic churches of Antioch, Jerusalem, or Alexandria. It was only by slow degrees that the papal claims, which have never been universally acknowledged by Christians, obtained a general acceptance from the churches of the west. The early Popes were mostly obscure men. They were not philosophers or theologians. They contributed nothing to the building up of church doctrine, and only with Gregory the Great entered the mis- *590-610* sionary field, which had been mainly left to the saints and visionaries of Ireland. If here and there a Pope was eminent, his capacity was displayed in the sphere of statesmanship, not of religion. Yet the Church of Rome was able to put forth credentials which in that age brought conviction to minds prepared to accept whatever was traditional, miraculous, or flattering to Roman pride. It was contended on the strength of a famous text, "Thou art Peter. On this rock I will build my Church" (Matt. xvi. 17-19), that Christ had given to St. Peter the primacy over the Apostles, that St. Peter, who is known to have preached and suffered in Rome, handed on his divine commission to Linus, the first bishop of the see, and that from Linus there had descended through an unbroken chain of bishops the sublime charge of safeguarding St. Peter's knowledge of Christian truth. Of Roman bishops we have no list earlier than Irenaeus (*circa* A.D. 180), but the belief in a secret reservoir of ultimate verity, in an oral tradition only to be communicated to the initiate, was widely spread through the pagan and Christian world. To this belief was added the strong conviction, shared not only by Latin but also by Greek Christians, that the city of Rome derived a peculiar strength and sanctity from the possession of the bones of St. Peter and St. Paul. St. John Chrysostom, the most eloquent of the Greek Fathers, has expressed in a powerful sermon the sentiments excited by the contemplation of the privileges which were thus accorded to the city of Rome. "For this," he writes, "it is I love Rome: though I might praise her on other grounds, for her greatness, her antiquity, her beauty, her numbers, her power.

her wealth, her victories in war; but passing over all these, I bless her because Paul, when living, wrote to the Romans, and loved them so much, and was among them, and spoke to them, and there ended his life. Whence also the city is more renowned for this than for all else; and like a great and mighty body, she has two eyes, the bodies of those two saints. The heaven is not so bright when the sun shoots forth his rays as the city of the Romans, shedding forth the light of these two lamps throughout the world. Thence shall Paul be caught up, thence Peter shall rise. Consider and be amazed! What a sight shall Rome then behold, when Paul suddenly shall arise with Peter from the tomb, and be caught up to meet the Lord. What a rose shall Rome send forth to Christ! What diadems are those two, with which the city is crowned, with what chains of gold it is girded; what fountains it hath! It is for this that I admire the city, not for its much gold, for its columns or any other phantasy, but because of these two pillars of the Church. Who will grant me to embrace the body of Paul, to cling to his sepulchre, and to see the dust of that body which 'filled up what was wanting' to Christ, which bore His stigmata, and sowed His teaching everywhere!"[1]

Had the emperors continued to reign in Rome the guardians of the Petrine tradition would hardly have escaped the servile destiny of the Byzantine patriarchs. The Popes would have been the agents of the emperors, and would have lost the moral authority which always attaches to the assertion of spiritual independence. From this danger, however, the Papacy was delivered by the two great political events which concurrently changed the face of western Europe—the breakdown of the imperial government and the barbaric invasions. As the emperor vanished from the west, the empty place was taken by the descendant of St. Peter. It was to the Pope that a bishop, condemned by a provincial council, was encouraged by the Fathers at Sardica (343) to appeal; it was the Pope and not the emperor who stood out as the champion of Italian civilization against the Huns and the Saracens, who defended Rome from the attacks of the Lombards, and upon whom necessarily devolved the power of writing letters or decretals on ecclesiastical issues which had the force of law. In the dark and troubled age of the barbaric invasions, in the days of Leo I and Gregory the Great,

---

[1] Hom. 32 in Rom., 2, vol. ix., p. 678 (75?). *Cf.* Chapman, "Studies in the Early Papacy," p. 97.

the see of St. Peter stood out in western Europe like a lighthouse in a storm.

The early Christians, though sharply opposed to many ancient practices, never set out to reform mankind. It is a mistake to imagine that any modern political label can be safely attached to them. They were neither socialists, nor communists, nor individualists. They had no philosophy of the state or belief in the regeneration of society through institutions. The idea that the framework of Roman politics or society could be transformed by the agency of their small and uninfluential congregations would never have occurred to them. They knew that the world was wicked, for they had learnt that man was fallen from grace and merited eternal torment, and rather than act wickedly some of them were willing to face a martyr's death. But they held that this evil world was not destined to endure for long. At the second coming of Christ, which many believed to be imminent and none thought would be long delayed, righteousness would be enthroned upon earth and all the flaws, wickedness, and imperfections of mankind be cleansed away. Why, then, should the Christian labour to abolish slavery, or war, or trade, or these great engines of physical force, which sustained the weight of the Roman Empire? All this was fated soon to vanish, and meanwhile each individual soul was confronted with the problem, at once awful and instant, of how best to avoid the everlasting torment which was the retribution of God for the original sin of Adam in the garden.

The Christians, then, accepted what they could not change. They offered up prayers for the Roman Emperor, though they refused to burn incense to his image. They accepted and condoned slavery. So far were they from generally repudiating force, that war among Christians became a melancholy feature of European society from the fifth century onwards. In none of their activities is it possible to discern any trace of class-conscious motives. Though the Christians of the apostolic age were poor, their religion spread so swiftly through every class that before the end of the first century it had even penetrated into the circle of the Emperor's family.

One grave danger the new Christian community was enabled to avoid through the worldly wisdom of a bishop of Rome. Callistus (219-223) showed himself prepared to absolve the fornicator and adulterer from sin. His decision, though it ran counter to a large body of Christian feeling, was epoch-making in its consequences. Based on exclusive doctrine a Church is strong, limited by exclusive morality it is weak. Many will subscribe to a test. Few will lead the life of virtue. A Church confined in its membership to the saints and offering nothing to the sinners would never have effected the conquest of Europe.

The position of the clergy in western society was greatly changed by the influx into the Roman Empire of wave after wave of Teutonic barbarism. In the tragical eclipse of lay education and culture the intellectual advantages of the Church became for the first time conspicuous. The cleric could at least read and write, was familiar with Latin, had enough arithmetic to calculate the date of Easter and was often accustomed to the sedentary toil which is necessary to the regular despatch of business. Moreover, as the attractions of the imperial service had fallen away, the Church had begun to draw men of the highest social standing into its service. In Gaul the bishops of the fifth, sixth, and seventh centuries were often noblemen of ancient lineage, of great wealth and widespread influence, who found in the discharge of official duties the only opportunity for the exercise of administrative gifts or the satisfaction of a public conscience. Accordingly it is not surprising that the Franks in Gaul and the Visigoths in Spain made a free use of this serviceable profession. The Teutonic sovereigns had a rich capacity for the pursuit of the boar and the stag and for the slaughter and pillage of their enemies. Without the aid of the Church they could not have governed.

The lively narrative of Gregory of Tours is sufficient to warn us against the temptation to idealize the Gallican Church in the sixth century. Its corruptions were numerous and flagrant. But comprising as it did all the little that was good in the French society of that time, it performed valuable functions which would not otherwise have been rendered. The fusion of the Latin and Teutonic elements in the state could not have been accomplished without the Church. The whole work of education was in its hands. If a river was to be embanked or an aqueduct was to be built, it was generally a bishop who supplied the initiative and controlled the funds. Despite much evidence of a cowardly compliance with wickedness, a bishop from time to time found the courage to rebuke or the authority to overawe a transgressing ruler. Nor in that age of violent autocracy was there elsewhere than in the Church a protection for the poor, the helpless, and the oppressed.

It is, indeed, to the circumstances of these turbulent centuries that we must ascribe the present position and authority of the priestly profession. The chaos of the Empire was the opportunity of the Church, the childish ignorance of the barbarian prepared the triumph of the priest. In an age when books were rare, everything depended on the voice and example of the teacher. The simple and superstitious barbarian was ready to tolerate a degree of interference in his private life which the cultivated Roman lady or gentleman would have resented as a vulgar intrusion. As the task of educating the barbarian world in the rudiments of the Christian Faith unfolded itself in all its vast and desperate proportions, the clergy became of necessity, like the school teachers of the United States during the spate of immigration from Europe, a well-marked and influential profession. In the sixth century it was ordained that the Latin clergy should wear a distinctive dress. While the German kept his tunic short and his hair long, the priest preserved the long robe and short hair of the ancient Roman.

The century which followed the conversion of Constantine is marked by the spread of monasticism through western Europe. Asceticism is a common feature of religious movements, and in Egypt, the original home of monkery, was apt to assume extravagant forms of self-torture and abasement. The good sense of the west avoided the eccentricities of the Egyptian solitary who, perched upon a pillar or a tree, exhibited the charms of his pious emaciation and squalor to the admiring pilgrim. The Latin genius was more practical, less speculative than the Greek. The rule of St. Benedict of Nursia (480-540) the great Italian visionary, who founded the monasteries of Subiaco and Monte Cassino, enjoined the intermingling of manual labour with study and devotional exercises, and as it became general through the west, enabled monasticism, which might otherwise have wrought nothing but evil, to make a positive contribution to human progress. It is to the credit of the Benedictine monks that they improved tillage and reclaimed waste land, that they undertook the work of relieving the poor, and that by preserving and copying manuscripts they rendered an important and necessary service to European culture. During the darkest age of Teutonic barbarism there was perhaps no other way in which the gentler natures of society might be turned to useful account.

The diffusion of Benedictine monasteries through the countries of the west proceeded during the next two centuries with a rapidity so amazing as to suggest that there must have been some special feature in the circumstances of that age to impel men and women to embrace in such great numbers a life of sheltered asceticism. Their motives, no doubt, were compounded of many elements, ranging from exaltation and heroic piety to cowardice, evasion, and hope of ease; but we can hardly doubt that what chiefly operated upon the imagination of those who were then drawn into the monastic movement was the difficulty of leading a Christian life in a world racked and disturbed by the barbarian invasions, a world of crime, lust, violence, and steadily increasing chaos. Their asceticism is intelligible; discerning little hope of improvement through human agencies, they withdrew from the darkness and turmoil around them into the tranquil light of the Christian paradise.

BOOKS WHICH MAY BE CONSULTED

C. Gore : Jesus of Nazareth. 1929.

E. Bevan : Christianity (Home University Library). 1932.

E. Bevan : Hellenism and Christianity. 1921.

L. Battifol : Primitive Catholicism. 1911.

J. Chapman : Studies in the Early Papacy. 1928.

F. H. Dudden : Gregory the Great—His Place in History and Thought. 1905.

H. H. Milman : The History of Latin Christianity. 1867.

Gibbon : Decline and Fall of the Roman Empire. *Ed.* Bury. 1896-1900.

C. Bigg. The Origins of Christianity. 1909.

C. Bigg : The Church's Task under the Roman Empire. 1905.

CHAPTER XV

THE NORSEMEN

Norse culture. The Norsemen on the Dnieper. Viking raids in the west. Danes and Norwegians. Raids on Ireland, England, France. Rise of Wessex. Alfred and his successors. Danish Conquest of England. Canute leads Scandinavia into the Christian fold. Edward the Confessor. The Normans in Normandy. Their acceptance of Latin culture. The Normans in Sicily. Splendour of Roger II. Exhaustion and poverty of Scandinavia.

ONE branch of the Nordic race, hitherto withdrawn from the zone of Latin and Teutonic influence, now made a violent irruption into the political scene, and for more than two centuries filled the world with noise and fury. The Norsemen were pagans. The ideas of conscience and sin, of virtue in the Christian sense of that term, were foreign to their ways of thinking. There was nothing in the cult of Thor, the God of Thunder, of Odin, the Lord of War and the inventor of song, or of Frey, the God of Fertility, that might bring shame to the murderer, the adulterer, or the pirate. The Norsemen loved war and women, wassail and song, pillage and slaughter. Their mythology, which was common to all the Nordic races, was distinguished for a spirit of fatalism, fierce as the northern seas, grave as the arctic skies. The gods they regarded not as guides to disciplined conduct, for of this they had no sense, but as friends and allies in a great adventure, leading, if a man was brave and fortunate, to death in battle and to a passage into the halls of Valhalla, where heroes slain in combat fight and feast to the end of time. Of false optimism there is no trace in the prose sagas which were written down in Iceland many centuries later. The Norsemen knew too much about the wild elements of nature and the furious passions of man to ask of life more than life could give. And so the old Norse literature, in which the record of this pagan civilization is faithfully preserved, stands out among the literatures of the world for its freedom from rhetoric and sentiment, its closeness to the facts of life, its abstinence from moral comment or literary embellishment, but above all for the picture which it gives of a society at once

A.D. 1150-1250

aristocratic and anarchic, violent and tenacious of the past, but ennobled despite all its lusts and cruelties by a manly veracity and a proud acceptance of inevitable fate.

To this very capable and strenuous race of mariners and shipwrights, yeoman farmers and merchants, woodmen and whalers, there was disclosed in the later half of the eighth century the exciting secret that great tracts of the globe offered the richest plunder on the cheapest terms. If the southward route was blocked by the Saxons and Franks, eastwards and westwards the paths lay open and almost undefended. While the Swedish merchants exploited the virgin resources of the Russian plain, the pirates of Denmark and Norway helped themselves, with more fighting but less effort, to the glittering treasures of the west. The Swedes established a factory near Lake Ladoga, and from that central and convenient station, close to the head waters of the Volga and the Dnieper, traded down the great Russian waterways to the Caspian and the Black Sea. Their settlements at Holmgarth or Novgorod, at New Garth or Kiev, became, in the midst of the unpolitical and disorganized Slavonic peoples, centres of guidance and authority. To Ruric, the Swedish leader, fame assigns the credit of having founded at Novgorod and at Kiev the original centres of a Russian state. So powerful was the Swedish influence, so patient and receptive were the Slavonic populations, who accepted Swedish rule, that the name (Ruotsi) by which the Swede was known to his Finnish neighbours was soon transferred from the master to the subject, and has become the common designation of the Russian people.

It is, then, to the Norsemen, and more particularly to a remarkable sequence of Swedish rulers in Kiev, that the Slavs of the Russian plain owe their first experience of state life. The Slavonic nature, dreamy, passionate, lethargic, imaginative, more Asiatic than European, needed then, as often afterwards, the shock and stimulus of an alien discipline. Such a benefit at the threshold of their history the Scandinavian adventurers conferred upon the Russian race. Nor is it less important that the Principality of Kiev, the chief centre of Swedish power on the Dnieper, was taught by its rulers to look for its civilization, not to the north, but southwards to Constantinople. To the Swedish governors of Kiev Russia principally owes its introduction to the art and religion of the Byzantine world. For these merchant pirates the Dnieper was chiefly to be valued as the waterway to Middlegarth, the wealthiest and mightiest of cities, which it was their ambition to conquer and despoil. Four times (860, 880, 907, 914) did their powerful fleets menace the capital of the eastern Empire. Four times were their attacks frustrated by arms or parried by diplomacy. In the end Swedish mercenaries entered the imperial bodyguard and by their valour and detachment helped to sustain the Byzantine state. But Russia's ambition to be mistress of Constantinople, first inflamed by the robber pirates of Sweden, has survived through the ages, and has been, until the late revolution, an important factor in European policy.

While the Dnieper Swedes were feeling their way to the Bosphorus, and the Volga Swedes were chaffering their wares with the Transcaspian subjects of the Caliph of Bagdad, the Danes and Norwegians had embarked upon a course of high-hearted rapine in the west. The monasteries of Ireland in particular, and in a lesser degree those of England and of France, were stored with gold and silver ornaments, with rich brocades and precious stones, and once discovered, were the first mark for Viking attack. A single shipload laden with the spoil of Lindisfarne or Noirmoustier is sufficient to explain all that followed. The Vikings were poor, the monasteries were rich. After the gloom of a northern winter it was a rare, and in the existing political distractions of the western kingdoms a not too dangerous amusement, to set sail with the first favouring breeze of summer in search of a quick fortune beyond the western sea. We need not look beyond common cupidity for the explanation of the Scandinavian expansion. The historians who descry in the Viking raids a pagan protest against the forced conversion of the Saxons by Charles the Great attribute to the Northmen a precise intolerance postulating a priesthood which they do not appear to have possessed, and in any case foreign to their cloudy theology.

Geography rather than design prescribed for these two plundering races differing routes and fields of activity. The Danes, being nearer to the Channel, threw themselves on Frisia, England, and France. The Norsemen, taking a wider and more westerly sweep, attacked the Orkneys and Shetlands, the Hebrides, and the Isle of Man, and effected settlements not only in these islands but in northern Scotland, Northumbria, and

Ireland. Thereafter, when their long clinker-built boats of stout Norwegian oak had been well tested in violent seas, these wonderful mariners performed feats more daring still, and never surpassed in the annals of seafaring men. Iceland and the Faroes were claimed and settled. The Atlantic was crossed. From Ireland as a base, the long Viking warships, driven by oar and sail, planted colonies on the bleak shores of Greenland and, six hundred years before the voyage of Columbus, explored the North American coast—the Vineland of Icelandic saga.

Apart from their skill in navigation the Vikings possessed the further advantage of alone understanding the value of swift movement in warfare. They would row up the Thames or the Loire, and, suddenly landing on some quiet inland field, seize the horses from the farms and scamper through the country burning, slaying, and robbing as they went, and be gone long before the slow-footed countrymen could combine to offer an effective resistance.

The long period of time during which these raids were successfully repeated, the immense havoc which they caused, and the panic which prevailed not on the seaboard only but in the heart of the continent, are a sufficient measure of the disorganization into which western Europe had fallen after the death of Charlemagne. Society seemed paralyzed before an enemy so fierce, so mobile, and so ubiquitous as within the space of a few years to attack Cadiz and Seville, Hamburg and Bordeaux, Valence and Pisa.

It is foolish to imagine that everything which happens on a great scale in this world is for good. The raids of the Vikings were purely destructive. In the first half of the tenth century they went near to bringing down in complete ruin the whole fabric of civilization in western Europe. The old Irish culture, once so distinctive and brilliant, never recovered from their widespread and persistent depredations, and with the sack of Iona, the principal channel through which Irish Christianity had flowed into England was finally obstructed. Yet such is human nature that great calamities provoke in the end countervailing efforts, and are found in the last account to have some compensations. The piracies of the Vikings led through conquests to settlements. If the Norsemen sacked the Irish monasteries, they founded the Irish trading towns. If they destroyed Armagh, they created Dublin and Wexford, Waterford and

Limerick. Nor were their insults to the Gaelic-speaking Highlands barren of distant benefits. By their control of the Western
Isles and the Irish Sea a barrier was interposed between Ireland
and Scotland, preventing migration, obstructing fusion, and
promoting the union of the Scottish people under a Scottish
king.

An even deeper impression was left by the Danish dealings
with England and France, by the startling shock of their terrible raids, by their conquest first of a Danelaw in England,
then of a Danelaw to be known as Normandy in France, and
finally by that critical period in the annals of our own country
(1013-1042) during which England was ruled by Danish kings
and became part of a great Scandinavian Empire. The Northmen, like the Anglo-Saxons and the Franks, were a Teutonic
people. In essentials of character they resembled the Saxons and
so much of the population of northern France as was Teutonic
and not Celtic in origin. For this reason the effects of the
Danish settlement of eastern England and of Normandy are of
more enduring importance than the Moorish settlement of
Spain. The conquerors and conquered influenced one another
in a permanent way, not because they were unlike, but because
they were like, and at one in the important particular of being
intelligent and receptive. The Danes in Normandy became
Frenchmen, the Danes in England became Englishmen. The
conquerors accepted Christianity and the Latin culture which
went with it. What they gave in return was an assemblage of
spirited qualities, which, when once the first passion of destructiveness had been exhausted, made first of the Normans and
then of the English the two leading peoples in the world.

To the student of English institutions the fundamental
similarity between Saxon and Dane is the key to many riddles.
The Anglo-Saxon people was distinguished above all other
branches of the Teutonic family for a copious and continued
output of written law. The stream which was eventually to
broaden out into the great river of the English common law
began under Ethelbert of Kent, at a time when Roman jurisprudence was speaking its valediction in the Institutes of Justinian, and received substantial additions to its volume under
the kings of Wessex. But the last and most comprehensive
Code of our island law, issued before the Norman Conquest,
was the work of no Saxon but of Canute the Dane. To him as to

the antiquarians of today it clearly seemed that while the differences of custom between Dane and Saxon were superficial the
resemblances were profound. The word law is Norse; so too is
that passion for litigation which is a distinctive feature of the
English character; but each race was accustomed to public trials,
to a procedure by oath helpers and ordeals, and to a tariff of
compensations for acts of violence to be paid in whole or in
part to the injured party. If the jury of inquisition is a Norman
innovation it has analogies in the practice of the Saxons and the
Danes.

A further consequence following the Danish invasions of
France and England was a strengthening of the state in each of
these countries by the emergence of a dynasty of efficient rulers.
In France, after many weary decades of weakness and disorder,
the house of Capet, first springing to eminence through its
defence of Paris against the Northmen, superseded the effete
epigoni of Charlemagne, and started upon a long career of
modest but steady aggrandizement. Not very dissimilar was the
course of events in England. Here at the climax of their destructive energies, with English government broken in Northumbria, East Anglia, and Mercia, and the fate of Saxon civilization trembling in the balance, the Danes met in the monarchs
of the house of Egbert a series of stubborn and valiant opponents. The contest was long, savage, and marked by abrupt
vicissitudes, but not wholly sterile. From it emerged the idea
of a national monarchy, centred in Wessex, the sole surviving
Teutonic power in the island which had escaped destruction at
the hands of the Vikings.

It was in 866 that the Danish raids on England, which for
thirty-two years had been steadily gathering in strength and
destructiveness, were exchanged for a definite policy of conquest.
In a brilliant and meteoric campaign Hingwar, the son of Ragnar
Lothbrok, one of the most famous pirates of his age, carried
everything before him from the Thames to the Clyde. The weak
kingdoms of Northumbria and East Anglia crumbled under his
hammer blows. He took Nottingham and besieged Dumbarton,
and when he crossed over to Ireland in 868, leaving Halfdan, his
brother, to continue his work, it seemed as if the whole island
might swiftly become a Danish prize.

There was, however, in the kingdom of Wessex, which now
extended from Land's End to the North Sea, a slow but stubborn

population of nobles, farmers, and peasants, which was capable under the strong leadership of a native king of offering a brave and dogged resistance to the enemy. It was in 871, when the Danes were in the heart of his country, that Alfred at the age of twenty-three succeeded to the formidable responsibilities of the West Saxon kingship. Everything which relates to the life of this great national figure is of interest to Englishmen: his early visits to Rome; his delight in the songs and literature of his people; his concern for education; his encouragement of learning through the translations which he commissioned of the most popular Latin books of the time, such as the *De Consolatione* of Boethius or the *Pastoral Cure* of Gregory the Great; his patronage of foreign artists, craftsmen, and divines; his interest in travel and geography; his widespread international relations; his intrepidity in war; his zest in hunting; his zeal, carried almost to the point of morbidity, in the cult of relics and the exercises of religion. But what makes his career significant is not this evidence of width and versatility, but the fact that he drove the Danes out of Wessex, and that in saving Wessex he secured the survival of Anglo-Saxon civilization and laid the foundations of a national state in Britain.

The triumph of Wessex under the leadership of Alfred is thus memorable for two distinct reasons. It was the first serious check to the great heathen onslaught from the north, and the beginning of that reverse process which led to the christianization of the Scandinavian races and their acceptance as members of the polity of Europe.

This is the ecumenical significance of Alfred's life. But it is also a landmark in the history of England. The saviour of Wessex has a claim on the loyalty of all men using the Saxon speech. Without any formal document, but from the march of events, he became the ruler of all that part of England which was not by express treaty ceded (878, 885) to the Danes. The fleet, the law, the capital of later England seem to be prefigured in his policies. He built long ships, issued a code based on Saxon, Mercian, and Kentish customs, restored a devastated London and incorporated it in his dominions.

Moreover, his work served as a foundation. From Wessex, as from a well-defended base, Alfred's son Edward reconquered the Danelaw, and his grandson Athelstan repulsed a combined attack from Ireland and Scotland in a battle so moving in its incidents and wide in its appeal (Brunanburh, 937) that it has inspired a great Anglo-Saxon poem and supplied a theme to one of the finest of the Icelandic Sagas. By 954 the king of Wessex ruled all England from the Channel to the Clyde.

So for seventy-seven years after the death of Alfred the Great the West Saxon monarchy preserved its predominance, extending its influence by steady degrees, ruling the Danelaw with a light hand, and with the help of the Church surviving the perils of a minority. Yet the unity of England, though proclaimed in theory, was still for various reasons insecure, and so remained till the consolidating work of the Norman Conquest. The Danish armies encamped and settled east of Watling Street, and the Norwegian armies who had established themselves in Northumbria were neither at one with one another nor completely fused with the Saxon population. The earlier traditions of the heptarchy were not altogether forgotten and under weak governance might again revive.

The crisis came under the long unhappy reign of Ethelred the Redeless (979-1016). The Danes now revived their attacks upon a country which after seventy-six years of comparative peace must, in contradistinction to the prevailing misery of the continent, have presented a spectacle of rare and tempting prosperity. To buy off these terrible enemies the government weakly resorted to the expedient of a danegeld, a tax so crushing in amount and so frequently imposed that under its weight the rural population lost its early character of freedom and, save in Danish East Anglia, sank into a condition of predial servitude. Some taxes are so heavy as to change the face of society, some are so lucrative that governments retain them long after the original occasion for their imposition has passed away. The danegeld belonged to both these categories. It promoted the development of feudalism and predial servitude. It was retained by Canute and William the Conqueror, and was the chief financial buttress of the Norman monarchy.

Heavy as was the danegeld it could not avert but only postpone a Danish conquest of England. Under Canute, the son of Sweyn, and the inheritor of his conquests, Britain became part of a Scandinavian empire, which ultimately included Denmark, Norway, and the Hebrides. A state divided by so wide a waste of stormy water could hardly hold together for long, and we may dismiss from the region of historical probabilities the vision of

Britain as a permanent part of a greater Scandinavia. The reign of Canute was but an interlude, more important for Scandinavian than for British history. Not for the first time did the conquered peoples make a captive of their conqueror. In becoming a Christian Canute crossed from the Nordic into the Latin world. He made a pilgrimage to Rome, he married Norman Emma, the widow of Ethelred, his Saxon predecessor, and ruled England not as a foreign, but as a native, king. To a man of his forcible common sense there could be no comparison between the fertile plains of England, with their gentle full-brimmed rivers, their rich harvests and thriving merchant settlements, and the wild mountain scenery of Norway, or the wind-swept undulations of Denmark. Britain was the pleasanter, the more cultivated land. Canute made Britain his centre, and from it determined to bring the religion of civilized men into his Scandinavian dominions. In this effort he was not a pioneer. As early as 830, St. Anschar, a Picard trained in the monastery of Corvey, voyaged through Denmark, Norway, and Sweden preaching the Gospel, a gallant adventure soon overpowered by the might of the pagan tradition. At the great temple of Upsala in Sweden worship continued to be rendered to Odin, Thor, and Frey, with an immense sacrificial slaughter, in every ninth year, of animals and men. Then, at the end of the tenth century, the miracle of the Roman Empire began to work among the wild peoples of the north. The Scandinavians of the Danelaw, who had gone over *en bloc* to the new faith at the Peace of Wedmore in 878, submitted themselves in increasing measure to the ministrations of the Saxon Church, so that traders from Norway and Sweden found in our English ports Christian men of their own speech and blood. From such encounters some rough seafarers were actually converted; in others the hostile prejudice against Christianity was broken down. A demand arose for English priests. By one of those consentaneous movements of policy, which through the force of imitation happen from time to time in history, the reign of Canute coincided with a development of Christian propaganda in Norway and Denmark, initiated by two kings, Olaf the Saint and Olaf Scotkonning, who owed their conversion to English missionaries, and carried on their work with English help.

That Canute should have thrown his weight into the same religious scale is of critical importance. Of all Scandinavians he was by reason of his mastery of England the richest and most powerful. Had he resisted baptism and appealed to the vast reserves of pagan sentiment in the hamlets of Norway and Sweden, he might have greatly retarded the settlement of Europe. He took the opposite course. In every way he was determined to show himself more Saxon than the Saxon, more Roman than the Pope, a pious and loyal member of the Christian polity. He restored St. Edmund's Bury in honour of the hero king who had been slain by the Danes, and sent English priests to Denmark to help the Danish Church. Though Thor and Odin were slow to die, his policy marks an end of the Scandinavian menace to Latin Christianity.

The historian will observe that the conversion of Europe to Christianity was, after the first heroic age of poverty and enthusiasm, mainly the result of material calculation or political pressure. The Goths, the Franks, the Saxons, the Scandinavians went over to Christianity, not as individuals directed by an inner light, but as peoples subject to mass suggestion and under the direction of political chiefs. That in every generation there were religious enthusiasts touched by the moral beauty of the Christian virtues or exalted by the contemplation of the Divine Nature will not be denied. There were conversions of the heart and of the mind. But the great mass of those who, under the Roman Empire or in the early middle ages, passed from Paganism to Christianity were little moved by considerations of pure religion or morality, and experienced no change of heart on conversion. It is well to remember that the acceptance of Christian beliefs by the barbarian world entailed no such profound and sudden change as the word conversion may seem to imply. Europe still remained the scene of fierce passions, animal lusts, and degrading superstitions. The great task of educating a savage society in the Christian virtues was hardly begun; and after centuries of toil is still uncompleted. Yet even in the rude society of mediaeval Europe human sacrifice was stamped out, polygamy forbidden, and slavery put down.

The Anglo-Danish kingdom was personal to Canute. His sons were not of the calibre to sustain so difficult a structure. Our island, which had led Europe in culture in the eighth century, lost nothing of its native character under the brilliant Dane, reverted soon after his death to its ancient loyalties and recalled the son of Ethelred from his Norman exile. The character of Edward

A.D 1042-66

the Confessor was neither so saintly nor so weak as it has been portrayed by monkish chroniclers. He was an honest, well-meaning, mediocre man, handicapped by a youth spent abroad, by foreign ways, and by a foreign speech, and confronted by powerful factions fostered under Danish rule, which he had neither the force to control nor the subtlety to undermine. Moreover, he was childless. The uncertainty attaching to the succession, entering as an exciting element into the manoeuvres of the time, increased the difficulties of government. To whom would the Witan allot the prize? Would it send abroad for the infant grandson of Edmund Ironside? Would it place the crown upon the brows of Harold, the son and heir of the most powerful and ambitious noble of the realm, Godwin Earl of Wessex? Or would foreign ambitions play a part in deciding the fate of the masterless land? There were two vigorous aliens to whom the throne of England was a matter of close personal interest. The first of these was Harold Hardrada of Norway, the second was William the Bastard, Duke of Normandy, a man of devouring energy and ambition, who, through the marriage of his aunt Emma to the father of King Edward, could claim a family relationship with the house of Egbert.

The Viking dispersion which in England, Ireland, and Russia quickened the life of commerce and the growth of towns, and led in the remote valleys of Iceland to a wonderful flowering of original literature, also gave Normandy to Europe. The Normans, as the Northmen settled since 911 in the Seine valley and its neighbourhood came to be called, grew to be the most brilliant of European races. All the virile energy of their northern origin they retained, much of the polish of the Latin races with whom their descendants mingled they succeeded in acquiring. Paganism was exchanged for Christianity, Danish for French, the tumultuous memories of the north for the defined traditions of the Latin world. They learnt to intone masses and to build churches, they listened to the *jongleur* as he recited the Chanson de Roland, and recalled in verses never to be heard without emotion the tragic death of the Paladin of Charlemagne. To the marine skill of the Scandinavians they added all that was then known of cavalry warfare and the poliorcetic art. The pastures of Normandy, like those of ancient Elis, were rich in horses. The Normans took as much pleasure in a horse as in a ship. So combative was their disposition that when they were not engaged in fighting a real enemy, they would slay one another, with the exhilaration of schoolboys at play, in the mailed encounters of the tourney.

Among the nominal subjects of the king of France none was so powerful as the leader of this strong and receptive race. The dukes of Normandy from their capital at Rouen were in a position to contend on even terms with the kings of France, whose headquarters were now fixed in Paris. Many a battle was fought over the Vexin, the disputed borderland between Normandy and the Île de France, but the ambitions of the Normans were not confined within the borders of the duchy. A passion for adventure was blended with their gift for close and cautious calculation. In the eleventh century they conquered Sicily and England, in the fifteenth they discovered the Canary Isles, and two centuries later the Norman voyagers were the first to descend the mysterious waterways of the Mississippi.

By the middle of the eleventh century Normandy had become, under a dynasty of vigorous dukes, the strongest and most coherent principality in western Europe. Here, as nowhere else at that time so fully, feudalism was organized and controlled for public ends. Military service was fixed by custom and rendered in respect of the tenure of land by feudal vassals. Private war was limited, castle building conceded only under ducal licence, the coinage made a ducal monopoly, the local administration entrusted to a *vicecomes*, or sheriff, who represented the ducal or public, as opposed to the feudal or local, interest. Even the Church, seldom more powerful in Europe than in the eleventh century, was in Normandy controlled by the duke. Nor did the old leaven of aristocratic anarchy, which was characteristic of Norse society, finally prevail against the dominance of the ducal house. The last formidable rebellion of the Norman nobles was broken by William the Bastard on the field of Val és Dunes in 1047.

It is the more important to note these facts, because the slow rebuilding of Europe into an organized society after the cataclysm which succeeded the death of Charles the Great was rendered possible only by the development of small, well-organized feudal states. Of these Normandy was the earliest and best example. The practice of Normandy was carried over the Channel to England, and to all those regions of France which the

kings of England and dukes of Normandy acquired by conquest
or marriage. It spread to Maine and Anjou, to Aquitaine and
Gascony, as well as to the islands of Scotland. In any part of
this wide area, the Norman Empire as we may perhaps call it,
justice came in the twelfth century to be administered with an
eye to common principles and in a form of provincial French
which would have been intelligible to every lawyer from the
Forth to the Garonne.

That the Normans had become Frenchmen for at least half
a century before the battle of Hastings was of great moment for
the reconstruction of Europe. Had they retained their Norse
language and ways and remained an insoluble element in the
social fabric of France, they would have exercised as little general
influence as the Basques or the Bretons, the Irish or the Welsh.
As it was they carried with them in all their enterprises the
attractive stamp of Latin civilization.

It is characteristic of this adventurous people that half a century before their conquest of England they had begun to hunt
for fortune under an Italian sky. Norman pilgrims returning
from the Holy Sepulchre in 1015 learnt that in the feuds which
distracted southern Italy there was an opening for the surplus
energies of many a younger son impatient of the dullness or
poverty of home, and anxious for travel, sustenance, and renown.
The news spread rapidly. Norman knights drifted southwards,
took their part in the local struggles of south Italy, and proved
their worth as fighting men. In 1030 the Duke of Naples accorded
to his valiant corps of Norman mercenaries the county of Aversa.
In his craft, courage, and domineering ambition, in his lust for
gain and munificence in spending, in his industry and endurance, in his love of gaudy clothes and command of eloquent
words, but above all in his mastery of the whole technique of
fighting, the Norman knight appeared to the motley south
Italian population, Greeks, Lombards, Saracens, Italians, and
Jews, to be at once a figure of glittering brilliance and a paragon
of efficiency. The prestige of these adventurers was out of all
proportion to their numbers. The conquest of south Italy and
Sicily was effected by a few hundred knights under the leadership of the twelve stalwart sons of Tancred of Hauteville.[1]

There are few more curious pages of mediaeval history than
those which recount the rise of this famous house, which wrested

[1] Genealogical Table B.

south Italy from the Greeks, Sicily from the Saracens, Antioch from the Turks, and challenged the might of the Byzantine Empire. The figures of Robert Guiscard, "a man of great counsel, talent, generosity, and daring," an expert cattle thief and a born, leader of horse, and of his youngest brother, Roger, the conqueror of Sicily, tall, handsome, eloquent, ambitious, live again in the pages of a Sicilian chronicler, who delights in abrupt vicissitudes of fortune. To this pious enthusiast it matters little that the sons of Tancred were capable of every devilry. The rough warfare of the Normans was redeemed by the possession of the Latin Faith. Though they handsomely defeated a papal army which was sent against them (1053), they made amends by the elaborate respect which they accorded to a captive legate. The Pope was quick to discern the advantage which might be derived from an alliance with this formidable body of muscular Christians, how they might rid Italy of the Greeks, redeem Sicily for the Faith, and make the Holy Father secure upon the Roman throne. A treaty was struck in 1058. Under the convenient authority of the forged donation of Constantine, Guiscard was accorded the duchy of Apulia as a papal fief. Forty years later his brother Roger received as the reward of his Sicilian crusade the singular honour of hereditary apostolic legate in that island.

So under the full glow of papal benediction these freebooters of the north laid the foundations of a civilized state in Mediterranean waters. With Norman flexibility the descendants of Tancred proved themselves equal to the responsibilities of conducting an organized government under new and difficult conditions and on original lines. In the kingdom of Roger II, who united the Norman territories on either side of the Straits of Messina, Europe witnessed a polity half-oriental, half-western, providing a shelter for Greek, Latin, Moor, and Jew, and better organized, seeing that it preserved the tradition of its Greek and Saracen past, than any other European government of that age. Among the orange groves of Palermo, Roger, the descendant of the Vikings, sat upon his throne, robed in the dalmatic of the apostolic legate and the imperial costume of Byzantium, his ministers part Greek, part English, his army composed as to half of Moors, his fleet officered by Greeks, himself a Latin Christian, but, in that balmy climate of the south, ruling in half-Byzantine, half-oriental state, with a harem and eunuchs, a true representative of his lovely island, shared then as ever between east and west.

Time has dealt kindly with this dynasty of gifted pirates. Mosaics, the best which Greece could provide, still embellish the walls of the noble cathedral of Monreale, which looks down upon the flowers and orchards of the Conca d'Oro. In that same earthly paradise an exquisite cloister still invites to repose, and the visitor, noting what he there sees of building and sculpture, of jewelry and decoration, must admire the splendour of the Norman princes now sleeping in tombs of dark porphyry, who in the twelfth century brought about so great an assemblage of the arts and crafts of their age.

Very different was the Scandinavian scene from which the Vikings had sallied forth to slay, to burn, and to conquer. No Monreale, or Caen, or Durham rose in the solitary valleys of Norway. There the Viking aristocracy bled to death in civil war. By the thirteenth century Scandinavia was empty of personal eminence. The days of her influence were over. A rude, unlettered peasantry extracted a sorry living from a barren soil.

BOOKS WHICH MAY BE CONSULTED

C. F. Keary : Vikings in Western Christendom.   1891.
B. S. Philpotts : Edda and Saga.   (Home University Library.)   1931.
Axel Olrik : Viking Civilisation.   *Ed.* H. Ellekilde.   1930.
Saxo Grammaticus.   *Tr.* O. Elton.   1894.
T. D. Kendrick : History of the Vikings.   1930.
Sir Charles Oman : A History of England before the Norman Conquest. 1910.
C. Plummer : The Life and Times of Alfred the Great.   1902.
G. M. Trevelyan : History of England.   1926.
C. H. Haskins : The Normans in European History.   1915.
C. H. Haskins : Norman Institutions.   1918.

CHAPTER XVI

SAXONS AND SALIANS

*Europe in 900. Germany and the Huns. Henry the Fowler and Otto I.
Foundation of the Holy Roman Empire of the German Nation in 962.
Its significance for Germany. Limitations to imperial power. Quarrel
with the Church. Revival of the Papacy after 1046. Leo IX. Hilde-
brand. The War of Investitures and the Concordat of Worms. The
Hildebrandine controversy. Its consequences for political thought.
German colonizing movements on the northern plain and middle Danube.
The Empire fails to profit. The hard Germany and the soft. No Franco-
German problem in the middle ages.*

WHILE the Northmen were thus assailing its outer fringes,
Europe began to develop those diversified political characteristics which led in modern times to the formation of the
separate nationalities of Germany, Italy, and France. At the
beginning of the tenth century no one of these countries possessed the organization proper to a state, and still less the conscious personality essential to a nation. There was a king of the
western Franks but no France, a king of the eastern Franks but
no Germany, a king of the Lombards but of Virgilian Italy
only a reminiscence. What is now known as France was a collection of fiefs, one of which, the Île de France with its capital at
Paris, was destined to devour its neighbours until its power was
co-extensive with the frontiers of the present state. Germany,
bounded on the east by the Elbe, was a loose assemblage of
tribal duchies—Saxon, Franconian, Bavarian, Swabian—under
the nominal rule of an elective king. The Italians, once the
proud and privileged members of a great empire, were parcelled
out into a congeries of dissimilar polities, a papal patrimony much
diminished by usurpation, a Byzantine province, Lombard fiefs,
independent cities. No Gascon or Breton would have pretended
to owe allegiance to France. No Venetian or Genoese would
have felt bound to follow the banner of a Marquis of Ivrea or a
Duke of Benevento. The Germans were more homogeneous.
Yet this violent and romantic forest folk, now so submissive to
authority, exhibited through the middle ages a surprising appetite for discord and rebellion.

Unlike France and England, Germany suffered little from the
Northmen. For her the Magyars, a Mongolian race who had
slipped into the empty Pannonian plain, dividing the northern
from the southern Slavs, constituted at the beginning of the
tenth century a more serious menace. Again and again these
formidable horse archers carried their devastations into the
heart of Europe, piercing even to the plains of Italy and France
and beyond to Andalusia. But as Wessex and Alfred stemmed
the onrush of the Danes in England, so Saxony and Henry
the Fowler gave a check to the Magyars. The Saxon hero was
not, like the West Saxon, a man of comprehensive genius and
vivid sympathy, but a good methodical German soldier who,
confronted with a novel form of attack, set himself down to
devise the best means of defence, and found in the construction
of well-garrisoned wooden forts and the use of the cavalry arm
the proper reply to the swift-moving levies of his enemy.
Henry's victory at the Unstrut in 933 brought glory to his
house and put a new heart in his people. He was succeeded by
a yet greater son, Otto I, whose victory on the Lech in 955 finally
liberated his country from the Magyar pest. What the soldier
began, the priest completed. In 1000 the wild Hungarian people
followed its royal shepherd into the Christian fold and, after
many centuries had elapsed, formed the south-eastern bastion of
the Latin faith against the conquering tides of Islam.[1]

In spite of these days of confusion the conception of an
organized world state co-extensive with the domain of a world
religion still floated vaguely in the minds of men. Even before
the victory on the Lech Otto had a claim higher than that of
any contemporary to be regarded as the temporal chief of Latin
Christianity. The tribal duchies of Germany had been brought,
not without fighting, to acknowledge his authority. He had
obtained the submission of Bohemia and had strengthened the
German powers of defence and offence along the Slavonic
frontier. Moreover, finding in 951 a pretext to intervene in
Italian affairs, he had assumed the Italian crown and had
appointed a deputy, Berengar of Ivrea, to represent him in
absence. To these striking achievements the great triumph over
the Hungarians furnished an impressive complement. Though
he came of a race which had never been included within the
Roman Empire and had only recently been admitted within

---

[1] Genealogical Table C.

the Christian fold, few would now dispute Otto's claim to be Roman Emperor should he care to advance it, for since Charlemagne no ruler had held a position of such widespread influence and prestige. Accordingly when in 962 Otto marched to Rome at the request of Pope John XII, and was by that unscrupulous pontiff crowned Roman Emperor, the world accepted the fact without a protest. So correspondent was his enterprise with the needs and ideals of society that the Holy Roman Empire of the German nation lasted till the nineteenth century, the embodiment of that aspiration after order and harmony which the reason of man is always pleased to entertain and his perversity as surely to frustrate.

So the Holy Roman Empire was founded; to some German writers a matter of pride, to others of poignant regret. There are those who reflect with sentiments of exultation upon an institution which in its mid-course excited the enthusiasm of Dante, in its decline the amused observation of Goethe. To such it is pleasant to recall how, when western Europe had reached the nadir of disorganization, the scene of the first concerted defence and political recovery was laid in Saxony by Henry the Fowler, how after that valiant prince had given security to his people, Otto, his still greater son, led all the German races against the Hungarians, redeemed Italy from degradation and helped to restore the Papacy to the respect of the western world. To this school of historical interpretation the revival of the Empire was not only a European but a German necessity. They dispute the notion that Germans were sacrificed to Italian influences. They contend that the imperial title gave to the German king a new prestige with tribes other than his own, that it developed national feeling and strengthened national pride, and that it was a means of securing for the service of the German monarchy the indispensable loyalty of the German Church.

With greater cogency it can be argued that the revival of the western Empire was unfortunate for the Germans. The area of Germany even in the days of Henry the Fowler was greater than that which a mediaeval monarch could conveniently control. The addition of Italy to that area meant that any real government of either country became impossible. The results of framing the permanent policy of the state upon a scheme too ambitious to be realized are what might be expected. Whereas

EUROPE IN THE TIME OF OTTO I.

Boundary of Germany proper
Territories tributary to Otto I.
B. Bohemia.
M. Moravia.
A. March of Austria.
Marches.
(Poland tributary in 963;
Pomerania to Germany 995.)
English Miles.
0   100   200   300

Kᴹ
OF
DENMARK

Saxony

Aachen

Lotharingia   Franconia

KINGDOM
OF
FRANCE

Swabia

Rhine

KINGDOM OF BURGUNDY

Rhine

Danube

Bavaria

Carinthia

KINGDOM
OF
ITALY

Rome

Pomerania

POLAND

B

M

A

HUNGARY

Danube

CROATIA

in the tenth century there was no part of the Carolingian
Empire which seemed more likely to be united under a single
monarchy, three centuries later Germany had become an anar
chical federation of principalities and republics.

A contributory cause of this great political calamity was the
elective character of the German monarchy. In England and
France, where the elective was succeeded by the hereditary
principle, the development of the state proceeded more or less
upon a continuous plan. In France the monarchy assumed an
absolute, in England a constitutional form, but in both countries
the kingship remained a fixed centre, and, being identified with
the government, exercised a formative influence on the national
life. In Germany things took a different turn. It was not convenient either for the Pope or for the tribal dukes and great
prelates in Germany that the monarchy should receive the
power which the adoption of the hereditary principle would
confer. Election, then, was retained. No dynasty was allowed to
take deep root. The Saxons were succeeded by the Salians and
these by the Hohenstaufens. Only after many vicissitudes
during which the imperial capital was transferred to points as
distant as Palermo and Prague, was a centre found in Vienna
and a long-lived dynasty in the Austrian Habsburgs.

The East Roman Emperor ruled over an organized state, a
strongly fortified capital and a subject church. No one of these
advantages belonged to Otto and his immediate successors. The
Holy Roman Emperor was a wanderer. His court moved from
farm to farm, from town to town, and as he travelled, administering such justice as he might with the aid of his attendant
clergy and nobles, his distant capital on the Tiber was in the
hands now of the Pope but more often of a camarilla of turbulent Roman nobles.

In theory the Empire was conceived of as world-wide; but no
Holy Roman Emperor exercised authority in France or Spain,
in Britain or Scandinavia, in Russia or the widespread dominions
of the Byzantine Empire. The influence of Otto's revival was
correspondingly circumscribed. For the unity of the German
and Italian peoples, for the fortunes of the Papacy, for the
growth of political thought in Europe, and for the fate of the
Slavs in the Baltic plain, the revival of the Empire as a German
institution was of the greatest moment. In central Europe
events and political speculations were for many centuries

ashioned or capriciously influenced by this singular institution.
Elsewhere its light shone with a fainter glow and the Holy
Roman Emperor was regarded as but a foreign sovereign whose
pretensions were remotely correspondent with his powers.

Grave as these disabilities were, they might but for one circumstance have been surmounted. In the middle of the
eleventh century the Empire came into collision with the Papacy
over two critical questions affecting the life of the Christian
church and the administration of the German state, the celibacy
of the clergy and the right of investiture. It had been part of
the policy of Charlemagne to endow the German church with
a lavish hand and to lean upon its help in the tasks of government. That policy was renewed by Otto and his successors.
With a liberality not unmingled with prudence they piled gift
on gift upon the German prelates, expecting in return that from
these royal and submissive nominees entertainment would be
provided for the royal court, subsidies for the royal treasury,
and a full complement of men-at-arms whenever the royal host
might take the field.

A very mundane Church of fighting archbishops and bishops
suited the convenience of a German king, and was indeed the
chief pillar upon which his government was based. More
securely than upon any tribal duke or feudal lord could he
count upon the secular assistance of German prelates for the
conduct of his administration upon either side of the Alps.

To this policy the Church, as soon as a clerical spirit revived
in Europe, was bound to take violent exception; and to such a
revival the Emperors themselves contributed. Secular though
these sovereigns might be in their use of ecclesiastical patronage,
they were nevertheless devout according to the measure of their
age, some, like the Saxon Henry II and the Salian Henry III,
attaining to a high level of personal piety. Moreover, they conceived it to be their duty as advocates and defenders of the
church to protect the Papacy against violence and indignity,
and if necessary to intervene when the pressure of turbulent
nobles or the choice of the clergy and people of Rome had raised
an unworthy man to the Papal Chair. In the interests of the
Holy See Otto I had hanged thirteen Roman nobles, and
Otto III, his grandson, a lad in his teens, had made two papal
appointments, one of which, though of a young man of twenty-
three, was respectable, while the other was Sylvester II, the most

distinguished savant of his age. But no Emperor rendered more
service to the Papacy than the devout Henry III, who at the
Synod of Sutri in 1046 deposed two or perhaps three bad Popes
and then proceeded in succession to appoint four good ones.

The effect of these four appointments was to clear the Papacy
from the scandals which had attached to it, to restore to it the
moral leadership of the Church, and to precipitate a quarrel
with the Empire which, lasting with intermissions for two hundred years, consigned Italy and Germany to centuries of political
confusion and helplessness. If it be asked how effects so far
reaching could be produced by the appointment of a succession
of elderly men to the bishopric of Rome, the answer is to be

1048-54   found in the fact that Leo IX and his successors brought to
the discharge of their office a doctrine of great explosive power,
long prevalent in Europe and capable under papal direction of
becoming a political force of the first order. They were Cluniacs.
They belonged, that is to say, to a movement which, starting in

910   the Burgundian monastery of Cluny more than a century before,
as a campaign for chastity, piety, and discipline in the monasteries, had widened out, as such movements are apt to do, into
a comprehensive programme of church reform. The earlier
Cluniacs had been content to preach the sublime virtues of
purity, self-discipline, and peace, and to introduce into the
mechanism of their order a system of central supervision and
control for the protection of these frail flowers of the Christian
spirit. The later Cluniacs were more ambitious. For them the
teaching of Christ would never be established on earth save
through the medium of an independent Church governed by
an omnipotent Pope. There were, indeed, differences of opinion.
Some were moderate, others extreme, but the general spirit of
the movement, which was passionate and unequivocal, was to
exalt the papal power and to insist upon a clear-cut professional
standard for the clergy. In Lorraine, on the Rhine, in Bavaria,
in North Italy, such theocratic ideas of every degree of refinement and crudity fermented in clerical brains, but more particularly among the monks, who, like the miners of modern
industry, lived a life apart and were thus peculiarly prone to the
acceptance of contracted doctrines in an enthusiastic form.

To this mass of exalted opinion the Papacy under the compulsion of Leo IX now gave the support of its authority. Leo
was a Cluniac. To the discharge of his high duties he brought

the spirit of the autocrat, the cosmopolitan, and the reformer. He regarded the Papacy, not, as so many of his predecessors had done, in the light of a local and lucrative dignity, but as a great international institution of unlimited authority and complete independence which had been entrusted with the spiritual mission to inspect, to reform, and to inspire. It was a symptom of his wide outlook and active spirit that he made Cardinals of foreigners, that he held synods in France and Germany, that he secured the South Italian Normans for his allies, and that under his rule papal legates were despatched far and wide through Europe on disciplinary missions. His immediate successors trod the same path of high papal doctrine. They supported the *pataria* or popular anti-German movement in Milan. They denounced heresy and lay patronage. In 1059 by a clever stroke of policy advantage was taken of an imperial vacancy to confide to the College of Cardinals the choice of a new Pope. The high clerical proceedings of the Curia were from that date inspired by the genius, at once fervent and subtle, of a squat, ill-favoured Tuscan peasant, first known to history as Cardinal Hildebrand and after his election to the Papacy in 1073 as Gregory VII.

To this stern and implacable idealist we may principally ascribe the spread through Europe of a theocratic philosophy as menacing to the nascent state life of the eleventh century as in our own times is the communism of Lenin to the capitalism of Wall Street. With imperious courage Hildebrand conceived of the world as a single Christian polity governed by an omnipotent and infallible Pope, a Pope bound by no laws, by whom an offending prince might be driven from his throne, cut off from the sacraments of the church, and severed from the allegiance of his subjects. Believing that the time had now come to reconstruct the militia of the Catholic church, he preached the doctrine of a celibate clergy under the undivided control of the Vicar of Christ. At one and the same time he was prepared in the interests of an autonomous clerical profession to break up the family life of the German clergy and to sap the power of the German king. His claims were exorbitant. The church was to retain its temporal possessions, its palaces and farms, its cattle and its money. No fragment of the vast wealth which made it in Germany the indispensable servant of the state was to be surrendered. But it was to be independent, an Empire within an Empire. As the soul was nobler than the body, as the sun outshone the moon, so was the spiritual superior to the temporal power. In a Roman synod held in Lent of 1075 the right of the lay prince to invest a prelate of the Church with the symbols of his office was denounced as an intolerable inversion of the divine law.

It seems certain that Hildebrand, who was perfect in all the parts of the ecclesiastical diplomatist, did not advance without carefully measuring his ground. He must have known that in openly denouncing lay investiture he was challenging the basis of imperial rule in two countries, he must have foreseen that his challenge would be taken up, he must nevertheless have counted on success. Nor was his calculation unnatural. Henry IV had only just succeeded to his father's throne after a long **1056-1106** minority, which had fostered all the elements of disobedience in his kingdom. He was young, inexperienced, headstrong. At the outset of his reign he was called on to confront a serious rising of the Saxon peasants who could not be brought to see by what right a Swabian prince pretended to establish a capital among their pleasant hills and to hold down a free population with his Swabian garrisons. He had won a victory, but still had many enemies on either side of the Alps, monks, peasants, princes, the anti-German rabble of the Lombard towns, who might under papal leadership be combined into a formidable coalition. In that age of superstition the Church possessed powers over the soul more mighty than armies. If it denied the validity of sacraments administered by married priests, if it threatened excommunication, if it proceeded in the last resort to depose a temporal sovereign, hearts were troubled, loyalties impaired, a great body of opinion was swung from its moorings. On all these harassing circumstances Hildebrand must have counted when he threw his fateful challenge to Henry IV.

The contest began with an exchange of blows which at once revealed the disparity between the moral resources at the disposal of the rival powers. The Emperor deposed the Pope and the Pope replied by deposing and excommunicating the Emperor; but whereas Gregory VII was little the worse for Henry's deposition of him, the consequences of excommunication were serious for a sovereign whom many of his more powerful subjects were already anxious to abase. At a diet of German princes Henry was flatly informed that unless he were absolved in the spring when the Pope was expected in Germany, his throne was forfeit. He knew better than to wait for a Roman judgment delivered in an atmosphere of German mutiny. Swallowing his pride and steeling his courage, he crossed the Alps in the dead of winter, sought out the Pope in the mountain fastness of Canossa, and doing penance there and receiving absolution returned to confound and amaze his enemies.

But the German princes were already too far gone in sedition to retreat. They proceeded to elect Rudolf of Swabia as anti-king, and when Rudolf fell fighting on the Elster (October, 1080), pursued the Emperor with their hatred to the end, replacing Rudolf by Hermann of Luxemburg, and finally, when Hermann was in his grave and Henry was old and grey, stirring up his two sons to unfilial rebellion. A German civil war contrived for the deposition of such a man as Henry could not fail to enlist the sympathy and, after no long interval, the active support of Hildebrand. Rudolf the anti-king was acknowledged by the Pope. Wibert, an anti-Pope, was set up by the Emperor. Instantly all Germany and Italy were ablaze. On the imperialist side were ranged the peasants and priests of the south-west, the lesser nobles of Franconia and Swabia, and the main body of the German townsmen. But Saxony, the most warlike of German provinces, under Otto of Nordheim, the most redoubtable of German nobles, rose against the Emperor, and only after the stiff Saxon neck had been again bowed beneath the Swabian yoke was Henry free to cross the Alps and to place his considerable military talents at the disposition of his Italian friends.

Little comfort did Italy derive from his intervention. Four times did he lay siege to Rome and as often was compelled to acknowledge failure. But neither had Hildebrand cause for gratification. To save his capital from the Emperor he invoked the aid of the South Italian Normans. The Saracen levies of Robert Guiscard were as little famous for clemency as was the Roman population for the Christian virtues of meekness and patience. The allies of the Pope met with a furious resistance in the streets of Rome and exacted a terrible revenge. To Hildebrand, dying in exile at Salerno (May 25, 1085), the ways of Providence must have seemed strange and bitter, for no Goth or Vandal had brought such destruction upon the city of St. Peter as this priest who had devoted a life to its service.

The war of the Investitures, outlasting Hildebrand and Henry, was brought to an end in 1122 by a compromise (the

Concordat of Worms) anticipated sixteen years before in the cooler atmosphere of Britain, under which the secular prince, while continuing to exact homage for the temporal possessions of the Church, consented to renounce the investiture by ring and staff, which were the symbols of spiritual authority. Each party claimed a victory. It was the cause of civil government in Germany and Italy which suffered a ruinous defeat from this protracted struggle.

There was nothing new in the Hildebrandine philosophy. The virtues of chastity and humility, of love and justice, had been continually preached to unheeding ears. The theory that the Roman Church, being founded by God, was "the mother and mistress of all Christianity," that it was infallible in doctrine, universal in dominion, and the sole means of salvation for erring and straying men, was no novelty in western Europe. Nor was Hildebrand the first to maintain that the Bishop of Rome was the supreme and autocratic ruler of the Catholic Church. What was novel in this extraordinary man was the ardour, the courage, and the persistence with which he carried on a critical campaign against the deep-seated corruptions of his age. It was not a battle of clergy against laity. The priests who were enjoined to break up their families, put away their wives, or abjure their concubines, were as much incensed against the Pope as the prelates who were subjected to his minute and harassing supervision. In Germany, where papal interference was at its maximum, the greater part of the clergy were opposed to the passionate crusade of the puritan autocrat. How can we be surprised? Celibacy is a hard virtue, the conquest of the natural love of woman a poignant human sacrifice darkening the sunlight of young manhood. The battle to which Hildebrand summoned his clergy was so long and desperate that victory was not finally won till the later years of the sixteenth century. But it may be asked whether it would have been won even then, if at one of the darkest hours of the Church's history, when the clergy were sunk deep in worldliness and vice, a great moral genius, commanding all the resources of the Papal Chair, had not forced upon his clergy, without fear or favour, and in defiance of the strongest secular power in Europe, the austere ideals of the celibate life.

Out of the Hildebrandine controversy rose a political debate which continues to this day. The clerical party contended that righteousness was set above material power, that temporal sovereignty was founded on contract, and that the unrighteous king might lawfully be deposed. The imperialist advocates argued otherwise. They disputed the social contract, denied the papal supereminence, and claimed for the Emperor an indefeasible, hereditary, and absolute authority. Few now read the rival tracts of Manegold, the papal, and Petrus Crassus, the imperialist, pamphleteer. Yet in these dry pleadings there is still a living core of interest. Is the state all in all? Is material power alone to be worshipped, or does Christianity divide the allegiance of the citizen? Less courageously than in the eleventh century, but still audibly, these questions are asked in Germany today (1934).

Meanwhile a great task was awaiting the German people which under happier auspices might have been turned to the advantage of the German monarchy. From the Elbe to the Niemen stretched a long level plain, now gleaming with thriving tillage and well built towns and villages, but then a waste of forest, lake, and marsh, sparsely occupied by tribes speaking a strange Slavonic tongue and worshipping heathen gods, such as Triglav of the triple head, and Redigast, and Svantovit, whose shrine at Arcona in Rügen overlooks the dark waters of the Baltic. To the bishops, the nobles, and the husbandmen of Saxony these vast mysterious spaces, whose eastern limit no traveller could fix, were as alluring as the plateau of the North American continent to the frontiersmen of Virginia and Massachusetts. Here beyond the Elbe was rich land to be had for the asking, forests to be cleared, marshes to be drained, villages to be built, and a heathen population to be converted, taxed, tithed, and reduced to bondage. "The Slavs," so runs a proclamation of the leading bishops and princes of Saxony, "are an abominable people, but their land is very rich in flesh, honey, grain, birds, and abounding in all produce of fertility of the earth when cultivated so that none can be compared with it. So say they who know. Wherefore O Saxons, Franks, Lotharingians, men of Flanders most famous, here you can both save your souls and if it please you acquire the best of land to live in."

The colonization of this northern plain was perhaps the principal achievement of the German people during the middle ages. Not without rebuffs, husbandry and commerce, church building and town building followed behind the axe of the German frontiersmen. By slow degrees at convenient spots along the bleak sea coast little fishing villages grew into great trading towns and ultimately into the powerful Hanseatic League, which covered the Baltic with its shipping and made of it the second commercial highway of the mediaeval world. Frisians, Flemings, and Walloons, hearing of the new empty country, in which farmers might live at their ease, pressed forward to share the advantages of the German pioneers.

> Naer Oostland willen wy riden
> Naer Oostland willen wy mêe,
> Al over die groene heiden,
> Frisch over die heiden,
> Daer isser een bettere stêe
> 'Als wy binnen Oostland komen
> Al under dat hooger huis,
> Daer worden wy binnen gelaten
> Frisch over die heiden ;
> Zy heeten uns willekomen syn.

> To the Eastland we will ride,
> To the Eastland we'll go too,
> All over the green fields,
> Gaily over the fields !
> There is a better place
> When to Eastland we are come
> Right under the high wall,
> There we shall be let in,
> Gaily over the fields !
> They will bid us welcome.

It is not to be pretended that this long and exuberant adventure was unattended by serious evils. The Saxon frontiersman of the middle ages, to whom rough nature imparted something of her own asperity, was as little disposed to be tender to the Abodrites and Wends as was the New England settler of the seventeenth century to the Red Indians who from time to time raided his holding. Only in Pomerania, where the native population were peaceably brought over to Christianity by Otto of Bamberg, one of the best of the German missionaries, was the onward march of the German people unaccompanied by the use of force. At no time, however, have great colonizing movements, involving the displacement of a weaker by a stronger population, been accomplished without serious injustice. The struggle between North German Christianity and Slavonic heathendom exhibits many, if not all the abuses which in a later age characterized the colonization by the white races of the western hemisphere. There was murder and treachery, expropriation and enslavement. The Slavs were not always patient under the hand of the despoiler. From time to time they rose in revolt (as in 983, 1018, and 1066) and overwhelmed the German settlements with fire and sword.

A similar colonizing movement, though more narrowly contracted, went forward in the milder climate of the middle Danube. Here the Bavarian pioneers were confronted by the stubborn strength of the Magyar nation and the hardly less intractable wilderness of forest and hill which on either side flanked their eastern advance. The conditions of the problem governed the mode by which it was attacked. The Bavarian Ostmark, established by Charlemagne against the Avars, renewed by Otto I against the Hungarians, extended by the campaigns of Henry III, was a military colony divided among nobles, bishops, and abbots, who were pledged to defend it, and populated for the most part by their Bavarian serfs. Thus while the vast spaces of the north-east were mainly won by free adventurers of the Saxon race, a greater measure of military organization was necessary for the making of that far smaller German territory which is known as Austria. The modern traveller who pursues his journey from the Dutch to the Russian frontier passes through a country peopled, save for a few Wendish villages, by Germans speaking the German tongue and penetrated by the German spirit. Only the ethnologist and antiquarian can bring to his notice the surviving relics of a different population long submerged or violently exterminated. In the south it is different. Whether the attack was softer or the resistance harder, the enemy was not absorbed. Not all the seductions of Vienna, for so many centuries the centre of German illumination in that backward corner of Europe, not the prestige of the Austrian Empire, nor the intolerance of the Catholic Church, nor the dominion of a German bureaucracy have broken the stubborn heart of the Czech and the Slovak, the Magyar and the Slovene. To this day they cherish a non-German mind and speak a non-German speech. Had the German monarchs of the middle ages been free from the distractions of Italian politics, they might, one would imagine, have secured for themselves an accretion of strength through the direction of these colonizing movements. This opportunity was not taken. No part of the territories wrested from the Slav was reserved for the domain of the German king. It fell to the Margraves of Brandenburg and the Bavarian Ostmark to reap the advantages which but for a long train of untoward circumstances, the acceptance of the imperial crown by Otto I, the war of the Investitures, the successful resistance of the Saxons to the attempt of Henry III and his son to establish in Saxony the seat of the German monarchy, might have been secured for the German state. In modern times the leadership of Germany has been shared between two great land colonies, Prussia and Austria. The growth of the movement out of which these states arose has little connection with the spectacular Italian and papal wars which form the central theme of mediaeval German history. Yet what in the German past can be more important than this immense and secular migration, this moving frontier of stalwart peasant families steadily advancing eastwards, clearing forests, reclaiming land, draining marshes, bringing in with their heavier ploughs a more intensive method of cultivation, and followed by monk and priest, trader and mason, peddling Jew and ingenious craftsman, the outpouring of a fecund and vigorous people, which has left enduring traces on the history of mankind?

A French historian has pertinently contrasted the eastern and western front of the German Empire during the middle ages—in the east the fighting Margraves on the Elbe, in the west the prelates and priests of the Rhine; in the east the German race at its hardest, its fiercest, its most enterprising, in the west the same people softened by clerical government or municipal affluence. As the tides of Germanism swept forward towards the east they receded in the west. The long intermediate territory which in the division of the Carolingian Empire among the sons of Louis le Débonnair had been assigned to Lothair, and had from him taken the name of Lotharingia, was an unstable compound, soon dissolved into a number of separate fiefs, principalities, and cities, of which some were Latin, others Teutonic, but all in the middle of the eleventh century included within the Holy Roman Empire. To this Empire belonged Alsace and Lorraine and the territories which are familiar as Switzerland, Franche Comté, and the Low Countries. Moreover, partly by bequest, partly by conquest, the Emperor Conrad II had come into possession of the kingdom of Arles, which comprised Provence, Dauphiné,

1024-39

and Savoy, some of the most classic ground of Latin civilization. But the hold of the German Empire on such part of this western area as was peopled by the Latin race was slight and precarious. As the French monarchy increased in strength, the Empire began by slow degrees to give ground, until by the end of the fifteenth century the valley of the Rhone, save for Avignon, had passed from the German to the French allegiance.

These changes were effected without great shock. A Franco-German war was not in the middle ages a political possibility. The German emperors, when they were not engaged in putting down rebellion in their own dominions, were occupied with Italy or the eastern advance. The eyes of the German people were turned towards the east where land was empty and conquest easy, and not towards the west where these conditions were reversed. Nor was there present that condition of geographical contiguity which is provocative of friction in the modern world. Between France and Germany ran a belt of principalities, duchies, and counties across which the two countries, though little love was lost between them, might shake hands. To these reasons may be added one yet more powerful. France was occupied in the west. For the better part of the middle ages she was involved with England in the greatest civil war of mediaeval history.

BOOKS WHICH MAY BE CONSULTED

C. R. L. Fletcher : The Making of Western Europe. 1912-14.
H. H. Milman : The History of Latin Christianity. 1867.
J. Bryce : The Holy Roman Empire. 1904.
W. von Giesebrecht : Geschichte der deutschen Kaiserzeit. 1881.
A. Hauck : Kirchengeschichte Deutschlands. 4 vols. 1904-20.
Cambridge Mediaeval History, Vol. V.
Zeller : Histoire d'Allemagne. 1890.

CHAPTER XVII

THE FOUNDATIONS OF ENGLISH GOVERNMENT

Prostration of France in the tenth century. Rise of the Capetians. Sources of their authority. The Norman Conquest of England. Its completeness. England becomes a province of the Latin world. England's debt to William the Conqueror. Preservation of Saxon customs. Consolidation under Henry II. French interests divert England from its proper tasks.

NOTHING in the condition of France during the tenth century indicated the strength or the unity which she was afterwards to attain. To the northerners who spoke the *langue d'oïl*, the *langue d'oc* of Provence and Aquitaine was only one degree less foreign than the Celtic of Brittany or the Norse of Bayeux. The country, which had become a chaos of warring fiefs, was rendered miserable by pillage, turbulence, and insecurity. Even in the north the Carolingian monarchs, though enjoying the superstitious prestige of legitimacy, were confronted by many vassals as powerful as themselves and little disposed to respect their authority. In Aquitaine and Gascony, or in the counties of Barcelona and Toulouse, the value of these phantom kings as guardians of peace or directors of policy was exactly zero.

From this state of political prostration France was ultimately rescued by a new royal dynasty which possessed, together with other valuable qualities, the merit of furnishing for a period of three hundred years a lawful male heir to the throne. There was among the vassals of the king a certain family which shone out above others for a remarkable tale of public service performed on a critical occasion and at a critical spot. Robert the Strong, Count of Paris, fought for ten years against the Northmen and died on the field of battle. The record of Eudes, his son, the hero of the famous defence of Paris against a great Scandinavian armada, was equally illustrious. For this exploit Eudes was rewarded by the dukedom of France, a dignity which the saviour of his country might in such an age of violent ambitions be emboldened to exchange for the monarchy itself. But the Robertonians were as distinguished for caution as for courage.

885-6

More than a hundred years passed during which the most powerful man in the kingdom was content to serve and wait. Then in 987 it so chanced that Louis V, the last surviving male in the direct line of the royal house, met with a fatal accident in the chase. Hugh Capet, with the encouragement and help of Adalbert, Archbishop of Rheims, seized the occasion and founded a dynasty which lasted eight hundred years. "I promise," he swore, "to grant to the people entrusted to my care justice according to their rights."

From the long duration of this famous house it might be tempting to conclude that its stability was never in serious danger. This was not so. The Capetians, indeed, enjoyed two great advantages over any feudal competitor. They held Paris and Orleans, and were thus stationed on the waters of the Seine and the Loire. No feudal vassal could boast of a domain so central or of a capital so populous, convenient, and easy to defend. The island city of Paris proved to be the key to supremacy, and this key valour and prudence had secured for the Capetians. But the election of Hugh, the most powerful by far of the French nobles and generally favoured by the Church, was not unanimous. The Counts of Flanders and Toulouse and the Duke of Aquitaine refused their recognition, a cloud in the sky foreshadowing the defiant ambitions and jealousies which continued to surround the throne of France.

A second resource, however, the Capetians possessed, the value of which became increasingly evident with the lapse of time. They were kings. By comparison with some of their feudatories they might be poor and weak, subjected to the humiliating defiance of robber barons even within the precincts of their own domain and hard put to it to make a living from their farms, but they had a reservoir of power peculiar to themselves. The King of France was the heir of the Roman tradition of empire, "the eldest son of the church and most Christian king," the head of that new feudal society which was at first so inimical to monarchy but afterwards, as its customs became defined, a source of regal prerogatives unknown to the ancient world. Upon each of these three foundations it was possible for the theorist to erect an imposing fabric of regal prerogative. To the feudal lawyer the king was the suzerain of suzerains, entitled to the homage and allegiance, the aid and counsel of his vassal, and the overlord from whom all land was immediately or mediately held. To the churchman consecration was an eighth sacrament, establishing the religion of royalty. To the Roman lawyer there was no limit to his prerogative. When Philippe de Remi, Sire de Beauvoisis, jurist and poet, wrote his *Coûtumes de Beauvoisis* in the thirteenth century, he echoed the famous maxim of imperial Rome that the princes' pleasure must be taken as law.

987-1108 Length of life, coupled with the wise practice of their house always to crown the son in the lifetime of the fathers, give to the first four monarchs of the Capetian house the better part of their claim to be counted among the benefactors of their country. They escaped the tempest of the War of Investitures, for the Pope, having the Germans on his hands, was too wise to force France into the ranks of his enemies by an over-close scrutiny of practices which were undoubtedly simoniacal. If these rulers achieved nothing sensational, at least they held their ground, governing mainly through the bishops, but themselves also active in a succession of miniature campaigns. One unfortunate calculation, to be ascribed to Henry I, had far-reaching consequences. In the struggle between Geoffrey Martel of Anjou and Duke William of Normandy, the King of France took the weaker side and was defeated on the fields of Mortimer and Varaville (1054 and 1058). These were the first exchanges in a duel which lasted nearly four hundred years.

The Church had helped to set up the new French monarchy. It was now to give its blessing to the establishment of a throne in England, which more seriously than any other power threatened the disruption of mediaeval France. William Duke of Nor-
1027?-87 mandy cannot be described as one of nature's clergymen. The rule of priests he refused to tolerate either in Normandy or in England; but, like other statesmen-conquerors, he neglected no influence, however remote, which was likely to advance his ambitions. The Roman Curia was offended with the condition, at once lethargic and independent, of the Anglo-Saxon Church. William, remote as he was from the acceptance of Hildebrandine ideas, saw in the Pope a convenient ally in an enterprise long and profoundly meditated, and the conquest and pillage of England by the Normans was carried out under the banner and sanctified by the authority of the Vicar of Christ.

In all particulars of military and political organization our island during the long reign of the monkish Edward had been allowed to fall behind the duchy of Normandy. There authority was concentrated in the hands of the duke, here the ambitions of the great earls of Wessex and Mercia, Northumbria and East Anglia filled the political stage. The Normans were skilled in the use of cavalry and bowmen. The English, absorbed in their own affairs and possessed by the sluggish spirit of conservatism which was then so characteristic of the national character, had failed to develop proficiency in either of these arms. The consequences of this disparity in preparation were astonishing. The force at the disposal of William the Norman for the subjection of a brave population of a million and a half can barely have exceeded twelve thousand. Yet after Harold's army, which was largely drawn from the south-eastern counties of England, had been defeated in the battle of Hastings and its commander slain, *1066* England, save for a few local revolts, ill-combined and speedily suppressed, lay prostrate beneath the heel of the conquerors.

No country has been more completely subjugated. If the English population expected to receive from William the measure of indulgence which had characterized the Danish conquest of the island fifty years before they were grievously deceived. The volunteer adventurers from Normandy and Anjou, Brittany and Flanders, who flocked to William's standard, were not so much on the duke's errand or the Pope's as on their own. If they donned their mail to put a Norman bastard on the throne of England it was in the confident hope that a handsome share of English land and loot would be available for themselves. They were not disappointed. As the island was conquered bit by bit, the properties of the Saxon thanes were dealt out to the hard-headed gentlemen adventurers from abroad. A new French-speaking aristocracy, in comparison with their Saxon predecessors most formidable, cruel, and versatile, dragooned the wretched peasants to its imperious ends, dominated the countryside, and gave from its imposing castles a new impulsion to the national life.

England became once more a province of the Latin world. In the palace and castle, in the law court, and on the hunting field, wherever the ruling class were brought together for business or amusement, the speech was that of northern France. The chance that this island, which had slipped out of the grasp of Rome in the fifth century, might develop without foreign admixture an Anglo-Saxon life of its own, or play a

part as a member of a Scandinavian empire, was now gone.
The Norman conquest drew England once more into full communion with the inheritors of Rome, with their theology, their
architecture, their poetical literature, their law, their social and
political organization, with all that was moving in the Roman
Curia or in the law school at Pavia, or among the active monasteries of Normandy, Burgundy, and Lorraine. Two great
Italians, Lanfranc of Pavia and Anselm of Aosta, held in succession the see of Canterbury, bringing to England standards of
scholarship, discipline, and philosophy to which the country
had long been a stranger. The cruelty of the conquest was mitigated by the culture of the conquerors. From the soil of the
plundered country vast cathedrals rose to the heavens, erected
by the labour of a subject peasantry and in scale as novel to the
Saxon ploughman as is the first towering vision of modern New
York to a poor lad fresh from a humble cabin in Connemara.

By what may seem to be a paradox the completeness of
William's despotism in England was a blessing in disguise. The
great evil which affected the life of Europe in the eleventh century and indeed throughout the middle ages was anarchy and
private war. The Roman system of government having been
broken down and the Carolingian system having also failed,
nothing effectual had by the time of the Norman conquest of
England been found to replace them. The Church indeed employed such influence as it possessed to relieve the society of
Europe from the incubus of perpetual war. It initiated local
" pacts of peace " and on a more general scale the Truce of God
for the protection of Sunday and the high feasts of the Church.
But influence is not government, and until the three cardinal
principles of government—a defined system of law administered
and enforced, a money revenue ascertained and collected, a
loyal force adequate to defence—had been reintroduced into
Europe the seeds of liberty would not flourish.

Such a government, harsh, despotic, but in the long run
salutary, England owed to William the Conqueror. With an
even hand he crushed Saxon rebels and Norman mutineers.
The great English earldoms were broken up, and the estates
of the Normans, whether by chance or prevision, were so widely
scattered as greatly to reduce the dangers of feudal opposition.
If, then, feudalism was promoted in the sphere of tenure, it was
deprived of its worst evils in the sphere of government. As in

Normandy, the barons held their land of the king and owed him military service in respect of their tenures; yet the main work of governing the country was never allowed to be monopolized by the nobility. The king was supreme. His commissioners travelled the shires. His sheriffs presided over the county courts. The Doomsday Survey, compiled in 1086 for the purpose of collecting the Danegeld, shows with what meticulous curiosity every source of revenue was explored by the agents of the Norman fisc. In the local jury the Normans possessed an instrument inherited from Carolingian times, which was soon shown to be serviceable not only in those fiscal enquiries to which it was first applied, but also in the determination of judicial issues. When the royal court in the reign of Henry II began to apply the jury to cases of disputed possession, the most frequent form of legal action in violent and uncertain times, its popularity was assured. Litigants frequent the court which promises them cheap and effectual redress. Such redress the Curia Regis in the twelfth century found and applied, and thus gathering to itself the main part of the legal business of the country, built up that imposing system of the Common Law by which the Anglo-Saxon world on either side of the Atlantic is to this day content to be governed.

The roots of that system lie deep in the soil of Teuton antiquity. It was a part of William's strength that he regarded himself as the lawful heir of Edward the Confessor, that he was crowned by the Witan, and worked through the old popular courts of the hundred and the shire. The primitive ideas of English citizenship, such as that men were bound to attend the courts, to follow the hue and cry after malefactors, to serve in the fyrd or militia, and to help with the bridges, the roads, and the forts were too essential to be discarded. Norman England could no more be governed without the active co-operation of the English people than British India can be administered without a numerous body of Indian officials. As Hindu caste survives under the British raj, the fabric of Anglo-Saxon law and custom has continued, despite some Norman innovations, and all the more effectually by reason of that taut system of centralization which the Normans introduced, to shape the life of the English people.

The task of centralizing the government was rendered easier by the fact that Norman England was a small country. Wales,

Scotland, and Ireland lay outside the confines of William's dominion. Northumbria, as a penalty for rebellion, was reduced to a wilderness. In an area so contracted the Norman sheriffs, who were the agents of the king, carried out the royal pleasure.

So, during the century which followed the Norman conquest, the foundations were laid for the construction of a free and well-governed state. Normans and English intermarried. Under the shelter of a government strong enough to keep the baronage in its place a rural middle-class, that valuable feature which most sharply distinguishes mediaeval England from its continental neighbours, maintained itself in rude comfort and respectability and in due course of time became a principal pillar of constitutional government in our island. Progress, indeed, was not continuous. There was tyranny under Rufus, anarchy under Stephen; but the tyranny of Rufus was contested by Anselm, the anarchy under Stephen was terminated by the strong rule of Henry II. Before this sovereign, whose brilliant power of thought and action amounted to genius, had finished his work, royal judges were going on assize as they have ever since continued to do, representing the authority of the king and the majesty of the law, the jury was fast superseding archaic methods of proof, such as the ordeal and the duel, and the king had established his position as fountain of justice and guardian of the public peace. Racialism was dead. In the old national militia, which was now recreated and revived, the King of England possessed a defence force more reliable than the feudal levies, cheaper and more popular than a mercenary force. In the exactitude of its treasury control only the Norman island of Sicily could stand comparison with the England of Henry II. Not a sixpence was allowed to go astray. In comparison with the loose financial methods of Germany and France the English exchequer was a marvel of efficiency.

In becoming King of England William the Bastard did not cease to remain Duke of Normandy. Neither to him nor to his followers or descendants was there any anomaly in the existence of a French-speaking state lying athwart the Channel. If Sicily went with Apulia, England could well go with Normandy. The King of England was in respect of his Norman Duchy a vassal of France. Many of his tenants-in-chief possessed lands, all possessed relatives, on the continent. To no one of them, in search of military adventure, were the hills of Wales, the moors of Scotland, or the bogs of Ireland as attractive as the familiar fields of France. So long, then, as any part of France remained annexed to England it acted more powerfully than even the Electorate of Hanover in the time of George II as a magnet upon English policy. But many years were destined to pass before the ruler of England could regard himself as an island king. Even after Normandy was lost in the reign of John, and together with this great province, Anjou, Touraine, and Maine, England still retained possession of Guienne, Auvergne, and Aquitaine, the important provinces in the south-west of France which Queen Eleanor, the divorced wife of Louis VII, had brought with her hand to Henry Plantagenet.

From this geographical interlocking, as also from the quarrels of seamen and traders, there resulted a chronic state of hostility between the Kings of England and France which lasted with some intermissions until the middle of the fifteenth century. Beginning as a French civil war the struggle developed into a clash between two distinct and self-conscious nations. No great armies were employed, no long campaigns were fought, no new philosophies were developed in this protracted and desultory struggle. Mediaeval warfare was partly a social convention, partly an amusement, partly a financial speculation, when it was not a crusade or the fruit of personal pique or injured pride. But however slight and frivolous this mediaeval fighting may seem measured against the sacrifice and slaughter of modern war, the wars between England and France in the middle ages had far-reaching consequences for both countries. Out of this struggle two nations emerged as sharply distinguished in social structure and personal temperament as they were opposed by a long tradition of envenomed hostility. France was victorious, but failed for many centuries to turn her victory to enduring account. England was defeated. She lost Rouen in 1204, Bordeaux in 1453, Calais in 1552. Every yard of French soil was surrendered, every end for which she had been fighting was sacrificed. The tombs of the Conqueror and Henry II lay in an alien land. Yet only after she had suffered this staggering reverse did she by slow stages find her way to the great tasks which were awaiting her, the union of the British Isles, the conquest of an Empire across the seas. Engaged in her struggle with France she had been blind to the true line of her advance. Opportunities had been neglected. Nothing had been carried through with persistence. Even Wales, conquered by Edward I, was not finally incorporated until the reign of Henry VIII. Not till after Charles Edward had been defeated at Culloden (1745) were the Scottish Highlands made truly subject to the British Crown. The spirit of the Irish Celt, often assailed, remains to this day defiant and insoluble.

BOOKS WHICH MAY BE CONSULTED

C. Petit Du Taillis : La Monarchie Féodale en France et en Angleterre. 1899.

H. W. C. Davis : England under the Normans and Angevins. 1905.

W. Stubbs : Constitutional History of England. 1880.

Mrs. J. R. Green : Henry II. 1888.

F. Pollock and F. W. Maitland : History of English Law before Edward I. 2 vols. 1898.

Chronicles of Benedictus Abbas. (Rolls Series.) 1867.

F. W. Maitland : Memoranda de Parliamento. (Rolls Series.) 1893.

A. F. Pollard : The Evolution of Parliament. 1926.

McKechnie : Magna Carta. 1905.

T. F. Tout : Edward I. 1893.

E. Lavisse : Histoire de France, Vol II. 1903.

Bainville : Histoire de France.

CHAPTER XVIII

THE EARLY CRUSADES

Struggle of the eastern Empire under the Macedonians, 867-1059. Points of weakness in Byzantine civilization. Rise of the Seljuks. Manzikert, 1071. Alexius Comnenus appeals to the west. Urban II and the Holy Places. Schism between the Greek and Roman Churches. Aims of the Sicilian Normans. Effects of Christian disunion. Circumstances in western Europe favouring the First Crusade. Its success. Increasing friction between Greeks and Franks. Rôle of the Italian cities. Franks and Syrians in Palestine. Fall of Edessa and the Second Crusade. Imperfect concert between Greek Empire and the Kingdom of Jerusalem. Conquests of Saladin and the Third Crusade. Results of Crusading movement.

WHILE the house of Egbert was struggling to preserve an Anglo-Saxon nation in Britain, a dynasty hardly less remarkable was engaged at the other end of Europe in defending the Byzantine Empire against the ring of enemies who threatened to destroy it. The resources at the disposal of the Macedonian Emperors (867-1056) were far superior to those which were at that time enjoyed by any sovereign in the west. They had a capital superbly fortified and inhabited by a population more numerous than the Paris of Philip Augustus or the London of Charles II, a trained civil service, an organized system of finance and law, an army widely recruited and strengthened by a well-disciplined force of axemen from the north, a navy which could draw upon the inherited maritime skill of the Levant, and a gold coinage (the bezant) which went the round of the world. But perhaps the most important characteristic distinguishing this old civilized government from the newer and ruder states of the west was its skill and experience in diplomacy. No European politicians were so well posted in barbarian psychology, no foreign office so well versed in the art of dealing with half-savage princes and people. In no capital of the world were diplomatic relations so numerous and extended as in the city in which Asia and Europe unite. And among the diplomatists who even more than the soldiers maintained the Empire must be numbered the missionaries of the Greek Church, exercising a compelling force upon barbarous minds not only by the con-

tent of their teaching but by the elaborate splendour of the
Greek liturgy, with its appeal to every sense through incense
and music, vestments and candles. Some barbarians were kept
loyal by gifts and pensions, others by marriages arranged with
ladies of the Greek aristocracy, others by high-sounding titles.
Upon all such as might be attracted to the capital it was hoped
that an elaborate court ceremonial devised to exhibit the Emperor as a divine autocrat raised high above the common clay
of humanity would make a suitable impression. Nothing certainly was more remarkable in this old and civilized government
than the skill with which it contrived to protect itself by distant
and outlying friendships and understandings, the knowledge
which it succeeded in acquiring of the wild peoples of the
steppes, and the promptitude with which it was able to embarrass its enemies by bringing into the field against them an
unsuspected ally.[1]

Moreover, the government, inheriting as it did the imposing
tradition of the Roman Empire, could never fail, when it fell
into vigorous hands, to cherish exalted ambitions. The four
fighting Emperors of the Macedonian house—Basil I, Nicephorus Phocas, John Zimisces, and Basil II—were soldiers whose
Spartan temper and inflexible will were well adapted to the
necessities of those iron times. Taking the offensive on every
front, they gave to the boundaries of the Empire an extension
such as it had not known since the days of Justinian. The
robber island of Crete was rescued from the Saracens by Nicephorus Phocas. Cilicia, Syria, and Palestine were overrun by
the armies of John Zimisces. Antioch and South Italy were
recovered, the distant mountain country of Armenia incorporated in the Empire. But of all the triumphs of this strenuous
dynasty none was so vital to the continued existence of the
867-1056 Byzantines as the reduction, after thirty years of fierce fighting
and adroit diplomacy, of the Bulgarian Empire by Basil II.
When Basil the Bulgar-slayer died in 1025, after wisely conceding to his conquered enemies their cherished customs, he left
his state stronger, richer, more influential, and better defended
than any state in Europe.

Byzantine history is a tissue of sharp and disappointing contrasts. Spells of high military energy are succeeded by periods
of civil turmoil and base intrigue. Learning and culture are

[1] Genealogical Table D.

often found combined in one and the same person with manifest cruelty or connivance in crime. We read of an Emperor
whom we are prepared to admire for his activity, his learning,
and his patronage of the arts, and then we are told that this
cultivated Byzantine composed scurrilous verses to be branded
with red-hot irons on the foreheads of three condemned heretics.
We study the works of a learned princess, who was familiar with
most of the Greek classics, who idolized her father, and composed an elaborate history in his honour, but was yet concerned
in a plot to assassinate her brother. The state whose craftsmen
wrought the mosaics of Ravenna and the gorgeous miracle of
St. Mark's at Venice, whose politicians were theologians and
whose theologians were politicians, whose poets were still
haunted by the echoes of Meleager or Callimachus, and whose
scholars were still dominated by the shade of Homer, produced
the most violent city mob in Europe and descended to the basest
mutilations—the blinding of the eyes, the cutting off of the
hand, the ear, and the nose—in the punishment of its criminals
or political offenders.

The modern critic, then, finds much to reprehend in the
Byzantine Empire. Its organization had defects. It lacked the
liberal institutions which are alone capable of giving to a population habits of self-reliance and initiative. Despite much well-
meant legislation it was unable to protect its agricultural population from the suction of the town or the *latifundia* of the acquisitive landlord. It suffered overmuch from the tempestuous pressure of monks and mobs. But in the ninth and tenth centuries
Byzantium was the undisputed queen of European culture. Even
in the eleventh century, though the west was then fast drawing
level, it could show a society easily superior to that of any western
city in art, learning, and civilized habits. Moreover, it performed
a great office in policing a vast miscellany of races, most various
in quality and many of them vile, savage, and dirty. It was,
therefore, a calamity that the death of Basil II in 1025 should
have been followed by fifty-seven years of feeble government and
civil strife during which the army was allowed to dwindle
through neglect. The results were serious. The Empire lost all
its holdings in south Italy to the Normans. More important
still, it was defeated by a new enemy, the Seljukian Turk.

Towards the end of the tenth century a body of Turkish freebooters, under the leadership of the sons of a certain Seljuk, rode out of the steppes of Turkestan with their short bows and curved scimitars to seek their fortunes by war and pillage. Embracing Islam with neophyte intensity and prospering in all their undertakings, the Seljuks grew from a company into a tribe and from a tribe into a people. So swift was their onward march to power that in 1055 Togrul Beg, their leader, having already conquered Khorassan and Persia, was proclaimed Sultan in Bagdad and loaded by the decrepit Abbasid Caliph with all the titles and honours which are indicative of secular pre-eminence in the Moslem world. The course of Turkish victories so brilliantly inaugurated by Togrul was continued by Alp Arslan, his successor. Syria and Jerusalem were wrested from the weak hands of the Fatimite Caliphs of Egypt, after which the invaders threw themselves upon the one formidable power which was left in Asia and gained an overwhelming victory. On the field of Manzikert (1071), north of Lake Van, in Armenia, the flower of the Byzantine army was mown down by Alp Arslan's horse archers, the Emperor Romanus Diogenes was taken captive, and all Asia Minor was laid prostrate before a pitiless foe.

The Byzantines had suffered many defeats at the hands of barbarous enemies, but none so serious as Manzikert, for the force of the Empire depended upon its control of those Asiatic provinces which a single battle had now delivered into the hands of the infidels. It was from the Anatolian provinces of Asia Minor that the Emperor had obtained his stoutest soldiers and most brilliant generals, from the Asiatic littoral that he had derived the best part of his fighting marine. Nowhere was the spirit of adventure more lively than on the frontiers of the Asiatic themes, nor a prouder tradition of service than among the great barons of Asia Minor, whose well-armed retainers and large resources, when not employed in mutiny, had constituted a powerful element in imperial defence. All these sources of power were now summarily cut off by the Sultans of Rūm,[1] who, establishing themselves first at Nicaea and then at Iconium, spread a belt of desolation across the fairest province of the Greek Empire.

To this tremendous challenge there was no immediate reply from Byzantium. The battle of Manzikert, which had been preceded by civil strife and unwise military reductions, was followed

[1] A shortened form of Rumania, or the East Roman Empire.

by a decade of political paralysis. Then, in 1081, a happy revolution brought to the Byzantine throne a man whose qualities were exactly fitted to restore an almost desperate situation. Alexius Comnenus, who belonged to one of the great soldier families of Asia Minor, was as resourceful as he was cultivated and courageous. In him the taste for theological disquisition was blended with the zeal of the educational reformer, the energy of the general, and the craft of the diplomatist. Finding disorganization in every department of the state, menaced by a Norman invasion from the west and by the devastating raids of barbaric tribes from the north, this temperate long-headed young sovereign brought to bear upon all the difficult foreign and domestic problems by which he was confronted the precise measure of skill which was necessary to solve them. Only when these preliminary obstacles had been overcome, when the army and navy had been to some extent re-created, when Robert Guiscard had been manoeuvred out of Dalmatia and the nomad hordes were driven back across the Danube was Alexius free to address himself to the grave menace of the Seljuks. He determined to appeal to the Latin west to come to the succour of the Christian Empire and suffering churches of the east. Jerusalem, Antioch, Edessa were already in the hands of the infidel. Constantinople would be their next objective. So a letter was written to Pope Urban II which had the effect of unloosing the First Crusade.

Twenty-one years earlier, Pope Gregory VII, in response to a similar request from an eastern emperor, had conceived with characteristic energy and passion of such an enterprise. But the plan of a crusade derives not from Byzantium but from Rome. The object of Alexius was to obtain western soldiers for the reconquest of the Asiatic dominions of the Byzantine Empire. The principal interest of Urban II, the theme of the great speech which he delivered at the Council of Clermont, the leading *1095* motive of the many orations which he afterwards addressed to his lively French compatriots, was the recovery of Jerusalem and the Holy Places. The two objects were not incompatible. but since each might be separately pursued there was from the first the danger that the recovery of the Holy Places, appealing as it did more powerfully to the imagination of the Frankish chivalry, might be preferred to the defence of the Byzantine Empire.

The danger was aggravated by the fact that, eighteen years before Manzikert, the eastern and western Churches had formally broken off relations. It is a common characteristic of the great quarrels of history that the deepest causes of variance are not those which are most openly disclosed. The rift between the Greek and the Roman Churches was ostensibly theological. Whilst both Churches accepted the fundamentals of the Christian Faith as laid down in the Ecumenical Councils, the Greeks objected against the Latins that they had added words to the Creed which described the Holy Ghost as proceeding from the Son as well as from the Father, that they used unleavened bread, that they fasted on Saturday, and that they caused their priests to shave their beards. But these grounds of dissension, favourable as they were to the production of interminable treatises, did not stand alone. Other causes rooted in political and ecclesiastical ambition, as well as in circumstances of national temperament and character, tended to envenom the quarrel and to frustrate every one of the thirty separate efforts which were made to compose it. The contempt of the Latin for the Greek, old as the days of Juvenal, had survived the barbaric conquest of the west and was repaid by the scorn of the virtuoso for the philistine, of the legitimist for the upstart. The Byzantines regarded themselves as the heirs not only of ancient Hellas but of imperial Rome. For them the Franks, the Normans, the Germans were members of the barbaric world, and the western empire of Charlemagne an impertinent usurpation to which the Popes of Rome had improperly lent their authority. A certain primacy they might be willing to concede to the See of St. Peter. Roman legates might be received in Constantinople, the judgment of the Roman Curia might occasionally be invoked; but the claim of Rome to exact obedience and to exercise disciplinary jurisdiction over the church was one which no Patriarch of Constantinople would for a moment admit. Nor is this unintelligible. The ninth and tenth centuries, which witnessed the obscuration of the Roman Papacy, were illustrious in the annals of the Greek church. Then it was that two Greek missionaries, Cyril and Methodius, translated the Scriptures into the Slavonic language and made them available in the Glagolitic script, that the Greek church was organized in Russia, and the Bulgarians rescued from the subtle invasion of the Latin rite. For a hundred and fifty years the Patriarchs of Constantinople profited by the brilliant conquests of the Macedonian emperors. Greek priests and Greek monks followed the victorious march of Greek armies to Apulia, to Cilicia, to the Armenian highlands, to the Danube, and, though the Macedonian dynasty came to an end and was followed by a period of political confusion and disaster, the proud spirit of empire still survived in the Patriarchs of Constantinople. To Leo IX, speaking the autocratic mind of the revived Papacy of the west, the Patriarch Michael Cerularius reaffirmed (1054) the autonomy of his Church and its detestation of the corrupt practices of Rome.

To the Latin world, then, Byzantium naturally appeared in a double aspect. On the one hand it was a Christian power confronted by non-Christian enemies and therefore deserving of Christian support. But on the other hand it was tainted by heresy, contumaciously defiant of Rome, and the foe of every Roman missionary enterprise in south-eastern Europe. That the schism between the two Churches was a misfortune, and that steps should be taken to bring it to an end, was a principle which the Greek and Latin clergy were always willing to salute, but for which they were never disposed to make any hearty sacrifice of prejudice or pride. The Latins, however, held that there were two avenues to theological peace—the way of agreement, difficult, but not under political pressure impossible; and the way of conquest. To the Normans in particular it seemed from the first that the shortest and most satisfactory method of dealing with the Greeks was to dethrone the Emperor, to capture Constantinople, and to subject the Greek Empire by force to Latin rule. That was the theory of Robert Guiscard, of Bohemond his son, of Roger II and William II of Sicily his kinsmen—in fact, of this whole race of northern robbers who had turned the Greeks out of southern Italy and dreaded nothing so much as a war of revenge. It was a doctrine which won recruits in many quarters, among the merchants of Venice, who saw in the Greek Empire incomparable occasions for commerce and loot, among vehement Latin theologians like St. Bernard, among monkish statesmen like Suger. There were even occasions (as for instance in 1108 and 1281) when the Pope was himself prepared to promote the destruction of the Christian Empire of the east.

It is difficult to exaggerate the disastrous effect of this profound estrangement between the two halves of the Christian world. The failure of the Crusaders to retrieve hither Asia from the

Moslems needs no other explanation. It was to this inveterate animosity, compounded of racial and religious feelings and quickened by political ambition and economic rapacity, that we must ascribe the most disgraceful act of mediaeval history, the diversion of the Fourth Crusade to the conquest of Constantinople and the mutilation and pillage of the richest and most civilized of the European states. In 1261, after nearly fifty years of Latin rule, the Greeks returned to Constantinople. If they had little love for the Latins before the conquest of their capital, it may be imagined with what sentiments of aggravated passion they viewed the authors of their bitter humiliation. It was in vain that piety and prudence counselled a union of Christian forces before the advancing menace of the Ottoman Turks. What was proposed by high dignitaries in ecclesiastical councils, as at Lyons in 1274 or at Ferrara and Florence in 1438, was violently repudiated by the monks and clergy of Constantinople. Great Latin victories over a common foe might have stifled their inveterate misgivings; but such victories were not forthcoming. The gulf which had been dug in 1054 by the rival challenges of Pope and Patriarch remained unbridged to the end. Thanks to the divisions of the Christian world the Turks established themselves on European soil, carried their arms to the Danube, conquered Greece and its islands, and finally in May, 1453, seized the last prize of political ambition, the unconquered city of Constantinople itself. Here, by grace of these same rivalries, the Turk is still permitted to rule.

These dark shadows, however, were not within the field of vision at the first excited and tumultuous launching of the Crusade. At rare moments of history the feeling of Christian fellowship overmasters the jealousies and hatreds by which the church of Christ is ever liable to be rent asunder. In the brilliant prospect of common action and common sacrifice for a cause held to be great and sacred, dividing memories are laid aside and petty suspicions are discarded. That such an exalted emotional experience was vouchsafed to the chivalry of western Europe as it took the Cross in response to the Pope's appeal is established by evidence and may be inferred from probabilities. For the time had now come when Europe, which had so long been exposed to barbarian attacks, could carry the war into the enemy quarters. The Saracens had been expelled from Sicily

and Crete, the navies of Venice and Genoa and Pisa ruled the
Mediterranean, the overland route to Constantinople had been
opened by the conversion of the Hungarians to Christianity
and by the incorporation of Bulgaria into the Byzantine state.
In Spain the Christians had conquered Toledo, from Sicily the
Normans had assaulted the Saracens of Africa; and while the
massive eastward movement of the Germans was rolling back
the worshippers of Triglav and of Svantovit, Scandinavia, long
the torment of the continent but now emptied of its unruly sons,
had withdrawn into the backwaters of history, where she lay
becalmed till Gustavus Adolphus came forward to give to the   *1630-2*
Protestant cause in Germany the glory of his sword and of his
name.

It is also to be remembered that in France, which more than
any other country was the soul of the Crusades, the Church had
already succeeded in giving to the military caste something of
its own code of aspiration. The institution of chivalry, as it was
developed at the end of the eleventh century, had the great
merit of laying stress upon the responsibilities attaching to the
possession of force. The young knight was initiated into his
knighthood with all the solemnities which the pious imagination of those days could devise. He must take a ritual bath, spend
a night of solitary prayer, make confession of his sins and partake
of the sacrament. The duties of knighthood were rehearsed to
him in a sermon. He must protect the Church, the widows and
the orphans, the desolate and the oppressed. He was already, in
all but name, enlisted as a Crusader.

The first military enterprise of united Europe was distinguished for its absence of organization. The Crusaders who,
in a wild fit of enthusiasm, first left their homes for the east
were empty of all that it most concerned them to know. They
knew nothing of the geography, climate, or population of
the countries through which they proposed to travel. They
were short of commissariat, cumbered by crowds of non-combatants, ignorant of hygiene, and contemptuous of discipline.
These large bodies of enthusiasts, recruited from north-eastern
France, Lorraine, and Germany, rushed off without leaders by
the land route to Constantinople and suffered a terrible penalty
for their violent marauding. Decimated during their passage
through Bavaria and Hungary, they were annihilated by the
Seljuks soon after they had set foot upon the Asiatic shore.

The great muster of western feudalism which started for Constantinople by four different routes in August, 1096, exhibited,
though in a lesser degree, the same deficiencies. There was no
unity of command. There was an abounding ignorance of
geography. The armies were burdened with long trains of camp
followers and disgraced by undisciplined pillaging. But here
there was a core of experienced soldiers, horse and foot, serving
under chieftains of skill and authority such as Godfrey of
Bouillon and his brother Baldwin, who led the men of Lorraine;
Bohemond, son of Guiscard, the captain of the Apulian Normans, with his brilliant nephew Tancred; and Raymond of
Toulouse, whose Provençal followers were of all that concourse
the best equipped. To this circumstance we must attribute the
surprising fact that the First Crusade succeeded in attaining its
objects, that the four armies, though not without serious
wastage, did actually meet before Constantinople, that being
conveyed across the Bosphorus they were able with Greek
assistance to capture the Moslem capital of Nicaea and to restore
to the Greek Empire not only the littoral but much of the interior of Asia Minor, that despite the molestation of the enemy
they accomplished in their leather coats and heavy chain
armour the long and thirsty march through Iconium to Antioch,
that they besieged and took that strongly fortified and famous
city and beat off a formidable attempt to recapture it, and that
these achievements were ultimately crowned by the capture of
Jerusalem itself. No succeeding Crusade rivalled these remarkable exploits. The armies of Godfrey and Bohemond founded
the Latin principalities of the east, which, though they have
now been extinguished for more than 650 years, are recalled to
the reader by the genius of Tasso and Walter Scott and to the
traveller by the superb shell of many a giant fortress, standing
proud and lonely among the pink hills of Palestine.

To these successive blows delivered by the Frankish chivalry
on the Turks and Saracens, the Byzantine Empire owes its continued existence for a further period of three hundred years. It
is seldom, however, that the allies in a coalition for war, even if
that war should prove to be successful, are inspired at the conclusion of their operations by feelings of gratitude for the help
that has been rendered or of satisfaction for the results that are
achieved. The Latins owed much to Alexius. Without the help
of Greek convoys, Greek supplies, and Greek guidance they

could never have accomplished their difficult journey from the Balkans to Syria. Equally great, if not greater, was the debt of Alexius to the western army, which drove the Turks from a capital (Nicaea) within easy reach of Constantinople, restored many flourishing provinces to his empire, and dispelled the haunting fear of a Seljuk conquest of European Thrace. Yet neither party was satisfied with the other. The Latins complained that the Greek Emperor had made use of the advantage which belonged to him as the head of a wealthy and experienced government to exact from their chiefs an oath of fealty. They accused him of having failed to give them a stipulated measure of military support, and with some reason averred that but for the timely arrival of sea-borne supplies from Europe, their victorious army would have perished ignominiously of famine when encamped before the walls of Antioch. Every victory they ascribed to their own valour, every reverse or miscalculation to the perfidy of the Greeks. A popular idea, widely disseminated in the west and reinforced by every subsequent disaster to crusading armies, was that the Greeks, out of the fear and hatred which they entertained for the Latins, deliberately made their overland passage to the east as difficult and dangerous as possible. Alexius on his side had good grounds for distrust and dissatisfaction. His first campaign as Emperor had been fought against the Apulian Normans who had occupied Durazzo and were openly bent on driving him from the throne. That Bohemond, the fierce Norman leader, had experienced a real change of heart was most improbable. The inference to be drawn from his conduct, as from that of most of his associates, was that they were far more concerned to achieve principalities for themselves than conquests for the Empire. It was natural, then, that Alexius should endeavour to secure, as far as security could be obtained from oath or treaty, that territories once belonging to the Greek Empire and hereafter recovered by the Crusaders should be returned to their former allegiance. The oaths were reluctantly sworn, the treaty (for treaty there appears to have been) was reluctantly signed. Oaths and treaty were alike disregarded, when Bohemond seized Antioch for himself and Godfrey of Lorraine was installed by his followers as the first Defender of the Holy Sepulchre. In the maintenance of states which had been thus created the Latins could not count upon Greek assistance.

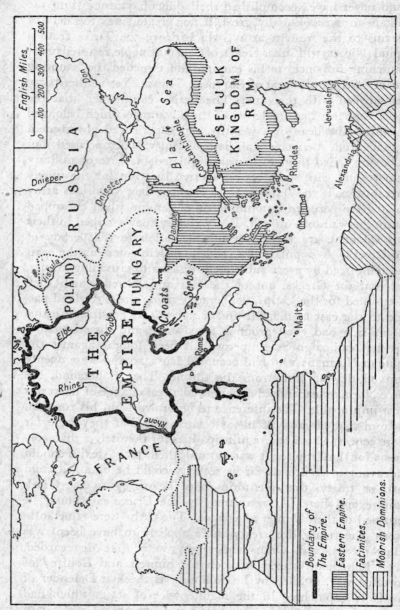

EUROPE AT THE TIME OF THE FIRST CRUSADE.

The bold experiment of the Crusaders in founding Christian states under a Syrian sky, though it was favoured at the time by the dissensions of the Moslem emirs, must, but for one circumstance, have broken down without delay. The great Italian republics were passionately interested in the extension of their eastern trade. Navies from Venice, Genoa, and Pisa co-operated in the sieges of the coast cities of Syria and were mainly instrumental in effecting their reduction. Yet even so the Christian states were in a precarious position. The Italians had no interest beyond the Syrian ports, the pilgrims from overseas no broader concern than a safe access to the Holy Places. The vital importance of conquering from the Moslem the whole of Syria up to its natural frontiers does not seem to have been apprehended and could not, in view of the slender numbers at the disposal of the Frankish princes, have been accomplished without permanent reinforcements from Europe. Such reinforcements were not forthcoming. For lack of numbers the vigorous Kings of Jerusalem were compelled to leave the eastern frontier in enemy hands and on that undefended and indefensible frontier were always exposed to attack.

The knights-errant who founded the kingdom of Jerusalem, the principality of Antioch, and the smaller counties of Edessa and Tripoli organized their new states upon a system of military feudalism such as they had known in France, but to which they were compelled by the special need of martial vigilance to impart an additional austerity. The Assizes of Jerusalem, a collection of customs compiled by John of Ibelin, a Cypriot lawyer of the thirteenth century, presents the picture of a society as rigorously dedicated to war as was ancient Sparta. In no instrument of the middle ages is the theory of feudal society so elaborately stated or the duties of military tenure so stringently defined. Institutions, however, depend upon the spirit of the men who work them. Under the seductive influences of an eastern climate, the rigidity of the Latin settlers insensibly relaxed. Syrian women, Syrian dishes, Syrian ways of life, began to appeal to these rude adventurers from the west and to temper their fanaticism. In Syria they found a society strange, to some extent abhorrent (for the Moslem women went veiled), but in many respects more refined and dignified than their own. Friendships were made between Frankish and Arab chieftains. The fierce religious intolerance of the Christian was softened by

the spectacle of pagan valour and courtesy. Even the half-
military, half-monastic Orders of the Knights Hospitallers and
the Knights Templars, which had been specially created for the
protection of the Holy Land, were not exempt from the
insidious infection of the east. The curious autobiography of
Ousama, an Arab prince, whose society was much affected by
the Templars, shows how deep by the middle of the twelfth
century had become the gulf between the polite and cynical

RESULTS OF THE FIRST CRUSADE.

tolerance of the permanent settler and the raw enthusiasm of
the newly arrived pilgrim from the west.

So long as the Frankish states were confronted with a ring of
small Moslem emirs, each acting independently of the other,
they were able, slender as were their resources in men and
money, to maintain an existence. But this advantage was not
destined to endure. Three capable Moslem rulers, coming one
after the other, altered in the course of half a century all the
weights and balances of the near east. Zanghi of Mosul con-

quered Aleppo and Edessa. His son Noureddin made himself master first of Damascus and later of Egypt, and finally, when Noureddin died in 1173, his place was taken by Saladin the Kurd, to whose brilliant and effortless gift of leadership the whole east between the Tigris and the Nile was in time made submissive.

The fall of Edessa in 1144, the first stage in this swift series of accumulating dangers, provoked an immense movement of agitated feeling in Europe. Edessa was a place in the imagination of the Christian world only less sacred than Jerusalem itself. That this home of early Christianity, the first of the new Latin states to be created as a result of the Crusades and the outlying bulwark of the Latin position in Syria, should be taken by the infidel, was regarded as terrible in itself and even more terrible for what it might portend. In an atmosphere of all-pervading excitement which the fiery eloquence of St. Bernard contributed greatly to inflame, Conrad III of Germany and Louis VII of France took the Cross and conducted their respective armies, still much encumbered by non-combatants, by the land route towards the east. A modest reinforcement of capable knights conveyed overseas in Venetian galleys would have been infinitely more effective than these imposing armaments led by the two principal sovereigns of the west.

The German army, save for a small fragment, wasted away in Asia Minor before it reached its destination. Of the French, who unwisely pursued the long and difficult coast route and were severely routed by the Turks in southern Phrygia, only the mounted knights, being transported by sea from Attalia, reached the scene of action. The Second Crusade was an un-relieved failure, marked by the needless wreck of two fine armies and the siege of Damascus, undertaken with half a heart and broken off after a few days by Baldwin II of Jerusalem, to the disgust of the princes from the west and to the infinite detri-ment of the Christian cause.

The west having thus signally failed to restore the situation in the east, it was natural that in due course the King of Jeru-salem should look for aid to Constantinople. The Greeks, should they care to exert themselves, might with their money, their fleet, and their greatly improved army, supply exactly that addi-tional force which was necessary to check the rising power of Noureddin. But Manuel Comnenus, their new ruler, was not too

1143-80

anxious to place the Latin kingdom of Jerusalem in a position of security. So long as he could recover Antioch, the prime object of his south-eastern policy, he was well content that the King of Jerusalem, to whom he had given a niece in marriage, should be kept quiet by the Arab on his flank. Seldom can there have been a keener sense of disappointment among the Latin residents in the east than when, in the summer of 1159, this showy and ambitious Greek Emperor marched a large army in and out of Syria without so much as a skirmish with the enemy. That Manuel preferred to treat with Noureddin rather than to fight him is probably to be explained by the fact that Antioch had been already surrendered to his rule.

Still, the Byzantine alliance was too valuable to be lightly thrown away. Amaury, who succeeded to the kingdom of Jerusalem in 1163, instead of concentrating his efforts upon the conquest of Aleppo and Damascus, was much taken with the idea of the conquest of Egypt and upon one of his four separate expeditions against that country received the assistance of an imperial fleet. His siege of Damietta in 1169 was a failure, but memorable for two reasons, alike as the last co-operative enterprise of Greek and Latin in the Crusades and as the first triumph of Saladin, the new Vizier of Egypt.

No Greek blood was shed in the battle of Hittin (1187), which sealed the fate of the short-lived Frankish kingdom of Jerusalem. The Greek Empire, to which the dynasty of the Comneni had given a century of prestige, had fallen once more upon evil times. Its main army had been defeated (1174) with huge losses by the Sultan of Iconium. It had quarrelled with Venice. In a mood of fierce suspicion against Mary of Antioch, the widow of Manuel and the Empress regent, it had disgraced itself by a *pogrom* against the French and Italian colony in Constantinople, and when Saladin's war cloud was ready to burst upon Syria, it was exposed to a deadly attack from the Normans, still faithful to their original thesis, that only a Latin power enthroned in Constantinople could finally settle with the Moslem world. There were no Greeks then on the field of Hittin. Only a force of some 1,300 Frankish knights and some 15,000 foot could be gathered together to oppose the great cavalry army of Saladin. What avail was brilliant courage against overwhelming numbers? The Latins were annihilated, the Holy Cross was captured, and the Holy Sepulchre, the dream of centuries and the first great prize of united Christendom, passed once more into paynim hands (1187) and so for 731 years remained.

At the news of this tremendous disaster a Crusade was organized, no longer by the Pope, but by the three foremost sovereigns of the west, Frederick Barbarossa of Germany, Philip Augustus of France, and Richard Coeur-de-Lion of England. But from these royal preparations, elaborated with all the improved knowledge and technique which a century of contact with the east had now made available, there was no result but the capture of Acre

RESULTS OF THE THIRD CRUSADE.

and a truce with Saladin granting to the Christian pilgrims free access to the Holy Sepulchre at Jerusalem. Here, indeed, was a shameful conclusion to an ambitious prelude and a damaging commentary upon the power of the Christian motive to fuse the energies of western Christendom and to direct them to a common end. In extenuation it may be said that the Third Crusade suffered one grave misfortune in the death through drowning in Cilicia of Frederick Barbarossa. Had that great German captain, the foremost soldier of the west, who had conducted his army across Asia Minor with conspicuous skill, and with an absence of casualties contrasting most favourably with the experience of preceding armies, survived to measure swords with Saladin, the result might have been different. As it was the Crusade served but to exhibit the national jealousies of France and England, the ill-will between Genoa and Pisa, and the intrigues and counter-intrigues of Conrad of Montferrat and Guy de Lusignan, the rival claimants for the shadowy throne of Jerusalem. Against this dark background of petty and paralyzing spite the military prowess and generous nature of Richard Coeur-de-Lion shines with ineffectual glory.

What remained of the conquest of the First Crusade was a line of Syrian ports of which Acre was the queen. These the strong material interests of Italian commerce were sufficient for a century to preserve. When Marco Polo started on his famous voyage to China the Italian mariner, as he approached the shores of Palestine, could still see the banner of the Cross floating from the citadel of his predestined port and hear across the waters the familiar salutation of the Christian bells.

Had the Crusaders been brought into contact with the best that Asia could give, and had they been able to absorb it, the Persian poetry of Omar Khayyam, the finest mind of the eleventh century, would have passed into the intellectual currency of Europe long before the days of Edward Fitzgerald. The Crusaders, however, never pierced to the best and most cultured peoples of the east. They saw nothing of the Persians, the Chinese, or the Indians. Their dealings were with the children of the steppes or the deserts, with the Turks or the Saracens, and with those softer peoples of the Levant who had suffered under Turkish or Saracen rule. Yet these limitations notwithstanding, the enlargement through the Crusades of western experience and material wealth was immense. Arts and crafts of the Orient, rich, intricate, and costly, strange lands and peoples were made familiar to a society, limited and largely barbarized by a long series of public calamities and only just emerging from the dominion of anarchy and fear. The new wealth of the east flooding into the Italian cities and thence distributed to northern Europe gave fresh strength and importance to the towns. Gains there were doubtless in the field of the spirit, a sense of the religious unity of Christendom which, once excited, was never wholly lost, a quickening of the romantic motive in vernacular literature, something of Arabic medicine, chemistry and accountancy, a larger and more exact appreciation of the non-Christian world than had hitherto prevailed. Of geographical knowledge, either directly resulting from the Crusades or indirectly from the missionary journeys to the far east to which the Crusades gave rise, there was a notable increment. The task of government, too, was perhaps made easier by the diversion of many turbulent spirits upon this distant quest. What, however, of the Christian religion? Candour compels the admission that the main effect of this vast movement of adventure and piety, curiosity and greed, was not to bring Christ nearer to man but to found the commercial empire of Venice in the Levant.

BOOKS WHICH MAY BE CONSULTED

Sir Charles Oman : A History of the Art of War in the Middle Ages. 1924.

W. Heyd : Histoire du Commerce du Levant au Moyen Âge. 1885.

O. Delarc : Les Normands en Italie. 1883.

C. H. Haskins : The Normans in European History. 1915.

H. Derenbourg : Ousâma ibn Mourkidh : Un Emir Syrien au Premier Siècle des Croisades. 1886.

J. Gay : L'Italie Méridionale et l'Empire Byzantin (867-1071). 1904.

G. Finlay : History of Greece, B.C. 146 to A.D. 1004. Ed. H. F. Tozer. 1877.

Cambridge Mediaeval History, Vol. IV.

F. Chalandon : Histoire de la Domination Normande en Italie et en Sicile. 1907.

CHAPTER XIX

FREDERICK BARBAROSSA

Blow to German unity through election of Lothair. Origin of feud between Guelph and Ghibelline. Frederick Barbarossa unites the rival factions, but makes no contribution to permanent German consolidation. His struggles with the Lombards and the Pope. His quarrel with Henry the Lion. A German federation based on respect for law alien to ideas of the time. Union of Germany and Sicily in 1186. Large ambitions and early death of Henry VI.

It was no good omen for the stability of the German state when, upon the death of Henry V, Lothair of Supplinburg was placed upon the vacant throne. Four generations of Franconians had succeeded four generations of Saxons, the crown passing from father to son by election during the father's lifetime with the unbroken concurrence of prelates and princes. And then in 1125, when it might have been expected that the principle of hereditary succession would have taken root in the political soil, the opposite principle, which placed the disposal of the crown in the hands of the great chieftains, was emphatically affirmed. So strong did the current now continue to flow in favour of free election that in 1156 the Princes Electors are spoken of as a substantive and important body in the state.

A yet greater misfortune, first manifesting itself under Lothair but growing to most formidable proportions under his successor Conrad III, was the feud between the Welf and Hohenstaufen families.[1] Of this historic quarrel which convulsed two nations and into which the most far-reaching issues of principle and policy were absorbed, the cause is no more dignified than the disappointed ambition of a south German clan. The Hohenstaufen were a powerful Swabian family who had good grounds for hoping that Henry V would be succeeded by the head of their house. In this hope they were bitterly disappointed. Lothair of Supplinburg, a Saxon united by friendship and afterwards by marriage with the influential family of Welf (or Guelf), was preferred to Frederick of Swabia, the near relative of the late king,

---

[1] Genealogical Table E.

the executor of his will, and the heir of his private estates. From such a decision Frederick of Hohenstaufen and his brother Conrad appealed to the arbitrament of arms. In pursuance of their ambition they did not scruple to involve their country in the familiar miseries of a civil war. Eventually, but not before every man, woman, and child in Augsburg had been destroyed, the king prevailed over the Hohenstaufen rebels. An interval of peace was procured, which, upon the death of Lothair, was followed by a renewal of the struggle. But now the parts were reversed. The Hohenstaufen were in power, the Welfs were in opposition, and it might seem that the resources at the disposal of the crown should have been sufficient to decide the issue. But if Conrad III was King of Germany, Henry the Proud was Duke of Saxony and Bavaria. What the king might do to abase the most powerful of his subjects, that Conrad endeavoured to contrive for the humiliation of Henry the Proud. He deprived him of Bavaria; he endeavoured to strip from him his duchy of Saxony. But there was an obstacle which Conrad, for all his Hohenstaufen *bravura*, could never overcome. The Saxon nation, which had little reason to love a Swabian, stood solid and staunch for the Welfs. Even when Henry the Proud suddenly died, leaving a lad of ten as his heir (*Henricus Leo, Dux Saxoniae et Bavariae*, as he afterwards styled himself), the people and princes of Saxony stood together to keep their duchy in the Welfic house. Conrad was compelled to acknowledge the unpalatable fact that his enemy was too strong to be broken and that only by a compromise peace, conceding Saxony but withholding Bavaria, could the country obtain relief from its domestic discords. The peace was struck (1142), but the animosities remained, casting a dark shadow over this unfortunate reign and threatening, unless some higher wisdom supervened, the disruption of the kingdom.

It was the great recommendation of Frederick Barbarossa, Conrad's nephew and successor, that his mother Judith was a Welf. With the blood of both factions running in his veins Frederick seemed marked out by destiny to bring the ruinous schism to an end. And this for a time he succeeded in doing, making friends with his cousin Henry the Lion and restoring to him the duchies of Saxony and Bavaria.

A chorus of praise surrounded the red-bearded king during his lifetime and has been echoed in tones of varying enthusiasm by subsequent historians. All the qualities most generally admired in the age of chivalry, courage, energy, good cheer, joy in battle, and love of adventure, the rough justice which goes with hearty common sense, and the geniality which accompanies superb physical health, belonged to Frederick. No German sovereign since Charlemagne possessed qualities so well fitted for the governance of the German people. He could both frighten and charm. Churchmen, nobles, peasants were prepared to regard him as the perfect knight.

To the modern mind it seems incredible that a ruler, succeeding to the government of a great country after a period of grave domestic struggles, should permit himself to be lured into distant enterprises of immense and unmeasured difficulty from which his subjects could not under any circumstances expect to derive a profit. But the German people did not then so reason. They were not disposed to blame a king who left his country to receive the imperial crown in Rome. To them the military expeditions of Frederick into Italy, costly as they were in blood and treasure, were no more reprehensible than the last quixotic crusading voyage undertaken in old age which led to the death of their sovereign in a distant Cilician stream. No German complained of Frederick that he governed too little. If in order to obtain assistance for his Italian wars he made reckless and extravagant concessions to the princes, setting up, for example, a duchy of Austria endowed with exorbitant privileges, no domestic critic raised a protest in the interests of central control. Frederick was the child of his age. If he moved in a mist of archaic romance, musing over Latin classics, fancying that he could revive the Roman Empire without the Roman legions, if he failed to appreciate the triple forces of the Lombard communes, the revived Papacy, and the Sicilian kingdom which were arrayed against him, he was not alone. The Germans, who would not have exchanged their brilliant knight-errant for the best organizer in the world, gave him their admiring confidence to the end.

In Italy the appearance of a German army was at no time regarded as an unmixed blessing. To Frederick it probably seemed a simple part of inherited duty that he should rescue the Pope from the newborn and violent republic of Rome, that he should receive the imperial crown, that he should put down his enemies and encourage his friends, and that he should recover for the Empire such fiscal rights as might have lapsed through the carelessness of his predecessor. But if he expected that these objects could be obtained easily and without resistance he was disillusioned on his first Roman journey. Then he learnt with what faint respect the republicans of Rome were prepared to treat the Emperor who had betrayed and the Pope who had burned Arnold of Brescia, their chosen leader. Hardly had the imperial coronation taken place when the German army was furiously attacked in the Leonine city and compelled to execute a retreat.

1155

But it was during his second Italian visit that Frederick provoked the great struggle with the Lombard communes which, beginning with the decrees of the Diet of Roncaglia in 1158, lasted until at the Peace of Constance in 1183 the Emperor was in effect compelled to acknowledge defeat. It is the practice of writers zealous for Italian nationality to represent this famous contest as marking the first stage in the growth of Italian liberty. Certainly a fine spirit of heroism and determination was shown in the struggle not only by Milan, which was a populous city, but by many a small Italian town which faced the formidable engines of the imperial army. The mere fact that Frederick at the head of his German chivalry was in 1176 routed by the townsmen of Milan on the field of Legnano was a notification to Europe that a new age was approaching in which statesmen would have to reckon with the military power of a middle class. Moreover, it was a novelty that a large number of Italian cities should combine in a league and enter into relations, as did the Lombards, with the Pope, with Sicily, with Byzantines and Venetians. Such a combination, even had it been unsuccessful, would have furnished a striking illustration of the weight to be attached to urban communities in the politics of Europe. But it is a mistake to suppose that this long-drawn struggle was at the time regarded as a contest between the German and Italian nations. The Italians, many of whom, especially among the northern aristocracy, were still conscious of their German origin, were divided. Some towns stood for the Emperor, others for the Pope. Nor would it have been fair to urge that the claims put forward by Frederick were those of a German usurper. The jurists of Bologna had affirmed that what Frederick demanded of the communes at Roncaglia was due to him as the heir of the Roman Emperors.

Closely mingled with the war of the Lombard League was a quarrel with the Papacy hardly to be avoided so long as Hildebrandine ideas survived in the Roman Curia and a resolute German Emperor was desirous of governing in Italy. At bottom the issue was always the same, " Which was supreme, Pope or Emperor?" or, as it was apt to be put in the feudal language of that time, " Did the Emperor hold his office as a fief from the Pope?" It is the part of wisdom in politics to avoid asking the largest questions, but as soon as this ultimate issue was raised a swarm of minor differences on points of procedure, of administrative convenience, of current Church policy came to life, as flies in the summer heat. Was the Emperor bound to lead the Pope's palfrey and to hold his stirrup? Could he nominate bishops or despoil their sees on vacancies? Could he claim provender for his armies or hospitality for his legates? On the first principle the German princes were of one mind. When at the Council of Besançon in October, 1157, Cardinal Roland, the eminent canon lawyer, acting as legate for Pope Hadrian IV, asked from whom did the Emperor hold his Empire if not from the Pope, the rash ecclesiastic barely escaped with his life.

Two years later this same cardinal, being known for his strong papal views, and having been concerned in bringing about a friendship between the Curia and Sicily, was elected Pope by part of the college and assumed the name of Alexander III. Other cardinals, either because they had been influenced by Germany or feared Roland and the Sicilians, elected the imperialist Cardinal Octavian, who took the name of Victor IV. Both Popes appealed to Frederick and by him were invited to submit their claims to a synod at Pavia.

And now Alexander III showed the world that the spirit of Hildebrand was still alive. He refused to attend the synod at Pavia. He declined to admit by his presence that the Emperor had any right to preside over a council of the Church or to dispose of the See of St. Peter. To the excommunication of the anti-pope, he replied by excommunicating the Emperor, by releasing his subjects from their allegiance, and by throwing himself upon the sympathy and hospitality of France.

The stars fought in their courses for this staunch and resourceful ecclesiastic. The Lombards rose against the oppressive German administration to which they had been submitted, with Venice, Sicily, Byzantium, and the Pope actively encouraging. The walls of Milan, which Frederick had razed to the ground, were rebuilt, the population which he had dispersed was re-

called. Then in the critical summer of 1167 a crowning mercy
was vouchsafed to the Church. Frederick had descended into
Italy with a large army, determined to strike at the two nerve
centres of rebellion, Rome, from which Alexander was now
guiding his coalition, and Sicily, which nourished the movement
with funds. At first fortune smiled on the imperialists. The
Romans were heavily defeated; the German army stormed into
St. Peter's; the Pope fled; the Emperor was crowned by his anti-
pope. A Pisan fleet appearing in the Tiber announced the impending conquest of Sicily. But in the course of a few hours the
August sun gave to Alexander an unexpected revenge. A
sudden fever struck the German army. Alone and unarmed
Frederick recrossed the Alps, leaving the flower of his chivalry
dead and withered on the Roman plain.

From this blow of fate Frederick never recovered. The army
which he brought into Italy upon his fourth expedition was too
small to re-establish his authority over an enemy which had
enjoyed seven years of respite from German attack. A small
force of German knights went down before the numerous
cavalry and pikemen of Milan upon the field of Legnano, and
their leader, reading the omens aright, determined to treat with
the Pope and to admit his claim. The meeting of Frederick and
Alexander in Venice on July 24, 1177, is commemorated by
three slabs of red marble in the porch of the cathedral of St.
Mark's indicating the spot where the Emperor knelt to the Pope
and received the kiss of peace. The scene made a deep impression. Not only to the Venetian crowd on the piazza did it seem
emblematic of the vanity of material force and of the triumph
of the spiritual principle in human affairs. Yet in truth
Frederick, while conceding no point of vital substance, had
gained the great advantage of peace.

From the decisive field of Legnano there was one important
absentee. For twenty-four years Henry the Lion had been permitted to govern his immense territories of Saxony and Bavaria
without let or hindrance from the Emperor. But now a cloud of
difference had arisen between the two men. Was it that
Frederick had bought Welf estates in Tuscany and Bavaria
which Henry coveted? Or that Henry was sated with Italian
adventures and preferred to be left free to deal with his own
difficult tasks in the north, where as a conspicuous tamer of
Wendish heathendom he has left a mark on the life of those

regions? Whatever the cause may be, Henry refused to help
his sovereign, and Frederick in consequence suffered the bitterness of defeat.

From this open variance there followed after an interval of
gathering hostility one result big with consequence for German
history. There were among the clergy and princes of Saxony
those who hated the imperious Lion and were waiting for an
occasion to pull him to the ground. A pretext was found, a
charge was levelled, but rather than appear before a hostile
court, Henry resorted to civil war. Stern punishment followed
upon his inevitable defeat and ultimate submission. He was
banished the country, and save for the two cities of Brunswick
and Luneburg stripped of his possessions. The great tribal
duchies were shared among lesser men, one of whom, Otto of
Wittelsbach, receiving part of Bavaria, founded a dynasty which
lasted till the German Revolution of 1918.

A tear of American learning falls upon the grave of ducal
Saxony. The vision of a German federal state, simple, orderly,
based upon the great tribal duchies each duly conserving its
customary law (*land recht* or state rights) and anticipating in
the heart of mediaeval Europe the principles of the American
republic, flatters the fancy of the transatlantic student. But such
ideas were foreign to the age of the Lion and the Redbeard.
The Lion was a great north German figure, honoured in the
sunset of his life, when his fighting days were over and he was
allowed to return from exile, as a patron of art and letters and
as the builder of the great cathedral of St. Blaise which still
enchants the visitor to Brunswick; but he was no more careful
of the rights of others than were the enemies who combined
to pull him down. Nor had Barbarossa, though his hand was
heavy on malefactors, and his rule was distinguished for its
penal legislation, a gift for creating institutions. When his
brilliant figure left the stage it was seen that his long reign of
stern repression and lavish gifts was but a disguised approach to
feudal chaos.

A wonderful glamour shines upon Frederick's last stage in
Europe through the marriage (January 27, 1186) of his son
Henry to Constance, the heiress presumptive of the Sicilian
kingdom. The rich and powerful island state which it had been

the Emperor's dream to conquer by arms was now to pass into the Hohenstaufen family on the easy terms of a marriage contract. Here, unexpectedly emerging from the diplomatic heaven, was the answer to the humiliations which Frederick had endured at the hands of the Romans and the Lombards, the Venetians and the Pope. Master of Germany in the north with its warlike feudal nobility, and of Sicily with its full treasury, its powerful fleet, its well-schooled Saracen army, the next Emperor would be well placed for imposing his will on refractory Popes and communes. But the very considerations which arrayed this conjunction in colours so pleasing to the Hohenstaufen made it a vital concern for the Papacy that their dynasty should be destroyed. The struggle once engaged was long and bitter. The Popes achieved their end. The offending dynasty was uprooted. But the cost of victory was a subservience to France which led through the Avignon captivity to an incalculable decline in papal prestige and so on to the Protestant Reformation.

The union of two countries so distinctive as Germany and Sicily, and divided from one another by the whole length of the Italian peninsula, presented a new range of difficult problems to the statesman. In Sicily the monarchy was hereditary, in Germany it was elective. In Sicily the King had acknowledged the Pope as his feudal superior; in Germany the claim of the Pope to be the feudal superior of the Emperor was hotly repudiated. It was now the established prerogative of the Archbishop of Cologne to crown the King of Germany. The Sicilian King was crowned by the Archbishop of Palermo. If it were deeply distasteful to the Sicilians to submit to a German sovereign, it was equally offensive to German pride to reflect that a time might come when their king might prefer the palms and orange groves at Palermo to the temperate climate of Aachen or Cologne, when the affairs of the Empire might be conducted by Saracens or Greeks, Englishmen or eunuchs, and German interests fatally postponed to those of a distant island.

That many of these difficulties were present to the acute intelligence of Henry VI is clear from some remarkable proposals which he made to the princes of Germany and to Pope Celestine III. His plan was that princes and Pope should agree to confer upon the Hohenstaufen dynasty an hereditary right to the German throne and that the Pope should crown his infant son Frederick King of the Romans. In return for these favours he proffered concessions—to the lay princes of Germany that their fiefs should be hereditary in the female and collateral line; to the prelates the renunciation of the *fas spolii*; and to the Pope, most important of all, an acknowledgment that the Empire was held as a fief from the Vicar of Christ. The rejection of this bold plan by princes and Pope effectually destroyed the project of an indissoluble union of the German and Sicilian crowns.

The historian is at once attracted and repelled by this hard and crafty son of the Red Beard who passed with his contemporaries as a scholar and died in 1197 after only seven years of rule, having already done many things that were wise, as well as others that were base and cruel, and who seems both in the scale of his ambitions and the novelty of his expedients to belong to the rank of creative politicians. But what principally matters in the context of events is not Henry's conquest of Sicily and designed conquest of Constantinople, nor his pacification of the Welfs, nor the meanness with which he exploited the captivity of Richard I to get money and power, nor that he sought the friendship of the Pope and planned a Crusade, but that he died young, leaving an infant to succeed him. During the long minority of Frederick II the political complexion of the world was profoundly altered.

BOOKS WHICH MAY BE CONSULTED

Cambridge Medieval History, Vol. V.
E. A. Freeman : Historical Essays. (Frederick Barbarossa.) 1892.
W. von Giesebrecht : Geschichte der deutschen Kaiserzeit. 1881-8.
Gregorovius : History of Rome in the Middle Ages. *Tr.* A. Hamilton. 1894-1900.
F. W. Thompson : Feudal Germany. 1928.
T. F. Tout : The Empire and the Papacy. 1903.
W. Stubbs : Germany in the Early Middle Ages. *Ed.* A. Hassall. 1908.
A. L. Poole : Henry the Lion. Lothian Historical Essay. 1912.

CHAPTER XX

INTELLECTUAL AND MONASTIC MOVEMENTS

Renaissance in the twelfth century. Medical studies at Salerno. Revival of Roman Law. English Common Law. Universities of Bologna and Paris. Origins of Oxford. Mediaeval university movements. The Monasteries.

WHILE the Crusades were thus powerfully affecting commerce and policy, another change, more profound in its effects, was coming over the intellectual life of western Europe. The twelfth century witnessed a renaissance of the European mind which, though more contracted in scope, is comparable in energy and creativeness with that great enlargement of custom and taste which divides the modern from the mediaeval world. The study of law and medicine, of logic and theology, received a new and powerful impetus. As conditions became more settled, travelling more secure, and the superfluities of life more easy to obtain, the thirst for knowledge, which is one of the primal appetites of man, began to assert itself afresh. Wandering students ranging from boys in their teens to grey-haired men might be seen on the roads travelling to such centres as were known to be distinguished by the presence of attractive teachers. Guilds were formed of learners as at Bologna, of instructors as at Paris, and after the manner of their kind evolved a body of rules and regulations for their guidance. From such associations arose the University, an institution which some mediaeval writers did not scruple to rank with the Papacy and Empire as an international force appointed by God for the direction and improvement of mankind.

It is a paradox that Italy, the seat of the Papacy, has been of all western countries throughout history the most secular. In contradistinction to the universities of the north, which grew up out of cathedral schools and developed their principal activities in the sphere of philosophical theology, the universities of Italy were founded by secular agencies and were mainly, though not exclusively, concerned with the prosecution of secular studies. The ancient University of Salerno was famous for a body of medical teaching based upon the writings of Hippocrates and Galen and the later experience of Jewish medical science. We may smile at this mediaeval medicine. It was devoid of the faintest knowledge of experimental anatomy. It was combined with astrology. It was prefaced by a careful study of the writings of Aristotle. Yet this is the principal root from which the science of the Renaissance was destined to grow. Nor can all value be denied to a course of training which gave to Dante his profound knowledge of Aristotelian philosophy and to Galileo his epoch-making interest in the stars.

More important in its immediate results was the revived study of Roman law (not that in Italy such learning had ever been allowed to die out) which is traced to the teaching of Irnerius during the early years of the twelfth century. The mediaeval expositions of the Digest, though characterized by learning and subtlety, were hardly more scientific, since they were devoid of historical background, than the contemporary science of the human body. Yet of all the intellectual influences affecting the politics and society of that time Roman jurisprudence was the most powerful, not only by reason of the infusion of its principles into the developing science of the canonist, not only by reason of the improvement which it was the means of introducing into the legal customs of Germany and France, but also because it was an arsenal of autocratic maxims. The great jurists of Bologna did not scruple to apply to the office of the Holy Roman Emperor the high prerogative which the lawyers of a long past age had ascribed to Diocletian or Constantine. In the struggle between the Empire and the Papacy the civilian lent the weight of his learning to the support of the imperial cause; nor was there a sovereign in Europe who was not prepared upon occasion to have recourse to those convenient maxims of absolute power which the learned doctors of the civil law were always so ready to supply.

There was, however, one striking limitation to the influence of this imposing system of jurisprudence. In England the teaching of practising lawyers was carried on, not at the universities, where both the Civil and the Canon Law were taught, but at professional schools, known as the Inns of Court, which were first set up in London in the reigns of the Edwards. To this circumstance we may principally ascribe the fact that the Common Law of England not only preserved its substantive existence, but was upon the whole a force making for liberty rather than for absolutism.

The University of Bologna, which in the twelfth century became pre-eminent as a law school, was managed by a guild of students, who hired the teachers, often failing to pay them their wages, and reduced them, in Dr. Rashdall's words, " to a most humiliating degree of servitude." " The professor," continues Dr. Rashdall, " was fined if he was a minute late for lectures, if he went beyond the time for closing, if he skipped a difficult passage or failed to get through in a given time the portions of the law-texts provided by the University. A committee of students—the *denunciatores doctorum*—watched over his conduct and kept the rectors informed of his irregularities. If the doctor wanted to be married a single day of absence was graciously allowed him but no honeymoon." From this iron and niggardly discipline the University was eventually rescued by the intervention of the city. Salaried chairs were established for professors chosen by the city, who being regularly and sufficiently paid came in time to monopolize the teaching. The civic university became popular in the prevailing secular atmosphere of Italy. By the end of the middle ages few considerable Italian states could afford to dispense with it.

Very different was the character and organization of the great University of Paris, which provided a model for the universities of the north. Here the prevailing study was not law but theology, the directing authority a guild not of students but of teachers. Originating from the cathedral school and subsisting under the shadow of the cathedral, the " Universitas " or guild of Paris masters was long treated with suspicion as an unlawful society, conspiring to undermine the authority of the bishop, his chancellor, and the chapter. For this suspicion some warrant may perhaps be found in the wild ferment of opinion which was excited by the free and fiery dialectic of Peter Abelard, the great Breton teacher (1079-1142), who first established the fame and popularity of Paris as a centre of thought and enquiry.

In truth, however, the orthodox Church had little to fear in that age from the speculations of academic philosophers. The voice of an isolated heretic was soon silenced in the lifetime of St. Bernard. Abelard was driven to recantation and a monastery, and when in the middle of the thirteenth century all the works of

Aristotle were made available for study in the west, this immense mass of ancient thought and knowledge was by a long process of devout and laborious gymnastic wrought into an exact and authoritative confirmation of the Catholic Faith.

Oxford derives from Paris, Cambridge from Oxford. If we would recall the turbulent life of those early gatherings of students and teachers out of which our universities arose, we must exclude from our field of vision the imposing buildings, the colleges, the libraries, the lecture rooms which now give to a university its fixity in space. The student of the twelfth century was like the Crusader, a pilgrim, travelling light and travelling often in quest of the Holy Grail of knowledge. Since there were no endowments to chain him to a particular place, since teaching was oral, and Latin the common language of the clerk all over the western world, teachers and pupils alike would wander from town to town and country to country. Sometimes they would voyage singly, sometimes in small groups, and sometimes, at the command of a sovereign or in a movement of protest or indignation, just as a modern trades union strikes against an employer, they would transfer themselves in large droves. Not seldom such a migration was the seed of a new university.

Such, at least, appears to have been the case at Oxford, though the evidence is not altogether complete. We know that in 1167-1168 a large body of English teachers and students were brought back from Paris by order of King Henry II as a result of his quarrel with the King of France; and it is clear that when later, in 1185, Giraldus Cambrensis read his *Topographia Hibernica* in Oxford there was already present in the city that organized body of teachers which is the sign of a *studium generale* or university. We have no direct evidence that the teachers and scholars who were brought back to England from Paris settled in Oxford. Yet it is probable that they did so and that the close and remarkable correspondence between the organization of the Universities of Oxford and Paris was due to this cause. Oxford, like Paris, was under the control of a bishop's chancellor, like Paris was originally organized in four nations with four proctors, and in time like Paris developed a system of residential colleges. Both universities were pre-eminent in scholastic philosophy and attractive to students from every part of Europe.

Compared with these two giants in the intellectual life of

mediaeval Europe, Cambridge, founded by a secession from Oxford in 1209, and even Orleans and Montpellier, the one renowned for law and the other for medicine, were of secondary importance.

In the ancient world culture and high birth went together. It was the grave misfortune of Europe in the middle ages that these two qualities admired of man were sharply dissociated. The business of the knight was to fight and hunt; the duty of the clerk was to pray and learn. The universities of the middle ages were not designed to civilize the fierce aristocracies into whose hands the conduct of European affairs was consigned as a consequence of the barbaric invasions. Rather they were the result of a spontaneous popular movement carried out under the shelter and direction of the Church and partly as a response to the growing need for doctors, lawyers, and an educated clergy. With all this clerkly hum and bustle, this busy talk about the real and the nominal, universal and particular, the fighting and hunting nobleman had little to do. The students who flocked in their thousands to the universities came, as they have always mainly come, from the middle and lower ranges of society. The poor and ambitious saw in the university a free career to talent. But how many endured to the end of the long course of five or six years in the arts and of twelve or thirteen years in theology which were required for graduation? The failed M.A.'s and D.D.'s of mediaeval Europe must have been almost as numerous as the failed B.A.'s of Calcutta University. Yet something was gained. A thin layer of education, a smattering of Latin and logic was widely spread.

Moreover, the university movement had the virtue of a steady growth in recognized importance and volume. It became the theory that it was the special and, indeed, sole privilege of the Pope or the Emperor to grant the *jus ubique docendi* which was asserted to be the hallmark of a *studium generale* or university. The age of apostolic poverty was succeeded by the age of lavish endowments. In 1252 Robert de Sorbon, the chaplain of Louis IX, founded the first of the sixty colleges which in the middle ages were built for the reception of university students in Paris. A few years later his example was followed by Walter de Merton at Oxford. The visitor to Paris may still see on the left bank of the Seine the Rue de Fouarre where Dante may have heard lectures. He may still enter the curious little Church of St.

Julien le Pauvre where the first Masters of Arts of the Paris University used to hold their meetings. But only a name attached to an uncouth modern building recalls the memory of the Sorbonne, and of the sixty mediaeval colleges of Paris not a stone remains. England has been more fortunate, and in the splendid collegiate foundations at Oxford and Cambridge preserves a memorial of the munificence and piety of a vanished age.

The European monasteries of the middle ages were often criticized and often reformed. In the west, Order followed upon Order, Chartreux after Cluny, Cîteaux after Chartreux, Prémontré after Cîteaux, but always with the same tale of high initial ardour and enthusiasm giving place to spells of laxity and imperfection. Yet the possible loss to society through the enforced celibacy of many of the best men and women in every generation was never a matter of comment in an age which regarded celibacy as the first and the hardest of the human virtues. Particular monasteries were assailed, now on grounds of moral scandal, now as hard and grasping landlords. To no one since Rutilius Namatianus in the fifth century did it occur to dispute the value of the monastic life or to regard it as squalid and degrading to man.

The reason is clear. Apart from the shelter which they afforded to devout and peace-loving natures against the rough gales of mediaeval life, the monasteries rendered services which we have now either ceased to require or can obtain more efficiently from other sources. In many cases the monastery was a missionary establishment, sometimes a bank of deposit, a hostelry for the refreshment of wayfarers, an improving landlord, a centre of education and scholarship, as well as of those arts and crafts which are enlisted in the conduct of any great establishment, a collector and recorder of current news, a storehouse of manuscripts, a depository of political knowledge, foreign and domestic, an organ for the reclamation of waste land and for the planting of civilization in babarous and pagan tracts. The services performed by the great German monasteries of Fulda and Corvey or by the Cistercian monks in Spain and northern England were of this pioneering character. They were at once missionaries, educators, and landlords. The expansion of civilized life in these regions is not a little due to the powerful and often ruthless impulsion of these organized bodies of dedicated men.

We owe much of our knowledge of the early middle ages to Latin chronicles compiled by monks. After the beginning of the thirteenth century historical writing escapes from the cloister and laymen begin to describe in the vernacular language the things which they have seen and the persons whom they have met. We have Villehardouin's sparkling history of the Fourth Crusade and Joinville's exquisite Life of St. Louis, and later the flowing chronicles of Froissart the Fleming and of Villani the Florentine. With the fourteenth century, too, we may dip into the English year-books or legal records and there come across a store, unexampled in volume, of the authentic talk of English litigants in the provincial French which was then the language of the law courts. But the chronicling of the age which lies between the barbaric invasions and the rise of the universities in the later half of the twelfth century was left mainly to the monks. Then the *scriptorium* of the abbey was the only secure centre for literary work and the monkish scribe the chief pillar of learning. If much of his work was poor, scanty, and unintelligent, some chronicles were vivacious and well informed, and here and there the monasteries produced a real historian. Posterity must not repudiate its debt to the mediaeval monasteries, to Monte Casino and Bobbio, to Reichenau and St. Gall, to Corvey and Fulda, to Bec and Mont St. Michel, to Jarrow and later to St. Albans. Much of our scholarship, not a little of our historical knowledge, is founded on the diligence of scribes, many of them nameless, who have toiled over crabbed manuscripts by a feeble rushlight in unwarmed cells in the hope that the labour of their pens might be acceptable to the Lord.

And now Europe has passed into a stage of civilization in which abbeys, while they may still live and function, are differently related to the facts of the age. No longer is the endowment of an abbey by prince or noble regarded as a short and simple road to the soul's salvation. No longer do men go to the abbey for news, for they have the daily press and the wireless; no longer for refreshment and shelter, for there is the inn and the casual ward. The task of education is performed by the universities and schools. Gone, too, is the function of the *scriptorium*, for the printing press multiplies books and the libraries store them; and gone the ministration of charitable relief. Long ago the temporal rulers have turned elsewhere for political counsel. It is with difficulty that the traveller, as he surveys the

shell of some ancient abbey, standing ruined and forlorn among
the sweet English pastures, can recapture in imagination the
distant hours of monastic influence when in a society much
simpler than our own and for a population less numerous the
abbey was a busy centre of social life and its strongest link with
the great world beyond.

Modern society is more willing to avail itself of the gratuitous
social service rendered by nuns. In Catholic countries religious
sisterhoods still perform much of the humanitarian work which
was expected of them in mediaeval times. They nurse the sick,
tend the poor, teach the young, console the dying. The education
of girls is largely in their hands. That which was purest and
best in mediaeval monasticism survives in these devoted women.

BOOKS WHICH MAY BE CONSULTED

H. Rashdall : Universities of Europe in the Middle Ages. 1895.
R. L. Poole : Illustrations of the History of Mediaeval Thought and
    Learning. 1920.
C. Mallet : History of the University of Oxford. 1924.
J. B. Mullinger : The University of Cambridge from the Earliest Times,
    1873-84.
C. H. Haskins : Studies in Mediaeval Culture. 1929.
C. H. Haskins : The Renaissance of the Twelfth Century. 1927.
Helen Waddell : The Wandering Scholars. 1927.
G. G. Coulton : Monastic Schools in the Middle Ages. 1913.
G. G. Coulton : Five Centuries of Religion. 1923-7.
G. G. Coulton : Mediaeval Studies. 1905-21.
G. G. Coulton : The Mediaeval Scene. 1930.

CHAPTER XXI

MUNICIPAL GROWTH

Growth and emancipation of towns. Civic feuds. Growth of commerce. Differing municipal development in different parts of Europe. The German Hanse and the Scandinavian countries.

By the beginning of the twelfth century the trade and industry of western Europe had sufficiently recovered from the interruption caused by the Saracens to permit of a sensible growth in municipal liberties. The great historic cities of the Roman Empire, whose population had been depleted through the destruction of sea-borne commerce, began to recover something of their former numbers and affluence. Villages grew into walled towns. Suburbs of merchants and craftsmen spread themselves round castle or borough. In France we hear of *villeneuves, sauvetés, bastides,* names which denote the movement towards new urban aggregations which was proceeding through the country. From such developments followed two consequences of great importance. The merchants and craftsmen organized themselves in guilds and began to demand conditions under which money could be safely made. In broad outline they claimed to be permitted to compound for their own farm or taxes (the *firma burgi*), to be permitted to make their own bye-laws, to be relieved of onerous feudal servitudes, to have their civil suits tried in their own courts and within their own walls, to be able to select their own officers, and that serfs resident for a year and a day within a town or borough should be regarded as free. Such is a rough epitome of the liberties and privileges which with infinite varieties of detail and liberality are to be found inscribed in the town charters of the twelfth century. It is less important to consider by what means such charters were obtained, whether as at Laon by a revolutionary struggle or as in London by a monetary transaction or by a peaceful process of permitted growth, than to note the point that in some way or other all the large and most of the small towns in Europe had by the end of the twelfth century obtained a positon of special privilege. At one end of the scale were urban republics, such as Venice or Marseilles and to a slightly lesser degree London : at the other end little country towns which had obtained no more than the right to compound for their taxes.

Man is an imitative animal. The privileges liberally accorded to one city were soon demanded by others less plentifully endowed; and the third estate, once it had arrived and had begun to organize its forces, steadily grew in power and influence.

Being small and insecure (London, a Leviathan among our English cities, can hardly have numbered more than twenty thousand inhabitants), mediaeval towns were everywhere fortified and organized for defence. M. Pirenne, writing more particularly of the Low Countries, tells us that up to the close of the middle ages a sum never falling short of five-eighths of the communal budget was expended on purposes connected with the maintenance of the walls and the provision of instruments of war. In Italy, despite the fact that she was now fast securing for herself the leadership of the world in craftsmanship and international commerce, the warfare of city with city was almost perpetual. · Cities would fight about diocesan boundaries and feudal rights, over tolls and markets, for the extension of their powers over the *contado* or surrounding country, or in pursuance of the long inherited feuds of the nobles within their walls. Mere contiguity was a potent cause of fiery and enduring hatreds. If Florence took one side in a quarrel, it was sufficient for Pisa, Siena, and Genoa to take the other; if Milan entered into an alliance with other cities, it would not at least be with Cremona and Pavia; and so long as the exploitation of Corsica and Sardinia was an open question between them, Genoa and Pisa were inveterate in rivalry. Accordingly no large principle of policy decided the alignment of the Italian cities in the great quarrel between Empire and Papacy. Since Florence was papal or Guelf, her neighbour Siena was naturally imperialist or Ghibelline; since Cremona was Ghibelline, Crema must be Guelf. The quarrel between the Empire and the Papacy enlisted, but did not create, the civic feuds of Italy. These animosities, the vendetta of the *consorzeria* or Lombard clan, the feud of aggrandisement and commercial jealousy, the feud arising out of personal slights, were active all over Italy before that universal issue was raised. The great political struggle of the middle ages only gave a new colour and intensity to rivalries already so sharp and warlike that in every city the inhabitants were organized as a militia of horse and foot.

Nevertheless trade and industry made steady progress. In the government arsenals of Venice and Genoa fleets were built for military and commercial purposes upon a scale and with a rapidity which would have astounded the generation that preceded the First Crusade. A constant stream of merchants from every corner of western Europe found their way to the six fairs of Champagne which by the middle of the twelfth century had established themselves as the chief northern centres for the exchange of goods and the settlement of international debts. The Charter of St. Omer in 1127, the first of a long series, marks the rising affluence of the Flemish towns. The wool of England, the cloth of Frisia, the fustians of Augsburg, the silks of Paris were beginning to obtain their international renown. Though the science of political economy was still in the far distance, the Counts of Flanders were shrewd enough to discern the value of a fixed coinage and a single standard of weights and measures. Ghent and Bruges, Cologne and Hamburg were rising into prominence. Lübeck was founded in 1143. Even to an Italian visitor the wealth and importance of the city magnates in London seemed in the reign of Stephen to be imposing. The Danube and the Rhine, the Rhone and the Seine were bringing the civilized world into a commercial relationship. The outlines of the European economic system, as it persisted until the discovery of America, were now fixed.

Very various was the ultimate fate of the cities of Europe, which in the twelfth century, thanks to the principles of self-help and free association, were making such progress in the arts of life. It was the destiny of the English boroughs to be incorporated in a national parliamentary system which, while it limited their independence, enlarged their usefulness. In France the communal movement, born of revolution, ended in royal control. But in Germany and Italy a strong central government was lacking. Here there was no monarch to control, no parliament to canalize and direct the manifold energies of urban life. It is accordingly in these two countries that the power and autonomy of the mediaeval city is most conspicuously illustrated, that cities grow into imperial states, form leagues for commerce and war, and are capable of subjecting the Emperor himself to a decisive defeat. And who, when he considers the variety and

brilliance of Italian city life or the vigorous contribution of the
Hanseatic League to the commerce and architecture of northern
Germany, will be prepared to say that the breakdown of central
government was in these regions an unmixed misfortune for the
human race?

The flowering time of the Hanseatic League lies in the fourteenth century, before the discovery of the New World had
revolutionized the commerce of Europe or the English had
developed a mercantile marine, and while the dominant merchant guilds in the Baltic cities were as yet unshaken by mutiny
from below. Then a golden opportunity to become the common
carrier of the north was spread before the German trader.
While the Edwards were ruling in England, many a North German merchant throve on the carriage of wool and cloth, of corn
and wine, of fabrics and furs for the wealthy or of pickled herring for all the world. Indeed long before the century had begun,
the " Easterling " was a well-known figure in London, so affluent
and long established in the *Hans* house or Guild Hall and so important as a factor in the foreign trade of the island, that
Easterling in its shortened form of sterling came to denote the
standard coin of the British realm.

Not that business in those days was a safe and easy matter
for the North German trader. There were pirates on the high
seas, bandits and toll-exacting nobles on the roads. More particularly there was the windy peninsula of Denmark, always an
uncomfortable blot on the German landscape, since it controlled
the Sound which is the channel between the North Sea and the
Baltic, and was therefore in a position to work much mischief
among the fishing fleets or trading vessels of the mainland.
How best to handle these troublesome Danes, to secure privileges for German factories in the Scandinavian countries and in
England, or to safeguard German fishing and commerce, were
problems too difficult for any one city to solve for itself. Self-
help and combination were imperative, for the Emperor was
distant and powerless, and the Saxon house which had once
been great had gone down with Henry the Lion. At last the
great mercantile oligarchies listened to the call of circumstance.
1241 There was a union between Lübeck and Hamburg which was
by degrees so widened out that every important northern town
from Novgorod to Bruges was included within its orbit. It was
a league of merchants. No noble or craftsman exercised power

in these trading republics, nor did any man of high political genius emerge from their parliaments. The merchants of the Hanse were only by accident politicians. There is no reason to think that they ever contemplated the onerous burden of a permanent federation for the political control of the Baltic. It was sufficient if, meeting at irregular times and with varying numbers, they were able to deal with the pressing commercial problems of the moment. Once only did the Hanseatic traders, coming into sharp collision with a tiresome Danish king, threaten to play a decisive part in the politics of the north. The two wars of the League with Waldemar III are famous in Hanseatic annals. The Treaty of Stralsund (1370), which gave to the victorious merchant republics the control of the Sound and the fisheries and a voice in the selection of the Danish King, appeared to point to the establishment of a traders' empire on the Baltic. Lübeck, wrote Aeneas Sylvius, a gifted Italian traveller, in 1458, "possesses such wealth and such power that Denmark, Sweden, and Norway are accustomed to elect and depose kings upon a sign from her." Nothing great came of it. The Hanse produced no Robert Clive. The temperature of co-operation in mediaeval Germany could nowhere and at no time be kept at a steady and effective level.

During the later half of the fifteenth century the League began slowly to decline in power and influence. The herrings, turning their dainty noses from the Baltic to the British coast, provided a gainful livelihood for generation after generation to English and Scottish fishermen. The Easterling was ousted from the British carrying trade. As the century advanced political development assumed a shape which was unfavourable to the "general company of German merchants." The prince out-topped the city. Loyalty to the territorial sovereign proved to be more potent than attachment to a league of merchant towns which, while they had several common interests, were always in the last resort rivals in trade. Brandenburg, Burgundy, Sweden, in their separate spheres of territorial influence, overshadowed the League. By the end of the century the cities on the inland seas had had their day.

To all this mediaeval development of North German trade, the Scandinavian kingdoms, had they been linked in a durable union, might have offered a serious counterpoise. But when has there been a real Scandinavia? Even when Denmark, Sweden,

and Norway were brought together under the Danish Crown at
the Union of Kalmar (1397-1523) Danish rule was never effectual
or uncontested in Sweden. At last the yoke was violently thrown
off, in circumstances calculated to brand deeply upon the
popular mind of Sweden a horror of the Danes. "The blood
bath of Stockholm" contrived by King Christian II (of that
German house of Oldenburg which had ruled in Copenhagen
since 1448) was the attempt of a hasty tyrant to found by the
pitiless massacre of his enemies a government which was lacking in every element of popular confidence and esteem. The
crime was speedily avenged. A young Swede came forward to
rally the peasants of his native land against the alien. His
name was Gustav Eriksson and he was afterwards known as
Gustavus Vasa. The war of liberation (1520-1523) led by this
Swedish counterpart of William Wallace of Scotland gave to
Sweden a national dynasty and ushered in the heroic period of
her history.

BOOKS WHICH MAY BE CONSULTED

W. J. Ashley : Economic Organisation of England. 1914.
H. Pirenne : Mediaeval Cities, their Origin and the Revival of Trade.
Tr. H. P. Halsey. 1925.
C. Gross : The Gild Merchant. 1890.
H. Zimmern : The Hansa Towns. 1889.
R. Lodge ; The Close of the Middle Ages. 1923.
D. Schaefer : Die Hanse. 1903.
H. Pirenne : Histoire de Belgique. 1909.
J. C. L. Sismondi : History of the Italian Republics. (Everyman's
Library.) 1907.

THE PONTIFICATE OF INNOCENT III

Zenith of the papal power under Innocent III. The evangelical revival.
St. Francis. Challenge to the Papacy from the Albigenses. St. Dominic.
Franciscans and Dominicans. The heresies of Joachim of Flora and
Siger of Brabant. The Church masters its critics.

As we cross the threshold of the thirteenth century the dream
of world dominion, which had died with an Emperor, springs
to life again in the policy of a Pope. We come to Innocent III,
the proud Roman patrician and trained canonist, who, reaching
the Papal Chair at the early age of thirty-seven years and profiting by a temporary eclipse of the Empire, brought the Papacy
to the summit of its power. This is the Pope under whose rule
the western Church was imposed on Constantinople, who dared
to place England and France under interdict, who launched the
most successful of the Spanish Crusades, who exacted from the
rulers of England, Aragon, and Portugal the surrender of their
respective countries as fiefs to be held of the Holy See, and did
not scruple first to excommunicate King John, and then, when
the culprit had made an abject submission, to set aside the
Magna Carta and to excommunicate the barons by whom it
was supported. It was this energetic ruler who cleared the Germans out of central Italy and Sicily, made himself master of
Rome, preserved against dangerous opposition the Sicilian
inheritance of his ward, the child Frederick, fomented a
terrible civil war in Germany, and then made and unmade
Emperors on terms most favourable to the Roman Church,
and lastly crushed out the formidable Albigensian heresy in
southern France, and with it the civilization of a brilliant
people.

The bare catalogue of these wide-ranging temporal activities
suggests a theocracy tyrannically worked and slavishly accepted.
Such an inference, however, would be false to history. There
was indeed no limit to the claims which Innocent was prepared
to make on behalf of his exalted office. It was his view that the
Pope was the Vicar of Christ, that he was as Melchisedec, prince

and king in one, that he had the " plenitudo potestatis," and
that he had the right, seeing that a Pope had transferred the
Empire from the Greeks to the Franks, to exercise his own dis-
cretion in the choice of emperors. But to the contemporaries of
Innocent there was nothing outrageous or tyrannical in these
opinions. It was common ground that the spiritual was above
the temporal power, that the Pope was supreme Head of the
church and the ultimate authority on all matters of faith and
ecclesiastical discipline. That he could excommunicate a
sovereign, that he could shake the basis of social order in a state
by releasing its citizens from their allegiance, or impose upon it
the extreme penalty of the interdict was not denied. The men
of the thirteenth century were agreed on the principle of a seat
of authority in religion, a supreme spiritual arbiter in temporal
affairs, an institution professing the rule of sanctity and justice,
an ultimate tribunal before which they might lay their causes.
The great multiplication of appeals to the Papal Curia under
Innocent III is proof that the Roman Court met the needs of the
time. Against all manner of local tyrannies and oppressions there
was in the last resort an appeal to Rome.

Yet under this apparent concord there was much variety of
belief and experience. The middle ages were neither so virtuous,
nor so orthodox, nor so stupid as is often supposed. There was
bestial immorality as well as stern asceticism, fantastic heresy as
well as compliant acceptance of the orthodox faith, and an intellectual ingenuity which, had it been directed to the cross-
examination of nature, would have anticipated by many centuries the benefits of modern science.

The problem before the Papacy in the thirteenth century was
how best to control a society greatly enriched in its experience
through the Crusades, more travelled, more acquisitive, more
pleasure-loving, but also, partly by reason of this opening-out
of the near eastern world and the tumultuous development of
lay interests which followed in its train, and partly owing to the
revival of intellectual life, more disturbed in its beliefs. The
pontificate of Innocent III corresponds with a brilliant development of vernacular poetry in Germany and France; a poetry
owing its impulses no doubt to the romance of the Crusades,
though its greatest themes are found in earlier history, and
giving ideal expression to the sentiments of chivalry which then
prevailed in the lay world.

It is during these years that the Minnesingers of Germany and the troubadours of Provence produced some of their best work, that Wulfram of Eschenbach wrote Parsifal, that Gottfried of Strasburg wrote Tristan and Isolde, and that the spirit of far-off German history is recaptured in the great epic of the Niebelungenlied.

The expression of the lay spirit in vernacular literature was one aspect of the sense of liberation which was now coming into Europe. An evangelical revival was another, a strong development of positive heresy was a third.

The evangelical revival, which starts with St. Francis of Assisi and St. Dominic the Castilian, was one of those profound and sacrificial movements of the heart, which long after its original purity of intention and practice has disappeared, continues to affect the lives of men. St. Francis, the son of a rich cloth merchant in a small Umbrian town, was born in 1181 or 1182. As a youth he was gay, careless, open-handed, in love with chivalry and ambitious of a soldier's career. Then he experienced a conversion. An illness contracted in prison in Perugia (for he was captured by the forces of that neighbour town in a skirmish) brought out the latent powers of an original religious genius, so loving, naïf, delicate and gay, so swift and instinctive in its response to suffering, so full of chivalry and poetic symbolism that it provides the sovereign charm which unites Christians of all denominations. One day meeting a leper he dismounted from his horse and kissed him. Later a voice ordered him to repair a ruined chapel near Assisi. He became a hermit, broke with his family, and lived on alms, rebuilding with his own hands the deserted chapels in the neighbourhood. Then on February 24, 1208, he heard the lesson of the day in the church of Portiuncula (Matt. x.): "As ye go, preach, saying, The kingdom of heaven is at hand. Heal the sick, cleanse the lepers, raise the dead, cast out devils: freely ye have received, freely give. Provide neither gold, nor silver, nor brass in your purses, nor scrip for your journey, neither two coats, neither shoes, nor yet staves: for the workman is worthy of his hire." The words struck home. Barefoot he went out into the world to preach repentance.

The religious prospect was troubled and uncertain. The great monastic foundations of the twelfth century, Grammont, Clairvaux, Prémontré, once the early fervour had died away, had

settled down to the management of their estates, the sale of their
wool, and the discharge of the multifarious responsibilities
which worldly endowments bring in their train.

The most powerful of the Popes was carrying out a great
secular design, not without much effusion of blood. The
contrast between primitive Christianity and the Church as it
had become, rich, secure, worldly, ambitious, affected many
minds. Prophecies floated about that a new age was at hand,
an age of love, dominated by the Holy Ghost in succession to the
past dispensation of law and of grace. Heresies were springing
up among poor, unlearned folk—there were said to be seventeen
heretical sects in Milan—by way of protest against sacerdotal
claims and even against matter itself, thought to be the creation
of the evil principle. Italy, racked by civil war and hatred, was
asking for something which the Roman Curia, so learned and
wise in Canon Law and so scrupulous in its judgments, but
also so remote from the poor and humble, had not yet been
able to give.

It was, then, wise of Innocent III to sanction, as after some
demur he did, the rule of St. Francis and to submit the saint
to the ecclesiastical tonsure. A great religious force which might
otherwise have been lost to the Church was now brigaded in its
ranks. The poor brothers of St. Francis (Fratres Minores,
Minorites, Grey Friars) wandered through Italy, preaching in
Italian as simple folk to simple folk, and going everywhere, as
well into remote hamlets as into the poor quarters of large
towns, with their call to poverty and repentance. The movement was the more effective because the early disciples were
neither churchmen nor schoolmen. The illiterate multitude
could understand a message, pure of all subtlety or artifice, and
delivered in the vulgar tongue by men and women who practised the doctrines of poverty and contentment, love and
humility, which they preached to others. By such manifest enthusiasm those who were merely orthodox before were tempted
to become religious now, and those who were heretical discarded
their heresies. That Italy was saved an Albigensian crusade may
be ascribed to the influence of St. Francis and his followers,
who gave in a form acceptable to the Church the satisfaction which many Italians were disposed to find in open
revolt.

Unlike Francis the founder of the Dominican Order was

trained for the Church and already a cathedral dignitary in
Spain, when a sudden turn was given to his life by an accidental
encounter with a heretic in Toulouse. To defend the orthodox
faith against the impassioned votaries of the Catharan or Albigensian heresy which was sweeping everything before it in
southern France became henceforth the central passion of his
life. During the eleven critical years (1205-1216) when the papacy
was at grips with this movement, Dominic was in the centre
of the fray, expounding doctrine, disputing heresies, and
gathering round him a band of preachers like-minded with him
self.

At an early stage of these operations the ardent Spaniard was
convinced that the enemy was only to be met by a moral force
equal to his own. The Cathari professed and to a large degree
practised an extreme form of asceticism. In the *consolamentum*
or rite of initiation, the initiate, who was invested like a
Brahmin with a sacred thread, swore to renounce the works
of Satan and the Holy Catholic Church. Believing that matter
was inherently evil, he condemned marriage, practised vege-
tarianism, and refused to countenance the shedding of blood
either in peace or war. Perfection in this hard school of mystical
self-discipline was not given to all, but it was attainable by a
few who upon death would assume a spiritual body without the
intervening delays of purgatory; and these elect and purified
souls it was the duty of the whole Church to venerate. Dominic
saw that the austere mystic of southern France would always
prevail over the soft-living legates and abbots who endeavoured
to convert him. Accordingly he took upon himself a life of
voluntary poverty and inculcated it upon his associates, not out
of mystical enthusiasm, but in his hard-headed Castilian way
as a means of influence. Meeting Francis later in Italy, he was
no doubt confirmed in his view that the renunciation of worldly
goods was, not in southern France only, where it could be employed as an instrument of war against an heretical Puritanism,
but everywhere, a source of unusual spiritual influence. He
determined to found an Order of Preachers bound by vows of
poverty and owing obedience only to the head of their Order
and to the Pope. To this project, too, Innocent III accorded his
assent.

The army which was then enlisted in the service of the
Papacy was an army very different from any which had

previously been enrolled under its banner. The begging Friars were ready to go everywhere and to do anything. No mission was too distant or too dangerous for these dedicated men, who stood outside every diocese and were independent of every bishop save only the Bishop of Rome. There was no country in Europe into which the Friar did not penetrate, bringing with him the stir of a religious revival. For work in heathen countries no missionary was more available. He was to be found in Morocco and Tunis. He preached to the motley crowds in Syrian seaports. He voyaged to Persia and India and to the distant parts of China. Nor were his energies wholly expended on the tasks of the missionary and revivalist. Dominic, rightly seeing that the time had now come when the faith must be defended against intellectual antagonists, was resolved that his Order should be studious. The old obligation of manual labour was replaced by the unfamiliar call to learning. The Dominican was charged to equip himself for intellectual combat and posted to the scenes of intellectual danger and activity. After a brief interval, the Franciscan, discarding the pious prejudice of his founder, elected to tread the same path of education and knowledge. He too frequented universities and made his contribution to theological science. If the Dominicans can boast of Albert the Great and Thomas Aquinas, the most original of mediaeval thinkers was a Franciscan from Oxford. So daring were his speculations and experiments, so forward reaching and comprehensive his mind, that it is a moot question to which of the two founders the genius of Roger Bacon would have been more disconcerting, to St. Francis, who distrusted the pride of learning, or to St. Dominic, who hated the poison of enquiry.

In theory the Friars were not permitted to own property. In practice bequests of land, houses, and money were made for their use to the Holy See, to the communities of towns, and to private individuals. Some endowment, bitterly as the principle of property was denounced by "the spirituals" of the movement, was probably essential to the effective and steady discharge of apostolic duty, more particularly in the cities; but wealth brought its familiar dangers. Before the end of the thirteenth century the Friars were sometimes accused of luxury and avarice. Nor were these the only charges. Popular preaching, no less than material wealth, has its special dangers. In his desire to impress and amuse, the travelling Friar often took leave of good sense and sound learning. The monks might be lazy, the parish priests might be dull, but in the eyes of the steadier villagers the Friar was a vagabond, an intruder, and a charlatan.

BOOKS WHICH MAY BE CONSULTED

Cambridge Mediaeval History, Vol. VI.
Sabatier : Vie de St. François d'Assise. 1931.
J. E. Renan : Études d'histoire Réligieuses. 1858.
H. C. Lea : History of the Inquisition of the Middle Ages. 3 vols. 1906.
E. Gebhart : L'Italie Mystique. 1906.

CHAPTER XXIII

THE FOURTH CRUSADE

Crusading policy of Innocent III. The Venetians divert the Crusade. Latin conquest of Constantinople. Weakness of the Latins. Rivalry between Venice and Genoa. Opportunity for spreading Greek culture squandered. Decline in religious motives and theocratic ideas.

NOTHING seems better to illustrate the limitations of papal power in the thirteenth century than the fate which befell the foreign policy of Innocent III. The object closest to the heart of that great Pope was the recovery of the Holy Land by a Crusade launched and directed by the Vicar of Christ. All quarrels were to be composed, all schisms ended. The joint force of the reunited Greek and Roman Churches was to be gathered together for the general overthrow of the Moslem power.

Of this ambitious programme, pursued throughout the whole course of his pontificate, nothing was accomplished. Europe was never united. The Holy Sepulchre remained in pagan hands, and the great Crusade which was set on foot to recover it was against the Pope's express injunction diverted by the Venetians for the capture of Constantinople. But perhaps the fact which is most striking is not that the strongest of the Popes failed to realize his hopes of the Crusade, but the obvious decline in the power of the religious motive which his failure implied. " You advise me," replied Richard to Fulk de Neuilly, the promoter of the Fourth Crusade, " to dismiss my three daughters, pride, avarice, and incontinence: I bequeath them to the most deserving: my pride to the Knights Templars, my avarice to the monks of Cîteaux; and my incontinence to the prelates." Neither Richard I of England nor Philip Augustus of France, nor the two contending Guelf and Ghibelline champions in Germany could be enticed to exchange their domestic interests for this distant adventure. By a chapter of accidents the task of directing the course of the Crusade lapsed to the Republic of Venice, upon whose good offices the valiant nobles of France and Flanders who had responded to the Pope's appeal were dependent for their conveyance across the sea. The atmosphere of the Rialto was very different from that of the Vatican. The Venetians, as the leading merchants of the Levant, had made too much money out of infidels actively to desire their destruction, and to the religious indifference and avarice of trade united the pride of a republic which had freed itself from Byzantium and was little disposed to accept dictation from Rome. In the necessities of the Crusaders who were short of money for their passage Enrico Dandolo, the aged doge, descried a prospect of more than ordinary advantage to his fellow-citizens.

The first idea of the Crusaders was to attack Egypt, from the conquest of which, seeing that it was the centre of Moslem power in the near east, the recapture of Palestine could be expected to ensue. The Venetians, however, thought otherwise. With Egypt they were so little disposed to quarrel, that they made a treaty with the Sultan under which they were assured a number of valuable privileges in the Egyptian markets. It was desirable then that the Crusaders should at all costs be headed off Egypt. A far more profitable objective from the Venetian angle was an expedition to overthrow Alexius III, the Greek Emperor who had been so unwise as to penalize the Venetian colony in Constantinople while lavishing privileges upon their hated rivals of Pisa. Fortunately the attack upon this Christian monarch, which was, in truth, but an extension of the commercial rivalry between two Italian cities, was capable of being represented in a specious guise to the simple minds of the Crusaders. Alexius III was vulnerable. He had imprisoned and blinded his brother Isaac Angelus, under whose negligent rule the Greek Empire had sunk to the last abyss of decrepitude. The son of Isaac, called, like his usurping uncle, Alexius, was on tour in the west, seeking to obtain support for the restoration of his father. The young Byzantine prince had little difficulty in enlisting the sympathies of Philip of Swabia, the King of the Romans, and of Boniface of Montferrat, the chosen leader of the Crusade. It cost this enterprising youth nothing to make promises flattering at once to the avarice of the traveller and the piety of the pilgrim. He would distribute 200,000 silver marks, would serve on crusade himself, supply 10,000 men for the reconquest of Palestine, and a perpetual force of 500 knights for the protection of the Christian establishments in the east. Buoyed by such glittering expectations, the leaders fell in with the Venetian scheme and resolved to dethrone the offending Emperor.

At first everything prospered for the imposing Venetian armada in the Bosphorus. Constantinople was taken, the cowardly Alexius found safety in flight, and Isaac and his son were solemnly crowned. The first objective of the Crusaders having been thus secured, it might seem that they should now have been free to accomplish the real purpose of their enterprise. But the expectation that the Greeks would rally round two princes, the one blind and incompetent, the other the reckless author of his country's recent humiliation, and both elevated to power by a hateful and insolent enemy, was too wild to be realized. A fierce rebellion broke out against the Latins and their protégés. A second siege of Constantinople was followed by a second capture, and from that moment the foundation of some kind of Latin state on the Bosphorus became inevitable.

1204

Had it been possible to impart to the new polity something of the concentrated vigour which England and Sicily received from their Norman conquerors, the main purpose of the Crusade might still have been achieved.

But the Latin masters of Constantinople were as little capable of promoting the papal policy as the effeminate Greeks whom they had so violently displaced. Weak in numbers, divided among themselves, hard pressed by the Bulgarians and by a Greek despot of Epirus in Europe, and confronted in Asia Minor not only by the Moslem power of the Sultan of Rum, but by the Greek states of Nicaea and Trebizond, the Latins of Constantinople, so far from being able to contribute to the rescue of Palestine, were only with great exertion enabled to maintain a precarious existence in the crumbling shell of the Greek Empire. Forces which might otherwise have been directed to Syria were required for the support of this new and unsteady creation. So perilous was the position that in 1209 Henry of Flanders, the second Latin Emperor of the east, allied himself with the Moslems of Rum against the Greeks of Nicaea.

Slender, too, was the satisfaction to be derived from the so-called union of the Greek and Latin Churches. That a Venetian nobleman should be Patriarch of Constantinople and that the Latin rite should be celebrated in Santa Sophia ministered to the pride of the Roman Curia. But there was no real reconciliation. The Archbishop of Athens and the principal Greek prelates, rather than acknowledge the Pope, surrendered their sees and fled to the welcoming court of Theodore Lascaris at Nicaea. From that not very distant exile the leaders of the Orthodox Church sustained the courage, the bigotry, and the hatred of their co-religionists.

The substantial profits of the enterprise were reaped by Venice, its chief artificer. In the division of the spoils the Republic of St. Mark received three-eighths of the city of Constantinople and there set up side by side with the much harassed administration a commercial establishment extending its filaments throughout Romania,[1] and governed by a *podesta* who described himself as despot and lord of a fourth and a half of the Empire. All the important maritime points which commanded the route to the Crimea in the north or to Egypt in the south, Zante and Cephalonia, the ports of Modon and Coron in the Morea, the Cyclades, Gallipoli, Crete fell by degrees into the hands of the Republic or of its adventurous nobles. The voyager among the isles of Greece may still admire the imposing fortifications which commemorate the harsh and soulless government of Venice, the first colonial power to establish itself in Europe during the middle ages.

Indeed, the key to the history of the Levant is the contest of rival Italian cities for commercial ascendancy, for as the Latin Empire was made by the Venetians, so nearly fifty years later, for motives of the same strictly commercial character, it was upset by a Greek restoration relying on the indispensable help of their rivals the Genoese.

1261

Not a single Greek manuscript is known to have been brought to Europe as a consequence of the Latin occupation of Constantinople and Athens, of Corinth and of Thebes. It would never have occurred to a Crusader, any more than it occurs to the modern Turk, that there is something to be learned from the literature of ancient Greece. A wonderful opportunity was therefore lost of opening out for the instruction of the west the splendid remains of Hellenic poetry and thought, and though some scattered rays of that great illumination penetrated to Europe during the thirteenth century they came not from Greece, but by the helpful mediation of the Arabs in Spain.

[1] As the Eastern Empire was then commonly called.

There is nothing so easy to follow as a bad example. The capture of the Fourth Crusade by the Venetians familiarized Europe with the idea that Crusades could be launched against a Christian and European power as well as against an Asiatic infidel. The seductive notion made rapid progress. The Saracens of Palestine and Egypt were not the only enemies who disturbed the peace of Innocent III. That active pontiff had theological enemies like the heathen Prussians, the Spanish Arabs, the heretical Albigenses, and he had also secular enemies like King John of England, who had refused to accept Stephen Langton as Archbishop of Canterbury. Against all these opponents of Roman theocracy Innocent found it convenient to preach a Crusade. Had the laws of currency been familiar to the thirteenth century, so astute a statesman can hardly have refrained from reflecting that indulgences, like bank-notes, may be over-issued and that no paper promise is apt more rapidly to depreciate than that of which there is an unlimited supply.

One thing was plain. Europe was not prepared to accept a theocracy. The trend of events was towards the making of national states, not towards the acceptance of a papal super-state. The great French victory of Bouvines (July 27, 1214) which enabled Innocent to crush Otto IV, the Guelf who had turned Ghibelline, helped to consolidate the national state of France, and since at the same time it foiled John's ingenious plan for the recovery of his lost French dominions, was good for the constitutional progress of England. To outward seeming the Pope had triumphed in his last duel with a hostile Emperor. Otto was down, renounced by Germany, routed by France. On his German throne was now seated that young Frederick of Hohenstaufen, who had been the Pope's ward, and from whom Innocent had lately extracted those large concessions with respect to the government of the German Church and the separate position of Sicily which he was wont to demand from candidates for the imperial throne. Yet beneath this brilliant surface there was muttering, challenge, uncertainty. There were Germans who asked what business the Pope had to interfere in their concerns. There were Englishmen who, despite the Pope's support of the versatile King John, were determined to defend their great charter; and there were Frenchmen who, notwithstanding the recent affair of Bouvines, were prepared to help them. Finally, there was the enigma of Frederick, master of Germany and Sicily, heir to the Norman and Ghibelline tradition. Despite all his paper promises, was it possible to believe that this half-Sicilian prince would act as a Guelf? The answer to this question was prompt, decisive, and important.

BOOKS WHICH MAY BE CONSULTED

Cambridge Mediaeval History, Vol. VI.
G. de Villehardouin : La Conquête de Constantinople. *Ed.* Bouchet. 2 vols., 1891.
L. Bréhier : L'Église et l'Orient au Moyen Âge. 1907.
A. Luchaire : Innocent III. 1905-8.
W. Miller : The Latins in the Levant. 1908.
E. Pears : The Fall of Constantinople. 1885.

CHAPTER XXIV

THE FALL OF THE HOHENSTAUFEN

Frederick II. His greatness and influence. Opposed by Gregory IX and Innocent IV. Goes on crusade. His Sicilian government and anti-papal propaganda. Deposed by Innocent IV. His dynasty destroyed. Consequences of the struggle. The interregnum in Germany. Loss of prestige to the Papacy. Boniface VIII challenges France and England. The Papacy destroys the Hohenstaufen only to become the captive of France.

FROM the cloud of contemporary detraction, the figure of Frederick II, the last of the mediaeval emperors, emerges temperamental and challenging, to a point of dazzling eminence. He was fluent in six languages, a lyric poet in the warm Sicilian manner, a munificent patron of architecture, sculpture, and learning, a skilful soldier, a statesman of infinite subtlety and resource but also of much careless hardihood. A passionate intellectual eagerness carried him into the fields of philosophy and astrology, of geometry and algebra, of medicine and natural history. He wrote a treatise on hawking, which marks the beginning of experimental science in the west, and travelled in the company of an elephant, dromedaries, and other arresting fauna from the tropics. The traditional inhibitions of his age, so strong in St. Louis, were no fetters for a man who had been nurtured amid the clash of race and creed in Sicily and could use and appreciate the Saracen and the Jew, though to gain political support he would burn a heretic as freely as a Dominican friar. The world marvelled at a prince who talked Arabic with his Saracens, supported a numerous harem, and was so detached from popular prejudice as to challenge the common belief in the ritual murder of children by the Jewish community. Had he not, it was rumoured, written a book entitled *De Tribus Impostoribus*, in which Moses, Mohammed, and Christ were branded as impostors? There was something uncanny in the prodigious energy of this realist in politics, this exquisite in art, this half-oriental at once mystical and sceptical, this daring revolutionary in method and opinion. His contemporaries called him the Wonder of the World, and so despite the lapse of centuries he remains.

Yet among the great men of history he is peculiar in this— that he belongs nowhere. Barbarossa means much to Germany, St. Louis and Napoleon to France, Simon de Montfort to England. No nation can rightly claim Frederick as part of its inheritance, neither Germany, though the instrument which founds German power among the heathen Prussians dates from his reign (1229), nor Sicily, though he chased the Moslems from the island. His work was undone, his dynasty uprooted. The greatest single human force in the middle ages passes in and out of history like a comet which shines and is gone. Only perhaps in the sphere of literature was his influence of enduring importance. Provençal troubadours fleeing from religious persecution found welcome in the tolerant court of Palermo and fired the emulation of Sicilian artists. Descending from the poetic circle which surrounded the poet king a rill of delicate Sicilian verse broadens out and deepens, and gaining richness from the Tuscan speech in its northward course, swells into the solemn music of the Divine Comedy.

The source of this comparative failure is to be found in the opposition of two remarkable Popes, Gregory IX and Innocent IV, the first a fiery zealot, the second a Genoese noble, learned in canon law, skilled in finance, and in the fierce excitements of conflict unburdened by scruple. The object of Frederick was to make of Italy and Sicily a united kingdom within the Empire. The settled purpose of the Papacy, supported by a revived and enlarged league of Lombard towns, was to frustrate this design. In the end the Papacy won the battle. The man was defeated by the institution, and with him passed away the last chance of an effective Roman Empire in central Europe or for many centuries of a united Italian kingdom.

The quarrel first broke out over a crusade which Frederick had in the enthusiasm of youth vowed to undertake, but repeatedly postponed. To the modern mind it seems strange that a young ruler, returning after an absence to a state disordered by a long minority, should be expected at once to depart upon a costly expedition overseas. So too it appeared to Frederick. Only after he had organized government in Sicily, brought Saracens, nobles, and cities to heel and founded the State University of Naples did he set sail for Palestine. He had already been excommunicated by Gregory IX for his delays. He was now excommunicated for his departure (1228). A crusade was even preached against the Crusader in his absence. He returned to the black displeasure of the Church. Yet what he accomplished, despite the papal opposition which was carried from Italy into Syria, was remarkable. Without waste of time, treasure, or blood, this most lukewarm but clear-sighted Crusader obtained from his friend, the Sultan, a treaty according to Christian pilgrims free access to the Holy Places for ten years. Such are the fruits of statesmanship when humanity and good sense are allowed for a moment to replace the blind fury of religious and racial hatred.

What Frederick had to offer to Italy was a cultivated and intelligent despotism on the model which he had succeeded in establishing in his Sicilian *regno*. There he had taken full control of criminal justice, had curtailed the liberties of the nobles, the clergy, and the towns, and built up a royal system of government only to be paralleled in Angevin England. In both countries there was the same concentration of power, the same efficient organ for the collection of taxes, the same system of itinerant royal judges, the same salutary intermixture of classes in the tasks of government. Indeed, the parliaments or general courts of Frederick II, with their representation of nobles, clergy, and townsmen, anticipate the later parliamentary development in England. But there was one significant difference between the two best governed states of the thirteenth century. Whereas the power of the English king rested in the last resort upon the support of a native militia, Frederick relied upon a standing army of Saracen and German mercenaries.

But in the passionate atmosphere of the Italian struggle the merits of this higher form of government were never appraised. The Lombard cities saw in Frederick the enemy of their liberties; the Pope viewed him as an apostate bent on undermining the authority of the Church. The Lombards had to be fought with an army. Against the Pope it was necessary to be equipped with a doctrine. The counsels of the Roman lawyer were reinforced by the dreams of the visionary and the astrologer. With true political instinct Frederick divined that to combat the material and worldly pretensions of the Papacy an instrument lay ready to his hand in the Franciscan doctrine of poverty. "It is upon poverty and simplicity," wrote this luxurious and intricate controversialist in 1227, "that the primitive Church was built in those days when she was the fruitful mother of saints. No one may presume to lay other foundations for men than those appointed by the Lord Jesus." As the contest proceeded, becoming fiercer and more bitter, with the Emperor capturing a General Council, and the Pope plotting, as was believed, the Emperor's murder, Frederick threw out dark hints of a new and better imperial Church to replace the corruptions of Rome. Was it nothing that he had been born at a town called Jesi, and was not his chief minister, Pierre de la Vigne, the true rock, forefigured in Scripture, upon which the Church of the Christ was to be built? The idea of a mendicant Church governed by an autocratic Empire was not one to appeal to the mediaeval mind. From his retreat in Lyons, Innocent deposed his antagonist and offered his crown with a patient and inveterate hatred to Robert of France, to a prince of Denmark, to Hakon of Norway, and ultimately to Henry of Thuringia and William of Holland.

The Hohenstaufen name still counted for much in Germany. Despite the activity of papal agents, the German princes and clergy, sweetened by concessions so lavish as to consort ill with the effective maintenance of royal power, remained loyal to the house and to the two young princes, Henry and Conrad, who were successively called upon to govern for their absent father. When the worthless Henry rebelled, Frederick had the main part of the country behind him in reducing the rebel to order. Even after the Council of Lyons in 1245 had solemnly deposed him, only a section of the German Church was induced to support the papal candidates, Henry of Thuringia and William of Holland, who were in turn put forward and elected kings.

The struggle was still proceeding when Frederick died in 1250, leaving behind him a reputation as great and as controversial as Napoleon's. To the Fraticelli "the hammer of the Roman Church" was a hero. By these ardent and revolutionary disciples of St. Francis, the great Emperor was remembered not as the luxurious half-oriental sovereign whose cause was supported by Saracen mercenaries in the south and wicked Italian despots in the north, not as the sceptic, the astrologer, the passionate love poet, but as the protagonist of a return to primitive Christianity. To the more orthodox he was Antichrist. Dante consigns him, alone among the Roman Emperors, to the pit of hell.

Nobody can outstrip his contemporaries at every point. Frederick, the most modern and wide-ranging of mediaeval sovereigns, was both in material resources and intellectual outlook the prisoner of his age. His largest army, which was smaller than a modern British division, was ill-matched against any well-defended Lombard town. Faenza, a city of the second class, defied him for eight months, Milan effectually spoiled his design for a united Italy. With pretensions which acknowledged no geographical boundaries, and with interests so wide that he has been called the first European, he was nevertheless unable to master even the Lombard plain. Again, though qualities belonged to him which in any age are remarkable—an immunity from the prejudices of colour and race, which puts most moderns to shame, an inexhaustible curiosity as to the operations of nature, and a strong sense of causality in the affairs of men—he combined with these rational promptings the superstitions common to his time, a blind belief in the oracles of astrology, an undue deference to the voice of sages, and an inability to distinguish between the type of question which can or can not admit of a precise scientific answer. Thus while some of Frederick's questions led to the discovery of truth, others could only be answered by an imaginative religious poet. "How many Hells are there? Who are the spirits who dwell in them? And by what names are they called? Where is Hell, and Purgatory where? Does one soul know another in the next life? And can a soul return to this life to speak and show itself to anyone?" To such questionings Dante was later to offer a confident reply.

Eighteen years elapse between the death of Frederick "Stupor Mundi" and the extinction of his dynasty through the cruel murder of his young grandson Conradin after the field of Tagliacozzo. During this tormented period the fierce duel between Guelf and Ghibelline continued to rage through Italy, dividing cities, classes, and families, but always dominated by the stern purpose of the Papacy to destroy the Hohenstaufen and to avert for 'ever the menace which such a power as theirs presented to the free expansion of the papal state. It is significant of the strength of Sicily under Manfred, Frederick's bastard son, and of the divided state of Italian feeling, that the Papacy was compelled to rely upon the foreigner for the means of bringing the war to a successful end. After two papal armies, financed by English money, had failed, Urban IV, the first Frenchman to

sit upon the papal throne, offered the Sicilian crown to Charles
of Anjou, the younger brother of Louis IX. To that wealthy and
ambitious prince the Sicilian kingdom was attractive not only
for itself, but as a stepping-stone to the conquest of the Greek
Empire. Under Clement IV, yet another French Pope, the contract was sealed, with the result that a French army, superior in
skill, discipline, and leadership to the levies which Manfred and
later Conradin were able to bring against it, secured for the
Papacy its final triumph, for the Guelf party a clear ascendancy,   *1268*
and for Charles of Anjou the Sicilian throne.

The effects of this long struggle may now be briefly summarized. Italy was lost to the Empire. The splendid civilization of
Norman Sicily, which had been one of the glories of Europe,
was destroyed by the French tyranny of Charles of Anjou, by
a tyranny so odious and penetrating that it led to the terrible
insurrection known as the Sicilian Vespers and afterwards to   *1282*
the severance of the island from the French kingdom of Naples   *(March*
and to its progressive decline in the scale of political influence.   *30)*
The French troops who had been called in by the Papacy to
give the final blow to the Hohenstaufen drove the German mercenaries and officials, upon whom the imperial system had been
supported in Italy, north of the Alps; but though this was a real
service, the cause of popular liberty was not thereby advanced.
Out of the incessant warfare which was at once the plague, the
amusement, and the occupation of Italy, there arose that peculiar
feature of Italian life, the civic despotism, often cruel and oppressive, but often distinguished for an enlightened patronage of
literature and art.

German unity was gone past recall. The long absences of the
Emperor Frederick, the lavish concessions which he had been
compelled to make in 1220 and in 1231 to the princes, lay and
ecclesiastical, and finally the furious civil war stirred up by the
Pope which had darkened the concluding years of his reign,
precluded the hope of any effective restoration of imperial
authority in Germany. How little concern was now felt by the
German princes for the Empire as an instrument of German
government was shown after the murder of William of Holland
in 1256. By a train of circumstances, which is still not entirely
clear, the choice of the King of the Romans had now become
vested in a college of seven electors, three ecclesiastics, and four
laymen. To these cynical dignitaries no qualities were more

desirable in a candidate for the Roman crown than that he should be a rich and negligent foreign absentee, knowing the value of a German vote, and able and willing to pay the price. The electors were divided, the majority deciding for Richard of Cornwall, the wealthiest man in England, the minority for Alfonso of Castile, the grandson, through his mother, of Philip of Swabia, and the favourite of France and the Papacy. Each of these princes was by his supporters declared to be duly elected as King of the Romans. Of the Englishman it may at least be said that his bribes were handsome, that he spent his money like an open-handed prince of whom much was expected, and that he made himself welcome among the Rhenish cities. The Castilian was wisely persuaded to remain in Castile. What the election proves is the fixed determination of the German princes to have no strong king over them and to treat the greatest piece of secular patronage in Europe as an occasion of private gain and international intrigue.

The terrible anarchy which prevailed in the land under the phantom rule of this English absentee might have been expected to suggest some doubts as to whether the real interests of Germany were served by its costly association with the Holy Roman Empire. When Richard of Cornwall died in 1271 it was open to the Germans to bring the Empire to an end and to attempt to found upon the model of their French and English neighbours a strong German state. The conservatism, the pride, the self-interest of the electors stood in the way. The question of ending the Empire was not even raised. After two kingless years the choice of the electors fell upon Rudolf of Habsburg, a Swiss nobleman from the Aargau, adjudged to be harmless but destined to be the founder of that famous house to whose mistakes in policy the Prussian critic ascribes the severance of Holland and Switzerland from the German Reich, the catastrophe of the Thirty Years' War and the outbreak of the great struggle of our own century which brought the Prussian and Austrian Empires to the ground.

In this dark and distracted period of German history there are only two points of bright light, the town leagues formed on the Rhine for the preservation of peace and on the Baltic for the promotion of trade, and the steady advance of German civilization eastward into Silesia, Bohemia, and at the expense of the rude and primitive Prussian race.

The papal victory had been won at a cost. Forced payments in support of international institutions, however valuable they may be. are always unpopular. If the problem of financing the regular work of the Papacy was grave, far more invidious was the task of procuring the resources necessary to the conduct of a papal war. Innocent IV shrank from no expedient likely to suggest itself to the rancorous fiscality of a hard-headed Genoese. To purchase influence he filled English benefices with Italian absentees and pluralists. To obtain money he laid crushing burdens on the clergy of England and France. In the pages of Matthew Paris, one of the best and most vigorous of English chroniclers, it is possible to trace the rising tide of indignation which these unprincipled extortions provoked in the land of all others famed for its obedience to the Holy See. Even Louis of France, whose country was more gently treated, reminded the Pope in a grave letter of protest that " he who squeezes too hard draws blood." The English clergy appealed in 1246 to a General Council. Though the plenitude of the papal power was still undisputed, the old spirit of affection and reverence had given place to anger and mistrust.

1243-54

Hildebrandine thunders no longer worked the old miracle. When they were repeated by Boniface VIII, in whom the pursuit of family advantage was so flagrant that he actually preached a crusade against the Colonna, his private enemies, the Pope met with stern and immediate resistance in England and France. Neither Edward I nor Philip the Fair would for a moment listen to the doctrine that a king was not entitled to levy a tax upon his clergy beyond the feudal aids (*Clericis Laicos*), or that it was necessary for salvation that he should be subject to the Pope. Each sovereign, in the most drastic manner available to him, made it clear that he was resolved to be master in his own house, and in this resolve was supported by his people. Even when Philip the Fair, in a transport of exasperation, sent his agent Nogaret to Rome, to kidnap the fiery old Pope and to bring him a prisoner to France, not a murmur of protest was heard from the subjects of the most Christian King. Six years later (1309) the Gascon Bertrand de Got, better known as Clement V, having through French influence been elected to the Papacy, set up his residence in Avignon and inaugurated the shameful chapter in papal history during which the Popes moved to the order of the King of France.

1294-1303

BOOKS WHICH MAY BE CONSULTED

Kantorowicz : Frederick the Second.   *Tr.* E. O. Lorimer.   1931.
Huillard Bréholles : Historia Diplomatica Frederici Secundi.   1852-61.
T. S. R. Boase : Boniface VIII.   1933.
E. Boutaric : La France sous de Philippe le Bel.   1861.

CHAPTER XXV

THE CATHOLIC MIND

St. Augustine. Siger of Brabant. Albert the Great. Aquinas. Dante.

AT the beginning of the thirteenth century the fabric of Christian belief in the west still retained the mould which it had received from the mind of St. Augustine. The City of God stood out sharply against the city of man, eternity against time, perfection against sin. The priesthood alone, while performing the miracle of their priestly function, participated in the blessedness of the angels, but as the century advanced, new intellectual and spiritual movements made themselves felt. Men of very different temper and intellect began to feel that the sharp contrasts of the great African father might not after all be so absolute, that even to fallen man it might be given to reach perfection on earth, that the spirit was more important than outward institutions, and faith and intellect than the sacraments or formularies of the Church. Had not Joachim of Flora, the Calabrian visionary (died 1202), proclaimed that the final stage of the world history was soon to open, when the Papal Church, which belonged to the age of the Son, would give way to the Spiritual Church, which belonged to the age of the Holy Ghost, when popes, priests, and sacraments would be unnecessary, and the Holy Spirit would fill every heart? Such dreams, in the enthusiasm created by the Franciscan movement, ran through Italy, inspiring among the Fraticelli the widest and most passionate hopes.

Philosophers, travelling by a different route, were reaching conclusions equally perilous to the sacerdotal order. Aristotle, now for the first time fully known and closely studied in the west, had become the serious concern of the University of Paris— Aristotle, who believed in everlasting time and uncreated mind, and in a divine intelligence working in man—and so we have eager Aristotelians like Siger of Brabant and his school maintaining such bold propositions as that the human intellect is eternal and the source of such perfection as is permitted to man, and that "a man directed to understanding is entirely disposed to eternal bliss."

These doctrines, the one of the self-sufficiency of individual faith, the other of the self-sufficiency of the individual intellect, struck hard at the heart of papal authority and discipline. Both were overcome by the forces of orthodoxy. The spiritualism of the Fraticelli, the metaphysics and psychology of Aristotle, were caught and harnessed to the chariot of the Church. But because the crisis was eventually mastered, because the doctors of Paris (1277) condemned the speculations of Siger, and because theologians were prepared to show that Aristotle was compatible with the Faith, it must not be imagined that the great opening out and agitation of the human mind which marks the thirteenth century was a matter of secondary consequence. The crisis was grave. The intellect of Europe was on the march. The tender conscience of spiritually minded men was stirred. Papal authority had not as yet been so sharply challenged. Many of the antecedents of the Reformation were already visible. If the Hundred Years' War had not supervened, arresting the development of the European mind and throwing back the progress of culture in the most advanced countries of the west, the forces making for freedom in education and politics would have captured new frontiers in the line of their advance.

At the critical moment Albert of Cologne (1193-1280) and his pupil, Thomas of Aquino (1226-1274), threw their massive intellects into the Catholic scale. These two Dominicans, the first a German, the second a South Italian, profited by the intellectual excitement created by the recovery of the physical and metaphysical works of Aristotle to build round the Catholic Church a powerful philosophic defence. The German was a vast encyclopaedia of knowledge, dominating by its mass. The Italian had a keener edge, a closer grip, a clearer method. Both welcomed the new knowledge, both believed that the essentially experimental philosophy of the pagan thinker could be reconciled with the cardinal doctrines of their Church. The weighty learning of the one, the close argumentation of the other, the vigorous orthodoxy and high character of each, impressed their thoughtful contemporaries. The intellect of the west capitulated to their combined attack.

In that age it was not expected of a philosopher that he

should approach the accepted doctrines of the Church with an open mind. Aquinas maintained that since faith and reason were both gifts of God, they must necessarily agree. The truths of revelation might transcend reason but could not contradict it. Faith was the assent of the intelligence at the bidding of the will to propositions which were seen to be possible and good to believe. Of the body of truth contained in revelation, truth inaccessible to reason but not incompatible with it, part only had been committed to writing. The remainder had been handed down by the Apostles, at the intimate prompting of the Holy Ghost, for the observance of the Church. By these unwritten apostolic precepts many a practice lacking scriptural authority, such as the worship of images, was justified. Nothing, then, which in the popular beliefs of that day was held to be orthodox awoke the rational misgivings of St. Thomas, neither the doctrine of transubstantiation, since a rational account could be given of the miracle, nor the eternal torments of the damned, for so did God cause the angels and saints to rejoice as they contemplated His justice and realized the evils which they had escaped. The grim doctrine of a fiery and everlasting punishment handed down from the Jews of the first century had lost none of its popular appeal with the lapse of time.

It was cardinal with St. Thomas that the possession of the true faith was necessary for salvation. *Extra ecclesiam nulla salus.* Salvation was neither for the unbaptized nor yet, save after confession and absolution by a lawfully ordained priest, for mortal sinners. The drunkard out of reach of the ministrations of the Church suffered the anguish of everlasting flame. Yet all was not thus dark and terrible in the religious landscape which presented itself to the mind of this laborious Friar. Visions of radiant beauty, forms of flawless saintliness and virtue, shone out amid the gloom and attested the goodness of the Creator. Prefigured in Aristotle's distinction of form and matter were the angels. On these consoling objects of philosophical speculation "the Angelical doctor" disserted with eager and enjoying prolixity.[1]

The third great figure in the Catholic firmament was a poet. Italy during the lifetime of Aquinas was in the throes of the political convulsion which tore the Hohenstaufen dynasty from its roots and led to the establishment under papal patronage

[1] See Appendix, p. 425.

of the Angevin house in Naples and Sicily. In that fierce struggle Florence, then a city of some 30,000 souls, and noted for its craftsmanship and advanced democratic feeling, espoused the papal side, expelled its Ghibelline or imperialist nobles, and after some sharp changes of fortune passed under the control of the Guelfic or papal party. The harmony of the victors was of no long duration. A personal feud imported from Pistoia clove the Guelfs into rival factions. There were White Guelfs and Black Guelfs.

That the Blacks eventually triumphed over the Whites with the help of the Papacy and the French is a matter only to be remembered because among many victims who were driven into exile by reason of that victory was the great figure of Dante Alighieri.

1265-
1321

Dante, who was then thirty-six, was already the author of a body of Italian lyrics, which marked him out as a poet of original genius. He had written the Canzoniere and commemorated his burning passion for Beatrice in the Vita Nuova. He had also mingled with characteristic vehemence and seriousness in the political feuds of the city and as one of the Priors of the Arts had borne a part in its government. His neighbours might note a man proud, reserved, studious, patriotic, and, since 1290 when Beatrice died, living under the shadow of a settled grief.

Exile delivered him from the clutch of Florentine politics and liberated his mind for continuous meditation. His reading was voracious and profound. The romances of chivalry and the lyrics of Provence, while they enchanted his imagination, failed to satisfy his deeper needs. He absorbed the philosophy of Aquinas, the history of Orosius, the astronomy of Ptolemy, the epics of Virgil and Statius. On problems of style, language, and metre he wrote more sense than anyone since the days of Horace and Quintilian, making himself the responsible champion of Italian as a literary language superior to Provençal, and deserving the encouragement of all men of patriotic will. In a passage of the De Vulgari Eloquentia, which has often been on the lips of Italian patriots, he urged that because Italy lacked a king she was not necessarily without a court. Her language was a kingdom in itself. Four centuries and more before Dr. Johnson, the bold truth was proclaimed that the greatness of a country depends upon its authors.

The Divina Commedia, the religious epic which Dante called a comedy mainly by reason of its style, but in part also for its happy ending, was perhaps suggested by the lovely passage of the Sixth Book of the Aeneid in which Virgil recounts the appearance of Dido to Aeneas as he moves through the underworld of shades. Dante, too, would see his love again. Beatrice would meet him in Paradise, and there, typifying divine theology, explain the hidden mysteries of God. To reach her he would descend to the nethermost pit of Hell and climb to the summit of Purgatory, guided in these two first stages of his visionary pilgrimage by Virgil, his master in poetry, and the supreme pattern, as it seemed to the men of that age, of earthly understanding.

Dante is not, then, the first, but is the most remarkable in that long list of apocalyptic writers (among whom Bunyan must be mentioned) who through the allegory of an imaginary voyage or vision have attempted to depict the destiny of the soul. The Divine Comedy owes much to the Dream of Scipio and to the Sixth Book of the Aeneid, but the theme of a descent into the nether world was neither original with Virgil nor was it principally confined to writers of pagan antiquity. There was a Κατάβασις of Heracles and a Κατάβασις of Orpheus as well as that Κατάβασις of Odysseus upon which the descent of Aeneas was modelled. On the Christian side the Pastor of Hermas, the Apocalypse of Peter, the Pistis Sophia, all of them belonging to the second century, exhibit, though with very notable differences, the same root of devotional enquiry into the mysteries of the future life which lies at the base of the Divine Comedy. The visions of the later middle age, such as the Visio Wettini in 824, the Vision of Alberic of Monte Cassino in 1107, and of the Monk of Evesham in 1196, are sufficiently numerous and widespread to dispel the notion that there is anything original in the ground idea of the Divine Comedy. The originality of the Divine Comedy does not consist in its apocalyptic character but in its genius, in the beauty of its language, the technique of its metre, the depth of its thought, the range and glow of its imagination. Of the mediaeval apocalyptic writers Dante alone was to any appreciable degree influenced by Virgil, and it is this fusion of the Virgilian spirit with mediaeval apocalyptic which, informing as it does the whole poem with a tenderness and humanity (not to speak of the learning) quite alien to the outpourings of the monkish visionary, gives to the Commedia its unique place in literary history.

Like all writers of the mediaeval period, Dante draws no clear line between ancient mythology and true history. Charon and Achilles, Tiresias and Nimrod, are to him as real as Cavalcanti, Virgil, or St. Francis; the miracles recorded by Livy and Lucan are true evidence that the work of the Roman Empire was divinely assisted. Ancient poetry was not history to be dissected but mystery to be divined. He conceived that allegory was a necessary quality of great poetry, or in Boccaccio's words that "poetical creations are not vain and simple marvels, as many blockheads suppose, but that beneath them are hidden the sweetest fruits of historical and philosophical truth, so that the conceptions of the poets cannot be fully understood without history and moral and natural philosophy."

This allegorizing and uncritical tendency makes much of Dante's epic remote and obscure to us.

The poet was without humour. Part of a famous speech delivered by Beatrice to Dante in the paradisal moon runs thus :

> "If you take three mirrors and put two of them at an even distance from the eyes and the third is placed between the two others just at a little greater distance, and you will place a candle behind you, you will see that if the largeness of the light reflected by these three mirrors is not the same, the intensity is."

Now this passage, the versification of which is a wonderful piece of dexterity, is pure prose. No modern poet would dream of introducing a chilly slab of scientific lecturing into the body of a passionate and mystical poem. But all through his poem, and more especially in the Paradiso, Dante does this frequently.

But if there is prose in the Divine Comedy, as there is violence, obscenity, and grotesqueness, there is no feebleness. Dante is never lax and talkative. He may be dry, tedious, difficult; it will never occur to the critic to describe him as pompous or verbose. The dulness of Dante is not due to a spell of intellectual fatigue, a mood of listless inattention, or to decay of interest, but always to the homiletic quality of a mind which sometimes found its lessons in difficult allegory, and sometimes in far-fetched interpretations of acted life. And it is a sufficient proof of this proposition that there is no part of the Commedia which has not for some quality or other attracted the admiration of good judges.

> " He was born," says Ruskin ("Stones of Venice," ix, 175), " both in the country and at the time which furnished the most stern opposition of horror and beauty and permitted it to be written in the clearest lines. And therefore though there are passages in the 'Inferno' which it would be impossible for any poet now to write, I look upon it as all the more perfect for them . . . and therefore I think that the 21st and 22nd book of the 'Inferno' are the most perfect portraitures of the fiendish nature which we possess."

Among mediaeval poets Dante stands closest to Virgil for the delicacy and minuteness of his observation. The storm crashing through the forest, the frogs slipping into the water from the snake, the lizard which crosses the road like a flash of lightning, the fireflies seen by the peasant in the gloaming, the old cobbler narrowly eyeing his needle, the boxers, their bare bodies gleaming with oil as they stand watching one another for their point of vantage, the duck dipping to escape the falcon, the mother who clutches her child on the alarm of fire, the gamesters crowding round the winner—here are pictures painted fresh from the life. And it is to the frogs, cranes, lizards, ducks, and falcons, to the sheen of fish gliding to their food in a tank of pure and still water, to the peasant who rises grumbling in a hoar frost, and then a few hours later when the world has changed its face, takes his crook and leads his flocks afield, it is to such pictures of the unobtrusive aspects of Italian country life only to be paralleled in Virgil that the poetical posterity of Dante owes its principal debt. He showed that no piece of real nature, if strictly observed, is alien to the making of poetry.

In common with Orosius, his master in history, Dante held the view that the Roman Empire was the divinely appointed instrument of government on earth, and that this was clearly proved by the double fact that Christ was born in the reign of Augustus and that during the same reign the world for the first time enjoyed universal peace. The De Monarchia is a Latin treatise written to prove, first, that a universal monarchy is a god-ordained necessity for man, second, that the Roman Empire was providentially designed to exercise this universal monarchy, and finally that the Roman Emperor held his title directly from God and was in no way subject to the Papacy. To modern eyes the reasons brought forward in support of these propositions may seem too far removed from the realities of political life to weigh with any sensible mind. But when we divest the argument of its scholastic integument and come down to the fundamental thoughts in Dante's mind we shall find that it is capable of being translated into the terms of an ideal which the world has never relinquished. That the highest activity of man is intellectual and that intellectual progress is arrested by war, that universal peace is the supreme end in politics, that it can be made secure only by the reduction of the whole world under a single government, that in every community there must be lodged somewhere a sovereign power, and that great evils have proceeded and will continue to proceed from the temporal ambition of spiritual rulers, these tenets would not be regarded as absurd, though they might be hotly disputed, by modern politicians. The universal monarchy of Dante is no more chimerical than Tennyson's Parliament of Man or than Mazzini's dream of the Republic. Aspirations, however distant they may be, play their part in the shaping of human affairs, and Dante's treatise was used as a controversial weapon in the next generation (when the quarrel broke out between Louis of Bavaria and John XXII) and received the honour of burning at the hands of a legate of the Pope.

Nevertheless, Dante's theory of the Empire postulated an order of things which every change in European affairs was involving in darker shades of obsolescence. The last faint hope of an Italy united under the imperial power vanished with the death of Frederick II in 1250, fifteen years before Dante's birth; and the lifetime of the poet synchronizes with a series of political changes every one of which was separately injurious to the restoration of imperial control. The downfall of the Hohenstaufen dynasty, the introduction of Charles of Anjou into southern Italy, the transfer of the imperial crown first to an Austrian and then to a Luxemburger, the steady growth in the territorial ambitions of the Papacy, and of the commercial strength of the Italian towns, these among other causes tended to loosen the bond which clasped Italy to the Empire and to confirm the political divisions of the country.

Amid much that is part of the civilized aspiration of every age, and much that was already archaic and obsolete in his own time, there is one characteristic of Dante's political thought and temperament which alternately loses and gains for him the favour of intellectual men. He was by temperament an aristocrat, by conviction an imperialist. It was not the Roman Republic which he idealized but the Roman Empire, not liberty but law. Critics have often noticed that neither in the Commedia nor in any of his scattered writings is there any sign of sympathy for the poor as a class, of such sympathy, for instance, as suffuses the earnest pleading of Piers Plowman or the early literature of the Franciscan movement.

But in claiming Dante for the aristocrats, the student should remember that to the mind principally occupied with the religious ordering of the universe, the competing claims of class and class which form the matter of political rivalry and meditation become specks of infinite insignificance. The arbitrament of God which peoples the circles of the Inferno and the Mount of Purgatory and the stars of Paradise falls with an equal hand on prince and ploughman. Great office does not screen the offender in that high court (for while there are several Popes in Dante's Hell, there is but one in Paradise), so that to the Italian of that age reading or listening to the Commedia the supreme impression must have been the vanity of all worldly things when measured against the divine graces of the soul. The Catholic Church is a great democracy. To Dante its power for good had been immeasurably injured by its lust for temporal dominion. As the city of Florence had fallen away from its days of early simplicity when ladies sat at the spindle and the flax and their husbands went in a skin jerkin, so the Church had been corrupted by wealth and power. In the beautiful eleventh canto of the Paradiso where St. Thomas recounts the life of St. Francis, the emphasis is laid upon the marriage of the saint with the Lady Poverty, who, reft of her first husband, the Church, had for a thousand years and more stood "despised and obscure, without invitation."

In such passages as these Dante confesses his enthusiasm for poverty as a religious ideal, hard and heroic, and yet never to

10

be lost sight of if the Church was to be kept pure of offence. The great epic of mediaeval Catholicism is the work of a humanist who was also a scholastic, of a mystic who was also a politician, of a churchman orthodox in belief but ardent in the cause of a puritan reformation.

BOOKS WHICH MAY BE CONSULTED.

E. H. Gilson : La Philosophie au Moyen Âge. 1925.

M. C. D'Arcy : Thomas Aquinas. 1930.

E. Armstrong : Italian Studies. *Ed.* C. M. Ady. 1934.

Dante : Divina Commedia. *Ed.* H. F. Tozer. 1902.

Dante : Opere Minore. *Ed.* P. J. Fraticelli. 1855.

Dante : De Monarchia. *Ed.* Dr. E. Moore; Introduction by W. H. V. Reade. 1916.

V. Nannucci : Manuale della litteratura del primo secolo della lingua italiana. 1883.

D. G. Rossetti : Dante and his Circle. 1892.

Mandonnet : Siger de Brabant et l'averroisme latin au 13me siècle. 1908.

CHAPTER XXVI

THE GROWTH OF MONARCHY IN FRANCE AND ENGLAND

Divergent constitutional developments of France and England. Growth of centralization in England. Contracted authority of French Crown. Louis VII and Henry II. Imperfect unification of France under Philip Augustus. Importance of the rural middle class in England. Parliament and States-General. Legal development in England and France. Louis IX and Philip le Bel. Absolutist tendencies in France. Constitutional tendencies in England. Magna Carta. Simon de Montfort. Edward I.

How sharply, despite all the unifying forces of civilization, are France and England now divided! The one a land of peasant proprietors, of small highly skilled craftsmen, of a large bourgeoisie, cultured, economical, and self-centred, with little or no interest beyond the frontiers of their own beloved country, the other a country of large landowners and tenant farmers, of big industrialists and crowded factory workers, of business men having interests all over the world, and with a population so much given to travel and adventure that few families cannot claim a relation who is settled beyond the ocean.

In the twelfth and thirteenth centuries the contrast between the two countries was less evident and of a different character. The Norman Conquest had made of England a province of French civilization. The language of the aristocracy, of the government, of the law courts, was French. It was from the Ile de France that England derived its Gothic architecture. A great part of France, first Normandy, then the Angevin Empire of Henry Plantagenet, was, until the beginning of the thirteenth century, ruled by English kings. Feudalism, chivalry, the Crusades, were French. The university movement, so far at least as England was concerned, originated in Paris. The general ideas about law and government, about society and religion, which prevailed on one side of the Channel were no less familiar on the other. So intermingled were the two countries that many English towns received charters upon a French model, and some of the terms most closely connected with the growth of English municipal liberties, such as mayor and commune, were imported from France. A traveller passing from one country to the other in the reign of King John would have found no very palpable contrast between the French and the English scene. He would see majestic cathedrals rising in either country, and would find upon examination that they were being built by corporations of master masons under the direction of a bishop or an abbot. He would find monasteries in either country obedient to a French rule, farming wide acres, and dispensing lavish hospitality; would meet monks travelling to fair, market, or tourney, or come across a knot of gaping rustics listening to the eloquence of a travelling Friar. England he would probably pronounce to be at once the rougher and richer country. But so indistinct were the spiritual frontiers between these two remarkable peoples that the barons of the charter did not scruple to invite the heir to the French throne, afterwards Louis VIII, to take the English crown, and that Simon de Montfort, the leader of the national revolt against Henry III, and the great popular hero of English liberty, was the son of the French nobleman who crushed the Albigensian Crusade. To the Frenchman of this period the German was a foreigner and almost intolerable. England was different. Though the commonalty spoke an unintelligible tongue, and for lack of vineyards were driven to a disgraceful beverage, the gentry were of a familiar world and could make themselves intelligible in their provincial French.

France, however, was not the only country by whom England was now influenced. The bulk of the English population was throughout the middle ages to be found in London, in Essex, and in East Anglia. It is in this region, as the Doomsday Survey shows, that a free agricultural population managed most easily to maintain itself throughout the economic disturbances consequent upon the Norman Conquest. Here was not only the most populous but the richest, and perhaps for this very reason the most liberty-loving section of the English people; for it was the quarter from which in after times Simon de Montfort and Oliver Cromwell drew their strength. But the bulk of the trade of London and East Anglia was not with France but with the Low Countries and Cologne, Scandinavia and the Baltic. Indeed, the greatest of all English mediaeval trades was done with Flanders. It was in the Flemish towns, in Bruges and Ghent, that wool from our famous English downs and pastures was worked up into cloth, and sent far and wide through Europe. Thus, while our aristocratic and literary connections were with a Latin people, our trading connections were mainly—though the trading connection with Rouen and Bordeaux was always important—with peoples of the same Teutonic stock as ourselves. In this area our English speech must have been always a better commercial language than French, and for that reason well worth keeping up in our trading towns which attracted then, as they continue to attract with even greater potency now, the most vigorous and enterprising sons of the village. It is significant that Chaucer, the father of English poetry, was a Londoner and a Commissioner of Customs.

The fact of the Norman Conquest, while bringing England fully within the zone of French civilization, was one of the causes which ultimately led England and France to pursue different lines of constitutional development. William I made of England a single state. That work was so well done that it was never undone. The period of feudal anarchy under Stephen was repaired under Henry II, to whose great series of administrative and judicial reforms England owes a centralization of justice for which France had to wait for many centuries. By the time of Henry II's death four great lessons had been instilled into the English people. They had been taught to pay taxes, a lesson which the French monarchy never succeeded in teaching the French people, and which even now is not fully learned. They had been taught that crime was an offence against the king's peace of which the king's court desired to have exclusive cognizance, save where benefit of clergy was claimed, in which case the ecclesiastical court tried the offender, but handed him over to the secular arm for punishment in the case of a conviction. They had learned that there was one law for the whole country, administered by one supreme court, the *Curia regis*, with its judges going on circuits through the country, and everywhere, when on these official errands, representing the power of the king. And, finally, they had become habituated to the disagreeable duty of co-operating in the task of government, either as tenants called upon to render knights' service in the wars, or as citizens called upon to follow the hue and cry, or as jurors for the assessment of taxes, the punishment of criminals, or the adjudication of civil suits in the county courts. The system continued to work under an absent king, like Richard, or under a bad king, like John, who in nothing more fully showed his remarkable ingenuity than in his capacity for extracting fleets,

men, and money from the national administration which had
been bequeathed to him by better men.

1100-37 Very different was the position of the King of France at the
beginning of the twelfth century. All that Louis VI could call
his own was a small domain on the middle waters of the Seine
and the Loire. Amiens was in Vermandois, Calais and Boulogne
in Artois, Lyons was imperial. Whereas in England there was
a national government, in France the King was confronted by
great fiefs (Flanders, Normandy, Burgundy, Guienne, Gascony,
Toulouse, and Barcelona) nominally subject to the French Crown,
but in fact independent. It is significant of the political weights
and measures of the country that Louis VI wisely concentrated
his energies upon the police of that little territory which was
directly under his own control. For him feudalism was the
enemy. In a modest way this active ruler was the founder of that
system of government through officials drawn from the middle
class, which, despite all subsequent political changes, has been
found congenial to the needs of France. His chief minister was
a monk of the name of Suger, a turgid historian, but as a man of
affairs, honest, capable, and trusted.

1137-80 All this progress was put to the hazard in the succeeding reign.
Louis VII, pious, charming, chivalrous, ineffectual, was brilliantly married to a lady who brought him as her dower the
Duchy of Aquitaine: but their tempers proved to be incompatible, and after fifteen years of married life Eleanor was divorced.
There have been few greater political blunders in the history of
mediaeval France. Eleanor married Henry Plantagenet, Count of
Anjou, and in accordance with the disastrous notions of that
feudal age, a vast area of south-western France (Guienne,
Auvergne, and Aquitaine) was now transferred from the control of her first to that of her second husband. When Henry
became King of England and Duke of Normandy, Louis was
confronted with a hostile kingdom stretching from the Cheviots
to the Pyrenees, and in every point of material strength stronger
than his own. "Your Lord, the King," he observed to Walter
Map, "wants nothing—men, horses, gold, silk, diamonds, game,
fruits: he has all in abundant plenty. We in France have only
bread, wine, and gaiety." A war broke out between the two
rival powers which was waged in the intermittent feudal manner
for a hundred years.[1]

[1] Genealogical Table F.

One advantage belonged to Louis VII which could not be claimed for his adversary. All through life the French King lived in the sunshine of clerical favour. In the struggle between Frederick Barbarossa and Alexander III Louis ranged himself on the side of the Pope, received him as guest, allowed him to behave as if he were the ruler of France, and in return for his submissive piety was presented with the gift of a golden rose. His aureole shone the more brightly by contrast with the dark disfavour with which Henry II was regarded by all the priests and monks of Europe. The English King who scribbled or chatted during Divine Service, who laid down that criminous clerks, if convicted, should be handed over to the secular arm to be punished, and that no appeals should go to Rome without the royal assent, who was for many years violently embroiled with Becket, his Archbishop of Canterbury, and commonly suspected of having directed his murder by the altar steps of his own cathedral, was regarded as the embodiment of the lay spirit in statesmanship, and of all that was most dangerous to clerical prerogative. The contrast between the pious and unfortunate Louis and the wicked, clever, prosperous Angevin presented the immortal problem of the equity of fate. Why were such things possible? Afterwards, when the English were driven out of Normandy by Philip II, the legend grew up that the murdered Becket had appeared to an ecclesiastic in his dreams, saying that he had chosen Philip to avenge his death.

Of this Philip, remembered after his death as Augustus, it may be said that he possessed the rarest of all qualities in a mediaeval ruler, concentration on the possible. Living in a world not of dreams, but of realities, he allowed nothing to divert him from the great object of driving the Plantagenets out of France, and of extending the boundaries of his kingdom. *Ampliavat fines regni* is the epitaph on this long-headed, unattractive figure who planted French power on the Channel and the Atlantic, gaining Vermandois by diplomacy, Normandy, Anjou, Maine, Touraine by war, and finally destroying on the famous field of Bouvines the army of an Anglo-German coalition, which would have robbed him of these conquests. *1214*

From this point the territorial formation of France proceeded without interruption until in the fourteenth century Edward III challenged the French crown. The English remained firmly *1337*

1179-1223

planted in Gascony: but Languedoc fell to France as the fruit of the Albigensian Crusade, Champagne, La Marche, and Angoulême a little later, and Lyons in 1312.

The making of France under the Capetian monarchs was wholly unlike the process by which political unity had been imposed on England through the policy of William the Conqueror. Even where the extension of the royal domain involved fighting, as when Philip Augustus evicted John from Normandy, it entailed none of those revolutionary consequences which followed upon the Norman conquest of England, neither transfer of property, nor the intrusion of a new nobility, nor the depression of the rural population. When the towns and castles governed by the troops of the English king had been taken, the province passed from England to France without further change, and, so to speak, with its soul intact. But in general there was no fighting. The King was felt to be the champion of order and justice, the defender of the weak and the poor against the wicked and the strong, the protector of religion from the Channel to the Pyrenees, and in a vague, unanalyzed way the suzerain and master of France. Even under Louis VII a sentiment of devotion to the monarchy is clearly apparent. The successful Philip watered the tender plant, and by an adroit exercise of his rights as a feudal suzerain extended the influence of the French Crown in the territories of his feudal vassals.

From this manner of growth by accretion, it followed that France was never in the middle ages so completely unified as England. The great fiefs were too much a part of the common heritage of France to be subjugated or transformed by the pressure of an iron despotism. They retained, therefore, even when annexed to the French Crown, much of their former independence, and as appanages created in favour of the younger members of the royal family, were more than once sources of peril to the monarchy itself.

A consequence of the greater measure of authority thus enjoyed by the great feudal nobles in France was the absence in that country of a rural middle class burdened by public responsibilities. In England the main tasks of local government were discharged by knights of the shire or country gentlemen of moderate fortune, who attended the county courts, presented criminals to the judges, bore the record of the country to West minster, where the doings of the shire court were challenged, acted as jurors in civil suits, and ultimately came to represent their respective counties in the national Parliament. In France there was no such amateur class of local jurors, justices, and administrators as the knights of the shire, and no such popular local institutions as the shire courts. The administration of the French monarchy was carried out by professionals. It was the achievement of Philip Augustus to have created in the office of *Bailli* or *Seneschal* an official of the royal government who, holding his post at the King's pleasure, might be trusted to do his will.

Here is the explanation of the fundamental difference between the development of France and England. In both countries the monarchy manifested itself as the chief constructive principle of the state, and in the thirteenth century developed representative institutions round the central nucleus of a royal council. In both countries these assemblies owe their being not to any abstract theory, but rather to the pressure of financial needs, or because business was thus most conveniently discharged, or as a means of reinforcing the crown in times of crisis.

In both countries insistence is laid upon the essential principle that the representative has full power to bind his constituents. But here resemblance ceases. In the great English councils of the thirteenth century, the Parliaments, as from the reign of Henry III they come to be called, knights of the shire took 1216-72. their place with burgesses and representatives of the lower clergy, and worked side by side with the prelates and barons, who were summoned by individual writ. The strength of this English body, the feature which gave it a permanent and continuous rôle in English government, was that it was in the main an assemblage of persons of an intermediate social rank, who were accustomed to the discharge of public business in their separate localities. The French States-General was not thus rooted in local government, nor closely fused by the presence of a class of representatives who, while they shared the country tastes and pursuits of the noble, were, in point of wealth and station, more nearly akin to the burgess. Consisting of three distinct orders, the nobles, the clergy, and the burgesses, the States-General failed to play a decisive and formative part in the moulding of French policy. So far from furnishing any continuous restraint upon the exercise of absolute power, these cumbrous assemblies met at rare and infrequent intervals and then spoke with a divided voice. It is significant that the total number of States-Generals known to have been summoned between 1300 and 1789 exceeds by two only the number of Parliaments summoned in the single reign of Edward III. The size of France was inimical to parliamentary centralization, and suggested the superior convenience of provincial assemblies.

There was no French common law. The great boon of legal unity secured to England through the judicial reforms of Henry II was not achieved in France till the days of Napoleon. Yet the first steps were taken on the road to legal improvement when the Parliament of Paris acquired in the reign of St. Louis a substantive and continued existence not many years after the foundation of the Inns of Court in London. This was not a political assembly, as the name might seem to imply, but a judicial corporation, the members of which in course of time acquired their positions by purchase or bequest. A great rôle both in law and politics was played by this legal institution, which numbered many illustrious intellects, and endured until, like all other privileged corporations, it was swept away by the French Revolution; but it was not the rôle of the English common lawyers who in the seventeenth century stood for Parliament against the King. The French lawyer of the island city breathed the air of Roman jurisprudence, and on every occasion might be trusted to support the prerogative of the Crown. Under the influence of the Papal Inquisition, the old Teutonic system of public trial which existed in France and continued to survive in England gave place to a secret procedure, better adapted perhaps to the detection and punishment of crime, but offering fewer guarantees to the accused and easily lending itself to the basest purposes of tyranny. Among the circumstances serving to differentiate the history of these two neighbouring peoples none perhaps is more important than the fact that the Papal Inquisition which was created in France never crossed the British channel.

Philip Augustus may perhaps be called the second founder of Paris. He authorized and supported the University, built the Cathedral of Notre Dame, and gave to the city pavements and hospitals, aqueducts and an enlarged circuit of fortifications. After his reign there was no question but that Paris must be

1226-70

the centre of French government. But how was France to be ruled? Louis IX, who attained to his majority in 1236, was a saint and mystic. No ruler of his time was more fully penetrated with theocratic ideas, more ardent in self-sacrifice, or, in matters where heresy was not concerned, readier to hearken to the voices of equity and mansuetude. It may be added that his personal courage was high and stainless, and that being exempt from many of the passions of his time, he often brought a shrewd and balanced judgment to the affairs of state. But the respect which we feel for St. Louis as a man must not blind us to his faults as a statesman and a strategist. On two critical occasions he left his country to go upon crusade. One good army was lost among the canals of the Egyptian delta, another in the torrid heat of Tunis. Neither sanctity, nor self-sacrifice, nor the administration of patriarchal justice under the oak of Vincennes could replace the advantages of a good and steady administrative routine, nor shield his subjects from extortion and misery. The good King returned from his Egyptian campaign to learn of the stern repression of the Pastoreaux, poor country folk, maddened with poverty and inflamed with injustice, who wreaked their hatred of the social order upon the prosperous bodies of the priests. The exquisite art of La Sainte Chapelle shone against a background of social wretchedness.

The moral beauties of St. Louis, better suited to a knight-errant than to a statesman, added lustre rather than strength to the Capetian house. It was given to Philip the Fair, his enigmatic grandson, to supply the ruthless and daring qualities which are absent in the composition of a saint. St. Louis was a feudal, Philip a national, sovereign. The one issued edicts for his domain, the other promulgated ordinances for France. The spirit of the grandfather was profoundly ecclesiastical. The civil order founded by Philip was pre-eminently lay, and even anti-clerical. St. Louis kept two grand objects constantly before his eyes, personal holiness and the happiness of his subjects, imperfectly as he was able to adjust his means to the achievement of that latter end. In Philip the two great problems were always, no matter at what cost, power and wealth.

There is accordingly something violent and revolutionary about the procedure of this energetic ruler, whose reign coincides with the final conquest of Syria by the Mamelukes and with the eclipse of all the hopes and aspirations which had been connected with the great age of the Papacy, and with the launching of the Crusades. Frederick of Swabia had captured a General Council, Philip the Fair, backed by his civil lawyers, did not scruple to lay hands upon the Pope himself. Nothing is more eloquent of the altered spirit of the time than the fact that when Boniface VIII ventured to interfere with the King's right to tax his clergy, and proceeded, as tempers rose, to claim supremacy over the secular power, Philip was able without **1303** affronting his people to have the Pope's person seized by violence, his Bulls publicly burnt, and to appeal to the States-General for its support against an interfering Bishop of Rome.

The same spirit of ruthless "laicity" characterizes Philip's dealings with the Templars. The King was needy, the Templars were rich. In that single circumstance is the explanation of an act of cruelty which prefigures, if it does not surpass, the robberies of the Reformation and the massacres of the Jews. For wealth was not the only crime of this famous Order, which had so long fought for the Christian cause under the Syrian sky, and was now fulfilling the office of banker to the King. The Templars incurred the even graver charge of general unpopularity. It is the habit of vulgar and excitable minds to find the explanation of great popular calamities in the treason of leading men. Again and again in French history the cowardly cry "Nous sommes trahis" has gone up in the hour of humiliation. It went up now. The Templars, it was said, had betrayed the Christian cause, which it was their special duty to defend. They had conspired with the Saracens. They were heretical, stained with nameless vices, devoted to secret and unmentionable rites. It was rumoured that they spat upon the Cross. Once let loose, the public imagination poured itself out in an unmeasured torrent of innuendo and attack. The Templars were deprived of an opportunity of reply. Many of them were tortured until from agony they made false confessions. Many were sent to the stake. With the disgraceful connivance of the Pope the Order was dissolved, and its vast resources in money and land were for the most part annexed to **1313** the use of the Crown.[1]

The want of money, which led to this, as to many other acts of unjust extortion, and notably to repeated debasements of the

---

[1] The Hospitallers, to whom the property was nominally assigned, obtained in France a very small part of it.

coinage, was a sign that the King of France was now attempting to govern his country. A study of the not altogether consistent legislation of the reign reveals Philip's underlying purpose: to draw money from the clergy, from the men-at-arms, from the nobles, and to administer the nation with the aid of lawyers of humble birth. Crown officials multiply their numbers, the organs of central government become differentiated as in England—the Parliament for legal, the *Cour des Comptes* for financial business, and at the end of the reign, the States-General, as an exceptional measure for the association of the three great orders in the state with momentous acts of royal policy. The government of this king was harsh, irregular, odious. The taxes were mostly farmed out with the inevitable result that the treasury received but a small fraction of the sums which were extracted from the taxpayer. The officials were indifferently and inter-mittently supervised. Still, despite all its defects on the side of publicity, and control, and fiscal science, there now emerges into the light of history a government of France, lay, auto-cratic, and, in so far as the conditions of that age permitted, centralized in the person of the King.

While the French monarchy was thus tending towards absolut-ism, England was set upon an opposite course. The Norman nobles who had conquered and pillaged this wealthy island did not long remain an alien and exclusive caste. They intermarried with the Saxons, merged with a population too vigorous to be permanently subjected, and came in the course of a century to regard themselves not as Normans but as Englishmen. After *1174* the last great feudal revolt had been crushed by Henry II, they were compelled to accept the national government of the crown as an established institution, in the working of which they were called upon equally with the knights of the shire and representa-tives of the towns to bear a part.

With this transformation in the character of the nobility from the position of an alien caste to that of a native aristocracy, the principal obstacle to the growth of an English nation disappeared. The tyranny of a bad king was sufficient to provoke a national opposition in which churchmen, barons, and townsmen were alike involved. The Magna Carta, extracted from King John, *June,* ranks as the first of our English statutes and is rightly regarded *1215* as the corner-stone of English liberties. That document, which played so important a rôle in the parliamentary struggles of the seventeenth century, was no revolutionary or philosophical manifesto, but a re-statement of the rights and privileges which were already assumed to belong to the Church, the nobles, the townsmen, and "the community of all the land." The barons of the charter were not concerned to make new law, but to prevent the violation by the Crown of existing rights. They had no theory of liberty as such. The liberties which they were concerned to defend were feudal, ecclesiastical, or municipal privileges. Against royal caprice they offered the bulwark of legal custom.

A later age saw in the charter the foundation of parliament and the jury system. The charter does not mention the word parliament, which first came into use in the succeeding reign, but lays down that no extraordinary aids or scutages are to be levied by the Crown save with the consent of the common council of the realm, an assembly of prelates, barons, and tenants in chief. Nor yet does it mention the word jury. What it says, however, in effect is that no free man should be imprisoned, dispossessed, outlawed, or exiled save by the judgment of his peers or by the law of the land. Those were lofty principles, and since the old methods of proof by ordeal and battle had been falling into disrepute, and were banned by the Lateran Council in 1215, they implied recourse to the criminal jury, an institution which may perhaps have its roots in the standing body of jurors sworn to accuse no man falsely, of whom we read in the dooms of an Anglo-Saxon king.

Much of this famous document, so largely concerned with the oppressions of the royal officers and with abstruse points of feudal law and custom, has now only an antiquarian interest. The importance of the charter is due to the fact that it is the first example in our history of a national protest against a bad government. The shape which the protest assumed, the details which it comprised, the manner in which it was drafted, are of less account than the co-operation of Stephen Langton, Archbishop of Canterbury, of the Mayor of London, and of the most politically minded barons of the land in a common effort to bring the King to account, and to force him to obey the laws and to study the interests of his people. The barons were in grim earnest. In the event of an infraction of the charter they were ready to carry their opposition to the point of civil war, and in proof of their resolute intent appointed twenty-five of their number to safeguard its provisions and to constrain the King, if necessary by the utmost use of force, to observe them.

This high example of constitutional obedience lived on in the national memory. The charter, in support of which a section of the baronage was even willing to put the English crown upon the head of a Frenchman, became a watchword. It was three times revised in the first decade of Henry III's reign. Its three forest clauses were amplified into a separate charter for the relief of those abuses of the forest law, which, of all the innovations of the Norman Conquest, were felt by the country folk of England to be the most oppressive. During the minority of the young King his wise counsellors, William Marshall and Hubert de Burgh, ruled in its spirit. But Henry III, once he had reached *1216-72* man's estate, showed himself strangely insensitive to the workings of the national mind. Devout, refined, artistic, the builder of Westminster Abbey was, like Charles I, in matters of public policy, blind, obstinate, and untrustworthy. The country hated the foreign favourites, Savoyards and Poitevins, upon whom he lavished power and wealth. It resented his subservience to the Pope. It saw no substantial advantage to English interests, but on the contrary a source of intolerable exaction in the King's ambitious project for securing the Sicilian crown for his young son Edmund. As the clergy were bled white to feed the ambitions of Pope and King, the tide of indignation mounted steadily. At last Henry was told plainly that redress must precede supply. At a parliament at Oxford (1258) he was compelled to accept a scheme of government which placed the conduct of affairs in the hands of the baronial party.

Had the Provisions of Oxford been observed in the letter and the spirit, there would have been no Barons' War. Henry never proposed to observe them. He could count upon the Pope obligingly to relieve him of an oath taken under duress in the papal cause. But he was now confronted with an opposition which was both widely supported and ably led. "The community of the bachelory of England," as the smaller landed gentry are called by a chronicler, was as ready to protest against the lukewarmness of the baronage as later to correct the backslidings of the King. The better part of the clergy, the students of Oxford, the burgesses of the chartered towns, joined hands with this section of the landed gentry in the movement to protect the country against arbitrary rule. Franciscans carried the popular

message through the towns and villages and acted as missionaries
of the cause. When the quarrel ripened into civil war, Simon de
Montfort, the alien Earl of Leicester, stood out as the champion
of the national interest. On the high down above Lewes he
routed the royal army (1264), and captured the King and Prince
Edward, his heir. Yet it is characteristic of the moderation of
the English civil war that the outcome of this brilliant victory
was not the deposition of the sovereign, but an attempt to bind
him in the eyes of the nation assembled in parliament to act on
the advice of a baronial council.

Nothing is more calculated to strike the public imagination
than the political employment of a victory in the field. Simon's
Westminster Parliament (January, 1265) marked an epoch. No
assembly had been summoned for so grave a purpose. None had
been so widely representative, for in addition to the clergy and
barons, the first numerously, and the second more sparsely summoned, every shire was invited to send two knights and many
boroughs two burgesses. The representation of the towns was
apparently an innovation. Upon the receptive mind of Prince
Edward, who was constrained in this widely representative
gathering of the constitutional party to swear to an unpalatable
peace, the lesson of such a gathering and of the strength to be
derived from it made an impression of enduring value to the
nation. The work of Simon, which seemed to be frustrated by
his defeat and death on the field of Evesham, was carried forward
by his conqueror and disciple, the more judiciously, and doubtless the more securely, since the legend of Simon as the hero and
sainted martyr of liberty and justice survived in the memory of
the English people.

1265

Edward I is the English Justinian. His reign is marked by
such legislative activity as this country has only twice witnessed
(in the reign of Henry VIII, and again under the Commonwealth)
before the Reform Act of 1832 opened wide the floodgates.
The Statute de Donis Conditionalibus, which settled our law of
entail, the Act of Mortmain, curtailing ecclesiastical endowments,
the Statute of Quia Emptores, which forbade subinfeudation, and
so limited the importance of tenure in chief, are among the legislative monuments of this clear-headed and industrious ruler.
The greatest, however, of Edward's titles to fame is that in his
reign parliament assumed its completed form and became an
established instrument for the transaction of public business

The grounds of this momentous change are not to be found in any development of political theory, or special distemper of the public mind, but in the practical convenience of dealing upon a national scale with national questions through a gathering representative of the nation. The development of trade and commerce, the expansion of public policy, the growing demands upon government for justice, police, and administration, had now far outrun the slight and dwindling capacity of the feudal revenue. The paltry income to be derived from aids and scutages, marriages and reliefs was an anachronism in an age when a London merchant buying wine in Bordeaux, or selling wool in Ghent, might out-top the rent roll of a baron or an earl. In his need for money Edward could no more afford to neglect the mercantile community than to spare the broad acres of the Church. To obtain a national revenue he found himself increasingly compelled to the expedient of summoning national parliaments.

The form of these conferences was for a long time fluid and uncertain; the word parliament, which means a talk or interchange of views, was originally applied to any meeting of the King's Great Council, and only by degrees confined to such meetings as were reinforced by representatives from the borough and the shire. The "Model Parliament" of 1295 was attended by prelates, earls, barons, and judges, summoned by individual writ, and by two knights from every shire, two citizens from every city, and two burgesses from every borough, summoned through the sheriff, and by representatives of the lower clergy, summoned under the terms of the writs addressed to the two archbishops. By degrees the lower clergy ceased to attend, having other and more pressing duties to perform. It was a lay House of Commons which voted the Reformation Statutes.

But there was no House of Commons in the reign of Edward I, nor yet that familiar procedure by which bills are drafted in the form of statutes, introduced, debated, and voted on in two Houses, and finally receive the royal assent in the House of Lords, as the Clerk looks over his shoulder at Mr. Speaker, humbly standing at the bar with his following from the lower House, and intones the magic formula *Le roy le veult*, at which the red-robed peers, representing the sovereign, simultaneously remove their archaic cocked hats. The division between the two Houses belongs to the fourteenth, the procedure by bills to the fifteenth, century. The main business of an Edwardian parliament was not so much to legislate as to vote supplies and handle petitions.

A vast miscellany of subjects, some important and others trivial, was brought by way of petition to the notice of this great inquest of the nation, which was termed a parliament. The judges were at hand to deal with such petitions as might involve issues of law. Matters of finance were naturally referred to the officials of the exchequer. The meeting of parliament afforded an opportunity of liquidating the current business of the kingdom. Here local grievances were ventilated and private wrongs redressed, arrears of pay settled, quarrels composed, foreign ambassadors received, and treaties drafted. Much of the work done in a parliament was legal, for the King's Council was still the highest court of justice in the land. The consequences were important. It is common knowledge that lawyers in a parliament of amateurs exert more than their fair share of influence. A mediaeval parliament was full of men learned in the law; and our statute book, which is singularly free from idle rhetoric or hysteria, bears the imprint of the most cautious, the most conservative, and the most insular of professions.

In the closing years of this great King's reign an impressive demonstration was given of that respect for law and constitutional usage which was fast becoming an ingrained political tradition of the people. Edward was a strong, straightforward, and, in the main, a popular ruler; but he was exacting and ambitious, and none too scrupulous in his methods. In the year 1297 he found himself at issue with the clergy, who had been told by the Pope that they were to pay no taxes without Rome's consent, with the general body of the nation, who groaned under the lash of his taxgatherers, and with certain pre-eminent members of the baronage who flatly refused to serve in arms beyond the seas. The King then learned that there were limits to his prerogative which he could not transgress without danger. He was compelled to confirm the charters, to permit amendments in his administration, and to admit that he could not increase the established customs on merchandise or raise aid or subsidy without parliamentary assent.

BOOKS WHICH MAY BE CONSULTED

H. W. C. Davis : England under the Normans and Angevins. 1905.

C. Petit-Du taillis : La Monarchie Féodale en France et en Angleterre. 1899.

W. Stubbs : Constitutional History of England. 1880.

E. Lavisse : Histoire de France. 1903.

F. W. Maitland : Memoranda de Parliamento. (Rolls Series.) 1893.

McKechnie : Magna Carta. 1905.

T. F. Tout : Edward I. 1893.

W. H. Hutton : Philip Augustus. 1896.

F. Perry : Louis IX. 1901.

A. Luchaire : Social France at the Time of Philip Augustus. Tr. E. Krebhiel. 1912.

CHAPTER XXVII

WALES, SCOTLAND, IRELAND

Predominance of England in Wales secured by Edward I. Quarrel com-
posed by Henry Tudor. Forces making for Anglo-Scottish Union. Policy
of Edward I. Growth of national feeling in Scotland. True greatness
of Scotland follows the union with England. The tragedy of Ireland.
Effect of the Scottish invasion and the French War.

EDWARD I was the first of our English kings to place in the forefront of his policy the reduction of Wales and Scotland. For a
comparatively brief interval (1259-1338) between two centuries
of profitless fighting in France, the union of the British peoples
under the English crown became an object worthy of steady
attention. In Wales the strategy of Edward was brilliant and
successful. The great mountain fastness of Snowdonia was surrounded and subdued. An English principality, created in favour
d. 1240 of the heir to the throne, divided into shires on the English plan,
and protected by a system of formidable castles, replaced the
north Welsh principality of Gwynnedd, which ever since the days
of Llewellyn the Great had been the heart of tribal Wales and the
principal sanctuary of the Celtic tradition. A political predominance of England in this wild land of narrow valleys and knotted
hills was thus secured; but no more than a predominance. The
Celtic tribes continued to fight among themselves in their mountain fastnesses and from time to time would carry fire and sword
through valleys up which the Lords Marchers, themselves often
married to Welsh women, were steadily pushing the tillage and
the tongue of the Saxon race. The Welsh uplands remained
much as Giraldus Cambrensis, himself half Welsh and half
Norman, had described them at the end of the twelfth century.
" These people are light and active, hardy rather than strong,
and entirely bred up to the use of arms; for not only the nobles,
but all the people are trained to war, and when the trumpet
sounds the tribesman rushes as eagerly from his plough as the
courtier from his court. They live more on flesh, milk, and
cheese than bread, pay little attention to commerce, shipping,
or manufactures, and devote their leisure to the chase and martial exercises. They earnestly study the defence of their country
and their liberty. For these they fight, for these they undergo

hardships, and for these they willingly sacrifice their lives. They esteem it a disgrace to die in bed, an honour to die on the field of battle."

The victory of Edward, though it was followed by wise measures for the pacification of the country, was powerless to alter the stubborn spirit of the Welsh people. In all essentials the Welshman remained as Giraldus describes him, warlike and flighty, jealous and eloquent, sensitive on points of family honour, quick to take up a quarrel and avenge an insult, temperate in food and drink, tricky and versatile in intrigue, and passionately devoted to poetry and song. It is true indeed that Anglo-Norman civilization, spreading from the great Welsh monasteries, and from the castles of the Marcher Lords, exercised an influence on this race of quarrelsome nightingales. English and Welsh families on the border mingled their blood. Welsh bowmen fought side by side with the yeoman farmers of England in the French wars of the fourteenth century, and contributed not a little, since the long bow was a Welsh invention, to secure victory for the King of England. Welsh gentlemen attended the University of Oxford, or, like Owen Glendower, learned their law at the Inns of Court. Wales took what England had to give, but yet remained as different from England as mountain is different from plain.

Long after England had adopted an orderly way of life, the little mountain land upon her flank remained a cauldron of seething and primitive passions. Just as the overspill of our modern Irish factions almost brought English politics to the point of civil war, so the fighting spirit of the Welsh Marcher Lords counted for much in the Wars of the Roses. But the quarrel between England and Wales was finally composed by Henry Tudor's victory on Bosworth field. A Welsh dynasty *1485* ruled over England for a century, incorporated Wales in the English parliamentary system, and made of England a Protestant country. It was a Welsh Prime Minister who brought the British Empire in triumph out of the great war.

The problem of Scotland was different in one important particular. All Scotland south and east of the highland line might equally, so far as its racial composition, its mode of government, and its legal customs were concerned, have been accounted part of English Northumbria. Saxons, Danes, Norsemen, with an

infusion of Celts, stronger no doubt in the northern than in the
southern region, but both north and south of the Cheviots subordinate to these stronger strains, constituted the population
alike of Northumbria and of the Scottish kingdom. Anglo-
Norman nobles held lands on either side of the border; Anglo-
Norman law and Anglo-Norman legal textbooks were as much
respected at Edinburgh as in London. It had been part of the
policy of David I, one of the ablest of Scottish kings, and himself the son of an English princess, to imbue his rude subjects
with some tincture of the more advanced civilization of the
south. In this design he had been successful. The traveller who
reached Edinburgh from York in the middle of the thirteenth
century would have found little in the speech, appearance, and
manners of the people, or in their military and ecclesiastical
architecture, to apprise him that in the course of his ride he had
crossed a frontier between deadly enemies.

1124-53

A political union between Scotland and England was therefore in itself a natural arrangement, more natural than the
union of England with Wales, Ireland, or Gascony. It was
Edward's object to accomplish it. By the Treaty of Brigham
it was arranged that Edward's son and heir should marry
Margaret of Norway, the heiress to the Scottish throne, and that
the two kingdoms should be brought together in a personal
union, each conserving its own rights and customs. Few
mediaeval treaties are wiser than this far-sighted transaction,
which, could it have been carried into effect, would have saved
Britain from centuries of border warfare, and Scotland from the
grinding poverty of its proud and desperate isolation. But it
was not to be. The Maid of Norway died at sea, the Treaty of
Brigham became waste paper, and Edward was driven to achieve
his object by other and more questionable means.[1]

1290

What followed afforded a signal instance of the characteristic
weakness of every mediaeval government, its inability to control the rapacity and maladministration of distant agents. A
dispute having arisen as to the claims of thirteen rival candidates for the Scottish throne, Edward was invited to the invidious task of arbitration. He decided, apparently without
sinister intent, that John Baliol had a better claim than Robert
Bruce. John Baliol was accordingly crowned king. But the
successful candidate had little cause to bless his benefactor. He

[1] Genealogical Table G.

was treated as the puppet of his English overlord. Indignation drove him to rebellion, and rebellion brought down upon Scotland the heavy hand of the English King. The land was conquered and governed as a province of the English kingdom.

And so, but for the tyranny and oppression of Edward's agents, Scotland might have remained. To the leading men of the country, whether lay or ecclesiastical, there was nothing in itself oppressive in the English connection. There was no literature of Scottish nationalism. In no respect was the southerner so alien as the Highlander from Argyll or Inverness. But oppression released new forces in the Scottish nature. The common people rose against the invaders and found in William Wallace, a man from nowhere, an inspired leader of revolt.

The birth of this little Scottish nation is justly accounted one of the cardinal facts of British history. The two founders, William Wallace, the guerilla leader, and Robert Bruce, the royal statesman, are acclaimed by their compatriots to this day as the architects of Scottish greatness. But to the critic who asks what use Scotland made of the independence so bravely won, so triumphantly secured on the field of Bannockburn (1314), the answer is less reassuring. The history of mediaeval Scotland is a tangle of savage broils and convulsions. Measured by the greatness of its statesmen and soldiers, its thinkers and divines, its authors and its artists, the greatness of Scotland belongs not to the era of mediaeval liberty and isolation, but to that less unhappy and distracted period which, following the personal union of the two kingdoms under the house of Stuart, witnessed the steady advance of the Scottish people in all the arts and accomplishments of peace.

Irish history is a tragedy. Often invaded but never subdued, the Irish have not been permitted either to build up an independent civilization out of their native stock of thought and feeling, nor yet forced to receive the discipline of a power stronger and more cultivated than themselves. Again and again the fatal words half-conquest are inscribed upon the annals of this gifted and unfortunate people. The Romans stopped at Anglesea. It was part of their prudence never to cross St. George's Channel, part of Ireland's misfortune that she lacked the convenience of Roman roads and never tasted of Roman

order. Centuries passed. The Irish received Christianity from
St. Patrick (432), and from their new religion acquired an impulse which at the darkest hour of European history brought
them to the forefront of Christian culture. But Ireland was not
long permitted to be a centre of world-wide illumination. Night
again descended with the Danish invasions, when all that was
brilliant and attractive in the social life of the people was
obliterated by a new barbarism; save for the Danish seaport
towns, nothing was left but an untamed wilderness. Then came
an event which was destined to exert an enduring influence on
the fate of the Irish people. England was conquered by a race
gifted beyond all others with the power of organizing conquest
and of turning it to civilized ends. But the Normans had no
eyes for the island across St. George's Channel. Sicily, Normandy, Anjou, distracted their attention; and when at last
with the formal encouragement of Pope Hadrian IV (the only
English Pope), it was resolved to conquer the island, the enterprise was not undertaken by King Henry II, who was far too
busy with the affairs of his wide Angevin Empire, but left to
the courage and appetite of private adventurers. Again the conquest was not complete.

1169-71   The Anglo-Normans who followed Richard de Clare, the Earl
of Pembroke, upon his Irish quest were brilliant soldiers. The
native Irish, divided among themselves by tribal jealousies, and
unprotected by body armour, were easily mastered by a picked
force of mailed knights trained in the best school of contemporary warfare. The Ostman towns passed into English hands.
But then the real difficulties began. The conquerors settled
down as Irish landlords. Many of them married Irish women.
Most of them learned something of the Irish language. Surrounded by the sights and sounds of Ireland, the Butlers and
Fitzgeralds, the De Courceys and De Burghs, took colour from
their environment and began to acquire Irish characteristics.
The old story of the victor taken captive by his victim was now
repeated. The ancient Ireland, with its tribal law and customs,
its language and literature, its evil leaven of a savage and
aboriginal population, but shorn of its ancient pride, continued
to exist.

These fundamental things the Anglo-Norman invasion had
done little to alter. What it did was to give to Ireland a new
aristocracy, which could hardly be described as fully English or

as fully Irish, but which partook of the qualities of both nations and occupied an intermediate position between them.

The overlord was an absent-minded absentee. Of our mediaeval kings Richard II alone was even disposed to treat Ireland seriously. The English settlers and traders in the sea-port towns, the Anglo-Irish nobility, the native Irish tribes, formed three separate communities, which only the wisest and most consistent statesmanship, and perhaps not even that, could have brought into stable and harmonious relations.

During the reign of Edward I, when England was free from continental entanglements, some progress was made in the development of Irish commerce and the spread of the shire system, the chief political export of the mediaeval Englishman. A century of peaceful penetration might have ended with the establishment of Irish unity. But again Ireland was dogged by misfortune. In the year after Bannockburn, Edward Bruce, the *1315* brother of Robert, seeking to cause the utmost annoyance to the hated Englishman, made a violent irruption into the island. In the next year he was joined by his brother. The invasion of the Bruces let loose upon the unfortunate country a war of savages. The tender plant of Irish prosperity withered away, the English influence was rolled back within the narrow compass of the Pale, and the progress of a century was suddenly arrested. These disasters were not repaired. With the outbreak of the Hundred Years' War the attention of the English government was diverted from the needs and bogs of Ireland to the more attractive and splendid quest of the French crown. Ireland sank back into its western mists, and when, in the sixteenth century, a serious effort was again made to reconquer the country for English civilization, there was added to existing sources of division the new and deadly fact of religious schism. England became Protestant, while Ireland remained true to the Roman Faith.

BOOKS WHICH MAY BE CONSULTED

P. Hume Brown : History of Scotland. 1899-1909.
A. Lang : History of Scotland. 1900-07.
Owen Edwards : Wales. 1901.
A. G. Little : Mediaeval Wales.
G. M. Trevelyan : History of England. 1926.
Mrs. J. R. Green : The Making of Ireland and its Undoing. 1908.
J. E. Lloyd : History of Wales. 2 vols. 1911.

CHAPTER XXVIII

THE HUNDRED YEARS' WAR

*The French War and English opinion. The English army. Strength
and weakness of France. The campaign of 1346. The Black Death.
The terrible decade. The Treaty of Calais. French recovery under
Charles V. French relapse. Burgundians and Armagnacs. Richard II.
The Lancastrians. Henry V and Agincourt. Treaty of Troyes. Defection of Burgundy. Joan of Arc. End of the war. Spirit and consequences. The Wars of the Roses. March of English genius.*

THE Hundred Years' War, which appears to a distant posterity
as a tissue of calamitous follies, was regarded with very different
eyes by the English subjects of Edward III and Henry V. To
our forefathers there was nothing fantastic in the idea that an
English King should claim the crown of France, or endeavour
to subject that country to his dominion. They made no protests
against the initiation of the war, nor demanded, even when
success appeared to be hopeless, a pacifist government to bring
it to a conclusion. The fountains of their wrath were reserved,
as in the popular risings in 1381 and 1450, for ministers who
were thought to be responsible for failure abroad or extortion
at home. Parliament met frequently, for without parliaments
the King could not obtain the taxes wherewith to nourish the
war; but no parliament refused the taxes. No critic rose to
point out that England was neglecting the tasks which lay to
her hand in Wales, Scotland, and Ireland to pursue a desperate
and sterile quest in France. A war with the French became
part of the national background, and, in the public mind of
England, though interspersed with taxes, almost assumed the
aspect of an ordinance of fate.

That it was thus popular may be ascribed to the fact that the
English, who were the aggressors, pursued their quarrel upon
enemy soil. While France sustained all the calamities of invasion, England enjoyed the advantages of successful rapine in
a bountiful land beyond the sea. The burden of heavy taxation
was offset for the commonalty of our island not only by the
glamour of foreign victory, but by the conviction that the war
was good for trade, that it enabled England to sell her wool in

Bruges and Ghent, to buy her wine from Bordeaux, and to find a continental market for her tin, her iron, and her hides. And this national and middle-class sentiment about the war was reinforced by the character of the English armies. The old feudal forces, based on tenure, were now discarded for a long-service army, raised by commissions of array, and so far as the infantry arm was concerned composed of English yeomen and of Welsh archery. An English army of the fourteenth century, unlike its French counterpart, was the mirror of a nation, not of a class. The cavalry was no longer the sole or even the most important arm. There now appeared for the first time upon the battlefields of the continent that steady British infantry, drawn from the humbler regions of society, which again and again has disconcerted the calculations of brilliant commanders. In the fourteenth century these stalwart countrymen were entrusted with a weapon which in range and hardiness outstripped all competitors, and in the use of which they had attained by devoted practice upon the village green an unequalled skill. The British yeomen who decided the day at Creçy and Agincourt were armed with the long bow, and, as the famous heavy cavalry of France advanced to the charge, aimed at the horses. A cloud of arrows brought the assault to a sudden standstill, and before a blow had been exchanged, the dismounted riders were floundering on the ground in their heavy armour, an easy prey to their assailants.

In the first decades of the fourteenth century France showed all the promise of a great nation. Her soil was rich, her vegetation was varied, her peasants and burgesses were economical and laborious. In no part of Europe, save perhaps in Venice, was the art of civilized life so well understood or so happily practised. The French were more refined than the English, more comfortable than the Germans, more open to world influence than the Spaniards, less afflicted by the violence of domestic discord than the citizens of Italy. For the last two centuries no country had given so many patterns to European thought as the land of Abelard and St. Bernard, of the Crusades and the Troubadours, of chivalry and scholasticism. Much also she owed to good fortune. The Capetian house, which for three hundred years had never failed of a male heir, had spared her the evils of palace revolutions and disputed successions. She had given dynasties to England and Sicily, and later had sent princes of the house of Anjou to reign in Hungary and Naples. The quixotic King of Bohemia thought that no place in the world was comparable to Paris. Even the Papacy had become French, for a French Pope, surrounded by a college of cardinals in which France exercised a predominant influence, was established at Avignon, and divided only from French territory by the breadth of the Rhone.

From this position of apparent strength there were three important deductions. The convenient shelter of the Capetian dynasty was not destined to be immortal. In 1316 Louis, the son of Philip IV, died, leaving only a daughter, but no male heir. He was followed by his brothers Philip V and Charles the Fair, the French lawyers obligingly discovering that, since females were excluded from the succession to a certain form of property under the law of the Salian Franks, they were incapable of sitting on the French throne. Then, in 1328, Charles died without male issue, and was succeeded by his cousin Philip of Valois. The title of the founder of the Valois dynasty was not accepted without challenge, for Edward III of England was the grandson of Philip the Fair by his mother Isabella, and claimed that a female, if she could not herself reign in France, was entitled to transmit the regal dignity to her male heir. Not for three hundred years had such a doubt been cast upon the legitimacy of a King of France.[1]

The second drawback was even more serious. All through the fourteenth century the nobility of France lived in a kind of feudal honeymoon, learning nothing, forgetting nothing, and foreseeing nothing. They waged private war, as if the state were not in danger. They oppressed their villeins, as if it were not through their labour that the life of the country was sustained. They were blind to the strength which came to their antagonists from the social fusion, which exposed the richest English barons and the poorest English yeomen to the equal perils of a soldier's life. Though the power of plebeian infantry to defeat the most aristocratic cavalry in the world had been demonstrated again and again, at Courtrai in 1302 and later on the moonlit field of Crécy, it was necessary for a French king to be brought as a prisoner to London, and for an English king to receive the crown of France in Paris, before the lesson was taken to heart. It is a curious illustration of the inability of a military caste to receive the teaching of experience that,

[1] Genealogical Table H.

lthough the English brought artillery upon the field of Creçy,
t was not until the battle of Formigny 104 years later that the
'rench were able to produce a culverin which outranged the
light of the English arrow.

Another source of weakness was so inveterate that only the convulsion of the French Revolution was able to effect a radical cure.
The French people, for all their brilliance, could neither impose a
good tax nor pay a bad one. Even under the best of her mediaeval
kings the fiscal system of France was deplorable. The taxes were
farmed, with the familiar result that more was wrung from the
taxpayer than ever found its way into the coffers of the state. The
gabelle, a salt tax, was crushing for the poor. The traders were
oppressed by an impost on sales, by constant tampering with the
coinage, and, under Charles V and his successors, by a ruinous
system of internal customs duties. The sale of offices, carrying
fiscal exemptions, was a vicious expedient invented by Philip the
Fair and revived by Charles V; and the poison of favours and
exemptions, once sanctioned, spread like a gangrene through
the whole system. It is characteristic of the fiscal weakness of
the country that the large ransom demanded by England for
King John of France, who was captured at the battle of Poitiers,
could not be otherwise met than by the sale of a French princess
to Galeazzo Visconti, the upstart and opulent Duke of Milan.

The struggle between France and England, which might
easily have been occasioned by a sailors' quarrel in a Channel
port, or by a foray across the border of Aquitaine, or, since
French aid was now (1336) openly given to the party of David
Bruce and the cause of Scottish independence, by some incident
in the course of that northern warfare, did, in fact, arise from
an event in Flanders. In 1336 all Englishmen travelling or resident in that country were, by the orders of Count Louis acting
upon instructions from Paris, arrested and cast into prison. The
outrage produced a reply from England which threatened to
bring the flourishing industries of Flanders toppling to the
ground. The export of English wool was forbidden, and the
English market was closed to the import of Flemish cloth.

At this critical juncture the course of western policy was
determined by the vigour and resolution of a Flemish brewer.
Jacob van Artevelde of Ghent preferred economic prosperity in
free alliance with England to economic ruin in feudal subjection

to Philip of France. He forced a rupture, and to quiet th
scruples of the Flemings prevailed upon Edward III to claim th
crown of France.

1340   The first serious action in the war was an English naval victor
at Sluys, so complete that for a space of thirty years it gave t
England the mastery of the Channel. Yet for six years no effor
was made to exploit this advantage. Why should England invad
France seeing that the danger to the English trade with Flander
had been averted, and the power of the French to land forces i
England was, for the time being, effectively broken? But th
embers of this quarrel were widely spread, and the flame whicl
died down in one quarter spurted up in another. A disputed
succession to the Duchy of Brittany brought England and Franc
into the field in support of rival claimants. Philip stood fo
Charles of Blois, and Edward for John of Montfort, the cham
pion of that part of the duchy which was Celtic in speech an
race, and therefore most strongly opposed to the invasive ir
fluences of the French.

    The outlines of a great panorama of war were now defined
In Flanders, in Brittany, in Aquitaine, in Scotland, the power o
France and England stood opposed. The idea of an Englisl
converging movement from Normandy, Brittany, and Aquitain
outlined itself in the mediaeval manner, not very distinctly o
with any close attention to detail, but nevertheless in such a wa
as to make 1346, the year in which the English sacked Poitiers
won Creçy, besieged Calais, and routed the Scots at Neville'
Cross, an *annus mirabilis* in the war. Yet from all these far-flun
victories there resulted only one point of permanent advantag
to the victors. Calais became an English town in 1347, and s
remained until it was lost under Queen Mary in the sixteentl
century.

    The year of the capture of Calais was marked by the adven
of a calamity more destructive than a century of mediaeval war
fare. The Black Death, a bubonic plague originating in the fa
east, swept along the lines of mediaeval traffic into every part o
Europe. It was conveyed from Asia Minor into Italy and Spain
entered France by Marseilles, England through Dorsetshire, and
swept eastwards through Germany and the Scandinavian coun
tries into Poland, Austria, and Russia. Mediaeval figures, upor
the basis of which it has been calculated by a modern writer tha

one-fourth of the population of Europe perished of this plague,
are notoriously untrustworthy. We have no complete means of
checking the statement of contemporaries that a hundred
thousand lives were lost in Venice, Florence, Paris, and London,
sixty thousand in Avignon, fifty-seven thousand in Norwich, or
that the death roll of Germany, which admittedly suffered less
than Italy and France, reached a figure of one and a quarter
million. But there can be no doubt that the mortality was upon
such a scale as to produce in its train those grave moral disorders
and far-reaching social consequences always to be expected when
mankind is overwhelmed by some vast natural calamity which it
is unable to forecast, to measure, or to mitigate.

It was observed of the plague that it sought out by preference
the young and the strong. Sometimes the enemy was merciful,
and slew by a sudden stroke; more often the patient was condemned to a few hours of hopeless agony. In Avignon, where
the plague raged for seven months, a creditable but forlorn
attempt was made to diagnose the cause of the malady. Bodies
were exhumed and examined by order of the Pope. But the
disease pursued its deadly course, working havoc among the
narrow, unclean mediaeval streets, and upon the decks of ships,
so that they drifted over the waters without guidance from their
lifeless crews, and stripping the fields of the labour which should
drive the plough, reap the harvest, or tend the cattle.

Among the moral results of this disaster the most shameful
was a series of attacks upon the Jewish population, who at Mainz
and other German-speaking towns were burned in their hundreds
or thousands by an infuriated mob in the belief that the plague
was a malignant device of the Semitic race for the confusion of
the Catholic creed. One consequence of some significance for
Europe ensued from this outburst of western barbarism. The
Jews who were persecuted in the Rhenish cities found now, as
on earlier occasions, an asylum in Poland. Casimir the Great   *1333-70*
took occasion to renew the protection which a predecessor had
accorded to this community in 1260; and the high proportion of
Semites to be found in modern Poland is not a little due to his
enlightened policy, pursued at a moment when no western Jew
was safe from the fury of Catholic mobs.

Other reactions to the calamity were less atrocious than these.
Some people, as in Boccaccio's famous description of the plague
in Florence, surrendered themselves to the pleasures of the

moment. Others, like the flagellants, who marched in melan
choly penitential processions, flogging themselves with rods
iron, fell into ecstasies of religious emotion. There were thos
again, who took to a life of reckless brigandage. But beyon
these passing excesses, which disappeared with their excitin
cause, the plague exercised certain durable effects, so that whe
it died down in 1350 (to be renewed at intervals by minor visit:
tions), and men resumed their normal habits of mind, Europea
society was not quite what it had been before.

The change was not catastrophic. Rather it would be true
say that the sudden destruction of life (which was specially ev
dent in the monasteries) had set in motion a series of small shif
ings, which, in their accumulated and accumulating effect
amounted to a revolution. In England, perhaps, the chang
were more noticeable than elsewhere: in the monasteries
marked decline in literary activity and discipline; in the in
poverished country parishes empty rectories and absente
priests; in the grammar schools the substitution, with a new rac
of teachers, of English for French; in architecture the spread
the Perpendicular style, simpler than the older forms of Gothi
more easily standardized, and better adapted to the capacity
a diminished band of travelling masons; and finally, in agricu
ture a marked acceleration of that process of converting labou
services into money payments, which led in time to the di
appearance of an unfree village population and to the break u
of the mediaeval system of tillage.

The last of these changes, which is not peculiar to Englanc
was due to the fact that owing to the dearth of labour the peasan
was able to demand a higher price for his toil, and the lord o
the manor was no longer always in a postion to secure the worl
ing of his demesne land save by the novel expedient of labou
hired from outside. The revolutionary possibilities of such
situation gave great alarm to the governing class both in Franc
and England. In France workmen were forbidden to take mor
than a third of their former wage. In England, Parliamen
called labourers and artisans to their old rate of wage and forbad
them to move from one county to another. Political economy
like nature, may be expelled with a fork, but it always return
The legislation of the Edwardian parliaments was unavailing t
arrest a process grounded in the economic necessities of the time
As the value of labour services to the lord steadily diminished

the convenience of a mobile labour supply, remunerated by money payments, became by sure degrees more clearly apparent. So the old manorial economy was gradually sapped by new forces, and as the villein became detached from his bondage to the soil, and began to sell his labour freely in the market, voices were raised challenging the whole social order and asking the question which in every virile generation is put to society by equalitarian men:

> ' When Adam delved, and Eve span,
>   Who was then the gentleman?''

The tragedy of the plague neither sobered the frivolity nor mitigated the ardour of the rival aristocracies of France and England. The national quarrel was revived at the earliest moment and prosecuted at the expense of the miserable peasantry of France with a barbarous and animated zest. The ten years (1350-1360) which follow the accession of John the Bountiful to the throne of France were written in flame and blood on the annals of his distracted kingdom. Petrarch, who travelled through the country four or five years after the battle of Poitiers, said that it had been so wrecked and ravaged by the English armies that he could scarce persuade himself that this was the same flourishing land which he had previously known. Arson and pillage, murders and rape, burning crops and mutilated cattle, marked the progress of the proud island race and their continental levies. In these methods of barbarism the Black Prince won a pre-eminence which has secured for him an abiding place in the popular memory of western France.

The experience of this terrible decade was the first impressive indication to the world that the remote inhabitants of England, whose defeat at the hands of the yet more savage Scots upon the field of Bannockburn was no distant memory, had now become a great military nation. In a series of unexpected victories, sometimes, as at Poitiers, obtained against overwhelming odds, these strange people had overthrown the ancient military glory of France. One English army led by the King had appeared before the walls of Rheims and Paris. Another, advancing from Bordeaux, had carried fire and sword through the olive groves and vineyards, the gardens and the tilth of Languedoc, wasting the richest revenue-producing areas under the French monarchy and involving it in the greatest embarrassment and distress.

It is difficult to imagine any form of humiliation to which this nation, only a generation before esteemed to be the proudest in Europe, was not now subjected. The King of France was a prisoner in England. A crushing tribute was imposed upon his people for a ransom. The disbanded marauders of the wars, gathered into free companies, pillaged the countryside, and dared to levy blackmail on the Pope. Even the patient tillers of the field, upon whose broad shoulders had fallen the principal burden of these cruel wars, rose at last against their enemies the nobles in a formidable revolt. The Jacquerie of 1358, which was characterized, as every rising of the desperate poor is apt to be, by great ferocity, was put down with ease; but the country was no stronger for that bitter victory, nor for the terrible social chasm which it left behind it. Save for one circumstance which impeached the completeness of the English triumph, France was prostrate. Paris had escaped the clutch of the enemy, and so long as Paris was French, France was not English. Yet even here a popular revolution, fomented by patriotic fury, public distress and disloyal intrigue, nearly succeeded in displacing the Dauphin by Charles of Navarre, that smooth and perfidious intriguer, who was the tool of England and pledged by a secret instrument to hold the crown of France as a vassal of the English King.

When at last the French had made the discovery that by the avoidance of pitched battles they could tire the patience of their enemy, it became part of British prudence to accept a peace. The Treaty of Calais, 1360, assigned Normandy to France, Aquitaine, Calais, and Ponthieu to England, an arrangement deeply humiliating to French pride, but permitting France to enjoy a few years of necessary breathing space. When the quarrel was renewed the balance was no longer tilted in favour of England. 1364-80 Charles V, now ruler of France, was a very different man from his prodigal and thriftless father. If a bad financier can ever be described as a good king, Charles the Wise merited that description. He had seen too much of mob rule during the evil days which followed the disaster of Poitiers to be enamoured of popular government, and it was not through the States-General, which he summoned once only during his reign, that he proposed to restore the fortunes of France. His main merit was that he divined the essential elements of victory, a navy which could dispute the seas with England, an army which would harass

EUROPE IN 1360.

**Boundary of
The Empire.**
Eastern Empire.
Ottoman Turks.
English Dominions.
Papal States.
Teutonic Knights.
to Aragon.
to Venice.

English Miles.
0   100 200 300 400 500

without engaging the enemy, and a people recalled to sentiments
of loyalty and hope. First of all the French kings he endeavoured
to give his subjects a sense of the sea, visiting himself, and causing others to visit, the ports and dockyards in order that money
might be more freely spent on the ships. Privileges for the
towns, titles for the townsmen, economy in administration conciliated the general favour. The country was rid of the plague
of the free companies or marauding soldiers from the disbanded armies, who were sent over the Pyrenees to die in
a Castilian civil war. As for the army, it was placed under the
Breton Bertrand du Guesclin, a great master of Fabian tactics,
who, in the campaign of 1369-1375, stripped England of all her
overseas possessions save Bayonne, Bordeaux, and Calais. Before
the end of the reign of this prudent and successful king, the
French sailors were ravaging the English coast, and a Spanish
navy had appeared in the Thames. Edward III and the Black
Prince were dead. In 1380 Richard II was a lad of thirteen. The
good fortune of the French monarchy seemed to be assured.
Indeed, but for the fact that King Charles had embarked upon
an attempt to conquer Brittany before he had finished with
England, the soil of France might have been completely cleared
of enemy occupation during his reign.

But then followed one of the most disastrous periods in the
history of France, during which all the gains which had marked
the later years of Charles V's reign were thrown away and the
continued existence of the French nation was again imperilled.
The source of this extraordinary relapse is to be found in an
accumulation of unexpected evils—a long minority, a mad king,
a spirit of fierce rivalry and faction among the princes of the
blood and their noble followers, and finally in the formidable
circumstance that for sixteen years England could rely upon
the active co-operation of the most powerful subject of the
French Crown.

It has already been noted that the kings of France had acquired
the habit of creating appanages or great territorial domains for
the princes of the blood, a method of decentralization often convenient but sometimes dangerous. Such an appanage John the
Bountiful, in his light-hearted and short-sighted way, had created
for his youngest son Philip, who had earned for himself by his
courage on the field of Poitiers the title of Le Hardi. To him
was accorded the Duchy of Burgundy, a splendid fief in itself,

1350-64

1363-
1404

famous for its wines and cookery, and French to the core, but destined by reason of three fortunate marriages to be joined to territories richer and more populous than itself, and for the most part estranged from France by race and language and by the potent affiliations of trade and politics. In a word, Philip espoused the heiress of Flanders and married two children into the Bavarian house of Wittelsbach, which ruled the greater part of the country now known as the kingdom of Holland. These were fateful alliances. It was doubtless the calculation of Charles V that the Burgundian dukes would bring the rich Flemish cities into the orbit of French influence. What happened was the opposite. Rich Flanders proved to be a more powerful magnet than poor Burgundy, Brussels a more attractive capital than Dijon, the preservation of English goodwill a more important consideration than a close friendship with France. As time went on the dukes of Burgundy began to feel the effects of their new environment. They became less French and more Flemish, and behaved as the ambitious masters of an independent and rival state established on the eastern flank of France.

If Charles V had been succeeded by a strong man no great evil might have resulted from the rise of this new power; but his successor, who ascended the throne in 1380, was an unbalanced and vicious boy, who, soon after reaching his majority, lapsed into a state of acute mania. The incapacity of Charles VI ultimately left the government of France to be disputed between Louis of Orléans, the King's youngest brother, and John of Burgundy, his powerful cousin. Louis was young, attractive, and through his Italian wife, Valentina Visconti, touched by the spirit of the Renaissance. John the Fearless was *1404-19* violent and of a rougher mould. The first stood for an energetic course of action against the hereditary foe, the second prudently recognized the economic interdependence of Flanders and England. On every question which divided France, and notably on the schism in the Church which was caused by the election of rival Popes, these two leaders took opposite sides. Louis stood for Benedict, the French Pope at Avignon; more wisely, since the support of the capital was vital, the passionate Burgundian espoused a policy of neutrality, which brought him the favour of the doctors, the students, and the rabble of Paris.

Then occurred one of those startling political crimes which in periods of great tension announce that patience is exhausted. One night in 1407 Orleans was murdered in a Paris street. There is no mystery about the origin of this crime, since it was avowed by the Duke, and defended by a don, nor any doubt of its importance, seeing that it split France sharply into two halves so furiously estranged that, by reason of their divisions, northern France, including Paris, passed into the control of an English king.

It was a sinister fact, which has often been repeated in the course of French history, that the full violence of the party contest was nowhere so fully felt as in Paris. The capital, which should have been the seat of order, was, on the contrary, the centre of the storm. It was so after the disaster of Poitiers, when the cause of constitutional reform was ruined by terror and treason; it was so again after the murder of the Duke of Orleans, when the intellectual proletariat of the University, in strange alliance with the powerful corporation of butchers, and supported by the Duke of Burgundy, besieged the Bastille and attempted to secure the persons of the royal family, enacting a series of revolutionary scenes which anticipate in many curious particulars the events of the French and more recently of the Spanish Revolution.

Neither in England had the course of politics run smoothly since the death of Edward III. The reign of Richard II, the son of the Black Prince, was happy only by reason of the fact that in it peace was eventually made and maintained with France. In other respects it was an uneasy reign, marked by fierce factions and by abrupt vicissitudes of policy, by widespread social discontent, and by a disquieting growth of heresy which challenged the whole fabric of the papal Church. But of all the issues which were calculated to endanger national peace none was so grave as the danger to the constitutional liberties of the country which disclosed itself in the last two years of Richard's reign. Whether it was by reason of his second marriage to Isabella of France and to the influence of French example, for, as we have seen, the French States-General met only once during Charles' reign, or from a strange fit of impatience and exasperation, such as may seize hold of temperamental natures, Richard in the last two years of his life showed a plain intention to discontinue parliamentary government. In this he seriously miscalcu-

1377-99

lated the temper of his countrymen. All through the French war, parliament, which had come in the course of the reign of Edward III to be divided into two houses, had been accustomed to meet and to vote supplies. The claim of the baronage and of the prelates, and, in a lesser degree, of the burgesses and knights, to take a hand in the burden of national affairs had by this time become established; and it was too late now to reverse the engines. Edward II had been deposed because he governed too little, Richard II was deposed because he attempted to govern too much. Without any serious convulsion in the national life, the last of the Plantagenets was displaced by Henry of Lancaster and murdered in prison, a lone, courageous, extravagant figure, more humane and enlightened than the fierce Gallophobe nobles around him, but pledged to a strange and unpopular cause.

The house of Lancaster stood for two principles which appealed to the Englishman of that time, religious orthodoxy and constitutional government. The policy of toleration which had permitted so great a heretic as John Wycliffe to die in his bed was exchanged for a course of persecution, which, in a very short time, frightened learning and respectability away from Lollardy, and reduced the movement to obscurity and ignorance. But while speculative liberty was suppressed, Parliament took full advantage of the new dynasty to press for the control of legislation and finance. The constitutional advance, which is marked under the Lancastrian dynasty, was not indeed maintained, for liberty depends upon the preservation of order, and the main characteristic of English governments in the fifteenth century was their failure to maintain the law. Yet the precedents first established by the Lancastrian parliaments were not forgotten, for it was to them that the common lawyers made their appeal in the great struggle between Crown and Parliament in the seventeenth century.

England has never been an easy country to govern. "A wondrous and fickle land is this," said Richard II as he lay in the Tower, "for it hath exiled, slain, or ruined so many kings, rulers, and great men, and is ever tainted, and toileth with strife, variance, and envy"; and Henry IV, a cheerless, cold-blooded *1399-* soldier, somewhat worn by his early campaigns in Prussia and *1413* Hungary, and soon falling ill of an incurable malady, found that the governance of England was no easy matter, what with the Lollards and the Scots, the Welshmen rebelling under Owen Glendower, and the Percies making such trouble on the north that they had to be beaten in a pitched fight at Shrewsbury. A prudent statesman succeeding to the heritage which Henry IV left behind him might well have concluded that what was truly needed for the establishment of the new dynasty was peace abroad. Henry V, however, was not built for prudent courses, but was all flame and martial ardour, as he lives in *1413-22* Shakespeare's verse. If England were not easy to govern, she presented in contrast to the divisions of France the spectacle of a united people. The baronage and clergy supported the Crown, the schism in the Papacy was no schism in England. Whatever inner dangers existed—and there was a party hungry for the property of the Church—were overcome by the animating prospect of war in France. Henry negotiated simultaneously both with the Burgundian and with the Orleanist or Armagnac factions. He was ready to offer himself to the highest bidder. Encouraged by the divisions of France he never for a moment doubted of victory.

1415   The capture of Harfleur and the battle of Agincourt were the first results of the young King's resolve to renew the glories of Crécy and Poitiers, and to show that in point of military prowess the house of Lancaster was worthy to succeed the Plantagenets. The French had neither army nor navy to resist the invaders. A section of the French nobility, almost entirely drawn from the Armagnac faction, sacrificed themselves vainly on the field of Agincourt, as French nobles had sacrificed themselves at Crécy and Poitiers, and later, fighting against the Turks, at the great slaughter of Nicopolis in 1396. But neither these victories nor Henry's later conquest of Normandy would have led anywhere had it not been for the vendetta between the rival parties in France itself. The Burgundians, who had stood aloof from the Agincourt campaign, and watched with unconcern the fall of Rouen, were swept into the war on the English side by a grave political crime. In 1419 John the Fearless was treacherously murdered on the bridge of Montereau by Tanneguy de Chastel, one of the Dauphin's intimates, and the flames of civil discord burst out afresh. For the Burgundians and also for the city of Paris, the Dauphin was henceforward impossible. They vowed to exclude him from the succession, and secured for Henry V of England (Treaty of

Troyes, 1420) the regency of France and the hand of a French princess.

All through the war with France the English had in great measure owed their military successes to French, Breton, and Flemish allies. The famous army of the Black Prince which won the battle of Poitiers was largely recruited from Gascony. One of the best of its captains was a Gascon nobleman. And now when Henry V had revived the association of France and England under a common crown, the governing factor in the situation was again the friendship of a continental faction. Everything depended upon the continued alliance of that party in the French state to whom no Englishman could be so odious as an Armagnac. So long as Philip the Good of Burgundy found it to his interest to support the Lancastrian cause, the small English garrisons which were posted to the towns of northern France were regarded as auxiliaries of a local faction, rather than as alien instruments of a usurper's rule. But when Burgundy changed sides (Treaty of Arras, 1435) the whole complexion of affairs was altered. It was thenceforward no longer a question whether England could maintain her footing in France. Without French support her position was untenable. Only the pace of her reluctant withdrawal remained to be settled.

Behind the great altar of the abbey church at Rheims lay the tomb of St. Remi and within the tomb a dove-shaped reliquary. In that reliquary was a crystal vase containing the sacred oil which a dove from Heaven had brought down for the consecration of Clovis, the first Christian King of the Franks. With this holy fluid, always by a miraculous dispensation maintained at its original volume, St. Charlemagne and St. Louis, and many Kings of France less illustrious than they, had been anointed, and at the solemn ceremony of their consecration had sworn to rule their subjects with justice and mercy. In the eyes of the pious it was a matter of doubt whether a King of France could be regarded as in a complete sense a lawful king if he had not undergone in the cathedral at Rheims this immemorial rite.

Henry V was never consecrated. He died prematurely in the full tide of his manhood (1422), poisoned, as the English soldiers maintained, by the magic verses of the Armagnacs, and leaving an heir of nine months, whose tender years would long preclude him from taking the solemn engagements of a newly consecrated King of France. The way was clear for the Dauphin Charles, chief of the Armagnacs and eleventh child of the mad king, a sickly, timid, pious youth, frightened of the English, still more frightened of the violent passions which raged around him as he held his fugitive court at Bourges, Poitiers, or Chinon, but still the head of the Valois house and the descendant of the Capets.

Joan of Arc divined that Charles must be consecrated at Rheims. Celestial voices spoke to the peasant girl as she plied her household tasks or tended her father's sheep at Domrémy, bidding her ride out of Lorraine into France and there relieve the city of Orleans which was besieged by the English, after which she must conduct the Dauphin to his consecration at Rheims. With a sublime simplicity of purpose Joan accomplished these two missions. Nine days after her arrival before its walls, Orleans, which had already endured a siege for more than seven months, was a free city. To the Dauphin, who doubted even his own legitimacy, she brought the warrant of her inspired confidence, and the political credentials which the rite of consecration could alone supply. It is idle to pretend that this girl of eighteen was a military expert. Good soldiers were at her side. Her strategy was spiritual. Ardent herself and clear of hesitations, she gave courage and elation to a disheartened cause.

May,
1429

The fear and hatred which she inspired among her opponents is a measure of her success. While the Armagnacs regarded her as a saint and a heroine, she appeared to the whole Burgundian and English interest to be a very wise sorceress and an unquestioned heretic. How else could they explain the sudden transformation of the whole war, the relief of Orleans, the defeat of Patay, the capture of Troyes, the coronation of Rheims, the threat to Paris, the exchange in the ranks of their enemies of a feeling of dejection for one of confidence and hope? A prophetess could only bring such victories to a bad cause if she were inspired by the Evil One. The University of Paris, which was Burgundian to the core, and had not scrupled to defend its Burgundian opinions by a pretorian band of butchers, was convinced that Joan was a witch.

After the consecration her task was accomplished. The work

of national deliverance to which she had given so strong an impulse could proceed without her. Having fallen into the hands of the enemy at Compiègne, she was handed over to the English chieftains, who, with the active and enthusiastic help of Pierre Cauchon, the Bishop of Beauvais, and of the doctors of the Paris University and of other notable French divines, burned her to death as a witch in the market place of Rouen. *May 28, 1431* It is to be remarked that Charles VII, who owed everything to this girl, never raised his finger to help her in her extremity. A young male peasant from the Gévaudan, professing also to be a visionary of pure and saintly life, had promised to bring Charles victory whenever he appeared, and the assistance of Joan was no longer indispensable. To her English enemies, whose views are enshrined in Shakespeare's " Henry VI," she was a wicked sorceress employed by bad men to make trouble for good, honest, valiant Englishmen who in a fair fight could always beat the " Coué," but were ill matched against the magic of a wizard.

The martyrdom of Joan gave to France a sense of moral unity such as the country had never yet known. One by one England was divested of all those advantages which had belonged to her in the earlier stages of the conflict. The Burgundians made their peace with France in 1435. Paris went over to the enemy in 1436. And meanwhile Charles, growing in prudence as he advanced in age, and being well served by able men of the middle class, such as Jacques Coeur the financier and Jean Bureau the first French expert in artillery, the arm with which Napoleon frightened all Europe, constructed an efficient instrument of government.

Under the Ordonnance sur la Gendarmerie of 1439, the King set up a regular force under royal officers, to be financed by a royal tax, the *taille*, while at the same time he struck hard at the inveterate lawlessness of the nobility, who were forbidden to tallage their demesnes, or to raise troops without royal licence, or to levy private war. It is characteristic of the great nobles of France that they rose in rebellion against a scheme of reform so essential to the strength and security of the French nation. The Praguerie was crushed. The Royal Army of France, *1440* cavalry, infantry, artillery, was formed in defiance of the feudal traditions of the Ancien Régime, and in the last campaign of this long war (1449-1453) made its first triumphant appearance on the battlefields of Europe, announcing that the age of artillery was come. Rouen, Bayonne, Bordeaux, fell in turn before the organized patriotism of France. Calais alone of all her French possessions remained to England after the peace was signed in 1453.

A curious feature of this long war was the persistence, despite cruel atrocities, of the spirit of the tournament. War, which was in practice an orgy of arson and pillage, was at the same time conceived of as the sport of kings, the matching of champions, and the ordeal of God. Edward III challenged Philip VI, Henry V challenged Louis the Dauphin to put all to the test of single combat. The display of personal courage and the observance of the conventions of chivalry were deemed to be obligations more binding upon the great Anglo-French military brotherhood than the obscurer virtues of clemency or discipline. On the evening of Poitiers, the Black Prince, who did not scruple to butcher the population of Limoges without regard to sex or age, waited at table upon the captive King John with ostentatious ceremony. The high-bred *camaraderie* between noblemen who spoke the same language, enjoyed the same sports, worshipped according to the same rites, and obeyed the same canons of social behaviour, brought some mitigation to the conflict, save only where it was waged by rough sailors on the unchivalrous sea. It is significant of the spirit of those times that in the year after Crecy the French widow of Earl Aymer of Pembroke founded a college at Cambridge, wherein French students were to receive a preferential claim to appointments, and that when the news came to Paris of Edward III's death, the King of France commanded a solemn service to be held in the Sainte Chapelle to the memory of a great hero, who was also his most dangerous and persistent foe.

A necessary effect of the long war was to end that close interpenetration of France and England which had helped through the Norman Conquest to fashion England and through the Angevin Empire to mould the administration of France, and had brought so much good and evil to both countries. In England the French language had given place to the native tongue in literature and the law courts, in parliament and the pulpit, in the official correspondence of kings and in the private letters of cultivated persons. The great contribution which English writers had made to the common literature of the two peoples was now brought to a standstill. French and English writers went their several ways, the English acknowledging the spell of French models, but also, under Chaucer's leadership, listening for the first time to Dante and the Italians. Between the two nations a steady feeling of bitterness and estrangement replaced the old relations of tolerance, which are reflected in the amusing chronicles of Froissart. The feudal age, leaving in Sir Thomas Malory's prose romance of Morte d'Arthur (1470) an imperishable after-glow, had passed away, and was now replaced by the clash of states.

A great war cannot proceed without far-reaching consequences for human life. There is nothing so efficacious in breaking the hard crust of custom as a sudden enlargement in the scale of state expenditure. The need for state money creates new problems, opens new horizons, establishes new claims, brings new men to the forefront of affairs, disturbs the economic relations of classes. The fiscal necessities of Edward III were the financial opportunities of the Florentine bankers and the constitutional opportunities of the English parliament. Out of the fear of war risks the English took to the manufacture of cloth and so established the first of their capitalistic industries. A fall in the value of money and a corresponding rise in prices was the natural effect of the disastrous currency policy pursued by the French kings under the pressure of war, and produced, not for France only, all the embarrassments which inflation inevitably brings in its train. As the existing taxes became insufficient, new sources of revenue had to be discovered; as price levels rose, the relations between the employer and the employed, the tradesman and the customer, the landlord and the peasant became difficult and embittered. In the decade between 1375 and 1385 a wave of popular discontent passed over western Europe. It was felt in Flanders, in northern France, in Ghent, and most seriously in the English peasant rising of 1381. Everywhere the ruling class was for a moment seriously alarmed. A new force had made itself manifest and given a shake to the obdurate fabric of European caste. The warrior aristocracy could no longer ignore the great underworld of thrusting ambitions which was now helping to shape society. It is significant that the English government which proposed the poll tax of 1381 was under the impression that all the wealth of the kingdom had passed into the hands of the artisans and labourers.

There was a further unexpected effect of these economic disturbances. Monetary inflation presented to the Popes of Avignon a problem of extraordinary difficulty. Whence were they to obtain the revenue necessary to support that imposing establishment which in the thirteenth century had supplied to Europe its active organizing principle, and was still regarded as a necessity of civilized life by Latin Christians? John XXII, the Frenchman from Cahorsin, invented Annates. That ingenious financier and theologian took the first year's revenue from every benefice. Other engines of extortion, notably the habit of papal provisions, were invoked in aid of the apostolic budget, and created, more particularly in England, deep resentment and formal opposition. The effects were far-reaching. Long before it had occurred to the common man to challenge the faith or impugn the credentials of the Papacy, the moral authority of papal government was gravely impaired throughout northern Europe by its corrupt and demoralizing methods of finance.

The English epilogue to this long French drama was the suicide of the feudal nobility in the Wars of the Roses. The nobles, to whom it had become a second nature to fight in the fields of France or among the hills of Wales, and for whom an affray at arms was little more serious than the pursuit of the deer and the fox, were not easily accommodated to the humdrum ways of peace. Many of them commanded little armies of liveried retainers, who could be entrusted to intimidate a jury, to despatch an enemy, or to help themselves without ceremony to the purse of the travelling merchant or to the goods of neighbours poorer and weaker than themselves. Against this evil of the "overmighty subject" the weak government of Henry VI was entirely unable to cope.

So two aristocratic factions, led by rival pretenders to the Plantagenet inheritance, fought out their public and private quarrels amid a people either heartily indifferent to the issue or honestly perplexed as to whether its interests were likely to be best served under the Red Rose of Lancaster or the White Rose of York. It was fortunate for England that this should be so. It was well that no question worthy to engage the passions of a great people was involved in this blood-letting of the old aristocracy. The two great movements which during the fifteenth century made for the welfare of the English nation, the growth of industrial and mercantile prosperity and the advancing cause of peasant freedom, were unaffected by the vendetta of the country houses. When the storm finally blew itself out it was found to have occasioned little damage. Rather the state profited by the elimination of forces which obstructed the working of government and the observance of law.

Though the loss of the French dominions was the subject of many bitter regrets, the English neither felt nor had reason to feel that they were inferior to their neighbours. They still cherished the belief that some day the glories of Crecy and Agincourt could be revived. They learnt from Sir John Fortescue to congratulate themselves upon the free constitution which it was their privilege to inherit, and to contrast the wellbeing and plenty of the English cottagers with the harsh lot of the French peasantry under their noble taskmasters. If they lost the long war, they none the less emerged a proud nation, hungry for action and consumed with restlessness within the boundaries of their small island. Nor had their development been confined to the arts of war. The contemporaries of Crecy and Agincourt had shown many forms of excellence more enduring than the prowess of their bowmen. They had developed a language so rich and flexible, and so happily compounded of Latin and Teutonic elements, that none is more fitted to express the thoughts and feelings of a poetic, imaginative, and humorous people. They had discovered in Chaucer and Langland two poets of genius. They had built the beautiful chapels of Winchester and New College. In needlework and the illumination of manuscripts, as also in the arts of the goldsmith and the carver, they had given evidence of possessing in addition to those robust and virile qualities by which they were generally known the rarer attributes of delicacy and taste. Nor had they shrunk from the arduous work of consistent philosophic thinking. John Wycliffe, writing without fear in the reign of Richard II, had drawn in anticipation the whole map of Protestant thought and belief.

BOOKS WHICH MAY BE CONSULTED

A. Luchaire : Manuel des Institutions Françaises. 1892.

E. Lavisse : Histoire de France. 1903.

W. Stubbs : Constitutional History of England. 1880.

Anatole France : Vie de Jeanne d'Arc. 1908.

Sir Charles Oman : The Great Revolt of 1381. 1906.

Sir Charles Oman : A History of the Art of War in the Middle Ages.
     1924.

Sir Charles Oman : Warwick the King Maker. 1891.

S. A. Armitage Smith : John of Gaunt. 1904.

Sir John Fortescue : The Governance of England. *Ed.* C. Plummer.
     1885.

Shakespeare : Richard II.

Shakespeare : Henry VI.

Bernard Shaw : Saint Joan. 1923.

N. Valois : La France et le Grand Schisme d'Occident. 1896.

Froissart : Chronicles. (Everyman's Library.) 1906.

K. H. Vickers : England in the Later Middle Ages. 1913.

Bainville : Histoire de France.

CHAPTER XXIX

GERMANS AND SWISS

Foundations of the Habsburg power. Louis of Bavaria. Growth of German towns. Decline of German literature. Emancipation of the Swiss. The Habsburgs lose Switzerland for Germany, but gain the Empire for themselves. Nullity of the Habsburg Emperor when the Turks take Constantinople.

THE election of Rudolf of Habsburg to be King of the Romans in 1273 marks the opening of a new era in the history of central Europe. The old imperial game of attempting to unite under a single effective sovereignty two countries so large and so dissimilar as Italy and Germany had come to an end with the death of the last scion of the last of the great imperial families, and the upstart Swiss noble who found himself suddenly lifted to the highest dignity in Europe felt no romantic or antiquarian scruples in abandoning to the Pope the Romagna, the Exarchate, the imperial claims in Tuscany, and the suzerainty over Sicily. Rudolf was not interested in Italy. The achievement of his vigorous reign was to wrest Austria from Ottokar of Bohemia (battle of the Marchfield, 1278) and to found the power of the Habsburg house in the valley of the Danube, where it remained an imposing and dominating influence till the world war.[1]

Political disunion nevertheless continued to be a prevailing feature of German life. The vigorous and intelligent Teutonic stock which had overrun the Roman Empire and given dynasties to Italy and Spain, France and England, and even to Russia, was stricken by a palsy at the heart and deprived of all weight and initiative in the affairs of Europe. The old principles of racial patriotism which promised in earlier days to supply some measure of moral coherence were now almost wholly effaced. Saxony and Bavaria had been dismembered by Barbarossa, the Duchy of Swabia had foundered during the minority of Frederick II. Germany was not so much a state as a field in which princes, prelates, and imperial cities, and thousands of small nobles claiming to hold immediately of the empire, pursued their separate ambitions with just so much political combination as might furnish the illusion of national

[1] Genealogical Table I.

greatness, and just too little sacrifice of personal convenience to enable the illusion to become a reality. Everybody fought for his own hand. So faint was the spirit of German patriotism that the crown was even offered to Edward III of England (who was prevented by his parliament from taking it), and that for a space of fifty years after 1346 the German people were content to have their affairs managed from the Bohemian capital of Prague.

The prime source of all these evils is to be found in the selfish policy of the College of Electors. For them every election presented a golden opportunity for rapacity and intrigue. If a candidate was uninfluential, if he was not heir to the last Emperor, if he was acceptable to France and the Papacy, if he had no great territorial position in Germany, and, above all, if he was lavish in his promises, then he was likely to be acceptable to the Electoral College. In these circumstances it is not surprising that the highest secular office in Europe sank steadily during the fourteenth century in dignity and repute.

There was but one exception to the general rule otherwise observed till 1742 against the choice of an Emperor with a great German territorial position. Louis of Bavaria was Emperor from 1314 to 1347. His election was disputed, and his reign embittered by civil war, by a long contest with the Avignon Popes, and by humiliating surrenders to France. Despite some engaging merits and a great territorial position, for the Rhenish palatinate, the counties of Holland and Hainault, the Tyrol and Brandenburg were, in addition to Bavaria, governed by the Wittelsbach house, this unfortunate prince died excommunicated by the Pope and deposed by the electors. Centuries passed by before the imperial dignity was again held by a prince whose territorial possessions were wholly situated within the confines of Germany. Charles IV and his son Wenzel were first and foremost Kings of Bohemia. Sigismund, the younger brother of Wenzel, was primarily King of Hungary. The long line of Habsburg Emperors from 1438 onwards were only as to the smaller part of their territories rulers of German-speaking people. It suited the convenience of the electors that the Emperor should be pushed into the uttermost corners of the Reich and closely occupied with non-German ambitions. For Germany itself they wanted not a national monarch, but an elective president of a Diet dependent on their favours.

It follows that the real interest of German history during the fourteenth and fifteenth centuries lies not so much in the action of the central royal government, which within the proper limits of Germany was seldom able to discharge even the most elementary duties of taxation and police, as in the rich and varied life of the people, in the growth of territorial principalities, in the free activities of great cities like Nuremberg and Augsburg, in the vast development of trading activity on the Rhine and in the cities of the Hanseatic League, or in the colonization and conquest of Prussia by the knights of the Teutonic order. The lack of political discipline, which is characteristic of this age, was consistent with a steady and indeed remarkable growth of material wealth. Aeneas Silvius, who visited Germany in 1458, reported that nothing more magnificent or beautiful could be found in all Europe than Cologne with its wonderful churches, city halls, towers, and palaces, that some of the houses of Strasburg citizens were so proud and costly that no king would disdain to live in them, that the Kings of Scotland would be glad if they were as well housed as the moderately well-to-do burghers of Nuremberg, that Augsburg was not surpassed in riches by any city in the world, and that Vienna had some palaces and churches which even Italy might envy.

The picture of the Italian visitor is the more remarkable when we reflect that in Germany private war was chronic, that no convoy of merchandise could travel safely without an armed escort, and that the imperial cities had only been able to win and maintain their prosperity by the armed vigilance of their citizens. In such circumstances an intense civic patriotism was strongly developed. The citizen of Augsburg, of Cologne, of Lübeck, or Magdeburg cared little for the claims of remote imperialism, but very greatly for the grandeur of his own city. For this his kinsmen had shed their blood, and for this he was prepared, if need be, to repeat the sacrifice. Beside such near and urgent loyalties his sentiment for the German Reich was faint and distant.

As often happens in an age of fierce violence and expanding wealth, the civilization of the German people was in the fourteenth century distinguished by an energetic materialism. It has been remarked by Döllinger that when Louis of Bavaria was engaged in his long-drawn controversy with the Popes, he was compelled, by reason of the lack of native jurists or theologians or of any German university, to call upon Englishmen and Italians to conduct his literary campaigns. No German poet was comparable with Chaucer for sweetness or humour, with Villon for passion, with Petrarch for elegance, or with the Minnesinger of the age of chivalry. The solid German middle-class inaugurated its conquest of a place in the sun by a salvo of inharmonious prose which the world has been content to forget. In a country so broken and disordered a standard or general level of excellence was not to be expected; but the soil of German human nature was nevertheless rich in its capacities, and from its confused but retarded vegetation rare plants emerged—here a mystic, there an inventor, an architect, a craftsman of virtuosity. The beer was excellent, the folk music good, and the people which stood so low in the scale of states-manship and literature produced the two discoveries which have done most in modern times to revolutionize human society. Gunpowder and the printing press came from Germany.

The crowning proof of Imperial weakness and impolicy in the later middle ages is the emancipation of Switzerland. The idea of secession was never present to the loyal hearts of this moun-tain people. The Swiss did not rise against the Emperor. On the contrary, they wished to be immediately dependent on him and to sweep away the intervening feudal tyrannies which plagued their lives and obstructed their access to his throne of justice. In all the Swiss leagues, from the first union of the three Forest Cantons in 1291 to the Treaty of Basel, February 22, 1499, which closed the final war of liberation, the rights of the Em-peror and the Empire were expressly reserved. But German statesmanship was wholly unable to harness the loyalty of this valiant people. Even when the Swiss pikemen and halberdiers had shown themselves again and again to be the most formid-able fighters in Europe, as at Morgarten (1315), Sempach (1386), and Näfels (1388); even when they had fought on even terms with the French and defeated the Burgundians, and had be-come the one great centre of military energy in the German Reich, so that it might have seemed to be a prime object of policy to assign them a large and important part in the govern-ing confederation, they were treated with studied neglect. The strongest community in the Empire had no voice in its counsels; and, so far as the imperial constitution went, might never have

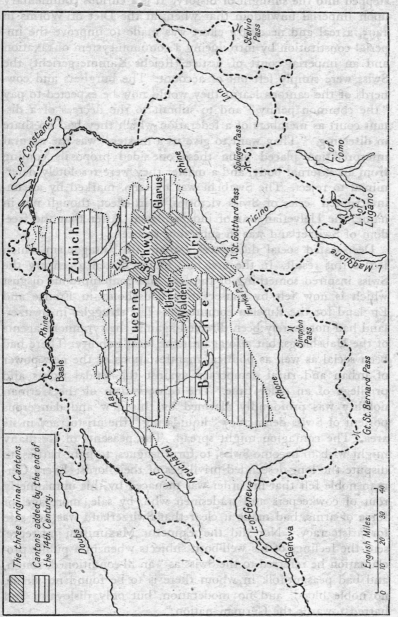

THE GROWTH OF SWITZERLAND.

The three original Cantons

Cantons added by the end of
the 14th. Century.

English Miles.
0   10   20   30   40

stepped into the sunlight of history. It is a curious commentary
upon Imperial unwisdom that when, at the Diet of Worms in
1495, a real and necessary effort was made to improve the imperial constitution by introducing a common system of taxation
and an imperial court of justice (Reichs Kammergericht) the
Swiss were simply left out of account. The burghers and cow-
herds of the cantons learnt they would now be expected to pay
" the common penny " and to submit to the decrees of a distant court as members of a federation which they had no share
in directing. " They want to give us a master " was the natural
interpretation placed upon these one-sided proposals coming
from an external body, and a master they were resolutely determined to reject. The Swabian war of 1499, marked by an uninterrupted series of Swiss victories, is in effect, though not in
name, the Helvetian war of independence. After that the freedom of Switzerland was in substance secured.

Deep-seated social differences explain the antagonism which
led to this result. In the first half of the fifteenth century the
Swiss inspired something of the fear and contemptuous disgust
which is now felt by conservative households in France and
England for the Russian communist. The struggles in Switzerland had not merely been directed against the tyrannous agents
of the Habsburgs, but also against the local nobility. There had
been social as well as political manifestations of the new power
of urban and rural democracy against the feudal rights and
privilege of an older time. The conservatism of the German
nobility was profoundly alarmed by this new and dangerous
portent of Swiss democracy " liquidating " the aristocracy in its
area. The contagion might spread. The peasants of Germany
might wish to become Swiss, to form leagues, to fight battles, to
dispute the long-descended privileges of their lords. Every German noble felt that his order was menaced by this unmannerly
rout of cowkeepers and tradesmen who, by sale, mortgage, or
force of arms, had made it clear that Switzerland was not safe
for aristocracy. Nor did the Emperor Maximilian misrepre-
sent the feelings of his well-born subjects when in a public proclamation he referred to the Swiss as " an ill-conditioned, rough,
and bad peasant-folk in whom there is to be found no virtue,
no noble blood, and no moderation, but only disloyalty and
hatred towards the German nation."

The liberation of the Swiss, which marks the first triumph of the democratic principles in Europe over an area larger than the city state, was the more remarkable by reason of the prevailing drift towards princely power and authority. The Swiss had no superfine ideas to give to the world. Their civilization was infinitely poorer than that of Italy, Germany, or France. They had contributed nothing then, as they have contributed but little since, to the stock of European science or culture. Yet few historical events have been more beneficial than the establishment of Swiss freedom by the valour and energy of a subject race and a divided people.

The Swiss not only gave lessons in the military art to all the armies of Europe: they helped to restore to the continent of Europe the idea of political liberty. This they showed to be a force capable of welding together peoples differing in speech and race and ultimately even in religion. And so through the age of despotism Switzerland remained the pattern of a *parvenu* state, governing its own affairs without the assistance of nobles or kings, and reminding Europe that the catalogue of political experiments was not yet exhausted. Here men could breathe freely and hither resort for the fearless discussion of questionable matters. Long before the loveliness of snow-flakes was discovered, and while its mountains were regarded with universal horror and aversion, Switzerland had become a place of refuge for the uneasy, anticipating on a miniature scale the later rôle of the United States, but with a greater influence on religious life.

The enemy in conflict with whom the Swiss cantons won their earliest and latest triumphs was the house of Habsburg. The cruelty of Albert I, the son of Rudolf of Habsburg, and of his oppressive agents, called into life the original league of the forest cantons. It was Habsburg pride which was abased on the fields of Morgarten, of Sempach, and of Näfels, and a century later in the last and decisive conflict of the Swabian war. All through the formative years of the Confederacy, the Swiss could count upon the steady hostility of this Austrian family, which, having sprung from a Swiss root, regarded the rebels with a peculiar and local malevolence.

If then the Habsburgs are the makers of Austria, they are also the makers, or from the German point of view the losers, of Switzerland. This was the great rebuff experienced by a family whose territorial aggrandizement and fortunate Empire-winning marriages have passed into a proverb. Save for this, everything on a long view turned out well for these steady, rather dull, acquisitive men. Even their failure to obtain the imperial crown between the death of Rudolf of Habsburg in 1291 and the elevation of Albert V to the Empire in 1437 was a blessing in disguise, for during that century and a half, undisturbed by imperial claims and duties, they built up for themselves the position of being the largest territorial holders in Germany. So when the Empire returned to them with Albert they were able to keep it with one brief intermission (1742-1744) until the end.

1440-93   There was something in the racial and geographical conditions of the Danube valley which seemed to demand such a dynasty, firm, steady, unintellectual. Frederick III, the first Emperor to show the famous Habsburg lip, and the last Emperor to be crowned in Rome, was as great a nullity as ever played an important part in history. Without any of the engaging gifts of Edward II of England, Frederick was just as little fitted as that unfortunate monarch for the despatch of business. A clever Italian diplomat like Aeneas Sylvius could twist him round his little finger. Yet this dull, obstinate bigot ruled in Vienna for more than fifty years, leaving no print of mind or will upon the conduct of affairs. The Turks conquered Constantinople and overran Hungary. The rôle of Austria as the chief remaining bulwark of Christianity against the Ottoman Turk became charged with a new significance, which could hardly escape the meanest intelligence. But no event, however startling, could ruffle the placidity of Frederick, no problem however grave could excite his sluggish mind, or the most alarming prospect inflame his torpid imagination. Inertia was the principle of his life. The most important station in Europe at one of the most critical moments in her history was occupied by a blockhead.

BOOKS WHICH MAY BE CONSULTED

Coxe : History of the House of Austria. 1847.

J. Bryce : Holy Roman Empire. 1904.

J. F. Kirk : History of Charles the Bold. 3 vols. 1863-8.

Aeneas Sylvius Piccolomini : De rebus et gestis Frederici III. *Ed.* A. F. Koller.

K. Dändliker : Short History of Switzerland. *Tr.* Salisbury. 1899.

W. T. Waugh : A History of Europe, 1378-1494. 1932.

CHAPTER XXX

CRITICS AND REFORMERS

Political ideas of Dante. Growth of scientific interest. The Papacy at Avignon. The Great Schism, 1378-1417. The Conciliar idea launched in the universities. Mystical movements of the fourteenth century. Wycliffe. Survival of Lollardy in England. Influence of Wycliffe on Bohemia. Progress of that country under the house of Luxemburg. Charles IV and the Golden Bull. The University of Prague and John Hus. Bohemian Puritanism. The Hussite Wars, 1417-1431. Compact of Iglau, 1436. Mixture of racial and religious animosities in the Hussite movement. Effort to reform the Church from within. The Conciliar Movement. Its failure. The Papacy triumphant over its critics, 1450.

WITH the advance of the fourteenth century the idea of a Christian Society organized under the joint authority of Pope and Emperor, though it still continued to haunt the imagination of men as part of the ultimate purpose of God, became increasingly divorced from the realities of European life. The Empire had ceased to command. The Popes in exchanging Rome for the pleasant retreat of Avignon had incurred the suspicion of every state in Europe which at one time or another was brought into opposition to the government of France. The age of pan-European movements was passing away. A new era of national consolidation had set in. To the sacerdotal pretensions of Boniface VIII England and France replied with a national manifesto, and the Hundred Years' War, the supreme political fact of the century, was the first of the national wars of Europe. Out of it emerged the two leading states of the west, each sharply conscious of its own superiority and of the other's deficiencies, and each inveterate in its rivalry with the other. In this long and cruel contest, the Papacy, ingeminating and enjoining peace, but always suspect of French sympathies, played a useful but mostly ineffectual rôle.

We have already seen how, in his Divine Comedy, as also in his Latin treatise on Monarchy, Dante sums up the regrets of a poet and a moralist upon a world which had swung away from its anchorage in the divine purpose. He saw the Papacy corrupted by wealth, the Empire broken and humiliated, his beloved Italy enslaved by foreigners. The universal monarchy designed for the rightful ordering of human society had been challenged and despoiled by the wickedness of men. Only in an imperial restoration and in the purification of the Church by the Franciscan spirit of evangelical poverty did he discern the hope of improvement. But the principle upon which it had been sought to organize the Christian world in the thirteenth century had now gone beyond recall. New men, new ideas, new forces, were pressing forward. The clergy no longer held the monopoly of learning and culture. The layman was coming into his own. Though European society still remained mainly agricultural, a wealthy middle class had been developed from the commerce of the towns, and was now beginning to patronize art and letters. We have reached the age of Chaucer, Froissart, and Boccaccio.

Even in those regions where thought was icebound in theology we become conscious, as we advance in the fourteenth century, of genial currents setting towards the illimitable ocean of scientific discovery. Led by the original genius of Duns Scotus, the Franciscans of Oxford, no home then of lost causes, but on the contrary conspicuous for its pioneering enterprise, challenged the power of the human mind to accommodate the claims of faith and reason. The mysteries of religion they pronounced to be unintelligible, the laborious travail of theology and philosophy to be an idle exercise of the spirit. Vain was the celebrated fabric of scholastic logic, vain the imposing and ingenious work of St. Thomas, harmonizing the newly found Aristotelian learning with the text of Holy Writ, as at the Cairene University of Al Azhar the Moslem doctor of today finds all science in the words of the Prophet. The human mind must feed on other pastures. The Oxford Franciscans and their French disciples of the University of Paris turned from the pursuit of theological subtleties to the science of observation and experiment. They touched upon psychology and optics; they affirmed that the celestial and terrestrial bodies were composed of the same matter and governed by the same mechanical laws. They made approaches towards a theory of gravity. To Nicholas Oresme, the French pupil of William of Ockham, belongs the credit of suggesting that our earth moved with the planets, and of contributing the first page to the vast body of scientific literature on the subject of currency.

Suddenly the warm current of lively scientific curiosity, after flowing freely for half a century, froze and was lost. The old scholastic logic resumed its sway at Oxford, as the quarrel of the orthodox Church with the Lollard heresy spread through the life of the English people; nor was it until the middle of the seventeenth century that the spirit of Roger Bacon and William of Ockham lived again among the gardens and quadrangles of Oxford, with Boyle and Mayow, Wilkins and Wren, Hooke, Petty, and Evelyn, and that the status of English science was secured by the foundation of the Royal Society.

It would be an exaggeration to say of the seven French Popes who ruled at Avignon from 1309-1378 that they were wholly untrue to the conception of their office. In France at least they worked for peace, in the near east fruitlessly for a Crusade. If they made the machinery of papal government odious by their exactions, they left it a good deal more effective than it had previously been. One of them was learned in theology, two were austere in conduct, a fourth organized an expedition against the Turkish corsairs, and by a rare act of courageous toleration at a time when the Jews were suspected of contriving the Black Death, extended his protection to these innocent but unpopular people.

But it would be idle to deny that the Papacy greatly suffered in public esteem by reason of the Avignonese captivity. All over Italy these French Popes were unpopular, first because they were Frenchmen, who filled the College of Cardinals with their compatriots, and secondly because they had deserted Rome for a city which, though not technically in France, adjoined the dominions and was exposed to the influence of the French king. The splendour and luxury of the papal court, to which the artists and scholars of Italy and France were attracted, the shameless nepotism with which the highest positions in the Church were lavished on the relatives of the Popes, and even upon boys, the grinding exactions of the papal tax collectors for the support of this magnificence, and for the prosecution of the temporal aims of the Papacy in the Italian peninsula, shocked scrupulous minds all over Euorpe. Even critics not remarkable for austerity commented on the clerical fortune-hunters, who crowded the streets of Avignon, whence all church patronage was dispensed, and where every office, so it was reputed, might be had for a price.

The flight of the Papacy to Avignon had been justified by the turbulence and insecurity of Rome. The return to Rome was prompted by the discovery that Avignon itself was not secure, but exposed to the ravages of the dangerous bands of hungry mercenaries, who, after the Peace of Bretigny in 1360, were loosed on the suffering population of France; and the return was undertaken the more readily since the papal state, which had now been reconquered, was awaiting a master, and might not wait indefinitely if the master failed to come. To the joy of every pious and patriotic Italian heart the move so vehemently advocated by St. Catherine of Siena was undertaken by Gregory XI, a Frenchman and the creator of eighteen French cardinals, in 1377. In the following year Gregory was dead.

Then ensued the Great Schism, which, lasting from 1378-1417, and dividing the Roman Church into two opposing camps, came near to destroying the unity of the Latin west. The real question had nothing to do with religion. The Italians wanted the Papacy for Italy, they wanted its money, its influence, its prestige. The French intended that the Pope, whether established in Rome or ruling in Avignon, should continue to be, as he had been during three-quarters of a century, the servant of their particular interests. The technical question as to which of the two rivals, Urban VI or Clement VII, was the rightful Pope was never submitted to dispassionate analysis. It was sufficient that Urban VI was the Italian, and Clement VII the French candidate. National passions and political alliances determined in each man's case which of the rivals was in truth the Vicar of Christ. France, Scotland, Savoy, and later Castile and Aragon were Clementine; England, Bohemia, Hungary, and later Portugal were Urbanist. The essentially political character of the struggle was illustrated by the fact that Clement endeavoured to entice the French to conquer Italy, and that with this endeavour in view he arranged the marriage of the Duke of Orleans, the brother of Charles VI, with Valentina Visconti of Milan, and caused Queen Joan of Naples to adopt as her heir Louis of Anjou. In these two transactions were rooted the French claims upon Naples and Milan, which, more than a century later, led to the French invasion of Italy by Charles VIII.

At this crisis Europe for the first time experienced the weight in public affairs of an organized body of academic opinion. The University of Paris, led by two vigorous and broadminded ecclesiastics, Jean Gerson and Pierre D'Ailly, was deeply concerned with the grave scandal which was undermining the discipline and affecting the honour of the

Church. In a sermon preached before King Charles VI of France (June, 1391), Gerson urged that if the schism could not be ended by the simultaneous resignation of the two Popes, or by arbitration between them, there was no method open but the summoning of a General Council of the Church. Once put abroad, and with the failure of each successive attempt to accommodate the rival obediences, the idea of a General Council attracted adherents, and as it grew in favour, became in the mind of its protagonists something a great deal bigger than a mere expedient for healing the schism. They saw in the General Council a divine instrument for the reformation of the Church in its head and members, and a means of subjecting the Pope to a permanent system of constitutional control.

The time was ripe for reform, for on this topic of the true ordering of the Christian Church Europe had long been full of uneasy questions. Was the Church, as the Fraticelli proclaimed, " the Great Babylon," and the Pope in truth Antichrist? Were the Apostles, as the Franciscans affirmed at Perugia (1322), empty of all earthly possessions, and should the Vicar of Christ tread in the same path of saintly piety? One such Pope had sat in the chair of St. Peter. Celestine V was an old, simple, destitute hermit. He had been driven from the throne by Boniface VIII, to whose ambitious secular policies it was customary to trace the abasement of the Papacy at Avignon. To the passionate idealists of Italy Celestine stood for all that was good, as did Avignon for all that was evil, in the Christian Church. It was not apparent to these simple men that institutions have value, and that they need for their support money and wisdom.

The Church has always found room for idealists and mystics; and the fact that in the fourteenth century mystics like John Eckhart and John Tauler conformed to its discipline, while repudiating its methods, has been put down to the credit of Catholic charity. But outside the Church, and in spite of the pitiless working of the Inquisition, the heresies of the puritan and mystical temperament flourished abundantly, taking different forms and colours (Catharists in Corsica and Bosnia, the Vaudois in the Alpine valleys and among the hills of Naples and Sicily, the Beghards in Germany), but united in their challenge to the pomp and ambition of the papal see, to its sacraments and ceremonies, and to the claim of the priesthood to a special measure of divine authority.

More important than these scattered and unlettered move
ments was English Lollardy. This was a protest against the
whole system of mediaeval Church teaching and practice
launched by a great divine, and supported during its formative
years by the influence of Oxford, then the most free and power
ful University in Europe, yet, despite its unsentimental appeal
to the scholarly intellect, carrying a simple message to the
hearts of humble folk, and a promise which all might under
stand of a regenerate society. We know little of the outward
history of John Wycliffe, the prophet of this movement for the
reform of the English Church. He was born in Yorkshire in
1324, he taught in Oxford, where he became for a time Master
of Balliol, and, on being expelled from the University in 1382
returned to Lutterworth, his cure of souls in Leicestershire
where he lived quietly until his death two years later. Within
these limits of time, Wycliffe anticipated all the main positions
of the Protestant Reformation.

He was one of those high-minded, energetic radicals who owe
nothing to the graces but everything to character. As he con
templated the manifold scandals of the Church, his plain, mas
sive Yorkshire brain was stirred by a sombre moral indignation
to the issue of a long succession of tracts and sermons in
Latin and English, often exaggerated in language, but stamped
with a courage and integrity which mark their writer as one
of the first English apostles of free thinking and plain speaking.
His great academic position in Oxford, won by a complete com
mand of the intricate dialectical art, then much affected by
learned men, gave him a prestige which the monks and friars
were unable, save with the outside help of king and archbishop, seriously to impair. But his message was not only, or
indeed mainly, to the wise. He believed in English preaching
and in an English Bible, in preaching based on Scripture, and
in Scripture made available for all. An order of poor preachers,
schooled by his models, spread the message through the countryside. The English Bible which bears his name was translated in
the circle of his disciples.

His first entrance into national politics was as the expert ally
of John of Gaunt, who, like many other parliament men at that
time, wished to see the Church disendowed and its broad acres
returned to the nobles and gentry. For this violent course many
plausible reasons could be assigned. The country was harassed

y taxation for an unsuccessful French War. The Church was
eported to possess a third of the land in the country. Many of
ts best benefices were under the odious system of Provisions,
nd, in defiance of the law, conferred by the connivance of King
nd Pope on non-resident Italians. Much of its wealth was drained
way from the country by papal taxation. From the remainder
t was contended that the state exacted an insufficient toll. The
lisendowment of the Church, then, was urged as a measure,
ot only good for clerical ethics, but also calculated to relieve
he laity from a crushing burden, and to strengthen the fiscal
evenues of the Crown. With these arguments based on national
onvenience Wycliffe was in accord. His outlook, which was that
f a patriotic English Erastian, was strongly opposed to the
osmopolitan theory of the mediaeval Church. In a pamphlet
ntitled *De Officio Regis* he claimed for the national sovereign
owers of ecclesiastical control and discipline in terms which
vould have satisfied King Henry VIII.

Once embarked upon a criticism of the Church as he saw
t at work in the reign of King Edward III, Wycliffe was drawn
n further and further until there was hardly a part of the
tructure which escaped his censure. The bishops, the Caesarean
lergy, as he called them, were too much engaged in affairs
f state to attend to their proper clerical duties. Monastic life
vas not so much abominable as useless. The Friars lowered the
vhole tone of the Church by the sale of indulgences for sin,
y their style of empty, sensational preaching. From his denunciations of the secular occupations of the Episcopate he was
ed on by an easy transition to condemn prelacy and to advocate
a form of Church government differing little from what was
ubsequently known as Presbyterianism. From the authority of
he Church he appealed to the authority of Scripture, and
inally launched an attack upon the central mystery of the
Catholic Faith. In an interesting treatise, *De Civili Dominio*,
Wycliffe argues with a logic impregnated with feudal conceptions, that "dominion" or power is founded on grace, or, in plain
language, that the claim to exercise any form of authority is
grounded on virtue, and disappears where virtue is not. From
these premises it followed that an unworthy priest could not
administer the sacraments, that the authority of the Pope belonged to him only in so far as he showed himself possessed of
the Grace of God, and that the claims made on behalf of the

ecclesiastical hierarchy as an institution possessing independent validity were invalid. By 1380 he had reached the position that Transubstantiation was a false doctrine, and that the priest had no magic whereby he could transform the substance of bread into the body of Christ.

It will be seen that the idea of a Christian Church which Wycliffe had gradually built up for himself was in abrupt contradiction to the world of belief and practice into which he had been born. Protestant in the fullest sense it was not, for Wycliffe retained his faith in purgatory, and did not refuse to the Virgin Mother a special place in the veneration of mankind. But in its repudiation of popery and prelacy, in its appeal to the authority of Scripture, in its denial of the miracle of the Mass and of the special claim of the clergy to be endowed with spiritual power, as well as in the rationalizing contempt with which he handled such established practices as compulsory confession and prayers for the dead, pilgrimages and the worship of relics the doctrine of Wycliffe was indistinguishable from that of the Puritan divines of the seventeenth century. Moreover, in the southern and more civilized parts of England these tenets were popular. Orthodoxy was still supreme, but ever since the Norman Conquest a stubborn vein of anticlericalism had been manifest in the English people. With this feature of the national character Wycliffe's teaching was in harmony.

Thus we may explain the fact that Lollardy survived the condemnation and death of its founder and outlived the persecution of the Lancastrian age. With the loss of Oxford, which was easily recovered for orthodoxy and once recovered was kept under an iron heel, the movement was deprived of the learned character which originally belonged to it, and became a religion of humble unlettered men and women, who met in secret to ponder Holy Writ, or to listen to the voice of a travelling preacher; but as such a religion it persisted until the sixteenth century, when it was merged in the tidal wave of the Protestant Reformation. We find it alive in London and East Anglia, among the poor charcoal burners of the Chiltern beechwoods, and in the country towns and villages of the west. Though there was yet no printing press to multiply copies of the Bible, or the tracts and sermons of Wycliffe, though transcription was a slow process and the possession of transcripts might lead to a fiery death, the English Lollards went on unsubdued, handling down from father to son the tradition of their simple Christian faith, and cherishing the memory of their heroic martyrs. We may conjecture that for every devoted member of this proscribed communion there were hundreds of an easier and more compliant temper who, while making their peace with the established order, had long ceased to render it a real allegiance. The English are a race slow to move. That they moved so far and so fast in the sixteenth century is due to the fact that for the first time since the conversion of the island to Christianity a religious alternative to the faith of Rome had been propounded by Wycliffe, and that, being in essentials congenial to the national temper, it had found adherents in many classes of society. Such is the justification for saying that the Protestant Reformation in England springs not from a German but from a native root.

The most important consequence of this English movement has now to be recounted. The kingdom of Bohemia was inhabited by a Slavonic people who had first received Christianity from an eastern and Slavonic source, but afterwards, coming under German influence, were compelled to accept the discipline of the Roman Church. Racial characteristics are deeply graven on this stalwart peasantry. The Czech, in becoming a Roman Catholic, retained, with the mysticism and excitability of the Slav, that aversion to the Teutonic temperament which is persistent in men of Slavonic blood. The Roman Church, alien in itself, and for its pomp open to the criticism of simple folk, was not made more acceptable by its association with the Germans. In the thirteenth century Bohemia was noted for its puritan heresies. In the later half of the fourteenth protests against the corruptions of the Church culminated under the quickening impulse of Wycliffe's writings in a great national movement, the first of its kind in Europe, for a new organization of the Christian religion.

In the thirteenth century little general notice would have been taken of the inner turmoil of a small obscure country on the confines of Europe. But the native line of the Přemyslids came to an end in 1306, and a new era opened for Bohemia with the advent of a foreign dynasty. The monarchs of the house of Luxemburg came from a region on the borders of France and Germany. They were members of that brilliant and adventurous French-speaking aristocracy, which had filled Europe with their fame during the Crusades, and in the fourteenth century furnished to Froissart the principal material for his vivacious chronicle.[1]

1308-13   The first of the family to rise to eminence is the brave and chivalrous Henry, one of the most accomplished knights of his age, who, being elected King of the Romans in 1308 (his brother being Archbishop of Trèves and therefore an elector) and afterwards crowned Emperor in the Lateran palace at Rome, appeared to Dante to be the ideal ruler appointed to bring peace and order to Italy. Only Barbarossa among the mediaeval German Emperors was more passionately loved and bitterly lamented than this valiant prince, who died suddenly, as he was marching against the King of Naples, poisoned, it was said,

1310-46   in sacramental wine through the malice of Florentine Guelfs. His son, John of Bohemia (for he had married the Slavonic heiress of that country), a blind Don Quixote, ever engaged in forlorn and perilous adventures, fought with the chivalry of France in the Hundred Years' War, and left his bones on the

1346-78   field of Creçy.

Charles IV, the son of John, though in a different fashion, was also remarkable. As prudent as his father was reckless, as concentrated as his father was dispersed, this hard-headed scholar of the Paris University was perhaps the first of mediaeval monarchs to see the world through plain glass. He also was present on the field of Creçy, but resolved that no vain sacrifice should wreck a promising career. To make sacrifices was not in his nature. The history of the mediaeval Empire had been a long tale of sacrifices, of German resources wasted uselessly in the endeavour to rule Italy from a northern throne, to compose Italian differences, to checkmate the remorseless opposition of Italian Popes. For such sacrifices Charles, becoming King of the Romans and in due course Emperor through papal favour, was not prepared. It was not for him to spend his energies upon the senseless feuds of Guelf and Ghibelline by which Italy was torn to pieces. Nor did he essay an impossible and heroic operation upon the complicated texture of the German Reich. A strong German monarchy was now impossible, and Charles knew it. On the other hand, a state of irredeemable anarchy in Germany was possible, and that Charles knew also, and by a wise precaution endeavoured to prevent. The Golden

[1] Genealogical Table J.

Bull of 1356, which is Charles' gift to the constitutional development of Germany, recognized the unhappy fact of German division, but by defining the College of Electors and securing that the electorates should be indivisible and should descend by the rule of primogeniture, minimized the evils incidental to this situation. Charles then refused to be drawn into heroic and forlorn adventures by the glamour of his imperial title. He declined to play the rôle of a mediaeval Emperor, distracted by the confluence of a thousand calls proceeding from every quarter of his vast dominions. What he attempted was the more limited but practical task of making his hereditary kingdom of Bohemia the strongest state of central Europe. In this he was successful. No matter what test be applied, Bohemia advanced in power and influence under the fostering care of Charles IV. Its territories touched the Danube in the south, and a point not far distant from the Baltic Sea in the north. Its expanding trade attracted German immigrants. Its capital became a centre of art, learning, and letters, the seat of an archbishopric, and of an academy which drew students from Poland and from every part of Germany.

The University of Prague, founded in 1348, at a time when there was no comparable institution in any German land, gave to the movement of religious reform in Bohemia a force and consistency which would otherwise have been lacking to it. One of the teachers in this University was a priest of humble origin, whose memory is the greatest national possession of the Czech race. John Hus was born in 1369. He was a man of rare purity and depth of character, studious, patriotic, of great eloquence as a preacher, who set himself in the first instance to attack the manifold corruptions of the Bohemian Church. The proclivities of his mind and nature drew him to the philosophy of Wycliffe, which for many years had been studied and admired in Prague. "O Wycliffe, Wycliffe," he exclaimed, "you will trouble the hearts of many." Eloquent sermons delivered in the Bohemian language, the character of which he greatly contributed to form, spread abroad the doctrines of the English teacher. The strength of Hus lay in the fact that he had no misgivings. When once he had grasped the idea that the ultimate test of Faith was Scripture, that only so far as he acted in accordance with Scripture was the Pope to be obeyed, everything else seemed to follow, the acceptance of clerical poverty, the doctrine of predestination, the condemnation of indulgences. These truths seemed so patent to him that he could not persuade himself that, once explained, they would not be equally compelling for others. He stoutly denied that he was a heretic. How could one be a heretic who persistently appealed to the very words and authority of Christ? The Council of Constance, to which he had been enticed by the safe conduct of King Sigismund of Hungary, decided to burn him. He went to the stake like a hero, kindling by his death the first of a long series of religious wars.

1415

Bohemian Puritanism, while full of religious mobility and vigour, was closely bound up with national pride, and with the ambition for political independence. It was a movement partly for the reform of a profligate, idle, and ignorant clergy, but partly, also, for a Bohemian Church on a national basis, and for the expulsion or subordination of the Germans. A light is thrown upon this last aspect of the struggle by a decree of King Wenzel in 1409, which transferred the control of the University of Prague from the Germans to the Bohemians. So passionate was the pride of the German masters and students that, rather than submit to the dominion of the Slavs, they emigrated in a body, founded the University of Leipzig, and spread far and wide through Germany their violent abhorrence of the Bohemian cause. The bitterness of the religious war was deepened by that intense racial animosity which is found when two mutually uncongenial races are intermingled in the same geographical area, and maddened by the jars of daily intercourse.

Even before the martyrdom of Hus, events had been rapidly moving towards a violent breach with Rome. Two scenes in particular which were enacted in Prague marked the rising feeling of the contending factions, the first the public burning, under the authority of a papal Bull, of 200 Wycliffite books, the second the execution of three young men, who, when the papal Commissary had set up a mart for the sale of indulgences in the city, had the audacity to denounce indulgences as an organized lie. That more blood was not then shed may in part be due to the policy of King Wenzel, who shielded the Hussites from the extreme measures of their antagonists.

In condemning Hus to the stake the Fathers of Constance roused the soul of a nation. The Bohemian nobles banded themselves together in defence of the new-found liberty of preaching. The grant of the chalice in the sacrament to the laity became a war-cry rallying every type of Puritan opinion. A fierce feeling that Christians had been deprived of their sacramental rights by the malignant jealousy of the priesthood was mingled with the denunciation of clerical wealth, in some cases prompted by the rapture of the ascetic, in others by the vulgar land hunger of the acquisitive squire. In 1419 the first blow was struck in the terrible twelve years' war which secured for Puritan Bohemia a special place in the Christian commonwealth. John Ziska, "Rhinoceros Ziska," as Carlyle calls him, a nobleman of Wenzel's court, marched to the town hall of the Neustadt in Prague, butchered the burgomaster, and "defenestrated" his Catholic associates.

Ziska was one of nature's generals. Under the rigid discipline of this stern and disinterested commander an army was formed of a type hitherto unknown in Europe. The followers of Ziska were religious and racial enthusiasts. They condemned games and dancing, music and drunkenness. To their fierce and sombre temper the flute, the drum, and the trumpet were as obnoxious as a foul oath, a loose woman, a rich wardrobe, or a German burgess. As they marched into action, with their huge flails and roaring the Ziska psalm behind the sacred chalice, they struck terror into armies whose inner moral principle was weaker than their own. The resourcefulness of their leader lent additional power to the stern enthusiasm of his ragged Puritan following. Ziska was the first European commander to make full use of the artillery arm, or to see the value of a mobile barricade of waggons as a factor contributing to the steadiness of a peasant army. Since Prague was too moderate to be relied on, he established a military capital on the lofty hill of Austi, which in the biblical phraseology of his followers was known as Tabor. So long as Ziska lived to lead them, the Taborites were invincible.

The Bohemians were right in thinking that only by arms and terror would they be able to secure the right to worship God and order His Church to their own liking. No help was forthcoming from the patronage of royal personages. Wenzel, the friendly but incompetent debauchee, died in 1419. His brother Sigismund, King of Hungary and King of the Romans, proved to be no friend but a bitter enemy, who had to be driven out of Bohemia by force of arms. The crown was offered to Poland, but the sovereign of that bleak and barren region refused from cowardice an opportunity, never destined to recur, of forming a great Slavonic confederacy, which might claim, with the help of Bohemian principles, the common allegiance of those who followed the Greek and Roman rites. In reluctant isolation, fighting as a reluctant republic with improvised generals and an improvised army, the Bohemians withstood five crusades, routed one undisciplined imperial army after another, carried fire and sword into the heart of Germany, and eventually compelled the Roman Church for the first time in its long history to sign a capitulation.

Against the Papacy and the German world the Hussites presented a united front. They asked that the word of God should be freely preached, and that the Communion should be administered in both kinds, that the temporal power of the Pope should be abolished, and priests be made to return to the apostolic life, and that the clergy should be subjected to secular penalties for crimes and misdemeanours (The Four Articles of Prague, 1420). But behind this common programme were violent divergencies of sentiment and opinion. The Utraquists or Calixtines[1] were moderate, the Taborites were extreme. The Utraquists accepted all seven sacraments, the Taborites only Baptism and the Eucharist. For the Utraquists any settlement with Rome would be tolerable under which a Bohemian layman might receive the Communion in both kinds. The Taborite went much further. He condemned prayers to the Virgin and the saints, he allowed laymen, and even women, to occupy the pulpit, he acknowledged no hierarchy in the priesthood. In one respect both parties were alike. Eloquently as they preached the doctrine of liberty, they practised against differing opinions a savage and consistent intolerance.

Two years after the death of Ziska in 1424 Bohemia was paralyzed by internal discord. Then from the ranks of the Taborites there emerged a figure hardly less remarkable for native military science and power of organization than Ziska himself. Procopius the Great was a priest, and, as a priest, took no active part in fighting, but, like Carnot, he was an organizer of victory. Moreover, he was clear-sighted enough to realize that the best defensive for Bohemia was an offensive on every front. Peace could be secured only by victory. At the battle of Tauss, August, 1431, the Taborites inflicted on the papal forces of

---

[1] So called because they claimed that the laity should receive the Communion in both kinds, the chalice as well as the paten.

Cesarini a defeat so thorough as to convince that great ecclesiastical statesman that only by the way of peace could the Bohemian question be finally settled. So, on November 26, 1436, after protracted and arduous discussions, a compact was signed at Iglau, and the Church for the time being recognized the Utraquists. At last Rome had been brought to concede a place in her system for an Evangelical Church, founded on the free preaching of the Gospel.

In the course of the struggle the Hussites had neglected no means of placing their case before the public eye of Europe. Their pamphlets were read far and wide, they had sympathizers in many lands. The spectacle of Rome defied in a series of savage battles exercised a profound and terrible impression upon Europe; but for the victors themselves the struggle was a great tragedy. In a wild outburst of vandalism the Taborites destroyed the wonderful monasteries and churches with which Bohemia had been endowed by the munificence of preceding ages. Wasted and impoverished, the little country faced an unfriendly future.

Years before the last shot had been fired in this civil war the early enthusiasm of the sectaries had died away. The famous Taborite army, its losses replenished by soldiers of fortune, had ceased some time before the peace with Rome to represent all that was best in the religious thought of Bohemia. In the long and bloody battle of Lipan (1434) it was annihilated by the Calixtines, and with it there passed out of Bohemian life that element of competent and fiery fanaticism which made the Bohemian name terrible and odious throughout Europe.

The Hussite wars, while they should primarily be regarded as the prelude to the Protestant Reformation, are also important as marking the reaction of a Slavonic race against the onward pressure and dominating influence of the Germans. The quarrel of Bohemia will not be understood unless we can enter into the emotions of a small people struggling to preserve its soul against a race more numerous and more advanced than itself. Passionate discipline and willing sacrifice made the Bohemians masters of their destiny; but the fruits of victory were snatched by a greedy nobility, and lost in 1620 at the battle of the White Hill, when the Protestant cause was overwhelmed, and the little country with its girdle of mountains was caught in the Austrian and Catholic net, from which it was only delivered after much fretting and uneasiness by the flashing scimitar of the great war. *1918*

The immense difficulty of getting Europe to work together for a common end, which is felt so keenly today at Geneva, was illustrated in a most signal manner during the fifteenth century by the failure of the Conciliar Movement to reform the Church. No reasonable person in that age denied that the Church was in urgent need of reform. Most educated people gravely feared the onward march of heresy. All were agreed that the schism in the Papacy was a scandal which should be ended without delay. To the deeper thinkers the lesson of the age seemed to be that the papal supremacy, which had been so flagrantly abused at Avignon, should henceforth be subjected to some system of regular supervision and control through the Councils of the Church. Accordingly councils met at Pisa, at Constance, at Pavia, and at Basel. The movement which began with divines ended by exciting the interest of statesmen. The questions to be discussed speedily outranged the original difficulty of two rival Popes each supported by a separate "obedience," and neither willing to give way to the other. And as the problems were numerous and grave, the attendance came to be representative and weighty, so that the assemblies of Constance and Basel wore at times the air of being not so much meetings of divines as congresses of statesmen and diplomatists gathered for the settlement of European affairs. Small, however, was the benefit which resulted from the stir and bustle of these famous gatherings. The council of cardinals summoned to Pisa in 1409 was not even able to put an end to the schism. So far from securing a vacancy in the papal office, it left Europe shamed by three competing Popes in place of two. It is to the credit of the larger and more representative assembly of Constance that it did eventually succeed in deposing two Popes and securing the resignation of a third. The schism was ended. There was at last a vacancy in the papal office. A golden opportunity seemed to have offered itself for the reformation of the Church, and for the imposition of such limitations as it might seem expedient to impose upon the power of the Pope. But the opportunity was not seized. When the council was called upon to decide whether it should reform the Church before it elected a Pope, or elect a Pope before it proceeded to reform the Church, it resolved, England and Germany dissenting, to postpone reform. This decision was just the kind of blunder which an assembly not very profoundly moved by moral issues was likely to make. The

1414

reform of the Church through a general council, difficult enough during a papal vacancy, would clearly be rendered far more arduous by the election of a Pope. By its choice of Odo Colonna, *1417-31* who took the title of Martin V, the council raised up a formidable rival who, alike as an Italian politician and as heir to the long tradition of papal autocracy, was bound to work for the frustration of its constitutional aims.

So the plan for a general reform of the Church fell to the ground. The Fathers of Constance burnt Hus and Jerome of Prague, and issued decrees providing for decennial meetings of general councils, for a council in five years' time, and for the convocation of a council always and automatically on the occasion of a schism; but as for reform it had capitulated to the Pope, whose main interest was in the establishment of his Italian principality, and who preferred to make provisional concordats with separate states rather than to work through the machinery of a rival authority.

The Council of Basel which met in 1431 was no more successful. All the main influences which combined to thwart the reforming zeal of the Fathers of Constance were equally powerful at Basel. Martin V, the Roman noble, had been succeeded by the Venetian Eugenius IV. To Eugenius, as to Martin, a general council, endeavouring to set itself above the Pope, to reform his finances and to limit his patronage, was abhorrent. From the first the Council of Basel could count upon the persistent hostility of the Pope. Moreover, though the Fathers of Basel did not, like the earlier council, divide themselves into nations, so that it was easier for the lower clergy to assert their influence and to put forward plans of radical reformation, the national spirit in Europe was as strong in 1431 as it had been in 1417. The French and the Spaniards were as reluctant as ever to countenance the idea of reform, and Eugenius, no less than Martin, saw that his best interest lay in coming to an agreement with national sovereigns rather than with the general council of the Church.

Yet it would not be fair to deny that one considerable achievement may be ascribed to the Council of Basel. It provided a theatre in which the theological differences beween the Hussites and Catholics could be, and were, examined and discussed. The theological debate between the leaders of the Hussite cause and the theologians of Basel is one of the most creditable episodes in a violent and intolerant age, and the council may be given the credit of having at last succeeded in securing a compromise-settlement, which, though violently resented by the Taborites, was acceptable to the main body of Bohemian opinion. In no other respect, however, was the Council of Basel able to advance the cause of Church reform or to limit the prerogatives of the Pope. This was through no lack of radical ambition. The council put out comprehensive decrees, such as that a general council should not be dissolved without its own consent, that an appeal from a general council to a pope was heretical; it attacked papal patronage, and by its denial of annates or firstfruits threatened the ruin of papal finances. It even went as far, in 1439, as to depose Eugenius, its enemy, and to elect a wealthy widower with seven children, who was both a duke and a hermit, to the papal chair.

In these proceedings the council clearly outstepped the limits of prudence. The public opinion of Europe was not prepared for so grave a reduction in the prerogatives of the papal power, and the prospect of a new schism added to the unpopularity of the council. Eugenius was not a clever man, but rash, headstrong, and limited. Nevertheless, he was clever enough to profit by the mistakes of his adversaries at Basel, and, circumventing the council, to treat with the French and Germans. It is significant of the new tendencies in European politics, of the growing influence of nationalism, and of the declining influence of the mediaeval Church unity, that the foundation of the liberties of the Gallican Church was laid in 1438, while the Council of Basel was sitting and behind its back, by a treaty between the Papacy and the King of France, known as the Pragmatic Sanction of Bourges, and that in the following year a similar treaty was made with the Germans at Mainz. The final and decisive blow to the authority of the council came in 1445, when Frederick III, King of the Romans, sold the liberties of the German Church to the Pope in exchange for a promise of the imperial crown.

The Councils of Constance and Basel had been largely promoted by the Emperor Sigismund. That mercurial and flighty statesman had been anxious to shine in the eyes of the world as a Church reformer, a cosmopolitan ruler, a pacifier of dissensions civil and ecclesiastical. He had espoused the Conciliar Movement in the hopes of arresting the spread of the Bohemian

1419-37

heresies, and of facilitating his assumption of the Bohemian crown, and so long as the Emperor stood by the councils, even though his authority was not undisputed in Germany, the councils were a serious power confronting Rome. Accordingly the treaties made between the Pope and Frederick III were of the utmost importance. The one secular authority from which the council might have expected effective assistance dealt a shattering blow to all its policies. By the final compact of 1448 Frederick restored to the Pope his revenue from annates and most of the rights of patronage of which he had been deprived by the stringent decrees of Basel. It was a crowning victory. The forces of reform were routed. The attempt of the Church to set its house in order through the medium of general councils had been frustrated by the underlying political differences of Europe, and most fundamentally by the opposition of the Pope, by the appetite of an Emperor, and by the determination of Italy never to accept the dominion of the barbarians of the north.

Once more the Italians were restored to their control of the papal office. With Martin V begins the long line of Pontiffs for whom the cares incidental to the management of an Italian state are a primary consideration. Martin V placed the Papacy before the Church, Italy before Europe, his Colonna kinsmen before everybody. His business it was to restore order to the city of Rome, which had been exhausted by civil war, to purge the Campagna of brigands, and to recall the distant provinces of the Church to a sense of obedience to the papal see.

The Papacy did not easily or at once adapt itself to the savage conditions of its old Italian home. If to some the papal restoration was a source of pride and profit, by others it was viewed with feelings of the strongest hostility and distrust. The Roman republicans hated the idea that the proud city of the Scipios should be placed under the humiliating governance of priests. They drove Eugenius IV into exile; they rose in arms against his successor Nicholas V. And the nobles of Rome and the Campagna, in whom generations of anarchy and bloodshed had made of disobedience a second nature, were even more dangerous than the Roman mob. The Restoration Popes did not feel themselves precluded by sentiments of Christian piety from applying to these disorders the harshest treatment which the refined cruelty of their mercenary captains and executioners could supply. They slew, tortured, hanged their opponents. Palestrina, the principal home of the Colonna family, was levelled to the ground by Vitelleschi, whose odious cruelties, exercised in the service of Eugenius IV and branded in the pages of Lorenzo Valla, cast a deep shadow of gloom over the rebirth of the papal state.

Thus sternly delivered from their local troubles the Popes advanced with a sense of triumph to meet the future. The difficulties, which ever since the schism had seemed so menacing to the continued authority of the Papacy, were now overcome. The Council of Basel, long a much reduced and discredited body, was finally dissolved in 1449; Felix V, the elderly antipope, had resigned. The German Empire under the lame and venal guidance of Frederick III had made its peace, renouncing the hard road of reform, accepting papal finance, patronage, and authority. The Bohemians, who had filled Europe with the terror of their name, were now quiet and apparently composed. No one murmured the name of Wycliffe. At the jubilee of 1450, Nicholas V, a scholar Pope, who had made of his court the principal centre of Italian learning and letters, and is famous as the founder of the Vatican Library, looked out, as it appeared, upon a subject world. It was the year in which the Spaniard, Torquemada, published a famous treatise (*Summa contra hostes ecclesiae*) which concentrated the orthodox reply to all the errors which had been afflicting the Christian commonwealth.

The great attack upon the fortress of papal power had been decisively repelled. Few would then have predicted that half a century later the onslaught would be renewed on a wider scale, with added power, and with results fatal to the unity of the Latin Church.

BOOKS WHICH MAY BE CONSULTED

G. M. Trevelyan : England in the Age of Wycliffe. 1909.

J. Loserth : Wycliffe and Hus. *Tr.* M. J. Evans. 1884.

M. Creighton : History of the Papacy during the Reformation. 1882.

R. L. Poole : Wycliffe's Tractatus de civili Dominio. 1885.

Ranke : History of the Popes. *Tr.* S. Austin. 1847.

Gregorovius : History of Rome in the Middle Ages. *Tr.* A. Hamilton. 1894-1900.

W. R. Inge : Christian Mysticism. 1899.

Lechler : John Wycliffe and his English Precursors. *Tr.* P. Lorimer. 1884.

A. S. Turberville : Mediaeval Heresy and the Inquisition. 1920.

E. Denis : Huss et la Guerre des Hussites. 1878.

CHAPTER XXXI

MEDIAEVAL SPAIN

Struggle of Christians and Moslems. Splendour of Cordova under the Ummayad Caliphs. The Christian opportunity in the eleventh century. Absence of Christian unity. The Reconquista, 1086-1266. Almoravides and Almohades. Long suspension of religious struggle. Iberian localism. Debt of mediaeval Spain to France.

THE history of Spain during the middle ages is that of a country in which two sharply contrasted civilizations, one Christian in religion and Celtiberian, Roman, or Visigothic in race, the other Moslem, Arab and Berber, are confronted with one another, and condemned despite much mutual influence and attraction to a long struggle for ascendancy. From this contest, which was closed only when, in 1492, the year of the discovery of America, Ferdinand and Isabella conquered the little state of Granada, the Christians emerged victorious. The Jews, and later the Moriscoes, were driven from Spain. By a singular act of intolerance, to be ascribed as much to the bigotry of the Christian mob as to the dark fanaticism of the queen, the country was rid of that part of its population which was most likely to minister intelligently to the advancement of its material needs, so that the way might be cleared for the undisputed predominance of the Catholic Church. Such was the *praeparatio evangelica* for a great period of conquest and colonization during which the arms of Spain were employed in the old world and the new for the defence and propagation of the Roman Faith. And it is from this close association of royal policy with religious intolerance that some are disposed to derive the decline and fall of the Spanish Empire.

For more than two hundred and fifty years the emirs and 755-1031 caliphs of the Ummayad house administered, from their populous capital of Cordova, a state which appreciated the values and possessed the luxuries of civilized life. The visitor to Cordova in the tenth century travelled through a land which bore abundant signs of the supervision of an improving government concerned to promote the interests of agriculture, trade, and industry. He found peasants tilling rice and sugar cane in fields which had been irrigated by Arab engineers, mechanics working delicately in glass, ivory, and leather, and scribes who had discarded parchment for paper. Entering the capital, he marvelled at the oriental eccentricity which required nine hundred public baths for the refreshment of the body and four hundred mosques for the elevation of the soul. The streets were paved with stone, fountains sparkled in arcaded courts, and hundreds of lamps, many of them of silver, illumined the columns of marble and jasper which sustained the greatest of the Moslem temples. Nor were these amenities the jealously guarded monopoly of the Arabian conquerors. Among the subjects of the Caliph were numerous Christian communities belonging to the conquered race who were permitted on payment of a tribute to multiply and prosper under the Crescent. The Mozarabs (would-be Arabs) formed an important part of the general community and together with the Jews constituted the principal channel through which the culture and knowledge of Arabia and Greece percolated to the Latin world in that age.

Until the beginning of the eleventh century the small Christian states which had been formed among the cold, damp mountains of northern Spain were wholly unable to cope with their powerful adversary. Their population was sparse. Their kings, devoid of a regular army or a revenue, were dependent on the favours of the nobles and the towns, which they purchased by extravagant concessions. The Arabs carried all before them. Under Abdur Rahman III and the famous Almansor, the dissensions of the Moslems were quelled, their armies organized, and their banners carried in victory into every part of the peninsula. Barcelona was conquered in 985, Santiago was despoiled in 997. Save for Leon and part of Catalonia (like Castile, the land of castles) all Spain was dependent on the Caliph.

Then ensued one of those revolutions of which the history of oriental despotisms provides many instances. From the death of Almansor in 1002 (*Mortuus est Almanzor et sepultus est in inferno*) there dates a swift declension in the political virtue of the Cordovian Arabs. Emir fought with emir, tribe with tribe. The caliphate disappeared. Cordova became a republic. The Christian opportunity had come.

At no point in the period of active warfare which now opened out were the Christian powers fully united against the enemy, or themselves secure from ruinous subdivision under the terms of a royal will. Alfonso VI of Castile first conquered Toledo in 1085. Alfonso I of Aragon wrested Saragossa from the enemy in 1118. These were important victories, entailing large extensions of Christian territory and influence, but they were the triumphs of independent sovereigns whose states differed from one another in speech, temper, and organization and found it quite as easy to quarrel as to agree. So inveterate indeed was the localism of Christian Spain that only the most powerful motive would have sufficed to overcome it. Such a motive was wanting. The period of the Reconquista must not be conceived as one of unremitting warfare between the Crescent and the Cross. The Arab in the age of his glory had been tolerant and civilized. The Christian had been amenable to friendliness and culture. There were spells of peace, intermarriages between royal and noble families, campaigns in which Moslems and Christians would be fighting side by side. The great legendary hero of mediaeval Spain, Rodrigo de Bivar, the Castilian nobleman who goes by *1034-99* the name of the Cid Campeador, was for many years before his famous conquest of Valencia in the service of a Moslem prince. On the Arab side a policy of wise toleration, which was seldom departed from, permitted Christians not only to dwell at peace in the territory of the Caliph, but to serve in his armies and even to hold high office in his administration.

It is thus no accident that the great period of the Spanish Reconquista, which begins with the conquest of Toledo in 1085 and ends with the conquest of Murcia in 1266, corresponds with the epoch of the Crusades. The enthusiasm generated by Urban II did not stop short at the Pyrenees. In the warm excitement of a general movement the barometer of Spanish fanaticism, which had often fallen to ruinous levels of indifference, mounted to an altitude of stable fervour. French, German, and Italian knights fought in the army of Alfonso VI and helped in the capture of Toledo. English and German adventurers on their way to the Second Crusade sailed up the Tagus, stormed Lisbon, and presented it as a gift to Alfonso Henriques, the first King of Portugal. *1147* The cult of St. Bernard, the inspired prophet of the Second Crusade, spread into Aragon, Castile, and Portugal. Monasteries were founded on the Cistercian model as pious outposts on the disputed frontier; and to these were associated by a momentous provision three of the four orders (Calatrava, Alcantara, Evora), half monastic and half military, which provided, in the campaigns that were to follow, the shock troops of the Spanish Crusades. The Order of Santiago, differently affiliated and even more illustrious, springs from the same motive.

While the Christians of the north were receiving a fresh impulse from the general stir of crusading enthusiasm, the position of affairs in southern Spain was completely transformed by two successive waves of immigration from Africa. If the Arabs of Cordova had lost much of their primal fierceness in the temperate warmth of an earthly paradise, the Berbers on the other side of the Straits of Gibraltar retained a full measure of Moslem zeal and barbaric courage. On the appeal of their Spanish co-religionists a powerful body of Almoravides from the Sahara swept into Mohammedan Spain and soon established a complete ascendancy over the Arab tribes who were disputing for its mastery. At the battle of Zallaca (October 23, 1086) Alfonso VI, the victor of Toledo, received a severe check at the hands of Yussuf-ul-Tashvin, the Almoravid. Much that had recently been gained for the Cross was now surrendered to the Crescent; and had the Almoravides been allowed to consolidate their position these territories would have been safely retained in Moslem hands. But there followed a second wave of immigration from Africa. The Almohades (Unitarians) of the Atlas mountains were even fiercer and more intolerant than the Berber tribes of the desert who had preceded them into the land of promise. They conquered Morocco, burst into Spain, subdued the Almoravides, and in the later part of the twelfth century rolled back the tide of the Christian advance. At the battle of Alarcos, Alfonso VIII of Castile was routed by an army of these formidable Berber mountaineers. Equally with the capture of Jerusalem by Saladin eight years earlier, Alarcos served to remind Christian Europe how imperfect was its organization for the conduct of a sacred war.

1195

The intolerance of the new invaders of Spain had one beneficial but undesigned effect. The more intelligent of the Jewish and Mozarabic communities, who set a value upon intellectual freedom, fled into Christian territory and were welcomed by the enlightened sovereigns of Castile and Aragon. Among the learned fugitives from the puritan bigotry of these Berber wanderers were some, like Averrhoes and Maimonides, who were destined to exercise a worldwide influence as disseminators of philosophical thought. Others were content with performing a more humble, but, at that stage of the world's knowledge, a most important intellectual function. By their translations from the Arabic they made available to the Latin west the science of the ancient world. It is not least among the titles of Alfonso VI that he encouraged the Jews of Toledo, a city which contrived under Christian rule to preserve its oriental character, to address themselves to this valuable task.

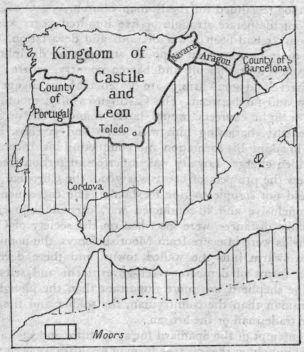

CHRISTIAN KINGDOMS OF SPAIN.

It is immensely to the credit of Innocent III that he never ceased to urge upon the little Christian kingdoms of Spain that they should lay aside their animosities and combine in a great forward movement against the enemy. In this endeavour he was ultimately successful. The forces of Aragon, Navarre, and Castile acting under the direction of Alfonso VIII, illustrated the value even of the most temporary coalition by winning the great victory

of Las Navas de Tolosa (July 16, 1212) which secured the preponderance of the Christian cause in Spain. There followed
fifty-four years, the most brilliant and critical in the military
annals of the country, during which under the direction of
James I of Aragon and St. Ferdinand of Castile victory after
victory crowned the arms of the Christian Crusaders. To the
prowess of Aragon there fell Valencia and the Balearic Isles;
to that of Castile, Cordova, Jaen, Seville, Xeres, Cadiz, Murcia.
Save for Granada, sheltered behind its lofty mountains, all Spain
was by 1266 reclaimed for the Roman Church.

The long desperate struggle of five hundred years was now
suspended. It had been a war of raids and devastation, waged
for the most part without supplies, strategy, or discipline, by
light cavalry over difficult and barren country, where " large
armies starve and small armies are beaten." Major engagements
were few and far between. The Castilian cavalry, mounted on
jennets or light coursers, would hover round their swift and
elusive enemy, harassing him with darts and javelins, in the
hope of breaking his formation and completing his discomfiture
by a sudden charge. Loyalty was imperfect, desertion frequent,
and unless the prospect of booty was good, the Christian *caballero*
lero would not scruple to ride for home. The consequences of
this inconclusive and ill-conducted war, carried on over vast
inhospitable distances, were inscribed on the society of Castile.
As the fields were insecure from Moorish forays, the population
began to swarm into the walled towns, and there developed
advanced forms of democratic self-government and self-sufficiency. The shepherd was more important than the ploughman,
the townsman than the countryman, the soldier and the priest
than the tradesman or the artisan.

The contempt of the Spaniard for agriculture and his calamitous belief in gold as the sole true form of wealth have been traced
to the wars of the Reconquista, which intensified the already
formidable difficulty of tilling the barren plateau of central Spain.

In the age of crusading zeal it seemed a possibility that Christian Spain might be able to overcome the deep divergencies
which separated its several units, that the lesson of Las Navas
de Tolosa might be learnt, and that, if unity was out of the
question, some loose form of Christian confederation might be
possible. The opportunity was not taken. The kingdoms of
Portugal and Castile, of Aragon and Navarre, went their several

ways, developed divergent interests, and were too busily occupied
with internal discords or foreign ambitions to conceive plans for
Spanish or Pan-Iberian unity. Navarre, which lay astride the
Pyrenees, had its heart in France. The heart of populous
Aragon was in Sicily, Naples, and Sardinia, in the Balearic
Islands, in the promotion of its Mediterranean trade, in its
manifold connections of culture and commerce with Provence,
but not in the acquisition of Granada (divided from it by Murcia,
now a strip of Castile) nor yet in the politics of its western neighbour. Portugal was an Aragon on the Atlantic, Lisbon a western,
but far less flourishing Barcelona. The little country lay behind
its mountains, its back turned on central Spain, and, therefore,
although often united by family bonds with the Castilian royal
family, only slightly by reason of that forbidding frontier
associated with the Castilian people.

As for Castile it stood apart, central, isolated, proud, priest-
ridden, digesting as best it might its spreading conquests, and
those burdensome legacies of its long crusade, the vast estates of
the military orders, the preponderant position of the Church, together with the Jews, the Moslems, the Mozarabs, whose presence
in a crusading state (now out of business) was to a nation of
proud and courageous aristocrats an unwelcome necessity. To
the difficult tasks of such a government the Castilian kings of the
fourteenth and fifteenth centuries were plainly unequal. So ill-
ruled was their country that the only effective force for the
maintenance of order was a league or brotherhood (Hermandad)
of cities. The student of language, literature, and art finds much
to excite his interest and admiration in the manifold energies
of the Castilian people during this period, in the gradual perfection of an aristocratic language, in the profusion of ballads and
of prose romances, *Libros de Caballeria,* reflecting the manners
and feelings of a knightly class, or in the great Gothic cathedrals which rose under the direction of French architects. But
what historian can examine the reign of Pedro the Cruel, when
French and English were called in to take part in a fratricidal
civil war, or study the turbulent reigns of his three successors
with any expectation of the renown which was awaiting
Castilian statecraft? It is not from these dreary struggles that
the greatness of Spain was to proceed, but from the work of
obscure cartographers in Catalonia and Majorca (the most
illustrious were Jews) who laid the basis of an oceanic empire.

The Moslem civilization of mediaeval Spain can only to an inconsiderable degree be ascribed to the genius of the Arabian people. The small band of bloodthirsty orientals who enabled Turk and Moslem to conquer Spain did not come into a waste or barbarous country, but into a land long settled by the Romans which still, despite the shock of the barbaric conquest, bore abundant signs of ancient opulence. Into this mould of established civilization the invaders injected currents of intellectual influence from Damascus, from Cairo, and from Bagdad. They introduced into Spain the Arab language and literature. They imposed the Koran. They were the means of reconnecting Europe with the eastern centres of art and scholarship at a time when the western channels between east and west were blocked. It was, however, the strength of the Moslems that their civilization was not racial but religious. The invaders of Spain, though they were cruel and licentious, were never so foolish as to attempt an exclusive ascendancy of the Arab race. It was not from Arabia that fresh Moslem immigrations were to be expected, but from the African Berbers who were close at hand; nor was it from Arabia that the Arab emirs furnished their harems, but from the households of Christian Spain, which it was their habit to raid twice a year for treasure and slaves. Purity of race, therefore, was never an object entertained or pursued by the Moslem conquerors of Spain. They married Spanish virgins, employed Jewish doctors, and were not ashamed to go to Byzantium for the artists and craftsmen who decorated their mosques and palaces. For the tillage of the soil they relied upon a native peasantry, whose pedigree, in Andalusia at least, must have reached back to Roman days.

As for Christian Spain, so rich in noble churches and monasteries, it was, in most of the arts, a province of France. In the eleventh century the Spanish religious houses obeyed the rule of Cluny, later they were subject to the house of Cîteaux. In all sacred architecture, save where, as in Catalonia, it was influenced by Byzantine or Lombard workmanship, French influence is predominant. The great cathedrals of Burgos, of Toledo, of Leon, were built by French artists after French designs. The Spaniards gave the commissions and paid the bills. Though a vast amount of building was done in Spain during the middle ages, it was only towards the end of the fifteenth century that Spanish architects became prominent. As for the decorative arts, carving and gilding, glazing and painting, these (without a twinge of self-reproach) the Spaniard was content to concede to the alien.[1] Later, when Madrid (which was only a hunting lodge in the middle ages) became the capital of a great empire, the patronage of foreign artists was extended upon a lavish scale by the sovereigns of the Habsburg house. Great models were then proposed for the imitation of the Spaniards. Titian could be seen at Madrid. El Greco worked at Toledo. But whether it was from some native vulgarity, which under-valued paint and canvas for their cheapness, or because of a certain strict and sombre religiosity in the Spanish temper, defining certain subjects only as worthy of the brush, there was no popular flowering of the painter's art in Spain. Perhaps there can be no such flowering save when thought and fancy can play in freedom. Velasquez was an exception, preaching no doctrine, constrained by no convention, and daring, a solitary among Spaniards of his age, to paint only what he saw.

1599-1660

[1] Royall Tyler, " Spain, a Study of her Life and Art."

BOOKS WHICH MAY BE CONSULTED

R. Altamira y Crevea : Historia de España y de la Civilizacion Española. 1902.

S. de Madariaga : Spain. (Nations of the Modern World Series.) 1930.

Louis Bertrand and Charles Petrie : The History of Spain. 1934.

H. Havelock Ellis : The Soul of Spain. 1908.

Cambridge Mediaeval History.

R. Tyler : Spain—A Study of her Life and Arts. 1909.

Dozy : Histoire des Musulmans d'Espagne jusqu'à la Conquête de l'Andalousie par les Almoravides. 1861.

R. B. Merriman : Rise of the Spanish Empire. 1918-25.

CHAPTER XXXII

MEDIAEVAL RUSSIA

The aloofness of Russia. The Greek colonies. The Norsemen on the Dnieper. Vladimir and Christianity. Influence of the Greek Church. Work of the Norsemen. Tatar invasion. The rule of the Golden Horde. Its lasting effects. The Grand Dukes of Moscow. Rise of Lithuania. Tatar defeat at Koulikovo, 1380, and birth of a Russian nation. Ivan the Great, 1462-1505, and the Byzantine heritage.

THE barbarous populations of the Russian plain were far withdrawn from the thoughts, ideals, and activities which, during the middle ages and afterwards, moulded the life of the Latin and Teutonic races. In this wild, half-Asiatic country there was no use of Latin or scholastic philosophy, no mediaeval analogue to the University of Paris or the Parliament of Westminster. The great movements which shook the west meant nothing to Russia. Here Popes did not quarrel with Emperors, setting alight in the process a flame of political discussion which laid bare the origins and credentials of the state. Here was no renaissance of classical learning, quickening into new life the intellectual ardour of a cultured people, no Protestant Reformation backed by princes and breaking and transforming the Catholic Church. And as the Russians pursued their way without Latin or scholasticism, without parliament or university, without a literature of political debate or a sustained challenge to religious tradition, so they were spared the wars of religion which for two centuries moulded the life and fashioned the moral being of western Europe. In these decisive spiritual experiences of the west, "Holy Russia," slumbering in oriental seclusion, had no share.

In part geography offers an' explanation. The vast inclement country, alternately parched by the summer sun, or buried under a pall of arctic snow, constituted a world sufficient to itself, uninviting to others. Unfriendly nature had here imposed a task so rigorous as to leave little energy over for the refinements of life or the higher types of social organization. In the forest zone there was no corn, in the arable zone no timber, in the zone of the arable steppes a treeless waste of

374

spring pasture. The goal set before the mediaeval Russian was the settlement and colonization of a land so vast that it always seemed empty, and so flat that it offered a perpetual temptation to movement, which only the invention of serfdom was able to arrest. How that goal was reached, we can but conjecture. The valiant labour of innumerable spades and axes goes unchronicled. Generation followed generation to the grave without leaving a mark upon the written page; yet in each generation forests were cleared, villages and towns were built of wood (stone being unobtainable in that unmountainous land), and burned down in some high gale and built again; rough lumbermen plied their trade upon the waterways, village communities tilled the rich black soil, which had been the granary of the ancient world, herdsmen galloped on rough little ponies over the heaving grasses of the southern steppes, war was waged upon the wolf, the bear, and the beaver, and a coarse, violent, emotional race of men lived, bred, toiled, quarrelled, and died.

The dawn of history in Russia broke on the shores of the Euxine. Here was a chain of Greek colonies (Olbia, Cherson, Panticapaeum, etc.), and in these a vivid life of commerce and art which did much for the culture of the rude Scythian tribes of the hinterland. But all this brilliant civilization which had left monuments of its taste extending over 800 years (400 B.C. to A.D. 400) was blotted out by successive tides of barbaric invasion. After the Sarmatians and Avars, the Goths and the Huns had done their worst and passed westward, who would have suspected that Homer had been recited, and Demosthenes declaimed by Greek, and probably also by Scythian, schoolboys in the ruined cities of the Euxine coast? The contact of the rude north with the literature and art of the classical age was abruptly broken and never renewed.

The Russian of to-day, then, owes nothing but a treasury of museum pieces to these ancient Greek colonies of the Euxine. The influences which first made a rudimentary state among the Russian Slavs were not Greek but Scandinavian, the sphere of their operation not the sea coast, but the great waterways which connect the Baltic with the Euxine. Here it would seem that German traders as early as the first century had built themselves stations, and here, after circuitous wanderings from south Russia to the Danube, and from the Danube to the Carpathians, the main body of eastern Slavs was by the eighth century collected, and engaged in the marketing of forest produce. The real story of Russia begins from the moment that the city states on the Neva and Dnieper, menaced in their trade by Turkish nomads, but also paralyzed by internal dissensions, called in a body of well armed warriors from Sweden to collect their taxes and defend their caravans.

The coming in 862 of Ruric and his Norsemen (or Ruotsi as the Finns called them) was decisive. The rivers and lakes from the Baltic to the Black Sea fell into the keeping of this valiant race of merchant warriors. They established themselves in Novgorod and Kiev, carried on an extensive slave trade, organized fleets, armies, and principalities, and plunging for the highest stakes, launched six attacks on Constantinople, and attempted the conquest of Bulgaria. The passive Slavs of the west were content to be called Russ, after the name of these convenient auxiliaries, who convoyed their cargoes down the seven cataracts of the lower Dnieper, enabled them to market their honey and their furs, and were of the mettle to beard the Emperor in his capital, and to extort commercial concessions from Constantinople at the point of the sword. From the Ruotsi or Varangians, they learnt the elements of state life, and by them were introduced to the sobering discipline of a state religion.

The conversion of Russia to Christianity was effected, it would seem, by a monster of cruelty and lust. That Vladimir (980-1015) was a fratricide, who maintained 3,500 concubines, has not prevented his canonization as a saint. All sins were forgiven to the man who made Kiev a Christian city and of the Russians a people obedient to the Christian rites. It is said that at some point in his violent career it occurred to this capable barbarian to examine the credentials of the leading religions. The Moslem creed, since it condemned strong drink, was rejected offhand. "Drinking," observed Vladimir, "is the joy of the Russes. We cannot exist without that pleasure." A papist who had the misfortune to observe that "whatsoever one eats or drinks is all to the glory of God" was curtly dismissed with "Our fathers accepted no such principle." When the Jewish apologist was compelled to confess that Jerusalem was in alien hands, the Varangian prince pertinently observed, "If God loved you and your fathers, you would not be thus dispersed in foreign lands. Do you expect us to accept that fate also?" There remained the Church of the Byzantine Empire, with its images and mosaics, its solemn music and swinging censers, its resplendent vestments and ordered ritual. A commission of enquiry, thrilled by the brilliance of a service such as only St. Sophia could provide, reported strongly in favour of the Greek religion. "When we journeyed among the Bulgarians, we beheld how they worship in their temple called a mosque, while they stand upright. The Bulgarian bows, sits down, looks hither and thither like one possessed, and there is no happiness among them, but instead only sorrow and a dreadful stench. Their religion is not good. Then we went to the Germans and saw them performing many ceremonies in their temples; but we beheld no glory there. Then we went on to Greece and the Greeks led us to edifices where they worship their God and we knew not whether we were in heaven or on earth."

The objective once determined, the business of conversion was carried through with the high hand of a pirate. Seizing Cherson, a jewel in the Byzantine crown, Vladimir threatened destruction to its inhabitants unless he was given the hand of a Byzantine princess. The blackmail was successful. The reluctance of a woman was overcome by the stern reason of state, and in that old Greek city the pirate from the north was wedded to Anne, the sister of the long descended Emperors Basil and Constantine (988). Returning to Kiev, the zealous neophyte submitted Nerun, the most popular idol of the Slavs, to a handsome flogging at the hands of twelve stalwart men, commanded the collective baptism of his subjects in the waters of the Dnieper, and set himself to make of Kiev a city of Christian churches and one of the architectural glories of the Byzantine world.

The acceptance of the Greek instead of the Latin form of Christianity is an event of capital importance for the history of Russia. In the Latin west, ecclesiastical was separated from secular power; in the Greek world, the church was a department of the state. Ideas of liberty were generated by the collision between church and state in the west. A passive subservience to Caesar was the fruit of all Byzantine teaching. The Greek Church brought with it many undoubted benefits, the music, literature, and architecture of a civilized people, a more developed conception of the state, the advanced notions of criminal law which were to be found in the codes of Justinian

and Basil, as well as those lofty ethical ideas, so sharply opposed
to Russian practice, which are distinctive of Christianity in all
its forms. That the uphill battle against Russian polygamy was
waged with a certain measure of success is to be attributed
wholly to the influence of the Greek Church. There was, too,
having regard to the backward civilization of the inhabitants,
an advantage in a church which used the native language in its
liturgy, and was admittedly national and not worldwide. But
for these advantages a heavy price was paid, in the isolation
of Russia, in its severance from the Slavs of Poland and
Bohemia, but above all in the failure of the Russian Church to
educate within the souls of the nation the power or the desire
to resist the despotism of its rulers or to fight the battle of the
downcasts and outcasts of society.

To the piratical rulers of the house of Ruric, princely power
over the new city states was an indivisible family heritage, distributed on a rota according to seniority. The older the member
the higher and more lucrative his command, so that at every
change in the personnel of the ruling family there were promo-
tions and occasions of heartburning and dispute. On such terms
it was hopeless to expect the construction of a stable polity on
the Dnieper.

After the death of Jaroslav the legislator in 1054, we enter
upon a period of endless family wars, mainly waged for the
purpose of deciding which among the large number of Ruric's
descendants was at the time the eldest, and consequently entitled to rule at Kiev as Grand Prince of the local confederacy.
In the course of these struggles Kiev itself, the city of 400
churches, was stormed, sacked, and ruined of malice prepense
(1169) by a member of the princely family, who was resolved
to remove the seat of power from the turbulent republic of the
Dnieper to a town of his own choosing in the heart of his forests.
The name of Andrew Bogoliouski of Souzdal is worth recording.
He is the founder of Vladimir, the second of the Russian
capitals, and was himself the first of a long line of Russian
autocrats. With him Russia makes a new start upon the poor
clay soil of the remote forests of the central plain, whither the
population of the west had been steadily trekking in search of
security from nomad raids.

With the fall of Kiev the first period of Russian history comes
to a close. The Vikings had achieved much and attempted more.

They had founded in the principality of Kiev a great Russian state, waged war against the Greeks and Bulgarians, against the barbarous Polovtsi or Kumans in southern Russia, and most persistently among themselves, and though Greek fire had again and again repulsed them from the Bosphorus, and the sword of John Zimisces, the first captain of his age, had decided once for all that there was to be no Norman conquest of Bulgaria, the fame of their exploits lived on in the ballads of ·the Russian Slavs. A fragment from the tale of the Armaments of Igor (1185) may be taken as emblematic of the age when the Varangian war bands, buccaneers and boatmen, controlled the western waterways of Russia and Kiev was the queen of Russian cities. "My own brother, my own bright light, thou Igor! We are both sons of Sviatoslav. Brother, saddle thy swift horses, mine are ready for thee saddled at Kursk beforehand. And my men of Kursk are experienced fighters, nursed amid trumpets, rocked in helmets, fed at the spear blades. Well known to them are the paths; familiar are the ravines; their saddle bows are strong; their quivers are open and their sabres are whetted. They themselves gallop like grey wolves on the field, taking honour for themselves and for their prince glory." Unlike the Normans the Varangians of the Dnieper never became landlords, but remained to the end fighters and traders, danegeld collectors and slave-dealers, following their occasions on land and water.

While the strength of the house of Ruric was wasting away in the internal struggles of a series of hostile principalities, Russia was invaded by the Tatars. Few catastrophes so great or so enduring in their effects have overwhelmed a young and struggling country. The Tatars were no undisciplined horde of feckless barbarians, but a force of some half a million trained light horsemen, representing an empire which in the lifetime of Jingis Khan, its creator, had been extended from Manchuria to the Caucasus at a cost of more than eighteen million lives. No empire had ever occupied so large a portion of the earth's surface as that of Jingis, or had been the cause of so much human suffering in the winning. No army had yet invaded Europe which in point of numbers and skill could compare with the cavalry of Batou, the grandson of Jingis and the nephew and lieutenant of the Great Khan Ogotai, who, in 1227, had succeeded to the throne of his father.

The princes of Russia, acting without combination or the

support of an armed peasantry, were no match for the hammer blows of these formidable orientals. The Russian chivalry of the south, of the centre and the north-west, was defeated in detail at the battles of Kalka (1224), the Oka, and the Sit (1238), and every important Russian town, Novgorod excepted, was burned or put to the sack. Not until they had ravaged Moravia and Silesia, had taken Cracow and Pesth, and menaced Vienna, was a check administered to these terrible adversaries of the west. The credit for precipitating the Mongol retreat has been variously assigned to the death of the great Khan Ogotai (December 11, 1241), to the valour of the Czechs, the Poles, and the Germans, who, if they did not win victories, at least offered resistance, or to the Russians, who had absorbed the main part of the shock and paid the chief part of the penalty. The real cause was geographical. The deliverance of central Europe from its great peril may be safely ascribed to distance and desolation.

The colossal empire of Jingis was shattered; not so the rule of the Golden Horde, which Batou had founded in the south-eastern steppes of Russia. For a space of two hundred years the Tatars of the Golden Horde, shaking themselves free of the Great Khan who succeeded to the power of Jingis, and embracing the Moslem Faith, continued from their capital of Sarai on the lower Volga to dominate the politics of Russia. The small Russian principalities and city republics were permitted to survive and to retain their customs, but on a footing of debasing subservience to their Asiatic masters. Compelled to seek investiture at the court of the Khan, to pay him a capitation tax in furs and money, and to furnish infantry contingents to his army, the Christian princes of Russia sank to the lowest depths of degradation. Even Alexander Nevski (1252-1263), famous for his victories over the Livonian knights, the Swedes, and the Finns, saw to it that Novgorod and Souzdal paid tribute to the Horde.

This long spell of soul-destroying servitude left a deep mark on the Russian people. It is to this period that we must trace the final estrangement of Russia from western Europe, and a retardation of culture which has never been repaired. It is now that the gloomy and pitiless despotism of the grand princes of Moscow was erected among the pine forests of central Russia, and that the last embers of Russian freedom were stamped out by the joint oppression of church and state. Only the monks and priests, being exempted from the Tatar capitation tax, profited from the general misfortunes of the country and built up for themselves, in that atmosphere of superstition and terror a position of territorial wealth and power, such as only the shattering convulsions of the latest Russian revolution could destroy.

No episode in the history of this tempestuous people is more shameful than the rise of the Muscovite power. The grand princes of Moscow overcame their neighbours and rivals, not by the vigour with which they attacked the enemy of their race, but by the success with which they courted his favour. If holy Moscow has grown into a great city from the small village in Souzdal, of which we first hear in 1147, it is because its princes in the fourteenth century obtained the assistance of Tatar armies against their Russian rivals, and constituted themselves the tax-gatherers and police agents for the Tatar Khans. It was the acquisition of this last lucrative but debasing monopoly which enabled Ivan Kalita (Ivan, the money bag) to *1328 41* distance all his rivals and neighbours and make a new central Russia in the heart of the great plain after the earlier and apparently more promising western Russia on the Dnieper had fallen into dissolution. The publican or tax farmer is an odious figure in every age, but it was reserved for Ivan Kalita, the first grand prince of Moscow, to distance all tax farmers in infamy by petitioning to discharge this invidious office for the benefit of the heretic oppressors of his race. This Ivan was a realist. He sought power where power lay, in the camp of the Great Khan, and determined that no other should share his prize. "It shall be for me to know the Horde," he said, " and not for thee." In the gallery of melancholy and formidable tyrants who built up the Muscovite power, this plodding, money-chasing man, who steadily extended his domains by purchase, seizure, colonization, or treaty, who did not scruple to use Tatar troops against his enemies, but who kept the peace and put down robbers, is a typical figure.

We cannot ignore him. By his policy of servile compliance he secured for his country fifty years of respite from Tatar raids. Under him Moscow, which was now at the very centre of the new colonial populace, became the seat of the Metropolitan of the Russian Church and the political capital of the country. He is one of the makers of the Russian state, dying after his career of extortions and economies in the habit of a monk with a tonsured head, like every other prince of his mediocre but serviceable line.

This Muscovite or colonial Russia was built on an agricultural foundation, and was therefore more enduring than the commercial confederacy of Kiev. The Viking princes of the west were military auxiliaries or *condottieri*, engaged by a chain of river republics, and limited by the appetites and traditions of an alien race already trained to the arts of civic government. These conditions did not prevail in central Russia. When the descendants of St. Vladimir trekked eastward into the forest lands of the Volga basin they found no ready-made cities, but a number of isolated river stations, freshly established in virgin soil by pioneering colonists and screened by vast spaces of impenetrable forest from the terrible nomads of the southern steppes, whose depredations had been the prime cause leading to the establishment of the Viking power on the Dnieper. In this environment of industrious and remote tillage the prince threw off his character of soldier, slave-trader, and bandit and assumed the quality of a colonizing landlord. The rota system of succession was abandoned as inapplicable to dispersed holdings and settled landed interests. The princely power descended in the direct line, and when it had become the practice of the Muscovites to assign to the eldest son the lion's share of the inheritance, the ground was cleared for the creation of a stable and expanding state.

Meanwhile a vast political change was overtaking all that western side of Russia, over which the Varangians in earlier days had established their power. Among the forests and marshes of the Niemen a fragment of the ancient and pagan Lithuanian race had contrived to escape the conquering thrust of the military monks of Germany, and to nurse, in solitary independence, the flame of political ambition. Suddenly this small nation sprang into the forefront of history under the impulsion of four capable and enterprising rulers. The conquests of Gudimin (1315-1340) and of Olgerd, his son (1345-1377), brought Lithuania to the Dnieper, made of Kiev a Lithuanian city, and subjected western Russia to the control of a power established in the distant Lithuanian capital of Vilna. A divided and prostrate people, still reeling under the shock of the Tatar invasion, was not in a position to make an effective resistance to these pagan

nvaders from the west. The Greek Christians bowed the neck
o the worshippers of Perkun, the God of Thunder, and preferred
he lax finance of the Lithuanian savage to the penetrating ex-
ortions of the Tatar.

It may be asked how so small a people was able to sustain
he burden of an empire thus widely spread and rapidly
cquired. The answer is that the Lithuanians were not long
inaided. A personal union of the Grand Duchy of Lithuania
vith the kingdom of Poland was effected in 1386 under
agellon I, who at the same time abjured his paganism and was
eceived into the Roman Church. Henceforward the Lithuanian
:mpire rested upon Polish swords and Roman missionaries.

So by the end of the fourteenth century, if we exclude the
iomad population of the southern steppes, two Russias stood
ace to face: the Russia of the west, Lithuanian and Polish in its
iolitical direction, Roman, Jewish, and Greek in its creed; and
he Russia of the east, all of a piece and Muscovite and Byzan-
ine to the core. The conflict between these two Russias, between
he Muscovite or Great Russia and the Lithuanian or Little
Russia, is one of the great themes of Russian history. From it
vas generated that bitter antagonism between the Russian and
he Pole, which, surviving into modern times, brought a Polish
irmy within reach of Kiev, and a Russian army of retaliation to
:he very outskirts of Warsaw, while Pilsudski was at the head of
Poland and Lenin still master of the Russian state.

1921

Planted between the Roman heresy of the west and the Tatar
heresy of the east, "Holy Moscow" steadily extended its influence. Churches, monasteries, convents, multiplied rapidly.
The metropolitan of Moscow stood side by side with the prince,
:orroborating and exalting his authority, and placing at the
disposal of the temporal power the tremendous engine of
religious fear. At last the time came when a Muscovite prince,
breaking a long tradition of dishonourable subservience to the
Tatars, struck a blow for Russian freedom. In 1380 Dimitri
Donskoi [of the Don], already renowned for domestic victories
and for his repulse of a Polish and Lithuanian invasion, smote
a great Tatar army on the field of Koulikovo. The spell was
broken. Though the Tatars returned soon afterwards and put
*he inhabitants of Moscow to the sword, it was shown that the
armies of the Horde were not invincible. The field of Koulikovo
witnessed the birth of a Russian nation, and of a new patriotism

largely founded on the possession of a common religious creed,
and owing much to the teaching of the Greek Church, which
had fused together the Slavs and Finns and all the minor tribes
and families of men who lived obscurely in the great dark plain.
Animated by this common spirit and equipped for the first time
in 1389 with cannon, the Muscovite forces were henceforth a
match for their oriental adversaries.

It is, however, to Timur, the great Tatar conqueror, even
more than to Dimitri, with his army of a hundred and fifty
thousand men, that the emancipation of Muscovy was principally due. Timour was not content with Christian adversaries
but pillaged and disorganized the Golden Horde. After his
destructive invasions (1390 and 1394), the task of the Muscovites
was easier and their success assured.

The Grand Dukes of Muscovy were the heirs at once of the
Tatar Khans and of the Byzantine Caesars. To the Khans they
owe an example of tyranny, a method of finance, and opportunities of emolument and power throughout that vital part of
the Russias which is drained by the Volga and its tributaries.
From Byzantium they derived the support of an ordered Church
and that profound doctrine of imperial authority which was
the legacy of the Roman Empire to the mediaeval world. So
when Constantinople fell into the hands of the Turks and the
last of the Palaeologi perished fighting for his throne, Moscow
became from the force of circumstance the capital of the Greek
Church in Europe, and its prince the heir to the Byzantine
Caesars. Was there not, it was asked, a divine dispensation in
accordance with which three cities were chosen in turn to be the
centres alike of a world empire and a world faith? Rome had
been followed by Constantinople. The high privilege and awful
responsibility now devolved upon Moscow. Such were the beliefs
and aspirations of the monks and priests of the Russian Church,
and such the historical logic which led Ivan the Great (1462-
1505) to call himself Tzar or Caesar, to take in marriage a
Byzantine princess and to blazon the two-headed eagle of the
empire on the arms of Muscovy. Here was a romance of history
and a dream of empire, running counter to the tumultuous
liberties of an earlier Russia, but destined to sustain a long course
of ambitious policy, which was shattered only by the disasters of
the great war and the well-knit dogmatism of a Jewish Communist from Germany.

1917

BOOKS WHICH MAY BE CONSULTED

A. Rambaud : Histoire de la Russie. 1884.
V. Kluchevsky : History of Russia. *Tr.* C. J. Hogarth. 1911-31.
Donald Mackenzie Wallace : Russia. 1912.
Makeef and O'Hara : Russia. (Nations of the Modern World Series.)
      1925.

CHAPTER XXXIII

RISE OF THE ITALIAN DESPOTS

Italian disunion. Commerce and war. Condottieri. The five states. Milan and the Visconti. Venice. Florence. The Albizzi. Rise of the Medici. Naples. Union of Naples, Florence, and Milan.

WITH the disappearance of the Hohenstaufen dynasty, Italy lost its last shred of political unity. Henceforward the visits of the Emperor were rare and fleeting, and had as little influence upon the government of the Italian people as the wing of the flying osprey upon the waves below. The country which was now left to find its own salvation was, if we except the kingdom of Naples and the papal domain, a medley of city states, each cherishing with a passionate tenacity its individual life and special commercial and political ambitions, making wars and alliances as the interest of the moment might dictate, and never scrupling to change its allegiance with a shift of the wind. In this scene of ardent rivalries and unstable combinations the fortunes of cities would mount and fall, now riding on the crest of the wave, now sunk into the trough, so that in the course of a single year the Venetians, being besieged by Genoa, were so desperate that they talked of refounding their republic in Crete, and again so exuberant that there was no bound to their ambition. And what was true of each city was true also of the living and turbulent factions within it. The picturesque towers of San Gemignano recall the days when the family feuds of the local nobility were waged within the city with a lordly disregard of vulgar convenience.

This amazing combativeness was the index of a vitality which found its expression in so great an outburst of commercial, artistic, and literary activity as to raise Italy far above any other European country in the scale of civilization. The northern visitor to the Lombard plain was astounded by the network of canals, the busy trade, the highly developed finance and skilled craftsmanship, the number of populous and wealthy cities stationed at so small a distance the one from the other, and by the many signs of public and private splendour. In the first half of the thirteenth century Fra Bonvesin da Riva, one of the early poets who wrote in the vulgar tongue, describes Milan as a city with two hundred thousand inhabitants, with fifty thousand men able to bear arms, with four hundred notaries, two hundred doctors, two hundred jurisconsults or *judices*, eighty schoolmasters, fifty copiers or sellers of books, sixty noblemen's houses, a hundred and fifty castles in the *contado* with dependent villages, with three hundred butchers and as many bakers, and a thousand farmers to cater for the population. The name of Lombard Street in the city of London records the fact that the Lombards were pioneers in banking, and that there was a time when the bankers and money-changers of Europe were called by this name.

The Italian despot was the necessary product of these two incompatible conditions of commerce and combativeness. Sooner or later every city felt the need of a strong hand either to avert some definite danger, or to keep the spirit of faction within bounds, or to maintain and extend its industry and commerce. Sometimes it would invoke the help of a successful soldier, sometimes that of a civilian magistrate from some other city, who, being unconnected with local feuds, might be trusted to act with impartiality. At first, since the spirit of liberty was vivacious and strong, these experiments were made with a tentative caution. The *podesta* was appointed for a year, or for a short term of years; but the convenience of having, more especially in difficult times, an authority capable of taking prompt action, of evading the restrictions of a popular constitution framed for narrow and local needs, and of exercising a vigorous policy, was found to be so great that the institution, once adopted, became rooted in the political morals of the country.

The despot who commands the Italian scene in the fourteenth and fifteenth centuries was the *podesta* made permanent and hereditary. One of the earliest members of his class was Can Grande della Scala of Verona, whose father was elected Capitano del Popolo for life, and who shines in history as the patron of Dante and Giotto, and as the pioneer in that distinctively Italian association of a stern tyranny, a sumptuous court, and a liberal, and indeed munificent, patronage of the arts.

The increasing concentration upon the arts of peace which produced as one of its results the *podesta* and the hereditary despot, also led to the substitution of mercenary for civic armies.

The Italian *condottieri* played their appointed part in the progress of civilization. They announced the advent of a new philosophy which regarded war no longer as the pride and privilege of the ruling class, but as butcher's work to be delegated to specialists. The merchant, relieved of his military obligations, was able to attend to the improvement of his fortunes and the government of his city, while the disfranchised noble—for under the constitutions of most Italian city states the nobility were excluded from any part or lot in the government—found in the life of the *condottiere* a congenial field for his tastes and activities. The development, therefore, of these mercenary armies, so far from being a sign of decadence, was an indication that in Italy, at least, a new and truer scale of human values was making itself apparent. It was realized that war was a necessary part of the political conditions of the age, but not so important that it should absorb the energies of men who were better employed in the amassing of fortunes, the building of churches, the painting of pictures, or the governing of states. Later on the system lent itself to abuses, to wars, which the well-paid combatants on either side had no interest in concluding, to expensive but bloodless battles, and to that general relaxation of civic and military fibre censured by the patriotic Machiavelli which, from the end of the fifteenth century, exposed Italy again and again to the insolence of foreign invasion.

There have been many instances in history of a despotism which numbs and abases the spirit of a subject population; but the Italian despotisms, though darkly stained by cruelty, craft, and caprice, do not appear to have stunted the free expression of the human spirit, or to have introduced habits of servility and abasement. The age of the despots in Italy is one of the flowering times of the human genius, during which, quite apart from the wonderful achievements of elect individuals, the energy of the popular will was still unimpaired and formidable, and those despots were most successful who, like the Medici in Florence, stood close to the people and understood their needs.

The process by which a number of independent city states were gradually merged into large units cannot be traced in a general history. It here must suffice to say that by the beginning of the fifteenth century the political affairs of Italy were regulated by the relations of five principal powers—the kingdom of Naples, the papal states, the republic of Venice, the despotism of Milan and Florence, which, though nominally republican, was in truth directed by the power of the Albizzi family. The long duel between Genoa and Venice for the dominion of the seas had been decided in the war of Chioggia (1378-1381) in favour of Venice by one of the most complete and sudden reversals of military fortune. Henceforward Genoa, always rent by internal factions, and narrowly confined between the sea and the mountains, is more important in the Bosphorus than in Italy.

In this complex of powers the central fact was the persistent rivalry of Venice and Milan, the first enriched by the trade of a great overseas Empire, the second by agriculture, by an incomparable breed of horses, by flourishing silks and embroideries, by its frontier at the base of a great commercial route across the Alps, and lastly by an industry in arms and armaments, which equipped fighting men all over the world and irrespective of creed. The master of such a city could easily make himself the richest man in Europe.

This is exactly what happened to the great Ghibelline family (Frankish in origin as was indicated by their ruddy hair and fair complexion) who obtained political control of Milan and absorbed most of northern and much of central Italy into their territory. The Visconti became the richest family in Europe, so rich that a Visconti bride was the most brilliant prize in the marriage market of Europe, and so successful in their royal marriages that they are connected through the female line with the five royal houses of Valois, Habsburg, Tudor, Stuart, and Hanover; though whether it should ever have been a source of pride to point to a Visconti descent may be doubted, for, while some princes of that family were men of integrity, others were cruel, treacherous, cowardly, and profligate.

Gian Galeazzo Visconti, the most conspicuous figure of the dynasty (1378-1402), was one of those fortunate men whose personal ambition, pursued without moral scruple but always with pertinacity, chimed in with the public interest at the moment. It suited well with the needs of a city, whose upper class was divided into the Guelf and Ghibelline factions, that there should be one master hand to compose disputes. It was agreeable to the merchants, the craftsmen, and the peasantry of the *contado* to enjoy the protection of a strong government; and though the cities under Milanese dominion might regret their independence, they were consoled by the solid advantages of a more economical administration and a more prosperous trade. Moreover, since it had become the habit of the Lombard nobles to live in the city, the master of Milan, as Commines observed, was the master of the state.

There was a certain bigness of vision in this fair-haired noble-man, the first hereditary Duke of Milan, which fixes the attention of posterity. He divined the foreign peril, and saw that without a strong and compact state in northern Italy, such as he proposed to found, Italian independence was insecure. Fine sentiments can hardly be attributed to a man whose character is deeply stained by craft and cruelty; but at least it will be conceded that Gian Galeazzo was a shrewd judge of political opportunity, who saw that with the Papacy distracted by schism, and Naples paralyzed by internal discords, the field was clear of the two most formidable obstacles which might thwart the expansion of his state. He had also, combined with the mean treacheries of his nature, the not uncommon ideal of a civilized and princely grandeur. He built bridges, castles, palaces. The *Certosa* and the University of Pavia are tokens of his ambition to shine as the patron of religion and learning.

As to his victories, they were due to no military skill of his own, for Gian Galeazzo was not a campaigner, but to Facino Cane, the very skilful leader of his mercenary army. Decisive and most alarming these victories were to the two neighbours who were most concerned to check his progress. Vicenza and Padua were wrested from Venice. The republic of Florence, despite the services of Sir John Hawkwood, a famous English *condottiere* whose monument may be seen in the Duomo, was caught in a noose of cities, Siena, Perugia, Assisi, Pisa, which found the road to safety in the acceptance of Milanese rule.

The half-century of northern Italian history which follows the death of Gian Galeazzo in 1402 is filled with the wars of Milanese ambition and Venetian and Florentine defence. The precious and irredeemable years during which it would have been possible, had there been a concerted Italian effort, to save Europe from the Turks, were consumed by three of the wealthiest and most advanced communities in the world in a contest which had no significance for civilization. The five wars between Milan and Venice, the last of which was protracted for seven years, effectually paralyzed concerted effort in the east, and when at last peace was made at Lodi in 1454 it was too late. The Turk was already master of Constantinople.

Neither did the Milanese realize their ambition. Even if there had been no Pope in the background, Venice and Florence were sufficiently wealthy, and therefore sufficiently powerful, to prevent the establishment of a northern Italian kingdom centred in Milan. Despite the skill of Filippo Maria Visconti, who after an intervening period of anarchy restored and enlarged his father's duchy, it was still very far from being the kingdom of his dreams, for Venice and Florence barred the way, and at Filippo's death in 1447 were holding a winning advantage.

The story of Venice, though marked by sharp reverses on sea and land, had been one of so much material prosperity and domestic peace as to give the impression of an almost miraculous sagacity in the management of affairs. No other Italian state seemed to be so contented or so fully assured of a stable and equable life. A blessed immunity from the two great plagues of Italy, exiles plotting ruin to the constitution or family feuds bringing storms and bitterness into politics, marked her out from less fortunate cities. Cheap and efficient justice, taxation bearing lightly on the poor, a brilliant round of spectacles and amusements, and a number of small, self-supporting, and self-sufficient trade guilds to keep the people happy and occupied, and to provide a modest theatre for the display of talent, were other elements making for harmony and content. Nor were these blessings purchased at the expense of national strength. The life appointment of the Doge was a guarantee of continuity, the wide powers accorded to the Council of Ten a pledge of administrative firmness. There was even a note of tyranny in the elaborate system of detection and espionage by which the government felt the pulse of the city and guarded itself against unpleasant surprises; but if a tyranny, the rule of the Doge was of all tyrannies the most paternal and benignant. As an example of the enlightenment of Venetian legislation we may note that children were forbidden to work in dangerous trades, and that there was a compulsory load line for ships, provisions which were not until late in the nineteenth century introduced into the statute book of Great Britain, then the leading industrial and sea-going country of the world.

Nature had placed Venice in a key position between east and west, and, using the favours of nature with skill, she outdistanced

Genoa and Aragon, her nearest rivals. The main part of the carrying trade of Europe was done in Venetian bottoms. Her galleys brought sugar and spices to England, supplied Flemish weavers with English wool, and Mediterranean towns with Flemish cloth. The long conflict with Genoa was not, like many mediaeval wars, frivolous and unnecessary, but a deadly, inexorable struggle for markets. Commerce shaped Venetian policy, and empire when it came was not so much an end in itself as an incident of expanding business. The sea was the element upon which the whole fortune of Venice was embarked and the exciting cause of all generous ambitions. The young Venetian noblemen went into the navy as the natural avenue to fame and fortune. Six fleets, each appointed to serve in a different area, but all built on a common pattern, so that the consul in every port could keep and provide spare parts, attested the enterprise and forethought of the Venetian government in everything which pertained to the administration of the marine.

More specifically the foreign policy of Venice had been long shaped by the triple need of securing the Dalmatian coast, of winning for herself a safe agricultural base in Italy, and a control of such alpine passes as were necessary for her convoys of merchandise. In the pursuit of these objects the republic had been brought into contact at different times with the Hungarian monarchy and with the masters of Padua and Verona; but in the first half of the fifteenth century her one dangerous adversary was Filippo Maria Visconti of Milan, who, with the aid of his famous *condottiere* general, Francesco Carmagnola, had by 1421 acquired for himself a dominating position in northern Italy.

Could Venice sit still while this ambitious rival consolidated his power? Could she trust him not to attack Verona at the moment most appropriate to himself? Was not attack the truest form of defence, and the extension of the Venetian rule over the Lombard plain the one sufficient guarantee of security? The case for the preventive war was vehemently urged in 1421 by the young Foscari and countered by the old Doge Mocenigo with arguments such as the wise in every age have brought against this immoral doctrine; and so long as that wise old man lived the preventive war was averted. But in 1423 Mocenigo died and Foscari took his place as Doge. The voice of peace was no longer predominant in the counsels of the Venetian Government; and

1412-47

with Florence pressing for war and Carmagnola deserting to her side, Venice entered the lists against Filippo Maria.

The republic of San Marco had little reason to be satisfied with her decision. There were in the military market other swords besides that of Carmagnola, and notably the sword of one Francesco Sforza, the son of a distinguished *condottiere* from the Romagna, himself a man of immense animal vigour and endurance, who was to prove himself in these long wars a fine and resourceful soldier as well as one of the most adroit politicians of his age. Carmagnola was no match for such an antagonist, and after some initial victories attracted the dangerous suspicions of his paymasters. When the Venetian fleet was destroyed in the Po in 1431, the government wished to know what their turn-coat general was doing, decoyed him to Venice, and there caused him to be secretly tried and publicly executed as a traitor. The iron courage of Venice in thus solemnly destroying a famous and popular *condottiere* chief was widely admired as evidence of an almost inhuman resolve to place the civil above the military power; but it brought neither victories nor wisdom in its train. When Filippo Maria died in 1447, leaving no male heir, prudence would have directed overtures of friendship to the new republican government, as yet weak and uncertain, which was set up in Milan. But in an evil hour, and under the impulsion of the same headstrong party which had been the source of all the trouble, Venice decided to strike down her rival. She had reckoned without the crafty *condottiere*, who had taken the precaution to wed the only daughter of the last Visconti, and this mistake was Sforza's opportunity. Coming forward as the defender of the young republic, he first defeated the Venetians on land and sea, and then, when Venice was so humiliated as to crave his alliance, turned against his old friends and employers and made himself master of the Milanese state. At the end of twenty-five years of almost incessant fighting Venice was faced with a Duke of Milan in comparison with whom Filippo Maria Visconti was an infant in subtlety and force.

It may be doubted whether Sforza could have accomplished his *coup d'état* but for the sudden revolution of policy in Florence. The Milanese *condottiere* was assisted by the long purse of his friend Cosimo de' Medici, a Florentine man of business, who in 1434 had been recalled from exile and had then made himself the *de facto* ruler of his state. It was the opinion of this cool observer that Venice, rather than Milan, was the true enemy of Florentine commerce.

Florence, the spiritual capital of Italy, the birthplace of Dante, of Petrarch's family, and of Boccaccio, was upon its material side renowned for banking, commerce, and the manufacture of cloth. In the great quarrel between the Guelfs and the Ghibellines, the Florentines, to whom the conception of imperialism in any form was anathema, embraced the papal, and consequently also the French side. And since Florence did not live on religious and political aspirations only, but had an eye to the main chance, she made money out of her papalism by becoming banker to the Roman Curia. To be a banker on a great scale is to be a diplomatist and a statesman. The banking business of Florence brought her into political relations with many governments in many lands. The great banking family of the Acciaiuoli, who may be described as the Rothschilds of the fourteenth century, provided a prime minister to Naples, a seigneur to Malta, a despot to Corinth, and a dynasty of Florentine dukes to Athens. Yet despite the development of cosmopolitan finance and big business, the spirit of the Florentine people had remained passionately and enviously equalitarian. While no family would admit the superiority of another, every family was ambitious to be first.

These fickle, jealous, and aspiring moods were reflected in a constitution which was entirely incompatible with efficient government. There was a rage for checks and counterchecks, for election and the lot, for short terms of office, and for the restriction of real power to the greater guilds or mercantile communities. If it were not that the nobles and the working class were alike disfranchised, one might describe the old Florentine constitution as a democracy doctrinaire to the point of insanity. The Gonfalonier of Justice, head of the signoria or cabinet, was allowed to hold office for two months only. Nor could any proposal of the signoria pass into law until it had secured a two-thirds majority in each of five separate committees or assemblies. It would be difficult to conceive provisions more calculated to impair the quality and check the momentum of government.

At the first serious test such a constitution inevitably broke down. When Florence began to be sensible of the menace of her neighbours, and as the conception began to prevail that the city itself was not enough, but that the acquisition of the surrounding country was necessary if trade connections were to be secured, the elaborate precautions of the old constitution, which was so popular that no one dared to propose to discard it, had simply to be evaded. The Parte Guelfa, a party organization, was the first body outside the constitution which seriously addressed itself to the task of violating the spirit, while observing the letter, of Florentine democracy. There was not much delicacy about the methods of this organization, which anticipated some of the worst practices of American gangsters. But Florence was never a tame or submissive city. The outrageous practices of the Parte Guelfa, combined with industrial grievances, produced the great popular revolution of the Ciompi (1378), which secured for the Arti Minori or Lesser Guilds a place within the pale of the constitution. But though the Parte Guelfa was henceforward stripped of the influence which it had abused, the constitution still remained popular and impossible, and the need for circumventing it correspondingly urgent.

At this juncture in Florentine history the control of affairs passed through a counter-revolution into the hands of a patriotic Florentine business family, who knew how to maintain and keep an effective measure of authority without manifest injustice or public odium. Maso and Rinaldo Albizzi were uncrowned rulers of Florence from 1382 to 1434. Their powers of efficient decision, their knowledge of trade, their enthusiasm for art and letters, their combination of liberality to the poor with their ruthlessness to dangerous men, their studious care to behave as ordinary citizens, and to conceal the springs of power, made them acceptable to Florence and her subject cities. Moreover, there was public danger. The rule of the Albizzi synchronizes with the development of the Milanese menace, when the *condottieri* of Gian Galeazzo and Filippo Maria were in the field, and a strong hand was needed at the helm.

Meanwhile another family, less oligarchic, more wealthy, but ever since the revolution of 1378 noted for its attachment to popular causes, was gradually coming to the front. The Medici were bankers. The opulence, the knowledge, the widespread influence in foreign courts and capitals which come to the great cosmopolitan banker, belonged in full measure to this gifted and remarkable Florentine family. So indispensable did their financial services ultimately become, that it was a generally recognized maxim, that a failure of the Medici banks would mean a collapse of the whole fabric of European credit. But while banking supplied the economic foundation upon which the Medici built up their rule in Florence, it was only one among many explanations of their success. If the Medici were bankers, they were also farmers, who could talk beasts or crops with the Tuscan husbandmen, connoisseurs in literature and art, and experts alike in the larger and more generous aspects of statesmanship, as in the sordid minutiae of political intrigue. Everything which had been done under the Albizzi was carried forward upon a greater scale and with a higher degree of imagination by a more gifted family. The taxes were still used to help friends and injure enemies. The elections were still jerrymandered. The letter of the constitution was still kept, while its whole drift and spirit were ingeniously frustrated. However frequently elections might be held, the result was invariably the return of the Medicean candidates. To these manifest irregularities the democracy of Florence turned a blind eye. A high capacity for government, a splendid court, a liberal and intelligent patronage of the arts, coupled with simple and popular manners, secured for Cosimo de' Medici and Lorenzo his grandson a brilliant period of substantial power.

Among the Italian states none should have been more powerful, but none was in fact less effective, than the military kingdom of Naples. The destiny of states has little connection with the charm of their climate, the romance of their scenery, or the long descent of their inhabitants. A political tragedy seems to brood over the lovely Italian land, " the favoured home of bandits and brigands," which was first touched by the sunlight of Greek civilization. Nothing has greatly prospered there for any long period of time. The soil is a palimpsest of broken and luxurious civilizations, of great achievements which have no sequel. The Normans were replaced by the Hohenstaufen, under whom Naples became perhaps of all the countries of Europe the most advanced and efficiently governed. But the power of the Hohenstaufen was broken, and the two Sicilies were transferred by the Pope to the alien rule of Charles of Anjou. From that date forward misfortune followed misfortune. Charles was a selfish and worthless tyrant. The Sicilians, with a spirit characteristic of their island, rose against him, massacred his officers, and placed their country under the house of Aragon, which could claim descent through the female line from Manfred, the bastard son of Frederick II.

Thenceforward Aragon was pitted against Anjou. The war was fierce, long, and, from the point of view of the Neapolitan Angevins, a failure. The island remained with Aragon, the third strongest naval power in the Mediterranean. But this was not the end of the troubles which continued to distract southern Italy. The Angevins were an ambitious and shallow race, more interested in show than in government. They were not content with the kingdom of Naples in addition to their French county of Provence. The elder branch of the family went to rule in Hungary, while the younger branch remained in Italy; and since no combination of territories was too fantastic for an Angevin, Lewis of Hungary invaded Naples in the hopes of uniting the kingdoms under his own sceptre. Even when this foolish project had been renounced, and Naples had been permitted to settle down under a cadet branch of the Angevin family (Charles III of Durazzo and his son Ladislas and his daughter Joanna II, 1382-1435), who, having no French possessions, were able more closely to identify themselves with Neapolitan interests, the monarchy rested upon uncertain foundations. The claims of the Durazzo house were disputed in Sicily and in Provence, and the sovereign was confronted with a baronage which found its interests best served by intrigue with a foreign pretender. In these circumstances the tasks of monarchy, which in England and France had been a source of national power, were gravely obstructed. A foreign dynasty, a succession of indifferent kings and bad queens, a distracting uncertainty and unrest arising from the disputed succession gave to Neapolitan politics under the house of Anjou an air of ruffianly melodrama. At last (1435) in the wise and charming Alfonso V of Aragon Naples found a statesman for its ruler, a true prince of the Renaissance, firm, munificent, cultured, and for the moment powerful. Alfonso saw that only by a close union with Florence and Milan could his house be securely protected against the French. That union he succeeded in effecting. It was the one triumph of Neapolitan statesmanship in the fifteenth century, its one contribution to the political welfare of Italy. After Alfonso's death the combination was broken by the treachery of Milan, and thereupon there was opened up a new chapter of troubles for Italy and for Naples, so vast in its consequences that for some historians it has been held to mark the watershed between the mediaeval and the modern world.

BOOKS WHICH MAY BE CONSULTED

Janet Trevelyan : History of Italy. 1928.

J. A. Symonds : The Renaissance in Italy (The Age of the Despots). 7 vols. 1875-86.

E. Armstrong : Lorenzo de' Medici and Florence in the Fifteenth Century. 1896.

Horatio Brown : Venice : A Historical Sketch of the Republic. 1893.

C. M. Ady : A History of Milan under the Sforzas. Ed. E. Armstrong. 1907.

P. Villani : The Two First Centuries of Florentine History. Tr. L. Villani. 1894-5.

G. Villani : Chronicles. Selections tr. R. E. Selfe. 1896.

W. F. T. Butler : The Lombard Communes. 1906.

J. C. L. Sismondi : History of the Italian Republics. (Everyman's Library.) 1907.

CHAPTER XXXIV

THE OTTOMAN TURKS

Weakness of the restored Byzantine Empire. The Catalan Company. Rise of the Ottoman Turks. The Janissaries. The Serbs. Kossovo. The intervention of Timur. Angora. The Hungarians. Early triumphs and final defeat of Hunyades. Christian disunion and fall of Constantinople.

THE Byzantine Empire, which for centuries had stood as the bulwark of European civilization against the Orient, was shaken beyond recovery by the Latin conquest. The Greek restoration of 1261, though productive of a late flowering of scholarship and literature, was followed by no revival of Greek power. The Emperors of the house of Palaeologus re-entered upon a shrunken and divided heritage, the acknowledged weakness of which was a perpetual invitation to insolent attack. While the great Anatolian recruiting grounds of the old Byzantine Empire had long passed under the control of the Turcoman Sultan of the house of Seljuk, who ruled at Iconium, the major part of the Balkan peninsula was in the hands of the Bulgars. Greece, save for a province in the Peloponnese, was a medley of Frankish fiefs. What remained to the Empire was a narrow strip of the Asiatic littoral, Constantinople and western Thrace, Thessalonica and the Thracian Chalcidice, the despotat of Mistra (in the Peloponnese), and a few islands in the Aegean. These, even if they were as valuable as Rhodes, which was taken by the Knights of St. John in 1310, the Emperor was unable to defend against serious attack.

There can be no better illustration of the deep-seated weakness of the Byzantine Empire during the early years of the fourteenth century than the strange story of the great Catalan Company. Everything relating to this fierce body of mercenaries seems charged with weighty premonitions of the future. It was recruited from that needy and ambitious nobility of Spain which was later destined to fill the world with its military renown. It was schooled in the wars of Sicilian independence (1282-1302) to meet on even terms the chivalry of Italy and France, and on the conclusion of that bitter struggle it embraced the service of the Byzantine Emperor. It was led by Roger de Flor, a pirate (incidentally the son of Frederick II's German falconer by an heiress from Brindisi), who was made a grand duke and even a Caesar, and was married to a Bulgarian princess. But compliments, which were cheap in Constantinople, meant little to these proud and quarrelsome strangers. The Catalans took the measure of their Greek employers, and came to the conclusion that no insolence was too gross for a government so weak and nerveless. Instead of settling down to a laborious campaign against the Seljuks, the Company preferred to quarrel with the Genoese of Galata, who supplied ships to the navy, and to fight the Alans, who were the *corps d'élite* in the army of their employer. Nor did they quit imperial territory until they had seized Gallipoli, the key fortress of the Hellespont, and beaten the Emperor himself in a pitched fight.

Meanwhile (1308) the Duchy of Athens, which had prospered for a century under the mild rule of a Burgundian family, had fallen to Walter of Brienne, the fiery son of a brood famous for its adventures in many lands.

In a moment as calamitous for himself as it was fortunate for the Emperor, the new Duke of Athens called upon the help of the great Company. The Catalans, who, when not quarrelling with others, quarrelled among themselves and were fresh from the butchery of eleven colonels, descended into Greece, fought for a year, and seeing that the land was fair, refused to accept their discharge, save on terms which the duke was unable to concede. As the traveller from Athens descends the hills into the lovely vale of the Cephissus, he beholds on his right the battlefield (1310) which brought death to Walter of Brienne and gave his duchy into the hands of the Aragonese for seventy-four years. The Catalans, six thousand four hundred strong, were stationed among the green March corn some way back from the coast road, a tempting mark for the superior numbers of their adversary. But between the Duke and his enemy lay a marsh, concealed and artificial, and here Brienne and his horsemen were butchered by the long Catalan knives as they lay engulfed and helpless on the sodden ground. The armies of Xerxes and Darius were civilized in comparison with the new Catholic masters of the Parthenon.

Beyond the Hellespont among the Bithynian hills there were men of a certain Turkish tribe who ruminated on this strange

Spanish portent. What marvels could not a small force of resolute men achieve, if only the infantry were disciplined! The Spanish lesson was not lost upon the grave and receptive Ottomans. The time was not far distant when they too would fashion an infantry army, seize Gallipoli, beat the Imperials, and tread the sacred soil of the Acropolis as masters.

The history of the Ottoman Turks is one of a family of simple shepherds and herdsmen, gradually gathering power and influence, and by patience and justice, mingled with a persevering course of cruelty and craft, attracting the most heterogeneous elements to its service until it was in a position to make rapid and gigantic conquests, and to fashion and support a mighty Empire. Othman, the founder from whom the race derives its name, prefigured, albeit upon a small scale, some characteristic features of the future policy of his line. The scene of his life work was the ill-defended frontier province of Bithynia, where he engaged in a guerilla warfare with the Greek Christians, first as an emir under the Seljuk Sultan, and after 1307 as an independent prince. His religion was deep and unaffected, his policy adjusted to the counsels of the holy men of his faith, his administration of justice remarkable in those venal and violent times for impartiality. But passionate as were his Moslem beliefs, he had the vision to discern that while the Moslem religion might be the creed of a great state, a Turkish tribe could not suffice for its foundation. Marriage, enslavement, the attraction of military renown must win adherents. So he chose his wife from Cilicia, seized a Christian damsel for his son, and employed as his *alter ego* in war Michael of the Forked Beard, a Greek apostate from the Christian faith.

The conquest of Bithynia which was begun by Othman was completed by Orchan, his eldest son. The two famous cities of 1326 Nicomedia and Nicaea passed at the cost of one inconsiderable battle against an imperial army into the hands of the Ottomans. So inexpensive were these conquests, so shameful had been the conduct of the imperial campaign that a mere soldier would have been tempted to pursue his military advantage and to attack the European possessions of his feeble enemy. But Orchan was no mere soldier. The twenty years following the victory of Pele- 1329-49 kanon, perhaps the most fruitful in the history of the Ottoman people, were spent at the beautiful Bithynian capital of Brusa in the organization of a state. Instead of leading his Ottomans

against the emirs of the Asiatic coast, or the populations of the
Balkan peninsula, the wise Orchan and his advisers employed
themselves in building mosques and colleges, hospitals and cara-
vanseries, in the establishment of a coinage, the prescription of
a national headdress (a plain cap of white felt), and, most important of all, in the organization of an army. It is to the period
of this momentous halt at Brusa that we must ascribe the foundation of those distinctive military institutions which made the
Ottoman Turk for many centuries the terror of eastern Europe
—the *akindji* or light skirmishers, the feudatory cavalry, the
Sultan's guard, and above all the famous infantry force, which
has now to be described.

The "janissaries," or new soldiers, were Christian children,
taken by force from their homes, and brought up as Moslems in
seminaries designed to efface all trace of their earlier affections
and affinities, and to make of them the pliable instruments of
the Ottoman state. Some, and these the most unfortunate, were
drafted off to serve as pages in the palace, others were employed
in the civil service, but the main body passed into an infantry
corps, so brave and devoted that no Turkish army with a
stiffening of janissaries failed to give an excellent account of
itself on the field. The janissary was a slave. The affections
which sweeten the character, the interests which expand the
mind, the ideals which give elevation to the will, were denied
him. An iron discipline effaced the past and impoverished the
future. He was made to forget father and mother, brothers and
sisters. He could never hope for wife or children. The barrack
was his home, fighting his trade, the Koran his religion,
and he went forth to slay the enemies of the Sultan and of
Allah with the inflamed and contracted fanaticism of a
monk.

The suggestion that this force should be recruited by a tribute
of Christian children is said to have come from Black Habil,
the proud Vizier of Orchan, and it is clear that without such
a tribute a regular recruitment could not have been maintained.
It followed, as a consequence, that the Ottoman Empire was
made and maintained, not only, or even mainly, by men of the
Ottoman race, but by the slave children of Christian parents,
who had issued through the seminaries of the janissaries, with
the appointed stamp of military subservience and the Moslem
faith. The most distinguished men of the Ottoman Empire

will be found to have passed from Christian homes through these institutions.

While an Ottoman State was thus forming on a new mould in hither Asia, a new power, profiting by the civil wars and corruption of the Greeks, had manifested a raw vehemence in the Balkans. A competent modern writer has described the Serbs as the Celts and the Bulgars as the Lowland Scots of the Balkan peninsula; and everything in Serbian history announces a brave, spirited, but temperamental people. Under Stephen Dushan, one of those great men who give aspirations to a race— 1333-55 a soldier, a legislator, and a statesman—the dominion of Serbia was extended from the Danube to the Aegean by the seizure of Albania, Epirus, and Thessaly, triumphs which, though they are deeply printed on the national memory of the Serbs, failed to satisfy the impatient leader of an impatient people. With an ambition which expanded with success, Stephen assumed the imperial title, and proposed as the goal of his endeavours the subjection of the Greeks.

A year after Stephen's death, with his last dream unaccomplished—it was the year in which France and England struggled 1356 at Poitiers—Suleiman, the heir and successor of Orchan, crossed the Hellespont under a harvest moon and founded on the Gallipoli peninsula the first Turkish settlement on European soil. A little later, while he was flying his hawks in a field near Bulair, Suleiman died from his horse's stumble, and was buried where he fell. "For a hundred years," says Von Hammer, "he was the only Ottoman prince who lay buried in European earth; and his tomb continually invited the races of Asia to perform their pilgrimage to it with the sword of conquest. Of all the hero-tombs which have been hitherto mentioned in connection with Ottoman history, there is none more renowned or more visited than that of the second Vizier of the Empire, the fortunate Caesar of the Hellespont, who laid the foundation of the Ottoman power in Europe."

With the accession of Suleiman's brother, Murad I, Europe 1359 at last discovered, what before it had not even suspected, the mighty force which had been steadily accumulating for more than a generation in the small Ottoman state beyond the Hellespont. Murad crossed to the Gallipoli peninsula and found himself invincible. Thessalonica and Adrianople, next to the capital the two principal cities of the Greek Empire, passed into his hands 1361 with such ease as to suggest that the last day of the Greek Empire was at hand. But as Orchan was cautious so was Murad. A pause was necessary to consolidate the European conquests, to convert Adrianople into a Moslem capital, and to set up that system of military fiefs which was necessary for the supply of the cavalry arm. When these objects had been achieved, and the supremacy of the Sultan had been established in Asia Minor, an advance might be made on Constantinople and Belgrade. The Emperor was pliant. The spirit of the Greeks was low and submissive. It was only in the north-west, on the side of Serbia, that the Christian cause was likely to find an effective champion. Stephen Dushan was dead, but something of his spirit still survived in the breast of King Lazarus, his son, so while the Sultan was engaged in a victorious campaign against his Turkish adversaries in Asia, a great confederacy of the Christian peoples of south-eastern Europe was organized under the leadership of the Serbian King for the destruction of the Mussulman power. Serbs and Bulgars, Bosnians and Albanians, Poles, Hungarians, and even Mongols from the Dobrudja, but nobody of the older European nations, not a Latin nor a Greek, gathered together in the Christian camp. It may be safely assumed that an improvised army, in which seven languages are spoken, will always, however high be the courage of its individual members, prove inferior to an experienced force which long and arduous discipline has fused into a unit. So it proved on the famous and hard-fought field of Kossovo, which is commemorated in the heroic poetry of the Serbs. The Turks were victors, but in the hour of victory Murad fell by the hand of a Serbian patriot.

1387

1389

Twelve years of continuous success followed the abasement of the Christian Slavs, years marked by the transfer of many loyalties, by the annihilation of a great crusading army from the west (Nicopolis, September 28, 1396), and by the extension of the Ottoman borders to the Danube and the Euphrates. The pitiless Bayazid, whose first public act had been the murder of the brother who had shared with him on the previous day the perils of Kossovo, seemed by the opening of the fifteenth century to have reached the climax of human fortune. Wherever the blood-red flag had waved, whether on the European or on the Asiatic front, it had brought victory. As the Sultan surveyed the scene from his voluptuous court at Brusa, as he reflected upon his vast harem, upon his Christian auxiliaries and slaves, upon the subjection of the Seljuks and the pusillanimity of the Greeks, and upon the strong network of his power, now extended over two continents, he felt that the time had come for one last inconsiderable operation, the replacement, whether in peace or war, of the Greek in Constantinople. In 1400 he ordered the Emperor out of the city, and meeting with a noble defiance, was preparing to deliver the lethal blow.

The impending stroke was averted in mid-air. A catastrophe supervened, which for many centuries made of Bayazid the standing example of the mutability of human fortune, and secured fifty years of respite for Constantinople. Timur (or Tamerlane) the Mongol, an old white-haired cripple from the far east, an intellectual specialist in chess, theology, and conquest, and perhaps the greatest artist in destruction known in the savage annals of mankind, was now approaching the confines of the Ottoman dominions at the head of his mammoth army of horsemen. Bayazid was rash enough to provoke the indignation of the master of Delhi and Samarcand, of Bagdad and Damascus, and paid the penalty for his presumption. On the wide plain of Angora the famous Ottoman army, the instrument of *July 20, 1402* so many conquests, was enveloped and destroyed by an overwhelming force of Mongol cavalry. Bayazid was made a prisoner, and as he proceeded in a closed litter upon his melancholy journey to Samarcand, the victors streamed westward to wreck his capital, and to ravage his country to the brink of the Hellespont and the Aegean.

The recovery of the Ottoman Empire after this overwhelming disaster is as remarkable as the inability of the Christian powers to turn it to account. When we consider that the Ottomans had lost all their Asiatic possessions, that their Sultan was a captive, and that his sons were fighting one another for his inheritance, the situation might well have seemed desperate. But what was lost in Asia was saved in Europe. Adrianople was now a Moslem city, in which were concentrated the resources of experience, courage, and perseverance necessary for the restoration of the state. Here for forty years was the nucleus of an effective government. Here were civil servants and soldiers, lawyers and dervishes, jurymen and law courts, seminaries for the education of janissaries, and leaders imbued with the old spirit of military pride. It was a good centre for the levying of Christian slaves;

and it was, in fact, from this capital of Adrianople, which the Greek Emperors neglected to assault, that Mohammed I and Murad II issued forth to restore their Empire.

It is characteristic of the unorganized state of western Europe that no serious effort was made to deal with the Ottoman problems until forty years after the battle of Angora. The golden moments, when the enemy was without soldiers or Sultan, were allowed to slip by. Nor was it until Murad II had recruited the army and refashioned the state, and was making life in Hungary intolerable by his slave-raiding aggressions, that western Europe woke up once more to its serious responsibilities in connection with the eastern danger.

The protagonist in the new Crusade was the nation which had most reason to fear and resent the revived power of the Ottomans. The Hungarians are among the bravest and most stalwart of the fighting races of Europe, exhibiting the steadfast qualities of the Turk, with whom they are racially allied, as well as others which belong to the more gifted and imaginative peoples. Under the rule of two spirited Angevin monarchs (1309-1382) this valiant but backward nation had advanced in military cohesion and in the arts of peace. Charles Robert and his successor, Lewis the Great, supplied exactly that form of stimulus which was best calculated to excite and regiment the disordered energies of a proud aristocracy. These princes, part French, part Neapolitan, introduced into Hungary much of the chivalry of France and something of the refinement of Italy. They set up a court, held tournaments, created a feudal army, and by the establishment of military orders, and the lavish bestowal of rewards, attracted to the service of their persons the wayward loyalties of their Magyar nobles. But the government of Hungary, which demanded the undivided energies of a vigorous man, was, soon after the death of Lewis, transferred to a son-in-law, who, of all the princes of Europe, was the least capable of concentrating his attention upon the necessary task of Hungarian defence.

Sigismund (1387-1437), husband of Mary of Hungary, was far too much distracted by the affairs of Bohemia and the Empire to give to Hungary the attention which a country "so dangerously placed in relation to the advancing power of the Ottoman Turks" imperiously demanded. After the disaster of Nicopolis, his policies in this area were half-hearted, shamefaced, and intermittent. He continued to rule, but ceased to govern, and the forces of Hungary, which, under a vigorous King, would have been deployed against the Turks, when their power had been shaken by the blows of Timur, were left unused.

With the death of Sigismund in 1437 the scene was changed by the appearance of a genius. It so happened that while Murad was engaged in his wars of recovery the Hungarians discovered a great soldier in John Hunyádi, reputed to be the natural son of King Sigismund by a Hungarian mother. The high military qualities of Hunyádi, which were exhibited in many a small affray with the Turks, attracted general attention. He was placed in command of the army of a confederacy so wide as to include not only Hungary and Poland, Serbia and Wallachia, but the Duchy of Burgundy, Genoa and Venice, the Pope in Rome, and the Emperor in Constantinople. While a fleet of Italian and Flemish galleys was despatched to the Hellespont, Hunyádi, at the head of the army of the league, crossed the Danube, chased the Turks out of Serbia, and routed them so handsomely both south and north of the Haemus, that for the first time in their history the Ottomans were compelled to sue for peace. 1444

This was the critical moment in the history of the near east. Two smashing victories had been won by the Christian army, which was now south of the Haemus, and within an easy march of the Turkish capital. The mountaineers of Albania were rising in rebellion under George Castriotis, soon to become famous as Scander Beg. Seljuk emirs were causing trouble in Asia Minor. It was the obvious duty of the Hungarian commander to press forward to Adrianople, and to clinch his triumph before the enemy had recovered from the stunning effect of his unexpected success. No such opportunity had yet been given to the Christian powers of the west to turn the Turk out of Europe, and 477 years were fated to go by before an occasion, equally favourable, was once more presented and declined.

In spite of his winning advantages, Hunyádi decided to break off the campaign and treat with his enemy. Whether he was influenced, as some say, by a Turkish bribe, or was acting under the impulsion of the Serbs, or whether there were other personal or military factors of the case, he gave to his shaken opponent the exact respite which was needed to assist his fortune. After

that unhappy choice, made in the dead of winter, things went
ill for a while with the great Hungarian commander. He connived at the perfidious breaking of a treaty, which, though insufficient, had nevertheless been signed and sworn to by King
Ladislas of Hungary, and so provided the Turk, for this time
only, with the rare advantage of the better cause. Late in the
year he advanced again to the Danube, and before the walls of
Varna (November 10, 1444) experienced a decisive defeat. But
though his army was routed and his sovereign killed, the spirit
of Hunyádi was still undaunted. Four years afterwards he was
again in the field at the head of a small but well-appointed army
of Hungarians and Wallachians: but the curse of Balkan disunion was upon him. At a critical moment in a three days'
battle, the Wallachians went over to the enemy on that very
field of Kossovo which had crushed out the hopes of Serbian
freedom. For a decade Hungary was eliminated from the ranks
of powers capable of taking effective offensive action against the
Porte.

1448

    We have now reached the last stage in that long course of
persevering ambition, which, starting in an obscure fastness
among the Bithynian hills, ended in the palace of the Caesars.
Constantinople was still a Greek and an imperial city. Its fortifications, though less strong than of old, had yet sufficed to
fend off an attack by Murad II, and since the city had never
been taken, a belief prevailed that it could never fall. Cities,
however, are not defended by beliefs, but by will and material
power. Had the Greeks been resolute and united, had the navies
of Genoa and Venice been placed at the disposition of the
imperial government, had there been among the Greek and
Italian peoples a common will to save Constantinople, saved it
would have been. But there was no such will. To most Greeks
the red hat of a Roman cardinal was even more odious than
the Turkish fez, to most Latins the heresy of the unmanly Greek
was less pardonable and more to be condemned than the false
worship of the conquering Ottoman. And while theological
animosities were strong, religious zeal was at a low ebb. To the
merchants of Ragusa, of Genoa, and of Venice, the rise of this
new Ottoman Empire presented itself not as a calamity to the
Christian Faith, but as an incomparable occasion for lucrative
commercial concessions. How could these astute traders afford
to quarrel with a state already so powerful and likely for many

years to control the political destiny of Asia Minor and the Balkans?

While Mohammed II was besieging Constantinople the Genoese merchants of the Galata suburb, who had all to lose in the Euxine, were negotiating arrangements for preferential trade in the Ottoman Empire.

Constantine XI, the last of the Caesars, though the nominee *1448-53* of Murad and his vassal, shines out in the final crisis of the Empire as a statesman and hero, prepared alike for compromise and for sacrifice. The Greek population of Constantinople, for whom the quarrels of monks were always more important than the clash of races, were unworthy of such a leader. While Mohammed's artillery was battering at the walls the public opinion of the capital was inflamed by denunciation of the Emperor who, in the desperate hope of winning the west to his side, had dared to recognize the Roman Church and to permit the celebration of Roman rites in the church of St. Sophia. To these wretched theological preoccupations we may perhaps ascribe the fact that the main part of the defence of the city was undertaken, not by the Greeks, but by Spaniards, Germans, and Italians. And as the defending force was not principally Greek, so the attacking army was not wholly Turkish. The levies of Mohammed were largely recruited from men of a Greek and Christian stock. So it happened that on May 29, 1453, by default of the Christians, the great city was breached and stormed, the last of the Byzantine Emperors perishing honourably in the death agony of the Empire.

The conquerors were Asiatic nomads and so remained. Sir Charles Eliot, describing the interior of the house of a Turkish gentleman in the nineteenth century, observes that it contained no more furniture than could be carried off at a moment's notice on a waggon into Asia.[1] A certain dignity of bearing, coupled

---

[1] "The very aspect of a Turkish house seems to indicate that it is not intended for a permanent residence. The ground floor is generally occupied by stables and stores. From this a staircase, often merely a ladder, leads to an upper storey, usually consisting of a long passage, from which open several rooms, the entrances to which are closed by curtains and not by doors. There are probably holes in the planking of the passages and spiders' webs and swallows' nests in the rafters. The rooms themselves, however, are beautifully clean, but bare and unfurnished. . . . The general impression left on a European is that a party of travellers have occupied an old barn and said, ' Let us make the place clean enough to live in; it's no use taking any more trouble about it. We shall probably be off again in a week.' "

with a grave exterior polish and a sense of humour and irony, were noted by western observers as favourable traits in the Turkish character, an abstinence in food and drink as a recommendation in their armies. But the culture of the west was not valued. The Turk remained an alien in Europe, having no part or lot in its traditions, and limited in his notions of imperial government to the philosophy of a slave-owning oligarchy in a world of potential slaves.

BOOKS WHICH MAY BE CONSULTED

G. Finlay : History of Greece. *Ed.* H. F. Tozer. 7 vols. 1877.

J. Von Hammer-Purgstall : Histoire de L'Empire Ottoman, Traduit de l'allemand M. Dochez. 3 vols. 1840-2.

H. W. V. Temperley : History of Servia. 1917.

C. G. Macartney : Hungary. (Nations of the Modern World Series.) 1934.

Gibbon : Decline and Fall of the Roman Empire. *Ed.* Bury. 1896-1900.

Cambridge Medieval History.

" Odysseus " (Sir Charles Eliot) : Turkey in Europe. 1900.

CHAPTER XXXV

NEW PERSPECTIVES

General lack of scientific progress in the middle ages. Growth of geographical knowledge. The realization of China. The circumnavigation of Africa.

WE have now reached a point in European history distant by some two thousand six hundred years from the civilization described in the Homeric poems. During that long period the mind of man had produced noble literature, great buildings, imposing systems of philosophy and religion, statues and pictures which have never lost their appeal. It had asked questions of the soul, the heart, the brain, the senses, of everything but nature, or if a question was sometimes put to nature, the challenge was not followed up, but remained as an example of a fruitless and brilliant intuition. Accordingly little progress was made in those arts and discoveries which increase man's power over the blind forces of matter and raise the general standard of well-being. Locomotion remained where it had always been. Three thousand years had not supplemented the speed of a horse or the force of the wind which filled the sail. The vast majority of Europeans continued to live in stifling cabins, their experience circumscribed by narrow boundaries, their lives shortened by malnutrition or disease. For any serious addition to the great prehistoric inventions such as the wheel, the sail, the plough, the world was condemned to wait until the age of steam, petrol, and electricity.

Yet in one important respect the Europeans had made a notable advance in knowledge since the period of the Crusades. They had obtained a fuller and more accurate acquaintance with the earth and the sea. It was now known that the earth was round, and that far away at the other end of Asia a traveller would find China, Japan, and the spice islands. The Genoese had crossed the Sahara to the Sudan and in 1336 had a settlement in southern China. The Portuguese, who had learned their seacraft from Genoa, were feeling their way down the western coast of Africa. The sailors of the Mediterranean, ever since the early years of the fourteenth century, when the Venetians launched their "Flanders galleys," had been taking to the Atlantic in

increasing numbers. Seacraft had become a branch of exac
knowledge, and in the Italian and Catalan *portolani* of th
fourteenth century had provided the mariners with scientifi
charts.

This expansion of geographical knowledge was due not only
or perhaps chiefly, to the spirit of adventure and curiosity whicl
is characteristic of Europeans, but also to the lure of wealth. Th
east supplied luxuries, which once tasted were ever afterward
objects of insistent pursuit. From the east came silk and spices
silk which as early as the fourth century had become so popular
through the Roman Empire that even the poorest women woulc
not go without it, and spices (cinnamon, pepper, nutmeg), a
precious cargo in a small bulk, which raised cookery to an ar
and gave to appetite a new incentive.

In the middle of the sixth century the silkworm was smuggled
into the Roman Empire. What weighty consequences hung
upon the transplantation of this trivial animal! A flourishing
silk industry was established first in Syria, then in Sicily, and
afterwards in Italy and Spain. In respect of this important com-
modity Europe was rendered independent of China, and deprived of one of the principal motives which otherwise might
have impelled her upon a course of far-eastern adventure.

As for the spices, they came indeed to Europe, but at what a
price! First the Indians, then the Arabs and Abyssinians, who
as early as the third century had closed the Red Sea route to
the Roman navigators, and after these the Mamelukes of Egypt,
exacted their toll before the precious wares reached the counters
of the Venetian merchant. To eliminate the exorbitant profits
of these oriental middlemen by the establishment of some direct
means of contact with the east became an inevitable object of
economic desire.

The overland route across Asia was 7,500 miles long, and for
much of the way difficult and dangerous, but it had been opened
for European travellers for more than a century by the tolerant
wisdom and policy of the Mongol Khans. During the hundred
years of the Tatar peace (1264-1368) technicians and missionaries
from the west were welcome in China. Then the veil suddenly
fell. The Mongol power was broken, the missionary stations
were obliterated, and with central Asia once more plunged in
chaos, China retreated into impenetrable darkness and the
sternest isolation. But the secret was out. The wonderful story

published in 1299, in which Marco Polo recounted his Asiatic voyages and his seventeen years' residence and travel in China, made an intellectual revolution in Europe, quite as important as that great expansion of human knowledge which two centuries later proceeded from the discoveries of Columbus.

It was now realized that the habitable globe was altogether unlike what it had been imagined to be, and that there was at the further end of Asia a country distinguished for its vast population, its imposing opulence, its paper currency, and for a standard of civilization and public order which equalled, if it did not surpass, the culture of Italy.

Such a discovery opened an endless series of suggestions and possibilities. In 1428 Don Pedro of Portugal procured in Venice a copy of Marco Polo's travels, and presented it to his brother Prince Henry the Navigator, under whose intelligent direction (1415-1461) Portugal was fast taking the lead in oceanic exploration.

Meanwhile the idea of the circumnavigation of Africa was beginning to claim increasing attention. It was no new project. The feat had been achieved by the Phoenicians, if we may trust Herodotus, in the sixth century before Christ; and achieved it would have been again, we can hardly doubt, under the Roman Empire, but for the fact that the Romans, having the command of Egypt and the Red Sea route, had no compelling economic motive to attempt it. But from the turn of the thirteenth century there was one city in the Mediterranean which experienced the force of such motives to the fullest extent. Genoa was the rival of Venice for the eastern trade. Venice was in league with Egypt, and by her compact with the Mamelukes possessed a monopoly in the distribution of such oriental wares as were conveyed to Europe by the Red Sea route. Of that monopoly she could be dispossessed only by one of two ways. Either her power might be destroyed in battle, or her wealth might be sapped at the source. The first method had been tried, and in the war of Chioggia had met with signal failure. There remained the second. A ship might sail round Africa and without let or hindrance from Arab or Turk fetch the spices overseas to Europe. This plan was first attempted from Genoa. In May, 1291, Ugolino di Vivaldo, a citizen of that republic, set out with two galleys to find his way to India by the ocean route.

Vivaldo was lost at sea off the African coast. The fourteenth

century came and went without an attempt to repeat his gallan
enterprise, but meanwhile the Portuguese, placing themselve
under the naval tuition of Genoa, had learnt to build and t
sail ocean-going ships, and by visits to the Canaries and voyage
in search of Guinea, were steadily equipping themselves for th
great achievement which, after a break of twelve hundred years
again let Europe into the Indian Ocean and so opened a new
chapter in the affairs of the world.

The modern historian sees in the capture of Constantinople
by the Turks, and in the almost contemporary discovery of
the Guinea coast by the Portuguese, two events of profound
significance, the first as firmly closing Europe's principal gate
ways to the east, the second as opening out the great period of
oceanic discovery and exploration which has spread European
domination through the planet and altered the economic weights
and balances of the world. Of these events the first alone was
regarded by contemporaries as marking an epoch; for who
could contemplate without emotion the conquest of the great
Christian capital by a Moslem power? By comparison how
trivial and inconspicuous was this new Guinea trade in gold,
ivory, and slaves opened out by the enterprise of the King of
Portugal! Even Zurara, the official biographer of Henry the
Navigator, is careful that the renown of his hero should not rest
upon activities so novel and inglorious as the organization of
maritime trade and discovery. Such is the way of the world.
The future passes under our eyes and we do not see it. As for
the English, who of all the peoples of the west were destined to
reap the greatest profit from the ocean-faring habit, they were
at this time still fiercely growling over the loss of their French
possessions and blind to the fact that, working from these
obscure voyages of the Portuguese, a good fairy was preparing
to place their remote island right in the centre of the habitable
globe.

BOOKS WHICH MAY BE CONSULTED

H. Prenne and A. Renaudet: La Fin du Moyen Âge. 1931.
C. R. Beazley: The Dawn of Modern Geography. 3 vols. 1897-1906.
G. F. Hudson: Europe and China. 1931.
H. M. Stephens: History of Portugal. 1891.
Horatio Brown: Venice: A Historical Sketch of the Republic. 1893.
Voyages and Travels of Marco Polo. (Everyman's Library.) 1908.

GENEALOGICAL AND CHRONOLOGICAL TABLES

CHRONOLOGICAL TABLE OF ROMAN EMPERORS
FROM 27 B.C. TO A.D. 476.

Emperors.	Year of Accession.	Emperors.	Year of Accession.
	B.C.		A.D.
Augustus	27	Diocletian	28
		Maximian, associated with Diocletian	28
		Constantius, Galerius ...	30
	A.D.	Severus	30
Tiberius	14	Constantine (the Great) ...	30
Caligula	37	Licinius	30
Claudius	41	Maximin	30
Nero	54	Constantine, Galerius, Licinius, Maximin, Maxentius, and Maximian reigning jointly	30
Galba, Otho, Vitellius, Vespasian	68		
Titus	79	Constantine (the Great) alone	32
Domitian	81	Constantine II, Constantius II, Constans	33
Nerva	96	Magnentius.	
Trajan	98	Constantius alone	35
Hadrian	117	Julian	36
Antoninus Pius	138	Jovian	36
Marcus Aurelius	161	Valens and Valentinian I ...	36
Commodus	180	Gratian and Valentinian I ...	36
Pertinax	193	Gratian and Valentinian II ...	37
Didius Julianus	193	Theodosius	37
Niger	193	Arcadius (in the east), Honorius (in the West) ...	39
Septimus Severus	193	Theodosius II (E.)	40
Caracalla, Geta	211	Valentinian III (W.)	42
Opilius Macrinus, Diadumenian	217	Marcian (E)	45
Elagabalus	218	Maximus, Avitus (W.) ...	45
Alexander Severus	222	Majorian (W.)	45
Maximin	235	Leo I (E.)	45
The two Gordians, Maximus Pupienus, Balbinus ...	237	Severus (W.)	46
The third Gordian	238	Vacancy (W.)	46
Philip	244	Anthemius (W.)	46
Decius	249	Olybrius (W.)	47
Hostilian, Gallus	251	Glycerius (W.)	47
Volusian	252	Julius Nepos (W.)	47
Æmilian, Valerian, Gallienus	253	Leo II, Zeno, Basiliscus (all E.)	47
Gallienus alone	260	Romulus Augustulus (W.) ...	47
Claudius II	268	End of the Western line in Romulus Augustus ...	47
Aurelian	270	(Henceforth, till A.D. 800, Emperors reigning at Constantinople).	
Tacitus	275		
Florian	276		
Probus	276		
Carus	282		
Carinus, Numerian	284		

CHARLEMAGNE'S ANCESTRY

Pippin,
Mayor of Austrasia; *d*. 639.

|

Begga,
m. Ansegisel.

|

Pippin,
Mayor of Austrasia, Neustria and Burgundy; *d*. 714.

|

Charles Martel,
Mayor of all Kingdoms; *d*. 741.

|

Pippin,
Mayor of Neustria, 741; King of Franks, 752.

|

Charlemagne

HOUSE OF TANCRED OF HAUTEVILLE

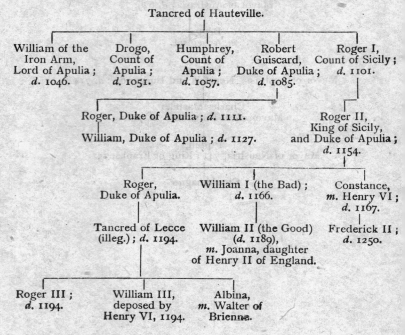

Tancred of Hauteville.

William of the Iron Arm, Lord of Apulia; *d.* 1046.

Drogo, Count of Apulia; *d.* 1051.

Humphrey, Count of Apulia; *d.* 1057.

Robert Guiscard, Duke of Apulia; *d.* 1085.

Roger I, Count of Sicily; *d.* 1101.

Roger, Duke of Apulia; *d.* 1111.

William, Duke of Apulia; *d.* 1127.

Roger II, King of Sicily, and Duke of Apulia; *d.* 1154.

Roger, Duke of Apulia.

William I (the Bad); *d.* 1166.

Constance, *m.* Henry VI; *d.* 1167.

Tancred of Lecce (illeg.); *d.* 1194.

William II (the Good) (*d.* 1189), *m.* Joanna, daughter of Henry II of England.

Frederick II; *d.* 1250.

Roger III; *d.* 1194.

William III, deposed by Henry VI, 1194.

Albina, *m.* Walter of Brienne.

SAXON AND SALIAN EMPERORS

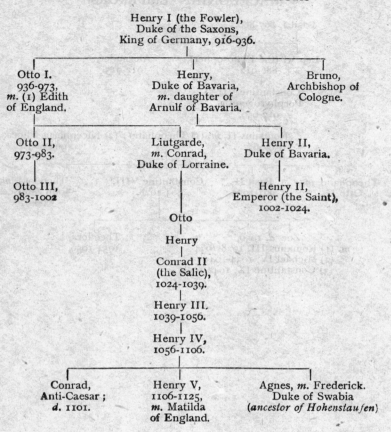

Henry I (the Fowler),
Duke of the Saxons,
King of Germany, 916-936.

Otto I.
936-973,
m. (1) Edith
of England.

Henry,
Duke of Bavaria,
m. daughter of
Arnulf of Bavaria.

Bruno,
Archbishop of
Cologne.

Otto II,
973-983.

Liutgarde,
m. Conrad,
Duke of Lorraine.

Henry II,
Duke of Bavaria.

Otto III,
983-1002

Henry II,
Emperor (the Saint),
1002-1024.

Otto

Henry

Conrad II
(the Salic),
1024-1039.

Henry III.
1039-1056.

Henry IV,
1056-1106.

Conrad,
Anti-Caesar ;
d. 1101.

Henry V,
1106-1125,
m. Matilda
of England.

Agnes, *m.* Frederick.
Duke of Swabia
(*ancestor of Hohenstaufen*)

MACEDONIAN EMPERORS

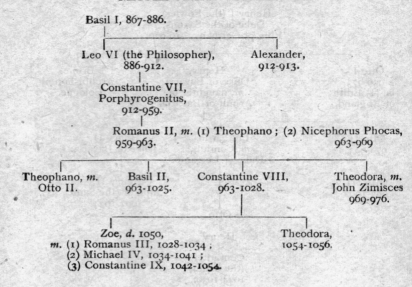

Basil I, 867-886.

Leo VI (the Philosopher), 886-912.　　　　Alexander, 912-913.

Constantine VII, Porphyrogenitus, 912-959.

Romanus II, *m.* (1) Theophano ; (2) Nicephorus Phocas, 959-963.　　　　　　　　963-969

Theophano, *m.* Otto II.　　　Basil II, 963-1025.　　　Constantine VIII, 963-1028.　　　Theodora, *m.* John Zimisces 969-976.

Zoe, *d.* 1050,
m. (1) Romanus III, 1028-1034 ;
　　(2) Michael IV, 1034-1041 ;
　　(3) Constantine IX, 1042-1054.　　　　Theodora, 1054-1056.

THE GUELFS AND HOHENSTAUFEN

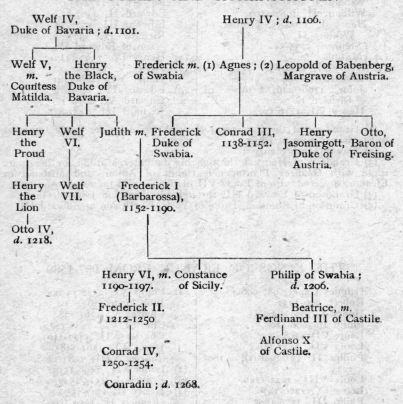

Welf IV,
Duke of Bavaria ; *d.* 1101.

Henry IV ; *d.* 1106.

Welf V,
m.
Countess
Matilda.

Henry
the Black,
Duke of
Bavaria.

Frederick *m.* (1) Agnes ; (2) Leopold of Babenberg,
of Swabia   Margrave of Austria.

Henry
the
Proud

Welf
VI.

Judith *m.* Frederick
Duke of
Swabia.

Conrad III,
1138-1152.

Henry
Jasomirgott,
Duke of
Austria.

Otto,
Baron of
Freising.

Henry
the
Lion

Welf
VII.

Frederick I
(Barbarossa),
1152-1190.

Otto IV,
d. 1218.

Henry VI, *m.* Constance
1190-1197.   of Sicily.

Philip of Swabia ;
d. 1206.

Frederick II.
1212-1250

Beatrice, *m.*
Ferdinand III of Castile.

Conrad IV,
1250-1254.

Alfonso X
of Castile.

Conradin ; *d.* 1268.

THE KINGS OF ENGLAND FROM 1066-1485

William I, 1066-87.
William II, 1087-1100.
Henry I, 1100-35, brother of William II.
(1) { Stephen, 1135-54.
(2) { Matilda.
(3) Henry II, 1154-89.
Richard I, 1189-99.
John, 1199-1216, brother of Richard I.
Henry III, 1216-1272.

Edward I, 1272-1307.
Edward II, 1307-27.
Edward III, 1327-77.
Richard II, 1377-99, grandson of Edward III.
(4) Henry IV, 1399-1413.
Henry V, 1413-22.
Henry VI, 1422-1461.
(5) Edward IV, 1461-83.
Edward V, 1483.
Richard III, 1483-85.

(1) Grandson of the Conqueror through his daughter Adela, married to Stephen, Count of Blois.
(2) Daughter of Henry I.
(3) Grandson of Henry I through his daughter Matilda, by her marriage with Geoffrey Plantagenet, Count of Anjou, and husband to Eleanor, divorced wife of Louis VII of France and heiress of Aquitaine.
(4) Grandson of Edward III, through his third son John of Gaunt.
(5) Grandson of Edmund, Duke of York, fourth son of Edward III.

THE KINGS OF FRANCE FROM 987-1589

Hugues Capet, 987-996.
Robert, 996-1031.
Henry I, 1031-1060.
Philip I, 1060-1108.
Louis VI, 1108-1137.
Louis VII, 1137-1180.
Philip II (Augustus), 1180-1223.
Louis VIII, 1223-1226.
Louis IX, 1226-1270.
Philip III, 1270-1285.
Philip IV, 1285-1314.
Louis X, 1314-1316.
Philip V, 1316-1322.
Charles IV, 1322-1328.

(1) Philip VI, 1328-1350.
John, 1350-1364.
Charles V, 1364-1380.
Charles VI, 1380-1422.
Charles VII, 1422-1461.
Louis XI, 1461-1483.
Charles VIII, 1483-1498.
(2) Louis XII, 1498-1515.
(3) Francis I, 1515-1547.
(4) Henry II, 1547-1559.
(5) { Francis II, 1559-1560.
Charles IX, 1560-1574.
Henry III, 1574-1589.
Margaret=Henry IV, son of Anthony of Bourbon.

(1) Son of Charles, Count of Valois, second son of Philip III. First monarch of the Valois House.
(2) Son of Charles, Duke of Orleans, and husband of Jeanne, the sister of Charles VIII. Afterwards married to Anne, Duchess of Brittany.
(3) Son of Charles, Count of Angoulême, married to Claude, daughter of Louis XII.
(4) Married to Catherine de' Medicis.
(5) Children of Henry II and Catherine de' Medicis.

THE SCOTTISH ROYAL LINE

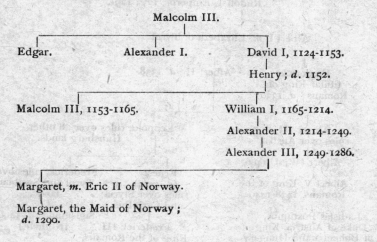

```
                            Malcolm III.
        ┌─────────────────────┼──────────────────────┐
     Edgar.             Alexander I.          David I, 1124-1153.
                                                      │
                                            Henry ; d. 1152.
                      ┌───────────────────────────────┴─────┐
          Malcolm III, 1153-1165.              William I, 1165-1214.
                                                      │
                                            Alexander II, 1214-1249.
                                                      │
                                            Alexander III, 1249-1286.
        ┌─────────────────────────────────────────────┘
Margaret, m. Eric II of Norway.
        │
Margaret, the Maid of Norway ;
    d. 1290.
```

CLAIMANTS TO FRENCH THRONE IN 1328 WHEN MAIN CAPET LINE ENDED

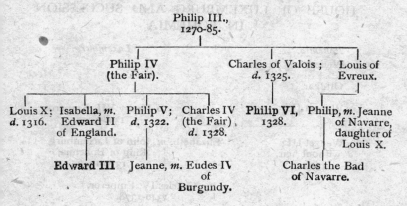

```
                              Philip III.,
                              1270-85.
        ┌──────────────────────┬──────────────────────────┐
     Philip IV            Charles of Valois ;        Louis of
    (the Fair).               d. 1325.                Evreux.
        │                                                 │
┌────────┬──────────┬──────────┐     Philip VI,    Philip, m. Jeanne
Louis X; Isabella, m. Philip V; Charles IV  1328.   of Navarre,
d. 1316. Edward II  d. 1322. (the Fair),            daughter of
         of England.          d. 1328.              Louis X.
             │             │                             │
      Edward III    Jeanne, m. Eudes IV          Charles the Bad
                        of                        of Navarre.
                     Burgundy.
```

423

THE HOUSE OF HABSBURG FROM 1273-1519

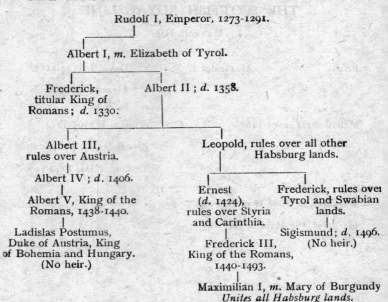

Rudolf I, Emperor, 1273-1291.

Albert I, *m.* Elizabeth of Tyrol.

Frederick, titular King of Romans; *d.* 1330.

Albert II; *d.* 1358.

Albert III, rules over Austria.

Leopold, rules over all other Habsburg lands.

Albert IV; *d.* 1406.

Albert V, King of the Romans, 1438-1440.

Ladislas Postumus, Duke of Austria, King of Bohemia and Hungary. (No heir.)

Ernest (*d.* 1424), rules over Styria and Carinthia.

Frederick, rules over Tyrol and Swabian lands.

Sigismund; *d.* 1496. (No heir.)

Frederick III, King of the Romans, 1440-1493.

Maximilian I, *m.* Mary of Burgundy *Unites all Habsburg lands.* 1493-1519.

HOUSE OF LUXEMBURG AND SUCCESSION IN BOHEMIA

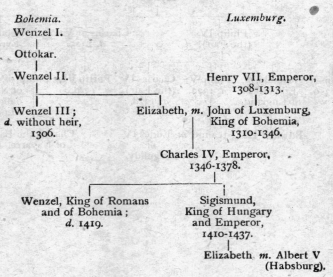

Bohemia.

Wenzel I.

Ottokar.

Wenzel II.

Luxemburg.

Wenzel III; *d.* without heir, 1306.

Henry VII, Emperor, 1308-1313.

Elizabeth, *m.* John of Luxemburg, King of Bohemia, 1310-1346.

Charles IV, Emperor, 1346-1378.

Wenzel, King of Romans and of Bohemia; *d.* 1419.

Sigismund, King of Hungary and Emperor, 1410-1437.

Elizabeth *m.* Albert V (Habsburg).

APPENDIX

A CATHOLIC friend, eminent in Thomist studies, comments as follows upon Chapter XXV:

"The Catholic student will have reason to be grateful for more than one passage in this chapter, with its challenging title of *The Catholic Mind*, but he will also dissent from certain of the judgments expressed or implied. You refer to Siger de Brabant. Surely the views which he is supposed to have supported were destructive of human personality and in the last resort of moral teaching. It was St. Thomas in the *de Unitate Intellectus* who defended the individual intellect and its rights against Siger. From your words his attitude towards reason might, I think, be easily mistaken. Though it is perfectly true that he held that faith and reason could not conflict, I am fairly sure that there is no place in his works where you will find him forcing his reason to follow faith against the evidence. His philosophy stands or falls on reason, and the best testimony to this is that modern scholars have agreed to accept him as one of the world's great thinkers, and they praise him for having accomplished a synthesis of the past, of Greek and Roman and Christian wisdom which has stood the test of time to the present day. You, I fear, may seem to hide the amplitude of his thought by giving as illustrations of it transubstantiation and the rejoicing of the angels and saints over the torments of the damned. I have no space to show that the philosophy of transubstantiation is not the crude, unscientific hocus-pocus one might suppose, but a piece of reasoning of the highest quality. The rejoicing of the saints over the sufferings of the damned has served as a gibe against Aquinas on more than one occasion. It is worth while looking at the chapter or article in which the subject is treated. There St. Thomas asks himself the question whether they rejoice over the suffering of the damned and urges first that it would be a horrible thing to take pleasure in the suffering of others. But he goes on to say that though this is true and no one should take pleasure in the pains of others as such, it is possible and even right to be glad

425

that a villain, for instance, is suffering the punishment deserved for his crimes. We all observe this distinction and are glad if the kidnapper and murderer of children is caught and punished. Why, therefore, this doctrine of Aquinas is held up for reprobation always puzzles me. I think the reason must be that many think in their hearts that the middle ages must have been cruel and superstitious and quite inferior to ourselves in thought and conduct, and so they seize on this text without reflection. Even you say of Dante that 'like all writers of the mediaeval period' he 'draws no clear line between ancient mythology and true history,' forgetting the kind of scholarship required for the verdict on the *de Causis*. If St. Thomas be representative there was a great passion for truth in his time, and it is this passion and the desire for reconciliation of the many-sided aspects of life rather than 'a feeling that the spirit was more important than outward institutions, and faith and intellect than the sacraments or formularies of the Church,' which lay behind the movements and current tendencies."

BOOK TWO
RENAISSANCE, REFORMATION, REASON

CHAPTER I

THE NEW EUROPE

Mediaeval and modern times. The wider world. Nationalism.
Capitalism. Artillery. The Protestant Reformation. Catholic rivalries.
Rapid spread of the Reformation. The age of religious wars. Their
effect on France and Germany compared. French diplomacy and
German Protestantism. Absence of religious war in England. Dying
down of the religious motive in politics during the eighteenth century.

No single date can be chosen to divide the mediaeval from the
modern world. The change was gradual and uneven, swifter and
more complete in one place than in another, and never so complete over the whole field as not to leave behind it mediaeval
patches, just as in the middle ages themselves we may find here
and there flashes of the human mind which appear to be
strangely unmediaeval, and to anticipate in ways which are almost uncanny the spacious outlook and complex sentiments of
the modern world.

Mankind is slower to move than city dwellers in the western
countries are always willing to allow. Modes of life and thought
rooted in deep antiquity still exercise their empire in certain
places and on certain minds. The belief in magical charms and
necromancy, in astrology and witchcraft is not yet extinct. Some
superstitions perpetuate themselves by a native and ineradicable
vitality in peasant homes; others are specially embalmed in religious rites. The elementary mysteries of nature, the waxing and
waning of the moon, the procession of the heavens, the secret
forces of reproduction and growth have from time immemorial
shaped the mythology of the European peasant. In Catholic
Churches swinging censers still wave their incense round the
coffin, as once they did, to chase away the demons who would
waft the soul of the dead to eternal fires. Still as in the middle
ages wonder-working miracles invite the pilgrim to be healed of
his rheumatism, his gout, or his broken limb. If the present age
has new shrines and other modes of locomotion, and Lourdes
has replaced Compostella and Canterbury, if the pilgrim no
longer trudges staff in hand, or rides at ease upon a palfrey, but
is whirled in excursion trains or motor-cars to his pious destina-

tion, the mentality of the votary remains unchanged. The mechanical conveniences of modern science convey a survivor from the mediaeval world.

In matters social, political and economic vestiges of this earlier period are hardly less notable. There is perhaps no part of Europe which has moved further from the middle ages than Great Britain, yet it was not until 1835 that the mediaeval constitutions of the English towns were reformed out of existence with all their picturesque and convivial abuses and made to give place to the common democratic pattern which suits an industrial and levelling age. Nor is the face of our rural landscape altogether cleared of mediaeval features. Here and there the traveller may still come across the open fields and scattered strips which were characteristic of mediaeval tillage, but which in England, earlier and more completely than elsewhere, gave place to the enclosures of improving landlords. And if such traces of mediaeval usage can be found in Britain, how much more numerous are they in the backward eastern parts of Europe where the priesthood has been long sunk in ignorance and sloth. Nor until the nineteenth century did the downtrodden peasantry of Galicia or the Balkans begin to experience any sensible change or improvement in their condition or mode of life. Within living memory the Prince of Montenegro would dispense a patriarchal justice to his subjects, sitting under a tree like St. Louis of old. Still the Albanian goes armed like the Afghan and lives the life depicted in the *Iliad*. Still do the Bulgarian villagers practise rites and superstitions which may have brought a smile to the lips of Euripides. A fine observer of modern Greece reports that the real spiritual equipment of the Greek people to-day consists in a number of ideas and superstitions, some of which are " disguised under a thin veil of Christian assimilation," while others may " still wear the classic garb unaltered." Gifts of money and salt and bread still propitiate the three Fates. Charon's obol is still placed on the lips of the dead. Nereids and vampires, goblins and demons still haunt the streams and mountains or send the mariner to a watery grave.[1]

In the fabric of peasant society in Europe there is thus even yet many an antique pattern which has been little altered by the lapse of time. But if the modern scene is not all rational illumination, neither was the mediaeval wholly black with superstition.

[1] Rennell Rodd, *The Customs and Lore of Modern Greece.*

There was Roger Bacon, the Oxford Franciscan, who laid down the axiom that nothing could be fully known without experiment, and first insisted upon a knowledge of chemistry as necessary to the training of a physician. There was Chaucer, whose close and whimsical observation of human eccentricities of character seems to prefigure the genius of Charles Dickens, and Villon, robber, murderer, and poet, in whose poignant lyrics, *1431* more than in Victor Hugo's *Notre Dame de Paris*, mediaeval Paris lives again with its irony and laughter, its sentiment and sensuality, its brooding melancholy and mingled moods of crime and penitence, wildness and culture, cruelty and romance. Life was uncomfortable for men of original genius in the middle ages. Bacon spent ten years in prison, Petrarch was prosecuted as a wizard at the instance of a cardinal for his undue addiction to Virgilian studies, but the spirit of modern science lived in Bacon as the spirit of modern humanism may be found in Petrarch. Even in the fourteenth century there were men so brave as in secret to dissect the human body. The great Vesalius, *1514-64* acknowledged parent of modern anatomy, had more than one obscure precursor in the age of Faith.

Yet, despite the inevitable gradualness of change, the broad contrast between the mediaeval and the modern emerges with sufficient plainness. A society divided between lay and cleric gave place to a society divided into rich and poor, an atmosphere hostile to free enquiry to one in which science could live and mature. During the early middle ages the Church was the sole depository of culture, the one supreme agency by which the barbaric tribes could be inducted into the great tradition of Christian and Roman civilization, the real inheritor of the political tradition of the shattered Empire of the West. Language, literature, politics, law, were all conditioned by the common educational mould which had survived the wreckage of the secular power. The use of Latin was universal among the literate class, and Latin was the *lingua franca* of western Europe. The spirit of the ancient Roman jurists lived on in the canon law, which was enforced by ecclesiastical courts in every quarter of Latin Christianity. The thinking of Europe, whether in the schools and universities or outside them, was carried on by tonsured clerks over a field of experience which was strictly confined by the sacred texts and their ancillary literature. Old knowledge was lost, and new knowledge was not acquired. Without the ballast of natural science, the human intellect fell a prey to extremes of rashness or timidity. To write in a vernacular language was felt to be a condescension which needed an apology. Even Petrarch preferred the *Africa*, a dull epic written in Latin, to the charming Italian sonnets which are his chief claim to immortality.

1304-74

The political theory of the middle ages was shaped by the surviving prestige of the Roman Empire and the overpowering authority of the Roman Church. It is true that the original unity of the Roman Empire had been broken by the shock of the barbaric invasion of the west. There was a western Empire which was Latin and an eastern Empire which was Greek. But the idea of an Imperial and Christian unity continued to survive. If the Greek and Latin churches could not be reconciled—and the hope that they might be reconciled was never wholly abandoned—the Latin church of the west was at least regarded as one indissoluble and immortal whole. The Pope was the supreme guardian upon earth of faith and morality. Above the chaos and violence of the temporal world his was the final oracle calling rulers and subjects alike to practise justice, to ensue peace, and to abide by the truths of revealed religion. In a poor and ignorant society mainly composed of soldiers, priests, and peasants, such a view of human governance found acceptance, the more readily since Christians lived for the most part in the shell of the ancient Roman Empire and were almost unconscious of the existence of wide tracts of the globe into which the name of Rome had never penetrated.

To this Roman and clerical outlook upon the world, the sixteenth century, the first age which may be regarded as distinctively modern, offers the sharpest contrast. The lay mind, fortified by the free use of the vernacular languages and by the full recovery of Greek and Hebrew, had come into its own. The close interrogation of nature, which was to lead to the development of modern science, had begun. Painters examined the human frame, surgeons dissected it. Verrocchio, the sculptor, was

1473-1543

also an anatomist. The discovery made by Copernicus, a Polish astronomer, that the earth revolved round the sun, steadily secured adherents. A new lay culture, aristocratic in origin, for it had chiefly grown up in the luxurious courts of the Italian despots, was made a general possession through the invention of printing. Strong and continuous as were the theological interests, they were now balanced by an exciting body of new knowledge, having no connection with theology, and the fruit of mental processes which theology was unable to turn to account. With a sharp gesture of impatience Europe turned away from the vast literature of commentaries and glosses, which the pedants of the later middle ages had inscribed "in letters of opium on tablets of lead."

An important part of this new knowledge was geographical. The Portuguese conquest of Ceuta on the African coast in 1415 had been the first step in that long and wonderful series of marine adventures which led to the circumnavigation of Africa by Vasco da Gama, to the foundation of the Portuguese Empire in the east, and to the discovery by Christopher Columbus, the *1492* Genoese sailor, of the new world beyond the Atlantic. The Mediterranean ceased henceforth to be the centre of the civilized world. The sceptre of commerce passed from the cities of Italy to the nations having easy access to the Atlantic Ocean, first to Portugal, then in succession to Spain, the Netherlands, France and England. A civilization which had sprung up in the river basins of the Euphrates and the Nile, and had spread round the littoral of the Mediterranean, was now carried far and wide on ocean-going ships to distant lands. Europe began to enter into that new phase of its existence, which is marked by the foundation of colonies and empires beyond the ocean, and by the gradual spread of European influences throughout the habitable globe.

The discovery of the new world, coinciding with the swift diffusion of printed books, taught the Europeans that "Truth" in Bacon's noble phrase "is the daughter not of authority but of time." The inhabitants of this continent had long known that the earth was round, and that if they sailed far enough to the west they would find the Indies. Nothing, however, had prepared them for the emergence of an intermediate land-mass of incalculable vastness and resources. If their expectations of the shape of the planet were confirmed, their estimate of its size was rudely overthrown. The world was far bigger than they had thought. The old notions of geography, taught for centuries by learned clerks and believed in all the universities, were suddenly shown to be in sharp contradiction to established facts.

The consequences were farther reaching than the additions

to positive knowledge resulting from the geographical discoveries. Insensibly mankind acquired a new attitude towards
knowledge itself. Authority no longer went unchallenged. The
past was no longer supreme. As the planet unfolded its unending wonders, generations grew up for whom truth was not a
complete thing already given in ancient books, but a secret yet
to be retrieved from the womb of time.

Not that among the many visions of the future which were
excited by the first impact of America there was present the
thought that some day this new continent would become the
receptacle for the overspill of Europe. America would have
many uses. It would bring a new spiritual Empire to the
Catholic Church and new temporal dominions to the masters of
Spain and Portugal. The mariner, the treasure hunter, the trader,
and the missionary would be drawn across the Atlantic. Dignified Spanish noblemen would administer law and justice among
the native Indians, and represent the majesty of the Spanish
Crown in its overseas provinces. But nothing either in the travel
tales of returned sailors or in the economic state of Europe during the early half of the sixteenth century encouraged the expectation that great blocks of European settlers would find new
homes in America. Even after a century of Atlantic voyaging
Francis Bacon, who was the prophet of scientific method and the
father of physical geography, warned his compatriots against
American colonization. If English emigrants there must be,
Ireland, that little neglected island across St. George's Channel
had the prior claim upon their attentions.

Meanwhile the political framework of the mediaeval Empire
had given way before the growth of national states. A universal
monarchy, supported by a universal church, though it corresponded to the aspirations of Europe during many centuries
was never closely adjusted to its needs or respected by its observance. The Empire had never secured a general allegiance. The
claims of the Papacy had often been countered by the will of
princes. By slow and painful steps, as feudal licence was brought
under the control of central power, national states were formed,
first of all in England, where the conditions were favourable,
then in the Christian states of the Iberian peninsula, in France,
and in the larger principalities of the German federation. By
the end of the fifteenth century national governments had been
established, not without the assistance of the new invention of

gunpowder, in England, France, and Spain. In England the suicide of the old feudal nobility in the Wars of the Roses was the prelude to the establishment of Tudor rule.

Framed against the background of mediaeval licence, the type of government which was now coming into vogue was remarkable for strength; judged by modern standards it was pitiably weak. The resources, moral, intellectual, and material, at the disposal of the most powerful monarchs of the sixteenth century were indeed paltry when we measure them against the disciplined social conscience, the organized national education, the powerful instruments for the accumulation and concentration of knowledge, the great military and naval establishments and vast revenues which support the fabric of a modern state. The papers which nourished the machine of English government during the whole reign of Queen Elizabeth would probably be outweighed in a month by the accumulations of the least important of our modern government offices. The strongest army put into the field by Francis I would have withered away before a single division of the army of Pétain or Foch. Even in the most advanced states of the sixteenth century the government lived from hand to mouth, improvising armies and navies to suit particular occasions, and driven to the most desperate expedients for finance. To recruit, to pay, to feed a national army were feats not only beyond the power of any government to execute, but beyond the scope of any statesman to conceive. Charles VII of France had asked of every parish in France that it should maintain an archer for the wars. The scheme broke down at once. His successor, Louis XI, fell back on a force of foreign mercenaries. The chronic insolvency of Charles V, judged to be the most powerful monarch of his time, is symptomatic of a weakness which afflicted all governments alike.

Nevertheless it is to this age, which witnessed the disruption of Latin Christianity, that we may ascribe the clear emergence of that more efficient form of social and political communion which claims the free yet disciplined loyalties of a nation. In the sixteenth century Europeans began, in larger measure than before, to think in nations, to act in national groups, and to render to the head of the national state some part of the loyalty which had previously been paid to the undivided Church. Roger Ascham, the schoolmaster and educational reformer who taught Queen Elizabeth, is a typical figure in the new lay educational movements which gave support to vernacular literature and national pride.

The formation of the strong continental monarchies ushers in a period of acute diplomatic rivalry which was governed by the conception of the balance of power. While the mediaeval sense of a common European interest had faded away, no country had acquired a measured estimate of its own strength and resources. Romantic ambitions, the legacy of the Roman and Carolingian ages, filled the minds of rulers who would have been better occupied in attending to the welfare of their subjects. Statecraft was still immature, political economy had not been invented, and the art of domestic comfort was neither understood nor intelligently pursued. In the absence of exact statistics the vaguest notions prevailed as to the wealth and population of the European States. It was a common belief that dazzling conquests might still be made and held within the old framework of European society.

Whether international states had international obligations was a question which no one at the opening of the sixteenth century was much concerned to ask or answer. Travel was difficult, the relations between governments were rare and intermittent. Every state tried to overreach its neighbour and to extend its borders. The greatest opportunity offered to Europe to undertake a grand work of co-operative civilization was thrown away. The discovery of the New World, which under wise direction and a happier temper of the public mind might have led to a harmonious subdivision of the new continent between the interested powers was, on the contrary, made the signal for an outburst of cruel war and piracy on the high seas which lasted for generations. All this was taken for granted. No political thinkers rose to the size of the vast events which were changing the face of the world. Sir Thomas More surrendered himself to the pleasant fancies of Utopia, while Machiavelli, the great Florentine publicist, had eyes for no bigger thing than an Italy liberated from barbarians.

Money, which has always been a power in human affairs, had become more plentiful in the later middle ages, and was destined to become more abundant still through the importation of Peruvian silver before the sixteenth century had run its course. In all the progressive countries of the west the growth of trade and commerce, which had received its first important stimulus during the Crusades, had created an influential middle class whose material interests were opposed to the continuance of feudal disorder. Capital was coming into its own. Great merchants and bankers, a Jacques Coeur of Bourges, a Fugger of Augsburg, a Dick Whittington of London, a Roberto Strozzi of Florence, out-topped many a great feudal noble in their command of free capital, and rose to positions of political influence. For many years the Empire was financed from Augsburg, while the Italian enterprises of France depended upon the support of the Strozzi Bank of Florence, with its branches in Lyons, Venice, and Rome. Capital then must be counted as a force in aid of those monarchical nation states whose consolidated power is one of the new facts distinguishing the Europe of the sixteenth century from the conditions of the feudal age.

Upon such a Europe, kindled by new knowledge and new horizons, and charged with the spirit of national pride and independence, fell the spark of the Protestant Reformation. A challenge to Roman doctrine was no new thing. It had been made by Wycliffe in England and by Hus in Bohemia. The problem how *1324-84* best to reform the manifest abuses of the Church had ever since *1373-1415* the first schism engaged the attention of serious minds throughout Christendom. Councils had met, deliberated, and dispersed, without effecting any serious improvement. The Pope, for whose sovereign authority no menace seemed to be more formidable than the recognition of a General Council as a regular and established organ of Church government, had been able to circumvent the conciliar movement by entering into separate and direct concordats with national governments. The ill-organized and tumultuous deliberations of an international assembly, whose members were divided from one another by race, language, and allegiance, were no match for the experienced diplomacy of the Roman Curia. A combination of the Papacy on the one hand, and the temporal powers on the other, might always be relied on to frustrate the endeavours of an ecumenical council. The Protestant Reformation, however, was neither initiated nor assisted by councils of the Church. It arose out of a passionate sense of the contrast between the simplicity of the Apostolic age and the wealth and fiscal exactions of the Roman Church; it was sheltered by the help and assisted by the appetites of certain temporal princes. And finally, in those regions of northern Europe in which it succeeded in securing a foothold, it was protected against the forces of Catholic reaction by a widespread confisca-

tion of abbey lands and the creation of a vested interest in the
spoils of the plundered church, which was in certain regions
so deeply rooted that neither war nor revolution was able to
disturb it.

This great religious convulsion divided Christian Europe at a
time when the Ottoman Turks had completed their conquest of
the Balkan peninsula, acquired Egypt, and created a formidable
navy. Yet so faint was the Christian motive as a shaping power
in politics, during the first half of the sixteenth century, that
Francis I and his son Henry II of France did not scruple to ally
themselves with the Ottomans against Charles V at the very
time when the head of the Habsburg house stood out as the
protagonist of Catholic orthodoxy against the heresy of Luther.
Indeed, it is to these national and dynastic rivalries, more acute
and powerful in the early part of the sixteenth century than in
any previous age, that we must ascribe the victory of Protestantism over a large part of northern Europe. It is a mistake
to suppose that persecution never succeeds. Persecution crushed
the Albigenses and the Lollards, and stamped out the seeds of
Protestantism in Spain, Italy, and Bohemia. If the temporal
powers of Europe had been united to put down the Lutherans
of Germany or the Calvinists of Geneva there is no reason to
think that they would have failed in their work. But they were
not united. The great duel between the house of Valois and the
house of Habsburg was the dominating issue of the age. The
heresies of Germany were far too embarrassing to Charles V to
be otherwise than welcome to Francis I, under whom was first
established that long French tradition of fostering heretics
abroad and suppressing them at home, without which all Germany might have been reclaimed for the Roman Church.

The course of the Reformation in England was similarly
governed by the great continental rivalry of the age. In the
critical year, 1527, when the continued allegiance of England to
the Papal See depended upon the Pope's acquiescence in Henry
VIII's repudiation of Catharine of Aragon, the Pope was in consequence of the Franco-Imperial war a prisoner in the hands of
Charles V, who was Catharine's nephew. Even had he wished to
be compliant, and there were papal precedents for the action
which was urged upon him by the English Court, Clement VII
was no free agent. He could not give his consent. The same

Habsburg and Valois rivalry, which ultimately helped to make north Germany Protestant, precipitated the breach between England and Rome during the reign of Henry VIII, and again sheltered the young Anglican Church from overthrow during the perilous days of Queen Elizabeth.

The religious disruption of western Europe was not effected without a terrible struggle. During the first half of the sixteenth century the great Habsburg-Valois rivalry absorbed the energies of the two leading Catholic powers on the continent. Protestant beliefs spread far and fast. They conquered the greater part of Germany and Switzerland; they were received into the Scandinavian kingdoms, penetrated into Italy and Spain, carried all before them in Scotland and Bohemia. According to the Cardinal of Lorraine, two-thirds of the inhabitants of France were infected with the new heresy in the reign of Henry II. For the *1547-59* space of a century the movement continued to gather force, and as happens when religious movements become popular and appeal to the plain man's jealousy of ostentatious power and ill-used wealth, the original core of true religious ardour was surrounded by a wide penumbra of selfishness, carelessness, and greed.

Then came a reaction. In 1559 Henry II of France, renouncing his dream of Italian conquests, and sobered, no doubt, by the defeat of his army on the field of St. Quentin, signed the Treaty of Cateau Cambrésis with the Imperialists, and resolved to devote himself to the extirpation of heresy at home. A new era opens. The dynastic struggle is suspended. The religious wars begin. Could the Lutherans hold Germany? Could the Calvinists win France? The Papacy, aided by the recently established order of Jesuits, embarked upon a systematic endeavour to reconquer the territory which had been lost to the Roman Faith.

The religious war in France lasted, with intermissions, from 1560 until the Edict of Nantes in 1598 secured for the Protestant Huguenots toleration and a privileged position, an *imperium in imperio*, within the French kingdom. It was fought with great bitterness and marked by many acts of mob violence and military atrocity; but it left no deep scar upon the social well-being of the French nation. At the end of her religious wars, France emerged more powerful than she had ever been before. Her army was the strongest in Europe, her diplomacy the best informed, her court the most resplendent. The seventeenth cen-

tury marks the zenith of the French monarchy. It was under
Richelieu and Mazarin that the foundations were laid for the
1643-1715 long, imposing dominion of Louis XIV.

Far otherwise was the effect of thirty years of religious war
upon the disjointed federation of Germany. When the Peace of
Westphalia in 1648 put a term to the quarrel, settling frontiers
for the rival confessions which have ever since been substantially
maintained, Germany was a ruin. Her population was depleted,
her treasuries were drained, her establishments of education and
learning were grievously injured, and her pride and confidence
sapped and impaired by a long succession of ruinous reverses
and humiliations. It is no fantastic conjecture that the Thirty
Years' War put the civilization of Germany back by two hundred years, or that the ease with which a people so virile was
subjected to the yoke of Napoleon in the first decade of the nineteenth century was due to the depressing effects of this tremendous calamity.

After a series of spectacular successes the Catholic movement
for the reconquest of Europe had been brought to a sudden and
general halt. The reunion of Latin Christendom under the Pope
of Rome had vanished from the category of possible things.
Too much blood had been shed, too many interests had been
created, competing loyalties had been too deeply engaged. The
Peace of Westphalia, the hard-won prize of a savage conflict,
inscribed the religious schism on the map of Europe. Catholics
and Protestants, their differences unbridged, their animosities
unappeased, remained entrenched in their war positions.

The result is the more surprising since Austria, Spain, and
France, the three leading countries in Europe, were true to the
ancient faith. Had these powerful States, each orthodox, each
anxious for the maintenance and promotion of Catholicism,
chosen to act in combination against the Protestants, can we
doubt but that they would have succeeded in imposing some
kind of religious unity, however mechanical and unreal, upon
the Continent? Heresy had been stamped out in Austria and
Spain, in Bohemia and Poland. Against a resolute and combined effort of the Catholic powers, could it have survived in
north Germany or the Netherlands? But the Catholic powers
were not combined. At the critical moment France, under the
guidance of Cardinal Richelieu, set herself to thwart first in-

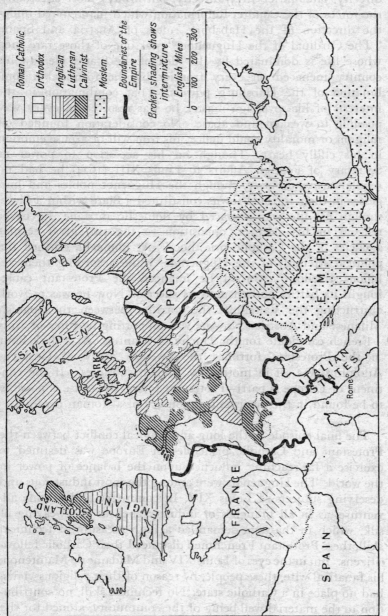

Legend:
- Roman Catholic
- Orthodox
- Anglican
- Lutheran
- Calvinist
- Moslem
- ▬ Boundaries of the Empire
- Broken shading shows intermixture

English Miles
0   100   200   300

SWEDEN

POLAND

OTTOMAN EMPIRE

DENMARK

SCOTLAND

ENGLAND

FRANCE

SPAIN

ITALIAN STATES

Rome

CATHOLIC AND PROTESTANT EUROPE, 1610.

directly, later (after 1635) directly, but always most effectually, the forces of the Counter-Reformation which manœuvred under the direction of the Habsburg rulers of Austria and Spain. "The Cardinal of the Huguenots" was one of those rare men whose life is dominated by the idea of the State. He saw his country menaced on every frontier by the formidable combination of the Habsburg powers. That combination in the interests of his sovereign master he was resolved in every way possible to weaken and abase. No consideration founded on religion or morality could deflect his iron will or arouse emotion in his chilly heart. Though on his accession to power as Secretary of Foreign Affairs to Louis XIII (1624) he had no regular army or navy, though the Huguenot nobles and burgesses in their fortified towns constituted a State within a State, though his life was menaced by domestic intrigue, he never relaxed in his sleepless opposition to the two great secular agencies of the Catholic priesthood. At home he crushed the political strength of the Huguenots, while according them religious freedom. Abroad he financed the Protestant cause, fought its battles and ensured its success. Now he was at work obstructing the Valtelline, the corridor between the Spanish Milanese and Austria. Now he was supporting by force of arms a French candidate for the Duchy of Mantua. At a dark hour in the Protestant fortunes the Swedish army of Gustavus Adolphus was set in motion by French subsidies. If the continent of Europe is partly Protestant today, the cause is possibly to be found in the persistent diplomacy of a Roman cardinal.

The final episode in the long and tragical conflict between the Protestant and Catholic principles in Europe was destined to exercise a far-reaching influence upon the balance of power in the world. The Huguenots were among the most industrious and deserving subjects of Louis XIV. In commerce and marine adventure, as in all branches of industry such as the weaving of silk, which in that age demanded a high measure of technical skill, these Protestant Frenchmen distanced their Catholic fellow-citizens. But in the eyes of Louis XIV and Madame de Maintenon, his fanatical wife, these people, by reason of their religious views, had no place in a Catholic state. No technical skill, no contribution to the material well-being of the community, atoned for the deadly fact of religious heresy. The Huguenots were first perse-

cuted and then expelled. The protection which had been assured
them under the Edict of Nantes was withdrawn in 1685, and a
community, which, if it had prevailed, might have given to
France the lead in colonial development, transferred its knowledge and skill to the more congenial soil of her Protestant rivals.

The fortunate island of Britain was spared the religious convulsions which tormented the continent. In the southern part of
the island a national Church, Erastian in government, Roman
in ritual, Calvinist in theology, was set up and firmly secured by
the end of the sixteenth century, not indeed without some bloodshed and local disturbance, but upon the whole with an astonishing measure of tranquil acquiescence on the part of an essentially
untheological people. The chance of a successful Catholic reaction, which was never very great after the nobles and squires
of England had been glutted with the abbey lands, vanished altogether with the ruin of the Spanish Armada. The Civil War
of the seventeenth century was fought, not over the issue of
Catholic and Protestant, though the fears of Rome, as a dark,
malignant, unscrupulous power, haunted the imagination of the
Roundheads, and gave a sinister meaning to every ritualistic
practice, but over parliamentary liberties and Anglican ceremonial. It is only in the later part of the seventeenth century,
when Louis XIV was beginning his persecuting career, that the
danger of a Catholic reconquest of the island became once more
an important factor in politics. Charles II was a secret, James II
an open, Papist. Both kings worked, the first with subtlety
and reserve, the second with gross and blatant unwisdom,
for a Catholic restoration in England to be established with
the assistance of an army from France. But the plot was defeated. It is permissible to doubt whether, even with the assistance of French bayonets, the Catholics of England could have
prevailed against the strong Protestantism of the City of London,
of the eastern counties, and of the fleet. When the final test
came, not a man was found to risk his skin for King James.

The revolution of 1688 which brought William of Orange to
the English throne was glorious because it was bloodless, and
bloodless because the country stood so solid for the Protestant
cause that it could afford to be clement.

The defeat of the Counter-Reformation in England ushered in
a new period of European history. In the eighteenth century the
rivalry of England and France continued, but tended to be fought

across the ocean, in Canada and India, rather than upon the con
tinent of Europe. Colonies and commerce became more impor
tant as motives of public policy than religious affiliations and
dynastic alliances. The Puritan of the second generation was ap
to be a shrewd, money-making man of business. Conservatism—
or, as it was then called, Whiggism—in politics, rationalism in
philosophy, an easy-going comfort in social life, were the mottoe
of the Hanoverian age. The wealth, the prosperity, and the liberty
of England began to attract the attention of foreigners. Though
the genius of Shakespeare was still a mystery, the idea began to
get abroad that much could be learned from the country which
had been the spearhead of the Protestant resistance to Louis XIV
Voltaire was the pupil of Bolingbroke. To Montesquieu it ap
peared that the English had discovered the secret of politica
freedom. The philosophy of Newton and Locke passed as a
formative element into the guiding minds of eighteenth-century
France. The small island became once more for a few decade
what it had been during the flowering time of mediaeval Oxford
the preceptress of Europe.

Such is the general trend of the story which has now to be re
counted. A religion widely held and strongly entrenched in the
social and political tradition of western Europe is roughly chal
lenged by new spiritual forces and over a large part of Europe
compelled to accept defeat. A "totalitarian" conception of the
social order loses colour and actuality as the Christian com
munity of the West dissolves into fragments which it is unable
to re-absorb. Views of life based upon freedom of thought, upon
the rights of the individual conscience, upon the self-determina
tion of states and even of small religious sects, corrode the ancien
fabric of the all-embracing church and give rise to trains o
revolutionary thought which in the end transform the institu
tions of Europe and shape the life of the modern world. The
more vigorous north falls away from Rome. The less vigorou
south, though only after inner convulsions, stands firm in the
ancient ways. In the long dispute which bathes Europe in blood
the basest and noblest motives are ineradicably blended. Cran
mer's Prayer-book and Milton's *Paradise Lost*, Loyola's *Spiritua
Exercises* and Pascal's *Pensées*, the Catholic music of Palestrina
and the Protestant music of Bach, may be taken as illustrations
of the depth of emotion aroused in religious men of genius or

either side of this great controversy. But the great mass of the European people has never been in any true sense religious. The dominant figures in the period of Europe's religious wars are the statesmen, soldiers, and adventurers, who make use of the raw enthusiasm of the masses to achieve their secular ends. A Wallenstein in Bohemia, a Marlborough in England, rises above the storm, shapes policies, directs armies, amasses wealth, and fills Europe with the fame and fear of his prowess. A Chinaman of the period, had he been in a position to survey the turbulent European scene during the sixteenth and seventeenth centuries, might well have asked himself whether the art of living was not better understood by a people which had no religious quarrels because they had no religion but only an ethical code of deportment, whether the vast liberation of human forces brought about by the Protestant Reformation with all its infinite consequences for art and music, science and letters, was worth the price of long and savage wars, and whether an attitude of mind towards the ultimate mysteries less aspiring, less heroic and less confident than that which prevailed among western Christians was not in effect more conducive to human comfort.

BOOKS WHICH MAY BE CONSULTED

Excellent short bibliographies for the greater part of the ground covered by this volume may be found in A. J. Grant, A History of Europe from 1494 to 1610 (1931), and in D. Ogg, Europe in the Seventeenth Century 1925). For more extended bibliographies see The Cambridge Modern History and the standard national Histories—e.g., Lavisse for France, and for England Froude, Gardiner, Macaulay, G. M. Trevelyan, and the composite Histories published respectively by Messrs. Longmans and Methuen.

THE ITALIAN RENAISSANCE

THE fifteenth century, which is intellectually so barren in
England, witnessed the effulgence of the Italian Renaissance
During two hundred years (1340-1540) the cities of Italy pro
duced an output of art, scholarship, and literature such as the
world had not seen since the glory of ancient Athens. But when
Italy passed under the political domination of Spain, and was
subjected to the religious rigours of the Catholic reaction, with
its Jesuits' Order, its Holy Inquisition, and its Index of prohibited
books, the broad and prodigal stream of Italian imagination
which had flowed so powerfully and so long, shrank into a feeble
channel. A sickly mystical sentiment replaced the robust virility
of the creative age. The great painters, who at Venice longer than
elsewhere continued to sustain the highest traditions of their art,
were not replaced as they passed away, and Italy, after having to
an incalculable degree enriched the intellectual life of Europe, and
earned for herself the permanent gratitude of mankind, descended
from her place of pre-eminence. The prose of France, the poetry
and drama of England, the music of Germany, henceforth
meant more to the world than all the studios and academies of
Florence and Venice.

It is natural that the rebirth of European art and letters should
have taken place in a land where the marbles of antiquity still
gleamed among the cypresses and olives, and the tradition of
humane learning, descending from classical times, had never
been wholly interrupted. Here too was the eager rivalry of com
peting cities and luxurious courts, and many a patron who would
pay high for a picture, or a manuscript, a secretary, or a tutor.
Here finally were ruins, inscriptions, coins, and medals, inviting

nd since the days of Petrarch attracting, the enquiry of the cholar.

The humanist movement, which had been gathering strength ver since the middle of the fourteenth century, acquired an stounding and brilliant velocity during the period of almost un- roken peace which divides the Treaty of Lodi in 1454 from the rench invasion of Italy under Charles VIII forty years after- wards. While Lorenzo dei Medici was master of Florence, and an ffective if uneasy accord between the four leading Italian states reserved Italy from foreign aggression, art and letters advanced with great strides. More particularly was this true of Lorenzo's wn capital on the Arno, which was already famous for the ames of Dante, Petrarch, and Boccaccio. Here was gathered ogether a constellation of illustrious men who made Florence he artistic and intellectual capital of Europe. When we consider hat a catalogue of great Florentines born and working during hese forty years would include the names of Michael Angelo, Donatello, Fra Filippo Lippi, and Sandro Botticelli, that to these great artists must be added Machiavelli the publicist, Guicciar- dini the historian, Ficino the Platonist, and Politian the Latin scholar, that Luca della Robbia and Domenico Ghirlandaio were Florentines, as well as Verrocchio, Perugino, and Leonardo da Vinci, and that Lorenzo himself showed genius alike as a poet, a statesman, and a virtuoso, we can form some faint impression of the blinding splendour of a society so led and quickened. It was a source of strength that the artists of the Italian Renaissance were not too highly specialized. In Florence, for instance, painters and sculptors belonged to the same corporation as the doctors and apothecaries, and were often instructed by jewellers, who combined science with trade and a wide acquaintance with the arts and crafts. Prodigies of versatility were not infrequent. Men passed and repassed from painting to sculpture, from sculpture to architecture and metalwork, and from these forms of energy to poetry, philosophy, and natural science. The classical examples of this omnicompetence are Michael Angelo, Leonardo da Vinci, and Alberti. The first is not only to be remembered for his statues and frescoes, but as a man whose skill in fortification de- fended Florence during a famous siege, as a man who took cap- tive the heart of his host in Bologna through his readings of Dante, Petrarch, and Boccaccio, and finally as one who, having passed the age of 70, composed a series of sonnets, whose note of rare and exalted passion had not been heard in Italy since the death of Dante. Leonardo, again, was not only the painter of Mona Lisa and the Last Supper, but architect, mechanician, and man of science as well. His notebooks reveal a mind eager to grapple with all knowledge and experience, curious as to the orbit of the sun and moon, theorizing on marine fossils found among the crags of the Apennines, concerned with problems of linear perspective and anatomy, and investigating the ultimate truths of mechanics. The same wide competence and curiosity were characteristic of Alberti, the first athlete and horseman of his age, who composed melodies, painted pictures, built churches wrote a comedy, and expounded the science of architecture in ten books, written in a prose so pure and elegant that it may be read with pleasure to this day. No branch of applied science seemed to be alien to Alberti, who devised machinery for raising sunken ships, and is said to have anticipated some modern discoveries in optics. Alberti's gifts are his own, but a spacious curiosity was a note common to the creative artists of his time.

The art of the Italian Renaissance, in its earliest Florentine as well as in its later Venetian manifestations, continued, since the Church was the greatest of patrons, to conform to a Christian tradition. For one subject taken from the classics, twenty were chosen from the Bible. Some distinguished painters, Fra Angelico, Fra Filippo Lippi, Fra Bartolomeo, were friars. But as time went on the painting of religious subjects lost much of the spiritual character which had originally belonged to it. The figures became less ascetic, less conventionally hieratic, and closer to the flesh and blood of human life. The Madonna of Titian was a handsome model, not an idealized vision of holy motherhood. On this, as in other branches of Italian activity, the lay and sceptical spirit of the age, nowhere stronger than in Rome itself, left its decisive imprint.

A love of personal glory was a feature of the age. Rich men commissioned portraits and statues and called upon painters and sculptors to give them an immortality in art. How magnificent and how swiftly renowned was Florentine sculpture, Englishmen who have never seen a statue of Donatello or Michael Angelo under an Italian sky may learn by a visit to Westminster Abbey, where the tomb of Henry VII carved by the chisel of Torregiano invites their admiration. And as the patron sought immortality from the artist, so the artist desired immortality for himself. The days of anonymous architecture, of Gothic cathedrals built by generation after generation of nameless craftsmen, were past. The architect of the Renaissance, basing his craft on the doctrines of Vitruvius, expected within his own lifetime to reap a harvest of fame from his completed work.

It is characteristic of the force and individuality of the Italians of the Renaissance that their architecture, though profoundly influenced by the writings of Vitruvius, was never a pedantic or servile imitation of ancient models. The Italians, while respecting the rules of their Roman master, were sensitive to the promptings of personal taste. The forms of the antique were adapted to modern usage, its rigours tempered to a new softness and luxuriance. A garden would enter into an architectural design, and complete, with its level parterres, its straight terraces, its rectangular lakes, and solemn lines of cypress or yew the imposing façade of the country house. Even Palladio of Vicenza, whose four books on architecture obtained a great authority through Europe, was not able to constrain to his severe classical proportions and measurements the profuse imagination of his compatriots. The Italian passion for decoration struggled with the stern canons of classical construction, and ultimately, in the baroque churches of the seventeenth century, obtained a mastery.

The architecture of the Renaissance, spreading outward from Rome, which was its centre, and claiming in the new St. Peter's its chief ecclesiastical triumph, covered Europe in the course of the sixteenth century with palaces and houses no longer built for defence but for the convenience and enjoyment of their owners. Azay le Rideau and Fontainebleau, Hatfield and Knole, announce the advent of a more luxurious age, when the fortified castle gave place to the country house, when town building began to sprawl at ease beyond the city walls, and the architecture of fear, which sprang from the barbarian invasions of the third century, yielded before the new social possibilities of composure, magnificence, and delight.

In the field of literature the main feature of the Italian Renaissance was a falling away from the scholastic and theological interests of the middle ages, and a compensating development of a passionate concern in the life and letters of pagan antiquity. Not all of this great movement of the human spirit was of equal value. Some who might have written passably in their native Tuscan thought it necessary to express themselves in frigid and

15

pretentious imitations of Cicero. Others threw ethics and religion to the wind. In general an excessive value was placed upon an easy command of Latin eloquence. Aeneas Sylvius, whose *Artis rhetoricae precepta* was written in 1456, rose to the Papacy on the strength of his Latin oratory. The humanist of the fifteenth century, like the Greek sophist or the mediaeval friar, was exposed and often succumbed to the temptations which in every age beset the popular preacher. So long as the classics existed in manuscript, only the humanist in possession of a codex held the key to knowledge, and could open or close the casket of marvels at his will. The travelling scholar, who lectured on Plato or Homer, read out the text and supplied the comment. It was through his brain and voice alone that his audience obtained access to the ancient mysteries. And when have audiences been more emotional, more ready to learn, or easy to lead? The humanist was orator, poet, scholar, teacher. The general would take him to the camp that he might deliver Ciceronian addresses to the troops; the government would employ him on solemn embassies, or to write despatches, or to make public orations upon occasions of state; the prince would receive him into his castle as wit, instructor, librarian, companion; men and women of every rank crowded to his lectures, wept at his eloquence, and lived upon his ideas. In such conditions profound and thorough scholarship was not to be expected.

Yet the achievement of the Italian humanists, despite the shallowness and artificiality of their Latin writings, was of great value. They led the way to the rediscovery of the true meaning and beauty of the ancient world, first of the Latin classics, and then of Greek literature itself. To them western Europe owes the recovery of Plato and a vast addition to its knowledge of classical texts. Having discovered that the past is as real as the present, and that the future will view the present as the present views the past, they began to think about posterity, and to imagine how their own age would look in the centuries to come. The great school of Florentine publicists and historians is distinguished by this new sense of historical continuity, leading backward to the past and forward to the future.

1403-72   So fast was the influx of new manuscripts (Cardinal Bessarion brought over 800 Greek codices from Constantinople) that there seemed no bounds to the possibilities of the future. Anything might come to light: the lost books of Tacitus, the lost plays of Sophocles, the lost decades of Livy; and the excitement was intensified by the difficulties of interpretation. A whole *apparatus criticus* had to be constructed from the beginning in the case of Greek, and nearly from the beginning in the case of Latin. Grammars, dictionaries, treatises on ancient art and archaeology, disquisitions on the meaning of terms, all the technical aids to culture were combined with the exposition of the rhetorical beauties of the new literature.

In this sudden crowding in of new tastes and fresh points of view, a place was found for scientific historical criticism. Its parent was Lorenzo Valla, whose bold treatise criticizing the *1405-57* authenticity of the Donation of Constantine opened a new epoch in European scholarship. Valla first of all argued on general grounds that neither would Constantine have made, nor Pope Sylvester have accepted, the Donation. He then proceeded to point out that if the Empire of the Western World had really been surrendered to the Pope, the gift would have been evidenced by the existence of papal coins. He observed that Eutropius, writing early after the alleged event, made no mention of this momentous transaction, that the original text had never been produced, and finally that the document was of a barbarous Latinity, betraying so clearly the system of the papal chancery as to bear upon its outer surface all the signs of an interested forgery. It is a remarkable evidence of the toleration which then prevailed in Italy that the author of this audacious attack upon one of the cherished privileges of the Papacy himself became the secretary of Pope Nicholas V.

In such an atmosphere of leisure and freedom the lives of scholars became interesting to others. The world, which has always been attracted by the doings of kings and captains, was now invited to read the biographies of men whose sole title to the regard of posterity was that they loved books and manuscripts and lived the life of disinterested culture. Here is a picture from Vespasiano of Niccolo de' Niccoli, whose private library of eight hundred manuscripts was one of the glories of Florence.

" First of all he was of a most fair presence, lively, for a smile was ever on his lips, and very pleasant in his talk; he wore clothes of the fairest crimson cloth, reaching to the ground; he never married in order that he might not be impeded in his studies; a housekeeper provided for his daily needs; he was, above all men, the most cleanly in eating and also in all other things. When he sat at table he ate from fair antique vases, and in like manner all his table was covered with porcelain and other vessels of great beauty. The cup from which he drank was of crystal or of some other precious stone. To see him at table, a perfect model of the men of old, was in truth a charming sight. He always willed that the napkin set before him should be of the whitest, as well as all the linen. Some might wonder at the many vases that he possessed, to whom I answer that things of that sort were neither so highly valued then nor so much regarded as they have since become, and Niccoli having friends everywhere, anyone who wished to do him a pleasure would send him marble statues, or antique vases, carvings, inscriptions, pictures from the hands of distinguished masters, and mosaic tablets. He had a most beautiful map on which all the parts and cities of the world were marked, others of Italy and Spain, all painted. Florence could not show a house more full of ornaments than his, or one that had in it a greater number of graceful objects, so that all who went there found innumerable things of worth to please varieties of taste."

It is now too that we begin to hear the praise of the best abused and most deserving servant of society. Vespasiano, who has painted for us the rounded culture of the scrupulous, old-world Florentine bachelor, has bequeathed to us also the portrait of a schoolmaster. Vittorino da Feltre stands as the pioneer of the educational movement which has resulted in the foundation of our English training in the humanities. He was a small, spare, gay man of a nature that seemed to be always laughing, a good horseman and gymnast, an indefatigable and devoted trainer of body, mind, and character. His school became famous through Italy, and among his posthumous disciples we may include Colet and Wolsey, John Milton and Charles Kingsley, and all our modern head-masters, so far as they seek to train mind and character through the instrument of fine literature, music, and art, and combine with this generous curriculum a care for the development of the body.

The rulers of Rome could hardly be indifferent to the lustre which shone upon the secular courts of Italy through the patronage of art and letters. The papal office, which had lost much of its spiritual prestige during the schism and the Avignonese cap-

1396-1446

tivity, was now usefully employed on the promotion of learning,
the collection of artistic treasures, and the embellishment and
restoration of a famous but long-neglected capital. Nicholas V,
the scholarly son of a poor bell-ringer, founded the Vatican *1447-55*
library, and gave commissions to Fra Angelico, Benozzo Gozzoli,
and Piero della Francesca. The brilliant Aeneas Sylvius, who
built the Piccolomini Palace at Siena, brought to the Holy See
the engaging gifts of a traveller, a man of letters, a diplomatist,
and a virtuoso, and even recovered as Pope Pius II much of the *1458-64*
antique zeal of a crusader.

To Paul II his successor, who collected gems and bronzes with *1464-71*
the ardour and knowledge of a Venetian connoisseur, is due the
restoration of the arches of Septimius Severus and Titus. And so
the Popes of the Renaissance continued, building, restoring,
decorating, collecting, and in pursuit of these cultivated tastes,
spending and taxing, until with the accession of Leo X of the
house of Medici in 1513 the papal patronage of the arts soared to
a climax of munificence and splendour, and with the crushing
cost of the new St. Peter's staggered the loyalty of half Christendom.

The visitor to Rome who enjoys the collections and buildings of
that age will find it difficult to condemn the Popes of the Renaissance for such enlightened, if expensive, activities. What is open
to censure is the naked and unscrupulous ambition by which
some of the Renaissance popes endeavoured to extend their temporal dominions at the expense of their Italian neighbours. When
we consider the gravity and imminence of the Turkish peril, and
the urgent need for the political combination of the Italian States,
the policy of a Pope like Sixtus IV, who in his ambition to found
a temporal monarchy built up a scientific system of nepotism,
and twice embarked upon war, stands high in the scale of political iniquity. Not least among the causes of the revolt from
Rome was the widespread feeling in northern Europe that the
Popes were Italian princes, to whom the advancement of their
temporal power was a more important interest than the furtherance of the spiritual welfare of Christendom.

For meanwhile the republic of Venice was confronted with
the new and formidable fact of the Turkish conquest of Constantinople. A short-lived peace (1454-63), more expeditious than
glorious, was followed by the outbreak of a difficult war from
which Venice emerged shorn of Dalmatia, Lemnos, and Morea.

and condemned to pay an annual tribute to the Sultan. The proud and adventurous aristocracy of Venice was not prepared tamely to acquiesce in so humiliating a conclusion. What had been lost in the east might be regained in the west. The disaster which had befallen Venetian arms in the Aegean might be repaired at the expense of Milan, Ferrara, or Naples. In a restless search for compensations Venice ultimately decided to inflame the appetites and invoke the ambitions of France.

Yet despite these political agitations the last half of the fifteenth century is memorable in the history of the Venetian renaissance. The Basilica of St. Mark, begun in 830 and completed in 1484, preserves more perfectly than any existing building in the territories once belonging to the eastern Empire the quintessential spirit of Byzantine art. It was a noble reply to the barbarous devastations of the Turk to complete upon the free soil of Venice a building which might serve as a perpetual memorial of the splendour and taste of the vanished Christian Empire of the east. But there was another side to the artistic and intellectual life of Venice which was not represented by Byzantine mosaics or by jewels recalling the designs of the Scythian goldsmith of antiquity. Venice was on the frontier of two worlds, Greek and Latin. St. Mark's is Greek. The exquisite art of John Bellini, one of the pioneers of Venetian painting, is wholly associated with the Italian schools.

The invention of printing, which in the north was destined to spread Luther's fiery prose through the length and breadth of Germany, was characteristically employed by the Italian race to further classical studies. The hero of Italian printing was Aldus Manutius (1449-1514), critic, grammarian, literary historian, moralist, the founder of the Aldine Press at Venice. In the annals of Italian humanism there is no finer or nobler figure. Aldus had suffered from one of the worst plagues of youth, a thoroughly bad school book. A platonist and educationalist, he came to see that the improvement of Italian education principally depended upon a supply of good and cheap literature. So he settled in Venice, a city which was secure from war alarms, where he could find a cultured society and count on the assistance of Greek immigrants, and there set up a printing press, which issued in swift succession classic after classic, in editions so cheaply and beautifully executed, so trim and handy, that they are still a pleasure to consult. The doom of the vast and cumbrous folio was pronounced. The Venetian gentleman slipping down the

Grand Canal in his graceful gondola could drink in the beauties of Homer from a tiny volume of the clearest print.

The humanism of the Renaissance, unlike those mediaeval types of piety or heroism which are embodied in the Gothic cathedrals or the Chansons de Geste, was not popular but aristocratic. The message of the humanist was to the elect. The soul of a people will never be greatly stirred by the religion of the artist or the savant. Philosophy, erudition, the critical examination of texts, the passionate pursuit of art for art's sake, these activities will always be confined to a small intellectual minority of the human race. So it is now, so it was then. If the humanist of the Renaissance elevated taste, he also enlarged the distance between man and man.

The Italian Renaissance, like most great movements of the human spirit, was the achievement of a comparatively small minority of gifted and creative men working in a sensitive and intelligent society. What they accomplished would have been impossible without the vivid Court life of Italy, the patronage of the Church, or the widespread Italian appetite for the enjoyments of the eye and the ear. In no other European country would the shops have been shut when a popular poet was reciting his verses or an artist's virtuosity have been permitted to condone a murder. Only in Italy was it expected of a nobleman that he should turn out a sonnet, appraise a picture, or read the classics. By comparison the French aristocracy, till Francis I showed a better way, were barbarians, dedicated to the camp, the tourney, and the chase. Not that Italian life, for all its civility, was either comfortable or secure. The country was unpoliced. Every man went armed against the sudden animal hatreds of his neighbours. Every palace, however resplendent with marbles and pictures, was a fortress, cold as the tomb in winter, and with few of those comforts which even the most modest householder in Islington or Putney now demands as his due. The autobiography of Ben- 1500-71 venuto Cellini depicts a society in which crimes of violence and acts of atrocious cruelty and treachery were almost too common to be seriously regarded. Such was the Italian temperament, as swift to anger and cruel revenge as it was sensitive to the subtlest enchantments of form and sound.

From this flowering of talent in Italy the fighting aristocracies beyond the Alps derived a new range of interests. Transalpine noblemen, their rusticity tempered by Italian travel, took to the

encouragement of art and letters. The gulf which divided mediaeval society into lettered clerk and illiterate fighting man began
to close up. Even for noblemen it became a fashion before the
end of the fifteenth century to frequent universities, to open
books, and, in the adornment of their homes, to study magnificence.

There was, for instance, in the England of the Wars of the
Roses no figure more generally detested for his ruthless cruelties
than John Tiptoft, Earl of Worcester (1427-1470), the instrument
(for he held the office of Constable) of King Edward IV's sharp
revenges. He was known as " the butcher of England " and " the
fierce executioner and beheader of men." Yet his cruelty, after
the Italian fashion, was blended with a high degree of cultivation.
Few Latinists in the island were more accomplished than this
ruthless aristocrat who had been educated at Balliol and had
afterwards mingled with the humanists of Padua and rifled the
bookshops of Florence. Tiptoft was a precursor. A long line of
Italianate Englishmen followed in his steps, " devils incarnate " as
it was the fashion in the days of Queen Elizabeth to describe
them, but having derived from their Italian discipleship, together
with many moral poisons, a range of taste, knowledge, and
experience which permanently enriched the culture of their
country.

Two ideas, destined to exert an enduring influence in the
sphere of politics and education, were bequeathed to Europe by
the Italy of the Renaissance. The first, that of the pure politician,
was contained in *The Prince* of Machiavelli, written in 1513, and
the second, that of the scholar-gentleman, in Castiglione's
Courtier, which was composed three years later. Machiavelli was
a Florentine diplomatist and an Italian patriot who employed an
exile's involuntary leisure in depicting the kind of ruler best
suited to liberate the soil of Italy from the profane presence of
barbarian invaders and to restore the glories of Ancient Rome.
What was startling in this brilliant treatise was its objectivity.
The Prince is an artist in " power politics," using without scruple
and remorse such measure of force or fraud as may enable him
to extend and secure his conquests. A realist who sees life
through plain glass, a close student of contemporary forces expecting nothing better of life than life can give, the Prince of
Machiavelli was far removed from the saintly ghosts who figured
in the manuals of mediaeval churchmen. The naked doctrine of

power politics stated without concealment or reserve, but representing what was in fact the practice of the age, came as a shock to public opinion. The world was not accustomed to a political treatise in which there was nothing either of morality or religion. That its hero was Cesare Borgia, the "nephew" of Alexander VI, an assassin Pope, and himself, despite brilliant personal accomplishments, widely known for successful assassinations and treacheries added to the challenge a further note of audacity.

Equally characteristic of the Italian spirit of that age was Count Baldassare Castiglione's *Cortegiano* or *Courtier*. The author, who had received his impressions of a highly cultivated Italian court under Duke Guidobaldo of Urbino, drew a picture of the ideal courtier which obtained a wide popularity through Europe. The courtier must be trained in the school not only of the court, but of the camp. He must be a man-at-arms and a sportsman, an athlete and an intellectual, a virtuoso in the arts and a citizen in the world, well read in Greek, Latin, and Italian, with some practical knowledge of drawing and music and a superficial and apparently effortless mastery of all the fashionable graces and accomplishments of his time. Such a conception of education chimed in with the mode of the age. The *Cortegiano* was rendered into many languages. To Sir Thomas Hoby's charming English version (1561) Milton's view of a generous education as that which "fits a man to perform justly, skilfully, and magnanimously all the offices both private and public of peace and war," is plainly indebted.

To the Greek orthodox world, whether living under the Sultan or the Tsar, all this prodigal outpouring of Italian genius was of no significance. The Italian Renaissance meant nothing either to the Russians or to the Turks. Save for a few scattered borrowings, a Venetian portrait in the Seraglio at Constantinople, the Kremlin in Moscow (taken from Milan), and some skilful touches in Agra and Delhi, the operation of Italian taste and intellect was confined within the limits of Latin Christianity. Russia was a world apart and not until the eighteenth century a factor to be reckoned with in European politics.

BOOKS WHICH MAY BE CONSULTED

Trenchard Cox : The Renaissance in Europe (1400-1600). 1933. Examples taken from the works of art in London Museums and Galleries.

M. Creighton : History of the Papacy during the Period of the Reformation. 1882-94.

Janet Trevelyan : A Short History of the Italian People. 1929.

E. Armstrong : Lorenzo de' Medici and Florence in the Fifteenth Century. 1896.

P. Villari : Life and Times of Girolamo Savonarola. *Tr*. L. Villari. 2 vols. 1897-8.

G. Vasari : Lives of Italian Painters, Sculptors and Architects. 8 vols. 1900.

B. Berensen : Central Italian Painters of the Renaissance. 1897.

B. Berensen : North Italian Painters of the Renaissance. 1907.

B. Berensen : Venetian Painters of the Renaissance. 1894.

M. von Wolff : Lorenzo Valla. 1893.

L. B. Alberti : Opere volgari. *Ed*. A. Bonucci. 1843-9.

L. von. Ranke : History of the Popes. *Tr*. S. Austin. 1847.

H. A. Taine : Philosophie de l'Art en Italie. 1865.

Machiavelli : Principe. *Ed*. L. A. Burd. 1891.

Vespesiano Da Bisticci : Vite de uomini illustri del secolo XV. *Ed*. L. Frati. 1892.

Cambridge Modern History, Vol. I.

J. Burckhardt : Die Cultur der Renaissance in Italien. 1869.

J. Morley : Machiavelli. Romanes Lecture. 1897.

J. Zeller : Italie et Renaissance. 1883.

H. Brown : The Venetian Printing Press. 1891.

J. A. Symonds : The Renaissance in Italy, Vols. IV and V. 1875-86.

A. F. Didot : Alde Manuce et l'héllenisme Venise. 1875.

The Book of the Courtier. *Tr*. Sir T. Hoby. *Ed*. W. R. Raleigh. 1900

W. Ormsby-Gore : Florentine Sculptors of the Fifteenth Century. **1930**

CHAPTER III

FRANCE AND BURGUNDY

Louis XI. He defeats the Nobles and buys off the English. His good fortune. Contrasted with Charles of Burgundy. Services of the Burgundian Dukes to Flanders. The Flemish art of the fifteenth century.

WHILE Italy was in a ferment of artistic creation, France was experiencing the arrest of cultural progress which is the natural result of great political calamities. The most splendid period in the artistic history of Florence coincides with the long and painful convalescence of France from the havoc of the English wars, with the sharp rivalry between the Burgundian duchy and the French kingdom, and with the stages by which a weak and harassed government in Paris staggered back through its own skill and the follies of its adversary to a sound and national foundation. During these anxious years there was no French patronage of Italian genius and little sign of native artistic talent. The great sculptors of the thirteenth century whose statues adorn the cathedrals of Chartres and Rheims had left no successors. Jean Fouquet, the painter, was from Brussels. It was not until their invasion of Italy in 1494 that the French became aware of the splendours of the Italian scene, and were prepared for a reception of the Italian renaissance. Verrocchio, silversmith, engineer, painter, lapidary, musician, and sculptor, and perhaps the central figure in the artistic development of the Quattrocento, had already been six years in his grave.

Charles VII, the king who had led France out of the miseries of the long English war and given to his country a government and an army, died in 1461. His son Louis XI, who had been a *1461-83* rebel and exile, continued the valuable but pedestrian work. In his shabby old hat and clothes this eavesdropping, cheeseparing, cautious monarch, who believed that everyone had his price, but was quick to strike off the head of an offending nobleman, and even to shut up a treacherous cardinal in an iron cage, seemed to be an enigmatic compound of craft, cruelty, and vice. Yet those who, like Philippe de Commines, the Burgundian, knew the man and understood the difficulties of the time, recognized in Louis an assemblage of gifts which, though they brought him no popularity with the foolish, illiterate, madcap nobles who were the pest of society, saved the monarchy of France from the worst humiliations. His native wit taught him that a statesman should be a good listener and greedy for information, that, so far as possible, everybody of real political importance, both in his own country and in neighbouring lands, should be known to him personally, that he should spare no pains to win over an enemy, harbour no grudges, exercise a long-sighted patience, always be willing to learn from his own mistakes, and, putting away pride, to retrace his steps. After a first ebullition of impolitic anger, natural in a returned exile, against the prominent supporters of the old régime, Louis thought better of it, and made it an object to win back the men whom he had wronged.

At a difficult crisis he showed more than once great resources of courage and skill. Soon after his accession he was confronted **1465** by a formidable coalition of malcontent nobles (the so-called League of the Public Good) led by Charles, Count of Charolais ("The Bold"), heir to the Burgundian Duchy, and supported by the Duc de Berri, his own brother, and by the Duke of Brittany. The enemy forces were on the outskirts of Paris. The loyalty of the capital was wavering. Any mistake might be sufficient to ruin the unpopular young man (so long a stranger) who had ejected from their places his father's counsellors and surrounded himself by a camarilla of his own choosing. But Louis never even stumbled. Throwing himself into Paris with a powerful force, he won over his opponents in the city by a wise clemency. With Paris at his back he could play with ill-disciplined enemies, avoiding a general engagement, but so harassing them with skirmishes that they were brought to the point of desiring peace. If, in order to obtain a breathing-space, within which to sow dissensions among his foes, Louis granted them terms (Treaty of Conflans) which were far too generous to be permanently consistent with French welfare, that too was part of his serpent's wisdom.

Had the Duchy of Burgundy been in strong hands, or if England had been able and willing to take an effective share in the conflict, the horrors of the Hundred Years' War might easily have been repeated. It is fortunate, perhaps, for Europe, and certainly for France, that Charles, by his headstrong attack upon

he Swiss, threw away the great position which four prudent
ulers had secured for the Burgundian house, and that the wars
)etween the Yorkists and the Lancastrians on the other side of
he Channel precluded any effective interference of England in
he affairs of the continent. An English expedition against the
•ld enemy was still possible and still popular, but its object was
to longer conquest but barefaced blackmail. Twice in twenty
years English armies were transplanted to the soil of France, and *1475*
withdrawn for substantial cash payments. Immunity from the *1492*
still formidable English archers was adjudged by Louis and his
heir to be cheap at the price.

In other ways Louis was helped by fortune. It was good for-
une that Charles the Bold had no male heir, so that on his death
n 1477 Burgundy, Picardy, and Artois reverted to the French
crown; good fortune again that René, the last King of Aix, died
with a similar lack of male issue, so that Maine and Anjou and
the Imperial fief of Provence became part of Royal France in
1480; and finally a crowning act of Providence that Francis,
Duke of Brittany, that old Celtic province which was so proud of
its independence and so rich in sea craft, had no son to whom he
could bequeath the ancient quarrel of his race. To these successive strokes of fortune is principally due the fact that France,
which after the accession of Louis XI seemed to be on the point
of disruption, was at his death compact, powerful, and well
guarded on every front.

In the brilliant narrative of Commines, Louis and Charles
stand out in clear relief as contrasted embodiments of wisdom
and folly. Louis by patient intrigue and with the least possible
waste of blood and treasure overcomes all his enemies, and leaves
his kingdom stronger than he found it. Charles from a restless
and costly military ambition throws away a great inheritance. It
is specially noted of Louis that he preferred to work with men of
the middle station. In his aversion from bloodshed, in his distrust of the nobility, in his preferences for mercenaries (he
brought the Swiss into the service of the French crown), and in
his encouragement of trade and commerce he typifies a new type
of statesmanship. Like his contemporary Edward IV, though to
a more conspicuous degree, he is a business king.

Taken as a whole, the work of the Burgundian dukes, though
it bears the stamp of coarse ostentation, is also significant as an

index of that deeper change from mediaeval feudalism to the
national state, which began in the fifteenth century to transform
the political complexion of western Europe. The Burgundians
were lavish, vulgar, flamboyant, cherishing as their ultimate
ideal the status of monarchy and the construction of a compact
polity in the valley of the Rhine and its affluents which should
comprise some of the wealthiest commercial communities in
Europe. Old traditions and loyalties meant little to them. Their
state was carved out, with little regard to the antecedents or the
affinities of its component parts, by the rude surgery of conquest.
A steady policy of aggrandisement, pursued for four generations,
brought this vigorous and pertinacious family within sight of
its goal.

1477　　　With the death of Charles the Bold before the walls of Nancy
the whole artificial structure fell to pieces. Yet the work of the
Burgundian dukes was not wholly in vain. They are the makers
of Belgium. To the county of Flanders, which is the kernel of the
modern Belgian kingdom, they gave a novel sense of independence and unity. Their ambitious policies, their meteoric triumphs, their happy mixture of the popular with the grandiose,
educated a school of publicists and historians of more than average merit. They made of Brussels, where they kept their court,
one of the most showy capitals of Europe. The commercial greatness of Antwerp owes much to their encouragement, and to the
restraint which they imposed upon the rival pretensions of
Bruges and Ghent.

In the conflict of economic interests, of which in that time of
rapid growth Flanders was the scene, the dukes could always
rely upon the rising commercial interest against the force of old-
fashioned industry, with its fettering monopolies and outworn
technique. It was their policy to make of Flanders, so far as this
was possible, an economic unity, to foster the fine arts as well as
the interests of trade and commerce, and to remove the internal
obstacles to the transit and exchange of commodities. French in
origin, in language, in tastes, they nevertheless set themselves to
learn the Flemish language, and were too wise to attempt what
indeed was impossible—the suppression of the Teutonic tongue
in which so much of the business of Flanders was transacted.

But if, having an eye to the main chance, they made Flanders,
where the memory of the old war comradeship with England was
still living, the centre of their dominion, the dukes never forgot

their original home. Brussels was the capital, but old-fashioned Dijon was the family burial-place. The art of the Flemish painters and sculptors spread westward through Burgundy into France, and there exercised a profound influence. And, as Flanders influenced France, so France, through the Burgundian dukes, influenced Flanders. The predominantly French character of Belgium today may be traced back to the period when Flanders under a French dynasty was for the only time in its history the heart and centre of an ambitious and conquering state.

Though it was encouraged by ducal patronage, the art of the Flemings, as of the Burgundians, grew naturally out of mediaeval soil. Whereas the renaissance in Italy was marked by an abrupt aversion from the mediaeval and the Gothic, and a clear-cut and vehement preference for the models of pagan antiquity, there was no such sense of conscious innovation among the artists of the Burgundian duchy. Quietly, insensibly, they glided out of the mediaeval into the modern world. The development of their painting owed more to close observation than to literary theory or intellectual preferences and aversions. Delicacy of feeling, fidelity to fact, scrupulous technique, were the distinguishing features of the Flemish art in the fifteenth century. From the Flemings who were its inventors the Italians borrowed the use of oils. And it is to the painting of this gifted people that the young, crude, and bustling principality owes the greatest part of its renown.

The art of the Netherlands, equally with that of Italy, springs from a vivid city life reposing on the base of material affluence. In the activity of their guilds, in their prizes for craftsmanship, as also in their public encouragement of literary and dramatic enterprises, the burgesses of the Low Countries vied with the inhabitants of Florence and Venice. The two great town systems of mediaeval Europe, that of Italy and that of the Netherlands, by the eclipse of which the civilization of the western world would have been fatally impoverished, grew up in substantial independence. The Flemish painters of the fifteenth century required no lessons from Giotto or his school in the art of painting the human form as they saw it. A native force of realism diverted them from Byzantine conventions. They painted from the life, but with a brilliance of colouring as if to challenge the gloom of northern skies and with a preference shaped by rich and secular patrons for domestic themes so portrayed as to exhibit every familiar detail with cameo-like distinctness. Their influence, like that of the Italians, was widespread. By the end of the fifteenth century northern Germany from end to end was an artistic colony of Flanders.

BOOKS WHICH MAY BE CONSULTED

A. W. Ward in Cambridge Modern History, Vol. I, chap. xiii.

C. de Cherrier : Histoire de Charles VIII. 1868.

J. F. Kirk : History of Charles the Bold. 3 vols. 1863-8.

C. Legeay : Histoire de Louis XI. 1874.

Sir W. Scott : Quentin Durward.

L. E. de Laborde : Les Ducs de Bourgogne. 1849-52.

C. Petit Dutaillis in E. Lavisse, Histoire de France, Vol. IV.

P. Fredericq : Essai sur le rôle politique et social des Ducs de Bourgogne dans les Pays-Bas. 1875.

E. A. Freeman : Historical Essays, First Series (Charles the Bold). 1892.

L. Battifol : The Century of the Renaissance. 1916

CHAPTER IV

THE GERMAN RENAISSANCE, 1450-1500

Intellectual progress of Germany in the later half of the fifteenth century. The spread of printing. Its effect in diffusing a popular interest in religion. Failure of Maximilian's attempts to reform the Empire. The real greatness of Germany at this time. The arts and crafts. Albrecht Dürer and Peter Vischer. Cusanus.

THE later half of the fifteenth century is marked in the history of Germany by a notable enlargement of culture, learning, and education, and also, as in Italy, by the development of the power of the territorial princes. The present reputation of the Germans as the leaders of the world in book learning may be traced back to this age, which witnessed the foundation of eight German academies, and the epoch-making invention in part due to John Gutenberg of Mainz of the art of typography. The immense revolution in the intellectual opportunities of mankind which followed upon this last discovery may be inferred from the speed with which, in an age unhampered by patents, it spread throughout Europe. Printing from metal types reached Italy in 1465, Paris in 1470, London in 1477, Stockholm in 1483, and Madrid in 1499. It has been calculated, but on an estimate which is probably too conservative, that by the close of the century some nine million printed books must have been in existence as against a few score thousand manuscripts which, up to that time, had contained the inherited wisdom and poetry of the world.

The credit of spreading the printing press through Europe must be principally ascribed to the Germans. Printing was known as the German art. The German printers and booksellers went everywhere in search of custom. By the end of 1500 they had more than a hundred presses in Italy and at least thirty presses in Spain. An immense missionary enthusiasm for the new art, and an intelligent appreciation of its significance for life, spread through the country. " As the apostles of Christ," wrote Wimpheling, a contemporary, " formerly went through the world announcing the good news, so in our days the disciples of the new art spread themselves through all countries, and their books are as the heralds of the Gospel and the preachers of truth and of science." It is a remarkable illustration of the keen eye of the German trader for these apostolic opportunities that in 1494, only two years after the expulsion of the Moors from Granada, three German printers were already established in that town.

The work of her early printers and bookbinders is one of the glories of Germany. Europe owes much to these inspired tradesmen, who were scholars and artists, as well as business organizers on an international scale, and even in a general history the names of the first great booksellers, of a Koberger of Nuremberg, or a Froben of Basel, may be recalled without impropriety. Some early German folios have, indeed, rarely been surpassed for beauty and magnificence. And if the main part of the literature which then issued from the German presses was theological, if during the first fifty years there were more than a hundred editions of the Bible and fifty-nine of the *Imitatio Christi*, this was due to the fact that here, as elsewhere, the clergy constituted the bulk of the lettered class, and were the chief patrons of the book trade. In the sixteenth century the printed book acted as a powerful inducement to liberating and critical movements of thought: but the first consequences of typography were otherwise, and are to be found in an awakening of popular religion and in a diffused interest in the reading and discussion of religious books.

It would not, therefore, be fair to urge that the period of German history which immediately precedes the Reformation was characterized by symptoms of degeneration and decay. There were, indeed, many grave faults in the political and social structure of the country. The Church, which is computed to have held a third of the landed property, was far too wealthy to be wholesome; the upper clergy too much given to idle ostentation or profligate expenditure. Private war was common, and, until the Diet of Worms in 1495, not seriously checked. The country, therefore, suffered from the irregular depredations of one of the idlest and most selfish aristocracies in Europe. Nor was there in the political framework of the German Empire any force capable of educating a firm body of patriotic and disinterested opinion, which might countervail the evils of class selfishness or petty localism. In this regard no episode is more instructive 1493-1519 than the career of the Emperor Maximilian, the founder of Austrian unity, the darling of the Tyrolese, the first of chamois hunters and "the last of the knights." Few German rulers have been more deservedly popular than this handsome, chivalrous, and most generous sovereign. None have been more energetic, more eloquent, more seductive, or more desirous of maintaining what he believed to be the true tradition of his high office and the honour of the German name. Yet despite all these admirable qualities Maximilian was unable to stir up the lethargic body of the German Reich to take effective action against the Turks in the east or the French in Italy. His attempts to provide an adequate reformation of the German Constitution at the Diet of Worms in 1495, and again at Augsburg in 1500, broke down against the solid opposition of the selfish interests. He could secure neither a standing imperial army nor a regular system of imperial taxation. His lieges refused to serve with the forces, or to pay the "common penny" (a graduated property tax), or to co-operate in the setting up of machinery for the enforcement of the decision of an imperial tribunal. Save for the fact that some slight improvement in the sphere of justice and police was secured by the proclamation of a perpetual land peace, by the establishment of a stationary imperial court, and by the division of the Empire into ten circles, the feverish attempts of this well-meaning and high-minded Emperor to make of the German Federation an effective power in the world were entirely frustrated. The Emperor had become a pathetic shadow. The real centre of political strength lay in the electors and princes.

There is, however, no necessary connection between political good sense and the spiritual and artistic progress of a people. The essential virtue of Germany lay, not in its empire or its great prelates and princes, and still less in its grasp of the essentials of public policy, but in the thousands of gifted and ingenious town workers, who built Gothic churches and cathedrals, developed the organ, wrought as carvers and sculptors in stone and wood and bronze, and by their engravings, paintings, and metal work secured a brilliant repute throughout the world for the craftsmanship of the German race. The drawings and engravings of Albert Dürer, and the noble array of bronzes which *1477-1527* for a space of fifty years were cast in the foundry of the Vischer family at Nuremburg are monuments of the virtuosity by which in the last epoch before the Reformation Germany partially atoned for the prevailing corruption of the Church and the violent confusion of her public life.

The development of the plastic arts in Germany, which with Peter Vischer the younger had reached a high point of virtuosity, experienced a sudden check in the third decade of the sixteenth century. The rich old vein of German craftsmanship seems to have worked itself out. Conventional patterns and ideas borrowed from the Italians replace the early German work which, though it missed the simple beauty of the Italian masterpieces, was sincere, strong and true to the native character. Nuremberg, which in the fifteenth century was the Florence of Germany, ceased to be a living centre of decorative art. With the coming of the Reformation an ill wind began to blow upon the sculptors and painters. It was not only that the country was poorer by reason of the discovery of the new oceanic routes, but that the swift onrush of religious and social anarchy turned the minds of the German people into other channels. Religion, not art, was the governing interest. It is significant that Holbein, finding Basel too uncomfortable for a German painter, fled to the shelter of the English court. It was not, then, in painting or sculpture, nor even in the gentle art of woodcarving, once, as is natural among woodland peoples, a universal pursuit, that the Germans found satisfaction for their artistic cravings. Luther's hymns pointed a new way. The Germans gave themselves to music. By the end of the eighteenth century they led Europe in this the most universal of the arts and the one common language of all religions.

This, however, is to anticipate. The person in whom, before the storms of the Reformation, the intellectual life of Germany is most fully represented, is Nicholas Krebs, later known as the Cardinal Cusanus from his birthplace at Cues in the Moselle valley. A strong vein of mystical religion, rooted perhaps in his early education with the Brethren of the Common Life at Deventer, was combined in Cusanus with the passion of a humanist, the eloquence of a statesman, and the laborious curiosity of a Teutonic scholar. As a young man he had studied mathematics and canon law in the university of Padua, and there mixed with a brilliant circle of Italian savants who were at that time skirmishing on the frontier of mathematical, astronomical, and geographical knowledge. Thereafter a timely piece of preferment opened many doors on either side of the Alps to the ambitious youth. Becoming secretary to Canon Orsini, an Italian intellectual and the Apostolic Legate in Germany, he

1401-64

found the chief stars in the Italian literary firmament shining on his path. Toscanelli, the geographer, Valla, the scholar historian, Poggio, the discoverer of Tacitus, became his friends. With the true grammarian's ardour he threw himself upon the monastic libraries of his native Rhineland, and before long was rewarded by the reappearance of twelve lost plays of Plautus. Thenceforward the name of Treviranus (for Krebs was from the diocese of Trèves) became famous in the learned world. A Deanery, a Tyrolese Bishopric, a cardinal's hat, rewarded the happy discoverer of a dozen salacious Latin comedies. In turn the oracle of the Council of Basel and the henchman of Pope Eugenius IV, Cusanus earned golden opinions by his substantial good sense, his omnivorous reading, and his high character. Whether he was transcribing Latin manuscripts in Germany, or bringing back Greek texts from Mount Athos, or commenting on the Koran, or composing an atlas of central Europe, this indefatigable student was inspired by the sentiments of a good Christian, a good European, and a good German. It is noteworthy that in a treatise on Catholic concord, written at the age of thirty, he attacked the abuses of the Church with severity, and advocated as a remedy against the terrible disorders of Germany the establishment of an Imperial army. It was not until after Germany had suffered the humiliation of Napoleon's conquest that the brilliant Goerres, another German publicist from the Rhineland, advocated, but again without success, the same plain remedy for the same obvious evil of German anarchy and helplessness.

As an ecclesiastic Cusanus is honourably distinguished for the vigour with which he assailed the immorality of the German clergy and the pagan superstitions still rife among the German 1450 peasants, as well as for his disbelief in the use of military force against paganism, and for his faith in the powers of knowledge, reason, and eloquence as binding forces in human affairs. It is not, however, either as humanist or as ecclesiastic that he is now chiefly remembered, but as the author of a book, *De Docta Ignorantia*, in which it is claimed that several guiding principles of modern philosophy and science may be plausibly discerned. To many a patriotic German Cusanus appears as the precursor of Copernicus, Descartes, and Hegel. It is not, however, to a corpus of mystical theology written by a busy ecclesiastical statesman that the world must look for pioneering work in the

sciences. If the cloudy folios of Cusanus are here and there lit
by a brilliant flash of intuition into the nature of the physical
universe, if his vision of an Absolute in which the contradictions
of the intellect are finally harmonized wears a modern air, the
method of the author was always mediaeval. Conclusions confirmed by modern science are reached by arguments which every
man of science would now repudiate as fanciful and foolish.
The real interest attaching to the work of this learned and
laborious Teuton is that in him we see a powerful intellect
moving on mediaeval and thoroughly German lines, but played
upon by the first enlivening aspersions of Italian science.

BOOKS WHICH MAY BE CONSULTED

J. Janssen : Geschichte des deutschen Volkes seit dem Ausgang des
     Mittelalters. *Tr.* M. A. Mitchell and A. M. Christie. 1896-1925.
C. Ullmann : Reformatoren vor der Reformation. *Tr.* R. Menzies.
     2 vols. 1855.
F. A. Gasquet : The Eve of the Reformation. 1905.
F. Paulsen : Geschichte des gelehrten Unterrichts auf den deutschen
     Schulen und Universitäten. 1885-96.
E. Müntz : Histoire de l'Art pendant la Renaissance. 1889-95.
W. B. Scott : Albrecht Durer, his Life and Works. 1869.
L. Geiger : Renaissance und Humanismus in Italien und Deutschland.
     1882.
A. D. Vandam : Social Germany in Luther's Time, being the Memoirs of
     Bartholomew Sastrow. 1902 (abridged). With preface by H. A. L.
     Fisher.
W. Bode : Geschichte der deutschen Plastik. 1885.
Cecil Headlam : Peter Vischer. 1901.
Sprenger : Albrecht Durer.
B. A. Daun : Ada, Krafft und seine zeit. 1896.

CHAPTER V

NEW MONARCHY IN ENGLAND

The Wars of the Roses. Their origin. Henry VI and Edward IV. Social and economic effects. The significance of Henry Tudor. The first English colony.

THE expulsion of the English from France in 1453 was followed two years later by the outbreak of the Wars of the Roses. It is difficult to imagine a combination of public calamities more complete than a long civil struggle supervening on the miscarriage of a foreign campaign. But the defeat and the civil war were blessings in disguise. Once the forlorn attempt to conquer France was definitely abandoned, England was able to find her true line of development in the enlargement of her influence over the British Isles, in the expansion of her commerce and industry, and in the foundation of colonies beyond the ocean. That she was able to play an effective part in such tasks as these was due to the fortunate and unparalleled thoroughness with which the feudal virus was eliminated from the body politic by the Wars of the Roses.

The contest between the rival houses of York and Lancaster is distinguished from the feudal insurrections upon the continent during the same period by one notable characteristic. Both English parties accepted the unity of the kingdom and the system of government by King, Council, and Parliament, which had been handed down from earlier times. The object of the Yorkists in the earlier stages of the war was not to shear away great provinces, as the League of the Public Good attempted to do in France, nor to reduce the kingship to a cypher as it was in Germany, nor to carry out any defined scheme of constitutional reform, but to storm their way into the Council, and through the Council to govern the country. Neither party can lay claim to a policy founded upon a disinterested concern for the public advantage. Private family feuds, and more especially the feuds of the Welsh marcher lords, war-restlessness, the need for occupying great bands of armed retainers, whom the cessation of the French wars had thrown out of work, were important fac-

tors in the Wars of the Roses. Yet it would be unjust to deny
to the leaders in this fierce contest any concern for the national
interest. The war between York and Lancaster was not wholly
frivolous, but arose out of the greatest of all public issues, that
of peace and war. Henry VI and his minister Suffolk were resolved to wind up the miserable French war, which Gloucester
and Richard of York were ardent to continue. The Treaty of
Tours (1444), negotiated by Suffolk, was felt to be doubly ignominious when it became known that it provided for the cession
of Calais to France, and for the marriage of the English king to
Margaret of Anjou, a woman of the enemy race. A fierce atmosphere of hatred and suspicion was generated by a quarrel which
in every castle of the land raised the burning issue of employment or idleness, adventure or war weariness, appetite or common sense, the forlorn endeavour to revive old glories, or the
ungrateful acceptance of inevitable defeat. Gloucester, the
special enemy of the French queen, and Suffolk, the popular
scapegoat for the pusillanimous peace, inaugurated by their sudden and violent ends the hideous period of assassination, judicial murder, and battle which disgraces the last age of Catholic
England.

If the Yorkists were the first to resort to arms, they could urge
in excuse humiliations abroad and mismanagement at home.
The Lancastrians were blamed for the loss of the French conquests, nor could the conspicuous piety of Henry VI, or his
noble educational foundations at Eton and Cambridge, atone in
the eyes of his contemporaries for an ignominious foreign policy,
a feeble character, a mind occasionally overclouded by insanity,
or for the acute unpopularity of his masterful French wife. After
his defeat at Towton (1461) the career of this blameless prince
lacked no element in tragedy. A bitter exile was succeeded by a
harsh imprisonment, and this by a cruel and violent death.

In contradistinction to the mild and ineffectual Lancastrian
saint, his murderer, the Yorkist leader, belonged to that more
modern and efficient type of statesmanship which was now
coming to the front in the progressive states of Europe owing to
the growing importance of industry and commerce. Edward IV
was not a virtuoso like Lorenzo dei Medici, nor a genius in diplomacy like Louis XI, but a good soldier with a handsome presence, affable manners, and the sound, middle-class instinct
which led the wiser heads of that time to appreciate the impor-

1461-83

tance of promoting the interests and enlisting the support of the money-making part of the community. Being intent on raising supplies with as little trouble to himself or others as possible, he was sparing in the summoning of Parliaments and preferred the direct method of a benevolence extracted from the wealthy to taxes collected by a cumbrous method and more widely diffused in their incidence. But with some attractive merits Edward combined certain grave faults. His morals, even judged by the standards of that age, were shamelessly loose, his industry irregular, his avarice inordinate, and to the crime of political murder (including fratricide) he added the supreme error, in a people dominated by social conventions, of finding a wife outside his class. The nobles of England, who never forgave Edward II for his addiction to the pursuits of a locksmith, a builder, and a waterman, took it ill that Edward IV should have secretly married into a family of thrusting upstarts. The beauty of Elizabeth Woodville was no compensation for the fact that her father, though the husband of a duchess, started life from the lowly grade of a knight. The Yorkist dynasty sank under the burden of the misalliance. When Edward died of his debaucheries at the age of forty, the children of the unpopular match evoked no protective sentiment of loyalty or enthusiasm. Their uncle Richard, who seized the throne, was well advised in thinking that the country was unprepared to make any serious sacrifice on behalf of Edward V and his young brother. Yet the heart of the English people was not so entirely hardened by the atrocities of the civil war as to acquiesce without a protest in the murder of the children in the Tower. Courage and ability did not save the unnatural uncle and the usurping king. His deposition was desired and plotted, not only by the Lancastrians, but by a large section of the Yorkist Party as well. On Bosworth Field, Henry Tudor, the son of a Welsh country gentleman, but *1485* descended through Margaret Beaufort, his mother, from John of Gaunt, and the sole surviving representative of the Lancastrian claim, made an end of Richard and his Yorkist following, and founded the strong dynasty which was destined to carry England through the religious and political troubles of the next age.[1]

The Wars of the Roses were ended. The English aristocracy had almost bled itself to death. But though the violent struggle

[1] Genealogical Table A.

was fought over a wide area of the country, and has been computed to have cost a hundred thousand 'lives, its social and economic effects were strictly circumscribed. No English town was sufficiently interested in the rival factions to stand a siege. The armies which hacked at each other with bills, or shot at each other with arrows, or less effectually and more expensively exchanged salvoes from their newfangled, and professionally manned cannon, were not drawn from the townsmen or the peasantry, but from the class of the great nobles and their liveried retainers. The social progress of the country suffered less from these disorders than might have been supposed. The quarrels of Mortimers and Percies, of Nevilles and Mowbrays, meant little to the villein, the craftsman, or the merchant. Trade pursued its even course. Fortunes were made. Wealthy men built houses of brick or stone for their personal use, or founded almshouses and colleges for the salvation of their souls. To Sir John Fortescue the position of the English peasantry appeared to be sharply distinguished from that of the peasantry of France by its prosperity. Villeinage was steadily dying out under the pressure of economic forces. Yet this long civil war was accompanied by one of the greatest evils which can afflict an organized society. It paralyzed the working, though it could not destroy the mechanism, of British justice. The royal judges still went on assize, the King's Courts still sat at Westminster, the Sheriff still held his tourn, and the Justices of the Peace still sat in their Petty and Quarter Sessions. Reluctant jurors were still summoned to serve on juries and punished for non-attendance. But wherever the interest of an influential land-owner and his retinue were involved, the course of justice was deflected by intimidation. The statutes against "livery and maintenance" were powerless to check an acknowledged evil but a popular practice. If two great families were involved in litigation at the Assizes, rival bodies of armed men, bearing the liveries of the lords by whom they were maintained, would ride into the county town and browbeat the jury and the judge. There was no rascal in the country so flagrant or notorious that he could not, if maintained and supported by a powerful noble, escape the merited retribution of the law.

Nevertheless, it is significant that, despite the anarchy and turbulence of the age, a writer like Fortescue finds it possible to exult in the laws and constitution of his country. The English vere then, as they have continued to be, a litigious people. Their lawyers were then, as they remain to this day, an influential and conservative profession, proud of their recondite science, and zealous for the honour and dignity of their calling. The violence of the civil war, and the frequency of judicial murders during that tempestuous epoch, did not efface the memory of the early Lancastrian days when Parliaments met frequently, and the law was administered, and constitutional precedents were stored up for future use. The tradition of parliamentary government survived, though the Parliaments under Edward IV did little but pass acts of attainder or connive at murder and confiscation; but local justice had broken down through local terrorism.

The restoration of the rule of law demanded the establishment of some new system of criminal equity, which should enable the great offender to be brought to his account, without the paralyzing incubus of those unhappy gentlemen of the jury whose verdicts were dictated by panic or by greed.

The significance of the reign of Henry Tudor consists in this, *1485-1509* that he reasserted the power of the national state over feudal indiscipline, and through his marriage with Elizabeth of York, the daughter of Edward IV, gave a signal to the country that the bitter feud between the two rival houses was henceforth to be composed. Save for an irreconcilable Yorkist remnant supported from Ireland and Flanders, and formidable only by reason of its foreign friends, the country welcomed the new men of peace. The risings of the impostors Lambert Simnel and Perkin Warbeck were successfully frustrated, and perhaps the more easily for the reason assigned by Bacon that "it was an odious thing for the people of England to have a king brought in upon them on the shoulders of the Irish and the Dutch." Henry Tudor had no standing army. Though he would have liked, as a Spanish ambassador observed, to govern England in the French fashion, he knew that he could not do it. From the first he was shrewd enough to see that without the good humour of the English people his dynasty could not survive.

To the student of politics nothing is more interesting than the process by which a nation, demoralized by a long course of rancorous strife, is gradually recalled to peace and sanity. To do this was the function of Henry VII. Many kings have been more spectacular, but none more valuable than this laborious

and frugal monarch under whose wise and vigilant treatmen
the poisons of the last feudal war were finally drained away
from the national system. If his rule was autocratic, it was free
from some of the worst autocratic vices, for there was no
jealousy of able men, no megalomania, no camarilla of court
favourites. The king's advisers were either the tried companions
of his youthful exile, or able lawyers, or men like Morton, Fox
or Warham, who had risen by force of brains and character
through the democratic avenues of the Church. It was better
frankly to commission Empson and Dudley to plunder the
nobles than to follow the French practice of giving to the whole
aristocratic class a privileged exemption from royal taxes. No
contemporary reproached Henry for his sparing use of Parlia
ments. In that age common justice was much to be preferred
to the arduous exercise of political liberty; and common justice
was improved. At last there was in Henry's " Star Chamber " a
court so powerful that it could strike fear into the heart of the
greatest noble in the land.

The advent of the Tudors did not and could not mean the
isolation of England. In self-protection Henry was obliged to seek
foreign alliances and to attend to English interests in Ireland
and Scotland, from each of which countries, as the story of the
Yorkist risings showed, an enemy attack might conveniently be
launched. So the heir to the throne was married to Catharine of
Aragon, and Margaret, the King's daughter, to James IV of
Scotland, while the long process of restoring English authority
among the Irish, which culminated in the Parliamentary Union
of 1800, was launched in 1494 by a measure (Poyning's Act) subjecting the Parliament of the Irish Pale to the Privy Council in
London.

Before the end of the century a certain Genoese mariner, by
name John Cabot, had sailed from Bristol under the king's
patent (1496) in a west country ship with a west country crew,
and had returned with the exciting news that he had struck land
on the other side of the Atlantic. Newfoundland, the oldest of
the British Dominions, dates from the reign of Henry VII, when
it is first perhaps possible to discern the outline of England's
future rôle in the world as a country exercising a predominant
influence in the British Isles, closely knit to the continent of
Europe, but also impelled by the spirit of commercial and maritime adventure to vast enterprises beyond the ocean.

BOOKS WHICH MAY BE CONSULTED

James Gairdner in Cambridge Modern History, Vol. I, chap. xiv.
Vickers : England in the Later Middle Ages. 1913.
Sir John Fortescue : Governance of England. *Ed.* C. Plummer. 1885.
Paston Letters. *Ed.* J. Gairdner. 4 vols. 1900-1.
J. A. Froude : Life and Letters of Erasmus. 1894.
P. S. Allen : The Age of Erasmus. 1914.
Erasmi Epistolæ. *Ed.* P. S. Allen. 1906-1938.
H. A. L. Fisher : History of England, 1509-47 (Longmans). 1910.
Francis Bacon : History of the Reign of King Henry VII. *Ed.* J. R.
    Lumby. 1876.
C. L. Kingsford : Prejudice and Promise in Fifteenth-Century England.
    1925.

CHAPTER VI

FRANCO-SPANISH RIVALRY IN ITALY

Charles VIII and Italy. The risk from Spain. Union of Aragon and Castile. Religious concentration and political expansion of Spain. The relations of Spain and Portugal. The treaty of Tordesillas. Spain linked by marriage with Flanders. Vast consequences for Europe and the world. The French invasions of Italy, 1494-1559. Alexander VI and the scandals of Rome. The new spirit of rationalism and Erasmus.

WE have now reached an episode in European history which proves how feeble are the affinities of religion, of race, and of culture, when weighed in the balance against the cupidity and war lust of mankind. Spain and France were, at the end of the fifteenth century, the leading Latin and Catholic countries of the West, allied in race, in religion, in their common possession of a Romance language and literature, and having reached a general standard of cultivation which, though sensibly below the Italian, was far higher than that prevailing in eastern Europe. Of this Latin and Christian civilization the Turk was declared the inveterate foe, and since he was master of the eastern Mediterranean, and threatened the shores of Italy and Spain, it might have been expected that the formation of a Latin League to oppose him would have been the dominating concern of western diplomacy. It was not so. Instead of combining against Islam, the Latin powers broke out into violent quarrels among themselves. Italy was the prize of victory and the scene of contention. It is one of the cruel ironies of history that this country, which had enjoyed a rare and almost unbroken spell of peaceful civilization, during which it had shown mankind new summits of artistic excellence, was now destined, for more than sixty years, to serve as the battlefield of French and Spanish armies.

For this the Italians were in part to blame, for the prime cause of the tragedy was Italian discord. The long peace, while effacing the memory of the savage realities of war, for the local struggles sustained by *condottieri* were almost bloodless, had brought the Italians no nearer to a common mind. Still as in the days of Dante, State plotted against State, and still there survived that pleasant Italian notion, proper to artistic studios, that battles might best be delegated to competing bands of mercenary troops. Whether the mercenary force was small or large, native or foreign, was hardly, in the low temperature of Italian patriotism, a matter of principle. Yet it was a grave thing for Italy and the seed of much future trouble when Ludovico Sforza, the powerful Regent of Milan, associated himself with the discontented subjects of Ferrante of Naples and appealed to Charles VIII of France to revive the old Angevin claim in the Neapolitan kingdom. Nothing could be said for Ferrante. He was a despicable and dangerous lout. But a French army, unlike the *condottiere*, would fight to kill, and since Ferrante was of the royal line of Aragon, though of a bastard branch, the fall of his house would not pass unnoted by the King of Spain.

At more than one juncture in her history the dangerous cry has gone up, "La France s'ennuie." It was so in 1494. The reign of Louis XI, so full of solid benefits, was not sufficiently spectacular to please an idle and adventurous nobility. A madcap rising, "La Guerre Folle," disturbed the wise regency of his daughter, Anne of Beaujeu, and warned her young brother Charles, the heir to the throne, that if he was to govern he must show the sport which a mettlesome aristocracy demanded of its king.

Of all adventures an Italian war was the most attractive. What could be more alluring to youthful ambition than the prospect of a cavalcade in glittering armour under the blue Italian sky, riding across a beautiful land which, by reason of its internal political divisions, seemed likely, failing the intervention of the chivalry of France, to fall a prey to the Turk or the Spaniard?

Expeditions of pleasure are never at a loss for a solemn excuse. The Turk had actually for a time flown his flag in Otranto. The Aragonese ruled in Naples, which had once been Angevin, while *1283-1442* the Emperor Maximilian, whose second wife was Bianca Sforza, was suspected of harbouring designs on the rich Duchy of Milan, which the princes of the house of Orleans had long regarded as their eventual prize.

Charles VIII of France, a young and licentious hunchback of doubtful sanity, was the master of the strongest artillery in Europe. Though every wise head in Paris was opposed to the Italian adventure, for the kingdom was ill-compacted, its finances uncertain, and the marine available for Mediterranean service of little account, the King yielded to the tempters, who flowed in upon him from Milan and Florence, from Rome and Calabria with their griefs, their aspirations and their bribes. He would descend on Italy, not merely as a conqueror, not merely as the claimant of his Neapolitan heritage, but with the star of freedom flaming on his banners. Italians suffering from oppression would flock to his camp and fill his treasury with ducats. He would restore a republic to Florence, drive the Aragonese from Naples, and then, perhaps, when a grateful Italy lay postrate at his feet, eject the Turk from Europe and place the Imperial Crown upon his victorious brow. His mounted gendarmerie, drawn from the nobility and gentry of France, his formidable body of halberdiers and pikemen from Switzerland and Germany, his Gascon cross-bow men, and the light, quick-firing artillery, which was the latest triumph of French mechanical ingenuity, would give Europe a sensation which it would not soon forget.

Diplomatic precautions were not neglected. Having through the good management of his sister, the Regent, espoused Anne, the heiress of Brittany (1491), he was secure against attack from the north-west. That he might cross the Alps with an easier mind he bought the acquiescence of Spain by the cession of Cerdagne and Roussillon (two provinces on the brink of the Pyrenees which had been pawned to Louis XI by John II of Aragon) and purchased quiet upon his eastern frontier by giving away Franche Comté to the Emperor. But despite these lavish concessions of territory, there was one eventuality against which Charles could not provide. Whatever treaties a Spanish king might sign, he would never tolerate the French in Naples. It was not merely a question of honour. The granaries of Sicily furnished a welcome supplement to the meagre harvests of Spain.

The risk of the Italian adventure, which was in any case great, for no populous and civilized country readily submits to the invasion of thirty thousand licentious foreign soldiers, was much increased by a momentous change which not long before had come over the political complexion of Spain. The maritime state of Aragon, whose sailors and merchants were known in every port of the Mediterranean, had been united with the kingdom of Castile by the marriage of Ferdinand and Isabella in 1469. A political union, founded on a marriage, cannot be expected to change the psychology of differing peoples. The inhabitants of

Catalonia, the richest and most important part of the kingdom of
Aragon, have never been assimilated with the Castilians, from
whom they are divided by speech and by all those profound
differences which distinguish landsmen from seafarers, merchants
from farmers, nobles from bourgeois, and a community stationed
on a great world thoroughfare from one mainly living in secluded
pride on a high inland plateau. But while Catalonia has always
chafed under the Castilian yoke, the marriage of Ferdinand of
Aragon with Isabella of Castile offered benefits of such a quality
that they have never been renounced. In virtue of that union
Spain became at once a great European power, strong by land
and sea, and rose to a position, which was maintained until the
close of the sixteenth century, of commanding pre-eminence in
the world.

The restless ambitions of Aragon, whose navies had won
kingdoms in the Balearic Islands, in Sicily, and in Naples, were
now to be supported by footmen drawn from the upland farms
and cities of Castile. The advantages which ensued from the
unity of Spain were inestimable. A mutinous and disorderly
people was reduced to some sense of discipline by the joint force
of a strong monarchy and a subservient church. By degrees the
spirit of a narrow and jealous localism was mitigated by a larger
outlook upon Spanish needs and world-wide opportunities. But
there was a reverse side to the medal. By inheriting the Italian
policies of Aragon, Spain was committed to a long series of
Italian wars, as deleterious to herself as they were mischievous to
Italy.

For Isabella, one of the narrowest and most influential women
in history, was a bigoted Catholic. The first exploit of the united
Spanish kingdom was the conquest of that little state of Granada,
which, under the enlightened rule of its Moslem sovereigns,
offered a spectacle of civilized luxury to be matched in no
other part of the Iberian peninsula, and in few even of the
most favoured regions of France and Italy. Whether the destruction of this Moorish polity was a blessing or a bane may be
variously debated; but it is at least reasonable to remember that
the Spanish Moslems, unlike the Ottoman Turks, were susceptible to the call of art, science, and philosophy, that their rule
was tolerant, their state weak and harmless, and that their expulsion from European territory, under the driving impulse of
Queen Isabella, was the first step in a steady course of religious

persecution which permanently impaired the strength and vitality of Spain.

Hateful as this policy may appear to a tolerant age, it aroused no antagonism among the Christian subjects of Ferdinand and Isabella. The doctrines of the Catholic Church were everywhere accepted. The principle that it was the duty of the Christian State to suppress heresy within its borders was nowhere denied. While local liberties were hotly defended, the sacred cause of intellectual freedom went by default.

A deep instinctive sense of political need helped to strengthen the forces of orthodoxy in a country whose foreign policy had for long worn the colours of a religious crusade. The union of Aragon and Castile had done so little to abate the inveterate localism of the Spanish provinces, the municipal and provincial privileges and institutions were still so jealously preserved and defended, that the assistance of the Church, as the one institution common to all Spain and held in universal veneration by its inhabitants, became of supreme importance to the government.

So successful were the sovereigns of Spain in securing the entire obedience of their clergy that no Protestant Church was ever brought into a more complete subjection to the temporal Prince than was the Catholic Church of Spain during the great epoch of the Spanish Empire. King and Church, Church and King constituted one indissoluble instrument for the propagation and defence of the orthodox Faith.

In sharp contrast to this austere religious concentration, which made Spanish rule everywhere synonymous with the persecution of differing beliefs, was a vast and sudden enlargement of the political and economic horizon of the country. France became an enemy, Italy a battle-ground, England an ally, the Holy Roman Empire and the Netherlands an annexe through marriage, the Atlantic Ocean a pathway to the Spanish dominions, illimitable and mysterious in the distant west. The harbours of Biscay and Santander, of Vigo and Ferrol, of Cadiz and Seville, woke to a new life with the expansion of oceanic enterprise. New adventures crowded in, new rivalries revealed themselves, new combinations were formed for attack and defence. Spanish diplomacy was compelled to work upon a large canvas. Nobody could say of Spanish politics, in the age which was now opening out, that they suffered from an undue concentration of purpose or an ignoble restriction of outlook. The danger rather was one of ex-

cessive distraction between ends as various as domestic reorganization and Italian conquest, the duel with France and the
colonization and settlement of the American continent.

Among the many policies of the Spanish monarchy a
developed naval imagination might have included the conquest
or incorporation of Portugal. This unneighbourly neighbour
was now leading the western world in marine enterprise. The
sailors of Portugal had tapped the wealth of Guinea, touched at
the Cape, were about to coast round Africa, and to open a new
way to opulence and empire in the Indies. The growing power
of the little state, its fine Atlantic seaboard, its noble harbourage
in the Tagus, might have tempted a keen rival in colonial enterprise to aggression. It might have been argued then, as it was
contended by a Portuguese writer in 1624 (when Portugal was in
fact united with Spain), that the true capital of the Iberian peninsula was Lisbon, its nerve centre the Atlantic seaboard, and the
first of its political objectives to destroy an enemy navy wherever
it might be found. Had such counsels prevailed at the close of
the fifteenth century, the beginnings of Atlantic exploration
might have been stained by a bitter civil war between the two
Christian powers of the Iberian peninsula.

Nothing of this occurred. Ferdinand and Isabella, who were
not greatly disturbed by sea-dreams, resolved to have Portugal
bound to them by ties of family alliance, strong enough to resist
the strain of colonial rivalry. So when Spain followed in the
wake of Portugal and claimed her share of the New World, conflict was precluded by the arbitration of the Pope. The award of
Alexander VI, under which all the lands and islands already
discovered or hereafter to be discovered "in the West, towards
the Indies or the Ocean Seas" were partitioned between Spain
and Portugal, has been assailed as a presumptuous infringement
of human liberty. It was one of those political arrangements
which, however useful as a temporary adjustment of the divergent interests, inevitably break down under the stress of facts.
Neither in France, nor in Holland, nor in England was this papal
arbitrament regarded as tolerable. What right, it was asked, had
a Pope, and least of all a Spanish Pope, to reserve the new world
for the Spaniards and Portuguese? And how could it serve the
Papacy that it should at this early date commit itself to the doctrine that India and America were for ever closed to the mariners
of the north? Yet an instrument, however imperfect, which

effects for a time a *modus vivendi* between rival states by defining their respective spheres of influence, cannot wholly be condemned. The five bulls of Alexander VI served a useful though momentary purpose. They became the basis of the Treaty of Tordesillas (June 7, 1494), by which everything east of a line drawn across the Atlantic at a point 370 miles west of the Cape Verde Islands was assigned to Portugal, while everything west of it was accorded to Spain. The line so drawn just enabled Portugal to claim Brazil.

It was the merest accident that Christopher Columbus made his famous discovering voyage under the Spanish flag. Portugal, England, and France had the offer of his cherished secret and burning ardour. A Spanish Commission sat upon his project for five years, and then rejected it, and it was only by the narrowest margin, and through the influence of a priest and a woman high in the Queen's favour, that this unfavourable verdict was finally reversed. Columbus was a brilliant sailor, raised to the point of greatness by the glowing resolution with which, despite rebuffs and difficulties, calculated to daunt men of average courage, he pursued his dream victoriously to the end. Crossing the Atlantic in three small caravels, he struck Watling Island, one of the Bahamas, on October 12, 1492, and named it San Salvador. He had sailed for five weeks over a lonely, unknown sea, stilling the mutinous misgivings of his crew by his unconquerable faith, until he had reached what until the end of his life he believed to be the eastern fringe of Asia. The discovery of the West Indies is his title of fame, the first voyage across the Atlantic his great contribution, for he had no gifts for the difficult problems of colonization or government on land, which embittered his later visits, and thought that nothing better could be done with the native Indians than to enslave them. To the commercial speculators who buzzed round the Court of Barcelona a few unintelligible slaves and a handful of gold seemed to be a poor reward for a sequence of expensive voyages, and a derisory substitute for the promised spices of the east. The great navigator was suspended from his command and sent back to Spain in chains, there to be confronted by the deep grudge of disappointed investors and the fiercer anger of returned colonists. In Spain, the country of his adoption, he died in 1506 a disgraced and humiliated man, but the discoverer of America and to be remembered till the end of time.

The discovery of the new world cannot rightly be regarded as originating in no higher purpose than the quest for spices and gold. Religious aspirations were blended with economic appetite. At the Vatican, and more particularly among the Franciscans, whose missionary enterprise was world-wide, the oceanic enterprises of Portugal and Spain aroused the strongest interest as likely to lead not only to the evangelization of heathen people, but also to an attack on the Moslems to be delivered from the east. It was known that the Negus of Abyssinia was a Christian, and it was believed that there still survived in India, as a result of the mission of St. Thomas, a Christian state ruled by a monarch known as the great Khan. From these distant oriental potentates it was fondly hoped that Catholic Europe would receive effective assistance in one last grand crusade against the infidel. Such was "the plan of the Indies" sketched out as early as 1454 by Nicholas V in a bull despatched to the King of Portugal. And it was in such an atmosphere of exalted expectation that Columbus himself set out to discover the Indies in the west.

Meanwhile the suction of remote events was drawing into one unnatural amalgamation three sharply distinguished States, Spain, the Netherlands, and the imperial federation of Germany. Two fateful marriages and five unexpected deaths changed the face of European politics. In 1477 Maximilian, son and heir of the Emperor Frederick III, married Mary, the heiress of Charles the Bold of Burgundy. Years passed. Mary died, Maximilian became Regent of the Netherlands, and then (1493), in succession to his father, Holy Roman Emperor. Philip, the son of his Burgundian marriage, a fine, handsome youth, grew to manhood, and, being heir to great wealth, was eagerly sought in wedlock. As early as 1491 there was talk of a union between the Flemish Archduke and Joanna, the third daughter of the King and Queen of Spain. The children were young, the negotiations leisurely, but in 1496 the match was made. Joanna of Spain became the wife of Philip of Flanders. Who could then have foreseen the violently contrasted fates of the happy couple, or the far-reaching consequences of their marriage, the early death of the handsome Philip, the madness of his wife, the long list of tragic funerals which brought her most unexpectedly to the throne of Spain, or the vast perspective of power and pride which opened out before her little child, heir to the government

of Spain and the Netherlands, and destined to follow in the foot-
steps of Maximilian, his grandfather, as the wearer of the Imperial Crown? While events were thus preparing for the empire
of Charles V, the main preoccupations of Spanish statecraft were
naturally with the old world rather than with the new.

The contemporaries of Charles VIII can hardly be blamed for
thinking that Italy, so far gone in political decomposition, and
yet so famous, opulent, and cultured, was a prize much to be
preferred to the freshly discovered islands on the other side of
the Atlantic, of which bronzed seamen were talking on the
quays of Barcelona and Lisbon. If a field for conquest was necessary, here was the field in which the harvest could most swiftly
be reaped. Yet it is deplorable that despite the needs of their
own subjects and the call of the new world, the rulers of France
and Spain should for a period of sixty years have wasted their
strength in a struggle for predominance in Italy, to their own
grave mutual injury, and to the abasement of a cultured and
relatively peaceful country, which was forced to become the
theatre of a savage war.

It has been urged in extenuation that but for the French and
Spanish armies Italy would have been conquered by the Turks.
It might as well be argued that these purposeless wars are justi-
fied by the heroism of Bayard or by the brilliant verse of Ariosto's
Orlando Furioso. Such shadowy conjectures may afford consola-
tion, but do not constitute a defence.

1494   Like all subsequent French invasions of Italy, the Italian enterprise of Charles VIII is the story of an early triumph followed
by a sudden and complete reverse. At first fortune smiled on the
glittering army with its mediaeval accoutrements and imposing
train of artillery. Ludovico Sforza, the ruler of Milan, who had
himself invited the expedition, was not the man to obstruct its
progress. Savonarola, the Dominican, one of those great Puritan
preachers who from time to time arise in the Latin and Catholic
south, welcomed the French as liberators to Florence, his adopted
city. Rome opened her gates. Without a blow struck Charles
was master of the Neapolitan kingdom. But then, when the
main objective of the campaign had been reached, the real difficulties disclosed themselves. The invading army, which was
partly German and Swiss, was not, as Savonarola's vision had
painted it, a flight of purifying angels commissioned to put an

end to luxury and lust and the abuses of the Papal Church, but was as ill-behaved, as licentious, and as brutal (though with some shining exceptions) as French and German levies of this period were wont to be. As the army passed southwards it left behind it a trail of burning indignation. An Italian league was swiftly formed to eject the invaders and bar their retreat. On the field of Fornovo Charles cut his way through the enemy, and with this victory to his credit, but with the loss of every yard of Italian soil, regained his native land. *1495*

Partly because of Fornovo, but still more because the French army lived on the enemy country and returned home laden with booty, the idea of an Italian war retained its lustre in France. When Charles died (1498), Louis XII, his cousin and successor, was drawn southwards by the same flattering mirage of Italian glory. The old story repeated itself. Facile successes were followed by grave complications, by defeats in Italy, at last even by the invasion of France. Milan was conquered and lost, Naples was shared with Spain and then lost, Venice was driven from her mainland possessions by a league of France, Papacy and Empire, and then restored by a papal confederation against France. In the unstable atmosphere of Italian diplomacy the friend of today became the enemy of tomorrow. Julius II, the warrior Pope, who assisted France against Venice, was soon afterwards the contriver of the Holy League to expel the French from Italy. Louis could count on no firm Italian friendships. His armies were beaten at Novara (1513), and, stripped of all his Italian conquests, he returned to France to deal with the English who had captured Tournai, and with the Burgundians who were besieging Dijon. Such were the final humiliations inflicted upon "the father of his country" by the lure of Italy. Milan, Naples, Venetia, were won and lost, and the soil of France invaded at two points. Still the lesson went unheeded. Francis I, the nephew of Louis XII, young, artistic, high-spirited, and self-indulgent, was not the man to forget that his uncle had been turned out of Milan by an army of base-born Swiss peasants. He crossed the Alps, confronted the Swiss mercenaries who guarded Milan, and by the brilliant victory at Marignano (1515) secured Lombardy once more for France, on a fleeting tenure. *1498-1513*

1515-47

Meanwhile conditions were becoming steadily more adverse to the prospects of an enduring French success in Italy. Spain was the rival, with an advantage at sea, with a stronger corps of

infantry, with the wealth of the new world beginning to find
1479-1516 its way into her coffers. Under Ferdinand the Catholic Spain
was strong enough to eject the French from Naples. Under
1479-1516 Charles, Ferdinand's Flemish grandson, the power of Spain was
made yet more redoubtable by the tribute of the Netherlands
and (after 1519) by the man power of the Empire. As time proceeded the opposition to France gathered force and was recruited
from every quarter. In the course of a generation the Pope,
Milan, Venice, the Swiss, Spain, Flanders, the Empire, drew the
sword to prevent a French hegemony in Italy. Yet Francis I
persevered in his Italian designs, and though he was defeated
and taken at Pavia in 1525, his countrymen did not desist from
their forlorn enterprise, or surrender their Italian claims until
Henry II signed the Treaty of Cateau Cambrésis in 1559. It was
a Spanish victory. The far-off result of Charles VIII's light-
hearted cavalcade was the deliverance of Lombardy and Naples
to the strict and solemn rule of the orthodox Spaniard, the
eclipse of the Italian Renaissance, and the obscuration under a
cloud of Spanish and clerical tyranny of that free play of the
Italian imagination, which is capable of spells of incomparable
brilliance, but equally of a cynical and patient acceptance of the
discipline of tyranny and defeat.

Italy had long exercised, if only through Rome, an influence
on northern Europe. In the fifteenth century scholars from
England, Germany, and France visited the country, studied in
its universities, and came back with cargoes of medical and
classical knowledge. Even if Charles VIII had never crossed the
Alps, the Italian Renaissance would in due course of time have
affected the life currents of northern peoples. But the wheels of
history run rapidly in war. Processes which otherwise might be
slow and gradual then become swift and vehement. Every campaign is a voyage of discovery, every diplomatic interchange a
revelation of foreign human nature. It was so with these Italian
wars. They accelerated, if they did not occasion, the spread of
the Italian Renaissance among the peoples of the north.

Among the figures on the Italian stage revealed to the general
eye of Europe as the curtain went up in 1494 was that of Rodrigo
1492-1503 Borgia, a wealthy Spaniard, who two years earlier had bribed
the Sacred College to make him Pope, and had assumed the name
of Alexander VI. Apologists can be found for anything. The

indulgent eye of modern criticism has withdrawn the gravest charges which were levelled against this Pontiff by his contemporaries. It is content to leave only as established sensuality and simony, worldliness, perfidy, and secret poisoning. There are periods in the life of any institution in which a rough bestial nature may have its uses. The stalwart Spaniard was not rougher, more licentious, or more cruel than the fierce families of Rome and central Italy with whom it was his business to cope. If he was a murderer and conspirator, he lived in an atmosphere of murder and conspiracy. A submissive papal state in central Italy, such as it was Alexander's object to create, could not be made by soft words and spiritual exercises, but by force and treachery, administration and finance. Here Alexander was in his element, working in part for the Holy See, but more obviously for the advancement of the Borgia family. How Cesare Borgia, the Pope's brilliant son, endeavoured to aid his father in the Romagna, and what resources of force and fraud he employed to this end, is recorded in *The Prince* of Machiavelli, who saw, as we have already noted, in the career of this unscrupulous adventurer the model of the new statecraft, unweakened by pity and uninfluenced by ethics or religious faith.

The spectacle of depravity presented by the Rome of the Borgias was deeply disturbing to spiritual natures. "The scandal," wrote Savonarola, "begins in Rome and runs through the whole clergy; they are worse than Turks and Moors. In Rome you will find that they have one and all obtained their benefices by simony. They buy preferments and bestow them on their children or brothers, who take possession of them by violence and all sorts of sinful means. Their greed is insatiable, they do all things for gold. They only ring their bells for coin and candles; only attend Vespers and Choir and Office when something is to be got by it. They sell their benefices, sell the sacraments, traffic in masses. . . . If a priest or a canon leads an ordinary life he is mocked and called a hypocrite. It has come to pass that all are warned against Rome, and people say, 'If you want to ruin your son make him a priest.'" In such language as this there may be some exaggeration, but in essentials the indictment was true. Though there was much genuine religious life in Catholic Europe at the end of the fifteenth and beginning of the sixteenth century, and though a genuine effort was made by good and able men, such as Hegius at Deventer in the Netherlands, or Nicholas of Cusa in Germany, or Dean Colet in England, to improve education and knowledge and to reform the abuses of the Church, Rome had definitely lost the moral leadership of Europe. No court had a worse reputation for avarice, corruption, and vice. In 1499 the probability that Germany and Spain would renounce their allegiance was freely discussed.

The spiritual declension of Rome was the more important by reason of the new spirit of rationalism which was springing up in northern Europe. Of this spirit, so far as it did not transcend the limits of Catholic orthodoxy, the herald and prophet was *1467-1536* Erasmus of Rotterdam. Few men have exercised a wider or more salutary influence upon his generation than this delicate, impecunious little Dutch scholar, who after a passionate course of self-education in the Netherlands and England, in France and in Italy, became to a degree unequalled until the days of Voltaire the acknowledged chief of European enlightenment. Erasmus, like every lettered man of his age, was influenced by the classics of Greece and Rome, which it was the glory of Italy to have recovered. Yet, differing from many Italian scholars, he was neither pagan, nor aesthete, nor metaphysician, but a plain, orthodox Christian, somewhat poor on the side of imagination, since Terence was his favourite poet, but abounding in those gifts of clarity and grace, good sense, moderation, and wit which were best calculated to commend his message to the world. For he was a man with a message, a prophet as well as a savant. His enemies were pedantry and superstition, ignorance and stupidity, violence and vice. Against these evils his long course of incessant literary activity offered a continuous and brilliant protest. Though he visited universities, and even for a time (1500-1513) held a Chair of Divinity at Cambridge, he was no college pedant, but a citizen of the world, interested in conduct above all things, and quite as much concerned with popularizing knowledge as with extending it. In particular he wished to see the Scriptures translated into every language. "I long," he writes, " that the husbandman should say them to himself as he follows the plough, that the weaver should hum them to the tune of his shuttle, that the traveller should beguile with them the weariness of his journey." Even his more technical works, such as his editions of the Greek Testament and of the early Fathers, illustrate his concern for the needs of the general reader. He resolved to get behind the Latin Vulgate to its Greek original, to turn from the subtle disputations of the scholastic theologians to the teaching of the Early Fathers, where he was disposed to find the spirit of the early Church pure and undefiled. That the true and primitive Christianity had been obscured by the intellectual detritus of succeeding ages and might be recovered by a great feat of careful and imaginative scholarship was the core of his grammarian's faith.

Apart from the new and fruitful direction which he gave to biblical studies, Erasmus stood out as the prophet of a humane, tolerant, and enlightened Catholicism. He did not scruple to pour scorn on the ignorant, idle, and vicious monks, on the superstitious worship of relics, on the evils connected with pilgrimages and the sale of indulgences, and on other notorious abuses of the Church; and his raillery, conveyed in vivid popular Latin, went the round of the republic of letters. Yet his critical spirit was never sharpened to the point of heresy or revolt. In the *Enchiridion Militis Christiani* he expounded the eternal gospel of that *1501* inner religion of the heart, which dispenses with the support of outward observance and ceremonials, and finds its nourishment in meditation on the holy texts. It is clear that he was not interested in the subtleties of theological doctrine.

The popularity of his writings was immense and unprecedented. His *Colloquies*, his *Praise of Folly*, his *Adagia*, were the earliest "best-sellers" in secular printed literature. The gift for persiflage was never more effectively employed. The priestly caste, once so formidable and dominant, was held up by this light and engaging satirist as an object of amusement and contempt. The wickedness of war, the ineptitude of the old educational methods, the prevailing hollowness of religious life, were denounced with an earnestness which was all the more impressive by its immunity from any suspicion of the ponderous, the fanatical, or the insincere. For a time he marched abreast with Luther. Then the two men diverged. Luther broke away from Rome. Erasmus believed that the Roman Church could be reformed from within. The violent and intolerant spirit of the Protestant Reformation was abhorrent to the humane and pacific temper of the Dutch scholar. While Germany was convulsed with religious strife, Erasmus from his quiet retreat at Basel (1514-35) was attempting through an elaborate series of editions and translations from the Fathers to revive for the direction of the Roman Church the thought and spirit of early Christianity.

The importance of Erasmus for the history of Europe consists in the fact that, in the age of the Reformation, he embodied, with a surpassing attractiveness and brilliance, that tradition of Christian and classical culture which was and remains the common possession of all Europe. In any list of good Europeans the name of Erasmus would rank high. He had the idea of a Europe organized for rational ends, true to its past, but purified of its abuses, and bound together in a perpetual bond of peace and fellowship. Such an inspiration is still cherished by the small band of humanists who in every country endeavour to sweeten the bitter waters of political life.

BOOKS WHICH MAY BE CONSULTED

J. S. C. Bridge : A History of France from the Death of Louis XI. 1921

H. Lemonnier in Lavisse : Histoire de France, Vol. V.

R. B. Merriman : The Rise of the Spanish Empire. 1918-25.

J. Fiske : The Discovery of America. 1892.

C. R. Markham : Life of Christopher Columbus. 1892.

E. J. Payne : History of the New World called America. 1892-9.

CHAPTER VII

THE TURKISH PERIL

Selim I and Suleyman the Magnificent. The capture of Rhodes. George Podiebrad and Matthias Corvinus. The field of Mohacs. Consequences for Austria.

FOR Mohammed the Conqueror the fall of Constantinople was not an end but a beginning. This able and ambitious ruler regarded himself as commissioned to conquer the world for Islam, just as Lenin, long afterwards, and by other and less warlike processes, aspired to convert mankind to the Communist faith. An obedient people trained to every hardship but that of independent thought, a skilled professional army, and a fine train of artillery gave Mohammed a commanding advantage against divided opponents. The roar of the Turkish guns was heard on the Euphrates, on the Danube, and on the Albanian coast. When the Sultan died in 1481, Asia Minor, Greece, and the main part of the Balkan peninsula had been subjected to his yoke, and the Turk was astride the Adriatic, holding the Ionian islands, Scutari, and Otranto, and menacing the security of Italy and Rome.

After the brief rule of the nerveless Bayazet the course of Turkish conquest was renewed by two of the most remarkable figures of the Ottoman house. Selim I, who dethroned his father Bayazet in 1512, is, next to Mohammed his grandfather, the principal architect of that wide Turkish Empire which endured the strain and stress of many centuries and was broken only by the tremendous shock of the last great war. It was Selim who conquered Syria, Egypt, and Arabia, and upon the resignation of the last Kaliph of the Abbassid line brought the Kaliphate into the Ottoman house. To him were solemnly tendered the keys of the Kaaba at Mecca, a symbol of supremacy over the Moslem world. From the days of Selim Stambul became the undisputed centre of Islamic power in three continents. Bagdad, which was the capital of the Abbassids and the principal scene of a civilization far beyond the reach of the Turkish mind, now sank to the position of a distant provincial city.

Three great victories specially distinguish the military record of Selim's strenuous successor, Suleyman the Magnificent: the capture of Belgrade from the Hungarians, the forced capitulation of the Knights Hospitallers in Rhodes, and the bloodstained field of Mohacs (1526), which sealed the doom of Hungary as an independent kingdom. Belgrade was the gateway into Hungary Rhodes the half-way house between Constantinople and Egypt and Hungary the last effective barrier between the Turks and the Austrians.

The effect of these triumphs was the more impressive by reason of the high military reputation of the Magyar nation, and the confidence which was generally reposed in the skill and valour of the Christian garrison in Rhodes. Under John Hunyades and his son, Mathias Corvinus (1458), the frontiers of the Hungarian kingdom had been triumphantly defended and the Turks more than once compelled to accept defeat. The reputation of the Knights Hospitallers of Rhodes was of a different order, for while the Magyars had only recently won their way into the fore-front of European history as the main defenders of the Christian cause on land, the Knights of Rhodes had ever since the Crusades been the easternmost spearpoint of Christendom against Asia and Islam. Rhodes was a small island. The Hospitallers in number and equipment were far inferior to their assailants. But they had survived so long that it was natural to think that they would survive for ever. That they were permitted to go down before the Turks, with the passive acquiescence of Genoa and to the unconcealed satisfaction of Venice, was a sharp advertisement to the west that the Turkish navy was mistress of the Aegean, and that the two great Italian cities which had conveyed the Crusaders to Palestine had now turned round and joined the enemy.

The collapse of Hungary was equally spectacular and for the history of Europe far more momentous. It has been one of the standing misfortunes of Europe that the Poles, the Czechs, and the Magyars have never been able to devise any durable form of political co-operation. An incompatibility of temper based upon differences of language, race, and religion has always proved stronger than the compulsion of political convenience or necessity. From Bohemia, the richest and most civilized of these three monarchies, Poland was estranged by religion, Hungary by religion, race, and language alike; and since the nobles of Poland Bohemia, and Hungary knew how to extract a full measure of

selfish indulgence from a weak and elective kingship, it followed
that at the very time when the princes of the west were consolidating their power, the states on the eastern border were under-
going the opposite process of feudal dissolution.

The last act of Bohemian and Hungarian independence was
marked by one of those rare opportunities which, once missed,
never return. In the spring of 1458 two remarkable men were
elected to the thrones of Bohemia and Hungary. George Podie- *1458-71*
brad was a Czech noble who had won the confidence of the
Bohemian nation by his successful defence of the Hussite faith
against a strong Catholic and Germanizing minority. His firmness, his moderation, his willingness to treat religion as a question
upon which the State might tolerate differing opinions, as well
as his success in putting down rebellion, gave him a position of
national authority such as no Bohemian ruler had enjoyed since
the days of Charles IV and no Bohemian ruler was destined to
enjoy again till the days of Mazaryk. The youth who almost
simultaneously mounted the Hungarian throne enjoyed a comparable advantage. Like Podiebrad, Matthias Corvinus was of *1459-90*
national stock. He was the son of that illustrious soldier John
Hunyades, who had driven the Turks from before the walls of
Belgrade, and he inherited much of his father's vigour and
activity. To the qualities of a soldier he added a perception of
the arts of peace. The conqueror of Vienna was also the founder
of Pressburg University, and the first to introduce among the
backward nobles of Hungary many of the accomplishments and
arts of Italy. A close alliance between two men, each in his ways
so remarkable, and each in his own country so popular as
Matthias Corvinus and George Podiebrad, would have been of
the greatest value. The conjunction of Hungary and Bohemia
under such rulers might have imposed a final limit upon the incursions of the Turk and averted from the two Christian monarchies of south-eastern Europe the destiny which was awaiting
them of absorption in the Austrian Empire. But the two men,
though united by marriage, drifted into a fatal antagonism
which proved to be ruinous to both kingdoms. Bohemia was
attacked by Hungary, and Hungary in its turn, unfriended and
alone, was allowed to go down before the Turk. The cause of the
sudden downfall of two kingdoms apparently on the high road
to stability and power was religion. George of Bohemia stood by
the Compacts of the Council of Basel, which accorded to the

Hussite Church in Bohemia the use of the cup by the laity in the sacrament. But to the papal Curia, which had never accepted the Compacts, the policy of the Hussite chief was impermissible.

1466

Podiebrad was excommunicated. It was determined in Rome to depose the heretic and to replace him by the Catholic Matthias. The Hungarian king yielded to temptation and joined forces

1468

with the Catholic malcontents of Bohemia. In the terrible civil war which ensued the Bohemian patriot held his own, but in self-defence was compelled to name as his successor a Catholic prince from the Polish royal family. In 1471, on the death of Podiebrad, Vladislav Jagellon succeeded to his throne.

The advent to power of this insufficient Polish alien who was in turn called to govern Bohemia and Hungary was a signal in each country for an outburst of aristocratic pretensions. Among the turbulent landowners of the eastern kingdoms the Pole was as helpless as a French master in a class of rebellious English schoolboys. He had neither army nor treasury, could do nothing without the Diet, and was expressly debarred from introducing any novelties into Hungary. Against the serried discipline of a Turkish army the feudal levies of such a monarchy were bound to fail.

The issue was tried upon the field of Mohacs (1526), a battle big with consequences for Europe, for after the Hungarian army had been defeated and Louis the last Jagellon king was killed, and the whole country up to the gates of Vienna had been overrun by the Turks, there was no life left in the proud Magyar aristocracy. The greater part of Hungary was seized and held by the Turks until late in the seventeenth century; the remainder fell to Ferdinand of Austria, the brother-in-law of Louis and the heir to his pretensions. The long subjection of Bohemia and Hungary to the Habsburg house, lasting until the Treaty of St. Germain after the recent war, was the direct result of that fatal day. Not until the Italian victory of Vittorio Veneto (1918) had sent the Austrian Empire toppling to the ground were the effects of the field of Mohacs finally undone.

For indeed there was born upon the field of Mohacs a new spell of life for the Holy Roman Empire and for the Habsburg house. The defence of Christian Europe against the Turks, which might otherwise have been conducted by the Hungarian nation, now devolved of necessity upon the Archdukes of Austria. Their "ramshackle Empire," built up by a succession of happy marriages, received a justification in the eyes of Christian Europe by reason of the fact that through the eclipse of Hungary it had become the necessary and only valid bulwark against a great and aggressive Moslem Empire. That it reposed on a multi-national basis was no matter of reproach in the sixteenth and seventeenth centuries. But as the Empire of the Habsburgs was made by the Turkish peril, so at each stage in the decline of Ottoman power it lost something of its original prestige and authority. In the end Turk and Austrian succumbed to the same enemy. The spirit of nationality born of the French Revolution first set aflame the Christian nations of the Balkans and then, spreading among the Croatians, the Czechs and the Poles, involved the Austrian Empire in ruin.

BOOKS WHICH MAY BE CONSULTED

Cambridge Modern History, Vol. I, chap. iii; Vol. III; chap. ix.

J. Von Hammer-Purgstall: Histoire de l'Empire Ottoman. Traduit de l'allemand par M. Dochez. 3 vols. 1840-2.

S. Lane Poole: Turkey. 1908.

L. von Ranke: The Ottoman and Spanish Empires in the Sixteenth and Seventeenth Centuries. *Tr.* W. K. Kelly. 1843.

F. Downey: The Grande Turke Suleyman the Magnificent. 1929.

La. Jonquière: Histoire de l'Empire Ottoman. 1881.

G. E. Hubbard: The Day of the Crescent. 1920.

G. Finlay: History of Greece. *Ed.* H. F. Tozer. 7 vols. 1877.

G. G. Macartney: Hungary (Nations of the Modern World). 1934.

Sir P. Rycaut: The Present State of the Ottoman Empire. 1668.

F. Palacky: Geschichte von Böhmen. 1844-67.

E. Denis: Fin de l'Independence Boheme. 2 vols. 1890.

H. F. Brown: Venice: A Historical Sketch of the Republic. 1893.

Zinkeisen: Geschichte des Osmanischen Reiches. 1840-63.

CHAPTER VIII

THE GERMAN REFORMATION

Causes of the Reformation. The new learning. The attractions of Protestantism. Literary power of Protestant leaders. Martin Luther. Indulgences. The ninety-five theses. The breach with Rome. Charles V and the Edict of Worms. Luther's auxiliaries. His partial success. He denounces the peasants. Zwingli and Luther. Lutheran successes in Scandinavia and Prussia. The rift beyond repair by 1541.

THE Protestant Reformation was a revolt against papal theocracy, clerical privilege, and the hereditary paganism of the Mediterranean races. On the one side it took the aspect of an insurgence of the lay spirit against clerical claims and immunities, on the other of a religious revival and an attempt to retrieve the original ways of the Christian Church. It occurred when it did partly because the abuses connected with the papal government and the Church were then felt to be specially grave and partly because the desire for a simpler and more spiritual form of Christianity, which at that time possessed many ardent minds, coincided with the appetites of secular princes, who, finding their traditional revenues inadequate for the growing needs of the state, cast covetous eyes on the wealth of the Church. It corresponded with the rising tide of nationalism, and was quickened by the conversion of the Papacy into an Italian state. A great movement of intellectual emancipation preceded its advent and accompanied its course. Thousands of separate little rills of doubt, criticism, and protest which had been gathering volume for a generation suddenly flowed together into a brawling river of revolt. The public mind recoiled from the discipline of the past. Old limitations upon thought and learning fell away. Reuchlin in Germany went back to Hebrew, Valla in Italy and Budé in France to the real Latin and Greek of antiquity. A spirit of brilliant forward-reaching enlightenment came into Europe, challenging traditional knowledge and shaming old abuses or superstitions by its scorn and mockery. Of the soldiers of light no country had a monopoly. Machiavelli and Valla were Italians, Von Hutten was German, Zwingli Swiss, Rabelais French, More English, Erasmus Dutch. Of these some were sceptics; others remained faithful to the Roman Church; others when the rift came went into revolt.

The enlightenment of the sixteenth century, though quite distinct from the Protestant movement, was one of the causes which helped it to succeed. The new learning weakened the traditional sentiment of reverence by which many of the beliefs, traditions, and customs of the Roman Church had long been supported. The layman could now read for himself. He could learn Greek and even Hebrew, getting behind the official Latin of the Roman priest to the original languages of Holy Writ. The Vulgate was no longer sacrosanct. There were texts older than the Vulgate, more sacred, at once unknown to the main part of the Latin priesthood, and accessible to the scholar who cared to learn. The thought inevitably sprang up that the virtuous layman could reach his God without the intermediacy of a priest. The movement appealed at once to that which was most lax and that which was most rigorous in the moral temper of Europe. There were those who, like the Anabaptists of Münster, threw off all the moral restraints of the old order. At the opposite extreme was that indwelling spirit of Christian stoicism which animated Calvin's polity at Geneva and Oliver Cromwell's New Model army, and out of which was fashioned the austere, money-making civilization of the New England colonies and their daughter states.

Against the aesthetic beauty of the Roman Church and the Roman ritual the reformers could offer two great popular attractions. The first was the delight of congregational singing, the second the interest of a service conducted in a language intelligible to the unlearned. Nor was there in this attempt to reach the common man any necessary vulgarity. Music often touched a high, language a sublime, level. Luther's Bible, Tyndale's Bible, and Cranmer's Prayer-book, Calvin's French version of his own *Christianae religionis institutio* are in their respective languages masterpieces of prose writing. Of Luther it may be said that a passion for music and prodigal gifts as a writer were almost as important a part of his equipment as deep learning and spiritual force. He counts as one of the makers of the German language, rich, copious, animated, but inferior in refinement to Tyndale and Cranmer. It is a fact of great importance for the history of the Protestant Reformation that among its earliest professors were certain writers of temperament and genius, whose words have still power to stir the heart. Few passages in our English Bible are more familiar than the wonderful thirteenth chapter of the first Epistle to the Corinthians. In substance the translation is the work of William Tyndale, who was burned as a heretic in 1537. The leaden literature of the Lollards and the Hussites may be searched in vain for so great an artist.

1483-1546   Martin Luther, the Saxon peasant to whom the German Reformation owes its origin and character, was one of those men who achieve a commanding position in the world not because they are original, but because they are representative. Luther was not a profound theologian; nor was he a philosopher. He did not believe in free enquiry or toleration, and so far from acknowledging the possibility of development in religious thought, held firmly to the belief that all truth as to the ultimate problems of life and mind was to be found in Holy Writ. It is not therefore from Luther, a savage anti-Semite, that the liberal and rationalizing movements of European thought derive their origin. Though he promoted a rebellion, he was not a revolutionary, but a self-experiencing religious genius who in his search for personal salvation was led by degrees to take up an attitude which made him the champion of the German nation against the claims of the Roman Church.

A great part of his power lay in the fact that he was German to the marrow. All the strength, all the weakness of the German character was reflected and magnified in his passionate temperament, its tenderness and violence, its coarseness in vituperation and old-fashioned Biblical piety, its music and learning, its conviviality and asceticism, its homely common sense and morbid self-scrutiny, its paroxysms of contrition and heady self-confidence. Not since Barbarossa had there been a German so typical of his age and race as this emaciated but very typical Saxon friar, with his rough combatant ways, his clear ringing voice, and unending command of words, jests, images, and arguments.

Let it not, however, be imagined that the German people, among whom Luther was brought up, were prepared for a Protestant theology or an heretical church. Had Luther in the first instance come forward with any such proposals he would have been the mark of almost universal animosity: but he did nothing of the kind. He denounced the sale of indulgences. The source of his extraordinary influence was due to the fact that he, an Augustinian monk, launched an attack upon those practical abuses of the Roman Church which every right-minded German, however much attached he might be to the Roman connection, regarded as morally and theologically indefensible. In so doing Luther spoke not only the mind of Germany but the better mind of the Church itself.

The idea that the Pope could issue indulgences for the remission of sins of every kind was rooted in the theory that there had been accorded to St. Peter and his successors the privilege of dispensing to the faithful an inexhaustible treasury of merit. Originally due to the sacrifices of Christ, the treasury of the Church was continually augmented by the merits of successive generations of believing Christians. The conception of merit, not as something ephemeral and personal, but as a store of spiritual wealth which could be accumulated for the benefit of the living and the dead, appealed alike to the religious imagination of the pious and to the pecuniary needs of the Popes. What could be more convenient to an embarrassed exchequer than the possession of a fund filled without effort, maintained without anxiety, and always capable of being employed to pecuniary advantage? As the financial attraction of the spiritual treasury disclosed itself, the moral judgments which had originally accompanied its administration were thrown to the winds. Confession and repentance were no longer insisted on. From Pope Julius II a plenary indulgence could be earned merely by a contribution to the rebuilding of St. Peter's. Pope Leo X went further still. To all who set out upon a crusade against the Turks he promised the everlasting bliss of heaven. *Claudo tibi portas inferni et januas aperio Paradisi.* Usurping the prerogatives assumed only to belong to the Almighty, the banker Pope (for Leo was a Medici) claimed not only to remit the temporal penalties for sin but even to expunge the sin itself.

The scandal worked to a climax in a great money-raising campaign for the new St. Peter's which was conducted, so far as the provinces of Mainz and Magdeburg were concerned, by the Dominican preacher John Tetzel.

"It is incredible," wrote a contemporary, "what this ignorant and impudent friar gave out. He said that if they contributed readily and bought grace and indulgence, all the hills of St. Annaburg would become pure massive silver, that so soon as the coin rang in the chest, the soul for whom the money was paid would go straightway to heaven." It was such effrontery which

provoked Luther to post upon the door of the castle church of
Wittenberg (October 31, 1517) those ninety-five theses which,
being swiftly circulated by a friendly·press, lit the fires of the
German Reformation.

By this time Luther had reached the fundamental convictions
which inspired his course of future action. Prayer, fasting,
scourgings had brought him no peace nor lightened by one
featherweight his agonizing burden of imputed sin. On the one
hand he saw the abject wickedness of man, on the other the
dazzling and unapproachable goodness of God. Where could he
find a bridge across the dark chasm? By degrees, first on a visit
to Rome, whose patent corruptions caused him to recoil, later at
Erfurt, through the teaching of Staupitz, he received a vision of
hope. Faith was the bridge. Man if he had faith could be saved,
despite his inherent and desperate wickedness. Works were of no
avail. Pilgrimages and ceremonies, the telling of beads, the lighting of candles, the worship of relics, were only obstructions on
the pathway to salvation. Faith, the condition of Grace, Grace,
the reward of Faith were all that mattered in the dark history of
predestined man. It was a graft from the tree of his master
St. Augustine, once unperceived, but, now that it was recovered,
ever afterwards held with fanatical tenacity.

Once embarked upon the ship of grace, Luther drifted far
and fast into tumultuous waters. If works were of no avail, of
what value was the monk's vow or the priest's unction? By 1520
he had come to the conclusion that every baptized Christian
was a priest, that Rome was Babylon, that the Pope was Antichrist, that priests should be allowed to marry, and that divorce
was lawful. In three famous treatises, the first an appeal in
German directed to the laity and urging them to take in hand
the reformation of the Church (To the Christian Nobility of the
German Nation respecting the Reformation of the Christian
Estate), the second a Latin treatise addressed to the theologians
(*De Captivitate Babylonica Ecclesiae Praeludium*), and the third
a curious letter "concerning Christian Liberty," directed to
Leo X, professedly as an eirenicon, Luther completed and made
irreparable his breach with Rome. "For your see," he observed
to the Pope, "which is called the Roman Curia, which neither
you nor any man can deny to be more corrupt than Babylon
and Sodom, I have indeed shown my detestation, and have been
indignant that the Christian people should be deluded under

your name and under cover of the Roman Church; and so I have resisted and will continue to resist so long as the spirit of faith lives in me." An Italian humanist may be excused for failing to discover any note of conciliation in such an utterance. Leo issued a bull excommunicating the rebel, and the rebel replied (December 10, 1520) by publicly burning the bull.

Meanwhile a grave Flemish lad of nineteen, having been chosen Emperor after a vast expenditure of money and intrigue, addressed himself to the novel and troublesome problem of dealing with a heretic who was also a national hero. Napoleon long afterwards charged Charles V with missing one of the great opportunities of history by refusing Luther's invitation that he should put himself at the head of the reforming movement in Germany. But how was it possible for Charles, a Habsburg, a Holy Roman Emperor, and a king of orthodox and Catholic Spain, to lead a national German rebellion against the papal see? The traditions of his house and of the imperial office, his own creed and upbringing, the conservative bent of his mind, the prevailing sentiments of his Flemish and Spanish subjects, made such a course impossible. Of necessity Charles was brought to view himself as the personal champion of the Papacy and as a shield and buckler of the established order.

So, amid a great commotion of the public mind and with a strong current of popular feeling running against the papal court, Luther was summoned to Worms to attend upon the *1521* young Emperor and his first Diet. He was charged to retract his writings. With a pride which must have been fortified by the sense of outside support he replied that, since Popes and Councils had often erred and contradicted themselves, he would withdraw nothing unless it were disproved by Scripture or evident reason. He lost nothing by his steadfast bearing. Though the Pope and Emperor entered into a league (May 8, 1521) to seize his person and to stamp out his opinions, he remained for a few more years the favourite of a great part of the German people, and more particularly of the middle class who plied their industries in the towns. The Edict of Worms, which made of him an outlaw, was, from the first, a dead letter.

Political conditions favoured the reformers. The Emperor, distracted between a thousand claims and drawn away from Germany in part by the war with France and by the necessity of suppressing the serious revolt of the Spanish Comuneros, was never in a position to apply the steady adverse pressure by which alone a middle class movement which had captured the printers could be brought into subjection. His brother, Ferdinand of Austria, having the Turks upon his hands, was in no better position to deal with the German heresy; and as for the French, for whom Charles was the most formidable of rivals and enemies, the Lutherans appeared to this orthodox but very political nation to be deserving of every encouragement as a standing source of annoyance to the imperial government.

One prophet does not make a church. Lutheranism owes much to a statesman, a scholar, and a university. Frederick the Wise, Elector of Saxony, was one of those men who, without being either powerful or in any way brilliant, influence history from the respect which they inspire, and by the opportune exercise of a kindly and paternal moderation. A mild, prudent, peace-loving ruler, proud of his chapel choir, his pictures and his castles, and of the University of Wittenberg of which he was the founder, and much occupied with pious Biblical exercises, Frederick gave to the new movement just that encouragement which was most necessary to carry it through the critical early stages of its growth. When Luther was proscribed both by the Emperor and the Pope, the old Elector saw to it that he was hidden away and sheltered from his enemies, and it was in Frederick's state, and with Frederick's support, that the fiery thoughts and hot passions of the great heretic were moulded into the fabric of the Lutheran Church.

The scholar was Philip Melanchthon. "I am rough, boisterous, stormy, and altogether warlike, I am born to fight innumerable monsters and devils, to remove stems and stones, cut away thistles and thorns, and clear away wild forests: but Master Philip comes along softly and gently with joy, according to the gifts which God has abundantly bestowed upon him." In these words Luther defined his relation to Philip Melanchthon, the gentle Greek scholar, who, in December, 1521, provided the new religion with its first elementary work on theology, the *Loci Communes*, the first book which, as Ranke observes, had appeared for several centuries in the Latin Church containing a system constructed out of the Bible only.

The University was that of Wittenberg, which became at once the principal seminary of Lutheran doctrines and a standing challenge to the traditional learning of the Sorbonne. Hither learners flocked from every part of Germany. Here was the great factory of Lutheran literature. It was in this little centre that the national mind of Germany, as it was affected by the passions and events of that tumultuous age, was first expressed in language which all Germans could understand. Hence, too, certain divines in the East Anglian University of Cambridge derived the evangelical doctrines which helped to make England a Protestant country, and gave to an obscure fenland seminary a new and sudden pre-eminence in the intellectual life of the English people.

Yet despite the initial tide of a boisterous popularity the reformers failed to make of Germany a Protestant country. The inveterate political divisions which had paralyzed this tempestuous people for centuries proved to be stronger than the widely spread indignation against papal abuses.

Some states accepted the new order, others remained faithful to the old. There was a League of Catholic States stitched together at Ratisbon (1524) and a counter-League of Protestant States set up at Torgau (1526) and enlarged at Smalkalden (1531). In the end, after a religious war which retarded the development of the country for two hundred years, Germany found peace, the newer civilizations of Saxony and Hesse, Prussia and Brandenburg embracing the Lutheran faith, while, broadly speaking, those parts of Germany which had been incorporated in the Roman Empire, notably Bavaria, Austria, and the Rhineland, remained faithful to Rome.

Thus the Lutheran movement, which had originally been national and popular, became in the course of a very few years neither the one thing nor the other. The new confession was restricted to certain principalities and free cities and everywhere was closely dependent upon princely and governmental favour. Great bodies of opinion, whole classes of society, were alienated and denounced. While the humanists, who had found much to admire in the denunciation of papal obscurantism, were estranged by the ascending scale of Luther's violence, Luther himself recoiled from the revolting peasantry (1525), and in a treatise which marks his breach with German democracy invoked upon the suffering toilers in the fields, from whom he was himself sprung, the condign vengeance of the princes.

From that moment the Lutheran Church ranged itself definitely on the side of civil order and authority. In principle the decision was wise. The ship of reform would have foundered in an ocean of anarchy. It speaks much for Luther's common sense that he stood out against every form of irresponsible lawlessness, whether of raving prophets or evangelical *condottieri* or anarchical Anabaptists. But the manner in which he dissociated his movement from the peasant rebellion, his failure to suggest points of accommodation and compromise, and the encouragement which he gave to a course of repression so savage that it left the German peasantry more defenceless and abased than any social class in central or western Europe, are serious blots upon his good name. The German peasants were rough men and rough fighters; but their grievances were genuine and their original demands were just and reasonable. That Lutheranism should have been associated with the reprisals of a hard and merciless landowning aristocracy, and with the degradation of the most deserving class in the community, proved to be a serious deduction from its vitalizing energies.

Of hardly less importance for the future of German protestantism was its emphatic breach with the Swiss Reformation. The Swiss were still the most famous mercenaries in Europe. Physically robust, but backward in all the arts and refinements of life, and separated by their mountains from the general movements of Europe, the Swiss were now (1522) for the first time swept into the reforming current and roused to a scrutiny of creeds and customs. The movement began in Zurich. It was partly moral, partly humanistic and patriotic, partly religious, and not a little, as all movements of religious revolt are wont to be, an impatient chafing at ancient and respectable restrictions. The Zurichers led by Ulrich Zwingli, a democrat, a republican, and a humanist, began to realize that it was not a very creditable thing for a self-respecting Zuricher to receive a pension or retaining fee from a foreign power. The fibre of latent nationalism began to vibrate among the burghers of this quiet lake city. "They would be neither French nor Imperial, but good Zurichers and Confederates." And with this determination to be at all costs Swiss there was combined a resolve to be on no account Roman. Zwingli denounced fasting in Lent, the celibacy of the clergy, monastic vows, the use of Latin in the church services, and the doctrine of the real presence. More radical, more enlightened, less mediaeval than Luther, the Swiss reformer drove forward without misgiving towards a complete breach with Rome.

By 1529 six of the thirteen cantons and some few towns in
southern Germany were captured for Zwinglian reform.

Philip the Landgrave of Hesse, the ablest German prince who
had embraced the Lutheran cause, saw how much advantage
would accrue from a junction of the Swiss and German forces,
and had politicians been in command of the two movements such
a junction would have been effected. Unfortunately Luther and
Zwingli were not statesmen but theologians, each resolute to
maintain every inch of the ground which he had taken up in
advance. It was in vain that the Landgrave prevailed upon the
contending divines to meet in conference at Marburg. Despite   **1529**
many minor points of agreement, on the central problem of the
eucharistic presence in the sacrament there was a gulf between
the disputants which no argument could bridge. For Zwingli
the sacrament was a symbolical ceremony. Luther, while rejecting the orthodox view that the body and blood of Christ replaced
the elements, held that they coexisted with them as fire is present
in molten lead. "*Hoc est corpus meum,*" he wrote upon the
conference table as he took his seat, and from the compulsion of
that plain text could see no escape. The dream of a wide Protestant confederation, comprising Swiss cantons, south German
cities, and north German principalities, was shattered on the
obstinate rock of those four words.

Lutheranism, then, made no conquests in Switzerland, and was
compelled to cede much of its original advantage in Germany.
But in revenge it conquered and still retains the three Scandinavian kingdoms; a low-temperature religion, agreeable to Erastian kings, and adapted to the long winters of the rigorous north.

The twenty years which followed the Edict of Worms are
among the most uncertain and critical in German history. Serious
men confronted with that welter of confused and conflicting
ideas must often have asked themselves whether the fabric of the
German Reich would survive so great a shock, and whether even
civilization itself would not be submerged in chaos. A hope persisted that the gulf could be bridged, and that if only a Council
were summoned the acknowledged scandals in the Church could
be put down and a basis provided upon which all true Christians
might be content to unite. To no one did the restoration of
religious peace seem more necessary than to the good and conscientious Charles V.

But the Emperor could do little that was helpful. Affairs in Spain, in Africa, in Italy, and in the Netherlands were for him more pressing than the composition of religious differences in Germany. Only once (1530) in that critical period of twenty years did this care-laden monarch show himself among his German subjects. Then, presiding over a Diet of the Empire at Augsburg, he was brought to reject a certain *Confessio*, or statement of belief, drawn up by the conciliatory Melanchthon, which, under its appellation of the Confession of Augsburg, has been ever since accepted as the classical exposition of the Lutheran Faith.

So without serious interference from the high powers the Lutheran Faith spread through northern Germany, and was even adopted in Prussia, where Albert of Brandenburg, the Grand Master of the German Order, decided (1525) to secularize his duchy and to hold it as a fief of the Polish crown, introducing at the same time the Saxon order of ritual and Church government. The consequences may easily be imagined. With every year the new system struck fresh roots in the soil, created new attachments, and became more difficult to dislodge. It followed that, when Charles returned to Germany in 1541, after nine years' absence, and again addressed himself to the task of reconciliation, the problem was, by reason of those vested interests, more difficult than ever. The last serious attempt at accommodation broke down at Ratisbon. By this time the differences between the Lutheran and Roman Churches were too wide, too deep, too numerous to be bridged.

BOOKS WHICH MAY BE CONSULTED

Cambridge Modern History, Vol. II.
T. M. Lindsay : History of the Reformation : Vol. I, in Germany ; Vol. II, in lands beyond Germany. 1905.
B. J. Kidd : Documents illustrative of the Continental Reformation. 1911.
T. M. Lindsay : Luther and the German Reformation. 1900.
The Table Talk of Martin Luther. *Tr.* and *ed.* William Hazlitt. 1848.
Luther's Primary Works. *Tr.* and *ed.* H. Wace and C. Buchheim. 1896.
L. von Ranke : Deutsche Geschichte im Zeitalter der Reformation. *Tr.* Sarah Austin, History of the Reformation in Germany. 1905.
L. Pastor : History of the Popes. *Ed.* F. I. Antrobus and R. F. Kerr. 1894-1933.
S. M. Jackson : Huldreich Zwingli, 1484-1531. 1903.
W. Oechsli : History of Switzerland, 1499-1914. *Tr.* E. and C. Paul. 1922.
E. Belfort Bax : The Peasant War in Germany. 1899.
E. Belfort Bax : Rise and Fall of the Anabaptists. 1903.

CHAPTER IX

ENGLAND'S BREACH WITH ROME

Henry VIII in youth. Humanism and orthodoxy. The temper of England. The social problem. Prestige of the monarchy. Absence of concerted opposition. Thomas Wolsey. The divorce. The Reformation Parliament. Thomas Cromwell. The Dissolution of the Monasteries. The Act of Supremacy. Henry's middle way. Thomas Cranmer. His two services to the Reformation. Edward VI and Mary. Reasons for her unpopularity. The Marian martyrs. The enemies of England.

A LAD of eighteen, tall, ruddy, handsome like Edward IV his grandfather, bursting with animal vigour, and skilled in all manly exercises, Henry VIII seemed in 1509 to be an accomplished specimen of the young Renaissance prince. With a passionate appetite for hunting, gambling, love-making, and jousting there was mingled a taste for the society of the learned and a fancy, not too seriously entertained, for a province in France and the Imperial crown. Soon after his accession he was married to a grave and gentle lady, Catharine of Aragon, six years his senior and the widow of his elder brother Arthur, who had died suddenly at Ludlow after four months of marriage, in his sixteenth year. A dispensation from Pope Julius II (1503) had sanctioned, despite the formal text of Leviticus, this union with the widow of a deceased brother.

Apart from the pleasures of the court and the chase, the young king was noted for two interests, hitherto not greatly observed in English monarchs. He was fond of the sea. He built the royal dockyards at Woolwich and Deptford, founded Trinity House, a school for pilots, supervised with the minutest attention the construction of a royal fleet, and laid the foundations of English naval power. He was the first English king to have a navy in any real sense or to make it fashionable. When the *Princess Mary* was launched in 1519 the whole court attended the ceremony, and Henry, as we learn from the French envoy who was present, ' acted as pilot and wore a sailor's coat and trousers made of cloth of gold, and a gold chain with the inscription *Dieu et non droit*, to which was suspended a whistle, which he blew nearly as loud as a trumpet." In this as in many other matters

509

the young king divined the moods and marched with the spirit of the English people.

His second interest was theology, then becoming, as economics in our age, a basic study for politics. He read and discussed the Thomists. He even wrote a treatise in refutation of Luther, which was published in 1521 and earned him the title of Fidei Defensor from Pope Leo X. And as he advanced in age and egotism his sense of theological security so developed that he seemed to himself on all high matters of theological doctrine to be a sole and sufficient judge, on intimate terms with the purposes of God and His special confidant. His views were papalist, and upon such fundamental subjects as the Mass or the celibacy of the clergy profoundly orthodox. It was as a champion of Pope Julius II against Louis XII of France that he first drew his sword in a foreign quarrel and won that victory of the Spurs and that other more famous victory of Flodden Field, which, though they were of no lasting importance, gave England the name once more of being a formidable power in Europe.

The English people, unlike their monarch and unlike the Scots, were untheological. Few countries had been so little touched by heresy or so widely noted for their devotion to Rome. Lollardy was a recent exception; but Lollardy had, at the time of the accession of Henry VIII, lost its hold upon the universities and country houses, and was now the faith of a scattered handful of obscure and humble men, plying a modest craft in some London alley or burning charcoal among the beech forests in the Chilterns. In the great doctrinal controversies over Predestination or Justification by Faith which rent the continent the manor houses and country houses of England were little interested. In the main the Englishman paid an uninstructed loyalty to the familiar things, and in particular to the Mass and the Roman liturgy. But in the universities, where the servants of the State received their education, and more particularly in the University of Cambridge, a certain doctrinal ferment had been created by contact with Lutherans and their writings. In the early days of Henry VIII such innovating opinions were confined to an elect academic circle.

But if the English people were prevailingly orthodox, they were also very generally anti-clerical. More particularly was this true of the laity in London and the trading cities. The new commercial class had begun to challenge the credentials of the old wealthy, and domineering Church. The English Ghibellines grudged the privileges and envied the possessions of the priests. They were indignant that the clergy should be immune from the criminal jurisdiction of laymen and that laymen should be subjected to the criminal jurisdiction of the Church. Why, they asked, should a murderer virtually go unpunished if he could recite a verse of the Psalms and so claim benefit of clergy, and what right had a bishop's court to condemn a layman to be burned for heresy without let or hindrance from the secular authority? These and other complaints, which had received some legislative interference in 1512, were passionately ventilated in the Parliament of 1515.

A *cause célèbre*, the mystery of which has never been wholly cleared up, inflamed the controversy to a white heat. Richard Hunne, a wealthy and charitable merchant tailor, was found dead by hanging in the palace of the Bishop of London. Laymen believed that Hunne had refused to pay the mortuary dues exacted by some avaricious priest for the burial of his infant son, that having lost his suit in the ecclesiastical court he had complained to the King's Bench, and that he had for this reason been foully slain by the officials of the bishop. The clergy took another view. While lay London was willing to believe anything evil of the priests, the bishop's court sitting over the corpse decided that the merchant tailor was an unrepentant heretic who had committed *felo-de-se*. His body was accordingly burned and his property declared forfeit to the Crown. The great issue was joined. In the atmosphere of angry recriminations roused by the death of Hunne all the ultimate issues of Church and State were canvassed and discussed. Only a prompt dissolution of Parliament saved an ugly and menacing quarrel.

But if opinion was for the most part lay and anti-clerical, it was not revolutionary. The course of the English Reformation was inflamed by no such widespread social bitterness as that which inspired the Peasants' Revolt in Germany. There were certain things which the English people could not stand. Overtaxation was one, a war with the Netherlands, which would ruin the wool trade, was another. The dangerous disturbance over the " Amicable Loan " in 1523, and the menacing tone of public opinion in 1528 when Henry projected war with Charles V, were the red lights of warning which showed the observant sovereign the limits of his power. But if the pockets of the landowners, the graziers and the cloth-dealers were respected the government had no great cause to fear. There was indeed a grave social problem which is at the bottom of all the popular risings of the century. Land was coming in an increasing degree to be treated from a commercial standpoint. Owing to the steady development of the cloth trade, which was England's premier industry, sheep became more profitable than corn, pasture fifty per cent. more remunerative than arable. The appetites of landowners and land speculators from the town were quickened. Big profits were to be made out of land and they might be made in many ways, by concentrating holdings, by enclosing common lands for arable or pasture, or by turning plough lands into sheep runs. These expedients had been practised in the fifteenth century. They were in no sense novel; but in the sixteenth century they were carried out upon a scale which occasioned widespread distress, alarm, and commentary. What was to happen to the yeoman who was deprived of his holding, to the many ploughmen on a farm who were replaced by a single shepherd, to the poorer commoners whose living was taken from them by enclosure? The problem of a dispossessed rural class, of homes broken up and villages dispeopled, of vagabonds tramping the roads and flocking into the towns, was serious in itself. It was rendered still graver by its association with a course of Church policy which turned every zealous Catholic priest into a potential leader of revolt, which threw the monks upon the labour market, and dislocated the mediaeval machinery by which relief was given to the poor.

It is possible that the evil was more serious in imagination than in fact and that the economic results of the enclosures have been over-estimated by contemporary writers. But that the immemorial tranquillity of English village life was now newly disturbed, and that a new sense of insecurity was very generally created among the rural poor, is beyond question. As generally happens in periods of economic disturbance, the rich were becoming richer and the poor becoming poorer. The power of the vested interests was sufficiently strong to frustrate the attempts of the government to apply a remedy.

It is remarkable that despite all these materials for discontent, to which may be added a steady rise in the price of the necessaries of life, the Tudor government was never seriously shaken by popular disorders. Without a standing army or a regular police, it was able on each occasion and with no great difficulty (using, however, in 1549, a chance force of foreign mercenaries who happened to be in the country) to master rebellion. For this there were three main reasons. The risings were local and disjointed. The nobles and gentry stood aloof from the poor. Of all the political sentiments of the people, respect for the crown and the dynasty ranked first. The spirit of political obedience was the more deeply implanted in the nation by reason of the freshly remembered dynastic war which had been brought to an end on Bosworth Field.

The Tudor monarchy stood between the country and a renewal of civil strife. The maintenance of peace and order, the enforcement of justice, the repression of aristocratic insolence, the protection of the poor, the encouragement to commerce were its attendant blessings. The dynasty survived the perils of a minority. The attempt to upset the rightful order of succession by calling Lady Jane Grey to the throne was defeated by one of the most instantaneous and spontaneous movements of English history. Though no woman had sat upon the English throne since Matilda, it was sufficient for Mary, as it was for her sister Elizabeth, that they were the children of a Tudor king. To the English people of this age, the exercise of constitutional rights did not present itself as an ideal. Their dominant anxiety was that the Tudor dynasty should rule and endure. So strong was the monarchical sentiment that Shakespeare could write of King John without mention of Magna Carta, and so strong in point of fact was the monarchy that, despite the crimes and cruelties of Henry VIII, it carried the country through this critical period of its annals without the convulsion of religious war.

For a period of fourteen years (1515-29) Henry was content to leave the real government of the country to Thomas Wolsey. The irony of this extraordinary man's career is that while all his ambitions were bound up with the Papacy, nobody did more to prepare the way for an Erastian state. By himself replacing the Pope in England as *Legatus a Latere* and by gathering up into his hands all the reins of ecclesiastical power, Wolsey superseded the mediaeval constitution of the native Church and taught Henry to be master in his own house. To the end he aspired to be Pope; yet even the Lutherans did not instil into the public mind so great an aversion from the foreign jurisdiction of the Papacy as did this cardinal, who in virtue of the bulls which he obtained from successive pontiffs established for himself a novel and odious form of ecclesiastical tyranny in England.

It has been argued that Wolsey was a great conservative reformer who, but for a fatal accident, would have saved the Catholic Church in England. Some reforms he partially carried out, such as the dissolution of the smaller monasteries, and the application of their endowments to the foundation of colleges in Oxford and Ipswich. Others, notably the establishment of thirteen new sees, he appears to have envisaged.

But it may be permitted to doubt whether a man who embodied in his own person almost every abuse which may be charged against the Catholic Church in the sixteenth century, who was a pluralist on a vast scale, who was loose in his private morals and notoriously neglectful of pastoral duty, had in him the heart of a reformer. Power, not reform, was the master passion in the breast of this son of the grazier of Ipswich, who combined in his own person the functions of Lord Chancellor, Archbishop of York, Bishop in succession of Bath and Wells, Durham and Winchester, Abbot of St. Albans, *Legatus a Latere*, and, in addition, farmed three bishoprics for non-resident aliens. But that such a man should have initiated reform was an omen of future changes.

He was the last of the great ecclesiastical statesmen to govern England. After Wolsey the laymen began to come into their own. But during his fourteen years of power he was, by permission of the king, autocrat of England, unchecked by colleagues, by Parliaments, or by Convocations. In the Star Chamber he bridled the nobles. As Chancellor he curbed the ecclesiastical courts. Presiding over the Court of Requests, he brought cheap legal remedies within reach of the poor. The king was content to delegate the hard work of government to a servant who was so able, industrious and submissive to himself.

As a prince of the Church he was not insular but European. It was from Rome that his ecclesiastical powers were derived; it was upon Rome that his supreme ambition was fixed. The fate of the Pope could not be indifferent to him. Alike as an English statesman and as a Roman cardinal, he was determined that the French should not enslave the Pope. If England's old enemy were once rooted in the *castello* of Milan, there would in time be a French Pope, a French College of Cardinals, a French

orientation of papal policy—a second Avignonese captivity no
less grievous than the first—and the Papacy would be as far
from his reach as the moon in heaven.

So it was resolved that England should take a full, showy,
and commanding part in the great European duel between
Charles and France, extracting profit from each rival, but when
it came to serious business siding with the Emperor against the
French king. The name of the great English king should rever-
berate through Europe. The foreigners should realize that the
island government was a force to be reckoned with, conciliated,
bribed. Wolsey spared no pains to advertise the splendour and
power of his master. An immense expenditure of money and
labour was put into the great international game. It may be
asked to what public advantage. The two continental powers
were already well balanced, and the idea that England, which
could not keep an army on the continent for more than three
months together, could seriously affect the European balance,
or disrupt the compact monarchy of France, was chimerical.
Moreover, events were destined to prove that the real danger
to papal freedom came not from France but from Spain. After
the capture of Francis at Pavia came the sack of Rome, and
two years after that (1529) the Treaty of Barcelona, which bound
Clement hand and foot to Charles. And meanwhile two papal
elections had been held and, despite the Emperor's express
promise, Wolsey was not Pope. By 1529 the diplomatic education of the cardinal was complete. The wool-dealers would not
allow him, for he had tried, to defy the Emperor, and the
Emperor was master of papal policy. As a prelate aspiring to
fill the Holy See he had backed the wrong horse. As an English
Prime Minister concerned for trade he could have backed no
other. But there was no compelling reason why he should have
backed either. When the great cardinal fell, his shrewder
master turned away from the continent and addressed himself
to the more immediate and feasible task of extending his
authority through the British Isles. Only in Wales was he completely successful. Meanwhile, out of that Spanish triumph in
Italy, which was sealed at Barcelona, came the fall of Wolsey
and the foundation of the Anglican Church.

Catharine had given Henry a daughter, who was christened
Mary, but no son. Again and again she had borne children, but
either they were stillborn or they died soon after birth, so that

the king, who was passionately desirous for a lawful male heir, on good political grounds began to conceive that there must be some curse upon his marriage. Perhaps the dispensation of Julius II was technically invalid? Perhaps the Pope had no power to dispense in such a matter? The more the king reflected, the more he was persuaded that he was a bachelor, a Christian and ill-used bachelor, and that the familiar papal machinery should be put into operation to admit of the setting aside of Catharine. He had no doubt that the thing could be done. Indeed, it had been twice recently done within the circle of his own family. His brother-in-law Suffolk had repudiated a wife, his sister Margaret had repudiated a husband, and both had married again under a dispensation from the compliant Clement VII. He was the more anxious after 1527 that the Pope should grant him this favour, having fallen in love with Anne Boleyn, and being determined, since such was her will, to make this young and wayward beauty his lawful wife.*

Spain was the obstacle. If the Pope had not been a weak Italian prince overshadowed by Spain, the marriage of Catharine might safely have been annulled. But Clement was helpless. Though Wolsey warned him that the whole Roman obedience of England was at stake, he could not affront the man whose troops had desecrated the shrines of St. Peter and stabled their horses in the Vatican palace. Under the contending pressure of King and Emperor, the wretched Pontiff turned this way and that, spinning out delays, suggesting expedients (even bigamy), but at last consenting to the establishment of a Legatine Court in London under Cardinals Wolsey and Campeggio, from which it appeared that a final decision might at last be obtained. Here Henry and Catharine appeared and pleaded. Here the vulgar but not unjust or inhuman populace of London was permitted to witness part of the great tragic drama which caught the imagination of Shakespeare. But nothing which was felt or pleaded in London mattered: not even the ardent popular feeling for the injured queen, nor the vehement hatred for the young woman who was destined to supplant her. Spain was all-powerful in Italy, and suddenly, under Spanish pressure, the king's case was revoked to Rome.

What followed is very significant. With a great flash of political insight, Henry summoned Parliament to assist him in

* As early as 1514 Henry desired to repudiate Catharine

his conflict with the papal see. Having managed to rule England without Parliaments (save for one brief exception) for fourteen years, he now called Lords and Commons to Westminster, kept them sitting for seven years and passed through Parliament the statutes which were required to secure the independence of the English Church from Rome and its subjection to the Crown. It has often been said that the House of Commons of 1529 was packed; but there is no evidence that this was so. Henry might safely reckon that an assembly of English squires and burgesses would not be unwilling to help him break the financial and legal ties which bound England to a foreign spiritual power. Had he asked them to renounce the Mass they would not have been so compliant. Had he been a Lutheran, as Anne Boleyn was commonly reported to be, his difficulties would have been insuperable. But in dogma he was a pillar of the old church, and Henry's orthodoxy was just as important as the revolutionary audacity with which in the sphere of constitutional relations he challenged Pope and Emperor to do their worst. The Protestant Reformation in England succeeded because it was carried through by stages and because the first or constitutional change was represented as being a reversion to the good old (mythical) times when kings were really masters of the English Church. Herein, too, Henry showed his shrewd sense, for nothing commends a radical change to an Englishman more effectually than the belief that it is really conservative.

The place left vacant by Wolsey's fall was in part filled by a layman who had been trained in the cardinal's service and had there learnt that the way to the king's favour was despatch, assiduity, and subservience. Thomas Cromwell looked at the world with the eye of a hard-headed adventurer who had campaigned in Italy and read *The Prince* of Machiavelli. He felt that the trend of events was making towards the secularization of politics. No man, prominent in England at that time, was less clerical or more remote from those appeals of sentiment and history, doctrine and piety which stir the hearts of religious men. He undertook the task of dispossessing the priests and uprooting the monks in the spirit in which an unemotional, unscrupulous solicitor handles a hard and intricate matter of business for a shady but important client.

Next to the management of the Reformation Parliament Cromwell's great task was the dissolution of the monasteries. He had promised the king that he would make him the richest sovereign in Europe, and though many religious houses were gravely burdened with debt, there was still a noble harvest ready for the reaper. There were other reasons for including an assault upon the religious houses in the strategy of an anti-papal campaign. The monks and nuns constituted the papal garrison. They were for the most part exempt from episcopal supervision. They were subject to a foreign superior. So long as they were tolerated it might be expected that every abbey or nunnery in the land would be a seminary of Catholic ardour and propaganda. Moreover, there was no better means of associating the propertied classes of the country with the great religious change than by a lavish distribution among them of the broad acres of the monasteries. We cannot say whether such a distribution was part of a preconceived plan. Neighbourly appetite made it inevitable. The wealth of the monasteries was no sooner garnered for the State than it was lavished upon the fortune-hunting squires and nobles of the country. Henceforth the strongest class in England had a vested interest in the Protestant Reformation. It was, designedly or undesignedly, the master-stroke of Henry's anti-papal campaign.

An air of spurious respectability was thrown over what would otherwise have appeared a naked act of spoliation by the evidence of immorality reported by Cromwell's Commissioners.

Immorality was, indeed, prevalent, as we know from less suspect sources; but the real grievance against the monastic institution was not vice which was perennial, but uselessness which was new. The abbeys had outlived their function. They had ceased to learn, to teach, to record, to illumine. Inspiration and initiative appear to have deserted them. At best they could pretend to an innocent and meditative repose. At worst they were the repair of the ne'er-do-well and the criminal. If their wealth had been applied to education, the general intellectual and moral tone of the country would have been greatly raised, but the Reformation would have been less secure, the Cecils, the Russells, and the Cavendishes would not have entered upon their princely fortunes, nor Thomas Cromwell have gone to the scaffold a millionaire.

These immense changes, which were felt in every village, were carried through with a ruthless expedition. An English government has never been more determined as to its course or more tyrannical in its methods. At the very opening of the Seven Years' Parliament clergy and laity were cowed by learning that having connived at Wolsey's legatine Commission they had exposed themselves to the dire penalties of Praemunire. The Act of Supremacy of 1534, which made the king supreme head of the Church, and more than the Annates Act or the Appeals Act or any other act of the Reformation Parliament embodied the central principle of the controversy, was taken as a test. To swear to it, as the king required, was to abjure the Pope. To refuse was death by the executioner's axe. Sir Thomas More and Bishop Fisher, the two greatest figures in that last age of Catholic England, went to the block rather than swear that oath; but their example was not followed. The terror, the admiration, and the loyalty inspired by the tremendous figure of the passionate king carried all before it.

Even D'Arcy, the leader of the Pilgrimage of Grace, the great northern revolt arising out of the dissolution of the monasteries, avowed that he would never have dreamt of drawing sword against the king. Nothing seemed to affect Henry's popularity, neither the repudiation of Catharine, nor the execution of Anne Boleyn, nor the death upon the scaffold of the best prelate and the most gifted humanist of the age.

The English Church was severed from Rome, the royal supremacy was affirmed, but there still remained the unsettled problem of the doctrine and the ritual. In the general fermentation of spirit which then prevailed these high and difficult matters might, but for one extraordinary circumstance, have led to a protracted period of confusion and chaos. That circumstance was the king. Henry was firmly resolved and to his own satisfaction adequately equipped to step into the place of the Pope and to prescribe to his people, under the most terrible penalties which an obedient Parliament could contrive, what they should and should not believe. It was the king who drew up in 1536 the first doctrinal formulary of the Church of England (Articles devised by the King's Highness to establish Christian quietness). It is owing to the king's influence that, despite Thomas Cromwell's desire for a religious and political union with the Protestant powers of Germany, England never accepted the Augsburg Confession nor was allowed to drift into the general orbit of German theology. It is to the king that we must ascribe the special colour and deliberate pace of the Protestant movement in its early stages.

The royal theologian was neither cosmopolitan, nor philosopher, nor idealist. He was resolved that the theology of the Church should be English, not German, and framed not by Philip Melanchthon, but by himself. Men of a finer temper in quest of a theology might have asked themselves what was true, or primitive, or best suited to advance the higher needs of man. Henry sought the settlement which at the moment appeared to divide his people least. In 1536 he advanced towards Reform. In 1539, warned by the Pilgrimage of Grace, he stepped sharply backward and enacted the Six Articles. At the end of his life, under the influence perhaps of Catharine Parr, he moved forward again. A general revision of service books was ordered and the Litany sanctioned in 1545. The "Great Bible," largely based upon the melodious translation of William Tyndale, was already by royal order placed in the churches and made accessible to all. To the end of his days, pursuing the *via media* which is dear to statesmen, he burned Lutherans for heresy and hanged Catholics for treason.

In the last fourteen years of his reign he was assisted by a man who has printed an enduring mark on the English Reformation. Thomas Cranmer was a Cambridge divine, married to a German wife, and already far advanced in his hostility to Rome when he rendered to Henry those services in connection with the divorce which laid the foundation of his future eminence and peril. In quiet times this refined and learned theologian would have passed a blameless and honourable career. His morals were pure, his religious feeling was deep and tender, and he was animated by a sincere desire to restore the Church to its pristine beauty. But he had no courage. In the sordid business of annulling a marriage the king could always rely upon the timid compliance of the Archbishop of Canterbury.

But despite this grave weakness Cranmer conferred upon the English Church two immortal services. He is the main author of the Anglican Prayer-book, to which he contributed the Litany and the Collects. A Catholic writer, who loves good English better than he loves Thomas Cranmer, thus eloquently acknowledges the quality which has given to the Prayer-book an enduring appeal: "Through the Litany, which is from his hand, through the Collects, through the Prefaces, through the admirable music of the special prayers, mainly due to his invention, he gave a strength to the newly established religion which it could never have drawn from any other source. He provided a substitute for the noble Latin on which the soul of Europe had been formed for more than a thousand years, and he gave to the Church of England a treasure, by the aesthetic effect of which more than by anything else, her spirit has remained alive, and she has attached herself to the hearts of men."[1]

His second service was the manner of his end. After a life of time-serving Cranmer died a hero and a martyr. He had been compelled by the order of Queen Mary to sign six recantations, and he knew that his recantations were published. As he went to the stake he threw them into the fire, reaffirmed his beliefs, and "finally stretching forth his arm and right hand, he said, 'This which hath sinned, having signed the writing, must be the first to suffer punishment'; and thus did he place it in the fire and burned it himself."

The interval which elapses between the death of Henry VIII and the martyrdom of Cranmer is marked by a continuation, though in a more violent form, of those oscillations of Protestant and Catholic influence which had been kept within limits by Henry's masterful will. During the reign of Edward VI the reformers gained control of the government, advancing by cautious stages under the enlightened rule of the Protector Somerset, but at a swifter and more dangerous pace under his successor Northumberland. But then ensued a sharp reaction. In 1553 the boy king died. Under his father's will the next heir to the throne was the Princess Mary, a woman of thirty-seven years, well set and well proven in her loyalty to the Roman faith. The accession of so staunch a Catholic was received by the extreme reforming party with eyes of dismay. They foresaw the undoing of all their work. The English liturgy would go, the Bible would go, the English Church would be reconciled to Rome, the Protestant bishops would lose their sees, the whole reforming connection would be exposed to grave personal risks. To avert these evils and also to secure his continued power Northumberland determined to alter the succession. His plot failed. The people of England preferred Mary Tudor to Lady Jane Grey, the grand-daughter of that other Mary who was sister to Henry VIII and married to the Duke of Suffolk. And then what was anticipated happened. The old worship was restored, the Church was solemnly reunited to Rome, and, save for the fact that not even a

[1] Hilaire Belloc. *Thomas Cranmer.*

Marian Parliament ventured to disturb the great vested interests created by the dispersal of monastic wealth, the work of the Reformation was formally demolished.

But though Parliament-men were very generally indifferent about religion, voting one way under Edward and the reverse way under Mary, there were in England two deep sentiments which were either unsatisfied or affronted by the government of this high-principled, unfortunate, and bigoted lady. The first was the sentiment of nationality. Mary by her own desire was married to Philip of Spain. Though the marriage contract was drawn up by Bishop Gardiner with the utmost skill and with the special view of safeguarding English independence, the match was unpopular. The Spanish king was not liked, nor his attendants, nor the thought that England was now an adjunct to a foreign country. There was even a rebellion against the marriage, led by Thomas Wyatt, and frustrated by the courage of the queen herself. And when it was known that the marriage would bring no heir, the thoughts of the people turned to the Princess Elizabeth, who was not the daughter of a Spaniard nor married to a Spaniard, but English or Welsh on both sides, the child of Anne Boleyn and Henry, and the fruit of that marriage which had brought about the disruption of the bond between England and Rome and let loose the great tide of the reforming movement.

The other was the sentiment of humanity. In moments of excitement the English were capable of great savagery, but they could recognize the face of virtue when they saw it. Their sympathies had been enlisted by the misfortunes of Queen Catharine. They were now excited by the still greater tragedy occasioned by the Marian persecutions. The number of Protestants condemned to the stake for their beliefs under Queen Mary did not probably exceed three hundred; but in this number, small as it was in comparison with continental standards, were included the chieftains of the reforming party and the men most eminent for virtue and talent in the country. The fires that kindled round Cranmer and Latimer and Ridley were not soon extinguished. In the Martyrology of John Foxe, in which the lives and deaths of the victims of Marian zeal are vividly recounted, the Protestant world obtained a record, deemed only less sacred than the Bible itself, of the high spirit which animated the fathers of their faith, and of the courage with which, rather than betray their convictions, they faced the fiery torments of the stake. Nothing so greatly served to purify and deepen the Protestant religion in England or to implant in the minds of the common people a horror of Rome as these ill-judged severities, undertaken against the prudent judgment of Charles V, on the initiative of a solitary and miserable woman. The memories of the divorce with all its sordid impurities were washed away in a clarifying stream of heroism and sacrifice.

The independence of England during this unsettled period was by no means secure. It was an open question whether the country would become a satellite of France or of Spain, or whether it would have the force to strike out on a course of its own. The master-key to national security lay in the union of England and Scotland. This truth was realized by Henry VII, who laid the foundations of concord in a royal marriage, realized again by Henry VIII, who planned the marriage of Edward VI with the infant Mary Queen of Scots, and again by the Protector Somerset, whose schemes for Anglo-Scottish union prefigured in many minor details the ultimate settlement. But the obstacles were formidable. The Scottish aristocracy, who controlled the course of policy in the northern kingdom, were as corrupt a body of jobbers as any in Europe, and would in smooth weather as lief sell themselves for a pension to London as to Paris. But they could not wholly unlearn the lessons of their national history, the centuries of raiding on the border, the haughty claims of the English kings, the long alliance with France, the traditional devotion to the papal see. Nor was their appetite for an English understanding improved when in the dark days after the defeat of Solway Moss (1542) Henry VIII revived the ancient claims of suzerainty which their ancestors had rejected, or when the same headstrong policy was continued under Protector Somerset, when their country was invaded, when Edinburgh was burnt, when a Scottish army was defeated at Pinkie. The elevated arguments addressed by the Protector to the Scottish people on the advantages of Union were not rendered the more persuasive by these operations. It is little wonder that the French party gained the ascendant. The child Mary, who was affianced to the young Prince Edward in 1543, was married in 1548 to Francis, the heir to the French throne.

This then was the cloud which overhung the political future of England. Scotland and France might eventually be united under the French husband of Mary Queen of Scots. In that event the Spanish alliance might be an essential condition of English security. But Spain was Catholic and the drift of English opinion was towards reform. A Spanish alliance might not always be obtainable, or might be forthcoming only at a price which England would not be prepared to pay. With a Catholic Ireland in the west and a Catholic Scotland in the north, with Spain doubtful and France hostile, a Protestant England would be in a position of dangerous isolation. That was the anxious prospect which led Somerset to press for the spread of reforming opinions among the people in Scotland; and that was the situation, modified only by the advance of the Scottish reformation, that the government of Elizabeth was called on to face.

BOOKS WHICH MAY BE CONSULTED

Histories of England : G. M. Trevelyan, 1926. C. R. L. Fletcher, 1905-23.
    J. A. Froude, 1856-1870. H. A. L. Fisher, 1906.
Cambridge Modern History, Vol. II.
A. F. Pollard : Henry VIII. 1913.
A. F. Pollard : Wolsey. 1929.
A. F. Pollard : A Life of Thomas Cranmer. 1926.
F. A. Gasquet : Henry VIII and the English Monasteries. 1906.
H. Belloc : Cranmer. 1931.
G. Cavendish : Life of Thomas Wolsey. 1930.
W. Roper : The Life and Death of Sir Thomas More. 1822.
Sir Thomas More : Utopia.
R. B. Merriman : Life and Letters of Thomas Cromwell. 1902.
R. W. Chambers : The Saga and Myth of Sir Thomas More. 1926.
J. S. Brewer : The Reign of Henry VIII. *Ed.* J. Gairdner. 1884.
R. W. Dixon : History of the Church of England. 1893.
W. Stubbs : Seventeen Lectures on the Study of Mediaeval and Modern
    History. 1900.
F. Seebohm : The Oxford Reformers of 1498. 1867.
J. B. Mullinger : The University of Cambridge from the Earliest Times.
    1873-84.
A. F. Pollard : England under Protector Somerset. 1900.
A. F. Leach : English Schools at the Reformation. 1896.
J. M. Stone : History of Mary I, Queen of England. 1901.
H. Forneron : Histoire de Philippe II. 4 vols. 1881-2.

CHAPTER X

THE EMPIRE OF CHARLES V

Its significance. Centres of opposition. Main objectives of Imperial policy. Charles popular in Spain. Financial difficulties. The Netherlands. Their financial importance. The Inquisition in the Netherlands. The circumnavigation of the globe. Mexico, Peru, and Greater Spain. Spain's treatment of subject races. Spanish victories in Italy. Clement VII and the sack of Rome. Doria brings Genoa over to the Imperial side. Charles at his zenith, 1530. The Spanish dominion in Italy.

THE Empire of Charles V constituted a political transformation of Europe which in the order of importance does not fall far short of Caesar's conquest of Gaul, or Charlemagne's inclusion of Germany within the realm of the Franks.[1] It was an empire which came to comprise countries so widely different in every particular of temperament and tradition as Spain and the Netherlands, Germany and Naples, the old civilization of the Lombard plain and the newly-conquered realms of Mexico and Peru. It was the occasion of wars, so wide in their scope that they may almost be called Pan-European, and of that direct rivalry between France and Germany for the hegemony of Europe, which ever since, in one form or another, has tormented the repose of statesmen. It gave to Spain, than which no country was more rigid in its conservatism, a passing supremacy in the modern world, which first in France and then in England was viewed as an international peril. It led to the extermination of Italian liberties and by a clear chain of cause and effect to the rejection of papal authority by the insular monarchy of England. To it we may trace the first stage in that gradual severance between the Netherlands (then closely united to Spain) and the German *Reich*, out of which, in due course of time, were developed the Protestant Dutch republic and the Catholic kingdom of Belgium. Equally well we may regard this widespread empire as marking the beginning of modern history or as the last grand attempt to recapture for the Roman Church the old mediaeval unity of faith and government. On every front, against the Lutherans in Germany and the Netherlands,

[1] Genealogical Table B.

against the Turks in Hungary and Tunis and Algiers, and in every quarter of the Mediterranean Charles was the appointed champion of the Catholic Faith, the secular arm of the spiritual power. The Spanish galleon, the Spanish pikeman, the Spanish military governor, the Spanish priest announced the assumption by the newly-soldered Spanish State of a missionary and imperial rôle.

But the heart of Europe was no longer one. France, which might have agreed with Charles the Catholic, was bitterly opposed to Charles the Emperor. Italy perforce (save for the faintest Lutheran sprinkle) accepted the control of a Latin power which might at least serve to shield the Italian coast towns against the Turks. But in the Teuton north the stiff, unintelligible Spaniard was an object of fear and aversion. Here the Lutheran states, supported by German pride and French hatred for the Imperialists, maintained their footing; and here, too, in the Netherlands an opposition was generated against Spanish control so fierce and persistent that among all the reasons which have been assigned for the decline of Spain, the revolt of the Flemings and the Dutch ranks as the foremost.

The head of this vast empire was a man wholly devoid of charm, magnetism, or chivalry. He was no soldier. He had no imagination. He was incapable of original thought on any subject. In appearance and manner he was ungainly, with a protruding Habsburg lip and a stutter in his speech. When, at the age of eighteen, he became a king he could speak French and Flemish, but knew nothing of Spanish, his mother's speech, or of Spain, his mother's land. But he was teachable, courageous, persevering. After the first ebullience of youthful indiscretion was over he grew old rapidly and developed a tough, persistent sagacity which enabled him to surmount difficulties that would have overwhelmed a baser nature. A Fleming by birth and heredity, he ended, having abdicated the throne, in a Spanish monastery. By insensible degrees finding that Spain was the real centre of his power, he became a Spaniard. Yet, however much he might endeavour to do justice to the different parts of his realm, he was never anywhere the complete master, never rich or powerful or able to fuse the incompatible peoples who owned his sway. To the end of the chapter Spain and Flanders, Wittenberg and Rome remained wide as the poles asunder.

Legend

- Boundary of the Empire
- Hereditary Possessions of Charles V
- to Hapsburgs, 1526
- M. Milan
- G. Genoa

English Miles
0 100 200 300 400

THE EMPIRE OF CHARLES V, 1525.

As against other Christian sovereigns, his policy was purely defensive. He proposed to keep what he had inherited or considered that he had a right to inherit. But the defence of an empire so new and formidable could not be accomplished without fighting. France was a necessary opponent, a rival over Burgundy, over Navarre (the little Pyrenean state which Charles had in 1516 promised to restore to its old French ruling family, the d'Albrets), over the Imperial election, over Milan. The prospect of a French state in the Lombard plain, or in the gulf of Genoa, intercepting the marine communications between Spain and Germany, was a menace which Charles felt bound to resist. Milan and Genoa must be imperialists if German *Landsknechts* were to be passed easily into Spain or Spanish pikemen to figure on German battlefields.

To wrest Milan from the French was not in Charles' eye an act of wanton aggression, but the restoration of an essential link in the chain of Imperial defence. The Turk was different. It was a sacred duty imposed on the Emperor by his historic office and by the common voice of Spain to assail the infidel on every front. Castile cared much for Navarre and nothing for Italy, Aragon cared much for Italy but nothing for Navarre. Neither Aragon nor Castile was interested in the Netherlands. But all Spain hated and feared the Turk, and with redoubled vehemence ever since Khaireddin Barbarossa the corsair went into the Turkish service, and from his lair in Algiers began to prey upon the Spanish coast. The Spaniard was schooled by history to the idea of a Crusade. So long as his Emperor was fighting the Lutheran or the Turk he was well content; for other parts of the far-flung imperial policy he showed a fainter concern.

The crown was popular. The revolt of the Comuneros which disturbed northern Spain after Charles first went to the country was so little republican that the chief treasure of the rebels was the person of the mad Queen Joanna. Their grievance was not that a young king had descended upon Spain from Flanders, but that he had come with a cortège of greedy Flemish attendants, had squeezed the country for money, and then had returned to the north leaving Spain to the tender mercies of Adrian, Bishop of Utrecht, an unpalatable Dutch prelate who knew nothing of the country or its speech. Even so, part of the Castilian aristocracy rallied round the king and defeated the rebels on the field of Vilagos (April 23, 1521), so that when Charles returned to Spain in 1522, his renown enhanced by the Imperial title, his orthodoxy proved by the Edict of Worms, with a good train of artillery and 3,000 German *Landsknechts*, he found a people prepared to obey, and, within limits, to vote him supplies. That he refused to shed blood brought him the admiring gratitude of his subjects, who (1522-9) were soon taught that he was prepared to learn their ways and to give them the kind of government which they wanted. Though the temper of Castile permitted of autocracy, Charles was scrupulous to respect the constitutional rights which were so dear to the Aragonese. He was quick also to see and acknowledge the power of the Spanish Church. The Moriscos of Valencia were told that they must accept Christianity or leave the country, an act of intolerant folly in the eyes of a modern economist, but of politic concession to the prevailing prejudice of that age. Welcome also as a defence against possible trouble in the west was his marriage to Isabella of Portugal, and a certain Burgundian magnificence, foreign to the frugal habits of the country but not thought unbecoming in a king who was also an emperor and the foremost sovereign in Europe.

The finance of a world-wide imperial polity presented a problem new to Europe, which Charles could not wholly solve even with the help of the Fuggers and Welsers, the two German banking firms whose loans were indispensable. At the end of his reign, despite the fact that the taxation of Spain had been roughly trebled and little had been spent on the country itself, there was a deficit of some thirteen to twenty million sterling and, what was a specially ominous feature of the Spanish budget, a steady increase in the *juros* or annuities granted out of the State revenues in return for ready money, than which there was no more unsound method of raising an internal loan. Worst of all, the nobles of Castile refused to be taxed (1538), and thereafter were excluded from the Cortes. Thus the difficulty of financing the empire, instead of developing parliamentary liberties in Castile, hastened their extinction. The Cortes, deprived of any representation of the landed interest, became a shadow, a Parliament of thirty-six town members.

Nevertheless the vast disjointed empire was kept together in a loose personal union under the Habsburg house. The provinces of the Netherlands were ruled first (1507-30) by Margaret, Duchess of Savoy, daughter of Maximilian and consequently aunt of Charles V, and afterwards (1531-35) by Mary of Austria, sister of Charles and widow of King Louis of Hungary. But Charles was always in the background. When the populous city of Ghent refused to pay its share of the tax which had been voted by the States of Flanders towards the war with France, and drifted so far into rebellion as to arrest the imperial officers and even to traffic with Francis I, Charles collected an army and inflicted condign punishment on the rebels. Thirty-two of the leading citizens were put to death, the constitution was abrogated, and the proudest republic of the Netherlands was degraded to the status of a town on the demesne and compelled to support an imperial garrison.

If an empire of any kind was to be kept together it was clearly necessary to resist the pretensions of a city like Ghent to determine whether it should contribute or not to the Imperial wars. But in truth neither Ghent nor any other Flemish or Dutch city was interested in the wide ambitions of the Emperor. They were proud of Charles. They were on a long view benefited by the policy which resulted in the addition of Tournai and Frisia, Utrecht and Overyssel, Gröningen, Deventer, and Gelderland to their loose formation. But what interest had they in Navarre or Milan or in the recovery of the lost duchy of Burgundy? The commerce of the Netherlands cried out for peace. The policy of Charles involved them in continual war. The burghers of the north were compelled to bear the main financial burden of the empire and were entitled to say that they got little in return, save a savage persecution of heretical opinion.

It is this religious persecution which is the chief blot upon the fame of Charles V. That he was himself a Fleming made him the more resolute to cleanse his native land from the taint of heresy. It was a sacred debt to God and country to stamp out unbelief. Finding, on his return from the Diet of Worms, that Lutheran opinions were spreading fast through the Netherlands, he introduced the Inquisition (1522) in the plausible belief that an instrument which had been so successful against the Moriscos in Spain would be equally efficacious against the Dutch and the Flemings. But the courage of the northerners was of the finest and most obdurate. When Henry de Voes and John Esch, the protomartyrs of the Protestant religion, were burned at Antwerp (July 31, 1523) they gave a foretaste of that indomitable spirit which, fifty-eight years later, triumphed in the establishment of the Protestant Dutch Republic. "As they were led to the stake they cried with a loud voice that they were Christians; and when they were fastened to it, and the fire was kindled, they rehearsed the twelve articles of the Creed, and after that the *Te Deum laudamus*, which each of them sang verse by verse alternately until the flames deprived them of voice and life."

It is claimed that some thirty thousand men and women perished for their beliefs in the seventeen provinces during the reign of Charles V. Of these, some were Anabaptists, rebels against the whole order of society as well as declared foes of the Roman Church, but others were Lutherans and Calvinists, whose sole crime was that they would meet together to read the Scriptures in their native tongue and were resolved to worship God after their own fashion. For the Anabaptists no penalties were esteemed too terrible. These poor sectaries, whose revolutionary beliefs were for the most part the fruit of social misery, were drowned, roasted by slow fire, burned alive, or put to other forms of exquisite torture. The scaffold or stake which sufficed for the Lutherans was held to be an inadequate reward for desperadoes who dared to denounce property as well as priesthood. Nevertheless, heresy persisted. The spirit of Lutheranism was too deeply implanted in the land of Thomas à Kempis and of the Brethren of the Common Life to be subdued by persecution, however severe. Persecuted, imprisoned, their conventicles banned, their Bibles burned, their preachers slaughtered, the Protestants of the Netherlands continued to offer a passive resistance to the government. When Charles resigned his throne in Brussels in 1555, his successor found in the northern provinces a people so fiercely settled in their Protestant convictions that with all the might of the Spanish empire he was unable to bring them to account.

In the year in which the Inquisition was introduced into the Netherlands, and while Luther was still hiding in the Wartburg, and it was reasonable for all good Catholics to hope that "the quarrel of monks," as the Lutheran nuisance appeared to be, would yield to a few years of firm government, the *Victoria*, a galleon of eighty-five tons flying the Spanish flag, under John Sebastian del Cano, cast anchor in the Guadalquivir after an absence of three years. This little ship had circumnavigated the globe. Starting as one of a fleet of five under the general command of Ferdinand Magellan, the *Victoria* had rounded Patagonia, crossed the Pacific, and, after Magellan's death among the Spice Islands, had fought her way across the long wastes of the Indian Ocean to the southern tip of Africa, and so home.

The young Emperor was exalted by this new proof of the manifold favours of Providence to the Habsburg house. Was it not clear that Austria was destined to rule the universe? *Austriae est imperare orbi universo*. The vision of a Catholic Austria governing a Catholic world rose before his eyes. Already Cuba was Spanish and already Hernando Cortes, starting from Cuba, had won Mexico for Spain. With a mere handful of Spaniards, but with the invaluable aid of horses and guns, this resolute and resourceful commander had overpowered the Aztecs, a race of bloodthirsty cannibals who here maintained a curious and mutilated civilization, knowing nothing of coinage, of beasts of burden, of cows or of goats, had kidnapped their king Montezuma and made himself master of their capital city. There have been few clearer examples in history of the power of prestige in war. The Aztecs were as innocent as they were cruel. They found in the Spaniard a source of bewildered amazement. His fierce animal energy, his horses, his guns were things outside the orb of their experience. They were ready to believe the fable industriously circulated by Cortes that the mysterious strangers who had suddenly dropped from nowhere with their uncanny attendant animals were demi-gods whom it was idle to vex or to resist.

The subjugation of Mexico or New Spain was only one among many manifestations of the exploring enterprise of the Spanish conquistador. He was to be met among the swamps of Florida and on the banks of the Mississippi and the Colorado. He founded Panama, entered Nicaragua, drew German financiers after him into Venezuela. But among the many great achievements of these daring pioneers none was so important as Pizarro's conquest of Peru. Here were to be found in abundance the gold, the silver and the precious stones which in the eyes of all materially minded Spaniards constituted the main object of colonial adventure. Here was Eldorado so long sought, so painfully secured; but so compelling in its attractions that it at once became the standard against which all other conquests and colonies were necessarily measured. Compared with the precious metals and jewels of Peru, Argentina, the greatest potential granary in the new world, was a country not worth the exploitation. Indeed, if the Plate River which waters that fertile country had the power to tempt the Spanish explorer, it was only because it appeared to be a waterway leading straight to the coveted treasures of New Castile.

Pizarro was an illiterate foundling who like many a poor Spaniard in those days took to the sea for a livelihood, having already tried other avocations. The autumn of 1522 found him in Panama, a needy fortune hunter greedy for enterprise and lucre. Here he learnt from one Pascual de Andagaya, a Spanish mariner, of a rich land on the Pacific coast of South America inhabited by a people known as Incas. Pizarro was one of those men who are devoured by greed as dipsomaniacs are consumed by thirst. The vision of great wealth easily got and easily handled filled his dreams and shaped his career. Gold was his religion. In search of gold he felt no fear and respected no scruple. He set off at once for the fortunate land with one ship and a hundred men. His expectations ended in failure. Two years later he renewed the attempt (1526) and was rewarded by the sight of well-cultivated fields and of natives wearing jewels and ornaments of gold. His purpose was thenceforth inexorably fixed. When his followers wished to take advantage of a relief ship and to return to Panama he drew a line on the sand with his sword, saying, " Friends and comrades, on that side are toil, hunger, nakedness, the drenching storm, desertion and death, on this side ease and pleasure. There lies Peru with its riches; here Panama with its poverty. Choose each man what best becomes a brave Castilian. For my part I go to the south." With these words he stepped south of the line and was followed by sixteen of his shipmates.

What he then discovered was a state the like of which has never exactly been repeated in any part of the globe. The vast empire of the Incas was remarkable for its application on a great scale of a system of despotic communism. Nobody was allowed to be idle. Nobody was allowed to overwork. Everyone was liable to transplantation, on evidence of overcrowding. The temples and palaces, the roads, aqueducts, canals and tillage of these opulent and ingenious sun-worshippers excited the admiration of the conquistadors. The gold and silver fired their greed. After a careful exploration of this wonderful land Pizarro returned to Spain and there obtained a commission from the Emperor (July 26, 1529), which entrusted him with viceregal powers over the country which he had still to conquer. In treachery and violence no conquistador surpassed Francisco Pizarro. Atahualpa, the unfortunate ruler of the country, was wickedly kidnapped, mulcted of his treasure, and after a mock trial burned to death in the great square of Casamanca (August 29, 1533). It was a sinister feature of this hideous crime that it was carried out with the applause and connivance of the missionary friars.

The conquest of Peru, the last and richest of the great colonial prizes which fell to Spain during the reign of Charles V, was not an unmixed blessing. No community has ever been ethically advantaged by participation in a gold rush. The Spaniards of the sixteenth century, who caught the gold and silver fever before philanthropic ideals had been properly organized and brought to bear upon the problems of industry, were no exceptions to this rule. They quarrelled among themselves and submitted the miserable and helpless natives of the country to a most grinding oppression. Money was mistaken for wealth and the true foundations of economic prosperity were ignored. Demoralized themselves, the treasure-hunters of Peru spread the taint of their merciless avarice through the body politic of Spain.

"Before the abdication of Charles, Mexico and Central America, Venezuela and New Granada, Peru, Bolivia, and Western Chile were organized possessions of the Castilian Crown. Argentina and Paraguay were still in the early stages of settlement, California and Florida in that of discovery." When it is considered that this great extension of Spanish empire and discovery were undertaken at a time when Spain was almost continuously involved in a war with the greatest of European powers, and often with the Turks, the achievement is astonishing.

That hideous oppressions were practised by the Spanish colonists is the dark blot upon this record. But it is due to Europe to point out that the weight of the Emperor was cast on the side of clemency, that when an issue arose, as it often did, between philanthropic missionaries and exploiting colonists, he was on the side of the missionaries, that largely as a consequence of the intervention of the home government the native populations of the American mainland were for the most part preserved from destruction, and that in the list of missionary heroes who have dedicated their lives to the relief of the subject races there is no nobler figure than Las Casas, the first priest to realize and denounce the iniquities practised by his compatriots in the Spanish colonies and the pioneer of all those later humanitarian move ments by which men have endeavoured to mitigate the exploitation of the new world by the old.

The Italian wars of Charles V are commemorated by the genius of Titian and Ariosto, but are of less enduring importance for the world than those distant conquests beyond the Atlantic Ocean. Yet to contemporaries few events seemed to be more big with the future than the overthrow of the French military power in Italy. It had been so sudden. It appeared to be so complete. The French were beaten at Bicocca in 1522; they were again defeated at Pavia in 1525 when their king Francis was taken captive and shipped off to Spain. Milan, wrested from the French, was handed over to Francesco Sforza as an Imperial fief, and became thenceforth under the thinnest mantle of disguise a Spanish dependency; and as through Milan Spain held the keys of the north, so through Naples and Sicily she was mistress of the south. To the poetic mind of Ariosto the Italian victories of Charles seemed to portend the world empire which was destined eventually to bring peace to mankind.

Such a demonstration of Spanish power was alarming to all those Italians who for one reason or another were concerned to prevent any one foreign state from obtaining a mastery over the peninsula. In particular it shot tremors of apprehension through the intelligent and well-informed statesmen who ruled in the Vatican. By birth, office and experience (for as Cardinal Giuliano dei Medici he had long been in the forefront of politics), Clement VII might have seemed to be well fitted to lead a great Italian movement against the Imperialists. Unfortunately, with all his skill in negotiation, his quickness and penetration, his subtlety and culture, he was devoid of those moral and intellectual qualities which are essential to leadership. He was one of those men who sweep so many small things into the field of vision that the big things are crowded out. When a clear decision was needed, Clement would hover between competing courses. When it was essential to enlist every Italian prince in a campaign against the Spaniards, he would throw away the aid of a powerful auxiliary by insisting upon the restoration of two paltry towns which the Duke of Ferrara had filched from the papal state. In a situation which required a world outlook and a resolute will this charming and cultivated Tuscan gentleman exhibited the parochial perspective of an Italian princelet and the nervous indecision of a fussy invalid.

Under such a leader no great scheme could come to fruition. Charles was aware of the Pope's intrigues with the Regent of France, with Venice, with Morone the Chancellor of Milan, he was aware of the Holy League of Cognac which was formed against him and of the army of the League which was gathering in Italy, and, being forewarned, saw to it that the imperial troops were so reinforced as to be able to deal with the situation.

The Pope was helpless and isolated in Rome. Even in the Vatican he was not safe from the Colonnas, that fierce Ghibelline clan, who never lost an opportunity of paying off old scores against a Pope. But there was a worse enemy to face than the Colonnas, under whose local and humiliating pressure Clement had been forced to withdraw his contingent from the army of the League. Twelve thousand Lutheran *Landsknechts*, marching without pay and living on the country-side (as was the manner of the Imperial forces), descended into Italy to chastise the Pope who had dared to affront their Imperial master. "The Pope," said George von Frundsberg, their leader, "is the Emperor's worst enemy and has begun the war. For the honour of God he must be hanged, though I have to do it with my own hand." In such a mood the formidable army of hungry Germans, joining hands with the imperial forces under the Constable of Bourbon, moved southward without molestation upon Rome. What then happened, though it was wholly undesigned, and in no sense the result of instructions from Spain, was a startling lesson to the priests of the danger of running counter to the Emperor's will. On the night of May 6, 1527, forty thousand wild and mutinous men, as fierce a body of troops as any in Europe, were collected outside the walls of the papal city. They forced an entry, drove the Pope into the Castle of St. Angelo and then for eight terrible days gave full vent to their cruelty, rapacity, and lust. All the churches and the monasteries were sacked. Friars and priests were beheaded; "many old nuns beaten with sticks, many young nuns raped and taken prisoner." The Church of St. Peter and the Holy Palace were turned into stables for horses. Two-thirds of Rome was left in ruins. To

some it seemed that this terrible punishment was a divine revelation. "In Rome," says a grave contemporary, "all sins were
committed—sodomy, simony, idolatry, hypocrisy, fraud. Surely
then what has come to pass has not been by chance but by the
Judgment of God." In Florence the lesson to be derived was
that the Medici might now be safely expelled and a republic
established in their place. To the world it was clear that more
than ever before the Imperial yoke was fastened on Italy.

Again, the menace of the Empire had become so great as to
provoke a coalition of powers against it. France and England
joined with Venice to reduce the Imperial pride and to free the
Papacy from the Spanish yoke. A French army under Lautrec
recovered most of the Milanese and passed uncontested through
Italy to the siege of Naples. The city, closely invested by
the French on land and by a Genoese squadron in the harbour, seemed in June, 1528, like to fall. Was all Italy to pass
from Spanish into French control? But then followed one of
those sudden changes of fortune which are specially liable to
affect small armies operating at a distance from their home. In
the south the army of Lautrec, decimated by casualties from
disease which it was unable to replace and demoralized by the
death of its commander, was compelled to abandon the siege of
Naples and to capitulate at Aversa. In the north the French
went down before a reinforced Imperial army at Landriano.
But more important still as affecting the permanent balance of
power in the Mediterranean was the defection of Andrea Doria,
the great Genoese seaman, from the French to the Imperialists.
A sailor of fortune, but also a Genoese patriot, Doria harboured
many grudges public and private against the French. It angered
him to see a French garrison in his native city. He viewed with
disfavour the commerce, growing too rapidly under French encouragement, of Savona, the neighbour and the rival. In the
very middle of the siege of Naples, when his defection would
be most injurious to the French and most helpful to their
enemies, Doria swung the whole influence of Genoa into the
Imperialist cause. The strongest Italian navy in the western
Mediterranean was henceforth enlisted on the side of Spain. For
Charles the alliance of Genoa brought three decisive advantages
It denied the Italian coast to the French, it opened the gateway
between Spain and Germany, and it gave to Italy a keen sense
of pride in the Imperial victories. In Ariosto's great epic, Doria

is singled out from among the paladins of Charles as the friend
who had brought him victory in every war.

Neither in this nor in any other Italian campaign did the
Emperor take a personal part. The Spanish victories in the field
were won by Spanish captains commanding disciplined Spanish
footmen who had been schooled not only to handle the pike but
in a skilful use of fire-arms. To Charles, however, belongs the
credit of securing the fruits of victory by a wise exercise of
diplomatic temperance. After Landriano he broke the hostile
coalition by a separate peace with France. He had something to
give and much to receive. Under the Treaty which was concluded at Cambrai (August, 1529) the Emperor surrendered his
claims to the Burgundian inheritance of his grandmother Mary,
while Francis renounced his claims in Italy and his feudal rights
in Flanders and Artois. Eleanor the sister of Charles was
married to Francis.

The Emperor was at the zenith of his power. He was master
of Italy. He had made a family compact with Clement VII, by
whom he was crowned at Bologna with the iron crown of Lombardy and the golden crown of the Empire. Ferdinand his
brother would succeed him as emperor, Philip his son as King
of Spain. And he had now received what was the prime condition for any successful operations against the Turks, a peace
with France. When in 1535 he led an army to Africa and took
Tunis, he shone out before Europe, despite the evil memory
of the sack of Rome, as the champion of the Christian Faith.

He had not finally settled his account with Francis I. That
accomplished but worthless monarch, who carried statesmanship
to such a point of cynicism that he encouraged heretics abroad
while he persecuted them at home and even offered the shelter
of Toulon harbour to the Turkish corsair Barbarossa, had not
yet, despite all that was written in the Treaty of Cambrai, relinquished his dreams of Italian conquest. The marriage of his
eldest son Henry to Catharine dei Medici, a kinswoman of the
Pope, was a signal that the French claims in Italy were still alive.
In effect war broke out over Milan in 1536, was stayed two years
later (Treaty of Nice, 1538), was resumed in 1542, and was finally
composed so far as Charles and Francis were concerned by the
Peace of Crespi in 1544. Nothing important was changed by
these two short struggles. Spain still remained mistress of Milan
and Naples. France, save for the loss of Boulogne to England,

maintained her frontiers. The diplomatic honours rested with Charles, who showed much skill in decoying Francis with hopes of the Milanese succession, and in his last war secured the assistance of England. But what was principally illustrated by this long duel for Italy was the sharp decline in the old conception of the Christian Commonwealth of Europe. Though the infidel was knocking hard at the gates, the army of the Holy Roman Emperor had sacked the churches of Rome, and the most Christian King was the declared friend and ally of the Turk.

The Spanish dominion in Italy, which was finally established in 1539, lasted until the end of the wars of Louis XIV. The brilliant intellectual agitation of the Renaissance was exchanged for a period of profound repose, during which the Jesuits, the Inquisition, and the Index combined to stifle the free movement of the mind and to mould it to the Catholic pattern. Life became more sedate and decorous. Hypocrisy replaced effrontery. The open parade of vice or atheism became dangerous and therefore unfashionable. There was a rally of all the virtuous elements in Italian society towards a reformed Church of Rome. Only among a small circle of Neapolitan intellectuals and in the Republic of Venice, which maintained its independence of Spain and kept the Pope at arm's length, was there any survival of that earlier liberty of thought and speech which had made Italy the preceptress of Europe in the previous age. The nimble-witted Italians laughed at their strong and solemn rulers, shrugged their shoulders, and, being relieved by these useful aliens of the burden of government and war, not unthankfully obeyed.

Among the terms of the family compact made between Charles and Clement in 1529 was the restoration of the Medici to Florence. The undertaking was carried out in the following year. The city was besieged by a large Imperial army under the command of the Prince of Orange, captured after a brilliant defence, robbed of its republic, and compelled to submit to Alessandro dei Medici, the bastard son of a mulatto slave woman. In the long annals of Europe the downfall of a short-lived Italian Republic may be of little moment; but circumstance gave to the eclipse of republican liberties in Florence a special significance. The city was the capital of Italian genius. The republic, which was the creature of a prophet's enthusiasm, had enlisted the hopes of a series of native historians whose grave pages still burn with classic ardour. Its walls were defended by Michael Angelo, its countryside by a patriotic militia realizing the dream of Machiavelli, and if it had survived it might have taught the Italian people that lesson of military self-help which alone could bring them safety, unity, and self-respect. But the city fell, and it is noteworthy that one of the causes of its surrender was the treachery of an Italian *condottiere* from Perugia, whose assistance had been unwisely invoked.

BOOKS WHICH MAY BE CONSULTED

E. Armstrong : The Emperor Charles V. 1902.
F. A. Mignet : Rivalité de François I et de Charles V. 2 vols. 1876.
H. C. Lea : The Moriscos of Spain. 1901.
Helps : The Spanish Conquest of America. 1900-4.
J. S. C. Bridge : A History of France from the Death of Louis XI. 1921.
Henri Lemonnier in Lavisse : Histoire de France, Vol. V, i ; V, ii.
R. B. Merriman : The Rise of the Spanish Empire, 1918-25.
R. Altamira y Crevea, Historia d'España y de la civilizacion espanola. 1902.
J. Fiske : The Discovery of America. 1892.
W. H. Prescott : History of the Conquest of Mexico. Everyman's Library. 2 vols. 1909.
W. H. Prescott : History of the Conquest of Peru. Everyman's Library. 1908.
H. M. Stephens : Portugal. 1891.
Janet Trevelyan : A Short History of the Italian People. 1929.

CHAPTER XI

CALVINISM

*The clarion of reform. The Evangel in Zurich. The field of Cappel.
Geneva. John Calvin. His stoicism and belief in predestination. Founds
a theocratic state. The democratic character of Calvinism. Geneva becomes the training ground for the reformed ministry. Far-reaching
influence of Calvinism.*

THE influence of Luther upon mankind was not restricted to that
German and Scandinavian area which was permanently won for
the Lutheran Church, but penetrated everywhere. His bold challenge rang through Europe. Was it true that the world had been
treading a false road for more than a thousand years, that the
Papacy was an imposture, the special sanctity of the priesthood a
fiction, and that rites, ceremonies, and institutions interwoven
with the familiar life of Europe were unnecessary and even harmful? Only the dullest indifference could fail to be startled by
such a message. Opinions might differ as to its value. Some
might think it very good, others very wicked. But no one could
deny that it was exciting. Poles, Czechs, and Magyars caught at
it in snatches. Spanish merchants carried it in little printed
quartos over upland roads to be rendered into Castilian prose.
Cambridge divines discussed it over their tankards; Oxford booksellers sold it across the counter. In Paris it was hawked about
under the noses of the doctors of the Sorbonne. If Erasmus more
than any other man aroused the great curiosity, it was Luther
who initiated the great revolt. In Switzerland and France, Scotland and England, countries in which reform assumed a shape
differing from the Lutheran model, it was he who sowed the seed
and prepared the ground.

Ulrich Zwingli went too fast. He tried by means of a trade
embargo to compel the five Catholic cantons of eastern Switzerland to admit the evangelical teaching which found favour in
Zurich and Bern, and paid for his temerity on the bloodstained
field of Cappel (October 11, 1531). With his soldier's death
Zurich lost its pre-eminence in the Swiss reforming movement.
In the eastern part of Switzerland which was mainly German in

race and language the old religion recovered its ascendancy. The results of that short six weeks' war have never been reversed. What was Catholic at the close of that struggle is Catholic now. The dream of Zwingli, that the evangelic faith might spread through the whole Confederation, that democracy might every where replace oligarchy, and that Bern and Zurich might acquire that weight in the affairs of the Confederation which their numbers demanded, was dissolved. The most gifted and attractive of the reformers, though in private morals far from flawless, failed from an impetuous under-estimate of the ardent peasant champions of the Virgin and the Saints, whose log cabins were strewn high among the Alpine pastures and forests and far removed from the heresies of town-bred men.

The direction of the Swiss reforming movement passed to Bern and then to a city lying outside the Swiss Confederation and containing no more than thirteen thousand inhabitants, but destined, partly through its geographical position—for it was placed on the confines of four nations—and still more through its association with one of the great religious leaders of the world, to become the capital of western Protestantism and for centuries a chief city of refuge for the persecuted minorities of that faith: it passed to Geneva.

For thirty years Geneva had been struggling to rid itself of the control of the Duke of Savoy and of its Prince Bishop. The struggle partook of the bitterness of a civil war. The Episcopal party were styled by their adversaries the Mamelukes. The party of liberty were known as the Eidgenossen (sworn companions), a name which, in its French form of Huguenot, was soon destined to be heard throughout Europe. But in the end (October, 1536), with the help of Protestant Bern, Geneva achieved its liberty and was prepared to give heed to certain French missionaries who with Bernese encouragement were spreading evangelical teaching through the Pays de Vaud. Of these none was so effective as the vehement William Farel, at whose instance a young French scholar travelling through Geneva on his private occasions in 1536 was prevailed on to stop and permanently to exchange a life of study for one of active ministration.

The young scholar was John Cauvin (Calvin), the son of a notary public, born at Noyon in Picardy in 1509, and already famous, though he was only twenty-seven years of age, for three remarkable publications—a learned commentary on Seneca's *De*

Clementia, an academic discourse, so full of evangelical enthusiasm as to necessitate his hurried departure from Paris, and an introduction to Biblical study entitled *Christianae Religionis Institutio,* which was published at Basel and dedicated to King Francis I.

Nobody could less resemble Martin Luther than this studious and polite young Frenchman, of the upper middle class, and never more at his ease than among men and women of noble birth, who had absorbed whatever Paris could give him of the humanities or Orleans and Bourges of law. Of Luther's vast animal power, of his gaiety and wit, his coarseness and humour, his wild vein of romance and crabbed scholasticism, his naïve peasant superstitions and morbid self-criticism there was nothing in Calvin. The Frenchman was quiet and reserved, lucid in thought and expression, always superior by reason of his ready store of patristic and Biblical learning to those with whom he was brought into controversy, and possessing the great advantage which comes to a man who has won his way to settled convictions with no visible scars of an inner conflict. A stern simplicity in the processes of his thought gave him a searching power over lax and uncertain minds. We may call him an intellectual athlete, or a saint without sentimentality, or simply a born director of the conscience. His work was to make of Geneva an evangelical republic and to lead the reforming or Huguenot party in France.

In accounting for his influence in France, Renan says that Calvin succeeded in an age and in a country which called for a reaction towards Christianity simply because he was the most Christian man of his generation. This is largely true, but not the whole truth. Calvin was a Christian. His private life was simple and austere; his passions controlled, his ends lofty. All his physical and intellectual powers were employed in the endeavour to bring back into the world the Christianity of the first three centuries, of which in his quiet, ardent, intellectual way he had constructed a convincing image. His correspondence was enormous. From his adopted home in Geneva he dispensed spiritual counsel to all the Huguenot congregations of France. Now he would strengthen the doubter, now prick on the slothful, now encourage the downhearted or rebuke the backslider. But neither his Christian piety nor the unflagging energy of his pen would have made him a power in France had it not been for the fact that he possessed in a very high degree the logical structure, the clarity and grace of phrase, the conciseness of statement and sense of measure which alone give to a French intellectual the ear of France.

"Your Serenity," writes the Venetian Ambassador to the Doge in 1561, "will hardly believe the influence and the power which the principal minister of Geneva, by name Calvin, a Frenchman and a native of Picardy, possesses in this kingdom. He is a man of extraordinary authority, who by his mode of life, his doctrines, and his writings rises superior to all the rest." And the influence of Calvin the man was supported by the singular prestige attaching to Geneva, a city in which the magistrates were chosen by the people, the ministers by their flock, in which there was no privileged church or aristocracy, but all were equal before the law as they were equal in the eye of God.

The editor of Seneca was, like his master, a stoic, believing that virtue should be practised for its own sake and without regard to future rewards and punishments. That stoical ideal, transformed by the teaching of the Gospels, lies at the heart of the Calvinist religion. Nor has its moral influence been weakened by that other doctrine of predestination, that some are pre-ordained to eternal life and others to eternal damnation, which Calvin could not have found in the Gospels, but deduced from the teaching of Paul and Augustine.

Indeed, among the European peoples none have been sterner in the practice of religion 'or more ruthless in the pursuit of wealth than the professors of a doctrine which seems to make all human effort unavailing and to invite to a life of apathy and ease.

Save for a period of three years (1538-41), Calvin lived in Geneva from 1536 to his death in 1564. Here he framed a new type of theocratic state which exercised an influence over the spirit and structure of the "reformed" churches throughout the world. The key to his organization was the discovery that during the first three centuries of the Christian era the unworthy were excluded from the Communion table. Calvin determined to revive that ancient discipline, and to confine the supreme privilege of the Church to worshippers of a proved and tested godliness. That such an end could not be achieved without a minute and irksome supervision into private life did not deter him. He welcomed conditions under which pastors and laymen alike would be subjected to a rigorous control, and though it was against his principles to invoke the lay power in aid of spiritual discipline, he was content that in Geneva the strong arm of the magistrate should assist the Church. What sacrifice was not justified to bring godliness back to earth? So a supreme Council, part lay, part clerical, was set up in Geneva to enforce a code of penalties on laxities of private conduct and belief. Adultery, blasphemy, and heresy were punished by death. It was a sombre, fault-finding, inquisitorial government which, being taken as a pattern in other lands, was a source of much cruelty and suffering in the New World as well as in the Old. In Geneva itself it led to the burning of Servetus, the Unitarian, with the concurrence and approval of Calvin himself.

Against this undoubted evil must be set the value to Europe of a new type of religious society, which, unlike the Lutheran Church, was independent of princely favour. Under the democratic system set up by Calvin each church was governed by an elective body of lay elders and deacons. Two important results followed. The first was the close association between Calvinism and a universal theological education, the second that Calvinism, unlike the Lutheran Church, never dried up when the original creative impulse was exhausted. How vital this creed still is, and how closely connected with a popular training in the Bible, may be realized by the visitor who enters any Welsh Sunday school today.

It was part of Calvin's greatness that he was not only the central figure in a wide European movement, but that, working intensively within the narrow circumference of Geneva, and against every description of obstruction, he made of it the high school of the reformed religion. During his long course of Biblical teaching he boasted in a valedictory letter addressed to the ministers of Geneva that he had never perverted a text of Scripture; and it is due to his exertions that Geneva became not only a well-educated city, but in a more specific sense, and particularly after the formation of the University in 1559, a training-ground for the Protestant or Huguenot ministry. Calvin found Geneva turbulent, divided, uneasy, immoral. He left it a Protestant Sparta, the soul of all that was valiant, devoted, and, it may be added, fiercely intolerant, in the evangelical movement of that age.

Of all the forms assumed by the Protestant Reformation, Calvinism has been the most far-reaching in its scope and the most profound in its influence. It made the Protestant Church in France, it fashioned the Dutch Republic, it was accepted as the national religion of Scotland. Before Calvin's death his creed had been received in the Protestant cantons of eastern Switzerland, in the Palatinate, and by the majority of those Hungarians who had broken with Rome. Even in England, where it was confronted with an overwhelming body of conservative sentiment, it exercised an influence over the Thirty-Nine Articles, which constitute the declared creed of the National Church, so palpable that Queen Elizabeth, little as she sympathized with the spirit of Geneva, was excommunicated as a Calvinist. Afterwards, but only for a time under the Long Parliament, and through force of arms rather than a change in national sentiment, Calvinism became a predominant force in English politics. With the Restoration it receded into the background, a minor but never a negligible element in the religious consciousness of the country. But if Geneva agreed ill with the merry court of Charles II, it was just the thing for the north American littoral. Here ever since the voyage of the *Mayflower* in 1621, and more particularly in the New England colonies, it has exercised a profound influence on church and state, reaching into the middle decades of the nineteenth century. From its harsh and gloomy teaching the reasoned optimism of the pragmatist, who exalts positive achievement, and the extreme idealism of the Christian Scientist, who negates the reality of pain and evil, are varying and characteristic reactions.

BOOKS WHICH MAY BE CONSULTED

Mark Pattison : Collected Essays. *Ed.* H. Nettleship. 1889.

T. H. Dyer : The Life of John Calvin. 1850.

H. F. Henderson : Calvin in his Letters. 1909.

A. Bossert : Calvin (Grands Écrivains Français).

Ch. Borgeaud : The Rise of Modern Democracy in Old and New England. *Tr.* Mrs. Birkbeck Hill. 1894.

Ch. Borgeaud : Histoire de l'Université de Genève. I, l'Académie de Calvin, 1559-1798. 1900.

L. Häusser : The Period of the Reformation. *Tr.* Mrs. G. Sturge. *Ed.* W. Oncken. 2 vols. 1873.

CHAPTER XII

GERMANY AGREES TO DIFFER

Balance of Catholic and Protestant forces in Germany. The first serious set-back to the Lutheran movement. Philip of Hesse. Charles V attacks the Lutherans. The inconclusive character of the war. France invoked by the Lutherans. The Peace of Augsburg, 1555. The Treaty of Cateau Cambrésis, 1559. France loses Italy but gains Metz, Toul, and Verdun. The new figures on the stage.

IF the Lutherans could not be peaceably recalled to the Catholic faith, could they be suppressed by force? In 1540 the big battalions were with the Catholic powers. The Lutheran religion was professed by a number of small German states, by Saxony, both electoral and ducal, by Hesse and Brunswick, by Brandenburg (since 1539) and Prussia and by a number of important cities in north and south. These Protestants, as they were called in virtue of a protest against Catholic claims drawn up in 1531, were organized, could put an army in the field, and had even won a military triumph against the Habsburg house by restoring to Würtemberg its banished Lutheran duke. But compared with the might of the Catholic states, had these been united or able to mobilize their resources, compared with Spain and France, Italy, Austria and the Netherlands, not to speak of the Catholic half of Germany, the military and financial resources of the Smalkaldic League were inconsiderable. Against an army even approximately representing the potential resources of Catholic Europe, any force which the German Protestants could have put into the field would have been inevitably destroyed. These conditions were never realized. Neither then nor at any other time has religion been an exclusive motive in European politics. Other motives, other elements have always been present. Charles was a sincere Catholic, but even Charles was often at variance with the Pope. Had the Catholic princes in the German Diet been asked to choose whether they would prefer a Germany united in the Catholic creed under a strong emperor or divided under a weak one, they would have chosen the second alternative. There was not a prince, Catholic or Protestant, who would vote for any scheme to mobilize the resources of the Empire easily and effectively for the pursuit of a strong policy whether Catholic or Lutheran. The princes were content that the Holy Roman Empire should continue, because it was ancient, elective, interwoven with their own privileges, so long as the Holy Roman Emperor did not presume to interfere with their internal affairs. So Diets met, and feasted and dissolved with nothing done except to recognize or ineffectually not to recognize the accomplished fact of religious disunion. The knowledge that the League of Smalkalden was organized for resistance and had friends abroad acted as a deterrent against a precipitate recourse to force.

The reformers had also, in all the earlier stages of their movement, the advantages which belong to an energetic body of earnest men carrying out a campaign against generally recognized abuses and for purposes of dialectical dispute better equipped than their opponents. The intellectual and moral attack was strong. The intellectual and moral defence, until the Jesuits came into the field, was weak. The ordinary forces of blind conservatism which might have been organized against the new movement were disarmed by its emphatic repudiation of the peasants and Anabaptists. Thanks to the regulative influence of Luther, who lived to 1546, the German reformers did not create the kind of panic which leads opponents to think that they are confronted with one of those perils to the ultimate decencies of life which at all costs and before everything else must be averted. Of all the forms assumed by continental dissent the Lutheran was the most conservative. Its church services were based on the Roman model. Its doctrine of Consubstantiation was not far distant from the Roman thesis of a change in the elements. Its original professors were not men standing outside the Church, but for the most part monks and priests of exceptional piety, who believed that they could bring the Church to its true and original ways. The line between Catholic and Protestant is now sharply and deeply graven. In the first generation of the reforming movements the outlines were more fluid, and intermediate possibilities more easily entertained. An Archbishop of Cologne was drawn towards the new doctrine, and at one time there was even an expectation that all three Rhenish Archbishoprics might go over to the Lutheran camp.

In all religious movements there is a period of danger. It

comes when the first passionate enthusiasm begins to die down, and the statesmen are called in to regulate and organize. The princes who succeeded the preachers in the control of the Lutheran movement were in point of morality little, if any better than the average of their age and country. One was apparently worse.

The first serious set-back to the Lutheran movement, the first incident which gave to its opponents a formidable handle of attack, was the divorce of Philip of Hesse in 1540. To those who had been fiercely assailed for their low moral standard, it was gratifying to know that the great Lutheran chieftain was no better than anyone else, that he was prepared to reject a lawful wife in order to marry another woman who had captured his fancy, and that in this profligate course he had been encouraged by Lutheran divines like Bucer and Melanchthon, and by the opinion of the great Dr. Martin himself that polygamy had the sanction of Holy Writ. Nor was the scandal lessened by advice of the divines that the second marriage should be concealed. Philip of Hesse had no intention of concealing his second marriage. He was not prepared, as Luther recommended, to tell "a great bold lie for the good of the Christian Church." But the fact that such advice was tendered cooled his enthusiasm for his Lutheran associates, drove him for a time into the Emperor's camp and advertised a rift in the Protestant ranks.

While the two German parties were watching one another with eyes of anxious hate, Charles made peace with France (September, 1544), and was thereafter free, should conciliation fail, to try the expedient of force against the Lutherans. There were many coherent arguments which might be used in favour of such a course, notably the recent triumphs of the Protestant faith in the Palatinate and in Cologne, and one influential firebrand, his father confessor, to advise it. But the Emperor was no great believer in a religious peace thus violently promoted, and only after long hesitation and with a significant attempt to conceal his true purpose, determined to gather an army, enlist allies, and to strike.

In launching an attack upon John Frederick of Saxony and Philip of Hesse, the two foremost leaders of the Lutheran cause, the Emperor was careful to found his action on considerations of politics only. The princes were to be punished not for heresy but for disobedience. Though the Pope was providing men and money, Charles knew that an open crusade against heresy would have little chance among the Germans. He was himself relying upon heretical aid, and notably upon the military talents of the wicked and aspiring Maurice of Saxony, to whom he had secretly promised John Frederick's electoral hat.

The war which ensued was marked by the inability of the Protestant generals to make use of a great initial advantage, by the paralyzing defection of Prince Maurice and by a crowning Imperial victory at Mühlberg on the Elbe (April 24, 1547). But the religious problem was no nearer solution for Charles' military success. The defeat of the Lutheran army, the capture of John Frederick and the unconditional surrender of Philip of Hesse made no alteration in the general balance of the opposing creeds. Nor were the Germans any whit the more disposed to help the Emperor to solve that evil of political anarchy which continued to be the curse of German public life. When Charles proposed a German league with permanent officers, a permanent revenue and a regular army, his suggestions fell stone dead upon the Diet. When he divulged a plan for making the Empire hereditary in the Habsburg house, it was at once rejected by the electors. Apparently the most resplendent figure in Europe, he was in Germany subject to every rebuff and humiliation. The princes distrusted him because he wanted power; the Catholics because he wished to reform abuses; the Lutherans because he believed in the Pope. A well-meant scheme for a religious *modus vivendi* known as the Interim (May 13, 1548) was everywhere denounced and nowhere observed.

Then followed an episode bringing immediate humiliation to Charles, still greater humiliation to Germany and leading through a long and connected chain of events to those two great Franco-German wars which have devastated Europe in the nineteenth and twentieth centuries. The leading actors in the drama were Maurice of Saxony and Henry II, the new King of France. Maurice had in 1546 sold himself to Charles for place and power. He wanted to rob John Frederick of the electorate and to transfer to his own (the Albertine) branch of the Wettin family the possessions which belonged to the Ernestine line. He wanted other things as well, for he was a highly appetitive adventurer, and some of these, though in the main his reward was rich, he had not received. He had won the electoral hat but not Magdeburg. Other grievances, of a less personal nature,

may have weighed with him, such as the continued imprisonment of his father-in-law, Philip of Hesse, and the violation by
the Emperor of the municipal liberties of certain Protestant
towns. Slipping swiftly from disappointment to distrust, from
distrust to anger, he began secretly to weave a coalition against
the Emperor, and being in search of a powerful ally turned to
Henry II of France. There is little favourable to be said of
this monarch save that he was brought to see that the true
interests of France lay not in Italy but on the Rhine. The
proposals of Maurice and his camarilla of Lutheran generals
chimed in with this intelligent appreciation of French needs.
By the Treaty of Chambord, 1552, it was arranged that Metz,
Toul, and Verdun, together with the city of Cambrai, should be
handed over to Henry as Vicar-General of the Empire in return
for his assistance to the German rebels. The entry of France
into Lorraine and Alsace dates from this memorable transaction.

While the French were occupied in seizing their prize, the
army of Maurice advancing on Innsbruck caused the Emperor
to flee suddenly for his life over the Brenner pass. From that
moment Charles exercised no further influence over the fate of
Germany.

Accordingly it was not by Charles but by his brother Ferdinand, one of the wisest rulers of the Habsburg house, that religious peace was given to Germany. Charles had worked for
comprehension based on compromise. Ferdinand accepted the
necessary fact of division. The guiding principle of the Peace of
Augsburg (September 25, 1555) was *cujus regio, ejus religio*. The
princes, without interference from the Emperor or the Diet,
were to be allowed each in his own territory to settle the form
and character of the Church. The idea, always cherished by
Charles, that the forces of a reunited Germany might be launched
against France was now recognized as an idle dream. Catholic
would not yield to Lutheran, nor Lutheran to Catholic. On the
most difficult question of all, Ferdinand decreed a compromise.
Catholic archbishops, bishops, or priests embracing Protestantism
should forfeit their sees or benefices; but no spiritual prince
should be entitled to impose the Catholic religion by force upon
his subjects.

The Peace of Augsburg cannot be reckoned among the great
liberating documents of history. It did not even assign a place
to those types of Protestant belief which flourished in Zurich or

Geneva. Still less did it enunciate the principle of religious toleration. But as a rough, serviceable solution of a grave controversy, it deserves to be honourably thought of, for, if it did not bring religious harmony, it kept war out of Germany for fifty years.

Four years after the religious settlement (April, 1559) there followed that other treaty signed at Cateau Cambrésis which closes the long struggle between France and Spain for hegemony in Italy. Proud and sensitive states do not lightly relinquish high ambitions. It may readily be imagined that it was not without pain and a certain humiliation that France renounced those dreams of Italian power upon which she had lavished blood and treasure for sixty years. But in the last stage of the struggle she had received two serious warnings. A French army led by the Duke of Guise, the most accomplished of her generals, and encouraged by Paul IV, the most ill-balanced of the Popes, had been defeated by the Spaniards in Naples and rolled back towards the Alps; and much nearer home, within a few days' march of Paris, another army composed of the flower of the French nobility and commanded by the Constable of Montmorency, the premier noble of France and the leading adviser of the king, was overwhelmed before the walls of St. Quentin by an Imperial army under Emmanuel Philibert the Duke of Savoy. Not since the days of Agincourt was such destruction wrought upon the chivalry of France. Never were so many distinguished noblemen made captives. The voice of the prisoners of war, among whom Montmorency was included, was raised for peace.

So the French, withdrawing from Piedmont and Savoy, left Italy to the Spaniards. But in the north they had their compensations. No one asked them to return the three bishoprics in Lorraine to which they were now able to add Calais, taken for good or evil in 1558 from the English. Henceforward the continental ambitions of France were drawn towards the Rhine.

The stage was set for new actors. The gallant Charles V had retired from his infinite labours, broken in health and broken in hope, to a Spanish monastery. The treacherous Maurice had fallen in action. Henry VIII, Edward VI, and Mary of England were also dead. Of the great figures of the past, one only, Ferdinand of Austria, now Emperor, was already well proven in war and peace. The new men were Philip, the exact, laborious, and very Catholic son of the retired Emperor, and Emmanuel Philibert of Savoy, the young victor of St. Quentin and the real founder of Turin and of that little sub-Alpine state in the north-west corner of Italy which in the nineteenth century united the Italian peoples under its rule. There was also in England a young woman named Elizabeth, as yet unknown but likely to count in the weights and balances of Europe, and at the Court of France a girl called Mary, daughter of James V of Scotland by Mary of Guise, and perhaps destined to wear upon her head the crowns of Scotland, of England, and of France. As for King Henry of France, he was killed in a tournament, soon after the great treaty was struck, leaving an Italian widow behind him whom the French called Catherine dei' Médicis. She, too, was cast for a conspicuous part upon the crowded stage.

BOOKS WHICH MAY BE CONSULTED

Cambridge Modern History, Vol. II.
B. Zeller : Histoire d'Allemagne, Vol. V. 1885.
O, Engelhaaf : Deutsche Geschichte im Zeitalter der Reformation.
P. Voigt : Moritz von Sachsen.
W. Stubbs : Lectures on European History, 1519-1648. 1904.
L. Häusser : The Period of the Reformation. 1873.
L. von Ranke : History of the Reformation in Germany. *Tr.* S. Austin. 1905.

CHAPTER XIII

THE COUNTER-REFORMATION

Ignatius Loyola. The Jesuit Order. The Council of Trent. The reforming spirit reaches Rome. Pius IV. Protestant strongholds. Bohemia and the Palatinate. Weakness of the Protestant movement. Occasions of conflict under the Peace of Augsburg. The ineffectiveness of German government. Maximilian II. Disastrous reign of Rudolf II. Jesuit education. Jesuit conquests in Austria and Poland.

ON August 15, 1534, the year in which Henry VIII broke with Rome, driving Thomas More to shed his blood for the old faith, and Jacques Cartier of St. Malo planted the cross by the gulf of the St. Lawrence, seven obscure students met together in the Church of St. Mary on Montmartre in Paris, and there swore oaths of chastity and poverty, pledging themselves to pass their lives in Jerusalem in the pursuit of those occupations which were regarded as most holy, the care of Christians and the conversion of the Saracens. The leader of the band was a lame Basque in middle life named Inigo Lopez de Recalde, but known to history as Ignatius Loyola. Another was Francisco Xavier. A third was Lainez.

Spain is a land of mystics and monks, of pilgrims and of soldiers. Loyola was a soldier and a visionary. In his sombre, fantastic, indomitable way he represents the religious and crusading genius of his countrymen, just as Luther embodies the old-world Biblical piety of the Saxon peasantry. Fighting in Navarre (1521), he received the wound from which he went lame for life, and thereafter during his slow and agonizing convalescence turned his thoughts to a new form of service, equally heroic, equally romantic, equally sacrificial, and offering to the schooled and dedicated heart opportunities of sublime distinction. He determined to be the soldier of Christ. No mortification of the flesh was too rigorous for this fiery zealot. He abjured his family, lived on bread and water, scourged himself several times a day, and by a rigorous course of prayer and physical repression educated his powers of communion with the Divine. Then, after a voyage to Jerusalem, there occurred to him an experience not often combined with the ecstatic temperament. He became self-convicted of ignorance and hungered for knowledge. In that quest he put himself to school, and eventually in 1528 was brought to Paris, the Queen of Universities. There he studied for seven years, there imposed his domineering will on a body of companions, and there conceived the idea of an enterprise of holy chivalry to be carried out by a company of elect and tested souls.

It was fortunate for the Roman Church that a war between Venice and Turkey frustrated the plan for a missionary life in Palestine to which Loyola and his companions were solemnly committed. In Italy their passion for the advancement of religion found a more practical field. They took vows of obedience, were ordained priests, called themselves the Company of Jesus, and eventually, September 27, 1540, obtained from Pope Paul III the Bull *Regimini Militantis Ecclesiae*, which establishes the constitution of the Jesuit Order.

The significance of Loyola's invention is that he provided the Papacy with a *corps d'élite* scrupulously trained to carry out its behests. The privileges of the Jesuits were large as their responsibilities were strict. They paid no taxes, they acknowledged no princely superior, they were exempt from the jurisdiction of all prelates not of their Order. Their organization was military and autocratic, for they were governed by a general elected for life, who was in all things subject to the Pope. Equally essential were those other characteristics of spiritual self-discipline and respect for education and learning which marked the riper years of Loyola's own life. The novitiate of the Jesuit was severe. The spiritual exercises devised by the founder were calculated to empty the mind of distracting images and to school the will to the dedicated life. But this wise discipline was not intended to be employed upon the perfecting of a race of anchorites. The aims of Loyola were as practical as they were visionary. It was the office of the Jesuit to preach, to hear confession, to educate. "Consummate prudence, allied with moderate saintliness, is better than greater saintliness and mere prudence"; and again, "If the Church preaches that a thing which appears to us as white is black, we must proclaim it black immediately." Such maxims illustrate the spirit of worldly compliance and absolute submission which gave to the Order its peculiar character. Wherever there was a policy to be shaped the Jesuit confessor was at hand with his counsel. Wherever there was educational work to be done, whether in Europe or in China, the Jesuit school and the Jesuit college, competent, well administered, and strictly controlled, were for more than a century important instruments of Catholic influence and propaganda.

To all intelligent Catholics it had been long plain that the Church had become a mountain of abuses. The need for reform had been acknowledged by Pope Adrian VI, who wrote of the many abominations practised in the Curia itself and of an inveterate and complex malady infecting the whole body of the Church, which it was idle to conceal; and the same theme was restated with greater fullness in a remarkable document (*Consilium quorundam cardinalium de emendenda ecclesia*) which was presented to Pope Paul III in 1538. Nowhere were these flagrant evils more evident than in the papal court and the city of Rome.

The Pope was an autocrat. To any proposal that church reform should be undertaken by national councils, or that an ecumenical council of the Church should have a free hand in making terms with heretics or in defining or limiting the prerogatives of the Holy See, Rome was, by reason of a long tradition of supreme authority, unalterably opposed. The Papacy had had experience of councils in the fifteenth century, and regarded them as evils much to be apprehended and only tolerable if they took their orders from Rome.

Nevertheless, after many delays and obstructions a Council was summoned to Trent, which, although it was sparsely attended and broken by adjournments, one of which was protracted for ten years, marks an epoch in the history of the Roman Church. Out of that Council the Church emerged with its doctrine defined, its discipline strengthened, and its services enriched by the exquisite music of Palestrina. The Papacy entered the Council exposed to many hazards. It issued victorious at every point. So far from being compelled to make concessions to the Lutherans, it had insisted upon putting dogma in the forefront of the discussion, and with its obedient majority of Italian bishops had secured during the early sessions clear-cut decisions upon the three fundamental questions—the authority of the Scriptures, the doctrine of justification by faith only, and the nature of the Sacrament—which divided the Lutheran from the Roman world. By these decisions it finally shattered the Emperor's hope of a scheme so contrived as to soothe the rebel temper of his Lutheran subjects. It drew the line sharp, deep and clear between the Catholic and the Protestant Confessions, ending the search for doctrinal compromise and beginning the period of open conflict. In the words of Lord Acton, a great Catholic historian, "it impressed on the Church the stamp of an intolerant age and perpetuated by its decrees the spirit of an austere immorality." What was then enacted by an ill-attended Council mainly consisting of Italian bishops dependent on the Curia has never been revised, and remains to this day the faith of the Catholic Church.

In the second period of its activity, which opened in 1562 after an intermission of ten years, the Council addressed itself to the problem of discipline and ecclesiastical education. It passed decrees against non-residence and for the establishment of seminaries for the training of priests, but evaded any proposal for meeting heresy half-way or for the abridgment of the papal prerogative. The critical spirit of the Venetian Paolo Sarpi has preserved for us a record of this extraordinary assembly, so unrepresentative of Europe as a whole, so disappointing to the believers in conciliar government, but so true to the tradition of Roman autocracy. The leading figure in the later debates and the man who again carried the papal cause to victory was Lainez, the second general of the Jesuit Order. In that scene of subtle intrigue, furious national hatreds, and open profligacy the stern, eloquent, and invincible Jesuit stood out like a giant.

Almost as important as the Council, and certainly of more immediate effect, was a notable improvement in the character of the occupants of the papal see, which begins to show itself with the accession of Paul III in 1534, and reaches a culminating point with the Pontificate of Pius V in 1563. The great Popes of the Renaissance were often splendid mundane figures, vigorous, nobly born, cultivated, munificent patrons of art and letters, who took a full and animated share in the political passions and rivalries as well as in the baser appetites of their age. They had "nephews" and "nieces," the offspring of their illegitimate unions, for whom it was one of their principal ambitions to provide establishments corresponding to their rank and position. They often promoted wars. They were patient of flagrant scandals. Their court was founded upon simony, plurality, and non-residence. In the long struggle between France and Spain for hegemony in Italy they could not avoid taking an active part. Paul III, of the great house of Farnese, who may be counted as the last of the Renaissance dynasty, was an irresolute supporter of France. Julius III was an imperialist; Paul IV, of the Neapolitan house of Caraffa, carried his insane hatred of Spain to such a point as to invoke the aid of the Turk against it. But meanwhile a change was coming. The reforming movement which had invaded France and Germany and England had begun to reach Rome itself. There was a feeling in the air that something should be done, and that while the whole world was crying out for change and reformation the Curia could not persist in its old ways. The intelligent and worldly Paul III responded to this new spirit, summoned a Council, and established the Order of Jesuits. The fiery and devout Paul IV felt it yet more strongly, and though he was a man consumed with the political passion of a Neapolitan aristocrat, the artificer of a wicked war to put France in control of his native land, and not above the vice of nepotism, he addressed himself seriously, being the first of the Roman Pontiffs to do this, to the detailed task of practical reform. But the most striking change comes with the Pontificate of Pius IV in 1559. This jovial, worthy Milanese was conspicuous for the absence of the special attributes which had for so long given a mundane quality to the Papacy. He was not well-born. He was neither politician nor war-monger nor nepotist. Indeed, he condemned the criminal nephews of his predecessor to death, his own nephew, Carlo Borromeo, being one of the saintliest figures of his age. As for the Council of Trent, he was agreeable that it should be recalled. "We wish for a Council," he said. "We certainly desire that it should be held and be universal. . . . It shall reform what wants to be reformed, even in our own person and even our own affairs."

But perhaps the Pontiff who more than any other typifies the new spirit of austere fanaticism which had come into the religious life of Italy in this age is the humble Michele Ghislieri, who ascended the papal throne as Pius V in 1565. The Roman populace admired the unusual spectacle of an ascetic Pontiff who walked barefoot through the streets, took no siesta, rose with the dawn, and cut down the expenditure of the Curia to the bone. A figure, he must have seemed, drawn from some mediaeval tomb as he called out that no quarter should be given to the Huguenots, gloated over the cruelties of Alva in the Netherlands or launched those Spanish and Venetian galleys which destroyed the Turkish navy at Lepanto.

Nothing counts like personal example. "It has contributed infinitely to the advantage of the Church," said Paolo Tiepolo in 1576, "that several Popes in succession have been men of irreproachable lives; hence all others are become better, or have at least assumed the appearance of being so. Cardinals and prelates attend mass punctually; their households are studious to avoid anything that can give scandal; the whole city has put off its old recklessness and is become much more Christian-like in life and manners than formerly." Yet the Popes were not yet perfect. The vigorous Sixtus V, under whose Pontificate these words were written, was not only a Philistine, from whose vandal hands no ancient monument, however beautiful, was safe, but also deficient in that gift of charity which is recommended by St. Paul. Learning that some banditti in the Campagna had died of the poisoned food which had been set out for them, this Vicar of Christ and editor of St. Ambrose showed notable satisfaction.

In a campaign for the reclamation of the Protestants to the Roman faith, Germany, where the schism had first arisen and whence it had spread far and wide through Europe, held the prerogative place. It was here that the new heresy appeared to be most firmly established. It was here that it was making most conspicuous progress. It was here that for lack of a strong central Catholic government it was most difficult to temper or repress. The north of Germany, which during the mediaeval struggles between Empire and Papacy had been noted for the ardour with which it espoused the papal cause, had become by 1570 an almost unbroken Protestant block. In the ecclesiastical territories of the lower Rhine, heresy, spreading south from Holland, spreading west from Saxony, spreading north from Switzerland, had gathered so great a measure of strength as to engender the apprehension that the great Rhenish Archbishoprics might, despite the ecclesiastical reservation in the Treaty of Augsburg, pass over to the Protestant camp. Calvinism had been established in the Palatinate, Lutheranism in Würtemberg and Baden. Ministers of the Lutheran religion were at work in the castles of the Bavarian nobility and in the towns on the Danube. While the Tyrol remained firmly Catholic, Styria, Carinthia, and the two provinces of the Austrian duchy were largely given over to Protestant rites.

The real strength of Protestantism in central Europe, though this was not clear in 1570, lay in two regions divided from one another by the whole breadth of the country. It lay in that ancient kingdom and electorate of Bohemia, where first the Hussites, then the Bohemian Brethren, and finally preachers from Lutheran Saxony had created among the Czech peasants, and to a large extent among the Czech nobility, a strong revulsion from Rome; and it lay also in the Palatinate, that beautiful region watered by the Neckar and the Rhine, where a succession of Calvinist electors, keeping in touch with their co-religionists in Switzerland and in France, and trading mercenary armies to the Huguenots, made a centre of Calvinist thought and teaching in their capital of Heidelberg and served as a binding link between the militant forces of the Protestant revolt in these countries.

But there were two weaknesses in the Protestant movement deeper than the geographical distance between Bohemia and the Palatinate. The more the Lutheran theologians examined their beliefs and dissertated upon them, the more necessary did it appear to these unpolitical pedants that Calvinism should be held at arm's length, as in many vital particulars clearly erroneous.

A formula drawn up to compose Lutheran differences (*Formula Concordiae*, 1580) traced the line between the two competing faiths in clear and unmistakable terms. Calvinists and Lutherans agreed to differ in theology; and so, when by exercising a joint political pressure upon the Emperor on the occasion of his demand for assistance towards the Turkish war, they might have extracted guarantees for the protection of their co-religionists, Lutheran Saxony took one road and the Elector Palatine another.

The second weakness was still more serious, for it was that lowering of spiritual tone which occurs in all revolutionary movements when the original fervour has ebbed. Luther left no successor. A hundred and thirty-four years barren of Lutheran genius divide his death from the birth of John Sebastian Bach. The age of the prophets and moralists was succeeded by a period of theological pedantry, servile abasement, and, in literature, of revolting and ignoble wantonness. No great thinker or scholar rose from the ranks of Lutheranism. No policies were swayed by this religion, acting as a public influence upon the imaginations and the hearts of men. Yet, in the pious family life of humble people and in its association with Church music, Lutheranism contained sources of inner strength which not even its Erastian

rganization and the widespread profligacy of German morals
vere able wholly to destroy.

The religious situation in Germany was still governed by that
ard-gotten, ill-drafted Treaty of Augsburg, which nevertheless,
ince it provided a kind of peace for more than fifty years, ranks
mong the more successful achievements of German statesmen.
Yet neither Lutheran nor Catholic was cordially prepared to
perate this compromise of exhaustion. The Lutherans had
ever accepted the principle of "the ecclesiastical reservation" in
ccordance with which an ecclesiastic, if he renounced the old
eligion, was also compelled to abandon the income and revenues
vhich he had so far possessed. The Catholics contended, and the
Lutherans disputed the contention, that the Roman Church was
ntitled to recover all ecclesiastical foundations confiscated since
552. The Catholic princes claimed the right to expel Protestants
rom their territory and otherwise to persecute them. In the eyes
f the Protestants, who were hardly less intolerant, this was a
lear breach of the Edict of Toleration, which they regarded as an
ntegral part of the settlement. It will be readily imagined that
t a time when the foundations of belief were fluid, when a
rince, a city, a cathedral chapter, or a prelate of the Church
night swing over from the Catholic to the Protestant side, raising
n each case the thorny question of the disposition of ecclesias-
ical endowments, the occasions of conflict arising out of the
dministration of this Peace of Augsburg were numerous and
ormidable.

Yet the evil was not irremediable. Though there was never
hat intolerable inflammation of the public mind which is excited
vhen good men are burned for their beliefs, Protestant ministers
vere expelled from Catholic territory, Protestant preaching was
orbidden, it was sufficient to be a Protestant to find every avenue
o public employment or to profitable livelihood bolted and
arred. But to the credit of the Catholic rulers of Germany it
hould be remembered that they refrained from imitating the
nethods of the Spanish Inquisition. In this they were acting
rudently. Had a Lutheran gone to the stake, German princes,
vith armies at their back, would have been compelled by the
lamour of their subjects to ask for redress.

The secret of this German collapse was lack of government.
There was no strong authority capable of determining the con-
roversies which arose out of the interpretation of the religious

treaty or of punishing the infraction of its provisions. The Diet
were slow, cumbrous, drunken, ineffective. The princes were far
more concerned with the pursuit of their several dynastic and
territorial aims than with a comprehensive and well-laid plan for
the solution of the religious problem in Germany. But there
remained the Emperor. He was a Habsburg, closely connected by
family ties with the powerful monarchy of Spain. He was King
of Bohemia, titular King of Hungary, though in effect, by reason
of the Turkish conquest, *de facto* ruler of only a small stretch of
that country, and ruler of the five duchies of Upper and Lower
Austria, Styria, Carinthia, and Carniola. No German prince
could vie with him in prestige or territorial power. Though his
constitutional powers in the Empire had been greatly attenuated
there was still latent in the German people a fund of imperial
sentiment to which a great man, had he been able to strike the
public imagination, to handle the princes, and to grapple man-
fully with the pan-Germanic problem, might have been able to
appeal. But the Habsburg Emperors of the later half of the sixteenth century were not men of this heroic stature. Ferdinand I
(1556-64) was a good and prudent Catholic, who, though he introduced the Jesuits into Vienna, succeeded during his lifetime in
securing reasonable conditions for his Protestant subjects. His
successor, Maximilian II, who has been praised by Stubbs as "the
first European prince of any religion who refused to persecute,"
who declined the invitation of Pope Pius to attack the Protestants
and the request of the Protestants that he should expel the
Jesuits, was none the less deficient in the qualities needed for the
situation. This attractive and amiable figure, who in youth listened to the teaching of Lutheran preachers, who in middle age
married his daughter to Philip II, who in his latest message to the
Diet declared that he was neutral in the religious question, and
refused the sacraments of the Church upon his deathbed, made
no positive contribution to the adjustment of the religious quarrel
in Germany. Tolerant himself, he acquiesced in the persecutions
enacted by his neighbours. Officially a Catholic, spiritually a
Lutheran, he lived balanced between the opposing creeds in a
state of ineffective indecision which precluded energetic and uncomfortable resolves.

There followed that critical and disastrous reign of Rudolf II
(1576-1602) which brought Germany to the brink of war. The
kind of man needed in 1576 for the conduct of the Empire was

one of large, genial, energetic temperament, fond of Germany and able to lay that foundation of easy friendship with the political leaders of the German people which was then the only road by which an emperor might recover a position of influence and authority. Rudolf was the opposite of all this. He had nothing in him of the boisterous, hard-drinking, affable German. Brought up in the formal atmosphere of the Spanish court, he had even as a youth, and before melancholia marked him for its own, evinced the fastidious temper of the student, the grandee, and the recluse. The passion for remoteness from the vulgar crowd grew into a deadly malady of the mind. While the Turks were harrying the Hungarian border and Germany was rushing onward to chaos and disaster, this eccentric and irresponsible celibate lived a life apart, far from the madding crowd of Germany, in the high castle which towers over Prague, consorting with astronomers, grooms, and chemists, and content so long as he might be free to enjoy his stables, his books, his mathematical instruments, and his mistresses, to delegate the dull business of conducting the Empire to a succession of incompetent valets. It was not by such a sovereign that the growing tumult among the German people could be composed.

Meanwhile the Counter-Reformation was slowly extending its conquests under the special encouragement of the Dukes of Bavaria and with the notable assistance of the Jesuit Order.

Ignatius Loyola, like all statesmen of the profounder sort, realized the truth that long-range changes in the spiritual direction of mankind must be based on the school. Seeing that the profligacy and ignorance of the Catholic clergy was a mainstay of the Protestant cause, he determined to mend this evil by education. He saw also that under the direction of the humanists a new scale of values had been insinuated into the teaching of the young, culture overshadowing theology, dogma giving place to freedom, and that society had lost that firm grasp of the dialectical defences of the Catholic Faith, which had been built up by the great scholastics of the middle ages.

For his immediate purpose it was more profitable to train the elect than to scatter his gifts to the multitude. The wheels of history are seldom moved by the poor. In the main the world is ruled by station, wealth, and intellect. The educational arrows of the Jesuits were directed, not at the rank and file, but at the pivotal persons whose gifts or position were likely to give them

an influence upon their fellows. Being gratuitous and conservative, their system was widely acceptable. They were far too wise
to discard the humanities, the teaching in the Greek, Latin, and
Hebrew languages which had now established themselves as cardinal requisites of the highest culture, and were careful, which
was also popular, to attend to the health and the manners of their
pupils. But even more distinctive than the technical excellence
of a method which trained the young to learn, to compose,
and to discuss was an iron routine of spiritual discipline. The
disciple of the Jesuits bore the print of their influence to the
grave.

In the fifties of the century the " Spanish priests," as they were
called, began to filter into Germany and there to found schools
and colleges for the restoration of the Catholic Faith. We find
them in Vienna, where they were given control of the University
in 1551, in Cologne and Ingolstadt in 1556, in Munich in 1559.
All along the Rhine and the Main, at Bonn, Mainz, and Speier,
as well as Würzburg, they established centres for teaching and
propaganda. With their high but narrow competence the
Lutheran schools in the middle of the sixteenth century were
ill qualified to vie.

Vienna was the key position. Ignatius Loyola could hardly fail
to see that if the Austrian provinces were not soon recaptured for
the Roman faith the heart of the Empire would be won by the
enemy. Accordingly to Vienna there was despatched one of the
greatest Catholic figures of that age, the strenuous and learned
Dutchman, Petrus Canisius, who as a mere youth had by his
ardour and eloquence saved Cologne for the Roman faith.
Canisius became the confidant of the emperor. It is to him that
the Counter-Reformation in Austria owes its strongest impulse.
He it was who procured for the Jesuits that ascendancy over
Austrian education which for many centuries was unbroken. Nor
was there among the German victories of the Order any more
notable than this, that Ferdinand of Styria, a cadet of the Habsburg house, having been saturated in youth with Jesuit principles, first drove the Protestants out of Styria, and then, as Holy
Roman Emperor, headed the forces of the Catholic reaction in
the Thirty Years' War.

But the greatest of the Jesuits' conquests has still to be mentioned. The kingdom of Poland was, after its union with the
duchy of Lithuania in 1389, larger than any state in western

Europe. In this desolate and empty land, where every pair of arms was welcome, the religious credentials of an immigrant had never been closely examined. Jews had fled to Poland in the middle ages from the bitter persecution of the Catholic west and had there been accorded the rights of hospitality, leaving behind them a progeny ever multiplying in numbers and supplying the main part of such urban arts as Poland possessed. More than half the population had always professed the Greek faith. Hussites had filtered in during the fifteenth century and been later followed by exponents of every variety of Protestant belief. Lutherans and Calvinists, Bohemian Brethren and Unitarians spread their propaganda with the greater ease since the power of the Catholic king was confined within narrow limits by the exorbitant privileges of the nobles. But the very fullness of religious liberty accorded to the Poles proved to be the ruin of the Protestant cause. There was no authority in the country to curb the luxuriance or to direct the flow of the differing religious opinions which had spread abroad as a consequence of Lutheran teaching. Compacts, indeed, were made. The Bohemian Brethren brought themselves to join with the Genevans in 1553, and these again to combine with the Lutherans in 1570, but these associations were too long delayed and too weakly compacted; for five years before the Lutherans and Calvinists had patched up their differences the Jesuits were in the field, and with the favouring authority of the Crown had been placed in control of the higher education of the country.

Then ensued a Catholic campaign, slow, sure, methodical, and eventually triumphant. By the end of the seventeenth century the Jesuits had made of Poland one of the most Catholic countries in Europe, a Latin outpost placed between Teuton Protestantism and the Greco-Russian civilization of the east. The voyager who today crosses the Polish frontier into the territory of the Soviet Republic forgets that the populations on either side of the line are united by a community of race. The Counter-Reformation has obscured whatever affinities may formerly have bound the Pole to the Russian. On the one side of the line are Roman churches bright with lights and rustling with the genuflexions of crowds of worshippers; on the other side the organized gospel of atheism by which the new Communist government of the Soviet Republic hopes to replace the age-long Byzantine image-worship of a superstitious and illiterate peasantry.

BOOKS WHICH MAY BE CONSULTED

L. Pastor : History of the Popes. *Ed.* F. I. Antrobus and R. F. Kerr. 1894-1933.

A. W. Ward : The Counter-Reformation. 1889.

L. von Ranke : History of the Reformation in Germany. *Tr.* S. Austin. 1905.

J. A. Froude : Lecture on the Council of Trent. 1896.

M. Philippson : La Contre-révolution religieuse du seizième siècle. 1884.

J. A. Symonds : Renaissance in Italy : The Catholic Reaction. 1886.

H. C. Lea : History of the Inquisition in Spain. 4 vols. 1907.

H. D. Sedgwick : Life of Ignatius Loyola. 1923.

W. Stubbs : Lectures on European History, 1519-1648. 1904.

W. E. Collins : The Catholic South (in Cambridge Modern History Vol. II, chap. xii).

A. Gindely : Rudolf II und seine Zeit. 1863.

G. Droysen : Geschichte der Gegenreformation. 1893.

A. Huber : Geschichte Oesterreichs. 1885.

CHAPTER XIV

THE FRENCH WARS OF RELIGION

Grave evil of this civil war. The situation in 1559. Catharine dei Medici. The Guises. The Huguenots. The Politiques. The initial compromise. The massacre of Vassy. The use of foreign mercenaries, and the appeal to foreign powers. Catholic victories at Dreux, Jarnac, Moncontour. Coligny restores the Huguenot fortunes, 1569. The Peace of St. Germain, 1570. Coligny's ambitious anti-Spanish policy. The Queen takes fright. The Massacre of St. Bartholomew. Henry of Navarre becomes in 1564 the next heir. Catholic apprehensions. Murder of the Guises. The last of the Valois. The resistance of the League. Triumph of Henry of Navarre. The Edict of Nantes, 1598. Henry's war policy and sudden death.

THE French wars of religion which occupy the later half of the sixteenth century were far more disastrous to the country than the Italian campaigns by which they had been preceded. The Italian policy had been unwise; among other reasons because it sacrificed the pioneering work of the Breton and Norman sailors in the New World, so that after much expenditure of blood and treasure this phase of French ambition ended in frustration. But the wars of religion very nearly broke up the hard-won unity of France, inflicting evils which cannot be measured by battle losses alone. Town was divided against town, village against village, family against family. Armed affrays and assassinations became incidents of ordinary life. Some murders were committed out of religious fanaticism, others in pursuit of private vengeance, others, as in all times when the hideous taint of espionage infects the body politic, out of senseless terror. The morality of the Huguenot saint was embarked upon a struggle which was largely carried on by the methods of the Irish gunmen. The wise French humanist stood aloof, like Montaigne, whose essays, published during the savage tyranny of the Catholic League, express the gospel of an enlightened Epicurean and charitable scepticism.

The position of France when Henry II died in 1559 was roughly as follows: the Genevan or Huguenot propaganda had made great progress. It had found friends in the army and in the Parliament of Paris, and in many country towns had secured a large following of devout adherents. Several persecutions had not checked the movement. Though the price of heresy was burning at the stake and eighty-eight humble Protestants had paid that price under Henry II, the new faith continued to make converts. Little French Bibles and psalm-books circulated surreptitiously and were read in the privacy of household gatherings. Teachers, trained in the fortifying school of Geneva, travelled about with their incitements to heroism and endurance. Nor were the French Huguenots kept in ignorance of the fate of their co-religionists in other lands. They learnt how Protestant women were buried alive in the Netherlands, how Queen Mary sent Protestant bishops to the stake in England, and how John Knox had raised his Genevan flag among the Scots. The congregations of the faithful were knit together in a confraternity of martyrdom. A body of heretical opinion, still imperfectly organized, but anxious, and inflamed, and strengthened by a sense of solidarity with Protestant communities in other countries, confronted the weak and impecunious government of France.

Against this gathering challenge to the ancient faith were ranged the long Catholic traditions of the French monarchy, the disciplined force of the Roman Church, the superstitious furies of the Paris rabble, and always in the background the power of Spain, great at sea, supreme in Italy and the Netherlands, and allied by the closest family ties with the house of Austria.

Had the French throne been occupied at this juncture by a strong, wise, and tolerant king, able and willing to take advantage of those strong feelings in favour of Gallican independence, which prevailed among so many prelates of the French Church, and prepared, like Henry VIII, to be undisputed master in his own house, the country might have been spared a long chapter of misery. But at this critical juncture the government of France devolved in succession upon three of the feeblest sovereigns who have ever sat upon a European throne. Of the sons of Henry II and Catharine dei Medici, the eldest, Francis II, was an invalid; the second, Charles IX, a nervous wreck, if not a madman; the third, Henry III, a degenerate. The real power lay with their mother, who suffered under the double disadvantage of being a woman and an alien.[1]

The position of this cultured and cynical Italian lady of the middle class, suddenly called upon to govern France amid the fierce rivalries which divided the court and country, was one of

[1] Genealogical Table C.

singular difficulty. A bold policy, which might have attracted a native king, was beyond the reach of a foreigner. An enthusiastic policy, which would have elicited the cordial support of either Catholic or Huguenot, was alien to her indifferent and essentially lay temperament. Encompassed by perils, and in a situation which required the utmost watchfulness, she resolved to preserve the enjoyment of the monarchy for her sons and for herself the substance of power, by the method which seemed to her to be most apt to secure that end, a religious peace based on compromise. The most divergent views have been entertained of her character. To one historian she is "specially distinguished for her genius for maternal love." To others she is the supreme embodiment of human craft and wickedness. Perhaps among her less charitable critics her youngest son is nearest the mark when he described his mother as *Madame La Serpente*. In her contempt for veracity, in her gluttony, and in the remorseless pursuit of private revenge she was an Italian of her age. Her great political virtue was the cool persistence with which she strove to secure a peaceful balancing between two fanatical parties. But though toleration was agreeable to her mind and temper, it was never with her an iron principle. A moment came when this fat, agreeable, industrious woman, whose taste in art was so delicate and true, who liked pictures and jewels and good books, who never forgave or forgot an injury, and was first of all the rulers of France to organize immorality as an instrument of political power, discarded her policy of indulgence and helped to engineer the Massacre of St. Bartholomew.

Overshadowing the Italian queen and her wretched sequence of sons were certain great aristocratic groups, for whom the control of the king's person and therefore of the government was a matter of ambition. Of these groups one was clearly Catholic and the other clearly Protestant, while the third occupied an intermediate position, being opposed to the Catholic leaders on the point of policy, and to Protestants in the matter of religious faith. The Catholic group was the party of the Guises. It was led by Francis, Duke of Guise, who was the idol of France by reason of his defence of Metz and his capture of Calais, and upon the ecclesiastical side by his brother Charles of Lorraine, the Cardinal Archbishop of Rheims, who would not have minded being the first patriarch of an independent Gallican

Church, but since this was proved to be impossible, constituted himself, at the Council of Trent, a most vehement and skilful advocate of extreme papal claims. The Guises, then, could boast of the first soldier and the leading churchman of the kingdom: but this was not the limit of their influence. A sister of Francis of Guise had been married to the King of Scotland. A niece sat upon the throne of France. With this close association with two crowned heads, with fifteen bishoprics in the family, and with properties widely scattered along the eastern border of the kingdom, the Guises represented the most powerful body of Catholic interests in the country. Spain and Rome, with whom they were in association, looked to this brilliant family to sustain the chief burden of Catholic defence in France.

The chieftains of the Huguenot party were the Bourbon princes, Anthony, King of Navarre, and his brother Louis, Duke of Condé, who was Governor of Picardy and had accepted the position of Protector-General of the Church of France. It cannot be said of either of these great noblemen that they were very deeply rooted in the Huguenot faith; but their influence in the west and south-west of France, as also in Normandy, was considerable, and drew many of the lesser nobility and gentry of these regions into the conflict.

A third group, originally led by the veteran statesman Anne, Duke of Montmorency, and specially strong in central France, were the Politiques. These were men who while adhering to the old faith had little love for the queen mother or for the Guises, and therefore occupied an intermediate position between the extreme groups. Montmorency was a strong Catholic, but his three nephews, the Châtillon brothers, took another line. They joined the Huguenots, and one of them, Gaspard de Coligny, Admiral of France, a man of unquenchable courage and deep religious convictions, became the leading Protestant General, and therefore the principal mark for Catholic vengeance.

In the passionate fermentation of these times the slightest incident might provoke a war. The execution in Paris of a Calvinist lawyer provoked in the Protestant underworld, but probably not without countenance from Condé, and even from Elizabeth of England, a plot to seize the king and the Guises at Amboise. The plot was discovered, the conspirators were cruelly punished, and the Guises, advancing from strength to strength, ventured to arrest Condé and to sentence him to death. But then came a sudden reversal of fortune. On December 5, 1560, the young king died. In the midst of their success the Guises found themselves stripped of influence at court, and their enemies established in their place. The queen mother became Regent for her son Charles, who was a minor, and with the help of the Chancellor L'Hôpital, one of the few great statesmen produced in that age, inaugurated a policy of amnesty and conciliation. Condé was released from prison, the Calvinists were amnestied, and the King of Navarre was brought into the Council as Lieutenant-General of the kingdom. An experiment was now tried by Catharine and her wise Chancellor which, in a cooler state of the public mind, might have laid the foundations for a provisional peace. After a colloquy between the leading divines of the contending churches had broken down, as such discussions invariably did, an edict was issued in January, 1562, which legalized, under certain not unfair conditions, the public celebration of Huguenot rites. But by this time tempers had risen high. Images were destroyed, churches defaced, priests were attacked on one side, preachers on the other; and eventually, after a barnful of worshipping Huguenots had been massacred by Guise's troops at Vassy, the civil war, which had been so long held down, blazed into sudden eruption.

It was a property of this quarrel not only that it was largely waged by foreign mercenaries, but that after a short spell of fighting peace would come, not because a settlement really tolerable to both parties was in sight, but either because money had run short, or because a leader had been killed, or from sudden dejection or weakness, or because, mingled with the fierce religious and personal rancours of the time, there was still the underlying sense of French unity as a treasure not lightly to be squandered. To these reasons is to be ascribed the fact that seven wars were found to be necessary before the quarrel between the Catholics and the Huguenots was composed in France.

Neither party scrupled to appeal for foreign aid. The Catholics turned to Spain, the Huguenots to England, even going so far as in the first war to put the English in possession of Havre and to promise them Calais. But one Protestant alliance was never made. Between the German Lutherans and the French Huguenots the gulf was insuperable. German Lutherans fought in the French wars, but they were to be found enlisted, for the most part, not in the Huguenot, but in the Catholic, ranks.

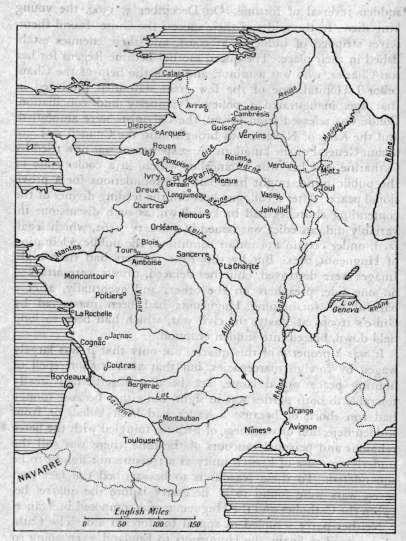

FRANCE DURING THE WARS OF RELIGION.

In the first war all the auguries appeared to point to a Catholic triumph, the possession of the persons of the king and queen, the support of Paris, the assistance of an efficient body of Spanish and German mercenaries, the capture of Rouen, and, finally, a Catholic victory at Dreux in Normandy over the forces of Coligny and Condé. But these advantages suddenly melted away when François de Guise fell by the hand of an assassin before the walls of Orleans.

Little good, however, did the Huguenots reap from this crime, for the murder was attributed to Coligny and supplied to the family of the murdered man a motive for revenge far more powerful than the strength of their religious convictions.

There followed four years of uneasy peace, during which Catharine and her sons toured the provinces. The suspicion of the Huguenot party was awakened by a meeting at Bayonne (May, 1565) between Catharine and her sister Queen Isabella of Spain, who was accompanied by the Duke of Alva. That Catharine's main object was to arrange a marriage between her daughter Margaret and Don Carlos, the son of Philip II of Spain, is clear; but other matters were also discussed, and notably the co-operation of France and Spain against the Netherlands. There was enough here to arouse the fears of Coligny, the most active spirit in the Huguenot party, and when Alva was found marching towards the Low Countries along the eastern border of France with a fine Spanish army accompanied by a French corps of observation, the Admiral felt that the time had come to emancipate the court from its Spanish toils. A plan was made to capture Charles IX, and, failing of success, precipitated a fresh outburst of fighting.

The next two wars, which, since they were divided by the short peace of Longjumeau, 1568, may almost be regarded as a single series of operations, are memorable on three accounts. It is now that La Rochelle first emerges as a great marine Protestant fortress, capable of successfully standing a siege. It is now that Henry of Navarre, the son of King Anthony, and afterwards destined to be Henry IV of France, is brought forward as a Protestant leader. But the most striking peculiarity of this period is that after an almost uniform sequence of Catholic victories, after Condé had been taken and killed at Jarnac, and some 6,000 Huguenot bodies had strewn the bloodstained field of Moncontour, the ultimate victory lay with Coligny. Executing a brilliant retreat from the Loire to the south, and then raising a fresh army, the amazing veteran marched upon Paris and finding the court empty of resources, confounded his enemies, dominated the king, and took control of the policy of France. Charles IX, who had had a Protestant nurse, was ready to treat. The Peace of St. Germain recognizes more fully than had been done so far the importance of the Huguenot party a a substantive and separate interest in France. The great nobles as before, were allowed to hold their Huguenot services in their castles for all who liked to attend them. The Protestant form of worship was to be maintained for all towns where it was actually practised, and in two towns in each administrative district in France. Safeguards were provided against judicial oppression Four places of great military importance, La Rochelle, Montauban, Cognac, and La Charité, were guaranteed to the party for two years as a security for the fulfilment of the treaty.

And now a new prospect opened out before the Huguenots Hitherto, largely owing to Guise influence, the French monarchy had been disposed to look to Spain for support in its defence of the Catholic cause. Coligny prepared a complete diplomatic revolution. His idea was to gain protection for his co-religionists in France by setting afoot a national war against Spain in the Netherlands. To this end he worked for a great confederation led by France, but helped by England, by the Dutch, by Venice and Tuscany, and possibly by the Turks, which would bring peace at home and add Flanders and Artois to the dominions of the French Crown. A defensive treaty with England, signed at Blois on April 19, 1572, was the first stone in the new diplomatic building.

Among the dealings of this period of Huguenot influence was a project destined to have a great effect upon the internal situation in France. A marriage was arranged and actually took place (August 18, 1572) between Margaret of Valois, the king's sister, and Henry of Navarre. The Bearnais, the little hook nosed rustic son of a Pyrenean knight by a fanatically Huguenot mother, was fished out of his remote province, and married into the royal and Catholic family of France. It was a mixed marriage, the first of its kind, and by all good Catholics heartily detested. Whither, it was asked, was France drifting under her light-headed king and Huguenot general? Into a war with the greatest Catholic power in Europe? Into a course which might place France under a Protestant king? Catharine was swift to read changes of temperature. She knew that though a third of the nobility might be Huguenot, the vast majority of the French people remained loyal to the old faith. She feared war, feared the might of Spain, feared Coligny's influence over her son, feared that if she remained inactive, the Guises would strike, and so obtain the mastery of France for themselves, and she was shrewd enough to see that no war waged to give France an inch of territory in Flanders would long be popular with the English government. She therefore resolved to have Coligny killed. The attack failed. The Admiral was wounded by a Catholic gunman, but not seriously (August 22, 1572). The position of the queen mother thus became critical. Paris was full of Huguenot gentlemen, drawn to the capital by the royal marriage, and furious at the dastardly attack upon their great and venerated chief. Lest worse befall, the queen determined to strike again, and this time not at Coligny alone, but in the secrecy of night at all the Protestant leaders. The weak king, fobbed off with the tale of a Huguenot plot, was persuaded to give his assent.

The Guises were eager for revenge, and behind the Guises and their bravos were the sleeping furies of·Catholic Paris. At dawn on August 24 (St. Bartholomew's Day) the bell of the Palace of Justice rang out the signal for the slaughter to begin.

Such a carnival of butchery as then ensued, not in Paris only, where some three or four thousand Huguenots were killed, but throughout the provinces, outran the fiercest anticipations of the court. The Parisians, whose trade suffered from the religious troubles, needed no incitement to massacre the Huguenots or to mutilate their corpses. They killed not the leaders only, but the rank and file, and their example was gleefully followed in the provinces. The head of Coligny was sent to the Pope, the golden rose was sent by the Pope to the king. At the news of the happy extermination of so many heretics the Pope ordered a medal to be struck and Philip of Spain commanded a Te Deum. So great a Catholic triumph had hardly been dreamed of. Coligny was dead. Condé and Henry of Navarre were in the king's hands, and thousands of Huguenot corpses attested the Catholic orthodoxy of France.

The conspirators who contrived the Massacre of St. Bartholomew acted in a panic, but may nevertheless have feared that a king who compromised himself too far with the Huguenots might be overthrown by a fanatical Catholic party controlled by the Guises and based on the Paris mob. Under Henry III, who succeeded his brother in 1574, that danger was very nearly realized. So far from extinguishing the Huguenots, the Massacre of St. Bartholomew had merely been the first act of a fourth war. From their western capital of La Rochelle the Huguenots, now helped by many Politiques, including for a time Monsieur, the younger brother of the king, defied the royalist forces and offered a menace to the unity of France. To the Catholics, and more particularly to the Catholic democracy of Paris, this fierce and continued obstinacy, so bad for business, so unpatriotic (for the Huguenots were in touch with England), was intolerable. The fanatics wanted war to the knife, and they found the king and queen mother still pursuing their familiar policy of offering a peace or a truce to the rebels on every occasion, still governed by the detestable idea that a place might be found for the free public worship of Huguenots in a Catholic state. The treaty of May 14, 1576, seemed to them little better than a capitulation. A Catholic Union was formed, commonly known as the League, with the Pope and the King of Spain as patrons, to stiffen the spine of Roman orthodoxy in France.

In 1584 Monsieur died. He was Catharine's youngest son and Henry's sole surviving brother, and since the king was childless, the next heir to the throne would be Henry of Navarre. "Better a Republic than a Huguenot King" was the principle of the Leaguers of Paris. Against the Guises, now supported by such an outburst of passionate feeling, Henry III was for many years very helpless. He hung on, protected by assassins, surrounded by a web of plots, while the real authority over Catholic France was wielded by the League. How weak he had become was shown on the Day of Barricades (May 12, 1588) when Paris, obedient to Henry, Duke of Guise, denied the royal troops an entry into the city, and again when the States-General, meeting at Blois under Jesuit influence, passed a series of enactments which, if carried through, would have drained the treasury of its resources and robbed the government of its last vestige of authority. From these humiliations the wretched king, "the worst ruler of the worst dynasty that has ever governed," sought relief by murder. On the approach of Christmas, 1588, the Duke of Guise and his

brother the Cardinal of Lorraine were cut down in the Castle
of Blois by the king's Gascon bravos.

The old queen mother was lying on her deathbed when her
favourite son brought her the news. "Now I am King of
France," he is reported to have said, "I have killed the King of
Paris." "God grant it may be so," was the answer; "but have
you made sure of the other towns?"

The last act of the long drama now opened. While the
Catholic League declared Henry deposed from his throne and
endeavoured to govern the capital and the country, the
thoughts of an increasing number of Frenchmen, neither
Huguenots nor Leaguers, were turning to Henry of Navarre, to
whom the succession in law belonged. The young southerner
had revealed remarkable military qualities. At Coutras he had
shown that a Huguenot army, well led, could beat the Catholic
levies of the Crown in a set battle. His good humour, his rustic
shrewdness, his numerous gallantries, commended him to the
common man. He was a Protestant, but a man, whereas his
cousin the king, who wore a pearl necklace and ear-rings,
though a Catholic, was a fop. The two cousins found it in their
common interest to attack the Catholic League, which had deposed the one and declared the other incapable of succession.
But while their armies lay outside Paris, the hand of Jacques
Clement, a crazy Jacobin, struck down the king (August 1,
1589), so ending the long Valois dynasty in France, and opening the way to the direct struggle between Navarre and the
League.

The Committee of sixteen who governed Paris for the League
under the supervision of the Duke of Mayenne, the younger
brother of Henry Guise, ruled like the Committee of Public
Safety in 1794, by a system of terror. Its apologists plead that it
saved France for Catholicism, which suited the people better
than Protestantism, and that its crimes were such as to disgust
the country with republicanism for two hundred years. During
its violent and unpopular rule France was brought round to the
view that the restoration of the hereditary monarchy would
divide it least. It would not accept an Infanta from Spain, or a
French nobleman elected by the States-General. The main
body of the French aristocracy rallied round the Bourbon
prince. But so persistent was fanaticism, that even after Henry
had abjured his Protestant faith in the Church of St. Denis

10

(July 25, 1593) he was compelled to wait eight months outside the walls of Paris before the resistance of the city was overcome.

The new sovereign brought with him one gift more precious than all the elegant accomplishments of the Valois. He cared for the common people of France and wished to see them prosperous and happy. The memoirs of his able Huguenot minister Sully, though on many points untrustworthy, are at least good evidence of the fact that the government of France under Henry IV was inspired by the idea of the public good. To put down anarchy, to promote agriculture and commerce, to restore peace to a country brought to the lowest point of misery by thirty years of civil war, were some of the aims which the French monarchy now resolutely set itself to pursue. Much was accomplished, as by great public works for the reclamation of marshes and the improvement of roads. The revenue was increased, the debt reduced. Finding the country burdened with a great deficit, Sully left its finance solvent.

But before these remedial measures could be applied in any fullness Henry was compelled to deal with two urgent problems, the Spaniards and the Huguenots. With some assistance from Queen Elizabeth he drove a Spanish army out of Amiens and compelled Spain (Treaty of Vervins, 1598) to relinquish the positions—Calais, and Blavet in Brittany—which she had been able to acquire upon French territory as ally to the Catholic League. The Huguenots presented a far more serious difficulty. These men of iron, who for more than thirty years had defied the French crown, and were at any time able to put an army of 25,000 into the field, were not easily to be subdued and were in a position to treat with the sovereign on level terms. The famous settlement known as the Edict of Nantes was no royal act of grace, still less a philosophic declaration of tolerance, but a treaty only reached after arduous and protracted negotiations and accepted with reluctance as a necessity, imposed by disagreeable, ineluctable facts. It gave the Huguenots freedom of worship in the castles of the nobility and in certain specified places, equality of civil rights, judicial protection, and for their better security the right of garrisoning more than a hundred fortified towns, including such great national centres as La Rochelle, Saumur, and Montpellier, at the cost of the French treasury. In effect a little Huguenot state, with its army, its fortresses, its civil government, was authorized to function in the heart of France.

The Edict of Nantes is notable in the history of civilization as the first public recognition of the fact that more than one religious communion can be maintained in the same polity. Long before religious toleration was recognized in England or Germany, it was, in virtue of this famous instrument, made part of the constitutional law of France. The strong arm of the Huguenot had extracted from his Catholic adversary concessions which no Roman would have conceded to argument.

The foundations were now laid for the most brilliant period of French history, during which the monarchy was exalted and revived, the field of industry and commerce notably enlarged, and the life of the Catholic Church stimulated and enriched by the challenge and juxtaposition of the Huguenot faith. These advantages narrow intolerance and martial ambition were destined to sacrifice. Scaliger, the great classical scholar, said of Henry that, despite his wit and shrewd knowledge of human character, he was incapable for a quarter of an hour of fixing his mind on the future. A more provident statesman would have endeavoured to govern with the assistance of the States-General, would have refused to recall the Jesuits, who in 1594 had been banished from France as corrupters of the young, disturbers of public order, and enemies of the king and the state, and would have put away from his thoughts the idea of an ambitious foreign war. Henry IV, who was the perpetual mark for the dagger of the assassin, lived on the improvisations of his ready talent. Despite his express promise, and confident in the wisdom of his advisers, he refused to summon the States-General, or to share with his subjects the educative burden of government. In religion he was tolerant and the inheritor from Catharine dei Medici of a system of toleration; yet he recalled the Jesuits, whose intolerant influence at the court and over French education was destined to lead to the expulsion of the Huguenots, and to the undoing of the Edict of Nantes, his greatest achievement.

In foreign policy he, for a time—after the peace of Vervins, 1598—vacillated between the idea of a sustained peace with Spain, to be cemented by royal marriages, and of an attack upon the Habsburgs; but eventually his thoughts turned to war and to a policy, such as that which Coligny had encouraged some fifty years before, of a grand onslaught on the Catholic Habsburgs to be assisted by Protestants from Germany and the Low Countries, and to end in the conquest of the Spanish Netherlands and the advance of the French frontier to the Rhine. The question whether the duchy of Cleves-Julich, which was on the eastern frontier of France, should become part of the Catholic or Protestant block, afforded a pretext for action. Without adequate diplomatic preparation, and being chiefly decided in his choice of the moment by his passion for the Duchess of Condé, who had been withdrawn by her husband to the shelter of the Austrian court in Brussels, he was on the brink of opening his enormous anti-Catholic enterprise when he fell by the knife of Ravaillac, a Catholic fanatic. The recall of the Jesuits had not disarmed the spirit of the League.

BOOKS WHICH MAY BE CONSULTED

L. von Ranke : Civil Wars and Monarchy in France in the Sixteenth and Seventeenth Centuries. *Tr.* M. A. Garvey. 2 vols. 1852.

L. Romier : Les Origines politiques des guerres de religion. 2 vols. 1913-14.

E. Armstrong : The French Wars of Religion. 1892.

P. F. Willert : Henry of Navarre and the Huguenots of France. 1893.

A. J. Grant : The Huguenots. 1934.

J. H. Mariéjol : Catherine de Médicis. 1920.

E. Faguet : Seizième siècle. Études Littéraires. 1894.

L. Batiffol : The Century of the Renaissance. 1916.

J. Delaborde : Gaspard de Coligny, Amiral de France. 1879-82.

A. J. Butler : Wars of Religion in France (Cambridge Modern History, Vol. III, chap. i).

Lord Acton : Lectures on Modern History (Saint Bartholomew). 1906.

H. Forneron : Les Ducs de Guise et leur époque. 2 vols. 1878.

A. Tilley : The Literature of the French Renaissance. 2 vols. 1904.

CHAPTER XV

THE RISE OF THE DUTCH REPUBLIC

Orthodoxy in Spain. Philip II. The Spanish army and navy. Spanish finance and economics. Importance of the Netherlands for Spain. Elizabeth elects for Protestantism. The queen's success in Scotland. "Mere English." Maintenance of national unity. The Church compromise. Philip and England. Granvelle in the Netherlands. William of Orange. Egmont and Alva. Orange and Alva. The Pacification of Ghent. Don John of Austria. The rift between north and south. Foundation of the Dutch Republic. The power of Amsterdam. The house of Orange. Causes of Dutch success. The distractions of Parma. The military skill of Maurice of Nassau. The Dutch make a truce with Spain (1609).

IN the great European conflict occasioned by the Protestant Reformation, Spain was marked out to be the foremost champion of the Catholic cause. While one species of Protestantism had established itself in northern Germany, and another was battling in a not uneven contest for its life in France, Spain behind her stiff, mountainous barrier was Catholic to the marrow. Here, as nowhere else in Europe, the defence and expansion of the Catholic Faith were identified with the growth and glory of the nation. The monks, nuns, and priests constituted a large fraction of the population. The Inquisition, which was controlled by the Crown, was regarded as a necessary safeguard. A great auto-da-fé at Valladolid (October 18, 1559) was the opening stroke in a repressive campaign, evoking only sparse and ineffectual protests, against the new beliefs which had come into Spain from Germany. The work which the Spanish Inquisition then did under the impulsion of Philip II was so thoroughly performed that heresy, in Spain a new and unfamiliar plant, was stamped out before it had begun to acquire strength. The Roman Church was henceforth secure. Not until the revolution of 1931 was its control of education successfully challenged by a movement originating in Spain itself and supported, as it would appear, by a majority of the Spanish people.

Philip II was a devout and dutiful Catholic ruler, who conceived it to be his principal mission in life to uproot heresy from his dominions and to support the faith of his fathers throughout the world. A grave, laborious, narrow man, unable to distinguish small things from big, and consequently incapable of delegating work to others, he allowed himself to be so much encumbered by minute duties that he was blind to the large aspects of state policy. Some dark stains rest upon his memory, the murder of an insane eldest son, the secret assassination of an ambassador from the Netherlands. There are few more pathetic pages in history than the life of this melancholy, conscience-stricken, dimly-lit autocrat toiling at his desk over the task, exceeding all human strength, of saving the Catholic empire of Spain from the new, unsettling thoughts and rapacious powers which were abroad in the world.

The strength of Spain consisted in its standing army. There were no infantry troops in Europe better drilled or better disciplined or more experienced in war than the famous Spanish *tercios*, for whom Italy was the appointed training ground. The gentry of Spain flocked to the standards, thinking it no penance to follow a military career under the pleasant Italian skies. During the second half of the sixteenth century the best officers in Europe were probably to be found serving under the Spanish king. Some, like Alva, were Spanish noblemen. But others were Italians, including the greatest general of the century, Alessandro Farnese, Duke of Parma. It is a tribute to Spanish statesmanship that it was thus able to attract to the service of the Spanish crown some of the best talent from the proudest families of Italy.

On the sea Spain was, for several reasons, less formidable. She was partly a Mediterranean, partly an Atlantic, power. In the Mediterranean she was confronted with the task of clearing the sea of Turkish corsairs, and of assisting Venice and the Knights of Malta in arresting the onward progress of the military navy of the Sultan. These were onerous and exacting duties. A mobile and enterprising enemy, based on Algiers and Tunis, raided the Balearic Islands and the Valencian coast. An ambitious monarchy, served by Greek seamen and established in Constantinople, offered a standing threat to the safety of Italy. Now, by the use of centuries, a form of warfare had grown up in these smooth Mediterranean waters which was wholly unsuited to Atlantic weather. The galley impelled by oars, the classic galley of the Roman republic and of the Roman empire, still survived. The tradition of rowing towards

your enemy, of grappling with him, and of deciding the issue
by a hand to hand infantry fight conducted on sea was as living
in the days of Philip II as it was in the times of Xerxes and
Pompey. The biggest naval battle in the Mediterranean fought
during the century, the battle of Lepanto (1571), when Don
John of Austria, King Philip's brother, inflicted a crushing
defeat on the Turkish army, was a galley battle, a clash of
military row-boats. Yet it did not follow that men trained to
fight in galleys would gain any experience likely to help them
in the ocean-going sailing ships or galleons which were now becoming an indispensable part of the Spanish naval equipment.
On the contrary, the tradition of the galley, surviving into
times when the galley was an anachronism, was positively
harmful. In the ocean and in the Channel a fleet manoeuvred by
fine seamen could always be trusted to beat an adversary whose
plans were dominated by the ramrod tactics of a galley fight.

Spain then was hampered by the fact that being compelled
to fight on two fronts, she was driven to employ at one and
the same time two different types of warship, one extremely
ancient and the other very modern, and that many of her seamen were trained in the ancient school. But these disadvantages
might have been overcome had there been at the centre of
Spanish affairs an intelligent appreciation of the value of sea
power in warfare. It is a curious circumstance that in spite of the
enormous stake which Spain had acquired in the new world,
she made no sustained effort to gain a mastery of the western
ocean. The emancipation of the Dutch republic from Spanish
control was certainly greatly assisted by the fact that the rebels
were left in undisputed command of the sea.

But the root of Spanish weakness lay in finance. No European government in the sixteenth century was financially
strong: but Spain is a conspicuous instance of a country owning a vast surface of the globe, both in the old world and in the
new, and having immediate access to the richest mineral resources then known to exist, which was nevertheless in perpetual straits for money, and often unable by reason of sheer
penury to perform the most elementary tasks of government.
The reasons for this paradox are to be found partly in an unintelligent general policy, partly in an ignorance of economic
laws and a vicious system of taxation, and not least in the absence
of any effective check on peculation and extravagance. The king

could raise but little money from Spain itself. Despite their vast wealth, the clergy were immune from taxation. In Castile the nobles, though often subjected to irregular acts of spoliation, were by long custom exempted from contributing to the regular revenues of the crown. In Aragon the Cortes voted a fixed and wholly insufficient sum. Of the immense wealth of Mexico and Peru, only a small fraction found its way into the royal coffers, for in the Spanish colonies peculation was universal. But what was even more serious, since fraud can always be remedied by a stricter method of control, the fiscal system of the Spanish empire was based upon a false theory of trade. What was necessary to its welfare was the greatest possible international exchange of goods. The policy which was, in fact, pursued was protection in its blindest and most extravagant form. Spain had no science and no manufactures. While she could not send her colonies what they needed, she forbade their trade with any power but herself. From such a policy only two consequences were to be apprehended, either a retardation in the material progress of the colonies, or the encouragement of smuggling on a large scale. Both consequences, in fact, ensued. And meanwhile the agriculture and commerce of Spain were hampered by innumerable internal tolls, and by the *alcabala*, a tax of ten per cent. on sales, than which it would be difficult to conceive an instrument more exactly calculated to paralyze the economic prosperity of a people.

If little money could be wrung from Spain, nothing could be expected from Italy. It followed that the most elastic source of material revenue was to be found in the Netherlands. Antwerp was now one of the wealthiest trading cities in the world. She was unhampered by guild restrictions. She had become a great centre of international dealings, easily distancing Bruges and Ghent in the wealth and freedom of her communications, and, owing to the development of oceanic trade, possessing an advantage over Flanders as a banking centre. And fast rising into prominence was the Hanseatic city of Amsterdam, whose prosperity, originally founded on the herring fishing, was now augmented by the growing wealth of all those European states which were situated near the Atlantic littoral. There was opulence in the Netherlands. Here was the fiscal heart of the Spanish empire.

Intimately bound with this Spanish Eldorado by long ties of

commercial intercourse was the island in which Philip II had for a time ruled as the consort of its native queen Mary. Philip, like his father before him, was well aware of the value of England as a friend and ally. He knew the worth of English trade to his Flemings and the evils resulting from any interruption of that intercourse; how a hostile England could molest the marine communications between Spain and the Low Countries, and a friendly England most effectually protect them. But he was a devout Catholic. Religion came before everything. The preservation of the friendship of England would in the long run depend upon the faith of the islanders.

Elizabeth determined to be a Protestant. It was a bold decision, for the north of England was Catholic and the Highlands of Scotland and the Irish, while in the Scottish Lowlands a French army under the Regent Mary of Guise was upholding the Catholic cause. But Elizabeth made it, with the concurrence of her great adviser William Cecil, Lord Burghley, and never receded from it. We may suspect that she may have been influenced by her early training and upbringing, which had been Protestant, and by the humiliations which she had endured under her Catholic sister's reign.

The statesmanship of the English government during the first few years of Elizabeth's reign was of an order of excellence higher than that which had yet been attained by any European government. A European war was happily avoided. The Church of England was placed upon a settled national foundation, without civil disorders and with a minimum of interference with liberty of thought. By a timely exercise of courage, for which the credit belongs to Cecil, an armed force was sent to Scotland, which liberated the country from the Regent Mary's French soldiers, who had there been upholding the Catholic cause, and cleared the Lowlands for John Knox and the Protestant religion. No English military exploit, not even Waterloo, has had results so far-reaching as the ill-conducted siege of Leith by an ill-disciplined English army, which resulted in the Treaty of Edinburgh. For the first time for centuries an English army had entered Scotland, not to put a humiliation on Scottish pride, but to advance a Scottish interest. In making secure the Protestant reformation in southern Scotland the government of Elizabeth, as some wise men then foresaw, took the first essential step to the union of the two countries. Foolish courses, which might have prejudiced the success of this great act of statesmanship, such as the revival of the old claim of suzerainty, or the marriage of Queen Elizabeth to a Scottish nobleman, were happily avoided. Skilful courses were pursued. The stroke was effected while England was quiet and France, with some surreptitious assistance to the rebels from the queen of England, distracted with the Amboise conspiracy.

The new queen prided herself upon being "mere English." She knew the prejudice of her island subjects against foreigners, and had seen it exemplified in the storm of disapproval which greeted her sister's engagement to the Spaniard. She did not propose to repeat her sister's error. But flirtation was second nature, and the grave entertainment of proposals of marriage a diplomatic duty which she owed to her country. In order to keep the Huguenot party in good heart she was prepared over a period of ten years to receive the suit of Alençon, nearly twenty years her junior and had his character been less contemptible, a mere figure of fun. But in her heart she shrank from sharing her throne with a foreigner. She would die as she had lived, a virgin queen and "mere English." At the end of her long life she said to her last Parliament: "Though you have had and may have many mightier and wiser princes sitting on this throne, yet you never had nor shall have any that loved you better." Englishmen knew that this was so. Vanities and caprices which would have made any lesser woman ridiculous, acts of meanness which would have tarnished any other reputation, never stood between Elizabeth and the romantic devotion of her subjects. They felt that she was a great woman, proud, mettlesome, and preternaturally wise, and that her life was dedicated to the service and honour of her country.

It was generally recognized abroad that a country so rich and powerful as England could never be conquered if it remained united. The hopes of the Guises and afterwards of Philip II and the Jesuits were founded upon the prospect of English disunion. But save for the rising of the northern earls in 1569, when Elizabeth had been on her throne for eleven years, there was no grave menace to national unity; and the call of the Catholic north came too late. The Lowlands of Scotland were already given over to the reformed church, and the main part of the population in central and southern England was satisfied with the Anglican settlement. When war eventually broke out with Spain there was

no English party like the French League willing to give support
to the foreign invader. London was Protestant to the core. A
Spanish garrison, such as that which held Paris for the League,
would have been unthinkable in the capital of England.

Foremost among the causes which produced this unusual composure of the public mind was the skill with which the Church
was settled upon its new foundations. There were no burnings.
The dispossessed Roman bishops were treated with consideration,
and though Parliament passed an Act of Uniformity, it was not
so administered as to make the profession of differing religious
beliefs a dangerous occupation. A convenient and calculated haze
shrouded the religious convictions of the queen and made it seem
possible that she might after all incline to Rome. If she objected
to the sacrifice of the Mass, she did not conceal her dislike of
married clergy. Candles should sometimes shine upon her altar
and give to the Catholics a delusive glimmer of hope.

Those who were disquieted by the fear that she would proclaim
herself Head of the Church, like her father, were consoled by a
new vague title, which might mean less, but might also mean
quite as much. What was there in this Church settlement that
could stir reasonable men to a revolt? The Liturgy, which was
Cranmer's Prayer-book of 1552 with some slight variations, was
avowedly based on Roman models. The government of the
Church was episcopal, the articles of belief very largely Calvin-
istic. To no one section of theological opinion was the settlement
entirely satisfactory. The English divines who had acquired their
theology in Switzerland thought it too conservative; the Catholics
regarded it as too revolutionary. To those who disliked surplices
or Communion tables, or found little warrant for bishops in the
Holy Writ, the Elizabethan Church fell far short of perfection.
But to the great body of the people, who were not theological,
there was nothing intolerable in this settlement founded on compromise. It was not until 1570, when the queen was excommunicated and deposed by the Pope, that the average Catholic was
compelled to ask himself the question to whom his ultimate
allegiance was really due.

To the King of Spain, England at the accession of Queen
Elizabeth appeared not in the guise of an enemy, but as a
country to be won over and conciliated. A pious Catholic, determined to root out heresy from his dominions, Philip was never so
much of a crusader as to sacrifice the solid political interests of

his country to religious propaganda. England was heretical, a grave misfortune, a terrible taint; but England's heresy would never have provoked Philip to attack her. On the contrary, he was well pleased to see an English army abate the pride of the Guises, Catholic though they were, in Scotland. As a Catholic he might be expected to welcome the prospect of a possible union of England, Scotland, and France under Mary Queen of Scots. As a Spanish king he could not but regard such a contingency as a catastrophe at all costs to be averted. And the politician in him was in the last analysis stronger than the priest. So it happened that at the great crisis which established the Protestant Reformation in Scotland and paved the way to the Anglo-Scottish Union Philip was friendly, not inimical, to his heretical sister-in-law. In 1560 Spain helped English Protestantism by her friendship, in 1588 by her enmity.

And now, as an additional reason for keeping well with England, Philip was confronted by serious trouble in the Netherlands. The government of the seventeen provinces had been delegated by the king upon his departure for Spain to Margaret, Duchess of Parma, the natural daughter of Charles V by a Flemish mistress. Margaret had character, intellect, and sympathy. She was a native of the country and could speak its languages, and had she been left to govern the seventeen provinces without interference from Spain and with the help of the native nobility, there is little reason to doubt that her reign would have been successful and popular. But the regent was not a free agent. Secret instructions bound her to execute the decrees against the heretics, and a *consulta* of three advisers was imposed upon her by the absentee sovereign, to whom all questions of policy and administration, great and small, were regularly referred. Of this Camarilla the Cardinal Granvelle, son of the great statesman who for thirty years had been chief adviser to Charles V, was by his industry, his accomplishments, and his vast capacity the acknowledged and all-powerful chief.

The real gravamen against the Granvelle government (for so it was then regarded) was not that it lacked ability or statesmanship, but that it was required against its own better judgment to carry out an odious policy dictated from Spain. The people of the Netherlands were proud of their chartered rights and provincial privileges. They detested the presence of Spanish troops and the cruelties of Spanish religious persecution, and were more partiularly apprehensive as to the effects of a new scheme for the creation of fourteen bishoprics, which was thought to portend the introduction of the Spanish Inquisition and yet sharper measures against reformed beliefs. Proud and wealthy native noblemen who had served the state under Charles V asked themselves how long these outrages were to be endured and when they were to be admitted to a legitimate share in the influence and spoils of government, from which they were excluded by the unpopular cardinal and his associates.

The two men who worked together to unhorse the cardinal from his high Spanish saddle were curiously different in temperament and character. Egmont was a generous, vain, somewhat unstable soldier, raised by his victories at St. Quentin and Gravelines to a pinnacle of popular eminence and smarting under the sense of ill-requited desert. William of Nassau, Prince of Orange, was made of tougher, if less showy, materials. The foundations of his character were pride, constancy, and compassion. The great aristocrat resented the pressure of Spanish troops upon Flemish soil, and was filled with pity for the suffering victims of Spanish tyranny. With few military qualities, save an unreadiness to acknowledge defeat, but with great tenacity of purpose and an infinite command of diplomatic resource, William found himself drawn by the course of events to lead a popular movement for severance from Spain. He is exposed to the charge of having been first a loyalist and then a rebel, first a Catholic, then a Lutheran, and finally a Calvinist. In truth he was an opporunist living on a thread of principle, and since he cared for liberty and hated fanaticism, and for these beliefs suffered like his friend Egmont a violent death, he is accounted among the principal champions of European freedom.

In face of the forthcoming signs of storm Philip resolved to drop the pilot. But the withdrawal of Granvelle under the pressure of Egmont and his friends (1564) only steeled the king in his resolve to stamp out the northern heretics. To the terror of the Spanish Inquisition and the rigorous enforcements of the "placards," or anti-heresy edicts, there was now added (August 18, 1564) the requirement that the population of the Netherlands should accept the doctrines of the Council of Trent. A solemn protest against these and other evils was drawn up in the Regent's Council under the influence of the Prince of Orange and taken in person by Egmont to the king (January, 1565).

THE REVOLT OF THE NETHERLANDS.

When it was found that Egmont's mission was all in vain and that the edicts and decrees against the heretics were to be strictly enforced, the temperature swiftly rose. Young nobles, some like Marnix unbending Calvinists, others like Brederode humane Catholics, banded themselves together to resist the Inquisition. This was the body who drew up the uncompromising document known to history as the Compromise, and took to themselves with pride from the lips of a despiteful enemy the appellation of "Beggars" (Gueux), just as certain British soldiers at a later date have not been averse to being known as the Contemptibles. To all this protest and effervescence, which Orange and Egmont endeavoured to moderate, as well as to a savage outburst of Calvinist iconoclasm, Philip was quietly preparing a deadly reply.

The reproach against this Spanish king is that he was neither open, nor intelligent, nor humane. The three men who in the recent troubles had most helped in the maintenance of order were Orange, Egmont, and Count Hoorn. But they had been acclaimed by the "Gueux" and secretly denounced by the regent. Accordingly their destruction was resolved on. Without so much as coming to the Netherlands for a fortnight to study the problem on the spot, the king sent Alva, his best and most intemperate soldier, with a strong army of Italian and Spanish mercenaries, to crush the heretics, and with a special charge to trap and execute the three men in whom a wiser monarch would have found the principal pillars of his rule.

The prudent Orange withdrew to the safety of his German home before the advancing storm, but in an hour fatal to Spain Egmont and Hoorn were taken by treachery and after a mock trial beheaded in the public square of Brussels. The murder of these two influential and courageous men was one of those political crimes from which governments do not recover (June, 1568).

During six terrible years Alva tried his doctrine of thorough upon the stunned population of the Netherlands. But there were four factors upon which he had not counted, which taken into combination turned his early success into a ruinous failure. The first was Orange. The prince was an outlaw, and having therefore everything to fear and nothing to hope from the Spaniards, embarked upon the bold course of raising armies against them. His campaigns were a failure. He was no general. His troops were ill paid and ill disciplined, and in a pitched fight unequally matched against the seasoned veterans of Alva. But if he could not beat the enemy in the field, Orange could put him to an intolerable expense. To pay his troops Alva was compelled to resort to a scheme of taxation exactly calculated to arouse a commercial community to a white fury of indignation. Catholic merchants who had not raised a finger to save a heretic from the stake or to protest against the wholesale butcheries of "the Chamber of Troubles" were furious when they were asked to pay a ten per cent. duty upon every sale. The argument that the tax was a feature in a Spanish budget did not appeal to them. The whole country, without distinction of class or creed, was united as one man against a government which levelled such a deadly blow against the trade which was its heart.

A third factor was the sea. The ships were in Protestant and pirate hands. A new brood of Low German or Dutch Vikings infested the narrow seas, intercepting treasure and supplies, plundering churches, murdering priests and monks, in exchange for barbarities which no land army raised under Protestant banners was yet able adequately to avenge. If the beggars on land were for the moment powerless, the "beggars of the sea" put a new heart into the struggle. With an open encouragement from English heretics like-minded with themselves and with the active countenance of Queen Elizabeth, the Dutch pirates seized the town of Brill and thus unconsciously laid the foundations of a new and famous European state.

April,
1572

Yet the Dutch Republic could never have been created from the sea alone. The Sea-Beggars imparted the original impetus which stirred the northern provinces to throw off the yoke of Spain and to invite William of Orange to lead them to victory. The seizure of Brill led immediately to the capture of Flushing in the north and of Mons and Valenciennes in the south; but, far more important, it opened out the campaign of sieges which has given to the history of Haarlem, of Alkmaar, and of Leyden an imperishable renown. If the Dutch were as yet unable to measure themselves with Alva's veterans in the open field, behind their city walls they fought with the desperate valour of men contending against an enemy who had proved again and again that in the heat of combat he spared neither age nor sex.

It was the cruelty and indiscipline of the ill-paid Spanish army which, in the autumn of 1571 and the spring and summer of the succeeding year, brought the Prince of Orange from the nadir to the zenith of his fortunes. Alva had been withdrawn, Requesens, his successor, had suddenly died, and a Spanish interregnum was a Flemish opportunity which so astute a diplomatist as the Prince of Orange was not likely to neglect. The lights of Dutch Protestantism had been burning low. The prince had lost an army and two brothers on the disastrous field of Mookerheede (1574), his forces had been driven out of the islands of Duiveland and Shouwen, his treasury was empty, he had been rebuffed by Queen Elizabeth, to whom he had offered the sovereignty of his northern provinces, and he knew well that without strong internal support his little Calvinist state, hardly yet in being, would be helpless before the might of the Spanish empire. Suddenly an unexpected beacon of help flared up in the Catholic south. The Spanish army, breaking out into mutiny for lack of pay, seized Alost, and from their bandits' lair carried fire and sword to the brink of Brussels. In the general state of public indignation and alarm William saw a golden opportunity to restore and enlarge the fortunes of his cause. Acting on behalf of Holland and Zealand, he entered into negotiations with the states of Flanders and Brabant for the exclusion of the foreigner and the settlement of religion. The terrible sack of Antwerp, known as the Spanish Fury, swept away the last cob- *Nov.,* webs of indecision which obstructed the Pacification of Ghent. *1576* The Catholic south and the Protestant north, the Low Dutchmen and the Walloons banded themselves together in a political union to deal with a common danger. When Don John of Austria, the new Spanish governor, entered upon his governorship, with all the lustre of his royal blood, and with the laurels of Lepanto not yet withered on his brow, he found it necessary to concede to a united demand that the country should be rid immediately and for ever of the foreign troops, and that the charters and liberties of the provinces should be maintained. Even more bitter to this proud and impetuous dreamer was the predominance of Orange. "The Prince of Orange," he wrote to the king, " has bewitched the minds of all men. They love him, and fear him, and wish to have him as their lord."

But the triumph of the prince was not sustained. The bonds of union forged in the flames of the Spanish Fury were too brittle to stand a serious strain. On the vital and unsettled point of religion the United Provinces were not at one. The Calvinists at Ghent, not without some unstatesmanlike encouragement from the Prince of Orange, rose in revolt against their government, imprisoned the Duke of Aerschot, who was the Catholic leader of the south, and aroused once more the seething passions of religious hate which had been composed under the sense of a common danger. It was upon a country thus inflamed and divided that there now descended at the head of a choice army of twenty thousand men the most accomplished diplomatist and soldier of the Spanish empire. The Duke of Parma was no bloodthirsty blunderer, like Alva; no chimerical dreamer, like Don John. He could soothe, cajole, conciliate; but while he disarmed suspicions, he could also strike. By his crushing victory of Gembloux he finally assured the return of the southern provinces to their Spanish allegiance.

June,
1578

By this battle it was decided that Holland and Belgium should lead a separate political existence, which, save for their brief and uneasy union between 1815 and 1830, has remained unbroken to this day. That Brussels and The Hague should now be so remote in spirit, though so near in space, is a circumstance chiefly to be ascribed to Alva, who crushed the southern Protestants in the sixteenth century, and to Parma who prevented their return and revival. These two foreign officers, the first of execrable, the second of most honourable, memory, are among the architects of modern Belgium.

It was with deep reluctance that Orange surrendered the dream of a united Netherlands and assented to the Union of Utrecht (1579), which his Protestant supporters in the north had framed as a counterblast to the Catholic Union of Arras. No choice was now open to him but to concentrate upon the defence of those hard-bitten northern Calvinists who, in Holland and Zealand, had placed their destinies in his hand and were willing to sacrifice everything for their beliefs. To this end he resolved, much to the grief of his best supporters, to invoke the aid of the Duke of Anjou, who, as heir to the French throne and an acknowledged suitor for the hand of the English queen, seemed likely to offer the best guarantees of effectual help. It was a bad speculation. Anjou was treacherous, his army mutinous, his protectorate hateful. Nothing useful was gained by his short-lived intervention. But a more powerful auxiliary in the fight against Spain was destined before long to disclose surprising resources.

The doctrine of political assassination was at this time so widely held, being specially, though not exclusively, commended by some Spanish members of the Jesuit Order, that it is no matter for surprise if the government of Spain resolved to remove its obstinate and formidable antagonist by murder. The prince was put to the ban of the empire (March 15, 1581), declared to be an outlaw and an enemy of the human race, and money, land, or a title were offered for his head. But there is a nemesis which attends the policy of political assassination. The victim may fall, but the cause survives, strengthened by the martyr's blood. On July 10, 1584, Orange was shot in the Prinzenhof at Delft by a young Burgundian fanatic named Balthazar Gérard: but though he was only fifty-one his murder had come too late. Three years before (July 26, 1581), the representatives of Brabant and Flanders, of Utrecht, Guelderland, Holland and Zealand, meeting at The Hague, had signed an Act of Abjuration, renouncing their allegiance to the king of Spain. So though William of Orange was now dead, out of the turmoil and tempest a state of his creating had already emerged, which was destined to cover the seas with its shipping, to build up an opulent empire in the east, to challenge the navies of England and the armies of France, and to earn the gratitude of mankind as an asylum of intellectual freedom, and as the home of a school of painters whose minute and delicate observation of the quiet beauties of life has permanently enriched the culture of Europe.

The new state possessed a constitution to all appearance most unfitted for the rough weather of European politics. It was a federation of seven tiny sovereign republics, each with its own estates or local parliament, and its own elective stadtholder or executive officer, and each claiming to exercise a direct share in the control of finance and foreign policy of the confederation. An assembly of delegates from the provincial estates, with the assistance of a council of twelve, dealt with matters common to the whole Union, and appointed the captain-general of the army, and the admiral-general of the navy; but since the real seat of sovereignty lay not with these central delegations but with the seven local estates. there was no constitutional security either for the coherence of the republic or for continuity and vigour in the conduct of its policy. At any moment, did they so choose, the peasants of Frisia, the canons of Utrecht, or the nobles of Guelders might frustrate by an adverse vote the well-laid plans of the burgher aristocracy of the trading cities.

From the ill consequences of these defects in its polity the republic was saved by three circumstances, the substantial homogeneity of the Dutch population, the pre-eminence of Holland among the provinces, and, most of all, by the special position, which during the first critical half-century of Dutch independence was freely accorded to the head of the house of Orange.

The bulk of the Dutch population, being concerned with trade, industry, and seafaring, shared a common outlook upon foreign affairs and a common understanding of Dutch needs and interests. Feudalism was dead. Noble and priest had given way to the urban middle class. A burgher aristocracy ruled the cities and the cities ruled the commonwealth. By a piece of good fortune, which greatly contributed to the stability and strength of the country, the chief centres of trade, learning, and politics were to be found within the ambit of a single province. Amsterdam and Rotterdam, Delft and Dordrecht, Leyden (the seat of the Dutch university) and The Hague, the political capital of the state, were all situated in Holland. Nowhere in Europe was there in the same area such a concentration of population and commercial power. Nowhere was trade more skilfully managed, or the art of city life so well understood. And as Holland was supreme among the seven provinces, Amsterdam was pre-eminent among its cities. In banking and commerce, in the size of its navy and the span of its colonial enterprise, this vigorous city distanced all competitors. The centralization which was lacking to the constitution was supplied by the force of economic preponderance. In theory local liberties remained unimpaired. In practice the course which found favour with the opulent rulers of Amsterdam was apt to commend itself to the weaker members of the federation.

To a policy thus divided and balanced the princes of the house of Orange supplied an indispensable unity of direction. In nothing was this dynasty more remarkable than in its wise regard for the jealous republicanism of the Dutch. Amid unending perils William the Silent made, and Maurice and Frederick Henry afterwards defended, the liberties of this people. Yet neither their success nor their wonderful record of service tempted them to overthrow the cumbrous forms of the federal constitution. The head of the house of Orange was content with the position of an elected magistrate. Stadtholder in five provinces, captain-general and admiral-general of the republic, he concentrated in his own hands by the free voice of the community the effective powers of the state. For seventy years an accumulation of elective offices gave to the chiefs of this remarkable family as large a measure of authority as was enjoyed by any hereditary sovereign in Europe during that aristocratic age. Then, after the death of William II (1650), came a long minority during which the conduct of the republic was vested in the hands of the principal civil official of its leading province, the Grand Pensionary of Holland. But the memory of the house of Orange was still alive in the hearts of the Dutch people; and in the hours of their greatest danger, when their small republic was menaced with destruction by the vast military power of Louis XIV, they called upon the great-grandson of William the Silent to save them, and did not call in vain.

Twenty-five years of warfare divide the death of William of Orange from the twelve years' truce signed in 1609, which advertised to the whole world Spain's final confession that she could not conquer the Dutch republic. What saved the Dutch was, firstly, the diversion of Spanish military effort against Elizabeth and Henry IV, and, secondly, the discovery by the United Provinces of a great statesman and a great general. When William fell by the hand of an assassin, the Duke of Parma was on the high tide of his triumphant career. One by one the cities of Flanders and Brabant fell before his victorious skill. He took Brussels, stormed Antwerp, threatened, unless help were speedily forthcoming, to overwhelm those last bulwarks of the Protestant cause, Holland and Zealand.

It is improbable that the small English army under the Earl of Leicester, which Queen Elizabeth threw into Flushing to restore the situation, would have permanently withstood the forces which the Spanish commander was so well able to assemble and inspire. But Parma's efforts were dispersed. He was commanded first to collect an army for the invasion of England, and, when this hope died away with the dispersion of the Armada, to forward his master's interests in the civil war in France. While he should have been mastering Amsterdam, he was directed to relieve Paris. While his troops should have been conquering Holland they were required for a futile occupation of Rouen.

and so, charged with miscellaneous and distracting military duties, this great soldier died with his task unaccomplished.

The Dutch constitution, like the American constitution today, was ill suited to bear the stress and strain of war. Every province was sovereign, and each province was tenacious of its accustomed ways. Fortunately, however, for the future of the republic, the province of Holland was, by reason of its wealth, its population, its energy, and the lion's share which it bore in the charges of the Union, the predominant power in the States-General. And for thirty-two years (1586-1618) the influence of Holland was wielded by its advocate John van Oldenbarnveldt.

To this wise, experienced, and liberally-minded man, who was for so long a period the real civilian head of the new republic, fortune supplied an admirable pendant in Maurice of Nassau, the soldier son of William of Orange.

It was the object of that accomplished officer and of his cousin, William of Nassau, to forge an army which could beat the Spaniards in the open field. This they did. In four brilliant campaigns Maurice liberated the soil of the federated provinces, and showed himself to be the first soldier of his age. There was no department of war in which he was not proficient. His siege dispositions were regarded as a masterpiece of caution and science. His handling of cavalry in action showed the eye of a master. His capture of Gertruidenburg, his cavalry pursuit of Varax during a winter night at Turnhout (1597), the daring and opportune charge which turned defeat into victory on the hard-fought field of Dunkirk, were regarded as supreme examples of the military art. And meanwhile on the sea the Spaniards were mastered. A great naval victory at Gibraltar in 1607 announced the definite superiority of the Dutch and impelled the enemy to think of peace.

There were three great difficulties obstructing agreement, independence, religion, trade. It was intolerable to Spanish pride that these Dutch rebels should be acknowledged as an independent state, that they should be permitted to prohibit the public celebration of Catholic rites, or that they should trade with that vast area in the new world which had been reserved to Spain by the Pope. A peace was found to be impossible: but eventually a twelve years' truce was signed at Antwerp (April 9, 1609). The delicate subject of religion was left unmentioned, but the Netherlands wrung from their reluctant antagonists the acknowledgment of their independence and of their right to trade in Spanish waters.

For during these five and twenty years the better part of the Dutch population had taken to the sea, leaving their land armies to be mainly composed of Germans, English, or Scots. A Dutch captain had wintered in the Arctic ice. A Dutch fleet had visited China and Siam. Dutch factories had been established in the Spice Islands. A Dutch East India Company, the first of the great chartered companies, had been established in 1601. The new-gotten wealth of an expanding world commerce nourished the war effort of this small and vigorous community, and now, after a generation of desperate struggle, enabled it to negotiate a victorious truce with the first military power in Europe.

BOOKS WHICH MAY BE CONSULTED

Motley : Rise of the Dutch Republic. 3 vols. Everyman's Library. 1906.

H. Pirenne : Histoire de Belgique. 1907.

F. Harrison : William the Silent. 1897.

W. H. Prescott : History of the Reign of Philip II. 1855.

Martin A. S. Hume : Philip II of Spain. 1902.

P. J. Blok : History of the People of the Netherlands. 1892-6.

J. E. Neale : Queen Elizabeth. 1934.

R. Altamira y Crevea : Historia d'España y de la civilizacion española. 1902.

R. B. Merriman : The Rise of the Spanish Empire. 1918-25.

A. F. Pollard : History of England. 1912.

F. W. Maitland : The Anglican Settlement and the Scottish Reformation (Cambridge Modern History, Vol. II, chap. xvi).

J. A. Froude : History of England. 1856-70.

A. Lang : History of Scotland. 1900-7.

J. Skelton : Maitland of Lethington and the Scotland of Mary Stuart. 2 vols. 1894.

P. Hume Brown : John Knox. 2 vols. 1895.

CHAPTER XVI

ENGLAND AND SPAIN

Commercial rivalry between England and Spain. Private enterprise and public caution. The Puritan sailors of England. The lure of the East. The first blow. Francis Drake. The Catholic rising in the north. Mary of Scotland. Union of Portugal and Spain. The Armada and its sequel. The passing of Spanish prestige. The expulsion of the Moriscoes. Beginnings of English colonization.

THE rivalry between England and Spain, which developed into open war in the reign of Elizabeth, while it undoubtedly helped to deepen the Protestant sentiments of the English people and had from the first some tinge of religious animosity, was, at the bottom, economic. The seafaring people of England were drawn by their appetite for adventure, for money, and for commerce, to challenge the closely guarded Spanish monopoly in the new world and in the Indies. The war did not arise out of religion. It did not come because the Spanish government was determined to force the Roman faith upon England, still less because Elizabeth was anxious to precipitate a quarrel with Catholic Spain. It came because English seamen, acting on their own initiative, but often not without the sympathy and connivance of the queen, were determined to make good their claim to share in the commerce of the new world.

1560-88 During the twenty-eight years succeeding the Treaty of Edinburgh, nothing is more remarkable than the contrast between the caution of the English government and the venturesome audacity of the military and seafaring section of the nation. While the official history of the government is singularly devoid of event, the unofficial and unauthorized activities of the people open up a new chapter in the history of the world. The object of the queen was to prevent religious disruption and to stave off a foreign war until such time as loyalty to her person had become a settled habit among all her lieges. Her policy, therefore, was to deprecate excessive vigour, and to disclaim responsibility for compromising adventures. To ardent Puritans like Sir Francis Walsingham such a course appeared to be a humiliating betrayal of the Protestant cause. They would have fought the enemy, not surreptitiously and on a system of limited liability, but openly and on every front, in France, in the Netherlands, and on the high seas. The queen's unheroic but statesmanlike avoidance of precipitate risk was little to their liking. For England had now become the first naval power in the world. She had the best shipwrights, the best ships, the best sailors. She had learnt the lesson of naval gunnery and the value of the broadside. Her ships, which were smaller than the Spaniards', could sail closer to the wind, and were easier to handle. Though the Royal Navy was small, amounting only to twenty-two ships of 100 tons and over in 1559, and to twenty-nine ships in 1603, there was always a large pirate and commercial navy in reserve which could be relied upon to co-operate with the queen's ships at a crisis. The growth of the nation's sea-power owed little to official encouragement. It was the result of the strong natural appetite of an enterprising marine population, who suddenly found themselves in the surprising position of being able to compete for the dominion of the world.

The mariners of England in the Elizabethan age, though all were not cut to the same pattern, were apt to possess certain common qualities. Sailorwise, they believed in an overruling Providence, governing the waves and winds and the fate of men. They were proud of England and their queen. They despised foreigners. They hated the Pope, the Turk, and the Devil, but perhaps most of all the Pope, who had allotted the East Indies to Portugal and the West Indies to Spain. Of international law, either as a need or as a fact, they had not the slightest suspicion. They regarded the high seas as a kind of no man's land upon which they might pillage and murder to their hearts' content. Only to a few more curious spirits did marine enterprise suggest the possibility of missionary work. No Protestant chaplain in an Elizabethan galleon was conscious of the noble rôle of the Catholic Las Casas.

Yet mingled with the baser appetites of the buccaneers was a certain largeness and simplicity of imagination which gave nobility to the seafaring movements of this age. The expansion of geographical knowledge and the discovery of Cathay, or the Earthly Paradise, were motives commonly felt, and not confined only to men of science or poetic dreamers. Audacity was bred of success. "There is no land unhabitable or sea unnavigable."

wrote Master Robert Thorne of Bristol (1527) recommending the northern passage to the Spice Islands to his sovereign with a *bravura* characteristic of that time.

For still those distant Spice Islands in the East Indies remained the primary quest. Willoughby and Chancellor tried to reach them by the north-eastern passage and opened up the trade with Russia. Gilbert, Frobisher, and Davis hoped to find the north-western passage and rediscovered Hudson Straits. But both passages were fatally barred by the ice and snow of the Arctic regions.

There remained no other course, if the wealth of the Orient were to be reached, than a direct invasion of the trade monopoly of Spain and Portugal in the South Seas. English sailors, like John Hawkins, who opened up a traffic in negro slaves between Guinea and the West Indies, knew that they could not so trade without the use of force. They armed their ships, were prepared to fight, and looked forward without misgivings to a breach with Spain. Only if a violent attack on an indefensible monopoly is itself indefensible, do these English sailors stand condemned. The question at issue was the trade of the world.

It was in 1567 in the Mexican port of San Juan de Ulloa that the first shot was exchanged in this great controversy. Here John Hawkins and his young cousin, Francis Drake, were sheltering from the hurricane after a successful course of trade and piracy on the Spanish Main, when a fleet of thirteen Spanish galleons, carrying on board the new Governor of Mexico, appeared in the offing. Hawkins, who had five ships only, but was in a position to deny an entry to the Spaniards, elected to treat. As the two little fleets lay side by side, and as their crews were fraternizing ashore, a treacherous attack was suddenly launched against the unsuspecting Englishmen. Many were slaughtered, three ships were lost, and it was only after a hard and gallant fight that Hawkins and Drake managed to extricate themselves from the mêlée. The story of Spanish treachery and English valour made a deep impression when it was known at home. "Military and seafaring men all over England," says Camden, "fretted and desired war with Spain. But the queen shut her ears against them."

For the next twenty-eight years the formidable figure of Francis Drake dominates the seas. There are some who think that his methods of buccaneering were not the best, and that he would have done well to establish a base for his piracies at Cartagena, or at some other spot on the Spanish Main. But he reached his object, which was by incessant and ubiquitous plunderings to drive Spain into war. Nothing was safe from him, neither the towns on the Spanish Main, nor the route taken by the Peruvian treasure across the Isthmus of Panama, nor the Pacific coast, nor the Spice Islands. In the year before the Armada sailed, he burned the shipping in Cadiz harbour. Before that, on his return from circumnavigating the globe, his compatriots called him "The Master Thief of the Unknown World," and his queen, who had gone shares in the loot, went down expressly to Deptford to knight the great discoverer, and the head of the pirates' profession.

Meanwhile, events had been moving forward to the outbreak of that open struggle which Philip and Elizabeth were so anxious to avoid.

The strength of England was now sufficiently manifest to convince its enemies that the country could be conquered only with the assistance of an English party desirous of overthrowing the queen and of establishing once more the Roman Faith. Such a party existed. Adherents of the Catholic Church were to be found scattered through the country, sparse in the south and east, numerous in the north, dominant in the Celtic regions of the British Isles. More particularly was their power to be apprehended in the poor and backward northern counties of England, where the feudal nobles were still strong, and where Scottish priests fleeing from the wrath of John Knox, and Catholic propaganda put about by English exiles in Louvain, combined to sustain the ardour of the ancient faith. In the politics of northern England, whether past or present, aristocratic pride has always played a part. To men like the Earl of Northumberland and Lord Dacre of the western marches, Protestantism was an odious innovation fastened on to the country by the middle-class counsellors who had unfortunately gained the ear of the queen. Relying on Spanish and Scottish help, which never came, they rose in revolt in 1569, destroyed the Bibles and Prayer-books in Durham Cathedral, and then, failing to find substantial support, were easily and ruthlessly crushed. The suppression of this premature and disjointed enterprise gave to Elizabeth a decisive advantage of which her enemies would have been wise to take note. The lesson was disregarded. The plots against the queen continued till the end.

For these Catholic discontents Mary of Scotland provided a steady and dangerous rallying point. The story of this unfortunate princess, had it been abruptly terminated during the summer of 1567, would have read somewhat as follows: Daughter of James V and Mary of Guise, Mary had been brought up in the profligate court of Catharine dei Medici where she was married to Francis, heir to the French throne and subsequently king. Her husband, a mere boy, died in Paris, her mother, Mary of Guise, in Leith. Being lawful queen of Scotland, she was invited into her kingdom by those members of the Scottish aristocracy who were principally concerned to defend the independence of their country from its southern neighbour. Here she was wedded to the young and profligate Earl of Darnley, who, thanks to his mother, had a claim to succeed to the English throne. But though the marriage resulted in the birth of the boy who became James VI of Scotland and James I of England, it was a tragedy deeply stained with blood. The queen had a favourite secretary. He was an Italian of the name of Rizzio, cultivated and agreeable, a pleasant contrast to the brutal Darnley and to the grim Protestant nobles who controlled the policy of the country. Darnley murdered him in Mary's presence. A year later Darnley was himself destroyed, as many thought with the complicity of his wife, who proceeded without delay to marry Bothwell, his assassin. The Scottish nobles, who were not squeamish, recoiled from the national disgrace of these transactions. They imprisoned Mary in Lochleven, intending to bring her to trial for her offence; but Mary escaped. With a reputation deeply tarnished in the eyes of her contemporaries, Catholic and Protestant alike, she crossed the border and threw herself upon the mercy of Elizabeth.

Had Elizabeth returned Mary to meet her accusers in Scotland, England would have been saved from many anxieties. But the Queen was outraged by the idea of rebellion, and had no sympathy with rebels, even when rebellion was helpful to the interests of her country. She hated John Knox, she scolded the Scottish nobles for the indignity which they put on their lawful sovereign, and she could never bring herself cordially to co-operate either with the Dutch or the Huguenots. So she kept

Mary in prison in England, and endeavoured to treat with her, suggesting terms of peace that were not unreasonable, as that she should resign her throne to James VI, and allow him to be educated in England; but Mary, who was set on revenge and flattered by ambition, preferred to play for higher stakes. In December, 1568, she was encouraged to hope that she might aspire to the hand of King Philip of Spain.

Accordingly, for nineteen years the captive queen was the 1568-87 pivot round which revolved the whirlpool of Catholic conspiracy and intrigue. Plot followed upon plot, encouraged by the King of Spain, by the Pope, who excommunicated the heretic queen and released her subjects from their allegiance, and by the English Catholic exiles abroad. A Protestant Association was formed to protect the life, so often menaced, of the great sovereign, who persistently refused, to the dismay and bewilderment of her Protestant subjects, to protect herself by bringing Mary to judgment. Eventually clear proof was forthcoming of the Scottish queen's complicity in a design to do away with her rival. When Babington's plot was divulged, both Houses unanimously petitioned for the execution of "the monstrous and huge dragon, the Queen of Scots." On February 1, 1587, after long and painful hesitation, Elizabeth signed the death warrant, than which there could have been no clearer defiance of the Pope, of Spain, and of all their works. Mary had long outlived the dark shadows of her passionate youth. She had become a heroine of romance, the champion of a faith, and was viewed by the whole Catholic world as a saint and a martyr. Elizabeth, greatly misdoubting, had given a precedent for the execution of a crowned and anointed queen.

Spain was in a position to take up the challenge. A disaster in Morocco, the death of King Sebastian of Portugal, and the 1580 failure of his line, had brought the Portuguese kingdom under the Spanish Crown. The fine Atlantic seaboard, the mines of Brazil, the rich Portuguese possessions on both sides of Africa, the factories and posts in the Spice Islands, the Azores, a half-way house across the Atlantic, and the East Indies, passed by an unexpected stroke of fortune into the hands of Philip II. Forty years later, when the nature of the contest between Spain and Britain was more clearly understood, a Portuguese publicist argued that the King of Spain should transfer his capital from Madrid to Lisbon, and thence launch a navy which should de-

fend India and South America in the British Channel wher
alone the great world issue could be decided. The advice wa
never taken. The Spaniard was never welcome in Portugal. Th
two countries were never brought to coalesce, and their uneas
marriage was dissolved after sixty years. By a singular irony o
fate, the period of Pan-Iberian union witnessed at once th
flowering time of Spanish literature and the gradual decline o
Spanish and Portuguese power. But in 1580, when the unio
occurred, it promised to Philip of Spain a vast accession o
strength which in England and France was viewed with eyes o
acute apprehension and distrust.

Still Philip hesitated. Though England gave support to Portu
guese discontent and to Dutch rebellion, the king shrank fron
the expense and danger of a direct attack on that island of fo
midable heretics. Eventually, while France was paralyzed b
the War of the Three Henries,[1] and after Mary Stuart ha
formally recognized him as her heir to the English throne, h
yielded his judgment to the sailors and the exiles and the priest
and, in the mood of Don Quixote pursuing a holy but impo
sible quest, commissioned his subjects to prepare the conque
of England.

The Spanish Armada, conceived in the spirit of a religiou
crusade, and prepared at an alarming cost, set sail from Lisbo
on May 30, 1588, under the Duke of Medina Sidonia, a foolis
and cowardly landsman, who was selected on the ground of hi
rank alone. The plan was that the fleet should proceed up th
Channel to Dunkirk and Nieuport, and thence convoy the arm
of the Duke of Parma to England, where Elizabeth was to b
deposed, and the Infanta of Spain set up in her place. A mor
chimerical or fantastic scheme it would have been difficult t
devise. Exiles are always bad counsellors, and the Englis
Catholics on the continent, who had the ear of the Pope an
the King of Spain, had not reckoned upon the change whicl
had come over the temper of the English people during the las
two decades. The Puritan spirit had grown strong: the Catholi
spirit had proportionately diminished. A generation of peac
and prosperity had consolidated the loyalty of the nation to th
crown. Persecution there had been, but not before the Pope'
Bull of deposition in 1570, and then upon a scale which con

---

[1] Henry III and Henry of Navarre against Henry, Duke of Mayenne
the leader of the League or ultra-Catholic party.

rasted favourably with the burnings of the previous reign, and
was far removed from the terrible holocaust of victims exacted
by Catholicism in the Netherlands, in France, and in Spain.
There was no party in the country which would have favoured
a Spanish landing or tolerated a Spanish queen. Even if Parma's
army had been disembarked in England with the military reinforcements · brought overseas from Spain, they would have
found themselves opposed by the united force of a high-mettled
and valiant people. But the whole scheme foundered on the incompetence of the Spanish navy. The vast galleons, crowded
with soldiers, and obsessed by the antiquated tradition of galley
tactics, were outmanoeuvred and outsailed in the Channel by
their nimbler opponents, beaten in a great sea battle off Gravelines, and finally ruined by the blustering gales of the North
Sea and the Atlantic. A Dutch fleet, hovering off Dunkirk, kept
Parma pinned to the shore, while Drake, Hawkins, and
Frobisher destroyed and dispersed the galleons of Spain.

The Spanish Armada was not the final but the first act of a
long war which outlasted Philip II and Elizabeth, and was only
concluded in 1604. On the side of Spain the continuance of the
struggle was marked by a great improvement in naval technique,
without which it would have been impossible for that country to
have preserved, as it succeeded in doing, its essential connection
with the new world; on the side of England by a number of
daring enterprises, of which the sack of Cadiz in 1597 is the most
memorable. On either side the struggle was carried on over a
wide field. England trafficked with the Moriscoes in Valencia,
with the adherents of Don Antonio, the Pretender to Portugal,
while Spain was in league with English Jesuits and Irish rebels,
and landed troops in Ireland to co-operate with O'Donnell and
Tyrone. The plantation of Munster under Queen Elizabeth,
effected at a fearful cost of Irish lives, was an incidental and
melancholy consequence of this phase of the struggle between
the Protestant and Catholic faction in Europe.

The fate of the Spanish Armada was the first notification to
the world that the Spanish empire was not invincible. The preparations for the invasion were well known to have been made
upon a scale which strained to the utmost the resources of the
country. The enterprise had the support of the Pope, the blessing
of the clergy, the prayers of the people. Yet by some Providence,
difficult to reconcile with religious pride, the great Armada had

been brought to nothing by the heroic seamen of the north and the wild blasts of heaven.

So, though the Spaniard was not ready to accept defeat and continued the struggle in France, in Ireland, in the Netherlands and on the high seas, the haunting fear of Spanish tyranny passed out of Europe. The victories of Henry IV showed that Spain could not maintain a foothold in France. The battle of Kinsale dashed her hopes in Ireland. In 1609 she was brought to the bitter point of acknowledging the independence of the Dutch. The anti-Spanish powers each made peace at the time most convenient to itself, the French deserting the English, and the English deserting the Dutch. When the English peace was made by James I in 1604 it contained concessions odious to the veterans of the Elizabethan age, for it was agreed that Spain might keep Englishmen out of the Indies and try them by the Inquisition: but in effect the Spanish offensive had been foiled. The Armada had completed the process which the Marian persecution had begun of making England a Protestant country.

A long succession of reverses experienced by a religious people may either shake or confirm them in the faith. In the agony of the great Channel fight the Spanish sailors exclaimed, "God has deserted us." Later the nation was brought to believe that it was punished because it had deserted God. The losses at sea, the miscarriage in Ireland, the failure of the plan to convert England or subdue the Dutch, were ascribed by the priests to a dark taint of heresy wickedly tolerated in Spain itself. In their view the first step to the revival of the country was no plan for fiscal or naval reformation, but the propitiation of an angry and jealous God. The Moriscoes must confess or leave the country. The advice was taken. The Moriscoes were disliked on many grounds : because they were dark in skin, because they were skilled and industrious, because they were thought to be at heart heretical and to sympathize with the African corsairs who raided the Spanish coast. Accordingly no act of Philip III was so popular with the Spanish nation as his expulsion of this deserving community, numbering half a million of the most skilled agriculturalists and artificers of the country, whereby Spain was rendered so much the less able to sustain the burden of her far-reaching empire.

By the end of the sixteenth century no serious effort had been made by England to colonize the new world. The sailors and gentlemen adventurers who singed the King of Spain's beard were not the stuff out of which colonists are made. Rather than face the hard and steady work of founding communities on the north American shore, the Elizabethan voyagers abandoned themselves to the excitement of discovery, pillage, and war. But the idea of colonization was in the air. It attracted men like Richard Eden and Sir Humphrey Gilbert, Sir Walter Raleigh and Richard Hakluyt, preacher and sometime student of Christ Church in *1553-1616* Oxford, whose *Principal Navigations, Voyages, Traffiques, and Discoveries of the English Nation* is the prose epic of this age of adventurers; and it led to the foundation in 1584 of a colony on the north American coast named, after the queen, Virginia, which for lack of adequate support was allowed to fade away and had to be founded anew in the succeeding reign. How colonies should be peopled, governed, or related to the mother country were questions which in the heat and excitement of the war with Spain were left unexamined; but it is plain that the idea of repeating in the new world the polity, privileges, and civilization of the colonizing state was foreign to that age. Even Gilbert and Hakluyt regarded a colony mainly as a means of promoting trade and of ridding the commonwealth of its unprofitable members. Nor had the Elizabethan fighting seamen any notion how to handle the gentle Indians of the North American continent. Sir Philip Sidney, who might have shone out before the world as the ideal colonial governor, setting a standard for others to follow, was stopped by Queen Elizabeth from taking charge of Virginia. Only by slow degrees in the eighteenth and nineteenth centuries did the English begin to learn those lessons of tact and clemency which have made their government of subject races tolerable to the world.

BOOKS WHICH MAY BE CONSULTED

Histories of England : Froude, 1856-70. Pollard, 1912. Fletcher, 1905-23. Trevelyan, 1926.

J. E. Neale : Queen Elizabeth. 1934.

G. W. Prothero : Select Statutes and Other Constitutional Documents. 1898.

M. Creighton : The Life of Elizabeth. 1896.

M. A. S. Hume : The Great Lord Burghley. 1898.

P. Hume Brown : John Knox. 1895.

20

G. Lytton Strachey : Elizabeth and Essex. 1928.

Conyers Read : Mr. Secretary Walsingham. 1925.

A. Lang : The Mystery of Mary Stuart. 1904.

J. Skelton : The Scotland of Mary Stuart. 1894.

R. Simpson : Edmund Campion : A Biography. 1896.

J. S. Corbett : Drake and the Tudor Navy. 2 vols. 1898.

J. A. Froude : English Seamen in the Sixteenth Century. 1895.

M. A. S. Hume : The Year after the Armada. 1896.

William Harrison : Description of England. *Ed.* F. J. Furnivall. 1877.

Daniel Neal : History of the Puritans. 5 vols. 1822.

W. B. Rye : England as seen by Foreigners in the Days of Elizabeth and James I. 1865.

W. A. Raleigh : Shakespeare. 1907.

G. Saintsbury : History of Elizabethan Literature. 1887.

For chief editions of leading Elizabethan authors, *cf.* Cambridge Modern History, Vol. III, chap. xi.

CHAPTER XVII

THE THIRTY YEARS' WAR

The main tragedy of German history. Ferdinand II. General character of the war. The rôle of Sweden. Protestant rebellion in Bohemia. The Defenestration of Prague. The Palsgrave and the Bohemian Crown. The responsibility of James of England. The fight on the White Hill. Catholic reaction in Bohemia. The punishment of the Palsgrave. The intervention of Denmark. Wallenstein. The Catholic menace in the north. Gustavus Adolphus restores the balance. His death at Lützen. Oxenstierna makes the Alliance of Heilbronn. The murder of Wallenstein, 1634, and the Peace of Prague, 1635. Religion goes out of the war. The triumph of Richelieu. The reverses of Spain. The Peace of Westphalia.

THE brilliant flowering of European genius which we associate with the names of Shakespeare and Cervantes was immediately succeeded by a catastrophe which plunged a large area of central Europe into an abysm of barbarism and misery. The Thirty Years' War arose out of a religious revolt in Bohemia which might have been isolated, but was allowed to spread until most European states were in varying degrees involved in the struggle. But though Denmark and Sweden, France and England, Savoy and the Netherlands, played a part in the tragedy, the main theatre of the war was always the German empire, and the chief sufferers the German and Bohemian peoples. Nature had already imposed a heavy penalty upon the Germans. By reason of their geographical position they were cut off from the colonizing enterprises which in the seventeenth century enriched the life of the oceanic powers. But to this geographical handicap there was now added the social depression consequent upon the devastations of a war waged with a ferocity to which history offers few parallels. It is indeed impossible to exaggerate the miseries which the helpless peasants of the German empire were compelled to endure in these iron times. There was marauding, there was starvation, there was even cannibalism. Whole villages died out, and, as is always the case in times of extreme and desperate calamity, moral restraints broke down and ceded to wild bursts of profligacy.

At the beginning of the sixteenth century Germany stood in

the forefront of European civilization. By the end of the Thirty
Years' War the country was barren of literature and art, burdened
by an almost unmanageable language, and in its social manners
and customs sunk to a Muscovite barbarity.

The *primum movens* was a crowned Jesuit. Judged by the
extent of the changes brought about by his personal initiative,
Ferdinand of Styria, afterwards the Emperor Ferdinand II. must
be regarded as one of the great men of action of the century. He
was the first pupil of a Jesuit college to mount the imperial
throne; and his intelligence, narrowed, embittered, and directed
by Jesuit teaching, was governed by a single passion and a single
purpose. He hated Protestants and determined to uproot them
from his dominions. By a resolute course of persecution begun
in Styria (1598), continued in Bohemia, and carried throughout
the length and breadth of his Austrian dominions he succeeded
in his object of "liquidating" the heretics and of bringing all the
religious and intellectual life of his realm under the iron rule of
the Jesuit Order. But the price was terrific; the violent subversion
of the whole fabric of Bohemian society and incidentally the
outbreak of the Thirty Years' War. Few men so honest, pious,
and consistent have brought upon the world so great an avalanche
of misery or have ensured for the intellect of a people so long a
period of theological constraint.

Yet the long and wasteful struggle was fought for no trivial
ends. It decided the issue whether Germany was to be reconquered from the Counter-Reformation, administering a sharp
check to the Jesuit advance, and saving for the Lutheran and
Calvinist Churches great tracts of central Europe. But religion,
though the most prominent and embittering element in the
quarrel, was not here, and perhaps has never been, the sole
motive operating in the minds of statesmen.

The Thirty Years' War negatived in the most emphatic manner
the idea that Germany could ever again be united under a strong
imperial constitution. It showed that even those princes of Germany who cared most for the Roman Church cared more for
their own territorial position, and rather than abet a restoration
of the Catholic Empire to a position of real authority in Germany
were prepared to be neutral or even to ally themselves with the
French, so that while the war perpetuated the religious divisions
of Germany, it also confirmed its political anarchy. There was
yet another political issue, entering largely into the motives of

that time and counting for much in the final settlement at the Peace of Westphalia (1648). To whom was the dominion of the Baltic to belong? The great days of the Hanseatic League were now passed. Lisbon and Antwerp, Amsterdam and London had, with the opening out of the new oceanic routes, long outstripped Lübeck and Rostock, Stralsund and Danzig. The serious competitors for supremacy in the Baltic were no longer the German republics of the League, but the rival kingdoms of Denmark, Sweden, and Poland, the first formidable by reason of its control of the Sound and by its occupation of the three southern Swedish provinces, the second for the energy and intellect of its remarkable kings, while Poland, which was ruled by a Catholic prince of the house of Vasa, appeared to portend that some day Sweden might be subjected to the alien bondage of the Jesuit and the Slav.

It is accordingly one of the characteristic features of the Thirty Years' War that the Swedes, while battling for the Protestant cause and making a decisive contribution to its ultimate victory, were also vitally concerned in securing the political and commercial control of the southern Baltic coast and the freedom of the Sound for their trade, that they made use of the religious struggle in Germany to reach their ends, and that at the close of the war they emerged masters of the Baltic and were endowed in virtue of their German conquests with a seat in the Diet and a large controlling interest in its concerns. The day of Russia was yet to come. Its Baltic provinces were wrested from it by the Swedes. As for the Hohenzollerns of Brandenburg, to whom the prize was ultimately to fall, they were cut off from the sea by Pomerania and held East Prussia as a Polish fief. It was Sweden's hour. For the first time since the Gothic migrations Sweden, a poor barren country numbering a million and a half inhabitants, stepped on to the stage of world politics and exercised an influence on the shaping of history. A great king, belonging to a dynasty exceptional for talent and energy and deeply rooted in the loyal affections of the peasantry, came forward as the champion of the Protestant religion, made Sweden a first-class power, and by a series of brilliant conquests, largely financed by France, converted the Baltic into a Swedish lake.

There are moments in the history of peoples when a variety of causes combine to produce a dangerous inflammation of the

public mind. The centenary year of the Protestant Reformation
(1617) was such a moment. For a long time past the quarrel of
the creeds in central Europe had threatened a general explosion.
There had been grave incidents, even little spurts of open war,
happily localized, as at Cologne in 1580, and a state of apprehension so serious as to justify the formation of an armed defensive
Protestant Union (1608) balanced by a Catholic League in alliance
with Spain. Only the murder of Henry IV of France prevented
the outbreak of a general war in 1610 over the succession to the
duchies of Cleves-Jülich. And then, in the centenary year, when
the pamphlet warfare was at its height, and the air was hot with
the recriminations of rival theologians, came the news that Ferdinand, the persecutor of the Styrian Protestants, was advanced
to the thrones of Hungary and Bohemia, and designed to succeed
his elderly cousin Matthias in the Empire.

The Protestants of Bohemia, though they were sufficiently
numerous and influential to extract from the Emperor Rudolf a
Charter of Toleration (the Letter of Majesty of July, 1609), were
not in command of the levers of government. They were condemned to see their cherished charter administered in a sense
adverse to their interests by the body of regents or royal ministers
who had been appointed by the Emperor Matthias to conduct the
government of the country. The Letter of Majesty had permitted
the nobles and royal towns of Bohemia, Silesia, and Lusatia the
right of building temples and of practising the Bohemian form of
Lutheranism. That right, so it was contended, had been denied
at two places, Braunau and Klostergrab, by the intolerance of the
Catholic clergy, backed by the imperial authority. The Protestant church at Klostergrab had been pulled down, the Protestant
agitators against Catholic persecution at Braunau had been imprisoned. If these things were done under Matthias, what hope
had the Protestants of fairer weather under Ferdinand? The
announcement that the persecutor of the Styrian Protestants was
now king and was shortly to be emperor had heartened every
Jesuit in the country. Under the leadership of a Calvinist noble,
Henry Matthias of Thurn, the Bohemian Protestants resolved on
rebellion.

To a royal decree forbidding Protestants to hold assemblies the
answer of the Bohemian nobles was that famous "Defenestration
of Prague" which lit the flames of the long war. There were two
Catholic ministers. Martinitz and Slawata. who bore the odium

of the royal policy and were specially connected with the late unpopular government. At a violent interview in the Hradshin, the great fortress-palace which frowns above the city, these two men and a private secretary were thrown from a window into the castle ditch, an act of premeditated passion designed to notify to all whom the affair might concern that the patience of Bohemian Protestantism was exhausted and that the Calvinists at last were prepared to strike.

A great opportunity was now open to the Lutheran Elector of Saxony and to the Protestant Union. If they had made it clear on behalf of this influential block of German princes that the Letter of Majesty must be respected, and had prevailed on the Electoral College to insist upon this as a condition precedent to the election of Ferdinand as Emperor, it is possible that Bohemia might have been tranquillized and the war averted. But the Protestant Union was not a brave or clear-sighted body. It neither discouraged the rebellion nor gave it active assistance, and Ferdinand mounted to the Empire with a free hand (1619).

Bohemian Protestantism was never a strong or united thing. It must seek allies or perish. In the east it looked to the Turk, to the Hungarian Protestants, and to the dubious help of a weird, barbarous Calvinist prince from Transylvania named Bethlen Gabor; in the south to the Protestants of Austria; in the west, since Saxony was inert and helpless, to that strong fortress of Calvinism, the Palatinate. Deposing Ferdinand, the Bohemians offered their crown to Frederick V, the Elector Palatine, or, as he was known in England, the Palsgrave.

For the Palsgrave was destined to become in the eyes of the now dominant English Puritans at Westminster the paladin of the Protestant cause on the continent. His mother was the daughter of William the Silent; his wife, the lovely Elizabeth, was the daughter of James I, the reigning English king. Every English Protestant of mettle was prepared to draw his sword for the English princess whose young German husband seemed marked out to lead the revolt against Austria and Spain. The popular idea in London was that Englishmen should be sent to help defend the Palatinate while the Palsgrave went to the rescue of Bohemia.

From this natural, heady, but essentially unwise, enthusiasm James I dissented. In some ways the royal pedant was more enlightened than his subjects. He believed in a thorough union

between England and Scotland, and thought that after the long
and bloody religious struggles it was high time that a little peace
and toleration should be brought into Europe. So he made an
unpopular peace with Spain in 1604, and was negotiating a no
less unpopular Spanish marriage for his son, being under the
spell of a finished and seductive ambassador, when he was sud
denly confronted with the Bohemian offer, and the unmistak
able sentiment of his subjects.

A wise and far-seeing statesman would have used every effort
to dissuade the Palsgrave from embarking upon a desperate
enterprise which would involve Europe in war from the Car
pathians to the Rhine. But James refused to exercise the in
fluence over his son-in-law which he undoubtedly possessed, and
accordingly bears a heavy share of responsibility for the evils
which ensued.

For the consequences were these. The Palsgrave, who was no
Paladin, but an inexperienced and somewhat timid youth, yielded
to the pressure of Calvinist hot-heads, and without counting the
cost, allowed himself to be crowned Bohemian king. One sharp
battle on the White Hill a few miles outside Prague (November
1620) was sufficient to settle his fate. A brave man might have
attempted to rally the fugitives. The young Calvinist only fled
with his lovely wife, leaving the Bohemian Protestants to the
tender mercies of Ferdinand. That monarch, who was now sup
ported not only by the Catholics of the League but by the
Lutherans of Saxony, saw no reason why he should be gentle
with rebels who had intrigued with Turks, menaced Vienna
and placed a heretic haled from the other end of Germany on
his throne. He determined to extirpate the Protestant religion
from Bohemia, and in this resolution obtained a success which
has rarely been equalled in the history of persecution. By a
system of widespread confiscation and ruthless repression the
country was brought under the Austrian heel. A German
ascendancy as intolerant as that of the English settlers in Ire
land was imposed upon the Czechs, and not seriously shaken
till the nineteenth century. German officials ruled in the
Hradshin, Jesuit priests controlled education from the Clementi
num. In the wake of the German nobles, fortune hunters, and
officials, of the Jesuit priests and the Capucin monks, came the
German lawyer expounding the autocratic principles of Roman
law. Under his rigid doctrine the Bohemian peasantry was

trodden down into serfdom. The first consequence, then, of the Palsgrave's enterprise was the manufacture of a servile state in Europe.

The second consequence was this. The emperor put the Palsgrave to the ban of the empire, and on his own authority transferred the Palatine territory and Electorate to Maximilian of Bavaria, the head of the Catholic League and the commander of the army which had won the battle of the White Hill. From such an act it necessarily followed that the quarrel was carried from Bohemia to the Rhine, and that it was given an entirely new lease of life. The Palatinate was the chief stronghold of Calvinism in western Germany. From the Palatinate armies had supported the revolt of the Huguenots in France and the efforts of the Dutch to throw off the Spanish yoke. Little as the Palsgrave deserved of his co-religionists, they were not prepared to see him ejected from his state in favour of a Catholic ruler, or his Electorate permanently transferred to the younger branch of the Wittelsbach house. The Diet of Ratisbon, sharing their feelings with regard to the Electorate, extracted from the emperor by way of compromise, that the gift of the Electorate to Maximilian should be limited to his life only: but the territories were otherwise viewed. These had been conquered for Rome, the Upper Palatinate (north of Ratisbon) by Maximilian, and the Lower Palatinate by Tilly, the skilful Walloon general of the army of the League, and these the Diet was content to have permanently subjected to Catholic rule. Such was the measure of the Roman triumph. First Bohemia, then the Palatine Electorate, had been successfully wrested from Protestant hands.

It was the more necessary that the Calvinists, if they were to recover these vital territories, should seek for allies, since a third consequence of the Palsgrave's adventure had been to throw Saxony and the Lutherans upon the Imperial side, and indeed to produce the dissolution of the Protestant Union. That Lutheran Saxony should have joined with Catholic Bohemia in fighting the Catholic battle for Ferdinand in Bohemia is a notable illustration of that deep antagonism between the Lutheran and Calvinist creeds which had prevailed from the first and was more than once fatal to the efficient conduct of the Protestant cause. But it is also significant of another important political fact, the strong conservatism of the Saxon Elector, his disin-

clination to give countenance to violent novelties, and his desire
to work with the Emperor so long as it was possible for him
to do so.

In their dark hour the fighting Protestants of Germany asked
and obtained the assistance of Christian of Denmark. The
motives which animated this Lutheran monarch to intervene
in the German quarrel were not so much an anxious concern for
the Protestant religion as a keen appetite for Catholic plunder.
Among the objects of his desire was a handsome provision for
his sons to be obtained from the revenues of certain bishoprics
in northern Germany, and since the appetite for ecclesiastical
property was by no means a Danish speciality but widely shared
by the Protestant princes of Lower Saxony, it was not difficult,
with some royal encouragement in England, to patch up an
alliance, to provide an army, and to plan a campaign.

While all this was brewing in the north an important change
came over the military direction of the Catholic forces. The
early triumphs of the Counter-Reformation in Bohemia and the
Palatinate had been won not by an Imperial army under Ferdinand, but by the German contingents of Maximilian of Bavaria.
That the emperor should be thus dependent for his protection
upon a neighbour who might develop into a rival was a situation
which could not long be regarded as tolerable in Vienna. An
imperial policy demanded an imperial army and an imperial
commander. Out of this necessity arose the powerful and enigmatic figure of Albert Wenceslas von Waldstein, Prince of
Friedland, commonly known as Wallenstein. The man was a
Bohemian noble, born and bred a Utraquist,[1] whose quality had
been proved in the Turkish wars. Of religion, unless astrology
may be so regarded, he had little or nothing; but of appetitive
desires a supply sufficient to make or mar an empire. His wealth
was enormous, for he made profit out of war, out of land speculation, out of everything he touched, and his ambition was equal
to his destiny. The vast palace in Prague, with its Italian statues
and portico, its long halls hung with showy candelabras, its
tapestries, pictures, and curiosities, survives as a memorial to the
taste, the splendour, and the success of Wallenstein. This man
now came forward with an offer to raise an army at his own
charges for Ferdinand, stipulating only that while artillery and

[1] Such was the name given to the Hussites of Bohemia, who had been
accorded the use of the cup in the Communion Service.

munitions captured in war should be handed over to the emperor, the booty should be reserved to the troops.

The Protestant campaign of 1626 comprised two separate enterprises, each of which ended in disaster: an attack to be launched in conjunction with the Prince of Transylvania against the Imperialists in the east, and an advance southward from Denmark against the army of the Catholic League. Nothing came of the eastern project, save the death, in a distant Bosnian village, of Mansfield, the best of the Protestant *condottieri*. As for the Dane, one smashing blow administered at Lutter in Thuringia (August 27) was sufficient to establish the predominence of Tilly and Wallenstein, to open Schleswig-Holstein to the advance of the Catholics, and to eliminate the Danes as a serious factor in the contest.

Once more the Protestant cause was sunk to its lowest depths, but once more the very completeness of the imperial triumph set in motion counteracting forces which were destined to give them check. In the elation born of victory the Catholic Electors conceived a natural but nevertheless unwise idea which was pursued with effects most injurious to the emperor's interests. A considerable body of ecclesiastical wealth, including in northern Germany two archbishoprics and twelve bishoprics, had, since 1552, passed from Catholic into Protestant hands. Of this imposing corpus of property part was honourably expended in maintaining the Lutheran church; part less honourably in the support of the necessaries and luxuries of the secular princes. All this spoil was now in virtue of an edict of March 6, 1629, to revert to its Catholic owners. It may be imagined how disturbing was this upheaval to Protestant administrators who were required under the tyrannical pressure of Wallenstein's troops to surrender property which they had for many years been accustomed to regard as their own. And even Catholics began to murmur when they learnt that Jesuit Fathers were filtering into abbeys where no Jesuits had been before, and that it was proposed on Wallenstein's advice to create out of four opulent north German sees a principality for a hereditary prince. What, it was asked by German Catholics and Protestants alike, was portended by the position and proceedings of Wallenstein? He was admiral of the Baltic, and Duke of Mecklenburg. His large army, recruited from every creed and country, pillaged Catholic and Protestant alike. Did he propose to make his master despot of Germany? Did he design to carve out a kingdom for himself? Was this furious zeal for the Roman religion only a cloak for a plot to subvert the liberties of Germany in the Austrian interest? These doubts passed through many a Protestant and Catholic mind in Germany. Maximilian of Bavaria was an honest Papist, but he had not fought Ferdinand's battle at the White Hill for the purpose of enabling a Bohemian *condottiere* to ride rough-shod over the German princes. At the Diet of Ratisbon (July, 1630) he pressed for Wallenstein's dismissal, and to the surprise of Germany obtained it.

Of this incipient revolt against the alarming predominance of Austria, France, under the guidance of Cardinal Richelieu, took prompt and skilful advantage. Disarming Bavaria by a secret treaty, she arranged to finance (Treaty of Bärwalde, January 23, 1631) a Swedish invasion of Germany to restore the fortunes of the Protestant cause.

In any computation of human excellence Gustavus Adolphus of Sweden should stand high. A brilliant linguist, for he spoke eight languages, a great soldier and trainer of soldiers, a statesman with wide but not impracticable ambitions, a sincere, passionate, and single-minded believer in the faith which he had inherited from his fathers, Gustavus out-tops the statesmen of his age in energy, simplicity, and integrity of character. Broadly speaking, he was governed throughout his career by the two great interests of country and creed. For Sweden he desired a safe, unmolested, and predominant share in the commerce of the Baltic, and to that end, as also for a shield against Poland and Russia, a long strip of south Baltic coast: for German Protestantism victory against the Catholics and a wider territory secure against attack.

His early manhood was consumed in warfare. He fought the Danes, the Russians, and later Sigismund Vasa, the Catholic King of Poland, a man of his own family, who dreamt of ruling in Sweden and of there spreading the Roman faith. In these hard wars under the inclement Polish skies Gustavus fashioned the military instrument which has made him famous in the annals of the military art.

The Swedish army, in which there was always a strong infusion of stalwart Scots, was chiefly notable for five characteristics. The men wore uniform. The regiments were small and

equipped for speed. A light, mobile field artillery, easy to handle
and brilliantly manoeuvred, reinforced the infantry arm. The
muskets were of a type superior to that in general use. The
cavalry, instead of galloping up to the enemy, discharging their
pistols in the Dutch manner, and then turning round and galloping back to reload, charged home with naked steel. To these
advantages the quality of the commander supplied an invaluable
supplement. Mastering every detail, sharing every hardship, taking every risk, seizing every opportunity, Gustavus inspired his
swift and mettlesome followers to endure, to obey, and, if need
be, to die.

Before the momentous treaty with the French, Gustavus was
already south of the Baltic, and established in East Prussia and
West Poland. If ever he had entertained doubts as to a campaign in Germany for the curtailment of the imperial power
they were dissipated by certain manifest signs of Ferdinand's
hostility. Holding that the throne of Sweden belonged by rights
to that Catholic member of the house of Vasa who was ruling in
Poland, the Emperor refused to acknowledge Gustavus by his
royal title. It required no great discernment to detect that behind
this refusal was a plan for engineering a Catholic restoration in Sweden through the person of Sigismund, the Polish
king.

So when Wallenstein had made himself master of North Germany, and further proceeded to lay siege to Stralsund, Gustavus
made up his mind that the time had come to strike hard for
Sweden and the faith. Ferdinand was an enemy on three separate
accounts, as the friend of Poland, as the protagonist of the
Roman Church, and as a direct competitor for power on the
Baltic—and all Germany seemed to be at Ferdinand's feet. But,
despite his generous and wide-ranging views for the formation of
a Protestant Federation in Germany, " that invincible monarch,
the bulwark of the Protestant faith, the Lion of the North, the
terror of Austria, Gustavus Adolphus," came no nearer than the
Dane to solving the vexed problem of bringing religious peace
to the Germans.

To students of the military art all over Europe, and not least
in England and Scotland, as the Civil Wars were destined to
show, the method of Gustavus served as a model. The quick,
victorious campaign in northern Germany, the crushing victory
over the overwhelming numbers of Tilly at Breitenfeld (Septem-

ber 17, 1631), the advance of the Protestant arms to Prague in the east and to Mainz and Worms in the west, the final defeat of Tilly on the Lech, and Gustavus' entry into Munich, constituted a dazzling achievement which long fixed the admiration of Europe. In less than two years the fortunes of the rival creeds had been violently reversed.

But there was more show than substance in the Swedish victory. An ill-paid foreign army subsisting on the country can never expect to be popular. The Protestants of Germany were backward in supporting a power of whom it was suspected on good grounds that one of its main objects was the acquisition of German territory. The Catholics, despite the hopes of Richelieu, were alienated by the systematic plundering of the blue and yellow brigades, and regarded them not as friends but as enemies, so that instead of throwing themselves against Ferdinand, Sweden and Bavaria attacked one another. From that conflict Gustavus emerged victorious. But there was an imperial army, now once more levied and led by Wallenstein, with whom a difficult account had yet to be settled, an army strong enough to drive the Saxons out of Bohemia, and after it had effected a junction with Maximilian's forces, reaching a figure of 60,000. At Nuremberg, Gustavus, pitted against the great Bohemian, experienced his first defeat; and though the honours were easy in the bloodstained field of Lützen (November 16, 1632), the courage of the Swedes was of little avail, for the king, without their knowledge, had fallen in the fight. "I am the King of Sweden," he is reported to have said to the cuirassiers who demanded his name as he lay on the ground mortally wounded, "who do seal the religion and liberty of the German nation with my blood."

The war continued, bereft of the last remnant of Protestant idealism through the death of Gustavus. Sweden was not prepared to discontinue a struggle which had given her the valuable bulwark of Pomerania, the sack of many wealthy cities, and a commanding voice in the councils of Europe. If Gustavus had disappeared, there still remained as regent of the Swedish kingdom during the minority of his infant daughter, the sagacious statesman, who, as the partner of his cares and dreams, had long borne the burden of civil government, and had gathered all the reins of foreign diplomacy into his hands. Oxenstierna was resolved to maintain for Sweden the leadership of Protestant Germany. The marshals of Gustavus, for whom campaigning was the salt of life, were at his call; and with their aid, supplemented by the efforts of the Franconian, the Swabian, and the two Rhenish circles (Alliance of Heilbronn, April 23, 1633), the Swedish Chancellor still hoped to be in a position to secure a peace of victory for the Swedish and Protestant cause.

With far less consistency of purpose Wallenstein also meditated a plan for settling the German question.

To the Jesuit Camarilla in Vienna, the conduct of the great Bohemian general after the battle of Lützen gave rise to the darkest suspicions. Wallenstein was inert in war, active in diplomacy. When it was expected that he would exploit to the full the consequences of Lützen, he remained idly stationed in Bohemia negotiating with the Saxons. Neither the capture of Ratisbon by the Swedes nor the alarm of Vienna provoked him to effective action. His thoughts, shaped by the weariness of ill-health and also by a treasonable ambition, turned to a general pacification of Germany to be accomplished through the operation of his unique prestige. The peace of Wallenstein would not have been a Jesuit peace. It would have been too Bohemian, too tolerant to please the Fathers. Perhaps, also, though this is not certain, it would have comprised as one of its conditions a Bohemian crown for himself. But nothing came of these imaginations. It was judged in Vienna that the man was too dangerous to live, and Irish dragoons were ready in the camp *1634* at Eger to do the butchery.

The first effective overtures of peace came from that quarter of Germany which ever since the beginning of the war had shown least appetite for the fight. Lutheran belligerency was a tender plant thriving only in the sunshine of Swedish victories. So when Bernard of Saxe Weimar and Horn, the two generals upon whom the mantle of Gustavus had devolved, were routed on the decisive field of Nördlingen, and all south-western Germany passed at one blow from Swedish into Imperial control, the Elector of Saxony led the Lutherans straight over into the Imperial Camp. The Peace of Prague (1635) was not a chivalrous transaction, for the Lutherans not only threw over their Swedish allies, but pledged themselves to help Austria to evict them from Germany; but peace is always wiser than war, and the Peace of Prague, which by the end of 1635 had been accepted by nearly all the important princes and free cities in the land, was as wise and good a settlement as the situation permitted. The Protestant signatories obtained a guarantee for their form of worship and for the retention for a period of fifty years of the lands and revenues which they had taken from the Roman Church.

But at this juncture, when it seemed that a general peace was in sight, the war entered upon a new and wholly secular phase, losing the religious character which had originally belonged to it, and becoming submerged in the struggle between the Bourbons and the Habsburgs for ascendancy in Europe. There was little indeed of the old theologians' spirit in a struggle in which Catholic France and Protestant Sweden were allied (Treaty of Compiègne, April 28, 1635) with the Protestant Dutch Republic against Lutheran Germany, Catholic Austria and Catholic Spain, in which Savoy sold its friendship now to one side, now to another, and when the stakes at issue were no point of doctrine or ritual, but whether Sweden should be permitted to keep Pomerania or France allowed to retain possession of Alsace. There was little of religion, but there was an intolerable amount of marching and countermarching, of sieges and sacks, arson, murder, and of all the horrors which savage and starving mercenary troops are able to inflict upon a helpless population. The chief contriver of this long spell of agony and chaos was, as has been seen, a cardinal of the Roman Church. For a period of eighteen years (1624-42) the political genius of Richelieu, the Prime Minister of Louis XIII, dominated the European scene. Many qualities essential to statesmanship were lacking to this imperious prelate. He knew nothing of economics or public finance. Despite his long spell of absolute power he never lifted a finger to remedy the confusions, the irregularity, and the oppressions of the French fiscal system which eventually brought that monarchy to the ground. To the whole humanitarian side of politics he was profoundly indifferent. But there was one cause and only one to which his lucid, ruthless, and logical intellect was persistently devoted. He worked with a single mind for the greatness of France as that phrase has been understood by a long line of French statesmen, by Mazarin and Louis XIV, by Danton and Napoleon, by Delcassé and Clémenceau, by Poincaré or his pupil Tardieu. From the outset he formed three projects, to destroy the political power of the Huguenots, to abase the nobility, and to make the king's name feared and respected through Europe. The first object he accomplished entirely, the second in part. To the third, which involved the unmaking of Germany and the downfall of Spain, he made an important contribution.

It is significant of his detachment from religious prejudice that in his great enterprise against the Huguenots he did not scruple to invoke Protestant aid. As a condition of receiving financial assistance from the French treasury the Dutch were compelled to help to reduce La Rochelle, the famous capital of French Calvinism. Odious as this task was felt to be in Amsterdam, there can be no doubt that on a large view of Protestant interests it was well that the Huguenots should be deprived of their power to molest the government of France. An armed minority holding a hundred fortified towns is a block of granite strewn in the path of national development. So long as the Huguenots were a state within a state, Richelieu was unable to marshal the Protestant princes of the continent against the Habsburg house. Only after he was rid of this domestic embarrassment (1629) did France step forward to take that commanding part in the direction of the Thirty Years' War which secured and perpetuated the religious schism in Europe. The nobles did not abash him. He had Montmorency, the first nobleman in France, executed for conspiracy. To balance the power of the aristocracy, he gradually built up the nucleus of a centralized civil service (the intendants) as well as an army and navy in the permanent service of the crown.

The student of diplomacy, if he may avert his eyes from human suffering, will admire the skill with which a Christian prelate prolonged a barbarous and unnecessary war, the apposite liberality with which the flagging enthusiasm of the indispensable Swede was refreshed with supplies of men and money, the subtlety with which the mirage of an impending peace was dangled before his eyes and the address with which his most to be apprehended rivals, the Danes and the Poles, were lulled into a neutral repose. If he notes that some schemes miscarried, such as that Rhenish Confederacy under French protection, which, again and again, under Mazarin, under Napoleon, under Poincaré, has been set up or attempted, he will applaud the span of a design which included the conquest of Roussillon, the invasion of Catalonia, the combination of Mantua, Parma, and Savoy against the Spanish power in Italy, a marriage alliance with England, and the acquisition of Alsace and Lorraine for the French monarchy. It has been pointed out that as a War Minister Richelieu had many defects, that he could neither create an army nor plan a campaign, that he was too jealous of superiority to place eminent men in command, and that it was not until 1643, when he was already in his grave, that Condé's victory at Rocroi announced that France was once more a great military power. All the more to be admired is the cardinal's diplomacy. The French armies made little out of their seven years' campaigning under Richelieu, but at the end of it France was mistress of Alsace, Lorraine and Roussillon, and had set a term to the conquests of the Counter-Reformation in Germany.

1-65   In this last section of the war, Spain, ruled by Philip IV and Olivarez, a nerveless king and a headstrong minister, suffered four staggering reverses, the destruction of her fleet, the revolt of Catalonia, the loss of Portugal, and an insurrection in Naples. The common root of all these disasters was the ambition of Spain, a poor, exhausted, ill-administered country, split by geography and history into distinct and opposing compartments, to play a commanding rôle in the theatre of European politics. A statesman unbewitched by the glamour of foreign war would have realized that for a state sunk so low as Spain at the accession of Philip IV, a long course of peace, retrenchment, and civil reform was imperatively needed. With her finances in utter disorder, her fleet of ocean-going ships reduced to a skeleton, with the Indies lost, with the American colonies held by the slenderest thread, with Portugal and Naples seething with discontent, with her coinage debased and the Netherlands practically gone beyond recall, Spain was no longer in a position to lead the Catholic forces of Europe against the Protestant enemy. Olivarez was able, vigorous, ill-tempered; but he was also a courtier with no foundation of political knowledge. His idle master was flattered by the suggestion that a great foreign war, managed by a capable minister, would restore the ancient lustre to the crown. But the policy inevitably foundered on the rock of finance. To conduct a war to a successful conclusion Olivarez required far more money than the people of Spain, acting through the five

Spanish Cortes, were accustomed to supply. Everywhere, but more particularly in Catalonia, the richest but also the most independent province of the Spanish Empire, he met with resistance. In an ill-judged moment Olivarez determined to break the Catalans, to abolish their privileges and to quarter a mercenary army upon them. But Barcelona was not like La Rochelle. It was, next to Seville, the richest port in Spain, and the capital of a population speaking a separate language, having ancient customs, which found it easier to fraternize with a Provençal than with a Castilian, and was in no circumstances prepared to be regarded as a province of Castile. In 1640 the Catalans rose in revolt, and the next year elected Louis XIII to be Count of Barcelona, and formally placed themselves under the protection of the French.

The Catalan rebellion had at once a serious reaction on the position in Portugal. Sixty years of union, so far from improving, had only embittered the relations between Portugal and Spain. The Portuguese chafed under uncomprehending Spanish viceroys, and complained that Cadiz had robbed Lisbon of its commerce. But a yet more deep-seated and legitimate grudge had made the whole connection in the highest degree detestable. Spain had lost Portugal her Empire in the east. The union had involved Portugal in all the enmities which the high-flying Catholic ambitions of the Spanish monarchy had attracted to itself. With these ambitions the sympathy of Portugal was restricted. A thousand times she would have preferred to be quit of a partnership which had led to the wastage of her most precious assets. To these acute discontents the centralizing policy of Olivarez, enforced by the odious Vasconcellos, added a grievance not to be borne. Learning that they were to be treated as a province of Castile, threatened with Castilian taxes, and fired by the example of the Catalans, the Portuguese rose in revolt, and called to the throne a noble of the house of Braganza.

The affair was a matter of three hours. The union was broken, and to this day the breach, widened by twenty-eight years of futile warfare (1640-68) has never been mended.

Olivarez and Richelieu were both right in thinking that a higher degree of centralization was necessary to the more efficient working of their respective states. The reason why Olivarez failed and Richelieu succeeded is that in France conditions were

favourable to centralization whereas in Spain they were adverse.
All ways in France led to Paris. No ways in Spain led to
Madrid. Iberian mountains and Iberian men are obstinate things.
Olivarez ignored the mountains and attempted to drive the
men. Against such an affront to its cherished quiet and seclusion no race in the world can be trusted to react with a higher
degree of mulish obstinacy than the Iberian. The Spaniard
dreamt imperially, but refused to pay for his dreams. Nothing
would persuade a Catalan that mediaeval standards of finance
went ill with the responsibilities of modern Empire.

The renewal of the war with the Dutch after the expiration
in 1621 of the twelve years' truce was another speculation which
came off ill for Spain. On the death of Maurice of Nassau, the
Dutch found in his younger brother Frederick Henry a statesman and a soldier well able to direct the work of national defence.
Under this admirable commander, and with the aid of the subsidies of Richelieu and a gallant corps of English adventurers,
the Dutch republic opposed a successful resistance to the land
armies of Spain.

The sieges of Hertogenbosch, of Maestricht, and of Breda
showed that in the art of poliorcetics the Dutch had lost none
of their ancient cunning. They could take cities and defend
them. In a war of position, as distinct from a war of movement,
no troops were more competent: but the swift marches, the
sweeping victories, and large scale operations of a Gustavus
Adolphus were alien to the genius of this slow and methodical
race. The Dutch maintained their positions. Even with French
aid, the task of crushing the Austro-Spanish defence in the
southern provinces was wholly beyond their strength.

The real genius of the Dutch people was shown not in this
land warfare, but on the waters. With the greatest intrepidity
they penetrated into the most remote and desolate portions of
the globe, exploring the Amazon, bringing tea into Europe from
Formosa, founding in Batavia the centre of an Eastern Empire,
and carving a Dutch State out of the vast bulk of Portuguese
Brazil. In estimating the causes which led to the downfall of
the united kingdom of Spain and Portugal, the attacks of the
Dutch upon the Portuguese settlements in Brazil and Ceylon
must be reckoned as substantial factors.

Against this steady accumulation of colonial activity the

united Iberian kingdom made on the eve of its dissolution one last gallant and forlorn effort. A strong fleet under Oquendo, one of the best of the Spanish sailors, was despatched to the Channel to dispute with the Dutch in their native waters; another Armada, partly Spanish and partly Portuguese, crossed the Atlantic to retrieve Brazil. Both these fleets were destroyed by the superior seacraft of their Dutch adversaries. The battle of the Downs (1639), in which Van Tromp defeated Oquendo, is famous in the naval annals of Europe; but the four days' fight of Itamarca, off the coast of Pernambuco (1640), was equally decisive. In combination these two Dutch victories, the first won in European, the second in South American, waters, sealed the doom of the Iberian empire.

The peace of Westphalia, which closed this long war, was the 1648 result, not of any inclination of the rival armies in Germany to force a military decision, for of such inclination—war being a most profitable calling—they had none, but of the common sense and humanity of Christina of Sweden, the fatigue of Spain, and the impatience of a congress, which had been sitting three years in two dull little Westphalian towns (Münster and Osnabrück), to bring its tedious and complicated work to a definite conclusion. But there must be no mistake about the undiminished gusto with which the soldiers, Swedish, French, and Imperial, carried on their trade to the end. Fighting and pillaging was the breath of their nostrils; and if the diplomatists had not come to an accord, being shaken out of their leisurely ways by the separate peace between Spain and the Netherlands in January, 1648, Wrangel and Konigsmark, Condé and Turenne, Collorado and Piccolomini, might have fought on until the time came for them to bequeath their war game to yet another generation of redoubtable captains.

The peace of Westphalia, corresponding as it did to the balance of religious and political forces of the time, settled for many generations the public law of Europe. Each of the protagonists obtained some form of mundane satisfaction, the emperor in the Bohemian crown, acknowledged to be hereditary in his family, France in the Landgraviates of Alsace, Sweden in western Pomerania and the bishoprics of Bremen and Verden, and Bavaria in the Upper Palatinate. For the future history of Europe by far the most important of these arrangements was the acquisition by France, as a reward for her intervention in the war of the Landgraviate, of Upper and Lower Alsace in full sovereignty. As one of her diplomats then saw and as Mazarin realized afterwards, it would have been safer for France, and less provocative to Germany, had Alsace been accepted as an imperial fief carrying with it a seat in the German Diet. But the error once made could not be retrieved. A challenge was thrown out to the German people, which at a later stage, when the sentiment of nationality had become strong, was taken up.

It was not to be expected that out of the passions of this exhausting war there would emerge the will to religious toleration. Neither side was prepared to tolerate: but at least a *modus vivendi* was found in the reaffirmation of that principle of *Cujus regio ejus religio* which had been the basis of the peace of Augsburg, and in its formal extension to the Calvinist faith. The northern bishoprics were saved for Protestantism. The Lower Palatinate gilded by an eighth electorate was conferred upon Charles Lewis, the son of the " Winter King," whose unwise assumption of the Bohemian crown had been the origin of so many ills; but Bohemia itself, and all the hereditary dominions of the Austrian house were surrendered to the Jesuits, and over this wide region the dream of Ferdinand was realized that no heretic should be allowed to worship or to preach.

A wide difference separates the Germany of Frederick Barbarossa from the weak federation of some three hundred and fifty states (each empowered to pursue its own foreign policy so long as it was not directed against the emperor) which emerged from the Westphalian congress. Then the emperor exercised a real though irregular authority in Germany. Now his power, though confirmed in Austria, Bohemia, and Hungary, was a shadow among the Germans. Then the Swiss and the Netherlands were imperial. Now the independence of the Swiss republic was formally recognized, and the Netherlands, though still nominally part of the Burgundian circle, had in effect broken into a Spanish province and a Dutch republic. Then Germany was a dominating influence in the world. Now it was little better than a cypher. Then there was one religious Faith, now there were three. Out of the distractions of Germany and the prostration of Spain there arose that opportunity for the development of French military ambition of which Louis XIV and Napoleon took full advantage.

BOOKS WHICH MAY BE CONSULTED

S. R. Gardiner : The Thirty Years' War. 1874. (A short masterly sketch.)

C. R. L. Fletcher : Gustavus Adolphus, King of Sweden. 1890.

A. Gindely : Thirty Years' War. 1882-3.

Hanotaux : Histoire du Cardinal de Richelieu. 2 vols. 1893.

G. D'Avenel : Richelieu et la monarchie absolue. 1884.

W. Coxe : House of Austria. 1847.

Lavisse : Histoire de France. 1900-11.

H. Belloc : Richelieu. 1930.

Hallandorf and Schuck : History of Sweden. 1929.

A. Gindely : Waldstein während seines ersten Generalats im Lichte der
    gleichzeitigen Quellen. 1886.

CHAPTER XVIII

THE TRIUMPHS OF MAZARIN

Ascendancy of France in Europe. Anne of Austria and Mazarin. The First Fronde. The revolutionary movements of France and England compared. The second Fronde. The depopularization of Condé. The influence of the Frondes. Diplomatic triumphs of Mazarin. Hugo Grotius and the Rhenish League.

THE Treaty of Westphalia, to a greater extent even than the Treaty of Versailles, might have been dictated by the ghost of Richelieu. Never has French diplomacy secured a greater triumph. Never before had the political map of Europe worn an aspect more favourable to French ambitions. As a military force capable of giving a serious check to French policies, Germany, a clumsy federation of powerless, impoverished, and mutually inimical states, was eliminated. So far from being a danger to France, she was, on the contrary, a prime factor in French security, a reservoir of political allies, a sphere of influence, a buffer against Austria, a prime condition of European equilibrium. To keep Germany thus powerless and divided was henceforth and until the French Revolution a prime object of French diplomacy.

In such an attitude there was nothing malignant. The French, having no fear of Germany, which was then prostrate and never likely to be strong, took pleasure in regarding themselves as the guardian angels and tutelary guides of an interesting, inoffensive, and much retarded people. They noted with pride the spread of French literature, French acting, and French fashions among the awkward and submissive Teutons, and regarded it as a wise dispensation of Providence that France was now able to resume, under the most favourable conditions, the civilizing mission of Charlemagne to the barbarians of the east.

But at the time the diplomatic triumph with its manifest opportunities went unperceived. While the diplomatists were signing the treaty at Münster, France was in revolution, and its government barely able to maintain a footing in Paris.

For at the head of affairs in France there were two foreigners, Anne of Austria and Cardinal Mazarin. Louis XIII, dying in 1643, had left an infant of five, whose Spanish mother, cleverly

shaking herself free from the Council which had been appointed
to guide her path, had assumed the Regency, and called her
Italian husband to share the burden. Everything about this
arrangement was odious to the princes of the blood, to the
nobles, to the Parliament of Paris, and to the mob. They disliked
Anne, the Spanish regent. They hated the principle of an omnipotent Prince Minister. There was no evil which they would
not believe of Mazarin, that he was a thief, a cardsharper, a perverted libertine, a low-born upstart, a pillager of the public purse.
The great diplomatic ability by which this undoubtedly rapacious minister sustained the tradition of Richelieu was lost in
a cloud of detraction.

The unpopularity of the government was augmented by the
taxes required to finance first the German and then the Spanish
war, which, even after the Peace of Westphalia had been signed,
dragged on for eleven years. Mazarin was as ignorant as his
master Richelieu of the first principles of finance. All his fiscal
expedients were bad; but two, since they injured Paris, were
dangerous, a tax upon the houses in the suburbs of the capital,
and a violent interference with the Parisians' favourite investment, the *rentes* of the municipal Hôtel de Ville.

Revolution was in the air. There was, in that year 1648, revolution in Naples, in Catalonia, in Portugal, in England, and how
could Paris fail to experience the general tremor? The market
women cried for Masaniello, the Neapolitan fisherman who had
dared to defy the King of Spain, while the greybeards of the
Parliament meditated the more substantial precedents set by an
assembly of like name to their own, which sat at Westminster and
had just brought the English monarchy toppling to the ground.

Out of these general conditions arose the two curious rebellions
which are known as the First and Second Fronde, rebellions which
exposed the monarchy to the gravest humiliations and spreading far and wide through the country at one time (1652) threatened to shake the fabric of the State to its foundations. Michelet
says that all the honest people in France were opposed to
Mazarin and that all the rogues were upon his side. This
is too absolute. Mazarin stood for the continuity of French
foreign policy and for the unity of the French state. His opponents in many instances cared neither for the one cause nor for
the other. What is true is that whatever sound and serious thinking there was in France either about financial reform, or about

constitutional checks on autocracy, or about "the condition of the people" question, was to be found in the ranks of the *frondeurs*, and particularly among the magistrates of the Paris Parliament, who took the lead in the First Fronde and gave it a dignity to which the second rising cannot pretend.

But in the quality and range of its appeal, as also in the character of the organ through which it was expressed, this body of valuable political thought was singularly bare of inspiration and power when we compare it with the passionate and enlightened intelligence, at once enriched and narrowed by religious emotion, which carried the Parliamentary cause to victory in England. A revolution, if it is to have durable results, demands some intellectual preparation; but in France there had been no considered movement for the reconstruction of the monarchy on constitutional lines. The States-General, which had met in 1614, after an appalling manifestation of aristocratic selfishness, dispersed without a message to the country. The Parliament of Paris, a hereditary corporation of magistrates, serious and honourable and able, through the right which it possessed to refuse the registration of royal edicts, to exercise a certain check upon the autocratic power of the Crown, was devoid of any general representative character. A privileged body, it spoke for a privileged class, and only on rare occasions, for brief periods, and by some accidental conjuncture of circumstances, voiced the general will of France. Such an occasion presented itself in August, 1648. The nobles, people, and Parliament were united in protesting against Mazarin's war taxation and in asking for civil liberty and constitutional guarantees. So hot was the feeling that when Mazarin imprisoned Broussel, the venerable protagonist of the Parliamentary claims, twelve hundred barricades rose in Paris and the government was brought to its knees.

Yet even in the First Fronde, when the constitutional issue was clearly defined and hotly felt, there was outside the Parliament no sustained interest in reform or organized attempt to secure it. The leader of the Paris mob, Paul de Gondi, was a born conspirator, fishing in revolutionary waters for a cardinal's hat. The fashionable ladies who played so active a part in this serio-comedy were actuated by motives as far removed as possible from the reform of the State or the improvement of the popular lot. Between the nobles, who wished for the States-General to confirm or extend their privileges, and the Parliament, which regarded that body as a dangerous rival, there was no bond but a common hatred of the cardinal. These differences among the *frondeurs* deprived the movement of all dignity or force.

The First Fronde was michievous and discreditable enough. A situation, which might have been dealt with by a few timely concessions honestly meant and steadily maintained, was allowed through ill-will and ill-faith so far to deteriorate that Paris was lost to the Court, and only recovered by a formal siege (Treaty of Rueil, March 11, 1649). But at least there was in the First Fronde a definite issue of real constitutional importance. Though the magistrates of Paris prejudiced their cause by their association with the mutinous nobility who stirred up the passions of the mob, they had a cause to which no wise ruler should have refused a hearing, for they stood for civil liberty and the introduction of a system of control over public finance. It is the great blot upon Mazarin's statesmanship that the concessions, which he was twice forced to make to the Parliament, were made in bad faith and withdrawn at the earliest moment.

There was less of principle and more of danger and disgrace in the Second Fronde. It began with the imprisonment of Condé, the victor of Rocroi and of Lens, and the commander of the Regent's army in the first rebellion. No man or woman could long endure the insufferable pretensions of this arrogant soldier. But it was a bold step on the part of Mazarin to imprison a man so wealthy, so formidable, and so famous. A violent spasm of indignation shook the country, bringing Turenne at the head of a Spanish army into Picardy, causing rebellion in Bordeaux, and ultimately leading to the liberation of Condé and the flight of Mazarin. But Condé, though he could count upon the support of *Jan.,* a mutinous faction among the nobles, was the last man, by reason *1651* of his infirmities of temper, to compose the differences of a political coalition. The combination of the nobility of the Sword and the nobility of the Robe was hardly formed ere it broke up. The wise Regent, inspired by Mazarin, set herself to the easy task of raising up against the vainglorious general, from the inner circles of the Fronde, an opponent as vainglorious and ambitious as himself. Paul de Gondi,[1] the leader of the priests and the rabble, went over to the Court for the promise of the cardinal's hat, and Turenne soon after surrendered to a bribe. Each of these recruits was in a position to make a contribution to the

[1] Afterwards Cardinal de Retz.

royalist cause, for Gondi was the uncrowned King of the Paris *canaille*, and Turenne, the son of a Dutch mother, was the most methodical soldier in Europe. In January, 1652, the situation was so far restored that Mazarin was able to rejoin the Regent at Orleans.

But there was still a formidable obstacle to be overcome before peace could be restored to France. Condé was in the field with friends among the rank and fashion in Paris, with a mutinous rout of nobles at his heels and the private fortune of a monarch, and Condé, though in technical skill inferior to Turenne, was the most fortunate of the French generals who had won their laurels in the Thirty Years' War. But Mazarin knew his Condé, and though the experiment was costly to France, realized that in due course of time that insufferable man could be relied on to forfeit his cheap popularity. As the prince, with some aid from Mademoiselle de Montpensier, a young lady of fashion in desperate need of an exalted husband, entered Paris (July 2, 1652) at the head of an army half recruited from Spain, the cardinal prudently withdrew beyond the frontier. At that, since Mazarinades were of no value without Mazarin, the fun and purpose of the insurrection seemed to evaporate.

Plain men began to ask why this disgraceful turmoil, so bad for trade, so dangerous for France, was kept on foot. They condemned Condé's treacherous treaty with Spain. They resented the presence of his Spanish troops and the outrages of his cut-throats. They asked themselves why Paris should be dragooned by this fantastic rout of idle nobles, smart ladies, street ruffians, and enemy soldiers. The game had been carried too far. It was unpatriotic; worse, it was ridiculous. Sensible that the tide of popular favour was ebbing from him, the prince abandoned his post and withdrew to Spain. On October 21, 1652, Louis XIV was once more in Paris and the Second Fronde was at an end.

The lesson of this fantastic rebellion was deeply graven on the mind of the young king. That is the chief importance of the Fronde for general history. Louis XIV never forgot the humiliations of his boyhood, when his mother was hunted from Paris, when the royal army was fired at from the Bastille, and the monarchy nearly destroyed by a rebellious nobility in league with an enemy power. From this experience he drew the moral that France needed the strong hand of an autocratic king, who would trust no grand viziers to transact his business, but would look into everything himself and put a curb upon the nobles. Thus the disorders of the Fronde led straight to the personal government of Louis XIV.

Mazarin lived on till 1661, supported by the victories of Turenne, and achieving in the later part of his life diplomatic triumphs hardly less distinguished than those which had marked his début as Prime Minister. The main business which now confronted him was that of bringing to a successful termination the dragging war with Spain. In a matter of such importance the cardinal allowed no consideration based on religion or ethics to affect his political action. He nourished rebellion in Naples, Catalonia, and Portugal, and did not scruple, in order that he might constrain his adversary to peace, to make alliance with the regicide English republic.

From that union (March 3, 1657) came the battle of the Dunes, when an English Puritan army, appearing for the first time on a continental battlefield, and fighting under Turenne, administered a last punishing blow in the duel between England and Spain, which ninety years before had been opened in the sunny waters of a Mexican port.

The Peace of the Pyrenees, following hard on the heels of the Anglo-French successes in Flanders, completed the territorial security of France. Catalonia, indeed, was abandoned to Spain, but not before she had shown an obstinate will to break off her precipitate federation with the French. But other conquests made at the expense of Spain—Roussillon and Cerdagne in the south, part of Artois, and a string of towns on the north-east frontier, in Flanders, Hainault, and Luxembourg—were retained under this instrument. That the English were installed in Dunkirk was from the French point of view the only drawback to a welcome peace. *Nov., 1659*

A royal marriage crowned Mazarin's work. The Spanish Netherlands, roughly corresponding to modern Belgium, had long been an object of French ambition. But how could they be won? The way of conquest was expensive and doubtful, the way of marriage cheap and secure. And since it seemed certain to Mazarin that Philip IV's little son by his second wife was too feeble to live, the way of marriage was open. It was the last of the cardinal's achievements that he effected a union between Maria Theresa, the eldest daughter of Philip IV, and Louis XIV. What brilliant results might be expected from this marriage!

Perhaps a deal for the partition of the Spanish Empire with Leopold of Austria, who had to content himself with the hand of the younger Infanta, or perhaps even, and still better, the union of Spain and France under a single crown. For Mazarin may have anticipated what proved to be the fact, that the dowry in respect of which Maria Theresa renounced her inheritance would never cross the Pyrenees.

How little can the wisest statesman forecast the future! The marriage, which gave rise to such flattering hopes, was the cause of an exhausting war out of which France and Spain, pitted against the Empire and the maritime powers of the north, emerged sensibly reduced in power and influence.

The terrible lesson of the religious wars did not fall altogether unheeded on the ear of humanity. It produced a great book and an interesting experiment. The book was that famous treatise the 1583-1645 *De Jure Pacis et Belli*, in which Hugo Grotius, a citizen of the Dutch republic, first envisaged in its full compass the modern Science of International Law. The experiment was a miniature League of Nations (set up in 1658 on the Rhine by Philip von Schönberg, an enlightened Archbishop of Mainz), the member states of which bound themselves to settle their quarrels by the method of conciliation. The classical work of the humane Grotius has had a lasting influence on the thoughts of peace-loving men. If it has been no more successful than the teaching of the Christian churches in preventing war, it has drawn distinctions which have affected the current moral judgments of states between just and unjust wars, between the position of combatants and non-combatants and between those modes of waging war which fall within or outside the limits of tolerated and conventional barbarity.

A far more restricted measure of success attended the Rhenish Federation. By admitting France into their union the Rhine-landers transformed a pacifist society into a confederacy coloured by the aims of a military and aggressive state.

BOOKS WHICH MAY BE CONSULTED

J. B. Perkins : France under Mazarin. 1886.
C. de Cherrier : Histoire de France sous Mazarin. 1868.
D. Ogg : Europe in the Seventeenth Century. 1925.
V. Cousin : La Jeunesse de Mazarin. 1865.
Lavisse : Histoire de France. Vol. VI.

THE GREAT REBELLION IN ENGLAND

WHILE the continent was racked with religious wars England passed through the crisis of the Reformation undisturbed by foreign invasion or grave internal tumults. By the end of Elizabeth's reign the main body of the English people were content to accept the state-made Church, neither Roman nor Presbyterian, which it was the achievement of Elizabeth to have sustained against the pressure of contending forces. The attack of the Counter-Reformation had been repelled. The Bull of Deposition, so unwisely issued by Pius V, by confronting the English Catholics with a cruel conflict of loyalties, had alienated from the papal cause that large body of Catholic opinion which was English first and Roman afterwards. Being identified with the enemy power of Spain, the popularity of the ancient Faith suffered an eclipse. The Jesuit plots to kill the queen had been foiled. So strong was the state that it could afford to be sparing in its penalties. Compared with the Protestants burned for heresy under Mary, the number of Catholics executed for high treason by Elizabeth was inconsiderable. Persecution is always deplorable, but these high-minded men were allied with a foreign power to upset the state.

Thus favoured by fortune, the English people received its education from Humanism, the Bible, and the sea. What was lost in the mechanical dislocation of schools throughout the Reformation was regained by the fresh tides of inspiration which passed into the life of the people through these three very different sources. In the Elizabethan age the English, though still rustic, had become a poetry-loving, music-loving, Bible-loving, and sea-loving people. The schools preserved that new discipline in the humanities the original impetus to which was found in the teaching of Erasmus and Colet. The nobles and squires sent their sons to Oxford and Cambridge, which now began to acquire their modern office of giving higher education to the laity. Ladies and gentlemen learnt Greek and Latin, Italian and French. The classics of Spain, France, and Italy were rendered into English. To travel in Italy, to write sonnets or blank verse after the Italian manner was fast becoming an object of educational ambition to the fortunate. Stories taken from all the world, from Boccaccio and Bandello and Saxo Grammaticus, as well as from remote Celtic antiquity, passed into the popular drama and furnished part of the new material for Shakespeare's genius.

This free artistic cultivation, spreading right through society, and owing more to the stir and vivacity of the court, the castle, the hostelry, and the playhouse than to the cloistered discipline of school and college, was prevented from degenerating into an Italian licence and triviality by the second great ingredient in the national education, the newly discovered wealth and majesty of the English Bible. For two centuries and a half before the advent of the cheap newspaper and the novel, the sacred books of the Jews furnished the staple intellectual and spiritual food of the poor and middle class of the English people. The authority of this austere and melodious literature was unique and universal. In every parish church the Bible lay free and open to all to read. Here was a people's university. Plunging into this vast miscellany, where all that is most solemn and sublime from the distant east is mingled with the records of a savage antiquity, the peoples of England wandered at their own sweet will, unshepherded and unfettered, and finding always by the way lessons for the conduct of life, some of infinite depth and beauty, but others prompting to gloom, pride, and self-sufficiency.

The third element in the English education of this time was the sea. The romance of geography seized hold of the people as if anything were possible to an age which had thus enlarged the boundaries of hope and knowledge. " Which of the kings of this land before Her Majesty," asks Hakluyt, " had their banners ever seen in the Caspian Sea? Which of them had ever dealt with the Emperor of Persia as Her Majesty hath done, and attained for her merchants large and loving privileges? Who ever saw before this regiment an English Ligier in the stately porch of the grand Signor at Constantinople? Who ever found English consuls and agents at Tripolis in Syria, at Aleppo, at Babylon, at Balsava, and, which is more, who ever heard of an Englishman at Goa before now? What English ships did heretofore ever anchor in the mighty river of Plate?" That in many ways, some clearly to be caught and noted, as in Marlowe's *Tamburlane* and Daniel's *Musophilus,* but others elusive, the sanguine spirit of the sailor-adventurer affects the mood of the Elizabethan poets with something of his own feeling of hopefulness, may be conceded. What is more important than any direct influence upon culture is, first, the discipline which the sea provided for all its votaries, and, secondly, the glamour which this age of adventure and discovery and maritime war cast over the sailor's life. Instead of being looked upon as a thing of horror, as it was by Horace, the sea was henceforward regarded as England's opportunity.

> And who in time, knows whither we may vent
> The treasure of our tongue, to what strange shores
> This gain of our best glory shall be sent,
> T' enrich unknowing nations with our stores?
> What worlds in th' yet unforméd occident
> May come refin'd with th' accents that are ours?

The forward reaching spirit of Daniel's *Musophilus* (1601) may be taken as a symbol of that new formation of the English mind which resulted from the combined action of the Renaissance and the Reformation. The Catholic had provided a coherent philosophy of life, moulded by the Latin genius and perfected in the thirteenth century. From this closed body of doctrine all the forces of humanism, of free Biblical study, and of maritime adventure were now withdrawing the better part of the nation. The centre of intellectual interest had changed. The prophetic genius of Francis Bacon was inviting the student to abandon Aristotle and the Scholastics and to turn to the obedient study of nature. Not by *a priori* reason but by induction were the secrets of the world to be unlocked.

The seventeenth century, which opens with the glowing dreams of Francis Bacon, closes with Isaac Newton's precise demonstration that the whole universe is one vast mechanism. Between these

21

two names lies a long and splendid chapter of English scientifi work, beginning with Harvey's discovery of the circulation of th blood in 1624 (reached only because he tested all his theories b experiment), carried on by Robert Boyle's epoch-making work i chemical science, illustrated by the foundation of the Roya Society, and giving to England a place in the intellectual life o Europe, which the insular reputation of a Shakespeare or Milton could not have secured. For at the death of Queen Eliza beth and right down to the days of Oliver Cromwell Englan counted for little in Europe. The great school of English dram and poetry which flourished under Elizabeth and her successo James passed almost unnoticed on the continent until Schlegel' translation of Shakespeare into German at the end of th eighteenth century, and even in England it suffered an eclips under the thickening clouds of the Puritan religion. Nor wa England, save under the Commonwealth, of serious account i the weights and measures of continental politics. The navy wa neglected under James, and despite Charles' greater interest i naval development was never, through the parsimony of Parlia ment, brought up to a strength in his reign such as even ade quately to protect the British seas from piracy. Valiant Englisl soldiers fought for the Protestant cause in the Palatinate, in th Low Countries, and in the armies of Gustavus. But there was n standing army; nor at any point was the course of continenta politics powerfully affected by English interference until Crom well converted England for the first time in her history into military state.

During this period of isolation and comparative obscurity th English people were wrestling with two great and interrelatec problems, the first religious, the second constitutional anc political.

The State Church of Queen Elizabeth was far from contenting the forward religious spirits who drew their inspiration from th advanced Protestant churches of Switzerland. To some the prin ciple of a State Church in itself was obnoxious, to others the insti tution of episcopacy, to a large section the use of the surplice, th eastern position of the altar, and a liturgy too closely correspon dent to Roman usage. The question therefore arose whether the Church could be so enlarged as to comprehend these widely ranging movements of Protestant thought and feeling, and, i not, what should be the position of the Protestants who should be left outside. Could there be toleration for Puritan scruples within the Church? Could there be toleration of any form of Protestant community recognized to be outside the Church? The first question was swiftly answered in the negative. Comprehension was rejected by James I, by Laud, by the Anglican divines of the Restoration. We may regret that this was so. We may be disposed to think that with a little more elasticity and allowance for the workings of the Puritan conscience in the matter of Church ceremonies during the reign of the first two Stuarts much trouble might have been avoided. But history took the other turning. When three hundred Puritan ministers resigned their livings in 1604 rather than conform to the Prayer-book, as they were required to do, the Stuart dynasty was confronted with the problem which brought Charles I to his grave.

For the idea of toleration, which was the true answer to the second question and the only solution of the whole problem, was foreign to the mentality of that age, and only at the end of the century, and at the cost of a civil war and a change of dynasty, in part established in an Act of Parliament. Under the long reign of the Roman Church, Europe had received no lessons in religious toleration, and amid the fierce passions released by the great disruption was slow to learn them. John Knox and William Laud were no more liberal than Ignatius Loyola and the Duke of Alva. So long as the great queen lived, the middle way of the Anglican Church was successfully defended, thanks to the firm administration of Archbishop Whitgift, against the Romanist on the one side and the Protestant sectaries on the other. But there could be no mistaking the drift of opinion within the Church : with ever-increasing volume it moved away from Rome and in the direction of Puritanism.

To this set of opinion James I, the strange offspring of Mary Stuart and Henry Darnley, and Charles, his son, were firmly opposed. Not that these two sovereigns desired to return to the Roman fold. The position of Supreme Governor of the Church of England satisfied all the claims of conscience and pride. But they were Episcopalians, and in varying degrees—for Charles was more pronounced than his father—sacerdotalists. "No Bishop, no King," said James to the leading Puritan ministers at the Hampton Court Conference in 1604, and this association of prelacy and monarchy, which became the corner-stone of the Stuart System, was given a kind of sanctification by a new doctrine vigorously preached by courtier prelates that the king held his crown by right divine. The theory was indefensible but convenient. The ministers of an Erastian Church hastened to applaud a philosophy which attenuated the mundane character of their establishment; and King James, whose claims to the succession were assailable, was well pleased to hear that the Stuart Monarchy was established by the will of God.

There is one great objection to making politics hang upon theology. A theocrat may not bend. Concessions and accommodations, which might otherwise ease the march of politics, are difficult for a king who believes that he is the mouthpiece of the unalterable will of God. If the doctrine of the Divine Right of Kings had been merely an amiable flourish, it would have done no harm. But when James told the leading Puritan ministers in 1604 that if they and their friends did not conform " he would harry them out of the land " it was no mere flourish. Rather than conform, three hundred ministers resigned their livings.

The inwardness of the battle thus early engaged between the Puritans and the Stuart monarchy can be understood only if we realize the strength of the anti-Roman feeling which then prevailed, not only among the main part of the clergy, but in London, in the seaports, and in the fighting class of the community. In these regions of public opinion fear and hatred of Rome were for many generations predominant emotions. The Marian Martyrdoms, the Spanish Armada, the machinations against the life of the great queen were recent memories when James I came to the throne; and before these recollections had time to fade came the Guy Fawkes plot (engineered by certain Catholic gentlemen) to blow up the Houses of Parliament, a crime the horror of which was so deeply printed on the public mind that the memory of it is still annually revived in a few English towns and villages by communal burnings of the Pope.

To these occasions of rancour and apprehension there was added the anxiety with which the wavering and uncertain fortunes of the Protestants upon the continent were viewed by their English co-religionists. The wars of the Huguenots, the long and desperate struggle of the Dutch, the catastrophe to the Protestant cause in Bohemia and in the Palatinate aroused the liveliest feelings of sympathy in England. In the war mentality which was thus generated little points of ritual and observance, which to a cooler and more indulgent age would seem to be trifles, acquired the most solemn and tremendous significance, so that many would leave hearth and home and face the storms of the Atlantic rather than see the Communion table in their village church moved to the east end, where it savoured of the abomination of the Catholic Mass.

The constitutional issue was whether the true seat of sovereign authority lay with the Crown or Parliament. It was perhaps well that this profound question of the adjustment of forces within the state was never viewed as a matter of philosophical theory, but fought out by practical men in reference to the day-to-day concerns of practical life and in the light of historical precedents. For this reason, being inspired by the stress of experience, the ultimate solution, a Cabinet of Ministers, at once advising the Crown and responsible to Parliament in all its actions, has stood the wear and tear of every kind of political weather, and has proved to be one of the chief contributions which the sagacity of man has been able to make to the science of free government. But the solution was complicated, obscure, unsupported by precedent. Even at the end of the eighteenth century the framers of the American constitution failed to understand the nature and function of the Cabinet system. That it should have been so long missed by the politicians of the Stuart age is no matter for surprise.

The paramount importance of this constitutional issue proceeds from the fact that the gentlemen of the House of Commons had now developed a strong and, indeed, passionate interest in many questions of public policy, and notably in religion, in foreign politics as a branch of religion, and in finance, as to which they found themselves placed in the strongest opposition to the Crown.

The old tradition of England was parliamentary. The Tudor despotism was a novelty, acceptable as the alternative to civil war and invasion, and commended by the prestige, the ability, and the skilful parliamentary management of the Tudor sovereigns. Until the danger of the Armada was overpast there was little disposition to challenge in Parliament the actions of the Crown. But at the end of Elizabeth's reign murmurs were heard which were premonitory of the rising storm. Once even, on the question of Monopolies (1601), when she deemed that the protests of the House of Commons represented the sense of the people, Elizabeth wisely saw that timely concession was the path of prudence. With a grand air, which unlocks the secret of her magic, she made her atonement. "Though God," she said to her faithful Commons, "hath raised me high, yet this I count the glory of my crown: that I have reigned with your love. This makes me that I do not so much rejoice that God hath made me to be a Queen as to be a Queen over so thankful a people."

With none of these captivating graces, and with a point of view sharply contrasted from that of the gentry and common lawyers, who sat in St. Stephen's Chapel at Westminster, James I soon succeeded in fanning the flame of a serious parliamentary opposition. The king was clever, learned, humorous, in many ways more enlightened and humane than the bulk of his people, but intractable through conceit and as bad a judge of a political situation as any man who has ever sat on the English throne. Everything which he touched went amiss. He raised a storm by his philo-Spanish foreign policy. He chose favourites — first Robert Carr and then George Villiers, Duke of Buckingham — who excited general animosity. He alienated the merchants of the city and affronted the fiscal creed of Westminster by endeavouring to raise indirect taxes ("impositions") by prerogative. He had the wrong theory of Parliament and the unwisdom to express it. He told Lords and Commons that their privileges were not of right, but dependent on the royal grace. He said that the House of Commons had "merely a private and local wisdom," and made it clear that while it was their business to vote supplies and to express the views of their constituents, the shaping of the national policy and the ordering of the national Church were high matters of state reserved for the sole consideration of the king. To this the Parliament of 1621 rejoined in a famous protest covering the essential ground of the great controversy that "the liberties, franchises, privileges, and jurisdictions of Parliament are the ancient and undoubted birthright and inheritance of the subjects of England: and that the arduous and urgent affairs concerning the King, State, and defence of the realm and of the Church of England, and the making and maintenance of laws and redress of grievances . . . are proper subjects and matters of counsel and debate in Parliament." These doctrines were so violently opposed to the king's view of the constitution that he tore the offending page from the journals of the House, dissolved Parliament, and impeached seven of its members. Among those who suffered was John Pym, the first leader of the Puritan revolution.

From the premise that Parliament was free to shape and challenge the whole course of public policy it followed as a consequence that it should also be free to dismiss ministers whose counsels were regarded as dangerous to the common weal. But how was this to be done? No better way suggested itself than the ancient and violent expedient, known as an impeachment, of a judicial trial in the House of Lords on charges preferred by the popular chamber. It was a clumsy, irregular, inappropriate method. The failures of statesmen are not ordinarily due to treason, felony, or misdemeanour, or to other faults which are the proper subject for judicial enquiry, but to errors of judgment, of temper, and of calculation. An impeachment, then, however useful in its political results, was almost always unjust in its procedure and its penalty. Yet during the seventeenth century the Commons resorted again and again to this expedient to obtain what seemed otherwise out of reach—the removal of unpopular or oppressive ministers. With the aid of this clumsy bludgeon the parliamentary leaders of that age levelled the path which led to the smoother and more regular methods of our modern parliamentary practice.

George Villiers, Duke of Buckingham, brave, lavish, affable, was a good companion, but in statesmanship a rash and wayward guide. He had been the favourite counsellor of James I during his declining years, and was the intimate friend and trusted adviser of his son Charles, who succeeded in 1625. Parliament distrusted him, criticized him, and in the end endeavoured to remove him by impeachment. So long as this showy and pretentious favourite stood near to the throne the leaders of the House of Commons could believe nothing good of the government. The quarrels of Charles with his first three Parliaments were, at bottom, due to the fact that the king was resolute to sustain a minister whom the Commons were determined to unhorse. No unwise act on the part of the young king was necessary to create an atmosphere of bitterness over and above his continuing friendship for Buckingham. The bitterness was bequeathed from the old reign to the new. At once Parliament broke with the traditional custom of granting to a new king tonnage and poundage (some £300,000) for life, and proposed this grant for one year only. Frugal to the point of parsimony and suspicious to the point of injustice, they would not trust Buckingham a yard with public money.

It is a fair criticism upon the early Stuart Parliaments, not only that they failed to take account of the shrinkage of the traditional revenues of the crown through the fall in the value of the currency, but that they were unwilling to pay the price of their own policies. They wished to fight the Spaniards, to save the Palatinate, to help the Huguenots against Richelieu, but were wholly indisposed to provide the supplies without which enterprises of this scale and character could not be maintained. Could they have controlled expenditure and administration, they would, no doubt, have been educated to a wiser generosity. As it was they grudged every penny. Their parsimony drove Charles to unconstitutional expedients for raising funds—to ship money, to forced loans, and eventually to a quarrel so hot that it led to a suspension of parliamentary government for ten years.

The quality of the English politicians who were fighting for constitutional liberty during this period was not to be paralleled in any country in Europe. They were for the most part country gentlemen, graced with a tincture of the humanities, who farmed, shot, and hunted, but at the same time took an active part as justices of the peace in the local administration of the shire. The main principles of the English Common Law were familiar to them, and though no body of men could be less doctrinaire, they were tenacious of legal principle. With something of that high religious seriousness which distinguished the Jansenist lawyers of the Parliament of Paris, they had a wider experience of life and a greater aptitude for the rough and tumble of politics. In the main they were grave, passionate men by whom deep issues were deeply felt, and though it had now become, through its system of committees, an instrument excellently adapted for the efficient despatch of difficult business, there were occasions when in the stress of its emotions the House of Commons would break down in a tempest of tears.

Charles was unable to handle these serious, energetic, and difficult men. Virtue and refinement are no substitutes for that buoyant and pliable common sense which alone keeps the statesman's craft above the stormy waters. A troublesome Parliament he would at once dissolve. A specially troublesome member he would commit to prison without trial. He had no conception of an honest deal with an honest opponent, nor any scruple in using his great influence with the judiciary in obtaining verdicts agreeable to the wishes of the Crown. Yet the danger signals were numerous. There were the fifteen peers who refused to pay the forced loan in 1626; there were the five knights who, equally refusing to pay that loan, were imprisoned "by special mandate of the king," and then pleaded in a famous case that even so they were entitled to a release under a writ of habeas corpus; there were the London merchants refusing to pay customs; and finally in the Parliament of 1628 the Petition of Right, drawn up on the pressure of no less a person than Sir Edward Coke, the Chief Justice of the Court of Common Pleas, which declared four practices of the government to be unlawful: commissions of martial law, the billeting of soldiers and sailors on private houses, loans and taxes without consent of Parliament, and arbitrary imprisonment. To no one of these signals would Charles attend. On March 2, 1629, passion exploded.

In the second session of the third Parliament the House refused to adjourn at the king's command. The Speaker was held down in the chair, and at the instigation of Sir John Eliot a resolution was read out to the house that whoever brings in Arminian or Popish innovations in religion, whoever advises the levy of customs before a parliamentary grant, and whoever pays the same, is an enemy to the kingdom and the commonwealth. At that the king dissolved Parliament and initiated a spell extended over eleven years of personal rule.

Chief among the political leaders who were concerned with the passing of the Petition of Right was Thomas Wentworth, afterwards Earl of Strafford. The motives which led this powerful and imaginative statesman first to side with the Parliament and then to transfer his energies to the support of the crown were less clear to his contemporaries than they have since become. Wentworth was accused of political apostasy; but in a war of movement he only can be called an apostate who renounces the better part of himself. This Wentworth never did. Royalism was in his blood, but also the passion for strong, just, and efficient administration. If in 1628 he was found leading the opposition to the Crown, it was because he distrusted Buckingham's policies, thought that the prerogative had been stretched too far, and believed that Parliament was "the great physician to effect a true consent between king and people." If he afterwards, first as President of the North and then during his Irish administration, appears as a forerunner of our long line of English proconsuls, it was because in the passionate stress of the parliamentary conflict he had come to the conclusion that the government of the country could be more safely entrusted to the king than to Parliament. "The joint well-being of sovereignty and subjection" remained throughout the grand object to be attained : but he had come to the conclusion that a firm hand or, as he phrased it, a policy of "Thorough" was the medicine for the distempers of the age.

In this enterprise Wentworth could count upon the zealous co-operation of the one second-rate Englishman who has exercised a wide influence upon the history of the world. The ecclesiastical policy of William Laud led to the foundation of the New England colonies and to the armed rising of Presbyterian Scotland against the Anglican Prayer-book, which precipitated the Great Rebellion. To have been the means of launching two movements of such magnitude on either side of the Atlantic as the foundation of New England and the overthrow of Charles I is a measure not of the statesmanship of Laud, but of the extraordinary resentment aroused by his policy. Yet his merits, though far less influential than his blunders, were undeniable. A strong but narrow intellect was in him combined with a deep and unaffected vein of piety, with a morbid sensibility of conscience and with a passion for minute and interfering activities. At Oxford, where he reformed the University and Colleges, he was in his true place. His attempt to harry the English people into the acceptance of ceremonies which at that time were believed to have a Romanizing tendency met with signal and inevitable disaster.

Light indeed as compared with the fierce persecutions in Spain, in the Netherlands, and in Bohemia were the penalties inflicted by this active and efficient Oxford don upon the recalcitrant spirits who refused to accept the uniform high church pattern which he was determined to impose upon the English Church. The Laudian martyrs were deprived of their livings and in some extreme cases sentenced to whipping and the loss of an ear; but they were neither burned at the stake, nor beheaded, nor tortured on the rack, nor condemned to work as slaves in the galleys. Yet the policy of the archbishop was sufficiently detestable to a large section of his countrymen to promote a stream of emigration to the shores of North America. Every year from 1629 to 1640 hundreds of English gentlemen and yeomen, farm servants, and ministers of religion, not dissenting from the Church of England, but desiring within the ambit of that Church to worship God after their own fashion, left their native land and settled upon the shores of Massachusetts. It is a curious result of the innovating policy of a pedantic Oxford prelate that from it sprang the New England states, the source, so it has been stated, of one-fourth of the population of the United States today. The greatest event in the English history of the Caroline age was the undesigned effect of a bad policy. The fugitives from Laud's repression carried with them to New England the institutions and character of their race. The New England colonies, which were closely settled, were always to be distinguished for three features: the Congregational church, the town council, and the village school. These aspects of our old English life were so firmly planted in American soil that when the age of steam erupted upon the American continent millions of emigrants from other parts of Europe they found a land where the inhabitants obeyed the English common law, spoke the English language, and maintained many essential characteristics of English government.

The Great Rebellion arose from the fact that the Lowland Scots, who were at once a military and a Presbyterian people, refused to accept the Anglican Prayer-book which Charles I and his unwise adviser Archbishop Laud attempted to impose upon them. To Charles, who knew nothing of Scotland, it was a complete surprise that the Scots, rather than accept the Anglican liturgy, would put an army in the field, to which the peaceful squires of England could make no immediate reply. The workings of the Presbyterian conscience were as mysterious to him as the readiness of the Scots to face ordeal by battle. While the English gentry had been farming, hunting, and administering the shires the military ardour of the Lowlands had been sustained by feudal broils, by the propinquity of the wild Highlanders, and by the professional zeal and knowledge of many a returned adventurer from the German wars. That the Scots, led by the Earl of Argyll, should presume at their Church Assembly at Glasgow to reject a prayer-book which was good enough for the English was amazing enough; it was still more disconcerting that this impoverished little country should be able at once to throw an army across the border which the King of England could not hope, without a special appeal to Parliament, to repel.

The experience of the Short Parliament, summoned to vote supplies for a Scottish war, but dissolved almost as soon as summoned (April 13–May 5, 1640) was sufficient to show the king that only if he were prepared to redress grievances could he expect to obtain supplies. Yet supplies he must have. The Scottish army under Alexander Leslie, a veteran of the German wars, crossed the Tweed, occupied Durham and Northumberland, and demanded as part consideration for its retirement a sum of money which could be obtained by Charles in no other way than by resort to a fresh Parliament. A remarkable group of country gentlemen, headed by John Pym and John Hampden, were determined that to this assembly at least members should be returned who should compel the king to redress the grievances of the nation.

The Long Parliament is famous not only in English but in general history as having put a final limit upon the autocracy of the English crown with the far-reaching consequences for the development of political liberties throughout the world which have flowed from that event. In its first session this assembly of earnest and angry men abolished the prerogative courts (the Star Chamber, the High Commission Court, the prerogative jurisdiction of the Councils of Wales and of the North), and solemnly affirmed the illegality of raising money, either by way of tonnage and poundage or of ship money, without parliamentary consent. The boundaries which were then set have never been disturbed. Irrevocably Parliament had then secured its right to control the finance and, through finance, the policy of the nation. Irrevocably also the civil rights of the subject were protected henceforth from the arbitrary interference of the crown.

But at the time nothing seemed less certain than that these essential principles should be fixed and embodied in the constitution. The air was full of alarming rumours, and the spectre of Strafford leading a savage Irish army upon London to restore the power of the Crown haunted the imagination of parliamentary leaders. So long as Strafford was abroad and free, Pym, the driving force of the parliamentary movement, could not reckon on English liberty. An impeachment was launched, and midway in the solemn trial, since a conviction seemed uncertain, was exchanged for the deadly process of attainder. Strafford was too formidable to expect justice from his opponents. The Parliamentarians who voted for death, the mob who howled round the royal palace of Whitehall or flocked to the execution of "Black Tom the Tyrant" on Tower Hill were not thinking of justice, but of safety. The execution of this valiant and intelligent man was an act of war, a stern and deliberate measure of precaution against a great political evil vividly apprehended as menacing the welfare of the state.

After that events moved swiftly towards open strife. Wringing the king's consent to a statute that it should be dissolved only with its own consent, Parliament, under Pym's leadership, and with the support of the City of London, where the tide of Puritan feeling was running strong, drove forward with a series of measures and proposals calculated to transform the character of the state. Since there was no class of man more unpopular with Pym and his friends than the bishops, it was proposed, with the novel support of a petition numerously signed in the city, that episcopacy should be abolished root and branch. A Puritan Church, managed by parliamentary lay commissioners, seemed to Pym much to be preferred to an Arminian Church controlled by royal nominees who favoured autocracy in politics and leant to ritualism in religion. But Parliament under the same strenuous leadership was not content with arrogating to itself the right to reform the Church. A terrible rising of the Irish Catholics, resulting in a great massacre of Protestants, brought the problem of army control into the forefront of English politics.

Despite all precedents, Pym was resolved that the army for Ireland should be officered, not by the king, but by Parliament. He was also determined that the king's ministers shall be "such as henceforth the Parliament may have cause to confide in." But if Parliament controlled finance, the Church, the army, and the Council, it ruled the nation. To this Charles was by no means prepared to assent. In an access of folly he determined first to impeach and then to arrest (January 4, 1642) the five members (Pym, Hampden, Hazlerigg, Holles, and Strode) who had led the parliamentary attack. But when, on January 4, he came down to the Commons "the birds were flown"; and six days afterwards Charles found it prudent to flee also from the tumultuous and hostile crowds of London.

In the course of these anxious and passionate debates the unity of the Long Parliament, which had been preserved so long as the question at issue was the restoration of the old balance between Crown and Parliament, was broken beyond repair. The moderate Episcopalians were drawn into the royalist ranks by the Root and Branch Bill attacking Episcopacy. Parties were formed, and party differences hardened as it became clear that Pym was no longer claiming what Parliament had claimed before, but was in effect aiming at ultimate sovereignty. It has been calculated that when the civil war broke out thirty members of the Lords and three hundred of the Commons espoused the parliamentary cause.

The English people, among whom there was a long and happy tradition of social harmony, only slowly and with painful reluctance ranged themselves in the opposing camps of Cavalier and Roundhead. The circumstances which generally lend bitterness to civil strife, or unduly protract its duration, were absent here. Class was not ranged against class, nor hunger against affluence, nor yet was the country sacrificed to the vested interests of marauding bands of mercenary troops. From beginning to end the flag of constitutional principle flew high above the combat, visible to all. The country gentry supplied leaders to both sides. The Earls of Essex and Manchester, Lord Fairfax and Oliver Cromwell, the principal generals on the Parliamentarian side, all belonged to the territorial class. A humane and enlightened aristocracy of sportsmen, slow to anger and quick to forgive, drained war of its more malignant poisons, and robbed it of some of its barbarity. The generous terms given to Oxford on its capitulation at the end of the war (June 20, 1646) were a fitting climax to such a controversy.

The war, which lasted five years, was in the end won by the Parliamentarians, who having behind them the fleet, the capital, the clothing towns, and the eastern counties, possessed a decisive preponderance of financial strength. Yet money, though it made ultimate victory secure, seeing that there was no failure of the Puritan morale, was slow to exert its full effect. In the campaign of 1643 the Cavaliers, being better prepared than their adversaries in the cavalry arm, and having in Prince Rupert, the king's nephew, an inspiring leader of horse, established an advantage so menacing to their opponents that Pym invoked the Scots to redress the balance. War ministers must take war risks. Rather than lose the war, Pym was prepared to face the possibility of a Scottish army dominating the political scene at Westminster. On the field of Marston Moor, the biggest battle of the *July 2,* war, his decision was justified, for a mixed army of Scots, York- *1644* shiremen, and East Anglians routed Prince Rupert's royalists, won the north for the Roundheads, and at one blow saved the parliamentary cause from the risk of disaster.

It was on that Yorkshire battlefield that Oliver Cromwell first *1599-1658* exhibited in a great action his outstanding capacity as a leader of horse. To the controlled momentum of his Ironsides, always impulsive but always in hand, the victory was due. Parliament recognized the genius of its new general. Though Cromwell was an Independent in religion, and on that score at issue with the intolerant Erastianism of Westminster, the parliamentary leaders cleared the way for his promotion and listened to his counsels. Once more, religious differences were ignored to achieve a military victory. The war, which under a lax direction, might have dragged on for many a year, poisoning the life of the country, was brought to a sharp and rapid end by the resolute and efficient men who succeeded Pym in the control of the parliamentary machine. The credit of victory is shared between Cromwell, who created, and the Parliamentarians who financed, that well-paid and well-fed professional force of zealous fighters known as the New Model Army, which won the fight of Naseby in 1645 and delivered the last hammer blows at the dismembered fragments of the royalist party. True to the maxim that the first duty of a war government is to win the war, the Puritan legislators threw their religious predilections to the winds, and helped Cromwell to forge the instrument which brought the king to the scaffold and the Long Parliament to a sorry and shameful end.

For this Parliament which won the war showed itself incapable of making peace. It persecuted the royalists by crippling fines, ejected the Anglican clergy from their livings, proscribed the use of the Anglican Prayer-book, and so threw away the chance of conciliating its beaten enemies. With an even more surprising measure of unwise intolerance the Puritan pedants of the victorious House of Commons alienated their friends. The triumph of the Roundheads in the Civil War had been due to the New Model Army, a body largely drawn from the small freeholders of the eastern counties, and distinguished from other parliamentary forces by its hospitality to every type of Protestant sectarian opinion. By persecuting the sectaries and refusing the army their just claims for pay, the Long Parliament prepared its own doom. An assembly which showed itself hostile to all that was most free and living in English Protestant opinion, and indifferent to the services of the army which had secured its triumph, was no longer fit to govern England. Oliver Cromwell and John Milton, the two greatest living Englishmen, were outraged by its narrow intolerance.

In the struggle between the Parliament and the army which now ensued, there is one circumstance highly illustrative of the English character. Neither party was prepared to dispense with the monarchy, but each strove to obtain possession of the person of the king, that it might strike a bargain and carry on the business of the country under the familiar old royal firm. In the triangular negotiations between Charles, the army, and the Parliament, each party stood for certain principles which the country needed and which, in their ultimate and necessary combination, furnished the pattern of a stable English peace: the King for monarchy and the English Prayer-book, the Parliament for Common Law and responsible government, the army for religious toleration to be extended to the nonconformists of the Protestant sects. But there was destined to be no restoration for Charles, neither by the army, whose fair terms he refused (not being disposed for the rôle of *roi-fainéant* over bishops without power and sectaries without rein), nor yet by the Scots, whose Presbyterian aid he did not scruple to invoke.

Playing Parliament against army, Scotland against England, and always hoping that by some happy turn of fortune he might master his opponents, Charles, "part woman, part priest, and part the bewildered delicate boy who had never quite grown up,"[1] let every chance slip by. The Second Civil War was the proximate cause of his end. The army could not pardon the king's engagement with the Scots, which brought the Duke of Hamilton's army raiding into Lancashire and threatened England with a Presbyterian monarchy to be introduced and supported by Scottish pikes. When Cromwell returned from the north, after the battle of Preston, his mind was attuning itself to the deliberate resolve of the army that "the man of blood" must be removed, and sweeping parliamentary obstacles from his path by the brusque method of Pride's Purge, he brought the king to that final scene before the Palace at Whitehall, which recalled the English people to their royal faith, and gave to Charles the

[1] John Buchan, *Oliver Cromwell*, p. 120.

Martyr, dying like a great English gentleman and a saint, a final absolution from his many faults.

The prophets who augured a short life for the regicides' republic failed to take a true measure of the energy released or of the organization promoted by the mere fact of a well-conducted war. The whole scale of English government had been enlarged by the ordeal through which the country had passed. To the surprise of Europe the new Commonwealth, so far from being enfeebled or exhausted by five years of domestic strife, was not only in every particular of financial resource and military power stronger than England had ever been, but was also aflame with a militant and aggressive ardour, foreign to its habitual mood. The age of the Commonwealth is filled with battle and blood shed. Ireland and Scotland were subjugated by Cromwell. An aggressive war was waged first against the Dutch, and then against the Spaniards. Jamaica and Dunkirk were conquered and annexed. For the first and only time in her history England became the chief among military states of Europe. " I have seen the English," wrote Turenne to Mazarin, on the eve of the battle of the Dunes, which gave Dunkirk to Cromwell; " they are the finest troops possible " (June 21, 1657). In tone, discipline, and experience no continental army could vie with Oliver's redcoats. His Irish and Scottish campaigns were part of a general design to secure the predominance of the Puritan Commonwealth throughout the British islands, so that neither Papist nor Stuart could hope to overset it. In a brief and cruel campaign (August to October, 1649) Cromwell wrote his name in blood in the annals of Ireland. Like Strafford, like James I, like Elizabeth, he desired to make of Ireland an English and Protestant people. Similar, but in proportion to his greater energy of conception more notably mischievous, was the measure of his failure. The Cromwellian settlement only aggravated the evils of Ireland. The native Irish, driven from their homes to make way for soldiers and land speculators from England, found a refuge among the desolate bogs of Connaught, where their descendants continue to this day, despite all that has been done for the congested districts, to afford a spectacle of material wretchedness nowhere else to be paralleled in the British Isles. So far from promoting the Protestant religion, the Cromwellian settlement deepened the aversion of the native Irish from a faith which had inspired the massacres of Drogheda and Wexford, and displaced

thousands of humble Celtic families to make way for an alien
territorial aristocracy. A short-lived legislative union, which
brought thirty Protestant Irishmen to Westminster, was no compensation for these evils.

The military subjection of Scotland, which was accomplished
in 1652, arose equally from the circumstances of the English
civil war. The Scots, though they had resisted the Laudian
Prayer-book, had no sympathy with the English sectaries who
had executed a Scottish king. They welcomed Charles II, crowned
him King of Scotland at Scone, and compelled that festive, intelligent youth, the most reluctant and evasive of converts, to
swear to their solemn league and covenant. The hopes of a Stuart
restoration to be accomplished through the incongruous help of
these grim Presbyterians were effectively shattered by Cromwell
at Dunbar and Worcester.

Sept. 3,
1650
Sept. 3,
1651

Then Scotland received its dose of Cromwellian medicine
which, though less drastic than the prescription made out for
Ireland, left nevertheless a bitter taste. Cromwell was a great
unionist. For the first time, under his Protectorate, England,
Scotland, and Ireland were brought under a single Parliament.
It was a new portent when the Protector stood out before the
world as the master not of England only but of Great Britain.
But a union baptized in the wine of violence cannot endure. The
work of Cromwell was undone before the harshness of military
conquest could be assuaged by the mitigations of civil policy. At
the Restoration the old Parliaments reappeared in Dublin and
Edinburgh, and the old animosities continued to pursue their
unpromising train. Even where religion was no barrier, real
union tarried. Where Catholic faced Protestant the black gulf
remained unbridged. Forty-seven years rolled by before Scotland
and England agreed to agree. Only in 1921, and after the convulsion of a world war, were England and Catholic Ireland painfully brought to the point when they could, at least for the time
being, agree to differ.

Across the North Sea lay the Dutch republic, bound to
the English regicides by the similarity of its democratic polity
and by a common interest in Protestant defence. The idea that
English and Dutch might coalesce in some form of political
union was so natural that it was actually the subject of negotiation. But the Dutch were rivals at sea, and rivals in trade, and
since they had married William of Orange, their late Stadtholder

(d. 1650), to Mary, the Princess Royal of England, they were on the whole favourable to the family from whom the English regicides had most to fear. Like ships struck by a rising gale, the two peoples, so nearly united, shot apart. With glowering rage the merchants of Amsterdam learnt that Westminster, aiming straight at the Dutch carrying trade, had decreed (Navigation Act, 1651) that no English goods were to be carried in foreign bottoms; and at Westminster, where the Netherlands were regarded as a nest of plotting and dangerous cavaliers, the feeling was no sweeter. To these occasions of ill-will the jealousies and jostlings of two equal navies in the Narrow Seas added a formidable item, producing a state of feeling in which a small incident might light the flame of war. The refusal of the Dutch to salute the British flag was the signal for a tremendous marine contest between great fleets commanded by brilliant seamen, in which Tromp and Blake enjoyed alternating fortunes, while the far-spread foreign trade of the Netherlands experienced a disproportionate loss. It was the first of three Anglo-Dutch wars which led to the decline of the Netherlands as a world power. Closing it by the treaty of 1654, Cromwell gradually felt his way to diplomatic combinations, which were more in accordance with the Protestant conscience. In the end, allied with Sweden and France, he resumed the classic conflict with Catholic Spain.

Critics have blamed the Protector for throwing the weight of English military and naval power into the scales against Spain. He should have seen, it is urged, the impending predominance of France, and endeavoured to check it. This he did not do. At the one moment when England was really strong, her strength was employed upon the wrong side. Wisdom is easy after the event. At the time there was much to be said for an alliance with a power, which, if hostile, could make mischief by its support of the exiled king, and was traditionally Protestant in its foreign policy. Moreover, the dangerous ambitions of Louis XIV were not yet deployed. Perhaps, had Cromwell lived for another decade, he might have stood out as the champion of Protestant liberties in Europe (anticipating the rôle of William III) against the aggressive intolerance of Catholic France.

One feature of the Cromwellian foreign policy was, however, in accord with the permanent interests of Great Britain. The Anglo-Portuguese alliance, offering to the English fleet the splendid harbour of Lisbon, dates from 1654. Lisbon is the key to the Mediterranean. English fleets, repaired and revictualled in Lisbon, ensured the defence of Gibraltar, and enabled England in the days before steam to figure as a Mediterranean power. With what prodigious *bravura* did she not make her début in this new rôle, when Blake's fleet, chasing Prince Rupert's privateers, called upon Tuscany and the Pope for indemnities, bombarded Tunis, and showed the flag at Malta and Venice, Toulon and Marseilles! Long before the need for a chain of naval ports along the sea route to India had made itself apparent, Blake, the soldier-sailor of the Commonwealth, whose portrait hangs in the Hall of Wadham College in Oxford, had shown with what ease such a feat might be accomplished.

The period of the Commonwealth and Protectorate, though rich in political debate and constitutional experiment, must be regarded rather as an interlude in the domestic history of the British people than as a contribution to its progress. What was attempted or achieved under the kingless government did not survive. Oliver, as had been well said, could neither rule with Parliaments nor without them. He was in the impossible position of being by nature a liberty-loving, constitutional ruler, compelled by the force of revolutionary events to carry on a military government, which had no roots in national assent. A free vote of the people, taken at any time after the execution of Charles I, would have restored the monarchy. But Oliver could not afford to permit such freedom. There were certain fundamentals, his own position, for instance, and toleration for the Protestant sectaries upon whom his power depended, which he could not, without risking the whole fabric of the state, open out for discussion; but it was just such questions which every Parliament desired to discuss. Had the Protector assumed the Crown, as most civilian members of his Council and many London Presbyterians desired, he would, from the point of view of the lawyers, have regularized a situation full of anomaly and embarrassment. A protectorate, even glorified by victories on sea and land, was a more dubious and uncomfortable thing in the eyes of a sentimental and conservative people than the old monarchy. But Oliver, though he recreated a phantasmal House of Lords, shrank, perhaps out of pride, perhaps out of prudence, or a critical sense of the fitness of things, from the traditional rite of a coronation. A Protector, then, this great man died, bequeathing, as perhaps the most durable memorial of his Puritan

1657

rule, that hatred of standing armies as inimical to civilian liberty, which long distinguished the English people, and is still enshrined in the constitutional practice by which the army is maintained on a yearly tenure.

The last years of Oliver's rule were bitterly unpopular. England was divided into eleven areas, each subjected to an officer with the local rank of major-general who was charged with the duty not only of keeping order, but of suppressing vice and encouraging virtue. The country did not soon forget or forgive the petty tyranny of these Puritan tyrants (many of them lowborn and ill-bred) who put down the people's sports and harried the gentry with new exactions. Long before the breath was out of Oliver's body, a pleasure-loving nation was yearning for release from the grim constraint of compulsory godliness.

BOOKS WHICH MAY BE CONSULTED

S. R. Gardiner : History of England.   1875.

G. M. Trevelyan : England under the Stuarts.   1904.

W. H. Hutton : William Laud.   1895.

Lady Burghclere : Earl of Strafford.

Lives of Oliver Cromwell : C. H. Firth, 1900.   John Morley, 1900.   John Buchan, 1934.

T. Carlyle : Oliver Cromwell.   1845-6.

T. Carlyle : Historical Sketches.   *Ed.* Alexander Carlyle.   1898.

C. E. Wade : John Pym.   1912.

W. Notestein : The Winning of the Initiative by the House of Commons (Proc. Brit. Ac., 1918).

CHAPTER XX

THE ASCENSION OF FRANCE

Louis XIV. Character of his Empire. Policy of Colbert. France little attracted by marine enterprise. Partial codification in France. Suppression of liberty. The Anglo-French alliance. The eastern frontier of France. The War of Devolution. The Triple Alliance. The Treaty of Dover. The Treaty of Nimweguen, 1678. Louis at his zenith. Charles II and Louis. Accession of James II to the English throne. Revocation of the Edict of Nantes. The English revolution of 1688. The success of William III and the miscalculation of Louis. The advantages of England. The War of the League of Augsburg.

THE autocracy of Louis XIV, reflecting the mounting ardour of French national feeling, is the dominant fact in the history of Europe from that king's assumption of power in 1661 until his death in 1715. As the Tudor dynasty brought peace to England after the distractions of a long civil war, and was the more welcome for that reason, so the long reign of Louis XIV inaugurated for France a period of security from foreign attack, and of exemption from the most dangerous type of civil disorder, which lasted till the revolution of 1789. No longer, as in the days of the League and of the Fronde, was the power of the crown confronted by a rebellious nobility headed by the king of Spain. The nobles of France still retained the fiscal immunities which divided them from the *roturiers* and the peasants: but their teeth were drawn. A splendid court attracted and held them within its glittering orbit. In the Byzantine climate of Versailles the proudest nobles put off their independence, lost contact with local affairs, and sank to the courtiers' level of intrigue, pettiness, and servility.

Louis was the first French sovereign to make of monarchy a serious profession. From the beginning he was resolved that no minister should exercise, and no favourite influence, the supreme direction of affairs. "The great, noble, and delightful trade" of royalty was too precious to be parcelled out; it was a divine office, entrusted by the providence of God to a divine agent, whose qualifications, as embodied in himself, merited, so he believed, the exalted trust. A dominating eye, a dignified bear-

ng, an assured grace in social commerce were combined in
Louis with a fixed habit of sustained industry, a strong memory,
and a capacity for using the brains of able men. Though the
tide of his animal passions was strong, he worked six hours a
day, and never allowed love-making to interfere with the discharge of public business. Duty always came first, duty conceived in the grand manner, as labour for great and spectacular
ends ministering to the splendour of France and the renown of
its sovereign; for the two were identical. "When the state is in
view," he observed to his son, "one works for oneself." And so,
if a smile was rarely seen to play on the grave, pock-marked
face beneath the long peruke, and if St. Simon, the hostile witness of his declining years, speaks of "the heart which never
loved anyone and which no one loved," it was because he was
the professional king, without a gleam of humour or a touch of
mystery, composed, laconic, reserved, egotistical, sustaining upon his sturdy and self-sufficient shoulders the main burden of
the state.

Counterbalancing this resolute sense of public duty were certain costly infirmities of temper. The best laid schemes were
often swept away by a fit of hot impatience and overweening
pride. The monarch, who at one moment seemed to be a miracle
of cool and long-headed calculation, at another was found to be
acting on a violent impulse proceeding from envy, ambition, or
contempt. Commenting for the benefit of his son upon his early
military campaigns, he wrote, "My natural authority, my hot
youth, and my violent desire to augment my reputation, imparted to me a strong feeling of impatience." He burned to
emulate the achievements of the great soldiers of his age and
"perhaps to surpass some undertakings which they had deemed
impracticable. Luxemburg, Namur, Mons, Ghent, and Brussels
were ever before me." Advancing years did not greatly abate
his vehemence. To the end he loved glory and hated Protestants;
passions which, however widely honoured by his fellow-countrymen, were nevertheless, since they involved France in forty years
of exhausting warfare, ruinous to his country and expensive to
mankind.

The scale, splendour, and organized power of the monarchy
of Louis XIV was something new in Europe. The empire of
Charles V, though wider in extent, was less compact, less efficient, less well calculated to strike the imagination of the world.

Nationalism, untempered by cosmopolitan association, and un-
perplexed by racial strains, now found in France its fullest expression; monarchy, as an art, its most brilliant exemplar; administration, as an educative and controlling force, its first real,
large-scale illustration. For this result the king was principally
indebted to the work of ministers who had received their training under an earlier régime. The first part of his reign is an
era of great public servants. In diplomacy Hugues de Lionne
(1663-71), in industry, commerce, and naval organization J. B.
Colbert (1669-83), in war Le Tellier and his son Louvois (1677-91),
were not merely able and efficient workers, but men of initiative
and improving zeal, who left the mark of their intelligence upon
the methods of the state. Louis himself, the willing victim of
unceasing adulation, was no judge of men. After the first race
of giants had died away, they were replaced by officials of
smaller stature and inferior metal. It is the nemesis of all autocracies that, sooner or later, for lack of the vivifying breath of
freedom, they cease to command the best services of the highest
and the best men.

Of the statesmen who adorned the early years of the reign,
the most unusual in range and distinction was Colbert. In his
comprehensive and devouring energy, in his grasp of detail, in
his power of surmounting obstacles and getting things through,
this cold, resolute, water-drinking nationalist was worth a whole
cabinet of ordinary men. "No one," says M. Jusserand, "had
before Colbert so clear an idea of the importance of the navy,
commerce, the colonies, of sound finance, of the improvement
of communications by roads, rivers, and canals." To the idle,
pleasure-loving nobles of Versailles he proclaimed the doctrine
that the greatness of a country depends upon wealth, and that
wealth depends upon work. It is one of his chief titles to fame
that during the long course of his active life he preached with a
pertinacious courage the unpopular truth that national strength
is to be measured, not by the showy uniforms of the household
troops, but by industry, commerce, and agriculture, by the service precisely of those classes in the community who were then
commonly regarded with condescension and contempt.

Unfortunately he laboured under the false theory common to
his age that the wealth of one country can be obtained only by
the impoverishment of another. He viewed international trade,
not as an exchange of goods and services from which both

parties profited, but as a money warfare, in which one country's gain was another's loss. Calculating that twenty thousand ships were sufficient to carry the commerce of western Europe, and that these were supplied in varying proportions by France, England, and Holland, he proceeded to the conclusion that French commerce could expand only through the reduction of the navies of her two commercial rivals. It is amazing that a man of commanding ability should have succumbed to so childish a delusion as to suppose either that the wealth of Europe was limited, or that it consisted of gold. It was also a disaster that from this erroneous philosophy of trade, Colbert was led to give his support to the Dutch war, which, provoking other quarrels, ruined the edifice of commercial prosperity which it was the main object of his life to erect.

It is to the credit of Louis XIV that he should have sustained until his death in 1683 this stern, managing administrator, whom Madame de Sévigné compared for his chill fixity of purpose to the north star. But the fervour of Colbert's nationalism was unmistakable. It was his aim to make the whole world minister to the glory of France and its king.

The methods by which Colbert endeavoured to carry out his spacious policy made a great impression upon his age, and stamped themselves deeply on the life of France. He had the superman's mania for regulation. Nothing escaped his watchful and supervising eye, neither art nor letters, neither industry nor commerce. His tariffs were drawn so high as eventually to stifle trade. His regulations were so minute as to take the spring out of industry. His vigorous arm stretched so far as to clasp the most distant settlements of the crown. It was in vain that the French colonist crossed the Atlantic to Canada, or beat his stormy way past the Cape to the tropical forests of Madagascar. He could not escape Colbert. A forest of regulations, devised on the banks of the Seine, disciplined the life of the royal colonies, and repeated in a wilderness the inequalities of feudal France. While the New Englander breathed the air of liberty, the society of colonial France was cabined and confined by the control of an ultramontane Church and an absolute monarchy. So little did Colbert understand the value of liberty in colonial development, that, even in Madagascar, natives and colonists alike were compelled to settle their disputes by the custom of Paris.

These drawbacks notwithstanding, a great impulse was given to colonization by Colbert. It is largely due to his energy and initiative that France, at the opening of the eighteenth century, found herself possessed of colonies in North America, of fisheries in Newfoundland, of plantations in the West Indies and in Madagascar, and of factories in India. It was a noble legacy imperfectly appreciated and defended. Had the spirit of Colbert continued to inform the shipyards of France, the tricolour might now be waving over the citadel of Quebec, and some part at least of India be numbered among the possessions of the French republic.

The evils of the French fiscal system were too deeply entrenched to be removed even by this capable minister. Colbert was forced to acquiesce in the customs lines which divided province from province, in the exemption of the nobility from taxation, and in that bad and inveterate practice of farming taxes and selling offices, which put a premium on peculation. Thus, while the revenues of the crown were greatly augmented by good management, they were collected in a manner most wasteful to the state and so assessed that the incidence of taxation fell most heavily on the class least able to bear it. The history of Colbert's efforts to raise money for his master's wars is, therefore, a dark chapter of misery and oppression, offering a sinister contrast to the glitter and frivolity of Versailles. While the nobles were hunting, dancing, and gambling, bloodhounds were tracking down the miserable creatures who smuggled salt, and hundreds of helpless tax collectors were suffering imprisonment for their failure to wring from an impoverished peasantry the appointed quota of the *taille*. Against the prime source of these evils Colbert was powerless to contend. Nothing less than a revolution was availing to introduce the principle of equity into French finances.

The moral of Colbert's rule is that no nation can be driven into paths which it does not wish to pursue. Because the Frenchman was content with a modest competence at home, because he hated and feared the sea, and did not care to risk his fortune on doubtful enterprises at the ends of the earth, Colbert's dream of a great marine empire and of a world trade promoted by joint stock companies was doomed to disappointment. He had hoped for a French Egypt, for a Suez Canal, for a line of naval posts on the sea route to India and the far east, anticipating, in fact, the exact policy which Britain afterwards pursued with success, and for colonies both populous and popular. His countrymen did not share his enthusiasms. The call to marine adventure fell on listless ears. The needs of the eastern frontier, so uncomfortably near to Paris, and so inadequately protected, and the lure of summer campaigning in the familiar European war theatre, where great captains had fought through the ages, and where real glory was always to be won, these were the things which fixed and absorbed the attention of the capital.

Another phase of Colbert's innovating courage is illustrated by his attempt to systematize French law. The "Code Louis," a series of elaborate ordinances dealing with Civil and Criminal Procedure, with Commerce and Marine, and with the negro population of the colonies (Code Noir) cannot, seeing that it maintains torture and excludes Jews and Protestants from the colonies, be reckoned among the humanitarian manifestations of the world. But the jurisprudence of this age is notable, not only as marking the first important step towards the legal unity of France which was afterwards realized under Napoleon, but as laying down the main lines in accordance with which French law courts still conduct their proceedings. Colbert did not succeed in codifying French law. A thick jungle of local customs throve with a kind of cumulative persistence until the revolution. But he bequeathed as part of his legacy to France the idea of a code and some important fragments from which such a code could in time be constructed.

The fierce military and clerical nationalism which dominated France in the reign of Louis XIV found no place for personal liberty. A stern censorship muzzled the press, and sealed the country against the perilous contagion of Dutch and English publications. Pamphleteering was made dangerous to life and limb. No impertinent Mazarinades, or organized protests, emanating, as in the days of the Fronde, from the Parliament of Paris, were permitted to impair the peace of the ruler. The comedies of Molière escaped censure, the wit of the dramatist atoning for the unchristian quality of his mind; but whatever was critical of the monarchy or suspect to the Church was rigorously suppressed. It is a grave detraction from the glory of Louis XIV that, despite his much advertised patronage of literary men, he did nothing to relax the rigours of a system which had made it impossible for Descartes, the greatest thinker of his age, to publish in his native country any one of the writings which announce a new epoch in European philosophy.

The power of France stood out on an eminence all the clearer by reason of the political dismemberment of Germany and Italy, the decline of Spain and the attitude of the Restoration Government in England. From 1661 to 1685 Louis was able in the main to rely upon English friendship. The Stuarts were partly French, for Charles was the grandson of Henry IV, and his sister Henriette (Madame) was married to the Duke of Orleans, who was brother to Louis XIV. Everything attracted them to France, French blood, French hospitality during exile, French splendour, French autocracy, French money, and, perhaps even more strongly than all these circumstances, the spell of the Roman religion of the French monarch, to which Charles was a secret, and his brother James an open, convert. To Charles, therefore, and still more to James, his successor, the friendship of the French was of great moment. With French help they might hope to secure toleration, perhaps ultimately ascendancy, for the old faith. With French supplies they might circumvent the niggardly spirit of English Parliaments. With French troops they might, in the last resort, should the crown again be seriously challenged, defend the prerogatives of the royal house. Save for one brief interval, England was, during the reigns of the last two Stuarts, a client of France.

In any appreciation of the causes which led to the overpowering ascendancy of Louis XIV, the Anglo-French entente which prevailed during the first half of his reign is of great importance. To the very Protestant, but also very commercial, cities of England it was more urgent at this time to reduce the Dutch than to challenge a power, which, though it was equally unpopular, was weaker at sea and as yet no serious rival in the marts of the new world. In the city of London the Dutch were regarded with feelings compounded of admiration, envy, and dislike. By their energy and thrift, by their practice of religious toleration and hospitality, as well as by the high average standard of their education and the low average standard of their tariffs, the Dutch had built up for themselves the largest carrying trade and the strongest commercial system in Europe. Nowhere was capital so cheap and abundant, banking so fully developed, shipbuilding so easy and inexpensive, or mercantile law so well adapted to the needs of a business community as in the Dutch Republic. These advantages, clearly apprehended by the English officials in Whitehall, were not as yet (1660) possessed by the England of Charles II. In the race for colonies and commerce the Dutch led, and on the assumption (at variance with the facts) that the world was not big enough for the Dutch and English to go their several ways and prosper, a sharp reduction in Dutch power was instantly demanded by their English rivals. To the jealously guarded Dutch monopoly in the Spice Islands and in West Africa, the Restoration Government replied (1660) by a comprehensive statute fencing off the English colonial trade from the foreigner. A quarrel ensued with important consequences. The two wars fought by Charles II against the Dutch Republic assisted the rise of the French monarchy, as the later wars fought in alliance with the Dutch under William III and Anne powerfully contributed to its decline.

Whoever deserved to rule the waves in Charles II's first Dutch wars, it was not Britannia. That slow-moving lady was still entangled with the notion that a titled landsman might command at sea, and that any ne'er-do-well swept up by the press gangs was ripe for service in the king's ships. After the four days' battle of June, 1666, when De Ruyter inflicted some eight thousand casualties on the English fleet, English sailors were found floating in the water dressed in their Sunday black just as they had been caught after church by the press gang. Pay was in arrears, food was short. So bad were the conditions of the lower decks that three thousand English and Scottish sailors actually preferred service with the Dutch. Stout and well-built as were the English ships, valiant and experienced as were many English mariners, that was not the way to rule the waves. Nor yet were it wise to leave an empty fleet lying in an undefended harbour as was done in June, 1667, when the enemy sailed into the Medway, bombarded Chatham, and with little loss to themselves delivered a smashing blow at the English navy. The shock was salutary. London, already scourged by plague and fire, did not soon forget the roar of the Dutch guns in the Thames. Clarendon, the chief minister, was driven out of the country. The Commons actually began to examine naval accounts. By the end of the reign the "tarpaulins" or old salts had come into their own, and an examination had been started for lieutenants at sea. From the rough schooling of the Dutch wars the Royal Navy emerged, a recognized profession.

1925 The problem of the eastern frontier of France, which the Treaty of Locarno has attempted finally to settle, was opened in its modern form in 1667, when Louis XIV, on the death of Philip IV of Spain, invaded the Spanish Low Countries on the plea that the rights of Spain in those territories had, by the Law of Brabant, devolved upon his own wife, the eldest daughter of the late king. The flimsiness of the pretexts which led to the so-called War of Devolution have often been exposed. Rarely has the peace of Europe been more wantonly disturbed. Yet there is some truth in the modern French contention that the Low Countries and Franche Comté, though politically annexed to Spain, were for the most part French in speech and culture, and that so long as they remained in enemy hands France was open to attack from the east. The term "a scientific frontier" belongs to the vocabulary of the nineteenth century, but the idea which it connotes inspired the policy of Louis and the work of Vauban, the great military engineer who perfected the defences of France on every front, and combined with the technical mastery of his craft the generous heart and wide vision of a patriot, a liberal, and a reformer. The War of Devolution, then, though aggressive, was not devoid of a purpose connected with the real interest of France. Turenne's campaign of 1667 gave his country a string of Flemish towns (Charleroi, Armentières, Tournai, Douai, Lille) which France retains to this day.

The French invasion of the Spanish Low Countries had one momentous consequence upon which Louis had not reckoned. It alarmed the Dutch. Swiftly composing its differences with England, the Dutch republic, under the leadership of John de Witt, a great civilian statesman, formed with England and Sweden a Triple Alliance (May, 1668), which, though short-lived, was sufficient to give a check to France and to induce Louis to evacuate Franche Comté (Treaty of Aix-la-Chapelle, 1668). To a vainglorious prince there was something particularly wounding in the reflection that a paltry republic of heretical merchants, which France had raised into life as a make-weight against a common enemy, should have the insolence to enter into a coalition against her. With England and Sweden Louis knew how to deal. They wanted money and could be bought. The Dutch were reserved for another fate. In an access of folly the French king determined to destroy the republicans of Amsterdam, who had given the first check to his military ambitions.

In this design Louis was now able to count upon the assistance of Charles II. As early as 1669 it was strongly held by a small and intimate circle in France and England that the king had been received into the Roman Church. The secret, being communicated to Madame, the king's sister, and consequently to Louis XIV, her brother-in-law, opened out large horizons of political and religious profit. A plot was hatched in which Madame, young, pretty, intelligent, and ardent, was assigned, or perhaps assumed, the leading rôle. The advantages of the French as opposed to the Dutch alliance were skilfully dangled before Charles. The elimination of the Dutch competition in commerce, the destruction of the Dutch military navy, the partition of Holland between England and France, the prospect of a royal army of foreign mercenaries to be stationed in the Netherlands, but to be available, if need be, for the protection of the crown against the Commons in England, and finally the restoration of the Catholic Church to its old place of authority on the island—these arguments, reinforced by the gift of a witty mistress, were instilled into the mind of the most recent royal convert by his enthusiastic sister. The plot succeeded. In 1670 two treaties were signed at Dover for a great Anglo-French attack upon the Dutch. Of these one (the Treaty of Madame) was secret, for it contained the religious compact. To ease his finances, to secure his monarchy, and to promote the Roman faith, Charles, the most charming and enlightened of men, was prepared to betray and ruin his Protestant ally and to endanger the parliamentary liberties of his country.

War is a series of surprises. By all the laws of probability the navies of England and the armies of France should have made short work of the small Dutch republic. But the expected did not happen. At sea the Dutch proved themselves a match for their English antagonists. On land they repelled the French from Amsterdam by flooding the country. The war which promised to be so short and so brilliant dragged on for six years (1672-8), widening out as wars are apt to do and revealing the sturdy spirit of resistance which the ambitions of France had evoked in the Teuton world. At the end of it the French obtained some part of their object, for they gained Franche Comté and a chain of towns on their north-eastern frontier (Treaty of Nimweguen, 1678-9), but the Dutch were unsubdued and more formidable than ever, for a revolution had overturned the republic and given power to a young prince of the house of Orange who, being married in 1677 to Mary, daughter of James, Duke of York, was afterwards destined, as William III of England, to be the soul of the European opposition to France.

Despite the favourable terms of the Peace of Nimweguen, that "French Peace" which the modern French historian finds good reason to applaud, the war presented many features which to a statesman more prudent than Louis XIV would have recommended a policy of moderation and restraint. The appearance of a French army on the Rhine had stirred up a great anti-French coalition in which the emperor and all Germany, save Bavaria, were leagued with Spain, Denmark, and the Dutch. Sweden, in whose famous valour Louis had placed the fullest confidence, was defeated in that decisive battle of Fehrbellin (1675), which first announced to Europe the tough metal in the Prussian soldier, and at once gave to the Great Elector of Brandenburg and to the Hohenzollern house of which he was the chief a position of pre-eminence in northern Germany. These were clear omens of coming trouble to France.

Louis, however, was not a man to take note of these gathering symptoms of European opposition. The military reforms of Louvois had given him a regular army of two hundred thousand strong, equipped with a regular commissariat, armed with the bayonet, and officered on the modern plan by professional soldiers. His navy, under the vigorous administration of Colbert, had grown from a squadron of fifteen to a fleet of two hundred, and though still having much to learn, had startled Europe, and more particularly England, by its full participation in the Dutch war. The work of expanding and consolidating the eastern frontier was therefore continued. Local courts, known as "Chambers of Reunion," were set up to decide upon the extent of the king's rights under the Treaty of Münster in Alsace, the three bishoprics, the Franche Comté, and, since the language of the guns was always ready to repair the silence of the law, the results of the antiquarian enquiry were satisfactory to Louis. The full sovereignty of Alsace was awarded to France and was completed by the military occupation of Strasburg

(September, 1681). From the brief war provoked by these high-handed proceedings Louis emerged with conspicuous success. The emperor, distracted by a Turkish invasion which pushed its way to the gates of Vienna, was in no position to add momentum to the operations of the Third Coalition; and the Truce of Regensburg (1684) left Louis in possession for twenty years of all the fruits (the Flanders forts, Luxemburg, Franche Comté, Alsace, Strasburg) of his long and connected endeavour to improve the eastern frontier of France. Here he should have stopped, for he had reached the climax of his fortune.

By this time the ambitions of Louis had given a serious shock to the public law of Europe as it had been fixed by the Treaty of Westphalia. Of that treaty France was a guarantor. By that treaty France was to an extraordinary extent a beneficiary. Nevertheless, to Louis the Treaty of Westphalia was altogether insufficient. He did not scruple to violate it, and with every fresh demonstration of his ambition alienated a friend and increased the muster of his enemies. First he alarmed Holland, then Germany, then Sweden. Finally he lost the friendship of England.

Ever since 1668 it had been one of the primary objects of French diplomacy to retain, if not the friendship, at least the neutrality, of the British. To that end money had been lavished on the crown, the court, the parliament, and even upon Presbyterian ministers. The policy was successful. Despite the national jealousy inspired by the spectacle of the amazing development of French naval and military power, England, led by Charles, remained at peace with France. The French ambassadors in London were, indeed, under no delusion as to the real feelings of the English people. From the first moment of Louis' invasion of the Spanish Netherlands the country was seized with panic, divined an enemy, and feared an invasion. Later, in August, 1677, Louis was informed by Barillon from London that the only friends of France in England were Charles II and his brother James, Duke of York. The earlier rivalry of Spain, the later rivalry of Holland, now seemed less formidable to the English people than the new military and commercial power of France. Yet with the help of French supplies, an expanding revenue from customs, and his own dexterity, Charles was able to surmount the formidable difficulties which the Whigs, led by the brilliant Earl of Shaftesbury, raised about his path. He saved his crown.

avoided war, and, defeating the movement to exclude his Catholi
brother from the succession, dissolved Parliament and broke th
Whigs. For the last four years of his reign he was able, thank
in part to the continued assistance of Louis, to govern Englan
without recourse to Parliament.

In a country still boiling with sectarian fury it was a grea
thing to have a king who brought so little heat and so muc
light to the handling of affairs as Charles II. His wit and charm
his easy manners and pleasant ways, his complete immunit
from all kinds of fanaticism, coupled with the play of his scien
tific curiosity, came like a cooling draught administered to
fevered patient. The open dissipations of his court were not in
compatible with spells of well-directed work. In many respect
his supple intelligence placed him far above the commo
standards of his time. Though he was compelled to acquiesce i
the persecuting measures of the Cavalier Parliament (1660-7), h
was in favour of religious toleration and excited the hostility o
his Parliaments by his endeavours to secure it by the use of hi
power to dispense with laws. Like Oliver Cromwell, he saw th
growing importance of overseas colonies and marine strength
The Navigation Laws passed under the Protectorate for the pur
pose of securing to the mother country a monopoly of the trad
with her colonies were during his reign worked up into a syster
of laws and regulations covering the whole field of colonial inter
course with the mother country.

A delicate sense of the drifts and eddies of public opinion, s
delicate as to be incompatible with true civil courage, kept hir
safe on his throne when a disclosure of his inner thoughts woul
have brought serious trouble. The country did not know, how
ever much it might suspect, that its constitutional king was a
heart an autocrat in politics and a Roman Catholic in belief. I
did not know that he was a pensionary of the French Crown
Charles kept silence. Even when Titus Oates was spreading mur
derous calumnies against his Catholic co-religionists he dine
with the villain and spoke no open word of reproach. It wa
not in his self-indulgent and circumspect character to take
chivalrous risk.

It would have required a stronger man than Charles II to stem
the tide of public interest in government which had been re
leased by the passions of the civil war. The nation was on it
feet, talking, disputing, reading news-letters, and watching the

Parliament men at their work. Marvell's letters to his constituents at Hull are symptomatic of a new age. So, too, was the development of the two party system, Whig and Tory, which first took a defined shape over the proposal to exclude the Duke of York (afterwards James II) from the throne on the ground of his religious faith. The country was strongly Protestant and parliamentary. Only the violent errors of Whig leadership, culminating in the support given to the mendacities of Titus Oates, gave to Charles the opportunity which he took with such brilliant address in 1681 of sending the Parliament about its business.

Charles died in 1685. James, an avowed and zealous Catholic, succeeded to the throne. His plan of action was to secure legal toleration for his co-religionists by packing Parliament with his supporters and by dispensing Catholics from the penalties to which they were subject by the law of the land. No policy either on its religious or on its constitutional side could be more repugnant to a Protestant and parliamentary country, more particularly since it became evident that its successful execution depended upon the support of France, of Ireland, and of a standing army, auxiliaries capable in the temper which then prevailed of ruining any cause with the English people.

James was almost as necessary to Louis as Louis to James, for the real alternative to James in England was not the Protestant Duke of Monmouth, whose ill-starred rising was crushed on Sedgemoor, but William of Orange, who had been married in 1677 to the Princess Mary, the Protestant daughter of the English king. To Louis, then, it was all-important that this Catholic king should be maintained upon the English throne and that his difficult and incalculable subjects should learn to bear his yoke with equanimity. So long as James was king of England there was no reason to fear that the English fleet would molest the West Indian colonies, which it had been the achievement of Colbert to develop, or an English army take part in continental operations against France. But William of Orange was of all France's enemies the most deadly and persistent, and the conjunction of England and Holland under his leadership was the contingency most likely to spell serious trouble for Louis XIV.

And it now happened that just when it was most important for the general success of French policy in Europe that France should show indulgence to her Protestant citizens, Louis revoked

the Edict of Nantes (1685). Though he desired to secure toleration for English Catholics, he withdrew the wise toleration which
his grandfather had accorded to French Protestants, prohibiting
their worship, proscribing their ministers, destroying their
churches, closing their schools, and so driving some two hundred
thousand of the best artificers of his kingdom into foreign lands,
there to create industries in competition with his own, and to
foment sentiments of enduring rancour against France. The best
excuse which can be made for this act of gratuitous folly is not
that it was counselled by Madame de Maintenon, the discreet,
elderly, and very pious lady to whom the king was secretly
married in 1683, but that it was popular with the clergy and
laity of France. The average Frenchman of the seventeenth century was apt to be at once orthodox in belief and anti-clerical in
policy. He was Gallican not Papal, Catholic not Protestant. There
was nothing which he feared so much as the renewal of the religious wars, which had broken so many homes, embittered so
many families, and left behind them a long train of poignant and
dividing memories. To the cool reasoner it must have been apparent that "the so-called Reformed Church" had, ever since
the days of Richelieu, ceased to present political dangers. It
possessed neither fortresses nor troops. It had been quiet during
the agitation of the Fronde. Its members served the state in the
army, the navy, and the magistrature, and had won for themselves an eminent place in the world of finance, commerce, and
industry. Yet so long as a million Huguenots lived in France
with their church councils and schools, their black-robed ministers and peculiar rites, the country felt uneasy. The sect was unpopular, had been dangerous once, and might, through the
attraction of clerical marriage, be dangerous again. Some envied
the Huguenot his money, others grudged his industry, others
were affronted by his rigour, and by the intolerance which he
showed to his Catholic neighbour in those regions in which the
reformed church had the upper hand. Why, it was asked, should
this obstinate and unreasonable sect, which repudiated a religion
which was good enough for the king of France, and belonged to
a Church which was shaped like a republic, be permitted to sustain its separate and unwelcome being in a Catholic and monarchical country? Year after year the Assembly of the Church
of France petitioned for the destruction of this foreign body.
Louis, who was not by nature intolerant, yielded to the pressure.

By a hundred differing forms of calculated cruelty and oppression it was sought to make the position of a Huguenot so intolerable as to drive him into the Roman Communion. The hateful policy was in a large measure successful. Huguenots, who had preserved their religion through twenty years of harassing but minor acts of persecution, went over in thousands when (1681-85) Louvois' dragoons were quartered in their homes, and pillage, murder, and rape became the price of continued loyalty to the faith of their fathers. When it was believed that the terror had done its work, that the resistance of these obstinate sectaries was broken, and that the conversion of a miserable remnant would be an easy undertaking, Louis revoked the Edict of Nantes. A paean of praise saluted the Christian hero who had at last, after so many vagaries, showed a true concern for the salvation of his soul and emulated the work of Constantine, Theodosius, and Charlemagne. "This," said Bossuet, the court preacher, "is the worthy achievement of your reign and its true character. Through you heresy is no more. God above has made this marvel." But however pleasing to French Catholics, the revocation of the Edict of Nantes was not the way to make James II popular in Puritan London.

The "glorious revolution" of 1688, which placed William III on the throne of England, was precipitated by the folly of James in attempting to force the Catholic religion upon his countrymen by unconstitutional methods. The revolution was glorious in that it was clement, and entailed no proscription of the vanquished party. Of land fighting the main part was in Ireland, and here the signal victory of the Boyne, followed up a year later *June 30 1690* by the surrender of Limerick, fastened the political dominion of Protestant England upon the Catholic Irish for two hundred and forty-two years, during which the long duel between France and England for colonial dominion was fought to an issue.

That England should have been able not only to effect this bloodless revolution, but to emerge all the stronger by reason of the triumph of parliamentary principles, was a result absolutely unexpected by Louis, and sharply opposed to the dominant political philosophy of the continent. France, had she exerted herself to do so, could have prevented William from landing at Torbay. But Louis, instead of using his army to make trouble for William in the Netherlands, sent it into the Palatinate, where it was effectually prevented from influencing the course of events. The explanation of this is that Louis counted upon the paralysis of England through a long drawn civil war, and looked with equanimity upon the prospect of his two principal antagonists, the Dutch and the English, being thus embroiled.

We need not be surprised that he was mistaken. The credentials of the Whig party in England, which made the revolution settlement, were not such as to inspire confidence in their moderation and restraint. In their struggle to exclude James from the Crown, the Whigs had stopped short of no extreme of factious violence. They had backed up the baseless and wicked calumnies of Titus Oates against the Catholics. They had given support to Monmouth's armed rebellion against James. Some of them had taken French money; but at the crisis of 1688, under the leadership of Halifax, the Trimmer, one of the great benefactors of the country, they listened to the voice of moderation. Louis could not have foreseen this, nor yet that the cold Dutch soldier-statesman, whom the Whigs had called in to save the state, would stamp upon the fires of party vengeance and succeed in the extraordinary task of making England a united, albeit a parliamentary, country.

On any comparison of man power the two countries which had now become combined under William III were immeasurably inferior to France. The population of England may have been five and a half million, of the Dutch Republic two and a half million, while the population of France was of the order of nineteen or twenty million. But in two respects an advantage lay with England. After the naval victory of La Hogue (1692) the English sailors established a definite superiority over the French marine, which had now lost the incomparable direction of the great Colbert. The second advantage was perhaps still more important. The form of government which England had secured at the Whig revolution was better adapted to stand financial stress and social change than the autocracy of France. Louis had discarded every constitutional check upon the royal power. He declined to summon the States-General. He confined the Parliaments to the exercise of their judicial functions. The government of the country was carried on by ministers and committees working with the king at the centre and in most provinces by intendants prefiguring the modern prefect. The fiscal privileges of the nobility, who were for the most part occupied at the front or attached to the court, were left unassailed, and despite the drain of incessant wars, and the vast authority enjoyed by the crown, nothing was done to remedy a system under which the main financial burdens of the state were borne by the poorest members of the community, while the contributions of the nobles and the clergy, who were by comparison wealthy, were wholly inadequate. An autocracy working in secret can endure only if it redresses social injustice. Failing to do this, and losing its initial momentum and efficiency with the death of the king's ablest minister and his own declining strength, the monarchy of Louis XIV left France as miserable as if victory had been exchanged for defeat.

But in 1689 the fabric of French government was the most imposing spectacle in Europe. Of English Parliaments it was mainly known that they were factious, capricious, venal, incapable, as it would appear, of steady direction. The fact that the revolution had transferred power from the crown into the hands of Parliament was interpreted as a sure sign of weakness by those who failed to perceive that Parliament would be governed for the next century and a half by a territorial and commercial aristocracy, which was neither inexperienced in affairs, nor careless of public interests, nor without the courage and sagacity which go to the making of statesmen. A parliamentary government was a new and untried thing. The Duke of Marlborough at Blenheim and Ramillies showed the world that such a government could conduct a European war, and put armies into the field which could rout the French in a fair fight. The admiration for English institutions which was so widely felt on the continent during the eighteenth century dates from the advertisement of these brilliant victories. The nation of civilians, which affirmed in the Bill of Rights that standing armies were illegal in time of peace, proved itself equal to all the demands of an exhausting war. In finance, banking, commerce, and the science and art of treasury control it stood far above its antagonists.

It was then with England no longer as a friendly rival but as an active enemy that Louis waged his next war for the expansion of France. It was a remarkable struggle, fought against great odds, continued for ten years (1688-97), marked by many victories, and yet ending in a serious check for France. It showed that Louis had taught Europe the art of progressive coalition, for the Triple Alliance had been succeeded by the League of Augsburg (1685), an imposing combination secretly supported by the Pope and comprising the Emperor and the Empire, Holland and Spain, Savoy, England, and Sweden. But it illustrated also the familiar truth that coalitions are rarely as effective in action as they are impressive on paper. The forces of the League experienced a humiliating series of defeats at the hands of the best armies led by the best generals then available in Europe. Catinat won Nice and overran Savoy. Luxemburg scored success after success over William III in the Netherlands. The Palatinate was twice subjected to a ruthless devastation, the memory of which is still among the causes of estrangement between French and German peoples. Nevertheless the Treaty of Ryswick, which closed the struggle, was a defeat for Louis. To win peace from his obstinate and unexhausted antagonists the French king was compelled to renounce his conquests, to accord to the Dutch the right of garrisoning the frontier towns of the Spanish Netherlands, to acknowledge the heretic king of England, and to consent that he should be succeeded by a heretic princess. In war, pitched battles do not decide everything. Ultimate success lies with that party to the controversy which can last the longest. That advantage, thanks to the steadfast Protestant mind of William III, lay with the first of the great European coalitions.

*Sept.,
1697*

BOOKS WHICH MAY BE CONSULTED

Macaulay : History of England. 1858-62.

Voltaire : Le Siècle de Louis XIV. 1753.

G. Hanotaux : Études historiques sur le XVIe et le XVIIe siècle en France. 1886.

D. Ogg : Europe in the Seventeenth Century. 1925.

D. Ogg : Louis XIV. Home University Library. 1933.

D. Ogg : England in the Reign of Charles II. 2 vols. 1934.

E. Lavisse : Histoire de France, Vol. VII.

P. Clement : Histoire de la Vie et de l'Administration de Colbert. 1846.

J. J. Jusserand : Instructions données aux ambassadeurs de France depuis les Traités de Westphalie. Angleterre.

CHAPTER XXI

THE SPANISH SUCCESSION

The Spanish Succession. The Partition Treaties. Opposition to the Partition in Austria and Spain. Louis accepts the undivided inheritance. The Grand Alliance. The English spirit. War of the Spanish Succession. Its character and duration. The Spanish " side-show." The Treaty of Utrecht. Marine supremacy passes to Britain. Jansenists and Jesuits in France. Pascal. The Bull Unigenitus. Continuance of the struggle in the eighteenth century. Decline of religious and dynastic motives. The seventeenth century. Spiritual hegemony of France.

MEANWHILE a question of vast general importance and affecting in particular the interests of the Dutch and English was hastening to a crisis. What was to become of the Spanish Empire on the death, so long expected and so long delayed, of Charles II, the imbecile invalid without hope of posterity, who ever since 1665 had been King of Spain? The idea that this was a question with respect to which the Spanish people might have a right to be consulted was foreign to the political philosophy of that age. A monarchy was still regarded as a family property, which could be devised by will or shared by agreement among the next of kin. And what a family property was this! The European possessions of the Spanish Habsburgs alone constituted a formidable empire, including, as they did, Milan, Naples, and Sicily, Sardinia, and the Balearic Islands, as well as the Spanish Netherlands and Spain itself. But the non-European dominions were even more imposing, the Philippines and the Canaries, Cuba, Mexico, Florida, California, and Panama, and save for the Guianas and Portuguese Brazil, the vast bulk of South America. Such an empire was too large for the peace of the world, too large for effective government. Its partition either under the will of the sovereign or by an amicable agreement concluded in advance by the interested parties was on all grounds to be desired as the only method of preserving Europe from a world war.

The possible claimants to the Spanish inheritance were in 1698 three young men, Philip, Duke of Anjou, the grandson of Louis XIV, Charles, the second son of Leopold II of Austria, and Joseph Ferdinand, the electoral prince of Bavaria, who was nephew to the King of Spain. Of these three the Bavarian, being the least formidable, was likely to be most acceptable to the interested powers and to offer the best guarantees for the preservation of the European balance.[1] Accordingly a Treaty of Partition was struck between France, England, and the Netherlands, which accorded to the young Prince of Bavaria the lion's share of the Spanish empire (Spain and the Indies) while providing for Austria and France substantial satisfaction from the remainder. These prudent arrangements were, however, frustrated in the following year by the unexpected death of the Bavarian. The problem had to be taken up anew and under far less favourable conditions.

So long as the Bavarian, a comparatively weak and uncontroversial figure, was alive it was possible that all the interested parties might be brought to accept a common plan; but with his death the problem became almost insoluble. An arrangement was, indeed, made satisfactory alike to Louis and the maritime powers. By the Second Treaty of Partition it was settled that the Netherlands should go to Austria (a capital point with the maritime powers), as well as Spain and the Indies, while France was to have Naples, Sicily, and Milan to be exchanged for Lorraine; and that Louis should have assented to such an arrangement is a singular illustration of his moderation at this period.

But unfortunately there were two powers, Spain and Austria, to whom the idea of partition on any condition was wholly inacceptable. It was natural that the king and the grandees of Spain should resent the idea of the dismemberment of the Spanish empire, but that Leopold of Austria, out of his desire for Milan, should reject the splendid terms offered him by the Second Treaty of Partition was a blunder only surpassed in the catalogue of costly Austrian follies by the ultimatum to Serbia of July, 1914. In face of these obstacles the wise policy of partition upon which William III and Louis XIV had expended great diplomatic ability was doomed to failure. When the Spanish king died in November, 1700, it was found that he had left a will bequeathing his undivided empire to Philip of France, with the provision that if the bequest was not accepted in its entirety the prize should be transferred to the Austrian Charles.

Louis could hardly have refused to take up the inheritance. It is true that he had only just signed the Second Treaty of Par-

[1] Genealogical Table D.

tition, which had awarded the heart of the Spanish empire to Austria; but Austria had not accepted that treaty, and England and Holland could not confidently be counted on to help France to enforce it. Had Louis refused the bequest to his grandson everything would have gone to Charles, and nobody can blame Louis if he shrank from acquiescing in the transference of the whole Spanish Succession to his Austrian rival. Had Austria been reasonable she could have had a magnificent accretion of power without a world war. Had Spain been prudent she could have escaped a foreign invasion at the cost of some outlying possessions. But since Austria and Spain would have nothing less than all, and since Spain rightly calculated that France would be more formidable as an enemy and more helpful as a friend than distant Austria, Louis found himself compelled, for fear of worse consequences, to accept the will. A Spanish cardinal controlling the death-bed of a royal half-wit had converted the French protagonist of partition into the shield and buckler of indivisible Spain.

Peace, henceforth, was difficult to preserve. Yet what made war inevitable was not so much the acceptance of the will by Louis as the new spirit of arrogant intemperance which the will created in his mind. At once he broke out into a series of wanton acts of aggression, exactly calculated to inflame the hostility of the maritime powers. He poured troops into the Spanish Netherlands, occupied the Dutch barrier towns, and compelled the Spaniards to make over to the French the *Asiento*, or right of trading in African slaves with the Spanish Indies. In face of such acts as these, English and Dutch felt that they must fight for their commercial existence. Even a Tory Parliament (February, 1701) invited King William to enter into negotiations with the Emperor and other powers to put a curb upon the French. In 1701, as again in 1793 and in 1914, the invasion of Belgium by a great power lit the flames of war in the spirit of the English peoples.

The foundations of the Grand Alliance, which fought the War of the Spanish Succession against France, were laid by the Duke of Marlborough, whom William wisely sent to The Hague to treat with Heinsius, the Grand Pensionary of Holland.

So practical were the aims of the Alliance, as originally defined, that after twelve years of costly strife they were substantially secured in the Treaty of Utrecht (1713). William was content that Philip should rule in Spain and the Indies so long as the Netherlands, Italy, and the Mediterranean islands passed from Spanish into Austrian hands. For this there were reasons grounded upon the maritime needs of the English and Dutch peoples. Unlike France, Austria was neither a naval danger nor a commercial rival. The merchants of London and Amsterdam could therefore safely trust her with possessions which lay along the great trade routes to the Baltic and the Levant.

The death of William III, who for hard upon a generation had been the soul of every European enterprise against France, made no difference to English policy. All his large designs—the Grand Alliance, the war against France, the capture of naval bases in the Mediterranean, the Protestant succession—were, as Professor Trevelyan reminds us, taken up by Queen Anne, the dull, devout, high church daughter of James II, who by a freak of fortune has given her name to a brilliant age. Though the Press had been freed in 1695 and party spirit ran fierce and high, there was enough of the mediatorial spirit in English politics to work parliamentary institutions. By a happy innovation, the germ of a great Civil Service, the Treasury experts continued from ministry to ministry. Whigs and Tories in turn advanced the welfare of the country. The Whigs carried through the Union with Scotland. The Tories passed the Act of Settlement which eventually brought the Protestant Electors of Hanover to the throne. The Whigs financed the victorious war, the Tories coming into full power in 1710 made the welcome peace. Fundamentally, for the worst sore was healed by a grant of toleration to the dissenters in 1689, the country was at one. The popularity of Marlborough with the queen, the skill of his diplomacy, the brilliance of his victories, coupled with the exasperation caused in every English Protestant heart when Louis recognized the Old Pretender as King James III, were causes sufficient to maintain the warlike spirit of the country. Security, commerce, the Protestant succession, were felt to be at stake. If the squires winced at the four shilling land-tax, which was the spine of Godolphin's war finance, they paid up to the end notwithstanding. Such was the English spirit. For the Dutch, robbed of their cherished barrier towns in the Spanish Netherlands, the war was a matter of life and death.

War in the later part of the seventeenth century was not the devastating curse which science and conscription have now combined to make it. It was waged by small mercenary armies, hibernating for half the year, and during the short campaigning season, no longer as in the Thirty Years' War living upon the country, but supplied by a regular commissariat service. Military movements were apt to be slow and deliberate, as befitted an age when even admirals wore full-bottomed wigs and methodical siege warfare constituted the most important part of military science. Commanders, heedful of the difficulty of replenishing their armies with fresh recruits, sought rather to avoid than to invite decisive encounters. Marlborough was exceptional. The English Prince Charming, who, but for the obstructions of the Dutch, could have driven the French from Flanders in the first two years of the war, was as anxious to manoeuvre his opponent into action as his opponent was in general desirous of avoiding it.

His hammer blows were decisive. After Blenheim and Ramil- *1704* lies the allies could have made a peace with Louis securing to *1706* them all the original war aims of the Grand Alliance. Blenheim had swept the French out of Bavaria; Ramillies had placed most of Flanders at Marlborough's feet. The brilliant Eugène, with some assistance from Victor Amadeus of Savoy, had established the supremacy of Austrian arms in northern Italy. Yet peace was delayed for seven years.

The cause of this needless prolongation of the war is ultimately to be traced to the beauty and convenience of Lisbon harbour as a port of call and repair for English vessels bound upon Mediter- ranean errands. England in quest of Mediterranean ports had need of the Portuguese alliance, but how could Portugal, a small power, be expected to enter the lists against France unless the Austrian candidate would come to Spain, rally his supporters, and with Dutch, English, and Portuguese support evict the Frenchman and establish himself in Madrid? In the Methuen Treaties of 1703, Peter II of Portugal insisted, as a condition of his alliance with England, that Charles, suitably supported by the allies, should make a bid for the Spanish throne. The bargain was struck. The war aims of the allies were enlarged to include the conquest of Spain for Charles, and an unsuccessful Peninsular War, extending over the best part of a decade, was the price by which England obtained the use of Lisbon harbour, without which the Rock of Gibraltar could not have been held or Port Mahon (in Minorca) wrested from Spain.

It was only by slow and reluctant stages that English politicians were brought to see that the Spanish "side-show" was a forlorn adventure, and that the proudest nation in Europe would never accept an Austrian sovereign imposed on them by odious northern heretics and even more repulsive Portuguese. The Catalans, indeed, inflamed by hatred of Castile, and encouraged by Peterborough's brilliant capture of Barcelona, declared for the Austrian Archduke, but Catalonia has never been an integral part of Spain. In language, in customs, in temper, this maritime province of Aragon had little in common with the inhabitants of the interior plateau. It was no passport to the affections of the Spanish people that Charles should have won the mercurial sympathies of the Catalans. The great bulk of the Spanish people was from the first, and throughout, favourable to the claims of Philip V.

The Austrian hegemony in Italy, which was not finally shaken until the days of Cavour and Garibaldi, dates from the Treaty of Utrecht (1713), which closed the war of the Spanish Succession. The Emperor, foiled of his designs in Spain, then received compensation in Lombardy, Sardinia, and Naples. The predominance in Italian affairs, which had belonged to Spain ever since the days of Charles V, now passed to a Teutonic government whose solid gifts of order and efficiency were unsweetened by qualities likely to engage the sympathies of a Latin people. It is curious to think of the extent to which the fate of Italy depended upon the brains of two Englishmen, Godolphin the financier and Marlborough the soldier, without whom the allied cause, despite all the military science of Prince Eugène, could never have prevailed.

For the greater convenience of the maritime powers the Emperor was required to rule in the Spanish Netherlands, in which the Dutch were accorded a line of barrier fortresses, a pledge that this valuable province would be defended against France, not by the Dutch alone, but also by one of the great continental monarchies.

Spain, the first prize of the competition, went to Louis. Philip V, who during the war had been twice ejected from Madrid and twice restored, lived to found a dynasty of Spanish Bourbons who survived the French Revolution and the empire, and, though now in exile, still carry the hopes of a royalist Spain. Though the crowns of Spain and France were finally separated,

1935

the close political association of the two Bourbon powers was
a feature of the political life of the next century, which came
into special prominence when Spain and France assisted the
American colonies to throw off the British yoke. The capitulation of the British at Yorktown was the answer to Blenheim and *1781*
Ramillies and the sequence of those victories of Almanza and *1707*
Brihuega by which Berwick and Vendôme planted French *1710*
rule south of the Pyrenees.

The long reign of Louis XIV did not, therefore, despite the
distress of the population during its concluding years, end in
failure. The medal "*clausa Germanis Gallia*" was justified; so,
too, though in a less literal sense, was that other saying of the
Sun King, "Henceforth there are no Pyrenees." That France was
free of invasion until the days of Napoleon may in part be
ascribed to the improvements in her eastern defences which were
effected in the king's early manhood and successfully retained in
the end.

England emerged from the struggle having secured not only
the original war aims of William III, but one advantage which
could not have been predicted. In her long war partnership with
the Dutch she had made the sea her special province, while the
bulk of the land armies who fought under Marlborough were
provided by her allies. As the war proceeded the English navy
grew and the Dutch navy, by comparison, declined. The marine
supremacy, which had been evenly divided between the two
nations in the middle of the seventeenth century, was by the end
of the war of the Spanish Succession definitely secured by
England. Meanwhile Britain had acquired new stations and
centres of power and colonization in the old world and in the
new, Gibraltar and Port Mahon, Newfoundland and Nova
Scotia. It was idle for the French, the balance of naval power
being what it was in 1713, to contest these acquisitions. They
passed to England under the Treaty of Utrecht, together with
the treasured right, known as the *Asiento*, of trading African
slaves (and incidentally other goods as well) to the Spanish Indies.

Though the four shilling land-tax was bitterly grudged by the
squires, England stood the strain of the war better than any
other belligerent. Expanding overseas commerce provided the
atmosphere of confidence in which individuals may lend and
governments may borrow. The Bank of England, the National
Debt, the exact practice of the Treasury, enabled England to

finance her allies. A European coalition, as in two other more recent war periods, was sustained by the might of British finance.

It was a further note of power that England was able to obtain from Louis XIV an acknowledgment of the Protestant Succession in the Hanoverian House.[1] In his last hours the aged persecutor of the Huguenots was compelled thus to salute the heretic city of London, where nothing was so greatly apprehended for its effect upon the Funds as a violent reopening of the old quarrel between Catholic and Protestant in England.

The suppression of the Protestants in 1685, while greatly impoverishing the religious life of France, failed to reduce it to a dead uniformity. Though the Jesuit had gained a victory and exercised a complete mastery over the court, he was not alone in the field. Within the Catholic Church itself, a movement drawing its nutriment from the same moral roots and, in part, from the same theological authority as Puritanism, challenged the fashionable theology of Versailles and powerfully helped in the first half of the eighteenth century to educate a political opposition to the crown. The Jansenists drew their name from Jansen, Bishop of Ypres (1583-1638), the author of three folio volumes on St. Augustine, which were condemned by the Pope in 1642. Few have read the learned work of this Catholic Dutchman; fewer still could have predicted that from such an unlikely source a stream of spiritual energy would descend upon France and there fertilize and refresh some of the finest religious natures of the age. It appears to be a long road from the pedantry of Jansen to the eloquence of Arnauld, the exquisite irony of Pascal, and the finished and contemplative beauty of Racine. Yet Arnauld, Pascal, and Racine were flowers from the same Augustinian stem, nourished upon the doctrine of Grace, which Martin Luther had found in Augustine, and by the light of which many had been brought to a belief in predestination, to an intimate personal piety, and to a repudiation of all easy and superficial ways of attaining salvation.

The bridge between the Dutch bishop and religious people in France was supplied by the appearance in 1643 of a moral treatise written by a young French priest against the notion that frequent Communion could atone for persistent ill living. Sincere natures were charmed by Antoine Arnauld's *De la Fréquente*

[1] Genealogical Table E.

Communion. Appearing in an age of widespread compliance with profligacy, this burning outburst of devotional eloquence represented the recoil of the Christian conscience from the mundane teaching of Jesuit confessors, who, in their endeavour to reclaim all sorts and conditions of men for the faith, sweetened the taste of religion to the palate of the worldling. An austere form of Catholic piety had long flourished in certain religious communities, notably in the nunnery of Port Royal, near Versailles, and was common among the grave magisterial families of the capital. To such *De la Fréquente* rang like a call to battle against the forces of laxity and vice.

The Jansenists, then, were the Puritans of the French Catholic Church. In beauty and integrity of character, as well as in a stern ardour of principle, perceptible in the rarest manifestations of the Latin genius from Lucretius to Condorcet, the Jansenists offered in their lives, as well as in their writings, an eloquent rebuke to a profligate age. Some went to great extremes. They condemned poetry and art, and preferred the melancholy decay of autumn to the vital exuberance of spring. All desired to return to the conditions of the Primitive Church and feared the onward march of science. To the pliant Jesuit, conscious that the Church could live only by adapting its teaching to the changing conditions of a changing world, the rigorous Jansenist appeared to represent a dangerous and impracticable sectarianism. The Jansenist thought the Jesuit too lax; the Jesuit thought the Jansenist too narrow. The one held that mankind would never be led up to the throne of God by a fierce and inhospitable virtue; the other that God would never accept a politic compact with vice. The one strove to make the way to heaven easy and accessible to the many; the other maintained that it must always be difficult and confined to the few.

The clash of opinion gave rise to Pascal's *Provincial Letters* (1656-7). In this famous controversial pamphlet every resource of light irony and passionate dialectic was deployed against the system of casuistry by which the Jesuits were said to obscure the plain distinction between right and wrong. The manifesto was the more important by reason of the fact that the author was not a professed theologian, but a mathematical genius, of amazing precocity and fertility of invention, who united the clarity and force of a first-class scientific mind with the exquisite scruples and sensibilities of a saintly and enthusiastic invalid. Feeling

deeply (for he had experienced two conversions) and writing
with an ease and simplicity which cleansed French prose of its
affectations, Pascal drew a great issue of moral theology out of
its hiding place among the folios and confessionals into the open
light of day, and exposed it with a merciless clarity to the view
of all.

The Jesuit has never quite outlived the force of his assault
and if the epithet Jesuitical still survives in common speech, as
denoting a subtlety fringing on fraud, the fact is largely to be
attributed to the *Provincial Letters*, which, while they gave to
Jansenism a fuller sweep and influence among the moral and
intellectual movements of the age, fixed upon the Jesuit Order
the stigma of debasing the moral currency of Christendom.

It was the Jesuit, however, and not the Jansenist, who during
the long reign of Louis XIV stood upon the steps of the throne,
and helped to mould the policy of the state. The Jesuits were
the king's friends. The Jansenists, from an early and unfortunate
association with some prominent members of the Fronde, were
marked out for his distrust. It was a Jesuit victory when, in
1653, five propositions doubtfully alleged to be contained in
Jansen's *Augustinus* were condemned by Pope Innocent X, and,
again, a Jesuit victory when, in 1661, the *Provincial Letters* were
burnt by the common hangman. Later on, in 1669, the Jansenists
made their peace with the Pope, and enjoyed a period of relative
immunity from persecution. But they were still without popularity or political influence. In the stiffly fought quarrel between
Louis XIV and Innocent XI, which developed out of the king's
claim to the temporalities of vacant bishoprics, the Jansenists to
their honour sided with the Roman Curia in its resistance to an
inexcusable abuse of the royal prerogative. This was the unpopular side. The tide of national feeling in France ran strongly
with the king in his defence of the liberties of the Gallican
Church against ultramontane interference.

The importance of Jansenism as a political influence was yet
to come. The concluding years of the king's life were marked
by a deep shadow of disaster abroad and gloomy piety at home.
Ever since Colbert's death the finances had been in disorder. The
short-term loans which had been issued to finance the war gave
way to a system of indirect borrowing, and this in turn to the
rise of a new class of middlemen, who defrauded the state, and
introduced a fresh poison into the atmosphere of the Court.

Louis was not a religious man, but he was deeply superstitious. To appease the wrath of the Deity, and to reverse the ill-fortune of his arms, he resolved upon a fresh attack on heretical opinion. He had already broken the Protestants. He was now prepared to listen to the advice of his Jesuit confessor, and to take steps against the Jansenists. The extraordinary brutality with which the campaign was conducted forms a bad page in the history of religious intolerance. The nuns of Port Royal des Champs were expelled, their convent pulled down, their cemetery violated. A French version of the New Testament, published in 1671, with an elaborate commentary by Pasquier Quesnel, a prominent member of the Jansenist party, was singled out to be the object of a combined attack, and since nothing was easier for a Jesuit than to find heresies in the book of an enemy, or to procure their condemnation in Rome, the work of the Jansenist leader was made to incur the censure of the Pope. Against the protest of fifteen bishops and with the lively opposition of the Parliament of Paris, the Bull *Unigenitus* found 101 heresies in a book which most readers regarded as a monument of evangelical piety laboriously erected by a Christian saint.

It was now the turn of the Jansenists to march with the Gallicans against ultramontane pretensions, an alliance which brought legal self-sufficiency and patriotic pride to the assistance of angular virtue. For one Frenchman whose religious beliefs were affected by the Jansenists, there were ten who resented the interference of the Pope, or were jealous of the power of the Company of Jesus. A struggle developed after the death of Louis XIV in which a great body of feeling and opinion, part Jansenist, but more largely Gallican, was arrayed under the leadership of the Parliament of Paris and with the support of twelve Provincial Parliaments, against the alliance of the Crown and the Jesuit Order. The struggle was protracted and violent, raising during its progress almost every political idea which afterwards led to the establishment of democratic government in France. Long before the appearance of Rousseau's *Social Contract* in 1762, the contest between the Crown and the Parliament of Paris, which had for its origin the papal condemnation of a Jansenist treatise, had familiarized the French people with a conception of constitutional government and of popular sovereignty. When the Jesuits were expelled from France in 1764 the stage was cleared for the movements which led to the French Revolution, and to that marked eclipse of papal authority and prestige which is one of the special notes of the revolutionary age.

In history everything is continuous. Yet the Peace of Utrecht may conveniently be taken as marking a point after which the religious and dynastic motives, which had previously played so large a part in the moulding of policy, sensibly declined in importance, while their place is taken by the struggle for colonies and markets. The long duel between England and France for colonial power which distinguishes the eighteenth century had not in it a particle either of religious or of dynastic interest. A new class had come to the front, which cared for none of these things, and was now sufficiently powerful to influence the policy of States.

By this time, too, science was swiftly coming into its own, largely in response to the material needs of a developing civilization. The mediaeval university, being the intellectual organ of the Catholic Church, was confined within the rigid limits of ecclesiastical orthodoxy. Reverence for authority excluded free investigation. The sacred texts of the Bible, the works hardly less dominant of Aristotle, were held to contain all that it was necessary to know, and all that it was safe to believe. What was present in these canonical writings was true, what was absent was unimportant, what conflicted was false. When at the beginning of the seventeenth century Kircher invited a brother Jesuit to look through his telescope at the newly discovered spots on the sun, the professor replied, "My son, it is useless. I have read Aristotle through twice, and have not found anything about spots on the sun. There are no spots on the sun." It was therefore heresy to maintain the Copernican theory of the planets, heresy to deny the creation of the Universe some four thousand years before Christ, heresy to frustrate the bodily resurrection by the destruction of a corpse. Such were the leaden inhibitions which shackled the learning of the mediaeval Faculties.

The world was wider than the universities. Sailors steering by the stars or marking the deviations of the compass, marine engineers reckoning with the tides, miners grappling with asphyxiation from gas or water below the ground, gunsmiths concerned for the durability of their muskets or culverins, built up by degrees a body of knowledge, part technical, part scientific, which lay far outside the university curriculum and was quite unaffected by university prepossessions. Navigation called for astronomy, led on to optics, and through the compass invited the study of magnetism. To frame tables of longitude it was necessary to ascertain the laws of the moon's movement; the determination of latitude implied a chart of the heavenly bodies. In view of the secular struggle between land and sea in the Netherlands it was natural that the first scientific chronology of the tides (1590) should be the work of Stevin, the Dutch engineer. As the art of warfare came increasingly to depend upon artillery, the mining of iron and copper received a fresh impetus with consequences of ever widening importance.

Mining is the prolific parent of science and technology. As early as the seventeenth century it was realized that an educated mining engineer must know triangulation and Euclidian geometry, the use of the compass, and the construction of apparatus for ventilation and pumping. Problems of aerostatics, of hydrodynamics, of mechanics, imposed themselves upon him. Alike the safety of the miner and the yield of the mine depended upon the laws of physical science.

Hardly less important was the train of scientific thought and discovery, which was opened out by the new developments in the art of war. As early as 1537 Tartaglia was at work upon the trajectory of the flight of a bullet. The most profound problems of physics were suggested by ballistics, the resistance of the air to a ball passing through it, the trajectory of a ball through a vacuum, the free fall of bodies under the influence of gravity. It is significant that Galileo opens his mathematical demonstrations with a compliment to the arsenal of Florence, the scene of so much activity and the storehouse of so much material for the scientific mind.

Meanwhile the strength of the ancient buttresses against the new knowledge had been weakened by the religious and political convulsions of the age. Europe was no longer undivided in faith. Monarchy was no longer unchallenged. The revolutionary and exciting discovery of the true nature of the earth's crust had created a temper favourable to intellectual innovations and contemptuous of the scholastic tradition. Intellectual life of the higher sort was no longer confined to the universities, but found organs appropriate to its needs in bodies like the Accademia del Cimente in Florence or the Royal Society in England, both founded in the middle of the seventeenth century and pledged to discovery and experiment. " Provare e reprovare," the motto of the Florentines, " Nullius in verba," the motto of the Englishmen, showed that the true spirit of science, which had been lost to Europe since the decline of the Greek city republics, was now again coming into its own among the Latin and Teutonic nations.

The seventeenth century witnessed the production of *Hamlet* and *Tartuffe*, of *Paradise Lost* and of Newton's *Principia*. It was the age of Rembrandt and Rubens, of Van Dyck and Hobbema, of Ruysdael and Franz Hals. It heard the first notes of Italian opera, the first strains of Purcell's music and of the Stradivarius violin. It gave the compass and the barometer to the mariner, the telescope and the microscope to the man of science, quinine and the thermometer to the physician, the shot gun to the sportsman. The comfort of daily life was enriched by the invention of the watch and the clock, and gluttony was robbed of half its grossness by the popularization of the fork. It was an age of growing wealth and of an expanding international trade in luxuries. The century of the Puritans and the Jansenists was marked by the discovery of ices and champagne, by the yet more beneficial importation of tea and coffee, and by the introduction of wax candles, the most beautiful of all forms of illumination, into the gorgeous saloons of Versailles. The first formal gardener, the first statistician, the first woman to pursue a professional career on the stage, belong to the later half of the seventeenth century. Yet the age which manifested its energy in these and many other happy ways, such as street lighting, and marine insurance, and the London penny post, was, despite its complex and advancing civilization, a period of almost uninterrupted war. In the policies which provoked war, and in the settlements by which quarrels were composed, little account was taken of public feeling. Democracy was uneducated and unorganized. The newspaper press was in its infancy. After the troubles of the Fronde and the Great Rebellion, the continent of Europe turned as if for safety to governments which became in increasing measure autocratic. In the science and art of hereditary despotism, Louis XIV set an example which was too dazzling for Scandinavia or Germany to resist. Nevertheless, despite everlasting war, the Europe of the seventeenth century held together. The sense of a common civilization and of a common European interest in the maintenance of a balance of power was far too strong to be obliterated by the summer activities of small heterogeneous and mercenary armies. Nine great diplomatic congresses, beginning with Westphalia and ending with Utrecht, attested the growing power of international action, and the passing away of that stage of European history when the office of universal mediator was among Christian people by common consent acknowledged to belong to the Pope.

It is also to be remarked that the wars against France, which fill the reign of Louis XIV, were in no sense waged in a spirit antagonistic to French culture. The intellectual and social prestige of the French monarchy, so far from being lowered in the eyes of its adversaries by the martial ambitions of Louis XIV, received from them an added lustre. French books were not the less read, French science not the less honoured, French fashions not the less followed, because half Europe was coalesced against the French monarchy. French civilization, illustrated by the brilliance and learning of its authors, ruled supreme and gave the law to every social group which aspired to the faintest tincture of culture, from the Russian border to the Atlantic Ocean. Nothing more clearly marks the distinction between the monarchical wars of this age and the national struggles of our own time than the continued spiritual hegemony of France, despite the bitter political opposition provoked by the domineering ambitions of her sovereign.

BOOKS WHICH MAY BE CONSULTED

Macaulay : History of England. 1858-62.

G. M. Trevelyan : England under Queen Anne. 1932-4.

J. R. Seeley : Growth of British Policy. 2 vols. 1895.

E. Lavisse : Histoire de France, Vol. VIII.

W. Coxe : House of Austria. 1847.

Winston Churchill : Life of Marlborough. 1934.

C. T. Atkinson : Marlborough and the Rise of the British Army. 1921.

Sainte-Beuve : Histoire du Port Royal. 5 vols. 1840-59.

E. Boutroux : Pascal. Tr. E. M. Creak. 1902.

Von Noorden : Europäische Geschichte im 18 Jahrhundert. Der Spanische Erbfolge Krieg. 1870-82.

D Ogg : Europe in the Seventeenth Century. 1925.

CHAPTER XXII

THE EIGHTEENTH CENTURY IN ENGLAND AND FRANCE

Prestige of England after 1714. John Locke. Voltaire. Montesquieu. The character of French philosophy. The physiocrats. English government in the eighteenth century. The age of George II. The disorders of France. Obstacles to reform.

THE English revolution of 1688, followed and confirmed by the accession of the Hanoverian dynasty, exercised a great influence on European thought. The spectacle of a revolution accomplished without bloodshed and unattended by any of those evils which were thought to be essential to popular government since the unfortunate upheavals of 1648, of a revolution resulting in such palpable benefits as religious toleration, the freedom of the press and parliamentary government, created a very general feeling of surprise and admiration. England, despite her revolution, had emerged richer and stronger than ever. On land and sea she had been the dominating spirit of the great alliance which had given check to Louis XIV. She could wage war and make peace and carry through the delicate operations of a change of dynasty without inner convulsion. Moreover, she had immensely strengthened her domestic position by her union with Scotland in 1707.

If ever a philosophy had been vindicated by events it was the Whig philosophy which lay behind the English revolution. John Locke was its great oracle. All the quintessential thought of the age of enlightenment is to be found in the writings of this humane and sober Oxonian doctor, the theory that ideas are not innate but reflected from the report of the senses (*Essay on Human Understanding*, 1690), the theory that civil government is founded on the consent of the governed, the view that the right to private property is based on labour, the doctrine of religious toleration, and of a rational education of the young. From Locke and his great scientific contemporary Isaac Newton, as also in a lesser degree from Henry St. John, Lord Bolingbroke, a body of rationalizing thought passed into France, where it was taken up, commented on and developed until, in its light, most of the established institutions of the country appeared to be shabby, outworn, and indefensible.

The man who was principally responsible for popularizing the new English ideas in France was a writer, so active, brilliant, long-lived, and influential, that he made himself the first figure in Europe. Voltaire, smarting from the tyranny and inequality which prevailed in his own country, for he had been thrown into the Bastille without trial for challenging a nobleman, came to England in 1726, and lived there till 1729. Here he was confronted with the astounding sight of a free, animated, and cultured people. He was introduced to Pope, read Addison and Swift, Bacon and Locke, Newton and Shakespeare. In his *Lettres sur les Anglais*, published in 1733, he explained to his compatriots the lineaments of this happy and surprising society, where a man was free to say or publish what he liked, where there was no torture or arbitrary imprisonment, where religious sectaries of all kinds were permitted to flourish, and among them a religious sect called the Quakers, who were so courageous as to denounce war as unchristian. "An Englishman," he writes, "goes to heaven by the road he pleases. There are no arbitrary taxes. A nobleman or a priest is not exempt from paying certain taxes. The peasant eats white bread and is well clothed, and is not afraid of adding to his hoard for fear that the taxes may be raised next year." A little later (1729-31) another great Frenchman came to England to study these instructive islanders. Montesquieu's report was no less enthusiastic. "England," he writes in his *Travel Notes*, "is the freest country in the world. I make exception of no republic. And I call it free because the sovereign, whose person is controlled and limited, is unable to inflict any imaginable harm on anyone." In the *Esprit des Lois* (1748), a philosophy of history which achieved a vast popularity and exercised a profound influence, he laid down (erroneously) that the true secret of English liberty consisted in the separation of the judicial, executive and legislative powers.

A leading feature of the movement of thought so inaugurated in France was its active concern for the regeneration of society. The niceties of metaphysical speculation did not appeal to the clear, practical mind of Voltaire, or, indeed, to any of the French thinkers of the Voltairian age. The metaphysic of Locke and of his French disciple Condillac was a sufficient instrument for their purpose, which was to apply the human reason, coolly and dispassionately, without theological predilections and restraints, to the removal of the intellectual detritus of the middle ages and to the amendment of man's estate. Accordingly there grew up in France a body of philosophical and humanitarian literature, of pamphlets and histories, philosophical and educational treatises, tragedies and comedies, culminating in a great encyclopedia in thirty-four volumes (1751-72) which rendered not only to France, but to all Europe, the incomparable service of attacking all that was cruel, all that was superstitious, all that was obsolete, unequal and unjust in the constitution of European society, and in the fabric of its religious and social beliefs. Some writers were frankly and blatantly irreligious. Voltaire and Rousseau, the most prominent of all, were anti-clerical deists.

This literature of opposition, passing into other countries through the medium of the French language, which had superseded Latin as the *lingua franca* of intellectual Europe, exercised an effect not the less important by reason of the fact that no European country save England was then ripe for parliamentary institutions. The atmosphere of Voltaire was breathed in the autocratic courts of Berlin and Vienna, St. Petersburg and Madrid. It was the age of enlightened despots. In the eyes of Frederick II of Prussia, of Catherine II of Russia, and of Joseph II of Austria, all that was needful to the improvement and elevation of society could be achieved by the paternal conduct of an autocratic ruler.

It was not, then, the advocacy of democratic government which gave to the message of the French philosophers its wide and commanding appeal. Voltaire was no democrat. What mattered to him and others was not the control of the levers of government, but freedom in all its shapes, freedom to think, to speak, to write, to act. Liberty was the universal remedy, the necessary mainspring of all progress, for given liberty all else would follow, the triumph of reason, the end of persecution, the disappearance of the superstitions of rival churches which obscured the face of that common religion which was believed to be natural to mankind. The prescription was valid throughout the world. It was a principle widely, though not universally, accepted among French thinkers that human nature was all of a piece in every age and every clime. How different the past was from the present was not clearly perceived, despite the great historical monuments of Voltaire and Gibbon, until the Waverley Novels had given to a later generation an imaginative vision of societies very different from their own.

The general trend of the French intellect in the eighteenth century was abstract, logical, cosmopolitan, much influenced by the exciting novelties of science and by the thought of the large perspectives of happiness for man which were expected to follow from the unimpeded application of common sense.

The fierce anti-clericalism of the French philosophers of the eighteenth century, like the militant atheism of the Russian Bolsheviks, sprang from the conviction that a tyrannical and obscurantist hierarchy stood straight in the path of intellectual and social progress. There can be little doubt that Voltaire, by assailing its manifest defects, improved the quality of French Christianity; or that the critical work of the philosophers, though often open to the charge of shallowness and unfairness, was amply justified by the very serious depravation which had come over the French Church. But the great objects aimed at by the French philosophical school were not negative but positive. Of these, many are now so fully secured in the institutions of the more enlightened parts of Europe that books which first issued from the printing press with the force of a revelation appear to the modern reader to be full of theories which it is worth no one's while to discuss. But there is one quality in this great body of French literature which retains its peculiar freshness and charm, and helps us to understand the spell which it cast upon the more intelligent and public-spirited of our forefathers. The literature of the *Aufklärung*, as the Germans call it, is the literature of confidence and hope.

If the philosophers had lost their belief in the doctrine of the churches, they had acquired a faith in the dignity and perfectibility of man. A great surge of optimism sweeps through the French political literature of the eighteenth century. A large number of intelligent people in the most intelligent country of Europe believed that if only the rubbish of the Gothic ages could be swept away with a strong broom, man, whose nature was good and susceptible of infinite improvement, would march from strength to strength. "If laws are good," said Diderot, "morals are good." Nobody was disposed to place limits upon the power of legislation to improve human nature indefinitely.

"It is the good legislator," says Helvetius, "who makes the good citizen."

Part of this sanguine literature was devoted to a criticism of those economic principles of state regulation which France had inherited from Colbert. The physiocrats were believers in the power of Nature, if left to herself, to bring men on to levels of prosperity not to be dreamed of under a régime of local or national restrictions. This doctrine, which had great influence, contained a profound fallacy and an important truth. The French economists held the theory that land was the sole source of wealth, and consequently that the needs of the state should be met by a single tax on agricultural values. That is a fallacy: for land is only one among many sources of wealth, and no one tax, however equitable, will meet the legitimate needs of a state. But they saw the important truth that all trade is an exchange of goods and services, and that the artificial obstructions placed by states upon the passage of wealth from one locality to another, or from one state to another, are injurious to prosperity. In their own country the doctrines of the physiocrats led during the revolution to the abolition of the internal customs duties in France, the ill effects of which were so graphically described by our observant English traveller Arthur Young. In Britain their teaching, coming from Quesnay, the physician of Louis XV, to Adam Smith, the famous Glasgow professor, led to results even more important and eventually to the adoption of that system of free trade, which during the century of our greatest prosperity and the years of our sternest trial was found to serve us well.

The literature which has so far been touched upon was marked by the qualities of optimism and rationality. But there was one powerful voice, more influential perhaps in the long run than any of that age, which sounded a different note. Jean Jacques Rousseau of Geneva was neither a philosopher nor a materialist, but a visionary. Though his intellect was pellucid, it was fed from the deep springs of his natural instincts and romantic emotions. He did not believe in progress or in the subdivision of labour or in any mechanical or material method of improving the lot of man, but finding the world full of cruelty, misery, and waste, and the vaunted civilization of Europe a mass of corruption and tyranny, set himself to draw the outline of a society in which a good man could live. That is

1712-78

the purpose of the *Contrat Social* (1762), which struck France with the force of a new gospel.

Rousseau's sovereign remedy for human ills is very simple. It is the application of virtue. The good state is one in which every member (duly educated for the civic life) contracts to conform his will to the general good. Only a society of virtuous citizens, each agreeing to do to others as he would be done by and spontaneously consenting to general laws framed not for the furtherance of particular interests but for the common advantage, could be called good. Such is the essence of Rousseau's political doctrine. The good state is based not on force nor on greed, but on the virtuous will of all its members.

The book worked like an enchantment. It was brief, eloquent, telling. The opening sentence alone, "Man is born free but is everywhere in chains," was a challenge to civilization. What again could be more seductive to the poor and the downcast than the vision of a society founded on the general will? Rivers of revolutionary sentiment were released by this single phrase. Yet it was too often forgotten that in Rousseau's mind the sovereignty of the general will was nothing else but the rule of virtue herself.

It has been said of Rousseau by Mme. de Staël that "he inflamed everything but discovered nothing." The phrase "he inflamed everything" points to an important truth, for to an astonishing degree he set France aglow with the ardour of his sentiments and his dreams. But is it equally true that he discovered nothing? In the aristocratic society of the eighteenth century he announced the virtues and believed in the sufficiency of the common man.

The English constitution of the eighteenth century, though far in advance of anything existing on the continent of Europe, was not the perfect model of enlightenment which the sanguine enthusiasm of the French philosophers imagined it to be. It had many grave defects. Its system of religious toleration, its system of parliamentary government, were both imperfect. The theory still prevailed that the state was a close Anglican preserve, permitting indeed the public profession of Protestant worship, but excluding the dissenter from any share of public power and responsibility and even from the enjoyment of the best educational opportunities. So tenacious were the Anglican

squires and clergy of their ascendancy that Parliament was no
open to Protestant dissenters till 1828, or the Universities of Ox
ford and Cambridge till 1871. The Tories of Queen Anne
reign wished to go further still. By the Occasional Conformity
Act they would have deprived the dissenter of the privilege o
sitting upon a town corporation, and by the Schism Act woul
have put down their schools and ruined their education. It i
one of the blessings of the Hanoverian succession that th
Whigs reversed this calamitous policy, that they repealed th
Schism Act, and by the passage of the annual Indemnity Act
released dissenters from legal penalties which they would othe
wise have incurred by taking municipal office.

Even thus limited, the blessings of toleration were not ex
tended to Roman Catholics, who, in England, were forbidden ti
1779 to practise their worship in public, while in Ireland, wher
they might brew political mischief, they were subjected to
system of special and cruel disabilities.

The government of England during the first two Hanoveria
reigns was an aristocracy. The great Whig families controlle
the House of Lords, and through their influence on the pocke
boroughs, returned the majority of the House of Common
The Tories, who were probably more numerous, though les
wealthy, suffered for more than fifty years the penalties attach
ing to parliamentary opposition by reason of their compromi
ing association with the Jacobite cause. But in the real govern
ment of the country, which was local and not parliamentary, i
the Quarter Sessions and Petty Sessions of the Justices of th
Peace, the Tory squire was allowed to exercise the full measur
of his social and political weight. In the execution of the gam
laws, the trying of poachers, and the punishment of vaga
bonds, these unpaid amateurs discovered a means of satisfyin,
their craving for public usefulness and importance, and were s
kept quiet and contented, while Whig magnates stood at th
wheel at St. Stephen's.

By an accident unforeseen in the days of William III an
Anne the supreme executive came to be vested under the firs
two Hanoverian kings in a Cabinet composed of the member
of a single party and responsible to Parliament. George I coul
speak no English, and after the experiment of conducting busi
ness in French with his ministers had broken down, absented
himself from the meetings of the Cabinet. The long and wis

administration of Sir Robert Walpole consolidated the Whig *1721-42*
party, confirmed the authority of the Cabinet, and established
the position of the Prime Minister. After that momentous administration the true principle of responsible government, that
is to say of government by a Cabinet responsible to a parliament
which is in turn responsible to the electorate, was established.

The success which attended the establishment of Cabinet
government may be ascribed to another historical accident. The
natural preference both of William III and of Anne was for
mixed non-party Cabinets. For the sovereign to draw advisers
from each party to his Council advertised the impartiality and
exalted the power of the crown : but this experiment of a coalition, only occasionally possible under these two reigns, broke
down when George I ascended the throne and learnt from his
Whig friends that the Tories were conspiring in the Jacobite
interest to drive him out of the country. From that moment
Whig Cabinets and Whig parliamentary majorities were the
order of the day. The custom was established that Cabinets
should be of one political complexion and that they should
really govern the country. It was an accident and a happy acci- *1770-82*
dent. During the ten years of George III's personal rule, when
Cabinet government was reduced to a shadow, England experienced the greatest political reverse in her history through the
loss of the American colonies.

Being, however, controlled by a wealthy territorial class, the
British parliaments of the Hanoverian age were not remarkable
for the gift of social compassion. The penal laws which were
allowed to remain on the British statute book until they were
reformed away by the efforts of Romilly and his friends in the
next century were a disgrace to a generally humane and good-
natured people. Nothing was done by the state for popular education. Town government remained corrupt, mediaeval, and
unpopular, until the great cleansing of the Municipal Corporations Act in 1835. The fact that the Glorious Revolution had
been primarily made to protect the ancient customs and charters
of the towns, as well as the prerogatives of Parliament, from the
innovating and autocratic invasions of James II, was a force
making for conservatism. The Whigs, exulting in their Revolution Settlement, were too apt to think that it had settled everything. This was an error. Parliament, in particular, was far from
perfect; but the Whigs who idealized Parliament were slow to

see that a legislature elected by forty-shilling freeholders in the counties and by small oligarchies in the towns was no true and sufficient mirror of national interests and opinions. Even Burke, the most imaginative of all Whig writers, saw no necessity for parliamentary reform. He was in favour of reducing the power of the Crown over Parliament, but not of widening the area of parliamentary representation. The eighteenth century was content that the great bulk of the middle class as well as the poor should be excluded from the sacred circle of the parliamentary Constitution.

Parliamentary corruption was another evil unnoticed by the French admirers of English institutions, and tolerated, despite opposition protests, at Westminster and in the constituencies. Bribes were offered and accepted by voters and members. There is reason now to think that this evil may have been exaggerated by contemporary critics. That it existed is certain. The expectation that even a small number of posts and pensions will be available for those who vote straight exercises an influence reaching far beyond the circle of those who are thus rewarded. Despite these defects, the country prospered and was happy. The sleepy Anglican Church, the sleepy and unlearned universities, the rosy foxhunting squires, and the top-booted, hard-drinking legislators at Westminster were not ill adjusted to the slow pace of that old agricultural society. There was no deep chasm between the classes; there were no difficult economic questions to vex the brain of Parliament. The Industrial Revolution had not yet begun to create in northern England a new population of bitter factory outcasts in vast inorganic aggregations of insanitary houses. The towns were still small. The sports and amusements of the countryside were generally enjoyed. An air of comfort and stability, typified by the stout red brick houses of the Georgian age, pervaded the country. In some sense, but for the horrid intervention of a Highland raid in '45, which had it been successful would have thrown everything back into chaos, England under George II must have seemed to all who were above the level of poverty to have reached a position of assured and fortunate inner peace. It was a society singularly free from disquieting and torturing doubts. It was harassed by no social problems, it required of Parliament no vast programmes, but was content with a small annual output of petty local legislation. Romance had not yet dawned upon a rational society, content to ask of life only what life could give, a society so stable and harmonious, so little superstitious or emotional, so sure of itself and apparently so well protected from the ruinous follies of the zealot that its like had not been seen in Europe since the days of the Antonines.

The English political literature of the eighteenth century bears the imprint of this felicity. Though it is spirited and combative, it has no quarrel with the foundations. Neither Swift nor Defoe, neither Addison nor Steele, neither Bolingbroke nor Hanbury Williams encourage their countrymen to believe that they are living under a régime of intolerable indignity and injustice. The quarrels of England are parliamentary, the disputes of political côteries, of the ins and the outs. Not even Wilkes, the radical, who opened new ground in the first decade of George III's reign, disputed the beauty of the Glorious Revolution or the value of the principles on which it was based. It was otherwise in France, where the persecution of an intolerant Church, added to the capricious and secretive tyranny of the state, provoked a literature of violent derision and contempt.

The internal problems of France which first in the later years of Louis XIV had begun to attract the attention of philosophic thinkers were primarily financial. No French government had dared to impose upon the whole French people a uniform and equitable system of taxation. Every government in its effort to conciliate followers in this quarter and in that had granted exemption from certain taxes. The nobles, the clergy, a large section of the bourgeoisie were dispensed from the *taille*, or property tax. Similar exemptions were enjoyed by many important provinces, especially by those which had recently been united to the French crown. The principle of privilege in taxation had been carried so far, and was bound up with so many class prejudices and traditions of provincial pride and autonomy, that it was exceedingly difficult to uproot. Only a strong government supported by a powerful body of popular opinion could successfully overcome the vast number of vested interests which were concerned to oppose its abolition. The old French monarchy, despite its immense prestige, was unequal to the task.

There were two possible avenues of approach, the method of constitutional reform and the method of autocratic action. The first method was inapplicable. A legislative assembly responsible to a popular electorate was wholly alien to French tradition. No statesman proposed it. No king would have accepted it. No government could have brought it into being without a violent convulsion. It was the nemesis of the long autocracy of Louis XIV that the habit of effective thinking on constitutional problems had been suspended, so that when, during the sombre last days of that vainglorious reign, Fénelon and others began to question the value of autocracy, their thoughts ran backwards to the older aristocratic constitution of France. They dreamed of more nobles associated in the task of government and dallied with the idea of reviving the mediaeval States-General, which had not met since 1614. The memory of this cumbrous and anachronistic body, without organization, without executive authority, without social cohesion, and without experience of affairs, blocked every fruitful avenue to constitutional reform. Its meeting in 1789 was not the beginning of government in France, but the signal for chaos.

Autocracy, at least, was in the later tradition, but was allowed no free sphere of action. The Parliament of Paris, restored by Philip of Orleans to its old position of authority, and supported by the twelve Provincial Parliaments, strewed the path of fiscal reform with insuperable obstacles. These lawyers had a horror of new taxes and new ideas. They burned philosophical books and voted down reasonable proposals for obtaining money from the public. But though they stood for obscurantism in thought and privilege in finance, they enjoyed an extraordinary measure of popularity as the sole organ of opposition to a profligate and discredited court. It argued high courage on the part of Chancellor Maupeou to suppress them in 1771. But the prospect of radical administrative reform to be undertaken by the Crown was hardly opened ere it was again blotted out. In 1774 the Parliaments were restored by a new king anxious to gain the love of his subjects. The compliance of Louis XVI with popular sentiment, though intelligible, was disastrous, for to any comprehensive and rational reformation of the French state a privileged oligarchy of hereditary lawyers could be trusted to oppose a stout and obtuse resistance.

BOOKS WHICH MAY BE CONSULTED

Lecky: History of England in the Eighteenth Century. 1878.
G. M. Trevelyan: History of England. 1926.

J. Locke : Essay on Human Understanding. *Ed.* A. C. Fraser. 1894.

Churton Collins : Bolingbroke, a historical study, and Voltaire in England. 1886.

John Morley : Voltaire. 1921.

H. Higgs : The Physiocrats. 1897.

Leslie Stephen : The History of English Thought in the Eighteenth Century. 2 vols. 1902.

A. Sorel : Montesquieu. 1887.

A. De Tocqueville : L'Ancien Régime et la révolution. 1860.

H. Taine : L'Ancien Régime. 1876.

F. Rocquain : L'Esprit révolutionnaire avant la Révolution. 1878.

Aubertin : L'Esprit public au Dix-huitième siècle. 1889.

The Political Writings of J. J. Rousseau. *Ed.* C. E. Vaughan. 1915.

Voltaire : Dictionnaire philosophique. 1765.

Voltaire : Lettres écrites de Londres sur les Anglais. 1734.

Lavisse : Histoire de France, Vol. IX.

CHAPTER XXIII

THE SWEDISH METEOR

The decade of Christina. The conquests of Charles X. The preservation of Poland and Denmark. The Northern War, 1700-21. Patkul and the anti-Swedish Coalition. Charles XII and Peter of Russia. Poltava. The downfall of Sweden.

THE triumphs of Gustavus and his marshals, which raised Sweden to a pinnacle of military renown, were followed by a decade of Swedish history less important, indeed, but hardly less arresting than the long story of marches and counter-marches, battles and sieges by which it was preceded. Christina, like her father Gustavus, was a creature of genius. For ten years (1644-54) this amazing and capricious young woman glittered in the eye of Europe, scattering her bounties with a prodigal hand, performing feats of physical endurance which the hardiest veteran of her father's army might admire, and charming by her brilliant and indefatigable curiosity the choice circle of philosophers and literati who had been enticed to Stockholm by the magnet of her sympathy, her favour, and her largesse. Then, out of feeling for the Roman Church, into which she was received, or from a sudden weariness and dislike for the routine of business, or desiring to create a spectacular effect, the "Pallas of the North" resigned her throne in favour of a cousin. Charles X was that dangerous thing a mere soldier. Campaigning was his master passion. To him is due the first of the two great northern wars which ultimately brought Sweden to the ground, raised Brandenburg to a position of predominance in northern Germany, and opened the gateway into western Europe for the portentous figure of the Russian Bear.

To this firebrand, questing for enemies, Poland and Denmark presented themselves as obvious targets for attack: the first a papistical country, ruled by that elder papistical branch of the Swedish house of Vasa, which had not yet given up its title to the Swedish throne; the second the old hereditary enemy, the kingdom which had once ruled all Scandinavia, which still held Norway and the three southern provinces of Sweden, and by its

position north and south of the Sound could command the trade
of the Baltic. Charles threw himself first on Poland, then on
Denmark. He overran Poland, he overran Denmark. There was
a point alike in the Polish and in the Danish campaign when the
military success of the Swedish army seemed to be complete and
unqualified. And yet it is instructive to notice that when peace
was signed at Oliva and Copenhagen (1660), and Charles, dying
prematurely, had ceased to trouble, Poland and Denmark were
not left as dependencies of Sweden, and that the most substantial
gains from the Polish fighting were reaped, not by Sweden, which
put out great efforts, but by the Elector of Brandenburg, who
without any troublesome exertion acquired the Duchy of Prussia
in full sovereignty as the price of his promised support of the
Poles.

1672

If Charles had emancipated the Polish serfs, he might have
counterbalanced the prejudice created in the minds of a pious
Catholic population by the sacrilegious behaviour of his Lutheran
troops. But he was not so intelligent as to anticipate Napoleon,
and, having nothing to offer the Poles but blows, insults, and
Protestantism, was turned out of the country by a national rising
assisted by Austria. It is important to notice the action of
Austria. That great Catholic monarchy could not afford to see
Catholic Poland under the heel of the Lutheran Swedes.

Just as the survival of Poland was an Austrian interest, so the
rescue of Denmark from the Swedish clutches was the concern
of Holland, England, and France. A Dutch fleet saved Copenhagen. A composite army of Dutchmen and Danes, Poles and
Austrians beat the Swedes at Fünen. When there seemed a
chance of the old familiar landmark of the Danish kingdom
being obliterated under the surge of Swedish militarism, a concert of maritime powers intervened to repel the flood. The trade
of the Baltic was an international interest. While the maritime
powers were well content that the Scanian Provinces (in south
Sweden) and the island of Bornholm should go as a prize to the
Swedes, the existence of an independent Denmark south of the
Sound seemed to them to be an international necessity.

Fifty years divide the peace of Oliva from the outbreak of the
second great northern war (1700-21), which was destined to seal
the doom of Sweden as a great power. Russia was rising; the
Hohenzollerns had schooled a redoubtable army in Brandenburg; but Sweden, sheltered by the powerful diplomatic support

of France, maintained her ground. So strong was the prestige of
the Vasa dynasty that after a minority of twelve years Charles XI,
a silent, boorish king, without magnetism or charm, but brave
and dutiful, and the hero of victories against the hereditary
Danish foe, was able to break the power of his nobles and with
the assent of burghers and peasants to establish an autocracy.
Dying in 1697, this enigmatic but successful sovereign left behind
him an army, a revenue, and an empire. The Swede ruled in
Finland and stood sentinel round the gulf of Bothnia. His flag
flew over the great ports of Reval and Riga. He denied western
Pomerania to Brandenburg, Bremen and Verden to Hanover,
the Scanian or southern provinces of Sweden to Denmark. He
held the little island in the river Neva, upon which Peter the
Great was soon to build with Swedish prison labour the Nevsky
Prospect in his capital of St. Petersburg.

1700

The prime mover in the undoing of Sweden was a member of
that Baltic baronage which shares with the landowning class in
Hungary the name of being the proudest and hardest aristocracy
in Europe. Johan Reinhold Patkul was a Livonian who
cherished a strong personal grudge against the Swedish Government. In common with others of his order, he had been attacked
in his private fortune by a comprehensive measure for the resumption of alienated crown property, had offered a vigorous
resistance, and had in absence been condemned to a traitor's
death. From that moment the fierce Livonian made it his object
to bring the Swedish Empire toppling to the ground. Passing
from capital to capital, he wove the network of a war coalition,
caught Augustus of Saxony, who had been elected King of Poland
and coveted Livonia; caught Peter of Russia, who, finding no
help in the west for his Turkish war, was turning his eyes to the
Baltic littoral; and, easiest of all, caught Frederick of Denmark,
who saw in a recent marriage of a Swedish princess to a Duke of
Holstein Gottorp a stab at the fatty part of the Danish anatomy.
The prudent Elector of Brandenburg refused to be caught, but
the coalition was full powerful without him. In May, 1700, the
Saxons invaded Livonia and started the long war which changed
the weights and balances of the north.

The moment appeared to be propitious. Charles XII of Sweden
in 1700 was an inexperienced boy of whom only it was known
that he had claimed and been accorded the autocratic power of
his father. That this tall, austere, intellectual lad would in the

SWEDISH POSSESSIONS IN 1662.

hour of his country's greatest peril reveal the qualities of a hero
of Scandinavian saga, that he would prove to be an inspired and
indomitable leader of men, that his decisions would be as swift as
his will was imperious and his courage sublime, that he would
think no enterprise too wild or too desperate and no labour too
exacting, that he would throw himself successively at Denmark
and Saxony and knock them out of the ring by a series of smashing blows and brilliant marches, and that his first encounter with
the army of Peter the Great, waged in a November snowstorm
before the walls of Narva, would be a victory so crushing that,
even if it had not been won against an army four times the size
of his own, it would be memorable in the annals of warfare; these
were developments which routed every calculation and appeared
to portend a transformation of Europe. With a speed which
seemed miraculous the young Swede broke through the circle
of his enemies and had them beaten on every front. Even Marlborough was prepared to salute him as a great master of war.

Unfortunately, he lacked sanity. While Marlborough was
always as cool as ice, Charles was in a constant blaze of excitement and indignation. For a nature so fierce and temperamental
the habits engendered by autocracy were not a blessing but a
curse, for when his judgment went astray, no force could deflect
it to the paths of common sense. Failures, hardships, defeats,
humiliations had no effect upon his inhuman confidence or unending resource. A fatalism, born of early success, carried him
buoyantly through every vicissitude, while Sweden, bled white
through his obstinate ambition, descended swiftly in the scale of
power until she forfeited for ever her place of command and usefulness in the affairs of Europe. His greatest mistake was to
underrate the Russians. Having defeated 40,000 raw troops at
Narva, Charles believed the Muscovites to be contemptible
fighters of whom he could always dispose at his leisure. Accordingly, instead of stiffening the Swedish defences in the Baltic
provinces, he devoted six critical years to the displacement and
condign punishment of his enemy the Elector of Saxony and to
the establishment of a nominee of his own on the Polish throne.
What he achieved was remarkable, but while he was capturing
Polish cities or carrying the war into Saxony, Peter of Russia,
who had reorganized his armies and discovered in Sheremetieff
a skilful general, secured the precious Baltic provinces (1701-4).
Good judges have opined that if Charles had been willing to

accept the Saxon offer of peace after his victory at Klissow in July, 1702, he would have saved, at least for the time being, this essential region of the Swedish empire.

However this may be, there can be no doubt that, having once lost the Baltic provinces, Charles took the wildest and least hopeful course for their recovery. After he had settled with Poland and Saxony and compelled Austria to give redress to her Silesian Protestants he marched off into the heart of Russia to dethrone the Tzar. Here in the vast roadless tracts of marsh and forest and in the pitiless cold of a Russian winter, his small army of superb veterans encountered an enemy far more formidable than the Russian Guard. Unprovided against frost, shrunk to half their original strength by disease and privation, and disappointed in their hopes of a great Cossack reinforcement in the south, the Swedes went into action against overwhelming odds at Poltava on June 28, 1709, and were annihilated. "Now by God's help," exclaimed the Tzar, as he saw the effects of his efficient French guns on the wasting ranks of the enemy, "are the foundations of St. Petersburg securely laid for all time."

The Tzar was right. He had secured on the field of Poltava Russia's window on the west. Charles, who had been disabled by a wound from directing the battle, escaped to Bender in Turkey, and had nine more years of romance before him. But though he stirred up the Turks to make war upon Russia (1711-13) and ultimately returned to his native country, reckless and uncompromising as ever, he never succeeded in reversing the decision of Poltava. That battle rang down the curtain on the Swedish empire. Poland reverted to Augustus of Saxony. Brandenburg seized the greater part of Swedish Pomerania. Peter added Riga and Reval to his Baltic conquests. The army of a powerful coalition, including Hanover and Prussia, as well as Saxony, Russia, and Denmark, forced the capitulation of Stralsund (December 23, 1715), the last remaining Swedish stronghold on the German coast, after a long and brave defence. Even so, Charles, escaping to Sweden, dreamed of victory. In the hope of fresh conquests as bargaining counters with the enemy, he invaded Norway, and there, laying siege to an obscure fortress, the wild, bare-headed figure in top-boots, who had swept through Europe like a tornado, calling for sacrifice after sacrifice from his Swedes, but never losing their support and devotion, met a soldier's end. Three years later (Peace of

Nystad, August 30, 1721) the Baltic provinces, the chief prize of the long contest, passed by consent from Sweden to Russia.

BOOKS WHICH MAY BE CONSULTED

R. Nisbet Bain : Christina of Sweden. 1890.

R. Nisbet Bain : Charles XII and the Collapse of the Swedish Empire. 1895.

Voltaire : Histoire de Charles XII roi de Suede. 1732. *Tr.* W. Todhunter. Everyman's Library. 1908.

Hallendorff and Schuck : History of Sweden. 1929.

D. Ogg : Europe in the Seventeenth Century. 1925.

CHAPTER XXIV

PETER OF RUSSIA

Russia in the seventeenth century. Reverence for the hereditary princi-
ple. The two dynasties. The rise of the house of Romanoff. Rivalry
with the Poles. Early western influence. Peter the Great. Azoff. Peter
turns westward. Foundations of St. Petersburg. Peter's reforms.
Russia takes part in western politics.

WHILE the contemporaries of Louis XIV in Paris and London
were enjoying the delights of a refined sociability, the subjects of
the Tzar of Muscovy were sunk in oriental barbarism and gloom.
Save for a few monastic schools there was no education. The
free life of the intellect was a thing unknown in a country where
illiteracy was general, and where a clergy ignorant, slothful, and
fanatical, instead of devoting any part of its vast wealth to the
advancement of knowledge, was prompt only to suppress the
first glimmerings of intelligent curiosity. There are certain primitive forms of entertainment which belong to all Asiatic peoples.
These the Russians possessed. They delighted in ballads and
hymns, in the song of the blind minstrel or in the eloquence of
the wandering story-teller, in dancing and buffoonery, and in the
epic poems of their race; but they had another amusement to
which the real Orient was a stranger. Nowhere was bestial
drunkenness so widely and patently practised, by women as well
as men, by statesmen as well as peasants, by the monks and
priests, no less than by the laity. Since women were kept in strict
seclusion, life save in the foreign quarter of Moscow was bare of
society. The humblest dairy maid in Brittany would have had
more to say for herself than the thickly painted spouse of a rich
boiar, her back flayed by the stripes which it was the habit of the
Russian husband complacently to administer, and of the Russian
wife submissively to accept.

The Tzar was the proprietor of his land and people. There
was no parliament, there were no free towns or corporations,
since the unfortunate extinction of republican liberty in Pskoff
and Novgorod at the end of the fifteenth century, nor was there
any organized social hierarchy. Justice was openly bought and

sold. The cancer of corruption, which is historically traceab
to the fact that the grand dukes of Muscovy chiefly rose
power not by force of arms but by their successful bribery
Tatar officials, had eaten so deep into the habits of the natic
that no efforts were availing to excise it. Taxation was litt
better than state brigandage. So backward was the country
economic development that most of its industry and commer
was in the hands of the Tzar. Western travellers visiting Russ
in the seventeenth century depict a violent, immoral, and shap
less society, jealously secluding itself from aliens, and hel
together only by a savage brutality. The Tzar flogged his boiar
the boiars and landlords flogged their domestic slaves and pr
dial serfs, the bishop flogged his priests, the abbot his monk
the husband his wife, and the father his children. In every pa
ticular of dress, deportment, custom, and law, there seemed t
be the sharpest distinction between Russia and the west. Th
Russian males wore long dresses and long beards. " To shave th
beard," said Ivan the Terrible, " is a sin that the blood of a
the martyrs cannot cleanse. Is it not to deface the image of Go
created by men?" The wildest cruelty and the most unspeakabl
forms of vice were here combined with the grossest superstitior
and with a steady aversion, encouraged by the black monks an
white priests, from every novelty, however harmless, importe
from the west. It is an indication of the Russian mentality c
this age that the one spiritual agitation which disturbed it
frozen stillness was a manifestation not of progress but of blin
obscurantism. The Raskoll (1668 ff.) was a widespread and pas
sionate movement of dissent against some trifling, but reasor
able, liturgical changes introduced by the Patriarch Nicon.

Russia, then, was the Orient. So little was the Russian peopl
regarded as an integral part of the European community tha
among the proposals mooted at the court of Henry IV of Franc
was a scheme for a great crusading movement of the west t
expel the Muscovites and Turks from European soil. The judg
ment of Olearius, an intelligent German, who visited Moscow ir
1636, is equally unfavourable. " If a man consider the nature
and manner of life of the Muscovites, he will be forced to allov
there cannot anything be more barbarous than that people. . .
They never learn any art or science or apply themselves to any
kind of study; on the contrary they are so ignorant as to think
that a man cannot make an almanack unless he be a sorcerer

ot foretell the revolution of the Moon and the Eclipses, unless
e have some communication with Devils."

This turbulent, but nevertheless conservative, people were for
period of over a thousand years governed by two dynasties, the
ouse of Ruric, originally Swedish, and the house of Romanoff,
hose chief recommendation was derived from a marriage con-
ection with that older line. It is a singular illustration of the
abitual reverence of the Russians for the hereditary principle
1at when Boris Godounof, a most capable usurper, secretly *1598*
1ade away with Dmitri, the second son of Ivan the Terrible,
nd the last offshoot of the family which had created the earliest
.ussian state on the Dnieper, introduced Christianity from
yzantium, founded the grand duchy of Moscow, and delivered
.ussia from the Tatar yoke, the people refused to believe that
)mitri was dead. How could it be that a family which had
eigned since the ninth century should thus suddenly disappear?
'alse Dmitris, first a renegade monk who became a Catholic
nd the husband of a Catholic, then a robber, appeared in turn,
aptured the enthusiasm of the peasants and Cossacks, and with
.elp from Poland and Sweden threatened to dissolve the state
nto its barbaric elements.

But then in 1612, at the darkest hour, when Sigismund III of
'oland was in Smolensk, and the Swedes were in Novgorod, and
'oles were in the Kremlin, there occurred an event memorable
n Russian history, and characteristic of an emotional and re-
igious people. The real question which Russia had to decide was
vhether it would submit to a Polish Tzar with such slender
;uarantees for the preservation of the Orthodox Faith as that
rospect held out. Letters went out from the monastery of
roitza putting the issue before the cities, and the nation rose
vith an emphatic reply. The leaders of the great patriotic up-
.eaval were a butcher and a prince, the butcher Minine of
Jischni-Novgorod and the Prince Pozharski. It is their glory
hat they raised a national army and drove the Poles out of
Moscow, and that as the result of their action, the assent of a
lational assembly was secured to the elevation of Michael
.omanoff, son of the Patriarch Philaret, to the Imperial throne. *1613*

Michael was an insufficient lad of fifteen, but of a family near
o the people, and strong in the benediction of the Church.
.ather than have a Pretender brought in upon the backs of the
'olish army, or see the Orthodox Church jeopardized by the

accession of a Polish king, the boiars of Moscow resolved to sup
port an inexperienced lad and the people to lay at his feet thei
childish and passionate loyalties. The admiration which ha
been paid to the house of Ruric was now transferred to th
Romanoffs.[1] The Tzar was the elect of God, the little father o
his people, the healer of the troubles. The dynasty took root and
flourished. It produced Peter the Great and Alexander II, and
other figures less stupendous, who shone in the forefront of
world affairs, and then, after three hundred years of power, the
Romanoffs perished suddenly, as they had suddenly emerged
among the storms of war and revolution. The blameless Nicholas
the kindest, the weakest, the most humane of the Tzars, the only
perfect gentleman in a long list of Russian rulers stretching back
to the ninth century, was forced off his throne and butchered in
the bloodthirsty carnival of a Bolshevist triumph.

1917

The new dynasty inherited a warfare with the Poles which had
been chronic since the fifteenth century. To the Russian mind
the peculiar malignity of the Pole lay in two circumstances, his
Roman religion and his political union (solidified at Lublin in
1569) with the grand duchy of Lithuania, which, unlike the little
Lithuanian republic of today, comprised vast tracts of territory,
once Russian, and since they were inhabited by the White Russians and Little Russians of the Orthodox Church, likely to
become Russian once more. The Pole, in a word, appeared to
the Muscovite to be a very violent kind of heretic and a very
dangerous breed of poacher. He was not only a Catholic, but he
was an aggressive Catholic. It was bad enough that he should
have Lithuania; it was worse that Polish Jesuits should endeavour
to seduce the Lithuanians by the modern compromise of a
"Uniate" Church, Roman in allegiance, Slavonic in ritual, when
they could not carry them bodily into the Roman fold. Moreover, there was no end to the airs and impudence of the Poles.
When Russia was in trouble the Poles had not scrupled to take
advantage of her distress. They had supported the Pretenders,
made themselves masters of Moscow, burned down part of the
city, and claimed the Russian crown. The Poles were cleverer
and more intellectual than the Muscovites; it was easier for
them to draw upon the military experts of the German wars;
but the nobles were madcaps; and the country had been greatly
weakened since the monarchy had been made elective in 1572

1610

[1] Genealogical Table F.

on the extinction of the male line of Jagello. There was a wild ferment in this nation of Hotspurs, as they pressed forward after objectives too variously contrasted to be successfully combined, an advance towards the Dnieper, an advance towards the Baltic, not to speak of a dashing thrust at the heart of Russia itself. One of the earliest services of the house of Romanoff was to curb this Polish-Lithuanian exuberance. In 1667, after a five years' war, Little Russia and the sacred city of Kieff returned to Muscovy.

The process by which the grand dukes of Moscow, who had first risen to power as the tax-collectors of the Tatars, gradually shook themselves free of their Asiatic masters, and working outwards from their forest capital, advanced to the Caspian, the Black Sea, and the Baltic, though little noticed in the west until the star of Peter the Great began to shine upon the horizon, was nevertheless always assisted by applications of western energy and science. Ivan the Great, who married Sophia Paleologus, *1462* niece of the last Greek Emperor, and doubled the extent of the *1505* grand principality of Moscow, attracted Greek and Italian architects and engineers to his court, and owes much of his success to Fioravanti degli Alberti, his Italian master of artillery. The historic victory of Kazan, which administered to the Tatars the greatest repulse of the century, and brought the territory of Ivan the Terrible (the first grand duke to call himself Tzar), to *1533-* the brink of the Caspian, was clinched by the indispensable help *1584* of a German engineer. The opening of the White Sea trade *1554* route was the work of English adventurers. In genius and energy Peter the Great was the wonder of his age, yet without the experience of western ways, which he gained as a youth through mixing with his Swiss, Dutch, and Scottish friends in the foreign quarter of Moscow, he would never have conceived his great ambition; as later, he would have been powerless to carry that ambition into effect had it not been for the opportune aid of western experts and western guns. The vast native powers of the Russian people needed for their release and control a shock from the intellectual batteries of the west.

Peter grasped the helm in 1689, violently displacing his sister Sophia who held the regency. He was then seventeen years of age, a Titan in physical strength, and possessed of all the gifts, including a strong dash of intimidating and capricious ferocity, which were needed to force unwelcome novelties on the Russian people. His temperament, which was one of astounding power and exuberance, led him into every extreme of fantastic tom-foolery and sullen gloom. For the first six years of his reign he was content to leave the dull work of government to others, while he held carnival with his boon companions in the Sloboda or foreign quarter of Moscow, devising fireworks, singing in the streets, building boats, arranging sham fights, or playing prac-tical jokes on his friends. Even when he began to take his work more seriously, it was never certain how serious he was. A wild, disconcerting vein of schoolboy irresponsibility, leading him, even as a man of fifty, to make an April fool of St. Petersburg, persisted to the end. His personal habits, save that his energy and curiosity were inexhaustible, were those of a drunken, dirty, Muscovite operative, happy in rough companionship and in the heaviest and even the most odious forms of toil, so that he per-formed, as occasion offered, and with abounding zest, the rôles of a bombardier, a pilot, a shipwright, and an executioner, not to speak of the more refined occupations of a dentist, an engraver, and an operating surgeon. No inhibition, moral, religious, or social, hampered his action. He immured his sister, discarded his first wife, exhumed and defiled the corpse of his uncle, and for fear that his westernizing policy might be reversed, murdered, after hideous tortures, his intelligent but reactionary son. Servile prostrations he abhorred and prohibited. He cared little for his own dignity, and whether out of an inverted pride or a hearty plebeian simplicity, thought no task or situation beneath him. It did not injure him with his people that his second wife was a common Livonian serving maid, that his profligacy was un-abashed, or that for days together he would be incapacitated for business by drunkenness. He was the epitome of his country, with its inconsequence in action, its tumultuous moods, its pas-sionate lusts, and generous fellow feeling. Yet when he died at fifty-three the sentiment of relief was universal. The mice, as a wit portrayed it, looked on gleefully at the funeral of the cat.

To a young ruler anxious for naval power and trade expansion no objective was more tempting than Azoff, the great Turkish fortress at the mouth of the Don, which could be reached by water from Moscow. Here, then, before the walls of Azoff, Peter gained his earliest experiences of war (1695), and here with the aid of a fleet, brilliantly improved after an initial failure, he reaped the reward of his patience, his energy, and his resource.

The capture of Azoff (1696) was justly applauded as the first victory ever gained by the Russians over the Turks. But the young Tzar, who was a realist, kept his head.

A nearer view of the Black Sea problem disclosed formidable difficulties to be solved only with the help of a western ally. For such an ally Peter searched the west, and, returning empty-handed from his travels, preferred the Baltic to the Black Sea in the order of his military objectives. It was easier to found St. Petersburg than single-handed to wrest the Crimea from the Tatar and the Turk. Sharply deserting the distant scene of his boyish triumph, the Tzar exhibited in a momentous decision the correct judgment of a statesman.

From the first blow struck at Sweden until his death in 1725, Peter was almost continuously at war; and it is against this warlike background with its campaigns against the Swedes, the Turks, and the Persians that his domestic work must be viewed. To make an army as good as the Austrian, a navy as good as the Dutch, and a Civil Service as good as the Swedish, and to wring from the peasants, upon whom he imposed more widely than before the bonds of serfage, the supplies which were necessary for the conduct of his wars, these were the most constant preoccupations of his unstable mind. There was nothing in his policy calculated to alleviate the burden of the poor or to promote the ends of social justice. What he wanted for his people was the science, the power, and the material amenity of western life.

The great achievement of Peter is that, clearly apprehending the superiority of the west, he succeeded by the sustained effort of a lifetime, and in the teeth of violent prejudices, in lifting his country on to a palpably higher level of civilization. To Lefort of Geneva, the boon companion of his youth, whose house in the German quarter was the scene of many unedifying revels, he probably owed his initiation into western ways, and it was beyond doubt Lefort who suggested the western voyage (1697) which marks a dividing line in the history of Russia. Thereafter Peter was never likely to forget the lessons which Amsterdam or Deptford had to give to the sailor, or Vienna to the tyro in military science. The westerners had learnt the art of life and the secrets of power. They could make ships, guns, and tools, they understood money and comfort and rational amusement, they read and wrote, mingled freely with women, and in their paved and lighted cities had created for themselves an existence which was neither savage nor cloistered. What could be done in the west, Peter resolved could and should be done in Russia also.

First of his compatriots he saw the value of a capital on the Baltic. St. Petersburg, the prize of a long war hastily undertaken, was a guarantee that the precious contact with the west would not be broken, and that Russian influence would make itself felt in western politics. It was more than a city, it was a flag. It stood for that stream of tendency in Russian life which welcomes and accepts the west, as against that other native philosophy, Slavophile in the nineteenth and Communist in the twentieth century, which, viewing the Russian as a civilization wholly divergent from the European, and not benefited by admixture with it, regards Moscow as the real heart of the Russian state and the proper centre for its government. To men of this type, Peter's city on the Neva appeared little better than a social centre for the Baltic barons and an outpost of Germany on Russian soil.

1698　A mutinous movement of the Russian pretorian guard (Streltzy or musketeers), easily suppressed, but terribly punished, created the initial atmosphere of panic required in the country for a reforming Tzar. With true insight Peter struck hard at those elements in the social life of the Russians which were most deeply rooted in tradition, the beards and gowns of the men, the seclusion of the women, the wealth and independent authority of the monks and priests. He even abolished the 1721　Patriarchate of Moscow, and placed the Church under a Holy Synod in which priests were represented as well as bishops.

After changes so revolutionary, it was a comparatively light matter to create vocational schools, to reform the currency and the calendar, to deduct eight letters from the alphabet, to set up a senate and a system of public offices, and to build a navy. The deep-seated corruption of the official world, though he had the satisfaction of hanging a fraudulent Governor of Siberia, successfully defied his attack. His second wife, Catharine, the Livonian, was an unblushing blackmailer.

To civilize a nation so deeply sunk in corruption was a task exceeding the span of any one ruler. Peter had no money for " the social services." His educational schemes, so ambitious on paper, came to little in practice. There were neither the funds, nor the teaching staff, nor the widespread disposition to learn, without which a great educational advance cannot be achieved. Nations do not grow new tastes to order; and education, like the sea, was a taste which the Russians were slow to acquire. Nor was Peter, who during a critical epoch of the Poltava campaign was blind to the world through liquor, the man to give to the Russian people a sense of administrative method. Could he have shared the sobriety of Charles XII or Napoleon, what feats might he not have accomplished! Yet it was a great achievement to have given to the Russians, as Peter undoubtedly did, the three primary constituents of a modern state, an army, a navy, and a civil service. Though there were western influences in the Muscovite court ever since Ivan III, it was he who first opened the western window wide upon the Russian world; nor since his day has that window been closed. The first Russian newspaper, the first Russian hospital, the first Russian museum derive from him.

Though he had taken no steps to secure the future, his work survived the ebb and flow of prejudice and passion. He was succeeded in turn by his widow, his grandson, his niece, and his daughter.[1]

Behind these figureheads stood capable Germans like Ostermann, for seventeen years foreign minister, or Munnich, the Commander-in-Chief of the Russian army under Anne of Courland, or else Russians of the Petrine school like Bestuchief, the principal adviser of Elizabeth. The old social and political isolation was broken down. A close alliance with Austria was, until the death of Elizabeth in 1762, the corner stone of Russian policy.

So by the enterprise of a barbaric technician of genius Russia was brought into the diplomatic system of Europe, where she occupied a position which was not wholly unlike that of England, being at once of the continent and yet attracted by distant interests in which the continent had no concern. Asia was at her back door. Only a low line of rolling pine-clad hills, first traversed by Yermack when Shakespeare was a youth, divided the Russians from the forests, the waterways, and the prairies of Siberia, where, save that the rivers run south to north, Nature seems to repeat on Asiatic soil the experiment which gives to Canada its charm and its challenge. But just because the colonial

[1] Catharine I, Peter II, Anne of Courland, Elizabeth.

empire of Russia had not to be sought across the seas, but was there for the taking, the Asiatic pull on Russian policy was not immediately evident, and only in the nineteenth century, when the Muscovite was brought face to face with Britain and Japan, a factor of paramount importance. In the eighteenth century it was not so much the East as the South and West that appealed to the framers of Russian policy. The West offered its technicians and its philosophy of enlightened despotism, the South a long succession of tempting conquests. There were the garden lowlands of the Caucasus, and the Crimea with its sunlit Riviera, and the Bosphorus, most enchanting of sea channels, which leads out of the grim Euxine to the warm water port of Constantinople and thence past the isles of Greece to the Holy Land. It is easy to understand the power which such prospects as these exercised over the Russian people. They wanted the warm water port and the access to the Aegean and the control of the old Greek city to which they believed themselves entitled as heirs of the Byzantine Empire. They were consequently compelled to regard the Turk as the power which stood between Russia and the sun and to adjust all their diplomatic relationships to that fact. The friends of the Turks were their enemies, the enemies of the Turks were their friends. Catharine II, the greatest of Peter's successors, understood this, though she was German by birth and French by education. For her too the Southern question dominated everything. It was in her reign that Poland was partitioned as a move in the game of Southern policy, the Crimea annexed (1783), and the Russian flag firmly planted on the shores of the Black Sea.

BOOKS WHICH MAY BE CONSULTED

Kluchevsky : History of Russia. *Tr*. C. J. Hogarth. 1911-31.
Rambaud : Histoire de la Russie. 1884.
A. Brückner : Peter der Grosse. 1878.
A. Toynbee : A Study of History, Vol. III. 1934.
Macaulay : History of England. 1858-62.
R. Nisbet Bain : Slavonic Europe. 1908.
R. Nisbet Bain : Pupils of Peter the Great. 1895.
K. Waliszewski : Pierre le Grand. 1897.

CHAPTER XXV

THE TURK AND THE CHRISTIAN

Strength of the Turkish army. Suleyman the Magnificent. The age of Turkish expansion. The Treaty of Torok, 1606. Tyranny and indulgence of Turkish rule. Divisions of Christendom. Turkish decline and revival. Austria as a Christian bulwark. Poland, its inner weakness and internal foes. John Sobieski. French opposition. Christian victories, 1683-99. Venetian conquest of the Morea. Christian nationalism. The real enemy of the Turkish Empire. Austria's internal problem and services to Europe.

THE immediate successors of Mohammed the Conqueror were not likely to forget that by a sustained effort of persevering valour a small and rude oriental tribe had been brought from the heart of Asia to the command of an empire stretching from Bagdad to Morocco, and from the Persian Gulf to the Crimea and the Danube. Superiority in arms had given them an empire, and they were wise enough to see that only by superiority in arms would that empire be maintained. The army, then, was the first object of preoccupation, and since for many years the Sultans possessed the only regular standing army of importance in Europe, they were able to make themselves formidable to their subjects and their neighbours. In gunnery, engineering, and the commissariat arrangements the establishments of the Sultan were above the average of the age; nor could any western state oppose to the Spahis and Janissaries, who were recruited by a tribute of Christian children, troops comparable for the fanaticism of their spirit or the prolonged severity of their training. For more than a century the Sultans reaped the reward of their military zeal and solicitude. A passionate loyalty to the Commander of the Faithful reinforced a blind and fanatical adherence to the Faith.

With such leadership and profiting by the divisions of the Christian world, the Turkish Empire continued to grow. Under the chivalrous and cultivated Suleyman the Magnificent, who reigned from 1520 to 1566, the Turks, as has been already noted, took Rhodes from the Knights Hospitallers, exacted a tribute from Transylvania and Moldavia, and robbed the

Austrians of seven-tenths of Hungary. These victories on sea and land against the appointed warders of the Christian Faith sent a shudder of apprehension through Europe. Never again, though a century later Candia was wrested from the Venetians, and Kameniek, a key fortress, from the Poles, was the Ottoman Empire so powerful as under the reign of this exceptional Turk, who combined with the energy of a soldier the gift for civil organization and an unaffected sympathy for art and letters. Thereafter symptoms of incipient decline began to reveal themselves. A succession of weak and profligate Sultans produced the evil results which are inevitable in a state where everything depends on the character of an autocrat. Corruption invaded the government, indiscipline the army. The Janissaries and Spahis were permitted to marry, and the tribute of Christian children began to be remissly levied, and then in the seventeenth century ceased altogether. The Treaty of Torok, in 1606, relieving Austria from a humiliating tribute and fixing the boundary between Turkish and Austrian territory, marks the point of time at which the first momentum of Turkish conquest in Europe comes to a stay, and the Turks, in a bargain with the enemy, bring themselves to concede a point of vantage.

So miserable had been the state of the Byzantine empire before the Ottoman conquest that by a large number of the Christian subjects of the Porte the strong rule of the Turk must almost have been regarded as a boon. The Christians, indeed, were excluded from political power, made subject to a special tax, and were on more than one occasion exposed to the risk of systematic extermination. They possessed, however, in the defects and limitations of their conquerors, the indispensable guarantees for a not intolerable existence. The Turk was cruel but indolent, overbearing but stupid. Having no aptitude for industry or commerce, he was content to allow the Christian to carry on the occupations of the shopkeeper, the merchant, and the artisan; and since he had no culture of his own to impart to others, the Greeks, the Bulgars, and the Serbs lived under his loose and irregular rule, practising their religious rites, preserving their ancestral customs, and offering to the Koran under the aegis of their Patriarch a quiet but inflexible resistance.

Two things, then, specially distinguished the Turkish rule in Europe, its tyranny and its indulgence. For the quarrels of the Christian churches the Turks exhibited a profound and con-

temptuous indifference. As soon as they had renounced their
intention of converting the world to Islam, they were content
to leave the infidels to stew in the juice of their irreverent wickedness. No course could have been more consonant with Turkish
interests. Many a Protestant in Transylvania and Hungary,
rather than come under the ferule of the Jesuit, elected to live
under the Crescent; and in the competition for Hungarian support, which characterized the Danubian wars in the later half of
the seventeenth century, there was no factor which weighed more
heavily in the balance for the Turks than their habit of religious
toleration, or more adversely to the Austrians than the declared
system of persecution which had already destroyed the Protestants of Bohemia and now menaced the lives and properties of
their Magyar co-religionists.

The empire thus widely spread and strictly organized for the
purpose of war had two main enemies, the Shiites of Persia, and
the confused and tumultuous forces of European Christianity.
During the whole course of their history the Turks have been
concerned to provide for a defence on two widely separated
fronts.

But for one circumstance their task would have been insuperable. The European world was incapable of a concerted effort.
It was the division between the Greek and Latin churches which
brought the Turks into Constantinople, it was the religious rift
in Latin Christianity, coupled with the rivalry of Francis I
and Charles V, which enabled them to consolidate and extend
their conquests, and it was the feud between the rival houses of
Habsburg and Bourbon, enlisting as it did conflicting loyalties
and sympathies in every court in Europe, which opened out to
them in the later half of the seventeenth century new prospects
of successful encroachment on Christian territory.

Happily for Europe, the epoch of the Thirty Years' War,
when Protestants and Catholics were making a shambles of
Germany, coincided with one of those spells of moral enervation
which from time to time come over the Ottomans. In virile
force and ruthless intelligence the house of Othman has been
one of the great dynasties of the world; but there have been
grave lapses from excellence, one of which covered the first half
of the seventeenth century. The Turks, however, possess a fund
of moral recuperation which again and again has confounded
their antagonists. Half a century of corruption and disorder

THE GROWTH OF THE OTTOMAN EMPIRE TO 1648

Legend:

Ottoman Empire in 1360
Added by 1519
Added by 1648
Eastern boundary of the Holy Roman Empire

English Miles
0   100   200   300

was followed by a sharp revival of tone and discipline. In the year 1656, during the long reign of the eccentric Mohammed IV, an elderly Albanian was summoned to take the post of Grand Vizier. Albania is a small country, but rich in characters as stern and dominating as its barren mountains. Scanderbeg was an Albanian; Mohammed Ali, the founder of modern Egypt, was an Albanian, and at this juncture, when the affairs of Turkey were in the gravest disorder, the empire was once more clamped together by the ferocious rigour of the Albanian Mohammed Kiuprili. For more than twenty years viziers drawn from the Kiuprili family enabled the Ottomans once again to play a vigorous and menacing rôle in south-eastern Europe, and to strain the defences of the western world.

The task of defending Europe from the Turks lay primarily with the Catholic house of Habsburg. The great rôle of Austria in European history, and one of the main justifications for the Austrian empire, lay just in the fact that it stood for centuries as the south-eastern support of Latin and Germanic civilization against Islam. But while the force of the Sultan was unified and *1658-1705* compact, Leopold of Austria was not even master of his hereditary states. In particular his authority was contested in Hungary, where a powerful body of nobles, hating German troops, fearing the prospect of German taxation, and above all resenting the intolerance of the Roman Church, were in active correspondence with the enemies of the empire. Bohemia, indeed, was crushed beneath the Austrian heel: but if troops were to be obtained from Germany, it could be only by the consent of the Princes of the Diet, and in face of the hostile diplomacy of France. Yet, even in the middle of the seventeenth century, mediaeval sentiment counted for something. At a real crisis of the Catholic faith, the Archduke of Austria, in his capacity as Holy Roman Emperor, could appeal to what remained of the crusading spirit in Europe, and as the head of Latin Christendom, might expect to receive the support of the Vatican, the prayers of the Church, and the assistance of an army, small, cosmopolitan, miscellaneous, and improvised.

His nearest ally, assuming that the golden persuasions of Louis XIV proved to be ineffectual at Warsaw, was the vast, tumultuous, and uncertain republic of the Poles. Ever since 1572, when the Polish nobles, refusing any longer to submit to the rule of a strong government, insisted that the crown should be made elective, the condition of this country had been one of complete moral and political disintegration. The king was a cypher. He had no machinery for collecting taxes, no standing army, and since any member of the Polish Diet, on any pretext, however slight, might impose an absolute veto on its proceedings, no means of effecting constitutional changes, or of procuring for his country any ordinary legislative progress. The Diets were biennial, but since they were composed of armed nobles, some in receipt of Austrian, and others in receipt of French, pensions, who rarely separated without tumult or bloodshed, they had none of the attributes which should characterize a national parliament. There was no nobility in Europe of higher metal than the Polish, no cavalry who rode into battle so magnificently and absurdly accoutred, but though diamonds were plentiful, discipline was scarce. The extent and composition of a Polish army at any given moment depended on the willingness of the nobles, or any section of them, to take the field with their retainers, and the same voluntary principle broke the spring of its efficiency. Even on campaign, obedience was measured by inclination, and the most successful commander might find himself weakened by voluntary withdrawals proceeding from pique, fatigue, or political machinations. The Lithuanians were diametrically opposed to the Poles, and the Poles to one another. A peasantry of predial serfs and a Jewish middle-class stood outside the pale of the constitution, despised, unfriended, and oppressed.

Two great calamities befell this unfortunate people soon after they had imprudently abandoned their old hereditary kingship. By calling (1587) to the Polish crown Sigismund Vasa, who thereupon was received into the Roman Church, they incurred the hostility of Protestant Sweden. That was a formidable liability. The quarrel with the strongest military power in the north was almost sufficient in itself to exhaust the defences of the Poles; but it did not stand alone.

All through the first half of the seventeenth century a spirit of indignant apprehension had been growing in volume among the Cossacks of the Ukraine. Jesuit missionaries had been attacking the Orthodox Faith. Polish absentee landlords had been employing despicable Jews to collect their rents. In 1648 the Cossacks could stand it no longer. They rose in revolt under Bogdan Kelmnitzky, their Hetman, and with the aid of the Russians and

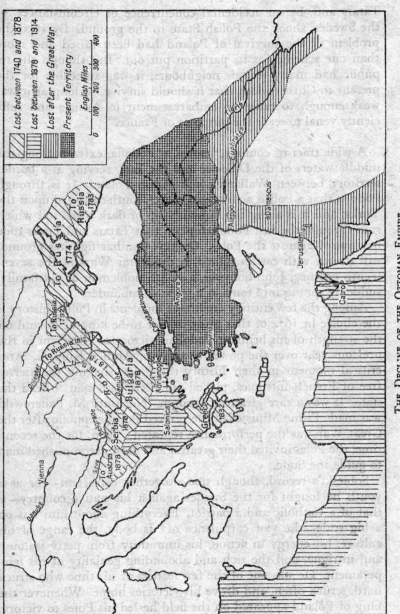

THE DECLINE OF THE OTTOMAN EMPIRE.

Lost between 1740 and 1878

Lost between 1878 and 1914

Lost after the Great War

Present Territory

English Miles

0   100   200   300   400

Tatars and, by an accidental concurrence of circumstances, o
the Swedes, shook the Polish State to the ground. By 1650 th
problem of the survival of Poland had been raised and mor
than one scheme for its partition put out. But though the re
public had many jealous neighbours, it was agreeable for th
present to Christendom that it should survive, so long as it wa
weak enough to cause no embarrassment to Austria and suffi
ciently venal to serve the purposes of France.

A wide tract of country, known as Podolia, extends along th
middle waters of the Dniester and the Bug, serving as a borde
territory between Wallachia and Polish Poland. It is throug
Podolia that a Polish army must march south-eastward upon th
Turks, and it is along the famous strip of dark black soil which
runs through the vast Podolian plain that Tatars and Turks rod
northward against the Poles. On this familiar fighting ground
still strewn with castles ruined in the Tatar Wars of the seven
teenth century, John Sobieski, a Polish nobleman of old family
suddenly sprang into fame as a great commander.

Among the few entirely creditable incidents in Polish history i
the choice in 1674 of that great soldier to be king of Poland on
the strength of his brilliant Podolian victory at Khoczim in the
previous year over the powerful army of Ahmed Kiuprili. At a
critical moment in their history the Poles, shaking themselves
free of French intrigues, picked out their best man to lead the
state. It was a rare gleam of wisdom. Not until M. Paderewski
was made Prime Minister of the revived Polish republic after the
Great War was the performance repeated. Then, for the second
time, the Poles invited their greatest and most accomplished man
to guide the State.

Sobieski's record, though not altogether consistent—for as a
youth he fought for the Swedes against his native country—is
that of a Catholic and a patriot. Everything about him was on
a big scale—the vast corpulence of his body, the range of his
culture, his energy in action, his immunity from petty jealousy
and intrigue, and the rich and abounding geniality of his temperament. He was one of the few leaders of his time who struck
hard, struck often, and drove his victories home. Whenever the
king of Poland appeared on the field he led his Poles to victory.
By 1675 he had forced the Turks to cede all Podolia (save for the
fortress of Kameniec) and two-thirds of the Ukraine to his

country; but his object was far greater than a local or Podolian triumph. He dreamed of a crusade to drive the Turk from Europe. "To give the barbarian," he said, "conquest for conquest, to pursue him from victory to victory over the very frontiers that belched him forth upon Europe; in a word, not to conquer and curb the monster, but to hurl him back into the deserts, to exterminate him, to raise upon his ruins the Empire of Byzantium, this enterprise alone is chivalrous; this alone is noble, wise, decisive."

All Europe was not of that mind. While Sobieski was endeavouring to stir up opponents all over the world against the Turks, Louis XIV was employing every artifice to secure the neutrality of Poland in the struggle which everyone knew to be impending. In this enterprise he was unsuccessful; but the patent rivalry of Paris and Vienna was one of the circumstances which contributed to the launching of a vast Turkish enterprise aimed immediately at Vienna and ultimately at Rome.

The repulse of the incompetent Kara Mustapha from the walls of Vienna in 1683 marks the beginning of that long process of Turkish decline which was sealed by the Treaty of Lausanne in 1923. The initial blows of Sobieski opened the way to a war for the control of the middle Danube, which was illustrated by a series of Imperialist victories. It was then that the old Austrian empire, employing commanders drawn from Germany and Savoy, rolled the Turks back across the Danube. It was in these campaigns that the Prince Eugène, the ally of Marlborough, and the darling of Protestant England, first made his renown. His crowning victory of Zenta led to the Peace of Carlowitz, under which *1699* all Hungary and Transylvania were ceded to the Austrians and all Podolia and the Ukraine to the Poles.

One Christian conquest which is registered in this epoch-making treaty was premature. The Venetians, stimulated by the Pope and encouraged by the Turkish repulse, had embarked on *1686-94* a campaign for the reconquest of Greece. With the aid of Hanoverian redcoats and other German mercenaries, they repossessed themselves of Dalmatia, drove the Turks from the Morea, and in a bombardment of the Athenian acropolis inflicted irreparable damage on the Parthenon. At the Peace of Carlowitz they were permitted to retain their spoils. But Greece was not destined to be a Venetian colony. After nineteen years of life under the Lion of St. Mark the Morea returned to its Turkish masters. The *1699-1718*

Venetians, who under Francesco Morosini were strong enough to conquer, were unable to retain their position. No Greek loves an Italian, nor any orthodox Greek a Roman Catholic; nor did the Aegean traders welcome the strict principles of Venetian monopoly. The mild rule of the republic perished without regret, having failed to excite enthusiasm in a population too deeply abased by centuries of oppression to respond to the spur of the Latin mind, and well content to regard the Sultan as its secular, and the Greek Patriarch of Constantinople as its religious, chief.

It was no call from the Vatican which rolled back the hosts of Islam in the eighteenth, nineteenth, and twentieth centuries. The last blast on the trumpet of Godfrey de Bouillon was blown by John Sobieski, while Catholic and Protestant factions were struggling for mastery in the court of Charles II, and Louis XIV was invading the Spanish Netherlands and subsidizing the Sultan. The real force which exploded the old Turkish Empire was not Roman, but Greek, not cosmopolitan, but nationalist. It was the determination of the depressed Christian peoples of the Balkan peninsula, of the Greeks, the Serbs, the Bulgars, the Roumans, to throw off the yoke of their Turkish oppressor and to enjoy an independent national life of their own. How this aspiration in the Balkan peoples slowly ripened, how it received steady encouragement from the Orthodox Church of Russia, from the Panslavists, and from the imperial ambitions of the Tzars, until finally Serbian nationalism, supported by Russia, and threatening to undermine the Austrian empire, led to the Great War of 1914, will be recounted later. Then also it will be noted how, when the Tzardom of the Romanoffs had fallen, and Russia was dissolved in revolution, France, reverting to her old diplomatic tradition, helped to preserve Constantinople for the Turk.

Meanwhile the victories of Prince Eugène, by hauling all Hungary back into Austria, left the Habsburg emperors with one of those desperate problems of internal government which, like the Anglo-Irish question, admit of no smooth and satisfying solution. The Archduke of Austria found in the elective kingdom of Hungary a proud Magyar nobility, exercising dominion over subject peoples of an alien race, speaking a language which few Germans knew, cherishing customs which no German shared, containing many families who were Protestant and many who for generations had sided with the Turk—a rude, semi-oriental aristocracy of landowning warriors temperamentally more akin to the Pole than to the German, and having little affinity with the musical and artistic côteries of Vienna. How was the Emperor to handle this difficult, mettlesome, half-pagan people? How adjust his relations to the Teuton and the Slav? How make of this miscellany of incompatible races a stable Catholic and monarchical State? Was it possible to centralize and germanize the whole mass after the Bohemian model? Was it possible to construct a federation in which each race should have its appropriate share of power? Or was the most workable expedient one which placed sovereignty in the hands of the Germans and the Magyars as the most virile and military races leaving each to manage his own barbarians?

The old Austrian empire, which attempted to solve these problems in the eighteenth and nineteenth centuries, and then, like the Ottoman empire, broke up after the Great War through the explosive force of nationalism within it, has many admirers and apologists among those who regard nationalism as the chief political curse of the human race. For such this Catholic State, guided in its religious policy by the Jesuits, and carrying out among its subjects, many of whom at the beginning of the eighteenth century were half barbarian and half pagan, a mission of religion and civility, exercises a great attraction. They see in it an attempt to realize upon a small scale that ideal of a Christian society, embracing all races and tongues, which it has been the professed aim of the Church to realize on earth. In the Pax Austriaca, as in the Pax Britannica—though if they are Catholics they prefer the Austrian to the British peace—they descry a form of polity superior to the national state, because it appeals from nationalism to some higher and larger principle of human association. They recognize the difficulties under which the old Austrian empire laboured, the oppressions which it exercised, the unpopularities which it typified; but they deplore its disappearance. Cumbrous, tyrannical, unintelligent as the Austrian Government often seemed to be, it nevertheless continued to hold together, over a wide and difficult area of Europe, excitable and incompatible peoples and to give them some aspersion of the Latin and Teutonic culture of the west.

Had the Austrian empire, like the United States of America, been the product of the free association of self-governing states, it might safely have defied the storms of time. The indispensable basis of assent was wanting. The state was the chance result of dynastic marriages, connoting nothing higher than allegiance to a family, reposing on no basis of common custom, achieving its religious unity by a persecuting force. Jesuits, soldiers, and police held together a polity which, for lack of such mechanical bonds, would have dissolved into its elements. In the old Austrian empire life was lived merrily, happily, fruitfully. It was a Catholic state, monarchical in its forms, conventional in its beliefs, having that full and exquisite enjoyment of art and science which may most easily be found where Jews are numerous, but wanting only a political soul and the breath of freedom.

This is to anticipate. In the early half of the seventeenth century Austria was the spear-head of the Counter-Reformation and the oppressor of Bohemian liberty. Later she rendered two services to Europe, as welcome to the spirit which prevailed in England as these earlier achievements were abhorrent: the re pulse of the Turks in the east, and in the west her indispensable and loyal support of the two Protestant and maritime powers in their stern struggle against Catholic France. So little may the policy of a state be deduced from the religious convictions of its citizens that the continued independence of the Dutch republic, the partition of the vast Spanish inheritance, and the successful establishment of the Protestant succession in England may, to no small degree, be ascribed to the spirited exertions of the old Jesuit-ridden Austrian state, which received its quietus by the Treaties of St. Germain and Trianon.

1919-20

BOOKS WHICH MAY BE CONSULTED

W. R. Morfill : Poland. 1893.
Dyboski : Poland (Nations of the Modern World). 1933.
N. A. de Salvandy : Histoire du roi Jean Sobieski. 2 vols. 1876.
J. B. Morton : Sobieski, King of Poland. 1932.
W. Coxe : House of Austria. 1847.
G. Finlay : History of Greece. *Ed.* H. F. Tozer. 1877.

CHAPTER XXVI

PEACE AND PRUSSIA

The Age of Reason. Anglo-French amity. The Spanish menace. Charles VI and the Pragmatic Sanction. The Polish War of Succession. France wins Lorraine. Walpole and Fleury. Character of eighteenth-century wars. The rise of Prussia. Geographical disposition of the Prussian state. The Hohenzollern house. Character of the Prussian. Frederick William I.

THE War of the Spanish Succession was followed by a period of relative tranquillity rare in the history of Europe and precious for the advancement of its civilization. The Treaty of Utrecht, based on a wise series of compromises, left behind it no immediate occasion for rancorous dispute. Though Austria and Spain were disappointed, all the belligerents had, in effect, gained by the division of the Spanish inheritance. To the weak and ill-established governments of Philip of Orleans, Regent of France, and of George I, King of England, peace was an essential condition of security. *1713*

It is fitting that the Age of Reason should have been heralded by the unusual spectacle of a political alliance between England and France, the two nations whose intellectual co-operation was the most important single fact during the eighteenth century. The joint armies of Britain and France have rarely failed of success from the days of Julian the Apostate to the triumph of Haig and Foch. Their joint diplomacy was now triumphant. For twenty-five years Europe was saved from a general conflagration. Wars, indeed, were not altogether avoided. There was conflict between Spain and Austria, between England and Spain, and finally, over the Polish succession, between France, with Spain and Savoy as auxiliaries, and the joint power of Austria and Russia. But it would seem as if the element of savage perseverance was wanting to these hostilities. To Fleury, who was a parsimonious bigot, as to Walpole, who was a robust economist, the lavish expenditure and waste of war were abhorrent. If war they must have, and they could not altogether avoid it, they were determined that it should be waged with economy, limited in scope, and at the first possible opportunity brought to a conclusion. *1713-39*

To those who consider the many reasons tending to bring France and Spain together, their common inheritance of the Latin and Catholic tradition, their colonies exposed to the rivalries of the English and the Dutch, their common subjection to the Bourbon house, and the removal of the one apple of discord which had so long poisoned their relations through the transfer of the Netherlands from Spain to Austria by the Peace of Utrecht, it may seem strange that at any period after that date France should have preferred the English to the Spanish alliance. But the relations of States are often affected by personal accidents.

1715 Louis XIV was succeeded by a child so delicate that it was long uncertain whether he would live to man's estate; nor was it until a Dauphin was born to Louis XV in 1729 that the succession in the direct line seemed to be secure. In the interval it was apprehended that Philip V, the first Bourbon king of Spain, might, despite a formal renunciation, lay claim to the French Crown. Nobody in Paris wanted Philip; and the unwelcome contingency that he might exchange Madrid for Versailles was for many years sufficient to sow dissension between the two Bourbon powers and to give support to the precarious friendship between England and France.

The first danger to the public law of Europe came from the ambition of Elizabeth Farnese, the second wife of Philip V of Spain, who was prepared to set Europe in a blaze, if she could obtain in the duchies of Parma and Tuscany an adequate endowment for her sons. The violent will of this masterful woman was seconded by the brilliant resource of the son of an Italian vine dresser, whose energy and inspiration, despite a grotesque and ignoble appearance, were long remembered by the people of his adopted land. If the dreams of Cardinal Alberoni had been fully realized, the Austrians would have been driven from Italy, the Hanoverians from England, and the Regent from France, while all three countries would have passed under the influence and direction of a revivified Spain. These far-reaching plans were frustrated by the effective accord of the French and English

1718 governments. One Spanish fleet was destroyed off the Sicilian coast by the English navy; another, carrying help to the Scottish Jacobites, was dispersed by storms in the Bay of Biscay. The conspiracy to kidnap the Regent was unmasked in Paris. The dashing Cardinal, who had not scrupled to attack the Austrians while with the encouragement of the Holy See they were engaged in a

war with the Turks, was forced by the joint pressure of England
and France to withdraw from the service of Spain. All his plans
had miscarried, and with his fall (1719) the first attempt drastic-
ally to revise the Utrecht settlement broke down in failure.

Undaunted and incurable, Elizabeth Farnese persevered in her
maternal designs. The ends which Alberoni had hoped to secure
by a direct attack on Austria, the Dutchman Ripperda, yet another foreign minister in the Spanish service, endeavoured to
obtain through a close understanding with the court of Vienna. *1725*
Again Europe was brought to the brink of a general war. Again
the spectre of Austro-Spanish hegemony raised for a time its
minatory head, and again the Hanoverian dynasty was threatened by a secret understanding between the Jacobite faction and
the foreign enemies of England. Yet once more a friendly undertaking between the prudent rulers of France and England saved
the peace of Europe.

At this time Austria was ruled by the man whom England at
a great expenditure of blood and treasure had vainly tried to set
upon the Spanish throne. Charles VI, unexpectedly succeeding *1711-40*
his brother Joseph in Vienna, was of the stiffest Habsburg clay,
at once ungrateful for past help and obstinately tenacious of past
pretensions. So stupid was he that, but for one circumstance, he
might have created as much trouble in Europe as Elizabeth
Farnese. Having no children but a daughter, who under the Salic
law was excluded from the Austrian succession, he was compelled
to solicit the assent of the leading powers of Europe to a family
statute known as the Pragmatic Sanction, which, notwithstanding the legal obstacle, provided for the accession of Maria
Theresa to the undivided inheritance of the Habsburg state. A
sovereign in quest of political favours from others is never in the
best position for pressing an advantage; and the astute diplomatists in London and Paris were not slow to appreciate the bargaining counter which chance had placed in their hands. Their price
was high. To Walpole Charles conceded the virtual suppression
of the Ostend East India Company, which threatened English
interests in the Indian Ocean. The French, holding their hand,
were even more successful, for out of the Emperor's necessities
Cardinal Fleury, their sagacious Prime Minister, wrung the
reversion to the duchy of Lorraine.

The occasion for this last concession was provided by one of
those brief and limited wars which are characteristic of this

period of diplomatic sobriety and material progress. The Polish War of Succession arose from the fact that Louis XV, who had married Marie, daughter of Stanislaus Lesczinski, desired on political and family grounds to replace his father-in-law on the Polish throne. It was a foolish policy, as Fleury saw, for Russia stood behind Austria in backing Augustus, the Saxon candidate, and had an army at hand, while the French were leagues away from the Polish scene.

It was idle, then, to suppose that the war aims of France could be achieved by operations in the distant plains of Poland. The imperial possessions in Italy and on the Rhine offered a nearer and more practical objective, and Italy was accordingly the main theatre on which the brief war of the Polish Succession was waged. Here France, with the ill-compacted aid of Spain and Savoy, succeeded, despite fluctuations of fortune, in delivering a sensible blow at her antagonist. A Spanish army under General Montemar drove the Austrians from Naples, and there established that ill-fated dynasty of Neapolitan Bourbons which for its tyranny attracted the scornful wrath of Gladstone and was at last sent about its business by Garibaldi's Red Shirts.

1733-8

1735

The conquest of the Neapolitan kingdom was the most important stroke in a war languidly conducted upon a limited and parsimonious scale and brought to a conclusion at an early opportunity. To the natural indignation of the Emperor, England and Holland refused to be drawn into the quarrel, and since imperial success in Poland was balanced by imperial failure in Italy, the court of Vienna listened to the overtures of Fleury. The treaty, known as the Third Treaty of Vienna, by which that aged ecclesiastic closed the Polish struggle, is justly regarded as a beautiful model of French diplomacy. Though he had spent little and ventured little, the cardinal was able to extract a brilliant advantage from an unreasonable and unpopular war. It was settled that Duke Francis of Lorraine should marry Maria Theresa, the heiress of the Austrian throne, and succeed to the reversion of Tuscany on the death of the last ruler of the house of Medici. In exchange for these shining prospects it was agreed that Francis should resign Lorraine to Stanislaus, and that after the death of the old Polish king the province should pass to France. French historians never cease to congratulate themselves on the skill by which, out of the bitter failure of French hopes in Poland, there emerged by a dazzling and unexpected feat of legerdemain the

1738

acquisition of Lorraine. But the miracle could never have been accomplished but for two things: Charles's need of the French assent to the Pragmatic Sanction, and the determination of Walpole to keep the peace. So the Polish War, which might easily have brought ruin upon Europe, passed away with little more than a few sieges and battles. Save that a Bourbon succeeded a Habsburg in Naples, and that the succession to Lorraine was secured for France, the political map of Europe was practically undisturbed. Diplomacy had been very busy for these twenty-five years. It was an era of congresses, of triple and quadruple alliances, of alarums of war, of conspiracies and intrigues of all kinds. Yet behind these endless agitations there was in Paris and London, by a rare stroke of good fortune, a steadfast will to peace guiding the actions of important persons. The Franco-British understanding, inaugurated by Stanhope, a gallant English gentleman, in conjunction with Dubois, a clever French rogue, was improved and consolidated by two far greater statesmen who continued their work. It would be difficult to conceive a sharper contrast than that between Cardinal Fleury, Prime Minister of France from his seventy-fourth to his ninetieth year, and Sir Robert Walpole, who for an even longer span dominated the political scene in England: the one an emaciated intellectual, wise, patient, serene, incomparable in diplomatic finesse, and raised above the passions and vices of the world; the other a coarse, pleasure-loving Norfolk squire, but the best financier and parliamentarian of his time. Yet so far as it might be given to two men to repress the combative instincts of Europe, that privilege was vouchsafed to these strange allies, each of whom, in pursuit of his own clear conception of the national interest, was compelled to tread the same pathway of international peace.[1]

The wars of the eighteenth century were not the product of great popular or racial movements, sustained and promoted by a powerful press. In general the peoples were condemned to bear the cost of wars which they had no part in promoting and in which they were but faintly concerned. Not that the governments of the eighteenth century, in pursuit of aims which were prevailingly dynastic, were altogether impervious to outside opinion. The French king listened to his fiery nobles. The Spanish monarchy might always rely on the support of popular

---

[1] This is consistent with the existence of a good deal of diplomatic friction between the two countries after 1731.

sentiment in an attempt to evict the English from Gibraltar. The great traditional hostilities, however unreasonable, however inopportune, such as the feud between France and Austria, or between England and France, were sunk far too deep in the national consciousness to be uprooted by a generation of original diplomacy. Walpole and Fleury between them had done their best to maintain the fabric of Europe as it had been settled by the peace treaties of Utrecht and Rastadt; but the lesson of European history is that Europe is never settled, but always restless and uneasy. In the declining years of Walpole and Fleury a new force of startling and unmeasured potency burst upon the scene and involved the continent in the havoc and carnage of a general war. That force was the Prussia of Frederick the Great.

England grew. Prussia was manufactured. Until the later half of the seventeenth century nothing in the political complexion of Germany announced the coming of this powerful state. Then the house of Hohenzollern, which had been ruling in Brandenburg since 1417, threw up for the first time a really remarkable man. Frederick William, known as the Great Elector, after his victory over the Swedes at Fehrbellin (1675), an affair slight in itself, but hailed as an augury of coming greatness, had conceived clearer notions of efficiency in government than were then commonly prevalent. Out of an unpromising, dispeopled, and divided inheritance he fashioned by his systematic encouragement of immigration and by his administrative and military reforms (for he regarded his people as material to be shaped and handled at will) the embryo of a modern State. There was nothing amateurish or haphazard about Frederick William's method. An army, a navy, a Civil Service, an improved postal system, a graduated income-tax, even an African colony, announced the quality of his ambition. All could not be realized. The colony went down before the powerful rivalry of the Dutch. The navy had to wait for Tirpitz and Kaiser William II, but the note of high ambition had been struck.[1]

1685-1713

1701

The Electoral title was no longer sufficient for Frederick William's successor. In consideration of favours to come, Frederick I obtained from the Emperor the right to be crowned King of Prussia, and to the horror of clerical Europe imposed the crown upon his own head in the cathedral of Königsberg.

[1] Genealogical Table G.

The alliance of the new Protestant kingdom was eagerly courted, and in the wars of Marlborough Prussian contingents played their part and watered the fields of Blenheim, Ramillies, and Oudenarde with their blood.

The weakness of the state lay in its geographical dispersion, for it was triply divided, with Brandenburg, Henry the Fowler's March against the Wends, at the centre, while away to the east across a block of territory once German, but between 1466 and 1660 subjected to Poland, lay ducal Prussia, and far westwards in the Rhineland the small duchies of Cleves, Mark and Ravensberg, over which since 1666 the Great Elector exercised full and acknowledged sovereignty. Between these divided members of an unpremeditated state there was no necessary or organic connection. Chance had brought them together under a common sovereign; chance might dissolve the partnership. The history of ducal or east Prussia had run one course, that of Brandenburg another. East Prussia had been part of a territory originally inhabited by a primitive, heathen, non-German people who, in the thirteenth century, had been driven into the Christian fold by the cold steel of the German Order of Knights, and by them governed for two hundred years, until the Order was shattered by the growing military power of Poland and East Prussia became a fief of the Polish crown. The early history of Brandenburg had been hardly less promising, for only with the coming of the Hohenzollerns did this region emerge from the humiliating vicissitudes of partition, repartition, and mortgage to which all German properties were exposed. The Hohenzollerns are among the able families of Europe. As Burgraves of Nuremberg they had lived in the sunshine of imperial favour and on the customs dues of a thriving city. In Brandenburg they had adopted artillery when it was novel, Lutheranism when it was assured, Calvinism in time to enable them to receive with open arms the industrious Huguenot refugees from France, and to compel their Lutheran subjects to a wise and profitable toleration of other forms of Protestantism than their own. One art, however, they did not possess. The Brandenburger could not win the good graces of East Prussia. It is noticeable that both in 1617, when John Casimir was admitted by the king of Poland to that Polish fief, and in 1660, when the Great Elector obtained the duchy in full sovereignty, the East Prussians manifested the keenest annoyance. Indeed, it was only by the use of force that the opposition of the East Prussian Diet was in that latter year overcome.

The Prussian is a distinctive European type. Goethe, who lived in Weimar and may be taken to represent the mid-German view of the Prussians, speaks of them as barbarians. There was an uncouth vigour and asperity about this remarkable people which jarred on the more refined susceptibilities of the Saxon, the Franconian, and the Rhinelander. To what causes the special characteristics of the Prussian race are to be attributed, whether to the Slavonic blood which flows through their veins, or to the harsh north German climate, or to the stern military tradition which nature imposes upon a state undefended by geographical frontiers or, if to all these causes, in what proportion: these are questions which admit of no precise answer. Let it suffice that before the eighteenth century had half run its course the world was aware that this vivid and masterful people, so sparingly furnished with the graces of life, presented by reason of their frugality, their discipline, their skill in arms, and heroic capacity for sacrifice a new and formidable problem for the statesmen of Europe.

In contradistinction to other Germans, the Prussians had a strict sense of service to the State. Their rulers could count, not upon their judgment, for the sturdy population of Prussia had no mind for politics, but upon a blind, ungrudging obedience to the word of command and upon a technical probity which ensured that every task would be faithfully discharged. It was a land of the Categorical Imperative, not only in the sense that Immanuel Kant, the apostle of the austere doctrine of Duty for Duty's sake, was Prussian to the marrow, but also because respect for duty was nowhere more savagely or successfully imposed. In this regard King Frederick William I, the father of Frederick the Great, set a notable example. No country could wish for a more economical sovereign or one who in his simple, dutiful, puritanical life more aptly illustrated the best characteristics of his people.

Prussia owes much to the peaceful rule of this homely but eccentric monarch—a large, well-trained army, a centralized administration, a good system of popular schools, closer tax-collecting and budgeting, and a full treasury. Yet the man had the mind of a drill-sergeant, the manners of a boor, and the moods of a savage. His army of giants was collected by the

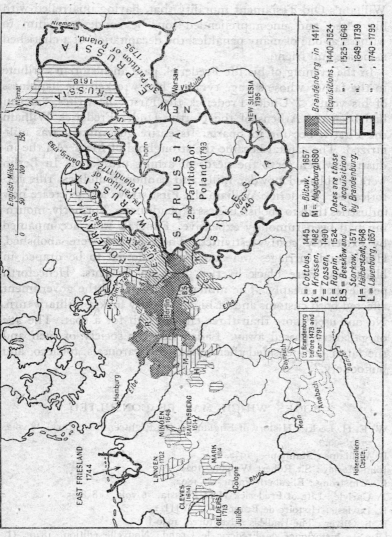

THE GROWTH OF BRANDENBURG PRUSSIA.

methods of a slave-driver. A tempestuous violence, tinged with insanity, wrecked the happiness of his home. It is characteristic of the brutal strain which was combined with Frederick William's Old Testament morality that, having quarrelled with his gifted and uncomprehended son, he condemned him to witness, as one of many penalties, the decapitation of a cherished associate and friend.

In the evening of his life Frederick paid an historian's tribute to the father whose savage tyranny had wrecked the happiness of his youth. "Under Frederick the First," he writes, "Berlin had been the Athens of the North. Under Frederick William the First it became its Sparta. Its entire government was militarized. The capital became the stronghold of Mars. All the industries which serve the needs of armies prospered. In Berlin were established powder mills and cannon foundries, rifle factories, etc. Frederick William the First strove less to create new industries than to abolish useless expenditures. Formerly, mourning had been ruinously expensive. Funerals were accompanied by extremely costly festivities. These abuses were abolished. Horses and carriages were no longer allowed to be draped in black, nor were black liveries given to servants. Henceforth people died cheaply. The military character of the government affected both customs and fashions. Society took a military turn. No one used more than three ells of cloth for a coat. The age of gallantry passed away. Ladies fled the society of men and the latter compensated themselves with carousals, tobacco, and buffoonery."

BOOKS WHICH MAY BE CONSULTED

W. E. H. Lecky : History of England in the Eighteenth Century. 8 vols. 1878-90.

B. Williams : Stanhope. 1932.

John Morley : Sir Robert Walpole. 1921.

E. Armstrong : Elizabeth Farnese. 1892.

T. Carlyle : Life of Frederick II of Prussia. 6 vols. 1858-65.

E. Lavisse : Histoire de France, Vol. VIII.

F. S. Oliver : The Endless Adventure. 1930-1.

Œuvres historiques de Frédéric le Grand ; Nouvelle édition, 1830 : II, Histoire de mon temps.

A. Sorel : L'Europe et la Révolution Française. 1885-1903.

P. Vaucher : Sir Robert Walpole et la politique de Fleury. 1924.

R. Lodge : Great Britain and Prussia in the Eighteenth Century. 1923.

CHAPTER XXVII

EUROPE AT WAR, 1740-63

The Silesian duel. The marine and colonial rivalry of England and the Bourbon powers. Frederick II and Maria Theresa. The War of the Austrian Succession. The interference of England and the re-entry of Prussia. The '45. The Peace of Aix-la-Chapelle. The diplomatic revolution. The impolicy of France. The Seven Years' War. William Pitt. Frederick's Annus Mirabilis. Reasons for Prussia's survival. England's colonial gains. Canada. India. The genius of Clive. The Peace of Prussia. War results for England and Prussia compared.

THE middle years of the eighteenth century are marked by a gigantic struggle which alike in its earlier and later phase revolves round two main international rivalries, the one, that between Prussia and Austria, startling from the shock of its novelty, while the other was of all European quarrels the most familiar. The War of the Austrian Succession and the Seven Years' War sprang from a common source. In 1740 Frederick II of Prussia drew the sword because he was determined to make himself talked about by the conquest of Silesia. In 1756 he launched a second war for fear that Silesia might be wrested from him. For twenty-three years, Silesia with its rich linen industry, undeveloped iron ores, and fine mercantile waterway, threw Catholic Austria into one scale, and the rude upstart power of Protestant Prussia into the other. Once kindled, the fire spread widely. Every political appetite was aroused. The most stable political frontiers were challenged. Almost all the continent was embroiled in a quarrel carried on at a huge cost of blood and treasure, and with many sharp vicissitudes of fortune. At one moment it seemed that Austria would be brought to the ground, at another that France would be dismembered, at a third that Holland and the Netherlands would be annexed by the French, at a fourth that Prussia would be overwhelmed by the Russians and Austrians. Yet, in spite of these violent oscillations, little change was effected in the political map of Europe, by fifteen years of hard fighting, beyond the transference to the Prussian crown of Silesia, a prize seized at the outset of the first war by an act of the blackest treachery, but defended against a world of enemies by the genius and pertinacity of a great soldier.

Meanwhile a controversy, springing from a different root and fraught with a more important issue, was proceeding between England and her commercial and maritime rivals France and Spain. The war between England and Spain, which broke out over the Spanish right of search in 1739, and was soon merged in the more critical struggle between England and France, was not made by statesmen in London, Paris, or Madrid. Wherever an Englishman met a Spaniard or a Frenchman on the high seas he espied a rival and a foe. It was a struggle not of courts and cabinets, but of men on the spot, of sailors and merchants, smugglers and privateers, of lumbermen, settlers, and free traders, of rival mercantile companies, brawling and quarrelling either along the Spanish Main or in Acadia and Newfoundland, or along the banks of the Ohio or the St. Lawrence, or under a burning Indian sky among the rice fields of the Carnatic, or the canes and mango trees of Bengal. Inevitably the unregulated competition for trade, colonies and dominion in Asia and America provoked innumerable collisions between the Anglo-Saxons and their Latin rivals. Unauthorized quarrels swelled out into unauthorized war. It was in vain that Sir Robert Walpole endeavoured to avoid being drawn into hostilities over the Spanish right of search in 1739. Popular clamour, echoed and reinforced by an eloquent opposition in Parliament, forced him into war. It was sufficient that English vessels, trading in the Spanish Main, should have been roughly searched for contraband by Spanish guard ships, and that English sailors loaded with chains should have been consigned to filthy Spanish prisons. In England the complaints of sailors and merchants always find a ready hearing, and the story that a wicked Spaniard had lopped off Captain Jenkins' ear sent the country into convulsions of fury, which only a declaration of war, as impolitic as it was unjust, was able to assuage.

The marine and colonial contest, which was thus inaugurated against the judgment of England's wisest statesman, lasted with little intermission (for when formal hostilities ceased, informal and local fighting none the less continued) until the Peace of Paris in 1763. Then it was made manifest that the sceptre of colonial dominion had passed from France to Britain. In India and Canada, thanks to the victories of Clive and Wolfe, British influence was triumphant and unchallenged.

This change in the balance of colonial power which, little as its true significance was appreciated at the time, constitutes one of the great revolutions in human history, could hardly have been brought about save for the continental war. The English ships, both of the commercial and of the royal navy, were more numerous than the French and the Spanish, because with England, though not with George II, maritime and colonial interests always came first, whereas with France and Spain the sea was neglected for the land. There are few errors in French history more calamitous than the decision which was taken in 1740 to join Frederick of Prussia in his attack on Maria Theresa. By that decision France became involved in an exhausting continental war, offering her so many temptations, exposing her to so many risks, and calling for so many sacrifices, that she could take little thought for her scattered settlers over sea. The French navy was accordingly neglected, and the error was not repaired until Canada and India had passed into British hands. It is one of the ironies of history that the blunder which helped England to become mistress of the seas also contributed to secure the predominance of Prussia in Germany.

It was not only a blunder but a crime. France had solemnly accepted the Pragmatic Sanction, which guaranteed to Maria Theresa the succession to the Austrian throne. But the government of France was always liable to be swept into war by the headlong passions of a military aristocracy. The prudence of the king and Cardinal Fleury was overborne. To Marshal Belleisle and his following of titled firebrands the prospect of wiping out old scores against the ancient enemy at a time when she seemed to be helpless and unfriended overbore every scruple of conscience and foresight. "What," they asked, "is an obligation to an opportunity?" Rarely has a sin against international good faith been in the end more amply punished.

No mist of ancient rivalries clouded the clear eye of *1740-86* Frederick II. That cool young realist, a bad German but a good Prussian, bore no grudge against Austria, nor were his passive and most unpolitical subjects lusting for conquests. But the field was clear for ambition. With a strong army, a full treasury, and an obedient people, the Hohenzollern was master of his fate. No loyalties restrained his freedom. He was prepared to throw his sword now in this scale, now in that, as Prussian interests seemed to demand. The manipulation of political forces, unhampered by religion or chivalry, by respect for engagements, or by any feeling for the German race, was the mark of his reign, and his equivocal contribution to the public life of Germany. That he saw himself and the world through plain glass, that he spurned delights and lived laborious days, viewing himself always as the first servant of the Prussian state, and that he possessed to an almost unequalled degree the gift of leadership in war and peace, are qualities which have compelled the admiration of the world. The German may find flaws in the sovereign who never affected to conceal his contempt for the language and literature of the Fatherland; but the Prussians are right in regarding the great Fritz as one of the master builders of their state. In the blaze of his transcendent service they readily condone the fact that he was an infidel in religion, a cynic in politics, and that in his intellectual outlook upon life he was a disciple of Voltaire. They see in him the sovereign who made the Prussian army feared through Europe, who founded the reputation of Prussia as a military state, and added new and important provinces to his Prussian inheritance. They honour him as a commander, generally victorious, but never greater or more resourceful than in the darkest hour of defeat, as a king who brought his country through great trials into peace and security, and raised it to a position of indisputable predominance in Germany. To the tender conscience shrinking from the long catalogue of dubious acts beginning with the perfidious seizure of Silesia, and ending with the first partition of Poland, by which Frederick attained his ends, they reply that such were the international morals of the age, and that the Hohenzollern was no worse than his contemporaries. The doctrine that the end justifies the means is a necessary part of the Prussian apology for Frederick II.

His ambition was high but not exorbitant. Asking much of his people, but always for a Prussian and a practical end, he was nevertheless not indifferent to the advantages of a balance of power. The Europe for which he fought was one in which Prussia strengthened by Silesia faced an Austria not otherwise aggrandized. Such a Europe was vouchsafed him by the Peace of Aix-la-Chapelle in 1748. By using the Prussian army as a diplomatic instrument, he had obtained his objective. Now it had been thrown into the fray, now suddenly withdrawn, now again launched against his old enemy. Alternately he had saved Austria from France by a treaty, and France from Austria by an attack. His interventions and withdrawals had been in each case decisive, so that of all the combatants in the eight years Frederick alone had reason to be satisfied. While everyone else went empty-handed, he had won Silesia. Yet there was a fly in the ointment, for another long war had yet to be fought before the proud spirit of Maria Theresa was brought to acquiesce in her loss.

In October, 1740, the Emperor Charles VI, dying without male issue, left to Europe an occasion for demonstrating that the principles of honour, chivalry, and good faith were not altogether banished from international relations. His daughter Maria Theresa was a young married woman, inexperienced in affairs. Her treasury was empty, her army weak. Her title to succeed to the undivided inheritance of the Austrian Habsburgs had been recognized by every important court in Europe (Bavaria excepted) and in most cases for value received. Yet neither her sex, nor her inexperience, nor the solemn guarantees which had been given to her father availed the Queen of Hungary. Within a year of her succession she was involved in a desperate struggle to save the inheritance of her ancestors from a rapacious coalition headed by the very powers who were specially pledged to respect it.

The first blow was struck by Frederick II, who, without a particle of provocation, swooped down upon Silesia, and on the field of Mollwitz, thanks to the steadiness of his Prussian infantry, advertised the weakness of Austria to the world. It was vain to suppose that after such an Austrian reverse the struggle could be localized. From every quarter of the sky the vultures came flocking to the prey. France wanted to rob Austria of the Netherlands and Luxemburg, Bavaria desired the Imperial Crown and an eastward extension of her boundary. The elector of Saxony, who was also king of Poland, was anxious to claim a share in an empire which was threatened with dissolution. In the anti-Austrian coalition, France, the old enemy of the Habsburgs, acted as the spearhead, believing that the moment had come, with the aid of this new and unexpected Prussian power, to establish once and for all her political predominance in Europe. For a time everything prospered with her designs. Her army penetrated into Bohemia and captured Prague, while the Bavarians threatened the safety of Vienna. It was arranged that the Imperial Crown, which for more than three hundred years had been accorded to the head of the Habsburg house, should be transferred to Charles Albert of Bavaria, who contested Maria Theresa's title and was resolved to assail her territories. At no time in her long and chequered history, until the last year of the great war, did the fortunes of Austria sink so low as in the early summer of 1741.

Then followed a remarkable reversal of fortune. In the hour of her tribulation Maria Theresa threw herself upon the loyalty of her Hungarian subjects, and found in that chivalrous and warlike aristocracy a fiery response. The Bavarians were driven out of Munich, the French out of Prague. By a singular irony of fortune Charles Albert, the new Emperor, was compelled to sign a treaty renouncing his pretensions to the Austrian succession, and ceding his hereditary dominions to the Queen of Hungary until the general peace. By the summer of 1742 the wheel had turned full circle. The aggressive policy of France had reacted upon her. The invader of Bohemia was now compelled to look to the defences of Alsace and Lorraine. England and Sardinia had thrown their weight into the Austrian scale,

June 1743

and a fortunate battle at Dettingen, the last in which an English king drew the sword, encouraged the idea that an invasion of France might now be successfully attempted by two armies advancing respectively from points situated upon the middle and the upper Rhine.

The main cause of this sudden revolution of fortune is to be found in the action of the King of Prussia. Frederick intended to keep Silesia, but was not prepared to squander an unnecessary Prussian thaler or Prussian life upon its acquisition. At any moment he was willing to treat with the Queen of Hungary, always provided that he was guaranteed his Silesian conquest. On that basis he went out of the war in October, 1741. On that basis again he went out of the war in July, 1742, this time taking Saxony with him from the ranks of Austria's opponents. Freed

July, 1743

by the Peace of Berlin from her most formidable opponent, and exhilarated by a surprising succession of victories, Maria Theresa resolved to exploit her success to the full. The most dazzling possibilities appealed to her ardent imagination, the annexation of Bavaria, the conquest of Alsace and Lorraine, the recovery of Naples and Silesia. The war which opened with a plan for the ruin of Austria passed into a war for the dismemberment of

France. In the heat of her indignation and the flush of her victories the Queen of Hungary scorned the notion of peace.

In this implacable attitude England, deaf to the advice of its wisest statesman, ranged herself by the side of Maria Theresa. Walpole, who had been opposed to the war with Spain, was no less averse from inviting a rupture with France: for he foresaw that the first consequence of such an entanglement would be a Jacobite rising, which might shake the Hanoverian dynasty to the ground. But peace had become unfashionable, and Walpole was driven from power to make way for counsellors who would respond more nearly to the excitable mood of the country and the king. Carteret, the most accomplished, but not the most prudent, of men, sprang into the saddle, and with his master, who was above all things a Hanoverian, committed the country to a continental campaign. A treaty signed at Worms between England, Austria, and Sardinia, revived the scheme of a grand alliance, fortified by English subsidies, against the ambitions of France.

Feb.,
1743

Sept.
1743

The allies had reckoned without Frederick. That astute sovereign had watched with growing anxiety the course of Austria's triumphs in the west. "It is a capital error in politics," he observed, "to trust a reconciled enemy," and Frederick reposed no trust in Maria Theresa. So far from believing that she was truly reconciled at the Peace of Berlin, he was convinced that the queen studied revenge. Accordingly, while an Imperial army under Prince Charles of Lorraine was occupied in Alsace, Frederick, throwing principle to the winds, broke the peace, invaded Bohemia, and seized Prague (September 16, 1744). At once the whole complexion of the war was altered. The re-entry of Frederick placed Austria again upon her defence, and liberated France from a grave peril. A series of most glittering prizes offered themselves invitingly to the government of Louis XV, the conquest of Belgium, the dethronement of King George, the establishment of a Catholic dynasty on the English throne. A French army under the skilful leadership of Prince Maurice de Saxe entered the Austrian Netherlands, and twice (Fontenoy, May 11, 1745, and Lauffeld, July 2, 1746) compelled an English commander to accept defeat.

That the great French plan miscarried was at bottom due to the preponderance of English power at sea and to the continuing affection of the English people for the Protestant cause.

Channel storms dispersed an invading fleet. English privateers ruined French commerce; and it was given to Charles Edward, who raised the Stuart banner in the Highlands in 1745, to experience the bitter truth that an unpopular Hanoverian king could yet command the passive support of a lethargic but very Protestant population. The Jacobite cause, which enlisted so many romantic hopes and loyalties, foundered on the field of Culloden (April 16, 1746), but was in ruins from the moment that it became evident that Englishmen were not prepared to rally to Prince Charlie as he made his southward progress from Carlisle to Derby. Scanty as were the claims of George II upon the affections of his subjects, his throne was too firmly established to be upset by a small army of wild Gaelic swordsmen from the Highlands of Scotland. The reckless adventure, which has been glorified by the genius of Sir Walter Scott, served to consolidate the Protestant monarchy, and to spread its power through many a wild and lonely glen to the northern tip of Caithness. The subjugation of the Highlands was the solid and enduring result of the '45. Marshal Wade's roads and Pitt's Highland regiments completed the Act of Union and opened out to the Catholic inhabitants of northern Scotland the lavish resources and manifold opportunities of a great empire.

In the eastern theatre of the war neither party gained a decisive advantage. If Frederick was compelled to relax his hold on Bohemia, he was still in a position to inflict such defeats upon his adversary at Hohenfriedberg and Sohr, that on the strength of these personal triumphs, and with the help of a useful victory won by his Saxon allies, he brought the Austrians to sign a peace at Dresden, which guaranteed him Silesia and Glatz.

Dec.,
1745

Equally fierce, equally indecisive was the bloody struggle for supremacy which proceeded south of the Alps. Here Austria and Savoy were pitted against the two Bourbon kingdoms. And here, as in Germany, the Austrians were in the end compelled to cede a point to the adversary. The Peace of Aix-la-Chapelle, which closed the war, allotted the duchy of Parma to Don Philip of Spain.

1748

To this war of sharp vicissitudes, in which no nation had won victories which were not offset by grave losses, there was finally an end, induced rather by fatigue than by satisfaction. Nothing was really settled by the Peace of Aix-la-Chapelle, neither the naval and commercial duel between England and the Bourbon kingdoms, nor the Silesian duel between Austria and Prussia, nor the struggle for hegemony in Italy, nor the fate of the Netherlands, perforce retroceded at the peace to Austria, but destined to be recaptured by revolutionary France. In India England had suffered reverses ere long to be brilliantly retrieved; in the gateway to Canada she had captured the strong fortified port of Louisburg, a base in Cape Breton Island, which pointed to ulterior designs.

Englishmen had never greatly liked this War of the Austrian Succession. The opposition, led by William Pitt, a fiery young orator, who was to become a great war minister, thundered against the subsidies to Hanoverian and Hessian troops, and alleged, not without cause, that the ship of British policy was steered by a Hanoverian rudder. The money power of England seemed to be ill employed in nourishing a continental war, the main purpose of which was suspected to be the protection of Hanover, and the main result of which was that the Netherlands were overrun by the French, and that England was invaded by the Highlanders. Neither was it agreeable to France to contemplate the ruin of her foreign trade, through the depredations of English corsairs, the reverses of her navy, the miscarriage of her Jacobite enterprise, or the long purse of the islanders, who, when their armies had twice been defeated on the plains of Flanders, were ready to hire a Russian army to redress the balance. Rather than face these thirty thousand Russians, the government of France was disposed to peace, and in exchange for the return of Louisburg, to withdraw her troops from Holland and the Netherlands.

Of all the practical arts diplomacy is the most conservative. In the War of the Austrian Succession fidelity to an old tradition had made England the friend and France the enemy of Austria. As it had been in the past, so it was assumed that it must always be. The memories of ancient quarrels, as when Turenne and Condé measured swords with the Imperialists or Marlborough and Eugène confronted the marshals of Louis XIV, coloured the imaginations of men and shaped their policies. But when it was found that a long and costly war waged upon this diplomatic pattern led to no decisive result, the question naturally arose whether the diplomatic pattern was not an anachronism. What had Austria got out of the English alliance? What reason had France to acclaim the aggrandizement of Prussia? Which of the two powers, Catholic Austria or Protestant Prussia under its soldier king, would be most helpful to England in her impending and inevitable struggle for colonial empire with France? From these doubts and discontents there emerged a diplomatic revolution. As early as 1751, letters were going from Maria Theresa to "Madame my very dear sister," the reigning mistress of the French king.

In diplomacy personality is always a factor. Frederick was a misogynist who found in the three dominant women of his day a perpetual invitation to scurrilous and well advertised wit. Maria Theresa, the devout, unforgiving Empress, Madame de Pompadour, the all-powerful mistress of Louis XV, Elizabeth, the licentious, vodka-drinking Tzarina of Russia, gave occasion to gibes which went the rounds of Europe, and lashed the courts of Vienna, Versailles, and St. Petersburg to a fury of indignation. If the reckless insults which Frederick hurled at "the Apostolic Hag" and "Mlle. Poisson" (for the Pompadour was said to be the daughter of a fish wife) did not make the diplomatic revolution, at least they helped it on its way. The Tzarina was tough. Yet even Elizabeth, in her intervals of sobriety, must have been roused by a nickname which consigned her to the worst depths of animalism, infamy, and vice.

The Austrian alliance, so violently opposed to the diplomatic traditions of France, was unpopular from the first, and since it led to disorders, helped to widen the gulf between the monarchy and the nation. Yet there is no reason to think that the French treaties with Austria were the result of the wounded vanity of a beautiful woman. The grounds for a Franco-Austrian alliance were sound enough, since it was reasonable to surmise that a German state so strong as the Prussia of Frederick had already shown itself to be was likely to be too strong for the comfort of France.

What, however, is open to criticism is not the original Franco-Austrian Treaty, which was defensive only, but the subsequent instrument which pledged France to an offensive and defensive alliance with Maria Theresa. The interests of France at this juncture of history were singularly ill served by another continental war. Her nationals were already struggling with the ancient enemy in the backwoods of America and in the plains of the Carnatic, and she would have been better advised to con-

August, 1756

centrate her efforts on the defence of her overseas possessions, which were already menaced by the formidable activity of their English rivals. It is, however, a remarkable fact how little public opinion in France was alive to the true character of the war into which her statesmen were leading her. So far from being concerned with India or Canada or the West Indies, the small section of France which was politically minded was passionately absorbed by the quarrel between the Crown and the Parliaments, between the liberalism of the Jansenists and the deists, and the persecuting Catholicism of the Jesuit Order, and with a wide range of constitutional problems suggested by the inevitable comparison between the free institutions of England and the secretive autocracy of France. So unpopular was the crown, so detested were the priests, and so violent was the spirit of criticism and revolt, that good judges, like the Marquis d'Argenson and the Earl of Chesterfield, writing in the middle of the century, discerned the signs of impending revolution. The vigorous and intelligent direction of a great war could hardly be expected in such an atmosphere. While the literary class was engaged in fighting the battle of toleration and freedom, the lawyers in the Paris Parliament offered a vigorous resistance to any attempt to enlarge the contracted basis of taxation. An imaginative grasp of war aims, a readiness to bear war burdens, a capacity to give to the people of France the unity of direction which is required by any great war effort, were wholly wanting to the quick-witted but short-sighted corporations of lawyers, whose busy and acrimonious contentions obscured the larger issues of the time.

The Prussian advance into Saxony (September, 1756) which launched the Seven Years' War has been compared to the invasion of Belgium, which lit the flames of a yet greater conflict. And if the parallel is not exact, for Saxony, though outwardly innocent, cannot be acquitted of meditating mischief, it is nevertheless true that Frederick's action in suddenly rushing troops into a peaceful neighbour state, in seizing its capital and treasure, and in incorporating its army forcibly with his own, appeared to contemporaries to be a flagrant violation of international law. The proofs of an anti-Prussian coalition discovered in Dresden did not weigh against the patent fact that the King of Prussia was the first to wreck the peace. The Aulic Council at Vienna deprived him of his dominions and titles and called upon the German Diet to send an army of execution against the criminal.

The dangers and difficulties which now confronted Frederick were enormous. A ring of powerful enemies menaced him on every side: in the south the Austrians, in the east the Russians, in the west the French and Imperialists, in the north the Swedes. Against such a combination, drawing as it did from almost limitless resources of man-power, and at once able to put into the field armies twice as numerous as his own, Frederick was at a serious disadvantage. Whereas the Russians and Austrians could replace an army which had been shattered in battle, Prussian casualties could not be made good.

Amidst a world of enemies Frederick found an ally in England. "The King of Prussia," observed George II, "is a mischievous rascal, a bad friend, a bad ally, a bad relation, and a bad neighbour, in fact, the most dangerous and ill-disposed prince in Europe." But the policy of England was now directed not by George II, but by William Pitt, in whose fiery imagination the Prussian king was magically transformed into the champion of the liberties of Europe and the pillar of the Protestant faith. Pitt did not send an English army into the eastern theatre of war; but English subsidies nourished the continental war, while English raids on the French coast, and English and Hanoverian support for Prince Ferdinand of Brunswick, who upheld Frederick's cause in western Germany, sensibly relieved the pressure which France might otherwise have exerted on his western flank.

Yet it is Frederick and Frederick alone who saved Prussia from obliteration. The Prussian army, though largely recruited from aliens, had been fashioned by its infidel commander into a unit religiously schooled to every sacrifice. As it marched into action, nerved by the inspired eloquence of its artist king, and warmed by the stirring music of a Lutheran chorale, it was persuaded that the Protestant God was fighting on its side. The most terrible losses, since they did not weaken the iron purpose of the leader, failed to demoralize the brave men who had fallen under his spell. Reduced to a third of its original strength after the fierce fighting of the opening year, the army of Frederick continued to defend against overwhelming odds the right of the Prussian nation to exist. It was of little moment that Berlin was plundered by an enemy raid in 1757, or that for many months in succeeding years a Russian army practised its notorious barbarities on Prussian soil. The soul of Prussia was not in a place but in a man, who beneath all his superficial gifts, graces, and accomplishments, his fugues and sonatas, his French verses and philosophic speculations concealed the ancient granite of his warrior race.

Never was his resistance more brilliantly exhibited than in the first year of the general fighting. His invasion of Bohemia ended in catastrophic failure. He was victorious at Prague, but beaten at Kollin, and compelled to withdraw the remnants of his sorely stricken army north of the Erz Gebirge. As the net of his enemies, French and Imperialists, Austrians, Russians, and Swedes, closed round him in the late summer of that year, his thoughts turned to a suicide pact with his beloved sister. But with the call to action the black mood of the man of temperament passed away. Hurrying westwards into Saxony to meet the French, he surprised the army of the Prince de Soubise at Rossbach, and there inflicted upon it a crushing defeat, duly celebrated *Nov.* at the Tabernacle in London by that eloquent Methodist preacher *1757* Mr. Whitefield as a crowning victory for the Protestant cause. Meanwhile Daun was in Silesia, and here on the hard-fought field of Leuthen, under a bitter December sky, Frederick routed *Dec.,* that sound Austrian general, who, a few months earlier, had *1757* compelled him to accept defeat.

The energy and skill with which, in this wonderful autumn campaign, Frederick drove the enemy from Saxony and Silesia, with an army shaken and decimated by earlier defeats, have compelled the admiration of soldiers in every subsequent generation. To Napoleon, the greatest of them all, the battle of Leuthen, "a masterpiece of movements, manoeuvres, and resolution," was alone sufficient to rank Frederick with the captains of undying fame.

The essential character of the war problem in the east was not altered by these triumphs. It could never be hoped that Prussia, a country vulnerable to an extreme degree on every frontier, could be effectively guarded against invasion. The only question was whether Frederick, the sovereign of this small, poor, ill-populated state, could keep an army in being against the united powers of two great empires, each able to bring into the field armies numerically superior to his own and infinitely more elastic. That the answer to this question was favourable to

Frederick was not only due to the military genius which enabled him again and again, as at Liegnitz (August 14, 1760), at Torgau (November 3, 1760), and at Schweidnitz (August 9, 1762), to attack and defeat the enemy, but also to the defective combination and mutual jealousies of his Russian and Austrian opponents and to certain ingrained defects of temperament of which he was able to take full advantage. If the morale of the Russians had been equal to the scale of their armies, if Fermor had not turned eastward after the drawn battle of Zorndorf, where he took heavy toll of Prussian manhood, if Soltikov had not surrendered himself to debauchery after his crushing victory at Kunersdorf, or if after that great Russian-Austrian triumph the Austrians under Daun had been prompt to pursue the advantage, Frederick would have been inevitably driven to take that fatal potion which was his alternative to a dishonourable peace. There seems, however, to be an inherent lack of orderly perseverance in the Russian character. In the Seven Years' War the Russians advanced again and again into Prussian territory. They seized Colmar and settled down in Prussian Pomerania. They penetrated to Frankfort-on-Oder and even to Berlin. They fought three savage battles with the Prussians and inflicted on them terrible losses; but they never clinched their victory. When the Tzarina Elizabeth died on January 5, 1762, a little, desperate, haggard man, his face unwashed, his clothes old and much soiled with grease and Spanish snuff, but with some leisure yet for the flute and French verses, and capable, as was proved on the field of Schweidnitz, of dealing a savage blow at his opponent, was still hanging on among the Silesian hills with a following of war-battered veterans as ragged and desperate as himself. Elizabeth's death was his salvation, for it put a friend upon the Russian throne in place of an enemy. Peter III was the king's ardent admirer. With the Russians withdrawn and the Turks menacing her eastern borders, Maria Theresa was at last compelled to sign the Peace of Hubertsburg (February 15, 1763). The idea that Prussia could be decreed out of existence by an Aulic Council, even if it were supported by the armies of the three greatest states in Europe, was shown to be an idle dream.

In the western and maritime area the sea power of England, directed by the genius of William Pitt, was destined to secure for the Protestant combination its greatest triumph. While the main result of the eastern or continental war was conservative, the consequences of the great conflict between France and England were revolutionary beyond all expectation. Frederick, by his great exertions, prevented a violent change in the balance of German power. He saved Prussia from destruction and secured his hold on Silesia; but England gained a new empire in the east and in the west. Here was a vast alteration in the weights and balances of the world. At the end of the war the North American continent had been secured for Anglo-Saxon expansion and India for Anglo-Saxon rule. The French, who had threatened to bar the western advance of the English colonists in North America, had been driven from their stations along the Ohio. The British flag flew from the fort of Quebec. The destiny of a huge continent was determined. In India Robert Clive, a young officer of the East India Company, had laid the foundations of that extraordinary polity which combines under the political direction of a northern and Protestant people more than three hundred million Orientals, whose almost infinite diversities of race, language, and religion present to their impartial masters an opportunity and a problem.

At first things went ill with the English. The French in Canada with their Red Indian allies had the advantage of the early exchanges. In the Mediterranean, Minorca was lost, to the rage and shame of a people ill accustomed to marine reverses. Calcutta fell into enemy hands. There was failure before Rochfort, and a British fleet disabled by storm before Louisburg. But then, as so often happens when the English go to war, the reserves of moral and material power began to accumulate, and, under the impulsion of a great leader, to tell on the result. *July, 1756*

A vast combination of offensives directed against France in every part of the world began to yield remarkable rewards. Louisburg (the key to Canada), Fort Duquesne (the French outpost on the Ohio, the link between French Canada and French Louisiana, and the kernel of a possible French empire in the middle west of North America) fell into English hands. So, too, did Goree, and with it the French West African slave trade. English subsidies and English soldiers were despatched to the assistance of Duke Ferdinand of Brunswick, who sustained the Protestant cause in the Hanoverian area, and in so doing found his task not a little lightened by the active raids of the English navy upon the French coast. A decisive victory over a more numerous *1758*

French army at Crevelt (June 23) announced that a new military talent of high quality had been enlisted in the Anglo-Prussian cause.

America was the principal goal of Pitt's effort. It is his supreme merit as a statesman that he divined its importance and regarded all other operations in the war as subsidiary to its conquest. It was the "fountain of our wealth, the nerve of our strength, the nursery and basis of our naval power."

Pitt's great design for the destruction of French power in Canada by a triple attack directed from west, south, and east, though incapable of exact execution, was indicative of a mind equal to the scale of its task, and was, in fact, successful. Wolfe's victory over Montcalm on the heights of Abraham (September 13, 1759) has never been reversed. French Canada, for ever impenetrable to the creed, the language, and the outlook of the islander, passed under English control, a fragment of ancient France embedded in northern ice. The sea power of England guarded the conquest.

Given the balance of naval strength which prevailed at that time, the result of the war, both in the west and the east, could hardly have been otherwise. The population of French Canada, though more effectively organized for war, was greatly outnumbered by the thirteen flourishing English colonies along the Atlantic Ocean. Two million men have an advantage over fifty thousand, which in the end is bound to assert itself. What was lacking to the English colonies was not courage or enterprise, but the power of combination. An English fleet, an English army, and an English plan of campaign mobilized resources which had long been present and enabled them to exert their due effect.

A share of the credit for the great marine and colonial triumphs of this time is due to the English Parliament, which provided a sounding-board for the passions, cupidities, and grievances of the sailors, merchants, and colonists. It was impossible for London, as it was not impossible for Paris, to forget the needs of its nationals beyond the seas.

English constituencies possessed colonial interests and affiliations. The members for Poole were the champions of Newfoundland. Devizes held a watching brief for the Carolinas. For Paris there was nothing of the kind. Wanting such an organ for concentrating the voices from the sea, the French marine administration was at the mercy of court favour. Good ministers like

Machault were allowed to fall without a murmur, bad ministers like Moras to rule without a challenge. In the critical year of 1759 the French Mediterranean fleet was crippled by Boscawen at Lagos, and the French Atlantic fleet in great part destroyed by Hawke in Quiberon Bay. Even if the campaign of Wolfe had miscarried, these two naval actions were sufficient to settle the issue of the American war.

In India, where the dissolution of the Mogul Empire afforded a free field for European ambitions, fortune first favoured, and then for similar reasons deserted, the French. Site for site, England was more advantageously placed than her rival. Bombay was a finer port than Mahé, Madras more central than Pondicherry, Calcutta more convenient for commerce than the French station at Chandernagore. But in the race for political influence and power the French at first drew ahead. During the War of the Austrian Succession, when La Bourdonnais commanded her fleet, and Dupleix from Pondicherry was working for an empire to be won through Indian alliances and a Sepoy army, and Bussy, a brilliant oriental linguist, was weaving diplomatic webs in Hyderabad, the influence of France was predominant in southern India. Madras even, for some years, passed into her hands.

1740-8

After the Peace of Aix-la-Chapelle the tables were turned. Of the two rival East India Companies the English was incomparably the stronger in commerce and finance. England had the better men on the spot and was prepared to give them more effective support and assistance from home. France withdrew La Bourdonnais and Dupleix, England discovered Robert Clive, Stringer Lawrence, and Eyre Coote. While French ships from their distant base in Mauritius refused to cross the Indian Ocean in the monsoon, there was no season of the year at which naval help was not available for the support of the English interest. The idea that a handful of Frenchmen could aspire to give the law to the Deccan seemed to politicians in Paris to be the wildest folly. A handful of Englishmen, inspired by Robert Clive, succeeded in demonstrating that a plan of political dominion even wider and more foolhardy could in effect be accomplished. The career of Robert Clive, the son of an impoverished squire, who started as a merchant's clerk in the employment of the East India Company and founded an empire, is one of the romances of the world. Clive died by his own hand at the age of forty-nine. His whole period of Indian service, which was broken by two visits to

1725-79

England, did not exceed twelve years. In his first spell he mad England supreme in the Carnatic; in his second he reconquere Calcutta from Suraj-ud Dowlah, defeated his army at Plassey defeated the Dutch, cleared the French out of Bengal and th northern Circars, destroyed their influence in Hyderabad, an established British power in the valley of the Ganges. In th third and not the least honourable period of his public service h organized and purified the civil administration of Bengal. Extra ordinary daring characterized his military enterprises. At the ag of twenty-six he led five hundred men to Arcot, the capital of th Carnatic, and there held a crumbling fortress against te thousand Indians with a stiffening of French troops for fift

1757

days. On the decisive field of Plassey he brought three thousan men into action, of whom nine hundred only were Europeans against a force of forty thousand infantry and fifteen thousan cavalry, and with a loss of less than a hundred men routed hi opponents.

With one exception all the great political secrets of Britisl rule in India were revealed to him. He saw that a Europear leader of Indian troops who was prepared to take extravagan personal risks could work miracles with his men; he realized tha no great political result could be obtained without Indiar alliances and co-operation; he set his face against corruption and contended that some day all the scattered possessions of the Eas India Company must be brought together under one politica head. The chief blot upon the fame of a bold but insensitive ma is that he perpetrated a fraud upon a Hindu blackmailer. Omi chund was a rascal, but even a rascal should not have been per mitted to provoke a signal display of British bad faith.

By April, 1761, the French had nothing left of their Indiar Empire. Their last Governor was an Irishman by descent, whe had fought for the Jacobites in the '45, and had still an unex pended balance of hatred to discharge against the Englisl people. Lally Tollendal had the impatient courage of his race but, knowing nothing of India or its people, and being of vehement and umbrageous temper, he outraged every suscepti bility and committed every mistake. Such an Irishman wa capable of wrecking any cause. The unfortunate Lally lost Indi for the French on the hard-fought field of Wandewash. There i no aspersion on his courage or loyalty; but in Eyre Coote he me a soldier hardly surpassed by Clive himself. Magnanimity in fac of disaster is not one of the special French virtues. Six years after the fall of Pondicherry (1761) a barbarous crowd gathered in the Place de la Grève to enjoy the last agonies of this passionate son of Erin as, under the clumsy axe of the Paris executioner, he expiated a proconsul's failure. To Clive a grateful but not uncensorious country awarded a medal, a statue, and an Irish peerage.

When the war was at last brought to an end by the Peace of Paris in 1763 the terms, though less favourable than Pitt would have had them, secured acquisitions of territory for England and her colonies on such a scale as to change the current of her history. Save for the few factories which she held in January, 1749, France was evicted from India. Canada and Senegal passed to England. Minorca was restored. Florida was surrendered by Spain. The constellation of the English West Indies was enriched by the addition of St. Vincent, Tobago, Dominica, and the Grenadines. Even though the French were allowed to retain fishing rights off Newfoundland and in the St. Lawrence, and received back some valuable West Indian islands, it was from the English standpoint a great peace. A contemporary not unjustly described it as "the most honourable peace this nation ever saw."

A vast increase of commercial prosperity enabled England to bear without distress the burden of a long and costly war, at the conclusion of which, as Adam Smith afterwards pointed out, "her agriculture was as flourishing, her manufactures as numerous, and her commerce as extensive as they had ever been before." Far otherwise was the position of England's ally on the continent. "Prussia's population," writes Frederick, "had diminished by 500,000 during the Seven Years' War. On a population of 4,500,000 that decrease was considerable. The nobility and the peasants had been pillaged and ransomed by so many armies that they had nothing left except the miserable rags which covered their nudity. They had not credit enough to satisfy their daily needs. The towns possessed no longer a police. The spirit of fairness and order had been replaced by anarchy and self-interest. The judges and the revenue authorities had given up their work owing to the frequency of invasions. In the absence of laws a spirit of recklessness and of rapacity arose. The nobility and the merchants, the farmers, the working men and the manufacturers had raised the price of their labour and products to the utmost. All seemed intent upon ruining each other by their

exactions. That was the terrible spectacle which the formerly s
flourishing provinces offered after the conclusion of the war. Th
appearance of the provinces resembled that of Brandenburg afte
the end of the Thirty Years' War." Forged in such a flame o
adversity, the Prussian will took on the hardness of steel, and b
the gentler courts of Germany, where the arts flourished, wa
regarded as something minatory and barbaric.

Compared with the terrible cost of Silesia, the English sacri
fices in the Seven Years' War seem to Germans to be a suprem
illustration of the harsh inequality of fate. Twenty European
only fell on the field of Plassey, one hundred and ninety-four a
Wandewash. The cost of the conquest of Canada, according t
Pitt, did not exceed one thousand five hundred lives. The bloo
price exacted from England for two great empires was multiplie
five times and more in many of the major actions in Frederick'
campaign. But if the initial cost, measured in lives, was low
plenty of trouble was yet to come. Before many years had passe
there broke out on American soil that formidable conflic
between the Mother Country and her colonists which led to th
foundation of the United States of America.

BOOKS WHICH MAY BE CONSULTED

T. Carlyle : Life of Frederick II of Prussia. 1858-65.

B. Williams : The Life of William Pitt, Earl of Chatham. 1914.

J. R. Seely : The Expansion of England. 1885.

A. duc de Broglie : Frédéric II et Marie-Thérèse. 2 vols. 1883.

A. G. Bradley : The Fight with France for North America. 1900.

A. C. Lyall : Warren Hastings. 1889.

A. C. Lyall : The Rise and Expansion of the British Dominion in India
    1907.

Macaulay's Essays (Clive, Warren Hastings, Chatham). 1852.

L. B. Namier : The Structure of Politics at the Accession of George III
    2 vols. 1929.

J. S. Corbett : England in the Seven Years' War. 1907.

CHAPTER XXVIII

THE WAR OF AMERICAN INDEPENDENCE

The consequence of the conquest of Canada. The English colonies in North America. Trade restrictions. Direct taxation. The obstinacy of King George. The Boston tea-party and the Philadelphia Congress. The misconduct of the British forces in America. George Washington. The entry of France and Spain. The peril of England. Illusions produced by her defeat.

PROMINENT among the causes of the War of American Independence were those very British victories which had been so lightly purchased. The expulsion of the French from Canada, and of the Spanish from Florida, by relieving the English colonists of two dangerous neighbours, weakened their dependence on the mother country. Having less need of English help, the colonists were the more ready to challenge English pretensions. Many had willingly borne arms in the great French War. Few were willing to take a share in liquidating its financial liabilities. When George Grenville proposed a stamp tax to defray part of the cost of an army for the protection of the colonies, motives niggardly and narrow were combined with others which belonged to the best political inheritance of the Anglo-Saxon race to frustrate the imposition.

1765

Of all the European settlements in the new world, the thirteen English colonies in North America enjoyed the largest measure of liberty. Though they were subject to the British crown and Parliament, they were in effect allowed to manage their own affairs with little interference from Westminster, save in one particular. Imperial trade was subject to regulation conceived to be in the mutual interest of the mother country and its colonial daughters. "Economic planning" on the grand scale is never likely to be successful over a tract of time, and the old English colonial system furnishes a good example of the friction which may be generated by a well-meant endeavour to regulate the commercial and industrial life of scattered communities from a distant centre. The colonies were forbidden to start factories which might compete with the industries of the mother country. They were compelled to ship their exports in British or colonial vessels manned to the extent of two-thirds by British or colonial crews, and in respect of a long list of enumerated articles, including many of their staple products, were constrained to discharge their cargoes in English ports. On the other hand Englishmen were forbidden to smoke tobacco grown elsewhere than in America or Bermuda, and bounties were paid to the lumbermen of New England to encourage the industry in naval stores.

1760   At the stage of economic development which had been reached by the English colonies at the beginning of George III's reign these regulations were not felt to be seriously burdensome. The time was not yet ripe for colonial factory development, and so long as the colonists were prepared to allow the mother country to provide them with manufactured goods it was no hardship to ship raw produce to English ports and to obtain in exchange the products of English factories.

There was, however, one restriction which caused the greatest irritation. If the piety of New England was founded on the Bible, its prosperity was not a little dependent on rum. The Molasses Act of 1733, by virtually prohibiting the importation of French-grown sugar, molasses, and rum, in the interests of the British plantations, struck a blow at the New England distilleries which, but for the enormous success of colonial smuggling, might have been sufficient in itself to produce a rupture. It is a singular reflection that had it not been for the activity of the bootleggers of the eighteenth century the primary impulsion which led to the foundation of the American republic might have been a restriction imposed by the port-drinking legislators at Westminster on the American trade in rum with the native Indians.

The rift came over direct taxation. The English have always quarrelled over money, and the English colonists in America (for the Irish element was then negligible) who resisted Grenville's stamp tax were faithful to the habits of their ancestors. On the old familiar fighting-ground "No taxation without representation" they protested against an impost which, though small in itself, was large in relation to their parsimonious budgets. It was an English issue dividing men of English race on either side of the Atlantic. America had its Tories or loyalists, England its Americans or Whigs. The three greatest British statesmen of the time, Chatham, Burke, and Fox, were opposed to the coercion of the colonies, and in their opinion supported by a substantial section of the British middle class. So domestic was the complexion of the quarrel in its early stages that officers of the king's army and navy could, without social stigma, resign their commissions rather than bear arms against their kith and kin across the ocean.

American historians now recognize that there was more substance in the English case than their predecessors had been generally willing to allow. The future of North America was not yet secure. There was always danger from the Indians. There might, given European complications, be a renewed attack from France and Spain. A colonial defence force, somehow provided, seemed to be a reasonable insurance against incalculable risks. Such a course the colonies out of mutual jealousies had hitherto been unable to finance, and there was no reason to think that an attempt which had failed in 1754, when the French danger was at its height, would succeed ten years later when the French had been decisively driven from the field. Was it, then, outrageous that the British Parliament in the exercise of its sovereign rights should impose a tax upon the colonists to be spent in the colonies upon an army exclusively designed for colonial defence?

The easy-going, pleasure-loving legislators of the British upper class, suddenly confronted with the strange problem of governing distant empires, were ill qualified to understand the rough democracy which across the Atlantic waste still cherished with fervour the ideals of the Cromwellian age. Even more serious, seeing that he had made himself master of Cabinet and Parliament, was the incomprehension of the king. In view of the violent outcry occasioned by Grenville's taxes, the most ordinary prudence counselled their abandonment and the surrender of any prospect of supplies from the colonies other than those which might be freely voted by the colonial assemblies. To George III, however, there was only one way to deal with mutinous colonists, the way of force. He would make no concession on the point of principle. The withdrawal of the stamp tax in 1765 was flanked by a parliamentary declaration that Britain had full right to tax her colonies, and a number of trifling duties on glass, lead, paper, and tea imposed (1767) by Charles Townshend, more for the purpose of illustrating a principle than of bringing in a substantial revenue, fanned the flame of colonial discontent to fever height. Even when it was clearly shown that the new taxes cost far more to collect than they were worth and were fast driving Massachusetts to rebellion, the king declined to surrender the point of dogma. By a majority of one vote the Cabinet of Lord North, while abandoning the other Townshend taxes, decided to retain the duty upon tea. It would be difficult to conceive an act of greater folly. At the utmost the duty was estimated to yield £16,000 a year; and the ministry, in order to conciliate public opinion, had expressly declared (May, 1769) that they did not propose to levy any further taxes upon America for the purpose of raising a revenue. The reply of the Americans was a war signal. On December 16, 1773, a body of men disguised as Mohawk Indians boarded three ships in Boston harbour and threw their whole cargo of tea into the water. The British Cabinet retaliated by closing the port of Boston, by remodelling the Charter of Massachusetts, and by an act enabling prisoners indicted on capital charges in that state to be sent for trial, should it appear that they could not be fairly tried in the province, to some other colony or to Great Britain.

The colonies rallied round Massachusetts in its resistance to these punitive measures. A solemn League and Covenant was formed binding the subscribers to abstain from commercial intercourse with Great Britain until their hated orders had been repealed. On September 5, 1774, delegates of twelve States met in Congress in Philadelphia to concert measures of resistance against the British Crown. Each side speculated upon the weakness and division of the other.

The British conduct of the war was no less unfortunate than the policy which had made war inevitable. There was in the colonies an important body of opinion actively favourable to the maintenance of the British connection, while an even greater number of colonists were indifferent or uncertain. To conciliate these friendly or wavering colonial minds, to respect the property of every friendly American, and wherever possible to enlist the help of American loyalists in the tasks of civil government should have been a prime object of British policy. Nothing of the kind was done. While the Indians, whose support had most unhappily been invoked by the British, alienated every frontiersman with their excesses, the army of Lord Howe, largely composed of Hessians and Hanoverians, pillaged indifferently the houses of friend and foe. It is a sufficient commentary upon their deplorable conduct that during the whole course of the war no more than 2,500 loyalist volunteers were enlisted in the British ranks.

Nevertheless, had not France and Spain entered the lists on the American side, the colonists might have lost the war. Even the genius of George Washington, by far the greatest man on either side, was unable to protect the American revolution from a series of crushing defeats. Long Island, Trenton, Brandywine were black days in the military annals of the "Sons of Liberty." There is nothing wonderful here. The American state was in the making. In Philadelphia, the capital of the young federation, where everything was raw and experimental, and state sense, state loyalty, and state cohesion had still to be created, the civilians could give no lessons to the soldiers. It was Washington, and he alone, who in the camp of Valley Forge, amid the dire hardships of a bitter winter, brought back a severely shaken and ill-provisioned army to a sense of disciplined efficiency and once more made of it an instrument of victory. So little was the revolution the work of a convinced and united people that at no time in the war did the army of Washington exceed twenty thousand men.

On October 17, 1777, an English army under General Burgoyne, advancing southwards on New York, was forced to capitulate at Saratoga. Stirred by this thunderclap, which sounded round the world, monarchical France, in a wild mood of jealousy, revenge, and enthusiasm, entered on a war for the establishment of an American republic.

Feb., 1778

For Louis XVI and Marie Antoinette no policy could have been more improvident, for not only did the American war give the final push to the tottering edifice of French finance, but the spectacle of republicanism triumphant and monarchy overthrown beyond the Atlantic kindled in every forward-reaching mind in France the vision of a Europe remade after the new American pattern of republican liberty. The fact that the emancipation of the American colonies was effected with the help of France and Spain made an enormous difference to the sentiment with which the struggle was regarded on either side of the Atlantic. The American war ceased to be a domestic and became an international quarrel. The colonists had appealed to the foreign enemies of England and secured their help. The colonial revolt, originally regarded as a small domestic quarrel, had widened out into a formidable coalition which taxed the resources of Great Britain in every quarter of the globe. As if the hostility of the Bourbon monarchies was not enough, the Dutch joined in against their old commercial rivals, and a league of neutral northern powers, headed by Catharine of Russia, menaced interference with the British Navy if it continued to molest neutral trade at sea. Great Britain had never been more isolated or in greater peril. If she was compelled to fight the Dutch on the Coromandel coast, in Ceylon, and in Sumatra, if Hyder Ali deluged the Carnatic in blood, if eight West Indian islands were lost owing to the greatly increased efficiency of the French Navy, if Minorca and Florida were wrested from her, the prime cause was the obstinacy of her own colonial children. Chatham was not the only British friend of the American cause who, when the aid of foreign powers was invoked by the insurgents, felt with a passionate intensity that henceforth there could be no word of surrender.

War is the parent of illusions. The French idealized without understanding the liberty and equality of a slave-owning republic. The Americans regarded the French, from whom they were widely separated in all fundamental points of character and temperament, as paladins of chivalry nearer to them and more congenial than the cross-grained English from whom the colonists had derived their race, their language, their literature, and their constitution. Another illusion was fraught with graver consequences. The defeat of England in the colonial war engendered a general belief that the history of the English was wound up. The Parliament of Westminster was compared to the Diet of Warsaw, the factions of English political life to the ruinous dissensions of the Poles.

That England's sun had set was the firm belief of rulers so powerful and intelligent as Frederick of Prussia, Catharine of Russia, and Joseph of Austria. The prestige of England, which stood so high in 1763, was depressed beyond all due reason by the capitulation of Yorktown eighteen years later. It has always been found difficult to take Britain's measure.

Proceeding upon a gross under-estimate of its adversary's power, revolutionary France, as Imperialist Germany in our own time, was destined to receive a serious shock.

From a purely political point of view there seemed much to justify this unfavourable estimate. There was nothing glorious or even moderately skilful about the English government (1770-1782) which lost the American colonies. Lord North, the Prime Minister, did not believe in the war, but allowed his will to be directed by the king. The Cabinet system was broken down. The Whig party was in decomposition. The fitful star of Chatham finally sank below the waters in 1778; the clear effulgence of his son's cold and powerful intellect had not yet risen above the horizon. The war was ill managed, unpopular, unsuccessful. Only the brilliant opposition speeches of Charles Fox kept alive a flame of political imagination in Westminster. Increasingly the country was becoming restless under a system which permitted so much corruption, so much incompetence, and so many failures. There was a cry for the political emancipation of the industrial towns; alternatively for a restriction of the king's power to corrupt Parliament. But when at last in 1782 the Whigs came into power once more and in the following year made the *Jan.,* Peace of Versailles with America, recognizing the independence *1783* of the American republic, the continent merely saw that an empire had been lost. It did not perceive that a constitution had been saved. Yet such was the case. The failure of the king's American policy involved the breakdown of the last effectual experiment in personal rule which has been tried in Britain.

A yet greater thing passed unnoticed. The defeated country was fast becoming through a series of unprecedented economic changes the workshop of the world and the principal centre of its finance.

BOOKS WHICH MAY BE CONSULTED

W. E. H. Lecky : History of England in the Eighteenth Century. 8 vols. 1878-90.

James Truslow Adams : The Founding of New England. 1921.

G. B. Hertz : The Old Colonial System. 1905.

G. L. Beer : Commercial Policy of England towards the American Colonies. 1893.

J. L. Hammond : Charles James Fox. 1903.

Sir George Trevelyan : The American Revolution. 1905.

S. E. Morison : The Oxford History of the United States, 1783-1917. 2 vols. 1927.

Cambridge Modern History, Vol. VII.

CHAPTER XXIX

ENGLAND BECOMES THE WORKSHOP OF THE WORLD

The foundation of English commercial credit. The Bank of England and the National Debt. Consequences for the Protestant succession and the growth of industry. Sea-borne timber and sea-borne coal. England becomes the workshop of the world. The bounty of Nature. The neglect of government. The Puritan spirit. The inventors. The improvement of communications. The new age of capitalism. The shadow side. The catastrophe of the French wars. Neglect of home conditions. Adam Smith and Karl Marx.

1697 AMONG the consequences of the English wars against Louis XIV were the establishment of the Bank of England and of the English National Debt, innovations bitterly contested at the time, but so far-reaching in their civilizing effects that without them a comparatively poor agricultural island could never, despite the brilliance of its mechanical inventions or the wealth of its mineral resources, have developed into the workshop of Europe and the principal loan market in the world. The sound system of bank credit laid down in the reign of William III enabled the economic consequences of the steam engine and the spinning jenny to be exploited to the full. Had the mechanism of finance in England been defective, as it was in France, this could never have happened. The engines of the Industrial Revolution, which made England so rich and powerful that she was able to stand the strain of the Napoleonic wars, were moved by the oil of finance; and at the heart of the English financial system stood the Bank.

Europe had long been familiar with banks and bankers. To change money, to store money, to lend money, are operations as old as the bazaars of Babylon and Egypt. The money changers of Greece and Rome, the Jewish usurers, who emerged after the barbaric invasions, the bank of Genoa, which financed the Crusades, the Lombards, who have given a name to a famous English street, the Medicis of Florence, who raised revenue for the Papacy, the Fuggers of Augsburg, who sustained the empire of Charles V, the goldsmiths of London, who stored the wealth of its merchants and made advances to Charles II, all these agencies in different degrees performed some of the functions of a modern bank, eased the operations of commerce, and promoted the accumulation of wealth. It was only, however, with the foundation of the Bank of Amsterdam in 1609 that the mechanism of commerce and finance began to assume its modern shape. In this populous and thriving city stocks and shares were bought and sold, " bulled " and " beared," currencies were exchanged, loans were made to governments, and a growing volume of commerce was passed through a machine which enabled it to be conveniently and expeditiously dealt with. Such an example could not fail to impress the people with whom the Dutch were brought into the closest economic relations. London beheld the strange spectacle of a small neighbouring country finding the means of financing navies, armies, and great commercial enterprises out of all proportion to its exiguous area and population. Sir William Temple, one of the wisest statesmen of Charles II's reign, realized the strength which Holland derived from a National Debt and a National Bank, and wished England to follow the Dutch example. The system had merits of incontestable value. It provided a safe investment for the savings of the ordinary citizen, and was therefore an incitement to private thrift. It enabled nations to raise money more easily, and consequently to sustain the burden of large undertakings. It furnished commerce with capital contributed by individuals who were not merchants. For a régime of financial caprice it substituted one of financial regularity. Before the introduction of banking and long term loans to the state, the governments of Europe were in continual default. Elizabeth, indeed, most parsimonious of queens, had furnished a rare and solitary example of solvency to her generation; but the Dutch, though large spenders, were solvent throughout the whole of the seventeenth century, because they had adopted a sound method of financing state expenditure.

The example of the Dutch was reinforced by the pressure of a disordered currency and an expensive war. The idea of a state bank, which had been pressed upon the government by William Patterson, a brilliant and imaginative Scot who had made his fortune in London, was carried out in 1694 by Charles Montagu, Earl of Halifax. Since a loan was required to finance the war, a corporation known as the Governor and Company of the Bank of England was formed to raise it, and guaranteed upon the security of the taxes an interest at eight per cent. Despite strong opposition, the Whig Bill for a Bank of England received the assent of Parliament; but so little were the doubts of politicians shared by the City of London that within ten days after the books were open, the whole amount of the loan (£1,200,000) was subscribed. Without it the British navy could not have gone to sea.

To the Tory squires the new system of Whig finance appeared to be an odious design levelled against the landed interest and certain to bring ruin on the country. But the Bank was too strong for its enemies. It survived the attacks of the goldsmiths and the competition of a land bank, which had been specially set up to bring it to the ground. It received the privilege of issuing notes (1697) and was then given a monopoly till 1810. Among the causes which promoted the Protestant succession, none was more powerful than the general belief that the Jacobites, were they restored to the throne, would repudiate the National Debt, which had made possible the victories of Marlborough. The first step on the road to the Industrial Revolution, which has spread the factory system over the world, and so multiplied its wealth and population, was taken when English credit was put upon a modern basis.

The forest-haunted music of Germany recalls to us an age when the material civilization of northern and central Europe depended almost entirely upon its woodlands. For more than two thousand years men lived for the most part in wooden houses, sailed in wooden ships, warmed themselves at log fires, and drew from the forest the materials out of which were fashioned the common utensils of domestic use as well as the instruments of agriculture and industry. Long after the Italians had shown the way in stone, brick, and marble, and the art of brickmaking so well known to ancient Rome had been rediscovered by the contemporaries of Caxton, the principal cities of northern Europe continued to be built largely of wood. It was a wooden London which went up in flames when Charles II was king, a wooden Moscow which burned itself to a cinder under the eyes of Napoleon. So persistent was the rural tradition that even the first steam engine was encased in a carriage of wood, as the first power loom was worked by a bull.

The problem of preserving forest timber had ever since the fifteenth century been a matter of intermittent concern, as trees were felled in abnormal numbers to meet some exceptional need, such as the mining of silver, or the manufacture of porcelain or glass. But to the maritime states of the west, as they developed in the seventeenth century, the timber supply was no mere local convenience, but a primary requisite of national power. After a million oaks had been felled to build the navy of the Commonwealth, John Evelyn, the most charming of humanists, asked in his *Sylva*, the most delightful of books, how soon by a scientific system of plantation the marine future of England was to be preserved. It is a tempting conjecture that the navy of Nelson was built out of timber which owed its existence to the providence of this engaging Surrey squire. But England in a matter so vital was not content to rely upon its home supplies. The virgin forests of Massachusetts were called in to save the antique glades of Windsor, of Hatfield, and of Selwood. In this, as in other directions, the new world was called in to supply the deficiencies of the old.

Meanwhile another source of fuel, known far back in the middle ages, had become a commercial proposition. In the seventeenth century, coal shipped from Newcastle came into general use in London. It was important for the new era of European history which was now to develop that the most forward maritime and commercial nation should have recently rebuilt its capital in stone and brick, should have founded a state bank of issue and deposit, and should by its free use of coal have given a far-reaching advertisement to the source of power which was about to transform the economic structure of the world.

Earlier by more than half a century than any other country in Europe, England assumed the character of a modern high farming industrial state. She ceased to be a land of peasant husbandry and small domestic industries, and of roads so bad that even on horseback, the sole sure means of conveyance, the journey from York to London occupied a week. The wasteful system of mediaeval tillage with its scattered holdings in the open fields increasingly gave way to the enclosures of improving landlords, practising with the novel aid of roots and grasses a scientific rotation of crops, which increased the food supply, and consequently the population. First water power, then steam power, transformed the conditions of economic life. The iron industry, which in Queen Anne's reign was faced with the imminent danger of a fuel famine, found in the rich coal measures of the midlands and north an unexpected impetus to vast developments. Wood gave place to steel, charcoal burners to pitmen. The age of fairs and travelling pedlars was succeeded by the development of a busy retail trade carried out all over the country in village and town shops. In half a century (1760 to 1821) the population of England rose from six and three-quarter millions to twelve millions. Such a scene as Britain presented after four generations of invention and activity had never yet been witnessed, a scene of communications rendered swift beyond the wildest dreams, of factories crowded with ingenious labour-saving machinery and polluting the pure air with their smoke, of industries which drew their raw material from one hemisphere and sent their finished goods to another, of huge and hideous towns, hastily constructed, and of a population whose lives from early childhood were ruled by the sound of the factory bell and constrained to a bleak and exhausting discipline of toil.

The causes which made Britain the pioneer of industrial capitalism were in part due to the bounty of nature. The climate was moist and therefore suited to the cotton industry. Of water power there was no lack in the northern and north-western regions of England. Most important of all there was abundance of coal and iron juxtaposed and convenient for transport by water. The coalfields of Britain were larger than any which had been opened out in France and Germany and closer to important harbours. On the basis of iron, coal, and textiles, Britain built up a type of civilization which has been copied all round the world.

That these natural opportunities were so fully utilized was due not to any high standard of popular education, but to an atmosphere peculiarly favourable to industrial invention and to the swift and ready exploitation of its results. The governing aristocracy of England, unlike the French nobility, was interested in commerce. Wanting money for the luxuries which money could command, the Whig lords were not the men to despise a fortune obtained through a factory or a mine or an Indian investment. Moreover, having successfully curbed the powers of the crown, they had no disposition to see an autocratic government revived in another form. The English parliaments of the eighteenth century may be criticized for doing too little: they can hardly be attacked for doing too much. To the self-sufficient, acquisitive spirit of a money-loving population they offered no obstacle which can be accounted serious.

In such an atmosphere of relative freedom—and it may be noted that Britain after the Scottish Union was the largest free trade area in Europe—the descendants of the Puritans came into their own. Excluded from an active concern with politics until 1828 the Nonconformists applied a grave and intrepid energy to the pursuit of opulence. Labour they regarded as a sacrament, pleasure as a sin, the making of wealth a sign that their service was acceptable to the Lord. Entering with a rugged determination into almost every form of industrial and commercial enterprise, but specially attracted to iron, they had a large share in the making of a new England, less tranquil and lovely, but richer, more powerful, and vastly more crowded than the old.

These changes, however, would have been impossible but for the inventions. A small handful of remarkable Scots and Englishmen, fewer than would be required for a football match, succeeded by their ingenuity in transforming the economic life of the country. No doubt they derived support and inspiration from the atmosphere of their age. Science had been spreading its influence ever since Francis Bacon preached the value of the Inductive Method, and some of the inventors, notably James Watt, who first gave a decisive industrial value *1736-1819* to the steam engine, were men of science. Yet more important probably than actual scientific training was the idea, which the Royal Society had so powerfully helped to spread, that knowledge was a growing thing, and that by observation and experiment new truths could be brought to light. Once aroused, the spirit of curiosity was inevitably turned upon the principal preoccupation of the British people. This was no longer, as in the Puritan age, religion, but the pursuit of wealth through industry and commerce.

Some of the great inventors were poor operatives without science or education, but guided by a mechanical tact in relation to the appliances of their own industry which amounted to genius. Such were Kay of Bury, who in 1733 by his invention of the flying shuttle more than doubled the work which the weaver could perform, besides improving its quality, and James

Hargreaves, whose spinning jenny (1754) multiplied eightfold
and more the productive power of the weaver. Such, too, were
Richard Arkwright of Preston (1732-92), inventor of the spinning
frame, founder of the English cotton industry, and parent of the
factory system. Few Englishmen have exercised a more profound influence on civilization than this vigorous Lancastrian,
who, after being successively a barber's apprentice and a wig-
maker, made a series of inventions for carding and spinning
cotton which rendered large scale production possible, and in
the factories which he set up to exploit his discovery, established
that system of massed and disciplined labour which is characteristic of the capitalistic age.

Being dependent on water for their power, the early textile
factories were erected by the side of waterfalls, generally on
some high desolate moor far from the natural centres of population. In such spots it is still a common experience to come across
the ruined shell of a gaunt, high-chimneyed building, once the
scene of busy activity, but long since deserted. The substitution
of steam for water as the motive power in cotton mills rendered
it profitable to concentrate factories in towns. Since power could
now be generated wherever it was convenient, it was no longer
necessary to transport workers to distant water. The village factory followed the cottage industry into the limbo of antiquities;
the application of steam to machinery led straight to the factory
town.

James Watt, the Greenock engineer, did not discover the use
of steam as a motive force, nor did he create the steam engine.
It was in brooding on the defects of an engine already fifty-
eight years old that this delicate, fretful, melancholy genius hit
upon the secret of the separate condenser (1769), which enabled
steam power to revolutionize industry. The Newcomen engine
had been employed for pumping in mines; but at deep levels it
was useless, and at all levels, through waste of heat and other
causes, defective in power and uncertain in operation. Watt
cured these defects by his device of a separate condenser. One
brilliant thought gave to mankind the empire of the mines with
all that followed from such a conquest, more power, more
machinery, more light and warmth, a higher standard of comfort for a large population. A subsequent invention of the rotary
motion, imitating the movement of the water wheel, brought
the steam engine into the cotton factories. This was in 1781, the

year of the British capitulation at Yorktown. All unnoticed, a new link more profitable than the broken skeins of imperial monopoly and preference was forged by the shy mechanical inventor between the United States and Britain. American cotton worked up in the mills of Lancashire went in the next century the round of the world.

These mechanical ideas were made effective only through the close association of the inventor with a great man of business, who had a faith in steam which no financial losses or anxieties could defeat. Without the help of Matthew Boulton, a hardware manufacturer of Birmingham, Watt's inventions might have been left to rest unused. Boulton, summoning Watt to his aid (1775), set himself to make steam engines for the market. He raised the capital, gathered the labour, erected the works, and eventually convinced the public. His sanguine energy and indomitable resource combined with the mechanical inventions of his sensitive friend accomplished in the space of a decade a revolution which in other circumstances might have taken a century. The first successful engine was turned out of the Soho works in 1776. Four years later forty engines were despatched to the Cornish mines. By 1789 steam had established itself as a dominating factor in most of the staple industries of England.

In the first half of the eighteenth century the great obstacle to industrial development in Britain was the state of the communications. While France possessed canals and roads which were the admiration of every traveller, the English roads, the supervision of which was confided to unpaid parish officers, were disgraceful, and English canals non-existent. So long as this state of things continued and many roads were impassable save in the summer months, while others, being too bad for carts or coaches, admitted only of packhorse traffic, no great industrial expansion was possible. But at last towards the middle of the century the British public began to take note of an evil which had been too long tolerated with an indulgent eye. Turnpike acts were passed under which improvements, substantial if unsystematic, were made. William Brindley, an illiterate genius, engineered the Bridgwater canal between Liverpool and Manchester; and then under the vigorous impulsion of three great engineers, Metcalfe, Telford, and Macadam, the long accumulated arrears were cleared away and the country was enriched by a system of roads, bridges, and canals, as good as any to be found in Europe. The age of packhorses receded into the past, the short-lived age of stage coaches began. "In the year 1770," writes Joseph Aston in his *History of Manchester* published in 1816, "there was only one stage coach to London and one to Liverpool, which went from Aston into Manchester, and these set out only twice a week. There are now seventy distinct coaches which run from hence, of which fifty-four set out every day, and sixteen others three times in the week, to their different places of destination. In the year 1754 a flying coach was advertised, and boasted that, 'however incredible it may appear, this coach will actually (barring accidents) arrive in London in four days and a half after leaving Manchester.' The mail coaches now constantly travel that distance in thirty hours, and on several occasions when Bonaparte was tottering to his ruin, and on the news of the terminating battle of Waterloo, the Traveller, the Defiance, and the Telegraph coaches came down in eighteen hours." That was the brief but golden age of English travel, immortalized in the pages of Pickwick, when the horse was in his glory and the traveller had time to relish the beauties of the country and the humours of the road. The coming of George Stephenson's railway (1829) closed that chapter in English history, and opened an era of greater mobility, greater wealth, and greater restlessness for mankind.

1815   By the close of the Napoleonic Wars the character of a capitalist society, such as has since become general, was already discernible in Britain. Capitalism in some form or other has existed since the dawn of history. What was distinctive of the new capitalism was that it was not, as in previous ages, mainly agricultural or mainly commercial, but to a predominant degree industrial. It involved a divorce between capital and labour over a wide sphere of economic work in which capital and labour had been generally combined. In the new factories which blackened the skies the operative had nothing but his labour to sell. The employing class bought labour, the working class sold it. For the old relations based on custom and sweetened by human sentiment there was now substituted the cash nexus between master and man.

The evils proceeding from this rapid and soulless industrialization were not brought home to the conscience of the nation till the forties of the nineteenth century. The problems were new and such as a Parliament dominated by wealthy country squires was ill fitted to appreciate. What was going forward in Lancashire and the Black Country, the sweated labour of women and small children, the shameful housing, the neglect of all amenities, the disparity between wages and profits, the uncertainty and impermanence of employment, failed to attract the interest or to stir the sympathy of the legislators of Westminster. Even Burke, whose flaming imagination embraced the Indian and American scene, and the vast significance of the French revolution, had no eyes for the urgent domestic problems of the Industrial Revolution. As the law forbade trades unions, Labour was unorganized and dumb.

The long war with France, though it had no effect in arresting the expansion of British industry and trade, was from every other point of view an unmixed misfortune for Britain and the world. The problems of the new industrial society, which were sufficiently novel and important to tax the undivided powers of a laborious and intelligent government, were by reason of the war deprived of any examination which was not positively unhelpful. While the government of England was struggling for its life with revolutionary and Napoleonic France, and the governing class were stricken with the fear of revolutionary danger at home, it was vain to expect that the needs of the new unknown, half-barbarous industrial population which had been so swiftly multiplying itself under the strange conditions of the factory in the northern part of the island would be sympathetically considered. Even William Pitt, who at one moment showed a real flash of interest and comprehension, recoiled from the task of alleviating the lot of the wage-earning population. The mentality which in and out of Parliament sustained the existence of the Slave Trade till 1807 was one element in the mental atmosphere of that time. Fear of the revolution was another. Both were unfavourable to a prudent handling of the social problems of the Industrial Revolution.

Adam Smith, saluting the dawn of the new industrial age in the *Wealth of Nations* (1776), exults in the vast accretions of wealth rendered possible under a régime in which trade is free, machinery general, and labour minutely subdivided. In his classic treatise, which is the Bible of Free Trade, the sagacious Glasgow professor discerns the tremendous economic powers latent in the British people which a system of liberty would release. The sober confidence of the Scottish economist was justified in the event. Free Trade paid: industrialism was a source of accumulating material prosperity; by whatever tests national wealth may be measured, its progression all through the nineteenth century was unimpeded. But ninety-one years after the publication of his *Wealth of Nations*, when the British capitalistic system had reached maturity, and was fast spreading through Europe, Karl Marx, a German Jew, resident in London, applied his critical intelligence to the examination of its result. Where Smith had seen only the sunlight, Marx saw only the shadows thrown upon the human scene by the unimpeded exercise of individual liberty, a subdivision of labour so minute as to stunt the intelligence and empty life of the craftsman's joy, an ever-widening gulf between wealth and poverty, a loss of that sense of stability and permanence which was characteristic of the older forms of society, and the relentless exploitation of the proletariat by their employers. The picture was overdrawn and in some important respects untrue to fact; but attention was directed to serious and undoubted blemishes, which, if they did not justify revolution, called imperiously for reform.

1818-83

BOOKS WHICH MAY BE CONSULTED

P. Mantoux : La Révolution industrielle au XVIIIème Siècle. *Tr.* M. Vernon. 1928. (Excellent bibliography.)

J. Aston : A Picture of Manchester, 1804. 1826.

Edward Baines : History of the Cotton Manufacture in Great Britain. 1835.

R. N. Boyd : Coal Pits and Firemen : A Short History of the Coal Trade and the Legislation affecting it. 1892.

R. E. Prothero : The Pioneers and Progress of English Farming. 1888.

R. H. Thurston : A Century's Progress of the Steam Engine. 1901.

S. Smiles : The Lives of the Engineers. 5 vols. 1874.

C. Beard : The Industrial Revolution. 1901.

J. L. and B. Hammond : The Town Labourer. 1917.

J. L. and B. Hammond : The Skilled Labourer. 1919.

J. A. Hobson : The Evolution of Modern Capitalism. 1894.

A. Toynbee : Lectures on the Industrial Revolution of the Eighteenth Century in England. *Ed.* Lord Milner. 1908.

GENEALOGICAL TABLES

A.—HOUSE OF TUDOR AND STUART: THE TUDOR AND STUART SUCCESSION.

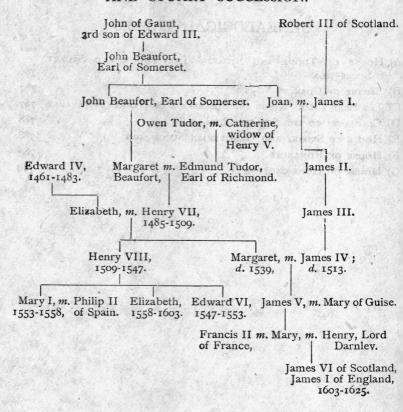

B.—EMPIRE OF CHARLES V.

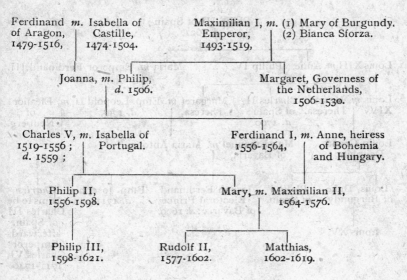

Ferdinand *m.* Isabella of Aragon, 1479-1516, | Castille, 1474-1504.

Maximilian I, *m.* (1) Mary of Burgundy. Emperor, 1493-1519, | (2) Bianca Sforza.

Joanna, *m.* Philip, *d.* 1506.

Margaret, Governess of the Netherlands, 1506-1530.

Charles V, *m.* Isabella of 1519-1556; | Portugal. *d.* 1559;

Ferdinand I, *m.* Anne, heiress 1556-1564, | of Bohemia and Hungary.

Philip II, 1556-1598.

Mary, *m.* Maximilian II, 1564-1576.

Philip III, 1598-1621.

Rudolf II, 1577-1602.

Matthias, 1602-1619.

C.—THE LAST VALOIS KINGS AND SUCCESSION OF HENRY OF NAVARRE.

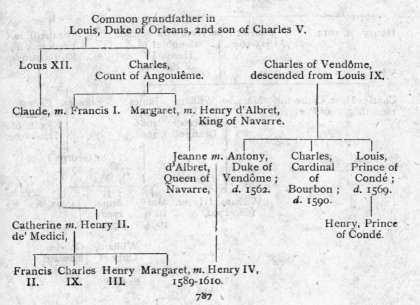

Common grandfather in
Louis, Duke of Orleans, 2nd son of Charles V.

Louis XII.

Charles, Count of Angoulême.

Charles of Vendôme, descended from Louis IX.

Claude, *m.* Francis I.   Margaret, *m.* Henry d'Albret, King of Navarre.

Jeanne *m.* Antony, d'Albret, | Duke of Queen of | Vendôme; Navarre, | *d.* 1562.

Charles, Cardinal of Bourbon; *d.* 1590.

Louis, Prince of Condé; *d.* 1569.

Catherine *m.* Henry II. de' Medici,

Henry, Prince of Condé.

Francis Charles Henry Margaret, *m.* Henry IV, II.   IX.   III.   1589-1610.

787

D.—CLAIMANTS TO THE SPANISH THRONE.

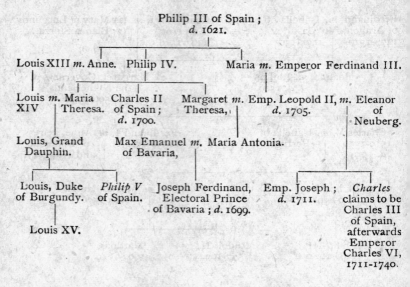

Philip III of Spain ;
d. 1621.

Louis XIII m. Anne.   Philip IV.   Maria m. Emperor Ferdinand III.

Louis m. Maria   Charles II   Margaret m. Emp. Leopold II, m. Eleanor
XIV   Theresa.   of Spain;   Theresa,   d. 1705.   of
d. 1700.   Neuberg.

Louis, Grand   Max Emanuel m. Maria Antonia.
Dauphin.   of Bavaria,

Louis, Duke   Philip V   Joseph Ferdinand,   Emp. Joseph ;   Charles
of Burgundy.   of Spain.   Electoral Prince   d. 1711.   claims to be
of Bavaria ; d. 1699.   Charles III
of Spain,
Louis XV.   afterwards
Emperor
Charles VI,
1711–1740.

E.—HOUSE OF STUART AND HANOVERIAN SUCCESSION.

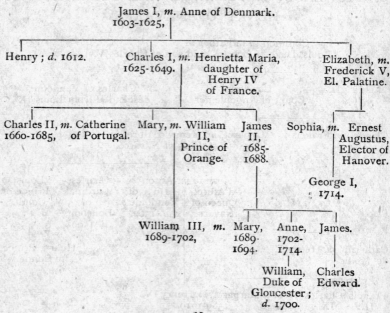

James I, m. Anne of Denmark.
1603–1625,

Henry ; d. 1612.   Charles I, m. Henrietta Maria,   Elizabeth, m.
1625–1649.   daughter of   Frederick V,
Henry IV   El. Palatine.
of France.

Charles II, m. Catherine   Mary, m. William   James   Sophia, m. Ernest
1660–1685,   of Portugal.   II,   II,   Augustus,
Prince of   1685–   Elector of
Orange.   1688.   Hanover.

George I,
1714.

William III, m.   Mary,   Anne,   James.
1689–1702,   1689–   1702–
1694.   1714.

William,   Charles
Duke of   Edward.
Gloucester ;
d. 1700.

788

F.—HOUSE OF ROMANOFF.

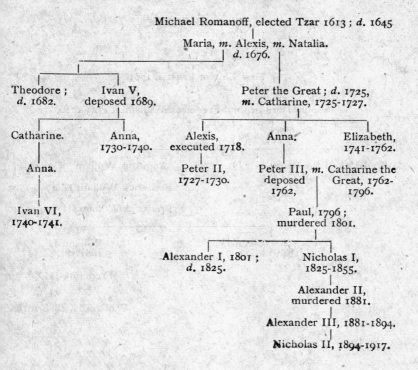

Michael Romanoff, elected Tzar 1613 ; *d.* 1645.

Maria, *m.* Alexis, *m.* Natalia.
d. 1676.

Theodore ;   Ivan V,   Peter the Great ; *d.* 1725,
d. 1682.   deposed 1689.   *m.* Catharine, 1725-1727.

Catharine.   Anna,   Alexis,   Anna.   Elizabeth,
         1730-1740.   executed 1718.   1741-1762.

Anna.   Peter II,   Peter III, *m.* Catharine the
                  1727-1730.   deposed   Great, 1762-
Ivan VI,   1762,   1796.
1740-1741.

Paul, 1796 ;
murdered 1801.

Alexander I, 1801 ;   Nicholas I,
d. 1825.   1825-1855.

Alexander II,
murdered 1881.

Alexander III, 1881-1894.

Nicholas II, 1894-1917.

G.—HOUSE OF HOHENZOLLERN.

Frederick William,
the Great Elector;
d. 1688.

Frederick I,
First King of Prussia, 1701,
1688-1713.

Sophia Dorothea, *m.* Frederick William I, 1713-1740.
daughter of George I
of England,

Frederick II the Great,
1740-1786.

Augustus William ; *d.* 1758.

Frederick William II, 1786-1797.

Frederick William III, 1797-1840.

Frederick William IV,
1840-1861.

William I,
1861-1888.

Frederick III,
1888.

William II, 1888-1918.

BOOK THREE

THE LIBERAL EXPERIMENT

STRANDS OF HISTORY

Liberty. Socialism. Industrialism. Nationalism. Revolution. War

It was important for the coming age that in an empty continent offering boundless opportunities for innovation and enterprise a new gospel of liberty and equality had been proclaimed as the slogan of a triumphant republic. The American declaration of rights gave the cue to every friend of liberty in the old world. What the Americans had made themselves by revolution the Europeans might become by a similar exercise of daring. The spirit of liberty took many forms, constitutional with Mirabeau, revolutionary with Danton, romantic with Schiller, Shelley, and Lamartine, prophetic with Mazzini, intellectual with Condorcet and J. S. Mill, practical with Cobden and Cavour, militant and adventurous with Cochrane and Garibaldi; but once aroused it embarked upon a contest which is still unconcluded. Surviving the crimes of the French Revolution and the terror of Napoleon, it succeeded by the end of the nineteenth century in founding parliamentary institutions in every important European country with the exception of Russia.

Like the Alexandrian age, the times which have now to be surveyed witnessed an immense increase in the scope, velocity, and complexity of events. In less than a hundred and fifty years the population of Europe grew by more than three hundred and fifty millions, and that of the United States by more than a hundred and thirty millions.[1] Cities became larger, governments became more powerful. Armies and navies, budgets and businesses, public revenues and private fortunes rose to a scale never hitherto imagined. New modes of transport enabled huge bodies of armed men to be conveyed hundreds of miles from their homes and to be provisioned with regularity for years together. New methods of communication annihilated distance, new methods of propaganda

[1] The population of Europe has been estimated by Dr. R. R. Kurzynski at 100 millions in 1600, at 152½ millions in 1700, at 173 millions in 1789, and at 525 millions in 1934.

schooled opinion. The information at the disposal of governments was brought to an extraordinary pitch of completeness. In a single day more business would pass through a Prime Minister's house than would have been concentrated for his handling during a year in the time of George III.

The immense increase in the population of Europe was due rather to man's increasing power over nature than to any surprising advance in the arts of government. Not that the age which we are about to survey was barren of political ideas or *1772-1823* happy improvements. The definition, elaborated by Ricardo, of rent as a surplus due not to labour or capital but to the original and indestructible powers of the soil directed attention to unearned increment in all its forms and supplied to socialism one of its strongest theoretical arguments. The discovery that trade prospered best when freed from fiscal fetters, and the complementary principle that in a world governed by competition labour must be defended against capitalist exploitation, led by two distinct and differing paths to a society in which material enjoyments were alike vastly more numerous and better distributed than ever before. Yet the problem of poverty was not solved. Every workman had a pistol pointed at his heart. A change of fashion, the bankruptcy of an employer, the failure of a distant harvest, the crash of a bank, the fraud or improvidence of a group of speculators, might throw him out of employment and reduce his family to want.

The problem of bringing happiness to the swiftly expanding democracy of hired town workers who begin in this period to constitute the main part of European society was far too vast and complex to be solved quietly or by any single body of statesmen. The alleviations which in course of time were provided by factory acts and the regulation of mines, by trades unions and co-operative stores, by state insurance and state pensions, by the public education of the young and the public assistance of the old, were only gradually discovered and partially applied. The "condition of the people question," though always of the first importance, was never steadily and continuously kept in the forefront of political attention. Other causes or diversions, more melodramatic and attractive, such as the rivalry of nations, the thirst for empire, the appetite for markets, were apt to ensnare the attention of statesmen or inflame the passion of mobs. The history of Europe, then, cannot be narrated strictly as the sequence of those multitudinous and almost insensible changes which transformed a society in which mill-owners and land-owners were predominant into one in which a town clerk, a borough engineer, a medical officer of health, or a schoolmaster may make all the difference to the happiness of a community. It would be too great a simplification of issues to regard the European story as nothing but a struggle of classes, a clash of economic interests. That would be to underrate the rich and varied stuff of human nature, the distractions of statesmen and the waywardness of events. In actual life even the most important social problems which press upon a generation are never removed into a laboratory, and after dispassionate examination there and then thoroughly and scientifically solved. The real nature of social ailments may for many years on end be com-pletely ignored. We may search the memoirs of Guizot, one of *1787-1874* the greatest Frenchmen of the nineteenth century, without find-ing evidence that he was aware of the soul of the underworld and of its many troubles.

Europe then, when confronted with the facts of the industrial revolution in England, did not say to itself, "The strange new things which are happening in England will in due course of time happen on the continent also. Here too factory towns will rise and belch their smoke into the air. Here too the labour of children will be exploited for gain, and nevertheless more and more children will be born into the world to be housed, fed educated, employed, and governed. Everywhere before many decades are passed English conditions will be repeated. Every-where society will be transformed by mechanism and capital, and everywhere governments, if they are to survive, will be com-pelled to make provision for a new population, owning no capital, uprooted from the stable economic conditions and ancient pieties of village life, without standards, without traditions, without loyalties, the flotsam and jetsam of rude and jostling competi-tion. We are entering in fact upon an industrial age. We must forestall its dangers, anticipate its needs, guide its course." Europe said nothing of the kind. So far from attending to the faint signals of the coming industrial democracy which were already visible in the sky, it plunged into the wars of the French Revolution and the Empire.

CHAPTER II

REVOLUTION IN FRANCE

Strength and weakness of France. Privilege. The food supply. The King's opportunity. The Deficit. The Estates General. The aspirations of France in 1789. Versailles and Paris. The first emigration. The fall of the ancien régime. The Proletariat and the Clubs. Mirabeau. The Constitution of 1791. The revolution and the Church. The revolution and private property. Gains of the peasantry. Varennes. End of the Constituent Assembly.

VICTORIOUS in America and nearly three times as populous as Great Britain, her vanquished rival, with enormous agricultural resources, a flourishing textile industry, splendid roads and canals, and a foreign trade which had increased five hundred per cent. since the death of Louis XIV, France was nevertheless confronted by grave domestic problems. The evil which was immediately obvious was financial. She was threatened, or believed herself to be threatened, by an appalling bankruptcy. What was more fundamental was that she lacked social equality, equitable taxation, political freedom, and an efficient executive. Privilege, mediæval and unprofitable, pervaded every portion of the body politic, privilege of the church, of the nobility, of the provincial estates or assemblies, of the judicial corporations and trade guilds. Privilege polluted justice, deflected the main burden of taxation on to the shoulders of the poor, and denied the prizes of the army, the navy, the church, and the magistrature to the most intelligent middle class in Europe. Privilege was now indefensible and odious. The higher clergy in France, who paid no taxes, had fallen far in public esteem by reason of their wealth, their worldliness, and their vices. The nobles, who were for the most part non-resident, had ceased to discharge any social function. They took their rents and feudal dues, exacted *corvées* or labour services, and, having no duties to perform, were a burden on the community. Exceptions personal and local were naturally to be found. There were good, improving landlords among the nobility, and in certain districts, notably the Vendée, nobles, living on their estates, after the manner of English squires, retained the devotion of their dependents.

But absenteeism was the rule. Publicists even thought and wrote of the French nobles as descendants of the Franks, as Teutons quartered on an alien soil and exploiting a subject Celtic population.

The revolution came because the monarchy was unable to solve the question of privilege, was not strong enough, in a word, to overthrow the remains of feudalism which, in France as in most other continental countries, cumbered the ground. Another problem of an economic order baffled the governments of the *ancien régime*. The food supply of the people, not yet reinforced by the potato, was insecure. Despite all the agricultural wealth of France, and the brilliant luxury of her upper class, sections of the population were from time to time exposed to the horrors of starvation.

This was not due to forced industrial development. Though in comparison with the Germany of that day France was highly urbanized, and Paris had even as many as 750,000 inhabitants, the methods of industry, as also of agriculture, were still for the most part mediæval. The proletariat of the French Revolution was not composed of nomad and uprooted factory hands, but of unorganized domestic workers and peasants. Such a society had no grievance against capital as such, or against ownership of land. What they wanted was bread, and bread, partly owing to archaic systems of cultivation and partly owing to internal customs duties, they were not able always to secure. The consequences were grave—chronic bread riots, and, in the large towns and many country regions, a mass of embittered destitution.

When Louis XVI mounted the French throne in 1774, the currents of European favour were running fresh and strong for enlightened despotism. Frederick of Prussia had set a fashion which others sought to follow. Even in Catholic Austria and Spain it was the experience that progress came from above, reaction from below, and that Kings and Queens were as liberal as their Diets were conservative. After the long and inglorious reign of Louis XV France was ready to welcome a new Charlemagne, who out of the plenitude of his wisdom would reform the state.

For such a rôle the young King was entirely unfitted. Louis had every private virtue, honesty, piety, amiability, good sense, but he could not govern. The clearness of mind, the decision of purpose, the sense of opportunity, the gift of steady application, which make the statesman, were denied him. Instead of directing events he drifted with the tide. Marie Antoinette, the Austrian was of stronger metal, but to the public the unpopular symbol of an odious alliance, and to statesmen the inspiration of all that was frivolous in the Court and obstructive of their frugal or innovating policies. Her beauty and charm brought no help. An enemy, she was too proud to conciliate or forgive. To the critics of Versailles she appeared to be the siren who was drawing the ship of state on to the rocks.

The best chance of forestalling revolution by reform was lost when the young King, in search of popularity, recalled the Parliaments and so raised up against the march of progress an obstinate barrier. An organized force will always defeat un- organized opinion. The better mind of France was with Turgot, the greatest of Louis' ministers, when he proposed to abolish the guilds and to free the corn trade: but the Parliament of Paris also was popular as the sole effective check on the Crown, and so when the King let Turgot go after thirteen months with nothing done but the memorable exhibition of frustrated reforms, there was no outcry, but a resigned conviction among thoughtful men that the promised reformation of France would not come from above, but must be sought elsewhere. Later the King summoned to his counsels the Genevan banker Necker, a Protestant and republican, who hit the humour of the time by financing the American War on loans, but fell under a dark shade of unpopularity as soon as he began to set up provincial assemblies, to relieve the Intendants of their administrative duties. Necker was dismissed in 1781, and thereafter the problem of finance dominated all other domestic issues in France. How was the deficit to be filled? Measured in cash it was not so formidable a task as it appeared to be, for an additional tax of six or seven francs per head could have enabled the country to balance its budget. But in terms of political psychology the balancing of the budget was beset by tremendous difficulties, for it meant the acquiescence of the privileged classes in a proposal that they should pay their proportionate share. Minister after minister failed to secure from the nobles the one concession which could have averted the storm. Calonne, the most daring and intelligent of the series, who had the happy idea of summoning an Assembly of Notables in 1787, failed like all the others, and with the more resounding crash, since he attempted to tell the country something of the real truth. "France," he wrote, "is a kingdom composed of separate states and countries, with mixed administrations, the provinces of which know nothing of each other, where certain districts are completely free from burdens, the whole weight of which is borne by others, where the richest class is the most lightly taxed, where privilege has upset all equilibrium, where it is impossible to have any constant rule or common will; necessarily it is a most imperfect kingdom, very full of abuses, and in its present condition *impossible to govern*." All expedients had now been exhausted save one, which was pressed on the Government from every side. On August 8, 1788, in an atmosphere of extravagant fears, suspicions, and hopes, the King summoned the States-General for the following year, and recalled Necker, the oracle on money, to his old office of managing the finances of France.

No great reform had ever issued from this archaic body, in which clergy, nobles, and third estate had hitherto deliberated and voted apart. None such was now expected by Necker. What that financier hoped of the States-General was money wherewith to balance the budget and close the yawning gulf of the deficit. No plan for constitutional reform had been prepared in advance by the Government, nor any directions for the guidance of an inexperienced assembly of twelve hundred men. Though it had been settled (January 24) that the numbers of the Third Estate were to be equal to the nobles and clergy combined, the Government had not even decided the vital question whether the Orders were to sit together or apart. The immense movement of resolute and excited political opinion which was evoked by the summoning of the Assembly to Versailles was a phenomenon which Louis had not expected, and could not diagnose.

Yet constitutional reform in some shape or other was clearly inscribed in the *cahiers* or instructions which were drawn up in every quarter of France or circulated by eminent men during the critical period. The mind of France as revealed in these documents was not republican; but that taxes should not be levied without popular consent, and that the *taille* should be abolished, was, despite many divergent interests, a common aspiration. One *cahier*, widely circulated, and drafted by a brilliant young ecclesiastic, sketched a constitutional monarchy very much on the lines of that which was established in France after the fall of

Napoleon. Its author was Talleyrand, Bishop of Autun, who was destined in 1814, after the turmoil of the revolutionary wars had subsided, to administer to France the very medicine which, wiser than many, he had in vain prescribed in his youth.

Once assembled at Versailles, the members of the Third Estate succumbed to the spell of crowd psychology. They had met together at a moment of vast excitement and measureless hope, and were resolved from the first to give France institutions which would be the envy and model of the world. Everything seemed possible to a generation which had seen in the first balloon an augury of the conquest of the air, and in Mesmerism a new and mysterious power over the operations of the human mind. Imbued with such a spirit, the members of the Third Estate were not disposed to tolerate the opposition of the privileged orders. They declared themselves to be the National Assembly (June 10), and at a famous meeting in the Tennis Court (June 20) swore that they would not separate until they had given a constitution to France.

The task was prodigious. The American Constitution was hammered out behind closed doors by a small body of highly competent men in the tranquil Quaker city of Philadelphia. The more numerous Assembly of Versailles carried on its deliberations in a country seething with anarchy and under the menacing pressure of the Paris mob. It was hard enough in any case wisely to reform the ancient structure of the French monarchy: but the task was rendered yet more formidable by the responsibility of governing France which events thrust upon the Assembly.

There was a camarilla at Court detesting concessions to the people, and passionate to curb the pretensions of the Assembly and the mounting disorders of the capital by a show of force. To them Louis so far yielded as to dismiss Necker, odious on a triple count as protestant, *parvenu*, and reformer, and to order the formation of a camp of regular troops near Versailles under the command of Broglie, a tried and famous veteran. For the moment Louis, who had himself volunteered reforms, was captured for the policy of the strong hand.

July 14, 1789

To this threat of reaction the democracy of Paris made the famous reply which France still celebrates as a national festival on July 14 of every year. The Bastille surrendered to a mob armed with the plunder of the Invalides, and probably financed by capitalists who saw in Necker the sole chance of financial recovery. There was little glory in an attack on a fortress whose guns were useless and obsolete, and much shame in the circumstances which preceded and followed its surrender: in the wild panic of the population of the capital, in the carnival of pillage, in the mutiny of some troops and the rowdiness of others, and in the brutal slaughter of a garrison which had surrendered on terms. But the capture and destruction of this ancient prison on the outskirts of Paris, though soiled by abominable crime, was a political masterpiece. All through Europe the fall of the Bastille was hailed as the end of secretive tyranny and arbitrary imprisonment, and as heralding the dawn of the age of freedom. Henceforward Paris steps into the forefront of history. Her Commune became a powerful government, her National Guard, in which many criminals were enlisted, the germ of a people's army, the grim brutality of her crowds a source of compelling terror in the dark days which were to come. The fall of the Bastille was a sharp advertisement to the Court that Paris did not intend the Constitution to fail, and that what Paris willed, France must accept. "This is a great revolt," said Louis, when he heard the news. "No, sir," replied the Duc de Liancourt, "it is a great revolution."

The eclipse of the monarchy was now complete. It could neither protect its friends nor overthrow its enemies. The wretched King was compelled to every indignity, to countermand the troops, to dismiss his ministers, to recall Necker, to bless in public the taking of the Bastille, and to accept in public the new tricolor cockade, which had been devised as the flag of the enfranchised nation by Lafayette, the liberator of America and the elected commandant of the National Guard. But still Paris was uncertain of its prey. So long as the King was at large he might be dangerous, resume, it was thought, his old reactionary tricks, collect troops, defeat edicts, plot a flight. The feeling grew that he would be safer in Paris, where he would be watched by the Commune and hedged in by the National Guard. A young woman of great beauty and much eloquence, wife of Roland, a grave inspector of mines, preached this doctrine to a circle of ardent friends.

By this time the machinery of revolutionary agitation was well understood in the capital. There were funds and organizers, simpletons and fanatics, and a plentiful supply of ruffians when rough work had to be done. In the first week of October there

26.

was also a pretext for a *coup*. The King had summoned the Flanders regiment to Versailles, had refused a decree, was said to be meditating flight. The Royal Guards had trampled on the tricolor. The spectre of reaction, laid in July, was again rearing its sinister head. Such beliefs, coupled with a shortage of bread (October 5), were sufficient to set in motion the famous march on Versailles, begun by a band of hungry women crying out for bread, but followed by the National Guard under Lafayette, which in the days of October brought the King and Queen back to Paris and to the bleak imprisonment of the Tuileries.

One night in July after the fall of the Bastille, when anarchy was rife, and the houses of the nobles were going up in flames, Talleyrand came secretly to the Comte d'Artois, the King's younger brother, and urged that Louis should dissolve the Assembly and restore order by force of arms. Out of humanity the King declined, and d'Artois, despairing of protection, fled across the border, leading the first of those successive waves of emigration which brought so much harm to France and to Europe. It is difficult to overstate the evils which proceeded from the presence beyond the borders of France of bodies of angry, energetic, empty-minded nobles, in league with the enemies of their country, and conspiring either through foreign war or domestic strife to uproot its new institutions. All the greater calamities which overwhelmed revolutionary France, the execution of the King and Queen, the mania of suspicion, the terror, the atrocities, the proscription of moderate and humane opinions, are not obscurely connected with the fears excited by the implacable hatred of the *émigrés*, by the power of their armed allies within and without the country, and, most disquieting of all, by the suspected presence in every part of France of secret sympathizers with the royalist cause.

Meanwhile the Assembly in a spirit of exulting confidence, as though the known oracles of philosophy would answer every riddle of the practical life, addressed itself to the task of framing a constitution for France. In one respect its work was marvellously simplified, for it had nothing to destroy. The castle of feudalism offered as little resistance as the Bastille itself. In the course of one feverish August night nobles and clergy, provinces, municipalities and corporations, abandoned in a paroxysm of fear and generosity their feudal rights and privileges. The old order crumbled away in the shock of a revolutionary emotion.

Aug. 4,
1789

which the Assembly in great part shared, but did nothing to originate or direct. Never has a famous society so violently renounced its historic past. If the monarchy had been vanquished and shamed in a desolating war, its humiliation could not have been more complete. After the fall of the Bastille everything was chaos: the administration, the Army, and, with serious results for the future of France upon the seas, the Royal Navy, which had acquitted itself so well in the American War. The peasants fired the muniments of their masters. Nobody obeyed the law or paid taxes. The National Guard, a great militia, devoted to the revolution, sprang up in every quarter of France to defend its cause. One thought flew through the country whispering its siren music in every heart. The people were Sovereign. The cumbrous monarchy of the old *régime* was a vast imposture. Frenchmen were no longer, and had never been, subjects. They were citizens, members of a free and equal confraternity, with the right to make peace and war, to conclude treaties, to administer justice, to regulate Church, Army, and Navy, to draft laws and impose taxes. No power could obstruct, none defeat the general will expressed through the National Assembly, its lawful organ. The *esprit de corps* of particular groups, whether provinces or municipalities, social classes or professions, trade guilds or corporations, must give way before the dictates of indivisible France. The charcoal burner at his furnace, the blacksmith at his forge, the farmhand following the plough, awoke to find himself part sovereign of France, as good a man as his lord, and endowed with impregnable rights, the right to be free, the right to own property, the right to speak his mind and to resist oppression. Such was the logic, such the sentiment, which captured France in the summer of 1789, and such the appeal of the new democracy to the subject peoples of Europe. Enshrined in the large, untested phrases of the Declaration of the Rights of Man, which was prefixed to the Constitution of 1791, this philosophy travelled far and wide, lighting lamps of pride and of aspiration in innumerable homes.

Against the seductive force of this democratic logic the voices of moderation and wisdom were of little avail. The belief in the essential goodness of human nature which underlay these theories was the source of most of the terrible disasters which now in swift succession assailed France. It was not a race of political angels, but a people needing, perhaps more than any other for the full development of its great qualities, the firm hand of authority, which was surrendered to its own devices by this sleek and optimistic theory.

Below the level of the bourgeoisie was a proletariat, starved in mind and body, and brutalized by neglect and the operation of unequal laws, a proletariat of smugglers, brigands, desperadoes, criminals. On the night of the taking of the Bastille women and children danced by torchlight round the decapitated heads of three blameless French gentlemen. The grim warning was not taken. The King and his ministers would not direct the Assembly, the Assembly would not govern France or police Paris. When King and Assembly were moved to the capital, the true centre of sovereignty was transferred to the political clubs, of which the most important was that of the Jacobins, soon to become the heart of a wide federation and the real ruler of France. To the operations of these revolutionary bodies, who terrorized the legislature and fostered mutiny in the army, no opposition was ever offered.

1749-91   History will always be interested in Mirabeau, adventurer, statesman, demagogue, publicist, as the man who endeavoured and failed to check the mounting surge of anarchy and to save the crown of France. To him, as to Mounier and other wise men, it was abundantly clear that only a strong executive could preserve France from the abyss. But where was strength to be found? It was not in the King, nor in his elder brother, the Count of Provence, nor in Lafayette, the vain, incapable commandant of the National Guard of Paris.

Every intrigue for the foundation of a powerful royal ministry foundered. All proposals likely to fortify the executive in the new constitution, such as a second chamber, an absolute veto, the right of the King's ministers to sit in the legislature, broke on the same rock of democratic doctrine. Mirabeau could not even count upon a full royalist vote, for many royalists were wreckers, bent upon making the constitution as bad as possible in order to discredit democracy. Concluding that nothing could be done with the Assembly at Versailles, Mirabeau secretly proposed to the court that they should retire publicly to Rouen. Of all his many expedients this perhaps was the least desperate: yet it came too late, for France, though she did not yet know it, was already at heart a republic. The constitution which finally

merged from the cauldron of debate retained that anarchical
dispersion of powers which the Assembly found and did nothing
to correct. The monarchy survived, but as a shadow only, for
the real power belonged to some forty thousand municipalities
which paid what taxes they chose to levy, and alone could call
out the National Guard. A fatal distrust of executive authority
evidenced by an overweening belief in popular election was one
of the most serious defects of the first attempt of the revolution
to organize France.

Another blemish proceeding from the same democratic logic
was the civil constitution of the clergy. It was a cardinal maxim
of the revolution that corporate bodies were dangerous to society,
and since there was no corporation so wealthy, so influential,
or with so long a record of intolerance as the Church, it was
specially marked out for the resentment of an anti-clerical
Assembly. Blow followed hard upon blow, first the abolition of
tithe without compensation, then a confiscation of all church
property, the suppression of the religious orders, the release of
monks and nuns from their vows, and a great reduction in the
ecclesiastical establishment. Yet since doctrine and worship were
left unaffected, these provisions, however drastic, might not have
caused an insuperable obstacle. The Church might resent the
loss of its wide acres and noble endowments and the arrangement
by which the clergy became the salaried dependents of a democratic state; but a state church had long existed in France, and
no Christian could condemn a measure which deprived the prelates of their superfluities and added to the scanty pittance of
the parish priest. The crowning offence which made the quarrel
irreparable was the requirement that the bishop should be chosen
by the electors of the department and the *curé* by the administrative Assembly of the district.[1] Catholic bishops and
Catholic *curés* might then be chosen by laymen who were
Protestants or even atheists. It was reasonable to surmise that a
church thus officered and recruited would drift far apart from
its ancient moorings, more particularly since at the same time
French citizens were forbidden to recognize the authority of any
bishop or metropolitan whose see lay outside the kingdom. It
was inevitable that the Pope, who had not been consulted at any
stage, should condemn the Civil Constitution, and that it should

[1] Such were the new administrative areas created to efface the old
local loyalties and privileges of France.

wound the conscience of the Catholic world. No error of the
Constituent Assembly was so far-reaching in its consequences as
this gratuitous affront to the religious convictions of the people.
At the beginning of the revolution the village *curés* had thrown
in their lot with the popular cause, and the value of their support
had been great. Now the clergy was split in two. The compliant
sort took the oath to the Constitution, retained their cures, and
drew their salaries; the braver sort rebelled. Rather than accept
a schismatic church they went out into the wilderness risking
starvation, imprisonment, and death, but carrying with them the
loyalty of a faithful flock. The *prêtres insermentés* became from
the first a formidable centre of opposition to the revolutionary
state. They were to be found in the Vendée and in Brittany, and
wherever the white cockade took the field against the tricolor.
In defeat and persecution they were yet triumphant, for out of
the purification of their sufferings the Church in France renewed
its moral life.

In all these provisions there was nothing of socialism. The
French Revolution attacked privilege, not property. The members of the Constituent Assembly reposed such belief in the
liberty of the individual that they assailed even those forms of
economic association such as trades unions which have been
found necessary in later times for the protection of the weak
against the strong. The peasant was enabled to cultivate and
sell as he pleased. Serfdom was abolished where it existed, qui-
rents disappeared, game laws were mitigated, the lord was deprived of his right over the commons. But if the incidents of
the land system were altered, the foundation remained the same.
The soil of France was still tilled by peasant holders, farming
tenants, or upon that system of metayer or share tenancy under
which landlord and tenant shared expenses and profits. A
scheme of agricultural communism or state ownership was never
even suggested.

A strong material tie, arising out of the very necessities of the
state, bound the peasantry to the revolution, and secured that in
part at least the work of the Constituent Assembly would not
be reversed. To govern France the Assembly required funds
and these it sought to find in the issue of notes or *assignats*
secured on the property of the Church, and afterwards on that
of the Crown and *émigrés* as well. An original issue of four
hundred million francs (December, 1789), which was regarded as

an advance on the proceeds of the sale of church property, was soon found to be insufficient. Further needs were met by fresh issues, with the result that inflation set in, that the assignat lost its value, and that land changed hands at a derisory price. The rapid degeneration of a nation's currency, while ruinous to many, always inures to the profit of some. The fall in the value of French assignats impoverished the Treasury, the *rentier*, and the townsman, and contributed to maintain revolutionary excitement in Paris by engendering an atmosphere of speculation and panic. But the peasant who acquired land for a mere song was a gainer, and for this reason, among others, he, together with many a land speculator from the town, had cause to bless the revolution and to dread the reversal of its work.

The prisoners of the Tuileries viewed with a helpless sense of horror and disgust the mounting tide of revolution, the violence of the Jacobin Club, the bloodthirsty incitements of the Press, and the incessant capitulations of the Assembly to the dictation of the mob. Where everything was distasteful, the civil constitution of the clergy appeared to the King as a crowning affront. He felt that he could never reconcile this enactment to his conscience or bear to receive the sacrament from a constitutional priest. On the Monday before Easter 1791 an event occurred from which it appeared that even the promptings of the private conscience were not to be respected. On that day the King and Queen desiring to make their Easter Communion at St. Cloud, were turned back by the mob. The indignity was decisive. The Royal Family resolved to escape to the frontier where Bouillé at the head of a royalist force could afford them protection. Before he left Paris the King drew up a manifesto abrogating the constitutional edicts which he had been compelled to sign, and requiring their amendment.

The fugitives were turned back at Varennes (June 21). From that moment the monarchy was doomed, for the King had come out as the open opponent of the constitution, at heart an *émigré*, a friend of the unsworn priests, a fomenter of civil war, and the ally of foreign counter-revolutionary Powers. For ten weeks he was suspended from his functions and a government, republican in all but name, allayed the fears that the removal of the monarchy would spell the dissolution of France.

When the Constitution was completed (September 14, 1791) the Assembly put an end to its own existence. Already by an act of abnegation, which did little service to France, it had decreed its members to be incapable of election to the new legislature. Lightly sacrificing the experience which had been garnered by two years of intense political application, the framers of the first French constitution were prepared to entrust its working to untried men. Nothing turned out according to plan. It was the fate of the expiring Assembly, which believed in Liberty, Fraternity, and Equality, and had worked for a democratic state safeguarded by a universal and democratic peace, to level the path for a military tyranny, and to sow the seeds of general war.

BOOKS WHICH MAY BE CONSULTED

For surveys covering the whole period the reader is referred to the following :

G. P. Gooch : Annals of Politics and Culture. 1901.
The Cambridge Modern History. 1902-10.
The Cambridge History of the British Empire. 1929.
A. J. Grant and H. Temperley : Europe in the Nineteenth and Twentieth Centuries (1784-1932). 1932.
Edward Fueter : World History, translated by S. B. Fay. 1923.
C. A. Fyffe : History of Modern Europe. 1924.
B. Croce : History of Europe in the Nineteenth Century, translated by H. Furst. 1934.
C. Seignobos : Political History of Contemporary Europe since 1814. 1901.

For the most recent books :

The Annual Bulletin of Historical Literature, published by the Historical Association.

For the first seven chapters of this volume the reader is referred to :

The Cambridge Modern History, Vols. VIII and IX.
L. Madelin : The French Revolution. *Tr.* Curtis. 1930.
Lord Acton : Lectures on the French Revolution. 1910.
A. Sorel : L'Europe et la Révolution française. 1889.
A. De Tocqueville : Ancien Régime. *Tr.* M. W. Pattersen. 1933.
H. Taine : Origines de la France contemporaine. 1876.
Carlyle : French Revolution. *Ed.* C. R. L. Fletcher. 1907.
J. M. Thompson : French Revolution : Documents. 1933.
A. Aulard : Histoire politique de la Révolution française. *Tr.* Miall. 1910.
Lecky : History of England in the Eighteenth Century. 1892.

Seeley : Life and Times of Stein. 1878.
Oman : Peninsular War. 1902-30.
H. A. L. Fisher : Napoleonic Statesmanship : Germany. 1903.
H. A. L. Fisher : Bonapartism. 1909.
E. L. Woodward : French Revolutions. 1934.
F. Masson : Napoléon inconnu. 1895.
Vandal : L'avénement de Bonaparte. 1902.
H. Houssaye : 1815. Waterloo. 1900.
L. G. Wickham Legg : Select Documents. 1905.
A. T. Mahan : Influence of Sea Power on the French Revolution. 1893.

Biographies

Mirabeau, by P. F. Willert. 1898.
Robespierre, by A. Matthiez. 1921, 1925.
Danton, by H. Belloc. 1928.
Talleyrand, by Duff Cooper. 1932.
Napoleon, by H. A. L. Fisher (1924), J. Holland Rose (1902), J. B. Fournier (1912), Jacques Bainville (1932).
William Pitt, by Rosebery (1910), J. Holland Rose (1925).
Burke, by John Morley. 1921.
Fox, by J. L. Hammond, 1903 ; Christopher Hobhouse. 1934.
Wellington (The Duke), by Philip Guedalla. 1931.
The Foreign Policy of Castlereagh, by C. K. Webster. 1934.

Imaginative Literature

Dickens : Tale of Two Cities.
Anatole France : Les Dieux ont Soif.
Stendhal : La Chartreuse de Parme.
Tolstoi : War and Peace.
T. Hardy : The Dynasts.

CHAPTER III

WAR AND TERROR

The Girondins. The outbreak of war. Its effects. Danton. The quarrel with Britain. William Pitt. The Polish Question. The influence of minorities. Fall of the Girondins. The Terror. The year of Robespierre. Thermidor. The persistence of a regicide government. The Directorate and Bonaparte.

THE leadership of the new Assembly fell to a body of young and eloquent men of the middle class, who, since they were drawn from the south-western area of France called the Gironde, soon became known, and are to this day remembered, as the Girondins. Of the art and science of government the Girondins knew little; but they possessed, and were able to communicate to others, a glowing enthusiasm for the republican idea, and a missionary impulse to spread it through Europe. Vergniaud and Isnard were the orators, Brissot the diplomatic adviser, the wife of Roland the Egeria of the party. The dazzling dreams, the sentimental enthusiasm, and the tragic end of the Girondins have secured them many friends. Upon them, however, must rest the chief responsibility for a long and terrible war, which destroyed the system of Richelieu and left France a permanently enfeebled member of European society, shielded from imminent danger on the eastern border only by heavy taxes and a universal and compulsory system of military service.

In the atmosphere of angry suspicion which prevailed in Paris the chief enemies of the revolution appeared to be the *émigré*, the non-juring priest, and the Austrian Emperor.[1] Upon these accordingly the Girondins concentrated their animosity, holding that nothing was more likely to make the position of the King and Queen impossible and to open the road to a Republic than a policy of sharp decrees against the *émigrés* and priests followed by a foreign war against the brother of the Queen.

Pretexts for a war were not lacking. Leopold of Austria could complain of French encouragement given to a revolution in

1747-92

---

[1] Technically until 1804 Archduke of Austria and until 1806 Holy Roman Emperor.

Belgium, of German princes dispossessed of feudal rights in Alsace, of Avignon snatched from the Pope and annexed to France, of the novel and disquieting principle that the people of a country have the right to determine their own allegiance, and yet more important than these other occasions of friction, of the dangerous position of his sister the Queen of France. To Marie Antoinette's entreaties that he should summon a European Congress to deal with the French Revolution and concentrate an armed force to give effect to its decisions he could not be altogether indifferent. After Varennes, he issued, in conjunction with the King of Prussia, a declaration from Pilnitz (August, 1791) which seemed to threaten France with the combined action of the European Powers, if Louis were not accorded the treatment which his status deserved. Yet the situation, though grave, was still not beyond repair. A cold, prudent, long-headed man, much occupied with the internal problems of the Austrian empire, Leopold had no desire to embark upon a quixotic crusade against the tumultuous democracy of France. Prompt to threaten, he was reluctant to act, and hoped that when Louis had accepted the Constitution the need for action had passed away. But as autumn melted into winter, and every week brought fresh news of revolutionary violence in Paris, the Emperor's mind turned more and more towards an armed intervention. On all sides he was pressed to stem the tide of militant French democracy; by the *émigrés* who were gathered at Coblentz, by Catharine of Russia, by Gustavus of Sweden, by the King of Spain, and more particularly by Marie Antoinette, who saw in an unsuccessful French defence against foreign invasion the one chance for the salvation of her husband's crown. But then, before his slow resolution ripened to action, Leopold unexpectedly died. His successor Francis, young, vigorous, and care-free, was prompt to take up the Girondin challenge. This took the form of a peremptory demand that the Elector of Trèves should dismiss from his territory the armed force of *émigrés* who were collected at Coblentz. It was a demand intended to precipitate war. Though the French army was disorganized, and Austria and Prussia were leagued against them, Brissot and his followers were confident of victory. At the shock of war the peoples of Europe would rise against their tyrants. Everywhere thrones would fall. The principles of liberty, fraternity, and equality would conquer the world. Robespierre,

1792-1835

an oracle of the Jacobin Club, reasoned otherwise, thinking that the war would restore prestige to the French Crown. But Robespierre's hour had not yet struck. A Girondin ministry, with the able Dumouriez at the Foreign Office, swept their country into war (April 20, 1792).

Then it was discovered that, if revolutionary France was to be effectively defended against the monarchies of unreformed Europe, Louis XVI must cease to reign and France submit to a strict form of tyranny very remote from that extreme dispersion of political authority which had found favour at the opening of the revolution. The war led straight to the fall of the Monarchy, the establishment of the Republic, and to the formation of the government of the Terror. It imparted a deeper note of savage apprehension and passion to the anxieties which had been caused by dear bread and soaring prices, by the widespread prevalence of disorder, and by the ceaseless agitation of the bloodthirsty press against counter-revolutionary activities. It was therefore the exciting cause of terrible crimes, and of a shameful fashion of bloodthirstiness which has been surpassed in modern times only by the communists of Russia. But the war had other consequences more profound and enduring. Revolution was identified with patriotism. For the first time the vast latent energies of the French people were deployed in defence of a cause which was regarded as the common concern of every citizen in the land. For the first time France emerged as an organic nation, its institutions based on popular assent, and maintained against a world in arms by a people in revolution, the masters and servants of a revolutionary state.

Another consequence was inevitable. As the military spirit of the French people was aroused, the idyllic professions of pacificism and cosmopolitan brotherhood which had decorated so many revolutionary speeches passed swiftly into the background. Old diplomatic principles, familiar objects of territorial ambition, resumed their empire. The ghost of Louis XIV returned to direct the counsels of the Jacobins. Fraternity was thrown to the winds. The Girondins were drunk with vainglory and the lust of conquest. They determined to isolate Austria, that they might rob her of Belgium, and bring the French frontier to the Rhine.

For the moment, however, the impolicy of the Girondins had launched France all unprepared (for the royal army was in dissolution) against Prussia and Austria, the two strongest military states on the continent. The result was what might be expected. The first hostile exchanges were sufficient to show that the revolution had no army upon which it could rely for the defence of the country. There was cowardice, indiscipline, failure, and, as invariably happened after every military reverse, the cry of treachery. It was during this period of agonized uncertainty, when the old army had proved itself incompetent, and before the new volunteers of the revolution had proved their worth, that the fate of the monarchy was decided. How, it was asked, could the war be made to succeed, while Louis, the friend of the enemy, reigned in the Tuileries, dismissing his Girondin ministers, refusing a decree for a big military camp near Paris, holding out, so it was believed, secret encouragement to the invader?

At this crisis, when the Prussian army was marching on France, and its chief was threatening Paris with destruction if the royal family was injured, a great, gross revolutionary figure rose above the tumult and took sudden command. The memory of Danton is red with violence. It was he who organized the attack on the Tuileries (August 10, 1792), when the gallant Swiss Guard were hacked to pieces, and the King and Queen were delivered over to captivity, and a Convention was summoned to proclaim a Republic; nor can he be acquitted of condoning the terrible September massacres in the prisons, which were planned to influence the elections to this new Parliament. Nevertheless more than any other revolutionary character of the time Danton was a statesman and a patriot, with an eye for essential needs, a mind clear of illusions, and a rare power for decisive action. He aimed at giving France a convinced republic instead of a disloyal monarchy, a centralized government in place of anarchy, and new armies highly disciplined and permeated by the revolutionary faith in place of the crumbling and doubtful fragments of the army of the Crown. The Girondin idea of a crusade against all the crowned heads of Europe soon struck him as fantastic. The man who pulled down the French monarchy became in diplomacy a pupil of the *ancien régime*.

To Danton as to all statesmen in time of war terror was a necessary instrument of policy. The one intolerable thing, as long as foreign enemies were on French soil, was disunion among Frenchmen. That such disunion existed was a suspicion widely entertained. Every misfortune at home and abroad, the high prices, the bad trade, the foreign war, the disquietude about the king and the priests, was calculated to swell the ranks of the malcontents. A counter-revolution was no impossibility. Such measure of terrorism as was necessary to cow the enemies of the revolutionary state Danton was always prepared to employ.

The birth of the Republic was signalized by a flimsy aureole of lightly purchased victories, which in the course of a few weeks (September 20 to November 7, 1792) placed Savoy and Nice, the Rhenish states, and the Austrian Netherlands, under the heel of the plundering armies of France. Goethe, who was present at the cannonade of Valmy, when the Duke of Brunswick's Prussian army, reputed to be the best in Europe, gave way, after trifling losses, before Kellermann, predicted the advent of a new era in human history. The democratic experiment was something more substantial than mere literature. The Prussian Guard had given ground before it. Better than any monarchy, so it appeared, the ragged distracted democracy of France had captured the real secret of power, which is never a function of mechanism but always an ardour of the soul. Moreover, the Republic was a government of conquest and propaganda. The compulsion of a universal doctrine, the constraint of an empty purse, combined to impel it to a course in which the rôle of the missionary was blended with that of the bandit. France could not afford the expense of peace. It must hold and exploit its victories. More particularly did Austrian Belgium present itself as a desirable acquisition. Here was a gold mine, rich in any case, but capable of yielding its full measure of tribute only were the Scheldt open to navigation and Antwerp revived as London's rival in the markets of the world. It mattered little to the Convention that this river had been closed by an international agreement to which France herself was a party. Such instruments, violating the law of nature, Republican France was prepared to treat as scraps of paper. So, declaring to the world that the Scheldt was open, and that France would offer assistance to all peoples struggling to be free, the Republic light-heartedly embarked upon the course which brought it up against the tenacious and formidable hostility of Britain.

Here was a nation, proud, compact, and wealthy, which was ruled by a government at once aristocratic and popular. The unity which France had now won through revolution, England

Aug. 20.
1792

had acquired in the twelfth century. Civil liberties intoxicating from their novelty in France were in England matters of long established usage. There was nothing which revolutionary France could teach Britain in the matter of Parliamentary government which was not better understood at Westminster than in Paris. There was no part of Europe in which the gospel of the Revolution was likely to be less attractive than Britain, for the reason that the best part of that which republican France had now to offer this conservative island already possessed.

William Pitt had been Prime Minister since 1783. He was a Whig by origin, a financier by taste, and a consummate master of that art of Parliamentary oratory which had never been more important in the history of Europe. It was his fate, while earnestly working for a long spell of peace and internal reform, to lead his country into the war which ended with Waterloo. Of that war he saw the first twelve dark and desperate years. In some respects he was not a great war minister, frittering away the nation's resources in paltry but very costly West Indian expeditions, and, save that he sent Nelson to the Mediterranean, showing little appreciation of the grand lines of martial strategy. But the French rightly discerned in Pitt their greatest and most persistent enemy. He was the soul of every European coalition against them, and as he rose from the Treasury Bench, night after night, and year after year, to put fresh courage into the gentlemen of England by his grave and lofty eloquence, he stood out as the personification of a collective will which could never accept the thought of defeat.

As in the days of Louis XIV, the long duel between Britain and France arose out of the settled policy of the island kingdom never willingly to acquiesce in the annexation of Belgium and Holland by a great continental power. Such designs revolutionary France had by 1793 clearly revealed. She had conquered Belgium, she was threatening Holland, she had torn up the Treaty of the Scheldt, she was inciting by her decree of November 19 the King's subjects in Ireland and elsewhere to rebellion, and on January 21, 1793, she outraged the feelings of the British people by executing Louis XVI. Without a navy she challenged the first naval power in the world.

The entry of Britain into the war introduced an element of single-minded and concentrated opposition to the revolutionary cause which had hitherto been wanting. The main preoccupation at this time of Russia, Prussia, and Austria was not France, but Poland. That unfortunate country, already diminished by a first partition, was about to endure at the hands of its acquisitive neighbours a second and yet a third operation of the same nature. At the time when the French Republic was proclaiming the generous doctrine of self-determination, the military monarchies of the East were busy in procuring the extinction of a nation. The story is one of the most shameful in the annals of the continent. On May 3, 1791, Stanislas Poniatowski, the King of Poland, had accepted a constitution which bade fair to remedy the chief weakness which had hitherto paralysed the Polish state. The *liberum veto* was abolished. The crown was made hereditary; the nobles were subjected to taxation. Varieties of religious belief were permitted. It was reasonable to suppose that, so reformed, Poland might yet play an honourable and useful part in the economy of Europe. But though the constitution was acknowledged by Prussia and Austria, the prospect of a strengthened Poland accorded ill with the voracious appetite of the Tzarina. In 1792 Catharine invaded Poland, and, having beaten down a brave resistance and abolished the Constitution, invited Prussia and Austria to a sharing of the spoils. By every consideration of honour these two Powers should have felt themselves precluded from upsetting a constitution which they had expressly guaranteed, and from attacking a country which they had undertaken to defend. Under the stress of temptation they were untrue to their engagements. In the partition, repartition, and extinction of Poland, Prussia and Austria, though divided by bitter jealousies, played a dishonourable and collusive rôle. They carried off their booty and smashed the patriotic rising of Kosciuszko. It was not until October 10, 1795, that the third Treaty of Partition blotted Poland from the map. For four critical years the gobbling up and deglutition of this vast territory had absorbed the main part of the attention of Austria and Prussia, had fatally impaired the effectiveness of their co-operation against France, and had enabled the Republic to establish itself firmly in the face of Europe.

The clue to the understanding of revolutions is that they are worked by small fanatical minorities. The French Convention, which proclaimed the Republic, executed the King, sent the Girondins to the scaffold, and established the Terror, was returned by the votes of some six per cent. of the total electorate.

The main body of the French people, after the first blaze of enthusiasm had died down, wanted nothing so much as to be allowed to manage their own concerns in tranquillity, and were well content to leave politics to the club men. Either because he was too inert or too busy, too selfish or too indifferent, too frightened or too disgusted, or too little capable of entering into combination with others, the average respectable citizen stood aside from the battle. In Paris, where political interest was most widely diffused, it would appear from the report of a careful

Partition of 1772
      "   " 1793
      "   " 1795

THE PARTITIONS OF POLAND.

observer that in every one hundred and thirty persons only one gave active support to the Terror.

The vast majority of the Convention, known as the Plain or *Marais*, belonged to that moderate, colourless, uncertain, but wholly respectable section of the French middle class, which constituted the strength of the nation. To such it was natural to seek guidance from the Girondins, who were returned a hundred and twenty strong, and were already established in parliamentary reputation. The Girondins were the last apostles of the liberal idea.

They believed in liberty local and personal. They had a vision of France settling down to a blameless and brilliant existence under a Republican Constitution the finest in the world. Being essentially humane, they were shocked by the crimes of August and September. But though they could make beautiful speeches, they were incapable of brave and concerted action. They attacked Robespierre, but did not imprison him; assailed the assassins of September, but did not prosecute them; realized the dangerous opposition of revolutionary Paris, but would neither close the clubs, nor curb the Press, nor provide the Convention with the necessary safeguard of an armed force on which reliance could be placed. One man might have saved them from destruction, and offered to do so; but the Girondins were too respectable to clasp the strong but blood-stained hand of Danton. To the average Frenchman no respectability remained to a party which had given a regicide vote, and when the Girondins through cowardice and ineptitude allowed themselves against their better judgment to be outmanœuvred by the Mountain into sending the King to the guillotine, they had decreed their own extinction. After that no moderate Frenchman would lift up a finger to help them.

*Jan. 21,
1793*

The spring which followed the execution of Louis was crowded with disaster for the regicide state. With England, Spain, and Holland added to the circle of her enemies, with her armies withdrawn from Belgium, with Dumouriez, her best general, gone over to the enemy, with insurrection ablaze in the Vendée and in Lyons, and with Toulon at the mercy of the British fleet, the Republic was fighting with its back to the wall. It was the stress of these terrible anxieties which swept the Girondins clean out of the political scene, and founded that firm and terrible instrument of autocratic rule which succeeded amidst much bloodshed and cruelty in restoring the military situation.

The Jacobin Government consisted of a small secret Cabinet or Committee of Public Safety for the general direction of policy, of a somewhat larger Committee of Public Security for police, of a revolutionary tribunal for the dissemination of terror, and of a plan for the strict supervision of generals in the field by civil agents of the purest fanaticism known as *représentants en mission*. The Convention, scornfully described by Dumouriez as a body of three hundred scoundrels and four hundred imbeciles, continued to sit, to debate, to legislate; but its authority was gone.

A *coup d'état* led by Henriot (June 2) had eliminated those ^{1793} Girondin orators whose eloquence had so often charmed and delighted the assembly. The party of these brilliant idealists had not even been able to defend its leaders from proscription or the scaffold. It could not police its debating hall. Paralysed by the publicity which its principles forbade it to renounce, it was overshadowed by the new Cabinet, by the Commune of Paris, by the Jacobin and Cordelier Clubs, and by the disciplined and vocal ruffians who dominated the revolutionary committees in the forty-eight sections or electoral districts into which the capital was divided. Other times required other methods. The stress of war had created an immense acceleration in affairs: swift and ruthless action in place of the interminable loquacity which had so long perplexed and arrested the march of government was the note of men like Carnot at the War Office and Jean Bon Saint-André at the Marine. The Jacobins, who saved the Republic, were giants of industry. Science came to their aid. On July 27 an order was sent from Paris to the armies on the frontier in a quarter of an hour. The semaphore telegraph, one of the secrets of an impending military Empire, had made its début in the service of France.

The man of the new era was Robespierre, the lean lawyer from $^{1758\text{-}94}$ Arras, who entered the Committee of Public Safety on July 28, 1793, and for one amazing year, memorable for its military glories and domestic shame, was the real ruler of France and the master spirit of Europe. What a catalogue of Jacobin triumphs belongs to the reign of Robespierre! The royalist revolution put down in Lyons, Toulon recaptured, the Duke of York beaten at Hondschoote, the Austrians defeated at Wattignies and Fleurus, Belgium reconquered, Holland invaded, French soil everywhere liberated from the invader. It is the year of the first *levée en masse* of the nation in arms, the year, though not the official natal year, of that system of military conscription which still brings a dark shadow into every Frenchman's life, the year in which Carnot began to organize the armies which made for Napoleon his instrument of conquest.

In Paris the year of Robespierre marks the culmination of the Jacobin Terror. The man was of the type of Lenin, a fanatical believer in an inspired text. As Karl Marx was to the Russian, so was Rousseau to the French revolutionary. Part of his power with the Parisians lay in his plain simplicity of purpose, and in a life reputed to be free from the taint of peculation. "You may laugh at him now," said a contemporary, "but that man will go far. He believes every word he says." The ease and malice of his oratory, the violence of his views, coupled with a great dexterity in the arts of political management, made him almost from the first a leader among the Jacobins. He was the master of the Paris revolutionary machine before he became a director of national policy. Scrupulously and elegantly dressed, well-mannered, ostentatious in his professions of republican virtue, he had for every dissenter from his narrow creed the one and simple remedy of the guillotine. In March he sent Hébert and Chaumette to the scaffold for their anarchy and atheism. In April the knife fell upon Danton and Desmoulins, who in the *Vieux Cordelier*, the one piece of real literature produced in the revolution, had advocated a return to clemency and modera-

June 10, 1794

tion. At last the man-eating tiger overreached himself by a law (the law of 22 Prairial) which threatened the life of every member of the Convention, for the legislators were deprived of their immunity, and the last feeble safeguards for the protection of persons accused for political offences were swept away. In self-defence even cowards may pluck up courage. There were men in the Convention led by Barras and Tallien who resolved that the tyrant should perish and saw that with a careful organization of forces outside the assembly the deed could be done. Meeting the Jacobins, not with eloquent speeches, but with their own weapons of calculated force, these capable men achieved a swift and easy victory. On July 28, 1794 (9 Thermidor by the Republican Calendar), the Hôtel de Ville was invested and stormed by a force largely drawn from the Section Lepelletier, a well-to-do quarter of the city. There Robespierre was found, his jaw shattered by a bullet wound, and thence he was hauled, all bleeding, to the scaffold that he might die under the knife, as his many victims had died before him.

The long nightmare was over. The hateful epidemic of butchery, which in Paris alone had cost two thousand six hundred victims, came to a sudden end. Moderates and Dantonists seized the wheel of power, abolished the Commune, closed the Jacobin Club, amnestied the Vendéans, and recalled the Girondins. The dark miasma of suspicion which had poisoned the political life of Paris passed away with Robespierre's fall and

ourdan's great victory at Fleurus. In her sudden deliverance June 25, 1794
rom fear and humiliation the country swung back into the
unlight of gaiety and hope. No more fanatical gloom! No
nore ravings of a bloodthirsty press! No more guillotining of
he brave, the good, the beautiful, the innocent! Frivolity
esumed its long-interrupted reign. But if France ceased to be
Terrorist, she remained revolutionary. The members of the
egicide Parliament could make no advances to the party of
eaction. For them it was a matter of life and death so to
nanœuvre that, whatever the future government of France
night be, regicides from the Convention should stand at the
wheel.

How that government should be framed was now a main pre- 1743-94
occupation. Condorcet, the best of the Girondin thinkers, had
devised a constitution, containing, like the German Constitution
of 1918, all the last refinements of democratic philosophy, but
plainly unworkable and never put into execution. Something
was wanted having in it less of a democracy and more of concentration and force, but at the same time securing the continued
predominance of that moderate revolutionary element which
had triumphed at Thermidor. There was one serious danger
obstructing the approach to a solution of the problem. The reds
of Paris, who had suffered the defeat at Thermidor, though
greatly weakened by the suppression of the Commune, were still
armed, still formidable, still in full possession of the technique
of a revolutionary *coup d'état*. On May 1 and June 2, 1795, they
attacked the Convention, but were on each occasion repulsed.
Then at last a decision was taken which, had it been adopted
earlier, might have saved the monarchy. The National Guard
was placed under a committee of soldiers.

The answer to the constitutional riddle was found in an imposture which survived for four years under the name of the
Directory. Since a dictatorship was as yet unthinkable, executive power was entrusted to a body of five men, elected for a
term of five years. It was thought to avoid mob rule by the
establishment of two chambers, the Ancients and the Five
Hundred, elected upon a limited franchise, and yet to secure
responsibility to public opinion by a requirement that every year
one-fifth of the executive and one-third of the Legislature should
be changed. But behind this pleasurable façade of moderate
liberty there was concealed the awkward fact that a government

of regicides could not afford to trust the people. The constitution
was accompanied by a decree, providing that two-thirds of the
new Parliament should be drawn from the Convention which
had voted the King and Queen to the guillotine. All the
moderates and royalists in Paris were up in arms against this
violent interference with electoral liberty. They had been happily delivered of the Terror; they now wished to be quit, once
and for all, of the politicians whose cowardice and fanaticism
had made the Terror possible. A movement was organized by
those sections of the city which represented wealth, respectability
or conservative opinion, to put an end to the regicide body. In
the first week of October twenty-six thousand men were said to
be mustered for the attack.

The new Directors were a motley body bound to one another
by a common complicity in regicide, but otherwise intentionally
drawn from different sections of the revolutionary camp. Rewbel
was a stiff Jacobin lawyer from Alsace, Carnot and Letourneur
were engineers, Lépaux a visionary Girondin. Barras alone, the
least estimable of the five, possessed a flair for political action.
At two critical junctures the vulgar, theatrical, peculating libertine from Provence showed himself to be a man of the moment.
In Thermidor he pulled down Robespierre. In Vendémiaire he
descried Napoleon Bonaparte.

This young Corsican general of artillery, who in the autumn of
1793 had distinguished himself at the siege of Toulon, happened
to be in Paris without employment in those anxious October days
when cries of " Vive le Roi " were again heard with acceptance
in the Paris streets, and the last Assembly of the Revolution was
trembling before the mutterings of a reactionary storm. There
he made the acquaintance of the most powerful of the Directors,
who discerned his worth, and entrusted him with the defence of
the threatened chamber. The military dispositions of General
Bonaparte announced the hand of a master. He sent Murat
galloping to Sablons for the guns, and against a tumultuous force
devoid of artillery established an immediate and decisive advantage. One brief cannonade efficiently directed cleared the
streets, rescued the government, and gave to its saviour an overwhelming claim to military promotion. He was at once made
general of the Interior, and in the next year received, again
with the favour and support of Barras, the hand of Josephine
Beauharnais and the all-important Italian Command.

Oct. 3-5,
1795

CHAPTER IV

THE COMING OF BONAPARTE

France and Europe. The lure of Italy. Bonaparte's Italian victories. Campo Formio. Consequences for Italy. Fructidor. Egypt. The second Coalition. Syria. The effect of the Syrian Campaign on French opinion. Siéyès. Brumaire. Survival of social equality. The Consulate. Marengo and Lunéville. The British attitude. Ireland. The Blockade and the Rights of Neutrals. The Peace of Amiens.

By this time the generals and diplomatists of the Directory had secured for France a position of tremendous ascendancy in western Europe. Holland had been overrun by Pichegru and converted into a client Batavian Republic, Belgium and all Germany to the Rhine frontier were annexed as integral parts of the Republic. Savoy was French. A French army was quartered on the Italian Riviera. Prussia, Spain, and Tuscany had withdrawn from the war. The stage was cleared for a conflict between the revolution and those two Powers in the world which represented in their strongest and most pertinacious form the counter-revolutionary spirit, Protestant Britain and Catholic Austria.

Behind her tutelary waves and winds Britain stood impregnable. Nature was her friend, sending storms to wreck Hoche's expedition to the Irish, and foiling every minor plan for the assistance of those latent rebellious sentiments which were assumed to exist in the English democracy. A direct attack upon this obstinate island could offer only slender encouragement to a brigand state in quest of quick returns. Such an attack must necessarily be naval, and therefore, since the old royal navy had been demoralized by revolution, highly speculative. The outlay would be large, the yield uncertain.

Very different was the prospect offered by Austria. One jewel of the Austrian crown little prized (by reason of its distance from Vienna) by its owner, who had more than once attempted to exchange it for Bavarian territory, had been conquered already. France had Belgium, and proposed to keep that rich coal-bearing and highly urbanized province, which lay adjacent to her frontier and within easy reach of her capital. But richer, more attractive, more romantic than Belgium were those wide provinces of the Italian peninsula, which acknowledged the direct rule of Austria.

or were content to follow in her wake. The Milanese with its famous constellation of Lombard cities was a province of the Austrian Empire. Tuscany was a Habsburg Duchy. Naples, though governed by a degenerate Spanish Bourbon King, followed the strong guidance of Marie Caroline, his Habsburg wife, and might on that account, for purposes both of plunder and propaganda, be added to the catalogue of France's enemies. In Italy then everything conspired to invite the military enterprise of the French Republic, old tradition, the charm of the climate, the variety and wealth of the crops, the opulence of the cities, the wonderful treasures of the galleries and museums, the reputed weakness of the enemy, and the assumed readiness of the Italian population to throw off the Austrian yoke.

There was yet a further incitement to an Italian campaign, which weighed heavily in the minds of the anti-clerical government in Paris. The Pope had made himself extremely difficult. He had refused to accept the Civil Constitution of the clergy, and had encouraged the resistance of the non-juror priests. Of all the counter-revolutionary forces in Europe, none had been more troublesome than the Vatican. Its hidden hand was found everywhere, among the *émigrés* of Coblentz, among the rebels of the Vendée and Brittany, and in every parish of France where a non-juror priest was held in honour by his flock. A French Ambassador had even been murdered in Rome. The condign punishment of this troublesome pontiff and the annexation of his backward and ill-governed state were accordingly among the favourite projects of the Directors, as, in plumed hats and gorgeous uniforms, they discussed the regeneration of Europe in the gilded halls of the Luxembourg Palace.

In the French armies, which now contained the flower of the nation, illusions persisted which had long faded away among the *parvenus* and profiteers who constituted the political society in Paris. The young men who followed Bonaparte across the mountains into Italy still believed that France had a liberating message to give to the world. The Italians they regarded with compassion, as a race completely outstripped in the calendar of civilized progress, but capable, under French tutelage, of learning the new way of life in which France was a pioneer. These thoughts, the young general, who may have in part experienced their attraction, thus expressed in an early proclamation to the Italian peoples : —

"Peoples of Italy, the French army comes to break your chains; the French people is the friend of all peoples; meet us with confidence. Your property, your religion, and your usages will be respected. We make war as generous enemies, and we have no quarrel save with the tyrants who enslave you."

Attached to the cause of the monarchies was that little Kingdom of Sardinia which carried all unseen the promise of Italian union. This kingdom, in the first month of the wonderful campaign which blazoned his military genius to the world, Bonaparte compelled to the Armistice of Cherasco and to a peace which it *April 28.* was never afterwards strong enough seriously to disturb. The *1796.* skill with which, striking at the point of junction between the allies, he split them apart, rolled the Sardinians to the northwest, and in a mountain campaign, conducted with lightning skill, brought them to acknowledge defeat, has always been acknowledged as a masterpiece of military art. To the larger and more formidable task of beating the Austrians he then, to the amazement of Europe, proceeded to address himself with an equal measure of success. The march to Lodi gave him the *1796-7.* Milanese; Rivoli, the last of a series of brilliant actions against relieving forces, produced the surrender of Mantua. The Archduke Charles was no more successful than Beaulieu or Wurmser, Quosdanovich or Alvintzy. Outmanoeuvred on the Tagliamento, and driven back into the mountains, he was glad enough to welcome the preliminaries of peace, which were signed at *April 18.* Leoben. *1797.*

All through the summer the young general kept state in the palace of Mombello, near Milan. His ambitions were no longer concealed. "Do you think," he said, as he walked in the gardens, "that it is to aggrandize the lawyers and the Directorate that I triumph in Italy?" Without reference to Paris he made war, drafted treaties, and created states. He had not scrupled, after defeating the Papal army at Ancona, to extort from the Vatican money, plunder, and the cession of provinces—Avignon and the Venaissin in France, the Legations in Italy. Lombardy was converted into a Cisalpine, Genoa into a Ligurian Republic, each of them equipped with constitutions on the French model, and devised as outlying bastions of the French Republic. Wiser than his Parisian masters, he declined to implicate himself in a Neapolitan campaign, seeing that peace was to be won not in Naples, but in northern Italy, and more particularly in Venice.

Austria, who had twice supped on the "eucharistic body of Poland," was now invited by the pupil of Frederick the Great to put aside her German scruples, to surrender Belgium and the Rhine frontier and Lombardy, and the integrity of the *Reich*, and to take in exchange a share in the famous but helpless Republic of Venice. To this corrupt transaction the Austrian government shamefully descended.

Oct., 1797

The Treaty of Campo Formio, which crowned Napoleon's first Italian campaign, seeing that it is based on the cynical partition of an innocent and independent state, arouses little enthusiasm in the breast of the moralist; but, morality apart, it was a great French victory. The leading conservative Power in Europe ratified the extraordinary conquests of the Republic. The chief secular protagonist of the Roman Faith consented to a vulgar act of brigandage. The official champion of the German *Reich* sacrificed its rights, and agreed that a Congress should be summoned to Rastadt to carry out such territorial adjustments as were consequent upon the advance of French territory to the Rhine. The triumph of Bonaparte was complete. He had made France supreme in Italy.

In the history of the Italian people the first campaign of Bonaparte marks the beginning of that resurgence of national feeling which is known as the *Risorgimento*. Bonaparte was not gentle to his Italian compatriots. He plundered their picture galleries and museums; he bled them white by his taxation and military requisitions; he repressed with merciless severity the slightest resistance to his authority; he murdered the ancient and historic freedom of Venice. But he was an Italian, cast in the imperial mould, and recalling by his exploits the glories of ancient Rome. Though he was severe, he seemed to come as a liberator, bringing with him the breath of a new freedom and wide-ranging prospects of Italian power. Much was forgiven to the young general who broke the Austrian strangle-hold on the Italian people, and invited them to work the institutions of a modern state. The Italian *literati* praised him to the skies; the best Lombards crowded to his court; and the Cisalpine Republic, though resting on French bayonets, acted for many years as a seminary of statecraft in a land where the tradition of public duty had long been atrophied by foreign rule.

With Prussia and Austria withdrawn from the war, France

and Britain stood face to face. Between them lay two questions, striking deep into the heart of politics, the Rhine frontier which Britain would never concede, the monarchy which the victorious armies of France would never accept. Moderate men there were in France prepared to give a trial to liberalism, and to explore the possibilities of constitutional monarchy and an English peace. Such, when once they were returned in numbers to the Councils, were adjudged by Barras, the Director in Paris, and by Bonaparte, his military friend in Italy, too dangerous to live. "I have come here to kill the royalists," said Augereau, the general's emissary, with characteristic frankness, as he brought his troops into Paris for the *coup d'état* of Fructidor. Suspect deputies were *Sept. 4 1797* seized in their sleep and shipped off without trial to Cayenne. Military commissions in the provinces dealt freely in sentences of death and deportation. The elections in 49 departments were cancelled. Among the victims of this September violence were some of the noblest names in France: Pichegru, the conqueror of Holland; Barthélemy, the diplomatist who signed the Prussian treaty; and Carnot, the organizer of victory. Barras, however, the ex-terrorist, was secure, and with him a Jacobin government so bad and purposeless that only fatigue and indifference could have preserved it, until Bonaparte was ready to seize command.

While cultivated Germans were delighting in Goethe's *Wilhelm Meister*, or reading a new plan for eternal peace put out from Königsberg by Immanuel Kant, the French Jacobins, relieved of dynastic opposition, had gained another lease of life, and persevered in their lucrative policy of plunder and conquest. They made the best of their opportunity. Revolutions were *1798-9* initiated in Switzerland, Rome, and Naples; and the Helvetian, the Roman, and the Parthenopean[1] Republics were added to the list of French dependencies. The politic scruples of Bonaparte, who knew the Latin peasant to be religious, and wanted his body for the wars, weighed little with the anti-clerical rulers of France. The Pope of Rome was treated with little more respect than the King of France. His person was seized and transported across the French border to Valence.

The year of Bonaparte's triumphs in Italy contains one of the *1797* darkest pages in the British calendar. In April and May the fleet upon which everything depended was paralysed by serious mutinies at Spithead and the Nore. The crisis was overcome by

[1] *I.e.,* Neapolitan.

that commixture of firmness and good sense which has often in the annals of England mitigated the penalties of long insensibility. The legitimate grievances of the sailors were redressed, the ringleaders were hanged, discipline was restored, after which with a swift and memorable resilience the navy proceeded to win the two victories of Camperdown and the Nile, which changed the history of Europe. In the first of these actions Duncan obliterated the Dutch navy; in the second Nelson destroyed the French fleet which had conveyed Bonaparte to Egypt, and so, by a swift cannonade in Aboukir Bay, secured for Britain a naval preponderance in the Mediterranean, which was never lost.

Oct., 1797

Aug., 1798

For in 1798 Bonaparte was in Egypt. Invited by the Directory to invade England, he had preferred, after a careful examination, to assail the enemy at that point in her world-wide sphere of influence where he expected that a French success might exercise a most shattering effect on her confidence and stability. Vast chimerical projects floated into a mind which was already fired by the fame and example of Alexander. From Egypt he would create an Eastern Empire, perhaps march on India, perhaps on Constantinople, and bring the shopkeeping island to a beggar's repentance by the destruction of its trade. In this design he was counting on the help of Tippoo and the Mahrattas. "You are," he said to his army, as he embarked at Toulon, "one of the wings of the army of England."

July, 1798

Modern Egypt, with its superficial glaze of French civilization, dates from the battle of the Pyramids, where Bonaparte destroyed the savage power of the Mamelukes. His expedition restored a long lost province to European civilization and advertised its archaeological interest to the West. From the valley of the Nile and all over the Aegean the Odyssey of the marvellous foreigner continued to inspire hopes of liberty and to furnish a pattern of civilized and ordered rule. It was a force in Greece, and penetrated to Albania, whence a great adventurer, whose Mosque still dominates the citadel of Cairo, came forth to lay in the valley of the Nile the foundations of a modern state. Among the many imitators of Napoleon none was more influential than Mehemet Ali, the ancestor of a line of Pashas, Khedives, and Kings, who, by his fiery and domineering energy, built out of Napoleonic ideas the Egypt which we know.

Nov., 1798

The news of Nelson's great victory brought into being the Second Coalition. From Naples, where the Queen and her friend

Emma Hamilton were thrown into wild paroxysms by the appearance of the conquering hero, the will to war passed swiftly through Vienna to St. Petersburg and to Constantinople, until it was moulded by Pitt's statesmanship and by British subsidies into a large design for driving France behind her ancient frontiers, and for the overthrow of her Jacobin government. The early successes of the allies were astonishing. In one brief summer campaign (1799) all that Napoleon had gained in Italy and all that the Directory had added to his gains was lost to the Republic. Suvoroff, a meteor out of wind-swept steppes, a Tatar peasant general, very old, very small, and very fiery, inspired into his Russian following a spirit as indomitable as his own. He beat Moreau at Cassano, helped to rout Joubert at Novi, and sent the little Franco-Italian republics clattering to the ground like a pack of cards. But the wild soldier of genius could not endure the pretensions of his pedantic and overbearing allies. There was nothing in common between Suvoroff's savage impetuosity and the slow deliberate formalism of Austrian warfare. Fortunately for France, before the next act of the Italian drama was played, the Tzar had broken with the Allies, and Suvoroff was far away in his native land. Meanwhile victories won by Masséna at Zurich and by Brune in Holland had saved France from complete disaster.

Aug. 15.
1799

With the entry of Turkey into the war Napoleon's dreams of an Indian expedition were replaced by the narrower objective of a Syrian campaign. With thirteen thousand picked troops he reached Acre, and was there stopped by two resolute men, Sydney Smith and Phélippeaux, his old schoolmate. It was a blessing in disguise. What was to be feared from the Syrian campaign was not the quality of the Turkish troops, which was low, but the vast and waterless spaces over which a Turkish army in retreat might succeed under skilful guidance in luring a pursuing foe. Only after the most serious losses was Napoleon able to extricate his army from Syria. That he could without disaster have led it over the highlands of Anatolia, if such was ever his intention, is hardly credible. From these dangerous temptations he was saved by a fortunate and humiliating repulse.

March.
1799

To the making of his career the Turkish war was of rare and unexpected assistance. If the invasion of Egypt was romantic, still more poetic was the glamour which attached to the Syrian campaign. Home-staying Frenchmen, however much they might mock at the Pope and the priest, read with a thrill the bulletins of the young French general who had taken Palestine, had set up his quarters in the Monastery of Nazareth, and had read the Bible to his officers under a Syrian sky in places sanctified by Christ and His apostles and made glorious in the eyes of Frenchmen by the exploits of the first Crusade. The recovery of Palestine from the Turk, which appealed even to the Baptist chief of a British Cabinet at the end of the Great War, was an idea which exercised a yet more powerful attraction for the countrymen of St. Louis, living under the sordid rule of the Directory. The name of Bonaparte was on everybody's lips. Before he returned to France, leaving his troops to fend as best they might, he was already the hero of a nation, and its uncrowned master. The news of a brilliant action against the Turks at Aboukir balanced the grim fact that a splendid army had been wasted on a profitless expedition.

July,
1799

After ten years of war and revolution France desired nothing so much as peace and ordered self-government. The country was tired of confusion and anarchy, of unrepaired roads and endemic brigandage, of schools without teachers and hospitals without nurses, and of the dragging royalist insurrection, which paralysed the life of fourteen departments. Even in the circle of Paris politicians there were men who saw that only a soldier's sword could cut France free from the entanglements of faction and establish an era of ordered liberty. One of these was a remarkable political figure, who, in the worst months of 1799, was brought into the Directory from the embassy at Berlin. His name was Siéyès.

1748-1836

No one was more deeply concerned in fixing the shape of the revolution, which he was now determined to transform, than this clear-thinking unfrocked priest, the champion of the Third Estate, the oracle of the Constituent Assembly, the creator of the artificial departments, the hammer of the Church, the adviser of the Girondins. That a thinker of such antecedents and of such authority should, from within the inner circle of the government, now decide to call upon the military arm was a fact of great significance. In the furtherance of his high ambition, Bonaparte, landing at Fréjus on October 9, could have wished for no more dexterous or effectual ally.

On a dull November evening the last scene of the French

Revolution was enacted in the orangery and park of St. Cloud. Thither on the false pretext of a Jacobin conspiracy the Councils had been transferred, there they were encompassed by armed men, and thence in the gathering gloom they were ignominiously dispersed at the point of the sword. The critical moment in a day of hazards and uncertainties was when Lucien Bonaparte, the young President of the Five Hundred, left the Assembly, and, on the fictitious plea that daggers had been raised against his brother, called upon the troops, who were mustered on the terrace, in the name of the law to clear the hall. Paris was unmoved by the imposture and violence incidental to the destruction of Parliamentary liberty. No tears fell over the Directory and the Councils. They had talked wildly and governed ill. All through France the *coup d'état* of Brumaire (November 9) was acclaimed as the dawn of a new era. A few weeks later the country by a vast preponderance of votes accepted a new Constitution, which gave to Napoleon as the first of three Consuls plenary authority over its destinies for the next ten years.

The Republic remained and not in outward form only. Bonaparte was a child of the revolution, equally in the sense that like so many other brilliant men he was enabled by reason of that great social convulsion to come into the forefront of affairs, as also because his youthful mind had been formed by the literature of criticism and revolt which had heralded the storm. A free career to talent could never fail to appeal to him. It was the essence of democracy, the mainstay of power, the secret of the military successes, which had made Europe tremble before the Revolution. This side at least of the revolutionary conquest Bonaparte resolved to preserve. Political liberty might go, social equality was vital. The amazing preponderance over Europe which France obtained during the Consulate and the Empire is not only to be explained by the genius of its leader, but is also due to the fact that by the destruction of privilege the best talent of the most populous of the highly civilized countries of the West was available for his service. Talleyrand was at the Foreign Office, Fouché at the Police. Men of science, a thing incredible at Whitehall, were given portfolios. The Council of State was the most efficient body of experts which Europe had yet seen. For the most part the marshals of the victorious armies had risen by merit from the ranks.

To the appeasement of France Bonaparte brought all the gifts

of skill, insight, and detachment which the problem demanded.
He was neither Jacobin nor royalist, but being raised above the
strife of factions could see the needs of the country as a whole.
Reasoning that the peasantry were religious, he restored the
freedom of Catholic worship and made a Concordat with the
Pope. The Vendée was pacified. The tyrannical laws of the
Jacobins were repealed. Gaudin, an able financier, was called in
to give France, which he succeeded in doing, a system of direct
and indirect taxes, at once fairly assessed and not too onerous,
changes which, coupled with the foundation of the Bank of
France in 1800, inaugurated a condition of financial stability to
which the country had long been a stranger. In all these necessary and welcome measures the First Consul marched with his
country's mind. For a time the voice of liberal opposition was
heard in a small assembly known as the Tribunate, which the ingenuity of Siéyès had intercalated into the Constitution for the
ventilation of grievances. Even this slight concession to freedom
was found excessive. The Tribunate, becoming inconvenient,
was suppressed in 1807, and perished without a murmur of
sympathy or protest.

The task of bringing peace to Europe was far more difficult.
Though Paul of Russia had withdrawn from the coalition, and
was fast bound in admiration to Bonaparte, Austria and England
were still in the field and obdurate to the First Consul's advances.
Austria, then, as the more vulnerable of his two opponents, was
singled out as the first object of attack, and with an ease which
offers a surprising contrast to the campaign of the previous year,
Austria was defeated. The single victory of Marengo (June 4,
1800), which threw France into paroxysms of enthusiasm, and
gave to the Consulate the necessary baptism of military glory,
was sufficient to bring toppling to the ground the ascendancy
which the Austrians had built up for themselves with Russian
aid during Napoleon's absence in Egypt. In Paris nobody cared
to observe that Bonaparte had failed to relieve Masséna in
Genoa, and that only by the sudden return of Desaix from the
south had he been saved from calamitous defeat at Marengo. It
was sufficient that like Hannibal he had crossed the Alps, boldly
thrown himself across the enemies' communications, and with
fifteen guns against two hundred, won a crushing victory. In the
next December the triumph of France was clinched at Hohen-
linden. The Austrians had not been fortunate in their com-

manders. Napoleon had been pitted against the aged Melas, Moreau against an Archduke of eighteen years.

Chastised by these two defeats the Emperor sued for peace, and at Lunéville (February, 1801) assented to a map of Europe which brought the French frontier to the Rhine, and recognized the four client republics, Batavian and Helvetian, Cisalpine and Ligurian, which had been set up as outlying spurs of revolutionary propaganda and influence. A Europe so constituted the Cabinet of William Pitt could never accept.

Feb. 9, 1801

The general outlook of Britain towards the French Revolution had been determined at its very outset by a dazzling political pamphlet, which was the more impressive since it came from the pen of an Irishman and a Whig. Burke's *Reflections* instilled into the Tory majority who governed the country a deep horror of the Revolution, which the advent of Bonaparte to power did nothing to diminish. A small minority of clear-sighted independent men like Charles Fox divined the great civil qualities of the First Consul. By the great mass of the nation they were unperceived. To them he was the creature of an odious and criminal movement, the last and most formidable of the revolutionary bandits, who had deluged Europe with blood, an ogre noted for a long carnival of Italian rapine, and more recently for alleged atrocities in Syria, the murder of Turkish prisoners who had surrendered on parole, and the poisoning of invalids whom it was cumbersome to save.

Nov., 1790

It is nevertheless an amazing instance of insolent fatuity that when in 1799 the First Consul expressed to the British Government his desire for peace, the reply came that the best guarantee which France could give of her sincerity would be the recall of her legitimate sovereign. Such an answer, as Talleyrand was quick to note, came ill from a German who sat upon the Stuart throne.

In the long controversy with France, Britain had experienced continual anxiety from the griefs, discontents, and conspiracies of Ireland. So it was during the war of the American revolt: so it proved again to be when the ideas of the French Revolution, alighting first among the educated Protestants of the north, spread sparks far and wide among the downtrodden and passive Catholics in the southern and western part of the island. Of all European peoples, the ignorant and priest-ridden Irish Catholics were most remote from the innovating and impious temper of

27

the French Revolution. But when men are told that they are
wronged; when they realize that they are disfranchised in their
own country; when they are invited in the name of liberty and
equality to throw off an alien yoke, and to take their lawful share
in the ruling of their native land, then, no matter how conservative they may be, the appeal will go home. This is what
happened in Ireland. The Protestants of the north led by Wolfe
Tone, the founder of the United Irishmen, called upon their
Catholic compatriots to claim the right to sit in the Parliament
of Dublin. The Catholics made their claim and were refused,
rose in rebellion and were crushed. Then Pitt, seeing many
difficulties and dangers resulting from the existence of two Parliaments under one crown, carried out the Legislative Union of
1800, under which a hundred seats in the House of Commons
and thirty-two in the House of Lords were accorded to Protestant
Irishmen. The constitutional change, though violently resisted
by the Protestant patriots of the Dublin Parliament, and carried
out only by extensive bribery, was for the moment effective.
Ireland gave little serious trouble during the Napoleonic wars:
but the Irish question, which is proverbially fatal to British
statesmen, closed the famous ministry of Pitt. That wise statesman had seen from the first that it was essential for the success
of the Union that Catholic Irishmen should be returned to the
Parliament of Westminster. He believed that Catholic emancipation was just; he argued that it was politic; he knew that it
was safe. The Catholic vote, which might be dangerous in Dublin,
would be harmless in the prevailingly Protestant atmosphere of
Westminster. But the King, out of respect to his coronation oath,
opposed an obstinate negative. That Pitt thereupon resigned,
and never thereafter presumed to press his policy, is one of the
major calamities of Irish history.

March,
1801

In his enterprise of striking England to the ground, Napoleon
hit upon the idea of a continental blockade. Starting from the
premise that England was a nation of shopkeepers, he concluded
that such a country could receive no wound more fatal than the
closure of every continental market to its goods. Accordingly
Spain was directed to invade Portugal, while a French garrison
dragooned the miserable Sovereign of Naples into a commercial
policy conformable to the French design. It was plain, however,
from the first that a Mediterranean blockade was in itself of
little value. If English merchandise could penetrate into Ham-

burg or Lübeck, or even into Stockholm or St. Petersburg, the blockade was broken and the game was up. The policy was not one which could succeed by halves. It must either succeed entirely or not at all, and what was formidable and ultimately ruinous to Napoleon was the fact that, drawn by the mirage of a universal blockade, he was condemned to the pursuit of a universal Empire. There was, however, a moment at the beginning of 1801, when this costly and exorbitant folly was nearer to success than at any subsequent stage of the war. Paul I of Russia was a half-crazy tyrant, whose brutality was partly redeemed by a whimsical enthusiasm for the Knights of Malta, and by a passionate admiration for the genius of Napoleon. In December, 1800, this strange Muscovite savage came forward as the champion of the higher morality in the maritime war. Gathering Denmark, Sweden and Prussia under his wing, Paul formed a League of Armed Neutrality for the protection of neutral rights, and with the special object of injuring Britain. It had been an old point of weakness in the armoury of that country that its navy in searching neutral vessels for enemy goods or contraband of war had often caused loss and inconvenience to their owners. How the right of search should be exercised, with what restraints and safeguards, courtesies and compensations, was and remains a thorny problem of international law. The doctrine of "the Freedom of the Seas," the view that neutral ships plying on their lawful occasions should be free from molestation from belligerent navies, was promulgated by Catharine II of Russia in 1780, was in 1800 revived by Paul, and to this day, though the American navy threw it to the winds in the latest phase of the Great War, remains a live issue which divides opinion. That Paul I should have succeeded in getting the Northern Powers to defend the principles of the Armed Neutrality was for Napoleon an unexpected piece of good fortune, which he was prompt to seize. But just as the combination was assuming a menacing shape, as the Prussians were marching into Hanover and Danish troops were taking station in Hamburg and Lübeck, the whole machine was shattered in pieces. In March, 1801, the Tzar was strangled in a palace revolution. In April the Danish fleet was broken by Nelson's guns at Copenhagen. Under the stress of this double shock the Northern League, which at one time promised to complete the continental blockade, came to a sudden and inglorious end.

These events, the assassination of the Tzar, the battle of Copenhagen, and the retirement of Pitt, prepared the way for the Peace of Amiens (March, 1802). It is the fashion of English writers to say that Addington, the new Prime Minister, who was not made of hard metal, surrendered too much. French writers take the opposite view. England at least retained her naval supremacy unimpaired, and of her many overseas conquests held on to Trinidad, which she had taken from the Spaniards, and Ceylon, which she had wrested from the Dutch. If it be true that the French could never have forced her to give up the conquests which she was prepared to surrender, it is also true that these overseas territories would easily be recaptured by a superior naval power on the resumption of war. The worst augury for future peace was the lack of a commercial pact. So long as English merchants in France were treated as enemy aliens, there could be no true understanding between the French and English peoples.

CHAPTER V

CONSULATE AND EMPIRE

Napoleon's civil qualities. The Concordat. The Codes. The University of France. Renewal of war. The Empire. The new Charlemagne. The camp of Boulogne.

NAPOLEON restored the respect for authority in France. He found chaos and left order, inherited mutiny and created discipline. For ten years the passions which rent the social fabric had raged unchecked, while those moral forces which helped to strengthen it had suffered a disastrous eclipse. The sentiment of reverence had been laughed away. Religion, antiquity, the long descended traditions of France, even the common decencies of life, had been made to appear as absurd and irrational survivals from a tyrannical past. Napoleon was a Voltairean, without formal religion or established morality, and with social manners of which the best that can be said is that while they were sometimes gracious, kindly, and dignified, they were often characterized by unfeeling brutality. But he was a man born for command, and quick to discern that union was the secret of national strength. Every force which tended to assist social cohesion found in him a champion; religion, because it was "the mystery of the social order," education, because it could be moulded to his will, the spirit of precision and science in government, because it ministered to power, outward decorum as a preventive against the biting wit of Paris. It was his task to reconcile the new France with the old, to rally priest and *émigré*, Jew, Protestant, Atheist, and Jacobin to the service of the state, and to compel them to minister to its grandeur. In his search for stability he ended by marrying into the proudest and oldest House in Europe. His government was of a form new to France, a scientific despotism based on the plébiscite. Three times, in 1800, in 1802, and in 1804, he sought and obtained authority from the people. In quick succession the popular voice made him First Consul for ten years, Consul for life, and finally Emperor. No European monarch could claim so good a title.

In according to Napoleon this remarkable and ascending

835

measure of confidence the French people expected him to give them in return the golden blessings of peace. This he did not, perhaps could not, achieve. On the contrary his advent to power led up to a war which, after nearly uniting central Europe under French rule, culminated in a military collapse so complete that, forfeiting even the earliest conquests of the Revolution, France was driven back within the ancient limits of the monarchy. It is one of the ironies of history that a family whose name is synonymous with martial renown actually diminished the area of France. The first Napoleon lost Belgium. His nephew, though he acquired Savoy and Nice by a diplomatic bargain, forfeited Alsace-Lorraine in an unsuccessful appeal to arms. It was given to a bourgeois Republic of black-coated lawyers and doctors to recover for France, with the aid of a wide circle of allies, some of the territory and most of the influence which was lost in the catastrophes of the Napoleonic house.

If the conquests of Napoleon were ephemeral, his civilian work in France was built upon granite. In every quality required for civil administration, in imagination and initiative, in propulsive power and minute attention to detail, in clearness of head and capacity for work, he stands supreme. With extraordinary speed the devastation wrought by the revolution was repaired. In the atmosphere of hope and excitement, which prevailed in France during the Consulate, prodigies were performed in every department of administration central and local for the improvement of the material condition of the people. The hampering conditions of the *ancien régime* were no longer present. There were no corporations, Parliaments, or Provincial Estates, no blocks of privileged citizens standing outside the general law. The prefect in his department, the sub-prefect in his arrondissement, the mayor in his commune, operating on a plain, unobstructed surface, executed the commands of the Head of the State.

July, 1801

The Concordat with the Papacy was not the least important part of Napoleon's policy of reconciling the new world with the old. Among the army chiefs who retained the acute atheism of the revolutionary period, as also among the political and intellectual Parisians, the change was distasteful and derided. It seemed to be the surrender of a gain for civilization, a relapse into the darkness of mediaeval night, an invitation to the priest once more to recover his lost empire over the mind of man. But Napoleon looked beyond the army chiefs and the intellectuals of

Paris to the vast mass of the peasantry, who formed the man-power of his conscript armies. He had divined the leadership of the priest in the revolt of the Vendée, had seen the Italian peasant kneeling before the little wayside shrine, and knew that religion was a power among simple men. The schism in the Church was an open wound, which, if not promptly healed, would corrupt and endanger the body politic. Napoleon therefore decided to make the plunge. In 1802, after protracted negotiations, con-ducted on his side with a brilliant mixture of force and fraud, he came to terms with the new Pope Pius VII.

Very different, however, from the Church of the *ancien régime* was the new Roman Catholic establishment which resulted from the Concordat and from the organic articles by which it was accompanied. The broad acres and remunerative tithes, the princely salaries and establishments, the imposing assemblies and vast social influence, which had belonged for many centuries to the prelates of the Gallican Church, were now things of the past. The Napoleonic bishop, an indifferently paid menial of a jealous state, was allowed neither to travel outside his diocese, nor to summon a synod, nor to correspond with Rome without the con-sent of the civil power. The Church indeed was permitted to live and to function. The Angelus again called the peasant to prayer, the white surplice of the priest again fluttered in the sunlight, the congregation of the faithful again clustered round the altar or kept the Sunday rest without fear of persecution. Once more bishops were nominated and consecrated after the practice of the *ancien régime*. But the Church had lost its independence, and sunk to the position of an impoverished and subservient client of the civil power. It was no longer the sole office of the priest to be the spiritual father of his flock, helping the sick, consoling the dying, instructing the young in the elements of religion. He was expected to read the army bulletins from the pulpit, to urge the laggard to the colours, and to instil into tender minds through the catechism of Napoleon the duty of implicit obedience to the Head of the State.

It may yet be asked whether it was necessary for Napoleon to come to terms with the Pope. A Gallican Church, orthodox in faith, but independent of Rome, was an alternative which in the prostration of religious life then prevailing, and with so many ardent priests killed in the civil wars, might have been accepted by the vast majority of the French clergy. But though Napoleon threatened the negotiating Cardinals with Gallicanism he did not adopt it. He had need of the Papacy. Low as that ancient institution had fallen, so low that in common with William Pitt and Thugut, the Austrian Chancellor, Napoleon believed its days to be numbered, he could not afford to throw away its support. "The old machine, which would crumple up of itself," might yet be of use in assisting him to regiment the Catholics of other lands.

The codification of French law, perhaps the most enduring of Napoleon's achievements, was a dream old as the fifteenth century, and an integral part of the revolutionary creed. But a period of torrential legislation is unpropitious to a task which demands a steady view of the legal landscape. The Revolution decreed that there should be a code, prepared numerous drafts, but in its feverish rush left nothing accomplished. Napoleon took up the suspended work, and by his personal energy and interest swiftly drove it to a triumphant conclusion. The Civil Code did not, of course, spring from the brain of one transcendent legislator. The main legal principles of the *ancien régime*, alike of the Roman Law which prevailed in the South, and of the Frankish *coûtumes* which governed the North, together with those parts of the revolutionary legislation which commended themselves to Napoleon and his advisers, were fused together and distilled into a volume, so beautifully clear that the layman may read it with enjoyment, and so succinct that it may be carried without embarrassment in the pocket of a great-coat. The merit of the Civil Code is not that it is exhaustive, or that it has prevented the growth of case law, or that it is flawless in form and substance; but that in firm intelligible outline it fixes the structure of a civilized lay society, based on social equality and religious toleration, on private property and coherent family life. The moment was opportune. A few years earlier the Code would have glittered with revolutionary extravagance, a few years later it might have been darkened by the shades of despotism. Drafted as it was in the fresh effulgence of the Consulate, when Napoleon was dealing out even-handed justice to all sections of French society, it presented, not only to France but to all Europe, a handy prospectus of a country faithful to a long tradition of family discipline and private ownership, but at the same time tenacious of the best fruits of a lay and liberal revolution. That is the chief European significance of the Civil Code. Through

1804

the institution of civil marriage and divorce it spread through
Europe the idea of a community capable of dispensing with
clerical aid. To the religious confessions marriage must always
be a sacrament. In the Code it is a civil contract which may be
cheaply made and cheaply revoked in the drab office of an un-
sanctified layman. For the first time since the acceptance of
Christianity by Constantine a settled and ordered European state
legalized in a code the thoroughly secular life.

From this it should not be inferred that Napoleon undervalued
the forces of religion and family discipline as elements in social
hygiene. The exact opposite is the case. The ideas of Napoleon
upon family life were of a Roman austerity. For him the
authority of the father could not be too strong or the subjection
of the wife too complete. " Do you not know," he said, " that the
Angel told Eve to obey her husband? Morality has written
this article in all languages. *A fortiori* should it be written in
French in the Code." But the tide of revolutionary secularism
was too strong to be resisted. Napoleon curtailed the facilities
for divorce, which had been provided by the revolution, but was
compelled to accept the institution.

It is a note of Napoleon's greatness that, not content with
launching the enterprise of the Civil Code, he took a substantive
and often a decisive part in the discussions upon the draft in the
legislative Committee of the Council of State. Minute technicalities did not interest him, but he had an eagle eye for any
issue which touched upon the broader aspects of sound policy,
and whenever these came into the field of vision he was prepared with a clear and forcible view. In general he wanted
France to be a land of moderate not too minutely divided properties, of despotic fathers and obedient children, and of a rightless
and dependent womankind. In all these particulars he succeeded
in stamping the impress of his powerful convictions on the law
of France.

More than any other influence the Civil Code spread through
Europe the fame of the institutions of the new France. Here was
the pith and kernel of the revolutionary philosophy in a shape
made practical for the use of men. Here was a combination of
fruitful innovation and ancient usage. Here was liberty combined with order. Not since the Institutes of Justinian has any
compendium of law been so widely copied.

There were four other Napoleonic Codes. Two of these, since

they were drafted under the Empire, and deal with the trial and punishment of crime, are defaced by the imprint of arbitrary power. A long list of savage penalties (including confiscation) shows that the framers of the Penal Code were far from reflecting the best thought of their time in the sphere of criminal legislation. The Code of Criminal Procedure is subject, albeit to a less degree, to the same reproach. Though it gives the accused the benefit of an open trial and a jury, these memorable advantages, the bequest of the revolution, were counterbalanced by other provisions, drawn from the jurisprudence of the *ancien régime* or from the imperial requirements of Napoleon, which were less favourable to the protection of the weak and innocent. Of these it is here sufficient to note the secret preliminary inquisition under the *juge d'instruction*, and the fact that the nomination of the jurors was entrusted to the prefects.

While this legal work was proceeding, a scheme of intellectual discipline for the Empire, rigorous as that of the Jesuit Order, was gradually taking shape in Napoleon's mind. The happy-go-lucky system prevailing in England, where young gentlemen whose real interests were in cricket and fives, battledore and peg top, were flogged into a smattering of Greek and Latin accidence by pedagogues who could not be dismissed from their posts even by King George himself. was wholly foreign to the Emperor's mentality. He would have regarded it as an act of political insanity to leave the education of a people to the chance play of private enterprise and endowment. Private schools must indeed exist, for in the stress of war there could be little public money for education, but private schools must submit to public control. Amusement was no part of education. Life was serious. The young should be educated for the polity and in a military Empire must be taught to serve, to march, and to die.

A University, controlled by the state, co-extensive with the Empire, and charged with the duty of organizing and supervising all branches of public instruction, was set up in 1808 to give effect to these ideas. The strange seed germinated in a soil prepared for centralization, and Napoleon's University of France, divided into local academies, survived with some transformations into the twentieth century. In all this there was little enough of democracy. Nothing was done for the primary schools, which were left to private agencies. Even in the sphere of secondary education the state *lycées* and colleges failed to cover half the ground. If, then, the reign of Napoleon is remarkable in the educational history of France, it is not because the state was generous to education, but because it was hostile to intellectual freedom. On the one side of the Channel was the careless, enjoying Etonian, repeatedly flogged and indifferently taught. On the other side, in a *lycée* which partook of the melancholy of a monastery and the rigour of a barrack, was a cheerless little boy in a tight uniform, drilled, spied upon, crammed with information, and, in the process of his rough adjustment to the Emperor's Spartan purpose, starved of the wholesome pleasures of youth.

It was a blot upon Napoleon's character for prudence that, having everything to gain by a prolonged peace, he should have so ordered his policy as to excite to the utmost degree the apprehensions of his rivals. In London it was noted that while English ships and English goods were rigorously excluded from French ports, the power of France was continually advancing. The English Cabinet was not indifferent to these changes. When it saw a French garrison established in Holland it began to reconsider its undertaking to restore the Cape. When it realized that Piedmont and the Valais were annexed to France, and that the Swiss and Cisalpine Republics had received new Constitutions, which brought them more clearly than before under French influence, it raised the question of compensations. When it learned that a great military expedition, more powerful than the avowed objective seemed to warrant, had sailed for the recovery of the black republic of San Domingo, it suspected, and with reason, that Napoleon was harbouring vast ulterior designs in the western hemisphere. But more sinister even than these disquieting symptoms was the evidence that the recovery of Egypt and the expansion of French territory in India still occupied a place in the schemes of the First Consul. A report from the pen of Colonel Sebastiani published in the *Moniteur* on January 30, 1803, and depicting the popularity of the French in the East, and the ease with which Egypt might be reconquered, confirmed the worst suspicions of the intentions of Napoleon. But if war were again to break out in the East, Malta with its superb harbour and famous fortifications was an essential point in the English defence. Accordingly, despite the terms of the

Treaty of Amiens, England declined to evacuate the island. Her decision, to which she was urged by the rulers of Russia and Turkey, each apprehensive of Napoleon's oriental designs, was technically incorrect. Yet in thus forcing a war can she be blamed? Secret instructions issued by Napoleon to General Decaen show that the project for French aggrandizement in India was already fully formed.

Before any serious blow had been struck in the war, a remarkable constitutional revolution took place in France. It was undoubtedly the will of the French people that the *régime* of Napoleon, which had brought France great benefits, should be protected against the opposite dangers of Jacobin violence and royalist reaction. These dangers, which were still acute, had since the general pacification of the Vendée taken the form of plots to assassinate the First Consul either by a bomb attack or by an armed affray. One such attack engineered by royalists missed its aim in 1800. Another, wider and more disjointed, since it included not only royalist fanatics such as Georges Cadoudal, but even famous generals of the Republic like Moreau and Pichegru, was, with the active and shameful connivance of some subordinate English ministers, in course of preparation during the autumn and winter of 1803, and in the spring of the following year. Napoleon was well served by his police and *agents-provocateurs*. He knew that famous Republican soldiers had been artfully entangled in the fringes of a royalist web, woven by the Comte d'Artois from his retreat in England, that Moreau had talked to Pichegru, that Normandy and Brittany were to be stirred to revolt, and that the whole conspiracy was timed to explode on the arrival of a Bourbon Prince.

Who was that prince? It so happened that the Duc d'Enghien, the last descendant of the House of Condé, was in March, 1804, residing at Ettenheim in Baden, close to the French frontier. Napoleon determined to take his life. Though Moreau, Pichegru, and Georges were already under arrest, and all immediate danger had therefore disappeared, this innocent young man—for d'Enghien had, as Napoleon knew before the end, no complicity in the plot—was kidnapped, haled off to Vincennes, and was there in the early dawn of March 21, 1804, hurriedly and secretly shot.

Carried out with a frigid determination, which shocked the conscience of the civilized world, the Corsican crime produced its designed effects. Never again did the Bourbon Princes meddle with a plot for the destruction of Napoleon, or the republicans suspect him of covert royalism. The blood of the innocent young prince was a pledge that the First Consul had ranged himself with the regicides. Even the most hardened Jacobins felt that hereditary power confided to a House now so irretrievably embroiled with the *ancien régime* could have no consequences likely to endanger the great conquest of equal rights, which it had cost so much bloodshed to secure. On April 23 Curée, a moderate regicide, proposed in the tribunate the adoption of the hereditary principle. The idea took form in a shape which commended itself alike to the ambitions of Napoleon, and to the classical taste of a people still largely revolutionary and dreading nothing so much as the restoration of the Kings. A *Senatus Consultum* of May 18, 1804, conferred upon Napoleon the title of Emperor of the French. The change received every species of confirmation which the constitutional repertory of the time could supply, the voice of the Senate, the vote of the people, the consecration of the Pope. Nobody can doubt but that it was acceptable to the nation, for the red light of the assassination plots was a signal which all could read that, failing heredity, one life alone stood between France and chaos.

Inevitably the name and example of Charlemagne captured the imagination of the new Emperor of the French. He would be the new Charlemagne, gathering the Latin and Teutonic peoples under his imperial crown, allotting client kingdoms and principalities to members of his family, treating the Pope as his chaplain, assembling in a brilliant court a new class of hereditary nobles, which, since they owed everything to his favour, would add security to the throne. At St. Helena he said, "I felt my isolation, so I cast anchors of safety all round into deep waters." Yet every anchor was a challenge to Vienna, the self-promotion *March,* of the Corsican to the imperial dignity, his assumption of the *1805* Lombard Crown in Milan, his significant visit to Aachen, the city of Charlemagne, that he might test the submissive loyalty of the Rhineland. It was clear that the Holy Roman Empire was doomed. That superfluous political cobweb was swept off the German ceiling by the strong broom of the new Charlemagne in 1806. Meanwhile a new hereditary Austrian Empire, created two years earlier, and destined to go down in 1918, had experienced a baptism of ruinous defeat.

The War of the Third Coalition was waged between England, Austria, Russia, Sweden and Naples, on the one hand, and France and her satellite Spain, on the other. It is characteristic of Pitt, who was the chief architect of the Coalition, that he contemplated, when the war was over and victory won, the summoning of a Congress to devise a federal system for the maintenance of a European peace. Napoleon, too, had a scheme for reorganizing Europe as a commonwealth of enlightened but unfree peoples under French hegemony; and there are some friends of European unity who still regret the frustration of his dream.

The campaign was to open with the invasion and conquest of England. In this island, so near, but so mysterious, Napoleon expected to find a down-trodden population, eager, when once a French army of liberation was in its midst, to shake off the tyrannous yoke of George III, as their American colonists had been enabled to do, also with French assistance, not thirty years before. At St. Helena he said that the *canaille* of London would have welcomed him, and that he would have set up with general acclamation republics in England and Ireland. Of the social cohesion of the English people or its new-born industrial strength he divined nothing. Had it been given him to witness the energetic preparations of the British Government, or the patriotic response of the people, he would have known that England would never become " a French island like Oléron or Corsica," and that, grave as were the risks of the Channel crossing, they would be surpassed by the perils awaiting an invader among the downlands or hopfields of Kent.

The narrow seas were never crossed. An army of 210,000 men, gathered in great camps along the North Sea and Channel coast, for two years awaited the order to embark. The signal did not come. Nelson was watching the Toulon fleet, Cornwallis was blockading Brest. Every French or Spanish squadron was under the close observation of an enemy as confident by reason of superior skill and numbers as his rival was dispirited. It followed that the one condition without which the whole enterprise was doomed to failure was never realized. Not for twelve hours was Napoleon able to concentrate in the Channel a fleet sufficiently strong to protect the transport and disembarkation of even a small detachment of his troops. Yet only when the news reached him in August, 1805, that Villeneuve, commanding the French-Spanish fleet, had run back into Cadiz harbour did the Emperor

abandon hope. The column at Boulogne, which still com
memorates his great ambition, recalls at the same time the heroic
vigil of English sailors, living hard on mouldy biscuit or salted
pork, and in all weather, fair and foul, keeping the seas in their
tossing castles of oak, that the independence of England, and
with it the liberty of Europe, might be preserved.

On a grey October day when all danger of invasion was passed *Oct. 21,*
and Napoleon was far away in the heart of Bavaria, Nelson won *1805*
the annihilating victory over Villeneuve which to the end of the
war established beyond challenge the British mastery of the seas.
Attacking in double column with twenty-seven sail of the line,
he destroyed the combined fleets of France and Spain which had
been lured out of Cadiz harbour to their doom. Yet the victory
of Trafalgar, though it placed the French and Spanish colonies
at the mercy of the British fleet, brought little pleasure to the
nation, for Nelson had fallen in action and a strong Austrian
force under Mack, a general of whom much was expected, had
only a day before capitulated at Ulm to the encircling army of *Oct. 20,*
the French. *1805*

CHAPTER VI

THE CONTINENTAL BLOCKADE

*The French hegemony in central Europe. Napoleon's diplomacy. Tilsit.
The continental blockade. The problem of Italy. Quarrel with the
Pope. The Spanish intervention. Importance of the Spanish War.
Bayonne. The royalism of Spain. Birth of Spanish Liberalism. The
Constitution of 1812.*

1805-7

NAPOLEON'S sea plans had failed, but the failure was followed by
that surprising sequence of victories at Ulm and Austerlitz, at Jena
and Friedland, which compelled first Austria and then Prussia
to sign an ignominious peace, and by an arrangement made at
Tilsit between Napoleon and Alexander of Russia, fastened upon
Central Europe the hegemony of the French Empire. Miracles
do not happen in history. But the effect on the political landscape of the campaigns of 1805, 1806, and 1807 has in it the
suddenness and completeness which partake of the miraculous.
As on every other occasion, Napoleon profited by the military
mistakes of his opponents, of which the gravest was the decision

*Dec.,
1805*

of the Austrians and Russians to force a battle at Austerlitz,
before the Prussians had thrown their weight into the war and
were in a position to menace his communications. Besides this
astonishing error of military judgment, there was present in this,
as in other coalitions, a fatal weakness arising from a long heritage
of political difference between the leading allies. There was little
friendship between the Prussians and Austrians. Having withdrawn from the war in 1795, Prussia, under the timid rule of
Frederick William III, was in no hurry to endanger the substantial advantages which she had derived from a policy of
peaceful neutrality, and only under the special pressure of the
Tzar, and as a consequence of the violation of her territory by
the army of the Rhine as it marched south-eastwards upon Ulm,
was she stirred into offering, under the name of an armed
neutrality, a show of opposition. It was then too late. The

*Dec. 22,
1805*

Austrians were knocked out of the ring at Austerlitz, before the
Prussian army was ready to strike.

During these years of dazzling victory the diplomacy of

Napoleon, while showing infinite ingenuity and resource, was open to serious reproach. France needed a friend. Talleyrand, a good European and a nice judge of diplomatic weights and measures, advised that this friend should be Austria. After Ulm, and again after Austerlitz, the wise Foreign Minister urged in vain upon his ambitious master a policy of conciliation, under which Austria might be assisted to aggrandise herself in the Balkans as a compensation for the losses which she would

THE CONQUESTS OF NAPOLEON.

be asked to accept in Italy and in the west. To these counsels Napoleon turned a deaf ear. Even the mutilating Treaty of Pressburg (December 26, 1805), which robbed Austria of three million inhabitants, and handed over her loyal Tyrolese to Bavaria, struck him as being too lenient. He had no measure to mete out to a beaten foe but an extremity of humiliation which left behind it a smouldering passion of revenge.

The humiliations put upon the Prussians were even more

serious. It is no pleasant thing for a self-respecting nation to be compelled by an alien power to rob a friendly neighbour with whom it has no quarrel, but to this signal sacrifice of honour the Prussians after Austerlitz were compelled to submit. Napoleon required them to take Hanover, and to declare war on England (Treaty of Schönbrunn, December 15, 1805). Honourable Prussians thought this disgraceful, and when a little later it was learnt
Aug.,
1806
in Berlin that Hanover was being secretly offered back to England, even the government of Frederick William III winced at the treacherous affront. Prussia declared war and suffered defeat on the fields of Jena and Auerstädt.

At Tilsit (July 8, 1807) the victor, undeterred by the eloquent entreaties of Queen Marie Louise, exacted the uttermost penalty, short of complete annihilation, which it was in his power to inflict. A new Duchy of Warsaw under the King of Saxony in the east, a Kingdom of Westphalia under Jerome Bonaparte in the west, were equipped with stolen Prussian provinces to keep the beaten enemy in check. Crushing indemnities, a burdensome army of occupation, a strict limitation of the native armed forces, completed the subjection of this stout and valiant people. At St. Helena Napoleon regretted his leniency, persisting in the bad delusion of conquerors that a vanquished nation can be permanently destroyed.

Meanwhile Alexander I, the pleasant, enthusiastic, new-found friend of Tilsit, appeared to offer to Napoleon advantages more solid than any which might be derived from the Austrian or Prussian alliance. The Tzar publicly acknowledged Napoleon's conquests, and in secret articles bound himself, should England decline to accept the mediation of Russia, to join in the continental blockade and to force Denmark, Sweden, Portugal and Austria to make war upon English commerce. With such powerful help Napoleon expected to rivet his dominion on the west.
June,
1807
He stood at the summit of his fortunes, delivered as by a miracle through the crowning victory of Friedland from a thousand perils. Austria and Prussia were at his feet. Russia was his ally. Pitt was in his grave. Could it be that the islanders under such a man as the Duke of Portland would dare to refuse him peace?

The islanders were most disobliging. Apprised of the secret
Sept.,
1807
articles of Tilsit, George Canning, the young Foreign Minister in the Portland Cabinet, seized the Danish Fleet at Copenhagen before it fell into the hands of his enemies. By this invidious

attack upon a weak and innocent nation Canning completed Nelson's work at Trafalgar and secured for his country the undisputed mastery of the seas.

The continental blockade, which was henceforth Napoleon's only bludgeon against England, involved, if it were to be exactly enforced, the political control of Italy and Spain. Of these two Latin countries Italy offered a problem altogether lighter than that which was presented by the fierce and obstinate nationalism of Spain. That Napoleon was an Italian in blood and speech was in itself a strong letter of commendation to a people which despite its inveterate political divisions yet cherished a sentiment of national pride. Moreover, Italy, unlike Spain, was long habituated to invasions from the north. If the French rule were foreign, it was no more foreign than the Austrian and Spanish domination by which it had been preceded. Rather it was more congenial. In the bustling cities of Lombardy the forward-reaching ideas of the French Revolution had made many converts before the ragged legions of Bonaparte had burst upon the Italian plain. Italy, then, was ill-prepared morally to resist Napoleon. She had neither a national monarchy, nor a national army, nor a national tradition. When once the spine of Austrian resistance was broken in the north, as it was after the double shock of Marengo and Austerlitz, it was a light operation to evict the weak Bourbon King of Naples, and to establish French governments in Florence and Rome. The exclusion of British wares, therefore, from the ports of Italy was a policy confronted, indeed, by many obstacles, as, for instance, attacks launched from Sicily with British aid, but nevertheless capable of execution with the resources which Napoleon had at his command. The serious difficulty was moral. The exact execution of the Italian blockade involved a breach with the Pope. It was an extraordinary lapse of judgment in a man of genius who was fully alive to the importance of conciliating Catholic sentiment in his wide Empire that, rather than tolerate the neutrality of the Vatican, Napoleon deported and imprisoned the Pope, annexed *May* his territories, and incorporated them into the departmental *1809* system of the French Empire. The Italians were probably of all the Mediterranean races the least religious, but the Papacy was one of the historical glories of their country, and they resented its abasement. Among Napoleon's grave errors there was none destined to shake so profoundly the fabric of his power, not in

Italy alone, but all over the Catholic world, as this gratuitous affront to the Papal See and to the Roman tradition.

While this sharp quarrel with the Pope was proceeding, Napoleon launched his attack upon Spain, a country the most religious in Europe, the least affected by ecclesiastical innovations, and despite a weak, inglorious, and ill-soldered government, proudly and quixotically patriotic. This he did, although he must have known the general character of the geography and climate of the Iberian peninsula, how the whole mountain and river system of the country lay athwart the path of an invader from the north, and how in that high tableland of central Spain, now parched with torrid heat, now frozen with the blasts of an Arctic wind, no large army could hope to support itself without a commissariat corresponding to its entire needs. But graver even than sun and frost, river, mountain, and waste was the obstacle presented by the psychology of the Spanish people. The Spaniards were withdrawn from the general life of Europe. They had different ideals, different thoughts, different customs. A certain negligence, half pride, half indolence, had impeded the development of the forms of material prosperity which elsewhere are found to be favourable to intellectual curiosity and enterprise. Only a third of the country was cultivated. Despite a vast overseas Empire, there was no Spanish commercial navy. Even the Mediterranean carrying trade was conceded to foreigners. Ignorance was general, poverty without reproach. The emancipating philosophy of the eighteenth century made no appeal to the peasants and monks, the priests and vagabonds, the smugglers and brigands, who constituted the greater part of the Spanish population. An enlightened monarch like Charles III, the best of the Bourbon Kings, who expelled the Jesuits, put down the bull fights, and endeavoured to stimulate the languishing industries of the country, so far from acquiring merit in the eyes of his subjects by reason of his salutary reforms, was on that very ground the object of their hearty dislike. On his death in 1788 the obscurantism which had never really been shaken in the provinces promptly recovered its sway in the court and the government. It may readily therefore be imagined how repugnant to Spain was the notion of a foreign anti-papal philosophy enforced by the bayonets of France. The Spaniards cared nothing for the rights of man, but everything for the Catholic religion and their provincial customs. The weights and measures

1759-88

of Europe meant little to this proud and serious nation of individualists, for whom Church was nearer than town, town than
province, province than kingdom, and kingdom than all the rest
of the world. So faintly were they impressed by Napoleon's
power that a little province like Asturias with an armed force of
eighteen thousand men did not hesitate to raise the standard of
revolt against the French Empire. The fact that Madrid, which
was the centre of the road system, was for many years in French
occupation, made no difference to the Andalusians of the south,
the Gallegos of the west, or the Catalonians of the eastern
littoral. The Spaniards did not fight on a nice calculation of
probabilities. Often as they were beaten by French generals, they
were never abashed by French prestige. Though their armies
were ill-found in guns and cavalry, though their discipline was
ragged and their *morale* uncertain, in the guerilla warfare most
suited to their country, and most harassing to their foe, they
were past masters. Always the French were in the neighbourhood of a savage, elusive, and persistent antagonist; nor was the
long line of their communications from the Pyrenees to Madrid
at any time secure from the Spanish sniper, the Spanish cut-
throat, and the Spanish ambush.

The Spanish insurrection, which was the first of a series of
national risings against the French Empire, was rendered vastly
more injurious to Napoleon by reason of the fact that it gave to
the small land army of England the theatre in which it could
most effectively deploy its resources. Up to the moment when
the Cabinet decided to give assistance to Portugal and Spain,
the English army had been frittered away upon a number of
disjointed enterprises, in the Vendée, in the West Indies, in
Holland, in southern Italy, which exercised no sensible influence
on the general course of the war. Now that they were confronted with the great task of driving the French north of the
Pyrenees with the aid of the national levies of Portugal and
Spain, English soldiers were able not only to bring their own
weight to bear upon the issue, but also to stiffen the resistance
of the Iberian peoples.

That this great opportunity was used to the full, that the
small English army in Spain was not rashly squandered, but so
husbanded that in unison with its local allies it was able to keep
a large French army pinned down in Spain. and ultimately to
drive it across the Pyrenees, is due to the prudent genius of a

1803

great co nmander. Arthur Wellesley had already broken the Mahratta power on the field of Assaye. The Peninsular War gave him the opportunity of showing that singular combination of military and diplomatic prudence without which the available resources of Portugal and Spain could never have been effectively directed against the common enemy. The tactics of his first

A no.
1808

were those also of his last European victory. At Vimiero as at Waterloo victory lay with the thin red line of steady British infantry, well posted and well concealed, who had been taught to reserve their fire until such time as it could be relied on to destroy the heads of the advancing columns of the enemy. That the line could be relied on to beat the column was the core of Wellesley's tactical philosophy, and the chief military lesson of the Peninsular War.

Of the manner of Napoleon's entry into Spain and the nature and consequence of the shock which was thus administered to the Iberian peoples, a few words may fitly be said here.

1806

On the eve of Jena, and counting on a flood tide of Prussian victories, Godoy, the unpopular favourite of the Spanish Queen and the real ruler of the country, ordered the mobilization of the Spanish army. The gross indiscretion, sinking deep in Napoleon's mind, was avenged with the finest Machiavellian skill. In place of an immediate and expected penalty Spain was

Oct.,
1807

compelled to sign a treaty at Fontainebleau, under which she promised to join in an attack on Portugal, the little country which had filled so many English cellars with its vintage, sheltered so many English fleets, and alone of continental markets was still wide open to English trade. But the conquest of Portugal, which was easily effected, was only a prelude to a larger plan. It was not sufficient that the Portuguese Regent had been driven from his capital and had taken ship for Brazil. Napoleon had determined to evict the Bourbons from Spain. Under the convenient pretext of the Portuguese campaign,

Feb.,
1808

French troops poured across the Pyrenees, seized the frontier fortresses, and advanced to Madrid. Indignation flamed up against the favourite, who had opened the gates of Spain to an infidel enemy. A riot broke out at Aranjuez, the spring residence of the King and Queen, when it was learned that they were meditating a flight with their favourite to the Indies. The miserable Charles abdicated the throne to save the life of Godoy, and his son Ferdinand was installed in his place. But by this time Murat was in Madrid, and Napoleon was master of the situation. He refused to recognize the new King, and Charles was instructed to withdraw his abdication. Eventually the whole Spanish Royal Family, King, Queen, and heir-apparent, were decoyed to Bayonne, and there compelled to renounce all claim to the monarchy of Spain. The vacant monarchy, after having *May,* been refused by Louis, was accepted by Joseph Bonaparte, while *1808* Murat, given the choice of Portugal and Naples, wisely decided *July,* to rule in Naples. *1808*

The Spaniards were monarchists and clericals. It is a measure of their backwardness that they accepted without a murmur the incapable autocracy of Charles IV. The Cortes had fallen into desuetude, the age of the newspaper press had not yet begun, and the riots and conspiracies which helped Napoleon to carry out the *coup d'état* of Bayonne were directed not against the principle of monarchy, but against the hated influence of the royal favourite. From this deep devotion to the monarchical principle the Spaniards were detached neither by the ineptitude of Charles, nor by the vulgar vices of Marie Louise, his wife, nor by the cowardice and treachery of Ferdinand, the heir-apparent; nor yet were they attracted by the liberal constitution which had been drawn up at Bayonne, nor by the prospect of a progressive and imperialist Government under Joseph Bonaparte. If Joseph had been an angel from Heaven, and the constitution of Bayonne had been verbally inspired, the Spaniards would still have persisted in their idealization of the despicable Ferdinand. All through the Peninsular War this wretched Prince remained the idol of the Spanish people. That he had cringed to Napoleon, that he had showed abject cowardice, that he had plotted against his father, that he was without a grain of intelligence, that he was treacherous to his friends, all these considerations counted for nothing in comparison with the single fact that he was the rightful heir to the Spanish crown. Accordingly the downfall of the Napoleonic *régime* in Spain was inevitably followed by the restoration of Ferdinand.

Nevertheless, though the old Spain came back with Ferdinand, the struggles and miseries of the Peninsular War had created in the country the elements of a liberal and national party. In the absence of the Crown, the Spaniards had been compelled to fend for themselves. They had set up a central Junta or Council, which had been constrained by the advancing tide of French conquest to retire first to Seville, and afterwards to Cadiz. Here a Cortes had met and a constitution had been drafted, and here for the first time a battle was joined on the fundamental issue of personal liberty which, giving rise to two political parties, known respectively as *Liberales* and *Serviles*, continued to divide the political mind of Spain all through the nineteenth century. The Constitution of 1812, though it accepted the principle of the hereditary monarchy, and confined the suffrage to Roman Catholics, was a document representing the radical opinion of the sea coast towns, and of some of the military leaders, rather than the stiff conservatism of inland Spain. It provided for universal suffrage, for a single Chamber, for Colonial representation, for the abolition of the Inquisition and the confiscation of its property. Its provisions were, therefore, too advanced for Spain, and never put into execution. Nevertheless this liberal instrument possesses an enduring importance in Spanish history. If it never became a machine of government, it was a flag of insurrection, standing as it did for the establishment of an all-Spanish Parliament, voting taxes, making laws, and limiting the monarchy and the power of the Church. From Spain, the most reactionary corner of Europe, the term "Liberal" came into English politics.

CHAPTER VII

NAPOLEON AND GERMANY

The Napoleonic government. Prussia resurgent. Goethe as a liberator. The German contribution to European letters.

THE Napoleonic government of Germany was a harsh but salutary episode in the history of the German people. Much useless detritus was cleared away. Many helpful ideas were scattered abroad. Both by way of stimulus and by way of reaction communities which had long marked time in torpid self-sufficiency were prompted to undertake serviceable reforms. A great simplification of the complicated political geography of Germany, involving the suppression of a hundred and twenty small states, was carried out in Paris in 1803 as a consequence of the compensations which had to be offered to the German Princes who had been compelled by the French conquest to forfeit their possessions on the left bank of the Rhine.

The Muse of History cannot afford to neglect these sordid transactions. Out of the Act of Mediation, as it was called, there emerged a Germany more manageable and easy to unite, and ultimately, therefore, more formidable to her western neighbour.

In broad outline Napoleon's scheme for Germany followed the classic lines of French diplomacy. A confederation of the Rhine *July,* under the Presidency of the French Emperor was formed as a *1806* makeweight against the two beaten and angry enemies, Austria and Prussia. Of this confederacy some member states were new creations carved out of conquered and enemy territory, while others, like Bavaria and Würtemberg, were ancient members of the *Reich*. Nothing better illustrates the difference which has come over Germany since those times than the ease with which this League was launched upon its course and the large measure of support which Napoleon received from the German Princes in the prosecution of a policy inimical to German nationality. He had indeed bribes to offer to the rulers— monarchies for Bavaria and Würtemberg, a grand duchy for Baden, as well as marriages into the charmed circle of the Imperial family; and after Austerlitz and Jena there was no

855

armed force among the Germans capable of standing up against the Grand Army. But the true explanation of a curious phenomenon is to be found neither in fear nor in corruption. The general play of popular sympathy, both in Bavaria, where the Austrians had long been regarded as a menace, and in the Rhineland, where the Prussian was little loved, was favourable to France until the pressure of Napoleon's blood tax turned favour into bitter hatred. No tears, then, were shed by the princes of this Rhenish Confederation when Austria lost her ancient place of pre-eminence in Germany, and the Holy Roman Empire received its quietus. No sympathy went out to Prussia in the hour of her abasement. Even in the Kingdom of Westphalia, where a strange mixture of Hessians, Hanoverians, and Brunswickers were forcibly combined under King Jerome, Napoleon's engaging but frivolous youngest brother, the best German families came forward to help the alien government.

Aug. 6, 1806

1807

There are some who think that a Germany so balanced and composed, with Prussia shorn of her Westphalian and Polish Provinces, with Austria extruded, and with a League of German Princes receiving its political direction from France, would have been a factor making for a more stable world. Be this as it may, the experiment was never tried in time of peace. Napoleon's Germany was from first to last an engine of war directed against England. Cut off from colonial trade, and at the same time denied an entry into French markets, held down by foreign armies of occupation who were far gone in the evil habits of pillage and peculation, drained of men and bled white for money, the Germans may be pardoned if, revising their first friendly estimate of the French, they ended by wanting nothing so much as a German nation strong enough to throw off the foreign yoke and ever after to defend the German Rhine. Only the Jews, liberated from the Ghetto and raised to equal citizenship with German Gentiles, continued to regret the downfall of Napoleon, their liberator.

When finally the reaction against alien rule took shape in Germany, the head and heart of the movement was found to be Prussian. In this kingdom, which had long been a magnet to attract able men from every part of the country to its service, the lesson of Jena had sunk deep in the minds of a small group of energetic and thoughtful patriots. It is the glory of Scharnhorst and Clausewitz, of Stein and Hardenberg, that the problem of Prussia was seen in its widest dimensions as one not merely of military reform but of national revival and awakening. Broadly speaking, the result of their work was to give a servile army and a servile nation some of the honourable characteristics of freedom.

Not often have the true lessons of a military *débâcle* been so clearly apprehended as lying in the moral field. Only a real statesman like Stein would have discerned that it was germane to the military resurgence of Prussia to grant a measure of self-government to the Prussian towns and to attend to the social condition of the peasantry. That he was not above taking lessons from the French, who had emancipated the peasantry in Poland and in Westphalia, is no disparagement to his prudence.

It is characteristic of the condition of the German Empire at the end of the eighteenth century that Goethe, who created the newer literature of his country, was neither Christian, hero, nor patriot. His long life, beginning in 1749 and ending in 1832, was contemporaneous with an age of violent and repeated change. He was a boy of seven at the opening of the Seven Years' War. He wrote *Götz von Berlichingen* in the last year of Louis XV, and *1774* immediately afterwards stormed the reading public of his own and other countries with *The Sorrows of Werther*. When the French Revolution broke out he was a man of forty, twenty years older than Napoleon, and already the most famous literary figure in Europe. The storms of the Revolution and the Empire swept over Germany without ruffling his marmoreal composure and his indifference to the fortunes of states. Living a sheltered life as an official in the little court of Weimar, he pursued self-culture as an end, deriving his inspiration, in so far as it was drawn from books, not from the tedious and lifeless work of earlier German writers, but from the vast romantic material of Shakespeare, from the dramatists and poets of Italy and Spain, and from the masterpieces of classical and oriental literature. Owing little to the German mind, and holding the Prussians in contempt for their barbarity, Goethe welcomed the genius and saluted the conquests of Napoleon. The defeat of the French Emperor at the battle of Leipzig came to him as a disappointment, and the greatest lyric poet of Germany makes no contribution to the literature of the War of Liberation.

Yet in a profound sense the army of German liberators

numbers no figure of equal stature. By his massive achievements in prose and verse Goethe freed the German people from the unintelligent subservience to French models, which, ever since the Thirty Years' War, had been a blight on the national intellect. His lyric poems spring fresh from a lover's passion. His prose, lucid, serious, elegant, is always the vehicle of positive knowledge or ripe meditation, never of abstruse metaphysic, or of ideas imperfectly grasped. To the narrow specialism of the Universities he opposed a vast curiosity embracing great tracts of art, science, and literature. He wrote on optics and botany, studied oriental tongues, and discovered the intermaxillary bone, bringing to science what is rarer and more valuable than the gift of accurate mensuration, the art of divination, so that his work is rich with ideas and suggestions, which in a later age have been found to be of value. The chief vices of German literature had been obscurity, pedantry, and lush sentimentalism. Goethe is often dull, but never obscure; often learned, but never pedantic; often governed by the passions inspired by his innumerable loves, but never to the extent of losing that chastening sense of form which is one of the properties of an accomplished egoist. Had he learned from the French the art of making a brief well-proportioned book, he would have added yet another to the many services which he rendered to the German people.

The idea of the French revolutionary writers that human virtue depends upon the legislator was not shared by Goethe, and is contradicted by the whole tenor of his teaching, which is the creed of a self-sufficient genius, untroubled by the fume and fret of politics and unconstricted by national prepossessions. To the French belief in legislation as the prime condition of human progress Goethe opposed the picture of a man of commanding physical and intellectual endowments, who, through love and letters, art, science, and administration, strenuously endeavoured to cultivate his soul. In the tiny courts and sheltered backwaters of Germany, where the stream of life flowed stilly through narrow channels, the prodigious energy of this multifarious, myriad-minded writer was a revelation of what an artist, under the application of no external stimulus, could from his own intellectual and emotional resources achieve. When all around at Weimar was stationary, Goethe's temperament was ever young and experiencing, his genius was always in movement, pouring out a flood of plays, poems, novels, treatises, and with so little adherence to type, that it turned from the mediaeval romantic drama, which inspired Walter Scott, to the severest Classicism, then plunged into the Orient, and finally survived to welcome the splendours of Byron. Working this perpetual and self-renewing miracle, Goethe the egoist and anti-patriot gave to the German people a new station in the intellectual hierarchy of Europe.

In this work he was not alone. Lessing, Schiller, Herder, and Heine are ranked with justice among the glories of German literature. Of these Heine was a Jew, and imbued even to a lesser degree than Goethe with the quality now so generally and doubtfully prized of hot German nationalism. Heine, *1799-1856* whose childhood was spent in Düsseldorf, when it was the capital of the Grand Duchy of Berg and part of the Napoleonic Empire, preferred the French to the Germans, and, like all German Jews, venerated Napoleon, the liberator of the Semite race. Schiller alone cherished political enthusiasms characteristically German; but even Schiller, most eloquent of German apostles, was compelled to seek his lessons in liberty from the *1759-1805* Dutch.

The tumultuous movements of the German mind which belong to this period, and the very considerable achievement of many German authors, were not generally appreciated until Madame de Staël published her brilliant book on Germany. Then it was *1810* discovered that the people who had been overrun by the Napoleonic armies, and treated with the contumely due to an inferior and subject race, were in fact the possessors of a treasure of contemporary poetry and prose, that in the range and depth of its perceptions, and in the richness and originality of its forms, surpassed any recent work which had been put out elsewhere on the continent of Europe. By 1815 Germany had found herself, not indeed as a political unity, but as a power in literature and science. The spiritual summit which she then reached, the range of spiritual influence which she then enjoyed, have never been recaptured. It is a remarkable fact that the zenith of German literature belongs to an age of political impotence and division, when Goethe and Schiller were friends at Weimar, and German patriotism stood at its lowest ebb. The old-fashioned picturesque imperial Constitution is not, then, altogether devoid of merit, or the victorious march of German nationalism immune from reproach. It may be asked whether, in the last analysis, Weimar has not done more for the human spirit than Berlin, and whether the system of small German states has not been more favourable to liberty and to the cultivation and refinement of the emotion than the modern *Reich*, assailed by the tempests of world politics and racked by the passions of internal strife.

CHAPTER VIII

THE DOWNFALL OF NAPOLEON

The first cracks. The Russian War. The German War of Liberation.
Reasons for the postponement of German unity. The campaign of 1813.
Napoleon's lost chances. His continuing military skill. Elba. The
return of the Bourbons. The Congress of Vienna. The re-settlement
of Europe. The triumph of legitimacy. Contrast with the Peace Treaties
of 1919-20.

WITH Napoleon's Spanish enterprise the first cracks began to appear in the fabric of the French Empire. The capitulation of 23,000 French troops at Baylen (July 19, 1808) was a clear signal that in Spanish nationalism a new force had emerged capable of upsetting the French Empire. Taking courage from Spain, Austria, under the advice of Count Stadion, determined to renew the struggle, and while Napoleon was chasing Sir John Moore back to Corunna, the Austrians were penetrating Bavarian territory. The speed with which Napoleon, having restored the situation in central Spain, rushed back to repel the Austrian *April* menace, the brilliance of the movements by which in three *1809* fiercely contested battles (of Abensberg, Eckmühl, and Landshut) he succeeded in crushing the Austrians on the middle Danube, the check which he experienced before Vienna, and the hard-won victory at Wagram, while illustrating his undiminished *July,* brilliance as a commander, bring out the increasing measure of *1809* the difficulties by which he was surrounded. The Austrian army with which he was confronted in these encounters was an altogether different instrument from the force which he had vanquished at Marengo and at Austerlitz. It was better trained, better handled, and in better heart. When soon afterwards Lainé objected to Napoleon that Austria was a spent power, he replied, "Then it is evident that you were not on the field of Wagram." Moreover, apart from the renewed activity of Austria, there were other indications that the Spanish example was infectious. A revolt in the Tyrol against the Bavarians, disjointed Prussian risings, slight in themselves and checked without great difficulty, were sufficient to indicate new strains and stresses in the fabric. In France, too, a certain lassitude was beginning to show itself. At a conference which Napoleon held with Alexander at Erfurt in 1808 Talleyrand had observed that Belgium and the Rhine frontier were the conquests of France, and that the further conquests were those of Napoleon alone.

Meanwhile Napoleon was gradually drawing forward towards that wild Russian adventure which, more than the Peninsular War or the British navy, brought the French Empire in ruins to the ground. The ostensible cause of the rupture was the open refusal of Russia in December, 1810, to close her ports to neutral ships, and her adoption of a tariff favourable to Colonial and adverse to French imports. Napoleon was not prepared to tolerate the defection of his Russian ally from the continental system. He had long been doubtful of that swift friendship which had been formed on the raft of Tilsit in 1807. He distrusted the Tzar, and knew that the distrust was mutual, that Alexander did not easily forgive his encouragement of the Poles or his Austrian marriage, and that the continued blockade, unpopular everywhere, was nowhere more irksome than among the merchants and nobles of Russia. He determined, therefore, to force the issue, hoping, perhaps, that, as at Friedland, a decisive victory won upon the border of the Russian Empire might produce a victorious peace, and cherishing also, for he was now ambitious to add to the rôle of Charlemagne the renown of Alexander, the dream of using Russia as a half-way house between Europe and the East. "People will want to know," he said, "where we are going. We are going to make an end of Europe, and then to throw ourselves upon other robbers more daring than ourselves, and to become mistress of India."

There was no second Friedland, and no peace, but by the middle of August, 1812, Napoleon was at Smolensk half way between Niemen and Moscow, without any decisive victory to his credit, and with his great army shaken by the loss of a hundred thousand men. It was then that, abandoning his earlier and more prudent plan for a two years' campaign, he determined to push on into the heart of Russia in quest of the smashing victory which might once again bring the Tzar to his knees; but as in Spain, so in Russia patriotism was a real thing. To make discomfort for the invader there was no sacrifice, even to the burning of Moscow, which the Russians would not endure. Though Napoleon was in the Kremlin, Alexander, with the Prussian Stein at his elbow, refused to listen for a moment to overtures of peace. It was then given to Napoleon to experience the answer which Russia will always make to the enemy who embarks on the unequal contest with a Russian winter. The retreat from Moscow, which began on October 18, finally destroyed the instrument by which Napoleon had fixed his domination on Europe, and gave the signal for that insurrection of the German peoples against his rule which brought in its train after an epical struggle defeat, abdication, and exile.

The German War of Liberation, while it is memorable as marking the destruction of Napoleon's power in central Europe, sowed the seeds of that strong sentiment of all-German loyalty which has transformed the politics of the modern world. For the first time the German peoples were possessed by a common passion. Every German had suffered from the rigours of Napoleon's blockade and from conscription. To free the Fatherland from the intolerable yoke of an alien tyranny and by some means to prevent the recurrence of the French peril were aspirations common to all, but more particularly strong in northern Germany, where poets, philosophers, and pamphleteers combined to proclaim the gospel of a German nation.

1813

As yet, however, there was no such nation, but only a hot ferment of national feeling by the help of which a nation under strong political direction might ultimately be built. That direction was not forthcoming. No German state was sufficiently powerful by itself to defeat Napoleon, and to rally all Germans under its leadership. In Prussia, where national feeling was strongest and leadership most enlightened, there was as yet no army sufficient for the purpose. The early defeats of the Prussians and Russians at Bautzen and Lützen were a sufficient indication of the fact that Germany could not owe her salvation to Prussia alone, even if she could count upon the support, which had been assured her by the Treaty of Kalisch, of a Russian army. It followed that the liberation of Germany could not be effected without active help from the Austrian Empire. Now the Austrian Empire was in the main a non-German power, which had steadily reduced its commitments in the west. It had abandoned Belgium and the Rhine frontier, it had given up its old possessions in Swabia, it had seen the disappearance of the Holy Roman Empire, not without a sentiment of relief, and it was more interested in securing a hold on northern and central

Feb.,
1813

Italy, and consequently upon the Vatican, than in resuming the dangerous and ungrateful task of sheltering Germany from French aggression in the west.

Austria, then, had no interest in the idea of a united Germany. Prince Metternich, who was now directing Austrian policy, had views as to the future of Germany which were diametrically opposed to those which were entertained by Hardenberg and Stein in Berlin. Whereas the Prussian statesmen wanted to evict Napoleon from Germany by force of arms, and thereafter to create a united German state, Metternich wished to impose his mediation on the contending parties, to negotiate Napoleon out of Germany, if possible, to detach the Rheinbund from their dependence upon France, and thereafter to form a loose German federation of equal states under the presidency of Austria. It was the Austrian view which prevailed, and the postponement of German unity until 1870 is due to the fact that, the military help of Austria being essential to the liberation of Germany in 1813, Austria was accordingly able, with the willing co-operation of the south German states, to frame a Germany according to her mind.

1773-1859

Prussian historians count it as one of the tragedies of German history that the national and liberal sentiments inspired by the War of Liberation were allowed to run to waste like an African river in the sands, and that as the result of the heroic efforts and sufferings of that time Germany emerged with a federal constitution so framed as to paralyse its action and to deprive it of any real power in the counsels of Europe.

The tremendous campaign which Napoleon waged in Germany in 1813 was not, then, fought against a united people, but against governments entering into the war at different stages, and not easily coalescing, despite common sentiments, into a common plan of action. Austria was jealous of Russia. The troops of the *Rheinbund* during the early part of the year still served under Napoleon's banner. Save for a common desire to be rid of the French, there was no ultimate political agreement between the governments of Vienna and Berlin. It was, however, common ground between Russia, Prussia, and Austria that Napoleon must give up his Polish and German conquests. This he declined to do. "What is it you wish of me?" he said to Metternich on June 26, 1813. "That I should dishonour myself? Never. I shall know how to die, but never to yield an inch of territory.

Your sovereigns, who were born on the throne, may get beaten twenty times, and yet return to their capitals. I cannot. For I rose to power through the camp."

It was this intractable spirit, rather than the military disasters which were soon to follow, which compelled Napoleon's abdica- *Oct.,* tion. Even after the crushing victory at Leipzig, where the last *1813* great Napoleonic army, raised by incredible exertions, was fatally broken, the allies offered to treat (November, 1813), on the basis that France should retain her natural frontiers, the Rhine, the Alps, and the Pyrenees. That offer was rejected. Later when France had been invaded, and one signal defeat had been inflicted on the defending army, the terms were harder, but even then (February 4, 1814), with the sacrifice of Savoy and Belgium, and the acceptance of the old frontiers of the French monarchy as they existed before the revolutionary conquests, Napoleon might have retained his throne. After this last chance had been rejected, there was no other thought in the mind of the allies but that he, like so many of his royal victims, must cease to reign.

That England would never permanently allow Napoleon to retain Belgium, nor France continue to obey him, if he relinquished this cherished prize of the Revolution, are positions which have often been advanced and plausibly defended. But when the history of the Revolution and Empire is presented, as a drama proceeding to an inevitable close by reason of this fatal conquest of Belgium, which Napoleon was inexorably bound to defend, and England determined by considerations equally cogent to contest, then it is pertinent to observe that even after Leipzig the allies were willing to contemplate a treaty in which Belgium was left to France. There can be no more impressive testimony to the respect which the military strength of Napoleon continued to inspire in the breasts of his enemies.

The issue of war depended less on numbers than on willpower. In his last two campaigns, the German and the French, Napoleon was faced with overwhelming numbers. Almost all Europe was leagued against him. Even Bernadotte, one of his old officers, now Crown Prince of Sweden, brought a Swedish army into the field against his former master with a view to securing Norway and possibly also the Crown of France when the spoils came to be divided. While in the German theatre of war Russia, Prussia, Austria, and Sweden were closing round

Napoleon, Wellington was driving the French across the Pyrenees. Yet, despite these formidable odds, Napoleon fought these last campaigns with a resilience and skill which have excited the wonder of posterity. Though his troops were for the most part young and untrained, his Marshals weary of war, his cavalry insufficient, his numbers inferior to those of his antagonists, he succeeded in defeating the main allied army under Schwarzenberg in the two days' fighting outside the walls

1813

of Dresden on August 26 and 27, and had he been, after his earlier fashion, prompt and effective in pursuit, might have compelled his adversary to consider terms. Afterwards he allowed himself, through some remissness of will, to be encircled and crushed in the terrible carnage of Leipzig. Yet the operations which he carried out in the following year, with a handful of raw troops, against the armies of Blücher and Schwarzenberg in the valleys of the Seine and the Marne, are accounted among his masterpieces. In these, acting on interior lines and striking now at the Prussians in the north, now at the Austrians in the south, he beat the enemy again and again by the swiftness of his movements and the impetuosity of his attack. It was all in vain. Blücher was an antagonist whose will was as fierce and pertinacious as his own, a general without nerves, indefatigable in anger and unflustered by defeat. Repulsed three times, the old Prussian fell back northwards on reinforcements, and, returning to the fray on the stiffly fought fields of Laon and Craonne, opened for himself and his allies the road to Paris. Outpaced, Napoleon followed westward, and, finding that the capital had been surrendered to the enemy, took station at Fontainebleau. There the Marshals, war-weary themselves and interpreting the

April,
1814

lassitude of the country, exacted abdication; and thence, after a farewell to the Guard, which made him a figure of sentiment in every cottage in France, he left for Elba, voyaging southwards amid the execrations and threats of the people. The making of history for the next ten months was left to other hands.

1754-1838

It was Talleyrand, a renegade priest and a married bishop, who persuaded Alexander I that the Bourbon House must be recalled to rule in France. Improbable as it might seem that France would willingly accept the government of a fat old gentleman, who for twenty-five years had lived in exile estranged from all the stirring events and glories of that time, there was, in truth, no alternative. Louis XVIII at least represented a principle, a tradition, a fragment of the political faith of France. He at least might be thought to promise repose and the goodwill of Europe to a much tried and deeply apprehensive people. After the escapade of the Revolution and the Empire the old monarchy seemed to be the least unsafe of expedients; but not even the pen of Chateaubriand, most eloquent of French writers, could make it glorious; nor the English-looking constitution imposed by the allies convert it into an instrument of wise and generous liberty. The white flag, by which the famous tricolor was replaced, was a fitting emblem of the family which returned to its home, having learnt nothing and forgotten nothing in an epoch of tumultuous change.

The terms accorded to the conquered country (Treaty of Paris, May 30, 1814) were marked by a politic moderation. No indemnity was asked, no foreign occupation was insisted on. There was not even a stipulation that the treasures of art which had been stolen from the galleries of Europe should be restored to their rightful owners. That the foreign conquests of Napoleon were surrendered went without saying; but it is noteworthy that despite the completeness of the allied victory and the length and bitterness of the war, Louis XVIII was accorded a territory slightly more extensive than that which had belonged to his brother before the revolution broke out. The simplest exercise of common sense was sufficient to show the allies that Louis, their client, would never keep his doubtful throne under the shadow of a Carthaginian peace.

The detailed settlement of Europe was left to a Congress summoned for November to Vienna. Here the aristocracy of the old régime, light-hearted in the moment of their great release, surrendered themselves to an orgy of brilliant dissipation. As Paris danced after Thermidor, and London after the 1918 Armistice, so through that autumn and winter Vienna danced while the Corsican was safe in Elba and the officials were working out the structure of a new Europe. In this circle of emperors and kings, princes, nobles, and diplomats Marie Louise, the faithless wife of Napoleon, was studious to display her tiny feet.

The new map was shaped by statesmen for whom revolution emanating from France was the greatest of all dangers to the well-being of mankind.

The eastern frontier of France was therefore lined by a series

of buffer states or provinces destined to protect the tender body
of central Europe from revolution: in the north a kingdom of
the Netherlands, which lasted till 1830, when the uneasy union
between Calvinist Holland and Catholic Belgium was dissolved;
in the south a Sardinian kingdom, strengthened by the incorporation of Genoa and Savoy, while the intermediate region of
the Rhineland was entrusted, mainly at the instigation of the
British Government, to the wardship of Prussia. Nobody then
foresaw the union of Germany under the Prussian crown, or
that change in the balance of European power which still
makes Germany formidable to her neighbours. Far otherwise
was the outlook in 1814. Then France was regarded as the
general enemy, and Prussia as the power best qualified to keep a
watch upon the Rhine.

With the same idea of recalling Europe to conservatism and
sobriety, the Austrians were accorded that dominant position in
northern and central Italy which soon provoked the conspiracies
and wars of Italian nationalism. They were given the kingdom
of Lombardy and Venetia, they recovered Trieste and the Dalmatian littoral, had the satisfaction of seeing an Austrian archduke reigning in Florence and an Austrian Archduchess in
Parma, and since Ferdinand IV, with whom they were connected
by ties of family, politics, and creed, was replaced in Naples
after the death of Murat in 1815, their influence was spread
from one end of the peninsula to the other. Indeed, out of the
wars of the Revolution and the Empire, Austria emerged with
the greatest share of the spoil, her population increased by some
$4\frac{1}{2}$ million, her control of Italy little short of complete, and as
the President of a newly established but loosely jointed Germanic Confederation.

These arrangements were reached without great expense of
controversy as part of a general design for repelling the influence
of France from those countries in which it had been spread by
the conquests of Napoleon. The principal difficulty arose in that
region of the middle east of Europe where the problem is still
most thorny. What was to be done with the Grand Duchy of
Warsaw, which Napoleon had carved out of the Polish Provinces
of Prussia and handed over to be governed by the Saxon King?
What was to be done with Saxony itself? Russia wanted
Poland, Prussia wanted Saxony, and had these two states been
left to their own devices, Poland and Saxony would have been

wiped off the map. Such a prospect, however, was most unpalatable to Austria and France, the one refusing to see her
Prussian rival so aggrandized, the other cherishing strong views
upon a liberated Polish state. It was a question which brought
the Congress to the brink of war. Eventually a compromise was
reached under which Prussia received some two-thirds of Saxony
and the Rhine provinces, while Poland was erected into a constitutional kingdom under the Tzar.

Talleyrand's formula of legitimacy summed up the spirit of
the settlement. It was legitimacy which restored the Bourbons
to France, saved Saxony for the Wettins, and confirmed the
power of the royal house of Sardinia. No respect was paid to
nationality or to the wishes of the populations concerned. In all
essentials, therefore, the statesmen who drew up the settlement
at Vienna were sharply opposed in aims and principles to the
artificers of the Europe in which we now live. The Peace Treaties
of 1920 constituted a democratic settlement made possible only
by the downfall of those very monarchies to which the Congress
of Vienna had entrusted the policing of Europe. The settlement
of 1920 created new Republics, redistributed frontiers, accepted
the dissolution of the old Austrian Empire, and built up a
Europe on that principle of self-determination which had been
preached by the French revolutionaries, but was afterwards long
lost to view. To the Congress of Vienna the principles of President Wilson would have been anathema. Guided by Metternich,
Talleyrand, and Castlereagh, it held that the well-being of
Europe was to be secured not by compliance with the assumed
wishes of the peoples concerned, but only by punctual obedience
to legitimate authority.

By a stroke of fortune for the conservative cause the allied
sovereigns and ministers were still gathered in Vienna when it
was learnt (March 7, 1815) that Napoleon was once more on the
soil of France. To wind up the work of the Congress, to proclaim
Napoleon suspect and outlaw, and to frame terms of military
alliance against him was the work of a fortnight. Before a blow
had been struck every diplomatic card had been taken from
Napoleon's hands. Had the issue on the field of Waterloo gone
otherwise, he would still have succumbed to the united strength
of Europe.

Yet of all modes of conducting his desperate adventure a
campaign aimed at Brussels offered the fairest chance of rallying

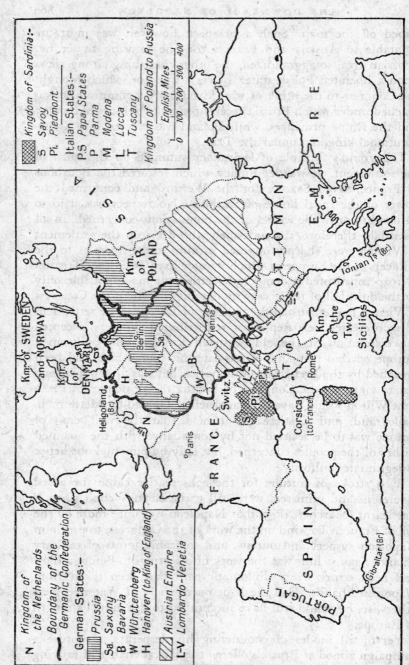

KEY (top-left legend):

Kingdom of Sardinia:—
S   Savoy
Pt. Piedmont

Italian States:—
P.S. Papal States
P   Parma
M   Modena
L   Lucca
T   Tuscany

Kingdom of Poland to Russia

English Miles
0   100   200   300   400

KEY (bottom-left legend):

N   Kingdom of the Netherlands
—   Boundary of the Germanic Confederation

German States:—
    Prussia
Sa. Saxony
B   Bavaria
W   Württemberg
H   Hanover (to King of England)

    Austrian Empire
L-V Lombardo-Venetia

Map labels:

Km. of SWEDEN and NORWAY

Km. of DENMARK

Heligoland (Br.)

°Paris

FRANCE

Switz.

Corsica (to France)

SPAIN

PORTUGAL

Gibraltar (Br)

Km. of RUSSIA

Km. of POLAND

Berlin

Vienna

Rome°

Km. of the Two Sicilies

OTTOMAN EMPIRE

Ionian Is. (Br)

EUROPE AT THE CONGRESS OF VIENNA 1815

the support of France. For centuries, seeing that it brought with it the great estuary of the Rhine, Belgium had possessed a symbolic, almost mysterious, value in the eyes of the French people. Over and over again the soil of this little country had been watered with French blood, nor had the ambition to acquire it ever failed to haunt the imagination of French statesmen. As the conquest of Belgium had been the first and principal glory of the young French Republic and its loss the most damaging commentary on the Empire, so its recovery now would be a prize than which none would be more welcome to the heart of France. Napoleon, then, was right to strike for Brussels, and Wellington, taking station on the field of Waterloo, was right to deny the road.

June 18,
1815

One long June day, memorable in human annals, decided the great duel between the revolution and the dynasts which had opened with the cannonade of Valmy twenty-three years before. Wellington's thin line, part British, part German, Belgian and Dutch, and powerfully aided as the shades of evening drew on by Blücher's Prussians, shattered the last army of Napoleon. Judged by the scale of modern battles the action was trivial.[1] Measured in terms of the spiritual exaltation which it occasioned there have been few greater victories, for Waterloo was the last act of a tragedy, the end of one age and the beginning of another.

It is much to the credit of British statesmanship that when, after the Hundred Days, a new arrangement had to be made with France, the vanquished country was still treated with moderation. If Prussia had had her way, Alsace and Lorraine would have been among the sacrifices required from the restored government of Louis XVIII. Wellington and Castlereagh, how-ever, saw that nothing would be more certainly calculated to undermine the authority of the Bourbons than a crippling loss of territory. It was to the interest of England, as it was to the advantage of Europe, that the old dynasty, despite the tre-mendous handicap of its estrangement from the military glories of the Napoleonic period, should nevertheless be helped to re-conquer and retain the loyalty of the French people. This, it was rightly judged, would have been a hopeless task if the full

---

[1] Wellington's army, " the worst equipped army with the worst staff ever brought together " in the view of its Commander, consisted only of 23,900 British, 17,000 Belgian and Dutch, 11,000 Hanoverian, 5,900 Brunswickers, and 2,800 Nassauer troops.

Prussian programme of spoliation had been sanctioned. France was, indeed, condemned to lose the Duchy of Bouillon and part of the Ardennes to the Netherlands, to hand over the forts of Saarlouis and Landau to Germany, to pay seven hundred million francs as an indemnity, to submit to an army of occupation for a period of five or three years, and to restore the art treasures which she was permitted under the earlier peace to retain. In these stipulations there was nothing intolerable to French pride, but the apprehensions of Alexander I, who doubted the wisdom of restoring the Bourbon House to France, were justified in the event. The plant of legitimacy failed to flourish upon soil still covered by the lava of revolution. The concert of Europe could neither save France from convulsions, nor prevent the return of Bonapartist ideas and the creation of a Second Empire. But with all its shortcomings it gave to Europe forty years of comparative peace.

CHAPTER IX

METTERNICH, CASTLEREAGH, AND CANNING

Aims of the Allies. The Concert of Europe. The Holy Alliance. Germany. The system of Metternich. Austria and England. The War of Greek Independence. Mehemet Ali and the Egyptian intervention. George Canning. Rôle of the British Navy in securing the independence of Greece and South America.

THE French Revolution and Napoleon had caused so much trouble to the governments of Europe that once " the Corsican ogre " had been shipped off to St. Helena and King Louis XVIII had been safely reinstated in Paris, the one idea dominating the sovereigns and ministers of the Great Alliance was that on no account must the French Revolution and Napoleon be allowed to recur. As in 1918 the exhausted peoples of the victorious *Entente* said with one voice " No more Prussian militarism," so in 1815 the conquerors came to a common resolve that there must be no more French revolution and that every germ of liberal opinion must be promptly killed lest it might develop into the malignant revolutionary fever. Behind the grim reaction which is the prevailing note of continental policy during the next twenty-three years was always the memory of what revolution had recently been and the haunting fear of what it might again become.

It was natural that these sentiments of resentment and panic should be most keenly felt by the three autocratic powers whose countries had been invaded and whose pride had been humbled by the armies of Napoleon. The monarchs of Russia, Austria, and Prussia had no difficulty in reaching the conclusion that it was their duty to Europe and to civilization to band themselves together against the spirit of revolution and to strike it down wherever it might show its ugly head. In this enterprise they hoped, but failed, to enlist the continuing sympathy and support of the British government.

Britain had emerged from the Napoleonic wars with a new industrial system and a new empire. She had obtained Malta, the Cape of Good Hope, Mauritius and Ceylon, and had successfully defended Canada in a war against the United States which had broken out in 1812 over the right of search on the high seas. She was developing a great trade with the Spanish and Portuguese colonies of South America which had taken the occasion of the Peninsular War to revolt against their respective mother countries. She differed from her continental allies by reason of the fact that she had large and expanding non-European interests, and that she had never been invaded by Napoleon. Moreover, even under her most reactionary governments, England maintained her parliamentary system and civil liberties. Castlereagh, the foreign minister who carried the country triumphantly through the concluding stages of the Napoleonic war, was denounced by his compatriots as the incarnation of all that was reactionary and obscurantist. Compared to Alexander of Russia and the Austrian Metternich, the English Tory was an angel of liberal and enlightened good sense.

Yet England, though differing in many respects from the continent, could not, having played so great a part in the war, refuse to take a leading share in the reorganization of Europe. The war had forced the country out of its insularity, had brought English statesmen into a close association with the political chiefs of other countries, and had created in the midst of the Great Alliance a diplomatic *esprit de corps*. A genuine feeling of mutual esteem bound Metternich and Castlereagh. Though Britain would not be a party to the Tzar's mystical Holy Alliance (a declaration of Absolutist and Christian principles which had no legal consequences) she joined a much more practical concert of Europe (November 20, 1815), in virtue of which the participating powers (Russia, Austria, Prussia, and Britain) pledged themselves to maintain the exclusion of the house of Bonaparte from France. A League of Nations was not contemplated by statesmen who repudiated the principle of nationality; but it was provided by the terms of the Quadruple Alliance that the contracting powers should meet together at agreed periods to discuss their common interests and matters affecting the peace and security of Europe.

At the moment nothing better could be devised than this concert of four great powers pledged to one another to protect the cause of European peace. It soon became evident, however, that the union of the powers was more apparent than real. Whereas Metternich wished the Quadruple Alliance to be an active instrument for the suppression of liberal movements throughout

Europe, Castlereagh took the view that it was no part of the duty of the four powers to interfere in the internal government of states. Castlereagh was a Tory, and in the eyes of his Whig opponents the incarnation of Tory tyranny, the tool of the Tzar's Holy Alliance, which he had refused to join, and the enemy of liberalism all over the world. But Castlereagh, while he wanted to strengthen Germany as a barrier against France and Russia, and valued the Austrian alliance as a prop of European conservatism, had no desire to see England drawn into the domestic broils of the continental states. Tory as he was, he knew his countrymen too well to suppose that they would permit themselves to be enrolled in Metternich's repressive police. The difference between the English view of policy, which was essentially liberal, and that of Austria, which was sternly conservative, steadily widened, until, with the death of Castlereagh and the accession of Canning to power, it led to an open rupture.

Aug.,
1822

Meanwhile a closer union of the three continental autocracies was formed in 1820 and continued till 1826, to give effect to the policy of resisting liberalism and revolution. It was this so-called Holy Alliance which muzzled intellectual life in Germany, stamped out the constitutional movements of Italy, restored autocracy to Spain, refused to recognize the insurgent democracies of South America and came into stark collision with the more liberal philosophy of England at the Congresses of Troppau, Laibach, and Verona. Goethe said, of this "Holy Alliance," that "nothing greater or more useful for mankind had been invented"; and the opinions of Goethe are entitled to respect. After the horrors and tribulations of the Napoleonic wars the statesmen of the victorious nations owed it to mankind that some method for the better organization of international relations should be essayed. Such had been the view of Pitt; such was the dream of Alexander of Russia, who flashed out now a mystic vision of Christian unity, now a less nebulous plan for a general league of the signatories of the Treaty of Vienna; such, too, was the intention of the cool and businesslike Castlereagh. The Triple Alliance of the autocrats fell far short of the Tzar's primal enthusiasms, of Castlereagh's liberally-minded caution, or of the conditions which should govern an effective organization of Europe. It reposed upon no foundation of public opinion, ran counter to the strongest popular aspirations of the age, and, being championed by the master of the Muscovite army, the most formidable in Europe, aroused suspicion in the western world. Yet as a practical instrument for bringing some measure of peace, order and decency into European society, the Holy Alliance, which was the system of Metternich, appealed to the disinterested intelligence of Goethe.

The idea that Europe could be ruled on principles of negative conservatism was wholly chimerical. The age of Scott and Byron, of Shelley, Coleridge and Wordsworth, of Froebel's experiments in child education, and of Robert Owen's adventure in socialism, was not one of intellectual inertia, but of rare imaginative achievement.

It was idle to suppose that a Europe stirred by so many dreams and thoughts, with its poets and romancers, its ardent university youths, its disbanded soldiers and sailors eating their hearts out for new enterprises, would long accept without a murmur and out of sheer exhaustion the peace settlement of Vienna. The peacemakers after the late war have been violently attacked for having paid too close a regard to the principle of nationality and the supposed wishes of the populations concerned. Still more general, but for the opposite reason, was the restlessness under the peace settlement of Vienna during the age of Metternich. The Italians and Czechs chafed under the Austrians, the Belgians under the Dutch, the Poles under the Russians and Prussians, the Serbs and Greeks under the Turks. The hopes cherished by Germans of the nobler kind that national unity and constitutional government would result from the vast energies of the liberating war were cruelly disappointed. There was no unity, but a Diet of thirty-nine states, each able to conduct its own foreign policy, and to frustrate by its solitary vote every important decision of the Federal *Bund*; no German cohesion, for foreign powers like Denmark and Luxemburg had seats in the Diet; no vigorous parliamentary life save in Bavaria and Baden, but a uniform spectacle of unenlightened, secretive despotism. Despite a formal promise of parliamentary liberty, the feudal nobility of Prussia saw to it that nothing like a parliament met in Berlin. German liberals, always a minority, envied, as they reflected upon the impotence and political sterility of their country, the brilliant debates of Paris and Westminster, and asked themselves whether the fatherland had gained anything of value from the great effusion of its blood and treasures in the Napoleonic wars.

The main root of the trouble was that the Germans themselves were not agreed upon any constructive design for the future of their country. Some wished for a Germany united under Prussia, some for a Germany owing allegiance to the Austrian Crown, others for a federation in which Austria, Prussia, and the lesser states might form mutually co-operating and balancing groups. To the outer world Germany seemed to move in metaphysical mists, and to be, as Michelet afterwards described her, " the Asia of Europe."

It was not only the denial of national rights which was secretly tormenting European peace. There was in the area controlled or influenced by the three autocracies a stern repression of opinions. All the apparatus of Papal control, the Jesuits, the Inquisition, the Index of Prohibited Books, was once more brought into play. In Italy the clericals supported by Austrian bayonets directed the schools. controlled the Press, and prevented any published deviation from the strictest path of Catholic orthodoxy. Under the restored Spanish monarchy, the Church with its vast endowments, its fiscal immunities, with the support of an ignorant and superstitious population, was in a position to direct the policy of the state. In half-Protestant Germany intellectual abasement was happily incomplete. The University of Göttingen, founded by George II and enjoying a relative immunity from government interference owing to its privileged position in the Electorate of Hanover, offered a welcome spectacle of academic liberty. Elsewhere after 1820 academic repression, under directions from Vienna, was the order of the day.

Over against this reactionary and non-national Europe was the spectacle, heartening to liberals in England, of the continent of America, in the north a powerful Republic which had achieved its freedom, in the south and centre a number of communities which under the inspiring leadership of Simon Bolivar of Caracás, and with not a little unofficial help from English seamen and merchants and most notably from the brilliant Lord Cochrane, were struggling to liberate themselves from their European masters. With these two Americas England in virtue of her advanced commercial development was in special contact, taking full advantage of the spread of cotton cultivation under the stimulus of the cotton gin (invented in 1793) in the Carolinas, and capturing all the European trade with the insurgent

states of the Latin South. Indeed, as one Creole state after
another threw off the yoke of its European master, as Cochrane
liberated Peru and then Brazil, as Bolivar declared the independence of Colombia and Iturbide of Mexico, it became plain
that a new commercial empire was offering itself to the fortunate
adventurers of Britain. An appeal went up from the merchants
of the City of London that the British government should
regularize an expanding trade by giving official recognition to
the rebel states.

The Englishman who had to deal with this South American
1770-1827 question was George Canning, a brilliant orator and wit, who,
though a member of a Tory government and a stout opponent
of Parliamentary Reform, was in foreign policy an exponent of
that new type of popular and liberal diplomacy, which, since it
descended to Palmerston, an adoring disciple, was for nearly half
a century a thorn in the flesh of continental autocrats. It was no
part of Canning's policy to abet a collective system for enforcing
discipline in foreign lands. If Austria with Russian and Prussian
assent chose to put down revolution in Naples and Piedmont,
that was her affair. If France sent an army into Spain to crush
a military revolt which had forced a constitution upon a clerical
1823 and autocratic king, that again was no matter calling for English
concurrence and support. On the contrary, the French invasion
of Spain was viewed in London with grave anxiety. What if the
French army, after crushing the rebellion, were to stay in Spain,
what if it were to invade Portugal, England's ally, what again
if it were to help the Spaniards to recover the Indies? Such
alarming contingencies Canning was determined to prevent. To
the horror and indignation of the autocrats, he recognized the
South American rebels.

Great as was the sensation caused by this radical announcement, it would have been greater still if the position of the South
American states could have been regularized, as Canning proposed, by a joint declaration from London and Washington.
The United States, however, acting on the advice of John Quincy
Adams, determined to make her own pronouncement. In a
1823 famous message to Congress President Monroe announced his
doctrine of America for the Americans and issued a solemn
warning to the old world that no fresh European settlements
would be tolerated on American soil. The " Monroe doctrine "
anticipated Canning's pronouncement, but what preserved the

South American continent through the greater part of the nineteenth century from European attack was not so much the excellent aspiration of the republican President as the efficient fleet of the British King.

The British fleet, which played so large a part in the emancipation of the South American colonies, next contributed to the liberation of Greece.

The struggle of the Greek people to liberate themselves from the Turkish yoke emphasized the two opposing tendencies in international life. To the Jesuit-trained nobles of Austria Greek nationalism was a disease, from the contagion of which, were it to spread into the Danube valley, they rightly augured the ruin of their state. The gentry of England had no such apprehensions. English nationalism they enjoyed, Irish nationalism they had suppressed, Indian nationalism was in a distant future. Education made them Philhellenes, public life made them parliamentarians, their sympathies as sportsmen went out to a small nation struggling to be free. When Byron died at Missolonghi, a martyr to Hellenic liberty, the romantic enthusiasm of the English for the Greeks spread out far and wide into the streets and taverns. No one stopped to ask how much of that ancient Hellas, which young men were taught to admire in the halls of Oxford and Cambridge, still survived in the herdsmen, the brigands, and the sea-pirates of Greece and its islands. The name of Greece was a talisman. Though Turkey was still the official friend and make-weight against Russian designs in the east, the mass of England was behind George Canning, when at last he was brought to recognize the Greek insurgents as belligerents, and joined with France and Russia to save them from extinction.

April 19 1824

The Greeks who made the war of independence were neither in culture nor in blood (save to an inconsiderable and hypothetical extent) connected with the countrymen of Plato and Aristotle. Descended for the most part from unlettered Slavs and Albanians, they were content that their minds should be in the keeping of the monks and priests of the Byzantine Church. They spoke Romaic, a form of Greek fashioned by the lips of goatherds and seamen, drawing freely from the vocabulary of the Turk, the Latin, and the Slav, and racy with all the mariner's slang of the Aegean. They used the Greek characters; but as an influence on the education of the liberators the poems of Homer and the tragedies of Aeschylus might almost as well have been written in Chinese.

Every national movement of the nineteenth century owes much to the inspiration of antiquity. The Serb went back to Stephen Dushan in the fourteenth century, the Italian to Dante and Virgil, the Bohemian to Czech ballads of reputed antiquity, the Irishman to Erse. Korais, a Corfiote schoolmaster, had the brilliant thought that the literature of ancient Greece might be translated into a tongue intermediate between the august original and the *argot* of the common speech. By creating a new language this industrious scholar helped to call into being a new nation.

The way for the Greek insurrection was prepared by a succession of shocks which in the opening years of the nineteenth century impaired the strength of the Turkish Empire and seemed to portend its approaching dissolution. Serbia rose in 1804, under Kara George, the swineherd, and claimed its independence. Ali of Janina made for himself an independent power on the Adriatic. Mehemet Ali, an Albanian adventurer, obtained control of Egypt. In these circumstances the wealthy Greeks of the Dispersion, who had founded (1815) under the name of Philike Hetairia a secret insurrectionary society in Odessa, discerned a new and flattering hope for the future of their race.

1769-1849

A first rising (1821) under Prince Alexander Ypsilanti, an aide-de-camp to the Tzar, being ill led and ill contrived, and failing to receive the Russian and Roumanian help on which it had counted, was easily crushed by the Turkish armies in Wallachia. The Greeks, however, possessed one advantage not ordinarily enjoyed by rebels against constituted authority. On sea they were superior to their adversaries. So long as the Greek navy had no enemy but the Turk on the water, the fire ships launched by the wealthy Greek islanders were able to keep the enemy at bay, and to land reinforcements where they were wanted on the mainland. For three years the Greeks of the Morea and the islands, aided by volunteers from the west, maintained a not unequal struggle, marked by horrible atrocities on each side, against their formidable antagonist. Then the situation was suddenly transformed by the intervention on the side of the Sultan of the powerful Pasha of Egypt.

Mehemet Ali, the founder of Egyptian independence and of the royal house which still reigns in Cairo, was an Albanian Moslem from Kavalla, and the exact coeval, since he was born in

1769, of Bonaparte and Wellington. A quick eye for the main chance, an extraordinary tact for circumstance, led him at each step of his energetic career to take the course, however treacherous and violent, which produced a margin of advantage for himself. He did well as a tax-collector, better as a tobacco merchant, best of all as a commander of an Albanian contingent in the Ottoman army. With the aid of this, the only reliable military force in the country, he made himself master of Egypt. The Turks were expelled, the British were beaten, the Mamelukes were slaughtered, the arms of the conqueror were carried victoriously to Mecca and Khartum. With a fleet newly purchased from the west, and an army largely recruited from the Sudan and organized by the experience of a French officer, the Pasha embarked upon a vast and ambitious policy, which, though originally calculated to obtain from the Sultan the island of Crete and the provinces of Palestine and Syria as a reward for the suppression of the Greeks, comprised among its secret and ultimate ends the total overthrow of the Turkish Empire.

At first the Egyptian intervention against the Greeks seemed to be an omen of utter ruin to their cause. The army of Egypt overran the Morea, the navy of Egypt dominated the Aegean. It was soon made known in the west that Greek captives were being sold as slaves in Cairo, and that the whole population of the Greek mainland was in danger of extermination. On that Canning intervened. Though he was a Tory by tradition and the member of a Tory government which viewed all rebels with disfavour, he was not prepared to see the most illustrious corner of Europe and the original home of its civilization settled by a population of fellaheen and negroes. Rather than acquiesce in the extermination of the Greeks he invited the intervention of the powers. Austria and Prussia refused, out of their steady hatred of liberty; Russia, having other subjects of quarrel with the Porte, and France, out of sentiment, accepted.

With Russia and France, then, Canning concluded the Treaty of London (July 6, 1827), which, since it contemplated an autonomous Greek state under Turkish suzerainty, to be obtained by a "pacific" naval blockade, is the real foundation of Greek independence.

Though Canning died in the next month (August 8) and was succeeded by Tory ministers wholly out of sympathy with any policy calculated to weaken the Porte or to strengthen the Tzar, his work was not undone. Out of the pacific blockade sprang the unauthorized naval fight in the bay of Navarino (October 20, 1827) when the Egyptian and Turkish fleets were utterly destroyed by the fleets of the Triple Alliance. After this, no matter what protests were made, the legitimate indignation of the Porte was inevitable. A British fleet appeared before Alexandria, a Russian army marched to Adrianople, a strong French force was thrown into the Morea. When the Tory government fell in England in 1830 and Palmerston, who was a Liberal, came to the Foreign Office, the way was cleared for the recognition of a new Greek state entirely independent of Turkey. Diplomacy, acknowledging perforce the irregular work of the soldiers, sailors, and adventurers who had taken part in the battles and forays of the war, threw a veil of royal respectability over the infant polity. A Bavarian prince was called to rule over a kingdom which, since it lacked Thessaly and Crete, was hardly workable and comprised but a fraction of the Greek-speaking race. Nobody could tremble at Otto's tiny monarchy. Yet the resurrection of Greece, little as it altered the balance of power in Europe, was a most significant fact. It was here that the first successful blow was administered to the autocratic government of Europe by Congress; here that the Ottoman Empire received its most sensible wound; here that the modern spirit of nationalism, afterwards destined to govern Italy and Poland, Bohemia and Ireland, and to bring the Austrian Empire to the ground, won its first romantic and resounding triumph. In the earliest Greek as in the latest Irish phase of nationalism, the human types recur: Kolokotrones and Michael Collins, Korais and Arthur Griffith, Canning and Lloyd George, the fighting conspirator, the literary dogmatist, the liberal statesman.

When we consider the terrible events by which the Greek wars of independence were marked, the ruthless massacre and mutilation of Turks by Greeks in the Morea, the extermination of the whole Greek population of Chios and of most of the inhabitants of the Greek quarter of Constantinople by their enemies, and further reflect upon the long series of savage encounters by which alone the national principle has, at last in our own days, been established in the Balkans, it is natural to ask whether Balkan nationality has been worth that price. If it be remembered that the position of the Greek population under Turkish rule was in the eighteenth century by no means intolerable, that the Greek Church under its Patriarch was allowed a full measure of liberty, that the commerce of the Levant was in the hands of Greek merchants, that the Greeks monopolized certain branches of trade and industry, and were accorded four of the great offices of state, it is clear that, without the ferment of the national idea, Balkan unity might have taken another turn which would have been entirely compatible with the material comfort of the Christian subjects of the Porte. Yet the price of greater quiet under the capricious and mutable tyranny of the Turk would have been great also, an estrangement from the progressive currents of western thought and a permanent temper of servility, incompatible with self-respect and cutting at the roots of self-improvement.

BOOKS WHICH MAY BE CONSULTED

C. A. Fyffe : History of Modern Europe. 1924.
C. K. Webster : The Foreign Policy of Castlereagh.
H. Temperley : George Canning. 1926.
Algernon Cecil : British Foreign Secretaries. 1927.
W. A. Phillips : The War of Greek Independence. 1897.
G. Young : Egypt. 1927.
W. A. Phillips : Mahomet Ali. 1907.
A. Toynbee : A Study of History, 3 vols. 1934.

CHAPTER X

THE REVOLUTION OF 1830

Britain and world trade. Spread of mechanical inventions. Relative backwardness of German industry. Survival of democratic society in France. The difficulties of French constitutional monarchy. Louis XVIII. Strife of French parties. Rising tide of liberalism. Charles X. The July revolution. Louis Philippe. Spread of revolutionary ferment. The birth of Belgium. The agony of Poland. Link between Poland and France.

FIVE years after Waterloo, Hegel, eminent among South German philosophers, wrote thus of the English: " The material existence of the English is based on commerce and industry, and the English have undertaken the weight and responsibility of being the missionaries of civilization to the world; for their commercial spirit urges them to traverse every sea and land, to form connexions with barbarous peoples, to create wants and to stimulate enterprise, and first and foremost to establish among them the conditions necessary to commerce—viz., the relinquishment of a life of lawless violence, respect for property, and civility to strangers." It was not, then, as masters of an empire that the English appeared to foreigners, nor so that they considered themselves, but rather as universal traders dispensing the abundance which mechanical improvements and mineral resources had newly created in their own country, and bringing back in return produce from every quarter of the globe. Though Australia had been discovered and claimed, though Canada had been successfully defended in a brief war against the United States, and Ceylon, the Cape and Malta had been added to the overseas possessions of King George, and though the old colonial system of preferential trade between the mother country and its daughter states had survived the successful revolution of the American colonies, nothing would have been more foreign to the English ideas of that time than that trade should be confined to the British possessions. The rich markets of the continent lay close at hand. South America, liberating itself from the yoke of Spain and Portugal, opened out vast possibilities to English trade. The coal, the pig-iron, the textiles of England were essential to the needs of the continent. Out of the exchange of

English manufactures with the food and raw materials of distant lands there arose a development of international trade such as had never previously been known in history.

It was the special note of the nineteenth century to spread through Europe and the outer world those mechanical inventions and that type of industrial civilization which were first developed among the Anglo-Saxon peoples. In 1819 the Atlantic was crossed by a steamship. The next decade witnessed the inauguration of the railway systems of Belgium, France, and Germany. In the forties, thanks to the work of Morse, the American inventor, the telegraph spread through Europe. The fifties brought submarine cables, the sixties the transatlantic cables. The seventies witnessed the formation of the international postal union and the development of the transatlantic grain trade, which made the harvest of the new world available for the populations of the old. The concluding decades of the century were remarkable all over western Europe for a growth in the size of towns, and for an alteration in the balance between urban and rural population. More particularly was this noticeable in Germany, a country which as late as 1871, when the Empire was founded, could be described as consisting mainly of free land-owning peasants and powerful cultivating squires, with few large towns and no considerable urban population, but which, through the combined influence of railways, overseas expansion, inventions in steel and electricity, and the exhilaration consequent upon the victorious war with France, quadrupled its urban population in the sixty years between 1849 and 1910.

The progress of industrialization, which had been so rapid in Britain, proceeded at a far slower pace on the continent of Europe, saving only in that small area of Belgium, which ever since the thirteenth century had been noted for its crowded and busy urban life. The revolutionary movements which broke out in various parts of Europe in 1820, in 1830 and in 1848 were not the product of factory discontent. There were, in truth, few great aggregations of factories, either in France or in Germany, during that period. It is noted by Dr. Clapham that between 1815 and 1848 two towns only in France, St. Etienne and Roubaix, grew rapidly, and that three-fifths of the pig-iron produced in the country came from hundreds of little charcoal furnaces scattered among the woodlands. In Germany the situation was not dissimilar. The Germans had many advantages over their English competitors. Their middle class was better educated, they were superior in the arts of design, they had more chemical knowledge, and could claim that the cutlery of Solingen had a wider market and a higher repute than any cutlery in Europe. Nor was there any country which had a larger heritage of metallurgical experience. Nevertheless the mind of Germany was so little occupied with the newer types and scales of economic development, and its industries, even such as were concerned with the exploitation of the rich mineral resources of the country, were so greatly retarded by lack of science, capital and enterprise, that it was not until about 1840 that the great Silesian coalfield, which has proved to be in recent years an apple of discord between Poland and Germany, began to be worked.

The restoration in France, though providing once more the spectacle of a King and a Court, made little change in the condition of the French people. The *ancien régime* had gone for ever. Society had been too profoundly altered by the vast convulsions of the Revolution and the Empire to recapture the irregularities, anomalies, and confusions which made the government of the old monarchy a mountain of abuses. The nobles never recovered their ancient sway. The episcopal grand seigneur was a distant memory becoming steadily fainter. All the main conquests of the Revolution, equality before the law, the liberty of the subject, the National Guard, the unity of the kingdom, the new judicial system, remained unaffected by the return of the Bourbons. Nobody had the power to repeal the Codes or to abolish the Legion of Honour or to dissolve the Napoleonic University. Even the Concordat, which was so offensive to clerical sentiment, was too strongly rooted to be torn up and cast to the winds. The restored monarchy, with its absolutist and clerical tradition, appeared ill adapted to a society which was now profoundly equalitarian and, in its middle and most influential region, prevailingly secular.

The experiment of a constitutional monarchy was started under every possible disadvantage. Not only was it hated by some and unfamiliar to all, but it implied a whole catalogue of political virtues which thrive only when men are not too bitter and implacable to adjust their differences. The constitution of England could be copied. The good-humour, the moderation, the pleasant give and take, the graded loyalties which made the working of that constitution successful were less easy to emulate. Whereas in England a newspaper of the period was full of sport and advertisements, in France, still trembling with the exasperation caused by the Hundred Days and by the White Terror which followed them, a newspaper was little more than a fierce political diatribe. The French legislator did not hunt the fox. No French Epsom or Newmarket sweetened the severity or abated the logic of his political meditations. He thought with a bitter clearness, spoke with a bitter violence. If he was a die-hard royalist, he assailed the Charter and the Concordat, and worked for the restoration of the estates which had been confiscated in the revolution. By the opposition school the noble and priest were hated with a rancour sharpened by apprehension, while the monarchy was denounced for its subservience to foreign powers, for its abandonment of the tricolor, and for its acceptance of a peace derogatory to the pride of a military nation.

The position of Louis XVIII, uneasily poised between two *1814-24* nations, two philosophies, and two traditions, was one of extreme difficulty. He owed his throne to the national humiliation of Waterloo. He had been brought back in the baggage of the allied armies, an inglorious, unromantic figure, to rule over a people thirsting for glory and romance. The tyranny of circumstances constrained him to drastic and unwelcome economies. He could not go with the ultra-royalists who dominated his First Chamber since they pursued the chimera of a return to the *ancien régime*. Equally he feared the revolutionary possibilities of liberalism. In the blinding violence of opposing factions the middle way was difficult to find and hard to keep. Louis both found and kept it. The electoral law of 1817, limiting the franchise to a narrow circle within the middle class, in its main principle governed France for thirty years.

It is to the credit of this sagacious and witty old gentleman that, after he had rid himself of his first impossible Chamber, which was more royalist than the King, he enlisted ministers by whose advice and support he was enabled to avoid the folly of extremes and to give to France a spell of peace and material prosperity, during which she put her finances in order, paid the war indemnity at a reduced rate, liberated her soil from foreign armies, and took a place once more in the Councils of Europe upon an equal and honourable footing. The names of Richelieu, of De Serre, of Decazes, and in a lesser degree of Villèle, a good financier who disliked adventures, deserve to be honourably mentioned in the roll of French parliamentary statesmen.

Outside a charmed circle of some 80,000 electors two opposing movements proceeded with accelerating velocity: first a renewal of the spirit and energy of the Roman Catholic Church, which set itself by a well-knit series of missions and by a determined onslaught on the universities and schools to reconquer for the Faith great tracts of French life which had lapsed into Paganism; and secondly a militant anti-clericalism, finding a new and secret organ in Carbonarism, a society derived from Naples, and aimed against tyranny in all its shapes. The liberalism of Europe was not, then, as Napoleon maintained, mortally stricken on the field of Waterloo. Not five years had passed before the conservative governments of the west were unpleasantly reminded that the spirit of revolution was still abroad. There was ferment among the university students in Germany, there were riots in Manchester, insurrections in Naples, Piedmont, and Spain, in Sicily a demand for independence, in Portugal the portent of a constitution, in Greece premonitory tremors of nationalism, in France a splutter of little Carbonarist revolutions, and the sensational murder in 1820 of the Duc de Berry, the King's nephew and the next King's eventual heir, by the dagger of Louvet, a fanatic. These movements were unripe, and even when most serious, as in Naples and Spain, easily put down by two obedient instruments of autocracy, the royalist armies of Austria and France. But when passions have once been roused to fever heat, wise government becomes more difficult than ever. After the Duke of Berry's murder, royalist feeling in Paris was too fierce to admit of a liberal ministry. To his keen regret Louis was compelled to dismiss his favourite Decazes, and to transfer his confidence to Villèle, the mainstay of the Right. The Press was muzzled. Heartened by an easy and almost bloodless progress across Spain, a French army, marching under the old royalist colours, put down the Spanish liberals, restored Ferdinand to power and freedom, and by this faint aureole of victory created in the old King's mind the illusion that all would yet be well with the legitimist cause in Europe. But already Canning was guiding British policy on liberal lines; already Brazil, Peru, and Greece had declared their independence, and no shrewd observer could doubt but that the tides of liberalism were fast rising in the world.

Shrewdness and observation were alike denied to the elderly bigot who mounted the French throne in 1824. Charles X, differing from his pleasant, easy-going brother, was a man of strict, autocratic, and clerical principle. " I would rather chop wood," he said, " than reign after the fashion of the King of England." He was deaf to all the calls of the future, obedient only to the voice of the past. A lively and sceptical generation, still largely pagan and becoming increasingly liberal and Bonapartist, learned with amused contempt how the new King had got himself crowned after the ancient rites at Rheims, how he had lain prostrate on velvet cushions and allowed his body to be pricked in seven places by a golden bodkin, that it might receive the blessing of the Holy Oil.[1] And when this mediaeval ceremony was followed by a law granting pecuniary compensation to the *émigrés*, by another law enacting stern penalties for sacrilege, and by a royal order dissolving the National Guard, who had demonstrated in favour of constitutional reform, amusement was succeeded by a gathering volume of impatience, irritation, and fear. The idea spread, fomented by the unconcealed desires of the ultra-royalist papers, that the King meditated a *coup d'état* to overturn the constitution and to bring back the *ancien régime*. That this was in effect his design was made plain to all, when, dismissing Martignac, an adroit and moderate statesman, who might have saved the Crown, Charles summoned Jules de Polignac to his side.

Polignac, a visionary professing to receive direct guidance from the Virgin, was reaction personified. He had been one of the original *émigrés*, had been imprisoned under the Empire, and had refused to swear to the Charter in 1815. His very name was a challenge, and when it was known that Bourmont, the General who had betrayed Napoleon before Ligny, was to be Polignac's Minister of War, a mark of ignomiay was added to the general distrust inspired by his Cabinet. Yet it is notable that under the last and weakest minister of her last and weakest legitimate King, France captured Algiers, inaugurating by that notable feat of arms the recovery of the north African littoral for the Latin races, and laying the foundation of the wide African Empire which she is now studious to support as a make-

---

[1] The popular belief that this ceremony took place may have been unfounded. What is certain is that Charles touched for the King's evil after coronation.

weight against the man-power of Germany. Paris, however, was not interested in Algiers, but in the nearer controversy between priest and layman, crown and people, which soon drew to a sharp climax. On July 25, 1830, ordinances were issued from the Royal Palace of St. Cloud, limiting the freedom of the Press, dissolving the Chambers, and altering the electoral law. The King and his favourite had shown their hands. It was plain that they meant not only to refuse the demand for an enlarged franchise, which had been gathering force throughout the year, but to tear up the Constitution itself and to blot out liberty in all its forms. The purport of the royal programme was no sooner apprehended than it was regarded as an intolerable insult. To the royalist *coup d'état* Paris responded by three days of fierce fighting, which drove the King from his throne and sealed the fate of the ancient monarchy of France.

July 27-9, 1830

The revolution of July is notable as the act of a single city. Paris decided the fate of France. Before the royalists in the provinces had time to open their eyes, the issue was decided against the White Flag at the Paris barricades. Not less surprising to the multitude was the government which emerged from the tempest. A large share of the street fighting had been done by men like Cavaignac, who wanted a republic, or else by the Bonapartist supporters of a Second Empire. Yet the progeny of the revolution was neither a republic nor an empire, but the bourgeois monarchy of Louis Philippe, the head of the House of Orleans and the son of that Philippe Égalité who had embraced the revolutionary cause, given a regicide vote, and perished on the scaffold. It was a good and ingenious notion cherished at that time by many men of liberal temper and notably by Thiers, a young Southerner of genius, then fast rising to the front in the sphere of history, politics, and journalism, that Louis of Orleans, who as a young man had fought in the revolutionary armies, and had afterwards tasted the sorrows and trials of poverty, would give to France the satisfying blessing of a democratic monarchy. None of the disabilities which had made Charles X impossible attached to Louis. He was a man of the new world, simple and homely in his ways, who would accept the tricolor and the lay institutions of a democratic state, and, since the precedent of the English revolution of 1688 was much in the minds of the little knot of politicians who made the July monarchy, he appeared as a French William of Orange fated to heal the disorders of the nation and to inaugurate a long and prosperous period of constitutional rule in a country ill used to tempered freedom. Before the population of Paris had realized what was afoot, the Prince had been brought by his adherents to the Hôtel de Ville. There publicly adopting the tricolor, and embracing before the assembled crowd Lafayette, "the hero of two worlds," and the "grand old man of the revolution," Louis Philippe obtained for his new and unsteady government a necessary baptism of popular applause.

Sparks from the Paris furnace flew fast and far among the unsound timbers of "congress Europe." The Belgians rose against the Dutch, the Poles against the Russians, the Carbonari against the priestly governance of the Papal States. A wild clamour for a war of liberation to be undertaken in the grand old revolutionary manner in relief of suffering peoples ran along the Paris pavements. There were serious riots. For more than a year the new French government trembled for its life. Eventually the storm was weathered. Louis Philippe would have nothing to say to the maniacs who would have involved France in a war with England over Belgium, with Russia over Poland, and with the Austrian Empire over Italian nationalism. It is his chief title to statesmanship that, keeping the peace with the great Powers, he gave to his country eighteen years of prosperous and advancing economic life.

1830-48

The revolution which broke up the ill-compacted Kingdom of the Netherlands started with a riot in Brussels on August 25, 1830. The Belgians had long chafed under the stiff rule of their Dutch masters. They hated the Protestant religion and the Dutch spirit of religious tolerance and racial monopoly. They knew themselves to be more numerous and eloquent; they believed themselves to be more cultivated and genial. Accordingly they regarded it as intolerable that Dutch should be prescribed as the sole official language, that the Walloon populations should thereby be excluded from public life, and that almost every important civil and military office should be given to a Dutchman. To the countrymen of Rubens these Dutch airs of superiority were intolerable. Inflamed by the example of Paris, they determined to throw off the alien yoke.

A monument in the Place des Martyrs in Brussels marks the burial place of six hundred Belgian volunteers, who died fighting

in the streets against the Dutch regulars in September, 183
Their sacrifice, which struck the imagination at the time, pr
claimed but did not secure the cause of Belgian independenc
The modern Kingdom of Belgium was made not by the militar
prowess of the Belgians but by Anglo-French diplomacy wit
some little help from the French army. Its architects wer
1784-1865 Palmerston, the new Liberal Foreign Minister in the Whi
administration of Lord Grey, and Talleyrand, the well-chose
ambassador of France in London. Palmerston's love of liberty
coupled with Louis Philippe's and Talleyrand's resolve never o
any account to reopen the old quarrel with England, enable
the issue to be settled on the lines of Belgian independence with
out a general war. Had Palmerston sided with the Dutch an
autocracy, or had Louis Philippe accepted the Belgian crow
which was offered to his second son, the old quarrel betwee
France and England would have flamed out anew with conse
quences which must have been fatal to Belgian freedom. The co
operation of the two countries localized and solved the problem
1790-1865 The Belgian crown was offered to Leopold of Saxe-Coburg, tha
long-headed, well-informed uncle of Queen Victoria, who, havin
taken his first wife from the English royal family, was now, a
evidence of impartiality, prepared to marry a French Princess
A wiser choice could not have been made. Leopold surmounte
all his difficulties, a dangerous Dutch invasion, a hardly les
dangerous French rescue, and the deep dissatisfaction of th
Belgian people at the loss of Luxemburg and Limburg, whicl
was imposed upon them by the Powers at the Conference o
London. The real triumph lay with the policy of Palmerston
Belgium was free from Holland, but equally free from the risl
of being incorporated in the military and commercial system o
France. A *régime* of perpetual neutrality was imposed on her
Under the famous treaty of 1839, which seventy-five years late
was described as " a scrap of paper," Belgian neutrality wa
guaranteed by five Powers, among which were numbered Prussi
and France, in addition to England, who by this expedient o
neutrality secured, as she thought, the prime political interes
which she had defended through many centuries with the bloo
of her sons.

Far removed from the protection of the liberal diplomacy o
the west the Polish insurrection of 1830 ran a very differen

course. The Tzar Nicholas, who had viewed with indignation
and alarm the July revolution in Paris, was preparing to inflict
condign punishment upon the insolent democracy of France,
when he was stopped short by a serious insurrection in Warsaw.
Here a body of Polish officers and landowners, ill relishing the
prospect of being marched off against their friends the French,
and hoping that something good might result for Poland from
the spread of the revolutionary flame, captured the government,
and, having the treasury and army of a small constitutional
state at their disposal, flung a challenge to the might of the
Russian Empire. For hard upon a year the Poles fought valiantly
against their giant opponent, receiving and inflicting heavy losses,
but eventually (September, 1831) succumbing in the unequal
contest. An end was then made of the last vestige of Polish
liberty. Congress Poland was deleted from the map, and absorbed
in the levelling and autocratic system of the Russian Empire,
gaining thereby in industrial strength, but losing, as Polish
historians assert, the spiritual virtues of ardour and faith which
result from freedom.

One consequence of this frustrated movement was an emigration of Polish artists and writers to Paris, which for many
generations after 1831 became the intellectual capital of the
Polish race. The early dispersion of Polish soldiers of fortune
was reinforced by a flight of professors, poets, and musicians
who advertised the claims of the Slavonic genius in the most
polite capital in Europe.

The Polish revolution, therefore, of 1830, though it appeared
to result in calamitous failure, was not altogether in vain. It
reminded Europe of the existence of a body of national sentiment, which was still strong, of national wrongs which were still
unappeased, and of a national temper which was bold to the point
of temerity. The French did not forget that the Polish rebellion
was a consequence of their domestic insurrection, that it had
been encouraged by prominent Frenchmen, and that at a critical
moment it had shielded them from the possibility of a formidable attack. To these considerations they remained sensitive. A
bond was formed between Poland and France which is still an
appreciable factor in the politics of Europe.

BOOKS WHICH MAY BE CONSULTED

Cambridge Modern History, Vol. X. 1907.
J. H. Clapham : Economic Development of France and Germany. 1921.
Lowes Dickinson : Revolution and Reaction in Modern France. 1892.
Chateaubriand : Bonaparte et les Bourbons. 1814.
P. Thureau Dangin : Histoire de la Monarchie de Juillet. 1884-92.
Memoirs of Beugnot, Chateaubriand, Guizot.
E. Faguet : Politiques et moralistes du XIX siècle. *Tr.* 1928.
H. Pirenne : Histoire de Belgique. 1903-33.
P. Guedalla : Lord Palmerston. 1926.
Duff Cooper : Talleyrand. 1932.
Ronan Dyboski : Poland. (Nations of the Modern World Series.) 1933.

CHAPTER XI

THE AGE OF PEEL

*The old Parliament and the new Society. Liberty of criticism. Advance
of public education. Whigs and Tories. Reform Act of 1832. Sir Robert
Peel and the foundation of the Conservative party. Repealers, Socialists,
Chartists, Free Traders. Steady growth of the Social Services.*

MEANWHILE England was slowly rising to a sense of the new and
formidable problems presented to her by the development of
factory life. It was a great misfortune, the consequences of
which are felt to this day, that for twenty precious years when
the whole mind of the governing class ought to have been given
to providing the new factory population with schools and public
hygiene, with good houses and well-planned towns as well as
with museums and libraries, parks and playgrounds, the country
was engaged in a bitter war with France, and that when the war
was finally brought to an end and Napoleon was banished to
St. Helena, the war mentality survived for many years, counsel-
ling fear, diffusing distrust, and standing in the way of any full
and dispassionate consideration of the "condition of the people
question." Of that continuing war mentality Lord Sidmouth's
"Six Acts" in 1819 may be taken as a last example.

It was a further unhappy circumstance that, under the long
Tory administration of William Pitt, the House of Lords assumed
that overwhelmingly Tory complexion which it has never since
lost. The reform of Parliament was in consequence delayed for
many important years and carried only in 1832 under the menace
of a special creation of Whig peers and in the midst of a political
ferment to which England had been a stranger since the civil
wars. The country, then, continued to be governed by the old-
fashioned machinery (which answered well enough to the requirements of a small rural population) of landlords at Quarter
Sessions and landlords at Westminster. The charmed circle of
Parliamentary life was not, indeed, and never had been altogether
closed to great fortunes, however made, or to shining talents
sponsored by noblemen. An Indian fortune gave the Pitts to
Westminster. The father and grandfather of Sir Robert Peel
were among the makers of industrial Lancashire. But while Old

Sarum returned two members to Parliament, Manchester and Birmingham went unrepresented.

The results were such as might have been expected. An aristocratic debating society was called upon to cope with the problems of an economic *régime* of which no country had any experience. The factory with its discipline, the huge industrial city with its swarms, the swift increase in the population, the spectacular growth of fortunes in the cotton trade, these were in truth portents announcing a new era in the conduct of human affairs, the full measure of which the unreformed Parliament was slow to seize. It was not therefore wonderful that Parliament went astray, that it interfered when it should have allowed things to slide, and that it allowed things to slide when it should have interfered, that it legislated, for instance, to prevent cheap corn and did not intervene to prevent cheap slums.

There was a great deal of untended and unnecessary misery in England during the years immediately succeeding the war. A ruined continent was in no condition to purchase the goods which England was anxious to export. While taxes and rates were high, wages were deplorably low, and as always happens after a war or when the march of scientific invention is abnormally swift, there was much unemployment improvidently dealt with. A badly administered Poor Law put a premium on rural idleness by its system of outdoor relief and family allowances. A vexatious system of Protection raised the price of bread to a hungry population and throttled foreign trade with a complicated machinery of duties. That smuggling should grow out of Protection and that a spirit of lawlessness should be bred by smuggling was as natural as that night should follow day. Violent habits may be softened by humane laws, but the state of the penal law, until it was reformed by Romilly and Peel, was exactly calculated to educate the poor in a spirit of reckless and sullen defiance. For a trivial offence, the theft of a cow, the burning of a rick, the snaring of a pheasant, some villager driven desperate by hunger might find himself sentenced to transportation or death.

Even as late as 1834, when Parliament had been reformed and a Whig government was in office, six agricultural labourers of Tolpuddle in Dorset were sentenced to seven years of transportation for administering an illegal oath to a branch of a Friendly Society.

As for the new factory population, it presented problems of such novel complexity that it would be strange if they had been promptly and adequately dealt with by the unreformed Parliament. Vast evil-smelling slums were allowed to grow up in which quick fortunes were made out of an ill-paid, under-nourished mass of immigrants from the villages. A window tax put a premium on dark and ill-ventilated rooms. But of all the deplorable features of English mill-life in the early post-war period, none was so hateful as the ruthless exploitation of little children. Even when at last in 1819 Parliament stepped in and passed a statute, notable as the first of the Factory Acts, for dealing with child labour, it did not do more than limit the hours of labour of children to twelve and a half hours and forbid the employment of children under nine in certain factories. So imperfectly educated was the public conscience that even this utterly insufficient Act was a dead letter for lack of inspectors to enforce it. Six years later, when another bill was introduced to protect the children, it was stated in Parliament that "in the best mills children were compelled to work twelve and a half hours a day and in others for fifteen or sixteen."

Nevertheless, in spite of much unintelligent reaction due to panic and many intolerable industrial conditions due to the cupidity of employers and parents, England enjoyed one precious advantage. The people were free to grumble aloud. Parliaments met. Newspapers criticized the ministers and the monarch. Juries returned verdicts against the Crown. Even in 1819, when reaction was at its height, there was a stiff Parliamentary opposition to Sidmouth's "Six Acts" for curbing the liberties of the people.

By slow degrees a notion began to spread abroad that the education of the masses was a national responsibility and not a matter which could be wholly left to the competing appetites of rival sects. Not that educational competition was valueless. The Church and the sects were first in the field. When no secular agency was available and at a time when it is doubtful whether any motive less powerful than religious zeal could have enlisted the necessary social effort to bring education to the poor, the unsectarian British and Foreign School Society and its rival, the *1812* Anglican National Society, occupied the ground. Their methods were bad, their resources slender, their teachers (for both societies believed in the monitorial system) were for the most part children in their teens. The story of their quarrels and jealousies cannot be read without a sense of shame. But at least they were pioneers in the greatest of the social services. The state has never wished to discard their work. It has never dared to build up in England a complete plan of systematic national education. Rather it has taken the existing elementary schools, Anglican, Free Church, Jewish, Catholic, as it has found them, and gradually, by assisting them with public funds, by inspection, and by the enforcement of higher educational standards and the institution of a regular scheme of training for teachers, brought them to a relative degree of efficiency. The process began in 1833 with a grant of £20,000 to the two societies and was carried to a further stage by the establishment of a committee of the Privy Council for education in 1839. Not till 1846 was there any state provision for the training of teachers.

Three great impediments obstructed a national advance against the fortress of ignorance: the guarded monopoly of the Established Church, the exorbitant claims of the factory, and a low and cheap view of the kind of education that was good enough for the children of the poor. Some of these obstacles had already been attacked before 1848. The University of London, founded in 1825, opened the gateways of the higher learning to non-Anglicans. A series of statutes beginning in 1819 and ending after a great political agitation in the Ten Hours Act in 1847 limited the hours of industrial toil for children and adolescents under eighteen, and established the precious principle that an industrial state must ensure some measure at least of leisure for its members. These were valuable conquests. So too was the foundation of the Mechanics Institutes for the spread of scientific knowledge among intelligent artisans. By the twenties and thirties of the nineteenth century it was beginning to be realized that education was a source of national power and the essential basis of a sound national life.

Much yet remained to be done. England had to wait till 1870 for universal compulsory elementary education, till 1891 for gratuitous education, till 1902 for secondary schools aided from public funds; but at least it is significant that as early as 1825 Henry Brougham, a great law reformer and by reason of his boisterous and innovating temper one of the most widely known and acclaimed of political figures, published his *Observations on the Education of the People*, which at once went through twenty

editions and led to the formation of the Society for the Diffusion
of Useful Knowledge.

The Whig party indeed suffered a long eclipse. Save for the brief
Grenville-Fox administration, rendered glorious by the abolition
of the Slave Trade, the Tories ruled England from Pitt's accession
in 1784 until Lord Grey in his old age came back to London
from his country home in Northumberland to carry the Reform
Bill which had been the dream of his youth. But the English
form of Toryism was very different from the Austrian—the kind
providence which has presided over English politics furnishing
the best Tory leaders with a measure of pliability and good sense,
without which the country would hardly have survived the
industrial and social changes of the nineteenth century, save at
the cost of revolution. William Pitt, whose long administration
fixed the Tory tradition during the early part of the nineteenth
century, was as far as possible removed from the mentality of
Metternich. He was suckled in the Whig religion of constitutional liberty, and though, as we have seen, under the stress of
the French war he found himself obliged to postpone the
enlargement of the franchise, never became a narrow or selfish
Tory. Like Disraeli afterwards, he divined the lamentable condition of the industrial poor. But for the King, he would have
had Catholic Irishmen sitting in the Parliament at Westminster,
and this fundamental generosity of outlook was shared by the
best of his successors, notably by Canning and Robert Peel and
Huskisson. Even the Duke of Wellington, the sternest of Tories,
was prepared in the end to assent to Parliamentary Reform.
The age of Metternich is not then a period of immobility in the
domestic history of England. On the contrary, it is one in which
great measures were passed, and great changes sanctioned, exhibiting the growing liberality of the English political mind.
Trades Unions were legalized in 1824, the tariff simplified in
1826. First the Protestant dissenters were admitted to office, then
the Catholics to the vote. Finally, the Reform Act of 1832,
passed in response to an overwhelming body of opinion in the
country, enfranchised the middle class, liberated the House of
Commons from aristocratic control, and led by a natural sequence
to the democratization of town government, to the reform of the
Poor Law, to the abolition of slavery, and to the removal of tariff
restrictions (1846) upon the food of the people. It is notable that
if Parliamentary Reform was carried out by a Whig, Catholic

Emancipation and Free Trade were brought in by Sir Robert Peel, a great Tory Minister, who was capable of adjusting his principles to the lesson of facts.

The peaceful acceptance by a domineering aristocracy of the democratic claims of an industrial age was largely due to the character of this strong Parliamentary statesman who for more than forty years (1809-50) strove in the forefront of the Tory battle. Home, school, and university combined to make Peel a Tory and to range him, when he entered Parliament in 1809, behind Liverpool and Wellington, the Tory leaders. But his was a mind powerful, honest, courageous, and "prone to receive the daily deposits of insensibly changing opinions." He moved slowly, for "he was converted with the conversion of the ordinary man," but he moved in the end and just in time, and, having once from conscience changed his convictions, had the nerve to speak his mind and to face what is always difficult for a born parliamentarian, the obloquy of the rank and file of his party. Most of the great measures which he either passed or accepted in middle age he had vehemently contested in his youth. He opposed, but afterwards himself carried, Catholic Emancipation and Free Trade. He opposed, but afterwards loyally accepted, the Reform Bill. In the Tamworth manifesto, which on the advice of Barnes, the editor of *The Times*, he issued to his constituents after the great defeat of his party on Parliamentary Reform, he announced a new life for a party no longer Tory, but Conservative. "My object," he explained in May, 1838, "for some years past has been to lay the foundations of a great party which, existing in the House of Commons and deriving its strength from the popular will, should deaden the shock between the two antagonistic branches of the legislature." This, then, was Peel's final contribution. Coming into office in 1841 at the head of a ministry of unparalleled ability, he made his government the instrument of a series of important social enquiries and reforms. If England during the latter part of the nineteenth century became a cheap place to live in, if her trade was world-wide, and the whole world was her granary, if a deficit had been turned into a surplus by the reduction of import duties, if her banking and currency had been placed on a firm foundation and her legal system relieved from many of the worst defects which had been pointed out by Jeremy Bentham, the great benefactor of legislators all the world over, the result is not a little owing to "the extraordinary abilities and ordinary opinions" of Sir Robert Peel.

It was an unquiet and tumultuous time. In Ireland, always on the fringe of revolution, Daniel O'Connell was pressing the claims first of Catholic Emancipation and afterwards of Home Rule. In England Robert Owen was demonstrating in theory and *1771-1858* practice the beauties of socialism, to be followed by the Chartists agitating for the six points of their Charter (universal suffrage, payment of members, the ballot vote, the abolition of property qualifications, annual parliaments, and equal electoral districts) in the hopes that a strict numerical democracy would cure all evils. And finally, more powerful than all, there sprang upon the scene Richard Cobden, the inspired salesman of calico, whose *1804-1865* crusade against the Corn Laws, preached with incredible vehemence and force, won for England cheap bread and free trade. It was the great service of Peel that, avoiding the extreme views of the radical doctrinaires on the one hand, and braving the wrath of the squires and the rectors on the other, he steered his country down the middle way of liberal reform.

So, while the continent was shaken by revolution in 1830 and again in 1848, there was in England a smooth and tranquil enlargement of liberty and well-being. The English did not look far ahead. Great risks were run and much suffering was caused through deference to vested interests and unchecked economic appetites. But in the moments of real emergency the right action was taken. When revolution threatened, the middle class was admitted to power. An epidemic of cholera produced the first Public Health Act, a potato famine in Ireland helped Peel *1846* to abolish the Corn Laws. By the time of Metternich's fall England had a reformed Penal Code, a beginning of state-aided education, statutes to promote hygiene and to limit child labour, and a fiscal system which bore lightly on the poor. Parliamentary statesmanship, though it had failed to provide a standard of education of which an intelligent German, like the Prince Consort, could approve, had nevertheless laid the foundation of that great system of social services which, more than any other force, has preserved the country from revolution.

The triumph of Free Trade in England was a victory of town over country, of the new manufacturing over the old landlord interests, of a middle class which while furthering its own material advantage incidentally promoted the interests of the poor. It was not only the long purse of the millowner which decided the day for Free Trade. If rural England had been united against the fiscal revolution, the result might have been otherwise. But rural England was not united. Landlords were on one side, farm labourers and cottagers were on the other. It was not least among the controversial advantages of the Anti-Corn Law League that in "the hungry forties" Cobden and his followers were able to represent the landlord not as the friend but as the oppressor of the poor.

Inevitably the policy of the cheap loaf postulated a navy which could rule the waves. If it emptied the villages, it crowded the towns and brought in its train a great development of population needing more food and raw materials from overseas, more markets for its exports, and more ships wherewith to supply its wants. A wide Empire, a great mercantile marine, a powerful navy could alone guarantee the food supply of a people so unevenly distributed between agriculture and industry and so numerous that it was idle to suppose that the tilth and pasture of a small island could ever again, save at a cost too ruinous to contemplate, suffice for its support.

Expanding material prosperity spread a strong tide of optimism through the land in the years immediately succeeding the abolition of protection. The profligate George, the fatuous William 1837-1901 no longer shamed the throne. Victoria was queen, bringing youth, decorum, and good sense to the discharge of her office, and by the happy accident of her sex bringing also the severance of England from the unpopular entanglement of the Hanoverian Electorate. The first international exhibition was held in London in 1851, in an atmosphere of exhilaration and hope. Had not a young poet nine years earlier dreamed of seeing—

> the heavens fill with commerce, argosies of magic sails,
> Pilots of the purple twilight, dropping down with costly bales;

dreamed also of a time when—

> the war-drum throbbed no longer and the battle flags were furled
> In the Parliament of man, the Federation of the World.[1]

1841   But Europe was not ready for internationalism. The Free Trade doctrine of Adam Smith was countered by the reasoned Protection of Friedrich List, the German economist. The example of

---

[1] Poems by Alfred Tennyson. In two volumes. London, 1842. 12 mo.

England in opening her doors to the imports of all the world was not followed. On the contrary, the next two decades witnessed an explosion of militarist nationalism on the continent which shattered the work of the Congress of Vienna and killed for the time being all those civilized aspirations for a better and more harmonious international order which free traders and poets were prone to entertain.

BOOKS WHICH MAY BE CONSULTED

G. M. Trevelyan : British History in the Nineteenth Century. 1922.
J. L. Hammond : Age of the Chartists. 1930.
W. Bagehot : Sir Robert Peel. (Biographical Studies.) 1907.
G. M. Trevelyan : Lord Grey of the Reform Bill. 1929.
G. M. Trevelyan : Life of John Bright. 1925.
George Peel : Life of Sir Robert Peel. (Dict. Nat. Biography.)
H. W. C. Davis : Age of Grey and Peel. 1929.
E. Halévy : Histoire du Peuple Anglais au XIX siècle. Eng. tr., 1926-35.
G. T. Garratt : Lord Brougham. 1935.

CHAPTER XII

THE JULY MONARCHY

Strength and weakness of the Monarchy. Revival of Bonapartism. Louis Bonaparte. Socialism. St. Simon, Fourier, Proudhon, Louis Blanc. The revolution of February. The Second Republic. The Days of June. The Coup d'État of December. The age of Nationalities opens.

Feb., 1848

THE monarchy of Louis Philippe, after a life of eighteen years, perished as it had been born, in a Paris revolution. It was a government of many virtues, directed by a prudent, experienced, and laborious King, and served by statesmen of talent, integrity, and force. Casimir Périer and Thiers, Molé and Guizot, were Prime Ministers whose patriotism and ability have never been challenged. Though the suffrage was limited to a narrow circle of two hundred and fifty thousand electors, the parliamentary oratory of France was never richer in volume and splendour. Trade prospered, there was a beginning of railway development, the work of consolidating and extending the Algerian conquest continued. The two besetting temptations of the French people, internal revolution and wild foreign military adventure, were successfully repressed. In Guizot France possessed a scholar-statesman who understood the need and prepared the way for a general system of state-aided popular education. Yet, for all its excellent qualities, and real services to France, there was never a government which fell with so little regret.

1883-6

The death of the Duke of Orleans, the popular heir to the throne, in a carriage accident in 1842 was not in itself sufficient to account for the catastrophe. To a logical people like the French there was a fundamental flaw in a *régime* which was neither true monarchy, nor true republic, nor true Empire, but a hybrid, without the historical glamour of the legitimate crown, or the democratic appeal of the republic, or the military renown of the House of Bonaparte. The very virtues of the government were a cause of offence, its policy of compromise, its desire to keep on good terms with England, its avoidance of flashy foreign risks. Lamartine, the leader of the romantic movement in literature, summed up the verdict of the people in the deadly phrase "La France s'ennuie." The kind bourgeois King with his large "sentimental umbrella" and his obtrusive domestic virtues was condemned by the common citizen as a bore.

Graver and more creditable reasons lay in the background. Alienating the Church by its laicity in education, the government took no pains to conciliate the intellectuals. It would neither enlarge the franchise nor advance proposals for improving the condition of the people. While England under the Reform Act of 1832 made rapid progress along the pathway of liberal legislation, abolishing slavery, reforming town government, and remodelling the Poor Law, Guizot, who directed policy during the last eight years of Louis Philippe's reign, steadily resisted even the most moderate demand for the extensions of the suffrage. In the ferment of opinion which prevailed a policy of flat negation was bound in the end to lead to disaster.

Eventually two currents dashed themselves with fatal force against the fabric of this drab, cautious, and uninventive administration, of which J. S. Mill truly said that it was " wholly without the spirit of improvement and that it wrought almost exclusively through the meaner and more selfish impulses of mankind." The first was Bonapartist. As the years proceeded, what was painful and ruinous in the policy of the great Emperor was forgotten, the grinding tyranny of the conscription, the destruction of the flower of French manhood, the foreign invasions, and the loss of territory, while poets, pamphleteers, and historians combined to decorate the wonderful epic of French victory which was recalled by the very sound of his name. Even the story of the Hundred Days during which Napoleon had appealed to the Jacobin spirit in the provinces and to the liberal intelligence in Paris was counted to him for righteousness. While Béranger sang of his wars, and Victor Hugo celebrated his victories in the *Ode à la Colonne*, the memories and conversations of the exile at St. Helena, being arranged with a view to the future of his dynasty, presented the Empire as a transitional fabric, designed to promote liberalism and nationality, but ruined through the malice of the dynasts before it had been able to display the full measure of its beneficent quality. This view of the Empire, not as a despotic but as a liberal and democratic thing, steadily gained ground. The legend of the little corporal, who, carving his own way to fortune, toppled over throne after throne, and then died a martyr to British tyranny in a wind-swept island in the Atlantic.

built itself up with many affecting and pathetic circumstances in the heart of the people. When in 1840 the ashes of Napoleon were brought back to be buried at the Invalides in Paris the second Empire was as good as made.

A Pretender was at hand. Louis Bonaparte was the son of the King of Holland and Hortense Beauharnais his wife, the nephew of the Emperor, and since the death of the Duc de Reichstadt in 1832 the head of the Napoleonic House. He was a strange, studious, ruminating young man, full of dreams and expedients, and possessed by a firm conviction that he was destined to revive his uncle's line in France. Twice, first in 1836 and again in 1840, he had made a dash for the French Crown. Twice he had experienced humiliating failure. Ridicule did not abash him or failure divert him from his course. In 1848 he was a needy exile in London, having seen life from many sides—as a *carbonaro* in Italy, as a fugitive in the United States, as a prisoner in Ham, as a journalist and pamphleteer—yet still nursing his imperial dream. In a little volume entitled *Idées Napoléoniennes* he had announced the entire programme of a Liberal Empire.

The second current was Republican and Socialist. The philosophy of 1789 had been egalitarian in its conception of political and personal rights, but had not attempted to abolish private property, nor to protect the artisan's standard of comfort, nor to interfere with the liberty of industrial exploitation. Trades unions were included in the general aversion from corporations as instruments of privilege which characterized the thought of that time, and since all associations were condemned, the artisan was deprived of the benefits which flow from the use of the strike or from the fixed habit of collective bargaining. These individualist ideas were now, however, fast giving way to a new view of society. The Assemblies of the Revolution had freed men from the fetters of privilege, but had left the problem of poverty as formidable and as unresolved as ever. The question was then asked whether poverty was really necessary or whether it was not possible so to reorganize society as to give to all, if not an equal, a reasonable, share of the world's material wealth. A remarkable body of political literature, which exercised a wide influence through Europe, grew up round this eternal problem. The followers of Saint-Simon preached universal peace, the abolition of the hereditary principle, the international organization of labour, and a system of distribution to each according to his capacity. Fourier proposed to abolish the State and to substitute *phalansteries*, or working cells. Louis Blanc advocated national workshops. Proudhon threw into the discussion the famous and dangerous epigram that "Property is theft." The words Socialism (invented by Pierre Lerroux in 1838) and Communism were minted and swiftly passed into the common currency.[1] An idea spread abroad in the lower ranges of Parisian society that a great upheaval was at hand when the valet would drink his master's wine and the lady's maid go in her mistress's finery. Amid much that was fantastic and violent one practical idea of far-reaching value was evolved. It is expressed in the title of a popular treatise written by Louis Blanc in 1837, *The Organization of Industry*: in place of the *laissez-faire* of Liberalism the *savoir-faire* of socialist doctrine.

Socialism, which is as old as poverty itself, takes different forms in different minds. To some it is the suffusion of industrial life by humane and Christian principles, to others the equalization of wealth and opportunity, to others again the public ownership and control of land and the instruments of production, while others—the disciples of Karl Marx—advocate the dictatorship of the proletariat to be won as the prize of a class war. There is guild socialism, municipal socialism, national socialism, in accordance with the view taken of the body most fitted to organize and direct industrial enterprise. To some, most logical of all, national socialism is not enough. These thinkers note the uneven geographical distribution of natural power throughout the world—in Europe, England, Lorraine, the Ruhr, Silesia; in America, Pittsburg. They ask whether it is just, for instance, that the raw materials for the equipment of a modern army should be available in Japan and not in China, or that Roumania and not Italy should have oil, and fail to see how world peace can be secured without some planned international distribution of the world's resources. In a word, they are international socialists. Soon after the end of the Great War, when American and English coal was selling at famine prices in Italy, an Italian delegate to the League of Nations advocated the international ownership of coal and other raw materials of industry.

Whatever form of socialism be preferred, the reorganization of industry on humane and scientific principles is obviously a task requiring the protracted and combined labour of many patient

[1] In England the word Socialist, used to denote a follower of Robert Owen, appears in the Co-operative Magazine for 1827.

and intelligent minds. The French socialist writers threw new ideas into the air and supplied to discontent an intellectual authority. What they did not do, and were not given time to do, was to prepare the minds of an experienced political class to work out concrete proposals. The revolution was upon them before they could school a generation of disciples. Heine has described the fiery atmosphere of Paris in 1842. "To-day," he wrote to a German newspaper, "when I visited some of the factories in the Faubourg Saint Marceau and discussed there what kind of reading matter was being spread among the working men, who are the most powerful element among the working classes, I thought of Sancho's proverb, 'Tell me what you have sown to-day and I will predict to you what you will reap to-morrow.' For here in the workshops I found several new editions of speeches by old Robespierre, Marat's pamphlets at two sous a copy, Cabet's *History of the Revolution*, Cormenin's poisonous little works, and Buonarotti's *Baboeuf's Doctrine and Conspiracy*—all writings which smell of blood. The songs which I heard them singing seem to have been composed in hell and had a chorus of the wildest excitement. Really people in our gentle walk of life can have no idea of the demonic note which runs through these songs. One must hear them with one's own ears—for example, in those enormous workshops where metals are worked and where the half-naked, defiant figures keep time to their songs with the mighty blows which their great iron hammers strike upon the ringing anvil. . . . Sooner or later the harvest which will come from the sowing in France threatens to be a republican outbreak." It is clear from Heine's words that what was in the minds of the Paris workers was not a Fabian or scientific transformation of society, but a violent and bloodthirsty political revolt.

In the summer holiday of 1847, Odilon Barrot, the liberal leader, having failed in the Chamber to extract concessions from the government, counselled a campaign in the country for Parliamentary reform. Banquets were held, speeches were delivered, toasts (not always loyal) were drunk. In a *crescendo* of defiance the demand was made that Guizot should be dismissed, that the Parliament should be purged of placemen, and that the franchise should be extended. Prominent among the orators was the romantic figure of Lamartine, the favourite poet, historian, and orator of France, the Adonis of every salon, and the prophet of republican idealism. The government resisted the appeal, forbade a banquet, and suddenly found itself confronted with a reformist riot in Paris, which by a sharp and unexpected turn of fortune, hinging perhaps on the chance volley of a frightened patrol, developed into a formidable republican rising.

It was on February 24, 1848, the second day of the street fighting, when the barricades were up in the workmen's quarters and *Vive la Réforme* had given place to *Vive la République*, that the King, very old, tired and humane, finding that the National Guard was against him and auguring wrongly that France was behind the National Guard, lost nerve, abdicated in favour of his grandson, and bolted to the safe refuge of a Surrey villa. As Louis Philippe faded out of France, Louis Bonaparte stepped in, a man of forty, at once mystic and Lothario, looking like an opium eater, and speaking French like a foreigner. A little later, finding the moment unpropitious, but having adroitly advertised his existence, he withdrew to England to await his call.

For the second time a revolution in Paris had determined the fate of France, but now it was a revolution which liberalism was unable to capture or direct. Under the violent pressure of the mob a Republic was proclaimed, and pending the summoning of a constituent assembly a provisional government was named in two newspaper offices, one socialist, the other radical, to administer the affairs of the country. The difficulties of the situation which confronted this small body of untried and widely differing men were immense. The city was in a state of delirious excitement, vast schemes of social organization being demanded by some, while others with equal fury and insistence called for an instant war against the tyrants of Europe. It is to the credit of Lamartine, the pacific Foreign Minister, that he refused to substitute the red flag for the tricolor and in place of a dangerous military crusade contented himself for the moment with a liberal manifesto. The social revolution was kept at bay by a brave but disastrous promise of employment for all, and by the establishment of national workshops for the relief of the unemployed.

The new Assembly was to be elected by universal suffrage. A truth was then discovered which, had it been divined by Louis Philippe and his ministers, might have saved the monarchy. In a land of peasant proprietors universal suffrage may well yield not a radical but a conservative result. An electorate of two hundred thousand well-to-do bourgeois guaranteed neither loyalty in the Chamber nor confidence in the country, encouraged corruption, aroused jealousies, deadened enthusiasm. But universal suffrage would have been for the monarchy a gilt-edged investment. On its first application after the revolution of February, the poll being the heaviest on record, it returned a Chamber of bourgeois, in which the republicans were only as one to eight. To the members of this Parliament, the first to be elected in France on such a system and therefore the first to reflect in adequate measure the antique pieties of the countryside, it was a matter of life and death to conquer the red peril in Paris. How precarious their position was, despite the tremendous weight and authority of the provincial vote, revealed itself on May 15, when a mob invaded the Chamber, decreed its dissolution, and declared war against the Kings of Europe. A desperate situation was then saved by the timely appearance and correct behaviour of the National Guard; but what if the attack were repeated? It was decided to grapple firmly with the evil at its source and, as a first step, to close the national workshops which had been running at a ruinous loss and had been the means of attracting a vast concourse of unemployed men into Paris. Upon that stern and necessary decision there ensued a struggle in the streets of Paris which suffices to explain, such was the deep horror which it inspired, the surprising political manifestations of the ensuing months. For four torrid June days the regulars and National Guard under General Cavaignac fought an insurrection, so formidable and desperate, though it was conducted without leaders and apparently without premeditation, that ten thousand casualties were the price of victory. The vast majority of the French population, having property in land or in the funds, acclaimed the triumph of the army, noted the scale of the peril and demanded of their future governors so to rule that the red spectre should not again dare to raise its head.

In the midst of these dreadful anxieties the Assembly produced a preposterous constitution, organized for deadlock and manacled against change. The new Republic was equipped with the rival autocracy of a single Chamber and a President, each elected by universal suffrage. The inspiration of America was obvious; but it was forgotten that while the powers of the American President are limited by the rights of the States of the Union, the new President of the French Republic, who was to be chosen for four years and not to be re-eligible, would be master of a bureaucracy which interfered with the life of every town and village in the land.

In the plébiscite which ensued (December 10, 1848) Louis Bonaparte was returned head of the poll, by more than four million votes, above Cavaignac the saviour of society, above Lamartine the orator, and despite his thirty-nine years of shabby inglorious exile. The name of Bonaparte was enough, standing in every cottage of the land for discipline, power, and renown.

Yet he was not a free agent, but confronted by a Chamber, fresh from the polls, conservative in complexion, and prepared, if Legitimists and Orleanists could compose their differences, to restore the monarchy; a Chamber in which he had no personal following and from which he could expect no loyal or enduring support. A liberal and nationalist by temperament he was compelled to trim his sails to clerical and conservative winds, and, abjuring his past as an Italian *Carbonaro*, to send aid to the Pope against the Roman Republic. The *coup d'état* of December 2, 1851, was his stroke for liberty and power. By that contrivance of consummate force and fraud, breaking an oath, violating a constitution, imprisoning many leading soldiers and politicians, and shooting some twelve hundred innocent citizens in the streets of Paris, Louis Bonaparte made himself master of France. The Chamber was dissolved, its members were imprisoned or dispersed, his own lease of power was prolonged; and yet, though the coup was denounced by Victor Hugo and Tennyson, on "the morrow of it," as has been well said, "Louis Napoleon appeared not as a tyrant but as a tyrannicide." As against the Chamber which had voted itself a salary, disfranchised three million electors by an electoral law the full consequences of which were perhaps not perceived, and refused revision, the President appeared well justified. "The people," said Broglie, "has the government it prefers and the bourgeoisie the government it deserves." To the Sardinian Minister the Prince President, who was now Emperor in all but name, observed, "Now I can do what I want. I shall do something for Italy."

A new page of European history was about to unroll itself, marked by the triumph of nationalism, with its brilliant idealism, its disciplined citizenship, its vivid political interests, but also with its blind passions, its great conscript armies, its wars of extermination, its standing threat to international harmony and peace. In the initial stages of that great movement of the human spirit, which has brought new perils into Europe, Louis Bonaparte played a decisive rôle. After attacking European reaction where it was at its worst in Russia, the author of the crime of December more than half achieved the union and the liberty of Italy.

BOOKS WHICH MAY BE CONSULTED

H. A. L. Fisher : Bonapartism. 1909.
Guizot : Mémoires. 1864.
E. L. Woodward : Studies in European Conservatism. 1929.
Lowes Dickinson : Revolution and Reaction in Modern France. 1892.
Louis Blanc : Ateliers Nationaux. *Ed.* Marriott. 1913.
H. Heine : Letters to the Augsburger Allgemeine Zeitung, 1840-3.
Odilon Barrot : Mémoires. 1875-6.
F. A. Simpson : The Rise of Louis Napoleon.
P. Guedalla : The Second Empire. 1932.
A. de Tocqueville : Souvenirs. *Tr.* 1896.
L. Blanc : Histoire de Dix Ans. 1843-5.
P. Thureau Dangin. Histoire de la monarchie de juillet. 1884-92.

CHAPTER XIII

THE RISORGIMENTO

Italy in ferment. Pio Nono. The Republican tradition. Mazzini. The Sardinian contribution. The Roman Republic. Venice and Manin.

EVEN before the fall of the French monarchy the fire of revolution which was destined to make 1848 a memorable year in Italian history was crackling among the rotten government timbers in Sicily and Naples. In that spring, as the flame spread northwards, constitutions came down in showers from the trembling hands of penitent or dissembling princes. The revolution touched Rome and Turin, Leghorn and Pisa, Florence and Milan, and when the news came that Vienna was in the hands of the mob and that Metternich himself had at last been chased from power, even unwarlike Venice took heart under Manin, seized the arsenal, and proclaimed a Republic.

In this wide revolt against prevailing conditions the primary and most generally shared emotion was the desire for those elementary political and civil liberties which belonged to England and had been secured by France, and of which, under the despotic but yet innovating and enlightened rule of Napoleon, the whole Italian population had been given a fleeting glimpse. To be free from police espionage, from arbitrary imprisonment, from an obscurantist censorship of newspapers and books, from harassing restrictions on travel, and, in those regions in which the rule of Austria prevailed, from a ruthless system of conscription which dragged the *contadino* from the village to serve in a foreign army and in distant lands, these were aspirations which Italians, otherwise differing in their political outlook, might agree to cherish. Italian unity was a different matter, for this involved as a preliminary step the expulsion of the Austrians by force of arms from Lombardy and Venetia, and at once raised the grave question how Italy thus liberated should be organized. It was because no single and certain answer could be given to this question in 1848, because some desired a federation under the Pope, others a unitary republic, and others again a monarchy under the Sardinian house, that the miscarriage of the Italian revolution in this year of turmoil and opportunity is principally to be attributed.

To most Italians the hopes of Italian liberation seemed at first to depend upon the rare and engaging portent of a liberal Pope. After the harsh tyranny of Gregory XVI there succeeded in the summer of 1846 a Pope who, having the heart of an Italian and a reformer, shone out the more brilliantly not only by reason of the contrast which he presented to his predecessor, but also because his spirit was in tune with a widely prevailing and honourable mood of liberal Catholicism at that time. All Italy was soon apprised that Pio Nono (Pius IX) had amnestied patriotic Italians who had been condemned to prison for political offences, that he had protested against the Austrian occupation of Ferrara, a town in his own dominions, that he had set up a civic guard, and that he was taking in hand the reformation of government in the Papal State. To many a devout Italian peasant and landowner the intelligence that the Pope was a reformer was a sufficient warrant that reform was good; and though the reforming zeal of the Pope was wildly exaggerated and was soon effectively checked by the course of events, it is difficult to overrate the advantage which his preliminary association with the reforming movement secured for the Liberal cause. Many conservatives who, had it not been for Pio Nono, would never have been drawn into the national movement at all, remained staunch to the cause of Italy after the Pope had abandoned it. Indeed, it may even be doubted whether the movement of Italian nationalism would ever have assumed such proportions as to make of the Italian problem one of the foremost political questions in Europe, had it not been for the original benediction of the Pope.

The enthusiasts for Italian liberty failed to foresee what was in fact inevitable, that the spiritual head of the Catholic Church could never encourage a war against the chief Catholic Power in Europe. Pio Nono cannot be blamed for declining (Allocution of April, 1848) to make war on Austria. Had he done so, he would have risked the defection of the German Catholics and compromised the unity of the Catholic Church. None the less his refusal to have part or lot in an Austrian war was rightly regarded at the time as a grave blow to the Italian cause, for of all the plans then put forward for Italian liberation a federation under Papal Rome was the least impracticable. Indeed, seeing that the union of Italy could not have been otherwise made in 1848, patriotic Italians and devout Catholics may rejoice together that the plans for making it were then frustrated.

Republicanism was a tradition deeply rooted in Italian soil, but it was a republicanism of the city, not of the nation, and consequently a memory which made for political disharmony rather than for national union. It was the office of Mazzini, the *1805-72* anti-clerical son of a Genoese doctor, to change the quality and direction of the nation's thought by preaching with rare and single-minded devotion the doctrine of the Republic one and indivisible. Mazzini is the saint of the Italian republican movement. That his country should ever accept the rule of a king, whether Neapolitan or Sardinian, seemed to him impossible, for the Neapolitan he knew to be corrupt and the Sardinian he judged to be retrograde. A republic alone, linked in perpetual and pacific bonds with free republics all over the world, was worthy of Italy. The dream was chimerical; characteristic of a conspirator whose hand was against all governments and who, like most liberals in '48, put his faith not in battlefield decisions but in the power of enthusiasm and reason to bring men to see political perfection. Yet if the Austrian white-coats needed something sharper and more material to expel them from Italy, it must not be concluded that Mazzini's life was a failure. The moral fervour of the nationalist movement was largely due to the teaching of this exalted visionary and of the Association of Italian Youth which he founded in 1831 in a garret in Marseilles to promote his ideas.

Meanwhile the heart of the Italian problem was the presence of the Austrians in Lombardy and Venetia. It was useless to talk of Italian unity so long as old Marshal Radetzky, with 75,000 white-coats and the strong fortresses of the Quadrilateral, dominated the situation in the north. The idea that such an army led by such a commander could be defeated by the untrained irregulars of the republican faith was shown in the event to be very wide of the truth. There was only one possible nucleus round which an effective and organized resistance to the foreign army of occupation could be organized, and that was the army of the Sardinian Kingdom. Naples and the Pope proved broken reeds. Such potential military resources as might have been latent in the province of Venetia were left undeveloped. Even the Lombards after the famous days of May, when the population rose

against their Austrian garrison and expelled it with heavy losses
played but a secondary rôle in the military operations of the
campaign. But the army of Charles Albert, slow though it was to
enter the fray and slow to grasp its opportunities, offered by so
much the most effective challenge to the enemy that when all was
over, after the army had been beaten at Custozza and Novara
and the broken-hearted king had abdicated his throne and fled
to a Portuguese exile, no doubt could be entertained by any
sensible man that it was from Piedmont if anywhere that the
liberation of Italy would proceed. If the army of the little sub-
Alpine kingdom had been ill led by its morbid self-tormenting
sovereign, at least it had fought to a finish and endured disproportionate sacrifices in a cause which concerned the whole Italian
people. This was not all. When Charles Albert abdicated, he left
his successor, Victor Emmanuel, to rule in Turin over a country
which, though beaten in war, had received in the *Statuto* the
blessings of a liberal constitution, so durable that it survived till
the days of Mussolini and so well-contrived that it provided a
framework within which Piedmont was able to become, under
the masterly guidance of Cavour, the most modern and progressive State in Italy.

Meanwhile the Risorgimento pursued a dramatic and memorable course in the famous cities of Rome and Venice. Pio Nono's
April Allocution had been an intimation to the world that a
Pope could take no further part in the unification of Italy. It
followed as a necessary consequence in nationalist logic that the
papal territories must be governed by a lay authority as an integral part of the new Italian State. It was hopeless to talk of a
United Italy if there intervened between the north and the south
the dominion of a temporal sovereign who discountenanced the
war of liberation and might feel himself free to support the Austrian enemy. The brutal logic of the new situation was felt by the
brutal Roman mob. Rossi, the enlightened minister whom Pio
Nono had summoned to his counsels, was murdered in open day
(November 5, 1848), and the Pope, fleeing to Gaeta from a situation which he was no longer able to control, left the Roman revolution to run its course.

The events which followed printed a deep mark on the
imagination of Italy. A Constituent Assembly was summoned
which deposed the Pope from his temporal power, proclaimed a
Roman Republic, and set up a triumvirate with Mazzini at its

head to govern the Roman State. Such an enterprise conducted in plain defiance of the Catholic Church and of the secular States which might arm in its support was doomed to disaster. A Roman Republic, however brilliantly defended, could not expect to prevail against a French Prince President angling for Catholic votes or an Austrian Emperor bent on recovering his supremacy in Italy. In fact, the Republic was crushed by the French (June 30, 1849). Yet though its life was short, the Roman Republic was for two reasons a memorable episode. "It was essential," wrote Mazzini afterwards, " to redeem Rome; to place her once again at the summit, so that Italians might again learn to regard her as the temple of their common country." Here was a flash of true political discernment. The establishment of the Roman Republic, which was defended with a fine light-hearted Italian gallantry against Oudinot's disciplined French army, awoke in the minds of the Italian people the idea that Rome might again become their political capital, an idea not realized until 1870, but ever since 1848 present to the political consciousness of that part of the population which cherished nationalist ambitions. Another reason has made the Roman Republic memorable in the annals of the Risorgimento. The defence was conducted by Garibaldi. *1807-82* This great blond leader of irregular troops, who hated priests, worshipped liberty and had returned from a wild life in South America to help to make his beloved Italy a free republic, now with his following of shaggy red-shirts burst into the very heart and centre of the Italian drama. Of political wisdom Garibaldi was utterly devoid. He was neither a master of Italian letters like Mazzini nor a profound statesman like Cavour, but as a daring captain of irregular troops and as a leader capable of inspiring rough followers with the elements of a simple and passionate political faith he had a certain Homeric grandeur. Four thousand volunteers, rather than capitulate to an enemy on Italian soil, followed Garibaldi out of Rome; and his retreat across Italy, with its many romantic episodes and tragic close, secured for him the confidence and admiration of Italian patriots.

The Venetian Republic, though it held out against its besiegers till October 24, 1849, had no real chance of survival after the Sardinian defeat at Novara (March 23). The lesson of the campaign was not lost upon Manin, the brilliant lawyer of *1804-57* Hebrew extraction who had been the soul of the Venetian defence and the guiding spirit of the Republic. It was clear to him through the failure of the movements in Rome and Venice that Italy was not to be unified on the Mazzinian plan, but only by the Sardinian Kingdom with the support of France. Charles Albert's doctrine that Italy could manage for herself had been exploded on two stricken fields. Isolationism was dead; so too was the idea that a strong regular army could be routed by republican guerillas. A new spirit of patriotic opportunism entered into the politics of the national party, replacing the improvident ardours which had led to the fiasco of the '48. Of this effacement of republican enthusiasm during the fifties there is no better illustration than the conversion of Manin, the creator of the Venetian Republic, to the idea of an alliance between Victor Emmanuel and Napoleon III.

BOOKS WHICH MAY BE CONSULTED

Bolton King : A History of Italian Unity. 1924.
G. M. Trevelyan : Manin and the Venetian Revolution of 1848. 1923
G. M. Trevelyan : Garibaldi. 1933.
W. R. Thayer : The Dawn of Italian Independence. 1893.
Mazzini : Essays, translated by T. Okey. 1894.
E. L. Woodward : Three Studies in European Conservatism. 1929.
J. A. Hübner : Une année de ma vie. 1848-91.

CHAPTER XIV

AUSTRIA AND GERMANY IN REVOLUTION

*Metternich's Austria. Kossuth. Democratic revolution. Slavonic and
Magyar aspirations. Reaction in Bohemia and Hungary. Victories of
Windischgrätz and Jellaçic. Statecraft of Schwarzenberg. The German
revolution. The catastrophe of Liberalism. The Parliament of Frankfort decides for the exclusion of Austria and the rejection of republicanism. Frederick William IV. Reaction triumphs in Berlin. Rivalry
between Prussia and Austria. Austria triumphs at Olmütz. Otto von
Bismarck. The Prussian philosophy of the State.*

THE government of the Austrian Empire, though sweetened by
negligence and frivolity, was slow, secret, arbitrary, and confused.
It was so tightly wrapped in layer upon layer of formalism, and
had been so effectively screened from the spirit of improvement,
that anomalies and abuses which had long been eradicated in the
West here flourished in undiminished vigour. While the nobility
of Austria and Hungary enjoyed every form of anti-social privilege, while they were exempt from military service, relieved of
taxation, and placed beyond the reach of the common law courts, *1835-c*
the peasantry were hard bound in the fetters of mediaeval subjection. Emperors came and went. The unintelligent Francis was
succeeded in 1835 by the imbecile Ferdinand. The peasant question, which involved a radical reconstruction of the local government of the Empire, was left unsolved. *Quieta non movere* was
the maxim of Austrian statesmanship under Metternich. A
police the most repressive and inquisitorial in Europe spied into
everything and endeavoured to defend the lively Viennese from
the insidious poisons of Western thought.

A system of this kind cannot last for ever. New formations of
opinion, sceptical and derisive, liberal and constructive, racial and
combative, began to manifest themselves as early as the thirties.
In Vienna it became the intellectual fashion to deride the
Government. Racialism rushed in with a sweep from Poland;
liberalism like a fine rain filtered through from Paris and
London. In Pressburg the Hungarian Diet drove forward with
its demand for the use of the Magyar language instead of Latin
in debate and for a comprehensive scheme of social reforms;
and as the racial temperature rose in Hungary it mounted also in

those areas of the Hungarian Kingdom which were inhabited by non-Magyar races, among the Croatians and Serbs of the south, among the Rouman peasants of Transylvania in the east, among the Ruthenes of the north and the Slovaks of the west, and stirred to a new point of impatience and aspiration the literary and antiquarian nationalism which in Bohemia was assuming a political shape among the Czechs. The archpriest of the new crusades was 1802-94 Louis Kossuth, whose brilliant powers as orator and journalist, first directed towards securing the substitution of Magyar for Latin in the Hungarian Diet and afterwards deployed in a passionate campaign for Hungarian independence, awoke in every part of the Empire the latent flames of a furious and disruptive racialism. By the spring of 1848 this powerful demagogue had been for eight years preaching his radical and nationalist doctrines to assemblies of his haughty and tempestuous fellow-countrymen.

Upon a Government thus corroded and assailed the shock of the February revolution in Paris fell with a shattering force. One day's riot (March 13, 1848) led by professors and students and supported by civilians put an end to the rule of Metternich, gave Vienna to the people, and dislocated for the time being the central administrative instrument of imperial rule.

Thereupon the difficulties peculiar to the composite Austrian State began to reveal themselves. Autocracy had capitulated. A Central Committee for the defence of popular rights ruled in Vienna. The old ministers had been cleared away. A parliament elected by universal suffrage for all Austria, Hungary excepted, was engaged on a Constitution. The main part of the army was busy in Italy. The cleansing tides of liberalism which were sweeping through Germany had touched all the capitals of the Austrian Empire, creating in the minds of educated men a common desire for constitutional or parliamentary government, for civil liberties, for the redress of peasant grievances, and for an end of autocracy. In such circumstances a thorough transformation of the Austrian State upon liberal and constitutional lines seemed to be entirely feasible. The spirit was hopeful, the good-will abounding, the moment apparently propitious.

In Prague and Pressburg as well as in Vienna there was an eager and confident expectation that in the abeyance of the Imperial power great and salutary reforms could be carried through; nor was that expectation altogether falsified. It is to the credit of

the men of '48, acting both in the Austrian and Hungarian legislatures, that they tackled the rural question boldly, that they
abolished the peasant servitudes and the legal distinctions between nobles and commons, and that in the course of a single
month they did more permanent good to the rural population of
the Austrian Empire than had been achieved since the days of
Maria Theresa.

But over this fair prospect of constitutional progress there
spread swiftly a terrible shadow. It was the special weakness of
the Austrian Empire and the strongest argument against innovation that to the grievances of individuals and of classes there was
added the factor of racial discord. No sooner, therefore, was the
constitutional question raised in Austria than every race began to
stake out for itself a position of safety in the new ground plan of
the Austrian State. The Court was powerless to resist or even to
influence these formidable developments. The control of the
army and foreign policy was granted to Hungary; to the Bohemians the promise of an independent legislature and local
institutions.

A new series of issues of far-ranging importance was at once
raised. There were many Germans in the Austrian Empire who
were well content to see power transferred from a secret Committee of Imperial Ministers to a free parliament elected on a
wide suffrage, so long as the predominant direction of policy
remained in German hands; but there were few who contemplated with equanimity the secession of Hungary or a constitution under which the Slavs of the Empire would exert an
authority corresponding to their numerical preponderance. Bohemian constitutionalism was all very well, but what German
could look with favour upon a Pan-Slavic Conference summoned
to Prague on June 2 to consider the possibilities of a union of all
the Slavonic races? Such a union, could it be effected, would
spell the immediate dissolution of the Empire. Ever since the
seventeenth century the subjection of the Bohemian Czechs had
been a corner-stone of Austrian policy, a prime condition of internal peace. That this peasant race, with its heretic traditions
and under the leadership of a few poets, philologists, and romantics should now aspire, not only to enjoy Home Rule, but to become the citadel of Slavonic influences and propaganda throughout the Empire was regarded by German Austrians, who had not
lost their old imperial pride, as a pretension at all costs to be

abated. Hungarian Home Rule stood upon a somewhat different footing, for the Hungarians had always been a ruling, never a subject, race; but that the Hungarians should be allowed to have an independent army, an independent paper currency, and an independent foreign policy was rightly regarded as a serious blow to the unity of the Empire and a palpable deduction from its strength. The miscarriage of the revolution was due to the fact that it brought such policies as these in its wake.

Reaction set in towards midsummer. On June 17, 1848, Prince Windischgrätz turned his guns upon the city of Prague and with one resolute cannonade, postponing for seventy years the realization of Czech liberties, crushed the Bohemian rebellion. Heartened by this triumph and with good news flowing in from Naples and Rome and from the victorious field of Custozza, the Court addressed itself to the far more serious problem of dealing with the Hungarians. In this enterprise, the natural difficulties of which were aggravated by the anarchical condition of Vienna, the Imperial Government was assisted by the desperate unpopularity of the Magyars among the Slavs and Roumanians, and more particularly in Croatia, the region in the Hungarian Kingdom in which the Slavs were best organized, most advanced in civilization, and most warlike. The feeling between Croat and Magyar had never been cordial; and at the Diet of Agram, which was the Croatian parliament, violent protests were wont to be made against the forcible adoption of the Magyar tongue. To turn the Croat against the Magyar, to invite the Slavonic and Roumanian inhabitants to pay back, with usury, the heavy debt of injuries which they had received from the dominant race, was no doubt a hateful policy; yet it was to this policy that the Austrian Government was driven, and to this policy that it owed its continued existence.

The anti-Magyar spirit of the Croatians was embodied in the person of Josef Jellaçić, a colonel of the Austrian army who wanted nothing so much as to force the Magyars into war, to crush them in the field of battle, and to restore the authority of the Empire. The Imperial Government was sensible of the value of this popular Croatian soldier, whose word alone was sufficient to ensure the loyalty of the Croatian troops serving in Italy and at whose behest the Croatians might be trusted to go forward against their Hungarian foes. Despite the protest of the Magyar leaders, Jellaçić was appointed Ban of Croatia and proceeded to march upon Pesth at the head of forty thousand men. War was now inevitable, and as the war passion mounted, Kossuth with his following of democrats seized the helm of state in Hungary, provoking at once a violent tremor of sympathy among the liberals of Vienna, who, seeing that Hungary was safely placed in the charge of radicals, regarded an active alliance between the two armed democracies as the last chance of saving the cause of liberty. But the forces of Austria were altogether too strong for their opponents. While Windischgrätz easily put down the Viennese, Jellaçić defeated on the plain of Schwechat a Hungarian force which was marching to their relief.

Oct. 30, 1848

With that double triumph reaction flowed back with a swelling tide. There was an end of democracy in Vienna, an end of constitutional progress, and with the execution of Robert Blum, a delegate from Frankfort, a sharp reminder to the Germans that Austria was set upon a backward course. The army had saved the Empire from disruption, and from the army there emerged a remarkable statesman by whose vigorous and daring initiative victory was driven home and secured in the constitution of the state; Count Felix Schwarzenberg came upon the scene in 1849 and died in 1852. In those three years this haughty and aspiring aristocrat procured the resignation of the imbecile Ferdinand, called Francis Joseph, his young and vigorous nephew, to the throne, broke with the help of a Russian army the Hungarian revolt, centralized the institutions of the Empire, and braving the risks of a Prussian war restored the old predominance of the Austrian Empire in the German Federation in accordance with the treaty of 1815.

Dec. 2, 1848

The emotions of western Europe were deeply stirred by the tragedy of the Hungarians, who, if they had acted oppressively towards their subject peoples, were yet in their traditional practice of public discussion, as in their passionate and tenacious struggle for personal liberty and responsible government, members of the fellowship of progress and freedom. As the valiant campaigns of Görgei and Bem, and the courageous radicalism of Kossuth, under whose guidance the Hungarians had established a republic, were followed with admiration, so the news of the capitulation of Villagos and of the terrible penalties which were exacted from the defeated army were received with indignation and horror. In the very excess of the Austrian triumph were seeds of future trouble. Not least among the causes which

Aug. 14, 1849

secured popular support in England for the Crimean War was the feeling of resentment against Russia for the sinister part which she had played in stamping out Hungarian liberties and in riveting the old Austrian fetters upon the Italian and German peoples.

In Germany, where there was no racial problem and no question of expelling foreign tyrants, the revolutionary impulse, which was as strong here as in Austria and Italy, assumed a unitary and liberal form. Though there were republicans, more especially in the south-west, and these heady and warlike, the party of the republic was in a clear minority. Most Germans were at the beginning of 1848 reformers, most reformers were liberals, and most liberals were believers in German unity. Distrusting the capacity or the willingness of the German Princes to grant constitutional reforms, and despairing of the Diet, they believed that Germany could be unified on liberal lines only through a Parliament of the whole German nation freely elected and entirely independent of the cumbrous and ineffectual assembly of delegates which had been imposed upon the country by the Congress of Vienna. Encouraged by the overthrow of Louis Philippe and without guarantees of support from the Princes, the leaders of German liberalism summoned a preliminary Parliament to meet at Frankfort to prepare for the election of a national assembly out of which it was hoped that a new Germany would arise through the peaceful process of discussion. That Assembly met on May 18, 1848. It contained some of the finest characters and noblest minds in Germany. It was patriotic, ambitious, laborious, quick to resent foreign injuries, solicitous to extend German power, and notable as having created the original nucleus of a German navy. After elaborate discussions characterized by a high seriousness it produced a democratic constitution for united Germany, of which there was no feature more valuable than a long array of scrupulous provisions for the protection of personal liberty. Yet its work was in vain. It is one of the tragedies of modern history that this Assembly, launched on a vast surge of national enthusiasm, was unable to accomplish its self-appointed task, and that the union of Germany was achieved, not by the give and take of Parliamentary argument, but by the blood and iron of civil and foreign war.

The causes of this catastrophe to German liberalism have now briefly to be enumerated. The Assembly, though it reflected the best mind of the learned, official and professional classes, failed adequately to represent either the nobles or the wage-earners or the big interests in business or finance. Defective in these respects and lacking tradition and party discipline, the Parliament was at once confronted with two problems of enormous complexity and hardly admitting at that time of a pacific solution. What was to be the shape of the new Germany? Should it include the whole Austrian Empire, or only that part of it which was German, or was even German Austria to be left outside the framework of the German state? The first question was readily answered in the negative. It was no great sacrifice to German legislators to decline to admit into the German family the Czechs, the Magyars, the Croats, and the Roumanians who were subject to the Austrian Crown. But to the proposal that German Austria should be shorn off from Germany there were at once violent and serious objections. How, it was argued, could it be tolerated that eight million men and women of German race and German speech should be cut out of the German *Reich*? The idealists who aspired to a pan-German state, the Roman Catholics who wanted their faith to be strengthened, the governments of the smaller states who were accustomed to look to Austria as a shield against the unpopular Prussians, were all ranged in opposition to the proposal. So formidable was the question felt to be that for the first five months the Parliament avoided the discussion of the framework of the future German Government. When everything depended on speed the legislators of Frankfort deliberately marked time. There was a second problem almost equally desperate. Germany was a federation of sovereign states each passionately concerned with the jealous maintenance of its rights and prerogatives. A new and stricter German Union could be reached only if the member states were willing to acquiesce in some curtailment of their sovereign powers. But would such a spirit of abnegation prevail? If it could be expected in the small states, would it be forthcoming in the monarchies? The Frankfort Parliament saw that it would get nowhere by the method of separately consulting the thirty-eight governments of the German Union. The delays would be infinite, the chances of agreement would be remote. Besides, it was fundamental to their position that they, as the duly elected representatives of the

German people, were commissioned to draft a constitution for the realm. What, however, if the governments were to prove refractory? It was a possible, indeed a probable, contingency. Wisely, though only by a majority of four, the Parliament, having decided that Austria was to be excluded and that Germany was to be an empire, resolved to enlist the strongest German sword in defence of their work and offered the Crown to the King of Prussia.

1840-61   King Frederick William IV of Prussia was a vain, versatile, romantic ruler, learned but without political grasp or stability, whose fitful gleams of youthful liberalism were soon overcast by the solemn maxims of Divine Right and by a gift, most fatal to an egotist, of misty homiletic eloquence. Ascending the throne in 1840, he toyed with liberal ideas and constitutional reforms. *1847*   Many schemes were proposed, but seven years passed with nothing done. Then the force of public opinion compelled him to summon to Berlin the first of Prussian Parliaments, which, being assembled amidst much unusual commotion of the spirit, claimed to make laws, to control finance, and to veto loans. These novel pretensions were abhorrent to Frederick William. The Diet was dissolved, and it was with a reputation much frayed by his inglorious first encounter with the parliamentary spirit that the Prussian King was called upon in March, 1848, to face a real revolutionary crisis.

In that month of almost universal disorder there was, in consequence of the King's delay in granting reform, serious rioting and much bloodshed in the streets of Berlin. The King, anxious to swing with the tide, stopped the fighting, withdrew the troops, promised a Parliament, and when quiet was restored (March 21) rode into the capital wearing the old German tricolor of gold, white and black, and announced that henceforth Prussia was merged in Germany. More than a rhetorical flourish was needed to identify Prussia with the great liberal movement for German unity which was going forward in the St. Paul's Church at Frankfort. The King was still at heart an autocrat, his army still staunch in its exclusive devotion to the Prussian Crown; his nobles still unconvinced that any good to Prussia could result from democratic movements, while always between Frederick William and German liberalism there ran, a source of bitterness and mistrust, the blood which had been shed at the Berlin barricades. Unfortunately there was nothing in the unripe democracy of the Prussian capital calculated to bridge the gulf. From his retreat at Potsdam the King watched with growing indignation the chronic disorder of the streets and the effervescent unwisdom of a hot-headed and inexperienced parliament. At last he gained, from the subjugation of the Viennese, the nerve to strike. On November 2, 1848, he embarked on a course of reaction, dismissing his cabinet ministers, dissolving the civic guard, dispersing the parliament, and all without a life lost or a shot fired, with the army solid behind him and with the acceptance of the most timid middle class in Europe. It was after this achievement, when he was once more master of his house, that Frederick William received the invitation to accept the Empire of Germany from the Frankfort Parliament.

The offer was refused. The King would accept no crown which *April,* was not tendered by the Princes, no constitution which the *1849* governments of Germany had not confirmed. In the proposals of the Frankfort Parliament he discerned a concession to the evil principle of democracy, an armed struggle certainly with Austria, probably with Russia, and many serious strains within the German Reich itself. Rather than assume the title of Emperor of Germany at the invitation of an Assembly which he had come to despise and distrust, which had enacted universal suffrage and the secret ballot, he preferred to remain undisputed master of his loyal Prussians, to shatter the work of the Frankfort Parliament, and to bring to a sudden end those designs for a liberal and united Germany which had inspired the aspirations and energies of so many honourable and patriotic men. The wheel of fortune had now turned full circle, and the Prussian army, stamping out revolution in Saxony, Baden, and Hanover, earned the gratitude of every German Prince who was trembling for his throne.

But now when the storms of revolution were cleared away the Prussian King found himself confronted by Schwarzenberg, the imperious master of a resurgent Austria. There ensued a memorable struggle between two contrasted policies which brought upon Prussia a deep diplomatic humiliation. Assuming that Austria was now outside the *Reich*, that the old German Diet was dead and done with, and that it was open to him to form by the voluntary association of German governments a fresh union under Prussian leadership, Frederick William had summoned a *Mar. 20,* federal parliament to Erfurt, propounded a federal constitution. *1850* and succeeded in gathering under his fatherly Prussian wing not, indeed, as he had hoped, any one of the four kingdoms, but twenty-eight of the minor German states. To all this policy Schwarzenberg was violently opposed. He refused for a moment to contemplate the exclusion of Austria from Germany, insisted on reviving the Diet under Austrian presidency, required at the point of the sword that Prussia should renounce her new league of Princes. At one moment in Hesse-Cassel, where Austria as the agent of the Diet espoused the cause of a tyrannous Prince, and Prussia was ranged behind his outraged subjects, the forces of the rival powers barely escaped collision. War, however, was avoided, since the Prussian army was judged to be unequal to the challenge, and at the price of complete submission at Olmütz Prussia purchased an inglorious peace.

Nov. 29, 1850

Among the spectators of these transactions was a young Pomeranian squire, a member of the Berlin Parliament, whose courage, eloquence, and conviction at this crisis gave him an authority often exceeding that enjoyed by the King's ostensible ministers. This was Otto von Bismarck, destined to be one of the greatest figures in Prussian history. Of vast physical strength, a powerful orator, a gay companion, a brilliant linguist, and born to every subtlety of the diplomatic art, Bismarck united all the qualities of the consummate politician with the breadth and simplicity of purpose which are essential to the highest forms of statesmanship. He, too, wanted German union, but not at the cost of the Prussian monarchy, the Prussian army, or the Prussian tradition. " We all wish," he said, " that the Prussian eagle should spread out its wings as guardian and ruler from Munich to the Donnersberg, but free we will have him, not bound by a new Regensburg Diet. Prussians we are and Prussians we will remain." The strong inherited conservative principles of a Prussian Squire taught him that the future of his country would be moulded, not by the speeches of liberal politicians aping English institutions, but by the hard discipline of the camp. The failure of the Parliament of Frankfort, the frustration of his own King's designs at Erfurt, filled him with a savage joy. He could not tolerate the idea of a Parliament raised above the Prussian King and qualified to move a soldier or a gun in the Prussian army. Against Radowitz, the Prime Minister, he counselled an Austrian peace, which, however ignominious it might be, would come as a welcome release from the insupportable prospect of the Prussian eagle moulting in the cage of a German League.

With the disappearance of Metternich and the emergence of Bismarck the rivalry between Austria and Prussia, which dates back to 1740 when Frederick II seized Silesia from Maria Theresa, was carried by swift and calculated stages to a violent climax. On the field of Sadowa the Austrians were defeated by 1866 the Prussians, the old world by the new. With a violent wrench the German *Reich* was shaken free from the ancient Austrian encumbrance which not even the mighty hammer of Napoleon had been able to crush. More effectually and finally than the Viennese revolution the Prussian needle guns swept the grand-motherly spirit of Metternich out of the German scene.

Yet the system of Metternich, seeing that it brought Europe peace for forty years, has secured for the Austrian statesman the plaudits of a generation which has recent knowledge of the tribulations of war. Metternich had many attributes of a great political leader, a brilliant and engaging presence, a cool head, a vast comprehension of affairs, a firm and patriotic will. His prestige as the liberator of his country and as the principal arti-ficer of the new Europe was immense; the confidence reposed in him throughout the German-speaking world almost unbounded. In the counsels of the autocrats his was the directing mind, so that the period between 1815 and 1848 has not unjustly been called the Age of Metternich. Yet this accomplished aristocrat, whose morals were so loose, whose principles were so strict, and whose influence was so wide, laboured under one of the greatest intellectual disabilities which can vitiate the judgment of a statesman. He saw no mean between revolution and autocracy, and since revolution was odious, he set himself to repress that which is the soul of humane life in society, the very spirit of liberty.

In a second respect the system of Metternich ran counter to a vital and growing tendency of opinion. The Austrian Empire was built on the negation of nationality. Its merit, as some would say, depended on the fact that it held together in the bonds of a political, religious, and fiscal union a number of races whose balancing antipathies were its surest support. The union had never been easy, and with the new spirit of nationality which the French Revolution had let loose in Europe it became more and more uncomfortable. "My nation," said the Emperor Francis II, "is like a worm-eaten house; if one part is moved one cannot tell how much of it will fall." Metternich was determined to take no risks. So long as he was responsible for the conduct of Austrian affairs, nothing essential was changed, neither in Italy, nor in Hungary, nor in Bohemia, nor in the Slavonic and German possessions of the Austrian Crown, nor was any precaution omitted against the invasion of novelty. The Catholic priest formed the conscience and shaped the mind; the Catholic policeman checked the infiltration of political literature from the West; the Catholic soldier was ready to defend with his bayonet a state which had been formed by the marriage of princes, and knew no political principle but obedience to a crown. There was neither a free Parliament, nor a free Press, nor a free University, nor even an enlightened bureaucracy, by whose means the people of the Austrian Empire might receive the rudiments of political education.

By contrast Prussia was more compact, progressive, and efficient. Industry indeed still remained for the most part on the old domestic footing, poor in coal, in capital, in organization, and so backward in its development that as late as 1840 less than 40 per cent. of the cotton looms in Prussia were driven by power. But conditions favourable to industrial and commercial progress had been laid. A Zollverein or customs union founded by Maassen in 1818 for the purpose of drawing together the scattered Prussian dominions behind a low tariff wall proved to be so seductive that, coupled with good Prussian roads and the happy Prussian immunity from obstructive tolls and customs, it succeeded in the course of thirty years in bringing all the German states within its net. By this great business achievement the foundations of a united Germany under Prussian control were securely laid.

Other credentials for the leadership of the German people became more evident as time went on. Austria was an agglomeration of polyglot states occupied with the thorny internal problems which the conciliation of differing races naturally brings in its train. Prussia, on the other hand, was almost entirely German. While Austria was becoming more and more drawn towards the East, the interests of Prussia were concentrated within the German *Reich*. Whereas Austrian policy under Metternich was directed to the simple object of repressing national and liberal tendencies, and to maintaining by a strict system of police repression the traditional ascendancy of an absolute monarchy and an absolute church, the policy of Prussia was inspired by a zeal for knowledge and by a practical and progressive business spirit. Between a Government whose creed was summed up in the precept of obedience, and one which was taking active steps towards the development of the material wealth and intellectual power of the people, there was no even balance. The period which elapses between 1815 and the Revolution of 1848, though it has little lustre, is significant as marking the preparation for the union of Germany under the Prussian crown.

Within that period a theory of the State was developed in Prussia by a great philosopher, which, since it was closely correspondent with the ethics and institutions of the Prussian people, quickly gained an ascendancy among them, and afterwards spread far and wide as an element in a comprehensive system *1821* of philosophical idealism. Hegel expounded with all the weight of his intellectual authority the doctrine that the State was "God walking upon earth," that States were superior to their pledges, that right must have might, and that might was right. Whereas Bentham, the English radical, argued that the object of the State was to procure the greatest happiness of the greatest number, Hegel maintained that individual well-being or happiness was of no account when it conflicted with the greatness of the State. Force, then, was justified, and since states were founded on force, war was a part of political well-being, the world was as it ought to be, and as the spirit rules the world all that succeeds must be good. The object of the State could never be universal philanthropy, but always its own special welfare. The only superior of the State was the world spirit, and the world spirit judged the State by its success.

It is easy to see how sharp a conflict there must always be between this mystical conception of the State as divinity and those theories deriving from Rousseau which regard it as the product of a social contract based on voluntary choice and consent. In Hegel's view God made Himself manifest in a noble or governing class whose authority could only be impaired by popular election.

Whereas French democracy derived from Rousseau, the cult of an omnipotent State which prevailed among the Prussians found full and explicit warrant in the teaching of Hegel. The logic of tyranny was gilded by the ethical beauty of sacrifice. The State was God. In the name of that abstraction millions must be prepared to work, to suffer, and to perish.

Such was the Spartan philosophy of the people for whom fate was preparing the leadership of Germany.

BOOKS WHICH MAY BE CONSULTED

Metternich : Mémoires. 1880.
J. Maurice : The Revolution of 1848. 1857.
Bismarck : Thoughts and Recollections. 1933.
J. W. Headlam-Morley : Bismarck. 1899.
H. von Sybel : Deutsche Geschichte im 19 Jahrhundert.
Leger : Histoire de l'Autriche Hongrie. 1920.
C. G. Macartney : Hungary. (Nations of the Modern World Series.) 1934.
F. W. Newman : Select Speeches of Kossuth. 1853.
C. Grant Robertson : Bismarck. 1918.
Hegel : Philosophie des Rechts. 1821. Tr. 1896.

CHAPTER XV

THE END OF THE IBERIAN EMPIRES

The revolt of the American colonies of Spain and Portugal. Character of Spanish rule in South America. Importance of the Jesuits. The part of England in the Wars of South American Independence. The restored Bourbon Government in Spain. The need of popular education. The Spanish Liberals fail to take account of the spirit of regionalism. Contrasts in Spanish history. Reduction of Spain's general influence.

AN important consequence of the revolutionary and Napoleonic wars was the rupture of the ties which bound Spain and Portugal to their possessions overseas. As the foundation of the United States was one of the greatest political transactions of the eighteenth century, so in the age of Castlereagh and Canning the severance of southern and central America from European control marks the further triumph of colonial liberty. Yet history never repeats itself. The story of the falling away of the Spanish Indies bears little resemblance to the circumstances attending the revolt of Massachusetts and Virginia. While the British colonists rejected the yoke of a country which a few years before had issued victoriously from a great European war, the first blows for South American independence were struck when Spain and Portugal had been sunk to the lowest pit of political degradation by Napoleon. The North Americans pleaded in defence the unjust and unconstitutional taxation of an autocratic King. The Spaniards of the Indies advanced no such apologies. So far from objecting to the autocratic powers of the legitimate sovereign of Spain, it was one of the original pretexts justifying their revolt that Ferdinand VII, who stood for old-fashioned autocracy, had been set aside for the democratic fashions of a French intruder. The Council of Castile, which *1814-33* ruled over the Spanish Indies, was a meddlesome body. The archives of the Vice-Royalties of Mexico and Peru were piled high with royal edicts testifying to its minute and paternal solicitude. Yet the colonists experienced no galling sense of vexation from an interfering despotism which was softened by distance, diluted by corruption, and evaded from sloth. Theoretically the most over-governed people on the planet, in practice the colonial Spaniards went much as they pleased. Individual governors might be oppressive. Of oppression exercised from Spain itself there was little sense.

The Spanish Empire had its dark spots, the forced labour in the Peruvian mines and on the great public works in Mexico. The liberal looks with disfavour upon a system which drove the Indian to the altar under the compulsion of the lash, and subjected the intellect of the continent to the tyranny of the Church. Yet peace, which is one of the supreme blessings, was preserved by the Spaniards over the whole of their vast dominions. A population part Spanish, part Creole, part Indian, and part Negro, was held together under a common system of policy and belief. South America has often been more disturbed and less content than during the last century of European rule. Indeed, the result of the revolt of the Spanish colonies was to substitute for the long *Pax Hispanica* an epoch of inter-state wars and domestic revolutions, which has not yet reached its term.

The United States was founded by a solid block of English colonists, all nourished in traditions of liberty, and many descended from ancestors who had left their native land in a movement of fierce indignation and despair. There was no such tradition of rebellion, no such inheritance of constitutional liberty, among the Spaniards and Creoles of the southern hemisphere. The Spanish Indies were regarded not as colonies to be peopled by free immigration from the mother country, but as royal domains, and settlement within them as a privilege only to be accorded by the Spanish Crown. The idea of exterminating the Indian population, or of making South America an all-Spanish country inhabited only by " hundred per cent. American-Spaniards " was wholly foreign to the Catholic philosophy of the monarchy. Spaniards were filtered into the Indies as the Jews now into Palestine, only with a laxer hand and a larger tolerance of evasion. It was an assumption of policy that the main part of the population would be Indian or half-caste, schooled in loyalty to the Spanish Crown by the unremitting propaganda of the religious Orders. In this task the Jesuits played a leading part. With their ejection in 1768 the Spanish Indies were deprived of the presence of the one powerful educational agency that steadily inculcated the duty of obedience to the Spanish Crown. This loss was not repaired. As the British conquest of

French Canada reduced the power of the motives which bound the American colonies to the mother country, so the abolition of the Jesuit Order four years later sapped the loyalty of the Indies to Spain.

England had her revenge for the assistance which Spain rendered to her revolting American colonists in the eighteenth century, for she played a large part in the liberation of the southern hemisphere from the Iberian kingdoms. An English fleet destroyed the best part of the Spanish navy at Trafalgar, and, when Junot invaded Portugal, conveyed the Portuguese royal family to its place of exile in Brazil. The first impulse to the revolt of Argentina was supplied by the landing of a British expedition at Buenos Aires in 1806. It was an English admiral, the brilliant Cochrane, who swept the Spanish fleet from the Pacific, and assisted in the liberation of Chile and Peru; an English force of six thousand adventurers which formed the nucleus of the army with which Bolivar, the liberator, gave life to the Venezuelan and Colombian republics; an English statesman, George Canning, who, to the delight of all the liberal drawing-rooms in London, announced, with his wonted *bravura*, as he gave recognition to the liberated republics, that he " called the new world into existence to redress the balance of the old." When Bolivar died in 1830, the southern part of the American hemisphere was, largely with the aid and connivance of the Anglo-Saxon peoples, broken up into a number of independent republics.

So the old feud between the Anglo-Saxon and Iberian peoples, which had begun under Queen Elizabeth, was continued on new lines. When the English stopped, the citizens of the American Union took up the pursuit. They annexed California and New Mexico in 1848, Cuba and the Philippines fifty years later. Spanish writers complain that of all the enemies of Spain, heretics of the Anglo-Saxon race have been the most redoubtable and fortunate.

The loss of an Empire, though it wounded the pride, did not injure the prosperity of the Spanish nation. Judged by every economic test that can be applied, Spain is richer and happier now than ever before. Her population has nearly doubled. Her internal resources have been immeasurably increased. The mediaeval Spain of the Peninsular War is fast disappearing from sight.

One consequence of the emancipation of the Indies was, however, of continuing importance. The falling away of the Indian revenue, which had been a substantial element in the old royal budget of Spain, confronted Ferdinand VII and his successors with a choice of evils. If the government were to pay the army, it must tax the Church, if it were to tax the Church it must offend the people. For the Church in Spain was not as in Italy an anti-national force, but on the contrary the very soul of Spanish nationalism. Whereas the Spanish liberals could never free themselves from the imputation of being imitators of the French radicals, atheists in religion and cosmopolitans in politics, the Church was regarded as the chief bulwark of the centralized and autocratic monarchy upon the preservation of which the strength and unity of Spain was thought to depend. Yet though the contending forces were thus unevenly mobilized, the preponderance of the Church was not unbroken. At recurrent intervals the poverty of the crown brought power to the liberals, for the army chiefs would intervene and at the point of the sword demand a livelihood for their soldiers at the expense of the priests.

Thus the political history of Spain after Ferdinand's restoration in 1814 illustrates the difficulty of establishing the principles and practice of free government in a Roman Catholic country. The seeds of liberty had indeed been sown. A Cortes had met at Cadiz in the crisis of the Peninsular War. A constitution had been framed. A certain body of liberal principles had secured the support of an active-minded minority in the seaport towns and in the army; and there were henceforth never wanting in Spain, even during the darkest days of reaction, men who would take risks for constitutional government, for the freedom of the Press, or for religious toleration. Yet so long as the Church controlled education, and through its vast social and material power dominated opinion, there was no possibility of framing a real political electorate in Spain. The long reign of Isabella II (1833-68), though nominally constitutional, was in reality a sequence of military dictatorships. The first Republic (1873-4), though adorned by the flaming eloquence of Emilio Castelar, broke down for lack of Republicans.

No mere change in political mechanism seemed able to give to the Spanish people that vigorous and sustained interest in national politics without which it is impossible to work free

1812

institutions. The Bourbons were recalled in 1874 and duly bitted and bridled by a specious constitution. Universal suffrage was introduced in 1910. Neither of these changes, seeing that sixty per cent. of the population was by reason of the ecclesiastical monopoly of education still illiterate, made a reality of Parliamentary life. In a population of more than twenty million there were, according to the estimate of Alfonso XIII, only some six thousand politicians.

In these circumstances the parliamentary life of Spain was a genteel mockery. Since the government in power " made the elections " it was expected of the sovereign that he should give to each party in turn the right of dissolving the Cortes and thus of determining the political character of the ensuing chamber. Ministry succeeded ministry with bewildering rapidity. A sterile system of rotation, arranged for the convenience of the politicians, deprived the government of any power of framing large and courageous policies for the benefit of the country and made Parliament impotent in a period of actual crisis. The real remedy for this evil was not a dictatorship, such as Alfonso XIII tried between 1923 and 1930, when the constitution was suspended and General Primo de Rivera was given full power to govern Spain, but the education in letters and politics of the Spanish people. This experiment, which the Bourbon monarchy never made, is now for the first time essayed, on paper at least (1931-), under the Second Republic.

The Spanish people has never been easy to conquer or to govern. Their restless and revolutionary temper, noted by Livy, has subsisted with little change to the present day. The parching sun, the dry, bitter, dust-laden winds seem so to work that afflictions of the soul such as communism and socialism, clericalism and syndicalism, develop in the Spanish climate in their most violent forms. And as in the climate, so in the temperament of the people, there is an absence of gentle gradation. Nothing is consecutive. Riot follows siesta, siesta follows riot. Long stretches of political passiveness are broken by sudden spasms of violent disorder. If thought about the welfare of the nation is underdeveloped, the sentiment of personal independence is high and the attachment to local liberties of an almost savage tenacity. It was one of the misfortunes of the Spanish liberal movement of the nineteenth century that, being influenced by French models, it took no account of that spirit of regionalism which is one of the strongest facts in Spanish character, strong particularly among the Basques and the Catalans, the first clerical, absolutist, mediaeval, the second fiercely radical and atheist. It was in vain that Ferdinand VII essayed to put down Catalan autonomy in a series of decrees (1828-33). The Catalan problem was not so easily disposed of. Again and again, in 1844, in 1863, in 1870, in 1874, a Catalan rising reminded the government in Madrid of these stiff, redoubtable opponents who, stationed on their eastern sea-board, thought so differently about men and things from their Castilian masters. Catalonia was no more to be suppressed than Catholic Ireland. The monarchy of Alfonso XIII and the Second Republic have alike been compelled to recognize its claims.

The particularism of the Basques, a smaller and less formidable people stationed on either slope of the Pyrenees, was made redoubt-able only by its association with the claim of Don Carlos and his descendants to represent the legitimate branch of the Bourbon house. The two Carlist wars (1834-9, 1872-6) were nourished by the vigorous animosity of the Basque for the Castilian. As the Jacobite cause in England was supported by the Highland clans, so the Carlists, who represented clericalism, autocracy, and re-action, drew the main part of their following from this primitive and valiant people, whose speech is thought by some to represent the original language of the Iberian race.

Ever since the peace of Utrecht Spain has played a secondary and distant rôle in the affairs of Europe. Once she was a central influence, a nursery of imperial statesmen and men of letters, a buttress of orthodoxy, a place of pilgrimage, a conduit of Arab civilization, and later the splendid metropolis of a great and powerful empire. The country which gave Trajan and Hadrian, Marcus Aurelius and Theodosius to the government of the Roman world, Quintilian and Seneca, Martial, Lucan, and Juvenal to the enrichment of Roman letters, was no remote appendage to the Roman polity, but close to the heart of its business and cul-ture. Even greater was the importance of Spain during the age of faith, when the theology of the Latin Church was on the anvil, and the shrine of St. James of Compostella was accounted among the holy places of Christendom, and during that long and fruit-ful interchange between Latin and Arab civilization which was brought to an end by the Christian conquest of Granada. During all these centuries Spain exercised a wide power, whether as a principal pillar of the Catholic faith or as the medium through which the thought of Aristotle and of the Arabians was diffused through the West. Out of Spain came Dominic, the hammer of the Albigensian heretics, and Averrhoes, the fountain-head of philosophic pantheism, and, when the tides of Protestantism threatened to submerge the rock of the Catholic Church, Ignatius Loyola, who bade the waves recede. Of the great movement which is described as the Counter-Reformation Spain was the spear-head. No part of Europe was untouched by its influence. The pen of Cervantes and Calderon, the brush of Velasquez and Murillo, shed lustre on a nation which for more than a century was feared and admired for its wealth, its power, and far-reaching ambition.

All this imperial magnificence is now a thing of the past. Under the Bourbon house Spain soon became a satellite of France and its colleague in the long colonial rivalry with England. Equally with France, Spain paid the penalty, emerging from the revolutionary wars too weak to reclaim the American Empire, which was fast slipping from its old moorings, and too much distracted by the clash of old and new philosophies to live at peace with itself. A succession of contemptible sovereigns—Ferdinand, Christina, Isabel—reduced its influence in Europe to a nullity.

For a long time past Spanish decadence has been a familiar theme in the pages even of Spanish scholars and historians. As they contemplate the vast possessions once held under the Spanish Crown and now lost, whether from indolence or pride or from incapacity blended with that mood of listless renunciation, as if nothing in this world very much mattered, which is part of the religious character of the people, and then think of the new French Empire in Africa or of the wide dominion of the Anglo-Saxon race, they are tempted to infer some mysterious decline in native vigour and efficiency. Yet of this there is, in truth, little evidence. There has been a change of orientation rather than a decay of the national character. Those who know Spanish history best find that in every age the Spaniard is true to type. A modern author reflecting upon the Spanish American scene, as it unfolds itself today, finds no grounds for pessimism.

"There has been no decadence," writes Azorin. "A world is newly discovered. Twenty nations are created. One single language effaces a multitude of indigenous languages. Vast works of irrigation are constructed. Roads are planned. Woods are cleared, land is broken up and cultivated. High mountains are scaled, rivers of immense breadth are overspanned. Multitudes are instructed and trained. Municipal institutions, all alike, are disseminated over thousands of towns and cities. Industry, commerce, navigation, agriculture, the care of flocks, all spring into life on a new portion of the planet, enriching peoples and nations. And who carried out this gigantic work? France, England, Italy, Germany, Austria, Russia, all united in one supreme and titanic effort? No. One nation alone; alone, with help from nobody: Spain. And how many inhabitants had Spain after founding the greatest of modern countries? We must not limit our view to the area of the peninsula. Spain is the peninsula and the twenty American peoples."[1]

Since the Great War Spain has drawn nearer to her daughter nations. There is no talk of a revival of the empire. The Spanish American peoples will not renounce their independence. Yet when the League of Nations meets every autumn at Geneva there is a renewal of spiritual intimacy between the scattered members of the Spanish dispersion. Confronted with the strange and complicated portent of Europe, Spain and her American daughters stand together.

[1] Azorin : *An Hour of Spain. Tr.* Alice Raleigh. The gifted virtuoso omits to notice English capital and German immigrants.

BOOKS WHICH MAY BE CONSULTED

Cambridge Modern History, Vol. X., chapters 7-10. 1907.
H. V. Temperley : Canning. 1926.
W. B. Stevenson : Twenty Years' Residence in South America. 1825.
Lord Dundonald : Narrative of Services in Chile, Peru and Brazil, 2 vols 1859.
J. W. Fortescue : Dundonald. 1895.
M. A. S. Hume : Modern Spain. 1923.
Bertrand and Petrie : The History of Spain. 1934.
Butler Clarke : Modern Spain, 1815-1898. 1907.
Sir C. R. Markham : History of Peru. 1880.
V. Cherbuliez : L'Espagne politique, 1865-73. 1874.
Y. Guyot : L'Évolution politique et sociale de l'Espagne. 1899.
L. Teste : L'Espagne contemporaine. 1872.

CHAPTER XVI

THE CRIMEAN WAR

English Russophobia. The defeat of Russia prepares the way for the triumph of Italian nationalism. The affair of the Holy Places. Lord Stratford de Redcliffe. The outbreak of war. The policy of Napoleon III. The conduct of the campaign. The French Emperor decides for peace. The Treaty of Paris. Cavour and Florence Nightingale.

By the middle of the nineteenth century the cause of nationality, which was destined to win its extreme triumphs in the peace treaties of 1920, had received a decisive and apparently irretrievable overthrow. What prophet would then have foreseen that within two decades the Germany of Thackeray's *Vanity Fair* would be united under the Prussian and the Italy of Pio Nono under the Sardinian Crown, or that Hungary raised from its bed of deepest humiliation would be accorded a place equal with the German in the constitution of the Austrian Empire? Against the possibility of such developments it would have been sufficient to point to the hatreds, jealousies, fears, and ambitions which had for so many centuries poisoned the political life of the German and Italian peoples, to the recent miscarriage of the universal revolution, and to the nature of the obstacles, now apparently more formidable than ever, which blocked the paths to the success of any similar movement in the future. And of these the greatest was Russia. The vast size of the Russian Empire, the scale of its armaments, its slow but apparently irresistible expansion over the Asian plateau, its reputed designs on Constantinople, created, more particularly in England with her Oriental interests, a vague but persistent feeling of alarm, which was combined with a vehement aversion from the whole political system of which Russia was the principal prop and pillar in Europe. To the contemporaries of Palmerston and Thackeray no feelings of admiration or regard mitigated the sinister impression aroused by the name of Russia. The genius of the Russian people in literature and art, in science, music, and dancing, had not yet become part of the common stock of European civilization. The engaging quality of the Russian peasant was unsurmised. It was only known that Nicholas I, Tennyson's "icy Muscovite" and "o'ergrown Barbarian of the east," who succeeded in 1825, had none of the liberal sentiments of his predecessor Alexander I; that he held his own subjects under the compression of a secret police, that he had crushed with merciless severity the insurgent Poles, that he had helped Austria first to muzzle the press of Germany, then to subjugate Hungary, and finally at Olmütz to humiliate his Prussian rival; that his government was, as De Tocqueville described it, "the corner-stone of despotism in the world," a fatal bar to the revision of treaties, to the liberation of nations, and to the revival of those generous hopes which had suffered eclipse in 1848. When Turkey, which had carried out some constitutional reforms, declined to hand over Kossuth and other Hungarian fugitives to Russian or Austrian vengeance, the Turkish Minister accredited to the Court of St. James for a time became the idol of the London populace.

Out of this mentality prevailing among the British people arose an unpremeditated war in the east from which Austria, outraging her Russian benefactor by an invidious neutrality, and, in the words of one of her statesmen, "astonishing the world with her ingratitude," emerged in a position of dangerous and friendless isolation. By smashing the strong links which bound Austria to Russia the Crimean War created the conditions which led to the liberation of the German and Italian nations. This is the chief political significance of a contest entered into without necessity, conducted without foresight, and deserving to be reckoned from its archaic arrangements and tragic mismanagement rather among mediaeval than modern campaigns.

The affair arose out of a dispute between Greek and Roman monks as to the custody of certain Christian shrines in Jerusalem, a quarrel paltry in itself, but deriving importance from the fact that the Greek claims were pressed upon the Porte by the Tzar, the Latin by the Emperor of the French. A troublesome, irritating, protracted dispute ended in a decision so hotly resented by Nicholas that he mobilized an army on the Pruth and sent to Constantinople a hectoring mission under Prince Menschikoff with a requirement not only for immediate satisfaction in Jerusalem, but for a treaty, exceeding all previous claims, which would in effect secure for him a protectorate over the orthodox subjects of the Porte. These proposals the Porte, contrary to the advice given by Stratford de Redcliffe, the British Ambassador, decided to reject.

The conditions have now passed away under which it is possible for an ambassador to involve his country in war. Telephone and telegraph make him the submissive instrument of Cabinet policy; but in 1853, the telegraph being imperfectly developed, a strong ambassador in a distant mission with clear views of his own and with a weak Prime Minister and Foreign Minister above him could, especially if he had reason to believe that his own views coincided with popular prejudice at home, take a line of his own and commit his country. Stratford de Redcliffe was believed to be in this position. His view of eastern affairs based on long experience was one of ruthless clarity. He admired the Turk, distrusted the Tzar, and may have thought that the time had come when Russia, whom he regarded as England's most formidable enemy, should be made to experience a great diplomatic or military defeat. Though he knew that Aberdeen his Premier and Clarendon his Foreign Secretary stood for peace, he was aware that Palmerston, the most popular member of the Cabinet, was on the spirited side of politics, and that the man in the street was blindly Russophobe. On these grounds it was long believed that Stratford de Redcliffe was the real author of the Crimean War. The despatches of the famous ambassador do not bear out this contention. Stratford urged moderation. But despatches never tell the whole story. The sagacious Turk knew well that he had a friend in the " great Elchi " and that British battleships were not far off. The mere presence in Constantinople of this able, high-minded, very temperamental diplomat was sufficient, apart from his formal despatches, to frustrate every successive proposal for the accommodation of the dispute. It stiffened the spine of Turkish resistance and wrecked the Vienna note, which could have settled all to the satisfaction of the French and English Governments, though the Tzar and even the Turkish Ambassador to the Austrian Court had expressed themselves satisfied with its terms.

When accordingly war broke out between Turkey and Russia, the Russians opening hostilities by the invasion of the Principalities, the Turks firing the first shots at Oltenitza (in Moldavia) and the Russians replying by sinking the Turkish fleet off Sinope, all Britain was aflame, as at a felon blow struck by a bully. Even to the more prudent section of the British Cabinet the Tzar's policy was deeply suspect since as far back as 1844 he had spoken to Aberdeen of the Turk as " a sick man " and had himself recently propounded to Sir Hamilton Seymour, the British Ambassador at St. Petersburg, the idea that Russia and England should unite in despoiling his estate. So after much hesitation, and with peace-seeking diplomacy still busy in Vienna, England decided to embark on the war (March 27, 1854).

In this enterprise of propping up the Turk, France stood by England's side. It would probably be unfair to suggest that Napoleon III's dominant motive was military glory. His people wanted and had been promised peace. "The Empire is Peace," they had been told. "We have immense waste territories to cultivate, roads to open, harbours to deepen, canals to complete, rivers to render navigable, railways to link up. Opposite Marseilles we have a vast dominion to assimilate to France." All this required peace. But in the foreign policy of Napoleon, which appears so fluid and opalescent, there were always a few fixed points. One was a revision of the treaties of 1815 to be obtained, if possible, from a European Congress; another some assistance to Italy; a third the avoidance of the specific mistakes which had led to the downfall of the first Empire. As the uncle had been overthrown by the sea-power of England, the nephew was resolved upon an English alliance. If that involved a war with Russia, so be it. The Russian was as good an enemy as anyone, unpopular with French clericals as a schismatic, distasteful to French republicans as an autocrat, and to the Emperor personally, by reason of the Tzar's insolence in denying him his proper title, a source of irritation. In the "Four Points" which stated the war aims of England and France there was much for England, since Russia was to be denied influence in the Balkans and warships in the Black Sea, much for the Austrians, since the Principalities and the Danube were to be freed from the Muscovite, but very little for France, though it was France that would contribute the larger part of the expeditionary force. Still, a joint enterprise with the solid Britons was calculated to give stability to an adventurous, new, and precarious throne.

Sebastopol, the great naval port of the Russian Empire in the Black Sea, was selected as the chief military objective in a campaign which was principally aimed at the marine forces of the enemy, and thither, since the Russians had evacuated the Principalities and there was no fighting to be done in the Danube valley, a motley armada of French, English, and Turks, the English some 26,000 strong, the French slightly more numerous, proceeded from the Bulgarian port of Varna in mid-September of 1854.

It was a mad enterprise. Since the Turks unaided had repulsed the Russians from the valley of the Danube, and since all risk of a Russian advance upon Constantinople was overpast, there was no valid reason why the allies should waste a man or a shilling upon a siege which, even if successful, would make no sensible impression on the huge resources of the enemy. And if the objective was insane, the methods were tragic. The English army, without ambulances or proper transport, marched into action clad in uniforms fitted only for a London parade ground, nor did it even occur to the government of the greatest engineering country in the world to ease the transport of supplies from the port of Balaklava to the camp by laying down the necessary five miles of light railway.

The landing was uncontested, the first battle (at the Alma) was a victory, and had the attack been pushed home, as Lord Raglan, the English commander, advised, there is some reason to think that the northern half of the city at least might possibly have succumbed to the allies. The disastrous decision was, however, taken to march away the troops, to sail round to the south where there was better harbourage, and thence to renew the encounter. The precious element of time squandered by the attacking was used to the full by the defending force. The fortifications were improved out of recognition, and Sebastopol was protected by the genius of Todleben, by the frosts and tempests of a Crimean winter, and, since the city was never completely invested, by the constant accretions of relieving troops. Eventually, but not before cholera and frost-bite had taken a heavy toll of all the armies, the French stormed the Malakoff fort (September, 1855) and the armies entered upon a wilderness of scorching ruins, which had once been and was again to become a thriving city.

Having won the crowning victory, Napoleon was entitled to call for peace, but now the high-spirited Palmerston was English Premier, and the war spirit of his countrymen, being at last thoroughly roused, and being ill satisfied with the meagre glories of Balaklava, Inkerman, and the Redan, called for a resolute prosecution of the war. An adroit shaft from the Emperor's diplomatic quiver pierced this warlike folly and brought peace in view. If the struggle were to continue, Napoleon explained, it must comprise among its larger objects the liberation of the Poles. At that devastating threat, unwelcome in London, abhorrent to Berlin, and full of evil omen in St. Petersburg, Europe was sharply recalled from foolishness to common sense.

The Treaty of Paris (March, 1856) secured for the allies all the objects for which they had professed to contend. The Principalities (Moldavia and Wallachia) were restored to their former position. The Danube was made free to navigation. Warships were forbidden on the Black Sea. The Sultan undertook to confirm the privileges of his Christian subjects, on the understanding that the Powers should not interfere with his domestic government. The Russian protectorate over the eastern Christians was abolished. As a reward for her neutrality the rights and privileges of Serbia, while still remaining as before under Turkish suzerainty, were guaranteed by the Powers. It was a further note of the allied victory that Russia was compelled to return Kars (in Asia), which she had recently wrested from the Turks, and to cede part of Bessarabia to Moldavia.

Such were the provisions, many of them of transitory value, which the allies were able to exact from the government of the new Tzar Alexander II. Though a fresh lease of life had been given to the Porte, the victors were unable to arrest the march of Christian freedom in the Balkans or the revival of Russian navalism in the Black Sea. Indeed, it was Napoleon who sponsored the new Roumanian kingdom when England, absorbed in the Indian Mutiny, was too busy to protest. As for the Black Sea clauses of the treaty, they were repudiated by Russia in 1870, all Europe acquiescing in a lawless but natural act which it was powerless to obstruct. For the moment, however, and for many years to come Russia was a disabled giant, crippled by the terrible effect of the long, hideous midwinter marches to the relief of Sebastopol, when ox-wagons sank deep in the snowdrifts and hundreds of thousands of honest peasants perished on the way.

Seated at the conference table at Paris was a stout, spectacled, whiskered figure, affable and fluent of speech, and full primed with technicalities of every sort—the Count Cavour, since 1852 Prime Minister in Piedmont. After the fiercest parliamentary tussle, this far-seeing statesman, gambling as the greatest statesman must often do for the highest stakes, persuaded the Turin

Parliament (January, 1855) to send a Sardinian contingent to the Crimea. Fortune favours the brave. At the cost of twenty-eight lives, lost when a division of his countrymen went into action at the Tchernaya, and some thousand casualties from cholera, Cavour earned the right at the end of the war to raise the wrongs of Italy at the council table of Europe.

Equally daring and decisive in another sphere was the action of a gently nurtured English Victorian lady, who, moved by the tales of suffering at the front, went out to nurse the troops at Scutari, and by her personal example and fiery energy then and thereafter raised the whole status of the nursing profession, improved the standard of public hygiene, and, more powerfully perhaps than any other single influence, won for the women of her country the right of entry into serious and useful callings. The extraordinary achievement of Florence Nightingale in defying the conventions of the age in her great work for the relief of human suffering is one of the few compensations for the waste and havoc of the Crimean War.

BOOKS WHICH MAY BE CONSULTED

P. Guedalla : Palmerston. 1926.
Sir Edward Hamley : The War in the Crimea. 1891.
A. W. Kinglake : The Invasion of the Crimea. 1877.
Pierre de la Gorce : Histoire du Second Empire. 1908.
Spencer Walpole : A History of England from the Conclusion of the Great War in 1815. 1890.
Sir E. T. Cook : The Life of Florence Nightingale. 1925.
W. R. Thayer : The Life and Times of Cavour. 1915.
F. A. Simpson : Louis Napoleon and the Recovery of France. 1923.
P. Guedalla : The Second Empire. 1932.
S. Lane Poole : Life of Stratford Canning. 1888.
English Historical Review, 1933. 1934.

CHAPTER XVII

THE UNIFICATION OF ITALY

England's miscalculation in the Near East. England and the Risorgimento. Cavour's debt to English Liberalism. The modernization of Piedmont. Austria in Italy. The interview at Plombières. The Italian campaign of 1859. The truce of Villafranca. National movement in central Italy. Ricasoli in Tuscany. The cession of Savoy and Nice to France. Cavour and Mazzini. Garibaldi in Sicily and Naples. Cavour and Victor Emmanuel march south. The retirement of Garibaldi. Concluding stages of the National movement. The Roman question. Italy alienated from France.

ENGLAND'S Crimean enterprise was based upon three mistaken estimates: an undue respect for the striking power of the Tzar in scenes of action far remote from the heart of the Russian Empire, a failure to appreciate the capacity of the rude Christian peoples of the Balkans to maintain a position of sturdy independence, and finally, despite many lessons of the past, a continuing faith in the power of the Turk to give to his Christian subjects, under appropriate western guidance, the benefits of a just and enlightened rule. These doctrines, which continued to inform British policy in the Balkans until they were rejected by the march of events in the eighties and nineties, cost the country twenty-five thousand lives in the Crimea and much subsequent alarm, perturbation, and waste of effort.

In Italy, whose achievement of unity under the House of Savoy is the next great episode of European history, the influence of England was more fortunately and inexpensively exerted. In the happy nick of time, when Italy was at the crisis of her fate, and the cause of Italian nationalism, threatened by internal dissensions and external peril, needed encouragement, every English envoy accredited to an Italian Court was the friend of Italian freedom. Wherever Liberals were gathered together in England, in the Universities, in the clubs, in the country houses, and in Parliament, the prevailing sentiment was one of hope that the cause of clericalism and absolutism, hateful to a Protestant and constitutional people and rendered yet more odious by Gladstone's revelations of the atrocities connected with the administration of justice in Naples, would suffer a complete overthrow.

More important still, Palmerston and Russell, each as strongly favourable to Italian liberty as the Queen and Prince Consort were adversely affected towards it, were at the helm of affairs in 1860, when at the least sign of encouragement from London, France or Austria might have intervened to prevent the junction of central and southern Italy with the north. The strong and open declarations of these two statesmen on behalf of Italian freedom and the uncertainty in foreign countries as to how the British Navy would be instructed to act, if any attempt were made from outside to bolster up the satellites of Vienna and Rome, were important contributions to the success of the Italian cause.

There is another respect in which the Italian movement was indebted to England. Cavour was a disciple of English liberalism. It was his ambition to create first in the little Kingdom of Piedmont and ultimately in the larger sphere of a united Italy the kind of polity which he found in England, a constitutional monarchy broad based on the practice of liberty and religious toleration, keeping the Church within its proper sphere, pursuing a policy of free trade, developing railways, and applying to the promotion of industry and agriculture all the scientific and technical knowledge of the time. French abstractions made no appeal to the practical intelligence of a man who had been a banker, a manufacturer, and a farmer before he rose to be a statesman. But if business was an essential part of his training, Parliament was the congenial theatre for the display of his larger powers. He excelled in debate, abounded in persuasion, invited and exulted in controversy. During his long administration (1851-59, 1860-62) the practice of responsible government took root in Italy; and of the foreign conquests of English liberalism, none has been so important as the mind of Cavour.

The state governed by Victor Emmanuel II consisted of four incohesive parts, of which one only (the recently incorporated Republic of Genoa) was in any way identified with the historic glories of Italy. Savoy on the French side of the Alps, albeit the original home of the royal house, was in language and sentiment to be reckoned as a province of France rather than an integral part of Italy. Piedmont was a poor backward sub-alpine region, with no claim on the admiration of Italians for its services in the past and with little prospect, so it must have seemed, of contributing to those particular spheres of literary and artistic excellence in which the Italians take special pride. As for Sardinia, it was a malarious and barbarous island. Genoa was different. Here was a city which had played a great part not only in the history of the Mediterranean, but in the marine enterprises of the world; Genoa, however, was in decrepitude, and being a recent member of the Piedmontese State and still chafing under the unfamiliar yoke, was a cause rather of anxiety than of strength to the government of Turin.

Out of these unpromising and disparate materials Cavour determined to build up a state which, alike for strength and efficiency as for its bold practice of Parliamentary government, should acquire and retain the direction of the Italian movement. In these designs he was assisted by a Parliamentary constitution inherited from the last reign, by a virile people, by a coarse, energetic, but thoroughly patriotic sovereign, and by the best army at the disposal of an Italian government.

The Piedmontese Risorgimento, as it was conceived by Cavour and his like-minded contemporaries, involved reforms which could be accomplished only at the cost of a sharp encounter with the Church. That encounter, despite the troubled conscience of the libertine king, was successfully carried through. The Siccardi law attacked ecclesiastical jurisdiction and the privileged position of the priesthood before the law. The Rattazzi laws curtailed the top-heavy ecclesiastical establishment, cut down the vast incomes of the higher clergy, and closed more than three hundred monasteries.

In the teeth of the most violent opposition from the Vatican civil marriage was enacted. By such enactments Piedmont in a very few years began to rank, not as before among the most retrograde states of Italy, its energies dispersed, its intelligence fettered by tradition and obscured by priestcraft, but as a modern emancipated and practical community. These improvements were confirmed by a balanced budget, by a series of commercial treaties, and by the steady application of the government to the expansion of railways, to the improvement of agriculture and of industry and to the building up of an army strong enough, should occasion arise, to drive the Austrians across the Alps.

Outside Tuscany and Piedmont the least badly governed part of Italy seems to have been those provinces of Lombardy and Venetia which were already administered by Austria. Nothing, however, which the Austrian government did for the improvement of the material condition of its Italian subjects could alter the fact that this alien power was the corner-stone of reaction throughout the peninsula, that it was under Austrian protection that the bad papal government in the Romagna was enabled to flourish and King Bomba to practise his notorious irregularities in Naples. Not for one moment would Mazzini, the arch-contriver of conspiracies, permit it to be forgotten that Austria was an enemy to be overthrown by fair means or foul. Weaving skein after skein of conspiracy, each more desperate than the last, this indomitable fanatic watered the soil of Italy with the blood of martyrs.

For Cavour also, Austria was the enemy, but while Mazzini thought in daggers and conspiracies, it was a primary factor in Cavour's plans that Italy should be liberated in open war by the joint armies of France and Piedmont. In Turin, then, all was martial preparation, while in Paris along the *coulisses* of the Tuileries there was an unceasing hum of expectation and intrigue.

At last in the July of 1858 Napoleon, always at heart a *Carbonaro*, but long uncertainly balanced between contending pressures, took a characteristic and decisive step. Secretly and without consulting his ministers, he summoned Cavour to meet him at Plombières in the Vosges, and there in the course of two conversations sketched out his plan for Italy without the Austrians; a north Italian kingdom stretching from the Alps to the Adriatic, a monarchy to be patched up for somebody in the centre, a Papal State (since clerical opinion would require that the Pope should remain in Rome), a reformed Naples, the whole perhaps bound together in some form of confederation with the Pope as President. That there should be a war went without saying, but it must be a war waged upon a pretext which would appeal to the Emperor's subjects, a war in which Austria would be made to figure as the powerful aggressor, Piedmont as the weak and innocent state battling for its mere existence. In some circumstances and always provided there were compensation for her sacrifice, the aid of France could be counted on. As an honorarium she would ask for Savoy and Nice, Savoy, the original home of the Sardinian dynasty, Nice, as it unfortunately happened, the birthplace of Garibaldi. A marriage would crown the political treaty. The Princess Clothilde, a child of fifteen, would give her hand to the Prince Jerome Napoleon, a libertine of thirty-seven years, who, if he laboured under a reputation of cowardice in the field, was praised for a sentimental fidelity to his mistresses. Perhaps this ill-assorted couple might reign together some day in Florence. A Bonaparte in Tuscany, a Murat in Naples, these were possibilities flitting in the opaque background of the Emperor's mind. With this bargain, no easy one for his royal master to digest, but with the comfortable knowledge that the French Emperor was henceforth his accomplice, Cavour returned to Turin to work for war.

At his next New Year's reception, Napoleon casually announced that he regretted that his relations with Austria were not so good as they had been. The vague words flew round Europe and were taken as an omen of impending war. Yet such was the balancing temper of the Emperor, such his belief in the method of international conference, that after all war might not come. Then, when things looked black for Cavour, the Austrians, who could always be relied on to play into the hands of an enemy, were so obliging as to issue an ultimatum demanding disarmament from Turin. The *casus belli* required at Plombières had been provided. Austria was the aggressor, and with a light heart and overweening confidence the paladins of France marched again under a Bonaparte into the plains of Italy.

For the student of military history the Italian campaign of 1859 is chiefly to be remembered as a catalogue of mistakes. It might have been thought that with their long warning of impending trouble the Austrians would have paid some attention to the development of their railways. The military mind, however, is slow to absorb technical inventions, and Watt and Stephenson might almost have lived in vain, so little were the potentialities of the railway discerned by the rival governments and their commanders in the field. A single line only connected Vienna with Trieste. From Trieste to Venice, a distance of seventy miles, there was no railway at all. To such an extent did the old leisurely fashion of campaigning still prevail, that although the Austrians forced the war and had their army massed on the Piedmontese frontier they made no effort to dispose of the Piedmontese before they had effected their concentration with the French. With a degree of incapacity almost inconceivable Giulay advanced into Piedmont, then retired, and passively conceded the initiative to his antagonist.

Despite the glamour of his name the Emperor of the French was no general. A plan of campaign regardless of railways, for it had been furnished by a veteran of the Napoleonic wars, stood in lieu of the promptings of native wit; and the obedient student of Jomini as he marched his army northwards across the enemy front should have been exposed to many an awkward thrust from a vigilant antagonist. Yet since the Austrians were even less efficient than the French, everything succeeded with the army of invasion, the march to the north, the advance eastward on Milan, the two fierce collisions, in which nothing seems to have worked out according to plan, at Magenta, and again at Solferino. By July, thanks to the courage of the rank and file, the allied sovereigns were masters of Lombardy.

At this point of the campaign (July 11, 1859), with the cries of the wounded of Solferino still echoing in his ears, Napoleon sought out Francis Joseph, the young Austrian Emperor, and made with him a truce at Villafranca. It was an act which then and afterwards laid him open to the charge of the basest treachery to the Italian cause, for without the consent of Victor Emmanuel and on the morrow of a definite military success he suddenly wound up the war, taking Lombardy for Piedmont, but leaving the Austrians established in Venetia. He was content for the moment, seeing that he had not fulfilled his share of the bargain, that the compensations should be waived. "You shall pay me the cost of the war," he said to Victor Emmanuel, "and we will talk no more of Nice and Savoy."

The fury of Cavour when he heard that these terms had been accepted by his King was such that he resigned his office. We can well appreciate the measure of his disappointment. He had been promised an Italy from which the Austrian power would be entirely eliminated, an Italy free from the Alps to the Adriatic, and now when Piedmont had made its war effort, when all Italy had been stirred to the boiling point, when two victories had been already won, when Milan had been recovered, and when a large French army was on Italian soil, a peace was made which left Austria as firmly established as ever in a famous Italian province, and as competent as ever from that point of vantage to maintain the whole fabric of clerical, autocratic, and anti-Italian interests against which the policy of Piedmont had been from the first an emphatic protest. From the moment that Napoleon made his peace at Villafranca, the whole sentiment of

Italy changed towards him. An aversion from the French, as traitors to the cause of Italian liberty, swiftly replaced the glowing enthusiasm which had greeted the liberators on their triumphal entry into Milan. Yet of all the actions of his career there have been few more judicious than Napoleon's sudden decision to close the Italian campaign after Solferino. His casualties had been heavy and there had been cases of cholera in his camp. In all those details which are essential to the successful conduct of a long campaign, in transport, in supply, in hospital equipment, his army was gravely deficient. His humanity, and humanity is always judicious, had been stirred by the terrible scenes of an actual battlefield. He reflected that the enemy, though shaken, was still intact, and likely, with the protection of the famous quadrilateral of the Venetian fortresses,[1] to oppose an obstinate and perhaps successful resistance to his advance. Even if there were no risk to be apprehended from Germany, it was still doubtful whether the allies would be able to conquer Venetia; but the German risk was grave. An urgent message came to him from Paris that a Prussian army was mobilized on the Rhine, and, if he did not promptly conclude with the Austrians, would be at the throat of France. Amply, therefore, was he justified, though on grounds obscure to Cavour and his friends, in staying the havoc. A conference at Zurich was to settle the future of Italy.

The episode which ensued was one of those spontaneous ebullitions of popular feeling which defeat all the calculations of statesmen. Central Italy, by the voice of the people, declared for Piedmont. The little Principalities, Modena, Parma, Tuscany, rose against their Princes. In Romagna, in Umbria, in the Marches, there was the same quick spasm of enthusiasm for the new kingdom of Italy which was burning in the north. Here was a situation unforeseen at Plombières, contravening the scheme of the French Emperor for a Tuscan Kingdom to be governed by Prince Napoleon, odious to the Pope, since it entailed the mutilation of his territory, hateful to Austria, whose princely clientèle was ejected from power and liable to be overset, either by the enthusiastic opposition of Italian republicans, to whom the rule of Piedmont was odious in every point, or by the intervention of foreign powers. The situation, however, was saved by three circumstances. Among the central States of Italy

Aug.,
1859-
March,
1860

[1] Verona, Mantua, Peschiera, Legnano.

by far the most famous and influential was the Grand Duchy
of Tuscany, which for a hundred and twenty-one years had been
ruled over with mild and distinguished sagacity by Princes of
the House of Lorraine. It was here, one would imagine, that particularism would be strongest, and that an easy hearing would
be found for arguments based on the long tradition of dignified
independence evolved by the Tuscan State, and the loss of
prestige attaching to the acceptance of Savoyard rule. By a
singular piece of good fortune, it so happened that when, under
the strong pressure of national emotion, Leopold II, the last of
the Lorraine Dukes, was expelled from his throne, the leadership
of the Tuscans passed with popular acclamation not to a hot-
headed and officious demagogue but to a nobleman of unblem-
ished character, ardent patriotism, and substantial good sense.
At the critical moment when everything might have gone
wrong in Florence, and if in Florence then in Modena and
Parma and other parts of central Italy, Benito Ricasoli brought   *1809-80*
the Tuscans firmly and decisively to· reject the solution of a
separate kingdom and to accept the House of Savoy. Among
the architects of Italian unity the name of this steadfast Tuscan
baron deserves to be remembered.

All this local movement, however, though ratified by plébiscites, might easily have been brought to nothing by foreign
intervention; but here Italy was helped by the warm sympathy
of the English government and by the fact that Napoleon was
already, through the conversations at Plombières, the accomplice of Cavour. That astute Piedmontese statesman was now
again, after a brief retirement, in charge of affairs (January 20,
1860). He knew the thoughts which were flitting in Napoleon's
mind, how he would like to see his cousin established in
Florence, a Prince Murat reigning in Naples, and the position
of the Pope safeguarded, but he remembered also that the
Emperor had first suggested, and then after Villafranca waived,
a claim for compensation. That claim Cavour was now willing
to satisfy, if Napoleon would accept the adhesion of the Italian
States to the Kingdom of his royal master. The bargain was
struck. The great formulae of democracy were observed and as
a plébiscite gave Tuscany and Modena to Italy, so, by the same
expedient of a popular vote, Savoy and Nice passed into the possession of France.

The transaction cannot be interpreted in terms of the outcry of patriotic Italians. The new Kingdom of Victor Emmanuel was rid of an obscurantist and priest-ridden province which it would have been difficult to educate and costly and impracticable to defend. But the transfer of Savoy, if for these reasons it involved no real deduction from the strength of the Italian Kingdom and was in any case handsomely paid for by the acquisition of the central provinces, was no unmixed blessing for Napoleon. Here, it was said in London and other European capitals, was the first modest beginning of a policy for extending the eastern frontier of France and for revising the treaties which had been framed by the victors in the Napoleonic wars to curb the torrents of French ambition. Queen Victoria complained bitterly that England had been made a dupe; and even his free trade treaty with Cobden, which cost Napoleon so much in domestic popularity, did not undo the unfavourable impression which the seizure of Savoy imprinted on the English mind. From that moment the capital of goodwill towards the French Empire began sensibly to decline in Europe, and Napoleon to be regarded as a disturber of the peace, an enemy of the existing order, who, even under the veil of a quixotic and sentimental crusade, worked always for the restoration of the continental preponderance of France.

Among the difficulties besetting the liberation of Italy none was greater than the problem of dealing with Mazzini and his school of republican conspiracy. For a statesman like Cavour, who believed in the action of regular governments, regular armies, and established forms of diplomatic pressure and inducement, nothing would have been more dangerous than open dealings with avowed conspirators or any apparent complicity in their designs. Yet it could not be denied on a cool view of the situation that conspiracy, however hateful, however criminal, however desperate, had at least the effect of advertising the discontents of Italy abroad, and of raising the political temperature at home. To have discouraged conspiracy altogether would have been tantamount to an assault upon the chief dynamic influence in the Italian movement. Cavour could not afford to throw away so powerful a weapon. His object was not to alienate the conspirators by rigour, but to attract them by seduction, and publicly to disown any activity likely to be ill viewed in Paris and in London. Conspiracy was met by conspiracy. In La Farina's National Society Cavour had under his hand an organization which, since it accepted power under the monarchy, complied with his main purpose. Above all he made a convert of Garibaldi, who, during the campaign of 1859, wore the King of Sardinia's uniform as commander of an irregular force of Hunters of the Alps, which had been formed for the express purpose of engaging the great guerilla leader in the work of the royal army of the north. The importance of this conversion was soon to be demonstrated.

While these great transactions were going forward in the north, Crispi, a hard-headed and subtle republican conspirator, was stirring Sicily to rebel against its Bourbon king. The man was formidable, the conspiracy wide, the temper of the island, being long attuned to rebellion, suggested the possibility of a flaming republican success. Crispi needed a sword. A soldier was required who could fan conspiracy into rebellion, concentrate rebellion into war, and out of war bring victory; and seeing that the sword of Garibaldi, the defender of the Roman Republic, was now idle—to what other quarter could Crispi more naturally turn? Once launched, the idea became everybody's secret; Garibaldi for Sicily and the liberation of the south.

There were many substantial grounds, fully present to the calculating mind of the wise Cavour, for postponing, if possible, the fusion of the south into the kingdom which had been so recently formed and was still so imperfectly compacted. The south was very different from the north, in racial composition, in social texture, in the degree of its education, in its aptitude for modern life. It had been long barbarized by bad government and the baser forms of superstition. Brigandage was endemic— societies secretly formed for crime were a cancer preying on the vitals of the nation; and to this accumulation of moral and political evils there was added the problem of southern destitution, with all its complex antecedents in the laziness of man and the niggardliness of nature. A premature assumption of these unfamiliar southern problems might break the back of the new Italian government with its capital in Turin. Postponement, however, was impossible. The revolutionary movement in Sicily was a thing altogether outside Cavour's capacity to prevent. It might be guided, but it could not be stopped. It might assume a dangerous republican form or be schooled into acceptance of the monarchy. The best hope rested on Garibaldi. On May 5, 1860, with Cavour's secret connivance, that great commander set

sail for Sicily. He had with him the uniform of a Piedmontes
general and used as his watchword "Italy and Victor Emmanuel.

The story of Garibaldi's amazing Sicilian adventure, how a
the head of a ragged and motley band of volunteers, bare c
treasure and with no serious military equipment, he landed a
Marsala, stormed Calatafimi, fought his way into Palermo, an
at the end of three months cleared the island of royal troops, i
even when full allowance is made for the cowardice and inept
tude of his opponents, and for the general sympathy of th
Sicilians, a great example of moral leadership in war. Havin
won Sicily he crossed the Straits. The great naval Powers wh
might have obstructed the passage, for one reason or anothe
let him pass, and then on the Neapolitan mainland among th
wrinkled Calabrian hills and on the shining levels of the Cam
pagna the same miraculous story repeated itself, of cowardl
enemies, dissolving armies, acclaiming crowds. The King di
not even defend the capital, but fled to Gaeta, leaving Naples t
the enemy.

The triumph of Garibaldi was almost complete; but it wa
perhaps fortunate, seeing that he dreamed of a brigand's dash a
Rome and Venice, that Bourbon garrisons in Gaeta and Capu
forbade a precipitate advance. A sharp fight on the banks of th
Volturno showed the Garibaldians that even a Neapolitan forc
sallying from Capua could sometimes show its ugly teeth.

The magical success of the Redshirts had from the first bee
watched from Turin with feelings of mingled anxiety and admir
ation. There was the risk that the whole movement of Siciliar
and Neapolitan liberation might break down in sheer anarchy
There was the further danger that Garibaldi, who had alread
been with difficulty restrained from attacking the Papal States
would now march on Rome and, colliding with the French, pro
voke a diplomatic difficulty of the gravest kind with Napoleon
In either event the cause of Italian liberation would be seriousl
compromised. It would be an ill start for the new Kingdom o
Italy to be compelled at the very outset to put down a nationalis
insurrection in Naples and Sicily. It would be not less disastrou
if Napoleon, in order to protect the Pope from a Garibaldiar
coup d'état, should be constrained to embark on a serious cam
paign in central Italy.

That these dangers were successfully avoided was due not onl to the remarkable qualities shown at a critical juncture by Cavour, Garibaldi, and the King, but also by a surprising demonstration in favour of the Piedmontese monarchy among the population of Naples. With great wisdom Cavour decided that the time had now come for Victor Emmanuel to show himself in central and southern Italy and to settle with Garibaldi before the Redshirts had time to set foot on papal territory and there to make mischief which could not be repaired. The programme, which was laid before Napoleon, was carried out with punctuality and despatch. A motley force of Papalists under the adventurer Lamoricière was dispersed by Cialdini at Castelfidardo (September 18), and with the surrender of this composite and cosmopolitan army the whole resisting power of the one central Italian territory which still stood for the old cause of foreign occupation and clerical control was broken beyond repair. A Parliament was then summoned to Turin to approve the policy of the Government and to press for the speedy adhesion of Naples and Sicily. When the plébiscite was taken, an overwhelming vote (October 21) announced the triumph of Cavour and the defeat of Mazzini. The danger of a southern republic balancing and defying the northern monarchy was overpast. The one man who could have fatally wrecked Italian harmony swallowed, when the great moment came, his personal griefs, prejudices, and vanities. Though at heart a republican, Garibaldi commended and accepted the cause of the King in whose name he had fought and whose uniform he wore. Together they drove in triumph into Naples. Together they had helped to make Italy a nation.

It was then that Garibaldi reached the apex of his renown. He had won and surrendered the south, he had held and resigned a dictatorship. He had been offered and had refused titles, wealth, decorations. Civilized respectabilities meant nothing to this child of the Pampas. He knew that wild fowl languish in the cage. With a sublime simplicity, taking with him some seed-corn, some vegetables, some salt cod, and a little borrowed money, he turned his back upon the plaudits and vanities of Naples and sailed away to a life of hard work and poverty in the island of Caprera. There among shepherds and goat-herds he meditated how best to complete the redemption of Italy.

For Venetia and Rome were still wanting to the Italian kingdom, the first to be gained only through the defeat of Austria, the second defended by France and, save in the event of a com-

31

plete reversal of French policy or of a sudden collapse of French power, unlikely to pass out of papal governance. Accordingly the final stages in the unification of Italy depend less upon the efforts of the Italians themselves than upon changes in the balance of European power greater than any which Italy was able unaided to effect. The acquisition of Venice was no fruit of Italian victory, but of a secret offensive and defensive alliance most prudently

THE GROWTH OF ITALY.

concluded with the Prussians in April, 1866. The Italians indeed took part in the war to which that alliance was by intention the prelude, but they gained no victories. Rather they were defeated by land and sea. The prize of Venetia was won on the field of Sadowa by the formidable Prussian army which had been organized by Von Roon, was led by Moltke, and was the instrument of the far-reaching policy of Bismarck.

Four years later the victories of that same Prussian army led

o the recall of the French troops from Rome and so opened the
way to the establishment of the new royal government of Italy
upon the Quirinal, where it has since remained, the embodiment
of the very spirit of Italian nationalism, throwing its challenge,
now loud, now low, to the priestly court and cosmopolitan rule of
the Pope.

That the solution of the Roman question should have been so
long delayed is a matter of surprise only if we refuse to recognise
the large part played in politics by implacable men holding
absolute and rigid opinions. To Antonelli, the adviser of Pius IX,
it was as inconceivable that any concession should be voluntarily
made to those who sought to abridge by an inch the full extent
of the Papal State, as it was intolerable to Garibaldi that a priest
should be allowed to subtract for the conduct of his own cosmopolitan and obscurantist policies an inch from the sacred soil of
the Italian people. But between these two extremes there were
intermediate opinions. Napoleon III, whose merit it was to take a
cool and detached view of heat-raising problems, advanced plausible arguments in support of the contention that, while the Papal
States, being notoriously mismanaged, should be sensibly reduced,
the Pope should retain Rome and the Roman patrimony. To that
view, which was equally repugnant to strict clericals and Italian
patriots, but was nevertheless grounded on a correct appreciation
of the balances of Europe, the Emperor of the French continued
to adhere.

Cavour, too, had a solution of the Roman question. In exchange for the Temporal Power he offered to the Church complete spiritual independence, but Cavour died in 1861, and the
Roman question continued to torment the government of Italy
and the conscience of Europe. Twice the irrepressible Garibaldi
essayed a thrust at his old enemy in Rome. Twice he was foiled.
At Aspromonte (August 29, 1862) he was turned back by the
Piedmontese, at Mentana (November 3, 1867) he was defeated by
the French while the royal army of Italy, which had undertaken
to defend the Papal State from every attack, looked on in helpless
neutrality.

Little profit was derived by Napoleon from the Italian blood
which was shed on this ill-starred field. "Les fusils Chassepot
ont fait merveille," wrote General de Failly of the new French
rifles—words which were not easily forgiven by a sensitive people

condemned to endure with such patience as they could command the defeat of their greatest living national hero under circumstances of peculiar humiliation. Out of regard for the clericals of France the Emperor had thrown away the prospect of a valuable alliance with a kingdom which he had helped to create and which stood deep in his debt. The result was serious, for there came a time in 1870 when, needing Italian help and failing to find it, he was obliged unfriended to face the formidable onset of Germany in arms.

Nearly a century has elapsed since the various peoples of Italy who, though they spoke the same language, inherited the same culture and occupied the same ground, had been wont to view one another with animosity and distrust, were brought together under the rule of the Piedmontese monarchy. The union that in its opening decades had seemed in the highest degree precarious has weathered the storms of time. The special differences between South and North have been reduced, the monarchy has taken root, a strong and even fierce Italian patriotism has burnt away the inveterate local prejudices of earlier times. No Italian would desire to see a return to the days when his country was divided and powerless.

This success of the unification of Italy is the more remarkable seeing that the monarchy was devoid of many of those supports which in other lands have assisted monarchical institutions. No ancient aristocracy surrounded the throne, no long-descended renown enhanced its prestige, no brilliant victories brought elation to its subjects. As the Italian reflected upon the unification of his country, he was forced to admit that but for the help of France and Prussia Italy could not have been made one. The Italian navy had suffered defeat at Lissa, the Italian army at Custozza. The Church, which in other countries was apt to throw the whole weight of its influence into the scale of monarchical authority, was bitterly hostile to the kingdom which had shorn it of its patrimony and deprived the Holy See of its ancient political pre-eminence. By the Bull *Non Expedit* (1874-1903) Catholics were forbidden to take an active part in the politics of the kingdom. In Rome itself the violence of the schism was most keenly apparent. The Pope regarded himself as a prisoner in the Vatican, the two courts were at daggers drawn and the two societies, the Black and the White, albeit living in the same city, might have belonged, so far as friendly intercourse went, to two distant hemispheres.

Nevertheless the monarchy survived. A remarkable body of conscientious statesmen stood round Victor Emmanuel II during the first decade of the kingdom, and working on the high tide of enthusiasm which had been engendered by the movement of the Risorgimento carried on the work of Cavour. Italy remembers with gratitude the names of Ricasoli and La Marmora, of Lanza and Sella, of Minghetti and Spaventa, as those of men who, when the new state was in the making, shouldered the hardest part of the initial toil. When in 1876 power passed from the Right to the Left the foundations of the new Italy had been soundly laid. The English example of Free Trade and the coming of the railways supplied an unassailable economic argument for political union. Even if separatist tendencies had been stronger than they were, steam and water power would have made return to the old customs barriers unthinkable. However much the Tuscan may have differed from the Piedmontese and the Venetian, or the Neapolitan from the men of the north, plain and unmistakable considerations of economic convenience forced them together and bowed them to a common yoke.

BOOKS WHICH MAY BE CONSULTED

Bolton King : A History of Italian Unity. 1924.

W. R. Thayer : The Life and Times of Cavour. 1915.

F. A. Simpson : The Rise of Louis Napoleon. 1925.

Pierre de la Gorce : Histoire du Second Empire. 1908.

H. von Treitschke : Historische und politische Aufsätze, Vol. II. (Cavour.) 1871.

G. M. Trevelyan : Garibaldi. 1933.

Bolton King : Life of Mazzini. 1912.

E. L. Woodward : Three Studies in European Conservatism. 1929.

CHAPTER XVIII

TOWARDS GERMAN UNITY

The strongest obstacle to German national unity. Otto von Bismarck. Circumstances of his rise to power. The Prussian army saved from the Prussian Parliament. The defeat of Prussian liberalism. Frustration of the Austrian plan for the reform of the German Empire. The Polish rebellion of 1863. Bismarck obtains the Russian alliance. The Danish Duchies. The War of 1864 and the Treaty of Vienna. The Austro-Prussian condominium in the Duchies breaks down in 1865. Napoleon III. His acquiescence. His Liberalism. His Mexican adventure. The Emperor Maximilian. Decline in French prestige. Bismarck reassures Napoleon at Biarritz. Universal suffrage offered to Germany. The Seven Weeks' War. Bismarck's moderate use of victory. The Treaty of Prague. Anger in France. The new German constitution. Contrast between Italian and German national states.

IT was unlikely that the triumph of Italian nationalism should fail to revive the hopes of German union which had been cruelly shattered in the ruin of the liberal revolution. What the little military monarchy of Piedmont had done for Italy the much larger and more powerful Prussian Kingdom might easily achieve for the Germans. That sentiment was widely diffused, and yet, though the Italian and German problems were separated by an important difference, Austria was in either case the enemy. In Italy the Austrian was an alien. Among the Germans he would never be so regarded. Rather he was bone of their bone, flesh of their flesh, an integral part of their corporate historic life, and to many, especially to such as lived in the south, much to be preferred to the Prussians. Many Germans who vaguely wanted German unity shrank with horror before the spectre of an Austrian war, many clamoured to make Germany a nation while averting their eyes from the odious but necessary price. No plébiscite of the German people, if taken at any time in the sixties, would have given a majority in favour of a war with Austria or for a Germany placed under the Prussian heel. Only a Government ruthlessly prepared to defy public opinion, to divide Germany, and to face the horrors of a fratricidal strife, could contemplate the undertaking. Only the most elaborate military and diplomatic preparations could ensure its success.

The titanic figure of Bismarck, who held that no man should die until he had smoked a hundred thousand cigars and drunk five thousand bottles of champagne, was Nature's lavish response to these exacting requirements. It is the special property of this extraordinary man that, while infinitely flexible in detail, he envisaged from the first the large conditions of the German problem and allowed no scruples of conscience to interfere with the execution of his plans. In 1862, a year after Cavour's death, he told Disraeli that he intended at the earliest opportunity to make war on Austria. "Take care of that man," said the wise Jew; "he means what he says." And exactly four years later, with all Germany dubious or hostile and with no following but the soldiers, Bismarck got the war which from the first he had seen to be essential to his political designs.

His wonderful administration, which lasted from September, 1862, to March, 1890, was marked at its outset by one of those rare constitutional struggles which are of enduring importance in the history of nations. William I, who had taken over the management of Prussia as Regent in 1858 on his brother's incapacity, was a plain, dutiful Prussian soldier who from his experience of the revolution had conceived a deep dislike of popular movements. There was nothing of German idealism in this elderly sovereign. It was sufficient for him that Prussia should be strong and never again through military weakness be compelled to swallow humiliation. In Albert von Roon the King *1803-79* found a War Minister to his heart. Together they worked out a plan for the enlargement and reorganization of the Prussian army. They asked for more regiments, for a three years' instead of a two years' term of service. The Lower House of the Prussian Parliament threw out the Bill. Neither side would give way. The deadlock was protracted, Parliament refusing supplies, Von Roon and his master ultimately raising fresh regiments as if supplies had been voted. A general election only returned a House less conservative and more determined to obtain control of the government than the last. It was now no longer a question of three years' service *versus* two. The claim was made that in Prussia, as in England, Parliament must be supreme, that army, finance, foreign policy should be governed in accordance with the will of the people as expressed through their representatives. If that claim had been conceded, the whole history of Germany and Europe would have taken a different turn.

That it was successfully resisted was due to the dominating intervention of Bismarck. Summoned by Von Roon to save the situation, the new Minister-President put heart into the King, who had actually written out his abdication, faced the blizzard of the politicians, and despite a tempest of obloquy maintained the position that in Prussia the army was a thing too sacred for the Legislature to control. When the war was successfully over in 1866, he obtained a parliamentary indemnity for the expenditure which had been incurred without authority; but there was no element of penitence in the politic gesture. Neither then nor thereafter was Bismarck prepared to accept the English system. The crushing victory in the Austrian war enabled him to defy with impunity counsels founded on the success of insular liberalism, and to grave deep upon the constitutional life of Germany the principle that, although a Parliament may vote new taxes and discuss laws, three things lie outside and beyond it. Neither may it prescribe the army, nor frame policy, nor, as in England, make or unmake governments. To the last days of the Hohenzollern Empire these principles continued to inform constitutional·practice in Germany.

It must not be imagined that the championship of responsible government in Prussia went by default. The German Liberals were for the most part well-educated and patriotic citizens, who, while they valued national strength, were equally concerned for the protection of national liberty. They had the sympathy of the Crown Prince and of his intelligent, enthusiastic, but unwise English wife; they were supported by the learning and authority of the Universities; and there was no argumentative missile drawn from the vast arsenal of English experience which they were not competent to discharge at the head of the opprobrious Junker who single-handed and defiant held the fort for autocracy. But Prussia was not England. It was more feudal, more military, and, since the factory system had hardly begun, much less industrial.

For all these separate reasons liberalism was in Bismarck's eyes an ineffectual force, safe to insult, easy to supplant. Englishmen he liked and respected; but English principles of government, transplanted to Prussia, would work ruin. A necessary prelude, therefore, to the Austrian war was the rout of the Anglophiles and votaries of freedom in Germany. Here Bismarck's triumph was complete and enduring. His success is blazoned across the history of the world. He led Germany into the path of long-ange policies of aggrandizement based upon long-range military and naval programmes. The State was Power. War, as Clausevitz taught, was the continuation of policy. End and instrument acted and interacted. As policies became more ambitious, armaments became larger; as armaments grew, policies expanded. The conversion of Europe into an armed camp was an inevitable conequence of the defeat of Prussian Liberalism in 1862. The road was safe so long as Bismarck was in control. Afterwards it became dangerous. The stakes rose, the risks increased, until it was at last possible for an emotional people to believe that by force of an irresistible destiny or mission they were called upon to play for world power or downfall.

At the very outset of his administration an obstacle, the more formidable because it was concealed, threatened to wreck his whole design. Austria invited a Council of Princes to meet at Frankfort to consider a scheme for the reform of the German Federal Constitution. On the face of it no proposal could be more specious. The German Constitution, seeing that it was the worst in the world, badly needed thorough-going repairs. Of that no one was more acutely conscious than Bismarck; but repairs carried out under Austrian direction and with Prussian complicity could have but one result. Austrian authority would be fortified in Germany. It was therefore essential in Bismarck's view that Prussia should not be represented at Frankfort, that the Austrian plan should be frustrated *ab initio*, and that the way should be kept clear for the constitutional reconstruction of Germany under Prussian influence. The old King of Prussia was slow to appreciate these implications. It was only after a protracted struggle that Bismarck extorted his reluctant acquiescence in the view that an invitation, delivered by a King on the instructions of an Emperor for the promotion of an object affecting the general interests of the German people, should be unceremoniously declined.

The year which witnessed this rebuff to Austria was also *1863* marked by an insurrection in Russian Poland which was destined to exercise a wide influence on international affairs. So far as the rebellion itself was concerned, it was quickly and cruelly suppressed. The cause of the Poles, however, had never been regarded in western Europe as a matter with respect to which humane and civilized governments could adopt an attitude of frozen indifference. In France and England and even in Austria public opinion was greatly stirred by the spectacle of a gallant people vainly trying to preserve the elements of its national life under an alien and oppressive yoke. The governments of these three countries accordingly agreed to present to Russia a joint note urging an amnesty and the establishment of Polish Home Rule; and in this not too hopeful diplomatic demand Prussia was invited to concur. There could be no doubt in Bismarck's mind that the answer to be returned to this invitation must be an emphatic negative. For the furtherance of his scheme for isolating Austria it was a brilliant stroke of opportunity that Prussia should be able thus sharply to dissociate herself from any plans calculated to embarrass the Tzar in the handling of his Polish problem. At a moment of high tension, when abuse from every quarter was raining down on the Russian Government, one Power extended the hand of friendship, refusing not only to join in the note, but signing a military convention which bore on the face of it the evidence of a common interest in the policing of a troublesome people. From that moment Bismarck had the Russian alliance, which was the corner-stone of his policy and the indispensable condition of its success. From that moment he could feel assured that in the prosecution of the wars with Austria and perhaps with France, which would be necessary for the completion of his great design, Prussia would be secure on her eastern frontier.

It was a further guarantee of the solidity of the friendship that it was based upon a congenial confraternity of repression. Britain had its subject Poles as well as St. Petersburg, and as the Irish problem vexed the conscience of English Liberals, so in western Germany and wherever German Liberals were gathered together there was a disposition to sympathize with Polish grievances and to entertain suggestions for their relief. All this philo-Polish sentiment was abhorrent to the Pomeranian squire whose receipt for the Polish problem was that the Poles should be converted into Prussians with as little delay as possible, that their language should be stamped out, their culture effaced, their traditions forgotten, and that the liberalism which sought to preserve some lineaments of the Polish nation should be countered by a resolute policy of assimilation. In this task Bismarck was as little disposed to tolerate interference as the Russians. " I would rather die," he said to General Fleury in 1863, " than permit our position in Posen to be discussed at a European Con-

gress. I would rather cede our Rhinelands." And indeed so long
as Russia and Prussia stood together, though the Liberals of
Europe filled the air with their protests and lamentations,
here was not and could not be the faintest hope for Polish
liberty.

Meanwhile a quarrel was boiling up in the base of the Danish
peninsula which was destined to give Bismarck his Austrian
war, to enable Prussia to build the Kiel Canal, opening out to
United Germany a new destiny upon the ocean. It is unnecessary
to burden the memory with the complicated details of the
Schleswig-Holstein question. The kernel of the matter is that
these two Duchies, Holstein being within and Schleswig without
the confines of the German Empire, but both since 1490 continuously governed by the King of Denmark, were now in dispute. They were desired by Denmark. They were desired by
the German Federation. They were desired and, without a jot
or tittle of historical or legal claim, taken by Prussia. The process by which this result was achieved was regarded by Bismarck not without justification as his political masterpiece; and
indeed there can be no more characteristic example of his craft.

The quarrel was by no means new. All Germany in 1848 had
trembled with indignation at the news that the Danes were
attempting to incorporate Schleswig, the most northerly of the
Scandinavian Duchies, in their monarchy, and to sever its connection, deemed among the legists and historians of the country
to be indissoluble, with the more German Duchy of Holstein.
In that year of revolution, when every issue in the national life
was put in question, there was no matter upon which German
opinion was more passionately unanimous than that the Duchies
must be subject to a single ruler, and he (after the death of
Frederick VII of Denmark, who had no male issue) a German
Prince. Such a Prince the German Diet was able to produce.
His name was the Duke of Augustenburg. We may here call
him the old Pretender.

A period of confused and inconclusive fighting was terminated
by the intervention of the Powers. By the Treaty of London in
1852 it was decided that Frederick VII should be succeeded by
Christian of Glücksburg, who should rule both in Denmark and
in the Duchies. The thorny problem seemed to be happily solved,
for since Austria and Prussia concurred in the treaty it was

difficult to believe that its provisions would be upset, and as for the old Pretender he accepted a handsome payment in commutation of his claims.

The quarrel, however, was not concluded. In Copenhagen there was a strong current of popular feeling in favour of bringing the Danish frontier southward to the Eider, and a disposition, hotly resented by the Germans, to interfere with the local privileges in the Duchies; and it was while German and Dane were snarling at one another, and the old embers which had been thought to be extinguished were sending out little hot jets of flame, that Frederick VII (March 30, 1863) issued a constitution incorporating Schleswig in his monarchy and giving home rule to Holstein. It was a very sensible solution. It was in principle the solution which was ultimately imposed by the Treaty of Versailles. It allotted the Danish-speaking Duchy to the Danes and gave to the German-speaking Duchy a practical measure of autonomy, but in Germany it was received with shrieks of horror. The Holstein Estates, which had not been consulted, appealed to the Diet, and since the Diet had been no party to the Treaty of London, it deemed itself free to work for the separation of the indissoluble Duchies from the Danish Kingdom and for their creation into a principality for a German Prince. Again a candidate was not wanting. With obliging hardihood, the son of the old Pretender, averring that he was not bound by his father's renunciation, again put forward the claims of his house.

On November 15, 1863, Frederick VII of Denmark died and was duly, and in accordance with the terms of the Treaty of London, succeeded by Christian IX, who under popular pressure brought into execution King Frederick's Constitution.

It is at this point that Bismarck began to inaugurate the series of diplomatic manoeuvres which ultimately gave to Prussia the Danish Duchies. He had no wish to march with the Diet. As a signatory of the London Treaty he was bound in advance to recognize Christian, on risk of giving offence to England and Russia. It was no attraction for him that the young Pretender, a liberal and a friend of the Crown Prince, should rule over a new German State which would certainly act as a check upon Prussia. He wanted the Duchies for his master. He determined therefore to act not with the Diet but with Austria, a co-signatory of the London Treaty, to acknowledge Christian according to the terms

of that treaty, but at the same time to present him with an ultimatum demanding the immediate repeal of the November constitution and couched in such a form that by no possibility could
it be accepted. Everything went forward according to plan. The
Danes, who had been encouraged to hope that the manifest
sympathy of England was no idle talk, rejected the ultimatum.
Austrian and Prussian troops invaded the Duchies (January,
1864), defeated the Danes and compelled Christian to sue for
peace. By the Treaty of Vienna the Danish ruler ceded his rights *Oct.,*
over Schleswig-Holstein and over the little Duchy of Lauenburg *1864*
to the two victorious German Powers.

A situation of great delicacy was now created. A condominium
is never a comfortable arrangement, and a condominium between
Austria and Prussia could not be expected to work without
friction. Sooner or later the two Powers were bound to determine
who should be invited to rule the territory of which they might
now by right of conquest dispose. Austria, with the sympathy
of the great majority of the German people, supported the claims
of the young Pretender which Bismarck was prepared to resist to
the end, except upon terms which would have made the Duchies
all but in name a Prussian province. The injudicious conduct of
the young prince, who settled down in Kiel, opened a little Court,
and with the obvious sympathy of the Austrian administration
promoted his candidature in the locality, increased the irritation
of Berlin. In the summer of 1865 the two countries were on the *Aug.,*
brink of war. Austria, however, was not then ready to take up *1865*
the Prussian challenge; nor was Prussian diplomatic preparation
complete. A Convention was signed at Gastein which plastered
over the cracks and provided a breathing space during which
the two Powers might organize their forces for a war. It was
arranged that the condominium should cease, and that Holstein
should be administered by Austria, Schleswig by Prussia, while
the Duchy of Lauenburg should be handed over absolutely to
the Prussian King.

So far Bismarck had been extraordinarily successful. Against
the predominant and even passionate opinion of the German
people, and despite the resistance of the Prussian Court and
Parliament, he had frustrated the Augustenburg claim. Without
interference from France or England he had carried the Danish
war to a successful conclusion; and now that victory had
crowned the first efforts of the newly organized Prussian army,

and that the old King's appetite for conquest had at last been
whetted by the acquisition of Lauenburg, he could look with
confidence to the future. With the endless possibilities of friction
still existing in the Duchies, it would always be possible at a
convenient moment to promote a rupture with the Austrians.
Meanwhile it was necessary to work for the complete isolation
of the enemy. On the eastern front Bismarck was secure. The
Russians could be depended on to observe a friendly neutrality,
but it was still necessary to secure if possible the neutrality of
France and the active co-operation of Italy.

Napoleon III, like Talleyrand and Briand, was a good European. Though he thought it necessary to give satisfaction to the
martial spirit of his people, he believed in peace, in nationality,
in government by Congress. He inherited the doctrine which his
great uncle had preached at St. Helena, that the formation of
large national aggregates was in the interest of European
stability. There is no reason to doubt that his sympathy with
the Italians and the Poles was genuine and disinterested; and
that, always provided that the balance of power in Europe was
not altered to the disadvantage of his country, he was willing to
contemplate and anxious to assist those large changes in the
map of Europe which were necessary to bring the political
boundaries of states more nearly in accord with national sentiments. The expansion of Prussia caused him no alarm. Not
only did he think it reasonable that the Prussians should have
the Danish Duchies, but even the prospect of a North German
Federation under Prussian leadership gave him no concern.
Would not the southern Germans lean on France? Would he
not, in a Prussian war against Austria, be able to repeat the
brilliant coup which had extracted Savoy and Nice from the
necessities of Piedmont? Would not such a war bring Venetia
to Italy? The heart of Napoleon, as Bismarck was quick to
observe, was better than his head.

The five years which had elapsed since 1860 brought with them
a sensible decline in the force and coherence of the French
Empire. The head of the state was no longer the man of the
coup d'état and the Crimean War. Incessant work and anxiety
had taken toll of a constitution which had probably been impaired by dissipation. A grave disorder, characterized by recurrent paroxysms of almost unbearable pain, weakened the will and
broke down the springs of enterprise.

And meanwhile, partly as a result of this physical deterioration, and partly that he might give effect to his uncle's doctrine that in due time the tension of autocracy should be relaxed and give place to the freer play of parliamentary institutions, he had begun to liberalize the Empire, permitting (November 22, 1860) the Senate and Legislative body to vote and debate an annual address in response to the speech from the throne, providing certain ministers without portfolio to explain and defend the government measures, and giving sanction to the publication of full shorthand reports of parliamentary debates. In the revival of parliamentary life which followed upon this measure the latent antagonisms of the French people burst into flame. The clericals blamed the Emperor because he had helped the Italians, the liberals because he had abandoned them. The manufacturers assailed his free trade, the Orleanists his confiscations, the adherents of the Legitimate branch his acquiescence in the expulsion of the Bourbons from Naples. The Emperor, who, after his Crimean and Italian trophies, had looked forward to a golden spell of honoured leisure during which he might shape an immortal biography of Julius Caesar, and further enrich his country with railways, telegraphs and banks, found himself exposed to competing and uncomfortable pressures, which it was difficult to resist. On the one hand he was pressed to do something for the Pope, on the other hand to redeem his early promise of Venetia to Italy. At last in an evil hour he was persuaded by his clerical advisers to embark on a crusade, part Catholic, part financial, in the distant land of Mexico.

In this country of chronic and passionate dissensions society was divided into two factions, one clerical and conservative led by Miramon, another progressive and anti-clerical which had ranged itself under Benito Juarez, an Indian remarkable for the integrity of his character, the clearness of his views, and the decision of his will, but regarded with vehement disapprobation all over the Catholic world for his vigorous and comprehensive measures to curtail the authority and wealth of the Church. Both parties resorted to arms, both parties borrowed money from Europe; and both parties were lavish in promises of repayment when once the fortune of war had declared in its favour. A Swiss banker in Paris named Jekker had lent money to Miramon and promised the Duc de Morny, the Emperor's half-brother,

30 per cent. of the profits. It was not, however, Miramon, but Juarez who won the war (1861).

To the clericals of France and notably to the Empress the overthrow of the sacrilegious Indians and the establishment in Mexico of a Catholic Empire under French tutelage appeared to be objects attractive in themselves and likely to result in financial profit. Mexico was, indeed, a distant country whose climate and geography were ill understood, but it was known to be large, was reputed to be fabulously wealthy, and, having been conquered by the Spaniards, was suspected, despite appearances to the contrary, of cherishing a steadfast affection for the Catholic Church and for monarchical institutions. Religion, finance, politics combined to point to a Mexican enterprise. It would please the Vatican, gratify the Bourse, exalt the Empire. Moreover, the moment was propitious. The United States was torn by the civil war between North and South. While the Anglo-Saxon Protestants were quarrelling over slavery and state rights, Napoleon might hope to establish upon the American Continent a Latin and Catholic state as an outpost of France and a barrier against the expansive movements of Western heresy.

1861-5

While these large ideas were taking shape in France, the Emperor joined hands with England and Spain in the more limited objective of a debt-collecting expedition. Ships were sent across the Atlantic, contingents were landed on the distant and malarious coast, and the new republican government of Juarez was sharply reminded that European creditors were not to be fobbed off by a two years' moratorium on the foreign debt. This proceeding was certainly high-handed; but far less open to objection than the decision of Napoleon, after his allies had withdrawn, to revolutionize the government of Mexico in the wild and erroneous belief that the people of that country, of whom little was known in Paris, were eager to exchange the new modernizing republic of Juarez for a Catholic and clerical monarchy.

Jan.,
1862

In no long time it appeared that the enterprise of forcing a sovereign upon the Mexican people was far more costly in troops and money than had ever been apprehended. To the person of the French nominee who was invited (July 10, 1863) to mount the Mexican throne no objection could be taken. Maximilian was the brother of Francis Joseph, the Emperor of Austria, and the husband of Charlotte, the daughter of the Belgian King. Tall, handsome, benevolent, with an honourable record of liberality as administrator of the Milanese, Maximilian was a ruler whom any people desirous of mild and honourable governance might have been content to obey. Unfortunately the Mexicans did not want him. They were eccentric enough to prefer their austere republican leader with his wild Indian blood to an accomplished Prince boasting the most famous lineage in Europe. Almost from the first it was clear that only French bayonets and French treasure could support the precarious throne of the unfortunate alien; but of such support there could, in the nature of things, be no indefinite continuance. In point of fact the end came suddenly and in a manner most humiliating for France, since the government of Washington, having vanquished the South in the civil war, peremptorily ordered the French out of Mexico and refused to acknowledge the sovereign who had been imposed on the Mexican people. That nothing might be wanting to a lamentable miscarriage of splendid hopes, the unfortunate Maximilian, who had been deserted by his French patrons, soon afterwards fell into the hands of his enemies and died facing a firing party at Queretaro.

June, 1867

It is difficult to exaggerate the loss of prestige sustained by the French Empire through the melancholy failure of the Mexican expedition. Everything had been miscalculated, the temper and courage of the Mexican population, the number of troops required to reduce the country, the obstacle offered by the climate, the prospects of the Northern cause in the American civil war. Even when they were at their greatest strength the French troops had only been able to police a tiny segment of the vast country; and meanwhile how many small but melancholy reverses, what serious wastage through disease had they not been compelled to endure! From the first the Mexican policy was sharply criticized by liberals who asked themselves what national interest was involved in the championship of the priests and monks of Mexico against the wholesome principles of the French Revolution, and complained that an army which would have been more usefully posted on the eastern frontier of France was squandered at a distance of five thousand miles in a quarrel fomented by priests and financiers. It was bad enough that the enterprise should have failed; it was worse that it should have been derided as "Duke Jekker's war" and denounced as a sordid operation undertaken to retrieve the gambling losses of a knot of influential speculators.

By the autumn of 1865 the failure of the Mexican war was an accomplished fact. The disappointment was keen, the humiliation palpable, and any prospect of obtaining in some other quarter of the political field compensations which might heal the sore and distract attention was eagerly to be desired. Such a prospect Bismarck offered to Napoleon at Biarritz. With the engaging frankness which made him so formidable a diplomatist the Prussian statesman put all his cards on the table; the war with Austria, the revision of the German Constitution, the acquisition of the Danish Duchies, an Italian alliance, and could he be assured of her neutrality a willingness to consider the enlargement of France. Nothing was made precise; nothing was committed to paper. It was sufficient for Bismarck's purpose that in exchange for vague hints of compensation, Napoleon had shown himself favourable to the Prussian plan and willing, in the event of war, to observe neutrality.

Emboldened by this precious, if shadowy, assurance, Bismarck could now complete his preparations for the war which had been so long designed and so artfully delayed. The military help of Italy was purchased by the promise of Venetia so that the enemy could be engaged on two fronts, and, since the Prussian railways were built, and the Prussian army, being divided into corps, each locally recruited and equipped with a full complement of cavalry, artillery, and engineers, had a fortnight's advantage in mobilization over its adversary, there was every reason to anticipate success. There remained, however, before the cannon were allowed to speak, one final precaution. It was part of the greatness of Bismarck that he saw the value of the moral element in war. Entering, as he proposed to do, into a struggle which was violently unpopular with the main part of the German people, he saw that the discovery of some pretext larger and more imaginative than the squalid and local quarrel in the Danish Duchies was a condition of permanent success. A Prussian victory was not enough. He must offer something big to the German people. What he offered was amazing. On the day after the Italian alliance was secured the arch-Tory came forward with a scheme for a general reform of the German Confederation and for a German Parliament to be elected by universal suffrage. It has been thought that he was influenced by Lassalle, the socialist. It is more probable that, like Disraeli, he had a deep conviction that though the middle class may be liberal, democracy is Tory.

Though it was pretended in Berlin that the final provocation came from Austria, there was no real doubt that it was Bismarck's war. Moltke, who was to command the Prussian army, told the bare truth when he said afterwards, " The war of 1866 did not take place because the existence of Prussia was threatened, or in obedience to public opinion or to the will of the people. It was a war which was foreseen long before, which was prepared with deliberation and recognized as necessary by the Cabinet, not in order to obtain territorial aggrandisement, but for power in order to secure the establishment of Prussian hegemony in Germany." This is no pretty story. " It must be confessed," said Bismarck to Treitschke, with engaging frankness, " that our linen was not always of the cleanest."

The war, which lasted seven weeks, was a revelation to Europe of the results which might be attained by the application of Prussian science and Prussian methods to the military art. The swiftness of the Prussian mobilization, the precision of the Prussian movements, the excellence of the Prussian needle gun, the clever use which was now for the first time made of railways, portended the advent of an era in which the great decisions of history would be governed by the relative capacity of states to make use of their technical and scientific resources, and the direction of war would more and more resemble the management of a vast and intricate industrial business. The ultimatum was delivered on June 15, 1866. In the first week of this war north-west Germany was under the Prussian heel; in the third (July 3) the main Austrian army was crushed at Sadowa (or Königgrätz), in Bohemia. The fight was stiff. The issue was long in doubt; and the day was won only when the army of the Crown Prince was in a position to attack the enemy right flank; but in proportion as the Austrian resistance had been obstinate, so was the catastrophe of their army, when that resistance was finally broken down, irretrievably complete. The way was open to Vienna. It was there that the old king, flushed with victory, decreed and determined to make the peace.

There is no more certain test of statesmanship than the capacity to resist the political intoxication of victory. Unlike

Napoleon I, who with every military success raised his diplomatic terms, Bismarck knew what he wanted and what he did not want. It was no part of his plan unnecessarily to abase or humiliate the Austrians, whose alliance or neutrality might hereafter be precious to his king and country. He did not wish for Austrian territory, or for fresh victories, or for a triumphal entry into the capital of the beaten foe. He was content if Austria would withdraw from Germany, acquiesce in Prussia's acquisition of the Danish Duchies, and in the formation of a North German Confederation under Prussian leadership. He would not even, out of consideration to the susceptibility of the South German governments, put any constraint upon them to join the North German Confederation. Rather he was prepared to acquiesce in a separate federation of the south, should this be desired. Though a great body of his compatriots clamoured for a united Germany, he shrank from such ambitious precipitation, calculating that a North German Federation would be as much as Prussia could then hope to digest or France be expected to accept. Before the war he had made up his mind that the Main should be his boundary, and from this prudent decision he refused to retreat. A pan-German movement was a counsel of desperation, a violent and doubtful expedient to be kept in reserve against the possible event of a Franco-Austrian alliance. It was far better not to force the southern issue, but to allow the South Germans to come into the Prussian Federation when and as they chose. He set his course to catch the breeze of their favour. Though they had fought against Prussia he would have no indemnities, and, on this crucial point eventually vanquishing his master, no annexations. His clemency was promptly rewarded, for before August was out Bavaria, Würtemberg, and Baden had signed military conventions with the government of the north.

On such wise and generous terms Austria was prepared to treat, and almost before Europe had recovered from its surprise at the news of Sadowa, it was faced (August 23) with the accomplished fact of the Treaty of Prague. The extreme expedition with which Bismarck, resolutely overcoming the opposition of the king and the army chiefs, wound up the war and made the peace was grounded upon the apprehension that, were the struggle protracted, he might be called upon to face the armed opposition of France. He had the more reason for anxiety since two days after Sadowa Napoleon made an offer of mediation which he felt himself compelled to accept. What was chiefly to be feared was that while the main body of the Prussian army was in Bohemia Napoleon would mobilize on the Rhine, and, as part of the general treaty settlement, demand compensation for France at the point of the sword.

That Napoleon entirely failed to extract any advantage for France out of the Prussian wars with Denmark and Austria was made a grave matter of reproach in the French Chamber. With sentiments of rage, jealousy, and apprehension France was condemned to witness the sensational victory which had enabled Prussia to swallow Hanover, Hesse Cassel, the Danish Duchies, to dominate all Germany to the Main, to add four and a quarter million inhabitants to her population, and to overturn the whole balance of power in central Europe, while not a gun nor a man had been moved by the Emperor to secure compensating advantages for his country. "It is France who has been defeated at Sadowa," said Marshal Randon bitterly; and it was a defeat which diplomacy was powerless to repair. Bismarck's blow had been too swift. The French search for compensations came too late. In the period which elapsed between the battle of Sadowa and the outbreak of the Franco-Prussian War the Emperor asked for every kind of solatium, for the Rhenish Palatinate and Hesse, for Mainz and the Saar, for Belgium and for Luxemburg. Such requests unsupported by force were rejected with impunity; but the evidence that they were made was carefully preserved and used at the proper moment with decisive effect to make French diplomacy odious to Bavaria and England.

Meanwhile the new North German Confederation received from the hands of its architect a Constitution which, while it contained little of English liberalism, was strong enough to endure the stormy weather of fifty-two years. The Reichstag or Federal Parliament, being elected by universal suffrage, was based upon a larger measure of democratic support than any English Parliament until 1918; but, in accordance with Bismarckian principles, it could neither make nor unmake governments, nor finance policies, nor control by an annual army act the scale of the military establishments. Accordingly it was not in this democratic assembly that the seat of sovereignty was allowed to rest. The real governing organ of the Federation was a Federal Council (Bundesrat) composed of forty-two delegates from the different States of the Union, which deliberated in secret under the presidency of the Chancellor, who was also the Minister-President or Prime Minister of Prussia. Such a council seemed to many critics to be unnecessarily cumbrous. Why, it was asked, should Prussia give to twenty little dynasties a separate representation in the supreme governing organ of the new State? Would not complete centralization be a simpler and more effective plan? Prussia had the power to stamp out these ineffectual relics of the past. It had dethroned the King of Hanover and put an end to his dynasty. Why, then, should it be at pains to keep alive a number of separate centres of political action and possible obstructiveness, and even, in the case of Saxony, to go so far as to permit a member of the northern Confederation to be separately represented by ministers at foreign courts? There can be no question that Bismarck was wise in resisting the temptation to make of modern Germany a unitary State. The dynasties were deep-rooted in the soil of German history and had a contribution to make to the tasks of government. From their wholesale destruction nothing was to be apprehended but needless difficulties in the north, and the development of a violent aversion among the South German peoples from any thought of closer union. Moreover, there was no risk to strong and efficient government in the federal plan. Prussia had an assured majority in the Council and Prussia was Bismarck. Under the original provisions of this unique constitution the German Chancellor, responsible to his king alone and untrammelled by a German Cabinet, was the working head of the Government in all its branches. Neither Bundesrat, nor Reichstag, nor Prussian Parliament could dismiss him from office or effectually challenge his will. Year after year the vast figure of the Chancellor dominated the scene, filling Europe with the thunder of his powerful oratory and reading to his wondering compatriots fresh lessons in the art of ruling mankind.

Great then was the contrast between the ordering of the two national states which owe their being respectively to Cavour and Bismarck. In Italy the triumph of nationalism was associated with the establishment of Parliamentary government on the English plan; in Germany with its decisive defeat. Yet the German polity, though so framed as to secure for Prussian autocracy the final word, refused it few of the lessons which are vouchsafed to the statesmen of Parliamentary countries. At regular intervals the cleansing tides of universal suffrage swept through the Reichstag and enabled fresh formations of opinion to make themselves felt in the political life of the country. These were not always favourable to Bismarck. While the national Liberals employed every instrument of popular propaganda to advocate German union and to give support to the new institutions of the state, Catholicism and Socialism bade him defiance.

BOOKS WHICH MAY BE CONSULTED

J. W. Headlam : Bismarck and the Foundation of the German Empire. 1899.
C. Grant Robertson : Life of Bismarck. 1918.
Bismarck's Thoughts and Recollections. 1899.
Pierre de la Gorce : Histoire du Second Empire. 1908.
H. A. L. Fisher : Bonapartism. 1909.
E. Ollivier : L'Empire Libéral. 1911.
F. A. Simpson : Louis Napoleon and the Recovery of France, 1848-1856. 1923.
P. Guedalla : The Second Empire. 1932.
Lord Edmund Fitzmaurice : Life of Lord Granville.

CHAPTER XIX

THE FOUNDATION OF THE GERMAN EMPIRE

Prussian war preparations. Uncertain policy of France. The temper of the French clericals. The Liberals, republicans, and socialists. Émile Ollivier. The Hohenzollern candidature. The Ems telegram. The war guilt. German superiority. Inferiority of the French higher command. Absence of trained French reserves. The campaign. The national rising. Léon Gambetta. The siege of Paris. The assembly of Bordeaux. The Peace of Frankfort and the contribution of Thiers. Alsace-Lorraine. The German Empire. Vast ambitions of Prussia.

1864 and 1866

WE now approach the last and greatest of the three wars which forged the unity of the German nation. First Prussia had forced a quarrel on the Danes, then on the Austrians. The final obstacle which appeared to stand between Bismarck and his ambition was France.

July, 1866

It was not to be supposed that Paris, which had been so greatly perturbed by the Prussian victory at Sadowa, would fail to resent, and within the measure of its strength to oppose, the expansion of Prussian power beyond the Main. A philosopher might have reflected that since some day or other German unity was bound to come, France would be wise to extend an early and cordial welcome to a change which she could not expect permanently to avert. But the ruler of a high-spirited, vain, and intelligent people cannot afford to be a philosopher. The moods, the fears, the foibles of his countrymen circumscribe his freedom, and when every *boulevardier* in Paris was certain that Prussia was henceforth the enemy it was impossible for Napoleon to behave as if Germany were the friend. The temper of Paris was well known in Berlin. To Bismarck and his military friends it was clear they could not reckon on completing the half-finished fabric of German unity without a violent clash with France. Strenuously, seriously, and methodically they pushed on the work of military preparation.

No such clarity or fixity of purpose was discernible in the counsels of the French Emperor. Here everything was opaque, genial, uncertain. War was thought of not as an inevitable stage in a national programme, but as an evil which might be circum vented by diplomacy. Alliances were projected with Austria and Italy. Conversations were held, visits exchanged, but nothing clinched. There was a vague expectation that in the event of war, Denmark, Hanover, Bavaria might welcome the chance of chastening Prussian insolence; but here again nothing was done. Important army reforms were projected but permitted to suffer defeat in an economizing Chamber, which, though it agreed that Prussia was the enemy, never for a moment imagined that the Prussians were a match for the famous professional army of France. Perhaps war might never be necessary. The friendship of France was precious, and like all precious things could be had for a price. In the interval which elapsed between Sadowa and the Franco-Prussian War French diplomacy was busy in the search for compensations which might appease public opinion at home and render it more easy to preserve the peace. There was the Rhenish Palatinate, there was Luxemburg, there was Belgium. These were foolish and dangerous quests. Nothing but harm came from them. When the Bavarians learnt through a French newspaper to whom the secret had been communicated by Bismarck that France had asked for a slice of southern Germany, they had no further scruple about joining the Prussians in the war. The scheme for the purchase of Luxemburg was withdrawn under pressure of fierce and open Prussian hostility. But most damaging of all was the claim for Belgium which Benedetti had been instructed to make in 1866; for when Bismarck, at the outbreak of the Franco-Prussian War, published the draft treaty in which this claim was made, British opinion, regarding Belgian neutrality as the Holy of Holies, veered sharply round to the German side.

Although to outward appearances the Court of Napoleon was still as glittering and lavish as ever, a disturbing sense of anxiety ran through the Tuileries. The Emperor was no longer capable of firm decisions. The heir to the throne was a boy. From every quarter the dynasty was assailed by a gathering volume of irritable and sardonic opposition. It was in vain that sacrifice after sacrifice was made to that great body of clerical opinion which had been the original mainstay of the Imperial power, that the Pope had been defended by a French garrison in Rome, that forty thousand good French troops had been sent upon a Catholic crusade in Mexico, and that Duruy, the greatest education minister of the century, had been ejected from power. The

clericals were not content. They could never forgive the
sovereign by whose initial intervention the sacrilegious Italians
had been enabled to eject the ancient and orthodox Houses of
Habsburg and Bourbon from Italian soil and to rob the Pope of
the greater part of his Principality. The influential Catholic
Bishops, the powerful ultramontane press led by Louis Veuillot, a
journalist of fiery temper, regarded it as the primary duty of the
French Government to support Catholic interests all over the
world and visited every backsliding with their steadfast censures.
In democratic nationalism they saw the arch-enemy of the
Church, and they applauded the syllabus of 1864, in which the
Pope condemned, among other features of contemporary civiliza-
tion, the institution of universal suffrage, and therefore by
implication an Empire built on the plébiscite.

If such was the temper of the clericals, it may easily be
imagined that the more progressive spirits found even less to
applaud in the Napoleonic régime. There was no glamour about
Fould, the Jew financier, or the lawyer Rouher, or the able but
unpopular Haussmann who drove the Boulevards through Paris
and made of it the modern city which we know. There was no
glory, but on the contrary a series of humiliating rebuffs in the
later foreign policy of the Emperor. The young men thought
that new blood was wanted in the government. The Liberals in
the Chamber, a growing body led by Émile Ollivier, a French
Gladstone but without the Englishman's courage, clerical, high-
minded, cultured, eloquent, clamoured for the enlargement of
the liberties of 1860 and for the establishment of responsible
government. After a long silence Republicanism recovered its
voice in Léon Gambetta, a young lawyer from the south who
openly preached the overthrow of the Empire. The socialists,
deriving prestige from an international institution, the exiles of
1852, released by successive acts of amnesty, added virulence to
the attack. Most alarming was the fact that during the last two
years of his reign, the Emperor was the mark not only of odium
but of ridicule. It was inconvenient that he should be denounced
as an assassin by the man in the street. More deadly was the incessant and brilliant raillery of *La Lanterne*, the organ of Roche-
fort, of all French journalists of that time the most gifted in
the art of cruel and irresponsible burlesque.

The situation was one of extreme danger. After the elections
of 1869 when, despite official pressure upon the electorate, the

b. 1825

opposition polled nearly half the votes of France, it seemed to many that there would be a race between internal revolution and foreign war. Either the Empire would perish from the blows of its assailants from within or by a successful vindication of French prestige abroad might secure for itself a fresh lease of life. There was a third way pressed upon the Emperor by Ollivier and ultimately, after many hesitations, adopted. Liberalism, such as had been found compatible with the existence of monarchy in England and Italy, might be applied to France. A homogeneous ministry, responsible to the popular Chamber, might relieve the Emperor of his crushing burden, satisfy artisan opinion, and by robbing revolution of its *raison d'être*, preserve the dynasty. The experiment was tried. On January 3, 1870, Ollivier found himself head of a Liberal administration. The constitution was reformed in a Liberal sense, the reforms were submitted to a plébiscite, and to the immense relief of the Court were accepted by a majority of nearly six million votes. Everything then seemed to point to peace, prosperity, and a fresh lease of power for the Empire. Lord Clarendon at Ollivier's suggestion began to open projects of disarmament with Bismarck. " On whichever side we look," declared the new French Premier, " there is an absence of troublesome questions; at no moment has the maintenance of peace in Europe been better secured." A month later, springing from the unsuspected source of a Spanish revolution and an empty throne in Madrid, the war broke out which swept away Napoleon and Ollivier and the Liberal Empire, and at the same time enabled the dream of German unity to become an established fact.

On July 3, 1870, Paris learned that Prince Leopold of Hohenzollern Sigmaringen, a distant kinsman of the Prussian king, the son of Prince Anthony who had been Prime Minister of Prussia, and the elder brother of the Prince of Roumania, had accepted, subject to the confirmation of the Cortes, the vacant throne of Spain. At once a situation of the gravest diplomatic tension was created. The Hohenzollern candidature had been discussed confidentially in Berlin in 1869, when the Prussians were apprised of the French objection to a plan which threatened to recall the Empire of Charles V and to alter the European balance to the detriment of France. How then did it come about that this obnoxious candidature was renewed? The French

government flew to the conclusion that Bismarck was at the
bottom of yet another plot to humiliate the French people, and
that, unless the candidature was withdrawn before the meeting
of the Spanish Cortes on July 20, France would be compelled to
draw the sword. On July 6 Gramont, the Foreign Minister, told
the Chamber that the honour and interest of the country were
involved. Even Ollivier, the liberal, the pacifist, the statesman,
who had openly declared (in a German print) that he would be
no party to resisting by force of arms the willing union of
southern and northern Germany, was stirred to a white heat of
indignation by this assumed exhibition of Prussian guile and
ill-will.

On this feverish disposition of the public mind there suddenly
dropped on the evening of July 11, like manna from heaven,
unofficial news that Prince Anthony of Hohenzollern had been
induced to renounce the Spanish throne in the name of his son.
Great was the surprise, greater the relief. It seemed that the
danger was overpast and that the representations of France had
produced their effect. The Emperor and Ollivier professed themselves satisfied. Surely this was not only peace but peace with
honour? The aged Guizot asserted that he could recall no
greater diplomatic victory for France.

The prize of peace, no sooner won, was sacrificed by a wanton
act of folly. Gramont, a diplomatist by profession and a great
deal more warlike than his Prime Minister, was not satisfied with
the bare renunciation of "Father Anthony." He must receive a
definite assurance from the Prussian King that the withdrawal
had his assent and that the candidature would never be renewed.
And he even went so far as to suggest to the Prussian ambassador in Paris that his master should express his regret for the
occurrence. Unfortunately Gramont was not alone in his unwisdom. In the Chamber, which had been worked up into a
mad fit of intractable passion by the events of the last few days,
a fool spoke of guarantees, and the cry for guarantees passing
from the Chamber to St. Cloud unnerved the Emperor. Behind
the back of Ollivier and his Cabinet he associated himself (July
13) with his foreign minister in instructing Benedetti to meet
King William at Ems, and there obtain from him an assurance
that he associated himself with Prince Anthony's withdrawal,
and would not authorize any renewal of the attempt to set a
Hohenzollern on the throne of Spain.

Though the Spanish matter had never been brought before the Prussian Cabinet, the French were right in their surmise that Bismarck was at the bottom of the intrigue. He had in fact left no stone unturned to counter the Franco-Austrian conversations by an alliance which should open Spanish markets to Prussian trade and secure for his country in the event of French hostilities a friendly power beyond the Pyrenees. He pressed the Hohenzollerns to accept the offer, pressed the Spaniards to renew it, pressed his royal master to regard it with favour and to treat it as a matter of strictest confidence, and, while carefully denying official cognizance of the affair, saw that it was discussed at a special meeting of the Council attended by the King, the Princes, and the War Lords. The utmost secrecy was observed, for it was hoped that, before the French were even aware that an offer had been made, the German Prince might be formally accepted in Madrid. Two consequences, each of them grateful to Bismarck, might ensue, a war between France and Prussia or, a degree less desirable, a war between France and Spain. It was, therefore, with bitter disappointment that Bismarck learnt (July 12) that "Father Anthony" had after all made the great refusal, that French diplomacy had triumphed, and that the insolence of the Paris Press was to go unchastised. In his *Thoughts and Recollections* he describes it as the greatest humiliation which his country had suffered since Olmütz.

Gramont delivered him from his dejection. When Benedetti met the King on the Promenade at Ems, the old gentleman was civil but firm. He would give no guarantee, broke off the interview, and, though twice subsequently requested to do so, would give no further audience to the French ambassador; but he sent to say that he had received an official communication from Prince Leopold withdrawing the candidature and that the withdrawal had his assent. That, in his view, concluded the matter. The relations between King and ambassador, both anxious to avoid war, were marked by perfect courtesy and good feeling.

The royal telegram from Ems recounting these proceedings reached Bismarck in Berlin when he was dining with Moltke and Roon. At once the great strategist saw that the enemy was delivered into his hands. With a little judicious alteration a statement could be issued to the Press embodying the substance of the telegram, but making it appear that the French ambassador had put an affront on the Prussian King and that the

King had been compelled to administer to him a sharp rebuff. When Bismarck's draft was read out to the famous soldiers, they were delighted. "It is a challenge," said Moltke. "It is good," said von Roon. Bismarck and the soldiers were right, for it was the Ems telegram which set Germany and France ablaze.

On the morning of July 14 Gramont burst into Ollivier's room with a copy of the *North German Gazette* containing the Bismarckian version of the Ems telegram. "They wish," cried Ollivier, "to force us into war." It was a day of anguished indecision, the needle of debate in the Emperor's Council pointing now to peace then rapidly swinging to war. At 4 p.m. it was decided to call out the reserves; at 6.30 p.m. to appeal to a congress; but after dinner opinion hardened against peace, and at midnight it was decided that war should be declared next morning. The Empress was present, a known but silent adherent of war, at the evening council when the critical decision was taken. The mind of Paris was unmistakable. "Even if we had no motive for war which we could avow," said the Emperor, "we should, nevertheless, be obliged to resolve on it to obey the will of the people." How little the people knew was evidenced by their street cries, "À Berlin!" and "Vive la guerre!"

If the war was popular in Paris, in seventy-one out of eighty-seven departments it "was accepted rather with hesitation or regret." It was an unnecessary, insensate war, for which the primary responsibility must rest upon Bismarck and Gramont, upon Bismarck for having engineered the secret candidature and for his alteration of the Ems telegram, upon Gramont for the headlong passion with which he deliberately broke the bridge of peace. King William and the Emperor are not absolved from censure. Against his better judgment, the King, who was the soul of honour, allowed himself to be persuaded to sanction the Spanish venture without consulting France, whom he knew to have an interest in the arrangement. Equally was the Emperor to blame for joining Gramont in the fatal demand for guarantees. That his position was made difficult by the intemperate heat of the Conservative orators of the Chamber and by the fiery tone of the Paris press is true enough, but a strong ruler would have kept his head, and it is noticeable that Thiers, the best politician in public life, was not afraid to speak against the war.

Everything happened with extraordinary celerity. Barely a

fortnight divided Europe from a state of profound peace and one of open war. In the dead of the summer holiday the electric telegraph and the newspaper press brought a wholly unanticipated quarrel to a climax, and convulsed two of the most civilized peoples of the world with savage hatred before reason or mansuetude could gain a hearing. On both sides the voice of the soldiers was violently given for war.

To the confusion of all the prophets the famous regular army of France, so far from carrying the war into southern Germany, was put out of action in a month. The result was due to no deficiency in the fighting quality of the French soldier, but to the fact that while the French military system was thoroughly inefficient, the German army was the most highly perfected institution in what was even then the best organized community in the world.

Most instructive is the comparison between the rival nations in the all-important point of mobilization. Whereas a German villager on being called to the colours found his arms and uniform at hand, a French soldier might have to travel across France or even to cross the sea to Algiers to join the depôt of his regiment. The result was that, while the transport of the German army to the frontiers proceeded with mechanical smoothness and regularity, the wildest confusion prevailed on the French railways, so that the Germans were on the frontier in superior force before the French were prepared to meet them. Since Napoleon's sole chance of bringing Austria into the war was a striking initial success, the shocking inefficiency of the French mobilization produced far-reaching consequences.

A second advantage belonging to the invaders is that they had studied with elaborate care, and in the light of the latest developments in field telegraphy and gunnery, the particular campaign which they proposed to conduct. While the French had never dreamed of the possibility that they might be called on to defend their own soil, the Prussian plan for the invasion of France was three years old. The roads were mapped, the carrying capacity of the railways was estimated, and few were the details as to the organization, equipment, and distribution of the units of the French army which were unknown to the General Staff in Berlin. To this carefully prepared fabric of knowledge, a moving screen of observant cavalry made, as the three German armies advanced into France, continual and hourly additions.

It might have been expected that the elaboration of the German military system would have stifled individual initiative. This was not so. It was the principle of the German General Staff to encourage the assumption of responsibility by subordinate commanders, and while the movements of the French armies were often hampered by an excessive deference to central control, no German general seems to have scrupled to march to the sound of the guns and to throw his men into the mêlée where the need was sorest. The brilliant initiative shown by subordinate German commanders is one of the most conspicuous features of the campaign.

In war everything depends upon the joint capacity of the civilian and military Higher Command to work together, to inspire confidence, and to give to the nation and the troops a steadfast and animating direction. In all these particulars France was most unfortunately situated in the summer of 1870. Nowhere either in the Higher Military Command or in the civilian control was there magnetism or method. Napoleon, an invalid racked by excruciating pain, Le Boeuf, his War Minister; Bazaine, his successor in the Supreme Command, were all in the highest degree technically incompetent. Behind them in Paris was a frightened civilian government, headed by the beautiful but ill-liked Empress and faced with the fast-rising floods of a popular revolution. To this spectacle of military mediocrity and civilian confusion Germany opposed a united nation, a deep-rooted dynasty, and the potent trinity of Bismarck, Roon, and Moltke, backed by an army of officers military and civilian who had been trained in the finest school of public service then existing in Europe.

One final comparison may be added. The Germans possessed a short service, the French a long service system. Whereas the Prussian system of two years with the colours, four with the reserves, and five and a half with the militia was calculated to produce a field army of five hundred thousand men and behind them a vast reserve of trained levies, the French plan of five years' service, convenient enough for colonial campaigns overseas, had no such result. The German regular army, if destroyed in the initial stages of a campaign, could be replaced by troops who had undergone the full period of training with the colours. But when the field army of France was destroyed or dispersed, the country was compelled to fall back upon levies who were for the most part raw and untrained. In the later half of the Franco-Prussian War this disability was severely felt.

The story of that late summer was one of unrelieved tragedy for France. The Germans with irresistible momentum carried everything before them. They defeated MacMahon at Wörth, Frossard at Spicheren, and by these two victories, one in Alsace and the other in Lorraine, each gained on August 6, only two days after the invading army had reached the frontier, they sent such a spasm of depression, indignation, and alarm through the country, that the Emperor resigned his command to Bazaine, and that honest, eloquent, timid Ollivier " with his light heart " was driven for ever from the stage of politics, to be replaced by (August 10) an elderly cavalry officer, the Count de Palikao, in whom the last confidence of the distracted Empress was capriciously reposed.

All these changes were unavailing. Bazaine was not the man to stem the onrush. His retreat was slow, so slow that he allowed the Germans to march round him, to hold him up at Mars la Tour, and after a bloody victory at Gravelotte (August 18) to drive him back eastwards to the shelter of the fortifications of Metz. There the commander of 170,000 men, containing the flower of the French army, permitted himself to be invested. There, with little effort to break through, he remained. There finally (October 27) he capitulated, releasing by his act of cowardice and treachery an investing army of 200,000 men to assist in the subjugation of his country. Meanwhile in those early days of August a field army of regular troops was collecting at Châlons under MacMahon, and it became a matter of crucial importance to determine whither this army, the last free and disengaged force of regulars, could most usefully direct its move-ment. Wisely, as it would appear, MacMahon counselled that the army of Châlons should avoid immediate contact with the enemy, fall backwards, and, rallying round it whatever scattered elements of military power remained, concentrate before the fortifications of Paris. But the Empress and her advisers would not hear of retreat. They urged that Paris required the relief of Bazaine and a victory in the east, and that, were the army of Chalons to yield ground, the people would rise and upset the throne. Reluctantly and against his better judgment the plain soldier complied, marching his army back to Rheims, and then, having heard that Bazaine proposed to break out towards the

3 2

north, turning north-eastwards towards the Belgian frontier.
Moltke was after him. At the little town of Sedan the French
army was encircled, broken by shell-fire, and compelled to
capitulate. Among the spoils of that supreme German victory
was the person of Napoleon. It was September 2; two days later
the Republic was proclaimed in Paris, and while Jules Favre
announced to the world that France would not surrender a stone
of her fortresses or a yard of her territory, the Empress secretly
made her way in the carriage of an American dentist towards
the classic home of political exiles. It was the end of Bonapartism, the system of monarchy based upon the plébiscite,
which, after nearly uniting all Europe under the sceptre of the
first Napoleon, ended by leaving France shorn of territory and
prestige and faced by a new and formidable rival.

The war against the Imperial army was concluded. The war
against the French nation was now to begin. A cool estimate of
the situation might have suggested that a good peace was most
likely to be obtained while Metz was untaken and the army of
Bazaine still unhurt. Passion, however, does not calculate, and
there are occasions in the history of every nation when the
manifestation, however blind, of the psychic forces of a people
is more valuable than a nice appreciation of profit and loss. The
national war, though it may have meant a harder peace, did
something to restore the self-respect of the French people and to
preserve their courage in the depressing years which lay before
them. Desperate, indeed, it proved to be, but full of embarrassment for the enemy, of difficulties perhaps greater than those
which confronted the invaders in the early and more professional
stage of the conflict. The area of operations was wider, the
lines of communications were lengthened and were frequently
threatened by *franc-tireurs*; the new French armies springing
up in all directions were less easy to measure and to locate.
If a substantial system of trained reserves had been available,
the French might have converted a grave embarrassment into a
serious menace.

The soul of this popular prolongation of the war was Léon
1838-82   Gambetta, the great republican orator from the south, who had
first sprung into notice in a *cause celèbre* as the bitter assailant
of the empire. Obstacles meant nothing to Gambetta. When
the Germans encircled Paris he escaped in a balloon to Rouen

(October 7), and by his prodigious and animating energy raised in the course of six weeks an army of 180,000 men. At Coulmier, near Orleans, the new army of Gambetta inflicted upon the Germans their first defeat, and had Bazaine still held in Metz it is possible that D'Aurelles, the victor of Coulmier, might have been able with the assistance of the Paris garrison to break the blockade. But the capitulation of Metz exercised a decisive *Oct. 27,* influence on the course of the campaign by making available for *1870* the Germans, at the hour of their greatest need, a large and powerful army. At every point the raw half-trained levies of Gambetta were met by forces superior in numbers, training, and equipment, so that D'Aurelles was thrice defeated near Orleans, Chanzy after a fierce three days' battle finally overwhelmed at Le Mans (January 10, 1871), and Faidherbe, who had won some initial successes in the north, defeated at St. Quentin (January 19). An attempt, too grandiose for success, to animate the south-east against the invader and from that quarter to create a powerful diversion by a raid into Baden, met with even greater calamity, for Bourbaki's army of 85,000 men, wretchedly equipped and defeated at Montbeliard, was pushed back over the frontier into the neutral territory of Switzerland and there ignominiously disarmed (February 1, 1871).

Meanwhile Paris experienced the unexpected hardships of a siege. Rage and humiliation possessed the inhabitants of this mercurial city who had lightly acclaimed the war with cries of " À Berlin!" and were now condemned to experience the bitter taste of defeat. The shortage of food, the frustration of every effort to break through the war circle, the horrors of the regular bombardment which began on December 27, when the Prussian guns were brought up and were directed upon the civilian population as well as upon the forts, contributed to create in the public mind " the siege fever," as the French called it, which passed by an easy transition into the mania of the commune.

At last, but not before the wild remedy of a *sortie en masse* had been tried in vain, Paris was willing to treat with the enemy. An armistice was granted, elections were held, an assembly *Jan. 1,* gathered in Bordeaux elected Thiers head of the executive and *1871* empowered him to negotiate with the enemy. On the main points Bismarck was adamant. He demanded Alsace, a great *Feb.,* part of Lorraine with Metz, and an indemnity which he con- *1871*

sented to reduce to 200 million pounds. The Prussian was in an
unassailable position. When Thiers proved obdurate Bismarck
threatened to treat with Napoleon. Only on one point of any serious
importance did he make a concession to the eloquent entreaties
of the Frenchman. If the German army might be accorded the
satisfaction of occupying Paris, he was willing that the French
should keep Belfort. The Peace of Frankfort (May 10, 1871)
which embodied these terms was imposed by the Germans
on the French, as the Peace of Versailles was later imposed
by the Allies on the Germans. The indemnity was a bagatelle soon disposed of, but no Frenchman gave more than
a forced and nominal assent to the cession of Strasbourg and
Metz.

1797-1877   Thiers, the fiery and patriotic statesman who negotiated on
behalf of his vanquished country the preliminaries of peace, had
warned his compatriots against going into the war and was now
freshly returned from a fruitless mission to foreign courts in the
hopes of obtaining their helpful intercession. The little man
whose impish form, egg-shaped head, and large spectacles were
the joy of the caricaturists, is one of the most considerable
civilians in the history of France. He made peace with Germany, suppressed the Commune, and more than anyone else,
though an Orleanist by conviction, created the Third Republic
which, surviving many perils of infancy, because of all forms
of government it divided France the least, was strong enough
forty-eight years later to reverse the verdict of the Franco-
Prussian War.

In asking for Alsace-Lorraine and for the great fortress of
Metz, Bismarck was perpetuating the quarrel between France
and Germany and laying the seed of a future war. It was the
greatest, the most serious, and the most far-reaching of the
errors committed in the course of a triumphant life. Alsace
was indeed essentially a German province, Lorraine was chiefly
French. The first of these provinces had been wrested from
Germany by Mazarin, the second had been acquired as part
of a general European settlement by Louis XV. To both provinces, but in fullest measure to Alsace, a German Empire could
claim an historical title. But the populations which had profited
by the social legislation of the French were given no opportunity
of expressing their will. Without the faintest interrogation of
local opinion, they were excised from a nation to which they

had become accustomed, and placed under the sterner yoke of the conqueror.

A few days before the fall of Paris the German Empire was *Jan. 18, 1871* proclaimed in the Hall of Mirrors at Versailles. The far-resounding victory of Wörth had been won by the troops of Bavaria and Würtemberg under the leadership of the Crown Prince of Prussia, and no sooner had Napoleon surrendered at Sedan than overtures were made by the South German States for admission to the Union. These advances were eagerly welcomed. Though there were many who thought that the moment had now come when it would be possible to establish in Germany a strong centralized State, Bismarck was not of that number. "We do not want an unwilling Bavaria," he said; "we want one which will join freely," and that Bavaria might be a contented member of the *Reich* he was ready to make wide concessions—the control of the army in peace, a voice in foreign policy, a separate Bavarian system of posts and telegraphs. There can be no clearer proof of his wisdom than that the King of Bavaria should have been brought to consent to propose that William of Hohenzollern should take the Imperial Crown.

It is difficult to exaggerate the enthusiasm and self-confidence which these remarkable events created in the German people. Though old-fashioned Prussians, like the King and Von Roon, had little relish for the new Imperial title, the fact that Germany after so many centuries of division and foreign danger had at last been united by a victorious war, that her armies had proved themselves invincible, that she had imposed her will successively on Austria and on France, and that by the recovery of two long-lost provinces she had established a powerful barrier against future danger from the west, filled every German heart with glowing emotions of pride and satisfaction. The Germans had long led Europe in music, in learning, and in the number, influence, and efficiency of their schools and universities. They were now without dispute the strongest military power on the continent. Was it unnatural that Prussian patriots, throwing their minds backward to the obscure origins of their state in a little military outpost of German-speaking men against a wilderness of Slavs, and thence tracing its successive developments, should discern therein the workings of a peculiar and flattering Providence? Was it unnatural that they should believe that the Prussian race,

by its frugality, its hardihood, its stern application, its formid
able and disciplined violence, was selected to accomplish an his
toric mission on earth, first as a missionary of German civilizatior
among the Baltic Slavs, then as the protagonist of the Protestan
Faith, and afterwards as the Power which delivered the Germar
peoples from their paralyzing connection with the Austriar
Empire and gave to them an arbitral position on the continen
of Europe? These reflections were widely sown from professoria
chairs. There were many also, bolder than the vulgar, who cas
their minds forward into the future and asked themselves whethe

THE GROWTH OF THE GERMAN EMPIRE.

an even greater destiny was not reserved for the Hohenzollerns
The world was wide, the salt seas beckoned to new adventures
Nothing was impossible to German heroism, neither marin
power, nor colonies, nor the ultimate dominion of the earth. To
the State which in an ascending scale of effort had vanquishec
the Danes, the Austrians, and the French there yet remainec
another ordeal. The Anglo-Saxon Empire, built up by a natior
of civilians, of frivolous amateurs, who had won the palm withou
the dust, was not immortal. Too long had these spoilt children
of fortune been permitted to disport themselves in the sun. The
time had come when Providence would reward the industrious

apprentice and transfer to solid merit the prizes which had fallen to the favourites of chance. Rome would wrest the trident from Carthage. Such in effect was the teaching of Heinrich von Treitschke, most influential of historical professors and publicists, from his chair in Berlin.

BOOKS WHICH MAY BE CONSULTED

Fyffe : A History of Modern Europe. 1924.
E. Ollivier : L'Empire Libéral. 1911.
Pierre de la Gorce : Histoire du Second Empire. 1908.
G. Rothan : Souvenirs Diplomatiques. 1882.
E. Bourgeois : Manuel Historique de Politique Étrangère. 1905-6.
E. Bourgeois and E. Clermont : Rome et Napoleon III. 1907.
J. Reinach : G. L. Gambetta. 1884.
Lowes Dickinson : Revolution and Reaction in Modern France. 1892.

CHAPTER XX

THE THIRD REPUBLIC

Unpopularity of Republicanism in the provinces. The Paris Commune. The struggle between Paris and Versailles. The foundation of the Third Republic. French Parliamentary Government. France and Germany. Jules Ferry. The problem of Clericalism. Instability of the Republic. Boulanger. The Dreyfus Case. French diplomacy.

DURING the years which followed the great defeat France gradually built up for herself a new political existence. She was heartily weary of plébiscites, dictatorships, and foreign adventures, and since the idea of a Republic had always been associated with war and revolution, the preponderant part of the population dreaded a constitution bearing that name. Out of the six hundred and fifty deputies returned to the Parliament of Bordeaux (February 8, 1871) four hundred were prepared to vote for a King.

Nevertheless it was not a King but a Republic which emerged in the end from this strongly monarchical and representative assembly. By slow degrees France came to realize that the monarchy was made impossible by the division between the legitimist and the Orléanist lines, by the obstinate refusal of the Count de Chambord, the head of the older branch, to acknowledge the tricolor, which was the symbol of democratic institutions, and by the manifest and violent aversion of the democracy of Paris from any attempt to bring back the Kings to France.

Paris was Republican and ardent for a revolutionary war against the Germans waged in the grand old manner of Danton and Carnot. It saw that the imperial campaign had been shockingly mismanaged, it believed that under brave leadership the siege might have been broken, and that a pusillanimous assembly of rural conservatives, recently (March 10) moved from Bordeaux to Versailles, had sold the birthright of the country to the enemy and was plotting to restore the evils and inequalities of the *ancien régime*. Rather than submit to the Versaillais, odious on the double count of royalism and pacifism, Paris would fight. The city was hungry, exasperated, wounded by the spectacle of German troops marching in triumph through the Champs Elysées and charged with revolutionary passions and dreams of every description—Jacobin, federal, socialist, communist, anarchist. The National Guard had been armed for the siege, and when the government of Versailles attempted to withdraw the guns from Montmartre it offered resistance. Baptized by the blood of two murdered generals, the Commune of Paris inaugurated its reckless and ruinous course.

The Paris Commune has passed into legend as the first fiery manifestation of the great revolutionary movement which throws from Russia a challenge to the capitalistic order of society all over the world. This, however, was not its original or dominating character. The genius of the Commune was rather that of Danton than of Lenin, its origin a sudden tempest of Republican patriotism rather than a deep-laid plot to overthrow society. As passion mounted, the movement, originally led by respectable burgesses, took on new colours. The dissolution of France into a Federation of Republics or even the destruction of the capitalistic *régime* throughout the world became for certain sections of the working-class Communards the watchword of the future. But there was no single creed common to the whole complex movement. The Commune of Paris did not even confiscate the gold reserve of the Bank.

Little old Thiers, in his tight frock-coat, was at the head of the government of Versailles, glinting through his large spectacles. Though nothing had yet been settled as to the ultimate constitution of France, for the royalists were in no hurry to take the helm, the provisional government was in fact republican. Yet the gifted, flint-hearted old gentleman showed no weakness. Collecting a strong regular force of 130,000 men, he applied himself with a steady and remorseless persistence to the reconquest of Paris. His severities then and thereafter were tremendous; but there was little compassion for the wild terrorists who had made a shambles of Paris and burned the Tuileries and the Hôtel de Ville. Rather it was counted to the government for righteousness that it had signed preliminaries of peace with the enemy and in "the week of blood" (May 21-8) stamped without mercy on the Paris Commune. A Republic, then, might after all be conservative and free from the terrifying associations of revolution and war, and so it came about that the Paris Commune had a bearing on the political evolution of France, for it showed that while the workers of Paris would always strain against a monarchy, the bourgeois could comfortably accept a Republic.

Thus the Provisional Government, "a republic without republicans," continued in being, gathering strength as it went along, rallying Gambetta, who was a big enough man to learn by experience, and eventually in 1875, when the constitutional statutes were under discussion, giving its sanction by a majority of one vote to the formidable word "Republic." The Royalists had missed the tide. The conservative Republic had triumphed by discharging the task from which through lack of courage and unity the royalists had shrunk. Their failure was merited and could not be retrieved. Two years later (1877), when Marshal MacMahon, the clerical and royalist President, endeavoured to obtain authority for a royalist ministry by dissolving a newly elected Chamber which was too republican for his taste, he received such a lesson from the electors that no subsequent President has ever since dared to exercise his right of dissolution. Not least among the causes of the Conservative *débâcle* that autumn was the belief that the Right under its military and clerical chief would plunge France into war.

The Republican constitution of 1875, which in substance governs France to this day, is inspired by a lively horror of the evils which a despotism founded on a plébiscite had brought on France. There are two Chambers, a Senate and a House of Deputies; and it is by the vote of these two Chambers in joint session and not by a plébiscite of the whole people of France that the President of the Republic is elected. Such a system is well qualified to shelter the country from the dangerous magnetism of sensational adventurers. The Chambers do not elect supermen; their choice falls upon the solid lawyer or man of business whose character and abilities have proved themselves in the Parliamentary arena. They are not in search of a force, but of a figurehead. Ever since MacMahon failed in his attempt to turn the presidential office to the account of the monarchy, nothing has been more injurious to a French President than the suspicion that he is seeking to make a policy of his own or to establish by speech or action a vital and independent contact with the mind of the country.

Parliamentary government, then, on the English model was the gift of the Constitution of 1875 to France. The keys of authority were confided, not to the President, who was elected for seven years, but to a Cabinet responsible to the popular Chamber. France became for the first time what England had been since the glorious Revolution, a strict parliamentary democracy, more parliamentary even, as the French contend, than England itself, since, whereas at Westminster the Cabinet controls the Parliament, in Paris the relations are reversed. In a legislature which may not be dissolved before its natural term party discipline is weak, and small groups, entering now into this combination, now into that, take the place of the great highly organized political combinations which struggle for power across the floor of the House of Commons. The French Cabinets, then, are short-lived, and since at any moment they may be upset by a new and unforeseen combination, they are compelled to devote to current parliamentary strategy much of the energy which might otherwise be employed upon long-range legislative projects. To these distractions, arising out of the group system, the great burden of patronage incidental to the government of a highly centralized state must be added. The tasks of an English Cabinet Minister are heavy, but at least he is not called upon to fight two hundred votes of censure a session or to canvass the claims of applicants for the village post office.

The French public can hardly expect to follow with reverential absorption a concern at once so kaleidoscopic in its changes and so largely occupied with triviality. The theatres, the salon, the *Académie Française*, the discussion and assessment of current literature, constitute a pleasanter and more absorbing interest. The parliaments of the Third Republic, despite the fire, eloquence, and ability of their debates, have never held a high place in the respect and admiration of the French people. Certain scandals, notably those connected with the financing of the *1888-92* Panama Canal, have spread an unfortunate impression of corruption. The prestige of antiquity is absent; and the loss has not been replaced by the renown of great ministers achieving with the support of powerful and sustained majorities policies which inflame the imagination of the people.

During all the years between 1870 and 1914 the most profound question for western civilization was the possibility of establishing friendly relations between France and Germany. Alsace-Lorraine stood in the way. So long as the statue of Strasburg in the Place de la Concorde was veiled in crêpe, every Frenchman continued to dream of the recovery of the lost provinces as an end impossible perhaps of achievement—for there was no misjudgment now of the vast strength of Germany—but nevertheless ardently to be desired. It was not a thing to be talked of. "N'en parlez jamais, y pensez toujours," advised Gambetta; but it was a constant element in public feeling, an ever-present obstruction to the friendship of the two countries, a dominant motive in policy, a dark cloud full of menace for the future.

Had the Germans been willing to grant a full measure of autonomy to the provinces, the tension would have been lessened; and there were some French statesmen who hoped that a cordial understanding could be reached by concessions of this nature. It was not so, however, that Bismarck viewed his duty. Alsace-Lorraine constituted in his eyes a necessary curb on the ambitions of a nation who would never forgive the humiliation of defeat. Bismarck had no trust in the pacific intentions of the Third Republic. He was alarmed by the economic resilience of France, by her swift and resolute adoption of a military system based upon Russian principles and calculated to yield a field army of 6,750,000 men and a reserve of half a million, and by the warlike language of some of her statesmen. But for the timely intervention of Queen Victoria and the Tzar, he would, not improbably, have impelled his country into a preventive war in 1875. Afterwards a cheaper way of soothing a restless neighbour occurred to his mind. He suggested that France should annex Tunis. "I have sent," he observed in his racy, idiomatic English, "the fiery steed of French ambition caracoling in the sands of Tunis. They will find it heavy going." It was his hope that, once launched upon a career of colonial conquest, France would brood less upon her lost provinces in Europe.

Among the rare glories of the French parliamentary scene was
1832-93
an ardent, unconquerable *député* from the Vosges named Jules Ferry, who, though he has left an imperishable mark upon the colonial and educational policy of his country, was pursued throughout his lifetime with the fiercest hatred and detraction. Under the Empire Ferry had been a pacifist and a radical. Afterwards he carved out for himself a course of his own as a colonial imperialist, a conservative republican, and, in the field of education, as a political anti-clerical. Storms of angry controversy gathered round this stout and combative figure, who outraged the cherished maxims of the radicals by his imperialism and of the clericals by his schools. France, it was urged, had no further need for colonies. The monarchy had involved her in the expensive adventure of Algeria, the Empire had committed her to a

distant colony in Indo-China. Her birth rate was falling; she had no surplus population to export; all her resources were needed to deal with the one problem which really mattered on her eastern frontier. Was not the lesson of Mexico enough? What was the value of Tunis or Tongking to a country whose prime duty was to the inhabitants of the two lost provinces of Alsace-Lorraine? Such were the views of Georges Clemenceau, the "Tiger," who, having tasted the defeat of 1870, was steadily set on revenge, and by no means anxious to throw Italy into the arms of the Germans for the sake of the cornlands of Tunis.

In such criticism there was a strong pith of good sense. The forward colonial movement led by Ferry contributed, as every such movement must do, to create new stresses and dangers for France. The friendship of Italy was lost over Tunis, peace with England was risked over Fashoda, the relations with Germany and Spain were seriously strained over Morocco. Yet when the struggle came in 1914 the French did not repent of their colonial empire, the second in the world, or of the African man-power which helped them to sustain their European struggle. The ambitious policy which covered "Le Tonquinois," as Ferry was called, with the ridicule of the boulevards was forgiven as the Algerian and Senegalese levies of the Republic took their place in the trenches as citizens of France.

In two other respects Jules Ferry stands out among the French statesmen of the Republic. He legalized trades unions and won the great educational battle which Duruy under the Empire had lost to the clericals. It is to him that France owes the system of universal, free, compulsory education. As Minister of Public Instruction in the de Freycinet Cabinet (1882), he caused the Jesuits to be evicted from their schools, and submitted other teaching congregations to strict regulations. Though out of regard to the colonial interests of France and to the feeling in the army, he was gentle with his antagonist, it was his view that clerical teaching was directed to undermining confidence in the Republic, and that the programmes of the Church schools were not up to the requirements of the age.

There can be little question that in both respects Ferry was right. If the greater part of the French population was illiterate in 1870, if the programmes of study were narrow and obsolete, it was largely by reason of the obstacles which clericalism had placed in the way of expansion of state education. Those obstacles still existed. The Senate opposed the attack on the teaching congregations; but the government, proceeding by decree, circumvented the Senate, dissolved the Jesuits, and so cleared the ground for the great development of education in all its branches, which has so far been the most remarkable domestic achievement of the Third Republic.

In the decades succeeding the Franco-Prussian War, the struggle of parties in France, though assuming many different forms as chance accidents, such as the Panama scandal, intervened, was at bottom the old quarrel between clericalism and the modern world. "Clericalism is the enemy," was Gambetta's war cry (May 4, 1877). The politicians of the Left feared the priest in politics, in the home, in the school. The great body of the industrial working class, though they accepted the rites of the Church in baptism, in marriage, and in burial, might be trusted always to give an anti-clerical vote. Tradition had enormous weight with them. In voting against the priest, they were voting, as they believed, against the *ancien régime*, against the return of feudalism, of inequality, of social oppression, evils which they had learned from their fathers to hate and to associate with the priests of the Catholic Church. A hundred years after the revolutionary terror, constituencies, formerly royalist, voted clerical, while those which had been Jacobin returned members belonging to one or other of the parties of the Left.

In the absence of a strong Protestant Church offering an intermediate body of feeling and opinion, the chasm between the two halves of France, the one religious, clerical, conservative, and military, the other pagan, anti-clerical, radical, and friendly to the empire of reason in the affairs of the world, was very deep and wide; and when the issue was squarely joined in an atmosphere heated by international tension it seemed as if France might flame up into civil war. The opposition until 1892 of the Catholic Church, the presence of the royalist and imperialist parties, the deep grudges left by the cruel repression of the Commune, and the steady growth of Socialist and Syndicalist opinion made the task of republican defence one of exceptional difficulty. Again and again the existence of the Republic seemed to be imperilled. Though concessions were showered upon democracy, though the centre of power in the Chamber moved steadily towards the Left, the dominant party being first conservative, then opportunist, then radical, and finally with Briand's advent to power (1910) socialist, yet always the question remained whether a parliament of bourgeois politicians, predominantly secular in their outlook and divided into bitterly hostile groups, would succeed in governing the mettlesome people of France and securing for it a commanding place in the world.

This inner instability of Republican France received two curious illustrations in the last two decades of the nineteenth century. In 1886, as the Presidency of the dull but respectable Grévy was drawing to a somewhat sordid end, the imagination of the country was caught by the figure of a handsome general riding a fine black horse. It was Boulanger, the late military *1837-91* governor of Tunis. Men, women, and children were infatuated by the brave spectacle of this plumed soldier from the African wars. Was he not the deliverer, the Mahdi, the chieftain, for whom France had long been waiting, and in any case an electoral asset of the first magnitude? The League of Patriots trumpeted the virtues of the favourite. Naquet, the Jew, organized his elections. In constituency after constituency, for his candidature was advanced wherever a vacancy occurred, the general was returned with handsome majorities. There could be no question that in 1886 and 1887 he was the most popular figure in France, at once Minister of War, mouthpiece of the nationalist or war spirit, and the advocate of a wholesale revision of the constitution.

Thrice, seeing that the voters of Paris were behind him, he might have ridden to the Elysée, dispossessed the President, and seized the wheel of government. But he was a man empty of real conviction and devoid of nerve, and as he allowed one chance after another to slip by, courage returned to the civilian rulers of France. It was resolved to bring him to trial, and the threat was enough. With a charge of high treason suspended over his head, the General fled to Brussels and there, taking his *1891* life, relieved the Republic of a great embarrassment.

Even fiercer were the furies which five years later raged round the name of Captain Dreyfus. It is difficult for those who did not live through the feverish years 1894-1903 to form a conception of the passions which were aroused by the fate of this young Jewish officer who had been condemned to deportation by a military tribunal on the charge of betraying military secrets to the Germans. Half France vehemently held that Dreyfus was guilty, the other half with equal vehemence that he had been cruelly wronged. Lifelong friendships were ruptured, the peace of families was ruined, the conscience of individuals was racked and tortured. A furious anti-Semitic campaign in the Catholic press, fortunately unaccompanied by the acts of terrible violence and injustice which have characterized anti-Semitic outbursts in central and eastern Europe, spread its venom through the land. How, it was asked, could this Jew be innocent? How could the soldiers be wrong? How could it accord with the national interest to impeach the honour of the army, which alone stood between France and the German peril? Of what account was justice to the individual when measured against the safety of the State? Morality eventually prevailed. The testimony of Paul Meyer the palaeographer, the denunciations of Zola the novelist, the confession and suicide of Henri the forger, and the courage of Colonel Picquart, a Protestant who risked his military career for the truth, established the innocence of Dreyfus and routed the military and clerical foes of the Republic. Fortified by this triumph of the civilian conscience, the Cabinet of Waldeck-Rousseau, radical at home and Jingo abroad, gave to Republican France its first long spell of firm and steady government.

Seen through enemy eyes the Third French Republic appeared to be deficient in soundness, stability, and repute. The revelation of incompetence in the Franco-Prussian War, the horrors of the Commune, the swift succession of weak ministries, the violence of party factions, the intermittent financial scandals, contributed to give even to the more experienced observers an unduly low opinion of the aptitude of the French people for the arts of government. The reorganization of the army by Freycinet, the brilliant work of soldiers, administrators, and explorers in Africa, the steady efficient mechanism of the Civil Service at home, the essential justice of the social system, went unperceived. It was felt that Frenchmen were being surpassed by the English, the Germans, the Americans. When Déroulède came to Renan in 1888 and asked him to join the League of Patriots, the old savant replied, "Young man, France is dying, do not trouble her agony." It was a common opinion at the end of the nineteenth century that the Latin races had outlived their glory; but the censure was premature.

From the Quai d'Orsay in Paris, a diplomatic service second to none in skill, tenacity, and accomplishments was quickly extending French influence through the world and weaving a network of alliances which recalled the shades of Richelieu and Mazarin.

Based on direct and manhood suffrage the Republic survived all attempts to overthrow it. No disfranchised class battered on the doors of the constitution. No privileged order as under previous *régimes* held the fort of authority against the poor. If the Chamber was not highly regarded, the press was free, the local government democratic, the trades unions ever since 1884 legalized and exempt from government interference. Whereas in Russia and Germany socialism was proscribed and therefore dangerous, the Third Republic could find a place for socialists in the Chamber, in the Cabinet, and even in the Elysée. Millerand, the first socialist to sit in a Cabinet (1899), ended an honourable political career as President of the Republic. Briand, borne to the highest places of the state by the seductions of his Celtic eloquence, showed France how a socialist Prime Minister could break a strike, and later become for many years indispensable at the Foreign Office. The fiery Viviani, one of the greatest orators of his own or any other age, was head of the Cabinet when the war broke out. So far from menacing the stability of the Republic, Socialism, robbed of its power to hurt by manhood suffrage, made a brilliant contribution to the Parliamentary life of France.

The more serious danger came from the Right. From time to time Frenchmen asked themselves whether these middle-class politicians were working for the safety and honour of France. Would they recover the lost provinces? Would they not cut down the army? Was not the whole system of lay, centralized education fatal to the development of those local and provincial pieties which nourish the normal strength of a nation? The sentiment of Catholicism, of royalism, of nationalism ranged itself against the free-thinking and secular atmosphere in which the affairs of the country were conducted. Jews, Protestants, cosmopolitans came under suspicion in accordance with the general law that in times of nationalist hysteria the minority creeds are made to suffer. Yet the Republic triumphed even over the nationalists. It broke Boulanger, defeated the anti-Dreyfusards, established the supremacy of the civil over the military power, and curtailed the influence of the Church in education. When the war broke out France was still a land of civilian freedom.

BOOKS WHICH MAY BE CONSULTED

Bainville : Histoire de France. 1924.
Hanotaux : Histoire de la France contemporaine. *Tr.* J. C. Tarver. 1903-8.
J. E. C. Bodley : France. 1898.
A. Rambaud : Jules Ferry. 1903.
F. C. Conybeare : The Dreyfus Case. 1895.
J. Reinach : Histoire de l'affaire Dreyfus, 6 vols. 1901-8.
Lowes Dickinson : Revolution and Reaction in France. 1892.
H. Poincaré : Au Service de la France. 1913-26.
A. Rambaud : Histoire de la civilisation contemporaine en France. 1932
A. Thiers : Notes et Souvenirs de 1870 à 1873. 1903.
A. Lavy : L'Oeuvre de Millerand. 1902.
J. Bainville : La Troisième Republique. 1935.

CHAPTER XXI

INTERNATIONAL CURRENTS

*The Vatican and Liberalism. The higher criticism. Lyell and Darwin
Herbert Spencer. Karl Marx. The Fabians.*

As the nineteenth century proceeded, the stock of ideas, beliefs,
and habits which European men had inherited from long distant
times underwent a profound transformation. History and
scholarship, economics and physical science, the zeal of reforming prophets and the profuse ingenuity of mechanical inventors,
made of Europe in many important respects a new society. Save
for one institution everything appeared to be in a state of flux.

The Vatican, a rock set among the swirling tides of the
Risorgimento, was immovable. The large and generous outlook,
the vast learning, the spirit of accommodation with the march
of events which distinguished the leaders of liberal Catholicism
in Germany and France were foreign to the Italian prelates who
stood round the Papal throne and helped, in face of the swift
encroachments of the secular power, to shape the policy of the
Curia. In a series of pronouncements, the bull *Mirari Vos* of
1832, the Syllabus of 1864, the Infallibility decree of 1870, and
the numerous encyclicals (1878, 1881, 1888, etc.) of Leo XIII, the
Vatican condemned the fashionable intellectual novelties of the
day and those free movements of the human mind which had
relaxed fidelity to Roman discipline. Socialism, Liberalism,
Communism, Bible societies, freedom of conscience, and freedom
of the Press were branded as erroneous. In a sweeping sentence
which gave great concern to liberal Catholics the Syllabus of
1864 laid it down as error to hold that "the Roman Pontiff can
or ought to come to terms with progress, liberalism, or modern
civilization." Assailed in his temporal possessions, the Pope
roundly defied the unheeding spirit of the age.

In the Protestant half of Europe religious beliefs were shaped
not so much by the authority of a developing church as by the
text of the Jewish and Christian scriptures. That ancient corpus
of sacred literature was now subjected to minute examination

The Bible began to be treated not as a thing apart but as any other book; it was submitted to those canons of proof and probability which the scrupulous conscience of the historical scholar applies to a classical text or to a mediaeval chronicle. The idea of biblical criticism was not new. Spinoza, the Jewish philosopher of Amsterdam, had already anticipated in his *Tractatus theologico politicus* (1670) many principles and conclusions which a hundred and sixty years afterwards found favour with the scholars of Tübingen, but it was not until the later half of the nineteenth century that this new way of treating the Bible began generally to influence the outlook of Protestant theologians, and even to win recruits among the modernizing spirits of the Roman Church. The stir created by *Essays and Reviews* in 1860 and by *Lux Mundi* in 1888 marks the stages by which in England first the Broad Church and then the High Church were brought to accept the conclusions of historical science. In France the most commanding literary figure was a religious historian who had broken away from the Roman Church altogether. In a series of volumes marked by extraordinary learning and insight Ernest Renan told the story of the origins of the Christian Church. An exquisite grace and lucidity of style gave to his work a wide appeal. "Who is this Monsieur Renan of whom everyone is speaking?" asked a young lady of the Parisian ballet (1863). "Is he a member of the Jockey Club?" A negative answer quenched further interest in the sentimental author of the *Vie de Jésus*.

A new sense of reality was imparted to biblical studies by the general adoption of historical methods, and although few scholars went so far as David Strauss (1835) and F. C. Conybeare (1909), who either doubted or whittled away the historicity of Christ, there was a general disposition to observe the valuable distinction drawn by Matthew Arnold, the English poet and critic, between literature and dogma and to find the distinctive character of the Bible not in the theological doctrines which it may be thought to define, but in the power which it shares with all sublime literature of filling and exalting the religious imagination of man.

It is seldom, however, that the work of textual critics attracts the attention of the general public. Mankind was not greatly affected by the discovery of the composite character of the book of Genesis or by the news that the story of the Flood might be traced to a Babylonian fable. The general abandonment of the old notions as to the antiquity of the world and the origins of man was the result, not of textual criticism, but of scientific discovery, and in particular of the work of Charles Lyell, whose *Principles of Geology* was published between 1830 and 1834, and Charles Darwin, whose *Origin of Species by means of Natural Selection* appeared in 1859, and was followed twelve years later by his sensational work on the *Descent of Man*.

In the face of this evidence it was no longer possible to accept the narrative of Genesis as other than a religious and poetical allegory. Geology banished the belief, which lingered for two generations in schoolrooms and rectories, that the world was created in 4004. Adam and Eve retreated before Darwin and the biologists. For the familiar story of the garden of Eden and the tree of knowledge there was substituted a picture of "Nature red in tooth and claw," of an unremitting struggle for survival, of a process continued over millions of years of biological evolution through the elimination of the unfit, and of the final emergence of man from the stock of the anthropoid apes at a late stage in the long chronicle of minute, accidental, and insensible variations. As a consequence of these discoveries and theories there was in the sixties and seventies of the nineteenth century a great falling away of intellectual men from the tenets of the churches.

Politics, too, were influenced by Darwinism. If biology was the clue to the understanding of the past, might it not also help to shape the future? Could the statesman afford to neglect the biological factor? Was it not his duty to encourage the stronger and to discourage the weaker breeds? Could a society survive which did not either by legislation or custom co-operate with nature in the elimination of the unfit? Was it not the necessary consequence of Darwinian principles that aristocracy was the only sound principle of government, and competition, economic, political, military, the only certain condition of progress? Many thinkers, oblivious of the fact that brilliant minds are not always united to wholesome bodies, thought that consequences of this nature flowed from the oracles of biological science. Huxley, one of Darwin's greatest disciples, did not thus err, but drew a clear distinction between the ruthlessness of the cosmic process and the essential charities of social life.

The influence of the new biological outlook was the more immediate and pervasive in England because it corresponded with a strong vein of individualism in native speculation and practice which had been evident since William Pitt read and was converted by *The Wealth of Nations*. A series of thinkers, remarkable for force, integrity, and direction, had given to one of the most freedom-loving communities of the world a philosophy corresponding to its needs and qualities. In prosperous times self-help is always a popular gospel, and England in the middle decades of the nineteenth century was a prosperous country, full of new fortunes and new men and ample rewards to ambitious industry. The dominant school of economic and political thinking flattered a society of self-made plutocrats and plutocrats in the making. It believed in freedom of trade, in the greatest happiness of the greatest number as the end of the state, and in the need of confining the interference of government within narrow limits. These were the sentiments of Adam Smith, the patriarch of Free Trade; of Jeremy Bentham, the reformer of English law and the seminal mind of English radicalism; of his disciples, James and John Stuart Mill; as well as of David Ricardo, the leading parliamentary oracle on questions of currency and public finance. Every carpet maker and cotton spinner, every millowner and speculative builder, every merchant and shipper was anxious for nothing so much as to be free of government meddling and to be allowed to get rich in his own way. The main weight of nonconformist opinion, always critical of government, was thrown into the same scale.

It was in fact from a scion of stiff English nonconformist stock that much of Europe in the later half of the nineteenth century was content to draw its intellectual guidance. Herbert Spencer, though little esteemed among professional philosophers in his own country, for he was self-taught, self-opinionated, and deficient in subtlety, became in his own lifetime a great European figure. In the eighties and nineties he was supreme in Paris and in most of the academies of the Latin and Slavonic world, nor was there any English philosopher of the century who spoke to so wide an audience. This immense renown was due to no grace of style, for Spencer, though a clear, was a clumsy, undistinguished writer, but to the fact that in a generation which had largely ceased to derive its spiritual guidance from the churches Spencer offered a confident philosophy grounded on natural knowledge. Fastidious people were repelled by this downright mining engineer, this radical agnostic from a middle-class home in Derbyshire, who handled English prose with such hearty in difference to its musical subtleties, who despised Latin and Greek, theology and history, who thought Ruskin barbarous and Dante over-ornamented, and wanted to turn the educational system of the country upside down. But for the ordinary man Spencer was a prophet. He took a naturalistic view of the universe. He propounded a synthetic philosophy which offered "a general theory of evolution as exhibited through all orders of existence." His contempt for received opinions, his vast, rambling, miscellaneous curiosity, and his extraordinary talent for generalizing about any fact, however trivial, which came within the range of his experience, made him an impressive figure. He wrote of the evolution of man, of the evolution of the family, of the evolution of social and ceremonial institutions. He offered as a general formula of development homogeneity turning into heterogeneity. He saw society passing from a military and despotic into an industrial and democratic phase. Ethics and politics were part of the science of life, a species of "transcendental physiology." In all this there was a kind of robust optimism, an absence of mystic involutions which flattered the philistine reader. Society, becoming industrial, could condemn the unreason and barbarity of war. Government itself, being a deciduous organ and a remnant of the predatory state, would, as civilization advanced, contract its functions. In time it would be seen that education had been hitherto based upon the most absurd lack of proportion, that "two local groups of facts and figures (i.e., Greek and Roman history), filling a relatively minute space in the genesis of the world, which is in itself but an infinitesimal part of the universe," had been allowed to dominate the field of vision, to the exclusion of the vital truths of physical nature.

People liked to hear all this. They felt that it was new, important, revolutionary. Moreover, they could understand, or believed that they could understand, this plain-spoken philosopher who criticized the accepted views so boldly and offered so large an assortment of confident opinions on every branch of knowledge. The middle class in particular were well disposed to a thinker who, so far from having a good word to say for socialism, was strongly opposed to any form of meddlesome interference by the state.

Yet for all his wide reputation Spencer was a voice crying in the wilderness. Despite his protest, the state interfered with industry, educated children, supported a church, organized public health. If on that side of his philosophy which offered a naturalistic interpretation of the universe he spoke for a large and constantly growing body of opinion, as the prophet of individualism in politics he made no converts. The whole stream of tendency was flowing swift and strong in the opposite direction.

The prophet of the socialist movement was a man as extraordinary for the glow and tenacity of his fanaticism as Mahomet himself. The name of Karl Marx (1818-83) has already been mentioned in these pages. He was the son of a respectable middle-class Jewish family from the Rhineland who sprang into sudden notoriety during the revolutionary troubles of the '48 with an epoch-making communist manifesto.[1] In this flaming document Marx put out a new philosophy of history, a new programme of revolutionary reform, and a new call for international action. He argued that the bourgeoisie had brought into existence its antithesis the proletariat, that the struggle between these two classes was the key to modern history, that the class conscious section of the proletariat were the communists, and that the communists would be content with nothing less than the "violent overthrow of the whole contemporary social order." Ten immediate reforms, many of them beneficial and since widely adopted by the bourgeois Parliaments whom Marx covered with his hatred and contempt, were then enumerated. But how could a revolutionary admit that desirable changes might be effected by national governments or middle-class legislation? Marx hated nationality with the rancour of an outcast, despised liberty with the arrogance of a despot, and throughout his life lost no opportunity of assailing the class from which he was himself sprung. The vital division of human society was not in the view of this fierce cosmopolitan atheist based on religion or nationality, but upon class. There was no common interest between German employers and German workers, but a common interest among the workers of the world to put an end to the capitalists by whom they were exploited. "Let the governing classes," he concluded, "tremble before the communist revolution. The proletarians have nothing to lose in it but their chains. They have the whole world to gain. Proletarians of all countries, unite."

After the failure of the revolutionary movement on the con-

[1] See Appendix A.

tinent Marx settled in London and there spent the last thirty-four years of his life, always in desperate straits for money, but at every crisis of his pecuniary humiliations helped from the generous purse of Frederick Engels, a German socialist friend and the son of a prosperous cotton spinner with a factory in Manchester. An inspiring presence, a clear, confident, powerful intellect, a fierce domineering temper, a brilliant gift of mordant conversation would have made Marx a distinguished, if disagreeable, figure in any company. "He combined," wrote H. M. Hyndman, " with his commanding forehead and great overhanging brow, his fierce glittering eyes, broad sensitive nose, and mobile mouth, all surrounded by a setting of untrimmed hair and beard, the righteous fury of the great seers of his race with the cold analytical power of Spinoza and the Jewish doctors." Writing in England and nourished by the material relating to English factory life which he procured in the reading room of the British Museum, Marx composed the weighty book on Capital which all the world over has been accepted as the Bible of the Proletariat.

Of the many million Marxists who are now scattered through Europe, few, it may be confidently surmised, have faced the labour of reading through the three long volumes which constitute the sacred text of the Communist religion. The influence of Marx does not depend upon the elaborate and untenable economic demonstration by which it is sought to prove that value is congealed labour, or that the surplus value created by labour over and above the return to fixed capital is always annexed by the capitalist as profit, or that as the rich become richer the poor become poorer. Marx, though a genius, was indifferent as a philosopher and economist, and as a writer had but an imperfect mastery over the English tongue. The power of this needy, passionate exile proceeds from the fact that he was always a prophet of revolution, attacking with concentrated fury the whole system of society which offered so sleek a surface to the sky and demonstrating with an arrogant confidence that throughout history the poor had been despoiled by the rich and were now by an inexorable law of human progress ordained in their turn to despoil.

Men are so constituted that they are prone to support a cause which they believed to be assured of victory. It was the achievement of this Jewish visionary that he persuaded the intellectuals of the proletariat in many lands that the hour of their triumph was at hand. He offered a formula of human progress suggested by Hegelian philosophy, but in some important particulars differing from Hegel, which seemed to set the past, the present, and the future of humanity in a logical and necessary sequence. Primitive communism had given way to feudal society, feudal society had been supplanted by the capitalistic bourgeoisie, the bourgeoisie were now to be expropriated by the proletariat. All history was a struggle of classes for the material goods of life. Class hatred, class war was the prime law of change. The dictatorship of the capitalists would be followed by the dictatorship of the proletariat, and this in turn by a classless society, which would be the ultimate end of the long and savage scramble for material things. As for capitalism, it carried within itself the seeds of its own doom. In a passage which has been often cited Marx describes the predestined overthrow of the capitalistic system, how as time proceeds businesses become larger, capitalists become fewer, and the mass of poverty and oppression, of degeneration and exploitation, becomes correspondingly greater. At last the system perishes of its excesses. The working class, which has grown in number, is developed, unified, and organized by the very mechanism of capitalistic production. As they contemplate the growing power of capitalistic monopoly and contrast the opulence of the fortunate with their own ascending scale of misery and want, the wrath of the workers explodes. The inevitable happens. "The centralization of the means of production and the socialization of labour reach a point where they prove incompatible with the capitalistic husk. This bursts asunder. The knell of capitalistic private property sounds. The expropriators are expropriated."

The course of European events was destined to give little comfort to those who placed their faith in a world-wide war of classes. The First International, founded in 1864 to bring the workers of many lands together, was feebly supported, riven with internal discords, and short-lived. Shattered by the Franco-Prussian War, it petered out after an inglorious thirteen years of squalls and squabbles in New York. The Great War was lethal to the Second International, a body rich in political talent,[1] the sinister influence of Moscow to the wider influence of the Third. The hope

---

[1] It contained Lenin, Mussolini, Briand, Ramsay MacDonald, Liebknecht, Laval, Vandervelde, Pilsudski, Bernard Shaw.

that internationally organized labour might avert national wars or improve the lot of the workers has been signally falsified in the event. National rivalries have proved stronger than class interests, patriotic and local sentiments than the loyalty to an economic grouping. Forces acting within the boundaries of individual nations, not the resolutions of international labour, have achieved whatever has so far been accomplished in the domain of social reform.

In England, the main scene of his labours, Marx was during his own lifetime almost a cypher. Here socialism did not spring from the brain of a prophet, but was the inevitable result of human compassion working on the circumstances of urban life. Parliament legislated to protect labour, labour organized itself in trades unions or co-operative societies to safeguard its standard of life, and intelligent municipal reformers like Joseph Chamberlain of Birmingham cleared out the slums, reduced the infantile death rate, and brought education and amenities within reach of the poor. While Marx was composing his indictment of English capitalism, measures were passed by Liberals and Conservatives which deprived the system of many of its evils. The great voices of Thomas Carlyle and William Morris stirred the social conscience. In the more pedestrian sphere of economics a band of able socialist thinkers, styling themselves Fabians,[1] noted the steady drift towards the collective regulation of industry which was proceeding around them and crowned the process with their applause. In a series of valuable publications the history of the trades union movement was narrated, the anatomy of the new industrial democracy was described, and the development of State and municipal enterprise heartily encouraged. Boldly attacking the Manchester doctrine of *laissez-faire* and the old Treasury tenet that money should be allowed to fructify in the pockets of the taxpayer, the Fabians advocated public expenditure for public ends. The country was told that the worker was entitled to a national minimum of education and health, of leisure and of wages. The *Zeitgeist* smiled on the generous doctrine. While the red star of Marx shone faint and distant through the English mists, the industrious Fabians, living in bourgeois comfort, and preaching " the inevitability of gradualism," stamped their thought again and again upon the pages of the English Statute Book.

1889

[1] G. Bernard Shaw, Sidney and Beatrice Webb, Graham Wallas, etc.

Even where the pinch of poverty was most bitterly felt the
Marxian doctrine of world-wide class hatred and systematic
atheism found little acceptance. Hyndman, the bluff well-to-do
Etonian cricketer turned Marxist who founded the Social Democratic Federation, was an inconsiderable figure when compared
with John Burns, the un-theoretical leader of the Dockers' strike,
or Keir Hardie, the Scottish miner and religious mystic, who, out
of the depths of his devout fanaticism, founded the Independent
Labour Party. British socialism was a characteristically native
product, deeply penetrated by evangelical feeling, and akin to
the popular religious movements, Cameronian, Methodist, Revivalist, which from time to time stir the religious consciousness
of the British people to new hopes and visions. The element of
fierce class hatred which inspired continental movements was
absent. "The working man," as Bernard Shaw observed, "respects the bourgeoisie and wants to be a bourgeois: Marx never
got hold of him for a moment."

Meanwhile the gospel of Marx was spreading fast among the
workers and intellectuals on the Continent. In Italy, in France,
and, above all, in Russia, Marxist doctrines began from the
nineties of the last century to captivate the imagination of
many of the foremost minds of the younger generation. Poets
and professors, teachers and artisans embraced the theory of the
class struggle, the iron law of wages, and of the coming triumph
of the Proletariat. Ada Negri, an elementary schoolmistress in
Lombardy, distilled socialism into her popular lyric verse.
Filippo Turati, another Lombard poet, founded a socialist
journal. Within the span of a decade Marx had dethroned
Herbert Spencer as the leading oracle of political and economic
wisdom among the Italians. His fame was bruited in the streets
and the factories; the general strike of 1904 attested his posthumous authority. While scholars were finding inspiration in
the classical verse of Carducci the Republican, and romantics
were entranced by the flowing eloquence of d'Annunzio, the
prince of poetical decadents and imperialists, the silk workers of
Milan found salvation in Marx. Indeed, the more backward the
country, the more likely it was that the influence of that revolutionary thinker would become decisive. In Russia, where the
standard of life was unsheltered by trades unions, the teaching
of Marx, once introduced into the factories and comprehended
in outline, speedily asserted its ascendancy.

BOOKS WHICH MAY BE CONSULTED

Seignobos : History of Contemporary Europe. 1909.
Leslie Stephen : The English Utilitarians. 1900.
Herbert Spencer : Social Statics. 1892.
Herbert Spencer : The Man versus the State. 1909.
Herbert Spencer : Autobiography. 1904.
E. H. Carr : Karl Marx. 1934.
Fabian Essays in Socialism. *Ed.* G. B. Shaw. 1931.
S. and B. Webb : History of Trades Unionism. 1920.
S. and B. Webb : Industrial Democracy. 1920.
Charles Darwin : Origin of Species. 1859.
Charles Darwin : Descent of Man. 1871.
Croce : History of Italy. *Tr.* C. M. Ady. 1929.
Acton : The History of Freedom and Other Essays. 1907.
E. L. Woodward : Three Studies in European Conservatism. 1929.
F. Nielsen : The History of the Papacy in the Nineteenth Century. 1906.

CHAPTER XXII

BRITISH RULE IN INDIA

WE have now in the course of our narrative to draw attention to two matters which, though falling outside the scope of a European History, deserve a brief note from the light which they throw upon the character of one of the chief European nations. The first of these is the British conquest and administration of India; the second the stand taken by Great Britain in the campaign against slavery and the slave trade. The conquest of India was never planned, but arose out of the need which English traders in that country experienced of creating the measure of order and settled justice without which commerce cannot flourish. The confusion of India which ensued upon the dissolution of the Mogul Empire gave the English an opportunity for which they had not sought, but were able to improve. As a great American moralist[1] has said, "India fell to British character." The English succeeded in conquering India because they brought with them peace and deliverance from oppression. Their achievement has been remarkable. They have preserved India from foreign attack, and given it the blessing of unbroken internal peace and freedom of trade. There is not an acre of British India the title to which is not inscribed in the books of the British administration and protected by the force of British law. Some forty million acres of desert have been reclaimed for cultivation by the art of British irrigation engineers. Though the number of Englishmen engaged on the administration has at no time exceeded five thousand, this alien people has so administered the country that the population has increased by more than 230 millions. Such measure of intellectual and political unity as may now be found in India is due to the English conquest and administration. The one common language which goes from end to end of the sub-continent, the one common medium of higher instruction, necessary, however

1707

---

[1] R. W. Emerson, quoted by the Marquis of Zetland: *Steps towards Indian Home Rule.*

egrettable, by reason of the great diversity of Indian tongues, is
he language of England. At every political gathering of Indians
debate is conducted in the idiom of the distant European island.
t has sometimes been charged against the British administra-
ion of India that ninety per cent. of the population (350
millions in 1921) are still illiterate. It is forgotten by those who
aunch this accusation that the spread of education in India is
subject to three crippling disadvantages which are not present in
any European country. The first and least important of these is
an extraordinary diversity of languages and creeds; the second,
the prevalence of child marriage, which so decimates the girl
population of India that there is a surplus of twelve million
males; and the third, the impossibility by reason of the social
customs of India of using unmarried women teachers in elementary schools. To anyone who surveys the landscape of elementary education in Europe and America, this last reason alone is
sufficient to explain the general illiteracy of the Indian people.

What, however, is most to be remarked as an indication of
English character is not the failure of this northern state to give
to Indians a complete system of elementary education such as
was only with difficulty established in England itself in 1870, but
its resolve to impart freely to the natives of India the benefits
of Western knowledge. Under the confident guidance of
Macaulay, the first legal member of the Council of the Governor-
General, it was decided that the peoples of India should be
educated in the language, the literature, and the science of their
European conquerors. The policy, though founded upon a defective sympathy with the intellectual tradition of the East, and
much overdriven, was nevertheless inspired by the generous
desire that India should participate in all that was good and
precious in the civilization of the conquerors. The results have
been surprising. A large class of intelligent lawyers, administrators, officials, teachers, and politicians have absorbed, with
uncanny facility, the language and the ideas of Britain. They
read English books, pass English examinations, act English
plays, cite English law cases, and both as pleaders and Parliamentarians give evidence of marked dexterity. The fruit of *1833*
Macaulay's famous minute on Indian education is the development in India not only of an excellent official class, some two
million in number, but of a body of educated politicians who,
having been taught out of English books to admire liberty,

argue that what is good for the English must be good for them
selves, and confront the ruling race with a challenge based upon
its own doctrines of freedom and progress.

A hundred years lie between the battle of Plassey and the end
of the East India Company. The India Act of 1858, which
brought the Indian Empire under the direct control of the
British Crown, acting through a Secretary of State, marks an
end of the period of conquest and inaugurates an era of con
solidation and peace. Yet, even during the century when the
British were extending their rule by force of arms through
central and western India and in the Punjab, their best repre
sentatives considered themselves as responsible for the welfare of
the native inhabitants. That was the view of Hastings and Wel
lesley, of Bentinck, Dalhousie, and the Lawrences. The Whigs
who passed the Reform Act of 1832 regarded Liberalism not as
an article for domestic consumption only, but as a recipe for
successful government all over the world. The Indian Charter of
1833 lays down the two great principles that "the interests of
the native subjects are to be preferred to those of Europeans
wherever the two come into conflict," and that "no native of
India or natural born subject of His Majesty shall be disabled
from holding any place, office, or employment by reason of his
religion, place of birth, descent or colour." After the Indian
Mutiny, when it might perhaps have been expected that the
Government would have been swept out of its steady course by
the tide of racial passion, the same attitude of paternal tolerance
was persevered in. A royal proclamation announced that the
rights of the Indian Princes would be respected, that equal pro
tection would be given to all religions, and that all subjects of
the Crown without regard to race and creed would be admitted
to all offices. Of these important engagements the first two have
been scrupulously observed, and the third conceded by slow and
guarded stages.

The substantial success of British government in India is
attested by the fact that there has been no widespread attempt
to overturn it. The Mutiny was not a general rising, but was a
military revolt, partial in extent, and quelled with the assistance
of Indian levies drawn from the Punjab. Though the outbreak
was marked by deplorable atrocities, not on one side only, which
left bitter memories, it was succeeded by a period of humane and
prudent administration, which, in its endeavour to soothe the

1857

religious susceptibilities of the people, erred, if anything, on the side of timidity. In the Great War, when the resources of the Empire were strained to the breaking point, the princes and peoples of India were loyal to the British connexion. Had the British Raj been harsh or oppressive, or adamant against the growing insistence of educated Indians to be admitted to a share in the government, Britain's peril would have been seized as India's opportunity.

Since the Mutiny British India has been ruled by a bureaucracy recruited by open competition. The advantage to India of a government exempt from irregularity, caprice, and corruption, and dealing out even-handed justice irrespective of caste and creed, has been generally acknowledged. The British members of the Indian Public Services have perhaps more nearly than any other ruling class realized the ideal of disinterested government which Plato thought could be secured only if the guardians of the State were shielded from the temptations of ownership and family. Their task has been exacting: to suppress crime, to provide for the needs of a modern state out of the scanty resources of a poor oriental community, to promote the unwelcome novelties of education and hygiene among a backward and superstitious peasantry, and to act as a buffer between hostile creeds and communities.

A political spectacle somewhat analogous to the Indian Empire in the decades before the war would be presented by Europe if we could conceive of it as being inspired for the most part by the mentality of a Tyrolean peasant, disarmed, formed into a single free-trade area, governed by a handful of intelligent and benevolent Chinamen, protected by Chinese junks on sea, and on land by an army mainly stationed on the Urals and consisting of about a hundred and fifty thousand European and seventy-five thousand Chinese troops. That a population of three hundred and fifty millions should be defended by a force not much greater than that which is required for the protection of Belgium is proof that the rule of the British in India commends itself to the great mass of the Indian people.

It has been among the wiser aims of British policy in an increasing measure to associate patriotic and educated Indians in the tasks of government. At first Indians were only admitted to subordinate posts. Before the war they held judgeships in the High Courts and were claiming half the places in the Imperial

33

Civil Service. The seed of parliamentary life, which has now flowered into a mighty tree, was sown as far back as 1861, when a few nominated Indians were summoned to the Legislative Council of the Governor-General.

An all-pervading passion of nationalism, quite foreign to the times of Clive and Warren Hastings, and foreign also to the generation of the Mutiny, has made the task of the Englishman in India more difficult than it was of old. The white skin which in the first century of British rule was a passport to veneration is now, in the eyes of many educated and semi-educated Indians, an affront. Colour feeling is more intense. The removal of the foreign element in the government has become, not indeed an unusual, but an ordinary object of ambition among that small fraction of the population which concerns itself with politics. The students dream of *Swaraj* at the college, and the pressmen and politicians are hot in its pursuit. From the success of the Japanese in their Russian war it is inferred that the Orient has no further reason to abase itself before the West.

1905

Indian nationalism is a fabric which, with infinite gradations of shade and colour, tends to assume one of two dominant patterns, the first western and constitutional, the second eastern and revolutionary. There is a school of intelligent Indians, who have been soaked in the philosophy of Victorian liberalism and have followed with ardent attention the course of the nationalist and emancipating movements in the West. They have noted the liberation of the American colonies, the grant of responsible government to the British Dominions, the ascending pressure and success of the Irish movement for Home Rule; and they conclude that what has been found good in other parts of the British Empire must be good also for the peoples of India. Their vision of the India of the future is, accordingly, that of a self-governing Dominion of the Crown, like Australia or Canada, equipped with democratic Parliaments and holding its own through the spread of Western enlightenment among the modern nations of the world. These men do not seek revolution. Believing that national independence is on its way, they desire, by the application of steady political pressure within constitutional limits, to accelerate its approach. G. K. Gokhale, the founder of the Servants of India and himself an accomplished Parliamentarian, was a protagonist, at once subtle and saintly, of this school of thinking.

d. 1914

Others place little value upon Western novelties and maintain that everything precious for Indian life is to be found in the Vedas. They believe in India as a nation but not in India as a Parliamentary democracy. Such was the philosophy of Dayananda, the founder of the *Arya Samaj*, an association for the revival of the ancient Hindu spirit, and such essentially was the outlook of P. J. Tilak, the formidable Brahmin who organized *d. 1919* a violent resistance to the British *Raj* in the Deccan during the nineties of the last century. It was characteristic of the extreme conservatism of this powerful revolutionary demagogue that he opposed the Age of Consent Bill which was designed to reduce what is generally considered to be the worst blot on the social system of India, the evil of child marriage.

It is possible that British administrators in India have been too stiff in their resistance to these new formations of opinion. Officials crushed by a heavy burden of work in a trying climate cannot be expected to welcome the shock of disturbing ideas such as may impair the efficiency of their smooth and intricate machine. The Indian Civil Service has presented a very cold shoulder to the politicians of the Indian Congress, who, since 1885, have been busy in working up a National Movement, and they have paid little heed to the unceasing attacks of the vernacular press. A certain contemptuous indifference, natural to the agents of a benevolent Power which has long usurped the rôle of Providence, has marked the relations of the official world to the effervescent nationalism of the young. Nevertheless, the Service has worked with characteristic loyalty the plans which liberally-minded Cabinets, Secretaries of State, or Viceroys have devised for the contentment of Indian politicians. Lord Ripon's Municipal Councils, the Morley-Minto non-responsible Legislatures of 1909, the dyarchy of the Montagu-Chelmsford Scheme of 1917, under which the nation-building services (local government, education, etc.) were transferred to Indian Cabinets responsible to elected Indian legislatures, while the security services (army, police, etc.) were retained in the hands of the officials, all these successive instalments of political liberty, however unwelcome to the bureaucratic mind, have been recognized as inevitable. That Indian nationalism must colour British policy in India is now a belief common to all sections of British opinion. Already the Parliament in Delhi makes an Indian tariff and checks the imports of British goods in the interests of the Indian producer.

Already "dyarchy," introduced as an immense concession in 1917, has failed to satisfy. A self-governing, all-Indian Federation, including the Princes,[1] and with certain safeguards for the maintenance of the Imperial connexion, is now the declared aim of leading statesmen in both countries and embodied in a statute. So far and so fast has Britain been prepared to advance along this perilous road, guided by the two lodestars of the Anglo-Saxon race, of which the first is that all government must rest upon consent, and the second that it is the office of statesmanship to avert revolution by reform.

"East is east and west is west." Indian character and Indian standards present always, in the last analysis, something which baffles the Western observer. In the religious atmosphere of India, where the things of this world are apt to be regarded as dust, the values of life experience an inversion. Otherworldliness ranks before efficiency, learning is in greater esteem than practical vigour. A saint who starves himself in public is widely honoured; a social reformer who clears slums, bridles usurers or battles with the plague is likely to encounter more opposition than applause. Lord Curzon left India an unpopular figure despite splendid services to agriculture, education, archaeology, and to the general welfare of the Indian people. The hero acclaimed among Indians during the last two decades is a man as different from the dazzling English administrator as it is possible to conceive. Mr. Gandhi has many qualities which, had his lot been cast in a Western land, would have brought him to the front of political life: great personal charm, ardent patriotism, brilliant dialectical ability, a keen eye for publicity, subtlety in attack and defence, a distinguished command of the English language. Such qualities, pertaining as they do to the Western category of political virtues, are easily appreciated by Englishmen. But this little Hindu lawyer who has given so much trouble to the British *Raj* as organizer of a boycott of British goods and as the leader in a campaign of civil disobedience, presents other aspects which perplex and elude. An indubitable saint yet as a member of the money-lending caste a friend to usury, an ardent patriot yet as a politician the beneficiary of the worst slum properties in India, a declared opponent of Western modernism yet not averse from availing himself of the conveni-

---

[1] The Native states, some 700 in number, cover nearly two-fifths of the total area of India.

ence of a Ford car, Mr. Gandhi is an epitome of those picturesque and baffling contrasts which offer so remarkable and
exciting a challenge to the patience and prudence of the West.

BOOKS WHICH MAY BE CONSULTED

A. C. Lyall : The Rise of the British Dominion in India. 1910.

T. W. Holderness : Peoples and Problems of India. (Home University
    Library.) 1912.

E. Thompson and E. Garratt : Rise and Fulfilment of British Rule in
    India. 1934.

Sir Courtenay Ilbert : The Government of India. 1913.

W. W. Hunter : The Indian Empire. 1893.

W. W. Hunter : The Marquis of Dalhousie. 1890.

T. Rice Holmes : History of the Indian Mutiny. 1898.

Marquis of Zetland : Life of Lord Curzon. 1928.

R. Temple : Lord Lawrence. 1889.

Indian Statutory Commission, 2 vols. Cd. 3568, 3569, XI, 1929-30.
    (Simon Report.)

CHAPTER XXIII

EUROPE AND SLAVERY

Slavery in antiquity. Mediaeval serfdom. Plantation slavery in the New World. Relative humanity of Spain. The English slave trade. Movement for abolition. The Emancipators. Importance of Parliament. The Wesleyans. The Economists. The Acts of 1807 and 1833. The fight against the foreign slave trade. Livingstone in Africa. The humanitarian note in modern legislation.

IN the history of Europe so far as it is known to us there are two chapters marked by a special note of infamy. The first was when the pillagers and pirates of the Roman Republic threw themselves upon the ill-defended opulence of the East, when the Aegean Sea was infested with slavers, and Delos (becoming a free port in 146 B.C.) obtained a hateful renown as the centre of the European slave trade, in which, if we are to believe Strabo, as many as ten thousand slaves would be bought and sold in a single day. But this period of rapine and wreckage, terrible indeed while it lasted, was fortunately short. The good government of the Empire put down slave-raiding; the gentle and humane philosophy of the Stoics softened and elevated the condition of the slave. If there was no movement to abolish slavery, the institution was gradually stripped of its worst evils, passing into predial serfdom and villenage in the fields, and becoming compatible with the exercise of many skilled and refined occupations in the cities. The Roman slave in the later Empire was often a freeman in everything but name. He had been taken into the social fabric of his masters, shared their studies and ideas, contributed to their arts and crafts, and often exercised a positive influence on the direction of affairs. Epictetus, one of the noblest and wisest of Stoic philosophers, endured without repining the status of a slave. The free play of human feeling in private life, the growing sense of responsibility in government, the influence of Christianity, the organization of the Asiatic and African provinces of the Empire, and the absence of those mechanical improvements which inevitably lead to mass production, continued to abridge the number, to improve the lot, and to lessen the industrial importance of the slave population.

Nor was there any serious recrudescence of the evil consequent on the break-up of the Roman Empire. In the middle ages, since agrarian serfdom was widely spread and the demand for urban labour was easily satisfied, the slave trade was a minor evil, flourishing chiefly along the coasts of the Black Sea, but on a scale which bears no comparison either with the slave-raiding operations of the Roman Republic or with the second great spasm of rapine which ensued upon the discovery of the new world.

It is a terrible commentary on Christian civilization that the longest period of slave-raiding known to history was initiated by the action of Spain and Portugal, France, Holland, and Britain after the Christian faith had for more than a thousand years been the established religion of western Europe; and it is the graver since the new slavery was worse and more inhuman than the old. In the ancient world domestic slavery, which was educative and often humane, was more important than the slavery of the mine and the plantation. In the new world this was otherwise. Mass production had come into its own. The demand of Europe for sugar, tobacco, and cotton was fed by the labour of African slaves, herded in barracks, working in gangs, and regimented, as they had been recruited, by soulless and mercenary violence.

Among the slave-raiding countries of the West who opened out this new chapter in human atrocity Spain is distinguished for a relative humanity. In the initial as in the concluding stages of her overseas Empire the cruelty of Spain towards her slave population in the American colonies was as great as that of any other country; but there was a long intermediate period during which the Roman Church honourably endeavoured to improve the lot of the labouring population in the Spanish colonies. The slave was baptized, prepared for the Mass, retained in his family group, and brought through his membership of the Church within the system of Spain. For the British colonies the Church of England made no comparable effort. "It is no more calculated for the negro," said Canning, "than for the brute animal that shares his toil." While the Spanish Church pressed forward on its missionary enterprise, the British planters looked with active disfavour on the attempt to spread among the blacks the disturbing ferment of Christian belief. To this attitude the Anglican Church offered no effective resistance.

The comparative inability of the Protestant religion to

moderate the horrors of this infamous traffic is the more serious by reason of the fact that of all European slave traders the British were the most successful and consequently the most guilty. It has been calculated that the total number of slaves imported into the English colonies from Africa between 1680 and 1786 was well over two millions. Statesmen like Chatham supported the trade as a pillar of national strength; to sailors like Nelson it was an essential prop of the mercantile marine. The prosperity of Liverpool and in large part also of Bristol was built on the slave trade. Formidable, therefore, was the task of attacking the immense vested interests bound up in slavery. In the eighteenth century no colonies were so valuable as the sugar islands of the West Indies, and, since these were cultivated by African slave labour, the whole West Indian interest was arrayed against any proposal to abate or destroy the traffic upon which its profits depended. When to this powerful group is added the number of Englishmen who were concerned with the slave-grown crops of the American continent, and the vast body of American opinion which, at any time previous to the severance of the tie between the American colonies and the mother country, could be mobilized in defence of American slavery, the prospect of uprooting the institution may well have seemed desperate.

Yet it was from Britain, the largest slave trader and the greatest offender, that the movement sprang which successfully abolished slavery in the British isles (1772), then the slave trade (1806), then slavery itself in the British Dominions (1833), and finally so worked upon the conscience of the world as to secure a large and nearly universal concurrence of action for the extirpation of the evil. The credit for securing from Lord Mansfield the famous decision in the case of James Somersett (1772) that the status of slavery was unknown to the common law of England was due to Granville Sharp, a civil servant, inconspicuous in wealth and station, but of a rare warmth of heart and persistence of character, who, once fired by the cruel usage of a negro slave in the streets of London, never rested until he had obtained the verdict which for ever afterwards rid the British islands of the taint of slavery. Thereafter comes a roll of English emancipators whose names even in a general history of Europe are worthy of commemoration: William Wilberforce, Thomas Clarkson, Zachary Macaulay, and James Stephen, whose preparatory labours, sustained over a period of twenty years, enabled Fox to carry the abolition of the slave trade; Thomas Fowell Buxton, the Parliamentary leader of the Abolitionists, who worked up the House of Commons to abolish slavery; and Brougham, who carried the torch through the country; Palmerston, who stopped the slave trade between Portugal and Brazil; and the noble group of missionaries, soldiers, and statesmen, David Livingstone, Charles Gordon, Sir John Kirk, and Lord Lugard, by whose efforts in large measure Africa has been opened up and rid of the curse of the Arab slave-raider. Lecky does no more than justice when he states that the crusade of England against slavery " may probably be regarded as among the three or four perfectly virtuous pages in the history of nations."

The cause of abolition was undoubtedly helped by the successful revolt of the American colonies, which removed a powerful body of pro-slavery opinion from the arena of controversy, and by the Irish Union, which brought into the English House of Commons a body of Irish voters who had no commercial interests to serve and were capable of responding to the abstract call of liberty and justice. These adventitious aids do not, however, explain how it was that a small body of men, none of them in the first rank of politics, were able to master the organized opposition of a lucrative trade which had come to be regarded as essential to national prosperity and naval strength. The fact could not have been accomplished without Parliament. It was because England possessed in the House of Commons an assembly in which hidden things could be brought to light and shameful things exposed in their shamefulness, that it was possible so to indoctrinate the nation with the hatefulness of slavery as to overcome the strong material forces enlisted in its support. It is not without significance that William Wilberforce, the Parliamentary leader of the Abolitionists, was known as the " Nightingale of the House," and that the abolition of the slave trade was carried in 1807 by Charles James Fox, the greatest Parliamentary orator of his time.

Behind this Parliamentary agitation was a movement proceeding from those deep religious and moral impulses which in the later part of the eighteenth century were specially distinctive of the Quaker and Methodist bodies. The committee of six which first (1783) organized a regular anti-slavery campaign in the country was a committee of Quakers. " The Clapham Sect," as the circle of Wilberforce came to be called, was deeply affected by the modes of quickened personal religious experience which John Wesley had preached and by his example recommended. Though other influences co-operated, though Adam Smith contributed his economic good sense, and Jeremy Bentham his rational humanitarianism, the predominant force which made abolition possible was a devout sense of religion and morality informing the lives and so dominating the consciences of a small knot of high-minded and energetic Englishmen that they could not rest until a great wrong had been righted.

The immediate effect of Lord Mansfield's judgment, the first victory in a long campaign, was to liberate some fifteen thousand negroes who had been introduced by their masters into England and were there freely bought and sold. The second stage in the operations was the more difficult and protracted assault upon the slave trade. Again and again, despite the combined influence of Wilberforce and Pitt, motions to abolish the trade were defeated by the slave-owning interest in the Cabinet, in the House, and in the country. Then Pitt died, and Fox, with the aid of the Irish votes, abolished the trade just before slave-grown cotton began to pour into Lancashire, and consequently before Lancashire was supplied with a motive for joining hands with the sugar interest in defence of slavery. The Act was passed in the nick of time, and in 1811 was made truly effective by a law which fixed upon slave trading the guilt of felony and the punishment of deportation.

When it is remembered that the slave trade was put down in the middle of a life-and-death struggle with Napoleon and that every sailor from Nelson downwards declared that its abolition would be the ruin of the British Navy, the courage of Pitt and Fox in utterly disregarding the advice of their naval experts and in steadily pressing even in war-time for the removal of this great outrage on humanity is truly to be admired. Not for the first or last time the wider wisdom of civilian leaders over-ruled the confident counsels of the fighting services.

It was then in her new and striking character of an abolitionist State that England entered the Congress of Vienna and there obtained from the eight leading powers a solemn declaration that the universal abolition of the slave trade was a measure "peculiarly worthy of their attention and conformable to the spirit of the times." To obtain the abolition of the foreign slave trade and of the institution of slavery in the British colonies became henceforth a main object of British policy, steadily and honestly pursued, and engaging the passionate interest of the serious-minded portion of the nation. Eventually Parliament, finding that it was useless to try to persuade colonial assemblies to abolish the institution of slavery, decided to legislate over their heads. In August, 1833, a Bill was passed for the abolition of slavery in all the British Dominions. A sum of twenty millions had already been voted for the compensation of the owners.

The effort to fight the foreign slave trade was, from the nature of things, far more difficult. Only in 1831 did France, only in 1835 did Spain, impose effective penalties against the offence of slave trading, and meanwhile Britain alone took adequate steps to ensure that the law against slave trading was strictly and continuously enforced. Owing to the fact that the United States objected to the exercise of the right of search by British vessels and provided no patrol of her own, most slave traders secured impunity by flying the stars and stripes. More particularly did the slave trade in Cuba flourish until Abraham Lincoln's decree of emancipation (1862).

Much was accomplished by the system of maritime patrols, though far less than would actually have been achieved had all the maritime Powers contributed their due quota. The destruction of the Portuguese slave trade with the western hemisphere was made possible only by the vigour of the British navy.

There remained the difficult and almost intractable problem of liberating Africa from the Arab slave gangs and the domestic slave trade which was carried on in the heart of the continent. A system of marine patrols, however excellent—and in the forties a sixth of the British navy was employed on African patrol work— was clearly inadequate to cope with so vast an evil. The career of David Livingstone, the Scottish missionary, who, mostly on foot and with few native companions, crossed Africa between 1853 and 1856, opened out a new epoch and pointed to a new way. Livingstone's African journeys brought home to the imagination of the British public the horrors of the Arab slave trade, which had its centre in Zanzibar, and led to a revival of Abolitionist activity, the first-fruit of which was the treaty between Britain and Zanzibar in 1873, which closed the great slave mart in that city. From this time a conviction steadily grew that unless the African continent were opened up, settled with farmers and missionaries, and brought under the control of the European Powers, the poison of slavery would never be fully eliminated.

The peaceful partition of Africa among the leading European States, which was perhaps the most striking achievement of European statecraft in the eighties and nineties of the last century, enabled this policy to be carried forward. Other European countries beside Britain were now prepared to take vigorous action for the suppression of slavery and the improvement of social conditions in Africa. The Brussels conference of 1889, convoked by King Leopold of Belgium on the suggestion of the British Government, and attended by the representatives of seventeen states, resulted in an act (ratified in 1892) which has been termed the Magna Carta of the African slave, so complete and far-reaching were the provisions which the participating states, which included Persia, Zanzibar, and the Turkish Empire, bound themselves to adopt. Yet still the evil persists, and still the European crusade proceeds, but now with an ever augmenting promise of success, against the eternal cupidity and cruelty of man.

The long battle against slavery and the slave trade is part of the general spread of humanitarian policy which has given rise to religious missions, expensive social services, and to the formation of societies for the protection of children and animals. Of all the features distinguishing modern from ancient society, this is the most encouraging, and to those who are rendered melancholy by the continuing spectacle of the crimes, the vices, and follies of mankind, the least dubious ground for solace and for hope. The democratic civilization of modern Europe has many flaws, but in the humanity with which it endeavours to shelter the weaker members of the community from the harsh effects of economic competition it offers a plea in arrest of adverse judgment, challenges the splendours of its scientific achievement, and outshines its advance in material wealth.

BOOKS WHICH MAY BE CONSULTED

W. E. H. Lecky : History of England.
R. Coupland : Wilberforce. 1922.
R. Coupland : The British Anti-Slavery Movement. 1933.
R. Coupland : Kirk in the Zambesi. 1928.
Livingstone : Narrative of an Expedition to the Zambesi.
Lugard : The Dual Mandate in British Tropical Africa. 1922.
P. M. Allen : Gordon and the Sudan. 1931.
H. Wallon : Histoire de l'esclavage dans l'antiquité. 1879.
M. Rostovtzeff : The Social and Economic History of the Roman Empire. 1926.

CHAPTER XXIV

WAR AND PEACE IN THE BALKANS

Despite the Dreikaiserbund Bismarck is nervous. The Austrian problem and the Dual Monarchy. The Pan-Slavonic movement. Its influence on Russian policy. The reforms of Alexander II. Bulgaria. The Balkan revolt, 1875. The Bulgarian massacres. The Russian invasion and the Treaty of San Stefano. Lord Beaconsfield and the Congress of Berlin. 1878. The breach in the Dreikaiserbund. Gladstone and Disraeli.

EVERYTHING in the years immediately succeeding the Franco-Prussian War announced the permanence and splendour of the German *Reich*. Its one serious enemy was shattered. It had no rivals within sight. A great population elate with victory supported the authority of the Imperial Crown and paid to the officer corps of the strongest army in the world a willing tribute of subservient admiration and respect. Nothing was to be feared from Russia and Austria, whose rulers were bound to the German Kaiser by cordial relations of personal friendship. When in 1872 the three Emperors met in Berlin and there agreed to defend the *status quo* in Europe, to work together amicably on Balkan questions, to chastise socialism, and to promote reform, the imposing edifice of the new German Empire appeared unassailable. What enemy would be so presumptuous as to flout the *Dreikaiserbund*? Yet Bismarck still shuddered at the spectre of French revenge, and it is interesting to note that before the decade was out Gambetta had descried in Serbia the Achilles heel which would bring the *Reich* to the ground. So early was it apparent that racial movements among the Slavs might threaten the principle of Teutonic authority and deliver a smashing blow at the conservative foundations of Europe.

The internal situation of the Austrian Empire, always difficult by reason of racial friction, had undergone many vicissitudes since the suppression of the Bohemian and Hungarian revolts in 1848 and 1849. There was first a decade of stern autocratic centralization with Germans everywhere, manning the Hungarian administration, officering the Hungarian army, controlling the Hungarian police, and with the whole intellect and education of the country confided (under the terms of a Concordat with the Pope, August 13, 1855) to the tutelage of the Catholic Church. It was, however, idle to suppose that the Slavonic and Magyar races would permanently accept as the beneficent ordinance of providence the hegemony of the German race. The system of centralized government devised and administered by Alexander Bach, a clever politician of Hebrew extraction, though not lacking in good will, efficiency, or the spirit of improvement, was regarded as an intolerable incubus by races to whom the German tradition, the German mode of life, and the German spirit of ascendancy were fiercely distasteful. It needed but the shock of a public calamity to show how slender was the basis of public confidence upon which the Government reposed and how widely spread was the spirit of disloyalty. When Austria went into the Italian War, the whole fabric of the Empire quaked as if it were built upon shifting sands. The Magyars and Czechs openly rejoiced at Austria's defeats at Magenta and Solferino. The war loan was a disastrous failure. Something, it was felt, must be done to check the mounting tide of racial discontent and to clamp the Empire together, before it was too late. Thereupon opened a period of constitutional experimentation (1860-67) which served only to show how difficult was the problem of combining in any stable form of political union the miscellaneous races of the Austrian Empire.

A half-hearted Federalism was a failure, a system of Parliamentary centralization was no greater success. The Magyars would no more come into a Parliament at Vienna to be voted down by Germans than Ulstermen would sit in a nationalist Parliament in Dublin. At last in 1865 Francis Joseph went to Pesth and invited the Magyars and Croats to table their proposals.

It so happened that at this crisis Hungary possessed in Deák a patriotic statesman of commanding abilities and moderate views, who, while holding that his country had much to gain from its association with Austria and sharply opposing the advocates of secession, was determined to secure for the Magyar races the essentials of political liberty and self-respect. That his task was sensibly lightened by the misfortunes of Austria in the Prussian War cannot be denied. Dejection at Vienna was opportunity at Pesth; but it is the task of statesmen to catch the flying skirts of opportunity, and it is to the credit of Deák that, profiting by the

Austrian defeat at Sadowa, he made with Beust, the Austrian Chancellor, the Dual Monarchy of 1867.

Feb., 1867

The relative permanence of this curious constitution is due to the fact that it accorded to the two strongest races of the Empire, the Germans and the Magyars, a parity of power. In Cisleithania, containing the seventeen provinces of Austria, the Germans were predominant, in Transleithania (Hungary, Croatia, Slavonia, Transylvania, and certain frontier districts) the Magyars. "You look after your barbarians," said Andrassy, the Hungarian, to Beust, the German, "and we will look after ours." Each part of the Empire had its own Parliament and local Assemblies, each its own official language. Though there were imperial ministries for war, finance, and foreign affairs, there was no imperial Parliament. Affairs of common interest to Hungary and Austria, such as the decennial commercial treaty, were discussed in two Delegations of sixty members each, meeting alternately at Pesth and Vienna, but deliberating and voting apart, and, by a precaution which is eloquent of the mistrust and alienation which prevailed, communicating with one another only through the exchange of written documents. That the sovereign independence of Austria and Hungary might be even more clearly marked, the *Ausgleich* or settlement was not an agreement between two peoples and governments, one with another, but a contract made by Austria and Hungary separately with the sovereign House of Habsburg.

Thus linked together in an uneasy compromise these two autonomous Powers faced the hard weather of fifty years, looking south-eastwards for their future, since the Prussian guns had driven them from Germany and Venetia, and therefore plunging more and more deeply into the Balkan vortex, while they accepted as an earnest of increased efficiency those principles of parliamentary government, religious toleration, and secular education, which had now become fashionable in western Europe. What vast changes had been accelerated by the Prussian victory! In 1867 Austria-Hungary became a constitutional monarchy, and a year later broke the educational monopoly of the Church.

One grave problem remained unsettled. Under the heel of the two dominant races was a restless underworld of Slavs. The Czechs of Bohemia, the Slovaks, Croats, and Serbs of Hungary, could not be expected to welcome the beautiful arrangement which had confided the destinies of the Austrian Empire to the proud Magyar aristocracy and to the German-speaking nobles and burghers of Austria. It is true that the Slavonic population of the Dual Monarchy was divided by geographical situation, by differences of dialect and custom, and in some cases by the deeper chasm of religion, that Czech was sundered from Slovak, Slovak from Serb, and all from Croat and Slovene, and that for many centuries these poor and scattered branches of the great Slavonic family had been conscious of no common ethnic personality. That state of things, however, was now passing away. A Pan-Slavonic movement had begun to stir the imagination of these rude and backward peoples, a feeling that, although they had been ground down under the wheels of history, some by the Turks, others by the Germans and Magyars, they were nevertheless members of a mighty society spread out from the Arctic Ocean to the Euxine, and from the Baltic to the Behring Straits. The movement started with Kollar, the Slovak poet, in 1824, and swiftly spread to Bohemia, where it was taken up by the Czech philologists and men of letters; at first out of a feeling for the common inheritance of Slavonic culture and a desire to explore and command the treasures of thought and emotion which belonged to Slavs all over the world, so that even the humblest peasant, as he toiled for an alien master, might feel himself to belong to a great common brotherhood with a distinctive and honourable contribution to make to the civilization of mankind. But then, as so often happens, the ideas liberated by poets and scholars passed into the domain of controversial policy. Pan-Slavism played a part in the Bohemian revolution of 1848; but Bohemia was a small stage, and the Bohemian revolution was soon over and done with. A larger theatre and a greater fortune were reserved for the movement. Some twenty years later, while Alexander II was Tzar of Russia, Pan-Slavic ideas entered as a directing influence into Muscovite policy. Then this new racial philosophy became a force of the first magnitude, challenging the whole authority of the Porte in the Balkans, and spreading a new restlessness among the many million Slavs who were living, in varying degrees of subjection, within the frontiers of the Dual Monarchy.

1855-81 While Miss Florence Nightingale was blazing new paths to freedom for Victorian womankind, the Tzar Alexander, equally as a result of the Crimean War, was carrying out with the assistance of a handful of enlightened noblemen and officials a great programme of domestic reform. Within the space of a decade he liberated the serfs, remodelled the judicial system, introduced local government, permitted a free press in St. Petersburg and Moscow, and accorded to the Universities a measure of academic freedom. Long afterwards the great work accomplished in the sixties by the reforming Tzar and his associates was looked back upon as the inspiring achievement of an heroic age. Much indeed was done to break the frost of tradition, and to lay the foundations of a sounder social and political system. But Russia is a land in which great ideas are more easily conceived than accurately executed. The measures were great, the men who were called upon to carry them out were not great enough. What was actually achieved fell far short of what was expected. There was an insufficiency of faith, skill, and integrity in the officials, a general aversion from steady political work, and an absence of support from the liberal members of the middle class, who, having been accustomed to tell themselves that no Tzarist government could do anything right, refused, even when great civilizing reforms were offered them, to vary their fixed attitude of opposition.

That would, however, be a very imperfect picture of Russia under Alexander II, in which the Tzar's great programme of reform was the only aspect visible to the eye. It was a reign of stern domestic tyranny, especially after the crushing of the Polish rebellion in 1863 and of protesting nihilism, a reign in which no suspect was safe from the secret police, in which houses were suddenly broken into and men and women transported to distant exile in Siberia, while conversely every member of the government from the Tzar downward was the mark for the dagger or the bomb. This was the time when the young intellectuals of Russia, impatient of the tardiness of reform and intoxicated with the new wine of physical science, began to assail the whole fabric of society with a savage recklessness, and, having nothing to suggest in place of all that they were resolved to destroy, earned for themselves the name of nihilist; the time depicted in Turgenev's *Fathers and Sons* and Tolstoi's *Anna Karenina*, when all the values of the old order were sharply challenged by the rising generation, and family harmony was often broken beyond repair as the traditional pieties of the old were confronted with the insolent atheism of the young. With all these revolutionary tendencies the Tzarist Government could have no truce. But with this spirit of domestic repression there were combined three other ideas: the unification of the un-assimilated peoples of the empire, the conquest of central Asia, and the liberation of the Slavonic nations of the Balkans from the Turkish yoke. Of these policies the first was futile, the second triumphant (for it was in 1868 that the Russians con-quered Samarcand), while the third, which was the creed of Pan-Slavism, was big with disaster to Russia, Europe, and the world.

The Pan-Slavic idea would have been well enough, had the Slavs of the Balkans been a united family, or the Powers willing to accept the hegemony of the Tzar in European Turkey. Neither of these conditions was realized. When the long Tur-kish tyranny was finally broken, it became apparent that there was no hate in the Balkans comparable to the animosity of Bulgar and Slav. Then to everyone's surprise it was learned that the people whom Russia had selected as being the leading Slavonic race in Turkey, and upon whom she had lavished years of propaganda and individual education, was, in fact, regarded by the south-western Slavs as an alien and an enemy, and that the establishment by Russian arms of a powerful Bulgaria, so far from putting heart into Pan-Slavism or contributing to the expansion of Russian influence, had the very reverse effect. The newly liberated Bulgaria created a counterpoise to the Muscovites and furnished the Serb with cause for bitter jealousy and offence. Of all this, however, there was no suspicion in the later seventies, when a crisis in the Near East threw Russia into a quasi-isolation and weakened the impregnable *Dreikaiserbund*, upon which the fabric of European stability had hitherto reposed.

In 1875 a revolt against Turkish misrule broke out in Bosnia and Herzegovina, a revolt of misery and irritation, springing straight from the heart of the peasantry. The storm spread apace to Montenegro, to Serbia, to Bulgaria. There was never so com-prehensive a manifestation of Slavonic nationalism in the Balkans, so large and resounding an advertisement of their wrongs. But the Turks were too strong. The army of Serbia and Montenegro withered under their attack, and the murder of some 12,000 Christians in Bulgaria by irregular Turkish troops (May, 1876) attested with characteristic emphasis the restoration of Turkish authority over the mutinous peasantry of the Bul-garian nation.

Russia was in no mood to acquiesce in the ruin of the Slavonic cause in the Balkans. She declared war (April, 1877), attacked the Turks alike in Asia and Europe, and after a temporary check before Kars and Plevna carried everything before her. On March 3, 1878, with Russian armies encamped before their capital, the Turks were compelled to sign a treaty at San Stefano, the main feature of which was the creation of a vast autonomous Bulgaria, to be administered under Russian tutelage, and to be garrisoned for two years by Russian troops.

In England, where the old Crimean spirit was much alive among the Tories, the Russian victories were received with a frenzy of indignant alarm. That Turkey should become a satellite of Russia seemed to imperil the whole position of Britain in the East. The Queen, the Metropolitan Press, the "upper ten thousand" were warlike. A silly song—

"We don't want to fight, but by jingo if we do,
    We've got the ships, we've got the men, we've got the money too!"

—captured the music-halls. Never was Europe closer to a great conflagration than in the early spring of 1878, when Lord Beaconsfield's cabinet came to Parliament for six millions, ordered the fleet to pass the Dardanelles, called out the reserves, and shed Derby and Carnarvon, the two ministers who stood for peace. Even Lord Salisbury, who had a few months earlier sensibly realized that Russia, with no fleet, no marine population, and a corrupt civil service, could never seriously menace Britain's position in the Mediterranean, was now willing to go to war, unless the Tzar were prepared to submit the whole treaty of San Stefano to the Powers and to vary its terms.

That the peace of Europe was happily saved was due to the good offices of Bismarck, to the brilliant dexterity of Salisbury, and to the readiness of Austria to follow the British lead.

Sensible of her isolation, Russia was persuaded to submit her treaty to the Powers, and to accept proposals which she might otherwise have regarded as wounding to her pride. At the Congress of Berlin (June, 1878) the whole question of the Near East was settled upon lines which safeguarded British interests, extended Austrian influence, and administered a severe check to the Pan-Slavist ambitions of the Tzar. While eleven million Christians were liberated from the Turkish yoke, and Bosnia and Herzegovina were handed to Austria to administer, the vast and sprawling Bulgarian state, the creation of which under the Treaty of San Stefano had been at once the chief fruit of Russian endeavour and the principal cause of British alarm, was reduced to more modest dimensions. For these enormous concessions Russia was compensated by the gift of Bessarabia and by the recognition of Asiatic conquests which the western Powers were in no position to contest.

Measured against Russia's great expectations, these were pitiful emoluments; and when it was learned that England, the principal rival, had secretly obtained Cyprus from the Turks on the pretext that with such a base she would be in a better position to defend the Asiatic possessions of the Porte, the whole mass of transactions could not appear to a Russian in any other light than as a decisive diplomatic defeat. Disguise it as they might, Beaconsfield and Salisbury had triumphed over Gortschakoff. They had given the Balkans a map devised on Anglo-Austrian not on Russian principles. They had confirmed their authority with the Turks, and throughout their enterprise they had received encouragement from Vienna and Berlin. When London acclaimed the two British statesmen who returned with "Peace with Honour," the Tzar could not but reflect how different the result would have been if his friends the Emperors of Germany and Austria had given him a full measure of diplomatic support. From that moment the *Dreikaiserbund* began to totter. A train had been fired in this Balkan crisis which was destined to split the union of the three Emperors and to throw Tzarist Russia into the arms of the French Republic. Of all the results of the Slav rebellion against Turkish misrule this was the most far-reaching in its effects.

Meanwhile England was convulsed by a domestic struggle of extraordinary and memorable intensity. It had been the tradition and pride of the Liberal party to espouse the cause of liberty and justice all over the world. Liberals had supported Italy against Austria, Denmark against Germany, and at the opening of the Franco-Prussian War had championed the treaty for the defence and neutrality of Belgium. To a party cherishing such traditions no European government was more odious than that of the Sultan, nor any people more cruelly wronged than the Christian subjects of the Porte. At the news of the Bulgarian atrocities the greatest of Liberal statesmen, suddenly emerging from his retirement, led a passionate opposition to the Turk-preserving policy of the Tory government. Gladstone was now nearing his seventieth year. He remembered Canning. He had served under Wellington. He had been a member of the first Reformed Parliament. He had fought ten General Elections. At forty-five he had been the author of a famous budget. At fifty-nine he became the head of a great administration (1868-74) which gave England universal education and the ballot, freed the Universities from religious tests, reformed the army, and levelled the first courageous blows at the injustices and anomalies inherent in English and Protestant ascendancy in Ireland. Though a strong Anglican, he had not scrupled to disestablish the Anglican Church in Ireland. Though a large landlord, he had passed the Irish Land Act against the interests of his class and for the relief of an impoverished and embittered agricultural democracy in the sister island. After a long course of unexampled Parliamentary activity he had retired to the noble woodlands of Hawarden, to fell trees, to re-read Homer, and to extend his favourite studies in theology. From these congenial occupations he was sharply summoned by the bitter cry of Bulgarian distress.

The campaign which he then conducted in and out of Parliament is one of the outstanding physical and oratorical achievements in English history. The Court, the aristocracy, the main part of the Press, the overwhelming majority in both houses of Parliament, the unthinking and shallow multitude who live for sensations, were passionately opposed to him. A fierce hatred of Russia, a traditional sentiment of friendship for the Turk, an enthusiasm for spirited and martial gestures, such as the summoning of Indian troops to Malta or the despatch of the fleet to the Dardanelles, obstructed his approach to the ear of the nation. Yet such was the splendour and force of his appeal to the moral sentiments of his countrymen that before three years were out he had talked down the reputation of Beaconsfield and Salisbury, talked the Tories out of office, and talked himself back to the leadership of his party and to the premier place in the counsels of the Crown. That English voters could not be indifferent to the general welfare of mankind was the main burden of his argument. "Remember," he said to the electors of Midlothian in a characteristic flight, "that the sanctity of life in the hill villages of Afghanistan among the winter snows is as inviolable in the eyes of Almighty God as can be your own." He had no fear of the big Bulgaria. With a sound instinct he declared that there could be no greater barrier against the advance of Russian influence in the Balkans than a nation of free men. Not many years afterwards his estimate of the situation proved to be correct. The two halves of Bulgaria, the separation of which had been the main object of British diplomacy in 1878, came together under the stress of national sentiment with the entire good will of Great Britain and to the intense chagrin of the Russian government.

The long duel between Disraeli and Gladstone (1852-80) is the central fact in the Parliamentary life of the mid-Victorian age. It was characteristic of England that the Tory party should accept the leadership of a Hebrew adventurer of genius, who chose the novel as his principal medium for the propagation of political ideas, while the Liberal leader was a High Church English squire, the fine flower of Eton and Oxford, who had begun his political life as the hope of the stern and unbending Tories. No one was more alien to the philosophical radicalism of his day than Gladstone, no one more responsive to atmospheric changes than Disraeli. The great scientific movement of the Victorian age left the mind of Gladstone, the Liberal, entirely untouched. Though he led the party of progress with utter fearlessness and unmatched Parliamentary resource, his was not one of the forward-reaching minds which pierce into the secrets of the future. There is more real grasp of the inner necessities of the time in Mill's *Political Economy* and in Disraeli's *Sybil* than in all Gladstone's political speeches. What gave Gladstone his special power was his unique control of the Parliamentary instrument. Never has there been a parliamentarian so ready for every emergency, so quick to divine the shifting emotions of his audience, and to confound them by the power and penetrating stroke of his response. Again and again, as he rose from the Treasury Bench, his dark eyes flashing, his wonderful voice rising and falling with the play of his emotions, and his athletic frame thrilling with the fervour of debate, he confounded his antagonists and restored the fortunes of his side. In extreme old age, and facing an unequalled array of parliamentary gladiators, he would fill the House with his dauntless eloquence and bring the members for Ireland to their feet, waving their order papers and cheering like maniacs till the rafters shook.

While under Gladstone's influence the Whig party became Liberal, Disraeli's contribution to English politics (1852-80) was

1885

to inject into the slow-moving Conservative party which had been shaped by the sober Peel something of his own swift spirit of romantic and democratic imperialism. In *Coningsby* he propounded for the benefit of Young England the doctrine of Tory democracy. He was not afraid to trust the people. Though he led the Conservatives, he was prepared to alienate many of his followers by admitting in 1867 the better paid artisan to the suffrage. Wiser than most of the landed gentry and big men of business, he saw that there was in the great mass of the English working people a fund of loyalty to the Crown and to the institutions of the country, and that to any well-grounded appeal of patriotic necessity the people of England would respond. That the Sovereign had yet a great part to play in the democratic civilization of England was another belief strongly held and justified in the event. He saw the Crown as a fountain of influence and a bond of Empire. As for the Empire, it was for him the more attractive since its principal jewel was in the East. India filled his imagination and inspired his policies. With India always present to his mind he saw Russia as the everlasting enemy, Turkey as the helpful friend. Thinking of India, he secured for his country a controlling share of the Suez Canal and 1875 added, with characteristic *bravura*, to Queen Victoria's royal style the title of Empress.

While Gladstone was always a religious preacher, Disraeli was an incurable romantic. Knowing her sentimental heart, he wooed Queen Victoria like a lover. Through the most strenuous years of his Parliamentary life he found solace in writing letters of romantic affection sometimes two or three times a day to Lady Bradford and her sister, only desisting when he found in *Endymion*, his latest novel, a fuller scope for his romantic pen.

His foreign policy, though much belauded at the time, and having the attraction which an imaginative and spirited Imperialism must always possess for the more mettlesome half of the British people, had elements of great unsoundness. He misjudged the Balkan problem and nearly involved England in a war to keep a Christian people under the Turkish flag. His Liberal opponents were right in fearing that his passion for prestige might lead the country into danger.

Imperialism, which exercised for the next half century so wide an influence over English political thought and action, owes to this Hebrew man of genius its original inspiration. Where Disraeli led, Kipling and Rosebery, Chamberlain and Milner, Balfour and Curzon followed after. Empire over Englishmen beyond the seas, in the strict old sense of British control, had been killed long ago by the success of the revolt of the American colonies. But a romantic and passionate belief in the excellence of British rule in India, and in the value of promoting closer relations between the Mother Country and her possessions and colonies overseas, passed with Disraeli's speeches into the faith of the Conservative party and greatly enriched its appeal.

Far other were the inspirations of Gladstone's wonderful and tempestuous old age. The sentiments evoked by the words Empire, prestige, war, domination, had little seduction for the religious leader of the Liberal party. So far from desiring to extend the British Empire, Gladstone was anxious wherever possible to limit his country's responsibilities. The satisfaction of national aspirations in the Balkans, in South Africa, in Ireland, were objects, quixotic as they appeared to many, for which he was fully prepared to stake his own and his party's fortunes. As a young man he had advised the restoration of the Ionian isles to Greece; as an old man he thought it just to return the Transvaal to the Boers.

Aug., 1881

His second administration (1880-85), though marked by the emancipation of the rural labourers and by an Irish Land Act which granted fair rents and fixity of tenure to the peasants, was clouded by failures in Egypt and the Soudan. Nor in the last and most desperate of his adventures was he more successful. Braving the Irish Protestant interest and the sentiment of the possessioned class in Britain, " the grand old man " proposed Home Rule for Ireland (1886); Chamberlain, Hartington, Goschen, the strongest of his lieutenants, refused to follow; but the loss of these powerful men and the knowledge that he had broken the splendid party instrument of his earlier triumphs did not weaken his purpose.

1893

At the age of eighty-three, after six years of opposition, the indomitable veteran returned to the charge and, by an extraordinary effort of physical and intellectual power, passed his Bill through the Commons. But the Lords refused to give way, and again the Irish Parliamentary party was disappointed of its hopes. Meanwhile the problem of Ireland had been attacked from a new angle under Salisbury's Unionist administration. A bold and original scheme of state socialism, suggested by Joseph

Chamberlain and carried out with courage and intelligence by *1887-91*
A. J. Balfour, showered material benefits on the country. But
the nation of dreamers refused to surrender its dreams. Good
government was not enough. The Catholic Irish wanted, as
Gladstone saw, to govern themselves. As time went on they
raised their demands. At last in 1921 a measure of independence was conceded to a party of violence greatly exceeding in
many respects those Gladstonian Bills which in the eighties and
nineties had convulsed politics and society in England.

The bitterness and intensity of the passion which the struggle
over Irish Home Rule infused into English politics at this time
can be understood only if we remember the manner in which
the Irish campaign was waged and the alarming perspectives
which it was thought to disclose. The Irish Home Rule League
which had been started in 1870 by Isaac Butt with a view to
obtaining by legitimate parliamentary pressure the concession of
Home Rule for Ireland was only part of a larger movement.
Fourteen years earlier a secret society known as the Irish Republican Brotherhood had been founded to sever Ireland once
and for all from Britain by force of arms. The constitutional
action of Irishmen at Westminster was flanked by revolutionary
movements outside, by the I.R.B. in Europe, by the Clan na Gael
in America, sworn and secret fraternities for whom the true
method of suasion was not talk but dynamite; and in the lurid
light thrown upon this darker side of the Irish movement by
Fenian outrages many an Englishman who would have voted for
a Parliament in Dublin if Ireland had presented herself in a
gentler guise recoiled from concessions. Moreover in Ireland
itself an agrarian agitation patronized by the political leaders
was prolific in the meaner sort of crime. It was in vain that the *Oct.,*
Government essayed to suppress Michael Davitt's Land League. *1881*
A Ladies' Land League continued the work.

Save for a handful of Protestants the Irish parliamentary
representatives were solid for Home Rule, and by a policy of
systematic obstruction set themselves to make Parliament in-
operative until such time as their policy was accepted. Fatigued
and exasperated by all-night sittings, assailed in their com-
placency by gibes and insults, outraged by Fenian crimes,
alarmed by the spectre of republicanism and perplexed by the
fact that the good intentions towards Ireland which they were

conscious of entertaining were met by an ingrained temper of hostility and distrust; the average English parliamentarians offered an energetic resistance to Home Rule.

It was, therefore, sanguine of Gladstone to hope, as in 1886 he seems to have done, that the Conservative party, realizing that there was now in consequence of a recent Redistribution Act a solid block of eighty-six Home Rule votes at Westminster, would take up the cause of Irish self-government. For a moment, indeed, Conservatives glanced that way, for there was a parley *June,* between Carnarvon and Parnell, the Nationalist leader, but *1886* nothing came of it. A problem which should have been dealt with by a coalition was left to the patronage of a depleted and mutilated fragment of the Liberal party.

Their task was not rendered easier by the character of the Irish chieftain. All the rebel traditions of Erin were embodied *1846-91* in the person of Charles Stewart Parnell. He was in touch with the secret societies of Ireland, England, and America, President of the Land League, Chairman of the Irish party in the House of Commons, the uncrowned sovereign of the Irish race. Every agency obnoxious to England recognized the mastery of this strange and mysterious being of ice and flame. In the House of Commons the proud, handsome, unsociable Irish landlord with his swarthy beard and dark flashing eyes, sitting still and saturnine among his obedient following, was regarded with a kind of awe. Descended though he was from an old and respected Anglo-Irish county family, he was known to be the foe of Britain. People thought him inhuman and none too scrupulous. *Oct. 12,* Indeed before ever Gladstone launched his first Home Rule Bill *1881* he had been compelled to put Parnell under lock and key.

From time to time phrases dropped from the formidable Irishman which disconcerted his Liberal supporters. "No one can set bounds to the march of a nation," he said once, and again, addressing an American audience (February 20, 1880): "None of us, whether we are in America or Ireland or wherever we are, will be satisfied until we have destroyed the last link which keeps Ireland bound to England." Faced with these declarations, Liberals could only hope that conciliation would kill conspiracy, that reform would avert revolution, and that the poison of violence would be strained away from the Irish system by the remedial action of a subordinate Parliament.

Yet Parnell survived the effect of his American speeches, survived also the formidable attacks of *The Times* newspaper associating Parnellism with crime. At last he was broken upon a point of domestic morals which offended the nonconformist conscience of Gladstone's following. The greatest of Irish statesmen was ruined by the love of a woman. Yet the disruption of the Irish party in the last years of his tragic life, though it temporarily retarded the advance of Irish Nationalism, made no difference to the ultimate fortunes of the movement. The desire of Catholic Ireland to be permitted to manage her own affairs and to lead her own life in her own way was too deep to be destroyed by the humiliation and death of a leader, by the schisms of party, or by vicissitudes in the game of parliamentary debate.

BOOKS WHICH MAY BE CONSULTED

Fyffe : History of Modern Europe. 1924.

Wickham Steed : The Hapsburg Monarchy. 1919.

C. G. Macartney : Hungary. (Nations of the Modern World Series.) 1934.

Seignobos : History of Contemporary Europe. 1909.

A. Rambaud : History of Russia. 1900.

Isenmann : Le Compromis Austro-Hongrois de 1867. 1904.

R. W. Seton Watson : Disraeli, Gladstone, and the Eastern Question. 1935.

John Morley : Life of Gladstone. 1908.

Monypenny and G. E. Buckle : Life of Disraeli. 1929.

E. Denis : La Bohème depuis la montagne blanche. 1930.

St. John Ervine : Parnell. 1927.

CHAPTER XXV

BISMARCK AND THE GERMAN REICH

Bismarck, 1870-9. Economic development of Germany. Bismarck adopts Protection. The German Insurance Acts. The policy of repression. The diplomatic revolution. The Dual Alliance of 1879. The Balkan crisis of 1885. Bismarck's relations with England. Bismarck's fear. Achievements of the German people after the Franco-Prussian War.

FOR nineteen years after the foundation of the German Empire Bismarck continued to direct the affairs of his country and to influence the fortunes of the world. After the great things which had been accomplished he was well content that Germany should be shielded from domestic change and foreign war. He had no wish for a colonial empire or for aggrandizement in the East, and it was among the cardinal maxims of his policy that the friendship of England should not be imperilled by a challenge on the sea. He was too much alive to the dangers of the situation on the continent to court new adventures. He saw France unappeased, Russia uncertain, Austria still harbouring griefs against Berlin. How to be friends with the Russians without alienating England, with the Austrians without estranging Russia—these continental problems kept his diplomatic powers on the stretch. The isolation of France, the domination of Europe by a powerful German army, and the maintenance of his own autocratic régime, were the guiding principles of his policy. Accidents of longevity amazingly contributed to his success. The Emperor William I, dying a nonagenarian in 1888, lived so long that when at last the Crown Prince Frederick ascended the throne he was an invalid stricken with cancer, and in his short reign of ninety days powerless to affect the course of events. With the tragic death of this liberally-minded sovereign the most formidable of all the obstacles to the general trend of Bismarck's policy was removed.

Meanwhile a change was coming over the economic life of Germany, similar, save for its greater velocity, to that which England had experienced in her industrial revolution. The decades which succeeded the Franco-Prussian War were marked by an astonishing expansion of German industry and commerce.

The country which had been poor became suddenly rich. The population which had been predominantly rural rushed in increasing numbers to the towns, and there multiplied until the balance between urban and rural Germany was decisively reversed. Leadership in two new and most important branches of industry, the chemical and the electrical, fell as a natural prize to the superior education of the German people. The output of coal went up by leaps and bounds, growing from thirty million tons in 1871 to a hundred and ninety million tons in 1913. A process invented in England and associated with the names of Thomas and Gilchrist, which enabled the basic ore of Luxemburg and Lorraine to be put to economic use, led to vast industrial developments and converted the Westphalian coalfield into a region comparable in the activity and concentration of its factory life to the English Black Country. In a single decade (the eighties) the German Empire doubled its output of steel and nearly doubled that of iron. And while industry was thus advancing and transforming the character and occupations of the German people a great impetus was given to marine enterprise. German ships began in swiftly increasing numbers to cross the Atlantic, to touch at African ports, to trade with the Levant and the further East. The old Hanseatic spirit was revived. In the twenty years between 1870 and 1890 the steam tonnage of the Empire multiplied sevenfold. The cry went up for colonies, for protection against American wheat and English manufactures, and for a spirited policy in every part of the globe. The pressure was such that no statesman, whatever his prestige, could have long held out against it. Bismarck was compelled to concede. In 1879 he adopted Protection as his fiscal policy, and three years later, making a virtue of necessity, started Germany on her colonial career. It may be noticed as an interesting coincidence that the formation of a colonial group in the *Reichstag* belongs to the same year (1883) which witnessed the birth of the A.E.G. (*Allgemeine Elektrizitäts Gesellschaft*), the huge electrical combine which established upon an impregnable foundation the greatest of German scientific industries.

In common with every other European country which experienced the effects of industrialism, the Germany of the seventies and eighties was confronted by the dark shadows of undeserved poverty and made anxious by the spectacle of a restless, miserable, and exploited proletariat. While Wagner was delighting the

fashionable music lovers of Europe by the operatic festivals of
Bayreuth, the workers in the German mines and factories were
exposed to hardships and uncertainties comparable with those
which afflicted the industrial population of England before the
passage of the Factory Acts. Bismarck was far too great a man
to be blind to the importance of the social problem. He saw that
if the edifice of his constitution was to stand it must content the
workers. He did not trust the unbridled play of private appetites
to work out the greatest happiness of the greatest number.
Paternalism, which was in the old Prussian tradition, received a
new justification and demanded a wider scope in the altered
circumstances created by the industrial revolution. The old must
be protected against want, the worker must be insured against
sickness and accident. Bismarck was no Shaftesbury. He passed
no Factory Acts, but in his great scheme for compulsory insurance against sickness (1883), accidents (1884), and old age (1889)
he was a pioneer, anticipating, save that he provided no insurance
against unemployment, the measures subsequently carried out in
England by Mr. Lloyd George as a member of the Asquith
Cabinet.

The German Insurance Acts constitute a landmark. Of all
the political inventions of the nineteenth century none was so
valuable a preservative of society as the discovery of a system
of insurance, dependent on the contributions of the state, the
employer, and the worker, and protecting the mass of the labouring population against the worst hazards of industrial life.
That revolution was so long staved off in Germany was partly
due to these valuable measures, by which Bismarck robbed the
Social Democratic party, despite its steady growth under persecution, of a compelling and irresistible appeal to the poor.

As the Iron Chancellor advanced in years he became more
fiercely intolerant of opposition. Taking advantage of two
attempts on the Emperor's life, he passed, and on three
subsequent occasions renewed, a law against the Socialists so
sharp that it placed the liberties of the subject under the heel of
the police. Only a country seized by a violent spasm of alarm,
or altogether lost to the virtue of political courage, could have
tamely submitted to the unjust and tyrannical acts of oppression
which were thus made possible. By consenting to this harsh
legislation the National Liberal party, which had been the mainstay of the German Empire in its early days, and the support of

the government in its struggle with the Clericals, declared itself bankrupt of true Liberalism. It was a nation far gone in the practice of passive obedience which entered into the next great European war.

The feeling of Bismarck with regard to France explains the whole of his foreign policy. He conceived of France as the irreconcilable and dangerous enemy of his country, always to be suspected, always to be weakened, always to be estranged from its European neighbours. The north African littoral, fast becoming an object of general ambition, served the turn of his anti-Gallican diplomacy. He encouraged France to take Tunis that she might quarrel with Italy, England to take Egypt that she might quarrel with France. The Anglo-Italian naval understandings which Lord Salisbury concluded in 1887 were fruits of the same long-sighted machinations with the object of leaving France without a friend in Europe. Nor was Bismarck indifferent to the play of political forces in Paris. A monarchist for Germany, he was a republican for France, a republic being, in his opinion, of all forms of government the weakest and the most discreditable.

In the east of Europe, the main diplomatic defence of Germany against a possible coalition fomented by the inveterate hostility of France was that alliance of the three Emperors which, as we have seen, was formed in June, 1873, and was still operative in 1878 when the Congress of Berlin, described by the Tzar as "a coalition of Europe against Russia under the leadership of Prince Bismarck," subjected it to serious strain. The *Dreikaiserbund* survived the crisis. The friendship was patched up. The alliance was renewed again and again; and every three years Europe was publicly informed that the rulers of the three great military monarchies of the east were bound together by fresh ties of comradeship and association. Manifest, however, as were the advantages of a good understanding with Russia, Bismarck never really trusted the Muscovites. He thought their friendship uncertain, their diplomacy tricky. From Gortschakoff, their foreign minister, he was divided by sentiments of fierce personal disesteem. If he were forced to choose between Russia and Austria, it would always be Austria that he would prefer, partly from the call of blood, partly because, were Austria for any reason to resume her old quarrel with the Prussians, she would advance historic claims upon Silesia, upon Alsace, upon the Danish Duchies, upon the very constitution of the *Reich* itself, which would put in dispute all the hard-won triumphs of the Hohenzollern house since the accession of Frederick the Great. And so, when the Balkan troubles of 1878 had been composed, Bismarck determined to make a secret treaty with Austria behind the back of his Russian ally. What he did then has been decisive for history. In the impending struggle against Pan-Slavism Bismarck ranged his country secretly and treacherously on the Austrian side. The Dual Alliance of 1879 became, by the junction of Italy in 1882, the Triple Alliance which lasted to the outbreak of the Great War. To the student of the diplomatic antecedents of that great event, as he works his way backward up the stream of history, the alliance which Bismarck and Andrassy negotiated between Germany and Austria-Hungary in 1879, against Russia and behind her back, presents itself as the original spring. From that moment it was fated that, should Austria and Russia come to blows in a Balkan trouble, the German army would stand side by side with its Austrian ally. "Should, contrary to their hope and against their loyal desire, one of the High Contracting Parties," runs the principal clause of this momentous treaty of 1879, "be attacked by Russia, the High Contracting Parties are bound to come to the assistance one of the other with the whole war strength of their Empires, and accordingly only to conclude peace together and upon mutual agreement." That the treaty was inconsistent with Germany's public undertakings to Russia was a sufficient ground for the special care which was taken to conceal it.

May, 1882

Bismarck did not want a war between Russia and Austria. It was his great ambition that such a war might be avoided. That there could be no greater peril for Germany, or for Europe, was a fact vividly present to his powerful imagination. Yet how easily might a spark be thrown among the inflammable timber of the Balkan States, which would set all Europe ablaze from the Neva to the Aegean! When Eastern Rumelia joined itself to Bulgaria in 1885, and the Serbs, greatly envying the sudden aggrandizement of their hated neighbour, rushed to arms and were defeated by King Alexander of Bulgaria on the field of Slivitzna, Europe was on the edge of war. Everybody knew, or, if they did not know, suspected, that the Serbs were acting on the impulsion of the Austrians. Everybody was aware that.

however distasteful the person of Alexander (a Prince of Battenberg by birth) might be to the Tzar, the Bulgarians were the special clients of the Russian Empire. Out of a quarrel between Bulgaria and Serbia, should it be allowed to drag to any length, it was easy to see that friction would arise between their respective patrons, that such contrariety might be succeeded by hostilities, and that with the first shots exchanged between Austrians and Russians all Germany would be involved. Such a war Bismarck strained every nerve to avoid. Such a war, since it was still his opinion that the Balkans were not worth the bones of a single Pomeranian grenadier, he in fact succeeded in avoiding. His word went at Vienna. While he soothed the ruffled feathers of the Russians, he did not allow the Austrians to get out of hand. Thanks to his skill, the Bulgarian crisis passed away without a general convulsion. An awkward little campaign was speedily brought to an end; a contentious vacancy in the Bulgarian throne was happily filled. From the inexhaustible resources of princely Germany there was drawn a sovereign who, while acceptable to Vienna, was not patently abhorrent to St. Petersburg. He was that long-nosed, long-headed, bird-loving Ferdinand of Coburg, " the fox of the Balkans," who eventually, despite all his craft and finesse, brought the Bulgarian people into the Great War on the losing side.

From the web of the anti-Gallican alliances England stood free " in splendid isolation." No government, liberal or conservative, dared to pledge the English people to continental entanglements. The island remained aloof, incalculable, and to continental people provoking and enigmatic. Its ambitions were pursued in regions far distant from the main centres of European life. A handful of Englishmen were ruling in India. A slight sprinkling were scattered over Australasia and the Cape. How solid such a fabric might be no German could readily tell. Trade, navy, empire he was bound to concede, but how accidentally had they been won, how cheaply were they kept by this race of happy, easy-going pirates! One thing only seemed certain to Germans: that English friendship meant Russian enmity. A secret treaty with England, sufficient to detach her from France without frightening Russia, was an idea attractive to some political Germans. Bismarck fished for it, first with Disraeli, then with Salisbury. But the English professed themselves opposed to secret treaties. They maintained that everything must be communi-

34

cated to Parliament and to Queen Victoria. Moreover, what faith could be placed in English governments, here today, gone tomorrow, and always the sport of electoral caprice? Could a Tory government answer for the actions of its Liberal successor? Salisbury was diplomatically doubtful, and Bismarck was willing to believe that democracies were unable to " deliver the goods."

No treaty then was made between Germany and England during Bismarck's lifetime. The great Chancellor, though he valued English friendship and desired, without too much advertisement of the fact, to draw England into the circle of his associates, was never able to obtain even from a Tory government the firm and secret pledges which alone could satisfy his need. Moreover, as Germany entered the colonial field, occasions for friction with England multiplied. There was friction over Fiji and New Guinea, over south-west and central Africa, over Jamaica and Zanzibar. Whenever German relations with Russia were good Bismarck could afford to bully England. That the islanders should be roughly handled gave general pleasure to the Tzarist government and the German people. But the game of baiting England was safe only when Russia was cordial. At the first touch of frost in Russo-German relations, England was restored to Bismarck's favour.

Still he felt insecure. Despite the *Dreikaiserbund* and the Triple Alliance, and the understanding between Italy and England, and further alliances of Austria-Hungary with the Serbs and the Roumans, and a secret reinsurance treaty concluded with Russia in 1887, Bismarck was afraid. The spectre of a war on two fronts haunted his mind. It is a melancholy commentary on the politics of power that in 1887, after twenty-five years of autocratic rule, Bismarck should have felt himself compelled to come to the *Reichstag* for an army of some seven hundred thousand men.

It is difficult to overestimate the achievements of the German people during the twenty years of Bismarckian peace, which followed the convulsion of the Franco-Prussian War. Great as had been the pace of economic progress, it had not outstripped the organizing power of the German mind. The foundations of public education had been wisely and truly laid. The schools were good, the Universities were numerous, and inspired with a zeal for the advancement of knowledge. Nowhere were the advantages to be derived from the marriage of science and industry more quickly, more generally, or more intelligently perceived. In the field of business the organizing instinct of the German people had led to the foundation of *Kartells* or combines for the maintenance of prices and the limitation of output. Scientific and learned treatises issued every year in prodigal abundance from the printing presses. No people in Europe read more widely or seriously. Music was everywhere—cheaper than in France, more universal than in England, and the best (save for Vienna) to be found in any quarter of the globe.

Almost equally impressive was the stamp of forethought in the handling of the grave social problems which the industrial revolution brought in its train. In town-planning, as in the chemical and electrical industries, the Germans were pioneers. While the creators of industrial England were permitted to toil and die in a sprawling and disorderly congeries of ignoble hovels, the Germans thought and planned beforehand. Their towns and suburbs were for the most part built to an intelligent design, and adjusted to the requirements of convenience and hygiene. The new urban generations were born into a world which had been prepared to receive them.

Darkening all this vigorous and manifold civilization was the thought of war, terrible to some, welcome to others, a preoccupation for all. Germany was at peace, but heavily armed, obsessed with internal suspicions and anxieties, fearing her neighbours and by her neighbours feared. The diplomacy of Bismarck had not tended to lessen the apprehensions of Europe. Too often had he used hectoring language and shown the glint of Prussian steel. Too often had he launched his reptile press against the English and the French, too often reminded the world that the *Pax Germanica* rested upon the bayonets of the German army. It was a serious blot upon his statesmanship that he believed in bad manners and double-dealing. But at least it must be accounted to his credit that he kept his country out of war, avoiding the three dangers which, under less skilful management, brought the Hohenzollern Empire to the ground; an alliance between the Tzar and the French Republic, a naval rivalry with England, and the outbreak of a quarrel in the Balkans so serious as to threaten the continued existence of the Austro-Hungarian Empire, and to precipitate a clash between the Slavonic and Teuton races.

BOOKS WHICH MAY BE CONSULTED

C. A. Fyffe : History of Modern Europe. 1924.

J. A. Spender : Fifty Years of Europe. 1933.

Lives of Bismarck, by J. W. Headlam-Morley (1894) and C. Grant Robertson. 1918.

E. Brandenburg : From Bismarck to the World War. 1927.

G. P. Gooch : Germany. (Nations of the Modern World Series.) 1925.

Bismarck : Thoughts and Recollections. 1899.

CHAPTER XXVI

THE END OF BRITAIN'S ISOLATION

Germany at the accession of William II. Character of the Kaiser. The Franco-Russian alliance. The continental balance. England. The Anglo-Japanese Treaty. Question of an Anglo-German entente. German hostility to England. British Imperialism. The South African question. The discovery of the mines. Majuba. Kruger and Cecil Rhodes. The Raid and the South African War. The Boers and the Kaiser. The construction of the German High Seas Fleet. Egypt—England takes responsibility. Charles Gordon. The reconquest of the Soudan. Omdurman. Fashoda. Death of Queen Victoria. The Victorian age. Edward VII. The Anglo-French Entente.

A STATE composed of soldiers and officials, a society dominated by the military caste, a people still drunken with the wine of victory, an imperial Parliament, elected indeed by universal suffrage, but schooled to vote the military budget at septennial intervals, and save for an insignificant and much persecuted body of socialists submissive to a government which it was unable to change, a Prussian Parliament elected on a narrow oligarchic franchise, and as obscurantist as when it was put forward in the reactionary crisis of 1850, and over all the towering, dominating figure of Bismarck. Such was the German scene in June, 1888, when William II, a young man of thirty-one, suc- *1888-1918* ceeded to his father's throne. "There is only one master in this country, and I am he," observed the new Kaiser. Rather than share his power with a Bismarckian dynasty William was prepared to break with the founder of the Empire. In March, 1890, the year in which David Lloyd George, an obscure Welsh Baptist, first stepped into the arena at Westminster, Bismarck was dismissed. Dropping the pilot who for twenty-eight years had steered the ship of state through the tempests, the impulsive Kaiser seized the helm, and found himself in control of the most powerful military engine in the world.

The new autocrat became at once a vital and disquieting force in European society. That he had some admirable and even brilliant qualities was at once apparent. His outlook on affairs was bold and spacious, his curiosity eager and comprehensive, his industry vast, his memory for detail powerful and exact.

He was pious, dutiful, patriotic, and sometimes, especially when he spoke of the sea, would rise to heights of moving eloquence. But with these shining qualities were mingled others of a baser alloy, an egregious vanity, an ungovernable temper, a love of theatrical ostentation which exposed him to ridicule, and a vein of malevolence which merited contempt. There was no flattery so base that he would not accept it, no barbarity so extreme that he would not in a spasm of fury invest it with imperial authority. A nervous excitability and impulsiveness, while it gave a certain zest and charm to his companionship, always made him dangerous as a ruler, so that, after experience of many alarums and excursions, his ministers began to ask themselves in trepidation whether the headstrong and loquacious master of Germany was not in fact deranged in mind.

It would be unfair to class him among the war-mongers. William kept his nation at peace for twenty-six years. There is no reason to doubt the sincerity of the pacifist declarations which at the beginning of every year he addressed to the Prussian *Landtag*. Yet the atmosphere of his court was steeped in militarism. The Kaiser never could forget that he was the supreme war lord, and in his innumerable orations to gatherings of soldiers and sailors made it a duty to inflame the martial ardour of the nation. The intemperance of his language, the unaccountability of his actions, and the numerous indications which he betrayed of a rash and unmeasured ambition, helped to raise the temperature of Europe and to create a climate unfavourable to the smooth and easy transaction of international affairs.

Not long after the fall of Bismarck a treaty was signed, the prevention of which was a principal object of the old Chancellor's diplomacy. Emerging at last from her long isolation, France found an ally in Russia. Here was a country needing armaments which France was willing to supply, railways which Paris (but not Berlin) was prepared to finance, and in view of eventualities in the Balkans (for the Tzar had been apprised in 1888 of the secret German-Austrian Treaty of nine years earlier) looking about for a friend who might serve as a makeweight to the Central Powers. Though there was no quarter of Europe in which the principles of 1789 were so little regarded as the Empire of the Tzar, the French could not afford to refuse the embrace of the Russian bear. The outlines of an agreement were signed in 1891, and on January 4, 1894, were completed by a secret military convention which bound both parties in the event of a German attack upon either to come to one another's assistance with a large army. The document, which provided for the consultation of the two general staffs in time of peace and for instant mobilization on the first news of the mobilization of the forces of any one of the Powers comprising the Triple Alliance, was of an extremely practical character. It was a soldier's document. "The available forces to be employed against Germany shall be, on the part of France, 1,300,000 men; on the part of Russia, 700,000 or 800,000. These forces shall engage to the full with all speed, in order that Germany may have to fight at the same time on the east and on the west."

The Triple Alliance of Germany, Italy, and Austria was now confronted by the dual alliance of Russia and France. Each combination was heavily armed, each ready to spring on the other at the first sign of hostile intentions, but which of the two in the event of a clash might prove to be the stronger no one at that time could confidently predict. It is possible that if the balance of power had so been left the peace of Europe might have been preserved. Meanwhile the secret of the Franco-Russian alliance was carefully kept.

England was an enigma. Her accession to either party might tip the balance. An equilibrium which was relatively stable while the two continental groups were thus massed the one against the other might, by the intrusion of this great naval power into the arena, be violently disturbed. Confidence would be heightened on the one side, apprehension on the other. In Germany the junction of England with the dual alliance might produce a nervous tension akin to claustrophobia, in Russia a mood of heedless and insolent temerity.

The Kaiser was the grandson of Queen Victoria. To that venerable lady he was always ready to pay the tribute of a grandson's respect; from that uncompromising pen, as from no other, he would accept a sharp but affectionate reproof. Having an easy command of the English language, and a large circle of English relations and friends, he would resort to his grandmother's island as to a favourite playground. To be received at Windsor, to sail his yacht at the Cowes Regatta, to wear the blue and gold of an English Admiral, to taste the plaudits of a London crowd, or to relax in the luxurious ease of an English nobleman's country house gave him great satisfaction. With part of his nature he admired England and its inhabitants, with another part he regarded them with envy and dislike.

In view of the division of the European continent into two rival combinations, a brisk competition between France and Germany for the favours of the island Empire might naturally have been expected. There was nothing of the kind. So far from being courted on the continent during the first fourteen years of the Kaiser's reign, Britain was regarded with a bitter, and sometimes perilous disfavour in France and Germany and Russia. Such was her isolation, and so dangerous did it appear, that in 1902, boldly departing from the tradition of Canning, Palmerston, Gladstone, and Salisbury, the Balfour Government took the momentous step of negotiating in secret and publicly concluding an alliance with Japan.

The swift and momentous assimilation of European knowledge by this distant Asiatic island is one of the miracles of recent history. Before the American Commodore Perry brought home to the Japanese (1854) the strength of Western armaments and the advantages of foreign trade, Japan was sunk in mediaeval ignorance. Two hundred and sixty-eight Daimios, or feudal lords, with their armed retainers or Samurai, ruled the country. There was no navy, no artillery or firearms, no merchant class, no public system of education or general code of law. The ethics of the people were those of a Highland clan in the days of Macbeth. Who then of Commodore Perry's crew would have dreamed that before the end of the century Japan would have abolished her feudal system (1871-3), centralized her government, provided herself with a modern navy and army, a modern code of laws, and a modern system of education, and would in all ways be prepared to play the rôle of a modern state? Yet under the long and memorable rule of the Mikado Mutzu Hito (1867-1912) these extraordinary things were accomplished with a swift and finished dexterity. Accordingly, when in 1902 England sought the alliance of the Mikado's Government, Japan was already the strongest naval Power in the Pacific. With a marine based on British and an army fashioned on German models, she had overwhelmed the Chinese in one brief campaign. So strong had she become by land and sea, so formidable was the combination of Western mechanism and feudal courage, that three years after the English treaty she emerged victorious from a war with Russia, whereat the whole Orient trembled with delight and the Occident began to talk of the Yellow Peril and to wonder whether the day of the Yellow Man might not be near at hand.

The rivalry of Britain and Russia was an old story. Fears for the safety of India, fears for Constantinople, fears lest a Russian navy might make its entry into the Mediterranean, were quite sufficient, apart from the rooted aversion of English democracy from Russian despotism, to estrange the two countries. An Anglo-German *entente* or even alliance was more easily to be conceived of.

Here there were no ancient deep-rooted causes of repugnance. English and Germans belonged to the same Teutonic family, spoke a language derived from a common foundation, and on many a stricken field had fought shoulder to shoulder. Rather than submit to a Catholic ruler the English had called in a German dynasty to rule over them. They had accepted the ugly German mistresses of George I, the frequent German absences of George II, the plain German wife of George III, and the handsome German husband of Victoria. As the reign of the great Queen proceeded, the threads of intercourse, economic, social, intellectual, multiplied between the two countries. Germany became the best foreign customer for English goods, England the most enthusiastic foreign customer for German ideas. Large bodies of intelligent Germans, some of them rebuffed by Prussian militarism, drifted into England, settled there in happiness and content, and contributed to build up the prosperity of Manchester in cottons, of Bradford in cloth, and of Sheffield in steel. The same phenomenon of easy and fruitful intercourse was repeated in the sphere of culture. While Oxford and Cambridge, once liberated (1871) from the thraldom of religious tests, reverberated with the echoes of Teutonic learning, the more eminent professors of Berlin or Göttingen could count upon a band of young English admirers, who, returning to their more civilized but less erudite compatriots, preached the majesty of German knowledge.

In view of such circumstances it is not surprising that some British statesmen, impressed by the dangers of "splendid isolation," should have turned their thoughts towards German friendship. "The most natural alliance," said Joseph Chamberlain (November 29, 1899), the powerful Colonial Secretary in Salisbury's administration, " is that between us and the German Empire." The Germans thought otherwise. To them the alliance which the British statesman described as most natural appeared an unholy and contaminating bond. A general howl of execration greeted the well-meaning overture and announced its inevitable doom.

It is not difficult to trace the history of the sentiments which produced this extraordinary explosion. The Prussians had thoroughly absorbed the lesson which the scribes of Bismarck had been sedulous to inculcate. They believed that liberalism, an English poison, after corrupting the aristocratic virtues of the island race, was now doing its devil's work upon the robust constitution of Prussia. From the momentous struggles which made Germany a united nation they noted that the English had stood aside in unhelpful neutrality, sympathizing hotly with the Danes, appreciably with the Austrians, and at last, when the guns of Moltke were playing on the streets and squares of Paris, openly and sentimentally with the French. The sentiments thus occasioned received yet further aggravation under William II. The new Emperor did not share the Bismarckian view that Germany was a sated power. Still less did his subjects. While the Pan-German League, founded in 1893, proposed that Austria, German Switzerland, and the Netherlands should be incorporated in the *Reich*, the Emperor was content to mark out for himself three new spheres of German influence in each of which he might expect to encounter the diplomatic opposition of England. The first was the Turkish Empire, the second the colonies, the third and most important the sea. Ships were the favourite toy of his boyhood. It was a misfortune for the German people that the construction of a battle fleet second to none was the ruling passion of the Kaiser's riper years.

The same lack of self-sufficiency was apparent in England. Here, too, Imperialism was running its burning course, with Rudyard Kipling for its prophet and Joseph Chamberlain for its advocate, and Africa following hard on the heels of India with dazzling invitations to dominion and trade. The English were established in Egypt, in Uganda, and in Nigeria. As usual they had secured the best places : far better than the Germans, better even than the French, who had Tunis, Algeria, and Senegal, or than the Belgians, who had been allotted the vast territory of the Congo. Yet the English were not content. Steadily during the sixties, seventies, and eighties they kept extending their tentacles, eastwards, westwards, and northwards from Cape Colony, until the two Boer Republics, which retained the quintessential spirit of the older Dutch colonial civilization, were ringed round, save for an outlet to Delagoa Bay, by a band of territory owing allegiance to the British Crown. The climax of British imperialism in this region was reached in 1889-91 when Cecil Rhodes, fortune-hunter and empire-builder, snatched Rhodesia. By no German were these developments viewed with a benevolent eye.

Yet the British Empire in South Africa had its Achilles' heel in the obstinate fact of Dutch nationalism. The Dutch settlers in Cape Colony were not imperialists, still less were the Dutch dispersion in the interior. The Cape Dutch, though they had learnt to live on amicable terms with the British, were at heart Republicans, looking forward to the time when, without any violent rupture, the tie with Britain might be severed, and a Federal State comparable to the American started on a course of splendid independence under the Southern Cross. What gave to this academic sentiment a point of danger was the attitude of the Dutch Republics north of the Colony.

In 1836 a body of Dutch farmers, having grievances against the British Government, which had abolished slavery with indifferent compensation to the slave owners, trekked away from the Cape Colony, and eventually founded two republics north and south of the Vaal River. On these sunny and exhilarating highlands the Boers hunted and farmed, flogged their Kaffirs and read their Bible, a rugged, patriarchal community belonging rather to the seventeenth than to the nineteenth century, and prizing the solitude of their vast air-washed spaces far above the rewards which a town could offer or the pleasures which townsmen may enjoy. Then a serious complication was intruded into the simple structure of South African society. First diamonds were discovered (1869-70), afterwards (1885) gold, the diamonds in unheard-of profusion at the place which came to be known as Kimberley, the gold within the territory of the Transvaal on that bleak range of the Witwatersrand where now stands the wide and wealthy city of Johannesburg. Into the solemn tranquillity of the veldt, where life had been wont to move at the pace of an ox-waggon, there suddenly burst a cataract of cosmopolitan town-dwelling fortune-hunters, bringing in their train the turmoil, the luxury, and the mechanism of urban Europe. It may be readily imagined that for the peasant rulers of the Transvaal the discovery of the greatest gold-field of the world created problems in government of unsuspected difficulty.

Meanwhile, before the gold rush to the Rand, the tension between the two white races had been increased by a singularly unlucky incident. Annexed in 1877 under a misapprehension by Disraeli, the Transvaal was restored to the Boers by Gladstone (1881) on the morrow of a serious reverse to British arms on Majuba Hill. It is wise to be generous after victory, but risky to be indulgent in the hour of defeat. By the ignorant Boer an act of magnanimity proceeding from the consciousness of strength was interpreted as a sign of cowardice and debility. Henceforward the Boers despised the Britons, and the Britons, galled by contempt and chafing under defeat, found less reason than ever to admire the spirit of the Boers.

Two remarkable men, one standing for the Dutch, the other for the British cause, dominated the South African scene: Kruger, the Boer Republican; Rhodes, the British Imperialist.

1825-1904 As a boy Kruger had shared in the great trek. His skill in marksmanship, his accomplished handling of horses and oxen, his great ability and physical strength, gave him a natural pre-eminence in youth. In riper age his ascendancy was confirmed by toughness, violence, piety, and craft. A rich gift of peasant humour, a capacity for homiletic eloquence, and a profound belief in the Divine guidance of his race added attraction to his rugged character. As he smoked his pipe in the stoep of his modest dwelling in Pretoria, chatting with back-veldt Boers, he seemed to be the embodiment of Republican simplicity. Yet the treasures of the Rand did not leave him unmoved. He was quick to discern the value of gold for his young Republic, how with the tribute levied from the mines it might dominate the railways, equip an army, and perhaps ultimately, as many young Boers desired, drive the British into the sea. For the moment he was on the defensive. The loud-spoken grievances of the Uitlanders, the foreign community in Johannesburg, convinced him that these wealthy and powerful men were plotting with the assistance of the British Government to overthrow his state.

1853-1902 Cecil Rhodes, with all the advantages of England and Oxford, was built on wider and more generous lines. Of sound country stock, he, like the Boers, loved the land. If he bent the main part of his energies to the making of money, it was not so much for its own sake as for the opportunities of power and influence which money would buy. As a young man he had dreamed of securing the permanent peace of the world by means of a great scheme of scholarships, which would bring Englishmen and Americans together in Oxford during an impressionable period of their lives; and this dream, modified, expanded, articulated, pursued him through life and fructified in a noble educational endowment. Unlike the typical Uitlander, he was no bird of passage. He lived and worked for South Africa, and for the harmonious co-operation of the two white races. The Dutch he held in deep and unaffected esteem. There was in them a slow simplicity which matched his own. But heart trouble made him impatient. The persistent clamour of the Uitlanders, the obstinate resistance of the President to reasonable reforms, affected the soundness of his judgment. In a disastrous moment he sanctioned a raid into the Transvaal, under his friend Jameson, to put down the Republic and to place the country under the Union Jack. It was in vain that the British Government disowned and denounced the Raid. The harm was done. A flame of racial passion enveloped the country, which under Kruger's fiery and obstinate leadership drifted steadily towards war. Sir Alfred Milner, the new High Commissioner, pressed for reforms. They were not conceded. Recent revelations of the bellicose temper of the young Boers at that time show how difficult it would have been to preserve the peace.

The grievances of the Uitlanders, though widely proclaimed in the London Press, were not in themselves calculated to stir the heart of the British democracy. Nobody had compelled these adventurers to settle in Johannesburg. Nobody proposed to obstruct their withdrawal. They had gone to the Transvaal to make money, and, notwithstanding the vices of the Republican régime, had made it, often on a lavish and spectacular scale.

A purely local quarrel in a South African mining city would have left the British public cold. But the quarrel was not local. It was suspected that President Kruger was using the wealth of the Rand to finance a wide-ranging anti-British conspiracy, and that in this enterprise he possessed the sympathy and counted on the support of the German Reich. Accordingly, when on the morrow of Jameson's defeat the Kaiser telegraphed his congratulations to Kruger, all England burst into a flame of indignation. The intervention was regarded as unwarrantable and sinister, bad for what it was, worse for what it portended. Fortunately it was not known in London that the Kaiser in his temerity had drafted an ultimatum which a wise ambassador declined to deliver, or that soon afterwards his government was at work plotting a continental alliance against England which broke upon the rock of French reluctance.

1899-1902 Three years passed. The South African quarrel grew into a serious war, which, while it brought volunteers from every part of the Empire to the assistance of the mother country, seriously strained its resources and exhibited to the military critics of the continent the numerous shortcomings of the British Army. Though it was the Boers and not the British who had declared war, the sympathy of the Continent was solid for the Republican armies. The skill, the tenacity, and the courage with which the Boer farmers resisted the professional forces of a great Empire were universally admired. To distant observers it seemed to be a contest between simplicity and luxury, liberty and despotism, God and Mammon. Every victory of the Boers was received with delirious enthusiasm, every setback to their cause by a corresponding measure of disappointment and gloom. In Germany and France the waves of anti-English indignation rose mountains high. Even the Tzar of Russia, whose domestic government was no model of freedom, proposed a general alliance of the continental powers against the unpopular and arrogant island.

Nevertheless Europe was powerless to intervene. With a stock of ill-will against England sufficient to launch a dozen wars, it was compelled to look on while Roberts and Kitchener retrieved the early reverses to British arms and wore down the Boer resistance. No continental power, no combination of continental powers, was in a position to challenge the British Navy. Supremacy at sea dominated the situation. Never so clearly as now had the Continent realized the inconvenience which ensued from Britannia ruling the waves. The lesson sank deep into the mind of the Kaiser and his advisers, impressing more particularly a vigorous young officer of the German Navy by name Tirpitz, who, coming forward about the time of the Jameson Raid, advocated the construction of a High Sea fleet. Accordingly two important consequences followed from the passions excited in

Germany by the South African War. First, the road to an Anglo-German alliance, which had been opened by Chamberlain, was for the moment decisively obstructed; second, an argument, which no German could fail to understand, was now supplied for the construction of a fleet which even the strongest naval power in the world would be compelled to respect. Aided by the lessons of the Boer War, the Kaiser pursued with headlong zeal his darling project. It does not seem to have occurred to him that England, whose very existence depended on sea-borne supplies, would feel herself endangered by the presence in the North Sea of a fleet as powerful as her own. Holding that any interference with his favourite plaything was an intolerable personal insult, and that no diplomatic weapon was more suitable for the English than the big stick, he pressed forward with a series of naval bills, for the passage of which it was essential to foment anti-British feeling in the country. That in view of the continental balance of Powers such a course was beset with peculiar dangers for Germany was a reflection which does not appear to have struck his vigorous but volatile mind.

Dividing France and England from 1882-1904 was the complex problem of Egypt. The English had by a fate which seemed to all Frenchmen to be singularly perverse and vexatious stumbled into the inheritance which France had marked out for her own. It was Napoleon who had recovered Egypt for Europe; it was Mehemet Ali, Napoleon's admirer and pupil, who had made of Egypt a modern state; it was de Lesseps, a French engineer of genius, who had in 1869 pierced the Suez Canal. All three were opposed by England. Yet it was England and not France who secured a dominating control of the canal by the purchase of the Khedive's foundation shares in 1875, and England, again, who from 1882 onwards directed Egyptian policy from Cairo. For all this France had only herself to thank. At Bismarck's instigation she had taken up in conjunction with England the cause of the Egyptian bond holders. The two powers had deposed Ismail, the extravagant Khedive, and entered into a *condominium* with the object of restoring the *1881* shattered finances of the country. From the exercise of that joint responsibility France deliberately withdrew, leaving England to quell the revolt of Arabi, a malcontent colonel of the Egyptian army, and to straighten out the financial and administrative tangle which the deposed Khedive had left behind him. It was a curious situation. The Liberal Government of Gladstone, hating Imperial commitments, anxious to be rid of Egypt at the first convenient opportunity, found itself compelled to plunge deeper and deeper into the Nile mud, while France, which had no compunction about Imperialism, and would have given her eyes for Egypt, had, in a sudden paroxysm of timidity, left the palm and the dust to her rival.

If the idea of a permanent occupation of Egypt was distasteful to English Liberals, still more abhorrent was the suggestion that any attempt should be made to conquer the Sudan. The Liberals stood for peace, retrenchment, and reform, aspirations difficult to reconcile with the despatch of a military expedition into a scorching wilderness against a wild horde of fanatical dervishes. Yet the new rulers of Egypt could hardly be indifferent to the fate of a territory which was subject to the Egyptian flag, garrisoned by Egyptian troops, and now menaced by one of those fierce movements of religious fanaticism which from time to time convulse the Moslem world. Of this strange and formidable insurrection the leader was one Mohammed Ahmed, nephew of a boat builder in Dongola, who in 1881 proclaimed himself the Mahdi or Messiah and announced as his object the conquest of the world.

A weak Egyptian army, straying into the wilds of Kordofan and there experiencing an annihilating defeat, gave to the prophet a baptism of victory, and since the commander of the defeated force was Hicks Pasha, an Englishman, created a perplexing situation for the British Government. That the province should be promptly evacuated was a counsel of prudence, that the Egyptian garrisons should be safely withdrawn was an obligation of honour. The first operation was easy, but how to evacuate the scattered Egyptian garrisons without a costly and dangerous expedition was a problem calculated to tax the wisest head.

In an unfortunate hour the Government listened to the *Pall Mall Gazette*. This journal suggested that there was one man who by his extraordinary magnetism and unique gift in the handling of Oriental peoples could rally the Sudanese against the Mahdi, deliver the garrisons, put down the slave trade, and, without the movement of a man or a gun from England, relieve the Cabinet of its anxieties. The man was "Chinese" Gordon, a visionary hero, who in the civil wars of China had borne a charmed life, leading armies, composing differences, and exercising by virtue of a certain spiritual intensity an irresistible spell over the wildest and most savage natures, and who had been since noted for a period of striking personal ascendancy in the Sudan. In a very few days Gordon became the popular favourite, "one of our national treasures," the man of destiny appointed to work the miracle. Nobody stopped to consider whether this brave and mystical figure possessed the steadiness and sobriety of judgment necessary for the accomplishment of so great a task. It was sufficient that he accepted the perilous mission. By February, 1884, Gordon was in Khartum, wherefrom there proceeded a continuous stream of telegrams, impulsive, inconsistent, confusing, and revealing the measure of the Cabinet's mistake in its choice of a Governor-General of the Sudan. A yet greater error was to follow. A year later (January 26, 1885) Gordon was allowed to perish under the spears of the Dervishes. A British army of relief, through the culpable delay of the Government, had arrived just too late to save the emaciated garrison of the beleaguered city and its indomitable commander.

The least important result of this tragedy was to sweep out of office the Government which was thought to have sent a brave man on an impossible errand and to have allowed him to perish at his post through remissness and delay. The wider and more enduring consequence was to inject into English policy a firm resolve to reconquer the Sudan. To the protection of the Suez Canal which was a serious British interest there were now added other reasons founded upon deep popular emotion against the evacuation of Egypt: retribution for Gordon, the liberation of the Sudan from barbaric tyranny, the restoration of military prestige. English ministers might declare that the official policy of the country was evacuation at the earliest moment, but the moment never came. Notable work awaited Englishmen in the Nile Valley. It was now that Evelyn Baring, later Lord Cromer, hiding dictatorial powers under the modest title of Consul-General, embarked upon the great course of administrative reform which made Egypt a solvent and prosperous country.

Eleven years passed. The Mahdi died, the Khalifa Abdulla el Taashi succeeded to his power: but change of rulers made no difference to the Sudan. The same fierce fanaticism, the   *1885-96* same barbarity, continued to distinguish the tribesmen who dominated this vast province. An Egyptian army officered from England was strong enough to defend the frontiers and to inflict a series of defeats upon the Khalifa and his lieutenants, but a greater and more systematic effort was required if the Sudan was to be delivered from the tyranny of the Dervishes. That effort was at last forthcoming, thanks to the careful preparations of Baring and Kitchener, the Sirdar or Commander of the Egyptian army. In 1896 Kitchener advanced to Dongola. Two years later, vanquishing distance by the railway and numbers by the machine gun, he annihilated his enemy on the field of Omdurman, entered Khartum, and there set up a joint government under the British and Egyptian flags. The victory of Kitchener was a triumph of order and method. For less than the cost of one of Ismail's more expensive entertainments this energetic and methodical engineer reconquered the Sudan.

1898

Hardly had this feat been accomplished when an unsuspected event threatened to undermine the whole British position in Egypt. A small body of French explorers under Captain Marchand had for three years been marching eastward through darkest Africa, and at last, in the late summer of 1898, reached Fashoda, a village on the Upper Nile, and there planted the French flag. The British government instructed Kitchener to meet Marchand and to demand his withdrawal.

Relations between the two countries became at once seriously strained. After the sacrifices involved in the Sudanese campaign England was not disposed to cede the upper valley of the Nile to France on the strength of the presence in Fashoda of a French exploring party from the west. On the other hand, French public opinion could be brought with difficulty to admit that France was not humiliated by the requirement that a brilliant French officer, after a remarkable voyage of exploration, should surrender a territory which he had been the first to reach. Fortunately Delcassé, the French foreign minister, was a statesman who declined to involve his country in a war because of a miserable little hamlet on the Upper Nile of which ninety-nine out of every hundred of his compatriots had never heard. Wisely he foresaw that France might before long be glad of the friendship of England. He determined to order the withdrawal. War was averted: but the fleets had been mobilized and war had come uncomfortably near.

Delcassé, who saved the peace in 1898, stood so clear of popular prejudice that, despite the furious Anglophobia which was occasioned in France by Fashoda and the Boer War, he dared to believe that an understanding between France and England was desirable and might be obtained. Happy always in his choice of instruments, he sent Paul Cambon to London to work for an *Entente*. On February 28, 1902, Joseph Chamberlain and Cambon were overheard at a party at Marlborough House talking of Egypt and Morocco. Having failed in his negotiations with Germany, the powerful English Colonial Secretary was turning his thoughts to an accord with France.

Queen Victoria's long reign had come to an end. The monarchy which she had found weak and discredited she left firmly rooted in the affections of the country. Indefatigable industry and weight of experience had given something of that unique authority to her judgment which belonged to Elizabeth in her later years. It was not, however, her ability in the despatch of affairs, with respect to which the nation knew little, and still less her cast of mind, which evoked the glow of a people's loyalty, but her Teutonic simplicity and warmth of heart, her ready and gushing sympathy, and her capacity for entering into the common griefs and joys of ordinary people, to whom more than to the intellectuals and aristocrats she was temperamentally related. That her court was clean of profligacy and scandal commended it to the esteem of her subjects, who had been outraged by the private life of George IV. In those days, much, even dullness, was forgiven to virtue. *Jan. 22, 1901*

This little old lady, who was so proud and imperious and yet so close to the ways and thoughts of middle-class housewives, ruled England during a period, extending over sixty-three years, which witnessed an extraordinary effulgence of the nation's genius. Thackeray and Dickens were writing in her youth, Meredith, Kipling, Hardy, and R. L. Stevenson in her riper years. She might have invited to her table, had it ever occurred to her to do so, such a galaxy of historians, beginning with Macaulay and ending with Maitland, as have never laboured under one reign. Among the major prophets the Victorian age may reckon Carlyle, Mill, and Ruskin; among the poets Tennyson and Browning, Swinburne and Matthew Arnold. In divinity Newman, in scientific discovery Darwin and Wallace, in exploration Livingstone, in medicine Lister, in romance Thackeray and Dickens, Anthony Trollope, Charlotte Brontë, George Eliot, and R. L. Stevenson, in the popularization of science and the rationalistic interpretation of experience T. H. Huxley and Herbert Spencer, in comparative law Henry Maine, stand out among many figures of commanding accomplishments in every category. But the Queen was not an intellectual. Vainly was the superb panorama woven by the imaginative genius of her subjects unrolled before her royal eyes, idle the appeal of their innovating enthusiasms. The Oxford movement, the socialist movement, the rationalist movement, the feminist movement, were all alike abhorrent to her plain and steadfast conservatism. A fiery English patriot and in English politics a fierce partisan, she retained to the end, despite shattering toil and responsibility, the sentimental heart of a German girl.

1901-10 Delcassé was in wait for Edward, her successor. The new King of England was made up of amiability. He had no enmities or grudges, other than a personal distaste for his bumptious German nephew, but a genuine desire that England should be in good relations with all the world—with Germany, with France, with Russia. France in particular, where Anglophobia was still so strong, he desired to soften and secure. As Prince of Wales he had amused himself in Paris and made many French friends. In its dealings with France the British Government could wish for no better emissary of good will than the King.

1902-4 Yet it would be wrong to ascribe to Edward VII a diplomatic revolution which was the work of the Balfour Cabinet. The King assisted but did not originate the *Entente Cordiale* with France. His official visit to Paris dispelled hostility and generated enthusiasm, but the *Entente* was due to the fact that the French and English governments had discovered that they were in a position to make a colonial bargain profitable to each. The essence of the transaction was that France recognized the special rights acquired by England in Egypt, while England acknowledged the special position of France in Morocco. The agreement was accompanied by a secret convention, which fixed the limits of the zone of French influence in Morocco in case of an understanding with Spain. At the same time the outstanding differences of the two countries in Newfoundland, Siam, Madagascar, and the New Hebrides were regulated. On the face of it nothing seemed happier or more reasonable than this mutual liquidation of vexatious colonial grievances. Cambon was jubilant over Morocco. The House of Commons was delighted with an arrangement which secured the position of England in Egypt, but Lord Rosebery, who noted that Germany, the strongest military power in Europe, had not been consulted over Morocco, was critical, saying in private that the *Entente Cordiale* with France would eventually lead England into a German war.

BOOKS WHICH MAY BE CONSULTED

J. A. Spender : Fifty Years of Europe. 1933.

J. L. Garvin : The Life of Joseph Chamberlain. 1932.

Lady Gwendolen Cecil : The Life of Robert, Marquis of Salisbury. 1921.

E. Brandenburg : From Bismarck to the World War, German Foreign
        Policy, 1870-1914. 1927.

H. N. Brailsford : The War of Steel and Gold. 1915.

J. Bryce : Impressions of South Africa. 1897.

Basil Williams : Cecil Rhodes. 1921.

D. Reitz : Commando. 1929.

S. G. Millin : Rhodes. 1933.

CHAPTER XXVII

LIBERAL REFORMS AND CLOUDS OF WAR

Peace of Vereeniging. English domestic politics. The Education Act. Liberal opposition. Temperance. Chinese Labour. Tariff Reform. The Liberal decade of 1905-15. Growing power of Germany. Morocco. The Anglo-French Entente. Anglo-German naval competition. Failure of the Hague Conferences. Anglo-Russian Entente, 1907. The Austrian coup d'état of 1908. Danger of war.

IT was difficult for the English, an insular and civilian people, fully to apprehend the significance of the diplomatic revolution which had brought to an end the long period of "splendid isolation." The Japanese Treaty, prepared in secret, made little stir; the *Entente* with France was regarded as a happy colonial deal, making for general harmony. The thought of a European war was far from men's minds. So rooted was the insular objection to a conscript army that there were Frenchmen like Clemenceau who regarded the *Entente* as a positive danger to France.

Moreover, England was absorbed in her own affairs. The beginning of the twentieth century found the country still grappling with the resistance of the Boers, who, despite the fact that Pretoria and Bloemfontein, the capitals respectively of the Transvaal and the Orange Free State, were in English occupation, persisted in keeping the field. Their mode of warfare, elusive, mobile, with every farmhouse in the country supplying food and shelter to the little groups of mounted riflemen who harassed an army altogether too small for effective operations over so vast a field, led to severities which attracted public censure. It was thought necessary to build blockhouses, to burn farmhouses, and to gather the evacuated women and children into concentration camps. Such expedients, however inevitable from the point of view of the soldier, were abhorrent to a good-natured population, and though the language of Campbell-Bannerman, the Liberal leader, who spoke of "methods of barbarism," was resented, the fact that such measures were thought to be required constituted an additional argument for the prompt termination of the war. The Government supported Kitchener in his desire for a negotiated peace as opposed to the requirement for unconditional surrender, which was favoured by Milner. The Treaty of Vereeniging was

May, 1902

a real effort at reconciliation. Though the Boers were required to come within the Empire, so far from being asked to pay an indemnity they were given three million pounds for the reconstruction of their farms. Soon afterwards General Botha, coming to London, found himself, not a little to his amazement, a popular hero. With cries of "Good old Botha" the sporting population of the metropolis of the Empire welcomed the most formidable of their recent enemies as a good sportsman, a good loser, and a friend.

An incident of the war which stirred English crowds to humiliating transports of jollity was the relief of an inconsiderable town on the western borders of the Transvaal. Little, perhaps, would have been made of the siege of Mafeking if it had not been defended by a man of genius whose happy resource and light-hearted sallies, telegraphed home while the siege was proceeding, made him a popular favourite with his countrymen. The name of Baden-Powell, which became known throughout the Empire for a feat of arms, was later celebrated for a civilian triumph. Out of his experience of the veldt the defender of Mafeking made a new and original contribution to the education of the young. The Boy Scouts have now become a world-wide institution and a welcome addition to the character-building forces in society. So from two English wars, the Crimean and the South African, something unexpected has emerged for the relief of man's estate. The Crimea gave Florence Nightingale to the nursing profession. South Africa suggested to Baden-Powell a form of moral training, well suited to the nature of average boys and calculated to correct the monotony of the urban classroom by the open-air freedom and discipline of the wilds.

The Tory party, which was governing England at the Peace of Vereeniging, had been returned to power in overwhelming numbers in the "Khaki Election" of 1900. The Prime Minister was Lord Salisbury, his principal lieutenants A. J. Balfour and Joseph Chamberlain, the one an accomplished humanist and philosopher with a special gift for parliamentary dialectics, the other a Unitarian from Birmingham, who, after a strenuous and successful career in business and in the municipal politics of his native city, had entered Parliament and, exchanging the radicalism of his early youth for an eager and constructive imperialism, was now the most commanding figure in the Unionist ranks. A poll taken in the heat and passion of a war is never indicative of the true balance of political forces, and when the Conservative Government, which had been returned with a mandate to finish with the Boers, proceeded to touch domestic questions, its strength swiftly and sensibly ebbed away. Nonconformity was alienated by its treatment of education and temperance, Labour by the introduction of Chinese labour into the South African mines, and commerce and industry by the initiation of a powerful attack upon the hallowed system of Free Trade.

The real author of the Education Act of 1902 was Sir Robert Morant, one of those powerful civil servants who often, more than their official chiefs, help to mould the policy of their country. It was a big, revolutionary, beneficent measure, transferring the local administration of education from school boards to special committees of the counties and boroughs—that is, to bodies elected by the ratepayers and possessing the powers and responsibilities in finance which such election confers. It was argued that a body which could levy a rate could do more and dare more for education than one which could merely advise. The Act in effect was a challenge to every borough and county to take pride in its schools and to develop them to the best of its ability. Nor was its operation confined to elementary schools. By a bold but necessary departure from existing practice it sanctioned the provision of public aid for secondary education.

Nevertheless, bitter offence was given to the Nonconformists, and therefore to the bulk of the Liberal party, by the fact that denominational schools were taken into the public system and made eligible for aid from the rates. "Rome on the rates," became a popular cry. How, it was argued, was it just, how was it compatible with the religious conscience, that a Baptist should pay rates for the support of a school pervaded by an Anglican or Roman atmosphere? Still more acute was the complaint that in single-school areas, some eight thousand in number, Nonconformists were compelled to send their children to church schools. The debate, which raged furiously through the country, brought out all the latent jealousy of Romanism, Anglicanism, and the domination of the squires. So keen was the feeling that many a pious dissenter "passively" resisted and would go to prison rather than pay his rate.

Temperance was another question much agitated wherever Liberals were gathered together. The evil of drunkenness was widely acknowledged; its connection with crime and social misery established. Every social worker regarded drink as the most potent obstacle to social reform. Many remedies were proposed: total abstinence, local option, the cutting down under a strict licensing system of redundant public-houses. It was therefore regarded as a distinctly retrograde step when an Act was passed in 1904 which treated the publican's licence as a property from which he could not be dispossessed without compensation (save in case of abuse) by the licensing justices. To the opposition which was gathering against the Conservative Government on the score of its education policy there was now added the indignation of all the temperance workers in the country.

All this, however, was nothing compared to the emotion excited by Chinese labour and the menace of a fiscal revolution. The English trades unions, which had built up for themselves a position of authority unequalled by any similar organization on the continent, saw in the proposal to import Chinese labour into the South African mines a menace to the standard of life which had been so painfully built up by the persevering effort of three generations. If a block of cheap labour could be transported from China to Johannesburg, would it not be equally open to capitalists to fill the mills of Lancashire and Yorkshire with inexpensive and submissive orientals? If that were done, what would be the position of British workers? The whole trades union movement would be ruined. Wages would fall, standards of life would decline, the gulf between employer and employed would be immeasurably widened. Though the danger that oriental labour would ever be introduced into England was remote and wildly enlarged by party passion, there can be little question but that "Chinese slavery" was an important ingredient in the great revulsion of feeling which returned the Liberals to power in 1906.

A larger and graver issue was raised by Joseph Chamberlain's campaign for Tariff Reform. During a visit to South Africa in 1903 the Colonial Secretary elaborated a policy which might distract the minds of his fellow-countrymen from sordid and trifling squabbles over church schools and public-houses and refresh the waning authority of the Unionist party by identifying it with the majestic theme of imperial consolidation. The votes which the Tories had lost over education, the publicans, and the Chinese might be recaptured by a bold policy of Imperial Preference.

Chamberlain returned to England resolved upon an onslaught on English Free Trade, and, resigning his place in the Cabinet, opened "a raging and tearing campaign" in the country. Meanwhile the Conservative Cabinet held the fort, the Prime Minister, Balfour, delicately balancing the pros and cons of the tariff question until such time as, the arrangements with France having been concluded, he felt himself at liberty to face the electorate.

The system of Free Trade had governed England for sixty years, during which time the country had experienced an astonishing expansion of national prosperity. While great industries had been developed and great fortunes had been made, the dietary of the people had been diversified, enriched, and cheapened by grains and fruits drawn from every quarter of the globe. The prosperity of the Lancashire cotton trade, depending as it did upon oriental markets sensitively contracting at the smallest rise of price, was thought to be endangered by any tax, however slight, which might tend to raise the cost of production. Again, shipping and shipbuilding, banking and coal-mining were staple industries which profited by freedom and could only be injured by the imposition of tariffs. That iron and steel should be as cheap as possible was regarded as axiomatic in a country where the uses of steel were so numerous and the application of machinery so widely diffused. The position of London as the monetary centre of the world, the strength of the mercantile marine, the livelihood of the mill hands in the cotton and cloth industries, were all believed to depend upon fiscal freedom. Though it was true that other countries had not followed England in her Free Trade policy and that two countries in particular, the United States and Germany, had notably prospered under protection, English goods still went all over the world. Despite high duties abroad, the old Free Trade maxim that foreign markets could be conquered by cheapness was still valued. The sacrifice of such indubitable advantages seemed to be a gamble, for it was only by a prosperous export trade, based on cheaper products, that Britain could rely upon being able to purchase the food which was required to support her population. When Chamberlain first opened his campaign the memory of the "hungry forties" was still a living thing in the country, nor was there any part of his policy which was more vulnerable to attack than the necessity which it involved. if a valuable preference was to be given to the dominions and colonies, of placing a tax on food.

Against such objections, based on the structure and conduct of British business, Chamberlain unfolded the vision of a great Empire bound together by fiscal ties. The home country was asked to place protective duties on imports, including food and raw materials, primarily in order that it might accord to the dominions and colonies a preference against the foreigner, but also as a shield against foreign competition at home. As the prophet of Tariff Reform, trim, beautifully dressed, an orchid in his buttonhole and a monocle in his eye, toured round the country expounding these views with incomparable vigour, now appealing to imperial sentiment, now pointing to the increasing severity of foreign competition, and in particular to the advance of German industry, he was followed by Asquith, the brilliant spokesman of the Free Trade Liberals. The debate, which raised the most wide-reaching issues, proceeded in every household. Its first political effect was to split the Unionist party, which was weakened by the secession of the Duke of Devonshire and Goschen; its second to contribute to the great Liberal victory of 1906. For the moment Tariff Reform was repulsed. Prosperity rather than dialectic had fought the winning battle for Free Trade.

The Liberal party thus returned to power governed the country for ten years. It stood for peace and Free Trade. It re- 1905-15 garded commerce not as a conflict of rivals but as a system of exchanges made for the mutual convenience of friends. It wanted to reduce expenditure on armaments and to promote the social services. Such grievances as the nonconformists cherished with respect to church schools and temperance, it was concerned to remedy. Colonial preference it rejected. The kind of imperialism which this party favoured was illustrated when Campbell-Bannerman, the new Prime Minister, gave responsible government to the Transvaal and the Orange Free State. There have been few more courageous acts in modern history than the decision to hand over the government of South Africa soon after a bitter contest to the defeated enemy. That "C. B.'s" confidence was not misplaced was shown eight years afterwards when General Botha, bravely suppressing a rebellion stirred up by a few old comrades in arms, led his people into the Great War on the British side.

By the irony of fate this peace-loving, peace-pursuing government fell straight into a European crisis. For the past two years the position of Germany in Europe had been strengthened by a series of events contributing to impair the value of the Russian alliance to France. The first of these was the outbreak of a war between Russia and Japan, the second a series of amazing Japanese victories, and the third a revolutionary convulsion in Russia, closely following upon the military collapse of the Imperial armies in the field. In 1905, while these troubles were proceeding, the moment seemed opportune for Count Schlieffen, the German chief of the staff, to propose that a war should be forced on France. The inhuman idea did not seem criminal or even indecent to the two sinister figures who now directed German foreign policy. It was common ground between Count Bülow, the plausible Chancellor, and Baron Holstein, the grim power behind the throne, that the time was ripe, even at the risk of war, for testing the strength of the Anglo-French *Entente* by a strong diplomatic offensive. Morocco was selected as the point of attack, for it was by permitting France a free hand in Morocco that England had purchased immunity from French molestation in Egypt, and it was rightly conjectured that unless the English were prepared to back the French in Morocco up to the point of war, English friendship would for ever lose its value in the eyes of France.

June, 1905

Jan., 1906

So the great offensive was opened. The Kaiser was sent on a mission to Tangier to assure the Sultan of his goodwill and support, and soon after the French were compelled to accept, under threat of war, the resignation of Delcassé and the summoning of a Conference to Algeciras. Little, however, did the Germans gain from the humiliations put upon their enemy by this clumsy and hectoring diplomacy. Sir Edward Grey, the new Liberal Foreign Minister, rightly judging that the honour of his country was concerned, gave to the French a full measure of diplomatic support at Algeciras, and, being impressed by the risks of a German attack upon France, authorized secret military conversations between officers of the French and English staffs.

The immediate result of the German pressure upon France in the matter of Morocco was to tighten rather than to loosen the Anglo-French *Entente*.

Though nothing was publicly known at the time, and most members of the British Cabinet shared the general ignorance of the public, a decisive step was taken when French and British officers were authorized to construct plans in view of an eventual

Jan.,
1906

war between Germany and France. Though it was carefully explained that such conversations could not pledge the government, which must always in the last resort be guided by the moral sentiment of Parliament and of the country, a presumption was created in the minds of soldiers on either side of the Channel that, in the event of European trouble, they would fight shoulder to shoulder. Mutual confidences had been exchanged, secret plans had been discussed. The initiation of these military conversations meant that the Anglo-French *Entente* was not merely an adjustment of colonial differences, but an understanding which, on sufficient cause and Parliament being willing, might lead to the participation of England in a European war.

Meanwhile the growth of the German navy had been long watched with anxious eyes by the English Admiralty. The Navy was not in England a party question. It was common knowledge that the protection of the country's food supplies in time of war was dependent on the possession of sea power, and that the coherence of the British Empire itself rested in the last resort on the ability of the British Fleet to keep the seas against its enemies. As a rough guide to Admiralty practice, it was part of the national policy to aim at a two-power standard, a navy capable of dealing effectively with the important navies of the two next strongest naval Powers in the world. But the rise of German navalism at once changed the outlook. No English sailor was disposed to undervalue the sea-going qualities of the German battleship, the skill of German gunnery, or the courage and sea-craft of German crews. Because the English sailor respected the German sailor, he was the more insistent upon the danger proceeding from German naval policy. What sailors thought, the Government and the country thought also. At whatever sacrifice, England must outbuild Germany. In 1906 two steps were taken which showed that the new Liberal government was alive to the danger. The first Dreadnought was launched, and the British Home Fleet was concentrated in the North Sea. The Germans responded by a new Navy Law. The race of naval armaments was now open and unconcealed. Nor did it escape the notice of the British Admiralty that the heavily armour-plated High Sea Fleet was constructed not for distant voyages, but for a conflict with a strong opponent in the North Sea.

The responsibility for this calamitous competition is not a

little to be attributed to the fallacious view held by the Kaiser and Tirpitz that there would be a period of time while the German navy was still relatively weak, when the English might be tempted to destroy it, but that once "the danger zone" was passed, all would be well. From this premise it followed that the more ships Germany laid down, the more swiftly would she pass through the danger zone, and the more certainly conquer the respect and acquiescence of her naval rival. From this ground of psychology and logic the Kaiser was not to be moved.

Any suggestion coming from the British side that there should be an agreed limitation, which would still leave England with more ships than Germany, was resented as an affront in Berlin. When Sir Charles Hardinge ventured (August 11, 1908) to broach the question of naval limitation at Cronborg, the Kaiser roundly told him that he would rather go to war.

*May,
1899 and
July,
1907*

The international atmosphere of Europe during these years was heavily laden with suspicion and fear of war. Two conferences summoned to The Hague on the initiative of the Tzar to promote peace and disarmament, so far from relieving, contributed to aggravate the situation. The Germans, who were firm set against military or naval reductions, noted with suspicion that while the Tzar proposed to limit effectives, in which Russia could always claim an overwhelming superiority, the development of Russian railways, which was greatly in arrears, was to be subject to no such curb. Britain, too, appeared in an equivocal rôle, on the one hand pressing earnestly for military reductions, on the other hand resisting the proposal upon which Germany and America were united, for according immunity to private property at sea. It was open, therefore, for Germany to say that, while the English were anxious that the continent should disarm, the strongest navy in the world still proposed to exercise its belligerent rights at the expense of neutral commerce in time of war. From these well-meant discussions little that was good resulted.

Meanwhile (1907) a combination thought in Berlin to be utterly impossible was translated into fact. England and Russia, the two rival oriental empires, adjusted their respective spheres of interest in the Middle East. The Anglo-French *Entente* on colonial questions was followed up by an Anglo-Russian *Entente* on Asiatic questions. Nothing could be more reasonable than that two countries should endeavour to eliminate occasions of diplomatic friction, and the Anglo-Russian *Entente*, though criticized by some as unfair to Persia, was generally applauded in England as an important further step towards the peaceful ordering of the world. Very different, however, were the views of this transaction entertained in Berlin. There the Anglo-Russian understanding was regarded as an additional indication of the Machiavellian design attributed to King Edward and Sir Edward Grey of encircling Germany by a ring of enemies.

Germany did not intend to be encircled. More particularly she was resolved to keep open for herself the Balkan route to the Near East and to the Persian Gulf. Since Austria, her friend and ally, held the gates, it was a cardinal axiom of German policy that nothing must be allowed to impair the close junction between Vienna and Berlin.

The strength of this necessary bond was soon to receive a striking illustration. The political map of the Balkans had, as we have seen, been arranged with infinite difficulty by a concert of the Powers in 1878. The Congress of Berlin had fixed the size of Bulgaria, returned Macedonia to the Turks, and invited the Austrians to administer under Turkish suzerainty the provinces of Bosnia and Herzegovina, whose populations were Serb in origin and in speech. The Treaty of Berlin was not ideal, for Macedonia under Turkish rule proved to be a chronic centre of oppression and disturbance, but at least it possessed the merit of being a settlement which had been agreed to by the Great Powers and could not safely or properly be varied without their consent. How great then was the consternation when it was learned that Austria, without even the knowledge of her German ally, had resolved to annex Bosnia and Herzegovina, *Oct.* and that the Bulgarians with Austrian encouragement had de- *1908* clared themselves to be a monarchy independent of the Porte! There was much to be said for these changes. Austria had borne the burden of administering the two Slavonic provinces for thirty years and her work had been good. Bulgaria was permeated by a strong spirit of national pride and independence. But if the objects were desirable, the manner in which it was sought to achieve them was a challenge to the public law of Europe, and a definite threat to peace. How could it be expected that the Serbs could view with equanimity the sudden incorporation of the Bosnians and Herzegovinians, peoples whom they regarded

as bone of their bone and flesh of their flesh, in the Habsburg
Empire? The annexation sent a flame of indignation through
Serbia which was the more dangerous since behind the Serb
stood the formidable might of the Russian Empire.

Again war seemed very near. Moltke and Conrad von
Hötzendorf, the chiefs respectively of the German and Austrian
staffs, urged that the time had now come to try conclusions with
Russia and France. Passions were high in St. Petersburg;
Isvolsky, who had been tricked by Aehrenthal, the Austrian
Foreign Minister, abounding in fiery denunciations of Austrian
duplicity, and every Russian feeling that by this sudden and
violent Austrian act the balance of power in the Balkans had
been decisively turned against the Slavs. But at this moment,
which might so easily have been critical for the fate of the Habsburg Empire, William of Hohenzollern stood by the side of
Francis Joseph. The Tzar was given to understand (March 23,
1909) that if he were to draw the sword in this Balkan quarrel
he must reckon on the opposition of the German Empire. The
threat was sufficient, the sense of humiliation remained. Next
year in Vienna the Kaiser boasted that in the Bosnian crisis he
had stood by his Austrian friend and ally "in shining armour."
It was unwise to flaunt before the world that only so had peace
been kept. There were those in St. Petersburg who vowed that
never again, were a similar crisis in the Balkans to arise, would
the Kaiser find a Russia so submissive to his will.

It is eloquent of the international neurosis of these times that
two second-rate men, Aehrenthal, the half-Semitic Austrian
Foreign Minister, and Isvolsky, a vain, empty, fire-eating Russian
diplomat, were able not only to bring Europe to the edge of
a general war, but by their furious personal hatred to infect
the relations between their respective Empires with a dangerous
measure of animosity. Meeting together at a country house in
Bohemia these two ambitious politicians had hatched a plot which
was to give Austria her two Balkan provinces and to open for
Russia the sea passage to the Mediterranean. The plot was secret
and, since it involved a double breach of the Treaty of Berlin,
deep-dyed with illegality. Moreover, even if Austria and Russia
had held together, the plan for opening the straits would have
been regarded by England as a challenge. But Aehrenthal betrayed Isvolsky. Before any steps had been taken to secure the
Russian objective, the Austrian conspirator published the news

of the Austrian annexations. The Russian was deeply mortified. The clever scheme which was to have earned him the eternal gratitude of his country had turned to dust and ashes, for Russia had lost the straits and Austria had won the provinces. Stung by wounded pride and frustrated ambition, Isvolsky was determined that the Austrians should pay heavily for their Aehrenthal. Among the war-mongers of the period this Russian diplomat ranks high, almost as high as the most fiery and persistent war-monger in Europe, Conrad von Hötzendorf, the fanatical chief of the Austrian General Staff.

Meanwhile, far away in London, Sir Edward Grey, much shocked by these lawless proceedings, proposed the summoning of a European Conference to regulate the situation. What England might do, were France to be drawn into war over the Balkan crisis, was a matter with respect to which neither Cabinet nor Parliament had come to a clear resolve.

BOOKS WHICH MAY BE CONSULTED

J. A. Spender : Fifty Years of Europe. 1933.
J. A. Spender : Life of Sir Henry Campbell-Bannerman. 1923.
Earl Buxton : General Botha. 1924.
G. B. Allen : Sir Robert Morant. 1934.
J. L. Garvin : Life of Joseph Chamberlain. 1932.
Von Bülow : Memoirs. 1931-2.
Grey of Fallodon : Twenty-Five Years. 1928.

CHAPTER XXVIII

SERBIA AND THE DUAL MONARCHY

Francis Joseph. Racialism in the Dual Monarchy. Croatia feels the call of the blood. The Serbian menace. Exasperation in Vienna. The Turkish revolution of 1908. Its real character. Turkish tyranny unites the Christian States in the Balkans. Agadir and Tripoli. The Balkan League of 1912. Its astonishing triumphs. A European War averted by the Conference of London. The second Balkan War. The defeat of Bulgaria. The Serbs become the leading people in the Balkans. Vienna apprehensive.

1848-1917 MEANWHILE Francis Joseph, the old Austrian Emperor, lived on in Vienna, diligently toiling at his desk, signing and reading, reading and signing, from early morn to night, a tragic figure, could he have felt tragedy, for his wife had fallen by an assassin's hand, his only son had committed suicide, and his nephew and heir-in-law had disgraced himself by a love-match, never forgiven, with a lady below his princely rank. But whether it was because all capacity for emotion had been drained out of him, or from an overmastering sense of the majesty of his public function, or simply because his nature was shallow and conventional, the old man went on his way unmoved, an ascetic, an automaton, yet acclaimed as the first horseman in his realm, and the first gentleman in Europe. A stiff ceremonial shielded him from the tumultuous world outside. A martial aristocracy defended his throne. An imperial bureaucracy supplied him with the ministers, fleeting and embarrassed, who endeavoured to cope with the anxious tasks of government. Under his long rule, the Austrian Empire had sustained so many shattering blows, the loss of Lombardy and Venetia, the rape of the Danish duchies, the exclusion from the German *Reich*, that it seemed to bear a charmed life, even when it was, in fact, fast moving to its dissolution.

Of all European States the Dual Monarchy had most to fear from the development of the racial and nationalist passions which were now sweeping through the world, potent in Japan, menacing in India, firing enthusiasm in the British Dominions, and finally transforming political life in the Balkans. For this composite State was based upon the entire negation of racialism. It proceeded on the assumption that eight and a half million Czechs, five million Poles, four million Ruthenes, five million seven hundred thousand Serbs and Croats, three million three hundred thousand Roumanians, and one million three hundred thousand Slovenes would rest content with a system under which the deciding influence was exercised in one half of the Empire by ten million Magyars, and in the other half by twelve million Germans. For many centuries that supposition had been justified. The Austrian Empire had held together under a common creed, a common army, a common crown, until men had come to regard it as an international necessity, a polity which, however anomalous and difficult to work, served so useful a purpose that, were it abolished, the nature of things would abhor the vacuum. But now the survival of the monarchy was jeopardized from within. Even between the two dominant races, the German and the Magyar, there was harassing friction, the Magyars seeking at every decennial revision of the *Ausgleich* to strip away everything which was substantial in the bond uniting Austria and Hungary, until only a bare personal union between the crowns was left. Still worse were the relations between the Magyars and the many non-Magyar peoples comprised within the Hungarian Kingdom.

All the bitterness which the Irish peasantry felt towards their English masters was experienced by the Slovaks, the Ruthenes, the Roumans, and the Serbs, towards the proud and privileged aristocracy which violently attempted to Magyarize the country, imposing its alien language, its alien schools, and so working the electoral system as to defraud the weaker peoples of their due share of representation in the national Diet.

The growing importance of social and democratic problems, the rise of international labour, the adoption in 1907 of universal suffrage, failed to soften the sharp divisions between the races of the Austro-Hungarian monarchy. When it came to the point, racialism was always the strongest factor in public emotion— stronger than creed, stronger than class, stronger than ties of professional or economic association. Every Parliament and provincial Diet tended to become a racial pandemonium. As an Austrian writer has put it, " the racial shirt was closer to the heart than the Imperial uniform."

Arising out of these serious discords was the prospect that the

Empire would be shattered by secessions. The Slovenes of Styria, and the Italians of South Tyrol, worked for severance. The Ruthenes of East Galicia strained against the ties which united them to the Poles in the western section of the Province. The peasants of Transylvania (a province of Hungary) were Rouman not in blood only, but in political sympathy. In Croatia, smarting under the enforced use of the Magyar language on the railway lines, a party was fast growing in numbers and influence which favoured a severance of the land from Hungary and its incorporation in a federation of southern Slavs, which should include Bosnia, Herzegovina, and Cisleithanian Dalmatia, and even, as some forward spirits dared to dream, the Serbian Kingdom. Such inspirations could not be lightly dismissed by the statesmen of the Ballplatz. Rightly the government of Vienna regarded the spectre of a Yugo-Slav or South Slav state with suspicion and alarm. The malady of Slavonic nationalism was not such as to admit of isolation. The Croatians were not merely a body of disappointed Austrian subjects who could be handled as a problem of domestic police. Though belonging to the Roman Church, they were Serb in speech and Serb in race. Loyally as they had served the Habsburg House, when Serbia was a downtrodden province of the Turkish Empire, they could not entirely resist the call of the blood. While Belgrade was Turkish, the devotion of Croatia went out to Vienna; but when Serbia became a free self-governing kingdom, able to hold its own against the Turk and the Bulgar, and standing out as the protagonist of the Slavonic race in the Balkans, the allegiance of the Croats flickered in division and uncertainty. On the one hand was a long and honourable tradition of service in the imperial army, of blood poured out on many a stricken field, of honours toilsomely deserved and generously accorded; on the other was the appeal which came from the presence just beyond their borders of a rugged, valiant, romantic people of their own blood and speech, who, albeit in a lower and more primitive stage of development, had won their way to political emancipation by the sword. It was an appeal which was strengthened by a common hate. To Croat and Serb the Magyar was odious. A wretched tariff war between Serbia and Hungary was the symptom of angry feelings, which winds sweeping across the wide horizon of international policy might blow into a formidable flame.

It is not then to be wondered that the Austrian Government regarded Serbia as an enemy. Here on the southern frontier of the realm was a state, small indeed in population and area, but armed, warlike, and enterprising, with racial affiliations spreading far and wide through Austria and Hungary, a standing centre of Slavonic propaganda, a possible spearpoint of Slavonic attack. It was no idle or extravagant hypothesis to imagine that a movement spreading outward from the Serbs to their kinsfolk in the Empire might produce a complete landslide of its southern provinces, with sympathetic reactions impossible to measure among the malcontent and emotional peoples of the centre and the north.

These Austrian suspicions and animosities were deepened by a terrible crime. There was in the Serbian army (1903) a secret society known as the Black Hand, at once revolutionary and nationalist, which had conceived a fierce abhorrence of the reigning Obrenovitch dynasty, not only in virtue of that old and bloody feud between the rival Houses of Obrenovitch and Karageorgevitch, which had for three generations divided the country, but also because Alexander, the reigning monarch, suffered from the reproach of being at once conservative and pro-Austrian. The officers of the Black Hand did nothing by halves. They entered the royal palace (1903), butchered the King and Queen, and ordered the Parliament to summon Peter Karageorgevitch, a mild and elderly exile, to ascend the vacant throne. It was little consolation to the Austrians to know that the new King of Serbia was an amiable gentleman, who had translated Mill *On Liberty*. They believed that he and his country were in the bloodstained grip of the Black Hand, and that this society, which was developing the idea of a union of all the southern Slavs under the Serbian Crown, would stop at no crime to effect its purpose.

Statesmen are human. There is a point at which, through the accumulation of worries, the nerve gives way. To that point in the early years of the twentieth century the statesmen of Vienna were steadily moving. Nothing went smoothly. On every side there were obstacles which no industry could overcome, discords which no art could appease, perils which no eye could measure. The atmosphere became charged with exasperation and impatience. To be quit of the Serbs, to read this upstart race of assassins and conspirators a sharp lesson, and to put every wretched Slav in his proper place became an obsession. Again and again the soldiers pressed for a preventive war. But for German discouragement it is probable, if not certain, that the civilians in Vienna would have hearkened to their advice.

In the spring of the year (1908) in which Aehrenthal made his successful but unfortunate coup, an astonishing revolution occurred among the Turks. That barbarous Asiatic people had not been altogether unaffected by their long association with the culture of the West. The American missionary, the French novelist, the Universities of Paris and Berlin, were combining to give to the wealthier sections of Turkish society a new outlook upon the world. A ferment of patriotic nationalism began to make itself felt in the corrupt and decadent society which had so long languished under the enervating and capricious rule of Abdul Hamid. By degrees patriotism took a practical shape. An association, styling itself the Committee of Union and Progress, was secretly formed for terminating the inglorious subservience of the Ottoman race to the western powers and for the creation of a modernized and efficient Ottoman state. It met first at Geneva (1891), flitted to Paris, and finally settled at Salonika (1908). Many of its members were lawyers and doctors, some were Jews, others soldiers. General enlightenment was the professed note of a body which represented, not the rough upland Turks of Anatolia, but the educated class which had been formed in the seaport towns by western culture. Among its members were Enver, a young officer who had learned soldiering in Berlin; Tálaat, a telegraph clerk from Salonika; and Djavid, a Jew financier. When the third army corps stationed in Macedonia had been secured for the cause, the Committee threw aside its disguises, proclaimed the Turkish constitution of 1876, and prepared to march on the capital.

To the amazement of Europe the revolution of the Young Turks met with instantaneous success. Startled into false professions of sympathy the Sultan accepted the constitution, summoned a parliament, disbanded his spies, and proclaimed the principles of liberty and equality. Soon afterwards (April 27, 1909) he recanted and was deposed. The Young Turks were masters of the state. The long Hamidian rule, founded on tyranny and espionage, was brought to an end. As Mohammed V. the new Sultan, mounted the throne, he was inspired to observe that the safety and happiness of Turkey depended on the "steady and serious application of the constitutional régime."

For a few weeks it seemed to western observers that all the popular notions about the Turks would need to be revised. Here apparently was a Moslem government prepared to repudiate every principle which had governed Turkey in the past, a government of liberals and democrats, of parliamentarians and humanitarians, of statesmen who were pledged to admit the Christian populations of the Balkans into a just and equal fellowship of privilege and power, and to give to the Turkish state all the benefits which modern civilization could confer. In England the Young Turks were acclaimed as idealists anxious to graduate in the school of liberty, and to found a Turkish Westminster on the Bosphorus.

All this was the wildest error. The Young Turks were very far from being liberals. The governing force in their movement was a hot and intemperate nationalism. Nothing was more foreign to their notions or to their practice than an attempt to conciliate the Christian peoples. A methodical and centralized tyranny was substituted for the slatternly extortions and numerous massacres of the Hamidian régime. Disorders grew, outrages multiplied. The state of Macedonia with its mixed populations of Bulgars, Greeks, and Serbs went from bad to worse. New taxes inflamed the Albanians. The union of Crete with Greece was forbidden. In less than two years the harsh government of these Turkish nationalists had achieved a miracle, such as no statesman could have foreseen. A vigorous and formidable Moslem tyranny, led by men who were determined upon one last desperate fling for Empire in an adverse world, suddenly healed the feuds of the Balkans and united the Christian populations into a military league.

The Balkan drama which had begun with the Turkish revolution in Salonika now entered its most critical phase. The scene for a moment must be shifted to Agadir, an obscure port on the Atlantic coast of Morocco. Thither the German Government, annoyed by the despatch of a French military expedition to Fez, despatched with great unwisdom the gunboat *Panther*. The demonstration provoked immediate reactions in Paris, in London, and in Rome. Mr. Lloyd George, the Chancellor of the Exchequer, in his Mansion House speech, went out of his way to warn the German Government that, were war to be forced upon France over such an issue, England would not be unmoved. In Rome the despatch of the German gunboat to the shores of Morocco acted as a spur to Imperial adventure, for Italy had caught the prevailing fever, and not content with nursing claims upon the Italian territory which was still subject to the Austrian yoke, dreamed of an African Empire. Her eye was on Tripoli, and she felt that if the Germans had designs on the North African coast, she had no time to lose. Even Giolitti, the finished Parliamentary artist, to whom adventures of all kinds were unwelcome, but who kept his ear close to the ground, realized the need for speedy action. With hardly a shadow of a pretext, he declared war on Turkey, and sent the Italian army into Libya.

*July,
1911*

It was clear that if ever the Christian population of the Balkans were to attack the Turks no moment could be more opportune than one in which the main strength of the Turkish army was locked up in Africa and engaged in a losing struggle with the Italians.

*March,
1912*

Nevertheless, the formation of the Balkan League was a surprising achievement, rendered possible by the violent maladministration of the Young Turks, but also by the emergence of a few men of outstanding political stature, of whom one was J. D. Bourchier, *The Times* correspondent in Bulgaria, while another was M. Venizelos, a Cretan hardened in the civil wars of his own island, and, as an islander, possessing a larger and more detached outlook on affairs than most of the politicians of continental Greece.

If the fact of the League was remarkable, its success was still more surprising. At every point the Turk was outgeneralled and outfought. The Greek Navy denied him the sea. The Bulgarians defeated the main Ottoman armies in Thrace, first at Kirk-Kilisse, October 23, 1912, and afterwards at Lule Burgas, driving the enemy in utter disorder behind the lines at Chataldja; and while the Bulgarians were achieving these astonishing results in the east, astonishing by reason of their completeness and their speed, the Greeks fought their way into Salonika, and the Serbs had the satisfaction on the hard-fought field of Kumanovo of wiping out the ancient memories of the great defeat of Kossovo, which had ruined the Serbian Empire in the fourteenth century. Such a victory, little as its implications were realized at the time, had a vital bearing on the difficult problem of maintaining European peace. It was one of those complete and unexpected

*Oct. 23,
1912*

triumphs which exalt the spirit of a nation, and was the more inspiring since it led on to the recovery of Uskub, the ancient capital of Serbia, and of Monastir, the key to central Macedonia. In a campaign of six weeks the Balkan League, which had put into the field more than 600,000 men, had practically destroyed all European Turkey outside Constantinople.

It may readily be imagined how disconcerting to Austria were these extraordinary events. Serbia, the chief source of Austrian apprehension, came out of this Balkan struggle with her reputation greatly increased, her territories enlarged, her aspirations inflamed. In the Conference summoned to London to settle a new map of the Balkans, it was Austria's prime object to deny to Serbia direct access to the Adriatic. The little mountain territory of Albania accordingly became a centre of intense diplomatic conflict. The resolution of Austria to keep Serbia out of Albania was matched by the determination of Russia that the Serbs should be given this access to the sea. Europe was brought to the brink of war, but war was averted. The Germans exercised a moderating influence over the Austrians, the English over the Russians, and the difficulty was solved by the erection of Albania into an independent state to be governed by a German Prince. *Dec., 1912 August, 1913*

While the Conference was proceeding in London, the Young Turks, led by Enver, carried through a revolution in Constantinople and reopened the war. The campaign which ensued was marked by two triumphs and one disaster. The Greeks took Yanina, the Serbs and the Bulgarians compelled the capitulation of Adrianople. But the hand of an assassin struck down King George of Greece, a wise ruler, who might, had he survived, have exercised a wholesome influence on his people. The Treaty of London (May 30, 1913) restricted Turkey in Europe to a small area covered by Constantinople and Gallipoli.

Hardly was the ink dry upon this instrument than an internecine quarrel broke out among the victors. Of the three allies who had beaten the Turk to his knees, the Bulgarians had contributed the largest contingent, had faced the most formidable opposition, and had incurred the most considerable sacrifices. It was the impetuosity of their attack which had broken the strength of the Turkish resistance, and had wrested eastern Thrace from the enemy. That Bulgaria was likely to become the predominant power in the Balkans seemed to most observers to be the likely consequence of the Balkan War.

There was a certain solidity in the Bulgarian character, which attracted travellers from the west and inspired confidence. They appeared to be less headstrong than the Serbs, less flighty than the Greeks, less ignorant and stupid than the Turks. In Ferdinand of Coburg they possessed an unpopular, but crafty and ambitious leader, who was known to be favoured in Vienna. Moreover, they were land-hungry and ill satisfied with the plunder accruing from their two campaigns. Not only had they failed to win Constantinople, but they knew well that, however weak the Turks might be, Russia would deny them access to the city on the Bosphorus. The great prizes of the war had been seized by their allies, by the Greeks who were in possession of Salonika, by the Serbs whose army was in central Macedonia, and they doubtless suspected, what was indeed the fact, that the Serbs and the Greeks were resolved to maintain their gains at all costs. Since there was a large Bulgarian element in the Macedonian population, the Bulgarians determined, in a moment of wild folly, to *August,* attack their recent allies. The Serbs and the Greeks were pre-*1913* pared for the onset, and, with the Roumans also invading from *Treaty of* the north, the Bulgars experienced a crushing defeat, and were *Buchar-* compelled to submit to a humiliating peace. *est*

The course of these tragical happenings in the Balkans had been watched with febrile anxiety and grave disappointment by statesmen in Vienna. The result of the Balkan Wars had been to shatter Bulgaria, the friend of Vienna, to weaken Turkey, in whom the Kaiser had found his most recent ally, and greatly to increase the power of the Serbs. The military triumphs won by this little people had been truly remarkable. They had defeated the Turks, they had helped to take Adrianople. They had materially assisted in procuring the humiliation of Bulgaria. Incontestably now they were the first people in the Balkans, heartened by triumphs, confident of Russian help, dreaming of the incorporation of their kinsfolk in Bosnia and Herzegovina and of a kingdom stretching along the Adriatic coast. Again and again the Austrian General Staff had urged on the Government that this dangerous little nation of peasant soldiers should be taught a sharp lesson before it became too powerful. Despite strong temptation, for Vienna was chauvinist, the soldiers' way had been rejected. What were the alternatives? A patient defence or a radical reconstruction of the Imperial constitution to meet the aspirations of the Slavs? There were wise heads who believed that a solution might be found by giving to the southern Slavs a fuller measure of autonomy and a larger share of influence in the affairs of the Empire. Would it not be possible, it was argued, to substitute for the dual monarchy, resting on the dominion of the Magyars and the Germans, a trialist state founded on the equal fellowship of Slav, Magyar, and German? It was rumoured that Prince Franz Ferdinand, heir to the throne, entertained some such ideas and that his policy ran sharply counter to the dreams entertained in Belgrade and Agram by fervent nationalists of the Serbian race.

BOOKS WHICH MAY BE CONSULTED

J. A. Spender : Fifty Years of Europe. 1933.
J. A. R. Marriott : The Eastern Question. 1924.
Lord Grey of Fallodon : Twenty-Five Years. 1928.
H. Temperley : History of Serbia. 1917.

CHAPTER XXIX

BRITISH AND IRISH DISCORDS

The House of Lords question in England. Increasing social friction. Growth of the social services. The English Labour movement. The Irish question. Nationalism and Ulster. The Irish Parliamentary Party and Sinn Fein. The spectre of Civil War. The Irish Americans. Party passion in England. War preparations. The psychology of peace persists.

THE Liberal party, which was returned from the polls in January, 1906, with a sweeping majority over Conservatives, Nationalists, and Labour men alike, soon found itself confronted with a serious obstacle. All the principal measures on the party programme, for temperance, for the spread of undenominational education, for Welsh disestablishment, for Irish Home Rule, were either thrown out or appeared likely to be fatally blocked, by the House of Lords. It seemed that, under a Constitution which was nominally democratic, no party, however numerous its majority, however fresh its mandate from the constituencies, could pass a Bill against the wishes of the hereditary Chamber. Liberals argued that in a democratic civilization such a veto exercised by such a body was an indefensible anomaly. In the last resort they held that the popular Chamber should decide. When the Lords took the unprecedented step of rejecting the Budget in 1909, Asquith, who had become Prime Minister in the previous year, determined to go to the country and to ask for a mandate to curtail the powers of the Second Chamber. Should the Lords prove obstinate, he was prepared to recommend the Crown to create four hundred peers. It was in the midst of this grave constitutional struggle, and after a vain attempt to bring the parties to accord, that Edward VII died and was succeeded by George V, his second and only surviving son.

May, 1910

The extraordinary vehemence of the passions aroused by the Second Chamber question may seem strange to a generation which has grown accustomed to the Parliament Act of 1911, under the provisions of which the life of a Parliament is cut down to five years and the Lords are deprived of the power of throwing out a Finance Bill or of rejecting any other public Bill thrice passed in the Lower House in the course of two successive sessions. It was not, however, then realized that a government of red revolutionaries would be unlikely to submit to the two years' delay required under the statute, since it could more speedily execute its purpose of ruining the rich by debasing the currency and of undermining order by corrupting the soldiers and police. The Conservatives believed that the Liberal plan of overpowering the resistance of the Second Chamber would open the floodgates to the tides of revolution which they saw surging through the world. They had been thoroughly alarmed by the Budget of 1909 with its plan for taxing the unearned increment from land, and they saw no limit to the fiscal spoliation of future Parliaments. More bitter still was the reflection that with the disappearance of the absolute veto of the Lords the last obstacle to the passage of Irish Home Rule would crumble. That changes of this magnitude should be forced by a Liberal Government which, having lost its majority of 1906 in two successive elections, was now so reduced as to be dependent on Irish and Labour votes, was regarded by the Conservative party as an aggravation of the offence.

There was some excuse for viewing the prospect with alarm. A movement of revolt against the social conditions in which the great mass of mankind was compelled to live was almost everywhere evident. It had led to the establishment of Labour governments in Australia and to a great spread of socialist and syndicalist movements on the continent in Europe. The workers were demanding a better wage and a better life, with more leisure, more amusement, more opportunity. In England class feeling was perhaps less violent than in Germany and in France, but it was growing in intensity as Marxist doctrines penetrated to the young men and with every successive demonstration of the fact that wage advances had to be wrung from the employing class by organized agitation. It is a measure of the economic friction in England between 1906 and 1914 that eleven million working days in a year were lost through industrial unrest.

How to build up a civilization in which want of money should not cut the people off from the amenities and refinements of life was a problem to which every progressive government in western Europe was then addressing itself with varying measures of success. Perhaps nowhere were the means of rational enjoyment so widely diffused as in Germany. Here town planning was a long-established institution. Parks and gardens, cheap theatres and concert rooms, bowling alleys and playgrounds ministered to the enjoyment of the shop assistant, the domestic servant, and the factory-worker. In the provision of inexpensive, accessible, and innocent recreations the Germans were at least a generation ahead of England. But soul-destroying and terrible as had been the results of the industrial revolution in the British factory towns, the latter half of the nineteenth century had witnessed a stirring of the social conscience, which had made a sensible impression on the life of the people. The Ten Hours Act, passed in 1847 under the influence of Lord Shaftesbury in the teeth of the fierce opposition of good men, was a recognition of the fact that human beings had a right to leisure, the Education Acts of 1870 and 1891 that they could claim of the State to be enabled to put that leisure to liberal uses. Yet despite the social legislation of the Victorian period, there were still great arrears to be overtaken. The British workman still passed his life "under a shadow," liable for no fault of his own, such as the failure of some crop in a distant quarter of the world, to be thrown upon the streets. Outside the operation of the Poor Law the State did nothing for the sick, nothing for the old, nothing for the relief of women in labour, nothing for the maintenance of a good standard of health in the child population. The individual exploitation of children, though greatly mitigated by the Factory Acts, was still a serious impediment to the growth of a happy and healthy community. The English country house was famous for its beauty, its comfort, and its elegance. But the great manufacturing towns had been allowed to grow up anyhow and were as desolate and forbidding as the peculiar English combination of rapacious money-making and grim Puritanism was able to make them.

During the eight years before the war a valiant effort was made to lessen these social evils by two able Liberal Administrations. Workmen were insured against sickness, accident, and in some cases also against unemployment. Pensions were given to the old. Three important statutes were passed to shelter the health and promote the welfare of children. By the Sweated Industries Act of 1909 Trade Boards were set up to fix a minimum wage in industries where wages were exceptionally low. The over-long hours of the shop assistant and the coal miner were shortened by Act of Parliament, and a Housing and Town Planning Act was passed. In the hope of increasing the agricultural population, the county councils were empowered to acquire land by compulsory purchase for small holdings and allotments. The Asquith government was not afraid to take lessons in Bismarckian socialism or to import into the statute book the revolutionary principle of the minimum wage.

To the Gladstonian Liberal, nurtured in the Gladstonian *laissez-faire* tradition, no less than to the Conservative, this great expansion of public benevolence and state interference seemed to strike at the roots of moral independence and to menace the financial strength of the country. Far greater was the storm of protest aroused by two other branches of Liberal policy, dealing with organized labour and Irish Home Rule.

While the Socialist parties on the continent came into being before the workers had received any industrial organization, in Britain the process was reversed. Here the trades unions had established themselves as a recognized and, indeed, necessary part of economic machinery long before an active Socialist party had entered the field of politics. In contrast to the French and Italian Syndicalists, who worked for the overthrow of the whole capitalist system by a revolutionary strike, the English Labour movement was a pattern of practical sobriety, preferring near realities to distant dreams, and far more concerned to obtain a minimum wage and an eight-hour day than to embark on violent plans for a wholesale change of society. Thus the Miners' Federation of Great Britain was formed in 1888 to protest against a particular method (the sliding scale) of remunerating labour in mines; while the object of the great dock strike of the following year, led by John Burns and Tom Mann, was to obtain an extra penny an hour for the London dock labourer. Even among those Labour leaders who, like Keir Hardie, had embraced the full socialist programme for the collective ownership of the means of production, distribution, and exchange, it was common ground that the revolution could be accomplished by constitutional means. Parliament was not an enemy to be destroyed, but an ally to be won. In 1888 Keir Hardie stood as Independent Labour candidate for Mid-Lanark, and five years later founded the Independent Labour Party. From that day forward the workers of Britain laid siege to the House of Commons, and the success which attended their campaign was one of the powerful barriers against revolution. A party of Labour men nearly fifty strong, from 1906 onwards, was sufficient to secure from the Liberal Government of the day a large measure of attention to social needs.

It was certainly prudent to make it easy for working men to enter Parliament. Indeed, it was a condition of orderly and constitutional progress that every legitimate grievance should be explored and debated, and that every legitimate political ambition should receive its satisfaction on the floor of the House of Commons. The Liberal Cabinets before the war realized this. They introduced payment of members, and strengthened the trades unions by exempting their funds from liability for torts or civil wrongs, and by empowering them to raise a levy for political purposes from the contributions of their members. These measures were passed only after bitter controversy. It was urged that the trades unions were now to be placed in a position of invidious privilege, which would enable them to exercise undue tyranny. That a new class should be helped to gain power for possibly subversive ends was thought to be a rash and wicked departure from the tried and ancient ways of English parliamentary life.

The schism in Ireland continued fatally and angrily to divide the leading political parties in the English Parliament. The Liberals were spurred on by the Catholic nationalists of the South, the Tories by the fierce Protestants of Ulster. The remedy of the one party was Home Rule, which meant a popish parliament in Dublin; of the other the maintenance of the Union, sweetened by light railways, land purchase, and general social amelioration. Since each Irish faction was implacable, neither consenting to give ground to the other, the good-humoured give and take of British politics was brought up against an abrupt and baffling obstacle. Home Rule refused to be killed by kindness. Nationalism rejected with scorn the idea of partition. Rather than come under a Dublin Parliament the Ulster Protestants, led by Sir Edward Carson, raised volunteers and prepared to fight. Each party had a case which it believed to be founded on the impregnable rock of justice. In Catholic and Celtic Ireland the bitter memory of ancient wrongs was combined with large aspirations for nationality, freedom, and self-determination. It meant nothing to the leaders of the nationalist movement that the practical grievances of the Irish people had been wholly or largely removed, that as far back as 1829 Catholics had been freed from civil and political disabilities, that the Protestant Church had been disestablished, that the peasantry had been given the land, that special measures had been taken to relieve poverty in the congested districts of the west, that eighty-five Irish members, a full complement, sat in Westminster, or that a career was open to talent for Irishmen in every part of Great Britain or the Empire. The pride of the Irishman was revolted by an administration centred within the grim walls of Dublin Castle, guided by an English Lord-Lieutenant and an English Secretary, and protected by the English army at the Curragh. Denouncing these emblems of foreign servitude, the Irish claimed as of right to be governed by an Irish parliament responsible to an Irish electorate. John Redmond and his following at Westminster were prepared to accept a jealously guarded measure for Home Rule within the Empire such as the English liberals were able to commend. Others went further and were not content with an Anglo-Irish parliament acknowledging the suzerainty of the British Crown and fettered by the terms of a British statute. The Gaelic League founded in 1892 made an appeal to the Ireland which lay beyond the British conquest, in mediaeval mists, and while Arthur Griffith, an insurgent remarkable for steadiness and integrity, stood for " Dominion status," a new party, styling itself *Sinn Fein*, dreamed of an Ireland violently severed from its British moorings and recapturing its native soul by the revived use of the Erse language and by a renewed familiarity with the ancient literature of the race. A brilliant constellation of scholars and poets threw a shimmer of aristocratic idealism over a movement which in its lower ranges enlisted the lout, the ruffian, and the gunman.

To all these movements the Ulstermen were inexorably opposed. In their eyes the three great causes, of Protestant education in the schools, of free trade with Britain, and of temperance, would be jeopardized by the legislation of a Dublin parliament. In Home Rule they discerned the first step towards secession, and to the establishment in Ireland of a government permanently hostile to the British connection and anxious to damage British interests in every quarter of the globe. As the fatal hour approached when, under the operation of the Parliament Act, it seemed inevitable that a Home Rule Bill would be placed on the Statute Book, arms were smuggled into Ulster. Then while the dark clouds of civil war were gathering in the sky the King summoned a conference to Buckingham Palace, but the quarrel refused to be resolved. Seldom has the public mind been racked by graver anxieties. Would the government have the nerve to use force against the Ulster volunteers? How could the Irish quarrel fail to divide England? Could England rely upon the support of the army? In July, 1914, it seemed as if the stout fabric of the British Isles was to be rent, as never since the seventeenth century, by civil strife.

It promised to be more than a local and insular quarrel. The Catholic Irish in Ireland were but a small fragment of an Irish population dispersed throughout the world. In every British colony and dominion Irishmen were to be found drinking happiness and freedom to the emerald island, and confusion to its oppressors. In every Australian parliament resolutions were passed in favour of Irish Home Rule. In America the Irish, whose forbears had for the most part emigrated in the middle of the nineteenth century when Irish misery and starvation were at their worst and before any remedial legislation had been applied, were numerous and powerful. They controlled Tammany, a great political machine in New York. They had captured Puritan Boston. They helped to create a strong anti-British opinion in the Middle West. In Chicago alone they numbered more than a hundred dollar-millionaires. It was to conciliate Irish opinion that the Hearst Press, a powerful syndicate of newspapers, consistently blackened British motives and British policy, and that American politicians, seeking for votes in constituencies where the Irish element was strong, were impelled to adopt the popular course of " twisting the British lion's tail." The vigour of the anti-British agitation among the American Irish was not affected by the fact that conditions in Ireland had been vastly improved since " the hungry forties." The memory of those terrible years still dominated the imagination and wrung from the poor Irish serving girls in Boston or New York their hard-won dollars for the Irish cause. It was to America that Parnell applied for financial help against England. It was from America that the Irish nationalists continued to draw their supplies. And as no motive was more powerful with the English Liberals than the desire to remove the Irish obstacle to Anglo-American friendship, so among the consequences to be expected from the frustration of their design none seemed more formidable than the sharp and certain alienation of the American Republic.

An extraordinary political effervescence prevailed in England during the period which lay between the Boer War and the fateful opening years of Armageddon. A spirit of fanaticism invaded a luxurious world which no longer felt itself secure. Pious dissenters broke the law rather than pay the education rate. Well-bred and delicate women smashed windows, scuffled with the police, and by one means and another got themselves sent to prison as a protest against a government which refused them votes. Party spirit ran so high in London over the House of Lords and Ireland that social relations were ruptured. To some Imperialism and tariff reform constituted a religious faith, pressed with sectarian fervour. By others these causes were denounced as synonymous with the exploitation of oppressed peoples by unscrupulous profiteers and the corruption of legislatures by sinister vested interests. The country was full of industrial unrest, the striking habit extending from the mines, the railways, and the factories to the schools. There was even, in the summer of 1914, a mutinous spirit among the officers of the Curragh, who feared that they might be required to march against Ulster. Was the British Empire touching the moment of its decline? Were the Spartan virtues preached by Kipling and derided by Shaw sinking into obsolescence? Indian students in Delhi gleefully noted the successful organization of the Ulster rebellion. To Germans Britain appeared to be a powerful and prosperous country in the throes of a disabling convulsion.

Yet the country had never been better equipped for war. Haldane, a lawyer and a philosopher, who had studied in Göttingen and translated Schopenhauer, had reorganized the army on principles which, while they owed much to German example, were yet adapted to an insular power which might be obliged to take part in continental warfare. To his administrative genius Britain owed the creation of a general staff, of an expeditionary force, complete in all its details, of a Territorial army, and of an Officers' Training Corps. The Navy had similarly been prepared by Sir John Fisher for an eventual conflict with the Germans at sea. Such was its concentration in northern waters that eighty per cent. of its guns were trained upon the German shores. Army, Navy, and the nucleus of a new force in the air, had been brought into correlation by a Committee for Imperial Defence. A war

book of secret instructions to be issued on mobilization prefigured with remarkable accuracy the initial needs of the country
in the event of a continental war.

Of these studied preparations little or nothing was known by
the man in the street. Mr. Lloyd George, " teasing the goldfish "
from his station at the Treasury, Sir Edward Carson defying
John Redmond, Mrs. Pankhurst and her turbulent train of
suffragettes, Bob Smillie and his obstinate miners, seemed to be
the most disturbing figures on the public stage. Otherwise all in
the midsummer of 1914 was peace. The technical preparations
of the war machine had no counterpart in the psychological
education of the public mind. Though some journalists rang the
alarm bell in London, the warning notes were but faintly audible
in the industrial north. Here nothing was nearer to the thoughts
of the average civilian than the summer holiday, and few things
more remote than the prospect of foreign war.

BOOKS WHICH MAY BE CONSULTED

D. C. Somervell : The Reign of King George V. 1935.

J. A. Spender and C. Asquith : The Life of Lord Oxford. 1932.

J. A. Spender : Fifty Years of Europe. 1933.

L. T. Hobhouse : The Labour Movement. 1893.

S. Gwynn : John Redmond's Last Years. 1919.

E. Marjoribanks and Ian Colvin : The Life of Lord Carson. 1932, 1934.

Richard Burdon Haldane : An Autobiography. 1929.

J. Ramsay MacDonald : The Socialist Movement. (Home University
Library.) 1911.

G. Elton : England Arise! 1931.

MENACING TENDENCIES IN GERMANY AND RUSSIA

The predominance of Germany in Europe. German militarism. Hatred of England. The unwisdom of the Kaiser. The British public and the British Cabinet. Efforts to improve relations with Germany. Closer relations with the Dual Alliance. Russia menaced with revolution. The experiment of Russian constitutional government. The weakness of Nicholas. The race between war and revolution.

AT the opening of the twentieth century Germany, by reason of the fixity of her purpose, the concentration of her means, the discipline of her people, and the power of her army, was the central figure in the European drama. Austria and Italy were her satellites. Sweden was an admiring friend. Turkey presented a sphere of growing political and economic influence. A world-wide trade, swiftly increasing in volume and importance and assisted by the Government as if it were an offensive operation of war, carried the German flag into every port. Nothing was left to chance. The state ran the railways, protected the home market, subsidized the exports and the ships which carried them. In military and economic strength no continental state compared with the German Empire. The keys of war and peace were in Berlin. The German Emperor could, in the course of a single morning, upset the delicate equilibrium of Europe.

In this remarkable predominance there were three points of danger. Every valid German male had been, was, or would be a soldier. The presence in the country of a large officer caste and of an immense body of men trained to arms diffused a wide professional interest in the art and technicalities of war. All young Germans expected, many young Germans hoped, that among the experiences which life would offer them would be a war for the Fatherland. Such a war they had been taught to regard not as a crime against civilization, but as a good and necessary medicine in the moral history of states. Accordingly they did not, as did so many English, dread, detest, and despise war as a relic of barbarism dishonouring to human nature. Rather they were disposed to welcome it as offering a supreme test of manhood, and the more readily since, judging from recent enterprises, they believed that the next war would be brief, exhilarating, and triumphant. If such were the feelings of the German general public, it may be imagined with what intensity the officer caste, grown restive under the retarded military promotion of a long peace, and its central organ, the General Staff, pressed for the adoption of spirited and provocative policies.

There was a second point of danger. Of all luxuries of the heart the most perilous is international hatred. The Germans, a naive and emotional people, were successfully encouraged to abound in this sentiment. Many years before the Boer War the popular hatred of England prevailing in Germany was so great as to wreck any prospect of a firm political understanding between the two peoples. Later on German statesmen, like Von Bülow, recognized this with regret, but it was then too late to reverse the engines. The anti-English propaganda had been running for half a century, and since it received a fresh stimulus with every Navy Bill, its work was not easily undone. In Britain, anti-German feeling, though vigorously expressed in certain anti-German organs, was, as well-informed Germans admitted, less general and deep-seated. In wide circles of society it was non-existent.

The character of the Kaiser was a further misfortune. His restless vanity, his political infidelities, his love of melodramatic display, and bursts of hysterical violence, maintained Europe in a high state of tension. The extraordinary series of letters which he exchanged with the Tzar Nicholas (the Willy-Nicky correspondence) shows that he was perfectly capable, while professing a warm friendship with England, of intriguing for a combination of continental powers against her. His public utterances were sometimes those of a madman. When some marines started for China in 1900 he adjured them as follows in terms which rang round the world: "You are about to meet a crafty, well-armed, cruel foe; meet him and beat him! Give no quarter! Take no prisoners! Kill him when he falls into your hands! Even as a thousand years ago the Huns under their King Attila made such a name for themselves as still resounds in terror in legend and fable, so make the name of German resound through Chinese history a thousand years from now." In private conversation he was equally dangerous to his country and to the world. It has been seen how vital it was for the preservation of the general peace that Austria should refrain from provoking Russia to a war over a Balkan difference, and accordingly, how important it was for Germany as Austria's ally to keep a restraining hand on Austrian foreign policy. Yet despite the most plain warning of the aggressive temper which prevailed in Vienna, and the fact that on two separate occasions, in 1908, and again in 1912, Austria had nearly involved Germany in a war, the Kaiser encouraged his ally to believe " that whatever came from the Vienna Foreign Office was a command for him." The record which Count Berchtold, the Austrian Foreign Minister, made of an interview with the Kaiser at the Foreign Office in Vienna on October 26, 1913, brings out in a truly appalling way the reckless unwisdom of this temperamental sovereign. He tells Austria that war between the east and the west is inevitable, that the Slavs were born to serve and not to rule, that the Serbs should be bribed or forced to place their army at the disposal of Austria, that alternatively their capital should be occupied and bombarded. He assures his ally that the Russians are not to be feared, since a German from the Baltic provinces had reported to him an observation of the Tzar to the effect that for the next six years war was impossible for Russia. " As often," says Count Berchtold, " as opportunity offered during our one and a half hours' talk to touch upon our relations as allies, His Majesty ostentatiously used the occasion to assure me that we could count absolutely and completely upon him." How calamitous these counsels and assurances were to Austria, to Germany, and to the world was very shortly to be made apparent.

It is a deep political instinct of the British people to range itself against the strongest European power. But at the opening of 1914 the ordinary Englishman expected nothing so little as that he might be called on to fight in a continental war. Though he had given a general assent to the understanding with France and Russia as likely to promote the cause of peace, and to improve the balance of power in Europe, he knew nothing of the military conventions, or of the international obligations to which his country might in honour be committed. The idea that England would ever be drawn into a general war by reason of a Balkan quarrel would have struck him as wildly fantastic, but the growth of the German navy, with the navy scares which it had from time to time occasioned in his own country, made him uneasy, and he would have felt it to be hardly decent or safe to look on with folded arms while Germany overran Belgium, destroyed France, and occupied the Channel ports. What he had learnt from the newspapers with regard to the German people's ambitions had not encouraged him to hope that, after such triumphs as these, the Germans would be tender to the British Empire. When France and Russia had been prostrated, would it be credible that the victors should refrain from settling their accounts with England? That the mind of the country, as yet innocent and unsuspicious, would thus react to the logic of facts was the calculation of Asquith, Grey, and Haldane, the three men who at this time were most concerned with the shaping of English policy.

It is perhaps a weakness of British Cabinets that they shrink from facing distant and hypothetical questions. What Great Britain would do in the event of a violation of Belgian neutrality, or a German attack on Morocco, or a general war arising out of the Serbian question, was at no time closely examined or narrowly defined in Downing Street. The theory was that the ultimate decision would lie with Parliament, and that Parliament would act according to its understanding of the moral issues, when the occasion arose. The Germans were, however, warned by Haldane in Berlin that a violation of Belgian neutrality would be gravely viewed in England, and Metternich, the capable German Ambassador in London, was given to understand by the same statesman that British public opinion would not permit the destruction of France. It has sometimes been contended that bolder and more emphatic declarations from the British Cabinet would have averted war. There can be no certainty on such a point. From 1912 onwards the real power in Berlin had not rested with the Emperor alone, but in an increasing measure with the General Staff. These able soldiers rated the possible war effort of England on the continent very low. That the English would be troublesome at sea was conceded. But Berlin was of opinion that, were war to break out, the campaign on the western front would be decided in a very few weeks. The presence of a British Expeditionary Force on the soil of France, though it would increase the casualty list, would hardly affect the time table.

Grey did not believe in the inevitable war. His hope was that while remaining faithful to her engagements to Russia and

France, England might notwithstanding succeed in improving her relations with Germany. More than once, but always with unfortunate results, the suggestion was conveyed to the German government that it should enter into a plan for the reduction of naval armaments. On this line no progress was possible. Offers made from London in the honest intention of creating a more friendly feeling between the two peoples were regarded in Berlin as parts of a Machiavellian design for perpetuating the supremacy of the British fleet. The pacific overture of Campbell-Bannerman was viewed in the red light of Admiral Fisher's Jingoism almost "as a threatening ultimatum." The Naval Holiday, or year's truce from shipbuilding, proposed by Mr. Winston Churchill, was stigmatized by the Emperor as "mere humbug." Equally fruitless was the Haldane mission to Berlin in 1912. The Germans were not content with an assurance that England would neither make nor join in an unprovoked attack. They demanded what the British government could not give, a specific pledge of neutrality in the event of war. Nevertheless the British Foreign Secretary persevered in his search for peace. In an atmosphere which had been greatly improved by the success of the Balkan Conference, an agreement between England and Germany with reference to the Baghdad Railway and the eventual distribution of the Portuguese Colonies was nearly completed in the early months of 1914. By that time, however, two steps had been taken, which made it almost inevitable that, were an attack to be made on France, England would be drawn into the war. By an agreement with the British Cabinet (1912), the French had concentrated their fleet in the Mediterranean, a redistribution of forces implying nothing less than the assumption by Great Britain of the naval defence of the Channel coast of France in the event of the outbreak of war. The second step was the authorization two years later of naval conversations with Russia.

Of the future course of that vast military Empire nothing could with certainty be predicted. The Empire of the Tzar was still standing. It had survived the students' riots of 1899, the peasants' revolts of 1902, the calamitous defeat of Russian arms in the Japanese War, and the rebellion of 1905, formidable among other circumstances for a general strike, the most complete so far achieved, and the first experiment in proletarian dictatorship to be tried on European soil. But could it long continue without the tonic of a successful war? Tumultuous forces from within were straining and tearing at the fabric. The student body at the Universities was honeycombed with disaffection. Middle-class liberalism nourished on western culture clamoured for far-reaching constitutional changes. The land hunger of an impoverished peasantry, the heady ferment of Marxist doctrines among the factory workers, the upward thrust of the oppressed nationalities, the bitter cry going up from Siberian exiles and other victims of arbitrary injustice, constituted a menacing body of opposition to the established order.

Assailed from every quarter and deeply discredited by its failure in the Japanese War, Russian autocracy made a pact with revolution. First, it summoned to the capital a central committee of the county councils; then, advancing further on the constitutional path, an elected Parliament or Duma. The news that Russia, the standing model of an unenlightened despotism, had borrowed the parliamentary system of the west caused a thrill of exhilaration among English liberals. There was scant cause for rejoicing. These Russian assemblies, which followed one another in quick succession, did little to mitigate the unpopularity of the Tzar or to assuage the violent clash of contending spirits. Indeed, since the government did not trust the Duma, or the Duma the government, the community failed to receive the benefits to be expected from the confluence of so many able and patriotic men in a legislative assembly. Nicholas was not the man to ride the storm. Like Louis XVI, he was made for private rather than for public life. A feeble though slightly obstinate disposition, a weak intelligence, an incapacity for grasping the size of events or the character of men, were combined in him with a vein of abject superstition, which was more than once harmful to the interests of the state. It was a misfortune for Germany that the Kaiser's personality was so strong; it was equally disastrous to Russia that the last of the Tzars was so weak, and that, though he was possessed of every private virtue, though he was a perfect gentleman, a loyal husband, and an affectionate father, he was incapable either of a firm comprehension of affairs or of a resolute course of action, but disposed to refer to an ignorant religious quack questions which demanded the balanced consideration of a statesman. In the choice of these blind and desperate expedients he was influenced by his tragic and melancholy wife, whose infatuation for Rasputin, monk, rogue, libertine, and impostor, forms a curious chapter of psychology.

The circle of soldiers and diplomatists who stood round the Russian throne were not pacifists. They wished to see Russia, since she had been forced to retreat in the Far East, established one day, as the result of a victorious war, in the great warm-water port of the Bosphorus. The foreign policy of the Tzardom had been aggressive in the past. It was aggressive still. For the moment, however, there was no urgent desire for war. The railways awaited development. If no intolerable affront were put upon the Serbs, the Russian government would maintain the peace. A serious strike in the St. Petersburg factories which broke out on July 8, 1914, and led to barricades and fighting in the streets, seemed to show that in the race between war and revolution it was revolution which would outstrip its rival and just pass the post.

BOOKS WHICH MAY BE CONSULTED

G. P. Gooch : Germany.   (Nations of the Modern World Series.)   1925.
Von Bülow : Memoirs.   1931-2.
J. A. Spender : The Last Fifty Years.
D. Lloyd George : War Memoirs.   1933.
Lord Grey of Fallodon : Twenty-Five Years.   1928.
Lord Oxford and Asquith : Memories and Reflections.   1928.
Winston Churchill : The World Crisis.   1923.
Paléologue : L'Empire des Tsars.

CHAPTER XXXI

THE OUTBREAK OF WAR

Development of a high common civilization in Europe. The murder of the Archduke. The Austrian ultimatum. Austria declares war on Serbia. Sazonov. The war responsibilities of Germany, Austria, and Russia. English feeling. The violation of Belgian neutrality. The responsibilities of Capitalism. General lack of Pacifism. Austria alone, supported by the German General Staff, wants war in 1914. The surprises of the Great War.

By the beginning of the twentieth century the peoples of Europe, save for a savage patch in the Balkans, had reached an unprecedented level of comfort and civilization. Representative institutions, though in many parts of the continent ill rooted, ill practised, and ill understood, were universal. The belief that the world was moving towards unity seemed to be growing in strength, despite the militant and nationalist movements of the time. By a unique exertion of provident diplomacy the concert of Europe had divided the African continent without a conflict between the imperial and colonizing powers. Recourse to arbitration for the settlement of international questions was becoming more frequent. The foundation of an international Postal Union (1875), of a common system of copyright, and of an International Office of Public Health (1907) are but examples of the manner in which governments were tending increasingly to co-operate in the management of their common affairs. It seemed as if statesmen had now at last learned the lesson that politics is the art of human happiness. Laws for the protection of the weaker members of the community had been passed in all legislatures. Unjust privileges had been eliminated from the budgets, mediaeval barbarity from the penal codes. In most parts of Europe education was general and progressive. Preventive medicine had greatly prolonged the duration of human life. In all the more advanced countries death from starvation had disappeared from the catalogue of social evils.

From one evil European society seemed to be effectively delivered. Though the physical force at the disposal of governments had been vastly increased by the march of science, there was a refreshing absence of intellectual coma. The Continent was awake from end to end. No writers had a greater vogue than those who assailed the existing order of society and essayed a revaluation of accepted values. In the Victorian age Matthew Arnold had employed his delicate and fastidious gift of ridicule upon the middle-class Philistine. Critics more powerful than Matthew Arnold occupied the stage at the turn of the century. Ibsen and Tolstoi, Nietzsche and Anatole France, Bernard Shaw and Wells spoke to wider audiences upon bolder themes. There was never a time when Europe was made more alive to its deficiencies or was more variously and brilliantly advised as to the means for their removal.

Electrical science had showered gifts upon mankind: light, heat, traction, the telegraph, the telephone, the cinema. The railway had been supplemented by the bicycle, the motor-car, and the aeroplane. Access to literature good and bad had been improved by the growth of public libraries, by the competitive enterprise of publishers, and by the advance in the mechanics of printing. A cheap newspaper press satiated the curiosity of a public whose intellectual discipline had ended with the primary school. But what, perhaps, was a more striking feature of the age immediately preceding the Great War was the growth of a belief that poor working men and women had the right to have enjoyments placed within their reach by contributions from the public purse. Never since the fall of the Roman Empire had public authority been so careful to provide for the common amusements of the people. Never had the human appetite for pleasure received such general satisfaction. Never before were the intellectual contributions of one country so quickly communicated to others. The music of Brahms, the plays of Ibsen, the novels of Tolstoi and Anatole France, the light operas of Gilbert and Sullivan, the popular songs of the English music-hall, were part of a general European stock. The obstacle of language was serious. Otherwise there was reason to hope that, given a century of peace, Europe, like the Aristotelian city, might be made one through the forces of culture and education.

This ascending process of civilized well-being was suddenly fractured by a crime. On June 28, 1914, Archduke Franz Ferdinand, heir to the Austrian throne, was shot by Gavrilo Princip, a young Bosnian fanatic, at Sarajevo. It was as if, at a moment of acute political tension, the Prince of Wales had been murdered in

A HISTORY OF EUROPE

Ireland. A storm of indignation swept through Austria-Hungary, where it was believed by many, and thought politic to assume by others, that the crime, though committed on Bosnian soil, was the work of the Black Hand and prompted or connived at by officials of the Serbian Government.[1]

Though a local enquiry conducted by Austrian agents found no direct proofs of the complicity of the Serbian Government, the Austrians were undoubtedly entitled to require a full and comprehensive enquiry into a conspiracy which certainly had roots in the Serbian kingdom as well as in Bosnia. Such an enquiry the Serbs would have been wise in their own interests to have instituted, but, whether by reason of the general election then proceeding, or because the Serbian Cabinet appears to have had information that some attempt was likely to be made upon the Archduke and to have failed to transmit the rumour to Vienna, nothing of the kind was done, and while the press on both sides of the Danube exchanged violent hostilities, opinion in Vienna, fortified by assurance of German support, moved rapidly to the need of war. On July 23 an ultimatum was sent to Serbia, of which Sir Edward Grey said that he "had never seen one state address to another independent state a document of so formidable a character." It was an ultimatum which, since it involved the abdication of Serbian independence, was intended to be declined and to lead to war, and it was issued at a moment when Poincaré, the President of the French Republic, and Viviani, the Prime Minister, were on the sea returning from a visit to the Tzar. Berlin stood behind Vienna. The German steamship lines were warned, and St. Petersburg, Paris, and London were notified that any interference between Austria and Serbia would be followed by "incalculable consequences."

It may be imagined what consternation this intelligence produced in the Chancelleries of Europe. At once the impression was created that this murder in the Bosnian capital was being seized as a pretext by the Austrian and German governments to deprive Serbia of its independence and perhaps to force on a general war with Russia and France before the Russian railways were ready. The impression was deepened when, after Serbia had accepted seven out of the ten points of the Austrian ultimatum,

[1] There is reason for thinking that the murder of King Alexander and Queen Draga in 1903 and the murder of the Archduke in 1914 were both the work of " Avis," the leader of the Black Hand.

Francis Joseph was nevertheless, on the advice of Count Berchtold, his Foreign Minister, persuaded to sign the declaration of war against the Serbs. The Austrian army, which had long been thirsting for war against the " nation of assassins," did not intend to be balked of its prey. *July 30, 1914*

It was not to be expected that Russia would look on unmoved while the Serbs were wiped off the Balkan map. Sazonov, the Foreign Minister, a man of too excitable a temperament for so grave a post, had conceived great alarm at the designs of the two central powers in the Near East. A German prince had been sent to rule in Albania, a German general to organize the Turkish army in Constantinople. If the Serbs were laid prostrate, what was to prevent the establishment of a German Caliphate running from Hamburg to Baghdad? Sazonov had little love for the Austrians. In spite of the fact that Russian arms had helped to establish Francis Joseph on the throne of Hungary in 1849, the Austro-Hungarian monarchy had crossed the Russian path again and again. While, therefore, he was anxious to find some means of preserving the peace, he was accessible to gusts of warlike temper and far too weak a man to resent the pressure of the soldiers, who, after the news of the bombardment of Belgrade came to Russia, forced a partial and then a general mobilization. *July, 1914*

The Kaiser had been naturally fired with indignation at the crime at Sarajevo. The Archduke was his personal friend. The assassination was a hideous, inexcusable crime. It was, nevertheless, most unfortunate that in his early communications with Vienna the Kaiser abounded without reserve in denunciations of Serbia and in protestations of his desire for her punishment.

The *Nibelung* loyalty to his ally on which he prided himself was the worst of counsellors at a crisis when the quality needed was not romance but cool common sense. In view of the character of the Austrian ultimatum, which involved the obliteration of a state previously independent, it could not be contended that here was a quarrel which could be isolated and in which no other country was concerned. The best service which the German Government could have rendered to Europe would have been to exercise a moderating influence on Austria. It is the gravamen against them that they did not begin to exercise any influence of the kind until it was too late and the Austrian military machine was in full motion. They neither supported Sir Edward Grey in his suggestion that the time limit to Serbia should be extended, *July 31, 1914* nor did they accept his proposal that the question might be considered by a conference in London. Throughout its intemperate proceedings the Austro-Hungarian government was given to understand that it could count upon the support of the German army. The one power in Europe which could have ensured peace refused its co-operation in the endeavours which were made to obtain it. The German government, which might have prevented the war, took the responsibility of declaring it. As for the German people, they had been so long taught that they were encircled by the Machiavellian concert of their enemies that they found no difficulty in believing that they were now called upon to defend the Fatherland from a wicked attempt to destroy it. More particularly were they apprehensive of the vast Russian armies on their eastern frontier. It was idle to suppose that in the fierce excitement of the moment they would recall the many occasions in recent history when their own government had sought to obtain its diplomatic ends by threat of war or the apprehensions which had been excited in foreign lands by its imperialism.

A yet greater responsibility rests upon Count Berchtold, the Austrian Foreign Minister. Although it was known in Vienna by July 13 that complicity in the crime of Sarajevo could not be brought home to the Serbian Government, he persisted in his policy of a punitive campaign, even in spite of the Serbian concessions, and even when it was clear beyond doubt that Russia would support the Serbian cause. That Austria had much to fear from Serbian revolutionary propaganda within the Empire may be admitted. It is difficult, however, to believe that she had anything to apprehend from the military power of a small country already shaken by two severe wars and faced with the troublesome problem of assimilating her new subjects in the south. Reckless of consequences, she chose the occasion of the odium excited by the Sarajevo crime to settle once and for all with this small but highly annoying neighbour state.

Had a strong and wise sovereign been seated on the Russian throne, it is possible that he might, at the risk of forfeiting the sympathies of the Balkan Slavs, have faced the unpopularity of deserting Serbia in her hour of need. He might have argued that Russia had as much territory on her hands as she knew how to govern; that foreign conquest could bring her nothing which would add to her strength; and that to waste blood and treasure for the sake of Serbia was a piece of idle quixotry likely to bring the fabric of the Empire to the ground. Nicholas, however, was not a strong man. A spirit of mystic resignation replaced in him, as in so many Russians, a capacity for sustained and energetic thought. Ingeminating peace and invoking the Hague Tribunal, he nevertheless permitted the General Staff, always eager for action, to extract from him the permission to order a general mobilization of the Russian army before Germany had taken the step of declaring war. In justification it may be said that his government had urged the Serbs to make those very concessions to Austria which the Kaiser, on first reading them, declared to be sufficient to avoid war.

England had striven consistently for peace during these fateful eleven days when the fortunes of Europe were at stake. The charge of war guilt certainly cannot be brought home to her. It was, however, inevitable, though the country did not realize it at the time, that on the outbreak of a war forced upon France, England, rather than witness the destruction of her ally, would be drawn into the struggle. Yet so little were the English people attuned to the idea of war, that, but for the German invasion of Belgium, cabinet, parliament, and country would have been divided. The unprovoked violation of an innocent country whose neutrality Prussia had solemnly guaranteed settled the mind of the Asquith Cabinet, dispersed the doubts of the Labour party in parliament, and satisfied the people that the war was justly undertaken. The Irish parliamentary party, led by John Redmond, were inspired by the affront put upon a small Catholic people by a powerful neighbour to offer its services in the German war.

The idea that the Great War was caused by the capitalists is a baseless fable. Everywhere, save perhaps in some armament centres, the leading business men were aghast at the prospect of a rupture of the peace. Yet neither they nor the socialist parties were strong enough to arrest the march of the great military machines. When the crisis came, international capital was as powerless as international labour. The socialists, forgetting their views of universal peace, voted the war credits in Berlin and Paris. A fierce and passionate nationalism over-mastered all other forces.

In no European country had policy been conceived on pacifist lines. Every Foreign Office cherished dreams which might be realized in war. France wanted Alsace-Lorraine. Germany wanted more colonies, a larger navy, and hegemony in the Near

36

East. Austria wanted the subjection of Serbia and a port at Salonika. Russia wanted the Bosphorus and Dardanelles. Serbia had designs on Bosnia and Herzegovina, Italy on Trieste and the Trentino, Roumania on Transylvania, to be obtained from Hungary, or Bessarabia, to be wrested from the Russians. Given a general war, all these ambitions would burst out in flame; but war was not inevitable or by any means generally desired. Neither France, nor Russia, nor England, nor Serbia desired war in 1914. There was, indeed, only one government which was wholly and entirely bent on breaking the peace in that year. This was Austria, encouraged and supported by the sinister and over-mastering force of the general staff in Berlin, which for months before the murder of the Archduke had been pressing upon the German Government the desirability of precipitating war without delay.

The stunning news that Europe was at war produced in the first instance an extraordinary quickening in the wheels of life. Everyone was busy, excited, exhilarated, hungry for new forms of energy and usefulness. The internal quarrels which had seemed so important a few days earlier suddenly died down before the grave danger to the national life. The strikers returned to their work in St. Petersburg, the suffragettes ceased to annoy in London. In Italy Benito Mussolini, who had just led a formidable revolutionary strike, urged intervention. Every nation believed that its cause was just, that it was oppressed by a malignant enemy bent on its destruction, and that the survival of a moral order in the world was dependent on the victory of its own side. The Germans, who regarded themselves as the exponents of the highest form of civilization as yet attained upon the planet, appeared to their antagonists to have exchanged the humane ideals of an earlier German generation for the Prussian doctrine of naked and unscrupulous force. The flames of the burning library at Louvain cast a lurid light upon the pretensions of the missionary of culture.

To few was it given to forecast the character or duration of the struggle which was opening in that golden August weather. The general impression was that it would be short and sharp and concluded by the clash of the forces by land and sea which had been so carefully prepared.

None of the governing factors of the war had been foreseen. Nobody anticipated that nearly all the world would be drawn in, or that it would be a war of peoples waged to the point of extermination, or again the degree to which science, mechanism, and industrial power would shape its character and determine its result. A Polish writer of the last century came nearest to the truth when he pictured the war of the future as a stationary process of deadly attrition in which that people would survive which could longest provide itself with food.[1]

The politicians were no more prescient than the peoples. The passiveness of Belgium, the neutrality of England, Italy, and Roumania had been confidently assumed in the German war plans. It was calculated in Berlin that the German armies would be in Paris in a fortnight and back on the eastern front in six weeks. In London the general staff made provision for four battles of three days each. Well-informed English politicians in the first winter of the war were inclined to the opinion that peace could hardly be delayed beyond the ensuing August for lack of finance. Alone among prominent men, Kitchener, the new Secretary of State for War, took a true measure of the difficulties, prophesying that his country must be prepared for a war of three years. An early estimate that Great Britain would be presented with a bill for a thousand million sterling seemed staggering, but the figure named was but one-tenth of the ultimate total.

It followed that the essential and distinguishing character of this new type of war was not at once apprehended. In England at the outset the popular cry was "Business as usual," the idea being that by carrying on its ordinary avocations as if nothing particular was happening the country could best help to finance the war effort of its allies. By degrees, however, it became apparent that in this clash of peoples the distinction between combatant and non-combatant disappeared, and that only from the fullest possible utilization of the human and material resources of a country was success to be expected. The moral results were truly astonishing. Never have armies suffered such terrific losses without yielding ground. Never have civilian populations thrown themselves with greater ardour and devotion into work for their country. Women showed themselves as heroic as men, in the munition factories, in the clearing stations and hospitals, or carrying their lives in their hands in the service of information. The

---

[1] Jean de Bloch. *La Guerre. Traduction de l'ouvrage russe " La Guerre future aux points de vue technique, economique et politique."* Paris, Guillaumin, 1898-1900. 6 vols.

idle notion that education and urban life were inimical to courage was shown to be ill-founded. Every record for valour previously established was here surpassed. Nor was anything more impressive than the superb social discipline which enabled the Germans so long to defy the depressing effects of the naval blockade and to present a solid military front to the enemy.

BOOKS WHICH MAY BE CONSULTED

Lord Grey of Fallodon : Twenty-Five Years. 1928.
Lord Oxford and Asquith : Memories and Reflections. 1928.
J. A. Spender : Fifty Years of Europe. 1933.
J. W. Headlam-Morley : The History of Twelve Days. 1915.

CHAPTER XXXII

THE WAR: FIRST PHASE

The German war plan. Early German successes. Joffre. Tannenberg and the Masurian Lakes. The allied victory on the Marne. The race for the Channel Ports. The defence of the Ypres salient. Trench warfare. Britain's expanding war effort. The British Navy. Easterners and Westerners. The Dardanelles. Italy joins the Allies. The Italian constitution. The Falkenhayn plan. Spectacular German triumphs in the East. Repulse of Allied attacks on the German front, in the West. Verdun and the Somme, 1916. The tanks. The success of Brussilov. Roumania enters the war. German conquest of Roumania. Economic hardships of the Central Powers and the naval blockade.

To Moltke, Chief of the German Staff and the mediocre inheritor of a great name, belonged the military initiative. His plan, which was founded on a design elaborated by Count Schlieffen, the Chief of the Staff in 1905, was, while guarding the eastern frontier with a few divisions, to put France out of action by a wide turning movement through Belgium and Luxemburg, and, when this had been done, to throw the full force of the German army against the Russians. It was confidently expected in Berlin that the French, even if stiffened by a British contingent of a hundred thousand men, as allowed for under the Schlieffen plan, could offer no effectual resistance to the impact of so great a force as four-fifths of the army of the German *Reich.* "Remember," said the Kaiser on two separate occasions to Sir Edward Grey, "we can be in Paris in a fortnight."

Nor was this a vain and idle boast. In every particular of discipline, equipment, and skill the German army of 1914 was the most formidable instrument of war which the world has ever seen. It numbered four million three hundred thousand fully trained and one million partially trained men. Its heavy artillery was overwhelming. The mobilization was a work of art. Thousands of trains, running to time, deposited their human burden on the long railway sidings which had been specially constructed on the Belgian and French frontier in anticipation of "the day." Though the resistance of Liège was an unexpected obstacle costing perhaps 40,000 casualties to the attackers, it did not seriously derange the time-table. The great army of field

greys flowed on, reaching Brussels on August 20, demolishing
with heavy howitzers fortresses such as Namur and Maubeuge
from which a long resistance had been expected, masking Antwerp, into which the Belgian army had retreated, by two army
corps, and pushing before it the French and English forces, who
in all too insufficient numbers and with an all too insufficient
equipment of machine guns, had endeavoured at Charleroi, at
Mons, and at Le Cateau (August 26) to offer an opposition to its
advance. On September 2 the army of Von Kluck, on the extreme
right of the German turning movement, was approaching Paris.
The government of France had fled to Bordeaux. The English
expeditionary force under Sir John French was pursuing its retreat. It seemed as if the fall of the French capital and the
successful conclusion according to plan of the first part of the
German military programme could only be a matter of days.

The French army was commanded by Joffre, a stout, good-
humoured man of inelastic mind, deliberate habits, imperturb-
able optimism, and steadfast will. The higher command had
committed every possible mistake. It had made no adequate
provision for the defence of the north-east. It had expected that
the Germans would come through the Ardennes. It had grossly
under-estimated their numbers through failing to anticipate that
reserve divisions would march with the field army, and, despite
the changes which had come over warfare through the invention
of machine guns and barbed wire, it had instilled into the only
too willing ears of its officers the disastrous doctrine of a fiery
offensive. Through these errors the French army had suffered in
the first fortnight of the war staggering losses. But though its left
had been driven back so far as to expose Paris to the enemy, the
right had held firm. Before Toul, Nancy, and Verdun the second
and first French armies successfully maintained their ground.

Meanwhile far away on the eastern frontier the cumbrous war-
machine of the Russian Empire had been urged into a precipitate
advance in the hope of relieving the menacing pressure upon
France. While the Grand Duke Nicholas drove forward into
Galicia against the Austrians, the armies (the one marching north
and the other south of the Masurian Lakes) of Rennenkampf
and Samsonov invaded East Prussia, spreading violent currents of
alarm through the length and breadth of Germany. Then all of
a sudden news came to Berlin of victories brilliant and complete
beyond all expectation. The army of Samsonov had been annihi-

lated at Tannenberg (August 25-31); the army of Rennenkampf
was heavily defeated at the Masurian Lakes (September 8-15). An
old Hanoverian general, who by reason of his local knowledge
had been forced out of retirement, and having for chief of the
staff a younger officer who had sprung into prominence at Liège,
had wrought this miracle, and by a series of incomparable
manoeuvres saved East Prussia. That they had worked upon a
plan supplied them by another[1] was not then known. The names
of Hindenburg and Ludendorff became from that moment talismans of victory.

Yet complete as was the catastrophe to their aims among the
drear Masurian woods and swamps, the Russians achieved at
least part of the purpose which their precipitate and quixotic
advance was intended to secure. To stem their onset two army
corps were transferred from the western front, whose presence in
the northern plain of France during the first week of September
might have converted a German defeat into a crowning victory.

For, turning back upon his pursuers in the valley of the Marne,
Joffre (September 4-9) won the decisive battle of the war. That
he was helped to do so by the counsels of Galliéni, the military
Governor of Paris, or by circumstances which he did not himself
control, such as the fact that the Germans had outmarched their
supplies, or that Von Kluck, in response to a request from the
second German Army, turned suddenly south-eastward to close
up a gap and thus offered a flank to an assault launched from
Paris, or that a German Staff officer gave the order for retreat in
the belief (widely accredited in England) that a Russian army
was descending on Belgium, does not seriously detract from his
credit. It is the business of the general to accept the good ideas
of his friends and to profit by the mistakes of his enemies. Only
a man of exceptional quality, after a retreat so long and humiliating, would have faced round, reformed his armies, and by a
properly concerted movement over a wide front suddenly inspired
his troops to victory.

Having failed to capture Paris, the Germans, by a strange
oversight, neglected to occupy, when it would have been easy for
them to do so, the Channel ports. Military criticism has been
busy with the reputation of Sir John French, a mercurial leader
of cavalry, who after Le Cateau would, but for the personal intervention of Kitchener, have withdrawn the British army from the

---

[1] Colonel Hoffmann, Head of the Operations Department.

line to refit. It should be remembered, however, that when the Germans had retreated from the Marne to the Aisne, and had then resisted all attempts to dislodge them, French of his own accord took a momentous decision. Skilfully moving the British army to the Channel (October), he outstripped the enemy and in a series of desperate engagements round the ancient Cloth Hall of Ypres repulsed attempt after attempt to pierce his lines. Few actions have been more tenaciously fought than the first and

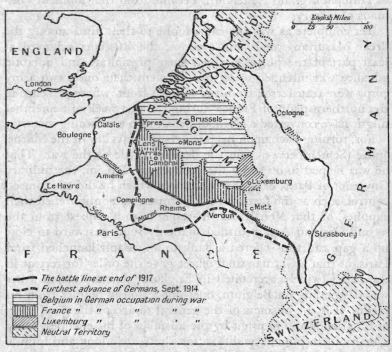

THE WESTERN FRONT, 1914-18.

Oct.-Nov., 1914 April-May, 1915

second battles of Ypres. Few have been more important in their results. Had the Germans been able to establish themselves in Calais and Boulogne, the quickest line of communication between France and England would have been cut and the whole plan of co-operation between the two countries seriously and perhaps fatally disordered.

The magnitude of the loss on either side attests the gravity of the issue. The old professional army of England and the young promise of the German universities withered away in the grim autumn and spring struggles for the Channel ports. But while the sacrifice of the allies, French and English, was not vainly made, the Germans had squandered a reserve of potential officers who could not be replaced, and in the last year of the war were greatly missed.

On the left of the British trenches the army of Belgium, under the command of King Albert, lined the Yser, and, partly protected by inundation, withheld until the end of the war a narrow strip of Belgian territory from the invaders. The Belgian army, albeit small and severely depleted by casualties, rendered an essential service. A little English force thrown into Antwerp in the nick of time had enabled it to withdraw from the beleaguered city and freed it to take its share in the defence of the ports.

By the winter it was clear that a profound change had come over the situation on the western front. A war of movement had given place to a war of attrition, a thrust at the vitals of France to a slow and exhausting siege of Germany. In long lines of trenches defended by wire entanglements and extending from the Channel to the Vosges the rival armies watched and fought, unable, despite prodigies of courage, to make more than the slightest dint in the rigid contours of the front. In this terrible and exacting duel the Germans possessed great initial advantages. They were more numerous and better trained; they had more machine guns and howitzers, more aeroplanes and flares, and they held the higher ground. They controlled the economic resources of Belgium and the rich industrial region of north-eastern France, containing 80 per cent. of its coal and nearly all its iron. Their flanks, resting on the sea and the Alps, could not be turned.

To the French and British governments it at once became apparent that only if a British land army far larger than the six divisions which had originally been thought sufficient could be raised and thrown into the battle would the balance be restored. Kitchener, the Secretary of State for War, called upon the country for volunteer armies. He contemplated seventy divisions to be formed within three years. His commanding figure and unique prestige secured for his message a special authority. From the first volunteers flocked to the colours, until the Kitchener armies, as they were sometimes called, reached a total of three million men. Even this figure proved to be insufficient. Conscription was resorted to in 1916, but it is doubtful whether any other country could have raised by volunteer effort so large a body of young men for service beyond the sea in a dull and murderous war. While these new armies were receiving their training and awaiting their equipment the chief burden of maintaining the western front lay upon the *poilus* of France.

Though she had been wholly unprepared for any such great military effort on land as was now demanded, Britain was mistress of the sea. Her fleet, which had been collected for manoeuvres in July, and by the wise prevision of Mr. Winston Churchill kept together when the manoeuvres were over, had taken up its war stations at Scapa Flow and Rosyth, and was supported in its operations by a large commercial navy most gallantly and skilfully manned. The tasks laid upon the Fleet were fully comprehended by the British Admiralty and by Jellicoe, the naval commander-in-chief. They were, in brief, the safe convoy of troops to any quarter of the world in which they might be required, the destruction of German ocean-going cruisers and overseas trade, the seizure of the German colonies, and the interception of food and munitions of war destined for the enemy countries. All these functions the British navy unobtrusively accomplished, with some assistance in Pacific, Indian and Mediterranean waters from Japan and France, and in the last stages of the war from the well-trained fleet of the United States.

The consideration of British strategy on land was necessarily affected by naval predominance. Alone among the combatant powers Britain was free to employ her armies in any quarter of the globe. No sooner, therefore, did it appear that there was likely to be a military deadlock in the west than a party grew up in the Cabinet which advocated the employment of British forces in the eastern theatre of the war. It was the argument of the easterners that the German lines in the west were almost impregnable, that in the endeavour to pierce them the attacking force always suffered far more heavily than the defenders, and that the true strategy of the *Entente* Powers was to remain on the defensive in the west, where a large application of men and munitions was comparatively ineffective, allowing the Germans to attack there if they thought it worth while to do so, and to seek a decision in the east, where the appearance of a comparatively small Anglo-French force might rally the Balkan peoples to an effective onslaught on the Austrian Empire or establish a safe channel for the munitioning of Russia. Of this eastern school of opinion Mr. Lloyd George and Mr. Churchill were powerful advocates.

The whole force of the French higher command was naturally thrown into the opposite scale. To a Frenchman no object was more imperative than the liberation of the national soil from the invader. The more guns and men England could pour into France, the lighter would be the French burden, and the speedier, so it seemed, the French release. Sir John French and Sir Douglas Haig, the steadfast Scottish cavalry officer who succeeded him in the English command, shared these opinions, and deprecated the dispersion of English war effort. In common with Joffre, they entertained the dazzling hope that a break through, with a great cavalry charge to thrust home the victory, was always possible and sometimes imminent. With the exception of Kitchener, most highly placed soldiers at home were of the same opinion, and pinned their faith to the western front.

Yet in the east an extraordinary event called for the attention of the *Entente* Powers. Russia was the secular foe of Turkey, yet in a war in which Russia, the enemy of the Porte, was co-operating with France and England, its immemorial friends, the Sultan would have been well advised to persevere in a neutral course. From such counsels he was eventually driven by the prestige and pressure of Enver Pasha, by the appearance before the walls of Constantinople of two German cruisers, the *Goeben* and the *Breslau*, by German largesse widely distributed, and by the vexation occasioned by the detention in British docks of two unfinished Turkish ships of war, the cost of which had been defrayed by public subscription. The final hesitations of a tremulous court were overcome by a masterpiece of craft and audacity. The great Russian port of Odessa was bombarded (October 28, 1914) by the *Goeben* and the *Breslau*, which had been fictitiously sold to the Turkish government, the more swiftly and surely to involve it in war. In mid-November, 1914, the Ottoman Empire had entered the struggle on the German side.

The consequences were momentous and far-reaching. Russia, though almost inexhaustible in man-power, was deficient in the industrial mechanism necessary for the nourishment of a modern war. By the autumn of 1914 she had already exhausted her reserves of ammunition and was only able to supply from her own resources one-third of the daily allowance required for the troops.

And now she was faced with the burden of a new campaign against the Turks in the Caucasus. On January 2, 1915, Kitchener received an appeal from the Grand Duke Nicholas for assistance to relieve the pressure on the Caucasus front. It was decided to send an expedition to the Dardanelles. With the Dardanelles blocked, Russia might be forced to fade out of the war for lack of supplies; with the Dardanelles opened, not only could shells and guns be poured into the country at every season of the year, but its discouragement might be arrested, its purpose confirmed, and the tactics of its armies perchance improved by the military lessons of the western war. Other considerations, hardly less attractive, pointed in the same direction. A British fleet before Constantinople would cut the Turkish army in two, open a way to the Danube, and make the lavish harvests of southern Russia available for the allies. The first and most striking diversion of military and naval effort was accordingly an expedition to the Dardanelles. In the background vast political and military issues began to take shape: the winning of all the Christian Balkan Powers to the allied cause, the possible emancipation of the Arab world from the Turks, the possible insurgence of the Moslem world against Britain, the destruction of British power in India and Egypt, or the end of the long Ottoman rule over the non-Ottoman peoples in Europe and Asia. The campaign in the Gallipoli peninsula was more than an expedient for putting new heart into Russia. It was the first strong blow struck in an eastern campaign, which, while failing of its primary object, so developed as to bring the Ottoman Empire to the ground.

In the execution of this hazardous enterprise there were many flaws. An attempt to force the straits by the fleet alone was foiled by an undetected minefield and unwisely, as some good sailors think, not renewed. The enemy were therefore fully warned and prepared when, after prolonged and avoidable delays, Sir Ian Hamilton was in a position to effect a landing on the peninsula. Thereupon the immense difficulties of the British undertaking declared themselves to every eye. The peninsula, which is bare of trees, slopes gradually downwards to the coast, providing almost everywhere a perfect field of fire for the defenders. The attacking force, which was too small, and entirely dependent for its supplies upon the fleet, was confronted with every obstacle which German science and Turkish diligence could supply. Nevertheless, not only were landings effected under withering fire at five

Mar. 18, 1915

points on the southern tip of the peninsula, but for many months the best part of the Turkish army was put to serious strain in defending its positions. There was even a moment when, after a substantial reinforcement, success seemed to be within reach of the British. On August 6 a new landing was made at Suvla Bay, which found the Turk wholly unprepared. Then a swift and vigorous advance might have given to Stopford's troops the Ana-farta ridge, which was the key to the position. But the oppor-tunity was missed. While forty-eight precious hours were lost by his assailants, Mustapha Kemal Bey, a young Turkish officer, collected a sufficiency of troops and, rushing to the vital point, saved the situation.

The withdrawal of the British forces from the peninsula effected, contrary to every prognostication, without the loss of a man (December 18, 1915–January 8, 1916) was a brilliant example of the naval efficiency which throughout had distinguished the course of the campaign. The enterprise, which had cost 120,000 British casualties, had failed of its main object. The attempt to open the southern waterway to Russia had been blocked by the stubborn resistance of the Germans and the Turks. Nevertheless, it would be rash to assume that the great sacrifice of British life and treasure on that wind-swept peninsula had no compensations for the allied cause. So long as the British, with the aid of mag-nificent contingents from Australia and New Zealand, were battering at the Turkish gateway, Russia had the strongest of all motives for prosecuting the war. The allies had promised her Constantinople, and by a miraculous twist of fortune Britain was engaged in a campaign which, if successful, would put the prize in her hands. Compared with such a gift no other gain to be expected from successful war counted with the Russian people. They cared little for Serbia; they had no appetite for western conquests, and were soon disabused of the belief that they could beat the Germans. But if Great Britain could have taken Tzari-grad, their huge losses in the Masurian Lakes, in Poland, and in Galicia were made good. So, though the Dardanelles expedition may be defended as having occupied and wasted the best divisions of the Turkish army, its most important military consequence was to keep Russia in the war.

Soon after the Gallipoli landing (May 24), Italy, having long balanced the issue, finally obeyed the call of ancient policies and came into the war against Austria, a much divided and unprepared nation. The lawless invasion of Belgium, though it made a sensible impression upon the generous Italian temperament, was less efficacious than the appetite for the Trentino and Trieste, for that "unredeemed" Italy which Austria declined to concede, but which the allies undertook to promise as the guerdon of Italian help. The secret treaty of London (April 26, 1915), which bound Italy to its new allies, was afterwards denounced as a sin against the gospel of self-determination, for it proposed to transfer the German Tyrolese to an alien master without their consent and in defiance of their wishes. Such, however, was the price of Italian help, and such the deviations from ideal justice to which necessity, knowing no law, constrained the democratic governments of London and Paris.

The effect of the Italian intervention was at once to open out a new field of struggle and anxiety for the Austrian army. If the Italians failed to pierce through to Vienna, they fought a long and even fight with their antagonists in the Alps, in the valley of Isonzo, and on the stony plateau of the Carso, losing in these encounters 280,000 men; and though afterwards they were routed at Caporetto and fled in such confusion as to suggest a national breakdown, there was yet in the Italian government and people a reserve of will and courage which even that great disaster was unable to destroy. Helped with a timely stiffening of French and English divisions, the Italian army under a new leader stood its ground on the Piave, and, gathering force and confidence from successive encounters, ultimately, in the last months of the war (October 30, 1918), delivered upon the field of Vittorio Veneto the decisive punishment to a crumbling and demoralized army, which brought the Austrian Empire to the ground. To this national triumph the Italians with pardonable exaggeration are wont to attribute not only the downfall of the Habsburgs, but the final victory of the allied cause. For a service so tremendous, and for losses greater in proportion to the population than those borne by any other continental Power, they opine that they received at the Peace a grudging and insufficient reward.

Meanwhile, on September 14, 1914, while Italy's attitude was still uncertain, Moltke, a broken and defeated man, gave place to the brilliant Falkenhayn. The strategy of the new chief of staff was at once bold and flexible. Though his autumn offensive in the west had failed of its main objectives, Falkenhayn was satisfied that the grey armies were now so well posted and entrenched in France and Flanders that they might be relied upon during the coming year to repel, with relatively small loss to themselves, any attack which might be made upon them. A decision, therefore, might be found in the East, where the Grand Duke Nicholas was still in Galicia offering a menace to Cracow and to the Austro-Hungarian kingdom. It was not enough that the Russian steam roller had been stopped by Hindenburg in the autumn fighting; it was necessary that it should be rolled back to Russia. The utter defeat of the Russian armies would have incalculable advantages. It would relieve Austria-Hungary of a mountain of anxiety, enable the central powers to help the Turks, to crush the Serbs, to bring over the Bulgarians, to confirm the wavering loyalty of the Greeks, and, should the Italians decide for the allies, to meet their attack with a more than sufficient force. The elimination of the Russian incubus by one powerful and sustained thrust would for the moment settle the affair of the East and clear the road from Berlin through Constantinople to Baghdad. This achieved, it would be possible to solve the more difficult question in the west. Here England was regarded as Germany's most malignant and dangerous foe, only to be constrained to peace by a combination of two methods, unrestricted submarine warfare by sea and the destruction of French man-power on land. The conclusion of the argument was that, when the east had been awed into submission, the German army should attack France at a point so vital that every sacrifice would be made to defend it. To this point the flower of French manhood would be attracted. Here it would be destroyed. The point ultimately selected for the great massacre of the French was Verdun.

An extraordinary success attended the early stages of this grandiose design. Mackensen blasted his way through the Russian centre in Galicia on May 2, 1915 (battle of Gorlice Tarnow), and having an immense advantage in gun power over his opponent drove him back with terrific losses to the Russian frontier. Lemberg, the capital of Galicia, Warsaw, the capital of Poland, Kovno and Vilna, the two chief cities of the Lithuanians, fell in succession to the heavy German howitzers. In the north von Bülow, one of the best of the German generals, sweeping through Courland, made a dash for Riga in the hopes of getting astride the military communications from Petrograd, for so St. Petersburg was now called, to the Russian front. So swift and irresistible was the German advance that by the beginning of

September it seemed as if the field armies of the Tzar might be cut off from their base and broken, and that the ensuing year might find the Germans established in Petrograd. Such a triumph was denied them. Russky in the north and Ivanov in the south achieved during that month successes which put a term on the German advance and shot a new flame of hope into the government of the Tzar. But if the momentum of the great German drive had exhausted itself, the results of the campaign were sufficiently impressive. The Russians had lost 325,000 prisoners and 3,000 guns, a blow from which the Tzarist army was never able wholly to recover.

The subjection of the Balkans followed. The Turk was assisted to repel the British attack in the Dardanelles; the Bulgars were won over (September 6); the Serbian army, whose campaigning in the previous autumn had been covered with glory, was driven headlong and with devastating losses into the snow-clad mountains of Albania, before a small allied force which had been landed at Salonika had time to render assistance. Whenever a German general appeared, he seemed to bring victory, Hindenburg in East Prussia and Poland, Mackensen in Galicia and Serbia, Liman von Sanders in the Gallipoli peninsula. And while these spectacular victories were being won in the eastern theatre of the war, the German front held its ground against the attacks of the French and British armies in the west. Here with an optimism ill-justified by the facts the allied command planned a series of offensives in Flanders, in Artois, and in Champagne, which, save perhaps in the successful surprise action at Neuve Chapelle (March 10-13), were vastly more costly to the attacking than to the defending force. The French command, proceeding on a false arithmetical theory, argued that in a war of attrition the advantages would be with the allies. The Germans knew better. Though they had gained nothing by their lawless employment of poison gas (April 22) after the first surprise at Ypres, on both fronts they had come out victorious in the fighting of that year.

The terrific losses endured by the allies both on the western and the eastern front in 1915 precipitated, as was only to be expected, changes in the higher direction of the war. English public opinion was so far disturbed by the lack of munitions and the evidence of failure at the front as to call for the formation of a Coalition government and for the substitution of Haig for

French in the military command. Far graver in its consequences
was the change in Russia. The Grand Duke Nicholas was relegated to the Caucasus and the Tzar with Alexeieff as Chief of his
Staff assumed the supreme command. Great as were the military
talents of Alexeieff, these changes were widely regarded in Russia
as signifying the triumph of all those influences in the government of the country which were considered to be most corrupt
and most hostile to the effective conduct of the war. The Tzar
was the creature of the Tzarina. The Tzarina was under the
spell of Rasputin, and Rasputin, an unclean profligate monk,
whose combined powers as visionary, healer, and voluptuary gave
him a magnetic influence over high-born Russian women, was
understood to favour a German peace. Since the Grand Duke was
the most formidable of this creature's enemies, his disgrace was
widely regarded as a triumph for the monk, a victory for the
Germans, and a blot of shame upon the scutcheon of the Tzar.
From this time forward the prestige of Nicholas, the Little
Father of his people, suffered a swift and uninterrupted decline.

The next year (1916) is specially memorable in the western
fighting for two battles on French soil, one extending over seven
and the other over four months. The attack and defence of
Verdun and the battle of the Somme rank among the greatest
achievements of human endurance and the saddest tragedies of
human waste. At the end of the year little seemed to have been
accomplished. The French had repelled their enemy and recaptured almost all the positions which they had held in the earliest
phases of the attack. The British, who had lost 60,000 men in
the first day's fighting on the Somme, had failed to break the
studied and intricate defences of the German line. Yet in reality
the two appalling butcheries had altered the balances of fortune.
When the French had repelled the invader from Verdun in July
and the sustained and heroic effort of the new British levies on
the Somme had died down in October, the old German army,
the best trained and most highly skilled body of fighting men
which the world has ever seen, was no more.[1] Hereafter the
Germans were compelled for the most part to depend upon
youthful levies whose military qualities were no greater than
those of their French or British adversaries. Another fact, calcu-

[1] The German losses at the Somme have been returned at 500,000,
the British losses at 410,000, and the French losses at 190,000.

lated to arouse deep anxiety at the German headquarters, was the appearance in the field of a numerous British army able to take over a large part of the line and capable at last of replying to the enemy with a bombardment as violent, as protracted, and as deadly as his own. It was at the Somme, too, that the tank, an armoured car on caterpillar wheels, which could push through wire, trenches, and other impediments, first made its appearance on the battlefield. It was a British invention, long obstructed by military obstinacy, and the key which was ultimately destined to unlock the riddle of the western front. At the Somme, however, this brilliant device made little difference, for it was employed in a manner which was partial, unintelligent, and premature. In 1918 it won the western campaign.

While German arms were encountering these serious obstacles in the west, fortune spun round and round on the eastern front. A brilliant westward thrust by Brussilov, probably the ablest of the Russian generals, demonstrated once more that, when reasonably well equipped and competently led, a Russian army was more than a match for the composite and disaffected levies of the Austro-Hungarian empire. In a campaign of ten weeks, Brussilov took four hundred and fifty thousand prisoners. His success, which shone out the more brightly by reason of the disasters of the preceding campaign, and seemed to remind Europe that a nation which could muster fifteen million men of fighting age was never at the end of its resources, encouraged Roumania to come into the war against the central powers. The adhesion of an ally, so rich in corn, oil, and other forms of natural wealth, was welcomed with acclamation by the peoples of the *Entente* states. But what appeared to be a blessing turned out in the event to be a disaster. The Russo-Rumanian generals were no match for Falkenhayn and Mackensen, who, sweeping all opposition before them, entered Bucharest on December 6. The swiftness and brilliance of the German campaign, the skill with which the two great soldiers, the one marching through the Carpathians, the other through the Dobrudja, combined their movements and ultimately converged upon the capital, gained the admiration of military observers. Henceforward the opulence of Roumania, save for the fact that the surface workings of the oil mines had been prudently destroyed by an Englishman, lay at the disposal of the German allies. By this means their power of endurance was notably enhanced.

The Germans had been quick to realize that one of their hardest problems would be to replace the raw materials and food-stuffs from which they were now debarred by the vigilance of the British navy. Walter Rathenau, a Jew eminent in science, business and letters, had undertaken the organization, on a methodical and ingenious plan, of the economic resources of the country. Substitutes were discovered for many popular articles of diet and many necessary raw materials, but despite all that science and organization could do the blockade told upon the nourishment and health of the people. There were signs of scarcity in 1915; more signs of scarcity in 1916, and, despite the welcome help of Roumanian supplies, the pressure became steadily more grievous. The population bore their hardships with an heroic stoicism, buoyed up by the continual noise of triumphs and the confident expectation of victory. When, after the failure at Verdun, *Aug. 28.* Hindenburg and Ludendorff, the twin giants, were placed in *1916* supreme control, the whole nation, imbibing fresh hope, braced itself to a supreme effort. By a long reach of public authority, the services of every citizen from fifteen to sixty were commandeered by the State.

From the beginning of the war the British navy had controlled the seas. The transport first of the expeditionary force and then of the new armies had been effected without the loss of a man. British troops had travelled to the Dardanelles, to Alexandria, to Salonika without let or hindrance. The German cruisers had been swept off the ocean, the German overseas trade stopped, the German colonies cut off from the fatherland, and exposed to inevitable conquest at the first convenient opportunity. Through the British navy the food, the raw materials, the munitions of war of the United States were made available to the allies, but not to their enemies. The task of this maritime police, however tactfully executed, was distasteful to neutral traders carrying wares destined for the continent of Europe. Whenever an American merchantman was stopped in mid-ocean by an English warship that her cargo might be examined, there was a fierce feeling in the American business community at the high-handed interference of a belligerent Power with the innocent rights of neutrals. The mutual esteem which united Sir E. Grey and Walter Page, the American Ambassador in London, did much to mitigate asperities which under less delicate handling might have resulted in serious trouble. But though it was a fair answer to American objections that, since the Germans were endeavouring to blockade the British coast with their submarines, Britain was entitled to retaliate, it was not to be expected that neutral traders would accept it as convincing. Not until America herself entered the war was the freedom of the seas consigned to oblivion, and the blockade, which had been tempered to American susceptibilities, exercised in its fullest rigour. Then the United States discarded its legal scruples with lightning speed. " Mr. Balfour," said Mr. Polk of the State Department, " it took Britain three years to reach a point where it was prepared to violate all the laws of blockade. You will find that it will take us only two months to become as great criminals as you are."

The traditions of the British navy had been dominated by the ghost of Nelson. "The Nelson touch," a brilliant and dashing sense of opportunity, a swift and certain tact in the manoeuvring of a fleet into battle, was supposed to be the special property of the great British seaman. The nation expected violent clashes in the North Sea, cutting-out expeditions, and a rapid and emphatic assertion of the naval superiority which Englishmen believed to belong to their fleet. Nothing of the kind occurred. The great fleet vanished into the mists of Scotland. Seven British cruisers were sunk by submarines. Months passed, the German battleships remaining safe behind their minefields, while the main British fleet appeared to show no anxiety to emerge from their lair and to engage the enemy. The new developments in naval warfare— the mine, the torpedo, the submarine, the smoke screen—created new perils and prescribed new cautions. A distant battle, off the Falkland islands, in which von Spee's cruisers, fresh from a victory off the Pacific coast, were sunk by Admiral Sturdee, gave encouragement not only because it finally cleared the enemy from the southern seas, but because it appeared to prove alike the good intelligence of the British Admiralty, the capacity of the admiral, and the accuracy of the gunners. It was not until May, 1916, that anything in the nature of a general action was fought. That, too, was a great and bitter disappointment to the British people. They had expected a decisive victory. They learnt of an encounter in which the Grand Fleet, though deprived owing to defective visibility of what should otherwise have been a triumphant advantage, had nevertheless lost twice as many men and twice as many ships as their opponents. The first news

Dec. 8.
1914

of the battle of Jutland, being received in London, created a May 31, 1916 sensation of unforgettable gloom. Was it true that the naval supremacy of the country now effectually challenged by the Germans was a thing of the past? Or was Jellicoe right in husbanding his resources and avoiding unnecessary risks? The answer came in the sequel. The High Sea fleet never again steamed out to join issue with the British Navy. If Jutland was a German victory, it had many consequences which in other naval campaigns proceed from a final defeat.

While the personnel of both fleets was, then, admirable in discipline and courage, the Germans were superior in technical preparations. Tirpitz had envisaged, as the British Admiralty had not, the exact nature of the problem presented by a naval action in the low visibility conditions of the North Sea. Unlike their adversaries, the German ships were designed neither for speed nor for long-range action nor for distant voyages, but for the limited objective of a clash in the home waters. They carried little coal; they provided only the most exiguous accommodation for seamen. But their shells were penetrating, their gunnery in the early stages of an action exact, and their steel protection so heavy that they were nearly unsinkable. While the inefficient British shells made little impression upon the thick steel plating of the High Sea fleet, the Germans were able, when a lightly protected British cruiser imprudently steamed within range, to pierce her insufficient armour and to send her with her splendid crew to the bottom of the waves.

One disadvantage, which later developed into a deadly malady, offset these superiorities. While the British sailor was always at sea, the German crews for the most part and save for short excursions were, for lack of accommodation on board, housed in barracks ashore. The effect of this arrangement was ultimately unfavourable to discipline. The sailor ashore catches every germ in the air. In the last months of the struggle a serious naval mutiny at Kiel paralyzed the German fleet and precipitated a general falling away from the further prosecution of the imperial war.

BOOKS WHICH MAY BE CONSULTED

The best short histories of the war are :

C. R. Cruttwell : A History of the Great War.   1934.

B. H. Liddell Hart : The Real War.   1930.

For longer histories the reader is referred to:

John Buchan: The History of the Great War. 1921-2.
Winston Churchill: The World Crisis. 1923-1931.

Most of the prominent actors have written memoirs. Of these the most important are:

D. Lloyd George: War Memoirs. 1933.
Concise Ludendorff Memoirs, 1914-1918. 1933.
Von Hindenburg: Out of My Life. *Tr.* F. A. Holt. 1920.
The Memoirs of Marshal Joffre. *Tr.* T. B. Mott. 1932.
Foch Mémoirs. 1931.
Jellicoe: Crisis of the Naval War. 1920.
R. Poincaré: Au Service de la France. 1913-26.
Sir Ian Hamilton: Gallipoli Diary. 1920.
Sir W. Robertson: Soldiers and Statesmen. 1926.
Admiral W. S. Sims and B. J. Kendrick: The Victory at Sea. 1920.
J. J. Pershing: My Experiences in the World War. 1931.
O. Czernin: In the World War. 1919.
A. Brussilov: A Soldier's Notebook. 1930.
Prince Rupprecht: Mein Kriegstagebuch. 1929.
Von Kluck: The March on Paris and the Battle of the Marne, 1914, 1920.
Huguet: Britain and the War. *Engl. tr.* 1928.
Huguet: Memoirs of Falkenhayn. Berlin, 1920.
Huguet: Memoirs of Hoffmann. Berlin, 1920.
Huguet: Memoirs of Conrad von Hötzendorf. Vienna, 1925.

The official English military histories are: Brigadier-General J. E. Edmonds (France), Brigadier-General C. F. Aspinall-Oglander (Gallipoli), Cyril Falls (Palestine and Macedonia), Brigadier-General F. J. Moberly (Mesopotamia); the official history of naval operations by Sir Julian Corbett and Sir Henry Newbolt; the official history of aviation in the war by Sir Walter Raleigh and H. A. Jones. A brilliant light is thrown on the campaign of 1914 by General E. L. Spears (Liaison, 1930), on the Italian fighting by G. M. Trevelyan (Scenes from Italy's War, 1919), and on the English attack on Zeebrugge by Sir E. Hilton Young (By Sea and Land, 1924). For the Arabian War see T. E. Lawrence, Revolt in the Desert (1927), The Seven Pillars of Wisdom (1935).

CHAPTER XXXIII

THE WAR—LAST PHASE

The U-boat campaigns and the entry of America into the war. The Russian revolution. The interlude of Kerensky. The Bolshevik triumph. Lenin takes Russia out of the war. Britain masters the U-boats. The defeat of Nivelle and the slaughter at Passchendaele. British conquest of Baghdad and Jerusalem. Obstacles to peace. The campaign of 1918. Victories of Foch and Haig. The German revolution. The Armistice. Consequences of the Great War for the world and the British Empire.

THE next year (1917) was big with two events each destined to exercise a far-reaching influence on the history of the world : the entry of the United States into the war, and the Russian revolution.

The German naval and military chiefs must accept the blame of provoking the hostility of the United States. With their eyes open, and discounting the risk, they dragooned Bethmann- *Feb. 1* Hollweg and the Kaiser into the adoption of " unrestricted U-boat warfare," which meant that the submarines would hereafter sink merchantmen at sight. They knew that they would by this open declaration of piracy bring down upon themselves the enmity of the United States, for a submarine not two years before had sunk the passenger ship *Lusitania* off the Irish coast, and nearly provoked a declaration of war from Washington; but they calculated that, before American soldiers could effectively appear on the battlefields of France, the U-boats would have starved England to submission. It was a great gamble, coming near to success, but in the end frustrated by the anti-submarine measures of the British Admiralty, and in its failure bringing utter ruin on the German cause. So reckless was the German Government in the opening of 1917 that it tried to tempt the Mexicans to attack their neighbours by the promise of Texas, New Mexico, and Arizona, three States of the American Union. The intelligence of this offer, which was intercepted by the British Admiralty and communicated to Washington, finally drove America into the war.

On a bright April morning of that year Londoners beheld *April 2,* with deep emotion the stars and stripes floating in the air from *1917* the Victoria Tower at Westminster, side by side with the Union

Jack. President Wilson had been deliberate, far too deliberate
for the leading Republicans of the eastern coast, who would
have come into the war as a protest against the violation of
Belgian neutrality. But the President, besides being a man of
peace, and compelled to pay regard to the strong feeling against
England which prevailed in many sections of the American community, had a vision of exhausted combatants invoking his aid
and calling upon him to propose some healing and beneficent
arbitrament. For such an arbitral rôle, as he projected himself
into the future, he believed that Providence had designed him:
that was the rôle he proposed to fill. Nothing short of the blind
stupidity of Ludendorff and Tirpitz could have moved him from
his position of cool and benevolent aloofness.

In the great stirring of American emotion which ensued, a
keen French observer has noted that a real, though unacknow-
ledged, factor was a latent sympathy for the parent stock whence
the larger portion of the American race derives its origin.[1]
Rather than allow England to go down, America would give up
her long cherished aversion from foreign entanglements.[2] The
sympathy for France, based on the memory of Lafayette, though
often more obviously displayed, was by comparison superficial.

Ultimately the consequences of America's entry into the war
proved to be decisive. The blockade was made more effective by
the assistance of the American fleet. The financial burden of
the alliance which had hitherto been mainly borne by Great
Britain was now not a moment too soon shared with the
wealthiest community in the world. And as American loans
relieved the financial anxieties of the *Entente*, so the appearance
on the western front of a great and well-equipped American
army in the last year of the war deprived the central powers of
their last chance of making a favourable peace. Armies, however, are not improvised in the twinkling of an eye. The
Americans, like the British before them, were slow in imparting
to their war effort an adequate momentum, and during the
months while their armies were in process of formation the
Entente experienced the gravest anxieties of the war.

[1] André Siegfried.
[2] In 1910 Admiral Sims of the U.S. Navy, speaking in the Guildhall,
said: "If the time should ever come when the British Empire is
menaced by a European coalition Great Britain can rely upon the last
ship, the last dollar, the last man, and the last drop of blood of her
kindred overseas." (Sims, *The Victory at Sea*, p. 65.)

For on March 15, a fortnight before Congress voted America into the war, the Tzar of Russia had been compelled to abdicate. The revolution, which had been long impending, burst out, not, as might have been expected, with a violent and organized upheaval, but in a series of apparently casual and unpremeditated protests, accumulating in volume and significance until it was clear that the whole country, nobles as well as bourgeois, the soldiers as well as the liberals and socialists, had fallen away from their allegiance to the Tzar. First there was a general riot in Petrograd (March 8), coupled with a general disinclination to work, then a cessation of newspapers; on the 10th a tram strike, on the 11th the mutiny of a regiment, on the 12th the defection of the household troops. The movement spread like a prairie fire. It was a revolution of hunger, misery, and fatigue, dashed with feelings of wild resentment as men called to mind the recent ruin of Russian armies, the long tale of military disasters, the four million Russian casualties, the malversation of supplies, the strong suspicion that the Tzarina under the influence of the profligate Rasputin had been playing into German hands, and finally the reactionary and oppressive methods of Protopopoff, the last and least intelligent of the Tzar's advisers. A Committee of the Duma headed by Prince Lvov endeavoured to govern the country and to conduct the war.

The Russian people were in no mood for such a government. The integrity of Lvov, the ability of Miliukoff and Guchkoff, the fiery eloquence of the social revolutionary Kerensky were of no avail against the Soviets, or workmen's and soldiers' councils, which formed themselves all over the country and were by the month of April gathered together in a central congress in Petrograd. A universal mood of mutinous inertia paralyzed government. Telephone and telegraph operators, typists and messenger boys, the props of sovereign power in a modern state, refused their services. In the Soviets themselves the clear-cut logic of the Bolsheviks, who were the extremists, swiftly mastered the tumultuous passions and confused thoughts of simple and hungry men. The plan of this party was large and seductive: bread for all, an immediate peace, the land for the peasants, and a dictatorship of the proletariat. So while Kerensky endeavoured to stir the army to renewed activities, the Bolsheviks set to work to corrupt discipline. Their success was complete and almost immediate. By the end of July, 1917, the Russian front had crumbled in face of the enemy. "No annexations, no indemnities," was the slogan of the new revolution.

Eloquence, and Kerensky had nothing better to offer, could not restore a situation so gravely compromised. The Bolshevik movement, despite a mistimed outbreak in July, steadily gathered strength through the weakness of the provisional government, the victories of the Germans, and the growing misery of the people. How could Kerensky, who could not save Riga and lacked the courage to execute revolutionaries when he caught them red-handed, hope to survive in such a storm? On November 7 (October 25 old style) the Bolsheviks struck their blow, which had been long prepared, and as the Red revolutionaries surged round the Winter Palace his provisional government fell like a pack of cards.

The organizers of the October revolution were two obscure exiles recently returned to Russia: Ulianoff, who called himself Lenin, and the Jew Braunstein, who had taken the name of Trotsky. Two more formidable or resolute adventurers have never seized the reins of power in a great state. Before three months were over they had taken Russia out of the war, ruined the rich and middle classes, and dispersed a representative assembly which had been convoked to frame a parliamentary constitution for a Russian Republic. Patriotism was as little to Lenin's heart as parliaments. At the Treaty of Brest-Litovsk (March 3, 1918) with the Germans he surrendered vast tracts of Russian territory[1] to the enemy without a twinge of shame or of regret.

It was no part of Ludendorff's plan for 1917 to renew the offensive on the western front. Withdrawing some miles to a position which had been fortified with elaborate care, and was known by the Germans as the Siegfried and by the English as the Hindenburg line, he proposed to allow his opponents to continue the costly assaults to which they were so strongly and religiously addicted. He was less disposed to waste men on aggressive tactics since he was confident that in six or, at the most, twelve months the war would be over on the sea. The U-boats would starve England to submission before the Americans could be convoyed to the shores of France.

The form of warfare to which the German nation, despite the

[1] Finland, Esthonia, Livonia, Courland, Lithuania, Russian Poland.

protest of many good citizens, was now committed, will for ever be condemned by the conscience of humanity. A merchantman or passenger vessel torpedoed by a submarine sinks with all hands. There is no means of rescue. Upon the brave U-boat commanders was laid the injunction, the most repellent to a naval officer which can be imagined, to discard the immemorial courtesies of the sea. Yet it cannot be denied that this new and lawless method of warfare contained the promise of success. At the end of April, 1917, there was only six weeks' supply of corn in Britain, and it became clear to the British Government that unless the rate of submarine sinking were promptly reduced the food supply of the island could not be guaranteed. The riddle was solved. Partly by the adoption (forced upon the Admiralty by Mr. Lloyd George) of the convoy system, partly by depth charges and improved hydrophones, and by other expedients too numerous to mention, the U-boat was subdued. A time came when very few of these submarines returned to their base, so completely had the British Admiralty mastered its problem. The courage of the German crews was great. Equally high was the spirit of the officers and seamen of the British commercial marine, whom no dangers, however certain, could frighten from the seas.

Ludendorff's hopes were frustrated on the water. The fighting on land, though nowhere decisive, clearly pointed to an ascending scale of German predominance. An attack on the Aisne, prepared with the utmost elaboration by Nivelle, an attractive and much acclaimed officer, who had been called to succeed Joffre in the French command, broke down with losses so murderous as to occasion a mutiny in part of the French army and a sudden lack of confidence among civilians and soldiers alike, which for a time threatened seriously to impair the military efficiency of the French nation. The situation was restored. Pétain, the hero of Verdun, stopped the rot in the French army. Clemenceau, the Tiger, coming to the head of affairs, put an end to defeatist intrigues in Paris. Yet the position remained one of great anxiety to the allied commanders. Fearing lest the shaken army of France might fail under a sudden strain, Haig was confirmed in the resolve for the remainder of the year to concentrate the attention of the enemy on the British front.

Oct., 1917

All that summer and autumn the rain fell pitilessly on the low-lying ground round the battered Cloth Hall of Ypres, where the British Army with a tremendous concentration of guns was endeavouring to force its way to the Belgian coast. Never were the penalties of bad weather more unevenly distributed. While the Germans, having the higher ground, were relatively comfortable, the British trenches were often waist deep in water. To the ordinary horrors of an intense and continuous bombardment, there was added the danger that men once wounded might drown in the water or suffocate in mud. Nevertheless, the battle of Passchendaele was continued with a dogged persistence, the Germans yielding little ground and suffering little by comparison, while the British casualties mounted up to the huge total of three hundred thousand. The dull thunder of the guns of Passchendaele heard in many a quiet Surrey village announced one of those national tragedies, which are all the more terrible because their necessity is questioned. It is pertinent to ask whether the French were only to be saved from destruction by so terrible a wastage of British life, or whether, seeing that an American army was expected in the following year, it was not an obvious counsel of prudence for Britain to husband her man power? Mr. Lloyd George advised strongly against the battle, but ceded his judgment to the earnest representations of the soldiers. The cost of Passchendaele was evidenced in Byng's November fighting round Cambrai, when a brilliant surprise attack launched with the aid of tanks failed to consolidate its swift and remarkable advance for lack of reserves.

The catalogue of allied reverses in this troubled year was completed at Caporetto (October 24), when the Italian army which had been destined for the capture of Trieste was driven back to the Piave with huge losses and in unexampled confusion. The catastrophe was the more alarming since it revealed the extent to which demoralization and war-weariness had gained ground among troops who were naturally intrepid and courageous. In truth the Italian Higher Command had paid little attention to the expedients by which an army submitted to the terrible nervous trials of modern warfare may nevertheless be kept in good heart. The Commissariat was irregular, the guns deficient in number and weight, and the facilities for amusement and education behind the lines which were so lavishly provided on other fronts were not available. In his rare intervals of leave the Italian soldier would return from the scorching limestone plateau of the Carso to find his family starving on a maintenance allowance from the state which was wholly insufficient for its needs. In such circumstances it is not surprising that his will to victory faltered, that he listened to the priests if he were a Catholic or to the Soviets if he were a socialist, and from each of these very different sources learnt that the war should be promptly stopped.

That after so great a deliquescence of military *morale* the Italian front should have been firmly re-established is a tribute to Cadorna's skill and to Italian resilience. The Piave was held and Venice saved. But when winter came it was still uncertain whether the Italian army, albeit under their new commander Diaz, and reinforced by French and British divisions, would repel with success a renewed assault.

While these disasters were sustained by the Allies upon the Russian, French, and the Italian fronts, a wide-sweeping British movement against the Turks in the East brought the famous cities of Baghdad and Jerusalem under British control. By these military exploits the Arab world was loosened from its Turkish moorings and the prestige of Great Britain in the East was restored. The conquest of Palestine was destined to have further consequences, the fruits of which were amply reaped before the close of the war. By proclaiming its intention to establish in Palestine a national home for the Jews, Great Britain rallied to the allied cause, at a time when money was urgently needed, the powerful and cosmopolitan community which, not from New York only, controls the loan markets of the world.[1]

The time had long passed since Germans were gaily speculating on vast annexations to be obtained at the expense of their rivals. But their arms had been so successful, their domestic war propaganda so encouraging and delusive, that they could not afford to offer a peace which the allies would accept. It was an axiom with the British Cabinet that Belgium should be evacuated, Alsace-Lorraine returned to France, and indemnities or reparations paid to the Allies. These terms the General Staff would not permit to be discussed. Holding that Bethmann-Hollweg, the Chancellor, was veering towards concessions, Ludendorff secured his dismissal (July, 1917) and became till the end of the war the real master of Germany. It was not the first injury the German people had sustained from their leading soldiers. It was the General Staff whose requirements had brought England

---

[1] That Palestine should neither fall to others nor yet cost money to Britain were also motives of the Cabinet.

and America into the war, and it was the General Staff who obstructed the fairway to a peace which would have left the Hohenzollerns and Habsburgs on their thrones. To the German navy in particular, which had been taught to believe that " a second Punic war " against England was inevitable, it was specially repugnant to abandon the convenient bases of the Belgian ports.

With forty divisions drawn from the Russian front Ludendorff was entitled to hope that a last bid for victory might yet succeed even in the West. The strategy of his campaign in 1918 was to deliver a blow at the point of junction of the French and English lines so crushing as to drive the two armies asunder and to enable each to be separately overcome. His tactics, which had been carefully rehearsed before Riga, were novel and brilliant. A creeping barrage of unexampled intensity sustained over a front of forty-three miles would blast a hole through which bomb-throwers, flame-throwers, and machine-gunners, specially picked and trained for the work, and rushed to the front in lorries, would stream forward without pause or intermission. Powerful trench mortars and enormous reserves were necessary for the success of the manoeuvre. These Ludendorff possessed.

The hammer blow fell on March 21. On that day a terrific avalanche of shells from 4,000 guns, the first salvo in a battle lasting over seven months, fell upon the Fifth British Army under Gough, which had just taken over part of the French line. Save at Arras on the extreme British left, the attackers, who were favoured by mist and hard ground, carried everything before them. The Fifth Army broke. In a few days German guns were playing on the railway line south of Amiens and it seemed as if Ludendorff's plan of severing the two armies was to be achieved. It was not to be. The Germans, who in the speed of their advance appear to have exhausted their original momentum, were held up before Amiens. The fatal thrust was not persisted in. It was decided by what appears to have been a departure from the original plan to make thrusts at other parts of the allied line. First the British were attacked on the Ypres sector (April 9-29) and pushed back twelve miles. Then (May 27) the French were heavily defeated on the Chemin des Dames. But these assaults, though formidable and destructive, were eventually stemmed. Strategists doubt their wisdom, for by the end of June the German line in France showed three great

ulges, each offering to an active opponent a convenient target
or attack.

In this menacing advance the Germans had sustained enormous losses such as are incidental to the free movement of
massed troops under heavy bombardment from the air and fire
from enemy batteries, gallantly and skilfully worked. Another
consequence might less easily have been foreseen. Whereas the
British army was the best-fed army in the war, their opponents
had long been on short commons. Accordingly, when the Germans overran the British lines and found them littered with provisions of every sort, they were seized with a sudden feeling of
hopelessness. Then, and only then, they perceived that the real
truth about the war had been withheld from them, and that the
enemy, who had been represented as being in the last stage of
want and inanition, was rioting in luxuries to which Germans
had long been strangers. By many channels this sudden aware-
ness of deception spread backward from the front and contributed to make the German revolution.

It was against an army already suffering from an infection of
hopelessness that the Allies began on July 18 the great series of
offensive movements which, to their surprise (for they had made
their plans for another year of fighting), brought the war to a
close on November 11. Everything now pointed to success. The
losses of the campaign had been more than replaced by the influx of some six hundred thousand fresh troops from America,
and though it was not until September that the American army
under General Pershing was able to take the field, individual
American divisions had fought with the French and English,
and at one action at Chateau-Thierry had greatly distinguished
themselves. In every particular of equipment, save trench
mortars, the Allies were now superior to their opponents. In the
air they had acquired a marked ascendancy. Hundreds of light
mobile tanks furnished them with an incomparable instrument
for piercing the defences of the enemy. Moreover, the most
serious defect which had marred their previous operations was
now remedied. Taught at last by the March disaster, the British
public acquiesced in the decision to submit its forces on the
western front to the supreme direction of a French commander.
The man chosen was Foch, an instructed soldier of great author-
ty, keen insight, and irrepressible dash, and the close friend of
Wilson, the chief of the British staff; but Foch did not stand

alone. With him stood the modest long-headed Weygand, as chief of staff, a living storehouse of facts and figures. The choice was justified. From July 18, when Mangin made a surprise attack upon the southern German bulge with three hundred light tanks and captured thirty thousand prisoners, till the last day of fighting in November, there was no moment of doubt that the power of offensive lay with the allies. But if any day in that long sustained struggle deserves to be singled out it is that which Ludendorff has described as the "black day of the German army." It was August 8, the day of Haig's surprise attack near Amiens, and it was black not so much because the Germans lost twenty thousand prisoners to the enemy, as because though in sufficient force they were evicted from positions which were held to be secure. From these premises Ludendorff drew the conclusion that demoralization had set in among his troops, and Haig that victory might be obtained by a concerted and violent offensive over the whole front. When the British army stormed the Siegfried line (September 29) the spine of the German resistance was broken.

On the next day Ludendorff asked his government to sue for peace. A month before the revolution broke out in Germany the chief of the General Staff had thrown up the struggle.

An astonishing succession of allied victories, crowded into a few weeks, brought the long and courageous resistance of the central Powers to an end. First Bulgaria, then Turkey, then Austria were so defeated as to sue for peace. Germany still remained, her army gravely shaken and depleted, yet in the gathering shades of autumn fighting a rearguard action on enemy soil with dogged tenacity. But the German people, who were hungry, miserable, and now plunged in despair, wanted peace, and peace at once; and since President Wilson, in whom Europe descried the arbiter of its fate, boggled at dealing even with a Parliamentary government in Berlin so long as the Kaiser was on the throne, they were well content that the Kaiser should go. It was understood that the allies would have no truck with German militarism. So when the fleet was ordered out to sea there was a mutiny of the Navy at Kiel, and soon afterwards (November 9) the Kaiser and the Crown Prince fled to Holland, and on the same day a republic was proclaimed at Berlin. Brave are the men who in the darkest days are willing to take responsibility for the government of their country. The middle

class German Socialists who now succeeded to the proudest
monarchy in Europe were brave and patriotic. Yet it was a
serious misfortune for the democratic cause in Germany that the
first inevitable act of the new Government was to accept an
armistice under which the Germans were compelled not only to
evacuate their conquered territory, but to surrender their aeroplanes, their guns, their rolling stock, and the best part of their
fleet.[1] All this is brought up against German democracy now.
But at the moment there was only one sentiment all over Europe
when at 11 o'clock on the morning of November 11 the firing
suddenly ceased, a sentiment of overwhelming thankfulness that
the long and hideous nightmare was at last at an end.

The war had been won by the democracies of the west. At the
end of it the three great military monarchies of eastern and
central Europe had disappeared. Though in the stress of the
conflict parliamentary debates were little considered, the leading
men had been fashioned in the parliamentary arena: Asquith,
Lloyd George, Churchill, Balfour, Bonar Law in England, Poincaré, Painlevé, Briand and Clemenceau in France. Again and
again it was made evident in Briand's witty words that " war is
too serious a thing to be left to the soldiers." The downfall of
Germany is not a little to be ascribed to the fact that she had
permitted the soldiers too great a place in the national life.

The temporary eclipse of personal liberty, coupled with a vast
increase in state control are necessary consequences of modern
war. Both evils were cheerfully endured. The English people,
less patient of regimentation than other nations, were nevertheless induced to accept conscription and the rationing of food,
and a measure of drink control which would have been thought
impracticable in time of peace. In every country it was considered
necessary to secure national solidarity by elaborate propaganda,
holding up the enemy to scorn and hatred. To the cruelty and
carnage of war there was added the evil of subsidized prejudice
and mendacity. In this respect no belligerent country can claim
to be exempt from guilt. As the anxieties and perplexities of the
war thickened, the men of violent and commanding will came to
the front and took control; Lloyd George in England, Clemenceau
in France, Ludendorff in Germany, Lenin in Russia. The Cabinet
convulsion in Britain in the winter of 1916 was characteristic of

[1] Appendix B

the growing concentration of authority which the stern circumstances of the time demanded. A small war committee sitting *de die in diem* under a dynamic chairman was substituted for a coalition Cabinet, very able but much divided in opinion, in which, in the words of Mr. Winston Churchill, one of its members, "every military decision had to be carried by the same sort of process of tact, temporizing, and exhaustion which occurs over a clause in a violently contested bill in the House of Commons in time of peace." It was this government which, under the direction of Mr. Lloyd George and with the occasional assistance of distinguished statesmen from the Dominions, ruled England and the Empire during the last two years of the war.

It might perhaps have been imagined that war, which is essentially inimical to liberty and justice, would have tended to arrest the progress of democracy in the belligerent countries. The bullet, however, is a great leveller. In England, where for many reasons, the absence of conscription being one of them, the equalitarian spirit was less developed than in France and Italy, class consciousness was shamed by the extremity of the peril voluntarily encountered for the general good by plain citizens. The stay-at-home landlord felt humble in the presence of his wounded gardener. The railway porter who had risked his life took on a dignity never to be obtained by the secure plutocrat. What, statesmen asked themselves, can be good enough for a population which is willing to stake its all for the country's safety? Even during the war the British Cabinet passed bills to extend education, to give votes to women, and turned its thoughts to providing "homes for heroes." The condition of the common man and woman was always present to their minds. It was not so with the British Cabinet during the Napoleonic wars.

With a surprising and instantaneous unanimity the British Dominions and colonies rallied round the mother country. Spurts of rebellion, soon suppressed, in South Africa and Ireland, indicated the presence of refractory elements, which were not, however, sufficiently strong to prevail against the momentum of a brotherhood in arms. India, its princes and peoples alike, stood by the Empire, and contributed to its war effort in France, in Gallipoli, and in Mesopotamia. New Zealand lost more men than Belgium. The conquest of German West Africa was effected by General Botha, of German East Africa by General

Smuts, of German New Guinea by an expedition fitted out from Australia. The French Canadians, who in another species of quarrel might have proved refractory, were content to serve in a war for the rescue of France. Yet the consequences of this widely spread enthusiasm were not exactly what might have been predicted. So far from leading up to a closer union of the Empire, the war had the effect of loosening the constitutional ties by which that great Commonwealth had previously been united.

Before the war men had talked of a Federal Parliament in London. Afterwards that solution of the imperial problem was so clearly unacceptable that it was never propounded. An exaltation of national sentiment, bred in some Dominions by the achievements and sacrifices of the war, and in others quickened by a spice of Irish or Dutch hostility, forbade the faintest suspicion of subservience.

The Dominions had made good as separate nations. As nations they signed the peace treaties and were admitted to the League of Nations, and as such they claimed equality with the mother country under the common Crown. As the Sovereign acted on the advice of British Ministers in Britain, so, it was contended, should the Governor-General, his Vicegerent, act on the advice of South African ministries in Cape Town and Pretoria, of Canadian ministries in Ottawa, of Australian Ministries at Canberra, and of New Zealand ministries at Wellington. The claim was conceded. A new picture of the Commonwealth, corresponding with the new aspirations, was enclosed within the framework of the Statute of Westminster (1931), and the war which had furnished to the world the most amazing example of imperial solidarity was at the same time admitted to have dissolved the Empire (India and the Crown Colonies for the moment excepted) into a free association of equal states.[1]

To an extent never previously realized the war was one of extermination. Whole populations were engaged in the combat and were regarded as legitimate objects of destruction. Though aerial warfare was in its infancy, it had so far advanced before the Armistice as to engender a hateful competition in the

[1] The position of the Dominions was thus defined by the Imperial Conference of 1926: " Equal in status, in no way subordinate one to another in any respect of their domestic or external affairs, though united by a common allegiance to the Crown and freely associated as members of the British Commonwealth of Nations."

bombing of cities and the destruction of civilian life. A bomb might fall anywhere, upon little children as they sat at their lessons, upon worshippers kneeling in church, or even upon nurses as they tended the sick. The rights of neutrals were little regarded. The German invasion of Belgium, the unrestricted U-boat warfare, the use of asphyxiating gas were all cruel acts of international lawlessness which may be charged to the German account. On the other side the interference of the British Navy with neutral trade, the appropriation of Corfu as an allied sanatorium, and the blockade of Greece by the French Navy, when it was feared that King Constantine might join the enemy, were in varying degrees actions for which no legal purist can find a defence. How little the humane counsels of international law influenced the conduct of belligerent nations was clearly, as we have already noted, illustrated by the case of the United States. Before she entered the war no country had more steadily or loudly proclaimed her devotion to the doctrine of the freedom of the seas. But once embarked on hostilities, once the rôle of the neutral was exchanged for that of the belligerent, the whole attitude of America changed. The blockade of Germany which a week before had been an international crime henceforward became an American virtue. The freedom of the seas was thrown to the winds, and the energetic American Navy addressed itself to the task of blockading the enemy with a completeness to which the British Admiralty had never ventured to aspire.

No words can paint the pangs and sufferings of this long-drawn agony of the European nations. Some men lost their reason, others were blinded, others were asphyxiated with gas or had their bodies torn and mutilated with explosions. Many came out of the war nervous wrecks for life. What is surprising and creditable to human nature was that the almost universal reaction to terror was not panic-stricken compliance, but indignant resolve. Every air attack upon England made recruits for the war, every bad week at the front redoubled the energies of the munition workers, every German severity in Belgium made an eventual German success less probable. One of the lessons of the war, if posterity cares to heed it, is the bankruptcy of terrorism as a policy directed against the wills of the progressive and civilized peoples of Europe. The population of Dunkirk, though the town was almost continuously attacked from the air, went about their ordinary occasions almost as in times of peace.

In those belligerent countries which were relatively civilized so long and cruel a war could be maintained only by an immense effort of massed propaganda. Recruiting was nourished by war speeches and war speeches by war fables. Even in England the gravest acts of injustice were committed against enemy aliens who were interned, deprived of their property, and in the concluding stages of the war deported to Germany. To weaken the *morale* of the army by distributing leaflets from the air became during the concluding stages of the struggle a feature of increasing importance. Germans endeavoured to inject mutiny into Russians; English propaganda led many Germans to doubt the justice of their cause and to impugn the veracity of their leaders. The dissolution of the ill-compacted army of the Austrian Empire was accelerated by skilfully devised appeals, prepared in London and distributed by air, to the subject races who had long chafed under Austrian rule.

Perhaps the most striking monument of the success of wartime propaganda is the sudden emergence from the wreck of the Austrian Empire of the Republic of Czecho-Slovakia. Most states have been fashioned by the sword or have grown out of colonization. Czecho-Slovakia is the child of propaganda. How two able exiles, Masaryk, the son of a Slovak coachman, and Benès, the son of a Czech peasant-farmer, set alight an agitation for the liberation of the Czechs and the Slovaks, with what wholesale desertions from the Austrian army their efforts were rewarded, how French and English brains were enlisted in their cause, with what enthusiasm the evangel of Czech liberation was received in Chicago (the second largest Czech city in the world) and with what sympathy by President Wilson, how 45,000 Czech war-captives in Russia formed themselves into an army, marched across Siberia, and were thence transported to their native country—the narrative of these events constitutes one of the most surprising chapters in modern history. It is not wonderful that the railway station in Prague is called, not after the name of any Czech general or victory, for there were no such names to be inscribed on the humble annals of this peasant and subject race, but after the American President who, impressed by the skilful propaganda of the two illustrious exiles, proclaimed that the establishment of a Czecho-Slovak republic was among the war aims of the Allied Powers.

CHAPTER XXXIV

TREATIES OF PEACE

The Legacy of War. Conditions which shaped the Peace. President Wilson. His great influence. The doctrine of self-determination. The Covenant of the League. Georges Clemenceau. David Lloyd George. The reparations problem, and the English elections. The Italian stand-point. Flaws in the Treaty of Versailles. The dismemberment of Austria-Hungary. The triumph of the Wilsonian doctrine. America withdraws. France allies herself to the Petite Entente. Organization of the League of Nations. Ideas embodied in the Covenant. Persistence of international rivalries. The war cloud of 1935.

THE situation of Europe at the time of the Armistice was one of unexampled misery and confusion. The vanquished Empires had crumbled to pieces and the new Republics had yet to acquire authority and confidence. And meanwhile, with government all over central and eastern Europe at its lowest point of experience and efficiency, with loyalties uncertain and divided, with frontiers fluctuating and unsettled, and with exhaustion as the last surviving ally of social order, a task was imposed upon philanthropists and statesmen calculated to strain and indeed to overpower the remedial resources of mankind. Eight million young men, the best and most vigorous of their generation, had been killed in the war. A greater number had been permanently disabled. Equally, if not more, serious, were the losses consequent upon starvation, malnutrition, and disease.[1] Particularly were these evils terrible in Russia, where the horrors of cholera, typhus, and food shortage were aggravated by revolution and continuing war : but they were great all through central and eastern Europe, in war-scourged Poland, where the peasantry were living on roots, grass, acorns, and heather; in Germany, where by reason of underfeeding the number of births in 1918 was actually below the number of deaths; in Austria, where since the factories were devoid of coal and raw material, every poor home was menaced by the spectre of famine; and in Serbia, where half the male population had been killed, and 35 per

---

[1] The total number of deaths attributable to the war has been estimated at 25 millions (Gilbert Murray : *Then and Now*).

cent. were suffering from recognizable tuberculosis. It is difficult to bring before the imagination the hopelessness and dejection which were produced by these dreadful conditions, or to estimate the consequences for the quality of the population of Europe of four years of nervous overstrain and malnutrition. The destruction of fixed capital through high explosives, save in so far as it was the occasion of want and exposure, was by comparison a negligible calamity.

These evils, though specially evident in Russia and the defeated countries, were by no means confined to them. Victors and neutrals also suffered. The losses of France calculated in dead and wounded, in farms ravaged, in factories, mines, and machinery destroyed were enormous. The privations of Italy through lack of fuel were great. Indeed, the ill consequences of the war were felt throughout the world, and nowhere more seriously than in those regions where a slight rise in food prices drives a whole population into want. Such was the case of India, where an epidemic of influenza which might otherwise have been relatively harmless carried off the enormous total of six million lives.

The extremity of these and other sufferings had produced in the public mind a pining for a world organized on a new and better plan, and, as often arises when desires are strong, a belief that such a world could be brought into being. The aspirations of Russia were centred round the person of Lenin. Western Europe looked for its salvation to President Wilson.

The Treaties of Peace were made under the direction of three democratic statesmen, each possessing astonishing prestige— Wilson, Clemenceau, Lloyd George. Yet while each of these remarkable men exercised his specific influence on the Treaties, so that we may say here is the trace of Wilson, here of Lloyd George, here of Clemenceau, the substance of the settlement was dictated by inexorable facts, which these men were compelled to accept, and which no other set of statesmen, however enlightened, would have been strong enough to vary or disregard had the big three been suddenly assassinated.

First of these shaping conditions was the fact that under the impact of war the old governments of Russia, Germany, and Austria-Hungary had disappeared and that the Poles, the Czechs, the Roumans, and the Serbs were setting up new national governments in their place. If the allied statesmen in Paris had desired to check these nationalist movements, they could have enforced their will only by armed force. And where could they have found that force? The French, the British, and the Italians were weary of war. There was but one fresh army available, and this had already accomplished its mission. Not for a moment would the United States have assented to the employment of even a single American division in a campaign to thwart the national aspirations of the Poles or the Czechs.

A second circumstance was the temper which then prevailed in the European belligerent countries, which had only by the nearest margin, and at the eleventh hour, been preserved from destruction. They held Germany responsible for the war. They observed that it was not the Serbs who had invaded Austria, nor the Belgians who had attacked the Germans, and that it was the government of the Kaiser which had declared war on Russia, Belgium, and France. They were angry, vindictive, unquiet. They wanted redress and safety. No statesman in a democratic age, however independent, can prevail against the clear and passionate wishes of his countrymen. Clemenceau would have ceased to represent France, Orlando would have ceased to represent Italy, if they had not worked for the weakening of the enemy powers, and for the better protection of their respective states. Lloyd George had received an emphatic mandate from his constituencies that the enemy must be made to pay, and if he had not already obtained the internment of the German Fleet at the Armistice would have been asked the reason why by the British people. Of all these statesmen, the one most naturally prone to take a liberal view of the situation, the British Prime Minister, was the most clearly committed to a course of retribution.

Thirdly, it was unfortunate that the Conference should have been held in a capital which was still reeling under the tragedies of the war and the shock of bombardment. In the inflamed atmosphere of Paris the ideals of appeasement fought an unequal battle with those of retribution. The cooler air of a Swiss city, as recommended by the British, would have been more conducive to a happy end.

To Paris, however, the Conference was summoned on January 18, 1919. It was a gathering unique in history, for the war, which had disturbed everyone everywhere, had quickened every resentment, revived every claim, fostered every vision, and sharpened every appetite, and with all these appetites, claims, visions, and resentments a handful of war-weary statesmen, each responsible to an exacting democracy in his own country and pestered by the ravings of a debased press, was expected to cope as best it might. The scene has been well described by a brilliant eye-witness. "The Paris of the Conference," writes Dr. Dillon, "ceased to be the capital of France. It became a vast cosmopolitan caravanserai teeming with unwonted aspects of life and turmoil, filled with curious samples of the races, tribes, and tongues of four continents who came to watch and wait for the mysterious to-morrow.

"An Arabian Nights touch was imparted to the dissolving panorama by strange visitants from Tartary and Kurdistan, Corea and Azerbeijan, Armenia, Persia, and the Hedjaz—men with patriarchal beards and scimitar-shaped noses, and others from desert and oasis, from Samarkand and Bokhara. Turbans and fezes, sugar-loaf hats and headgear resembling episcopal mitres, old military uniforms devised for the embryonic armies of new states on the eve of perpetual peace, snowy-white burnouses, flowing mantles, and graceful garments like the Roman toga, contributed to create an atmosphere of dreamy unreality in the city where the grimmest of realities were being faced and coped with.

"Then came the men of wealth, of intellect, of industrial enterprise, and the seed-bearers of the ethical new ordering, members of economic committees from the United States, Britain, Italy, Poland, Russia, India, and Japan, representatives of naphtha industries and far-off coal mines, pilgrims, fanatics and charlatans from all climes, priests of all religions, preachers of every doctrine, who mingled with princes, field-marshals, statesmen, anarchists, builders-up, and pullers-down. All of them burned with desire to be near to the crucible in which the political and social systems of the world were to be melted and re-cast."

In this scene of confusion the American President shone at the opening of the Conference with the lustre of a Messiah. At one time he had been violently unpopular with the belligerent nations. He had recommended the "neutral mind" as though ethical differences did not exist, and "peace without victory" as though war held no resentments. But now all this was forgotten. The Princeton professor had brought America into the war. In a series of lofty and eloquent speeches he had defined the aims of the allies and indicated the new political formations in Europe. He had noted that the enemy was "Prussian militarism," that the aim was "to make the world safe for democracy." It was from him that the allies learnt that they were fighting not only to restore Alsace-Lorraine to France, but for a revived Poland with an access to the sea, and for a new republic of Czecho-Slovakia. It was he who had formulated "the fourteen points,"[1] who had negotiated with the German Government, who had insisted on the military armistice. His country wanted no territory and no indemnities. Even in Germany he was widely regarded as an oracle of disinterested morality and wisdom, as a prophet sent by the New World to cleanse the impurities of the Old. But whereas other prophets had been voices crying in the wilderness, Wilson was the master of a powerful state. The Allies were dependent on America for their food supplies and finances. While the young manhood of France and England were lying beneath the sod, two million fresh American troops were encamped upon the soil of France.

One weakness in the President's position, obvious to Americans, was not appreciated at the time in Europe. He did not represent his countrymen. He was a Democrat and an idealist. The people who mattered most in the United States at that time were neither the one nor the other. The Republicans had a majority in the Senate, and the Senate in the last resort controlled American foreign policy. It would have seemed, therefore, an obvious counsel of prudence for the President, when once he had decided to go to Paris in person, to have invited the assistance of certain eminent Republican statesmen. But the President was in temper an autocrat and in home politics a bitter partisan. He went to Paris without the Republicans, and the Republicans in revenge upset his plans.

For the Peace Treaties bear Wilson's mark. The new map of Europe was drawn according to that principle of self-determination (a phrase borrowed from the Bolsheviks) which the President had proclaimed as the clue leading through a labyrinth of evils to justice and peace. Over the Poles and their Corridor, as over the Czechs and the Slovaks, he cast his peculiar benediction, perhaps desiring to right the errors of history, but perhaps also recalling how useful was the Polish vote at home, and how numerous and weighty were the Czechs in the city of Chicago.

[1] Appendix C.

Americans have no right to argue, as some do, that in this fundamental aspect of the peace-making, American idealism was upset by the wickedness of Europe. The new political frontiers of Europe are Wilsonian, and so drawn that three per cent. only of the total population of the continent live under alien rule. Judged by the test of self-determination, no previous European frontiers have been so satisfactory.

In another important respect the treaties are Wilsonian. But for the American President the Covenant of the League would not have been drafted then, and placed within the framework of the Treaties. The idea of a League of Nations was not original with Wilson, but was an Anglo-Saxon conception, foreign to the Latins, which had germinated during the course of the war in many peace-loving minds, both in England and America, and had led to the formulation of definite proposals, the most important of which were drafted by Lord Phillimore and General Smuts. But it is one thing to draft proposals and quite another thing in a vast press of competing claims to carry them into execution. Wilson took the Phillimore-Smuts drafts, insisted on placing the problem of the League in the forefront of the Peace discussions, himself presided over the commission which drew up the Covenant, and with his great authority pushed the work to a conclusion. So resolved was the President to force the Covenant on his Senate by making it an integral part of all the Peace Treaties that two precious months went by before the Conference addressed itself to the real work of peace-making.

It is not, therefore, true to say that the Peace Treaties are lacking in idealism, or that they are destitute of principle. They contain an ideal in the Covenant. They follow a principle in self-determination. But the ideal was not one generally shared on the continent; and the principle, albeit just, was full of danger and innovation, for it led to the erection of five new states all of questionable stability, and to large transfers of territory and population at the expense of the Teutonic and Magyar races.

The war against the German Empire ended in a radical and revolutionary peace drawn up by democratic politicians. It recognized the liberation of nations, canonized new republics, provided for the protection of minorities. The general trend of Europe towards nationalism and democracy, which had made itself felt ever since 1848 with steadily increasing emphasis, seems to culminate naturally in Mr. Wilson's peace.

The French Prime Minister was Clemenceau, a rude, sensible, witty octogenarian, utterly empty of illusions, but faithful throughout his violent Parliamentary and journalistic career to three affections, science, France, and liberty. Save that he liked and understood the Anglo-Saxon race, and realized more perfectly than his fellow-countrymen the value of Anglo-Saxon friendship, Clemenceau was the mirror of logical and realist France. The ghosts of immemorial policies, of Richelieu, of Mazarin, of Louis XIV and of Danton, lived again in this brilliant and fiery republican. He had seen his country twice invaded, and now saved from utter destruction only by alliances never likely to be repeated; and knowing that by 1940 Germany would have twice as many men of military age to put into the field as France, he doubted whether any league would avail to protect her. Is it wonderful that his mind should have been filled with two things only, reparations for the past, security for the future, or that when Marshal Foch, with the aureole of victory on his brow, asked in effect for the bridgeheads of the Rhine, Clemenceau, who put no faith in Germans, should have vehemently supported the claim? But here France was countered by the two Anglo-Saxon statesmen, who argued that to detach the Rhineland from the *Reich* was to create another Alsace-Lorraine and to lay the seeds of a future war.

On this Mr. Lloyd George was adamant. What was offered to France in exchange for the Rhineland was the abolition of conscription in Germany and the fixed reduction of the German army to a hundred thousand men, a demilitarized zone on the right bank, and a treaty of guarantee signed by Wilson and Lloyd George pledging their respective countries to defend the soil of France against aggression. Clemenceau bowed to the Anglo-Saxons. But when the American Congress refused to ratify the treaty of guarantee, France felt that she had been induced to part with the Rhineland for a scrap of paper. The French army, it was said, had won the war, but Clemenceau had sold the peace.

As for the English Prime Minister, he brought back trophies for his country such as even Chatham might have envied; the bulk of the German Fleet (surrendered at the Armistice and afterwards sunk in Scapa Flow), and of the German commercial navy, a sphere of influence in Mesopotamia, Palestine, Tanganyika, the most valuable of the German colonies (while other less important colonies were secured for the South African Union, the Commonwealth of Australia, and the Dominion of New Zealand), a share in German reparation payments, and the recognition of the Dominions as qualified to take part in the treaty making and to be separately represented in the League of Nations. Every point in the negotiations which could be won for the British Empire Mr. Lloyd George was successful in gaining.

Judged by the conventional standard of power-politics no triumph could have been more complete. Yet despite his brilliant war-leadership, and all the lustre of his country's achievements by sea and land, Mr. Lloyd George went into the Conference under a handicap. There had been in England the unescapable calamity of a General Election. A rare mood of vindictive passion, strengthened rather than assuaged by the new women voters, had convulsed the electorate. The cry went up that Germany should pay the whole cost of the war, that the Kaiser should be hanged, and that all Germans who had violated the laws of war should be brought to trial and punished. The doctrine had been so assiduously preached that war was a crime, the sinking of passenger ships by submarines was so fresh a memory, that the rank and file of the British electorate may be excused for thinking that the authors of such a war should suffer the fate of criminals. Politicians, of course, knew better, and to statesmen this intense manifestation of national fury came as an embarrassing surprise. Speakers at the election were thrown off their balance. The Prime Minister was no exception. By sheer pressure of popular sentiment he was driven from the noble appeal for national reconstruction with which he had launched his electoral campaign. "Homes for heroes" failed to interest. His audiences were set on the punishment of the enemy. An orator is sensitive to an audience. The Prime Minister's tone hardened. He enlarged on penalties. Though he was careful to make some wise reservations and to disclaim responsibility for the astonishing figures which were recommended by an expert committee, he propounded the legal view that the beaten party pays the costs, and certainly led the country to believe that a very considerable sum could be and should be extracted from the enemy. Afterwards he discovered the truth that Germany's capacity to pay might be more nearly assessed at 2,000 millions than at the fantastic figure of 24,000 millions, at which one British committee of experts had put it. But in the atmosphere of chimerical hopes which then prevailed, the announcement of so low a figure would have been received as an outrage. No figure, then, was put into the treaties. By a wise and statesman-like provision it was left to a Reparations Commission, on which the United States was invited to serve, to decide what the reasonable figure should be.

The unsettled condition of the Reparations question caused great bitterness of feeling and undoubtedly helped to weaken the German Republic and to retard the economic convalescence of Europe. But it was a transitory evil. Sooner or later, as the British Prime Minister foresaw, business men would meet together and, with or without American help, fix a scale of payments which it was possible for the debtor country to make and profitable for her creditors to receive. The event proved this to be the case. Frontiers are seldom altered without force, but money payments are susceptible of infinite adjustments. By degrees, though not before they had been the cause of much heartburning and confusion, Germany's reparation payments were scaled down until eventually at Lausanne (1932) they were reduced to negligible proportions.

While England agreed with France in thinking that German militarism was the danger, and was willing that Germany and Austria should be stripped of non-German territory, in two vital particulars she parted company with France. Her trade interests demanded a convalescent, a prosperous Germany. Her political interests required that Germany should be peaceful and content. The influence, therefore, of Mr. Lloyd George was cast in the scale of mitigation. He was opposed to the suggestion that the Rhineland should be severed from the *Reich*, or that the whole of the rich industrial district of Upper Silesia should be handed over to the Poles, or that the Allies should be entitled, under the Treaty, to occupy German territory for fifteen years. Collecting the Imperial Cabinet round him in Paris, he secured that the destination of Upper Silesia should be determined by a plébiscite of its inhabitants.

The attitude of Italy was strictly national. No wide philanthropic ideas obscured the vision or warmed the heart of the realist politicians of the Monte Citorio. The League of Nations, which almost consoled many Anglo-Saxons for the war, excited little interest in Milan or Rome. Did it not even, thought the *papalini*, invade the immemorial prerogatives of the Vatican to impose its mediation on conflicting nations? A frontier running up to the crests of the Alps and a line of ports on the Adriatic were more to be valued than a Parliament in Geneva. Italy said to herself: "France is getting Alsace-Lorraine, England is getting the bulk of the German colonies, what do we get?" In the end she was allotted the Trentino, Trieste, and Zara, and helped herself to Fiume, the Hungarian port at the head of the Adriatic sea, by the "coup de main" of d'Annunzio the poet. But even so, she was bitterly chagrined: the Dalmatians, who had been evangelized by Italian missionaries and civilized by Italian artists, were allotted to Yugo-Slavia.

When the terms of the draft treaty were made known to the Germans, they were regarded as staggering in their severity and impossible of fulfilment. The whole scheme seemed designed to keep the country in perpetual subjection. While Germany was to be stripped of her armaments and left naked before her enemy, the allies were entitled to ask for impossible sums, and to occupy German territory as a gage of payment. Loud complaint went up that the instrument differed widely from President Wilson's fourteen points and subsequent speeches, upon the faith of which Germany had, as it was contended, laid down her arms. The prospect of a crushing tribute spread over two generations, and of a long military occupation, the forced destruction, under the eyes of an allied commission, of the mechanism and equipment of the German national army, and the abolition of conscription, were humiliations difficult to bear. Most obnoxious too were the arrangements for the eastern frontiers, the revival of Poland, the Polish corridor to the sea severing East Prussia from Brandenburg (though these were among the fourteen points) and the cession to Poland of a large slice of the industrial area of Silesia which, but for German brains and German capital, would never have attained to its swift and imposing development. That the conquests of the great Frederick should be thus abandoned through compulsion was of all the conditions of the Treaty that which German pride found it least easy to accept. The loss of Alsace-Lorraine, always a troublesome problem, was comparatively light to bear, and the temporary relinquishment of the Saar valley as a compensation for the injury done by the German army to the French mines a *bagatelle*.

It is for the Republic of Poland to justify, by its prudence, justice, and toleration, the confidence which was reposed in the Polish nation by the signatories of the Treaty of Versailles.

On its economic side the Treaty was much too harsh, and prejudicial to the stability of the Republican *régime* in Germany, which it should have been the aim of the Allies to assist. But while Englishmen blamed the pact of Versailles for its severity, the prevalent view in France was that Clemenceau, in his endeavour to meet the Anglo-Saxons, had still left the enemy too strong for the peace of Europe and the world.

The Treaty of Versailles has often been condemned as having been imposed and not negotiated. All treaties struck between conqueror and conquered are made under constraint. The Treaty of Bucharest, which the Germans imposed on Roumania, and the treaty of Brest-Litovsk, which they dictated to Russia, are savage exemplifications of that genus. When it is remembered how vast and complex was the ground covered by the treaties, how essential was despatch, how impatient were the war-weary armies for the hour of demobilization, and how easily protracted discussions might have jeopardized a settlement, the desire of the Allied and Associated Powers to proceed as they did become intelligible. To the written German criticism of the draft treaty, an allied reply containing some concessions was delivered in writing. For a more generous, open, and elastic proceeding, no allied statesman in that tense and passionate Parisian atmosphere was prepared.[1]

Austria, the prime mover in the war, was the greatest sufferer through its miscarriage. Dynasty, army, empire disappeared in the whirlwind. The Hungarians declared themselves independent and were invaded by the Roumans. The Czechs and Slovaks broke away. The Serbs exploited their victory in the south. In the end a small republic of six million souls, specifically forbidden under the terms of the Treaty of St. Germain to join itself with Germany, save with the consent, only to be obtained by a unanimous vote, of the League of Nations, was all that remained of the famous polity which had ruled over fifteen races and given the law to central Europe. With a capital city many times too great for its contracted needs, with a Civil Service framed for a wide Empire, with enemy neigh-

[1] In the freely negotiated Treaty signed with the U.S.A. in 1921, Germany accepted many provisions, including the " War Guilt " clause to which she now objects.

bours killing its trade with their tariffs, with a city population
bitten with Bolshevism, and a peasantry as mediaeval and superstitious as any in Europe, Austria was plunged into the pit of

EUROPE REMODELLED BY THE PEACE TREATIES.

despair. In the face of the fierce nationalism of the new states a
Danubian Zollverein was impossible to impose or to sustain. In
the dark landscape there were only two gleams of light, the

opera in Vienna and the remedial action of the League of Nations, which at the crisis of its fortune (October, 1922) saved the new Republic from bankruptcy.

The treatment of Hungary under the Treaty of Trianon is of all parts of the peace settlement that which has aroused most misgiving. The Hungarians were stripped of Slovakia, which was transferred to the Czechs, of Transylvania, which was conquered by the Roumans, and of Croatia, which now became part of Yugo-Slavia in the Serbo-Croat-Slovene Kingdom. Some six

AUSTRIA, AFTER THE PEACE TREATIES.

hundred thousand men and women of Magyar race, some four and a half million of former subjects of the Hungarian crown, passed under alien domination.[1] To the proud Magyar aristocracy the spoliation of their ancient kingdom by peasant democracies without lineage or distinction seemed an intolerable affront. Lost, too, was the lovely mountain region of Transylvania, where the Magyar noble was wont to take his pleasure in sport. His sentiments may be imagined. As easily would the

[1] These figures are probably too favourable to Hungarian claims. According to the official Hungarian census figures of 1910, the number of Magyars incorporated in the new states was 2,945,273.

owner of a Scottish deer forest welcome the news of its forced partition among the Irish immigrants in Lanark.

The treaty, then, has left sore places. There is the little republic of Austria, too weak to live comfortably by herself, yet debarred by the peace treaties from joining Germany without the consent of the League. There are the transferred Magyars, there is President Wilson's Poland with its special points of irritation in the Corridor and Silesia, there is the subjection of some 230,000 German Tyrolese and 1,300,000 Yugo-Slavs to Italian rule. To a smaller yet sensible degree the Germans resented the cession of the little woodland districts of Eupen and Malmédy to Belgium, and the temporary submission of the Saar district to the League of Nations. Yet viewed in proper perspective and despite these defects, the political map of Europe is drawn more closely than ever before in accordance with the views of the populations concerned.[1]

Nevertheless, when the Treaty of Versailles was finally signed in the *Galerie des Glaces*, where half a century earlier the Hohenzollern Empire had been proclaimed, everybody felt that a great opportunity had been missed. The statesmen had not been equal to the grandeur of events. They had made a peace which was no peace. American idealists, who were well content that the doctrine of self-determination should be violated in respect to their Red Indians and Africans, joined with English idealists, who were not proposing to march out of India or Egypt, in denouncing the lapses from the high doctrine of self-determination which were noted in the treaties. Human nature, it was widely felt, had failed. Europe had not been made safe for democracy. The bright exhilaration of victory was soon blotted by the fog of disillusion, resentment, and despair. *June 28 1919*

It is too soon to pass a final verdict on the work of the treatymakers. They will be judged by the success of the states which they brought into being or greatly augmented, by the new Poland, the new Czecho-Slovakia, the new Roumania, the new Yugo-Slavia, and the new Greece. A hundred years hence the historian will know. We who are passing through the zone of maximum friction and uneasiness, when the war passions are still alive and the minorities are wincing under new masters, and before the oil of habit has begun to smooth the springs of the newly-made chariots of state, can hardly with any show of confidence formulate a guess.

[1] See Maps in Appendix D.

It was a common hope and expectation among the Allies not only that America would sign the Treaty, which had been so largely shaped by the President's ideas, but that she would join the League of Nations, which was perhaps the most characteristic and remarkable contribution made by that great American

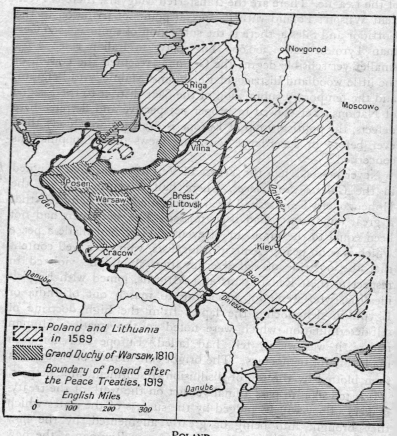

POLAND.

statesman to the problem of international order. In both these respects the United States falsified the expectations of Europe. America neither signed the Treaty nor joined the League. All the hopes, therefore, which had been founded upon American co-operation in scaling down reparations, upon an Anglo-American guarantee to France, upon the assistance which

America might render as a member of the League in bringing economic pressure to bear on a peace-breaker were suddenly dissipated. The disappointment was extreme. Yet a close knowledge of American history and the American outlook might have warned Europeans that it was as natural for America to withdraw from Europe, as for England to require the Germans to evacuate Belgium, or for France to demand the restoration of Alsace-Lorraine. The Americans did not come into the war when the neutrality of Belgium was violated, nor when the *Lusitania* was sunk. They decided to fight only when their merchantmen were sunk by German submarines. That outrage they were determined to punish. When the punishment was inflicted they reverted to that policy of withdrawal from European entanglements which they had inherited from George Washington. President Wilson indeed was an idealist; but in his own country he was almost alone.

There the Republican reaction was in full spate. With a sharp swing away from Europe and its miseries "the hundred per cent. American he-man" now coming into fashion was content with the glories of his own nation, enriched beyond the dreams of avarice, and towering above an exhausted and impoverished world.

A terrific problem then disclosed itself. The Central Powers had been beaten by a combination, such as was never afterwards likely to occur, of twenty-seven states, including the United States and the British Empire, two civilian nations who had by superhuman efforts improvised vast armies while the war was in progress. That combined military effort, and nothing less than that effort, had for the moment destroyed the German military machine and made it powerless to alarm the peoples of the continent. But now America had withdrawn, England with a rare unanimity of sentiment had abandoned conscription and curtailed her army and navy, and Italy was racked with civil trouble. France felt herself deserted; faced with a Germany disarmed indeed, but angry, defiant, and full of immense possibilities of mischief, she regarded herself as the gendarme of Europe, the maintainer of the public order established by the Peace Treaties. At Geneva she found friends. These were Belgium and Poland, and the three states which had benefited by the fall of the Austrian Empire, and now were leagued together in the *Petite Entente*. With these states France entered into close political relations. Together they formed a combination to replace Russia as an eastern counterweight to the central races of Germanism.

It was not so, however, that the English and Scandinavian advocates of the League of Nations regarded the future of Europe. The peril which they were anxious to avoid was the division of Europe once more into two rival groups of powers, each arming and plotting against the other. That the small powers of the east, so new, so unstable, and so close to the incalculable forces of Republican Russia, should provide themselves with armaments seemed natural enough. But it was unsatisfactory that this necessity should exist. Under a rational organization armaments would be subject to collective control and disputes would be settled by resort to arbitration or conciliation.

While all countries stand to lose by war, to no country is war more injurious than to Britain, which can feed its population only by the profits of international trading. Here, more even than in France, was the doctrine preached and believed that this was a war to end war. The dream so often entertained, so often frustrated, of a world organized not for war but for peace, once more became alive in the thoughts of men. After the torments of the war the Covenant of the League of Nations furnished to most Englishmen a gleam of consolation and of hope.

The importance of the League of Nations is that it offers to the world as much world-government as the world can stand. The framers of the Covenant saw that it would be idle to create a super-state to override the national governments. Accordingly they rejected the idea much favoured in France of a League army, or of a League police, or of any other predetermined mode of coercion by which a member state might be compelled to bow to the will of an external authority. Rather than violate by one jot or tittle the sovereign rights of the nation states, the founders were prepared that their League should be an association of nation states, each, however insignificant, entitled to equal justice and consideration, and protected from invasion of its domestic prerogatives by the requirement that any decisions of the League should receive a unanimous assent.

How often in the past had men of good will met in conference to promote the cause of peace, and after much eloquent talk and virtuous resolve separated with nothing done! The League of Nations was to be altogether different from these ephemeral and ineffective manifestations. It was to be a permanent organ, supported by national governments, for the transaction of international affairs, with an Assembly of delegates from all the member states, meeting once a year for a month in Geneva, and a Council, originally of nine delegates (five from the larger states), meeting more frequently, while the business of Assembly and Council alike was prepared and executed by an international Civil Service or Secretariat. Other organs were subsequently added, an International Labour Office, for the levelling up of Labour conditions throughout the world, and a Court of International Justice at The Hague. Of this carefully planned machinery for world government the nations were free to make as much or as little use as they chose.

The pith of the Covenant consists in the obligation assumed by every member-state to submit his quarrel to the League before resorting to arms. The Covenant does not exclude the possibility of war, but provides tribunals (the Council and the Court) before which member-states undertake in advance to lay their disputes, and prescribes a period during which, should the decision of the League prove to be unacceptable, the aggrieved party undertakes to preserve the peace. Were the League universal, and were its members prepared to obey the Covenant in letter and in spirit, these provisions for conciliation, arbitration, and delay would be sufficient to rid the world of the spectre of war.

Another function entrusted to the League was to obtain, if possible, from its member-states an agreed and progressive reduction of armaments. The evil of competitive armaments was generally admitted; their burden universally deplored; the theory that no state should arm in excess of its strict needs for home defence and the discharge of its international obligations was conceded by all reasonable men. The difficulty was to translate these principles into action, with Germany chafing under her compulsory disarmament, and with France nervously feeling that perhaps after all she was not sufficiently secure from a German attack. It is a measure of the strength and vitality of international fears and animosities that, despite the steady efforts of the League, the load of armaments pressing on

Europe in 1935 was actually heavier than it was on the eve of the war.

Among other fruitful ideas embodied in the Covenant is the need for fostering international co-operation of all kinds in time of peace. It was not sufficient that the member-states should abjure war, practise open diplomacy, or reduce their armaments. They must learn to work together through the League not only in the great tasks of humanity, but in all matters of common interest, such as the protection of the standard of life among the workers, or the campaign against the traffic in women and children, or the regulation of the opium trade, or the framing of measures of international hygiene. Perhaps it is in this humanitarian sphere that the League is destined to achieve its most certain triumphs.

At the end of the Napoleonic wars the Congress of Vienna had taken up the question of the abolition of the Slave Trade. In a like spirit the framers of the Covenant took note of the fact that European states had obligations not only to the racial and religious minorities in their midst, but also to the weak and backward peoples in other continents who had come under their control. The principle of trusteeship, the idea that the power of the governor should be exercised for the benefit of the governed, had long been familiar to the British Empire. This principle (under a term borrowed from Roman law) it was now decided to affirm in connection with the territories taken by the allies from the Germans and the Turks. The crudity of conquest was draped in the veil of morality. The annexed territories (with some exceptions) were regarded as mandated by the Allied and Associated Powers, and the annexing States as mandatories obliged at fixed intervals to give an account of their stewardship to a League Commission. That such a requirement was made and assented to was a clear advance in international morality.

A league of peace, comprising ultimately all the nations of the world, and having the Anglo-Saxon race as its solid nucleus and the governments of the British Empire and the United States as the principal instruments of its activity and influence, such was the vision which filled the minds of President Wilson and his English associates, as they sat down in Paris to work at the framework of a new international order. These large hopes were swiftly killed. When the first Assembly of the League met in the autumn of 1920 in Geneva forty-four states only were represented. Russia stood aloof. Germany, Turkey, and other ex-enemy states were not yet deemed ripe for admission: but the gravest blow of all was the absence of the power whose concur-rence was essential to the enforcement of economic sanctions against offending members, and upon whose impartiality great reliance had been placed. The work of President Wilson had been repudiated in his own country. America had refused to join the League.

The League of Nations can be no better than the member states of which it is composed. If they wish for peace, the League provides machinery by which peace may be the better secured and maintained, but League or no League, a state which is resolved on war can always have it. Not till the mind of man is filled with the conviction that modern war offers a peril for civilization so great that it is a crime, certain to be visited by condign punishment, for any state acting in pursuance of its own national interest to initiate it, will mankind be effectually rid of this menace. At present the world neither entertains nor is prepared to act upon these salutary and intelligent beliefs.

Meanwhile the League transacts so much international busi-ness for which there is no alternative machinery that if it did not exist it would be necessary to invent it. Statesmen have become acclimatized to the strange atmosphere of cosmopolitan consultation which prevails at Geneva. The secretariat has been so composed as to inspire confidence. The work grows, the area of international co-operation extends. For the first few important years the ideals of the League were expounded to the Assembly with authority and conviction by Robert Cecil, one of the framers of the Covenant. At the annual meetings at Geneva the leading statesmen of the smaller nations can make their contributions to international wisdom. Here Hymans of Belgium, Branting of Sweden, Nansen of Norway, Motta of Switzerland, Benès of Czecho-Slovakia, and Politis of Greece have rendered service to the Commonwealth of Europe. More important still is the opportunity which the League meetings afford for the formation of friendships, the comparison of ideas, the enlargement of knowledge, and the adjustment of differing points of view. Amid the rough jolts and jars of international life the annual month of cool conciliation at Geneva, though little respected by the warlike idealists of Japan, is like Christmas Day and our nearest approach to the mediaeval truce of God.

Yet many as have been the services of the League during the first fifteen years of its existence, it has brought, as we have seen, no moral or material disarmament to Europe. Though much labour has been expended on the problem of how best to reconcile the French demand for military security with the German claim for equality of treatment, the problem has in fact, given the greater population and higher birthrate of Germany, resisted solution. Save in Great Britain, there has been no serious effort to reduce land armaments. British pacifism has not been shared by the governments of Paris or Berlin, of Rome or Moscow, of Tokio or Prague. The Fascist master of Italy has never scrupled to express his belief in force. The Soviet Republic, though lately reconciled to the League, keeps on foot an army nine hundred and forty thousand strong. Japan and Germany have marched out of Geneva. In 1935 the Third German *Reich*, after more than a decade of secret and illegal arming, openly reverted to conscription and came before the world once more as a military power of the first class.

1931,
1933

A general agreement as to political objectives is the only sure basis for a policy of disarmament. Such an agreement was reached with regard to the problems of the Pacific in 1921 by the United States, Great Britain, France and Japan, and furnished the groundwork for the only substantial measure of disarmament which was reached by diplomatic methods during this period. When the four great naval Powers discovered that they were at one in desiring the policy of the open door in China and the preservation of the territorial integrity of the Chinese republic, naval disarmament became a relatively easy problem. Foreseeing no occasion of political variance, the four Pacific Powers found it easy to agree upon naval ratios, to curtail the size of capital ships, and to provide against the fortification of new naval bases in the Pacific. But when in 1933 Japan broke away from her allies, and by unilateral action seized a province of China, the whole plan for naval disarmament contained in the Treaty of Washington was placed in peril. In point of fact, Japan lost no time in announcing that she did not propose after 1936 to renew the treaty. She was developing a bigger and very controversial policy in China and was resolved upon a bigger navy with which to support it.

As yet there is no agreement as to political objectives in Europe. Germany wishes to absorb Austria. Italy and France are resolved that Austria should maintain her independence. A deep chasm of sentiment and policy sunders Nazi (National Socialist) Germany and the Communist rule of the Soviets. The year which witnessed the return of the Saar to Germany, so far **1935** from ushering in a happier period of international relations, has seen darker storm clouds over Europe than any period since the guns stopped firing in the Great War.

BOOKS WHICH MAY BE CONSULTED

Winston Churchill : The World Crisis. 1923.
Harold Nicolson : Peace Making. 1919.
F. H. Simonds : How Europe made Peace without America. 1923.
J. M. Keynes : The Economic Consequences of the Peace. 1919.
H. Wilson Harris : The League of Nations. 1929.
A. Toynbee : Survey of International Affairs, 1920-23.
H. Temperley : History of the Peace Conference at Paris. 1921.
E. M. House and C. Seymour : What really happened at Paris. 1921.
E. J. Dillon : The Peace Conference. 1919.
Colonel E. M. House : Intimate Papers. 1926.
Prince Max of Baden : War Memoirs. *Eng. tr.* 1928.
Ten Years of World Co-operation. (Issued by the Secretariat of the League of Nations, 1930.)
F. J. Berber : Locarno. A Collection of Documents. 1936.

CHAPTER XXXV

THE TRANSFORMATION OF TURKEY

Venizelos. The Greek landing in Smyrna. Mustapha Kemal. The pact of Sivas and the Greco-Turkish War. The Greek disaster in Asia Minor. New aspect of the Near Eastern question. Fall of the Lloyd George Government. The Treaty of Lausanne. The New Turkey.

AMONG the brilliant figures who were drawn to Paris for the peace-making was Venizelos, the Cretan. Few statesmen of that age had surmounted greater difficulties, whether as a leader of irregular troops among his native hills, or as the main artificer of the Balkan League, or as the advocate of an alliance with the *Entente* Powers in the Great War, when the whole influence of the Athenian Court, of the Peloponnese, and of the Ionian islands was thrown in the opposite scale. His horizon was wide, his eloquence and charm were compelling, audacity and finesse were at the service of his ambition. From the first he was certain that the Allies would win the war and that the true interest of Greece was to espouse their cause. It was not his fault if Greek divisions did not fight side by side with the British at the Dardanelles or later come to the rescue of the Serbian army before it was driven to its final disaster in the Albanian hills. And if in the end, after King Constantine had been expelled by the French fleet, a quarter of a million Greek troops took a share in the final allied victory against the Bulgars, the credit belongs to Venizelos, who of his own initiative settled down upon Salonika and there created a pro-Ally Greek Government and pro-Ally Greek army while Court and Cabinet in Athens were still obstinate in their adhesion to the German cause. For such services Venizelos, coming to the peace-making in Paris, was entitled to expect a high reward.

It was an axiom of Allied policy that whatever could colourably be regarded as of Greek speech and race in European Turkey should be assigned to the Greeks. Thessaly, Macedonia, eastern Thrace presented no difficulties. The crux lay in Asia Minor. Here, widely dispersed in the coast towns and over the upland country were some million merchants and bankers, seamen and shopkeepers, tobacco growers, vine growers, rice growers, and carpet makers of the Greek race, whose situation gave cause for great anxiety. The Turkish power in Anatolia was still alive. Though Syria, Palestine, and Mesopotamia had been wrested from the Turks by British arms, and Allied forces controlled Constantinople and the Straits, in Asia Minor, which was the real Turkey, the hatred of the Christian races was awake and armed. A million Armenian lives had been sacrificed to the Crescent since the inception of the war. And as it was to be expected that the Greeks would be the next victims, Venizelos obtained from the Prime Ministers of Britain and France leave to land forces at Smyrna, suspecting that otherwise the city might fall to the Italians, and hoping that if the worst came to the worst a refuge might here be provided for the Asiatic members of his race. It was an ill judgment. Italians might perhaps have been tolerated in Smyrna, but that the despised flag of Greece should wave over any part of Asia Minor was regarded by every patriot Turk as an intolerable affront. The Greek landing (April 15, 1919), disgraced by crime, roused all that was fiercest and most determined in the Turkish temper and offered to Mustapha Kemal, "the Saviour of the Dardanelles" and the most brilliant officer in the Turkish army, the chance of creating out of the shattered fragments of the vanquished empire a new and independent Turkish State.

Mustapha was now thirty-eight years of age, a fierce, disagreeable, quarrelsome figure, with a frame of iron (for though born at Salonika he came of stout Anatolian peasant stock), and a will of steel. If his debaucheries, which were sordid, callous, and violent, belonged to the tradition of his race, his clearness of head, his independence of judgment, his gift of military and political leadership were all his own. Turkey for the Turks was his motto through life. As a youth he had joined in the plot to overthrow Abdul Hamid, not out of love for constitutional liberty, but because he saw that under the Red Sultan his country was decrepit, spy-haunted, and the prey of foreigners, and that only by the destruction of that paralyzing *régime* could it hope to become strong and free. Fighting in many fields—in the Lebanon, in Tripoli, in the Balkans, on the Syrian front—gave him a wide experience of men and things. He was jealous of Enver, the brilliant pro-German, and shrewdly critical of the policy which had made of Turkey a German tool and involved it in the German ruin. So intelligent a man could not be blind to the larger significance of contemporary events. The moral which Mustapha drew from the Great War was that Turkey had been defeated because she had permitted herself to be entangled and bullied by the Western Powers, because she had remained un-progressive and barbaric and had overtaxed her strength in endeavouring to control non-Turkish races. The cure was emancipation from the foreigner, internal reform, and the educa-tion of a self-centred Turkish nationalism in the original Turkish homelands. The old ambitious imperialism of Enver and his gang had broken down in irretrievable ruin. The Turks had been driven from the Canal, from Mesopotamia, from Palestine and Syria. The British fleet was in the Dardanelles. The Sultan was a puppet in British hands. There remained only Asia Minor, and here, too, the west had made a lodgment. Four days after the Greek landing in Smyrna, Mustapha set foot on Asiatic soil, holding a military commission from the Sultan. His mind was made up. "I will stay in Anatolia," he said, "until the nation has won its independence." On September 13, 1919, a representa-tive assembly of Turks, meeting at Sivas, signed a pact to con-tinue the war until the soil of Asia was free of the invader. All that was most virile in the Turkish race rallied round Mustapha Kemal and the National Pact. He set up a Government (April 24, 1920) at Angora, snapped his fingers at the Sultan in Constan-tinople, and resolved to build up a new life for his people in the bracing uplands of Anatolia, where the ancestors of the Turkish race, far from the miasmal breezes of the west, had first displayed their steadfast valour to the world.

In the war which ensued everything after some preliminary successes went awry with the Greek cause. At home there was a series of misfortunes and convulsions, abroad a notable breach in the allied front against the Turks. Who could have predicted that young King Alexander of Greece would die suddenly of a monkey's bite or that in the plébiscite which ensued a wave of royalist feeling would sweep Venizelos from power (November 14, 1920) and bring Constantine back with his pro-German follow-ing? These events were not without their repercussions on the Asiatic front. The Greek army, spurred by the old king to a rash advance on Angora, suffered a heavy defeat on the river Sakaria (August 23–September 13, 1921) and, being further weakened by the dismissal of many tried Venizelist officers, was in no fit state to offer an effective resistance to the Turks. Little help was to be expected from the Allies. While the Italians hated the Greeks, the French made a separate peace with the Turks (October 20, 1921). The proposal of the Athenian Cabinet that the army of Thrace should be permitted to occupy Constantinople (June, 1922) was negatived by the Powers. Indeed, of all the prominent Allied statesmen, Mr. Lloyd George alone was conscious of responsibilities to the Greek people and eager that the task of finally crushing the Turk, which had been so brilliantly initiated by Maude and Allenby, should be completed by the levies of Hellas and her islands.

The Greeks, then, were left alone to weather the storm. They were unequal to the test. Shaken by defeat, paralyzed by schism, and distrustful of their higher command, they crumbled under the next hard blow delivered by the enemy (August 26, 1922) and streamed back, a disorderly rout, to the coast. Stern was the vengeance of their enemies. Entering Smyrna on the heels of the fugitives, the Turks fired the city and massacred all whom they could find of the Greek tongue and blood. More than a million Christians, fleeing that terrible wrath, were rescued from Asia Minor in Allied ships and by a great feat of benevolent organization distributed through Greece and its islands.

Out of the burning wreck of Smyrna there arose an unfamiliar and more hopeful East. Two monarchies disappeared, the Greek and the Turkish, the one an alien institution of some ninety years, the other rooted in the immemorial traditions of the race of Othman. Greece became, by reason of its industrious Asiatic immigrants, richer, stronger, more populous than before. A like concentration of national power marked the new Turkish republic of Mustapha Kemal. Accordingly, the problem of Christian minorities, which had so long vexed the conscience and shaped the policies of the western world, ceased to haunt the chanceries. The minorities had been massacred or driven away, and by the very extremity of that calamity the chief occasion of Greco-Turkish hostility was paradoxically removed. Wise arrangements for the exchange of populations on European soil further assisted the establishment of friendly relations between the governments of Angora and Athens. Thus did the principle of self-determination work itself out through fire and sword in the half-savage East.

Lloyd George, the Gladstonian Philhellene, went down with his Hellenic friends. The rank and file of the Tory party were restive under a leader who so far carried his radicalism into foreign policy as to treat with rebel Ireland, to encourage the Greeks, and to propose the defence of the Dardanelles against the exultant Turks. Alarmed by the spectre of a new war, the Tories gathered in the Carlton Club and dismissed the Prime Minister, "a daring pilot in extremity," who for six years had exercised in peace and war a greater influence on public affairs than any subject of the British Crown since the Duke of Wellington. The fall of the Coalition in Britain set the seal on the triumph of the Turk. Providentially delivered from the ghost of Mr. Gladstone and the aeroplanes of Mr. Lloyd George, Mustapha Kemal, beneficiary of the Carlton Club, quietly crossed the Dardanelles.

At Lausanne in 1923 the Allies were compelled to ratify the political results of the Turkish victory. Everything which symbolized the old *régime* of Western supervision was swept away— the capitulations giving special privileges in justice and finance to the Western merchant, the right so often conceded to the Powers to protect the Christian subjects of the Porte. The Turk was resolved to be master in his own house. The last effulgence of Lord Curzon's eloquence could not undo the effects of Mustapha's victories. The Crescent still flies at Chanak and Stamboul.

The field was now cleared for the series of audacious reforms which, though long debated in the private counsels of the Young Turks, have given to Mustapha the name of a genius and to Turkey the aspect of a modern state. The Caliphate was abolished, the women were compelled to abandon the veil, the schools were laicized, the Koran was ordered to be rendered into Turkish. By an astounding breach with tradition it was decreed (1928) that the Moslem faith should no longer be the official religion of the Turkish Republic. Small things as well as large attracted the innovating zeal of the Ghazi, or "Raider of the Christians," and, lest the devout should persevere in the practice of touching the ground with their foreheads in the course of their devotions, they were compelled to substitute the rimmed hat of the European for the traditional fez. These and other modernizing changes, such as the abolition of polygamy, the introduction of the Latin script, and the adoption of Western codes of law, were accepted without a murmur. The dervish, the chiromancer, the magician, the dice thrower and amulet seller were decreed out of existence. It was sufficient that such changes were recommended by the Ghazi.

When a doubt was expressed in the Grand National Assembly at the breach of tradition involved by the abolition of the Sultanate and the Caliphate, Mustapha argued that the last of the true Caliphs had been murdered in A.D. 924, and thus proceeded: "Sovereignty is acquired by force, by power, by violence. It was by violence that the sons of Othman acquired the power to rule over the Turkish nation and to maintain their rule for more than six centuries. It is now the nation that revolts against these usurpers, puts them in their right place, and carries on their sovereignty."[1] At the end of his speech there were shouts of, "Vote, vote!" One single voice was heard declaring. "I am against it," but this was drowned by cries of "Silence!" Stupefied with admiration, the Turks, a nation of private soldiers, wheeled to the word of their general's command.

[1] A speech delivered by Ghazi Mustapha Kemal (October 15 to 20, 1927), Koehler, Leipzig, 1929.

BOOKS WHICH MAY BE CONSULTED

A. Toynbee : Survey of International Affairs for 1925.

K. Krüger : Kemalist Turkey and the Middle East.   1932.

H. C. Armstrong : Grey Wolf.   1932.

Mustapha Kemal : Speech delivered from October 15 to 20, 1927. Koehler, Leipzig, 1929.

W. Miller : Greece. (Nations of the Modern World Series.)   1928.

A. Toynbee and M. P. Kirkwood : Turkey. (Nations of the Modern World Series.)   1926.

H. Nicolson : Curzon : The Last Phase.   1934.

CHAPTER XXXVI

NEW DICTATORSHIPS AND OLD DEMOCRACIES

*New dictatorships and old democracies. Declining belief in Liberty.
The challenge to Capitalism. The Bolshevik religion. Lenin. The War
of the Reds and the Whites. Russia and Poland. The battle of Warsaw.
Communism in Italy. Benito Mussolini. The Fascist revolution. Adolf
Hitler. The Weimar revolution. The French in the Ruhr. Stresemann
and the policy of fulfilment. Delays in disarmament. The crash of
1929. Racial philosophy of the Nazis. Victory of Hitlerism. Post-war
Britain. Foundations of British policy. The scare of Europe. The
Refugees. Stalin. Peace and Freedom.*

WITH the passing of Europe under the harrow of war there passed
also by insensible degrees out of the average thinking of average
men that strong belief in civil liberty and peaceful persuasion
which had been a distinctive feature of the nineteenth century.
Before the war there were good reasons for believing that parliamentary institutions would supply the sovereign formula for the
coming age. No country in the world claiming to be civilized—
not even Russia—had been able altogether to withstand the
public pressure in favour of responsible cabinets, representative
assemblies, and democratic electorates. The Austrian Empire
possessed a parliament elected by universal suffrage. The Congress party in India were clamouring for parliaments. It was a
general assumption that the path of political progress lay along
the line of extending the franchise, educating the voters, and
improving the machinery of parliamentary government. This at
least was the Liberal faith which Conservatives were compelled
with varying degrees of readiness to accept. That every citizen
should be able to think as he liked, to speak as he liked, and to
vote as he liked was widely regarded as the mark of a civilized
polity. Some dangers there might be in the practice of liberty,
but they were nothing to the risk of allowing discontents to fester
under a system of repression.

A doctrine of *laissez-faire* in the sphere of economics was often,
and most strongly in England, allied to this widespread faith in
political freedom. The peace-time structure of European society
had not been shaped by governments. It was no government

which had made the prosperity of Lancashire or the Ruhr, no government which had built up the financial wealth of the Rothschilds, nor any assemblage of governments which had enabled the population of Europe to increase by more than three hundred and fifty millions in a hundred and thirty years.

The capitalist structure of European society had been due to individual invention and individual enterprise, to a liquid fund of cosmopolitan capital accumulated from individual savings and flowing freely from country to country in obedience to the magnet of private gain. The richest country in Europe was that in which government interference in trade and industry had been confined within the narrowest limits, and the best advertisement for the value of economic liberty was supplied by the trade returns of the British people.

On the other side of the Atlantic was a society of European stock which in the course of the nineteenth century had experienced a fantastic accretion of numbers and prosperity. The social and economic history of the United States of America from the declaration of independence in 1776 to the great slump in 1929 was one of unexampled and continuously ascending prosperity; but, swift as had been the growth of the population, the resources of the continent had been equal to the expanding demand. The vast fortunes accumulated by a Vanderbilt, a Rockefeller, and a Ford were compatible with the enjoyment by the whole American people of the highest general standard of comfort ever reached in the history of mankind.

Apart from the favours of nature this staggering prosperity had been due to a long tradition of individual enterprise. From the earliest colonial days, when every constitution wore "the engaging air of a prospectus," private enterprise in money-making was the note of American society. Everything was made easy for the immigrant, the settler, the pioneer. He was invited to come "right in," could purchase public land in small lots at low prices, was offered free education for his children, and knew that wherever he might settle all the private rights and constitutional privileges belonging to the oldest state in the Union would in due course be his. America was "the land of the dollar." No American citizen was debarred by law or public sentiment from amassing dollars. In the absence of an hereditary aristocracy or any widely respected political class, and since any American citizen might aspire to opulence, inequality was robbed of half its bitterness. Wealth was the prime object of national veneration, not least because it was easily come by and easily lost. The astonishing spectacle of this material paradise was not lost upon Europe. If amid the rush and fever of the American scene voices were sometimes heard denouncing the financiers of Wall Street or the magnates of oil and steel, nobody before the great slump doubted that it was in America, where the acquisitive faculties of man were least impeded by law, that the problem of poverty had been most successfully solved.

Meanwhile in Europe, as the tides of political liberty surged forward, the tides of economic liberty tended to recede. It was reasonable for James Mill in 1820 to think and write of government as a bad thing, because English government at that time was controlled by a small and privileged class and open to the charge of corruption and jobbery. But it was less reasonable to take this disparaging view of government when the whole people had been admitted within the pale of the constitution. A democratic government might not always be wise; but at least it might be expected to protect the interest of the public as a whole. The interference of such a government might be positively conducive to human happiness.

Such a government in particular might be expected to arrest the evils of the capitalistic system. These evils were patent, the wastefulness of competition, the soullessness of limited liability companies, the pressure of sinister influences on legislation, the exploitation of the weak, the great disparities of wealth between man and man. In the years after the war the world was faced with the strange phenomenon of dire poverty existing in the midst of unexampled plenty. While millions went short of food and clothing, crops were actually destroyed as being in excess of remunerative demand. What was the world coming to? It was freely contended that parliaments were bankrupt, that democratic civilization had reached its term, and that *laissez faire* must give place to " planned economy," all along the line. Even in England a complete reconstruction of the fabric of society was demanded (1919) by the voice of organized labour.

One major evil resulting from the war was the collapse over a great part of Europe of social discipline. The trust in authority was undermined, the fabric of custom broken, and while everywhere the defeated peoples, loosened from their old moorings, watched for new leadership over uncharted seas, this was specially true of Russia. There government was found at its worst and weakest. There the soil of revolution had been most fully prepared, and there too, more swiftly and decisively than in any other region in Europe, emerged at the crisis of disorder a man, a doctrine, and a faith.

The doctrine, derived from Marx, was the substitution, deemed to be the inevitable climax of a long historic process, of communism for the accepted order of capitalist society. It challenged property, the belief in God, the social hierarchy, the middle class, and all the ideas of art, morals, and philosophy on which that class had been nurtured. The deep evangelical piety of the Russian went out to meet a new religion, which, apart from its offers of peace, bread, and the land, proceeded on the maxim that the last should be first and the first last. For though Russian communism denounced religion as "the opium of the people," it bore, like Islam, the marks of a religious faith. It was cosmopolitan, militant, propagandist. Lenin was its prophet, and the Communist Party its Church.

Lenin was a fanatical visionary whose effective power was multiplied threefold by an inner conviction that he was designed by fate to be the commander of a victorious Russian Revolution. Without wealth or station, this obscure conspirator, who had spent much of his life in Siberian prisons, or in cheap lodgings in London or Switzerland, was confident that it would one day be given to him to overturn the old *régime* in Russia, to "liquidate" the bourgeoisie, and to establish the dictatorship of the proletariat. Great animal vigour, a powerful and saturnine mind, a gift rare and precious among Russians for succinct speech, clear-cut views, and despatch in business, coupled with an almost unequalled capacity for making himself disagreeable, secured for him an ascendancy among his revolutionary following, comparable in character to that exercised by Charles Parnell over the Irish Parliamentary Party. The German General Staff, with an intelligent appreciation of his uncanny gift, arranged that he should be conveyed to Russia from Switzerland (1917) in order to poison the *morale* of the Russian army. The poison worked, but before the year was out the poisoner was a Tzar more formidable, more destructive, and more creative even than Peter the Great.

Lenin had no scruples or inhibitions. He was a humanitarian

on so large and comprehensive a scale that he could look wit
composure upon the wholesale destruction which was demande
by the establishment of his system. Famine and war appeare
to him not as enemies but as friends, famine because it enrage
the peasants against the Tzar, war because the armed conflict c
capitalist nations would merge into the yet more terrible civ
war between classes through which alone the world could b
brought to the Communists' peace. Communism for Russia firs
and then for the rest of the world, was his programme. Th
writings of Marx constituted his Koran. But though he was
doctrinaire and man of the book, he was not without the grai
of statesmanship.

In defiance of theory he permitted private trading in 192
when he saw that unqualified communism was leading to di
aster. Nor was he insensible of the value of foreign capital fo
the support of Russian industries. The wild scheme of Trotsk
and Zinovieff for an intensive campaign of revolutionary prop
ganda in foreign countries did not win his approval. It wa
better, he thought, first to consolidate the system in Russia itsel
with such aid as the capitalist countries could afford. In 1921
commercial agreement was made with England, in 1922 wit
Germany. He dreamed of a Russia in which every peasant coul
read and write, and had his cottage heated and lit by electricity

The instruments of his power were, firstly a highly organize
communist party, second a secret police inherited from th
Tzarist régime, and thirdly the Red army. If there wa
terrorism there was no peculation. Lenin and his commissars o
ministers drew small salaries and practised the rigid an
laborious asceticism which they preached to others. The countr
honoured their loyalty to the people's cause.

To Lenin, in particular, who ruled Russia for six critical year
and in that time transformed the life and institutions of th
people, semi-divine honours were readily paid. Everything wa
forgiven to the Liberator, the dull and angry pedantry of hi
voluminous writings, the pitiless rigour of his system, the ir
human glee which he derived from the sufferings of rich o
comfortable men. Devout pilgrims to Moscow even yet defile i
an unending cortège before the embalmed corpse of the grea
revolutionary figure, once so violent and rugged, who lies ther
in the peace of death, while his will and mind continue t
fashion the ideals of the Russian state.

On the threshold of its career Russian Communism was confronted by the great evil of a civil war supported by the allied and associated powers. The motive of the Allies was to keep Russia in the war against Germany by giving assistance to those elements in the Russian population who were still willing to honour their engagements entered into by the Tzarist government. From every quarter of the compass, from Siberia, from the Black Sea, from Archangel and Murmansk, from Estonia, the Bolshevik Government was placed on the defensive. In the east, Kolchak overran Siberia. In the south, Denikin marched upon Moscow. But as formerly in the Vendée, so now in Russia, the mere fact of foreign interference consolidated loyalty to the revolutionary *régime* and made the reputation of its defenders. The White armies were everywhere repulsed, as much by their own disorders, tyrannies, and follies as by the merits of their opponents. A brilliant Jew who had graduated in petty crime gained renown as an organizer of victory, and Trotsky was hailed as the Russian Carnot.

The Bolshevik Revolution was a portent transcending in magnitude any movement of the kind of which Europe had experience. Its efficacy, its ruthlessness, the wide span of its ambition gave it a strange fascination. Even in conservative England, the Labour leaders talked of workers' councils, of the supersession of Parliamentary government by direct action, and of the General Strike.

All over western Europe statesmen asked themselves how far this conflagration would spread. In Finland the Reds were ruthlessly suppressed by the Germans, in Hungary by the Roumans. But who could forecast the effect of Bolshevik propaganda in the cordon of new states, some of them very small, others still unsettled and confused, which had been set up by the Peace Treaties? In 1920 there was a moment of extreme danger for Poland, upon which even in a general history we may be permitted to pause.

Few people had suffered so grievously during the war as the Poles. Their country had been the principal battlefield of the eastern campaigns. It had been drenched in blood and blasted by explosives. It had been the scene of butcheries such as no pen can describe, of butcheries inflicted and endured by subject peoples. Some Poles had fought in the Russian, others in the

Austrian, and others again in the Prussian armies. All had fought under compulsion. Then by an extraordinary turn of chance the partitioning Empires were simultaneously overthrown, and the Poles, war-wracked and impoverished, found themselves, after more than a century of subjection, masterless and free.

It is little wonder that the champagne of liberty went to their heads. At Paris they were like children asking for the moon. In the east they were like visionaries in search of the Holy Grail. Under the leadership of Joseph Pilsudski, an austere socialist conspirator, and one of the great war figures of his age—for ever since the Russian Revolution of 1905 he had been secretly composing the elements of the national Polish army—they resolved to renew the ancient glories of the seventeenth century and to water their horses in the Dnieper. But low as Russian pride had sunk, it had not sunk so far as to tolerate a Polish government in Kiev. The rash invaders were driven back, and Poland in turn was overrun by a Bolshevik army. The roar of the Communist artillery was heard in the streets of Warsaw, and in every capital in Europe it was assumed that nothing was left for this rash and unfortunate people but to make the best terms possible with a powerful enemy. But the history of Poland is a series of surprises. Aided by General Weygand and a staff of French officers, a Polish army under the command of Pilsudski won a victory of amazing completeness. With few casualties on either side, the Russians were pushed back across the frontier and driven to negotiate a peace. By his decisive manoeuvre in the bloodless battle of Warsaw, Pilsudski earned the gratitude of Europe. He had saved Poland from Bolshevism. How far, but for the miracle which he wrought on the Vistula, that contagion would have spread no man can say.

Two other services Pilsudski has rendered to his country. The Poles had no experience in the art of self-government. Suddenly emerging from their long servitude into the full sunlight of liberty they equipped themselves, as was perhaps natural, with a Parliamentary constitution of the most modern and extreme democratic type. They adopted proportional representation and universal suffrage for both their Houses, and as they had no less than fourteen parties, none of them closely adjusted to the needs of the novel situation which had arisen from the war, efficiency in government was made almost impossible. Ministry followed ministry with bewildering speed. There was neither continuity in policy nor coherence in thought, nor guarantee of technical ability. At a critical moment a peasant prime minister might be away on his farm carrying hay, and the ship of state, which had narrowly escaped disaster from the Bolsheviks, might very easily founder on the rock of Parliamentary confusion.

So things continued in Poland going from bad to worse until Pilsudski, emerging from retirement, rode into Warsaw on May 4, 1926, and stopped the fooling. What he then did is proof of a sagacity and moderation rare in the politics of central Europe. He refused to be President of the Republic, but promoted a much respected professor to the place of power. He neither abolished the Diet, nor endeavoured to form a Fascist party. The veteran soldier of Polish liberty, the honourable inmate of Siberian and German prisons, did not propose to turn dictator in his old age. The Diet should continue to meet, to discuss, to educate itself and the people; but it should not be allowed to turn out the Government. Pilsudski held that the business of Parliament was not to break Cabinets, but to learn from them. Accordingly a council of proved technicians was chosen to direct the wheel of state. Their permanence was guaranteed. It was enough that they were known to have the support of Pilsudski, who held the portfolio of war, commanded the devotion of the troops, and still retained the gratitude of the Polish people.

A second benefit conferred upon Poland by this remarkable man is a good foreign policy. Non-aggression pacts signed with Russia and Germany have brought a sense of security to a nation which dreads nothing so much as a renewal of war in Polish territory. Wider commitments are feared. Poland is heavily armed, but for defence only. After an initial burst of disconcerting temerity the Republic of Pilsudski has learnt to put safety first.

1933
1934

That Bolshevik propaganda made so little progress in the new states which were created by the treaty is undoubtedly due to the fact that almost everywhere the peasantry were enriched by agrarian legislation of a most far-reaching kind. In Poland, in Czecho-Slovakia and in Roumania, as also in the little Baltic states, larger properties were divided up for the benefit of the peasants. There were many who lamented the disappearance of the great country houses, which had played their part in the art, letters, and politics of the middle east for so many centuries. But one of the results of this wide agrarian revolution was that a strong cordon of peasant owners was drawn between Russian communism and central Europe.

The effects of so great a convulsion as the Russian Revolution could not, however, be wholly circumscribed. The period in which we are now living is still dominated by the shade of Lenin. It is not in Russia only that Europe beholds the spectacle of an armed doctrine enthroned in the seat of power, of a totalitarian state ruthlessly repressive of liberty and set upon the creation by a system of increasing pressure of a new type of human being and a new type of society. The grim logic of the Russian Communist has been accepted elsewhere. The maxims of despotism have been imposed by violence and propaganda on the submissive populations of Italy and Germany, at a moment when their will-power was at its lowest. Though Leninism is cosmopolitan, while Fascism, both in its Italian and its German garb, is fiercely nationalist, all these governments are united in their opposition to human liberty. Communists and Fascists alike have given up the idea that political problems should be settled by discussion, that the rights of minorities should be considered, or that an appeal to reason is always preferable to a recourse to violence. The new dictators are as absolute as any Tzar or Pope. The new slavery is penetrating to a degree never previously experienced. Inhumanity, bred of war and revolution, is a feature common to totalitarian tyranny in all three forms.

The fear of the Russian infection played an important part in the politics of Italy. Here, too, the end of the war produced a general feeling of lassitude and disillusion. Italy, it was felt, had suffered so much and gained so little. Revolutionary propaganda had been strong in Italy before the war and had played its part in procuring the _débâcle_ of Caporetto; and when victory at last came, and was found to bring nothing but high taxes, dear food, and scanty fuel, Italian working men asked themselves what they had gained from the exertions of the country. A mood of sharp revulsion against existing governments seized the factory hands of the north. The name of Lenin was popular. The portrait of the Russian prophet was circulated. Strike followed upon strike. Old soldiers of the war were mocked in the streets. Since Parliament was elected by proportional representation, the groups were many and the Cabinets weak. Speech was free, debates open; but there was nothing in the government of the country to rally opinion, to strike the imagination, or to prevent the degeneracy of the patriotic spirit. Many of the parliamentary statesmen were able and single-minded, but much of the energy which should have been devoted to the consideration of great national problems was wasted in the barren dialectic of debate or the ceaseless manoeuvring for position.

This apparent dispersion and paralysis of national forces explains the meteoric rise of Benito Mussolini. He came from outside the parliamentary class, for he was the son of a blacksmith at Forli. Before the war he had edited a Socialist paper. His opinions were too violent for Switzerland; nor could anybody in Italy have been more justly considered a standing menace to the social order But then war broke out between Germany and Russia. The German Socialists, despite their loudly advertised pacifism, voted the war credits. Mussolini recognized, as in a flash, what this meant. He saw that at the real pinch country comes before everything. The Socialists had not even protested against the violation of Belgium. It was not for him to be more Socialist than his German leaders. With a sharp swing he urged Italy's entry into the war, took arms himself, endured wounds, and "came out at the end burning with patriotism and bursting with ambition, a *condottiere* of fortune, prompt, fiery, clear-headed, shrinking from no violence or brutality, a born master of conspiracy." His first step was to form a party of action. He called it the Fascisti, having in mind the Roman rods, or *fasces*, which were carried by the lictors before the chief magistrate of the State as emblems of authority. It was to be a party of discipline, strict, Spartan, virile, and it was to rule the state. His organization, founded in a Milanese newspaper office (March 23, 1919), grew. It controlled the streets. Sometimes the Fascisti, wearing the black shirt of the *arditi*, or storm troopers, killed their opponents; at other times beat them or degraded them through the forced administration of castor oil. Sometimes in the old-fashioned manner of Italy they sacked the house of a liberal politician from floor to rafter. In the old soldiers of the war, chafing under neglect, the party found material for its militia. On October 30, 1922, Mussolini marched on Rome and, preserving the nominal primacy of the King, took on the conduct of the state.

b. July 29, 1883

The development which followed was extraordinary. The Fascisti grew till they absorbed the whole people. No other opinion was tolerated. The Press, the professors, the *litterati* were compelled to conform to the new doctrine. The phial of castor oil, the dungeon, or exile to an island were the penalties of disobedience. The convenient assassination of Matteotti, the leader of the parliamentary opposition, was an advertisement that the old liberalism of Italy was at an end.

In violent reaction against proportional representation, the "Duce" divided Italy into fifteen constituencies (November, 1923) and decreed that the party which obtained the majority should be awarded two-thirds of the seats. That party was his own.

Catholic, anti-feminist, national, authoritarian, the Fascist party was opposed at every point of prejudice to the liberalism which, during the long abstention of the Papalists from active policy, had become the guiding spirit of Italian parliamentary life. By a bold rupture with his past, Mussolini, who had organized a general strike in 1914, declared that strikes and lock-outs were forbidden. Under his Law of Corporations every industry in the country became part of a great public scheme directed with an eye to the protection of the interest of the worker on the one hand and to the prosperity and solvency of the businesses on the other. In the Liberal countries of the west the high-handed persecutions of the Italian dictator were received with sentiments of hostility and alarm. The silencing of the universities, the schooled obsequiousness of the Press, the destruction of parliamentary life, the substitution of brute force for persuasion in every department of national life, seemed to run counter to all those tendencies which had been judged to be most promising in human affairs. Yet humane Italians were found, even from the first, to applaud a movement which, despite the ferocity of its repression, brought into the political life of Italy a sentiment of grandeur recalling the Imperial age. The glowing genius and devouring energy of the "Duce" communicated itself to every part of the body politic. An entirely new standard of efficiency was required of every branch of the Public Service. The trains ran to time. The peculation of officials was severely punished. Great public works were undertaken. A new momentum was given to archaeological exploration, to the rebuilding of Rome, and to the reclamation of malarial regions of the south. By degrees Fascism, which had at first been viewed as the violent dream of a lunatic, was received with respect and admiration. It was not only a policy, but a creed. It opposed to the militant faith of international communism a faith not less combative and persecuting, a fervent national socialism, interpreted, preached, and imposed by an organized political party. Every force which tended to unite the nation it respected; every influence which tended to divide or perplex or to illumine it was brutally suppressed. The crucifix was restored to the schools, the State reconciled to the Church (February 11, 1929). All antagonism—local, provincial, religious, sectarian—disappeared in a common worship of the "Duce," recalling in its lavish and unbroken expressions of homage the cult of Alexander or of Augustus. If the price was the loss of liberty, it was a price which the Italian was prepared to pay. Again Italy had produced a man of the Caesarean mould, a tyrant with the *bravura* of an orator and the broad sympathies of a man of the people, but a tyrant who was content to give strength and unity to his own nation and did not, so it was long supposed, seek, like Napoleon, to impose his will upon foreign lands.

The remarkable character of the Italian leader, the way in which he succeeded in correcting the fatigue and despondency of the Italian people and in harnessing to the use of the State all the military virtues which had been educated by the war, his skill in striking the popular imagination, in generating enthusiasm and confidence, and his success in overcoming industrial unrest, attracted sympathies in other countries and led to the formation of Fascist groups or parties.

There was a certain lance-corporal of the sixteenth Bavarian Infantry reserve division lying blinded with gas in a German hospital on Armistice Day, who, when he had recovered from his war disabilities, felt that the German answer to the Communists and the Allies must take some such shape as that which the "Duce" had ordained for Italy. He was the son of a small Austrian customs official, and a house painter by calling. His name was Adolf Hitler. Waking up after the victorious *camaraderie* of the front line to find the Fatherland brought low, the army broken, the spirit of revolution abroad, and the social democrats installed in power, this obscure young man set himself to found a German party on the Italian model. He was a tough, resentful, visionary figure, half crazy

b. April 20, 1889

with anti-Semitism, as an orator violent, abounding, and hysterical, but disinterested, patriotic, and charged with Teutonic pride. Knowing how great Germany had been, he felt that she had but to will to be great once more. As a middle-class front-line man and a fanatical racialist, he had no use for social democrats, communists, Jews, or liberals. The classic German doctrine of the State as power, the doctrine of Hegel, of Bismarck, of Treitschke, was fixed in the very marrow of his being.

His friends, some of whom were selfless idealists, while others were ruffians of the lowest character, called themselves National Socialists, and were known for short as Nazis (about 1920). They demanded the union of all Germans in a centralized German State, the abrogation of the peace treaties, the return of the German colonies, the disfranchisement of the Jews, the foundation of a national army, and the communalization of the large shops. They attacked pacifism, cosmopolitanism, capitalism. A fanatical German patriotism, which refused to abandon the will to power, marked them out for eventual success. In *Mein Kampf*, a spiritual autobiography mainly written in 1923-4, Hitler sounded his very German defiance of the Jewish race and the Christian virtues: "The great revolutions of this world would have been inconceivable if their driving force had been the respectable bourgeois virtues of peace and order instead of the fanatical—nay, the hysterical—passions which they in fact displayed. And yet our world is moving towards a great revolution, and there is only one question at issue: Will that revolution be the salvation of Aryan humanity, or will it be merely another source of profit for the eternal Jew? The true National State must make it its duty to develop a suitable system of education for its youth so that it may maintain a race of men prepared for the last and greatest decisions of this globe. The first nation to take this road will be the conqueror. The whole character and education of the true National State must find its apex in its racial instruction. It must brand the sense of race and the feeling of race in the instincts and the understanding of the hearts and brains of the youth entrusted to it. No boy and no girl shall be permitted to leave school until he or she has been initiated into the deepest knowledge about the inner necessity and essence of blood purity."

The German Republic had been founded in the dark hour of frustration and defeat. Republicans had set their signature to the Armistice, and Republicans again had signed the Treaty of Versailles. Though the Weimar Assembly, which met on February 6, 1919, to draft a constitution, was elected by so great a preponderance of the German nation that it is idle to contend that the Republic was not the deliberate act of a free people, the sufferings which accompanied its birth and the hardships and humiliations which attended its early course were things not to be forgotten and by some Germans difficult to forgive.

High gales burst upon the Republic from the first. On the one side the Communists and Spartacists, on the other the Reactionaries and Royalists worked for its overthrow. Nor was either opposition a force to be despised. All over Central Europe, and nowhere more than in Germany, the story of the Russian revolution had made a deep impression on the manual worker. The brutalities and miseries which had been associated with the rise of the Bolsheviks to power could not counteract the prodigious fact that in Russia, of all countries in the world, the people had overthrown their masters and were governing a vast empire in the interests of the poor. Spartacism, then, was widely diffused among the industrial workers. It possessed a sacred creed in Marxism and a literature of revolt in the burning pamphlets of Rosa Luxembourg. But Spartacism, though full of sound and fury, lacked military leadership, discipline, organization. Against it was ranged a government which, albeit shaken by the events of the war, could yet command the service of officials and officers of the regular army. More fortunate than the broken Kerensky, President Ebert found to his hand strong and capable instruments. Of these one stood out above the rest—Noske, the Commandant of the National Guard. By stern and timely measures Noske suppressed the Spartacists and enabled the Republic to survive.

There was little sympathy for the Kaiser. To a nation of soldiers it was a sufficient condemnation that in the hour of defeat he had deserted the army. Yet there was enough of military, aristocratic, and imperial sentiment in Germany to embarrass a raw Socialist government which had accepted a peace of compulsory disarmament. Dr. Kapp's "Putsch" in 1920 was an illustration of the ease with which in the uncertain youth of the Weimar Republic a bold *coup de main* might capture the citadel. Kapp, a royalist of no account, seized Berlin with his naval brigade, and frightened the Government away to Stuttgart. Yet the wounds of the imperial war were too fresh to admit the restoration of royalism in any form. The German people stood behind their saddler President, and Kapp was defeated, not by a clash of arms, but by the democratic and effectual weapon of a general strike.

There remained an even greater danger. The deepest feud in Europe was deep as ever. Over against the German people, hungry, exhausted, abased, disarmed, yet still conscious despite the sharp deception of its hopes of great achievements and a shining destiny, stood France at the head of the victorious alliance, brandishing the Treaty of Versailles and demanding the exact fulfilment of its terms. The representative of the retributive spirit in France was Poincaré, a blunt, solid, very able and industrious lawyer, and of all the political figures on the French stage during the crisis of the war and afterwards the most commanding. The idea that the exchange of a militarist empire for a Socialist republic denoted an improvement of the German heart, or the British argument that the whole continent would suffer from the ruin of Germany, did not impress this stern lawyer from Lorraine. He wanted reparations and security—reparations at once, security always—and since he did not believe in the German protestations of poverty, but thought that the Germans were fraudulent debtors, seeking by every dishonest ruse to evade their liabilities, he was resolved that they should feel the full weight of a military occupation. So, to the burning indignation of the Germans, black colonial troops were quartered in the Rhineland towns, and, when even thus deliveries were backward, Poincaré marched an army into the Ruhr.

The occupation of the Ruhr, against which every British party protested, was one of those extreme historical misfortunes which, when suffering has reached an intolerable point, supply their own correction. In 1921 the Reparations Committee under French and Belgian influence fixed Germany's reparation debt at 6,600 millions. As one means of evading a fantastic and impossible obligation, the Germans decided to depreciate the mark. But inflation is a tricky sprite, which, once invoked, is apt to evade control. By January, 1923, when the French first entered the Ruhr, 80,000 marks were necessary to purchase a sovereign; by October the sum had mounted to the astronomical figure of 112,000 millions. Great fortunes shrank to a pittance. The whole upper and middle class, and all wage-earners whose livelihood depended on fixed money payments, were plunged in destitution.

And while the scale and character of this monetary tragedy were such as to attract the attention of the world, the general economic situation became increasingly difficult both for France and Germany. On the one hand, the French army in the Ruhr strangled German industry; on the other hand, the passive resistance of the German miners and mineowners, which was financed from Berlin, obstructed the exaction of those "productive pledges" which it had been the prime object of the French invasion to secure. The bitter struggle could not proceed indefinitely. In the autumn the

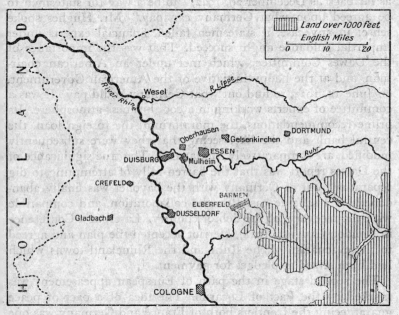

THE RUHR.

Germans gave way over passive resistance and suddenly in the early summer of 1924 reformed their currency. The French, sobered by a fifty per cent. fall of the franc, threw out Poincaré and called Herriot, the radical leader, to the helm. The stage was then set for the three acts which, taken in combination, improved for a time the political atmosphere of Europe: the Dawes Settlement of 1924, the Locarno agreement of 1925, and the entry of Germany into the League of Nations in 1926.

The war had brought about a complete revolution in the economic relations of America and Europe. Before the war

America was Europe's debtor; afterwards she was a creditor upon an undreamed-of scale. At the close of 1923 (the year of the Ruhr) the United States Treasury held obligations of foreign governments alone amounting to the huge total of 2,360 millions, principal and accrued interest, of which sum no less than 920 millions were owed by Great Britain. How could the Government in Washington fail to be interested in the solvency of debtor countries from whom such payments were due? " There ought," said Mr. Hughes, the United States Secretary of State, as far back as December 29, 1922, " to be a way for statesmen to be agreed upon what Germany can pay." Mr. Hughes spoke sense; in any case, if statesmen failed, financial experts under impartial guidance might succeed. That was the importance of the Dawes Committee, which met under an American chairman, and at the happy initiative of the American Government, on June 14, 1924, to find out what Germany could pay. It was a committee of experts working in a cool business atmosphere. Its prime recommendations, the moratorium, the foreign loan, the central bank and the like, seeing that they were subsequently modified, are comparatively immaterial. The true significance of the Dawes report was that the barren folly of attempting to dig reparations out of Germany with the bayonet was finally abandoned for a scheme based on the collaboration, and compatible with the recovery, of the debtor country. Later, at a Conference in London (August, 1924), Herriot accepted the plan and agreed to the evacuation of the Ruhr and the Rhineland towns which had been seized as pledges for payment.

1925

The second stage in the path of European appeasement was marked by the Pact of Locarno. The idea of a pact of peace guaranteeing the frontiers both of France and Germany was one so violently opposed to the military prejudices of the hour that it seemed hardly possible that it should ever be embodied in a Treaty. In 1922 it had been roundly rejected by the French, and in 1925 it was carried through only by the happy coincidence that in Stresemann, Briand, and Austen Chamberlain the three nations principally concerned were represented by statesmen who were prepared to take risks for the furtherance of European peace. It needed some courage on the part of Stresemann (a dissembling imperialist) to put his hand to a treaty which renounced Alsace-Lorraine; some courage on the part of Chamberlain to pledge his country to oppose France, if she invaded Germany, and Germany, if she invaded France; nor was it entirely easy for Briand, in view of Paris opinion, to renounce the cherished dream of a permanent offensive and defensive alliance with Britain against the ancient enemy across the Rhine. The risks were faced. The Treaties were signed. The war frontier between France and Germany was placed under the guarantee of Britain, Italy, and Belgium. A pledge was given by Stresemann that, while Germany was not content with the eastern frontiers, which had been assigned to her by the Peace of Versailles, she would not endeavour to change them by force of arms. " *À Locarno*," said Briand, " *nous avons parlé européen. C'est une langue nouvelle qu'il faudra bien que l'on apprenne.*"[1]

After Locarno the way seemed clear for Germany's entry into the League. She had undertaken to pay reparations, she had accepted her new frontier on the west, and had pledged herself against warlike adventures in the east. That she should take her seat as a permanent member of the Council on an equality with the victors was a stipulation of the Treaty and regarded by all good Europeans as a matter of course. Yet at the last moment the entry of Germany into the League was obstructed by a series of humiliating and discreditable intrigues. The prospect of the admission of a new Great Power to a permanent place at the Council table aroused the jealous susceptibilities of the secondary states. The claims of Poland, of Spain, and even of Brazil, were hotly urged, and the admission of Germany having been once vetoed, to the exasperation of Europe, by the Brazilian vote, was at last secured only by an enlargement of the Council, which abridged its authority and influence.

What Geneva might do for Germany remained to be seen. A revision of the war frontiers was not to be expected from an assembly governed by the rule of unanimity: but the grievance of unequal armaments was one which fell directly within the province of the League to adjust. Despite its great economic advantages, the disarmament imposed on Germany by the Treaty of Versailles had never willingly been accepted by a nation of soldiers; and the Germans were entitled to claim, either that they should be allowed to rearm, or that a reduction of armaments should be seriously undertaken by their neighbours. With a rare

[1] " At Locarno we spoke European, a new language which we ought certainly to learn."

unanimity of passionate emotion, the youth of Germany claimed equality of treatment, and protested against the continuance of a system which left them helpless before the aeroplanes, the tanks, and the heavy artillery of Poles, Czechs, and Frenchmen. A problem was raised of the greatest delicacy and complexity, the solution of which was not rendered easier by the military propaganda of the German Press, and by the general and well founded belief that Germany was secretly supplying herself with forbidden instruments of war. The League's progress toward an agreed all-round system of disarmament was necessarily so slow and so steadily obstructed by the grave apprehensions of the heavily armed Powers, as to suggest the suspicion that nothing serious was intended. Years passed, Stresemann died in 1929, an irreparable loss to the Republic. Still there was no disarmament. The long delays of the League militated against the authority of the Social Democrats who stood for fulfilment of the treaties, and had been prepared to make sacrifices for European peace. For seven years Germany had wooed Geneva, and wooed in vain.

All this time a menacing civil war feeling had been steadily growing in intensity within the limits of the German *Reich*. The revolution of 1919, while it had put an end to the rule of the Court and the aristocracy, had done nothing to impair the position of the great magnates of industry and finance. The chasm between wealth and poverty was never so painfully evident as during the period of the catastrophe of the mark, when vast fortunes were made by fortunate speculators in a time of general misery. It is not, therefore, surprising that communism, which is the fruit of envy and despair, made rapid strides among the German workers.

Meanwhile an economic calamity, the sharper since it supervened upon a series of shattering experiences, brought the Republic to the ground. The miseries of the inflation of 1923 had been succeeded by five years of ostentatious prosperity, when under the stimulus of some seven hundred and fifty million of foreign loans, industries were extended, banks and factories were built, and a wild orgy of extravagant spending announced the advent of a new race of profiteers. There followed in 1929 a great financial crash in New York. At once American money was recalled from Germany with results which were calamitous to German business. Banks closed, factories turned off their hands, revenue diminished. The enormous problem of finding work for

he six million unemployed, and of endeavouring to balance the
budget, confronted the unfortunate Cabinet of Social Democrats,
which had just lost in Stresemann its outstanding statesman.

At the crisis, when the bitter cry of the workless was in every
ear, and the red flag of Communism waved freely in the streets,
the country was swept by a brilliant propaganda which expressed
all the resentments and voiced all the hopes of a leaderless people.
Adolf Hitler has already appeared in these pages as a front-line
soldier, the apocalyptic organizer of the Nazi party. His object
was to clear Germany of the Jews, to stamp out Communism,
and to revive the military renown of the German people. Having
failed to win power by a military " Putsch " in 1923, he applied
himself with conspicuous ability to a constitutional campaign.
He was a great natural orator who could voice in short, vibrating,
intelligible phrases the passions good and bad of his countrymen.
No arts of the modern impresario were lacking to the conduct
of his propaganda. At the end of fourteen years' campaigning   *1933*
his little Austrian Messiah had infused so strong a blast of
courage and confidence into a dejected and distracted people,
had organized terrorism with so high a hand, and had obtained
so complete a mastery of the streets by his brown-shirted storm
troops of ruffianly bullies,[1] that he became Chancellor of the
Reich and master of the German state. The Government had
been too weak to suppress the private armies wearing shirts of
different colours who paraded the country and menaced the
peace. Not least among their sources of weakness was the fact
that von Papen, a rich Catholic Westphalian nobleman and   *June,*
royalist, hoping to bring monarchy back on the crest of the   *1932*
movement, had captured the President of the Republic, the old
and illustrious von Hindenburg, for the Nazi cause.

The Weimar Republic, which had long laboured under heavy
seas, foundered in the great Nazi storm of 1933. Little indulgence was felt for the parliamentary institutions which had failed
to bring hope and prosperity to the country. The Reichstag, an
assembly of inflamed, bewildered and inexperienced men, was
too bitterly divided in opinion and too barren of teachable conservatives to constitute an effective instrument of government.
Even Brüning, the last true republican chancellor and a Catholic
socialist, had been driven to govern by emergency decrees.

Yet the Weimar Republic had rendered services to Germany

[1] Known as the S.A. (Schutz Abteilung).

which it was convenient to forget. In a dark hour it had restore
the currency, liberated the Fatherland from the occupation
foreign troops, brought Germany into the League of Nations
a first-class power and obtained from the Allies a reduction
the reparation debt to a nominal figure. The first difficult step
towards the restoration of Germany to her place in Europea
society had been taken under the Republican government before
Adolf Hitler, aided by Goering the airman and Goebbels th
*Jan. 30.
1933*
propagandist, stormed his way to power and threw an audaciou
challenge to the four greatest forces in modern civilization, th
Catholics, the Protestants, the capitalists and the Jews.

The philosophy of the naïve and reckless Nazi ruler is based o
the view countenanced by Wagner and Nietzsche and preache
before the war by Houston Chamberlain that race is everythin
and that all the great achievements of the world have bee
accomplished by the Nordics. It is argued that Christ, Dant
Thomas Aquinas were certainly Nordic, and that the Goth
who were of the same Teuton stock, did more for civilizatio
than the Romans. Adolf Hitler, then, is a racialist. No Jew ca
be a German citizen. The Old Testament and the Crucifix ar
suspect; the one is a Jewish publication, the other a Jewish sym
bol. It is, indeed, as the more constructive thinkers of the move
ment have already discovered, difficult to harmonize the Chris
tian gospel with a philosophy of the state which derides th
brotherhood of man, expels professors of liberal or cosmopolitan
principles from the Universities, and deliberately extirpates th
spirit of liberty and charity from the educational system of th
country.

Wotan, not Christ, is, as many of them proclaim, the real Goo
of the Nazi religion.[1] Fortunately, as by the method of ter
rorism the party has now been made coterminous with the state
there are many who wear the colours without adopting the creed
Nor is German Christianity utterly effaced. Alike in the Protest
ant and Catholic Churches brave men have protested in publi
against the humiliations put upon their faith.

The internal revolution in Germany accomplished by Hitle
and his national socialist party is an extraordinary psychologica
phenomenon. The dread of communism, the hatred of Jews and

[1] " At the moment we Germans are the people which has freed itsel
furthest from the teachings of Christianity." (Ludendorff on his 70t
birthday. *Times*, April 9, 1935

profiteers, the desire once again to be feared abroad, the need of a government stronger, more progressive, and more sanguine than the Republic, which would repudiate the Peace Treaties and once more launch Germany on the course of ambition and honour, all contributed to make Hitlerism possible. As in Italy with Fascism, so in Germany with Hitlerism, the old soldiers, who had served their country in the trenches and felt themselves miserably needy, and often despised by Jewish profiteers, joined the movement in great numbers. The Germans are always thorough. The significance of Hitlerism is that of all forms of nationalism yet invented or devised it is the most thorough-going. There are to be no classes, no parties, no trades unions, semi-autonomous states, or relics of the old German Federal system, but one centralized corporate state made up from top to bottom of Nazis, wearing shirts of the same colour, giving the same salutes, repeating the same catchwords, holding the same faith. And this uniform, standardized Germany, taking its orders from a single chief, is to regard itself as self-sufficient. One of the first acts of the new chief, when his storm troops had made themselves masters of the streets, was to march his country out of the League and the Disarmament Conference (1933).

In this violent affirmation of Germanism there is much that is familiar. The foreign policy of the Nazis is broadly that of the Pan-German League. They wish to see all European Germans united under the German flag, and to win fresh areas for the German people. The militarism of the Nazis is no new thing in Germany, nor their worship of force, nor their desire for expansion. Nor does it surprise the student of German history to learn of the ease with which German Liberalism was overthrown by Hitler, for since Schiller the Germans have had no great teacher of Liberalism, and since 1848 German Liberalism has been a weak, unprosperous plant. What is new in the National Socialist movement is that centralization replaces the ancient federation, that the old civil service which had weathered the storm of the first revolution is broken down, and that militarism is no longer associated with an Empire or with an aristocratic caste, but becomes enforced as the creed of an equalitarian democracy. The kind of revolution which made France formidable as a military state in 1792 makes Germany a nation in arms (so far as the will to arm is concerned) in 1935. This is the new fact of which Europe and the world must take account.

The Hitler dictatorship, though it favours social equality, is the inverse of democracy. It makes of the citizen not only the servant but the slave of the state. The great democratic maxim that the state should aim at securing the greatest happiness of the greatest number is replaced in the Nazi philosophy by the theory that the end of the individual is to maximize the material power of the nation. The prime function of women is to breed for the state, of men to fight for it. The supreme death is death in battle, the supreme virtue the heroism which faces the enemy and the torments of war. That a population of over sixty-five million Germans should even nominally accept such a philosophy of life is a note of that lack of balance and moderation which goes with the character of this remarkable people, at once the most virile and enthusiastic, the most industrious and submissive, the most methodical and sentimental in the world.

President von Hindenburg died in August, 1934. By an overwhelming majority of votes the German people, acting under strong governmental pressure, accorded to Adolf Hitler, "the Leader," that full supremacy over the totalitarian state which was the goal of his ambitions. His past was not counted against him, neither the early years of ruthless terrorism, nor the suspicion, which a public trial has done nothing to abate, that he had secretly caused the burning of the Reichstag (February 27, 1933), in order to spread fear of the Communists, nor "the blood-bath" of June 30, 1934, when the leading gangsters of his party (including Captain Roehm, one of his earliest allies) were suddenly butchered and their bodies burned,[1] nor the murder of Dr. Dollfuss, the Chancellor of the Austrian Republic, which was engineered by Nazi bands from Munich. These atrocities, reminiscent of the Roman Empire in the third century, were condoned. It was sufficient that Hitler, the wild hero of a Wagnerian opera, stood for a Germany proud, united, and defiant. When in the spring of 1935 he suddenly restored conscription in breach of the Versailles Treaty, an hysterical paroxysm of delight shook the country.

A prophet, but not an administrator. Unlike Napoleon and Mussolini, Hitler is devoid of the specific administrative gift. Behind his mesmeric speeches and the Nazi propaganda so debasing in method, so effective in result, quiet soldiers, bureaucrats

---

[1] The official number of butcheries is 77. It seems probable that some 1,200 perished.

and captains of industry are reassembling their forces. When the leader goes the old hands will be found placed on the levers of policy, but the policy will not be altogether old. Some items, such as the Second Punic War with England and the war of revenge on France, are no longer regarded as likely to be remunerative. Far more promising as a means of augmenting the territory of the Third *Reich* is the expédient of the plébiscite, inaugurated by the French in 1799 and lately in 1935 exercised with fortunate results in the Saar. What might not be expected from plébiscites in Austria, in German Switzerland, in Schleswig, in Silesia? It is natural that the Nazi should cherish such hopes. The Germans of the dispersion are his natural associates. The enemy is red Russia. The spectre of that vast, populous, highly-armed, propagandist state, which holds, it is said, the secret spiritual allegiance of seven million German hearts, haunts the directors of German policy, and more than any other single cause ensures the solidity of the Third German *Reich*.

It will be seen then that three forms of government, new in the twentieth century, Russian Communism, Italian Fascism, German Hitlerism, confront the Parliamentary democracies which have their roots either in the English Revolution of 1688 or in the French Revolution of 1789. The doctrines of Hegel and Marx oppose the philosophies of Locke and Rousseau.

These Parliamentary governments are not perfect. In France the executive is too weak, the legislature too strong. The average duration of a French ministry between 1918 and 1934 has been eight months and twenty-five days. Such discontinuity is inconsistent with firm and consecutive government, and though the remedies are well known, and by no means revolutionary (the abolition of the standing committees which usurp the functions and impair the authority of responsible ministers and the right of the Prime Minister to call for a dissolution of the Chamber without the consent of the Senate being the most important), it does not follow that they will be easy to secure. Lesser men may not succeed where the venerable and respected Doumergue, an ex-President of the Republic, taking office amidst unusual applause at a crisis when the prestige of the 1934 Chamber was gravely shaken by the Stavisky frauds. was miserably frustrated. Reforms, however beneficial to the public, are difficult to carry, if they require the assent of bodies who imagine that they will be injuriously affected by their passage. In this respect the amendment of the French legislative system is in the same category as the reform of the English House of Lords.

While on the continent of Europe one throne has fallen after another, the British monarchy has advanced in strength and popularity. The unaffected simplicity and strong sense of public service exhibited by King George V and Queen Mary, and noticeable also in the wide circle of their family, have made a deep impression on the minds of the nation. The rising generation are not growing up republican. The remarkable manifestations of loyal enthusiasm on the occasion of the King's Silver Jubilee in 1935 made it plain to any intelligent observer that a constitutional monarchy has a place to fill in a democratic and equalitarian society.

Parliamentary government holds its ground. The attempts to disparage its value or to demand its supersession have brought discredit upon those who have made them. There is no sign of any desire to depart from the salutary British principle that the Cabinet is responsible for the government of the country to the House of Commons and through the House of Commons to the electorate. It is true that in the growing complexity of affairs Parliament delegates work to the administrative departments or to newly formed statutory bodies like the Port of London Authority or the British Broadcasting Corporation, and there are signs that this process may be carried further; but there is always a Minister of the Crown responsible to Parliament for these agencies. The delegation of functions is not permitted to impair concentration of responsibility. Meanwhile it is before the legislature of Westminster that the great panorama of imperial business is annually unrolled, and there that the largest issues of policy are discussed. Never has there been a measure so long and intricate nor one affecting so many million human beings as the Government of India Bill which was introduced by Sir Samuel Hoare in 1934. The debates upon this unusual and difficult theme have been worthy of the best traditions of English Parliamentary life.

The rise of the Labour party, though it has accelerated the eclipse of the Liberals, already divided among themselves by the unhappy cleavage of 1916, when some Liberals supported the coalition under Mr. Lloyd George while others went into opposition with Mr. Asquith, has agreeably disappointed the alarmists. The leaders of British labour, Mr. Ramsay MacDonald, Mr. (afterwards Lord) Snowden, Mr. Arthur Henderson, Mr. Thomas, Mr. Clynes, were as far as possible from being revolutionaries. Mr. Ramsay MacDonald, though a pacifist, was by temperament a poetical Highland Tory, Mr. Snowden a robust Yorkshire Radical, Mr. Thomas a full-blown Imperialist. To no one of these men did the example of Russia offer any encouragement. In 1931, when the over-lavish expenditure of the Labour Cabinet had brought the country within sight of a commercial crash, these three men joined with the Conservatives and Liberals in a National Government to balance the budget and to restore the credit of the country.

Contrary to general expectation, an apprenticeship in the Trades Union movement proved to be an excellent preparation for the assumption of high political responsibilities. The Labour leaders had much experience in the art of handling troublesome and disagreeable men. They had negotiated with employers, mingled with foreigners at international conferences, and they knew, as most members of the House of Commons did not, how the vast majority of men and women in the country really lived. The party, then, despite great deficiencies of knowledge, contained men of ripe human experience and ability. Mr. Ramsay MacDonald and Mr. Henderson made good at the Foreign Office. Mr. Snowden won golden opinions at the Treasury. Elsewhere the faults of inexperience were largely corrected by the loyal help of the Civil Service. Though Labour in its two brief administrations has achieved little in the field of legislation, it has taught the country that political capacity is no longer the monopoly of the upper or middle class.

The Hitler revolution is a sufficient guarantee that Russian Communism will not spread westward. The solid German bourgeois holds the central fortress of Europe. But there may be secrets in Fascism or Hitlerism which the democracies of the West will desire, without abandoning their fundamental character, to adopt. That the peoples of England and France will ever, save under the actual spell of war, surrender liberty is difficult to believe.

Ever since " the glorious revolution " Britain has been the most wisely governed of the European states. Cabinets have made mistakes, but never of such a character as to provoke a

serious protest under arms or to compromise the future. The
nation of civilians stood the shock of war, financed its allies,
and accepted without a murmur, and in defiance of a long
tradition, the odious burden of military conscription. The
troubles of the peace, graver in most respects than those which
assailed France, were surmounted by patience and skill.

Five million men trained to arms found their way back into
civilian employment without a shot fired. A police strike, a
railway strike, and a coal strike successively disturbed Mr. Lloyd
George's coalition government and were each in turn overcome.
A nine days' general strike in 1926, at once firmly and generously
handled by Mr. Baldwin's government, was no more successful.
The great mass of the people of the country sided with the
government, which was aided in its struggle by the petrol engine
and the novel invention of broadcasting. Workers' insurance, too
often miscalled "the dole," was, since it kept starvation at bay,
the great safeguard against social despair.

The relative peace of the country was the more remarkable,
since, partly owing to the normal increase of population, and
partly owing to the stoppage of emigration in the war, Britain
had three million more mouths to feed. With less capital for
the support of labour, there was more labour to support. A
chronic burden of unemployment, far in excess of the normal
rate, strained the resources of the Insurance Fund, and
strengthened the case of those who wished to revise the Free
Trade system, which had carried the country through the war.
It was given to Mr. Ramsay MacDonald, the leader of the
Labour party, to discard, as head of a National Government in
1931, the policy of fiscal liberty introduced in 1846 by Sir Robert
Peel, under which Britain had enjoyed a spell of national prosperity which up to that moment had no parallel in the world.

At this time the British people bore without repining a burden
of taxation heavier than that of any European country. The
annual service of the debt charge alone amounted to more than
300 million sterling. Fifteen years after the end of the war the
state levied 4s. 6d. in the pound on the income of the tax-payer
irrespective of the super-tax on incomes exceeding £2,000 a year.
Yet it is characteristic of the democratic spirit which prevailed
in the country that, despite bad trade and crushing taxation,
the level of the social services, higher than that which prevailed
in any other country and more expensive, was not seriously

lowered. That the health, the education, and the housing of the people should be well cared for was common ground with all parties in the state. No class in Britain at any time since the war experienced the terrible collapse of fortune which came to the Germans through the catastrophe of the mark, or to the French *rentier* through the sudden collapse of the franc. In the areas of unemployment there was great depression and hopelessness. Otherwise, taken by whatever test may be applied, the returns of savings banks, the expenditure on films, holidays, and travel, the boots of school-children, there was evidence of a community not too ill provided with those little superfluities which sweeten the grim monotony of the worker's life.

The old economic ascendancy which was enjoyed by the inhabitants of Britain during the first three-quarters of the nineteenth century was no longer theirs. Other countries had learned to manufacture for themselves and behind the shelter of protective tariffs were supplying their own needs. The trend towards economic self-sufficiency was greatly increased by the war, and by the six thousand additional miles of tariff frontier which were imposed upon the map of Europe, as a consequence of the peace. Over-production, unemployment, and a great falling off in the volume of international trade, were the consequences of this unwholesome development of economic nationalism. To no country was it so injurious as to Great Britain, a third of whose population is concentrated in seaport towns.

It was natural that in these altered circumstances the thoughts of many Englishmen should revert to the possibility of developing, apart from the continent of Europe, and in a happy indifference to its perils and complications, a life of economic and political self-sufficiency in conjunction with the Dominions and colonies of the Empire. The policy of colonial preference was put into action at Ottawa in 1932. The further and more attractive scheme of a Free Trade Empire has failed to evoke a response from the highly protected Dominions of the Crown. But strong as is the sentiment which unites the various portions of the British Empire, it is no longer possible for Great Britain to disengage herself from the politics of the continent, or to confine her trading interests within the borders of her colonies and Dominions. Were there no other argument against a revival of Lord Salisbury's "splendid isolation" the development of aviation would be sufficient. Britain is no longer an island. If it was a British interest before the war that Germany should not overrun Belgium, or take the Channel ports, or dominate France, it is even more important for national security that these changes in the European balance should not happen now.

As a member of the League of Nations, as a guarantor of the Pact of Locarno, as a Power vitally interested in the preservation of European peace, Britain is compelled to make her contribution to the welfare and tranquillity of the continent. That, despite Ottawa, her commerce will continue to be world-wide, and that her traders will make money out of Argentine and Brazil, out of China and the United States, is one of the few prophecies to which the student of markets may safely subscribe.

Wise men on the continent everywhere agree that it would be a calamity were Britain to withdraw from Europe. It is not that the British are popular. Their superficial defects of manner and bearing are far too obvious to the foreigner, but at least Englishmen are not so unpopular in France as the Germans, not so unpopular in Germany as the French. It is recognized that these eccentric, incoherent, apparently stupid people desire peace, support the League of Nations, and that they are able to exercise a mediatorial office which no other first-class European power can well fulfil.

If the greatest of all present political problems, that of disarmament, should ever be happily solved the result will be largely due to the consistent efforts of British Cabinets, and of statesmen drawn to Geneva from every part of the British Empire, to bring about a better international order, and to prevent a recurrence of the fatal competition in armaments, which led, and could only lead, to an explosion.

For a commercial island peace is a prime necessity. With few exceptions British statesmen have recognized this fundamental axiom of policy. It may also be claimed for British foreign policy that a vein of humanitarian sentiment, sometimes quixotic, sometimes capricious, but always genuine, and deriving through Wesley and Wilberforce from the Puritan tradition of the seventeenth century, mingles with the coarser stuff of economic or political calculation. No other country in Europe so swiftly or lightly conceives a passion for the oppressed in other lands. Pro-Vaudois, Pro-Catalan, Pro-Émigré, Pro-Slave, Pro-Hellenic, Pro-Italian, Pro-Bulgar, Pro-Armenian, Pro-Serb, Pro-Boer, Pro-

Belgian, the English idealist, recking little of material profit and loss, helps in shaping the policy of his country and can never be wholly neglected. Across the waters of the Atlantic, another branch of the Anglo-Saxon race exhibits in its public dealing the same concern, not always logically blended, for great humanitarian causes and closely calculated economic gains: an identity of outlook not without consequence for the world. Hence it is that in the hour of her greatest naval triumph, Great Britain was prepared without a murmur to accept the claim of American naval parity, a claim which for centuries past she would have denied with all her might and main to another power. Whatever may be the fate of the European continent, it will at least be the aim of British policy to uphold the Anglo-Saxon peace.

It is reasonable to hope that one ancient cause of friction between the American and British peoples has since 1921 been sensibly diminished if not entirely removed. The subjection of Ireland to the British yoke can no longer be an occasion of offence to the citizens of the United States. Save for the six mainly Protestant counties of the north-east which desired to retain the British connection, Ireland is as free as Canada. The Lord Lieutenant has vanished from Dublin Castle, the Chief Secretary from the lodge in Phoenix Park, the troops from the Curragh and the Royal Irish Constabulary from the streets. The Irish Parliament in Dublin passes laws and the Irish executive endeavours to carry them into effect. The Irish *Seorstat* or Free State flies its own flag, sends its envoys to foreign courts, its delegates to Geneva, its representatives to the Imperial Conference. The new Dominion imposes duties on British goods and may, since the Statute of Westminster, pass laws which are inconsistent with the statutes of the Imperial Parliament. From a recent decision of the Privy Council (1935) it is plain that the Dail, as this Dublin Parliament is called, may even legislate away the provisions of the treaty of 1921 which called the Irish Free State into existence.

If Mr. De Valera, the Republican leader of to-day, quarrels with the present position of his country under the treaty, it is not because a republic would bring to Ireland a larger measure of liberty or well-being than that which it is now open to her to enjoy, but because for ideal reasons he wishes to see a united

Ireland standing altogether outside the British Empire. Having
fought for a republic in 1916 and again in 1921, he does not
lightly abandon his dream of a republic of saints, nourished on
the Erse language, spurning material things and living withdrawn from the world in mysterious isolation and self-sufficiency.

1921
The Cabinet of Mr. Lloyd George which made the Irish treaty
did not exclude from its consideration the possibility of granting to the republicans of Catholic Ireland the full measure of
their demand. It would have been in accordance with the principles of self-determination which governed the continental
settlement if the Catholic counties of Ireland which demanded a
republic had been encouraged to secede from the Empire, while
the Protestant counties continued to remain an integral part of
the British state. But quite apart from the military and naval
dangers to be apprehended from secession (and the objections
which appealed to Abraham Lincoln in America carried equal
weight with the British Cabinet in London), the injuries to Ireland resulting from such a severance were not easy to contemplate. How could a policy converting Irishmen into aliens fail to
press hardly upon the numerous Irish residents in Britain or on
Irishmen desiring to make their careers in the Empire? As a
British subject the Irishman is at any time free to better his
fortunes in Liverpool or Glasgow; as an alien he might easily
find himself excluded. The idea of making foreigners of a people
who had played so large a part in the building up of the British
Empire, who had given and continued to give so much to
English letters and who were bound by so many ties of family
connection to the British people, was deeply repugnant. The
decision which was then taken may have been erroneous, but it
was founded upon an honest belief that the position of complete
freedom under the British Crown and within the British Empire
offered to Catholic Ireland the best prospect of well-being and
was of all courses that which was most likely in the end to bring
about the reconciliation of the Irish and English races throughout the world.

June,
1935
Europe still bears her scars. The rulers of Germany and
Russia, Italy and Turkey have won their own way to power
through blood. With every roar of the Nazi tiger, the small
powers tremble for their lives. Greece is cleft by the deadly feud
between the Venizelists and their largely monarchical adver-

saries. The new republican government of Spain treads uneasily on burning lava. Refugees from tyranny flock into the free countries, Greeks in flight from Asia Minor, Jews in flight from Nazi Germany, Russians who crowd into Prague and Constantinople, Paris and London, rather than endure the rigour of the Soviet rule. Venizelos, the liberator, is a fugitive in Italy. The voyager in the Tyrrhenian sea as he views the low line of the Lipari islands, etched against the flames of the setting sun, may reflect that on those barren strips of rock sprinkled in a waste of waters are immured the last champions of Italian freedom, the last inheritors of the great liberal tradition which made Italy one.[1]

Still the revolutionary governments hold their ground, even the government of the Soviets whose speedy end in the early days of Lenin was so often and so confidently predicted in the west. There is no reason here for surprise.

The durability of the Bolshevik régime in Russia is due as much to its conservative as to its innovating character. The Russian people have long been inured to tyranny. The stern repression of the Soviets, which so deeply offends the liberal susceptibilities of the west, does not shock the notions of this half Asiatic country. The government of Stalin, the rude son of a Georgian cobbler who graduated in revolutionary politics as a train bandit and a homicide, is not more ruthless, not more savage than the rule of Ivan the Terrible or Peter the Great. The real novelty in Russia would have been not a communist tyranny, but a Parliamentary Republic working in an atmosphere of liberty and conducting affairs by free untrammelled discussion. When Lenin destroyed the Constituent Assembly he decreed that Russia should turn her back on the political innovations of the west and revert to the well-tried technique of the Tzars.

Yet there is this of novelty in the Soviet system. A living religion is enforced by the massed large-scale propaganda of a scientific age, by machine guns and aeroplanes, telephone and telegraph, printing press and film, broadcasting and the regimentation of all the arts. A hundred and sixty million human souls are by a gigantic system of governmental pressure hermetically sealed against the invasion of unwelcome truth. All

[1] Since these words were written George of Greece, recalled to the throne by a Coup d'État, endeavours to appease the strife of factions.

previous experiments in tyranny recorded in human annals pale beside this colossal achievement.

A planned economy, seeing that in some shape or other it is implied in any scheme of socialism, is not an idea peculiar to Russia. What is impressive here is the scale upon which this grandiose project is now being carried into effect by the Soviet government, the risks which have been run, the opposition which has been overborne, and the sufferings which have been ruthlessly imposed and patiently endured. To predict in any year the varying economic needs of a vast and expanding population is a task calculated to strain to the utmost the abilities of the most experienced government in the world. To adjust economic production and distribution to meet these demands is still more difficult. Yet both these gigantic operations are attempted by the Communist rulers of Russia over the immense territory stretching from the Polish frontier to the Pacific Ocean which is submitted to their sway.

The spectacle of a great people working out a new way of life for itself and boldly defying the accumulated prejudices and traditions of the past is one which cannot fail to arouse interest and curiosity. The core of the new Russian state is a political party of two or three million men and women selected by cooption upon definite qualifications of political belief and rigorously purged from time to time of those members who seem to fall short of the prescribed requirements of knowledge, zeal and fidelity. It is this Communist party, a body dedicated to poverty and obedience and organized in a hierarchy of committees or Soviets, which controls the beliefs and persecutes the vagaries of the Russian people. It is by service to the Communist party that the ambitious man may rise to the forefront of affairs, become a people's Commissar, or Cabinet Minister, or, holding the modest title of Secretary-General to the party, exercise supreme control over the policy of the state. A wide franchise offers to every Russian citizen from eighteen years upwards many fields of public activity. The citizen may speak and vote as a politician in one committee, as a producer in another, as a consumer in a third. One thing is refused him, the liberty to deviate from the Communist faith.

No fair observer will deny certain merits to the Soviet experiment. Education is now general and since 1928 divested of its wilder eccentricities and normally planned. Intelligent concern has been shown for public health and public recreation. Though it has been found necessary to devise special rates of pay for skilled labour, the wounding sense of social inequality which prevails in the industrial towns of the west is removed from the Russian body politic. The natural development of a backward country has been greatly assisted by the continuance of that vigorous programme of mechanization which had been initiated in the later years of the Tzarist régime. New towns have sprung up, new industries have been introduced, a systematic attempt has been made to Americanize, without enlisting the motive of private profit, the industrial system of the country. Seeing that everywhere labour is in the last resort compulsory, there is no unavoidable unemployment. At the cost of its civil liberties a vast population is enabled to enjoy a prison ration of the goods of life.

Two questions, then, inevitably suggest themselves to the observer of contemporary Europe: Will the peace be preserved? Can liberty survive? These questions have often been asked before, but never with the implications which they must now carry, for to each question there is today attached an aspect which is entirely novel and unprecedented. Aviation has come into war. A new scientific technique and apparatus for propaganda has come into politics. Antiquity has never beheld despotisms so penetrating and all-pervasive as those which with the help of modern mechanism it has been so easy to set up in Russia, in Italy, and in Germany. It is a light matter now for any government with the tremendous means at its disposal to decree and to enforce the spiritual servitude of the totalitarian State. Equally, it will be a light matter on the outbreak of hostilities for any Power well served in the air to lay whole cities in ruins almost before the enemy population has woken up to the fact that it is at war. Yet the Europeans, in respect of whom these two questions are necessarily asked, may recall before it is too late that they are trustees for the civilization of the world. For centuries the nations of this continent have lived together in a loose kind of society, often quarrelling fiercely and ignorantly, but always, in the fields of religion and philosophy, science and literature, art and music, giving and taking, lending and borrowing the one from the other. The common heritage of European civilization is the most splendid possession of man. No issue now dividing the nations of Europe is so great as to warrant its destruction.

BOOKS WHICH MAY BE CONSULTED

Arnold Toynbee : Survey of International Affairs.

W. H. Chamberlin : Russia's Iron Age. 1933.

Lord D'Abernon : The Eighteenth Decisive Battle of the World. 1931

Luigi Villari : Italy. (Nations of the Modern World Series.) 1929.

Lord D'Abernon : An Ambassador of Peace. 1929.

D. C. Somervell : Reign of George V. 1935.

J. S. Barnes : Fascism. 1931.

H. J. Laski : Communism. 1927.

H. J. Laski : Liberty in the Modern State. 1930.

Rudolf Oeden : Stresemann. Tr. R. T. Clark. 1930.

Vernon Bartlett : Nazi Germany Explained. 1933.

H. F. Armstrong : Hitler's Reich. 1933.

F. H. Simonds : How Europe made Peace without America. 1927.

Hitler : Mein Kampf. 1932.

Sidney and Beatrice Webb : Soviet Communism. 2 vols. 1935.

CHAPTER XXXVII

EPILOGUE

AFTER some twenty million years of life upon this planet the lot of the major part of humanity is still, as Hobbes once described it, "nasty, brutish, and short." Of its two thousand million inhabitants some hundred and fifty million are still living very close to the hunger limit. But with all that human misery which prevails in the vast spaces of Asia, Africa, and South America, where thousands of millions of men and women have lived, worked, and died, leaving no memorial, contributing nothing to the future, these volumes are not concerned. Here I have only attempted to convey in the briefest outline a general idea of the story of that section of the human race which, being favoured by the temperate climate of Europe, has so prospered that not only has it peopled new continents with its offspring, but that out of its exertions and conflicts, its dreams and aspirations, standards of well-being hitherto unconjectured have been reached and maintained and widely communicated through the globe.

Only once in this long period did civilized Europe enjoy the blessings of a single government. The Roman Empire, and the Roman Empire alone, held for three critical centuries all that was precious in European life within its clasp. But then the greatest of calamities happened. The political framework of this majestic polity was broken by the mighty hammer of the Teutonic world. The Empire perished, leaving behind it as legacies of its greatness the voices of Virgil and of Cicero and of Horace and Augustine, the institution of the Roman Church, and the imposing fabric of the Roman law. But the prize of unity, the secret of discipline, the freedom and humanity of the ancient world were lost. Civilization had to be built up again almost from its foundation in a scene of predominating barbarism. East was severed from west, the Greek Church from the Latin. The Papacy, strongest of the institutional forces bequeathed by the Empire, was unable to keep the peace among the combative and passionate peoples who

had made the new chaos. Society splintered into minute par
ticles, fief warring upon fief, town upon town. Gradually out o
this welter of lawlessness nations emerged centred round the
hereditary dynasties of kings.

Within each nation there grew up by degrees a rude system o
justice and police; but between nation and nation there was no
common ground of law, save in so far as the Roman Church wa
able to supply it. But even that agency, which had been al
through the middle ages the helpless spectator of the crimes, the
vices, and the quarrels of men, was weakened at the Reformation
To the ecclesiastical rupture between Greece and Rome there
was henceforward added the division between Protestant and
Catholic. The wars of religion in the west were succeeded by
the dynastic wars of the seventeenth and the colonial wars of the
eighteenth century. But from these came no better chance of
European cohesion, rather a deepening of the cleft which divided
the continent. Yet never was the human mind so widely or
sensibly affected by large humanitarian ideas or by the thought
of man as a citizen of the world as in the half-century which
preceded the French Revolution. Could there once again be upon
the continent of Europe a common political framework for a
common Latin civilization? The rise and fall of Napoleon provided the answer. Since the break-up of the Roman Empire so
much of Europe had never been brought together under a single
sceptre. But it was too late; the nations of Europe were too
strong. There was to be no *Pax Napoleonica*. A coalition of
powers, of which Great Britain was the spearhead, shattered the
dream of French hegemony. The revolutionary and Napoleonic
wars left Europe exhausted, but were distinguished from other
European struggles by the birth of an idea—a permanent Concert
of Powers against a permanent revolutionary danger. A long
peace of exhaustion rather than of good will was followed by
those exciting nationalist wars which made Italy a kingdom and
Germany an empire. But still Europe was not at rest. Germany
was ambitious of world power, France studied revenge; the partition of Africa and the decay of Turkey illumined ambitions.
And all the time in the heart of Europe there was fermenting the
poison of suppressed nationalism. It threw fever among the Irish
and the Poles, among the Czechs and the Roumans, among the
Croats and the Serbs. An atmosphere was produced in which the
least spark might fire an explosion.

The tragedy of the Great War was that it was fought between the most highly civilized peoples in Europe on an issue which a few level-headed men could easily have composed, and with respect to which ninety-nine per cent. of the population were wholly indifferent. The main problem of statesmanship is to avert the recurrence of so great a catastrophe: the more so since the place of Europe in the world is no longer what it was in the seventies of the nineteenth century. Then the civilization of this continent seemed to repose upon a basis of unassailable security. The products of European skill found their way with ease into the markets of the East and the West, and purchased in return cargoes of food and raw materials produced under the law of increasing returns. Then there seemed little reason to doubt that despite a staggering birth-rate the standard of the wage-earners would be maintained and improved. Real wages were rising, and countries like Germany, where life had been hard and frugal, were swiftly advancing in affluence and luxury. Then the United States was open to European immigrants and provided a market, remunerative and almost illimitable, for European capital. Taking from Europe her surplus men and sending to Europe her surplus supplies, America was an integral factor in the prosperity of the Old World.

Now things are otherwise. The Latin nations of the Western Hemisphere no longer dispense their large hospitality to needy fortune-seekers from the Apennines. The doors of the United States since 1924 have been more than half closed to European immigrants. The law of diminishing returns has begun to operate in the farmlands of the West. The secret of the machine is no longer a European monopoly, for India and Japan import machinery from Europe or make it themselves. Mass production in the United States, cheap labour in the Orient, menace from opposite quarters of the globe the standard of the European wage-earner. Even the original home of British industrial strength is invaded. The Lancashire mill hand walks in stockings which are made in Japan.

The fact that Europe is entering into a period when competition may be expected to be sterner than in the past should be taken, not as a discouragement, but as a challenge. The old world, though handicapped by wars and rumours of wars, by tariffs and quotas, by class struggles and strikes, and by every folly which the demon of economic nationalism can contrive, is charged with industrial excellence. It must take its stand on quality. It must live on its taste, its ingenuity, its good sense. Then, with a better spirit at home and abroad, with less bitterness or unrest, and with a shedding of the encumbrances which now manacle progress, European quality will tell in every market. Not otherwise can we expect to safeguard the workers' standard of life, which, though far lower than we would wish it to be, is still the foundation upon which our hopes of a higher civilization must depend.

Europe, then, has now reached a point at which it would seem, as never so clearly in past history, that two alternative and sharply contrasted destinies await her. She may travel down the road to a new war or, overcoming passion, prejudice, and hysteria, work for a permanent organization of peace. In either case the human spirit is armed with material power. The developing miracle of science is at our disposal to use or abuse, to make or to mar. With science we may lay civilization in ruins or enter into a period of plenty and well-being the like of which has never been experienced by mankind.

In the meantime the war has left us an evil legacy. The moral unity of Europe is for the time being broken. Nordic paganism assails Christianity. An insane racialism threatens to rupture the seamless garment of civilization. May future generations close the rents, heal the wounds, and replace our squandered treasure of humanity, toleration, and good sense.

CHRONOLOGICAL AND GENEALOGICAL TABLES

PRESIDENTS OF THE FRENCH REPUBLIC

Date of Election.

August, 1871. Marie-Joseph-Louis-Adolphe Thiers.

May, 1873. Marie-Edmé-Patrice-Maurice de Macmahon, D. of Magenta, Marshal of France.

January, 1879. François-Paul-Jules Grévy. Re-elected 1886. Resigned 1887.

December, 1887. Marie-François-Sadi Carnot. Murdered 1894.

June, 1894. Jean-Paul-Pierre Casimir-Périer. Resigned 1895.

January, 1895. François-Félix Faure. Died 1899.

February, 1899. Émile Loubet.

January, 1906. Armand Fallières.

1913. Raymond Poincaré.

1920. Paul Deschanel.

1920. Alexandre Millerand.

1924. Gaston Doumergue.

1931. Paul Doumer.

1932. Albert Lebrun.

II

PRIME MINISTERS OF ENGLAND

GEORGE III, 1760-1820.
John Stewart, Earl of Bute, First
Lord of the Treasury, 1762-3.
George Grenville, First Lord and
Chancellor of the Exchequer,
1763-5.
Charles Wentworth-Watson, M.
of Rockingham, 1766.
Augustus Fitzroy, D. of Grafton,
1766-9.
Frederick, Lord North, 1770-82.
Marquis of Rockingham, 1782.
William Petty, Earl of Shel-
burne, 1782-3.
William Bentinck, Duke of
Portland, 1783.
William Pitt, 1783-1801.
Henry Addington (Viscount Sid-
mouth), 1801-4.
William Pitt, 1804-6.
William, Lord Grenville, 1806-7.
Duke of Portland, 1807-9.
Spencer Perceval, 1809-12.

GEORGE IV, 1820-30.
Earl of Liverpool, 1812-20,
1820-7.
George Canning, 1827.
Viscount Goderich, 1827.
Duke of Wellington, 1827-30.

WILLIAM IV, 1830-7.
Charles Grey, 1830-4.
Viscount Melbourne, 1834.
Sir Robert Peel, 1834-5.
Viscount Melbourne, 1835-7.

VICTORIA, 1837-1901.
Viscount Melbourne, 1837-41.

Sir Robert Peel, 1841-6.
Lord John Russell, 1846-52.
Earl of Derby, 1852.
Earl of Aberdeen, 1852-5.
Viscount Palmerston, 1855-8.
Earl of Derby, 1858-9.
Viscount Palmerston, 1859-65.
Earl Russell, 1865-6.
Earl of Derby, 1866-8.
Benjamin Disraeli, 1868.
W. E. Gladstone, 1868-74.
B. Disraeli, 1874-80.
W. E. Gladstone, 1880-5.
Marquis of Salisbury, 1885-6.
W. E. Gladstone, 1886.
Marquis of Salisbury, 1886-92.
W. E. Gladstone, 1892-4.
Earl of Rosebery, 1894-5.
Marquis of Salisbury, 1895-1901.

EDWARD VII, 1901-10.
Marquis of Salisbury, 1901-2.
A. J. Balfour, 1902-5.
Sir Henry Campbell-Bannerman,
1905-8.
H. H. Asquith, 1908-10.

GEORGE V, 1910.
H. H. Asquith, 1910.
D. Lloyd George, 1916.
A. Bonar Law, 1922.
S. Baldwin, 1923.
Ramsay MacDonald, January 22,
1924.
S. Baldwin, November 4, 1924.
Ramsay MacDonald, June 8,
1929 (National Labour, August
25, 1931).
S Baldwin, June, 1935.

III

CHANCELLORS OF THE GERMAN EMPIRE

WILLIAM I.
P. Otto von Bismarck, 1871-88.

FREDERICK III.
P. Otto von Bismarck, 1888.

WILLIAM II.

P. Otto von Bismarck, 1888-90.
C. George Leo von Caprivi, 1890-4.
P. Chlodwig von Hohenlohe-Schillingsfürst, 1897-1900.
Count and Prince von Bülow, 1900-8.
Theobald von Bethmann-Hollweg, 1908.
F. von Michaelis, 1917.
Count Hertling, 1917.
Prince Max von Baden, 1918.

IV

KINGS OF ITALY

Victor Emmanuel II, 1862 (1849)-78.
Humbert I, 1878-1900.
Victor Emmanuel III, 1900.

GENEALOGICAL TABLE A

BELGIUM—HOUSE OF COBURG

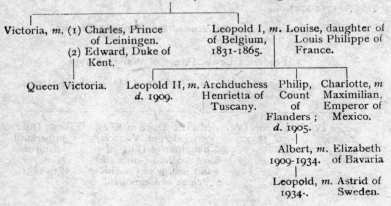

Francis Frederick, Duke of Coburg.

Victoria, *m.* (1) Charles, Prince of Leiningen. (2) Edward, Duke of Kent.

Queen Victoria.

Leopold I, *m.* Louise, daughter of of Belgium, Louis Philippe of 1831-1865. France.

Leopold II, *m.* Archduchess d. 1909. Henrietta of Tuscany.

Philip, Count of Flanders; d. 1905.

Charlotte, *m* Maximilian, Emperor of Mexico.

Albert, *m.* Elizabeth 1909-1934. of Bavaria

Leopold, *m.* Astrid of 1934-. Sweden.

GENEALOGICAL TABLE B

THE BRITISH ROYAL FAMILY SINCE GEORGE I

George I, *m.* Sophia Dorothea of Brunswick-Lüneburg.
1714-1727.

George II, *m.* Caroline of Brandenburg-Ansbach.
d. 1760.

Frederick Lewis, Prince of Wales; *d.* 1751.

George III, *m.* Charlotte of Mecklenburg-Strelitz.
d. 1820.

| George IV; *d.* 1830. | William IV; *d.* 1837. | Edward, Duke of Kent, 1767-1820; *m.* Victoria, daughter of Duke of Saxe-Saalfeld-Gotha and and widow of Charles, Prince of Leiningen. | Ernest, Duke of Cumberland, King of Hanover, 1837-1851. |

Victoria, *m.* Albert of Saxe-Coburg-Gotha;
d. 1901. *d.* 1861.

| Victoria, *m.* Frederick III. | Edward VII, *m.* Alexandra *d.* 1910. of Denmark. | Alice, *m.* Louis IV of Hesse. |

William II of Germany.

Alix, *m.* Nicholas II of Russia.

| Albert, Duke of Clarence; *d.* 1892. | George V. *m.* Victoria Mary of Teck. *d.* 1936. |

| Edward, Prince of Wales, afterwards Edward VIII. Abdicated December, 1936. | Albert, Duke of York. Succeeded as George VI.; *m.* Lady Elizabeth Bowes-Lyon. | Mary, Princess Royal | Henry, Duke of Gloucester. | George, Duke of Kent. |

| Elizabeth Alexandra Mary | Margaret Rose |

APPENDICES

APPENDIX A

THE immediate reforms advocated in the Communist manifesto are:

1. The expropriation of landed property and the use of rent from land to cover state expenditure.

2. A high and progressively graded income tax.

3. The abolition of the right of inheritance.

4. The confiscation of the property of all emigrants and rebels.

5. The centralization of credit for the needs of the state by the establishment of a state bank with state capital and an exclusive monopoly.

6. The centralization of transport in the hands of the state.

7. An increase in the state ownership of factories and instruments of production and the redistribution and amelioration of agricultural land on a general plan.

8. Universal obligation to work and the creation of labour armies especially for agriculture.

9. The unification of agriculture with industrial labour and the gradual abolition of the difference between town and country.

10. The public education of all children. Abolition of factory labour for children in its present form. Unification of education with economic production.

Then after detailed criticism of contemporary socialist movements, which now possesses only an historical interest, the Manifesto proceeds to its famous peroration, ending with the slogan which had already figured on the title page of the *Kommunistische Zeitschrift*:

"The communists consider it superfluous to conceal their opinions and their intentions. They openly declare that their aims can only be achieved by the violent overthrow of the whole contemporary social order.

"Let the governing classes tremble before the communist revolution. The proletarians have nothing to lose in it but their chains. They have the whole world to gain.

"Proletarians of all countries, unite!"

(E. H. CARR, *Karl Marx*, pp. 52-3.)

APPENDIX B

THE terms of the Armistice which had been drafted by the soldiers and sailors were discussed at great length by the Supreme War Council in Paris as early as October 5-7 and the conditions finally approved by the Council on November 4. Mr. Lloyd George communicated the terms to the War Cabinet in London on November 5, mentioning that Foch thought that the Germans would decline them but was confident that in any case the enemy would be overpowered by Christmas. The terms were drawn upon the principle that the enemy should not be in a better position to resume the combat, if peace negotiations broke down. Thus the naval demands (6 battle cruisers, 10 battleships, 8 light cruisers, 50 destroyers of the most modern type and 160 submarines) were based upon the fact that if no demands were made on Germany she would end the war with 25 battleships " of which twelve would be the most modern and powerful in the world " (Admiral Hope) and would be a source of constant anxiety to the Grand Fleet. The arrangement finally agreed to was that the ships to be surrendered should be interned preferably in some neutral port under Allied supervision. The battleships were eventually brought to Scapa Flow (November 21) and sunk by the Germans. The naval authorities had pressed for surrender, not internment. The civilians, considering that the military and naval terms were very stiff and that it would be difficult for the German Government to accept them, decided for the milder alternative.

APPENDIX C

THE Fourteen Points were, in brief:

1. Open covenants and no secret diplomacy in the future.

2. Absolute freedom of navigation in peace and war outside territorial waters, except when seas may be closed by international action.

3. Removal as far as possible of all economic barriers.

4. Adequate guarantees for the reduction of national armaments.

5. An absolutely impartial adjustment of colonial claims, the interests of the peoples concerned having equal weight with the claims of the Government whose title is to be determined.

6. All Russian territory to be evacuated, and Russia given full opportunity for self-development, the Powers aiding.

7. Complete restoration of Belgium in full and free sovereignty.

8. All French territory to be freed and the wrong done by Prussia in 1871 to be righted.

9. The readjustment of Italian frontiers on the lines of nationality.

10. The peoples of Austria-Hungary to be accorded an opportunity of autonomous development.

11. Roumania, Serbia and Montenegro to be evacuated; Serbia to be given access to the sea, and the relations of the Balkan States to be settled on the lines of allegiance and nationality.

12. The non-Turkish nationalities in the Ottoman Empire to be assured of autonomous development and the Dardanelles to be permanently free to all ships.

13. Poland to be an independent State with access to the sea.

14. A general association of nations to be formed under specific covenants for the purpose of affording mutual guarantees of political independence and territorial integrity to great and small States alike.

When the Fourteen Points came to be considered at the Supreme War Council (Nov. 3, 1918), Mr. Lloyd George protested against Art. 2, M. Hymans (Belgium) against Art. 3, and Signor Orlando (Italy) made reserves as to Art. 9. Mr. Lloyd

George was emphatic in his opposition to the American doctrine of the Freedom of the Seas, saying, "The English people will not look at it. On this point the nation is absolutely solid." He also laid stress on the importance of demanding reparations for injuries done. Accordingly the following message was sent to President Wilson:

"The Allied Governments have given careful consideration to the correspondence which has passed between the President of the United States and the German Government. Subject to the qualifications which follow, they declare their willingness to make peace with the Government of Germany on the terms of peace laid down in the President's address to Congress on January 8, 1918, and the principles of settlement enunciated in his subsequent addresses. They must point out, however, that Clause 2 relating to what is usually described as freedom of the seas is open to various interpretations, some of which they could not accept. They must therefore preserve to themselves complete freedom on this subject when they enter the Peace Conference. Further, in the conditions of peace laid down in his address to Congress of January 8, 1918, the President declared that the invaded territories must be restored as well as evacuated and freed. The Allied Governments feel that no doubt ought to exist as to what this provision implies. By it they understand that compensation will be made by Germany for all damages done to the civilian population of the Allies and their property by the invasion by Germany of Allied territory by land, by sea, and from the air."

November 3, 1918

APPENDIX D.

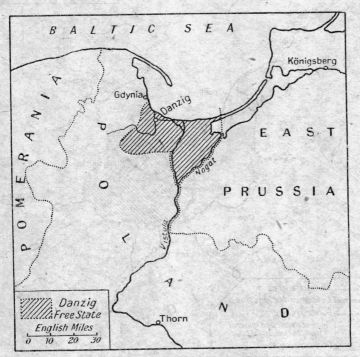

DANZIG AND THE POLISH CORRIDOR.

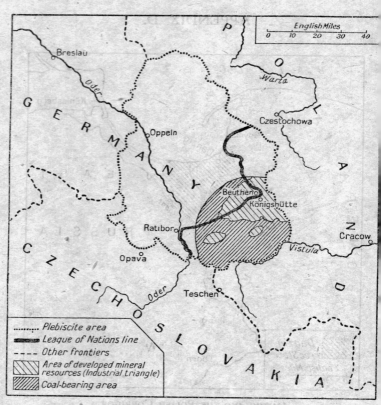

THE SILESIAN TRIANGLE.

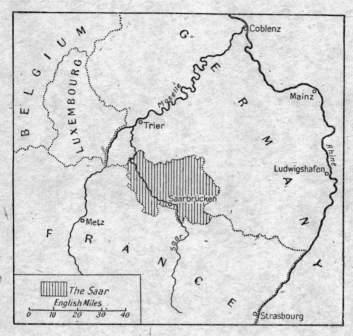

THE SAAR.

INDEX

Yorktown, British capitulation at, 687, 772, 781
Young, Arthur, cited, 700
Ypres battles, 1126, 1148
Yser river, 1127
Yugo-Slavia, 1165
Yugo-Slavs under Italy, 1169
Yussuf-ul-Tashvin, 368

Zachary, Pope, 155
Zallaca battle, 368
Zama battle, 59
Zanghi of Mosul, 230
Zante, 269

Zanzibar, 1033, 1034, 1056
Zara, 1165
Zealand, 593-5
Zeno (philosopher), 45
Zeno, Emp., 120
Zenta battle, 733
Zimisces, John, Emp., 379
Zinovieff, G. E., 1188
Ziska, John, 357
Zola, E., 1006
Zorndorf battle, 760
Zurara cited, 414
Zurich, 542, 551; battle, 827
Zwingli, Ulrich, 498, 506, 541